OXFORD HANDBOOK OF

THE BRITISH SERMON 1689–1901

Edited by
KEITH A. FRANCIS
and
WILLIAM GIBSON

Consultant editors:
ROBERT ELLISON,
JOHN MORGAN-GUY, & BOB TENNANT

UNIVERSITY PRESS

Great Clarendon Street, Oxford, OX2 6DP,
United Kingdom

Oxford University Press is a department of the University of Oxford.
It furthers the University's objective of excellence in research, scholarship,
and education by publishing worldwide. Oxford is a registered trade mark of
Oxford University Press in the UK and in certain other countries

© Oxford University Press 2012

The moral rights of the authors have been asserted

First Edition published in 2012

Impression: 1

All rights reserved. No part of this publication may be reproduced, stored in
a retrieval system, or transmitted, in any form or by any means, without the
prior permission in writing of Oxford University Press, or as expressly permitted
by law, by licence or under terms agreed with the appropriate reprographics
rights organization. Enquiries concerning reproduction outside the scope of the
above should be sent to the Rights Department, Oxford University Press, at the
address above

You must not circulate this work in any other form
and you must impose this same condition on any acquirer

British Library Cataloguing in Publication Data

Data available

Library of Congress Cataloging in Publication Data

Data available

ISBN 978–0–19–958359–1

Printed in Great Britain by
MPG Books Group, Bodmin and King's Lynn

Acknowledgements

We would like to thank the contributors to this handbook for their work and their efforts to ensure that we could hit our deadlines. It might seem foolhardy even to attempt to get thirty-two contributors to submit work by a specific deadline but the majority did so. This handbook could not have been published without the help and support of three consultant editors, Dr Robert Ellison, Dr John Morgan-Guy and Dr Bob Tennant. Robert Ellison acted as final arbiter in matters of citations and saved us from the inconsistencies of the Harvard style of which humanities scholars remain wary. John Morgan-Guy and Bob Tennant were able to attend a working editorial conference in Oxford in March 2011 which turned into a symposium and from which emerged much of the final shape of the volume and the introductory and concluding essays. Their collective wisdom lies behind much of this volume.

William Gibson is grateful for the award of a visiting fellowship at the Armstrong Browning Library at Baylor University in Texas in 2009 and a visiting fellowship at the Lewis Walpole Library at Yale University in 2011; both considerably aided his research on sermons. Keith Francis is grateful for the award of a visiting fellowship at Oxford Brookes University and the help he received at the British and Bodleian Libraries.

Finally, our thanks to copy editor Tom Chandler, and to Tom Perridge, Elizabeth Robottom, and their colleagues at Oxford University Press who have been exemplary publishers, supportive, encouraging, and stimulating.

Keith A. Francis
William Gibson

Contents

List of Contributors   xi
Preface   xiii

PART I INTRODUCTORY ESSAYS

1. The British Sermon 1689–1901: Quantities, Performance, and Culture   3
   WILLIAM GIBSON

2. Sermons: Themes and Developments   31
   KEITH A. FRANCIS

PART II COMMUNITIES, CULTURES AND COMMUNICATION

3. Parish Preaching in the Long Eighteenth Century   47
   JEFFREY S. CHAMBERLAIN

4. Parish Preaching in the Victorian Era: The Village Sermon   63
   FRANCES KNIGHT

5. Preaching from the Platform   79
   MARTIN HEWITT

6. The British Quaker Sermon, 1689–1901   97
   MICHAEL GRAVES

7. The Sermons of the Eighteenth-Century Evangelicals   114
   BOB TENNANT

8. Sermons in British Catholicism to the Restoration of the Hierarchy (1689–1850)   136
   GEOFFREY SCOTT

9. Preaching in the Churches of Scotland   152
   ANN MATHESON

10. The Sermon and Political Controversy in Ireland, 1800–1850   169
   IRENE WHELAN

11. Sermons in Wales in the Established Church   183
   JOHN MORGAN-GUY

12. Preaching in the Vernacular: The Welsh Sermon, 1689–1901   199
   D. DENSIL MORGAN

13. Order and Uniformity, Decorum, and Taste: Sermons Preached at the Anniversary Meeting of the Three Choirs, 1720–1800   215
   ANDREW PINK

PART III OCCASIONAL SERMONS

14. The Sermon, Court, and Parliament, 1689–1789   229
   PASI IHALAINEN

15. The Defence of Georgian Britain: The Anti-Jacobite Sermon, 1715–1746   245
   JAMES J. CAUDLE

16. Preaching, National Salvation, Victories, and Thanksgivings: 1689–1800   261
   WARREN JOHNSTON

17. Sermons in the Age of the American and French Revolutions   275
   G. M. DITCHFIELD

18. 'This Itching Ear'd Age': Visitation Sermons and Charges in the Eighteenth Century   289
   WILLIAM GIBSON

19. Consecration Sermons   305
   COLIN HAYDON

20. The Protestant Funeral Sermon in England, 1688–1800   322
   PENNY PRITCHARD

21. The Victorian Funeral Sermon   338
   JOHN WOLFFE

PART IV CONTROVERSIES, AND THE DEVELOPMENT OF IDEAS

22. Hard Labour: Institutional Benevolence and the Development of National Education — 357
    BOB TENNANT

23. Sermons for End Times: Evangelicalism, Romanticism, and Apocalypse in Britain — 374
    KEITH A. FRANCIS AND ROBERT J. SURRIDGE

24. Rationalism, the Enlightenment, and Sermons — 390
    NIGEL ASTON

25. Preaching the Oxford Movement — 406
    JEREMY MORRIS

26. Sermons and the Catholic Restoration — 428
    MELISSA WILKINSON

27. Paley to Darwin: Natural Theology versus Science in Victorian Sermons — 444
    KEITH A. FRANCIS

28. Preaching the Broad Church Gospel: The *Natal Sermons* of Bishop John William Colenso — 463
    GERALD PARSONS

PART V MISSIONS AND IDEAS OF EMPIRE

29. From Barbarism to Civility, from Darkness to Light: Preaching Empire as Sacred History — 481
    ROBERT G. INGRAM

30. Eighteenth-Century Mission Sermons — 497
    ROWAN STRONG

31. The Sermon in the British Colonies — 513
    JOANNA CRUICKSHANK

32. Church of Ireland Missions to Roman Catholics, *c*.1700–1800 — 530
    ANDREW SNEDDON

33. 'Go ye therefore and teach all nations.' Evangelical and
    Mission Sermons: The Imperial Period 548
    JESSICA A. SHEETZ-NGUYEN

PART VI SERMONS AND LITERATURE

34. The Poet-Preachers 565
    KIRSTIE BLAIR

35. Tradition, Preaching, and the Gothic Revival 579
    STEPHEN PRICKETT

36. The Sermon and the Victorian Novel 594
    LINDA GILL

PART VII CONCLUSION

37. Sermon Studies: Major Issues and Future Directions 611
    KEITH A. FRANCIS

Index 631

List of Contributors

Nigel Aston is Reader in History at the University of Leicester, UK.

Kirstie Blair is Senior Lecturer in English at the University of Glasgow, UK.

James J. Caudle is the Associate Editor of the Boswell Papers at Yale University, USA.

Jeffrey S. Chamberlain is Director of the Frederik Meijer Honors College at Grand Valley State University, Michigan, USA.

Joanna Cruickshank is Lecturer in History at Deakin University, Australia.

G. M. Ditchfield is Professor of Eighteenth Century History at the University of Kent, UK.

Robert H. Ellison is Visiting Assistant Professor of Literature, Marshall University, West Virginia, USA.

Keith A. Francis is Visiting Research Fellow at Oxford Brookes University, UK, Executive Secretary of the American Society for Church History, and Assistant Adjunct Professor at the University of Maryland University College, USA.

William Gibson is Professor of Ecclesiastical History and Director of the Oxford Centre for Methodism and Church History at Oxford Brookes University, UK.

Linda Gill is Professor of English at Pacific Union College, California, USA.

Michael Graves is Professor of Communication Studies at Liberty University, Virginia, USA.

Colin Haydon is Reader in Early Moden History at the University of Winchester, UK.

Martin Hewitt is Professor and Head of the Department of History and Economic History at Manchester Metropolitan University, UK.

Pasi Ihalainen is Professor of History at the University of Jyväskylä, Finland.

Robert G. Ingram is Associate Professor of History at Ohio University, USA.

Warren Johnston is Assistant Professor of History at Algoma University, Canada.

Frances Knight is Associate Professor of Theology at the University of Nottingham, UK.

xii LIST OF CONTRIBUTORS

Ann Matheson was Keeper at the National Library of Scotland and is currently Secretary of the General Council at the University of Edinburgh, UK.

D. Densil Morgan is Professor of Theology and Provost of Lampeter at the University of Wales Trinity Saint David, UK.

John Morgan-Guy was lecturer in Church History at the University of Wales Trinity Saint David, UK.

Jeremy Morris is Dean, Fellow, and Director of Studies in Theology at King's College, Cambridge, UK.

Gerald Parsons was Senior Lecturer in the Department of Religious Studies at the Open University, UK.

Andrew Pink is an independent scholar, UK.

Stephen Prickett is Regius Professor Emeritus of English Language and Literature at the University of Glasgow and honorary professor at the University of Kent at Canterbury, UK.

Penny Pritchard is Lecturer in English Literature at the University of Hertfordshire, UK.

Geoffrey Scott, OSB, is Abbot of Douai, UK.

Jessica A. Sheetz-Nguyen is Associate Professor at the University of Central Oklahoma, USA.

Andrew Sneddon is Lecturer in International History at the University of Ulster, UK.

Rowan Strong is Associate Professor of Church History in the School of Social Sciences and Humanities at Murdoch University, Australia.

Bob Tennant is honorary research fellow in English at the University of Glasgow, UK.

Irene Whelan is Professor of History and Director of Irish Studies at Manhattanville College, New York, USA.

Melissa Wilkinson is an independent scholar and author of *Frederick William Faber* (Gracewing Press 2007), UK.

John Wolffe is Professor of Religious History at the Open University, UK.

Preface

The emergence of a discrete field of Sermon Studies has occurred over the last two decades. That is not to say that there were not distinguished studies of sermons and preaching before this, but a new interdisciplinary endeavour of historians, literary and linguistic scholars, theologians and rhetoricians has developed in response to recognition of the importance of religion in this period. As the editors of a companion volume to this book have argued, 'the landscape of sermon studies has been transformed'.* That transformation has renewed the interest in sermons as literary, political, religious and controversial performances. In all cases, sermons were inextricably linked with the public sphere in Britain; they were intended to be heard and read, and were written and performed with the intention of having an effect in the minds and actions of the audience. The element of the sermon as a performance, as well as a text or in other printed forms, is integral to preaching. While there is some comparatively fragmentary evidence of the reception of the sermon, it is tiny and highly individualistic. So like other performances, theatrical, liturgical and political, sermons are fossils: their real substance has gone, they can only partially be recovered in the disturbance of material around them and in the changed forms in which they survive. Nevertheless the palaeontology of sermons shows how pervasive their influence was.

Perhaps the dominant claim that can be made for this volume is that it reveals the degree to which the period 1689–1901 can be regarded as a 'golden age' of sermons. It was a period in which the religious culture and polity of Britain was largely defined by the sermon: Britain was a sermonic society in which preaching was one, if not the principal, shared experience of all classes and conditions of people. Anglicans, Catholics and Dissenters of all hues saw themselves reflected in, and defined by, the sermons to which they listened. Methodism without field preaching, Nonconformity without extempore preaching, the Church without the parson in his pulpit would not exist. Consequently this volume seeks to restore the centrality of the sermon in this period. It does so by tracing the key trends in the study of the sermon in this period. These trends include the connections between sermons and politics, sermons and communities of believers, sermons and ideas and literature, and sermons and identities. The period 1689–1901 is often regarded as divisible into the 'long eighteenth century' and the Victorian period. However the sermon culture transcends this periodization by historians. The divisions adopted by historians of 1800, 1815 and 1832 do not represent any natural division in the history of the sermon.

*P. MacCullough, H. Adlington, and E. Rhatigan, *The Oxford Handbook of the Early Modern Sermon*, Oxford: Oxford University Press, 2011, xiv.

The organisation of the volume reflects the character of the sermon in this period; it played a key role in communities and cultures, in political, state and local occasions, in controversies and the development of ideas, in the spread of empire, and in literature. The essays in Section Two, on 'Sermons: Communities, Cultures and Communication,' consider the sermon in its most popular form: the non-elite sermons which most people heard each Sunday—or more often—in the churches, chapels and meeting houses up and down the country. These essays, for the first time, map the terrain of the sermon in its most diverse forms, devised to accommodate congregations in different areas, with differing identities, theologies and even languages. Drawing on printed, manuscript and recalled sermons, they show preaching to be the 'stem-cell' of religious performance, able to mould and adapt itself to the circumstances of the men, women and children in the pews and sometimes beyond them. The authors also demonstrate the astonishing volumes of energy and inventiveness that preachers devoted to their sermons: this made sermons easily the most widespread and sustained form of intellectual activity in the country in this period.

Section Three, on 'occasional sermons,' shows the sermon in its least representative, but often most influential, form. 'Occasional sermons' were frequently elite performances, by and for the leaders of church, state and society. The essays in this section are testimony to the central role preaching played in the rituals and formal social occasions of British society in this period. Political moments, victories on land and sea, ecclesiastical ceremonies and rites of passage were all marked by sermons which emphasised the intensely religious character of British society. Sermons were the occasion of expressions of political and religious identity and coherence. In controversy, victory, defeat, disaster, relief and bereavement people sought leadership and solace from the pulpit.

Section Four considers the ways in which sermons contributed to change in British intellectual and social life in the period. Sermons were always prone to be controversial but in the period 1689–1901 they became the engines of national debate and intellectual innovation. Sermons caused and reflected changes in education, theology, society and science. They were also occasions of furious controversy such as Henry Sacheverell's sermon of 1709 and Hoadly's Bangorian sermon of 1716. If these sermons represented revolutions in thought, they should not detract from the many evolutionary sermons, showing the gradual emergence of trends and movements, and it is on these that the essays in this section principally focus.

The essays in Section Five show the ways in which the sermon both preceded and followed the flag into Britain's colonies and possessions across the world. These essays demonstrate just how adaptable the sermon form was. Not only could missionary-preachers use their sermons to convert, indoctrinate, and teach but also to inculcate, they hoped, a sense of Britishness and belonging to the Empire. Furthermore, and ironically, because the sermon form was so malleable it could be adopted by the colonized and transformed into something indigenous and nationalist: consequently sermons could sometimes be used to challenge the imperial project. The essays in this section consider the ways in which the colonizer and colonized used sermons.

Section Six demonstrates the intimate relationship between the sermon and literature in this period. Sermons were, in many respects, the precursors of the novel and popular literature. As fiction grew as a percentage of the print output, the sales of the sermon contracted. Nevertheless these two literary forms were not necessarily in competition with each other and in some respects they were complementary. Sermons employed the forms of literature being poetic and lyrical as well as imaginative and speculative, and they were, like other aspects of everyday life, frequently featured in novels.

Inevitably, perhaps, for such a volume the goal of comprehensiveness is elusive. Individual sermons, and preachers undoubtedly justify their own studies but they have not formed the principal approach for this collection. Instead these essays seek to focus on the trends represented by sermons and preachers and their goals and objectives. Consequently the approach is not predominantly biographical, though this plays an important part in sermon studies. The aim of this volume is to serve as a research tool for both experts and students of religion, politics and society in this period.

It is important to acknowledge that the genesis of this collection was the idea, possibly the dream, of a 'British Pulpit Online,' making all the bibliographical data—and perhaps even page scans—of the published sermons of this period searchable. While one reviewer of the project outline admitted that they found sermons 'dull', it is hoped that this volume will have disabused them of this misapprehension. It is also an aspiration of the editors and consultant editors that this volume will make the case even more strongly that much more information is needed for a thorough quantitative analysis of the sermon in the eighteenth and nineteenth centuries.

K. A. F.; W. G.
November 2011

PART I
INTRODUCTORY ESSAYS

CHAPTER 1

THE BRITISH SERMON 1689–1901: QUANTITIES, PERFORMANCE, AND CULTURE

WILLIAM GIBSON

The sermon genre is unique in modern British culture: sermons were performances as well as texts but differed from other performances in four important respects. First, they were produced for liturgical use. Secondly, as confessional performance texts, with the audience palpably involved, there was only a single speaker. Thirdly, they were often critical acts—exegetical exercises on Scriptural texts—whether composed as ethical teaching or as an expression of collective worship and confession (Hebert: 130–8; Lose: 3). Fourthly, occupying the central ground in a largely Protestant society, they had an extraordinarily miscellaneous nature: within the defined contextual limits of liturgy and pastoral ministry there was hardly an area of contemporary human concern or enquiry which was unexplored in terms of the Church's spiritual mission. Consequently the sermon was unique in its creation and occupation of public space.

The dates of this volume, 1689–1901, are a conscious attempt to identify a particular period in British sermon culture, framed by the Glorious Revolution and the death of Queen Victoria. Those two events mark natural boundaries in the life of sermons in Britain. The year 1689 may reasonably claim to mark the end of two traditions in pulpit literature: the 'baroque' sermons of the seventeenth century, represented by such preachers as Donne and Andrewes, and the Puritan sermons of preachers such as Hall and Smith (McCullough). For some, the Puritan practice of sermon note-making was dying out though it remained a feature of spirituality in Dissent into the eighteenth century. The year 1689 also signalled the emergence of the Tillotson era of preaching and of the antecedents of sermons adopted by Evangelical preachers. These styles have been described as 'pervasive' and long lasting (Edwards: 405). The death of Queen Victoria, in contrast, while not marking the demise of the sermon in Britain, certainly coincided with a sharp decline in its printed form and with a rise in serious questions about the value of sermons when other—often leisure—activities were competing with them for the time and attention of both the working and middle classes.

The decline of the sermon in the nineteenth century took a long time. As early as the 1830s Archbishop Richard Whately of Dublin had asked whether preaching damaged some aspects of devotion and faith: authoritative sermons quashed private judgement, talented preachers could ignore pastoral needs, and an undue focus on the sermon could detract from the everyday Christian life (Poster: 92). The Congregationalist J. Baldwin Brown asked in 1877 'is the pulpit losing its power?' Though he claimed that the Evangelical pulpit had saved Britain from revolution in the late eighteenth century, it had decayed, even though few Evangelical meetings occurred without a sermon. 'The power of the pulpit is manifestly on the wane', he wrote, partly because of the availability of cheap religious and other publications. Charles Spurgeon and visiting American revivalists were exceptions, but could not prevail against what Baldwin Brown called 'the scientific mind' (Baldwin Brown: 304–13). Three years earlier another author in the same journal asked:

> what the pulpit actually does towards furthering the religious and moral life of the enormous number of persons constantly exposed to its influence?…There is no doubt the pulpits of our churches, considered as spiritual motors of the time, is [sic], with few exceptions, all but powerless. Whatever [the sermon] may have done in the past, it now does nothing which can be reckoned amongst those large elements that give tone and character to society. ('English Pulpit': 67)

Evidence of the decline was found elsewhere: in a survey of sermons on 'hospital Sunday' in London in June 1873, the *Times* reported that it looked 'in vain' for evidence that the preachers had seized the opportunity to strengthen Christianity (*Times*). The problem seemed to contemporaries to be a 'supply side' problem:

> The large congregations, consisting in a great part of men, which gather beneath the dome of St Paul's and within the walls of Westminster Abbey every Sunday, show that there is no lack of interest in the message of the pulpit. Perhaps the general public never looked so earnestly as they do now towards the assistance and furtherance of the religious life by its means. ('English Pulpit': 69)

Both the rise and the decline of the sermon in the period do not mean that there were not continuities: parish preaching did not change immediately in 1689 or 1901, but it was subject to gradual changes which altered it in content and form. Whether 1689–1901 forms a coherent 'period' in sermon studies may be controversial. Nevertheless this period saw preaching reach its highest point in terms of popularity and influence; it also saw sermons diversify and specialize. Preaching became fissiparous and moulded itself to almost every cause and sectional interest. There were mission sermons, preaching before societies, sermons with specific purposes such as to raise money for the anti-slavery movement, university and school sermons, sermons for the army and navy, sermons for the young, and many others evidenced in this volume; these were forms of specialization which meant that, while preaching remained popular, fewer people had such a communal or shared experience of it. The audience for sermons, as it grew, became increasingly extensive rather than intensive. The official control of sermons, through the licensing of preachers in the Church of England and the 'testing' of candidates for orders in Dissenting churches, also became less effective, so that preachers could break the bounds of preaching which was officially sanctioned by the authorities. Thus the diversification of sermons is an important feature of the nature of pulpit literature in this period and one of its most significant characteristics.

The period 1689–1901 may be said to represent a 'golden age' of sermon culture in Britain. As Bishop Sprat said in 1695, 'the sermons preach'd every Sunday…are more excellent compositions of that kind than have been deliver'd…throughout the whole Christian world' (Sprat: 19). And John Trusler, who rarely withheld criticism of any object he disliked, wrote in 1809 'sermons of the present age are in general much improved, as much improved as the age itself' (Trusler: 195). Sermons were important factors in political and social change: the Sacheverell sermon and the following trial almost certainly determined the outcome of the election of 1710, and preaching directed much of the demand and resistance to religious and political change as well as fuelling movements such as that against slavery. Preaching could be deployed for political purposes and one historian has claimed of the clergy that 'in their Sunday sermons and in their weekday conversations with their parishioners they were quite capable of swaying the votes of entire villages' (Pruett: 164). In 1827, *The Monthly Review* contained an article which claimed that sermons and novels were the two most widely published forms of literature, and likened books of sermons to birds flying from one end of the country to another, 'ample demonstrations' that 'the desire of sound knowledge and religious instruction has kept fully pace with the appetite for sentiment and description and heroic story'. Nevertheless, preaching rarely attracts the attention in scholarly circles that its significance in the period justifies. The popular attention given to sermons is something that could not be discovered from studies of the history, literature, and theology of the period. In short, sermons, while they contributed in a remarkable degree to the experience of everyday life in this period, have largely been ignored by scholars. The aim of this handbook is to correct that imbalance.

It might reasonably be asked, what constituted a sermon? While initially this seems a facile question, it is more complex than might be assumed. Did sermons have to take place in churches? Clearly not, as Methodist field preaching, sermons at Paul's Cross, and other places indicate. In the Victorian era theatres were sometimes used for preaching. Charles Spurgeon hired the Surrey Gardens music hall in 1856 because it held over 10,000, whereas he had been forced to turn people away from Exeter Hall, which held only half that number ('Preachers and Preaching': 689–93). Some secular buildings were built as auditoria with preaching in mind. So the 'sacred space' of pulpit, church, and chapel were incidental to the sermon, though preachers sometimes intentionally sanctified open spaces, making them church-like. Did a sermon have to be called a sermon? Again, this is not the case. Preaching was sometimes delivered and published as discourses, addresses, charges, and lectures; this is especially the case in sermon controversies, in which clergy replied and responded to one another on contentious issues. Did a sermon have to be preached by a clergyman? Again, no; laymen and women preached in the Methodist and Nonconformist traditions and in Anglicanism later in this period. Sermons were not even exclusively Christian. Nor were they even written as sermons: in one case in 1755, the Revd Henry Stebbing told his friend Edward Weston, a layman, that he had read a letter from Weston 'instead of a sermon of my own,... to let them see... that the preaching [of] virtue and sober Christianity was not merely the trade of parsons' (Stebbing 1755).

Sermons also spilled over into forms such as 'exhortations' (which were very common in Evangelical circles), orations, and 'witness'—all of which often enabled those with less education than clergy and ministers to speak publicly to congregations. Sermons were sometimes printed to be read alone, or in small household groups, so even the public aspect of the performance of a sermon was not integral to it. The sermon in this period therefore adopted many forms and guises, but the essential element was its confessional purpose: teaching, exposition, exhortation, and the propagation of the Christian faith. The contributions to this volume bear witness to the extraordinary variety in both form and content. In doing so they demonstrate that this period was one in which religion was full of energy and vitality and exercised an extraordinary pull on the minds of the people of Britain. Here too, the relative silence of scholars is regrettable. Sermons were perhaps the dominant literary form in Britain between 1689 and 1901, and yet this is hardly acknowledged by scholars of history, literature, theology, and ideas.

Quantifying the Sermon

Preaching, taken collectively, contributed to the development of British culture throughout the world and the determination of religious identity at all levels of society. Thus the questions of an accurate assessment of printed sermon numbers, and their relative densities by place, occasion, and subject, are especially important. The numbers are clearly so large that the printed sermon constituted not only a major pastoral and intellectual enterprise by the Church but also a major part of the output of the print industry and a significant element in the cultural fabric of the country. It is likely that in the eighteenth century about eight pages of sermons were printed for every one page of fiction; sermons were popular, mainstream literature. While imaginative literature replaced some religious literature during the eighteenth century, sermons remained enormously popular and held their market share (Shevlin: xlii). The eighteenth century's best-selling sermon, Henry Sacheverell's *The Perils of False Brethren* (1709), became a staple of conversation in coffee-houses and salons; its market penetration—its readership's proportion of the literate population—must have approached saturation. 40,000 copies were produced by Sacheverell's first publisher, Henry Clements, alone (Cholmondley), and it was extensively reprinted and pirated. The assumption that each copy was read or heard by at least ten people is probably a conservative estimate.

However, published sermons were a tiny minority of those delivered. If the term 'sermon event' is used for the experience of a congregation hearing a preacher, a simple calculation makes the scale of the churches' preaching apparent. Given that most of the ten thousand or more Anglican parishes heard at least one sermon every Sunday, and many heard two on a Sunday and one or more during the week, between 1689 and 1901 therefore the Church of England alone encompassed at the very least 110 million potential Sunday sermon events (and possibly double that figure). If the established churches of Scotland and Ireland and the Dissenting churches in the three kingdoms are added this number can with certainty be doubled, without including preaching in overseas territories, the army and the navy, and other institutions like schools and colleges. Colonial sermons were hardly negligible in the nineteenth century, with the Anglican parish and missionary system alone gradually extending throughout the empire. If the hundred SPG (Society for the Propagation of the Gospel in Foreign Parts) missionaries of 1800 are taken as a median figure, the eighteenth and nineteenth centuries witnessed a million potential sermon events from them alone. To these may be added the major Church festivals which fell on Sundays only one year in seven (Christmas Day, saints' days, and the rest—perhaps another 10 million sermon events) and funerals: most deaths in Britain would have occasioned a Christian funeral and possibly a sermon. Occasional sermons (assizes, parliamentary, charity schools, hospitals, lecture series) would have constituted only a small addition of a couple of millions to the aggregate numbers. In total, a quarter of a billion potential sermon events between 1689 and 1901 is probably an underestimate.

As sermons were frequently repeated and even borrowed by clerical colleagues, if this total of pulpit events is divided by ten to accommodate such practices, perhaps 25 million unique sermon performances may be a reasonable estimate for this period. Chamberlain has also suggested that the general practice existed of the destruction of manuscript sermons on their authors' death, so that posthumous reuse was restricted. John Wesley was a critic of the 'common practice' of clergy burning sermons every seven years, recalling that some he had preached thirty or forty years earlier were among his best (Heitzenrater 1999: 105).

It might be thought, in contrast to problems of making an estimate of sermon events, that the number of published versions is easy to determine. Unfortunately, this is not the case. Sermons were published in various forms, and each presents difficulties to the scholar. Many sermons were published as single items and issued as pamphlets. Others (and a significant percentage, perhaps as high as 80 per cent) appeared only in collections, often in the 'complete' or 'collected' sermons of an individual, and sometimes in multi-author anthologies, or in, for example, the annual series of Boyle and Bampton lectures. Increasingly in the nineteenth century, sermons were published in liturgically, doctrinally, or theologically thematic collections, such as those of Robertson and Liddon. Others exist only as fugitive items in the miscellaneous sections of authors' collected works. This last category, although probably numerically small, is especially intractable, as items can only be discovered by physically inspecting whole libraries of books.

Singly-published sermons can be elusive as they were often published variously as 'sermons', 'lectures', 'discourses', and 'homilies', or with titles which fail to indicate their origin in the pulpit. Collections, although less fugitive, have a peculiar difficulty: that catalogues usually contain their titles but not the discrete items in their contents. This makes analysis laborious and systematic analysis impossible for the time being. A further difficulty is cataloguing practice. Even where items, and whole libraries, have been catalogued according to Library of Congress protocols, there is wide scope for divergent, and professionally legitimate, practice within those protocols. This means that an item may appear in different catalogues in different forms. Thus Henry Sacheverell's 1709 sermon could be catalogued correctly in short form as *A Sermon Preached Before…the Lord-Mayor*, as *A Sermon Preached…at the Cathedral Church of St. Paul*, as *A Sermon Preached…on the 5th of November, 1709*, or as *The Perils of False Brethren, both in Church, and State* (its running title). Experience shows that, when cross-checking between catalogues, about 5 percent of items cannot be safely matched without physical inspection. As an example, an online search of major library catalogues is currently likely to turn up about ten sermons published in 1815–16 on the Battle of Waterloo. However physical inspection of sermons over a period of years has identified two dozen.

John Gordon Spaulding's posthumous *Pulpit Publications, 1660–1782* (1996) was the result of more than three decades' work in an era without developed software. Sermon scholars are deeply in his debt. *Pulpit Publications* aspires to identify every published sermon, listed by author, scriptural text, and date of publication, although the last is very unreliable. Spaulding's catalogue is partly derived from the collections of Letsome (1753) and Cooke (1783). For the period 1660–1782 Spaulding lists about 34,000 sermons and claims 99 per cent completeness for Church of England sermons and 82 per cent for those of Dissent (Spaulding: 1:xiii) as well as unspecified proportions from Scotland, Ireland, and the colonies. These claims, if aggregated to the 212 years of the present volume, give a potential of 58,000 published sermons. It is fairly easy to make additions to Spaulding's lists and sampling suggests a slow but distinct acceleration of publication rates well into the nineteenth century. Allowing for this and the present intractability of quantifying the more fugitive categories of sermon publications, it seems reasonable to estimate 80,000 individual printed sermons for the period 1689–1901 as a conservative approximation: this figure includes all publications in the British empire and colonial America.

An accurate assessment of sermon numbers is important for two issues: the relationship between preaching and published sermons; and the ways in which the latter were received by publishers and readers. Both of these are complex issues. It is obvious that the numbers of sermons which were published constitute a tiny and unrepresentative sample—eighty thousand compared with the 250 million unique sermon events. Consequently, consideration of parochial preaching will remain the prerogative of critical investigation rather than the statistician's enquiry. The relative numbers of published and unpublished sermons is important. The tiny percentage of all preaching that is constituted by the printed sermon means that any claim for the latter to be representative must be regarded with caution. Moreover the only way in which scholars can attempt to recover the spoken sermon is through accounts by its hearers. But this is naturally problematic for scholarship. So there must be a contingency in the understanding of the wider corpus of sermons delivered but not recorded.

On the narrower question of sermon publishing and public events, such as the Exclusion Crisis, the Monmouth Rebellion, the Glorious Revolution, and the 1715 and 1745 Jacobite rebellions, there was a varying response by the printing industry (Claydon; Tennant). Sometimes topical sermons simply displaced other sermon publications from the production process (consequently gross numbers were virtually unchanged) and on other occasions additional production displaced non-sermon pamphlet production. Occasionally a crisis was accompanied by, and presumably caused, a hiatus in the publication of collected sermons, but sometimes not, so that the division between the production of cheap duodecimo pamphlets and expensive quarto and octavo books was made porous by wider events.

Between 1689 and 1901 there was a general increase in the production of printed material, raising the question of the sermon's market share. From time to time there was a step change in the gross production of sermons. For example, the plateau of about 75 singly-published sermons annually in the 1680s and 1690s rose abruptly to about 140 annually by 1712 (Tennant). Such changes are unlikely to have been the result of increased productive capacity in the industry—this would more naturally be plotted by growth curves, not step changes—but, more likely, of the trade's reassessment of the buoyancy of the sermon market and the extraordinary controversies of the first decade of the eighteenth century. These comments seem plausible also if applied to collections of sermons. Research into these phenomena is at present almost entirely lacking but possibly an annual output of 300–350 sermons in all forms was attained by 1715 and maintained, or increased somewhat, thereafter. It is likely that the peak of production was reached early in Queen Victoria's reign and that it was not until the 1870s that numbers started to decline from the mid-nineteenth century.

In the eighteenth century, the singly-published sermon was obviously not proportionately representative of preaching. The occasional sermon predominated in the published corpus, but was drawn from a few hundred events a year, compared with many hundreds of thousands potential sermon events in the three kingdoms, vanishingly few of which were published. The published genre was therefore always disproportionately weighted towards the occasional sermon and its authors tended to be the clerical and political elite, positioned at the cutting edge of theological and cultural observation. In contrast, the parish sermon, preached by virtually the whole body of clergy, would often tend to express the prevalent religious culture, perhaps even that of their authors' student days. Sermon studies that utilize such published sermons therefore may represent national history and high culture, but may not necessarily claim coverage of popular or local cultures.

Performance in the Pulpit

As is clear from the comparative figures on performed and published preaching, the vast majority of sermons in this period were performances in front of congregations. Yet these were for the most part ephemeral experiences, rarely recorded and only surviving in the hearers' memories. Memories of specific sermons lingered longer than might be thought: on one occasion a sermon preached at Wallingford in the 1770s was recalled thirty years later by some members of the congregation (Trusler: 324). Sermons were comparatively long—probably between thirty minutes and an hour was the norm—though there is some suggestion that sermons were becoming shorter by the end of the seventeenth century (Green: 212). However a sermon of 5,000 or 7,000 words probably took at least an hour to read and there are many such parochial sermons published in the eighteenth century. In 1738 one Oxfordshire parson shortened his sermons from a usual half an hour in response to his parishioners' request, but this was exceptional (Jenkins: 17). Nevertheless there are many examples of very long sermons. In 1834 Gerald Noel preached at Farnham for two and a quarter hours, and a visitation charge and sermon of Archdeacon Hare lasted four hours; the late seventeenth-century Presbyterian Daniel Burgess apparently preached for three hours, and it is said that the Welsh Evangelical Daniel Rowlands once preached from morning to sunset. Even Wesley and Pusey preached on occasion for two hours or more (Ellman: 156–7; Ditchfield: 229; Wood 1960: 48; Quiller Couch: 351; Downey: 206). University sermons might, perhaps, be expected to hold the attention of a clerical and educated audience longer, but Edward Tatham tested this with a two and a half hour sermon in 1803 (Bennett: 416). By the mid-nineteenth century however advice to clergy was for preaching to last no more than twenty to thirty minutes (Heeney: 136). Naturally some clergy could not devote such length to their sermons especially if they had more than one church to serve. Jonathan Swift claimed that as a young curate he sometimes

> Within an hour & eke a half
> I preach'd three congregations deaf
> Which thundering out with lungs long-winded
> I chopp'd so fast that few there minded. (Swift)

Preaching, irrespective of length, often drew huge audiences. In Piccadilly, where Thomas Secker was rector of St James's in the 1730s and 1740s, it was said 'when Secker preaches the church is crowded' (Downey: 90). Sensational preachers drew people from other churches: Daniel Rowlands drew large numbers of people from other churches in Wales whenever he preached in the mid-eighteenth century (Wood 1960: 46). Even an unpopular parson, such as Skinner of Camerton in the 1820s, found that when he preached his church was packed, often so that 'the church could not contain them' (Coombs and Coombs: 167). Fashionable London preachers in the second half of the eighteenth century, such as Richard Harrison, could even attract large crowds on weekdays and even at burial services. Word of mouth often spread news of a gifted preacher. Martin Madan, by training a lawyer, having become chaplain to the unfashionable Lock Hospital (for venereal disease), found that, when he preached in the parlour to the 'poor loathsome patients', people gathered in nearby rooms and even outside the building to hear his sermons (*Pulpit Elocution*: 27, 67). In some cases the appetite for sermons seemed unquenchable. In the heightened atmosphere of the Cambuslang meetings in

Scotland in 1742, George Whitefield preached at 2 p.m., 6 p.m., and 9 p.m. to vast crowds; he was followed by Mr M'Culloch at 1 a.m., and even after that the crowds would not depart in the hope of hearing another sermon (Wood 1960: 120). Despite the satire of Hogarth's 'Sleeping Congregation' (1736) and the *Tatler's* claim in 1709 that a sermon was 'as good as an opiate' (*Tatler*), such episodes were probably unrepresentative. John Newton was exceptional, as an Evangelical, in needing to round up his parishioners before a sermon with his riding crop (Elliott-Binns: 151). On occasion, John Wesley expressed disappointment when people would not rise at 5 a.m. to hear a sermon before they went to work (Heitzenrater 1999: 94).

Congregations were clearly discriminating, with high expectations of preachers, and some made their views apparent. Gilbert Burnet's coronation sermon for William and Mary in 1689 was met with applause, as was Samuel Horsley's performance before the House of Lords in 1793 when the whole congregation stood for the last minutes of the sermon (Farooq: 33; Abbey and Overton: 465). On some occasions congregations gave a hum of approval for the sermon (Carpenter: 35). One commentator at a Methodist chapel in the late eighteenth century witnessed 'a lengthened moan' of approval emanate from the congregation and in North Wales there were examples of people jumping with enthusiasm at popular sermons (*Pulpit Orator*: 93–4). Most criticism of sermons was that there were too few. Between 1662 and 1750, of 127 prosecutions of clergy in Salisbury diocese, only ten were regarding preaching, and that from Laverstoke in 1689 was because the parishioners wanted more than one sermon a week (Spaeth: 114, 189). In Leicestershire at the start of our period, few clergy were prosecuted for poor preaching (Pruett: 45). Congregations could be impressively respectful, as in Churchdown, Gloucestershire in the 1870s when it remained customary for men to stand throughout the sermon (*Notes and Queries*). And Methodists attending Parson Skinner's sermons in Camerton in 1822 did the same (Coombs and Coombs: 222). Occasionally, as happened in St Andrews Plymouth in the mid-eighteenth century, a parson might punish his parish by withholding sermons (Woodland).

Even poorly educated congregations could become discerning; a largely illiterate congregation in a Southey poem was said to be able to identify a sermon read by their parson from the works of Sanderson, Taylor, Barrow, or South (Ditchfield: 235). When the preachership of St Giles in the Fields was decided by election in the 1760s William Sellon, an enormously popular preacher, was elected by an overwhelming majority by the parishioners (*Pulpit Elocution*: 42). Nevertheless since London lecturers were dependent on preaching fees, a parson might find the process of soliciting subscriptions from his congregation embarrassing, especially when they did not wish to pay (Trusler: 35). Moreover parishes might come to take excellence in the pulpit for granted: Francis Dawes, the rector of Solihull in 1763—who had been the incumbent since 1749—was noted by a traveller to be the best preacher he had heard; a member of his congregation agreed but said 'we have heard him so often we are tired of him' (Trusler: 191–2).

Some congregations could be demanding. Mr Linklater, who preached in Shadwell in 1869, said he 'never preached to a more exacting congregation' by whom 'fervent sermons were especially welcomed' (Ellsworth: 111). Talented speakers could hold the attention of congregations: one preacher in the 1780s commanded 'the most profound silence in the church, and the people are almost afraid to breathe, lest they should lose a word' (*Pulpit Elocution:* 15). Some parishioners, drawing on the example of seventeenth century Puritan sermon note-making, were keen to reflect on the sermon afterwards; the eighteenth century Sussex shopkeeper, Thomas Turner, often wrote his reflections on the week's sermons in his diary (Vaisey). Rich's shorthand system was invented in the seventeenth century specifically to enable people to make sermon notes for reflection afterwards (Mitchell: 35). Lady Abney, a Dissenter, was assiduous in summarizing sermons, keeping copious notes: in nine months in 1722–3 she summarized forty-six (Abney).

Sermons had a clear catechetical purpose, and were widely used in Anglicanism to prepare people for confirmation and in other churches to inculcate the teachings of the denomination. Such catechesis was the foundation of popular understanding of sermons, since many preachers assumed their audience's prior knowledge of essential doctrine and church teaching that was usually contained in catechism. Thus sermons appear to offer evidence of the success of catechizing—in contradiction to some more pessimistic accounts of religion in the eighteenth and nineteenth centuries. If the churches failed in their objective of catechizing in this period, why did so many sermons clearly assume high levels of knowledge of religious teaching? Some catechetical sermons, such as Thomas Secker's *Lectures on the Catechism,* were published and reprinted frequently in the eighteenth century. It is also clear that some clergy, like the incumbent of Fairford in the early eighteenth century, composed prayers to complement the specific content of their sermons (Fairford).

Clergy were alert to the popular appeal of sermons. William Sherlock in the early eighteenth century noted that 'many who have little other religion are forward enough to hear sermons, and many will miss the prayers and come in only in time to hear the preaching' (Abbey and Overton: 464). The sermon seemed all. One writer in 1692 commented

> many men have taken up the notion…that the principal end of their going to Church is to hear a sermon; that if there be no sermon, they have nothing to do there: or if the preacher be such as either they do not like, or cannot, as they fancie, edify by, they may well be excused for staying away. (*Two Letters:* 29)

The sermon seemed to blot out the rest of church services. In Henry Fielding's *Tom Jones* of 1749 church services were referred to as 'sermon time', which Thackeray referred to in *Vanity Fair* also; and in George Crabbe's poem of 1807, *The Parish Register*, he referred to the church bell as the 'sermon bell'. Consequently, sermons were sometimes a way to exert a pull on people. The vicar of Kinlet, Oxfordshire, introduced Sunday afternoon sermons to 'keep his parishioners from going to (the) dissenter meeting' (Marshall: 108). Skinner of Camerton chose to preach on fraudulent claims to miracles in June 1828 because a 'ranters camp' had been established locally and he wanted to prevent his parishioners from attending it (Coombs and Coombs: 336). In Kidderminster between 1778 and 1813, Thomas Robinson won back many Dissenters to the Church of England

by his popular preaching (Elliott-Binns: 302). In the nineteenth century wily Tractarians, such as Edward Munro, regarded sermons as 'bait' to attract the poor to the sacramental services they offered and to daily prayers (Heeney: 40–4). This tactic was not new: John Clubbe, rector of Whatfield, Suffolk, had used sermons to bring people to frequent communion in the mid-eighteenth century (Clubbe: 2:19). Very occasionally an event in the pulpit sparked the imagination of large numbers of people, as when John Oakes died in the middle of preaching a sermon in London in 1689, for which his eulogist asked of his congregation 'was he not thus stricken for your rebellion against his calls?' (Oakes: 22).

There were also cases of disappointing preachers. Thomas Ken was grievously and surprisingly disappointed by Tillotson's sermon at Queen Mary's funeral in 1695 (Ken). Thomas Haweis was equally disappointed by James Hervey's preaching; Hervey's sermons sold well but his performance in the pulpit was 'whining… canting and unoratorical' (Wood 1957: 52). Even John Wesley was found to be disappointing by some including Horace Walpole (Heitzenrater 1999: 98–100). James Murray, attending a Methodist meeting in Founders Hall in the 1760s, was disappointed to find the sermon 'dull and tedious', and Edmund Burt visiting Scotland in the mid-eighteenth century found that Calvinist preaching went straight over the heads of the congregations. Disorder was not unknown; Boswell recorded in 1778 at Carlisle that he could not hear the assize sermon because 'the crowd made such a disturbance' (van Eijnatten: 349, 355, 367). During the anti-ritualist disturbances in London, Anglo-Catholic preaching in Protestant neighbourhoods could sometimes spark off violence (Ellsworth: 110). Some clergy feared the response of their congregations: Hugh Stowell Brown, a Baptist minister, was anxious that his congregation might laugh at his early attempts at preaching in the 1840s.

There were of course wide variations in congregations, and sermon performances had to accommodate these. The benchers of Lincoln's Inn were said to be a particularly discriminating audience, whose education made particular demands on a preacher (Baker: 73–4). Tillotson often preached an erudite sermon to them on a Sunday and then, stripped of its learning, Latin, and legal language, preached it to a parish later in the week (Brown: 29). Equally university sermons were often pored over by scholars; one Oxford student made a close analysis of 364 sermons between 1704 and 1707 (Bennett: 387).

An important debate throughout this period was whether sermons should be written and read or delivered extempore. At the Restoration Charles II had sought to suppress the reading of sermons in favour of memorized or extempore preaching but, despite an injunction issued to Cambridge University, it was impossible to enforce. Gilbert Burnet, who had travelled extensively in Europe in the 1670s and 1680s, regarded English preaching as 'incomparably better' than that he had heard abroad; he also regarded the practice of reading sermons as 'peculiar to the English nation'; but the quality of sermons which were read was so high that 'a mean composition will be ill heard' (Mitchell: 394; *Essay on Preaching*: 6). While reading sermons was common in the seventeenth century, and continued well into the nineteenth, there were strong views on both sides. Jonathan Swift loathed preachers who, because they read their sermons, kept their faces within an inch of the text and did not look at their congregations (Pruett: 124). Hugh Blair claimed that 'the practice of reading sermons is one of the greatest obstacles to the Eloquence of the Pulpit in Great Britain, where alone this practice prevails' (Deconinck-Brossard: 121). But in 1785 the author of *An Essay on Preaching* reasonably concluded neither extempore preaching nor reading 'can be generally recommended to all'; each had its advantages and disadvantages. The essay made clear that learned sermons, such as those for assizes or visitations, ought to be written and read, and clergy generally should respect the taste of their congregations for reading or extempore preaching (*Essay on Preaching*: 6–20).

Written sermons had the advantage of being a safeguard against heresy and eccentricity. Some bishops, like John Sharp and Edmund Gibson, routinely invited clergy to bring their sermons to them so that they could be checked (Jacob: 258; Sykes: 145). Written sermons, however, required considerable preparation and thought; indeed in 1785 it was acknowledged that extempore preaching was much less costly in time (*Essay on Preaching*: 16). By 1874 the time taken to write sermons was regarded as eroding the effectiveness of the clergy ('English Pulpit': 86). Mark Pattison claimed that it took him six weeks to write one particular sermon. John Wesley as a young parson found that composing one of his first sermons took him three weeks (Heitzenrater 1970: 111). Over a career, the volume of work entailed in writing an hour's sermon twice a week could mount up: when Matthew Postlethwayte, rector of Denton, Norfolk, died in 1795 and his manuscript sermons were burnt, they weighted 120 lb (Hartshorne: 56). John Welsh of Newchurch composed and preached 103 original sermons between 1726 and 1732 (Snape: 175) and this took considerable intellectual effort and research. For younger clergy therefore, many bishops recommended that they began by reading the published sermons of leading preachers to their congregations, as they learned and developed their skills, and only gradually wrote their own. This was often described as laying up one's stock. Given the effort involved in their composition, sermons were sometimes reused or recycled. Tillotson often cannibalized old sermons for new occasions (Brown: 33). Not to do so invited criticism; Wesley accused Whitefield of not developing his sermons, having written most of them in his youth and become over reliant on them, so that his preaching was the same as many years before (Elliott-Binns: 371). One clergyman, either due to its popularity or his lack of originality, preached the same sermon between 1722 and 1746 on twenty-five occasions (Osborn).

A rare insight into the practice of a clergyman survives in the preaching records of John Longe, vicar of Coddenham, Suffolk, from 1787 to 1832. In the first two years of his incumbency Longe wrote thirty-seven sermons. But it is clear that he also drew on an extensive collection of published sermons; he owned a library of thirty-eight authors some of which were multi-volume collections. These enabled Longe to blend his own compositions with those of published sermons and his father's stock of sermons which he inherited. In April 1789 he preached a sermon 'partly from Sherlock and the rest my father's'; in June 1794 he preached one by 'myself assisted by my father'; in November 1798 a sermon 'partly from Fothergill'; in 1800 one 'altered from Mr Gardemau's'; and in 1803 one 'compiled from various sermons'. Longe was a slow writer, taking a month in 1826 to compose a harvest sermon, and he often used the long winter months to write sermons. Nevertheless occasionally an event was sufficiently significant to demand an immediate response in the pulpit: a murder in Suffolk in July 1831 was one such an event on which Longe preached twice (Stone: 171–4).

A detailed study of manuscript sermons also shows something of the practice of writing and delivering sermons. Parsons clearly developed a sense of the specific seasonal qualities of preaching: one wrote on a sermon 'proper at any time especially after Xtmas & ye Sunday before Lent' and other 'after confirmation'. Manuscript sermons which were passed from hand to hand were by no means static, they were fluctuating and changing; an inheritor or purchaser of a collection of sermons would often amend, delete and add to a sermon in the margins and elsewhere on the page—in many cases the back of a page was reserved for such additions. In some cases pages were added and stuck into the manuscript with supplementary material. From these additions it is clear that the variables accommodated by such changes were the congregation, the circumstances of the preaching, and the ideas and tastes of the preacher. Thus manuscript sermons often developed a patina of subsequent users. Favourite and popular sermons were often re-preached; in one case a note on the front of a manuscript sermon noted 'Learn of me for I am much copied'. Others were not preached in propitious circumstances, as when a parson noted 'the last two leafs and that inserted p27 were omitted because 'twas dark' (Beinecke sermons c550, c410, c420, c104).

Clergy made considerable efforts to customize manuscript sermons even when they were their own. In one case a parson developed a suite of funeral sermons and added to each a one-page summary of the life of the specific individual to whom it related. Preachers added prayers to their sermons, so that the sermon complemented the liturgy as a whole. It is also clear that preachers introduced their sermons with an explanation of how the current sermon connected to earlier preaching and related to the circumstances of the parish. Henry Newcome, rector of Middleton, Lancashire, responded to events such as the first Quaker meeting in the village with a sermon entitled 'A Caveat Against Quakers'; he also ensured that his sermons were congruent with the hymns for the service, saying to his parishioners 'we sing a psalm before sermon, yt our minds may be more composed to receive ye impressions of divine truths'. It also seems likely that suites of sermons, on such themes as the Lord's Prayer, with a catechetical theme, were more common than might be assumed. Some preachers asked questions from the pulpit with the same goal. Sermons were clearly integrated by clergy into the spiritual advice they offered to their parishioners, which can be divined from sermon notes (Beinecke sermons c88, c247, c250, c264).

The alternative to writing sermons and reading the published sermons of others was to beg or borrow the work of other clergy. In Lincolnshire in the eighteenth century a group of clergy met together regularly to exchange sermons (Downey: 7; Walsh). John and Charles Wesley shared sermons which they had composed and used a specific cypher and unique shorthand to record them (Heitzenrater 1970: 113). In 1742 Richard Hurd asked John Potter to lend him his sermons as he found himself painfully unable to write his own. He promised not to lend them to anyone else or preach them outside his own parish (Brewer: 72–81). In such circumstances this led to a problem of originality: Thomas Sharp abandoned one charity sermon as it was on the same text as one by a previous preacher and might therefore be assumed to be identical (Deconinck-Brossard: 113).

Extempore preaching was sometimes favoured because it was thought to be closer to primitive practice in the early church (*Two Letters*: 8). It had been widely used in seventeenth century Nonconformity, but the Anglican preference for a settled liturgy led to a similar partiality for written sermons. Extempore preaching attracted people by the immediacy and emotional nature of the experience. Leading Evangelical preachers quickly realized its power. Emotion became a key ingredient in Evangelical sermons: George Whitefield stamped his feet, cried aloud, beat his breast and choked his voice in tears, so that at the end of the performance he was often exhausted. The experience of extempore preaching could be shocking: Whitefield called people, to their faces, 'half-beasts, half-devils'; he punctuated his comments with personal asides and anecdotes to establish an intimacy with his audience; his sermons also contained as many as sixty questions designed to make the hearer question the depth of their faith (Downey: 165, 174). This was the preaching of the heart rather than of the mind. Such histrionics attracted criticism from observers like Samuel Johnson (Lessenich: 141–2) and Wesley also, who disliked what he called mere 'gospel preaching', which he regarded as 'unconnected rhapsody of unmeaning words' (Heitzenrater 1999: 100). Southey attacked the postures and grimaces of such preachers (Downey: 23).

Between the two poles of the read and the extempore sermon was the *memoriter*, or remembered sermon. Francis Atterbury and Samuel Wesley Sr both committed sermons to memory so that they could preach them without notes (Jacob: 260). James Fordyce, preacher at the Monkswell Meeting House in London in the 1780s, also preached from memory and an observer commented 'he must have a memory the most tenacious, to retain so much matter, perfectly new and original, every week, the delivery of which requires a full hour each time' (*Pulpit Elocution*: 38). There were, however, preachers who simply couldn't sustain extempore or *memoriter* preaching: the great Tillotson's only foray into extempore preaching was a disaster and he had to leave the pulpit after just ten minutes (Carpenter: 30); while he attempted to memorize sermons this 'heated his head so much, a day or so before & after he preached that he was forced to leave it off' (Tillotson: 134). Charles Wesley was so uncertain about his ability to preach extempore that he only tried it in front of a small congregation (Elliott-Binns: 238).

By the nineteenth century it had become settled dogma that extempore preaching had greatest impact on the poor and a polished read sermon went down better with the educated classes (Heeney: 44). But this was not entirely uncontested; as early as 1707 *The Pulpit Fool* versed:

> At first, He that extempore will Preach
> Is a bold fool—and what can blockheads teach?
> All Serious Preaching must come from the heart
> When they are fools that think not—yet exhort
> Words spoke at random, have not half the grace
> As a word ranked in its proper place.
>
> (*Pulpit Fool*: 6)

The issue of how to preach to the ill-educated preoccupied preachers; Tillotson was said to read his sermons to an illiterate old woman who worked in his house to see if they would make sense to her (Campbell: 304–5). John Wesley even advised a preacher to listen to the women in Billingsgate market to learn how to be more direct in his sermons, and believed that preaching was much better than theology for instructing the poor (Elliott-Binns: 369; Heitzenrater 1999: 94). Certainly it was by no means a foregone conclusion that a congregation of labouring people would 'prefer a sermon from a poor illiterate stroller, who perhaps, a few days ago threw away his awls' (*Fashionable Preacher*: 13).

Guidance on preaching was available throughout the eighteenth century from sources such as Richard Baxter's *The Reformed Pastor* (1656), Swift and Burnet's books, and, in particular, John Wesley's *Directions Concerning Pronunciation and Gesture* (1749) which became the Methodists' rhetorical bible. But during the nineteenth century sermon preparation became an element in clerical training and in the curriculum of theological colleges, which assumed the role that university sermons had in the eighteenth century of modelling preaching styles.

The greatest preachers of the day were a phenomenon. When Archbishop Dawes of York visited Leeds in 1719 'not only the church galleries were throng crowded with people, but even the little windows facing the pulpit a little below the high roof' (Oates: 73). George Whitefield was said to have driven fifteen people mad during his preaching in London in 1736 and in consequence his sensational sermons created a huge demand for transcripts (Edwards: 432). David Garrick, the actor-manager, attended Monkswell Street Meeting house in the 1780s to learn from the remarkable performances of James Fordyce (*Pulpit Elocution:* 38); and he envied the amplification of Whitefield. Such preaching could be spellbinding: Lord Chesterfield once heard Whitefield preach at Lady Huntingdon's chapel, where he spoke on the blind beggar who staggered near the precipice of a cliff and, as Whitefield acted out the event, Chesterfield shouted 'Good God he is gone!' and fell forward himself (Downey: 171).

A reputation as a preacher became important for many clergy. John Wesley found that many pulpits that had been closed to him early in his career were open to him once he had achieved a degree of celebrity in preaching (*Pulpit Elocution*: 53). But there remained prejudices against over-theatrical performances: Adam Clarke advised against making jokes, adopting odd postures and such ploys as waving a handkerchief (A. Clarke: 16–17). The danger was, as Richard Graves indicated in *The Spiritual Quixote,* that a congregation might convert when they heard a dazzling performance but relapse when the words were forgotten (Lessenich: 125). Reputation for dramatics was not the only eminence that preachers obtained: John Jago, perpetual curate of Helston and Wendron in Cornwall, gained such a reputation as a funeral preacher that he delivered and recorded fifteen, including discourses on child deaths and suicide, in the first decade of the eighteenth century (Jago).

Such celebrated preachers drew historically large audiences, occasionally dwarfing even those that came to Spurgeon's sermons in the mid-nineteenth century. Whitefield, preaching in Hyde Park in 1737, drew a crowd of 80,000 and it was said to be the largest gathering in the country since the battles of the Civil War, and a year later in Boston, Massachusetts, he preached to 20,000, then the largest gathering in North America (Edwards: 433).

Preaching—especially to large audiences outside buildings—took enormous vocal power. Benjamin Franklin did not believe that Whitefield could project his voice to 20,000 until he saw it for himself (Downey: 174). In the mid-eighteenth century David Lloyd of Llwynrhydowen in Cardiganshire was said to be able to be heard up to a mile from where he preached, such was the power of his voice (Evans: xviii). John Wesley preached to a crowd of 60,000 in the natural hollow at the base of a hill in Leeds in 1755. But one historian has doubted his claim that he could be heard at a distance of 140 yards, which would mean he could be heard by 134,000 people. Wesley recognized that vocal power and acoustics were vital, checking whether he could be heard at the back of a church and deliberately deciding where to aim his voice (Heitzenrater 1999: 92).

The Material Culture of the Sermon

The dominance of preaching in British culture and public life was expressed in a vibrant material culture. Its clearest expressions were in architecture and publishing. From the late seventeenth century the 'auditory church' came to dominate Britain; whether in temple form, baroque, palladian, eighteenth-century gothic, or circular, the pulpit dominated them. Such churches and chapels were designed principally as the settings for sermons, with single chamber buildings which gave equal, and often greater, attention to the pulpit than to the altar. Wren's St James's Piccadilly (1684) became the model for such churches in London and was emulated by many others, such as Gibbs's St Martin in the Fields (1726). Wren made careful calculations of acoustics from the pulpits of his churches and architects regarded the pulpit as a central feature of the architecture of the buildings they designed (Friedman: 99). In New England St Michael's Marblehead, Massachusetts (1714), introduced this style to North America. Such churches contained elevated pulpits from which preachers could comfortably address pews and galleries. In All Saints, Newcastle (1786) this arrangement was emphasized by pews that extended radially from the pulpit. Three-decker pulpits, with parson's pew, reading desk and pulpit extending vertically, lifted the sermon physically as well as liturgically. Such pulpits remained popular into the nineteenth century with an excellent example at St Mary, Bylaugh, Norfolk built by Sir John Lombe in 1801. In some churches the pulpit was placed on wheels so it could be trundled into position for the sermon, though in Shrewsbury hospital chapel it was placed in a different position every three months so different parts of the congregation in turn were closest to the preacher (Friedman: 102). The importance of the pulpit in the churches of this period has been thoroughly considered by historians (Addleshaw and Etchells; B. F. L. Clarke). Testers, sounding boards, lecterns, and cushions were all part of these pulpit-focused churches. The need for effective acoustics for the sermon to be preached was also important for church builders (Gibson 2001: 173).

But some variations in practice have not yet been fully considered. For example, while many Anglican churches had both a reading pew and a pulpit, in Welsh Nonconformity there were chapels in which there were two pulpits, one for exhorters and witnesses and one reserved for the sole use of the ordained clergy (Davies: 6). In short, the sermon shaped the architecture of churches across Britain throughout the period under review. Parson James Woodforde even moved his pulpit in 1775 so that it had greater prominence (Jacob: 257). The placing of the pulpit was a central concern in the arrangement of churches; at St Peter's Leeds in 1714 it was moved twice during the renovation (Oates: 41).

In London in the second half of the eighteenth century preaching was such a successful activity that builders began to construct proprietary chapels on a speculative basis. John Trusler, a popular preacher, was offered an appointment at such a chapel in Bloomsbury on the basis of £100 salary or buying the lease and taking a percentage of the income in preaching fees, with the option to buy the chapel in the future (Trusler: 17).

By the mid-nineteenth century, population growth was such that even large auditory churches could not accommodate the most fashionable preachers of the day. Consequently, theatres entered the market as preaching venues. By 1856, Charles Spurgeon complemented the use of Exeter Hall, which only accommodated 5,000, with hiring the Surrey Gardens music hall, which could hold over 10,000 people. Seven years earlier seventy people were killed in a Glasgow theatre, which had been rented by a preacher, when a fire broke out ('Preachers and Preaching': 690). Nevertheless there were some, like Pusey, who regarded the use of theatres for preaching with horror (Heeney: 38). Outdoor pulpits clearly had a long heritage in Britain, going back to St Paul's and other preaching crosses when they were often used as a means of disseminating officially sanctioned sermons. They underwent a revival in the nineteenth century, both in Britain and North America, and were usually attached to a church and accessed from the interior. They enabled a preacher to reach many more people than the church alone could accommodate, but required a much stronger voice. In 1833 George Cruikshank sketched 'St Swithin's chapel', a parody of a preacher addressing a congregation in Clerkenwell in the rain which was obscured by massed umbrellas. The vogue for outdoor pulpits in London quickly proved to be impractical for all but the shortest sermons. Others found the familiarity, function or status of the pulpit important. John Wesley may have preached in fields and on top of tombs in graveyards but more often he spoke from a portable pulpit made of wood and canvas, suggesting that he saw the need to appear to speak from a pulpit (Heitzenrater 1999: 92). In the nineteenth century Jonathan Titcomb, incumbent of Barnwell, also made a folding iron pulpit for outdoor use when he preached to large numbers in his fast-growing parish (Prior).

The greatest contribution the sermon made to material culture in this period was in printing. Religion outsold all other genres in the eighteenth century and remained a central plank of the printing industry well into the nineteenth. Consequently 'sermon paper' was the name given to foolscap quarto writing paper because of its widespread use for sermons. The Society for Promoting Christian Knowledge (SPCK) became a major publisher in the eighteenth century because of widespread demand for books of sermons and other devotional works. There were natural peaks in sales, especially in the first two and last decades of the eighteenth century (Feather: 35). But events could lead to a surge in demand for sermons. When an earthquake hit London in 1750 there was a strong run on sales of religious tracts and sermons (van Eijnatten: 358). On 6 February 1756, the day appointed for the sermons and prayers on the Lisbon earthquake, Henry Stebbing wrote that 'Never were the churches so thronged as they were... in this city nor more serious and devout attention paid to the duty of the day' (Stebbing 1756). And sales of the sermons were strong. Nevertheless there were also times of glut, as seen in Fielding's *Joseph Andrews,* published in 1742, when a bookseller claimed he could not sell sermons unless they were fashionable items preached on popular occasions such as 30 January.

In general booksellers regarded sermons—both new and second-hand—as a staple of their trade, and this was in part due to the ubiquity of demand. Johnson said they were as likely to be read in the coffee house and inn as the country house library (Wickham Legg: 5). Boswell regarded a library as 'very imperfect' if it did not have a stock of sermons (Elliott-Binns: 400). He meant, of course, the gentleman's or country house library; but sermons also formed the core of parish libraries and were an important constituent of circulating and subscription libraries. With the growth of provincial printers booksellers' early profits were often dependent on the publication and sale of sermons (Ferdinand: 434). For some consumers there was almost a bewildering array of sermons on offer; the *Monthly Review* in the mid-eighteenth century struggled to keep up with reviews of them (Forster: 634). By 1861, when excise duty on paper was removed, there was a boom in the sales of all printed material, sermons included. Consequently sermons could be printed more cheaply in different forms including in large print editions for those with poor eyesight.

Some preachers made considerable amounts of money from their work; Laurence Sterne made more from his sermons than from *Tristram Shandy* and boasted of his earnings (Downey: 104; Raven: 316). Naturally therefore the copyright in sermons was valuable. Archbishop John Tillotson's widow sold the rights to print her husband's sermons for £2,500 in 1695, a record sum which established Tillotson as the most prolifically published preacher of the century. One hundred and sixty items of Tillotson were printed, some with print runs of over 2,000 copies, and by 1719 the copyright was worth £2,000 (Dixon: 154–69). The market for his work extended to translations into Welsh and Irish. As late as 1716 shares in the copyright of Donne's sermons were sold; and after his death Bishop Sherlock's widow raised money by selling the remaining stock of her husband's sermons (Belanger: 281; Blagden: 248). Preachers' stock could rise with their reputations: Hugh Blair sold the copyright of his first volume of sermons for fifty pounds in 1777, but his reputation became such that his last volume sold for seven hundred pounds in 1794 (Trusler: 225). Publishers knew their market well and there is evidence that some kept prices of sermons low to create high-volume sales (Raven: 301). But for the most popular preachers high-volume sales were assured, especially when directed at both the British and American markets. The first volume of Charles Spurgeon's sermons in the USA in 1857 sold 15,000 copies and sales of later sermons rose from 20,000 to half a million (Spurgeon 1857: 2:vii, 19:11). By 1860 the popularity of Spurgeon's sermons in the USA was such that he had difficulty defending his copyright and had to make public statements of who his official publisher was, so widely were they pirated (Spurgeon 1860: vii–viii). Classic sermons were frequently reprinted; the 'Pocmanty Sermon' by Mr Row in 1638 was reprinted in Scotland well into the eighteenth century. Demand was not limited to the English language; there were frequent requests for sermons in Welsh in Wales and also from the settlers in the American colonies (Clement). Later in the eighteenth and nineteenth centuries the diversification of the printed sermon noted earlier led to publications for particular social groups including, for example, for women, children, townspeople and countryfolk. Unsurprisingly in the second half of the eighteenth century, Rivingtons abandoned their publication of theology in favour of popular sermons (Raven: 272). Some clergy became prolific authors: the unorthodox Anglican parson Charles Voysey sold more than one and a quarter million copies of his sermons, published in *The Sling and the Stone* series in just a few years after 1865 (Reynolds).

Charitable printers produced cheap sermons which they sold for the benefit of the poor. Henry Hills, a Blackfriars printer, sold many of these, often for a few pennies, though he had to constrain them into sixteen pages, so the font often became progressively smaller in order to accommodate lengthy sermons. Others were similarly motivated: Edmund Pyle, Bishop Benjamin Hoadly's chaplain, wrote in 1753 that Hoadly 'is going to put forth a volume or two of sermons...I believe Mr Knapton must pay well for the copy, for 'tis certain they will sell fast enough. And I believe that the money will be given in charity to some grandchildren of Bishop Burnet, who...are left in distress' (Hartshorne: 191). Single works controlled the popular end of the market, while volumes of collected sermons, such as the Boyle lectures or Rolls Chapel sermons, were 'top end' items (Rivers: 592–93). There were some who straddled both poles: Spurgeon, who issued his sermons in the 'penny pulpit' series, also produced a sixty-three volume complete collection of his 3,600 sermons (Francis: 274).

The publication of sermons was especially important to Dissenters. In John Cooke's *The Preacher's Assistant* of 1783, 81 per cent of the sermons he listed were Anglican and 19 per cent were from Dissenters (Rivers: 591). This was a disproportionate representation of Dissent, and suggested perhaps that printed sermons were a means of maintaining the identity of Dissent in a religious world dominated by the Church of England. By distributing sermons across the country, Dissenters had physical confirmation that they were not alone in their parishes facing the dominance of the Anglicans. Moreover sermons were a critical ingredient in Dissenting worship.

For the clergy, preaching was complemented by guides to sermon writing. Swift, Doddridge and others published guides for young clergy on how to develop their skills in the pulpit. Sampson Letsom's *Index to the Sermons Published Since the Restoration* was published in 1734 as a way of helping clergy find inspiration from other sermons. It supplied the texts for 24,295 sermons published since the Reformation; Thomas Sharp used his copy to develop a database of sermons, interleaving his copy of Letsome with annotations. Similarly William Beveridge in 1710 published *Thesaurus Theologicus* in four volumes which aimed to help clergy compose sermons by providing outlines for the preacher to flesh out. In 1802 Charles Simeon published *Helps to Composition* with 600 sermon outlines for clergy to 'fill in'; it included a 200-page guide to preaching. It went through three editions in England before 1810 and was published in Philadelphia in that year. In 1832 Simeon's *Horae Homiletica*, outlines from all sixty-six books of the Bible, was written with the intention of promoting Evangelical sermons in parishes up and down the land. William Enfield's *The Preacher's Directory; Or a Series of Subjects Proper for Public Discourses* (1771) provided Dissenting ministers with 'assistance in the choice of subjects and texts' (Deconinck-Brossard). Such guides also encompassed the style and demeanour required when preaching: Adam Clarke's *A Letter to a Methodist Preacher on His Entrance into the Work of the Ministry* of 1800 included a section entitled 'Concerning your behaviour in the Pulpit' (Clarke: 16–24). They institutionalized the gradual changes in preaching style during the century, including that of the Evangelical movement, and spread the fashions begun by Whitefield and Wesley.

Equally useful for the laity were the published guides to where and when to hear preachers. John Patterson's *Pietas Londiniensis* (1714) gave details of the sermons delivered each Sunday and weekday in the London churches. So did John Stowe's *Survey of London* (1722) which included the dates of special sermons at each church and also of monthly preaching in preparation for a subsequent service of Holy Communion. *Pulpit Elocution* (1782) was a guide to the most fashionable preachers in London, with gossipy snippets about each and a description of their strengths and weaknesses in the pulpit. Guides to preaching indicated the sophistication and differentiated nature of the 'consumption' of sermons by their audiences.

A key issue is the degree to which printed sermons resembled the text delivered in the pulpit. Clergy were sometimes accused of amending their sermons between the pulpit and the printer—among them Benjamin Hoadly (Gibson: 2004: 155–6). Some made no bones about it: John Wesley certainly published sermons which bore little or no resemblance to those he delivered, whereas George Whitefield was furious when a printer mangled one of his so that it was not identical to the original (Whitefield, 3: 406–7). Sermons could of course become 'mummies', lifeless carcasses of the original without enlivening intonation and gesture, or the excitement of the congregation (Elliott-Binns: 367). But there were clergy such as Thomas Sherlock who made few, if any, changes to the sermons they had preached when preparing them for publication (Sherlock). Spurgeon made clear that his sermons were transcribed from the pulpit and the publications were the work of 'a very busy man' and consequently he was 'frequently unable so much as to glance at the proof-sheets' so errors inevitably crept in (Spurgeon 1857 3:v).

Starting with John Trusler, a clerical publisher in the 1770s, there was a growing trade in the sale to clergy of imitation or faux manuscript sermons, with the intention that a preacher would pass them off as his own. Trusler was described:

> He grinds divinity of other days
> Down into modern use; transforms old print
> To zig-zag manuscript, and cheats the eyes
> Of gall'ry critics by a thousand arts.
>
> (Downey: 8)

Augustus Toplady was offered a set of sermons by a bookseller and when he sternly rejected the offer was surprised to be told that he had sold them to more than one bishop. And in 1802 the trade in sermons was managed circumspectly with advertisements in the *Courier* in Latin (Johns: 202–3).

By 1869 the periodical *St Pauls* devoted an article to the sermon trade. At this time the usual cost of such a sermon was 1/3d; at the rate of two a Sunday this amounted to £6/10/- for a year's supply. Vendors promised that special care was taken 'to prevent their being detected' and that no duplicates were supplied 'to preclude the possibility of the same sermons being preached in neighbouring parishes', and there was a strict ban on lending the items to others. *St Pauls* estimated that there were about a dozen dealers in the trade, and if each had fifty clients, about 1,200 sermons a Sunday were supplied (Littlewood: 594–8). By the end of the nineteenth century the trade in sermons had grown significantly. B. G. Johns wrote that the trade was highly profitable with 'the cool impudence of the vendors...only exceeded by the transparent folly of the clerical customers'; the sermons he claimed were worthless. Johns identified the source of the trade in the absence of clerical training in preaching and the need for young clergy to build up a stock of sermons quickly. He outlined the 'incredible extent' of the trade as contained in advertisements. Some newspaper announcements offered the sermons only to the clergy, some by regular subscription, others in whole sets. There were offers of sermon-writing services with bespoke items costing up to a guinea and guaranteed to be unpreached. Vendors claimed that their sermons were written by distinguished clergy, even college fellows and prize winners. In some cases executors sold a deceased parson's manuscript sermons, in one case offering 600 for sale, and in another case offering them to publishers. Some advertisements included the theological 'tone' of the sermons, such as 'moderately high church' and 'sound evangelical' in content (Johns: 197–207).

Passing off other people's sermons as one's own always presented the opportunity for embarrassment: the Revd Jack Russell once preached a sermon at a funeral written by the deceased, and Spurgeon preached a sermon which referred to powdered hair, something long forgotten in the mid-nineteenth century (Turner: 186; 'Preachers and Preaching': 692). Charles Girdlestone, a prolific Victorian Anglican preacher, once heard one of his sermons read by another parson as his own (Matthew).

The publication of sermons was not the only part of the economy dependent on preaching. Sermons spawned a separate culture of accessories and accoutrement. There were lavender preaching gloves worn or carried at formal events, last seen in the middle of the nineteenth century (Oman: 50), and candles were increasingly needed for lighting churches during afternoon or evening sermons (Barry and Morgan: 27). Churches also installed hour glasses to enable the preacher and his congregation to keep track of time. Printed sermons were integrated into the growing culture of coffee houses, being borrowed, sold and read in them (Suarez: 21). The emergence of booksellers was often dependent on the sales of sermons; one in 1734 admitted that they made up three quarters of his sales (Briggs: 400). Some pulpit products became highly specialized: in 1853 Hodson, a leading bookseller, advertised cases made of black roan for protecting paper sermons. In addition printers benefited from the production of invitation cards for public and charity sermons. Medals were also struck, such as those to commemorate Henry Sacheverell's sermon in 1709, to mark the funeral sermons for Queen Mary II in 1694, and to celebrate John Wesley's and George Whitefield's preaching. There were even plaster and china plaques such as that produced to commemorate Orator Henley's sermons around 1734. By the nineteenth century the most popular china figures of John Wesley showed him preaching or in a pulpit.

Sermons were also an important means of raising money in this period. A sermon would often be the occasion of a collection for a particular cause or charity. James Folds of Bolton sometimes preached in aid of the local farmers' society (Greenhalgh: 37–47) and the charity school movement in the eighteenth century was heavily dependent on sermons for fund raising (Lowther Clarke: 69). Fashionable London preachers were in demand for their fund raising skills. In 1782 it was said that when Colin Milne at St Sepulchre's Snow Hill was asked to preach to raise funds 'a handsome collection was made and the subscription (for the Humane Soc) was enlarged' and that 'people, when they go elsewhere to be entertained must pay' (*Pulpit Elocution*: 13, 16). John Trusler, another popular London preacher, claimed to have received two or three invitations to preach each week and to have given sermons in most London churches. But such invitations were sometimes mischievous as the etiquette was that a refusal to preach should be accompanied with a donation to the cause, so that issuing numerous invitations was itself a means of raising money (Trusler: 33–6). In some cases tickets to attend a public sermon would be sold in aid of a charity and, when aristocrats attended, they often paid high prices for the best seats. The abolition of slavery and other movements owed considerable income to the sale of sermons. Such campaigns even extended to suppression of duelling, which was the subject of a sermon by Thomas Jones before Cambridge University in December 1791.

It is perhaps inevitable that the material culture of sermons gave rise to a healthy stream of parodies and satires. In 1720 Thomas Browne's *Works* included a satire on a Quaker sermon, including a woodcut of a Quaker meeting. In 1729 Jacob Gingle published a poetic satire on Joseph Beatty's sermon before the University of Oxford, called *The Oxford Sermon Versified*; it quickly ran to three editions. The libertine John Hall-Stevenson published political attacks in verse which he dressed up as sermons entitled *A Pastoral Cordial, or, an Anodyne Sermon* (1763) and a year later *A Pastoral Puke. A Second Sermon Preached before the People called Whigs*. The clergy as a whole were made the object of the anonymous *Visitation Sermon, A Satire*, published in 1788 in Bristol.

By far the most potent satires were images of sermons. Hogarth's *Sleeping Congregation* of 1736 is perhaps the best-known image of the sermon in this period along with *Credulity, Superstition and Fanaticism* (1762), which seem to make opposing fun of the pulpit occupants. Much more entertaining is *Preaching Portraits* by Woodward and Cruikshank (1796) in which a series of twelve caricatures of preachers say such phrases as 'I shall divide my discourse my patient brethren into sixty three parts, all of which I shall touch upon in the course of the evening'; 'I am sent to comfort you; you'll all go to the devil' and 'like the voice of a shrill trumpet I shall tell you what I think of you'. This was one of many such books of caricatures 'lent out for the evening'. The height of such satires was

Pulpit Extravaganzas, published by William Holland in October 1789. Across three pages twelve clergy are depicted each with the parish clerk sitting below the pulpit at the reading desk. As each parson speaks the clerk responds with an expression or action which perhaps mirrors those of the congregation. So as one parson says 'I could never be tired of this subject' the clerk below yawns widely; as another preacher says 'what a heavenly countenance' the parish clerk below is picking his nose; as a third says 'I shall now draw to a conclusion' the clerk rubs his hands in relief and as a fourth says 'fly from those baleful schools of fanaticism that spring up like mushrooms in every quarter of this city' the clerk looks at his watch.

Methodists and Evangelicals were especially likely to be lampooned, with Cruikshanks's *The Field Preacher* of 1796 showing a shabby youth addressing 'an unpolite declamation' to 'an unpolite congregation'. In *The Mischief of Methodism* by Woodward *c*.1790 a Methodist preacher tells a parson how all the tradesmen neglect their businesses to hear his sermons; to which the parson replies that in his parish 'everyone minds their business'. *The Clerical Manoeuver, or the Way to Finish a Charity Sermon* by William of 1815 showed how evident it was that charity sermons were becoming a vehicle for fund-raising with an embarrassed congregation grudgingly giving funds at the end of a sermon as requested by the preacher.

Even the style of printing of a sermon was a point of ridicule. In 1890, a Reverend Omnia Omnibus published *The Extension of the Indefinite. A Sermon of the Times* at Bittercider Press, Nobridge by Tootoo, Utter & Moonshine Publishers. Omnibus was claimed to be rector of the Church of St Latitudinarius, Broadwalk, Beamends, Fellow of the Antediluvian Abrogation Society, and author of *An Inquiry into the Limitations of Lunacy*. The sermon included a request from his parishioners to publish the discourse (the names of the parishioners are M. T. Sounding, T. Bell Brass, and A. Tinkling Cymbal). An amusing April Fools' joke, but clearly written by someone who had studied the format employed by authors and printers for a published sermon.

Perhaps these parodies and satires summed up the essential ambivalence towards the sermon. Powerful and dominant as it was, and perhaps because of this, it attracted the cynical and sardonic. The arch-cynic Horace Walpole wrote parodies and mock sermons for friends and sent Lady Hervey 'a tract to laugh at sermons' and regarded sermons as 'the dullest of all things'. But he also attended sermons regularly, bought them for his library and sent copies of published sermons to his friends (Lewis 31:113–14, 423, 34:115).

Conclusion

The ubiquity of the sermon between 1689 and 1901 is an aspect of contemporary experience that has been largely forgotten. Yet if a single cultural experience can be said to have been shared by all classes and conditions of people in Britain and throughout her empire it was that of sitting below a pulpit hearing a sermon. The conversations and debates, other than in print, that they engendered have, of course, been lost like most such experiences. In comparison with politics, economics, warfare, crime, and perhaps even sex, sermons probably occupied more of the attention of people.

This raises the question of the degree to which Britain in this period can be said to be a secular society. The saturation of culture and popular experience with preaching created an ambient focus on faith and belief that are quite at odds with the claims to secularization. Whether bought from a bookshop, borrowed from a coffeehouse or a library, or heard in church, sermons were part of a persistent voice of religion in the streets, houses and ears of the period. Clearly secularization is not the same as the decline of faith, or worship, or even religious culture. The growing challenge to the meta-narrative of secularization in the eighteenth and nineteenth centuries is certainly supported by the evidence from the demand, consumption, and culture of sermons. This theme is considered in more detail in the concluding chapter 'Sermon Studies: Major Issues and Future Directions'.

Before the dominance of novels, sermons were the best-selling literature and provided the literary and intellectual enjoyment and stimulation for most readers. Preaching even invented the serial form, later adopted by the novel. Serial sermons were common in the eighteenth century, often written to be preached, or read, in a cycle in the run-up to major festivals such as in Lent. They were also sold to be read in families and formed a record of particular suites of preaching. The degree to which sermons contributed to the growth of literacy and a literate culture in the seventeenth and eighteenth centuries is of course also significant. Yet what cannot be overlooked is the overwhelming numerical predominance of the spoken sermon. Oracy rarely finds adequate representation compared with diaries, letters, and the written record. But if there is an obligation on scholars arising from this volume it is to remember that some of the commonest words heard collectively by most people in this period were those of the sermon.

Acknowledgements

I am grateful to Dr Bob Tennant for his advice and guidance on sections of 'Quantifying the Sermon'.

References

Abbey, C. J., and Overton, J. H. (1887). *The English Church in the Eighteenth Century*. London: Longman & Green.
Abney. Sermon summaries. Yale University, Beinecke Library, Osborn c516.
Addleshaw, G. W. O., and Etchells, F. (1958). *The Architectural Setting of Anglican Worship*. London: Faber.
Baker, W. J. (1981). *Beyond Port and Prejudice*. Orono: University of Maine Press.
Baldwin Brown, J. (1877). 'Is the Pulpit Losing its Power?'. *The Living Age* 133: 304–13.
Barry, J., and Morgan, K. (eds.) (1994). *Reformation and Revival in Eighteenth Century Bristol*. Stroud: Bristol Record Society.

Beinecke Sermons. Yale University, Beinecke Library collections of manuscript sermons in: c550, c410, c420, c104, c88, c247, c250, c264.
Belanger, T. (1975). 'Booksellers' Trade Sales 1718-1768'. *The Library,* 5th Series, 30-4: 281-302.
Bennett, G. V. (1986). 'University, Society and Church 1688-1714', in L. S. Sutherland and L. G. Mitchell (eds.), *The History of the University of Oxford,* 5: *The Eighteenth Century.* Oxford: Oxford University Press, 99-128.
Blagden, C. (1951). 'Booksellers' Trade Sales 1718-1768'. *The Library,* 5th Series, 5: 243-57.
Brewer, S. (ed.) (1995). *The Early Letters of Bishop Richard Hurd 1739-1762.* Woodbridge: Boydell Press.
Briggs, A. (2009). 'The Longmans and the Book Trade, c 1730-1830', in M. Suarez and M. L. Turner (eds.), *The Cambridge History of the Book in Britain,* 5: *1695-1830.* Cambridge: Cambridge University Press, 398-407.
Brown, D. (1958). 'The Text of John Tillotson's Sermons'. *The Library,* 5th Series, 13: 18-36.
Campbell, G. (1807). *Lectures on Systematic Theology and Pulpit Eloquence.* London: Cadel & Davis.
Carpenter, S. C. (1959). *Eighteenth Century Church and People.* London: John Murray.
Cholmondley MS, Cambridge University Library Cholmondley MS 67/9.
Clarke, A. (1800). *A Letter to a Methodist Preacher on His Entrance into the Work of the Ministry...* London: Longman, Brown, Green.
Clarke, B. F. L. (1963). *The Building of the Eighteenth Century Church.* London: SPCK.
Claydon, T. (2000). 'The Sermon, the "Public Sphere" and the Political Culture of Late Seventeenth-Century England', in L. A. Ferrell and P. McCullough (eds.), *The English Sermon Revised: Religion, Literature and History 1600-1750.* Manchester: Manchester University Press, 208-35.
Clement, M. (1973). *Correspondence and Records of the SPG Relating to Wales, 1701-1750.* Cardiff: University of Wales Press.
Clubbe, J. (1770). *Miscellaneous Tracts of the Revd John Clubbe, Rector of Whatfield.* Ipswich: J. Shave.
Cooke, J. (1783). *The Preacher's Assistant.* Oxford: printed for the editor.
Coombs, H., and Coombs, P. (eds.) (1984). *The Journal of a Somerset Rector 1803-1834.* Oxford: Oxford University Press.
Davies, J. D. (1996). *The Reverend Peter Williams, 1722-1796.* Carmarthen: Carmarthenshire County Council.
Deconinck-Brossard, F. (2009). 'The Art of Preaching', in J. van Eijnatten (ed.), *Preaching, Sermons and Cultural Change in the Long Eighteenth Century.* Leiden: Brill, 95-133.
Ditchfield, P. H. (1908). *The Old-Time Parson.* London: Methuen.
Dixon, R. (2007). 'The Publishing of John Tillotson's Collected Works, 1695-1757'. *The Library,* 7th Series, 8-2: 154-81.
Downey, J. (1969). *The Eighteenth Century Pulpit.* Oxford: Clarendon Press.
Edwards, O. C. (2004). *A History of Preaching.* Nashville: Abingdon Press.
Eijnatten, J. van (2009). 'Getting the Message: Towards a Cultural History of the Sermon', in J. van Eijnatten (ed.), *Preaching, Sermons and Cultural Change in the Long Eighteenth Century.* Leiden: Brill, 343-89.
Elliott-Binns, L. E. (1953). *The Early Evangelicals.* London: Lutterworth Press.
Ellman, E. B. (1912). *Recollections of a Sussex Parson.* London: Skeffingtons.
Ellsworth, L. E. (1982). *Charles Lowder and the Ritualist Movement.* London: Darton, Longman and Todd.
'English Pulpit' (1874). *The Living Age* 120: 67-86.

Essay on Preaching; Wherein is Considered The Expediency of Using or of Laying Aside A Written Preparation for the Pulpit. (1785). Leicester: J. Gregory.

Evans, G. E. (1908). *Lloyd Letters (1754–1796) Being Extant Letters of David Lloyd, Minister of Llwynrhydowen; Posthumous Lloyd, His Brother and Charles Lloyd, His son…* Aberystwyth: William Jones.

Fairford. Sermons. Yale University, Beinecke Library, Osborn c414.

Farooq, J. (2006). 'The Politicising Influence of Print: The Responses of Hearers and Readers to the Sermons of Gilbert Burnet and Henry Sacheverell', in G. Baker and A. McGruer (eds.), *Readers, Audiences and Coteries in Early Modern England*. Newcastle: Cambridge Scholars Press, 28–47.

Fashionable Preacher; or Modern Pulpit Eloquence Displayed. (1792). London: Thomson and Drury.

Feather, J. (1986). 'British Publishing in the Eighteenth Century: a Preliminary Subject Analysis'. *The Library*, 6th Series, 8: 32–46.

Ferdinand, C. Y. (2009). 'Newspapers and the Sale of Books in the Provinces', in M. Suarez and M. L. Turner (eds.), *The Cambridge History of the Book in Britain*, 5: *1695–1830*. Cambridge: Cambridge University Press, 434–47.

Forster, A. (2009). 'Book Reviewing', in M. Suarez and M. L. Turner (eds.), *The Cambridge History of the Book in Britain*, 5: *1695–1830*. Cambridge: Cambridge University Press, 628–41.

Francis, K. (2010). 'Nineteenth Century British Sermons on Evolution and the *Origin of Species…*', in R. H. Ellison (ed.), *A New History of the Sermon: The Nineteenth Century*. Leiden: Brill, 269–309.

Friedman, T. (2011). *The Eighteenth Century Church in Britain*. London: Yale University Press.

Gibson, W. (2001). *The Church of England 1688–1832: Unity and Accord*. London: Routledge.

—— (2004). *Benjamin Hoadly 1676–1761, Enlightenment Prelate*. Cambridge: James Clark & Co.

Green, I. (2000). *Print and Protestantism in Early Modern England*. Oxford: Oxford University Press.

Greenhalgh, J. D. (1879). *The Sayings and Doings of The Revd James Folds, Otherwise Parson Folds, Lecturer of Bolton Parish Church 1755–1820*. Bolton: G. Winterburns.

Hartshorne, A. (ed.) (1905). *The Memoirs of a Royal Chaplain 1729–1763*. London: John Lane.

Hebert, A. G. (1961). *Liturgy and Society*. London: Faber and Faber.

Heeney, B. (1976). *A Different Kind of Gentleman: Parish Clergy and Professional Men in Early and Mid-Victorian England*. Hampden, CT: Archon Books.

Heitzenrater, R. (1970). 'John Wesley's Early Sermons'. *Proceedings of the Wesley Historical Society* 37: 110–28.

—— (1999). 'John Wesley's Principles and Practice of Preaching'. *Methodist History* 37-2: 89–106.

Jacob, W. (2007). *The Clerical Profession in the Long Eighteenth Century, 1680–1840*. Oxford: Oxford University Press.

Jago, John. Sermons. Yale University Beinecke Library, Osborn b246.

Jenkins, A. P. (ed.) (1991). *The Correspondence of Bishop Secker*. Oxford: Oxfordshire Record Society.

Johns, B. G. (1892). 'The Traffic in Sermons'. *The Nineteenth Century* 31: 197–207.

Ken, Thomas. (1695). Undated letter. Yale University, Beinecke Library, Osborn c183.

Lessenich, R. P. (1972). *Elements of Pulpit Oratory in Eighteenth Century England (1660–1800)*. Vienna: Bohlau Verlag.
Letsome, J. (1753). *The Preacher's Assistant*. London: printed for the author.
Lewis, W. S., et al. (1961–5). *The Yale Edition of Horace Walpole's Correspondence*. New Haven, CT: Yale University Press.
Liddon, H. P. (1890). *Passiontide Sermons*. London: Longmans, Green.
Littlewood, H. (1869). 'Sermon Trade'. *St Pauls* 3: 594–8.
Lose, D. J. (2003). *Confessing Jesus Christ: Preaching in a Postmodern World*. Grand Rapids, MI: William B. Eerdmans.
Lowther Clarke, W. K. (1945). *Eighteenth Century Piety*. London: SPCK.
McCullough, P., Adlington, H., and Rhatigan, E. (eds.) (2011). *The Oxford Handbook of the Early Modern Sermon*. Oxford: Oxford University Press.
Marshall, M. (2009). *Church Life in Hereford and Oxford, A Study of Two Sees 1660–1760*. Lancaster: Carnegie.
Matthew, H. C. G. (2004). 'Charles Girdlestone 1797–1881', *Oxford Dictionary of National Biography*, Oxford: Oxford University Press.
Mitchell, W. F. (1932). *English Pulpit Oratory from Andrewes to Tillotson, a Study of its Literary Aspects*. London: SPCK.
Notes and Queries (30 September 1871): 232.
Oakes, J. (1689). *The Last Sermon and Sayings of that Most Pious and Reverend Divine, Mr John Oakes, Minister of the Gospel in the City of London,...* London: J. Conyers.
Oates, J. (2006). *The Memoranda Book of John Lucas, 1712–1750*. Leeds: Thoresby Society.
Oman, C. (1941). *Memories of Victorian Oxford*. London: Methuen.
Osborn. Anonymous Sermons. Yale University Beinecke Library, Osborn c652.
Patterson, J. (1714). *Pietas Londiniensis, or the Present State of London*. London: Joseph Downing.
Pope, A. (1714). *The Rape of the Lock*. London: Bernard Lintott.
Poster, C. (2010). 'Richard Whately and the Didactic Sermon', in R. H. Ellison (ed.), *A New History of the Sermon: The Nineteenth Century*. Leiden: Brill, 59–115.
'Preachers and Preaching'. (1856). *Tait's Edinburgh Magazine*, New Series, 23: 689–93.
Prior, K. (2004). 'Jonathon Holt Titcomb 1819–1887', *Oxford Dictionary of National Biography*, Oxford: Oxford University Press.
Pruett, J. H. (1978). *The Parish Clergy Under the Later Stuarts, The Leicestershire Experience*. Urbana, IL: University of Illinois Press.
Pulpit Elocution: Or Characters and Principles of the Most Popular Preachers Of Each Denomination in the Metropolis and its Environs. (1782). London: J. Wade.
Pulpit-Fool. A Satyr. (1707). London: n. p.
Pulpit Orator, Being a New Selection of Eloquent Pulpit Discourses... (1804). Boston: Joseph Nancrede.
Quiller Couch, L. M. (1892). *Reminiscences of Oxford by Oxford Men, 1559–1850*. Oxford: Clarendon Press.
Raven, J. (2007). *The Business of Books, Booksellers and the English Book Trade 1450–1850*. London: Yale University Press.
Reynolds, K. (2004). 'Voyse, Charles (1828-1912)', *OD,NB*. Oxford: Oxford University Press.
Rivers, I. (2009). 'Religious Publishing', in M. Suarez and M. L. Turner (eds.), *The Cambridge History of the Book in Britain*, 5: 1695–1830. Cambridge: Cambridge University Press.

Robertson, F. W. (1859). *Expository Lectures on St. Paul's Epistles to the Corinthians*. London: Longman, Green.
Sacheverell, H. (1709). *The Perils of False Brethren*. London: Henry Clements.
Sherlock, T. Yale University, Lewis Walpole Library, Weston MSS vol 3, 24 July 1746.
Shevlin, E. F. (2010). *The History of the Book in the West*, 3: *1700–1800*. Farnham: Ashgate.
Snape, M. (2003). *The Church of England in Industrialising Society: The Lancashire Parish of Whalley in the 18th Century*. Woodbridge: Boydell and Brewer.
Spaeth, D. (2000). *The Church in an Age of Danger, Parsons and Parishioners 1660–1740*. Cambridge: Cambridge University Press.
Sprat, T. (1710). *A Discourse Made by the Ld Bishop of Rochester to the Clergy of His diocese…* London: Nutt.
Spurgeon, C. H. (1857). *Sermons of Rev. C. H. Spurgeon of London*. New York: Funk & Wagnalls Co.
—— (1860). *Sermons Preached and Revised by the Rev. C. H. Spurgeon*, Sixth Series. New York: Sheldon and Co.
Stebbing, H. (1755). Yale University, Lewis Walpole Library, Weston MSS vol 4, 19 March.
—— (1756). Yale University, Lewis Walpole Library, Weston MSS vol 4, 7 February.
Stone, M. (2008). *The Diary of John Longe, Vicar of Coddenham 1764–1832*. Woodbridge: Boydell Press.
Suarez, M. (2009). 'Introduction', in Suarez, M. and Turner, M. L. (eds.), *The Cambridge History of the Book in Britain*, 5: *1695–1830*. Cambridge: Cambridge University Press, 1–24.
Spaulding, J. G. (1996). *Pulpit Publications, 1660–1782*. New York: Norman Ross.
Stowe, J. (1722). *The Survey of London*. London: Churchill.
Swift, J. Yale University, Beinecke Library, Osborn c150 f78.
Sykes, N. (1926). *Edmund Gibson*. Oxford: Oxford University Press.
Tatler, 20 September 1709: 2.
Tennant, B. (2009). 'John Tillotson and the Voice of Anglicanism', in K. Duncan (ed.), *Religion in the Age of Reason*. New York: AMS Press, 40–65.
Tillotson, J. British Library, Add. MSS, 4236 f.134.
Times, 16 June 1873: 13.
Turner, E. S. (1998). *Unholy Pursuits*. Lewes: Book Guild.
Trusler, J. (1809). Yale University, Lewis Walpole Library, MS 71, Trusler memoir.
Two Letters to a Friend Containing Certain Considerations Relating to the Pulpit. (1692). London: Thomas Bassett.
Vaisey, D. (1994). *The Diary of Thomas Turner, 1754–1765*. London: CTR Publishing.
Whitefield, G. (1771). *The Works of the Reverend George Whitefield*. London: E. Dilly.
Wickham Legg, J. (1914). *English Church Life from the Reformation to the Tractarian Movement*. London: Longman.
Walsh, J. D., and Taylor, S. (eds.) (forthcoming). *The Papers of the Elland Society 1769–1828*. Woodbridge: Boydell and Brewer.
Wood, A. S. (1957). *Thomas Haweis 1734–1820*. London: SPCK.
—— (1960). *The Inextinguishable Blaze*. London: Paternoster.
Woodland, P. (2004). 'Alcock, Thomas (1709–1798)', *ODNB*. Oxford: Oxford University Press.

CHAPTER 2

SERMONS: THEMES AND DEVELOPMENTS

KEITH A. FRANCIS

Publishing Sermons

In 1860 the Brighton publisher Charles E. Verrall included the following advertisement in one of the books he published: 'Charles E. Verrall begs to call the attention of Ministers, Authors, and others, to the facilities *peculiar to his Establishment*; in which are united all the various departments necessary to the Reporting, Printing and Publishing of Sermons, Lectures, Addresses, Reports or works of a more extensive character.' Having touted the wide range of facilities his business could offer, Verrall drew attention to the quality of service provided: 'The whole is under the personal superintendence of the Proprietor; who is a *Practical* Printer, and *Professional* Reporter.' After explaining that his business could handle '*every description of Printing*', Verrall assured his clerical readers that 'Confidential and special arrangements [could be] made with Clergymen and others for *Reporting* Sermons, etc.' and that 'Accurate and verbatim Reports of Sermons, Lectures, Discussions, Speeches, etc., [could be] supplied for publication or private perusal' (Bidder 1860a: 160).

In an age when sermons are still preached regularly but preachers and preaching are not as important culturally as they once were, it is easy to forget how significant a social event the sermon once was. Leaving aside religious considerations, as noted in Chapter 1 the publishing of sermons was an important and lucrative business in the two hundred years before 1901. A portion of the offerings of John Murray, the publisher of several of Charles Darwin's important scientific works including *On the Origin of Species*, were published sermons, for example. In the case of Verrall, it was a business which required a proprietor to stay ahead of his competition in any way possible: promising clergy that the published version of their sermons would be an authentic copy of the sermon they had preached was one way to do this.

What Verrall promised was significant. Disputes could and did arise over the reporting of sermons or, more precisely, the accuracy of the published sermon as compared to the preached sermon. In 1829, a reporter, Robinson Taylor, complained in the preface to a sermon about aspersions cast on his recording skills by noting that

> certain individuals, with a zeal worthy of a better purpose, have industriously promulgated an opinion (which they hoped would prove prejudicial to the publication of this Sermon), that the Reporter has acted either under the influence of some unkind feeling towards the Rev. Mr. Byron, or has been prompted by those who have been denominated his enemies. (Taylor: iii)

In fact, Taylor reminded readers, he had only recorded the sermon because a number of people had asked him to. Defending his version of the sermon, Taylor stated that he only wanted 'to exercise himself in a useful art'. Further, he could affirm that 'his notes will be found a faithful record of the original Address, though the Reverend Speaker in the course [of] his delivery, evidently laboured under great mental excitement, which occasionally rendered his voice almost inaudible at the conclusion of several of his periods' (Taylor: iii–iv). Clearly, poor or bad reporting of a sermon could result in a loss of reputation and revenue for the Taylors and Verralls of the nineteenth century.

It is worth telling more of Charles Verrall's story because it is representative of a bygone age. His publishing business was not equal to Rivingtons, a London publisher with a sizeable catalogue of published sermons, but it was profitable. Located in 4 Prince Albert Street, it was a five-minute walk from Brighton Pier and a ten-minute walk from Grand Parade, one of Brighton's major thoroughfares: ideally situated to take advantage of the crowds going to the market or summer visitors to the town. He named his catalogue of published sermons, understandably, the Brighton Pulpit. The business was successful enough that in 1860 Verrall had to employ additional workers (Bidder 1860*a*: 160).

Despite the financial success, Verrall made it clear that his publishing of sermons was not simply a commercial exercise. Commenting on the accuracy of a group of sermons he had published, Verrall added:

> One who desires to be an humble instrument, in God's hands, of promoting in any way, which may be in accordance with His holy will, the welfare of His Church, has caused these sermons to be published … and if the God of all grace should, in mercy condescend to make use of them, either as an arrow of conviction in His hand, to cause some of His chosen people to cry out, 'Men and brethren, what shall we do?' or for the comfort and edification of any of the Church of Christ, to Him alone shall be all praise. (Bidder 1860*b*: 4)

In another volume of sermons, Verrall explained that his objective was larger in scope than ministering to the here-and-now; the sermons could be 'a source of edification and consolation to the living Church of God—even to many yet unborn' (Bidder 1860*a*: 3). Furthermore, his enterprise, being evangelistic in nature, was one in which others who felt the same concerns as he, could participate: 'Every Christian should feel interested in spreading as much as possible sound gospel Sermons, which, under God's blessing, are calculated to promote the welfare of Zion', he noted in another volume of sermons (Bidder 1861: iii).

Verrall's approach to his publishing was a combination of sound business sense and a passionate commitment to putting copies of sermons into the hands of as many people as possible. It is not a surprise that he combined his resources with a London publisher, H. J. Tresidder, in order to optimize the potential for more sales. Though Verrall was not the first nor the last person to combine capitalist acumen with his Christian beliefs, he could only have operated successfully in a society which took the preaching and reading of sermons very seriously: the demand for the sermon seemed to be a permanent and necessary fixture of life.

In the period covered by this volume which includes the Victorian age—commonly accepted as one which was religious—the age of Wesley and Whitefield, and the post-Restoration period with its battles over the relationship between the Church and monarch as well as Church and state, the evidence for the importance of the sermon is widespread. On the other hand, it seems a hard task to argue that the sermon was more important in post-Restoration British society than in early modern Britain or in the late medieval period, particularly given the work of Peter McCullough or Gerald Owst (McCullough; Owst). Did the sermon occupy an increasingly significant place in British society in the years after the Reformation? In a word, the answer is yes. The difference may not have been qualitative but it certainly was quantitative. Not only did the British population grow in each succeeding century but the technology of publishing improved also and with it the proliferation of reading material and literacy. No matter the importance of the sermon in late medieval Britain, the opportunities to read a sermon outside a church service were limited; by 1901, it was easy to obtain sermons to read in the home, for example, and such activity was commonplace (although declining from an earlier high, being supplanted by the reading of weekly or monthly serials of novels). Even in the great pamphleteering age of the early eighteenth century, when published sermons could and did provoke numerous reactions in print, publishers would have found it hard to imagine an enterprise as large as Charles Spurgeon's Penny Pulpit, one in which a single preacher had a new Sunday sermon printed and ready for distribution by Tuesday every single week.

This is why the story of the publisher Charles Verrall is noteworthy. It was not unique: it was commonplace. Verrall was doing what many other contemporaries were also doing. Furthermore, as in the case of the Unitarian minister John Page Hopps (1834–1911), preachers unable to find or unwilling to wait for a publisher for their sermons could do the job themselves (Hopps). Though, as noted in Chapter 1, in the modern era the ratio of published sermons to sermon events preached is quite small, these sermons reflect a phenomenon that was a central part of British life. It is appropriate then that one theme of the following chapters is the ways in which preached and published sermons enable scholars to understand major events and developments in the period up to 1901 better and more clearly.

Sermon Topics and Sermon Types

Given their central place in British life, their quantity and ubiquity, knowing the subject matter or topics of sermons makes it possible to examine and analyse the concerns of the British—at least with regard to matters of religion—over a period of more than two hundred years. Even the roughest classification can provide a wealth of material for a cultural history of the British people. Did ministers preach more sermons on the judgements of God during periods of war or poor harvest? How compelled did ministers in different eras feel to speak about the politics of the day in the pulpit? In what ways did the content of sermons—and the style in which preachers delivered them—change over the period? The essays in this volume are attempts to answer these and other related questions.

The eighteenth century was the great age of classification in the biological sciences with naturalists such as Carl Linnaeus creating methods to make it easier to find and organize species: the same task needs to be performed for sermons in the modern era. Asking questions about the literary styles of sermons or doing an analysis of the occurrence of words or phrases is the beginning of an attempt to develop a taxonomy of published sermons. (Again, such research must acknowledge the wide gap between 'sermon events' and the number of sermons in print or available in manuscript form.) The constituent parts of that corpus, the division of the whole into the subject matter covered by preachers, is an equally important task in the classification process. And while chronological divisions cannot be ignored, a simple separation into the late seventeenth century, the eighteenth century, and nineteenth century will not suffice. Taking natural theology as an example, some late seventeenth-century sermons had much in common with those preached in the nineteenth century. A similar point could be made about the use of poetry in eighteenth- and nineteenth-century sermons.

Subject matter then, or the topics of sermons, is an important consideration in any attempt to classify sermons. Naturally, all sermons were religious in some sense but, given the social and political history of Britain in the two centuries before 1901, it is less surprising that many sermons might be labelled 'not very religious'. The Civil War, the Glorious Revolution, and the Jacobite rebellions resulted in the preaching of overtly political sermons (as had been the case during the sixteenth century). The consequences of the sixteenth-century reformations and the attempts to create the United Kingdom in the eighteenth and nineteenth centuries means that a volume such as this one would be deficient without a consideration of the national and cultural context of sermons. Preaching and sermon writing in Wales, Scotland, and Ireland is an obvious area of investigation but there is also the even more complicated and complex question of the difference between sermons preached in Britain and those preached in the British colonies. Furthermore, there is the question of the social dimension of sermons. Even if matters such as class and enfranchisement were left aside—the rights of Christians in India from various castes or the role of women who accompanied their missionary spouses—the influence on sermons of great social movements such as the labour and union movements or the development of mass education cannot be ignored. Last, religious controversies could be considered a separate topic for sermonizing: the Oxford Movement, the restoration of the Catholic bishoprics, and the debate over liberal theology elicited comment in the pulpit long after the initial events which triggered the controversy had occurred. All of these topics will be examined in the following chapters.

On the other hand, in one sense, the classification of sermons for the period 1689–1901 is very simple. There were two groups of sermons. The first, and the vast majority, were sermons on the Christian life and Christian doctrine. Preachers instructed their congregations on the responsibilities of being a Christian and how they should live their lives. As Henry Stebbing put it in the preface to his father's *Sermons on Practical Subjects*,

> In making this selection, the Author has chosen those Sermons only which point out and enforce the duties of a Christian. Contested and abstruse points of divinity, are subjects highly proper to be treated at certain times; but at present the intention is, to speak to all, on subjects with which all ought to be well acquainted.

In other words, if a clergyman intended to publish his sermons these written versions ought to, in the main, 'inculcate the Christian Religion, by instructing the ignorant, and persuading the more learned of their duty' (Stebbing: 1:vi). The more general versions of these pedagogical sermons had titles such as *The Duty of Praise and Thanksgiving*, 'The Christian Race', *Confidence in God*, or *Spiritual Lethargy* (Burscough; Dunbar-Dunbar: 17–28; Paget; Andrews). Or, the preachers would explain some specific aspect of Christian doctrine to their congregations. 'Jehovah: In Persons Three; In Essence One, Justified by His Grace', *The Doctrine of Grace Clear'd from the Charge of Licentiousness*, *A Sermon on the Ascension of Our Lord Jesus Christ...*, or *The Doctrine of a General Resurrection...* are sermons which fit into this category (Bidder 1860b: 34–45; Walsham; Gill; Goe; Beconsall).

The second group, a very small minority compared to those on Christian life and doctrine, were all the other sermons. A section of this Handbook is correctly entitled 'Occasional Sermons', sermons preached on historic or social occasions, be it a victory, charity school or society meeting, opening of Parliament, or a perceived threat to religion or the state; conversely, one way to analyse the content of the sermons is to recognize that the term 'occasional sermon' is a misnomer. Any sermon which was not about the Christian life or Christian doctrine was an occasional sermon.

Even the opportunity to preach a sermon on an occasion such as before the monarch did not always result in much deviation from the standard fare. When George Bright, the Dean of Asaph and a chaplain to William III, preached a series of sermons before Queen Mary he stuck to his usual habit of presenting 'the Duties and Doctrines of our Religion plain and reasonable' (Bright: preface). Thus the Queen heard sermons on the dangers of 'evil communications', the need for a Christian to keep good company, the importance of confessing sin, the certainty of the existence of God, justification, and sanctification (Bright). Edward Cobden, the Archdeacon of London, preached a sermon entitled 'A Persuasive to Chastity' to George II on 11 December 1748 for which the author claimed he received 'some unjust censures', but he consoled himself in the hope that the published sermon might convert one sinner from the error of his ways (Cobden: Advertisement). A century later, in December 1846, Samuel Wilberforce avoided references to certain types of sins—those of a sexual nature such as adultery and fornication—but exhorted Queen Victoria to reflect on the successes and failures of the past year in order to turn 'past failings into earnest resolutions...past sins into deeper acts of penitence and seeking after [God]...and find in every past deliverance an argument of [God's] faithfulness and a reason for our trust in the great Unknown' (Wilberforce: 55).

Periods of controversy certainly resulted in sermons which focused on particular points of argument. There were, for example, hundreds of sermons preached for and against Benjamin Hoadly's position during the Bangorian Controversy, and the clergy seemed preoccupied with these disputes in the pulpit. However, although this was the case, there were also Bangorian sermons with titles such as 'Mutual Charity, A Most Perfect Bond of Christian Unity'. Thomas Hayley, a canon of Chichester and chaplain to the King, noted that 'so long as there is any obscurity in any parts of Divine Revelation' there would be disputes among Christians but, as Hayley stressed repeatedly, the 'true foundation' of Religion was in the heart, not the head, and so Christians should strive to live in peace with one another (Hayley: 8, 9–10, 28–31). The published sermons of Jabez Bunting do not leave the reader with a strong sense of the numerous controversies, doctrinal and organizational, in which the Wesleyan Methodist leader was involved despite William Thornton, the editor of the two volumes, noting that they fix 'the attention, and [keep] it fixed on those vital doctrines which some of our contemporaries seem anxious, above all things, to cast in the shade' (Bunting: 1:7). Nor would anyone reading Charles Spurgeon's published sermons for the years 1886, 1887, and 1888 be aware of the controversy swirling about the preacher and the Baptist Union—the so-called Down-Grade controversy. Unless singularly perceptive, it would be difficult to recognize that the sermons 'To Those Who are Angry with Their Godly Friends', preached at some time in 1886, 'A Sermon for the Time Present', preached on 30 October 1887, and 'No Compromise', preached on 7 October 1888, were significantly different from any of the other sermons of admonition that Spurgeon had preached in the past (Spurgeon: 32:613–24; 33:601–12; 34:553–64). When he published his sermons—in contrast to other publications such as his monthly magazine *The Sword and the Trowel*—Spurgeon adhered to his oft-spoken mantra to uplift Christ alone.

The apparent dissonance between the turbulent events in the lives of Bunting and Spurgeon and the sermons they preached suggest that most sermons, those that constitute the millions of sermon events referred to in Chapter 1, almost certainly addressed the nature of the Christian life and how to live it. Thus they were both a contribution to the 'conduct literature'—often attributed in the eighteenth and nineteenth centuries to entirely secular literature—and an expression of religious (and therefore human) values. These rules and obligations or ethical norms were relatively constant and stable during the period 1689–1901 and less susceptible to change. A congregation in 1901 could have heard a sermon preached in 1701 on a topic such as the ethical obligations due to one's neighbours and not regarded it as anachronistic. Indeed this explains why so many nineteenth-century clergy frequently recommended and praised sermons of the previous century. It also explains why the training of clergy and the curriculums of the newly formed Anglican theological colleges drew so heavily on sermons published in the eighteenth century by such preachers as Butler, Secker, Burnet, and Tillotson.

In contrast, commentators in the twentieth century noticed the way in which the sermon had changed since the nineteenth century. Gaius Glenn Atkins, the Congregationalist minister and professor at Auburn Theological Seminary in New York, when editing his *Master Sermons of the Nineteenth Century*, remarked that the nineteenth century was one which 're-explored and recast almost every province of human thought' but a reader could not deduce this from the best sermons of the period. He added: 'One could probably reconstruct a good deal of twentieth century storm and stress from twentieth-century preaching. But one cannot write a history of the nineteenth century from these sermons. They belong for the most part to the timeless and with little mutation would be true anywhere at any time. They possess a timeless modernity' (Atkins: xi). Of the thirteen representative, and best, sermons Atkins chose, seven were British and six American. Three of the British preachers he chose were the 'usual suspects' preaching on the usual topics: the romantic spirituality of John Henry Newman in 'The Invisible World', the transcendentalism of James Martineau in 'The Witness of God with Our Spirit', and the down-to-earth bonhomie of Charles Spurgeon in 'Everybody's Sermon' (Atkins).

In contrast, the content of sermons that focused on occasional events and religious behaviour was much more prone to change over time. The repetitively taught principle that obedience was due to a ruler, so often preached in the late seventeenth and early eighteenth centuries, would have sounded very odd to congregations full of voters after the three parliamentary reform acts of the nineteenth century. Similarly, the teaching on the need for 'national humiliation' and repentance of sin in response to natural disasters, common in the first half of the eighteenth century, would be unlikely to sound reasonable to people in the last years of Queen Victoria's reign. The plea on abolitionist medals and in anti-slavery sermons, 'Am I not a man and a brother?', would have sounded incongruent to most ears of the late seventeenth century. The same is true of sermons advocating the abolition of cruelty to animals, popular from the 1820s onwards. Despite preachers' duty of the cure of souls, an obligation which dominates sermons in this period, the ways in which their sermons interpreted that cure evolved and developed with society.

Sermons were a chameleon form of literature, able to acculturate themselves to a wide array of settings and forms. They were adapted to new situations and circumstances and adopted new forms and modes. Some of the sermon forms examined in this volume emerged, developed, and declined between 1689 and 1901: sermons on victories and thanksgivings, visitation, and humanitarian campaigns show something of the extraordinary adaptability of the sermon. This adaptability is one of the explanations for the success of the sermon in both spoken and written form.

Occasional sermons reveal the specific concerns of the churches and preachers and their responses to events and trends. What the faithful were expected to think or believe about such occasions and events are contained in their pages. Consequently, they are a valuable window into the minds of the British people. Different from the political speech or polemical tract, the occasional sermon came closest to the desired popular religious response to events. Thus, in the published sermons of Henry Stebbing, despite the disclaimer written by his son in the preface, there are sermons with titles such as, 'Considerations on God's Judgments, and the Proper Improvement of Them Pointed Out'—a commentary on a hurricane in Jamaica, 'The Miserable End of Profligate Sinners'—a commentary on a high-profile forgery case, and 'On Occasion of the Suppression of Riots in 1780' (Stebbing 2:135–46, 3:257–72, 3:339–48). These sermons are more like a diary entry or letter on a particular event: the latter would not be generalized to represent opinions in society in general. Nevertheless, published occasional sermons form the shadows which enable us to perceive the dimensions and proportions of the sermon corpus as a whole.

The Purpose of Publishing Sermons

What did those clergy who published their sermons, and those who published the clergyman's sermons after he had died, hope to achieve? If most sermons were 'teaching moments' and clergy believed this to be an important activity, it is surprising that many more sermons were not published (thus increasing the opportunities for further learning to take place—in this case, outside of the church or religious service). On the other hand, a sermon is so time-specific—it is preached on a particular day, at a particular time, to a particular congregation or group—that publishing any sermon is, in a sense, a rather odd activity. The moment has passed and those who were not present have missed it (and even those present cannot really recapture it). According to his wife, Charles Kingsley preached a sermon about ghosts in 1856. What was noteworthy about this sermon, according to Fanny Kingsley, was the fact that Kingsley did not believe in ghosts; to present-day scholars what is more intriguing is the fact that Fanny Kingsley thought the sermon important enough to mention in Kingsley's biography but there is no extant copy of it: the emotion of whatever Kingsley had said could not be captured in a recitation of the sermon's words (Kingsley: 2:2). Thus it may be hard, for example, to discern Spurgeon's feelings about the Down-Grade Controversy from reading the sermons he preached from 1887 onwards but the congregations who heard the sermons may have witnessed the poses and the gestures or, perhaps more significant, heard the tone and the way Spurgeon expressed the words: these visual and verbal cues would have told far more than the bare text ever could. Similarly, the contemporary reader is hard pressed to explain why John Wesley's sermons were so captivating from reading them or to detect the well-known, even notorious, humour of Samuel Wilberforce from reading his published sermons. These weaknesses of the text suggest that the clergy and others must have had compelling reasons for wanting or allowing the publication of something that could never be the verisimilitude of what had been preached.

In fact, the desire for an authentic recapturing of a moment was one of the major reasons for publishing a sermon. Without discounting the evangelistic fervour of a Charles Verrall, clergy often published sermons because those who had heard the particular sermon wanted a copy of it. Thus it is that the words 'Printed at the Request of the Congregation' or a similar phrase appear on the title page, or thereabouts, of numerous sermons. (Fortunately for scholars, when the phrase was 'Printed for Private Distribution' these instructions were frequently ignored.) For those congregations which wished to share the sermon with others, the comment of the Unitarian minister Lawrence Holden is typical: 'Having been requested by you to print and publish the following sermon… I here present it to your serious reconsideration; trusting to your candour, and hoping that it will not wholly disappoint your expectations' (Holden: 3).

Fans—to use a modern word which is apt for this phenomenon—of a particular preacher were eager to obtain copies of his sermons, whether legally or illegally. In the nineteenth century copyright rules for author ownership were lax compared to the present day: it was not difficult to turn a reporter's notes or a transcript into a published sermon (and this became easier as printing technology improved). The reasons Charles Spurgeon published his sermons so regularly were to meet continual requests for them and, equally important for his finances, to prevent illegal copies of them circulating. William Paley, being aware of the fan problem, included in his will a limit on the number of his sermons which would be published and the number of copies of the final volume. The number Paley had in mind proved too small and the editor of Paley's sermon collection, George Stephenson, confessed that it was 'impossible to adhere to that intention'; only by publishing a greater number of Paley's sermons could the executors of Paley's will prevent 'surreptitious sale' of those supposed to remain unpublished (Paley: Advertisement).

It is hard to rule out an element of egotism in the clergy who had their sermons published—having already been a kind of oracle when preaching the sermon their words now acquired a permanence—but there are also numerous examples of clergy who seemed genuinely surprised at their hearers' request. The Bishop of Antigua, William Walrond Jackson, noted in the preface that his sermon 'Childhood' preached for the Ladies Society for Promoting Education in the West Indies on 10 June 1860 'was not written with the remotest idea of publication'. In fact, 'it was preached on the Sunday before the Writer left London for his distant Diocese, and was composed in a few hurried hours snatched from the pressing preparations for his departure'; that being the case, some might complain about the style and structure, Jackson added (Jackson). Stephen Bridge, later rector of Droxford in Hampshire, was even more blunt: 'Why print this Sermon?' he asked. Not because 'the Writer ever meant it whilst preparing it, or because he wished for it now' he answered. 'It is done simply at the urgent and repeated request of many among all classes, whose opinion he values and whose piety he respects. *They* think it may be *useful*; if it be so, that is all the Preacher prays for or desires' (Bridge: preface). This was hardly a problem new in the nineteenth century: William Lyng, a minister in Yarmouth, made a similar point about a sermon he preached in Norwich Cathedral in 1703 (Lyng: Epistle

Dedicatory). For some clergy it was gratifying to be asked; others were so reluctant that the sermon had to be metaphorically wrung out of them.

As most sermons were attempts to teach, some clergy took advantage of the opportunities that publishing provided. They could emphasize important ideas, be they doctrinal, moral, or ethical. When William Fraser, curate of Alton in the diocese of Lichfield, published a group of eight sermons which focused on judgement, he commented in the preface:

> The Sermons which make up this little volume were selected from among a great quantity of Parish sermons, principally because they appeared to be listened to with some attention when they were preached. I had often been led to think…chiefly from the immense number of sermons which are now preached every week in England [that] the final end and object of preaching had…dwindled down to the simple fixing the attention of the hearers. The sermon which failed of doing this, seemed to me to fail of its object; and the sermon which did this, did as much as a sermon could fairly be expected to do, in congregations so thoroughly mixed, as ours for the most part are. (Fraser: v)

While correctly drawing the attention of scholars to all they have lost, Fraser's assessment was not quite accurate. Even if his congregation had not listened carefully to his sermons, they had another opportunity—whether they desired this chance or not—to 'hear' them again. Joseph Jowett, a contemporary of Fraser's and the rector of Silk Willoughby in Lincolnshire, was even clearer about the pedagogical use of sermons. 'In this age of enlarged benevolence, many pious Christians are in the habit of giving or lending to their poorer neighbours such works, as may convey spiritual instruction in a form suited to their capacities', he noted. It was sermons in particular that were 'occasionally read aloud by those, who visit, for the most benevolent of purposes, the cottages of the ignorant' (J. Jowett: vi). The published sermon could teach long after its preacher was dead and buried.

The notion of reaching past the initial impact of the 'sermon event' was evident in a third objective of those who published sermons: the sermon could contribute to the memorializing of an event, series of events, a person, or a group of people. The publishing of occasional sermons was an example of this type of memorializing but not the only one. In fact, one of the commonest examples of this type of memorial was the farewell sermon. Leaving was a normal part of the clerical life—whether moving to another parish, church, or circuit, retiring, or departing this life. Congregations who wished to remember their minister asked for these farewell sermons to be preached and published. When James Walker, the future Bishop of Edinburgh, resigned from St Peter's, Edinburgh, in order to concentrate his efforts on the professorship he held at the Episcopal Theological College, he ended his preface to the published version of his last sermon with the words 'Finally, Brethren, Farewell' (Walker: Advertisement). That kind of intimate shared moment was typical of farewell sermons: William Milton, the rector of Christ Church in Nottingham, included a history of his twenty-one-year incumbency written by himself, copies of letters of appreciation from members of the congregation and a list of parting gifts that he had received with his farewell sermon (Milton: 28–32). It could be seen in eulogistic sermons for a beloved minister—Robert Baynes's sermon after the death of Samuel Wilberforce, then Bishop of Winchester, in a horse riding accident—or in the desire to collect the minister's sermons as George Salmon and J. Dowden did when William Lee, the Archdeacon of Dublin and a lecturer in divinity at the University, died unexpectedly of pneumonia in 1883 (Lee). Again, the permanence of the published sermon meant that a significant moment could be shared repeatedly.

Different from the memorializing sermon in motivation, but similar in that repetition was necessary for it to best achieve the preacher's objective, was the charity sermon. Collecting money from believers has been an essential part of the preacher's task since the beginnings of Christianity. It made sense to publish sermons in which the preacher had appealed for funds for a particular cause: others who were not present could be asked to contribute and those who had already given could be persuaded to give more. So regularly were these sermons preached in the period 1689–1901 that they could be described as a type of sermon as well as being a reason for publishing. All ranks of clergy preached them and they spoke on behalf of an exceedingly wide range of causes. Joseph Butler, better known for his contribution to philosophy, preached a sermon for the London Infirmary in 1748 (Butler). Charles Harbin, the incumbent of Hindon in Wiltshire, preached a sermon in 1834 to raise money for a barrel-organ for the church (Harbin). In 1861, Edward Wilkinson made one of his sermons do double duty: it memorialized his daughter and the proceeds of the published version were used to support the Women's Benevolent Institution of Leeds (Wilkinson).

A final reason for publishing a sermon which needs to be mentioned was much more self-centred than the altruistic charity sermon. Clergy, their friends and devotees, published sermons in order to add to the corpus of their works and advance their careers and reputations. Though both men were very popular preachers, it is naïve to think that Samuel Wilberforce and Charles Spurgeon started publishing their sermons early in their careers solely out of concern for the spiritual health of their congregations: publishing their sermons was one way to be noticed (with the concomitant possibility of advancement). Spurgeon stands out as the 'master publisher' but, though not nearly as prolific, his contemporaries John Henry Newman, Charles Kingsley, R. W. Church, and H. P. Liddon were equally well known for their volumes of published sermons. In the preceding two centuries men such as John Tillotson, Edmund Calamy, Benjamin Hoadly, and John Wesley were similarly well known for the number of sermons they published.

The relationship between a publisher and clergyman was very important. Sermons were published as single pamphlets and in collections. The successful preacher–publisher partnership produced both. If the sales merited it, the same sermon could appear in different volumes as well as in second, third, and more editions. (Having a good reporter/taker of notes and being a good editor were critical also, hence Charles Verrall's advertising of his company's skills.) The clergyman with a good eye for a selling point could do well also. Despite his disclaimer that the sermons were intended to 'dispel the delusions of the Working Classes' there is little doubt that Francis Close took advantage, very cleverly, of the visit of Chartists to his church in Cheltenham on consecutive Sundays by publishing the sermons he preached on those days (Close 1839a: iv; Close 1839b). Perhaps it is a little discordant to focus on the pecuniary motivation but Arthur Winnington-Ingram, a canon of St Paul's Cathedral at the time, and the publisher Wells Gardner, Darton & Co. must have been aware of the opportunities provided by the outpouring of emotion at the death of Queen Victoria when Winnington-Ingram's four panegyric sermons preached about the life of the Queen were published in 1901 (Winnington-Ingram). Even if seemingly unconcerned about sales, these collections of sermons could reflect the zeitgeist or the anxieties of the time and still make money for the preacher and the publisher; this was the case with T. M. Morris's *Sermons for All Classes*: though no publication date is given on the title page, the repeated references to the Religious Census of 1851 and the need for sermons which interested the working classes date the collection to the 1850s and 1860s.

Obviously there was a wide and differentiated demand for these collections but an astute clergyman or publisher could create a niche in the market. The regular publishing of sermons 'for the people', or town, or town and country, or village are examples of this kind of market positioning. The Baptist minister Alexander MacLaren went one step further when he published three volumes of sermons he had preached at Union Chapel in Manchester (MacLaren). The sermons of Benjamin Jowett, the reforming Master of Balliol College, on historical figures such as Ignatius Loyola, John Bunyan, and Blaise Pascal were collected and published after his death, as were the sermons of J. B. Lightfoot, Bishop of Durham, on famous northern religious figures such as St Oswald, St Cuthbert, Bede, and Joseph Butler (B. Jowett; Lightfoot).

It may be a little cynical to suggest that anything that could sell would end up as a published sermon in the period 1689–1901 but the need to market and sell sermons led to the wide diversity of sermon types and sermon topics. As noted in Chapter 1, the preaching of sermons all over the country on every Sunday confirms the sermon's ubiquity in British life. From the smallest village parish to the open air at Epsom Downs sermons were preached, the British came to listen to them, and publishers published (some of) them.

Studying the Sermon

These introductory chapters have drawn attention to the difference between the sermon as a spoken event and as a written object. Put simply, the published sermon served a very different purpose from the preached one. While the focus of scholars up to the last decade or so has been on the history of preaching and preachers, the emerging field of sermon studies has the text, both manuscript and book, as its object of interest: individual preachers' biographies and matters of preaching style are less important. That is not to say that the field can ignore personal stories and rhetoric—in fact, such approaches are central to some of the essays in this Handbook—but the modus operandi of sermons studies scholars is more holistic. The disciplines of history, theology, literature, rhetoric, psychology, sociology, and economics are all necessary in order to understand the sermon.

What makes the published sermon so interesting as an object of study is the fact that it could be used in ways that the spoken sermon could not. It could be 'preached' in the absence of a minister or clergyman. It could be preached again and again both by its creator and by imitators. It could be read as part of a family's worship or for an individual's personal devotion. It could be permanently polemical because print did not die. These are some reasons why a multidisciplinary approach is needed in order to understand the role and impact of the sermon on British society in the period 1689–1901. Sermons mattered then and, for scholars examining the history of Britain in the modern era, sermons matter now.

References

Andrews, E. (1829). *Spiritual Lethargy. A Sermon...* London: Ebenezer Palmer.

Atkins, G. G. (1949). *Master Sermons of the Nineteenth Century.* Chicago: Willett, Clark & Company.

Baynes, R. H. (1873). *The Chariot of Israel, and the Horseman Thereof. A Sermon...* London: H. S. King & Co.

Beconsall, T. (1697). *The Doctrine of a General Resurrection...* Oxford: Leonard Lichfield.

Bidder, W. (1860a). *Second Number: Containing Six Sermons Preached by Mr. William Bidder...* Brighton: C. E. Verrall.

——. (1860b). *Six Sermons Preached by Mr. William Bidder...* Brighton: C. E. Verrall.

——. (1861). *Third Number: Containing Six Sermons Preached by Mr. William Bidder...* Brighton: C. E. Verrall.

Bridge, S. (1858?). *Dress. A Sermon Preached...* London: Wertheim, Macintosh, and Hunt.

Bright, G. (1695). *Six Sermons Preached before the Late Incomparable Princess Queen Mary...* London: Walter Kettilby.

Bunting, J. (1861). *Sermons by Jabez Bunting, D.D.*, W. Thornton (ed.). London: John Mason.

Burscough, W. (1715). *The Duty of Praise and Thanksgiving. A Sermon Preach'd...* London: Samuel Crouch.

Butler, J. (1751). *A Sermon Preached before His Grace Charles Duke of Richmond...* Newcastle upon Tyne: M. Bryson & Co.

Close, F. (1839a). *The Chartists' Visit to the Parish Church...* London: Hamilton, Adams, and Co.

—— (1839b). *The Female Chartists' Visit to the Parish Church...* London: Hamilton, Adams, and Co.

Cobden, E. (1749). *A Persuasive to Chastity: A Sermon Preached...* London: J. Lodge.

Dunbar-Dunbar, J. A. (1877). *Six Sermons Preached in the Church of S. Salvador's.* Oxford: A. R. Mowbray and Co.

Fraser, W. (1855). *Parish Sermons.* Oxford: John Henry Parker.

Gill, J. (1751). *The Doctrine of Grace Clear'd from the Charge of Licentiousness ...*, 2nd edn. London: G. Keith.

Goe, F. F. (1872). *A Sermon on the Ascension of Our Lord Jesus Christ...* London: Seeley, Jackson & Halliday.

Harbin, C. (1837). *The Grounds of Duty of Praise*... Salisbury: W. B. Brodie and Co.
Hayley, T. (1718). *Mutual Charity, the Most Perfect Bond of Christian Unity*... London: Timothy Childe.
Holden, L. (1812). *The Nature, Spirit and End of a Christian Association*... London: A. Grant.
Hopps, J. P. (1892). *The Message of the Church to the World. Six Discourses*... Croydon: The Free Christian Church.
Jackson, W. W. (n. d.). *Childhood. The Annual Sermon for the Ladies Society*... London: Wertheim, Macintosh, and Hunt.
Jowett, B. (1899). *Sermons Biographical & Miscellaneous*..., W. H. Fremantle (ed.). London: John Murray.
Jowett, J. (1828). *Sermons, Preached Before a Village Congregation*. London: R. B. Seely and W. Burnside.
Kingsley, C. (1879). *Charles Kingsley: His Letters and Memories of His Life*, abridged edn., F. Kingsley (ed.). London: C. Kegan Paul & Co.
Lee, W. (1886). *University Sermons*... Dublin: Hodges, Figgis, and Co.
Lightfoot, J. B. (1890). *Leaders in the Northern Church*..., J. R. Harmer (ed.). London: Macmillan and Co.
Lyng, W. (1703). *A Sermon Preach'd in the Cathedral Church of Norwich*... London: Owen Peartree.
McCullough, P. (1998). *Sermons at Court: Politics and Religion*... Cambridge: Cambridge University Press.
MacLaren, A. (1871). *Sermons Preached in Manchester*... London: Macmillan and Co.
Milton, W. (1860). *Christian Mercifulness: Its Nature and Reward*... London: Wertheim and Macintosh
Morris, T. M. (n. d.). *Sermons for All Classes*. London: Elliot Stock.
Owst, G. R. (1926). *Preaching in Medieval England*... Cambridge: Cambridge University Press.
Paget, T. B. (n. d.). *Confidence in God; A Sermon*. Doncaster: R. Hartley.
Paley, W. (1808). *Sermons on Several Subjects*, 2nd edn. London: Longman, Hurst, Rees, and Orme.
Spurgeon, C. H. (1863–1911). *The Metropolitan Tabernacle Pulpit*. London: Passmore and Alabaster.
Stebbing, H. (1788). *Sermons on Practical Subjects*, H. Stebbing (ed.). London: C. Dilly.
Taylor, R. (1829). *Report of a Sermon, Preached at the Independent Chapel, Lincoln*... Lincoln: Edward B. Drury.
Walker, J. (1829). *A Farewell Sermon*... Edinburgh: Robert Grant.
Walsham, C. (1866). *'Justified by His Grace.' A Farewell Sermon*... London: Morton & Co.
Wilberforce, S. (1877). *Sermons Preached on Various Occasions*... Oxford: James Parker and Co.
Wilkinson, E. (1861). *'For Me to Live is Christ, and to Die is Gain.' A Sermon*... Leeds: Thomas Harrison and Son.
Winnington-Ingram, A. F. (1901). *The After-glow of a Great Reign*... London: Wells Gardner, Darton & Co.

PART II
COMMUNITIES, CULTURES AND COMMUNICATION

CHAPTER 3

PARISH PREACHING IN THE LONG EIGHTEENTH CENTURY

JEFFREY S. CHAMBERLAIN

It is surprisingly difficult to paint a full picture of parish preaching in the long eighteenth century; very few have even tried. In recent years there have been concerted attempts to understand the nature and effectiveness of the Anglican Church in the localities, but one searches in vain for an in-depth treatment of parsons in the pulpit (Gregory and Chamberlain; Spaeth). When the issue is broached at all, it is usually either from the vantage point of case studies (Deconinck-Brossard; Sykes) or from published sermons (Claydon; Albers: 94–102). The main reason for this is that, despite the fact that there were 10,000 parishes in England, each of which presumably had a sermon or two preached in them weekly, there are very few extant manuscript sermons. This would initially seem to be counterintuitive—wouldn't preachers want to leave a legacy of the works they crafted for public consumption? The fact remains, however, that unless sermons were published, they were seldom preserved. In fact, it was not unusual for parsons to stipulate in their wills that their manuscript sermons be destroyed. For instance, Thomas Newhouse, the rector of Duncton (1718–73) and Nuthurst (1736–73), both in Sussex, was so determined that his manuscript sermons be burned, that his executor and executrix were each to forfeit £100 of their inheritance should they fail to fulfil his wish (Newhouse). It is often thought that copying and preaching sermons written by others was a common practice (Downey: 5–6). Is this why parsons had their sermons destroyed? Perhaps in some cases, but certainly not in all. There are cases of preachers destroying their sermons during their lifetimes. John Egerton, rector of Ross-on-Wye in Hertfordshire and, successively, Bishop of Bangor, Lichfield and Coventry, and Durham, did this, with the clear indication that he wasn't pleased with those he burned (Egerton). But this does not explain why so many had the entire corpus of their lives' work destroyed at their demise.

Even some of the few large extant collections are problematic. Richard Rawlinson, the non-juring clergyman and antiquarian, gathered hundreds of manuscript sermons up until his death in 1755, but his collection, now housed in the Bodleian Library at Oxford, is limited in its usefulness: first, many of the authors are unidentified; second, many may not have been intended for preaching in parishes; and third, a significant portion of them were by Dissenters, and using a Nonconformist sermon as illustrative of Anglican parish preaching is clearly unhelpful.

The paucity of manuscripts, therefore, means that we are hindered in reaching definitive conclusions about parish preaching in the period. But there are enough sources available to make some tentative conclusions. This chapter will offer some of these by adducing evidence from as many manuscript sermons as possible, and supplementing it with commonplace books, correspondence, and printed materials.

The first thing that should be said is that sermons were written out longhand and read from the pulpit. There seems to have been virtually no extemporaneous preaching in the Church of England between the radicals of the mid-seventeenth century and the advent of the Methodists. Even in the nineteenth century, most parsons were still writing out their sermons, though some began to take note that they used the text (and presumably the general themes of the sermon), but they spoke it 'extempore' (Herefordshire Preacher).

Before about 1730 or so, preachers usually used small (duodecimo) booklets to write out their discourses. Not long after 1730, most were using booklets closer to octavo in size. As might be expected, parsons had very different styles of handwriting—some hands were careful and precise (even beautiful), some were crabbed or shaky, and some were so poor you can hardly imagine how the preacher himself could read it. Prior to the adoption of the larger booklets, much of the writing was tiny; unless a pastor had extremely good eyesight, he must have held the manuscript very close to his face as he read it. Many used a large number of abbreviations, too, which saved space on the page. Sometimes preachers wrote on both sides of the booklet; sometimes just the right-hand side. It was not uncommon for the writer to underline words which he evidently intended to emphasize in preaching: Thomas Birch's sermons are replete with such markings (Birch).

The format of sermons was quite uniform—logically developed using divisions (or 'heads') in order to explicate, confirm, and apply a short text, or passage of Scripture (Wilkins: 5; see also Lessenich). The preacher gave a bit of introduction or background (usually a page or two), and then enumerated the points that he wished to get across, as we see in Gilpin's suggestions for structuring a sermon (Gilpin: vi–vii). The following from the 1750s is a fairly typical example:

> Mark 13 chap. V. 37
>
> And what I say unto you, I say unto all, watch.
>
> There are two comings of our Lord mention'd in Scripture: the former of them in Mercy to save the world, the latter of them in Majesty to judge it. Some of those who had liv'd in the time of the former had mov'd a Question to our Saviour concerning his latter coming. When will the Coming of the Son of Man be? Now our Saviour in

> way of answer to this question layeth down Both the certainty & uncertainty of his second coming. The certainty that it shall be, the uncertainty when it shall be; that wch is wont to be said of death, is most true of Judgment, nothing more certain & nothing more uncertain;... In speaking to this I shall observe 1. What it is to watch. 2. Why we ought to watch. 3. The manner how we must watch. 4. The means whereby we must watch. (Hertfordshire Preacher)

It might be worth noting at this point that, unlike modern talks or sermons (and unlike some contemporary printed sermons), there was no attempt at humour, and few if any personal illustrations. In fact, it appears that most preachers used mainly biblical language and biblical illustrations. The main points were then often broken down into subpoints. So in the section from the sermon quoted above about 'Why we ought to watch', the preacher enumerated three reasons:

> Sin is a spiritual sleep & repentance is an awaking out of this sleep, saith the Apostle; awake to Righteousness & sin not, & this is the watch that Christ doth exhort us to; it is the duty of a Christian diligently to watch & take heed that he is not overcome of sin...
>
> 2^{ly}...a Xtian therefore has need to be always on his guard because his Adversary the Devil continually lies in wait...
>
> 3^{ly}, A Christian has need to be vigilant because our prowess in well doing is most necessary, the promise was thus, He that endures to the end shall be saved: a Christians course is compar'd to a race, thus run with patience the race that is set before us. (Hertfordshire Preacher)

How did the clergy craft their sermons? It is unlikely that parsons simply sat down and wrote via a stream of consciousness, though that is how the finished product often appears. The only example of drafts that I have discovered appears in Bishop George Berkeley's manuscript collection. There he outlined his sermon on pieces of paper before he wrote it out. In a sermon on Romans 8:13 about fasting, he started with a brief outline, then wrote down examples that he might use, then listed 'species of Fast', and described the type of 'exhortation' he might use. On the basis of this, he then developed an even more detailed outline with eight separate points (Berkeley). Examples of his 'skeletons' of sermons were published in 1871 (Fraser). Once the outline was completed, Berkeley—and presumably all sermon-makers—apparently wrote out the discourse from start to finish. This is really quite remarkable when one thinks about it. In some ways it was akin to composing on a typewriter, since there was little opportunity to change or revise. Some sermons have revisions written into the text—words scratched out and others substituted above them—and there are a few where the authors pinned in a new section (Stanley: sermon 2). Occasionally, clergymen seem to have avoided writing on the opposite page in the booklet so that they could add emendations (Stanton). But overall, once the thinking and planning were completed, parsons wrote out their sermons and did very little editing later.

How did clergymen decide what to preach on? There was, of course, a liturgical year, but this played a surprisingly small role in the topic of the sermon. Christmas sermons addressed the nativity, and Easter sermons focused on the resurrection, but sermons on those topics could also be preached in other seasons. Parsons wrote specific sermons for Fast days, usually proclaimed during wars or natural disasters, and days of thanksgiving, prompted by positive events of national significance. Fast-day sermons continued throughout the century to emphasize sin as the cause of disaster (Deconinck-Brossard: 118–19). In the second half of the century, though, there was a bit more ambivalence or uncertainly about this. Note in the following sermon, preached during the Seven Years' War in 1757, how the parson tries to allow for both natural causes and the visitation of God for sins:

> In this, as in all other Matters relating to God's Providence & his Governmt of the World, we cannot speak in universal Terms... These Evils go, wch we are mentioning, when they happen to a Nation, are not always perhaps inflicted upon it as Punishmts, and on the other Hand, when God punishes, He does not always make use of those Means: because there are other Methods of Scourging & Chastising a rebellious People.... And whenever they happen, no Nation Is so righteous as not to deserve them, but it does not from hence follow, that they are always occasioned by its Sins___ But notwithstanding this, it is certain from my Text that sometimes & probable from Reason, that for the most Part these Calamities are sent from Heaven upon a People for their Transgressions, or are the natural Effects & Consequences of them___ That there are national Sins & that they call for national Punishmt is too manifest to be questioned. (Garstang Preacher)

The preacher then called for repentance, but how certain could the congregants be after hearing this that their penitence was necessary or beneficial? Sir Adam Gordon, rector of Hinxford, in Hertfordshire, preached a thanksgiving sermon late in the century in which he felt obliged to argue strenuously that King George III's illness was indeed visited upon him because of the sins of the people (Gordon: 224–43). People were clearly questioning the causal connection.

Fast and thanksgiving sermons could also bring out the emotions of the preacher. Though the following is David Renaud's thanksgiving sermon from 1787, it is filled with lament:

> God has heard our former petitions—& has restored to us, after so long—so Bloody, so destructive—& in one part, I may say so unnatural a war, the Blessing of peace—ought we not, to return our most ardent Thanks & praises to that Almighty Being, who has still ye raging of ye sea & the madness of ye people.— ...

> But that wch ought to be ye 1st in our Thoughts—is the Various & continual Toils & Hardships, yt such Numbers of poor Creatures must endure, exposing ymselves in defence of others;—The Loss of so many Thousands or Lives by Sickness & in battle;—The Grief of many Relations & Friends, the Miseries of so many destitute Families; —Part of these our Fellow: subjects' & not a few of them possibly very dear to one or other of us.— ...

> Wn we seriously consider these & indeed many & grievous Calamities, wth wch wars are attended, we must be stript of all Humanity & natural Affection indeed, if we are not moved wt a compassionate sense of such afflicting miseries—& rejoice at any tolerable conditions & agreemt, for putting an end to such misery. (Renaud: item 25)

Here we can experience the power that an eighteenth-century sermon could have. The choice of words, sentence construction, and repetition convey profound pathos—both pain for suffering and joy for the approaching end of the suffering. Contrary to the perspective that the ethical preaching in the period was devoid of passion, emotion is very common in parish sermons (Brinton).

Fast and thanksgiving sermons seem to be the main occasions where the focus was on external events. There appear to be very few 30th January or 5th November manuscript sermons, though they continued to be preached and printed (Burdett; Weinbrot), and almost no references to politics or controversial issues. This may have been largely because it was thought improper (Lessenich: 46–7), but it also may have been because time-specific references would limit the repeatability of the sermon. Most of the printed sermons appear to have been preached at special occasions (like Fast days or visitations). The few that were not are also quite generic. This would seem to indicate that, though printed sermons might have contributed significantly to the development of a 'public sphere' (Claydon), parish sermons rarely did, or, at least, that preachers connected parishioners to the nation only in the sense that they were preaching similar things.

There is one other common type of sermon: the funeral sermon. The interesting thing about this genre is that there is almost never any eulogy. Printed funeral sermons often incorporated a tribute (Newlin; Oliver). Perhaps manuscript sermons had the eulogy separate, so that the preacher could use the sermon at other funerals—even some printed sermons had the eulogy added in at the end (Hayley). Certainly some preached a given funeral sermon multiple times (Evans). Congregants sometimes heard sermons preached in church that they guessed had originally been funeral sermons (Vaisey: 99). But it is clear is that most preachers used the occasion of a funeral to make the sermon a *memento mori*. As one parson put it, this was a proper occasion to contemplate the 'necessity of entertaining our Minds wth ye freqt Considerations of our latter End will be of great Advantage to us' (Finsthwaite Preacher).

Other than these particular occasions, parsons seem to have chosen a topic they thought important or relevant to their congregations, then found an appropriate biblical text, and developed a sermon—John Sharp sometimes matched texts to his sermons, rather than vice versa (Deconinck-Brossard). It was not unusual to preach a two- to five-part series based on the same text, but there seems to have been no long-term plan or pattern in the theme from week to week. Samuel Rand, rector of Hardwick and Shelton in Norfolk in 1683–1714, left us a priceless description of the reasons he chose to preach on the topics that he did when he collected his sermons together:

A.D. 1700 The Contents of this Book

4 Eph. 26 A discourse concerning anger, occasioned by ye many feuds & animosities among my parishioners of Hardwick & Shelton

13 Heb 4 A discourse agst fornication & adultery occasioned by yt great lewdness of yt kind in my parishes, especially in Hardwick

5 Levit 1 An exhortation to detect witnesses agst, & bring to punishmt, yt sin of swearing: yt be wt may help yt Magistrates in suppressing it

2 Chron 32:33 A discourse occasion'd by ye death of K. Wm yt 3rd of blessed memory

5 John 14 A discourse occasion'd by a very sickly limp [?] wch many were sick, but most Recovered

148 Psal 8 A discouse occasion'd by a dreadfull wind & tempest wch did very great damage both at land and sea

1 James 27 A discourse occasion'd by yt patent granted for yt relief of ye fatherless children & widows of ye seamen & others who perished in ye terrible & dreadful stormy wind Nov. 26th & 27th 1703

4 Hosea 4 A discourse occasioned by ye many causeless contentions of my parishioners of Hardwick & me ye Minister

13 Nehem 17 A discourse agst profaning ye Sabbath day

1 Acts 12 A discourse showing to a Sabbath days journey

12 Deut 13:14 A discourse shewing ye reasonableness of frequenting ye publick places of God's worship

8 Prov 34 A discourse exhorting persons to a constant attendance upon ye publick worship & service of God

5 Eccles 1 A discourse exhorting persons to behave ymselves decently & reverently at church, or in the house of God

4 Mark 4 A discourse exhorting persons wt doctrine they hear, entertain, & embrace

8 Luke 18 A discourse directing how to hear ye word of God

26 Math 40 A discourse agst sleeping at church

7 Luke 5 A discourse occasioned by her Majys patent for collecting of moneys towards ye directing & building a church for ye exercise of the Protestant Religion… in the Duchy of Berg, within the Empire of Germany

2 Gal 10 A discourse exhorting psons to remember ye poor in times of hardship & Difficulty

25 Prov 18 A discourse agst bearing false witness agst or neighbours. (Rand: 6)

It was probably quite common that parsons used the pulpit to correct or chastise their parishioners—the Sussex congregant and diarist, Thomas Turner, sometimes felt that his pastor addressed congregants in pique (Vaisey: 125–6). There is no question that they often had conflicts and felt that the people to whom they ministered were backward and godless (Spaeth; Chamberlain 2003: 85–7).

Samuel Rand was stern and direct in his sermons against the sins of his parishioners, but at least he did not point fingers from the pulpit. In his sermon against fornication, he began:

> Lewdness and debauchery being soe predominant in this age, yt filthy & smutty discourses from ye tongues of most persons; fornication & adultery are complained

of in most [areas?], ye presenting & trying ye cases of bastardy is most of the business of ye sessions, & ye murdering of base begotten children brought before ye judges at most Assizes, doe make a discourse upon such a subject as ys to be...highly necessary: especially from us Ministers of ye Gospel who are required (as we find 38 Isaiah 1) to cry aloud, & not to spare to lift up our voices like a trumpet, & shew or people yr transgressions & sin,...In my discourse upon the subject, I shall not reflect upon the particular persons who are guilty of the sins spoken agst in my talk soe as to expose ym; but shall endeavour to perswade ys who are guilty of ym to repent & to reform from yr abominations, & soe escape ye severe judgment of God at last. (Rand: 6:34)

Despite the fact that parsons like Rand sometimes wrote for very specific reasons, the majority of parish sermons seem designed for timelessness. Clearly they were written to be used on many different occasions. Clergy frequently gave the same sermons every few years. For many, it appears as if they wrote all of their sermons in the first year of their ministry and never wrote another one again (even John Sharp seems to have stopped writing early in his ministry) (Deconinck-Brossard: 111–12). Most parsons made notations on their manuscripts regarding when and where they preached a sermon. The durability of these sermons is amazing, since they were not infrequently preached across a long span of years. Consider the following two examples. One clergyman in Norfolk preached sermons repeatedly from 1689 until 1728, often in the same parish, but sometimes in neighboring parishes (Norfolk Preacher). Revd Francis Stanley, rector of Eastwick and vicar of North Weald, Essex, in 1764–85, started preaching his sermons in 1764, and continued using them every few years until 1821—a time span of nearly 60 years. Clearly his message to his people did not change one jot or tittle, since the manuscripts show very little alteration or emendation (Stanley). Since he had two parishes, his usual practice was to preach a sermon in one parish in the morning, and then the same sermon at the other parish in the afternoon. It was not uncommon, either, for neighbouring clergymen to visit each others' parishes and preach (Vaisey: 186). When George Woodward of Berkshire went to Kent for a visit in 1756, he clearly took some sermons with him because he records how he was ready at a moment's notice to preach for his 'brethren' (Gibson: 87).

Daniel Renaud provides a good illustration of preaching the same sermons in rotation. In 1766 and 1767, Renaud, rector of Whitchurch, Herefordshire, in 1728–72, carefully copied all of his sermons (or, at least, all that he thought worthy) in three bound volumes (Renaud: 1–3). These three volumes comprise 104 sermons. It is clear that he had already been preaching them, because preserved along with these volumes are identical sermons written into the standard booklets five or six years earlier (Renaud: 4–10). And it is clear that he planned to continue preaching them, since in each volume, he put in a chart with the number of the sermon on the x axis and the years, written out from 1766 to 1773, listed along the top of the y axis.

There is another important point to be made from the Renaud collection. One of Daniel Renaud's sons—David—became a parson in a different parish in another county, serving first as rector of East Chelborough in 1765–8, and then as vicar of Havant, Hampshire, in 1768–88. Daniel's sermons were passed along to David, and were preserved together with many of David's sermons. But there is no evidence that David preached his father's sermons. The son wrote his own discourses, and preached each one many times, but he did not even use the same texts as his father. So not every clergyman was willing to use others' sermons.

In fact, among the extant manuscripts, there seems to have been little sharing of biblical texts at all. As we will see below, many themes were very similar if not identical. But parsons evidently did not like to use the same texts. Out of hundreds of sermons consulted, only one or two were based on the same text and virtually none of the manuscript sermons used the same texts as those published in John Tillotson's sermons (Tillotson), despite that fact that Tillotson was held up as a paragon of preaching (Downey: 10). It may well be that many clergymen were preaching other people's sermons, but the ones who were writing their own did a significant amount of original work. When a Sussex pastor, John Latham, wrote a book to discourage young men from going into the priesthood because of the manifold trials of the clerical life, one of the reasons he gave was the intensive work involved in writing a sermon:

> For here he may by weekly Labour, by plodding, and torturing and racking his Brains, squeeze out something (whether coherent or incoherent, it is no Matter) which with much adoe (by changing and exchanging, and the Assistance of some necessary tho' very indifferent Helps) may be lick'd into the Model of a Thing commonly called a Sermon'. (Latham: ix)

In terms of what those 'Helps' were, we get hints from some sermons as well as other sources. A few sermon-writers actually put references in the texts of their manuscripts. Occasionally they would quote these to their congregants—Daniel Renaud cited classical authors such as St John Chrysostom and Numa Pompilius (Renaud: 2, sermon 7), and William Stanton, educated at Balliol College, Oxford between 1693 and 1697, mentioned Chrysostom, Bonaventure, and Hugo Grotius (Stanton). The sermons preached in Chiddingly, Sussex, probably in the late seventeenth century, were replete with marginal notations to Church Fathers such as Augustine and Lactantius (Chiddingly Preacher). Commonplace books reveal that clergymen were using a wide variety of sources from which they undoubtedly drew inspiration or theological reflections. John Henry Ott, who served as vicar of Bexhill, Sussex in 1722–39 and rector of Crumhill and Gameston, both in Nottinghamshire, in 1739–43, wrote down more quotes from John Tillotson's sermons than anything else, but he also had observations from a wide variety of other sources: Barrow's, Clarke's, Wilkins's, and Scott's sermons, Jean-Pierre de Crousaz, and even the *Spectator* and *Tatler* (Ott). Sermon notes from Lancashire around 1780 include quotes from William Laud's Diary, Quesnel's *Moral Reflections*, Jeremiah Seed's *Sermons*, as well as the *London Magazine*, the *Gentleman's Magazine*, the *Critical Review*, and the *London Review* (Lancashire Preacher). In the late eighteenth and early nineteenth centuries, John Longe, vicar of Coddenham in Suffolk, kept a sermon book where he carefully noted down the 'Author made use of'. He still used Tillotson and

Francis Atterbury, and not infrequently adapted sermons published more recently by William Gilpin, John Hewlett, and others. He also used some manuscript sermons of his contemporaries (Stone: 171–4). George Woodward read many collections of sermons. In a letter in 1757, he recorded his impressions of Bishop Conybeare's discourses:

> I think (as you do) that they are very good and rat[ion]al, but they are very long; and in my opinion he is too apt to labour a point, that wants no proof;...his style is by no means elegant, neither is his manner of reasoning so concise and striking, as Bishop Sherlock's. (Gibson: 100)

This gives us a lot of insight as to what clergymen thought made a good sermon—logical (but not abstruse), elegant, and not too long (usually around 30 minutes—see Gilpin: viii). Most sermons did not delve heavily into theology. There are certainly hosts of printed sermons that plunge into theological controversies and issues (Adams), but looking at most extant manuscript sermons, you would hardly know that there were theological disputes during most of the long eighteenth century. John Frewen, vicar of two Sussex parishes—Fairlight in 1726-43 and Guestling in 1736-1743—left papers that demonstrate that he was very concerned about Socianism (J. Frewen, *b*), yet nothing of this appears in his sermons. Even in Daniel Renaud's sermon on 1 Timothy 4:16 ('Take heed to thyself & to thy Doctrine') it is impossible to tell what doctrines one should stay away from. The gist of the discourse was that parishioners should follow the lead of the minister of the parish because he, as a 'Dispenser of God's Word' and a 'Teacher of Righteousness', would lead them into truth (Renaud: F63/2: 63). Though there are exceptions—for example, the sermons of Thomas Dalton, rector of Harting, in Sussex, in 1773-1822 (Dalton)—for most parish clergymen, the detailed theology seems to have been reserved for the catechism. Daniel Renaud's catechetical lectures were preserved along with his sermons. These covered the theology of each of the Thirty-Nine Articles in six separate discourses, and, though the discussion of each article is brief, the lectures are packed with theological meaning (Renaud: 17). John Frewen also catechized using his own *Commentary on the 39 Articles*, which went into much greater theological depth than his sermons (J. Frewen, *a*). Late in the century, William Gilpin recommended keeping sermons much simpler and less detailed than treatises (Gilpin: vi).

The most common themes of parish preaching appear to be obedience to God, avoidance of sin, and coping with a difficult life in hopes of a better life to come. The word 'duty' looms large in almost all of the sermons, as if preachers were taking their cue from *The Whole Duty of Man*. But this was not the genteel, worldly moral preaching that has often been depicted as dominant in this 'enlightened' age (Downey: 10–12)—it was based squarely on biblical warnings and the fear of eternal punishment. The pervasiveness of preaching against sin and vice was also mirrored in some parishioners' diaries (Vaisey: 24–6, 32, 39, 99, 125–126, 140, et. al.). The emphasis on obedience and the threat of punishment (even hell) is so dominant that, were it not for the liturgy of the Book of Common Prayer and the theology taught in catechism, a congregant might easily miss the theology of the atonement.

It is undoubtedly no accident that when Daniel Renaud recopied his sermons into his compendia, he began with the sermon on repentance. He explained that repentance 'comprehends in it all that change of Life, Whereby a Sinner forsakes his Evil Way, & becomes obedient to the precepts of the Gospel'. Then he added that 'the Remission of Sins is made a consequent to Repentance, so this Repentance must include in it Faith & Good Works, the Whole Duty of a Christian' (Renaud: 1:3). The theology that comes through over and over again in this period was the brand expressed by Archbishop Tillotson, that, in essence, sanctification preceded (or at least coincided with) justification (Chamberlain 1993). Justification was by faith, but if sanctification was not present in a person's life to the very end, that person could not be assured of going to heaven.

So preachers emphasized works, duty, and obedience, and they did not hesitate to threaten their parishioners with God's judgement if they did not manifest good works. The preacher at Chiddingly, Sussex, made the contrast stark in a sermon on Romans 8:13 ('For, if ye live after the flesh, ye shall dy; But, if ye through the Spirit do mortify the deeds of the body ye shall live.'):

> There are in the Text two parts.
> 1. A threatning, and
> 2. A promise.
>
> The threatning is as old as the sin of Man. You shall dy. The promise is as old as the Faith, and Obedience of man. You shall live.

That death, he went on to say, was twofold: a death here, and the 'death of Condemnation hereafter'. The preacher pleaded with his parishioners to be holy with Christ's help, and 'so live here, That we may live forever hereafter' (Chiddingly Preacher: f. 2).

The Revd Peter Lancaster, rector of Stanford River in Essex, proclaimed in a sermon on Colossians 3:8 that 'we should put off all these, anger, wrath, & malice, because unless we doe so we cannot be sure of ye pardon & forgiveness of our own *sins*'. Then he added this chilling comment:

> our souls will continue forever what we make them in this world, such habitts & dispositions as we carry from here will remain with us in ye other state, & consequently since god in his owne nature is infinitely pure & holy, & since our chiefest good & happinesse will consist in union & communion with him to all eternity all our unmortifyed affections, our vicious habits, our unruly lusts & passions not reputed of & subdued will hinder us from enjoying god with that inward delight & agreable satisfaction, which is necessary to make us happy even in heaven itself. (Lancaster: ff. 38, 52)

With the pervasiveness of such 'hellfire and damnation' preaching, one wonders what happened to the Enlightenment 'reasonable religion'. The answer is that it continued alongside—these preachers held dear the Enlightenment values of rationality and responsibility at the same time that they railed against sin. They emphasized Reason and talked about being able to discern God from nature. They maintained that God made humans to be 'rational souls' whose end was happiness (Birch: 4329 f. 88b; Deconinck-Brossard: 114; Davies).

It was undoubtedly because of their unabashed confidence in human nature that they could not fathom why people around them were so utterly profligate. After all, Reason itself taught people that holiness was the wise course of action (Keble: f. 1). People were responsible for their actions, and had the ability to live holy lives if they wished (Birch: 4327, sermon 2, and 4329 f. 80; Woodforde). But more often than not, they failed to follow the dictates of their consciences. Clergy throughout the century, therefore, often expressed their astonishment that sin was so pervasive and that people could so freely scoff against religion and swear blasphemously (Lloyd). Thomas Dalton preached in 1785 and after that 'the Bulk of Mankind are so hot in ye Pursuite of perishing Trifles that they can find no Leisure seriously to examine their Spiritual Condition' (Dalton). As William Stanton put it,

> 'Tis not now a days strange, by reason of ye universall commonness to see how securely people advance in all kind of wickedness, & impiety; even making the whole scene of their lives, one intire debauch: There reason is knock'd under, & ye brutell parts of men onely act their parts of life; & there remains nothing besides their shape to distinguish their body from worst of ye creation, & pest of ye world, & ye lumber of nature. (Stanton: f. 23)

He even waxed lyrical about the danger facing humankind: 'For, do we not see ye world dance (as it were) on ye very brink of ruin, & destruction? And as constantly running their causes in ye road to Hell, as ye Sun, does [lying] in ye circuit of Heaven?' (Stanton: f. 22). Late in the century David Renaud was echoing the same sentiment in his sermon on Jonah 1:6, a text which called on the sleeper to awake: 'It is a stupid Thing to be secure in ye midst of Danger. There are too many amongst us who are Insensible of our Danger, who live as in a Deep security even when we are ready to be swallow'd up by ye Indignation and wrath of ye Almighty' (Renaud: 48).

Thomas Birch, rector of St Margaret Pattens and St Gabriel, Fenchurch, London in 1746–55, tried to explain the perversity of people by talking about God hardening their hearts. He was at pains to explain this text, though, because he could not accept the idea that humans lacked freewill. Instead, Birch put the blame squarely back on sinners themselves—they had hardened their own hearts by wilfully turning away from Reason (Birch: 4327, f. 2). He never explained, however, why rational souls would do this in the first place.

There certainly were many temptations and enticements by which the devil lured people away from reasonable behaviour. Another significant reason pastors adduced to explain why people sinned against all logic was that punishment for sin was not swift. Yet even this was illogical, as John Ward, rector of Stoke in Hertfordshire in 1690–1734, made clear to a number of congregations in his sermon on Ecclesiastes 8:11:

> ...it is therefore a strange and most amazing thing that men should not consider what a grievous crime it is to make Gods forbearance of us an occasion to persist in our impenitency, that the continuance and larger share of his tender mercies should

> not molliefye our flinty hearte, but rather cause us to adde more fuel to the fire, how ungratefull & withal how dangerous a matter this is may we in time consider, otherwise justice will take place, Heaven will not be mocked by our delays and vain pretences, if we doe neglect the means of Grace, we may be assured that we shall bring down the divine vengeance upon our selves. (Ward: sermon 4)

And judgement coming upon sinners unexpectedly was a frequent theme (Hertfordshire Preacher; T. Frewen: ff. 2–9; Hutchinson).

So parsons often felt as if they were voices crying in the wilderness against sin (they were often successful in convincing parishioners too, as witnessed in Thomas Turner's diary (Vaisey: 137)). As far as they were concerned, the Church—indeed civilization itself—continued in danger throughout the entire period. But the danger was not principally from false doctrine or polity, it was due to the wickedness of the people. According to John Courtail, vicar of Burwash in Sussex in 1768–1806, previous ages were ungodly because of superstition; the contemporary one was bad because of sin which bred infidelity (Courtail: 17–18). David Renaud saw himself as a latter-day Abraham pleading to God not to destroy Sodom for the sake of a few righteous:

> You will say, peradventure, wt Hope is there of a general Reformation? The Whole Head is sick and ye whole Heart faint, and we are all overwounds and Bruises and putrified sores. Wt Fruit then can we expect fm a Handful here present. I answer let us do our Duty,... We cannot tell how far ye Intercession of a few faithful persons may avail to avert yt Cloud of Judgmts yt hovers over us. (Renaud: 48, sermon 1)

Even the most 'latitudinarian' preachers like Thomas Birch and Parson Woodforde continued to emphasize the folly of looking to this world for succour (Birch: 4327; Woodforde). The promise of heaven and the consolation of the afterlife were, therefore, constant refrains of parsons. The overwhelming majority of sermons were otherworldly in that they emphasized the difficulty of earthly existence and the rewards of heaven (Povey; Brownsword). As Thomas Frewen, rector of Sapcote, Leicestershire in 1732–78, proclaimed, 'And let us remember that this world was only allotted to Mankind, in order to a sincere preparation for the next' (T. Frewen: f. 8b). Focusing on the things of this life would result in misery, both here and in the hereafter, but focusing on God and our Christian duty would bring great joy. As Daniel Renaud put it, 'True Religion causes true joy & a sincere gladness, a joy, infinitely transcending the delights of sin;—and such gladness as heaven hereafter will improve' (Renaud: 1: 22). There were such rewards in Heaven: Thomas Evans, vicar of Bassaleg and curate of Caerleon, Wales, maintained that the trials and tribulations of this life were well worth it:

> Not one Injury or Affront we ever forgave but it qualifies us for the obtaining ye Forgiveness of our infinitely more heinous offences agst God. Not one Pang or Sickness we have patiently gone thro & with Xtan Resignation, but it will be repaid with Interest in perfect tranquility & Joy for evermore. (Evans)

Thomas Dalton preached a tender sermon on Matthew 11:28:

> When we attempt to think of that exalted Happiness, we can do little more than remove from it in our Minds all those afflictions, Evils, & grounds of Discouragement which we at present feel... All their Burdens shall drop with their naturall bodies, none of them can pass beyond the Grave. Then Faith & Hope shall become sight & Enjoyment; then Love more perfect shall cast out Fear; & nothing shall remain of all these former Trials, but ye grateful Remembrance of that friendly Hand which supported them, & hath [replaced] their light & momentary afflictions with ye far more exceeding & eternal Weight of Glory. (Dalton)

Parsons continued to have an unshakeable confidence in the divine pattern of rank and order (Bridgen; Lewis). Daniel Renaud told his congregation that 'Societies & Communities are erected in the World by the Will & Providence of God, for the Preservation & Security of Mankind, & that every one is bound, according to his Ability & Rank to help & contribute to their Maintenance' (Renaud: 2:27). People ought not to try to rise above their station in life, but to be content with their lot, a view repeated in Thomas Dalton's sermon on 'Submission and Divine Providence' (Dalton).

It is hard to get a good handle on the delivery style of parish sermons. Parishioners did not seem to object to their pastor reading the sermon, though it did make a difference whether there was 'warmth' in the preaching or not (Vaisey: 131, 186; Lessenich: 132–50). There is little doubt that people flocked to the Methodists and evangelicals when they emerged on the scene. The emphasis of the evangelicals on grace and faith rather than works must have seemed like a breath of fresh air (note the stark difference of emphasis in the sermons of John Stuart, who 'gloried' in being one of 'that sect' (Stuart: 49). Their delivery was often much more dynamic too (Lessenich: 132–42). When John Egerton gave his first visitation sermon after becoming Bishop of Bangor in 1774, he addressed his clergy about the threat of the Methodists. Evidently many of his hearers were not vibrant preachers, because he made a point of saying that eloquence was not required of ministers of the Gospel—some men had the quality and some did not. Rather, parsons should win people over by being good examples, caring diligently for their parishioners, and making cogent arguments (Egerton). Preaching took on even greater importance with the encroachment of Methodism, but so did the individual approach and demeanour of the parson (Courtail); this was the same approach as that advocated for Dissenters some decades earlier (Hargraves). The clergy may have redoubled their efforts, but they evidently kept on preaching the same sermons—perhaps they felt the age-old message was the solution.

In conclusion, though this chapter is based on a limited number of manuscript sources, those sources do span the entire long eighteenth century, and contain samples from many different regions. The manuscripts are consistent enough that it is reasonable to come to some basic conclusions. The majority of parsons developed a corpus of sermons that they used over and over. Those sermons focused on sin and judgement, obedience to God, hardships in the here and now, and the rewards of the afterlife. The fabric of the rhetoric of these sermons was stretched across a frame of logic and scripture, but often woven with redolent words and judicious, powerful phrasing. Parsons could fulminate, but they could also console. At their worst, parish sermons were repetitive and rudimentary, but at their best, they could be rhapsodic and soaring, and undoubtedly moving and meaningful to congregants. They were clearly an important part of worship, because it was a truism that people were more apt to attend a service with a sermon than prayers alone (Secker). If eighteenth-century parish sermons come across to modern readers as dry or stale, that is doubtless because we cannot hear them in the same context and with the same perspective as parishioners of the period.

References

Adams, G. (1752). *An Exposition of Some Articles of Religion which Strike at the Tenets of the Arians and Socinians. Likewise at the Infidels, Romanists, Lutherans and Calvinists. In Several Sermons and Dissertations*. London: Clarke, Johnson, Owen.

Albers, J. 'Seeds of Contention: Society, Politics and the Church of England in Lancashire, 1689–1790'. Ph.D. dissertation, Yale University, 1988.

Berkeley, G. Manuscripts. British Library, Add. MS 39,306, ff. 142–5.

Birch, T. Manuscript collection. British Library, Add. MS 4327–4330.

Bridgen, W. (1713). *The Duty and Power of the Magistrate in Matters of Religion Vindicated. In a Sermon Preach'd at East Grinstead [...]*. London: n. p.

Brinton, A. (1992). 'The Passions as Subject Matter in Early Eighteenth-Century Sermons'. *Rhetorica* 10.1: 51–69.

Brownsword, W. (1704). *A Sermon Preach'd at Steyning*. London: J. Nutt.

Burdett, C. (1760). *A Sermon Preached before the Honourable House of Commons*. London: John Knapton.

Chamberlain, J. S. (1993). 'Moralism, Justification, and the Controversy over Methodism'. *The Journal of Ecclesiastical History* 44–4: 652–79.

—— (2003). 'A Regular and Well-Affected Diocese: Chichester in the Eighteenth Century', in J. Gregory and J. Chamberlain (eds.), *The National Church in Local Perspective*. Woodbridge, Suffolk: Boydell Press, 73–98.

Chiddingly Preacher. Manuscript sermons. Bodleian Library, MS Rawl. E. 90.

Claydon, T. (2000). 'The Sermon, the "Public Sphere" and the Political Culture of Late Seventeenth-Century England', in L. Ferrell and P. McCullough (eds.), *The English Sermon Revised: Religion, Literature and History 1600–1750*. Manchester: Manchester University Press, 208–34.

Courtail, J. (1760). *The Expedience and Necessity of Wisdom and Innocence towards a due Discharge of the Ministerial Office*. London: J. Whiston and B. White.

Dalton, T. Manuscript sermons. West Sussex Record Office, Par 98/7/115.

Davies, T. (1776). *Rational Religion Recommended; or, a Caution against the Evils Attending the Want of Understanding in Religious Matters. A Sermon*. London: William Lee.

Deconinck-Brossard, F. (1993). 'Eighteenth-Century Sermons and the Age', in W. M. Jacob and N. Yates (eds.), *Crown and Mitre: Religion and Society in Northern Europe Since the Reformation*. Woodbridge, Suffolk: Boydell Press, 105–21.

Downey, J. (1969). *The Eighteenth Century Pulpit*. Oxford: Clarendon Press.

Egerton, J. Sermons and papers. Hertfordshire Archives and Local Studies. HALH, AH 1993.

Evans, T. Manuscript sermons, 1759–1773. Ashmolean Museum, JE/A/6/3.

Finsthwaite Preacher. Funeral sermon for Mrs Mary Backhouse of Jollyvertree, Finsthwaite. Lancashire Record Office, DDPD 26.

Fraser, A. (1871). *Life and Letters of George Berkeley, D. D.* Oxford: Clarendon Press.

Frewen, J. (*a*). *Commentary on the 39 Articles*, East Sussex Record Office, FRE 687.

Frewen, J. (*b*). Manuscript papers and sermons. East Sussex Record Office, FRE 519.

Frewen, T. Manuscript Sermons. Bodleian Library, MS Rawl. E. 5.

Garstang Preacher. Anonymous sermons, but preached in the town of Garstang in the 1750s. Lancashire Record Office, PR2435.

Gibson, D. (ed.) (1982). *A Parson in the Vale of White Horse: George Woodward's Letters from East Hendred, 1753–1761*. Gloucester: Alan Sutton.

Gilpin, W. (1799). *Sermons Preached to a Country Congregation, to which are Added a Few Hints for Sermons*. Lymington: J. S. Rutter.

Gordon, A. (1790). *Sermons on Several Subjects and Occasions*, vol. 2. London: A. Gordon.

Gregory, J., and Chamberlain, J. (eds.) (2002). *The National Church in Local Perspective*. Woodbridge, Suffolk: Boydell Press.

Hargraves, J. (1724). *A Sermon Preached in LAMBETH-CHAPEL*. London: J. Stagg.

Hayley, W. (1699). *A Sermon Preached in the Parish Church of St. Giles in the Fields. At the Funeral of Bernard Connor*. London: Jacob Tonson.

Herefordshire Preacher. Bundle of anonymous sermons. Herefordshire Record Office, B47/H131/1.

Hertfordshire Preacher. Bundle of anonymous sermons. Hertfordshire Archive and Local History, D/EHx F107.

Hutchinson, T. (1746). *A Sermon Preached in the Parish-Church of Horsham in Sussex*. London: Jeremiah Reason.

Keble, J. (1778–1813). Manuscript sermons. Lambeth Palace Library, Keble 7/4.

Lancashire Preacher. Sermon notes c. 1780. Lancashire Record Office, PR 2851.

Lancaster, Peter. Manuscript sermons, Bodleian Library, MS Rawl. E. 135.

Latham, J. (1736). *A Short View of the Difficulties and Discouragements Attending those who Enter into Holy Orders*. London: W. Parker.

Lessenich, R. (1972). *Elements of Pulpit Oratory in Eighteenth-Century England (1660–1800)*. Cologne and Vienna: Böhlau Verlag.

Lewis, G. (1719). *Submission to the Divine Will Recommended, in a Sermon, Preach'd at Westram in Kent*. London: Jonah Bowyer.

Lloyd, J. (1713). *The Egregious Folly and Sinfulness of the Most Detestable Crime of Scoffing and Derision*. London: Henry Clements.

Newhouse, T. Will. Public Record Office, Prob 11/998, 195 Bargrave 1774.

Newlin, T. (1736). *The Crown of Righteousness. A Sermon Preached at Wiston in Sussex, at the Funeral of the Reverend Mr John Hart, Rector of the Said Parish*. London: W. Parker.

Norfolk Preacher. Manuscript sermons of anonymous preacher. Norfolk Record Office, COL 7/9.

Oliver, R. (1700). *A Sermon Preach'd at the Funeral of George Payne, Jun*. London: Arthur Bettesworth.

Ott, J. H. Commonplace book. British Library, Add. MS 27, 617.

Povey, J. (1698). *A Sermon Preached in the Colledge Church of St. Katharins*. London: J. Mayos.

Rand, S. Sermon Books. Norfolk Record Office, COL 7/6–8.

Renaud, D(aniel). Manuscript sermons and papers. Herefordshire Record Office, F63/1–24, 25–48.

Secker, T. Letter to Samuel Dugard, 27 Feb. 1766. Lambeth Palace Library, Secker Papers, vol. 6, f. 197.

Spaeth, D. (2000). *The Church in an Age of Danger: Parsons and Parishioners, 1660–1740*. Cambridge: Cambridge University Press.

Stanley, F. Manuscript Sermons. Hertfordshire Archive and Local History, D/P 44/3/8.

Stanton, W. Manuscript Sermons. Bodleian Library, MS. Rawl. E. 34.

Stone, M. (ed.) (2008). *The Diary of John Longe (1765–1834) Vicar of Coddenham*. Woodbridge: Boydell Press for Suffolk Record Society.

Stuart, J. (1753). *The Necessity of Faith in Prayer. Two Sermons*. London: Charles Breed.

Sykes, N. (1939). 'The Sermons of a Country Parson: James Woodforde in His Pulpit'. *Theology* 38–224: 97–106.

Tillotson, J. (1673). *Sermons Preach'd Upon Several Occasions*. London: S. Gellibrand.

Vaisey, D. (ed.) (1985). *The Diary of Thomas Turner 1754–1765*. Oxford: Oxford University Press.

Ward, J. Manuscript sermons. Herefordshire Record Office, B47/H131.

Weinbrot, H. (2010). 'The Thirtieth of January Sermon: Swift, Johnson, Sterne, and the Evolution of Culture'. *Eighteenth-Century Life* 34–10: 29–55.

Wilkins, J. (1646). *Ecclesiastes, or, A Discourse Concerning the Gift of Preaching as it Fals under the Rules of Art*. London: Samuel Gellibrand.

Woodforde, J. Manuscript sermon. Norfolk Record Office, WKC 7/168, 404 x 9.

CHAPTER 4

PARISH PREACHING IN THE VICTORIAN ERA: THE VILLAGE SERMON

FRANCES KNIGHT

'True,' said Dorothea. 'It is hard to imagine what sort of notions our farmers and labourers get from their teaching. I have been looking into a volume of sermons by Mr. Tyke: such sermons would be of no use at Lowick—I mean, about imputed righteousness and the prophecies in the Apocalypse.'

George Eliot, *Middlemarch*

AMONG the many bound volumes of printed sermons which survive from the Victorian era, it is likely that the largest discrete category is that of the village sermon. Numerous collections of village sermons steadily rolled off the presses from the 1820s to the early years of the twentieth century. Their authors were largely, though not exclusively, Anglican clergymen, and they spoke from every theological perspective from the premillennial to the advanced Tractarian. This homiletic genre was remarkably popular and well understood during the nineteenth century, by preachers, by publishers, and by the purchasers of printed sermon collections. Yet, in common with much else about nineteenth-century preaching, it has been totally neglected since. It is hoped that this investigation of the village sermon will allow us to understand more about the mind-set and the practice of the nineteenth-century preacher in his parish setting. What was it about publishing sermons addressed to villagers that he found so compelling, and how did he visualize his village? What did he expect of the villagers, and how did he approach them? How were village sermons typically constructed? How did preachers use the Bible, and what reference did they make to Christian themes and the seasons of the Church's year?

This study is based on a sample of 150 volumes of village sermons located in the British Library catalogue that were published between 1804 and 1906. In order to qualify for inclusion in the sample, the volume of sermons had to have the words 'village' or 'country' in its title, and it had to be a collection of such sermons; no single items were included. In most cases the author is identifiable, and in all cases where the author is identified, he is the sole author of the entire volume; no edited collections of village sermons from multiple authors have been discovered. Some authors produced multiple volumes of village sermons, but later editions of earlier works are excluded. The sample includes some anonymous works, such as *Twelve Plain Sermons Preached in a Village Church* (1833) and *Plain Sermons for Country People by a Clergyman* (1862), the criteria for inclusion being the words 'village' and 'country' in the title. The rigid insistence on a narrow range of titles filtered out the numerous collections of 'plain' or 'parochial' sermons which also exist, but which are not overtly directed at village audiences. It also excluded collections of sermons which were 'preached in the parish of X', even when 'X' would have been considered a 'village' at the time of preaching. Thus the 150 volumes analysed here are undoubtedly an underestimate of the true number of what were considered village sermons that were printed in the nineteenth century. They constitute a comprehensive, but not a complete, survey. The definition of what qualified as a village sermon was made deliberately narrow in order to prevent the sample from becoming an amorphous collection of parish preaching, in which the focus on the rural community of the 'village' was obscured.

Who Published Village Sermons?

Anglican clergymen of all types published collections of village sermons: it was not associated with any particular churchmanship or ministerial pattern. Some clergy prepared their village sermons for publication at a very early stage in their careers—in the case of the pre-millenarian Evangelical Alexander Dallas, just a year after his ordination, and in the case of George Butler (better known later as the husband of Josephine Butler) just three years after his ordination. Among those who, unlike Dallas, are presumed not to have been imminently expecting the second coming, it was more common to wait. Clergy might reasonably expect to gain experience in their rural parishes, and to hone their sermons on their congregations, as well as in the study, before rushing into print. It was also very common for a volume of village sermons to be assembled by a relative, and published a year or so after the preacher's death, both as an epitaph to his time in rural ministry, and as evidence of his ability to communicate clearly, something which, as we shall see, was very highly regarded.

In analysing village sermons it is important to appreciate that the date of publication is not indicative of when the material was preached. Thus R. W. Church died in 1890, and his *Village Sermons* were published in three volumes between 1892 and 1897, with a later edition in 1913. The sermons originated in his Somerset parish of

Whately between 1853 and 1871, and within this date range it is impossible to know when they were created. Similarly, Thomas Arnold died in 1842, and in 1878 his daughter published the sermons he had preached at his Surrey parish of Laleham in the 1820s. (Some of his village sermons had been available earlier, but she decided to publish them systematically 'for a fresh class of readers', believing them to have retained their 'freshness and force' over the intervening half century.) It is only occasionally possible to pin down a village sermon to a particular time of writing or preaching, which makes it harder to make generalizations about changing styles of preaching as the decades pass.

Well-known clergy had little difficulty in seeing their works into print in the nineteenth century, and many of the authors of village sermons were well known. Of the ninety-nine named individual authors in the sample, twenty-nine are included in the *Oxford Dictionary of National Biography*. The fact that the genre was favoured by men of all ecclesiastical standpoints (or their executors) is easy to see: famous Evangelical authors of village sermons were Thomas Scott and T. R. Birks, the Broad churchmen included Thomas Arnold and J. W. Colenso, moderate High churchmen were John James Blunt and Thomas Thorp, and the Tractarians included John Keble and R. W. Church. However, when the Tractarians issued ten volumes of their sermons between 1839 and 1848, Thomas Keble successfully lobbied for having the title changed from *Village Sermons* to *Plain Sermons*, although his reasons are not known (Ellison 2010: 36–8). Other very well-known authors of village sermons were Sydney Smith and Charles Kingsley, and among top-ranking theologians may be noted F. D. Maurice, B. F. Westcott, and F. J. A. Hort. Several more, like Thomas Kerchever Arnold, Edward Berens, and Charles Heurtley, were reasonably prolific authors who were well known in the Church of their day, although now they are seldom remembered. Some are today principally known as hymn-writers, such as Henry Alford and Sabine Baring-Gould (who is also remembered as a prodigious novelist, religious writer, and folk-song collector). Nevertheless, about two-thirds of the sample is composed of parish clergy whose lives remain fairly obscure, and a few were well-known Nonconformist ministers, such as the Independent George Burder and the Baptist Jabez Burns.

Twenty-two volumes of village sermons in the sample were published in the 1820s, as the earlier trickle turned into more of a torrent. *Sermons Preached Before a Country Congregation* was a title much favoured at this period, with authors and publishers seemingly indifferent to the fact that other works were appearing with identical or almost identical titles: something which seemed of little consequence for the next eighty years. Edward Berens, who became one of the early 'specialists' in village preaching, published the first of his seven collections anonymously in 1820. Thomas Scott's executors produced *Village Discourses, Composed From Notes of Sermons, Preached at Aston Sandford* in 1825. Scott had served Aston Sandford, Buckinghamshire, from 1801 until his death in 1821, and had belonged very much to the world of eighteenth-century Evangelicalism. As the title makes clear, the sermons were reconstructed from the notes of his hearers; he had not left his sermon material neatly with the intention that it should be brought to publication. Most of the other authors from this decade come within the category of 'obscure clergy', indicating that it was a genre that was developed by ordinary country clerics and then adopted by the more famous, rather than the other way round.

Village sermons continued to be published at a steady rate until the early years of the twentieth century. The 1850s were a particularly prolific decade, seeing the publication of twenty-eight of the volumes in the sample. It was also the decade when the majority of the British population began to live in towns for the first time, when public health reached an all-time crisis and when for many the 'village' was becoming more of a memory, or even an imagined community, rather than a reality. In the second half of the century, the output began to slow, but only very gradually. Seventeen volumes were published in the 1860s, eleven in the 1870s, fifteen in the 1880s, and fourteen in the 1890s.

The Allure of the Village

To a greater extent than is often appreciated, the idea of the village parish burned brightly in the mental world of the nineteenth-century Anglican cleric, and it continued to burn brightly, even as Britain accelerated into an urban and suburban transformation. Should we interpret the continuing enthusiasm for village sermons as a sign of dogged refusal to take note of these changes, and of a desire to retreat into the nostalgic evocation of small-scale, compliant communities where Dissenters were few, free thinkers were unthought of, and the vicar was perceived as king of all he surveyed? It is impossible to escape entirely from this conclusion. On the other hand, as I have argued elsewhere, the extent to which much of nineteenth-century Britain continued to remain rural tends to be overlooked, and country churches continued to provide a loud heartbeat for Anglican experience (Knight). With this in view, the continuing market for village sermons becomes more explicable. Clerical experience at the *fin de siècle* was as much about wondering how the century's finest theologians had communicated the gospel in the ordinary parish as it was about being shocked by Oscar Wilde or the 'new women' who wanted divorce on demand. Moreover, few village sermons were dependent for their success on the rurality of the location; they could equally well be read profitably by those preaching in towns or cities.

The 1850s saw a sharpening of interest among clergy in the life of the village. Not only, as we have seen, was it the peak decade for the publication of village sermons, but it also witnessed the rapid spread of harvest festivals, and the publication of material designed to advise clergy on some of the associated developments, for example John Thomas's *How Shall the Parish Feast Be Dealt With?* (Thomas). Vastly ambitious in its conception of what a clergyman should do in his country parish was the anonymous *Village Development Based on Practical Principles or, the Old Vicar's Advice* (1854), which was couched in the form of an extended letter from an 'old vicar' to a young priest setting out on a rural incumbency. The opening advice on how he should conduct the services was unremarkable enough: 'be punctual...don't mumble...avoid wearing creaky shoes'. It was in the lengthy section on 'The Village' that the work moved into a different realm. The author advised the young priest that he should consider the village 'as your farm...it should be your business to improve [it] in every possible way, towards what your ideas of a model village should be' (*Village Development*: 35). Many of the instructions which followed related to improving the physical appearance of the village, for example using the parsonage garden to grow plants which could be given to parishioners to fill window boxes, keeping a supply of paint for them to use for decorating, and advising them to move their manure heap away from the cottage door. Clearly influenced by Prince Albert's model cottages at the Great Exhibition, the author advised the priest to commission the village carpenter to make some cheap and useful furniture, and then 'make a sort of little exhibition' (*Village Development*: 37) so that the parishioners could see and gradually adopt the furniture, for example replacing huge and unhygienic curtained bedsteads with neat smaller beds with built-in chests of drawers. Rather than merely advising parishioners on how to improve their homes, the priest should set up a range of village institutions and services. These should include a village library with tea room attached, a playground and park, village allotments, village shows for flowers, vegetables and poultry, a parish savings bank, an emigration fund, a charity shop (for the disposal of bulky old furniture), a lodging house, a temperance hotel, a village hospital, and a public kitchen (building on the already common institution of the public bakehouse). Careful instructions are provided on how each of these facilities should be established and managed, although very little is said about how they should be paid for, or how the priest should handle objectors or vested interests. A somewhat vaguely constituted monthly meeting of parishioners is envisaged, which 'will also be in some measure your fund and security in monetary arrangements...the clergyman is not expected to do more out of his own pocket than give a moderate subscription' (*Village Development*: 70–2).

The anonymous nature of this publication means that it is impossible to link it with any particular parish in order to assess the extent to which its author succeeded in practising what he preached. It is not clear whether there ever was a village exactly like the one he described, or whether it was an extended fantasy on what would be desirable in an ideal world. But whether or not it was all true is beside the point. What the book reveals is the allure which the English village held in the mid-nineteenth century clerical imagination, and the possibilities which it was thought to hold for instilling social harmony and material well-being. Nor was it all hopelessly idealistic. There were many parishes in which at least one or two similar schemes were successfully put into practice. At Fenny Compton, Charles Heurtley successfully organized a small company to provide a proper water supply for the village. At Eversley, Charles Kingsley established a lending library and ran adult education classes on three nights a week. He also ran several parish savings schemes, and doled out bread and soup (Chitty: 96). What is striking, however, is the extent to which the clergyman is placed so firmly at the centre of the village, a benevolent autocrat retaining his ancient status as the only educated gentleman in the community. The motto at the front of the book, to the effect that men are simply boys grown big, a sentiment repeated in the text, tends to reinforce the infantilizing of the male villagers and the distance between them and their modern, omnicompetent parson. For Anglican clergy, the village represented the ideal community, in which 'all the inhabitants [are]…admitted into the Church of Christ by the same common baptism…meeting together in the same sacred edifice for public worship, and walking in the house of God as friends' (Berens: 215). The ideal of unity is a factor in explaining the popularity of village sermons, although the reality of religious difference at this date could not be ignored. Berens went on to insist on the duty of obedience to the parish minister, and to compare 'schism in a parish, when its inhabitants are split into religious parties, some choosing one teacher, some another; some resorting to church, and others to a meeting-house' (Berens: 219) as being reminiscent of the Church at Corinth.

As a homiletic category, the village sermon is to be distinguished from other major sermon categories, including the visitation sermon, the cathedral sermon, the university sermon, and the public school sermon, volumes of which were also published during the nineteenth century. Robert Ellison has considered some of these categories in relation to Tractarian preaching, although he does not discuss village sermons, in part at least because of the Tractarian fondness for the terms 'parochial' and 'plain' (Ellison 2010). University sermons were obviously intended for an educated audience, and public school sermons for an audience that was being educated; many of the same assumptions—from the duties and opportunities weighing on the hearers' lives to their comprehension of phrases in Latin and Greek—could safely be made. 'Town' sermons also exist, but in such small numbers that it is difficult to do more than make a couple of tentative suggestions about them. The first is that they may sometimes have tackled more challenging themes than would have been typical in the countryside. Charles Hardwick's *Twenty Sermons for Town Congregations*, which were preached in London in 1851 and 1852, included 'The Fall of the First Man', 'Rachel Weeping for her Children', 'The Real Object of the Athanasian Creed', and 'The Rich Man his Doom'. Hardwick seems to have had a relentless willingness to tackle difficult material in the city. This may also be true of Charles Kingsley's urban offerings, although his *Town and Country Sermons* usually fail to make clear which were preached in the town and which in the country, so it is impossible to draw any firm conclusions. Hardwick's town sermons tended to be more topical, and it is significant that he had them published just a year after they were preached—a very rapid turnaround by the standards of contemporary sermon publication. He expected his hearers to be familiar with current events, as seen in this extract from a sermon entitled 'The Papal Monarch Not Founded on the Rock', which was preached on St Peter's Day 1851 as a commentary on the setting up of the Roman Catholic hierarchy in the previous year:

> It is superfluous to remind you that a foreign power; inhabiting what I may call the mother-city of the west, inherits the ambitious and aggressive spirit of the ancient Romans, when their eagle flew victorious to the limits of the earth…The present age has seen her bracing on her arms afresh, and publishing in all the world, in west and east alike, her long-exploded claims to universal empire. But her engines, as you know, have been especially directed to this country. (Hardwick: 174)

This little snippet, evoking as it does a world far beyond the parish, is of a different character from the village sermons we shall consider shortly. In contrast with preaching aimed exclusively at educated upper and middle-class males, or at more sophisticated urban audiences, village sermons were seen as being timeless and simple. Indeed, it was their timelessness which was an important factor in making them publishable many years after their initial preaching. There was an unspoken assumption that the countryside, and country people, did not change.

The Preparation of the Village Sermon

The incumbent of the 'developed village' discussed in the previous section would presumably have had little time to prepare his sermon, in the midst of his many practical projects. The author advises the following:

> Let your sermon be short, and to the purpose. A sermon should be an explanation and a familiar application of a certain portion of Scripture, not simply a verse, which, after a few slight observations, gradually merges into a long discussion of the individual clergyman's favourite doctrine. No; let your sermon advocate Christian, manly energy, based on our Saviour's mediation and forgiveness, social improvement, and love and good-will to our fellow creatures, assisted by familiar illustration, which will recall the precepts in their domestic duties; prefer a text from the Sermon on the Mount rather than the Apocalypse. You will find the former more practical, and therefore, more beneficial. (*Village Development*: 16)

Some of the key elements in this advice—the virtue of relative brevity, clarity, and the importance of a coherent exposition of an identifiable portion of scripture—were repeated by all who offered thoughts on the art of village preaching. A preaching time of half an hour, producing about ten printed pages, was generally considered to be quite sufficient. There was a difference of opinion as to how the sermons should be pitched, with some preachers seeing their rural congregations as very simple, and others appreciating that they comprised a cross-section of intellectual ability and experience. Hort regarded his Hertfordshire congregation at St Ippolyts as 'a very simple class of hearers' (Hort 1900: ii). In contrast, J. J. Blunt warned against underestimating the understanding of the congregation:

> It is a mistake…in to which many young preachers fall, that they reckon upon the simple people they have to address as loving simplicity over-much, and on this account dilute their divinity till it is really too small for babes…In almost all congregations there are *some* persons of liberal education, *many* of shrewd natural parts; and it must be always borne in mind that the Bible and what relates to it is the whole compass of *every* poor man's literature. (Blunt: 149)

Meanwhile, William Jackson reminded his readers that 'village congregations usually contain a diversity of ranks, for each of which meat should be provided in due season' (Jackson: v). Harvey Goodwin expanded on the feeding metaphor: 'This mixture of people, who are to be fed with the same food, does in reality constitute one great difficulty of sermons, whether in town or country, as regards not words only, but other matters as well' (Goodwin: 112).

William Gresley admitted that one of the major challenges in preaching came from the mixed nature of the congregation (in wealth, status, and age, as well as in intelligence). He thought that this could be overcome if the preacher had a detailed knowledge of his hearers, and tried his best to adapt his message to their circumstances (Gresley: 3, 27). Gresley believed that a different tone was needed for country and town audiences, which gives some substance to the notion that the village preaching style was indeed different from its urban counterpart:

> Plain and homely sayings, and common illustrations which would suit a country congregation, are inadmissible before a more refined audience. You might quote 2 Peter ii 22 in the country, but perhaps in town it would be better to seek for some other illustration, than to apply to your congregation the homely proverb—'the dog is turned to his own vomit again, and the sow that was washed to her wallowing in the mire'. Undoubtedly quaint, or even homely expressions, will sometimes 'hitch' themselves in the mind, and be remembered when more serious matter is forgotten. (Gresley: 349–50)

All, however, agreed that 'plainness' was a sermon's chief virtue. A plain sermon was, Goodwin insisted, 'not plain in the sense in which that adjective is applied to the human face, namely in the sense of uninteresting and unattractive' but plain as in clear and well thought out. Nor should the use of very simple language be confused with plainness. He warned that an abstract thought would remain unintelligible, although expressed entirely in words of one syllable (Goodwin: 114, 119). The Sermon on the Mount was held up to readers as the model of plainness. J. J. Blunt, Lady Margaret Professor of Divinity at the University of Cambridge, and formerly a village parson in Shropshire and Essex, published posthumously in 1856 the lectures which he had given to divinity students as *The Acquirements and Principal Obligations and Duties of the Parish Priest*. It was a work which has been judged to have been almost immediately obsolete,

> not simply because of its donnish tone but because the book presupposed a readership of university-educated country clergy (it recommended extensive reading for the preparation of sermons), whose parishioners were mostly agricultural workers: the industrial revolution and problems of the church in large cities might not have existed. (Pickles)

In fairness to Blunt, all other writers on homiletics at this period also urged extensive reading as a preliminary to preaching. Blunt did, however, attract some criticism with his suggestion that sermons should consist as far as possible of Anglo-Saxon vocabulary:

> So far then as it is worth while to deliberate upon a choice of words, those of Anglo-Saxon origin...are to have a preference over those of Latin or French extraction, where there is room for selection; and still on the same grounds as before, for the sake of *taste* and of *plainness*. The most refined of your congregation will hail them as English undefiled, and the most illiterate will understand them, as their mother-tongue. (Blunt: 172)

The notion that the parishioners of Great Oakley, Essex, had been struggling to comprehend common words which had been in circulation for hundreds of years does seem faintly ridiculous, and Goodwin thought so too:

> Even to a village congregation I do not know that Saxon substitutes could easily give you such words as these: *congregation, educated, possible, edifying, squire, vulgarity, intended etc.* What is needed is a grasp of idiomatic English. The humblest auditors are familiar with Bible English, so a copious vocabulary is ever at hand. (Goodwin: 113)

A plain sermon was one which the preacher had prepared himself. William Gresley gave considerable space to insisting that all clergy—even the most inexperienced—should write their own material, even if it seemed less impressive than what was available in printed format. 'A moderate sermon of your own will have twice the effect of a much better one written by another' (Gresley: 2; for more on Gresley, see Skinner, *passim*). Young clergy needed to be reassured on this point, for 'sermon culture' retained an immensely powerful hold in Victorian Britain, and the clergy continued to be judged very largely on the basis of their performance in the pulpit. The temptation to preach other people's sermons was considerable, particularly for those who had had no training in homiletics, and who were lacking in confidence. According to Gresley, there were many reasons for preferring one's own productions. For one thing, only one's own sermons could be individually tailored to meet the particular needs of the congregation. Second, a sermon should be heart-felt, rather than impressive: a man could only be eloquent when he was speaking his own thoughts. Third, by studying in preparation for a sermon, a preacher formed his opinions and increased his stock of knowledge: 'a preacher of printed sermons is not in general of a very studious turn' and his doctrine was likely to be inconsistent. 'He may be an Arminian one Sunday, a high Calvinist the next'—the head of John Calvin clapped on the shoulders of Wesley, or vice versa. 'The worst thing you can do is make a patch-work of your sermon, by taking part from one place, and part from another.' Gresley concluded candidly: 'If you must steal, steal it all, and all from the same place; but the better way is not to steal.' Finally, there was the risk that the congregation would find out that the words were not the preacher's own, condemn him as idle, and abandon his church (Gresley: 5–8).

What then was the justification for publishing so many sermons, if all they did was create a dangerous temptation? Gresley believed that they could be read, but only in private. Charles Heurtley agreed, but only at a fairly late point in the sequence of preparation for a sermon, which should begin with prayer, and then proceed with study of the text in the original Greek or Hebrew, followed by the judicious use of a commentary. Only after these stages had been completed should printed sermons on the same text be consulted (Heurtley 1879: 143). Many of the editors of the sermons in the sample made comments in the preface about the hoped-for usefulness to other preachers of the work being published: naturally, none suggested that their works should be read out *in extenso*. Some were clearly designed for private reading only, and as a help for the house-bound, such as George Burder's *Twelve Sermons to the Aged, in Large Type* (1829). The printed sermon volumes considered here were very different productions from the individual sermons printed in copper-plate, which were designed to be taken into the pulpit and passed off as the author's own work.

The Use of the Bible and Moral Exhortation

All of the sermons that have been considered in this study were linked to a biblical text, which was printed at the beginning. The manner in which the sermon writers used their portion of scripture varied considerably. Most may be located somewhere on a spectrum which had biblical exposition at one end and moral exhortation at the other. Those at the 'biblical exposition' end spent the bulk of their sermon discussing what the text might mean, how the characters involved might have reacted, and how other parts of the Bible might shed further light on the matter. They tended to intersperse this with fairly brief passages of application. Those at the 'moral exhortation' end spent much of their sermons issuing warnings about the eternal fate of the lost, and urging their hearers and readers to repentance, faith, and good behaviour. They tended to use the chosen text as little more than a garnish or a motto, a hook which allowed them to move very rapidly into moral teaching, although sometimes they would pile on other, but unrelated, scriptural references. Most preachers were somewhere in the middle of this spectrum, interspersing observations about the Bible with observations about the temptations and shortcomings of nineteenth-century people, and they moved quickly back and fro, from sinful behaviour in the Bible to sinful behaviour in the local community, and then pointing to virtuous behaviour among biblical characters as an exemplar for the congregation's own conduct. The balance tended to vary very much from sermon to sermon.

Those who were, or were destined to become, professors tended towards the biblical exposition end of the spectrum: Westcott and Hort, their minds steeped in biblical scholarship, evoked the worlds of the Old and New Testaments easily and interestingly. Once they had evoked them, there they tended to stay for the duration of the sermon. Indeed, Hort was vastly happier in the world of first-century Palestine than he ever was at St Ippolyts, where he preached from 1857 to 1872 (with a two-year pause when he had a breakdown). But although he is reckoned to have struggled to express himself in the pulpit, in printed form his sermons are lucid. On the assumption that, as Goodwin and Blunt stated, the Bible's major themes and language were well known amongst the mid-nineteenth-century rural population, Hort's sermons should have been encouraging and thought-provoking, rather than baffling. He pointed out Old Testament allusions and parallel texts. He carefully explained that words in Hebrew and Greek might have meanings other than those conveyed in the English of the King James Version, and he drew out alternative readings. He tried to come up with striking local analogies, on one occasion explaining how different the tribes of Israel were from the 'county' sensibility existing in Hertfordshire and neighbouring counties. He always deployed scholarship in ways which were intended to be relevant to his audience. This may be clearly seen in the text he took for his first sermon at St Ippoltys, Luke 4:18–19 'he hath anointed me to preach the gospel to the poor', in which he referred to the nineteenth-century preacher's favourite text, the Sermon on the Mount:

> It is worth notice that there is...a difference in the beginning of the two Gospel accounts of the Sermon on the Mount. According to St Matthew Jesus said, 'Blessed are the poor in spirit, for theirs is the kingdom of heaven': according to St Luke He said, 'Blessed be ye poor, for yours is the kingdom of God.' The 'poor in spirit' of St Matthew answer to the 'meek' of Isaiah. Now we must not go away with a notion that one of these meanings is right and the other wrong: rather, by comparing them boldly together, we may find more exactly the full meaning of Scripture. The Hebrew word in Isaiah means both 'poor' and also 'meek,' but—mark this—it is especially used when it is wished to speak in one word of those who are both poor and meek. By the 'poor' is not here meant simply those who are in want of money or other property, but all who are in any way depressed or beaten down low in any way, whether by what we commonly call poverty, or cruelty, or tyranny, or any other sore burden. (Hort 1897: 9)

In 1868, after years of preaching in the accustomed way on single texts, Hort decided to change tack and deliver a series of sermons on the Bible as a whole. He wanted to deepen his congregation's understanding of the Bible, and had concluded that sermons on single texts had

> one great disadvantage: they help to keep up that mischievous notion which is everywhere so common, that the Bible is nothing but a collection of texts, in which we put our hand and draw out at random whatever we please without troubling ourselves to think where it came from...And many of the most precious truths of the Bible are not to be found in any text at all; they come into our minds only when we think of whole chapters and books together'. (Hort 1897: 130)

Hort devoted twelve sermons to a systematic introduction to the contents of the Bible. When Hort left the biblical world to return to the present he tended to dwell on psychological or religious difficulty: the weariness that comes with 'unchanging sameness'; in a Good Friday sermon, the difficulty attendant upon aligning one's moods with the solemnity or thankfulness appropriate to the Church's seasons: 'sometimes, feeling how difficult that is, we give up the attempt, and rest in a half-sullen and unprofitable gloom, and long for the day to be over' (Hort 1897: 102). Although Hort's sermons also contained some of the conventional pieties of his day, there is sometimes a note of shocking honesty which marks him out from many of his contemporaries.

Edward Berens is an example of a preacher at the other end of the spectrum. Berens (c.1777–1859), who became Archdeacon of Berkshire, produced six volumes of village sermons between 1820 and 1852. He described his works as 'of the humblest description...[whose] only object was to impress upon the hearts and consciences of a Village Congregation plain and acknowledged truths, with reference especially to the practical effects, which those truths ought to produce' (Berens: vii–viii). Berens's desire to stress 'practical effects' may account for his relative lack of attention to biblical sources. His *Twenty-Six Village Sermons* are strongly hortatory, with only seven being intended for the seasons of the Christian year, and the other nineteen being concerned with themes relating to conversion and Christian behaviour. His sermons warned repeatedly of the danger of hell and of being only interested in religion when ill or facing death. Titles include 'Conversion, on Turning to God', 'Death-bed Repentance', 'Time is Short', 'Folly of being Wicked', 'Government of the Heart', 'Behaviour in Church', and 'On Joining Audibly in Public Worship'. The sermons have been arranged in a way which would make them a logical sequence for a reader in search of a course of instruction on how to be saved. Berens's thesis was simple: 'This *change,—*or *conversion,—*…is absolutely necessary in order to our being received into Heaven; and consequently, since there is no middle state, it is absolutely necessary in order to our escaping the punishment of Hell' (Berens: 4). The sermons were certainly not devoid of biblical material: his sermon 'Time is Short' (1 Corinthians 7:29–31) goes into some detail about the Corinthian Church, and his sermon on 'Zeal' (Galatians 4:18) begins with an explanation on the Galatian context, before warning of the dangers of lapsing into formalism. But in treating many themes, Berens was completely focused on his contemporary situation, and used biblical allusion simply as a form of seasoning. For his sermon 'On Joining Audibly in Public Worship' he took as his text Romans 15:6 'That ye may with one mind and one mouth glorify God, even the Father of our Lord Jesus Christ'. He complained that in many congregations 'The voice of the minister is heard, but in the many instances it is responded to by the voice of the parish clerk alone, the rest of the people preserving the silence and stillness of sleep.' But equally, he wanted to discourage ostentatious parades of devotion, lest the congregation become like the hypocrites praying on street corners—a reference which deftly moved the context from Shrivenham to Matthew (Berens: 261–2).

If Hort and Berens represent two very different sermon styles, other preachers tended to switch back and forth between the Bible and moral exhortation, although there is much more work that could be done in order to analyse how this process occurred. William Jackson, curate of Bodle Street Green, East Sussex, tended to heap biblical passages upon each other, producing a florid weaving of texts. He also tended to move readily from his text, in this example Genesis 2:8–9, to imaginative descriptive passages (in this case the Garden of Eden) and then to a contemporary message of social conservatism:

> Adam laboured, and you labour: but Adam ate freely, and without restraint… whereas you are often compelled to eat sparingly…I dare say it seems sometimes very hard that you should turn the stubborn soil, preparing it with much labour for the precious seed in its season, your children gathering out the noxious weeds; and again at harvest time should reap the ripe corn, and store it in the barn for another; seeming yourselves to have but a scanty portion for your toils. Does this seem hard, my brethren? Would your own hearts sometimes persuade you to believe what wicked men would teach you, that this order of human society is unjust and wrong? Let not your own too easily perverted hearts, let not any subtle teacher of evil, persuade you thus to doubt the ordinance of God, who has appointed by His Divine

Providence the various ranks of men, and declared in His sacred Word that 'the poor shall never cease out of the land'. (Jackson: 89)

The overwhelming majority of the sermons that have been studied here have as their primary purpose exhortation and warning. Hort was scathing about this type of preaching:

> There is no congregation in the whole Church which needs nothing but warning and exhortation; all need teaching likewise. It is not enough to be told what we should feel, and think, and say, and do. We want to have the story of God's wondrous dealings with men in past times impressed on our minds; and many of us will never be able to understand it unless it is explained to them. (Hort 1897: 131).

For theologians less gifted than Hort, it was however always easier to condemn and threaten fornicators or thinkers of impure thoughts (something which Berens did in virtually every sermon) than to explain how the various parts of the Bible interrelated.

The Use of the Lectionary, Themes, and Seasons

Most of the volumes of village sermons studied here contain a mixture of material for the seasons of the liturgical year and on particular themes, with the thematic material in the ascendant. What is noticeable is how infrequently preachers preached on the readings laid down in the lectionary printed in the Book of Common Prayer. This raises the question of whether they actually read the appointed lessons, or substituted their own readings to fit their sermon. No evidence either way has been discovered on this, although the very strong strictures which existed concerning the full and correct use of the Prayer Book would make the abandonment of the appointed readings seem unlikely. If this is the case, then it must have been that the sermon was seen as a free-standing item, and no attempt to relate it to other parts of the 'ministry of the Word' was thought necessary.

William Gresley, in his advice to young preachers, did not suggest that their choice of subject or scripture should be informed either by the lectionary readings or by the Church's year. Instead, he advocated a 'chain of topics', a formula for all sermons into which biblical and contemporary material could be inserted. He explained it thus:

> The chain of topics is briefly this—we are by nature under God's wrath; how can we escape? Only through the atonement made by our Redeemer. How shall we attain an interest in this atonement? By faith. How be sure we have faith? By holiness. How obtain holiness? By the aid of the Spirit. How obtain the aid of the Spirit? By watchfulness and prayer. These are the grand staple topics of the preacher. You will see that, at any point in this scale, an infinite number of minor topics will branch out, and a copious store of materials will be found to illustrate any one of them. You will find it better to preach on a precise and limited subject, than on a general one: but on whatever

> subject of detail you choose to preach, you should constantly refer to these first principles. Thus if you preach about a sin to be avoided, you should not make avoidance of it the sole object, but speak of it as incompatible with Christian holiness, grieving the spirit of God, and frustrating his gracious purpose of saving us. Christ crucified as the means of salvation should be mentioned in every sermon. (Gresley: 365–6)

It is apparent that preachers who were mainly concerned with warning the congregation about their eternal fate, such as Gresley and Berens, had no obvious interest in lectionaries or liturgical seasons. Preachers like Hort, who had followed F. D. Maurice in rejecting the doctrine of eternal damnation, were much more likely to have what Anglicans would see as the 'modern' approach of linking preaching to the set readings and the liturgical season. Nevertheless, Hort's approach to the lectionary was hardly slavish. In Lent 1861 he devoted three Sundays to the temptation narrative in Matthew 4, which had been the Gospel reading for the first Sunday. In 1858, he preached on Romans 5:8 on Good Friday and on 1 Peter 1:3 on Easter Sunday. R. W. Church's 1899 collection, *Village Sermons Preached at Whately*, contains thirty-seven sermons in total, of which twenty-three were preached on identified Sundays and holy days in the calendar. But only seven of the twenty-three used that day's lectionary reading: even impeccable Tractarians were little bothered by such matters.

Only four of the fifteen sermons printed in Charles Heurtley's *Parochial Sermons Preached in a Village Church* (1851) can be linked to specific Sundays, but none used the lectionary readings. In his advice on sermon preparation, he suggested that there might be occasions when explaining and applying the gospel of the day would be appropriate, but he preferred taking an easily remembered biblical narrative, and using biblical episodes to illustrate present-day shortcomings and sins. Examples included 'the danger of presumptuous self-confidence in the prospect of temptation' illustrated from Peter's denial; or 'the sinfulness of shutting our eyes to the claims of others...upon us for succour or courtesy' from the parable of the Good Samaritan (Heurtley 1879: 137). In his own sermons, he ranged widely in his choice of arresting narratives, selecting Exodus 14:30, 'Israel saw the Egyptians dead upon the sea-shore', for Easter Sunday. He mentioned the resurrection in his second paragraph, linking the Israelites' deliverance from tyranny with the deliverance brought in Christ, but the sermon's major theme, as so often in the nineteenth-century village, was the snares and temptations of everyday life. The majority of village sermons were thematic, free-floating compositions, which did not require to be preached at any particular season. Sub-themes, such as tidiness or punctuality, sometimes made an appearance. They had little to do with the Bible, but much to do with ensuring good order in nineteenth-century society.

Conclusion

Neither the popularity of the printed village sermon, nor its extent as a preaching genre, has been appreciated hitherto. They were, in fact, preached in their hundreds of thousands, and published in their thousands, over a period of about one hundred years.

Although they required from their audience a solid knowledge of biblical stories, they were intended to be simple forms of communication, whether they were read or heard. What Robert Ellison has described as the 'ornamented oral rhetoric' of the seventeenth and eighteenth centuries had given way 'to a plainer, more natural, more literary approach to sacred speaking' (Ellison 1998: 28). Among the theological elite, the continuing ability to write plainly in clear, sparse prose was shown through the publication of village sermons. It also indicated that although the author's natural habitat might have been the university or the cathedral, he had still believed it important to communicate with rustic audiences, and had believed in upholding the village community.

The sermons reveal the village clergy as (in this limited sample with the notable exception of Hort) an autocratic body—rectors in the ancient sense of rulers—maintaining a somewhat unrealistic vision of rural unity, in which they were themselves at the centre. They preached a message based on salvation by faith, expressed through unwavering self-discipline and good behaviour. It is a world of bridled tongues and patient forbearance, of continual watchfulness and temptation lurking at every turn. It is striking how seldom the love of God is ever mentioned. A village congregation was more likely to hear a themed sermon on 'Sloth' or 'Signs of Declension in Religion' or 'The Reward of Forsaking all for Christ' (all by Heurtley) than anything relating to the calendar. But even in an Easter Day sermon, Heurtley's message remained joyless and depressing: 'Snares succeed to snares, and temptations to temptations. Like the waves of the sea, no sooner is one past than another approaches' (Heurtley 1851: 122). The village sermon has much to tell us about how the understanding of what constitutes a Christian life has changed in the intervening years.

Acknowledgements

I am grateful to Sara Kincaid of Baylor University for undertaking the initial investigation of the British Library catalogue, which allowed me to identify the village sermons.

References

Berens, E. (1836). *Twenty-Six Village Sermons*. London: Rivington.
Blunt, J. J. (1856). *The Acquirements and Principal Obligations and Duties of the Parish Priest*. London: J. Murray.
Chitty, S. (1974). *The Beast and the Monk: A Life of Charles Kingsley*. London: Hodder and Stoughton.
Ellison, R. (1998). *The Victorian Pulpit: Spoken and Written Sermons in Nineteenth-Century Britain*. Selinsgrove, PA: Susquehanna University Press.
—— (2010). 'The Tractarians' Sermons and Other Speeches', in R. Ellison (ed.), *A New History of the Sermon: the Nineteenth Century*. Leiden: Brill, 15–57.
Goodwin, H. (1879). 'What Constitutes a Plain Sermon?', in C. J. Ellicott (ed.), *Homiletical and Pastoral Lectures Delivered in St Paul's Cathedral*.... London: Hodder and Stoughton, 105–31.

Gresley, W. (1835). *Ecclesiastes Anglicanus: Being a Treatise on the Art of Preaching.*... London: Rivington.

Hardwick, C. (1853). *Twenty Sermons for Town Congregations.* Cambridge: Macmillan and Co.

Heurtley, C. (1851). *Parochial Sermons Preached in a Village Church*, First Series. Oxford: John Henry Parker.

—— (1879). 'The Preparation of Sermons for Village Congregations', in C. J. Ellicott (ed.), *Homiletical and Pastoral Lectures Delivered in St Paul's Cathedral*... London: Hodder and Stoughton, 135–57.

Hort, F. J. A. (1897). *Village Sermons*, A. F. Hort (ed.). London: Macmillan and Co.

—— (1900). *Village Sermons in Outline*, A. F. Hort (ed.). London: Macmillan and Co.

Jackson, W. (1854). *Sermons Preached in Village Churches.* London: J. & C. Mozley.

Knight, F. (1995). *The Nineteenth Century Church and English Society.* Cambridge: Cambridge University Press.

Pickles, J. D. 'Blunt, John James (1794–1855)', *ODNB.* Oxford: Oxford University Press.

Skinner, S. A. (2004). *Tractarians and the 'Condition of England'*... Oxford: Oxford University Press.

Thomas, J. H. (1858). *How Shall the Parish Feast Be Dealt With?* London: John Henry and James Parker.

Village Development Based on Practical Principles... (1854). London: George Cox.

CHAPTER 5

PREACHING FROM THE PLATFORM

MARTIN HEWITT

Introduction

Despite its huge popularity with contemporaries, nineteenth-century religious lecturing—as opposed to sermonizing from a pulpit—has largely passed from view. Some attention has been given to its American history, but scarcely any to its British. Biographical studies rarely attend specifically to the lecturing activities of even the most prominent lecturers. General histories tend to dismiss lectures as part of an 'evangelical consensus', the orthodox repertoire of ancillary activities which included tea meetings, Sunday School trips, and fund-raising bazaars, or to subsume them into preaching.

There is some justification for this. For one thing, it is not easy to identify a distinct object of study. Not only did the term 'lecture' remain common parlance for specific preaching establishments, but it was regularly used interchangeably with 'sermon'. Lectures were, as one popular lecturer put it, 'a somewhat freer form of preaching' (Young 1920: 30), often delivered by the same people in the same chapels to the same congregations. For another, lectures, for all their popularity, attracted little direct contemporary attention. Victorian homiletics offered no theory of lecturing as distinct from preaching. It is possible to infer such a model from ways in which accounts attempted to define the limits of the pulpit, but the lecture always remained merely as a residual category (Ellison: 18–19). The Victorians never entirely escaped the anxiety that, in speaking to the intellect and not the conscience, lectures were a dangerous distraction from the task of preaching salvation. John Angell James's 'apprehensions and convictions that we are in danger in the present day of allowing the lecture to encroach upon the sermon, science to supersede religion, and the labour to inform men's understanding and to gratify their taste, to take up the time and enervate the vigour which should be devoted to the conversion of their souls' were widespread (James: 282–3).

Yet, even if they derived from gravitational pull rather than clear demarcation, as James's anxieties indicate, there were distinctions between lecture and sermon arising from enduring assumptions about the 'the dignity and gravity of the pulpit' as Thomas Guthrie put it (Guthrie and Guthrie: 156). At times contemporaries applied precise functional discriminations. The preacher taught how to live, and the lecturer what to think. Lecturing offered scope for illustrations and dramatizations unthinkable in a sermon, 'more freedom of expression' as Silas Hocking explained: 'In the pulpit one had to...observe all the conventions.' The platform 'was like a gallop across the open country rather instead of running between fences' (Hocking: 8). Above all, in those denominations without traditions of lay preaching the lecture provided a platform for those who were not ministers, both men and women.

It is impossible in the short compass of this chapter to attempt more than an exploration of the main outlines of the nineteenth-century religious lecture, its critical moments and prominent practitioners. The focus will be on the lecture in its popular and public manifestations, and lecturing as culture and practice, rather than on lectures as texts or embodiments of thought. In this way, it is hoped to help rescue the lecture from its obscurity and provide a context for further detailed work.

Preaching Lectures

In the early nineteenth century the remnants of the Puritan lectureships of the Reformation provided endowed or subscription lectures in many London parishes and more irregularly elsewhere. The lecture provided a means of evading the legal restriction to licensed venues of acts of worship, and so remained one way of Dissenters gathering a congregation, or a basis whereby Evangelical clergy were able to establish a foothold in London. In the 1820s it was still not uncommon for subscription lectureships on Sundays or weekdays to be attached to parishes. Within Old Dissent, evening lectures were delivered by local ministers in those places where separate subscriptions could be raised. Thomas Binney recalled that getting one guinea for a Sunday evening lecture kept him afloat in his early ministerial years ('Multum in Parvo': 6).

The subsequent history of these lectureships is obscure. Many Sunday foundations seem to have survived as (slightly anomalous) elements of the regular worship of Anglican parishes, especially in London. In the late 1840s Robert Bickersteth held the Limborough Lectureship, at Christ Church, Spitalfields, while curate at Clapham. Other models existed: Exeter had a Sunday Evening Lectureship, delivered *gratis* by local clergy at a number of churches. Where the duty of electing a lecturer devolved on the Vestry, it could be used as a means of disputing with the incumbent, as was the case at St George's in the Fields in 1858 (when the election of the extravagant Puritan, the Revd Hugh Allan, led to anti-Ritualist disturbances). The general tendency, however, appears to have been for the consolidation of lectureships into the parish, with any foundation used to contribute to the salary of a curate, as in the case of the Barnstaple Old Church Sunday Evening Lectureship, whose occupant resigned in 1861 to make way for a curate. The weekday lectureships were more resilient, although they struggled to sustain attendance. One or two became lucrative and sought-after appointments. The Haberdasher's Company Jones or 'Golden' Lectureship, based for most of the century at St Margaret's, Lothbury, was worth nearly £500 p.a. by 1850. By the end of the century, however, only the Merchants' Lecture seems to have garnered any general public attention.

During the first third of the century the sermon lecture became an increasing feature of congregational worship, especially on Sunday evening. Unitarians often led the way. Anglicanism soon followed. The years before the accession of Victoria saw the steady spread of lecturing both on Sunday afternoon and Sunday evening. (Scotland was an exception to this pattern. There it was very common for a lecture to be delivered in the morning, with a sermon in the afternoon.) In Manchester in 1837 in response to the spread of Owenism, ten Anglican parishes had Sunday evening lectures (*Manchester Courier*). It was said of Robert Halley's Sunday evening lectures in Manchester that 'he saw that something fresh was necessary' and 'ventured to enlarge the field from which the topics of the pulpit are taken', looking into 'obscure nooks of Church history' and 'characters of earnest but almost unknown Christian labourers' ('The Late Dr Halley': 648). Over the century most of the leading Dissenting preachers engaged in Sunday evening lectures, often giving extended exegetical series on individual books of the Bible.

At the same time, weekday congregational lectures became increasingly common. There is no neat narrative. When Basil Woodd introduced a weekday lecture at Bentinck Chapel, St Marylebone, in 1785 'it was pointedly opposed, and many objections were raised', although fifty years later the practice seemed quite conventional (Woodd: 169). The lectures took a variety of forms. Congregational instruction by catechetical lectures, especially held in Lent or Advent, was common by the 1850s. Eugene Stock recalled the Thursday evening lectures of the Revd George Allen at St Thomas, Islington, which regularly attracted 300 and more, as remarkable, expounding 'Epistle after Epistle, verse after verse; so that numbers of people, especially young men and women, really knew the letters to the Galatians, the Colossians, or to Timothy' (Stock: 69–70). Another form was the 'cottage lecture', a simple address, often with Bible reading and prayer, held in private homes or occasionally houses taken especially for the purpose, which were central to Walter Hook's renovation of the Anglican parochial model in the 1840s. Cottage lectures could help serve scattered hamlets in large rural parishes, as Charles Jerram intended at Witney in the 1830s, although this kind of activity was hard to sustain. Biblical history was the most popular field. Ralph Wardlaw, the Scottish Presbyterian minister, left a collection of over 300 manuscript lectures on leading characters of Scripture history.

These weekday lecture-sermons were aimed primarily at those with established religious affiliations. At Witney, Charles Jerram noted that the weekday lectures attracted a 'select congregation' requiring 'something more of simplicity of statement, and familiarity of illustration, as well as a detail of matters more intimately connected with the trials, and difficulties, and corresponding supports and encouragements of the Christian life, than can be so profitably brought before a more mixed congregation' (Jerram: 331). In many cases they were expository lectures, offering sustained and systematic instruction rather than conversion.

As the period progressed weekday lecturing initiatives were more and more designed to appeal beyond the congregation. Special Sunday evening lecture series within Dissent, even when they took place in the chapel, seem generally to have attracted a distinct audience from the morning services. (It was said of Halley's lectures that 'the chapel was crowded, up to the pulpit stairs, with a congregation drawn not from Manchester alone, but from all the country round' ('Death of the Rev. Robert Halley': 3)). Even Lenten lectures were advertised by handbills, or placards outside the church. It was hoped the throwing open of pews would bring the 'unchurched' into the building. Henry Scott Holland's Passion and Holy Week lectures at St Saviour's, Hoxton in 1873 were one such attempt; the addresses considered 'current objections against religion' and questions were invited. But as Holland noted, 'Only a few outsiders ever turned up: we used to beg them a little, in the street, to come: but they won't go to a church, I think' (Paget: 68–9).

In the Church of England the norm was probably the occasional lecture, though there were plenty of exceptions, like Spencer Thornton, Rector of Wendover, who by the 1840s was delivering seven weekday lectures each week in addition to his other classes (Bebbington: 11); but by the later 1850s congregational life in much of Dissent had become a wearing round of lectures and tea meetings. Nineteenth-century Methodism sustained an particularly vibrant congregational lecture culture. The case of Peter Mackenzie is particularly illuminating because although he did also appear on general lecturing platforms, he was overwhelmingly a denominational lecturer, and although never entirely respectable, in Scotland and the rural north he became one of the fixtures of Methodist culture. In the last three decades of his life Mackenzie was reputed to have travelled over 360,000 miles; in March 1893 he had over 600 future lectures and sermons booked. 'His preparation...was almost entirely meditative rather than literary' (Young 1904: 26). But what he offered was the full drama of the lecture platform, and the full play of the greater freedom it offered, especially in the introduction of action, comedy, and illustrations (J. Dawson 1896). Surrendering himself completely to the characters he was presenting, Mackenzie 'transformed' Scripture stories 'from a dumb shadowy record of the past into a speaking, moving picture of the present'; contemporary analogies opened up Bible history: Old Testament saints became circuit superintendents (J. Dawson 1897: xiv; Bamford). Props were improvised from whatever came to hand: the bass fiddle of the singers would become the jawbone of an ass wielded by Samson. 'His power of grimace was simply extraordinary. He could *look* more than most men could say' (Young 1904: 19).

Extension: Education, Agitation, Confrontation

By the time Mackenzie commenced his ministerial career, the context for congregational lecturing had already been transformed by the progressive opening out of the lecture platform. Thomas Binney, arriving in Huddersfield in February 1856, was 'much struck... by the number of large bills announcing different lectures. There seemed to be lectures on everything' ('Lecture on... the Life of the Apostle Paul': 6). This development can be traced to early-century radicalism and free thought. The Sunday lectures of the Revd Robert Taylor at Salter's Hall and the Rotunda in the later 1820s and 1830s, and in the Owenite Halls of Science, were a direct challenge to religious orthodoxy. Even the expansion of scientific lecturing created a platform for the articulation of new discoveries in geology, astronomy, and the natural sciences whose heterodox tendency could not entirely be disguised by the widespread convention of avoiding direct consideration of matters of religion or politics. During the later 1830s and 1840s a dense network of literary and related associations emerged in London at which religious questions were aired in a sceptical or at least questioning environment. From May 1844 until March 1846, W. J. Fox, the minister of the South Place Chapel, who in the 1810s had opened his former chapel for evening lectures on 'great public and social problems' (Conway: 39), delivered and published a series of Sunday Evening Popular Lectures to the Working Classes in the National Hall, Holborn. For figures like Fox, the lecture was part of a broader educational aspiration to challenge the hegemony of the parson's sermon. 'Pulpit instruction', Fox suggested, 'to attain any power of usefulness, must extend... into moral speculation, into civil and political life, into the investigation of institutions and manners' (Conway: 80). At the same time, figures like George Dawson and R. W. Emerson were challenging traditional restraints on the use of the lecture platform to raise controversial questions of belief and morality. Emerson's understated delivery and complex thought set him apart from the crowd-pleasers, but could not disguise the profound impact of his 'short crisp sentences which rattled about the hall like bullets. I can hardly believe that many were hit, but those who were carried the marks for life' ('W.B.': 658).

Isolated responses to these challenges are visible from the beginning of the century. In the 1830s there was a growing recognition in the Church of England that 'the Clergyman of a Parish should be its "Educator", as well as Spiritual Guide' (Myers: vii). Congregational mutual improvement societies, reading rooms, and classes proliferated. At Leeds in 1838 Walter Hook developed experiments already commenced at Coventry, attempting to establish reading rooms in various parts of the town, with magazines and weekly lectures, each under the superintendence of a clergyman. A few years later Derby Congregationalist James Baldwin Brown began his long-continued practice of delivering a series of winter lectures to his congregation and neighbourhood. By mid-century it seemed to Charles Kingsley that work in the lecture room was vital to gain the attention of the intelligent working men, and ministers were taking to the lecture platform in increasing numbers. F. W. Robertson at Brighton achieved first local and then national prominence through his lectures to his Working Men's Institute, his own popular congregational preaching, and various special ministries, such as a weekly lecture in his vestry for the poor.

Inevitably, the lecture was seized upon as a powerful agitational weapon. Abolitionists were using full-time itinerant lecturers like George Thompson to mobilize a moral community through lectures in chapels and meeting rooms from the later 1820s (Garrison). The success of the lecture campaigns of the Anti-Corn Law League, in which ministerial lecturers like W. J. Fox had been prominent, spilled over into the politics of Nonconformity: disestablishment, national education and temperance. Although eventually in the 1880s the heat finally ebbed from the disestablishment movement, for several decades Liberation Society lectures helped constitute the unruly fringes of the religious lecture platform, where audiences might be showered in soot and speakers with stones. W. B. Carpenter remembered Liverpool in the 1840s being 'steeped in a controversial atmosphere' in which 'great debates were carried on, now in newspapers, now in lectures and sermons'. Like many, Carpenter was wary of controversy, but recognized that he 'gained much from hearing all kinds of theological questions ardently debated. We listened with breathless attention as each side was argued, and we gained experience in argument, [and] some knowledge of the past history of doctrine' (Carpenter: 75).

The dangers of controversial religious lectures were most visibly demonstrated by nineteenth century anti-Catholicism. As Dennis Paz has noted, sectarian lecturers were 'fixtures of mid-Victorian public life [combining] entertainment (sometimes of a most prurient nature) with edification (sometimes of a most sanctifying nature)' (Paz: 26). While leading figures like Alessandro Gavazzi occupied public halls, a broader subculture was sustained, especially through open-air preaching, where sectarian lecturers often shared the ground with temperance orators, secularists, and home missioners. The Christian Instruction Society and later the Christian Evidence Society both placed considerable emphasis on open-air addresses (Johnson). Around 1870 the vehement anti-Catholic lectures of William Murphy prompted riots in a number of towns. Open-air lecturing brought a particular intense interaction with audiences, and often a constant battle to assert control. Open-air preachers met all sorts of opposition: in Salford Joseph Guttridge faced a deliberately organized dog fight, a handcart driven through the crowd, even a horse rider with a pint of beer he offered to share. The flow of people around the fringes offered opportunities to try and draw new hearers in (Guttridge: 52–4, 29). At the same time, national Protestant societies provided a steady supply of lecturers for congregational platforms, and pioneered a number of developments including co-ordinated schemes of lectures and examinations, and the use of lantern displays. For example, in 1870 the Scottish Reformation Society was sponsoring courses of Lectures to Young Men followed by prize examinations claiming thirty-three series in London and around forty in the provinces.

The 1840s and 1850s brought an explosion of opportunities for lecturing. Figures like Brewin Grant and Thomas Cooper were able to carve out a niche as itinerant lecturers, lecturing up and down the country in chapels, public halls, schoolrooms, under the informal patronage of local ministers. Others like Edwin Paxton Hood and George McCree were able to combine periods as a Congregational minister with an extensive lecturing and writing career, embracing purely religious platforms, temperance associations, mutual improvement societies, and other mixed lecture courses. An increasing number of organizing secretaries and lecturing agents undertook tours which sustained a lecture culture even where regular courses were not viable. Thomas Cooper's lecturing efforts were prodigious. From 1858 to 1863 he claimed to have lectured 468 times in Scotland and 852 times in England (*The Freeman*). But it was Henry Vincent, formerly an influential Chartist speaker, who most fully demonstrated the new opportunities, offering Nonconformist audiences not only single lectures on the heroes of Dissent, but also longer series of up to six lectures on the history of the Reformation, or commentary on contemporary movements, from the revolutions of 1848 to the American Civil War. By the 1860s he and George Dawson were described as the two most prominent professional lecturers in Britain. He could fill Spurgeon's Tabernacle with 8,000 for an oration on Garibaldi, and between 1866 and 1875 he made four extremely successful tours of the United States (Dorling; 'Such is Popularity': 6). Preaching at times on Sunday evenings, before delivering more secular lectures from the same chapels during the week, Vincent epitomizes the 'reverse' colonization of the pulpit by the platform.

YMCA and General Lecture Platform

From the 1850s lecturers like Vincent found increasing opportunities for lecturing in the more stable environment of formal winter courses of lectures organized by Young Men's Christian Associations and the like. One of the earliest of these was organized in Glasgow in the winter of 1840–1; twelve lectures were delivered to audiences of 1600–1700 men, and subsequently published. With the establishment of the London Young Men's Christian Association in 1844 the British religious lecture platform entered a new phase. From 1846 to 1864 the Exeter Hall lectures, delivered to audiences of several thousands and widely circulated as individual pamphlets and in annual volumes, were the pinnacle of the religious lecture platform. Lectures delivered at Exeter Hall were usually redelivered to the provincial associations which sprouted in the larger towns and cities and quickly overseas. The YMCA lectures came to typify 'that type of moral instruction which, without invading actually the domain of the pulpit, approximates very nearly to its teachings' offering addresses 'familiar and interesting, apart from the grave and solemn prestige of pulpit ministrations' (Waddel: 258, 288).

The Exeter Hall lectures became embroiled in controversy in the 1860s, and were abandoned in 1864. Nevertheless, most of the associations (187 in England and Wales in 1876, and 239 in 1884) sustained lecture courses at least for some of the 1850–1900 period, sometimes both weekday and Sunday courses. The movement was particularly strong in the north of England, but the YMCA or a close variant (Catholic, Protestant, or Church of England Young Men's Associations, Church Institutes, and the like) provided the basis for lecture courses in smaller towns and villages across the country. Beneath these was a less visible culture of Congregational institutes and recreational associations, which had proliferated by the final decades of the century, many of which made do with the occasional lecture from local ministers, but some of which themselves attracted nationally prominent lecturers (Yeo).

The YMCAs and kindred societies helped develop a distinct culture of religious lecturing, less lecture-sermon and more lecture-entertainment. Although some associations faced initial opposition from local Anglicanism, the YMCA circuit created and sustained a corps of 'star' lecturers drawn from all denominations, many of whom were known primarily for their lecturing—figures like the Baptists William Landels, Hugh Stowell Brown, and Arthur Mursell, the Methodists William Morley Punshon and Gervase Smith, the Congregationalists Thomas Binney and Edwin Paxton Hood, secessionist ministers like George Gilfillan and David Macrae, and also a lesser number of Anglicans including Hugh Stowell, John C. Miller, and Hugh R. Haweis. Lay lecturers did appear, and tended to become more frequent as the century progressed, as programmes became more miscellaneous, including the scientist Edwin Lankester, and John B. Gough, the American temperance orator. Gough was one of a number of American visitors; another was Henry Ward Beecher, who enjoyed a triumphal lecturing visit in 1887 (Pond).

For the first rank of popular lecturers, each lecture became an entity, a performance in itself. Frequent repetition merited considerable care in composition. Landels and Punshon corresponded with each other before picking topics for a new lecture. William Landels's repertoire encapsulates the major themes of the YMCA platform. These included topics in British Protestant history, conduct lessons ('How men are made', 'Business is Business'), as well as Christian apologetics and celebrations of the Bible. The historical lecture could slide into crude anti-Catholicism, but Gervase Smith's 'Wycliff' was more typical: a vivid 'historical review', offering a restrained celebration of the manifest destiny of Protestant Britain, and a final peroration which called for men who would 'live as to impress their Christian character upon coming populations...who are prepared to chastise with a more vigorous hand the vices of the times' (Smith: 83). Conduct lectures often offered observational humour, drawing lessons from ridiculing stock character types. David Macrae's 'Characters' lecture poked fun at different styles of salesmen, the varieties of chairmen of public meetings, the personal and moral character types to be avoided—the intellectual bully, the inveterate punster, the meandering bore, the mole (living in the dark, eschewing the light), the mule (obstinately sticking even to clearly erroneous opinion), the monkey (the imitator)—concluding with the desired character traits of 'the man' ('The Rev. D Macrae on Character and Characters': 4).

Punshon was the pre-eminent YMCA lecturer, the touchstone by which others were measured. A Punshon lecture was a major event. Tickets were feverishly sought, and could change hands at a considerable premium. Shops were shut early. Crowds gathered at the entrance and pew holders needed to be ushered in by the side door. The roots of his success were elusive even to contemporaries. Punshon's delivery was sedate, his voice not immediately memorable, the matter often conventional. But his highly prepared and polished lectures, likened to a musical score, were full of dramatic power and vivid scene-painting: during his 'Wilberforce', the audience, it was said, 'could almost hear the baying of the bloodhounds on the fugitive's track' (Jennings: 53). His dramatic delivery played on the emotions of his audience, evoking laughter one moment and tear-filled stillness the next. His 'John Bunyan' at Exeter Hall was indicative of his powers. As one hearer recalled:

> He spoke with his usual captivating elocution, and with immense energy and force. Feeling amongst the audience grew; enthusiasm was awakened, and gathered force as he went on. At last, at one of his magnificent climaxes, the vast concourse of people sprang simultaneously to their feet, and oh! what a scene of excitement! Hats and handkerchiefs were waved; sticks and umbrellas were used in frantic pounding of the floor; hands, feet, and voices were united in swelling the acclamations; some shouted 'Bravo!' some 'Hurrah!' some 'Hallelujah!' and others 'Glory be to God!' (McCullagh: 69–70)

Although the YMCA platform was not exclusively male, female lecturers were very much the exception, and few courses were explicitly addressed to women. Clara Balfour, the most successful female lecturer at mid-century, appeared almost exclusively on the secular circuit (Cunliffe-Jones). Other occasional lecturers included the women's rights activist Emily Faithfull, and the social purity campaigner Ellice Hopkins, and female lecturers like Emma Hardinge Britten, the Spiritualist, operated on the fringes of the religious platform. Only one, 'Marianne Farningham' (Mary Anne Hearne) became an established figure. Farningham, a prolific writer of manuals on girlhood, piety, as well as moralistic tales and other devotional material, was a regular of YMCA courses in the 1880s, lecturing in social conservative vein on 'Women of Today', as well as offering conventional advice about family life addressed—unusually—particularly to wives and mothers (Farningham).

As the century progressed the boundaries between the YMCA and secular lecture platforms began to disappear. While retaining a moral ambition, programmes became more miscellaneous. In places, the secularization of the main course might have been associated with parallel provision of Bible lectures, lessons for Sunday school teachers, and occasionally branch lectures of a more religious character. But there was a definite shift in tone: in the 1880s and 1890s the repertoire of popular YMCA lecturer Mark Guy Pearse included 'Hugh Latimer', but he was better known for his lectures such as 'The Old Folks at Home', anecdotes about West Cornwall characters 'played shamelessly for laughs' (Williams: 124). In many ways both the porosity and shift of emphasis were exemplified by the career of Lydia von Finkelstein, a naturalized American who made a number of extensive tours of Britain during the later 1880s and 1890s, lecturing on topics related to Palestine and Bible history, whose increasingly elaborate costumed tableaux created a minor sensation. Many of her early lectures were delivered in chapels (including both the City Temple and the Metropolitan Tabernacle) under the auspices of local

Sunday School Unions. Yet by the mid-1890s her performances, now styled 'lecture-entertainments', although still on biblical topics, had taken on a much more commercial character.

The Lecture as Special Sunday Service

The YMCA lectures had never made any meaningful claim to religious outreach, and the 1851 Religious Census convinced contemporaries that reaching the 'unchurched masses' would require lectures of a different sort. In the following years much of this impetus coalesced around attempts to draw the working classes into religious observance on Sundays. Hitherto, attention has focused on the Special Services for the Working Classes held in public halls and theatres in London and provincial towns which were organized in the wake of the 1855 Religious Worship Act. However, in a number of Northern towns these attempts were anticipated and then paralleled on the lecture platform. By 1853 Liverpool Baptist Hugh Stowell Brown was holding monthly Sunday evening lectures in the Concert Hall. The lectures were soon every Sunday afternoon, with open-air addresses in the summer attracting 7,000 to 8,000 ('The Working Men's Sabbath Addresses': 6). On occasions in 1857 so great was the number excluded that the lower hall was opened up and Stowell Brown's lecture read to an overspill audience by one of his assistants. During 1857–8 this movement spread rapidly especially in the industrial towns of the north, but as far afield as Norwich and Barnstaple.

The peculiar characteristics of these Sunday afternoon lectures attracted considerable criticism. They were held in secular halls and lecture rooms. Admission was free (with a collection) and seating generally unreserved. The lectures were widely advertised in the local press and via placards and handbills, and the more popular lecturers also printed their lectures as penny pamphlets. They had titles rather than scriptural texts, sometimes impeccably biblical, often simple, but mildly enigmatic phrases, such as 'Merry and Wise', 'Roots and Fruits'; and at times the sort of dramatic cries like 'Fire! Fire! Fire!' adopted by Arthur Mursell at the Free Trade Hall in Manchester that were assailed by critics as 'claptrap'. The style was familiar, conversational, and, in seeking to speak to working-class audiences in their own idiom and to attract them with humour, open to the inevitable charges of vulgarity and poor taste. Critics were more sympathetic to the lecturers' attempts to focus on ethics rather than doctrine, and root their appeals in the ordinary circumstances of working-class life. Stowell Brown, who was generally excluded from the most outspoken attacks, was praised for his 'clear, straightforward, upright, downright, hammer and anvil sort of production' ('English Correspondence'). His most famous outing, 'Five Shillings and Costs', dwelt on the various costs of wrong-doing—not just fines and court costs; but the physical costs, the cost of domestic wretchedness, the cost of character, the encouragements to lewdness and dishonesty of drunkenness, offering guidance in practical ethics rather than salvation (Stowell Brown).

Most of this Sunday afternoon lecturing was short-lived. Stowell Brown continued to 1869 at least, and four volumes of his lectures were reissued in 1869–70. But by the time Mursell gave up his regular Free Trade Hall series in 1864, most of the other series had ceased. Nevertheless, the model had been established as part of the potential repertoire of the churches, and was frequently revived, both by the original lecturers and their imitators. The Congregationalist Robert Stainton was active in Sheffield from 1866 to 1878, and the 1870s saw the establishment of enduring non-denominational series in Bristol's Colston Hall, and also the early work in Birmingham of Charles Leach, who became the most prominent of the later Sunday afternoon lecturers. In a number of volumes with titles like *How I Reached the Masses* (1887) Leach promoted the efficacy of the model, arguing that conventional religious sensibilities had no place in a genuine attempt to reach non church-goers; and that in fishing for the 'careless, the indifferent, the ungodly and the prayerless', preachers must bait their hook accordingly.

Leach's occupation of the Birmingham Town Hall was caught up in controversy in the winter of 1880–1 when the council refused to extend its permission to the local 'Sunday Evenings for the People' to use the Town Hall for lectures. There had been a Sunday Lecture Society in London since 1869, and belatedly in the 1880s societies and courses were established in various provincial cities. But this was a different sort of Sunday lecturing. The London society emerged out of the Victorian religious crisis, drawing its support from the capital's deists, positivists, and agnostics. The lectures of the 1870s included contributions from Thomas Huxley, John Tyndall, and Max Muller, espousing the sort of vague anti-denominational deism associated at points with the 'creed of science', championing religious freedom and freedom from religious interference. Among the many clerical speakers attracted to this platform in the 1880s and 1890s were figures such as Stewart Headlam, the Christian Socialist. The movement prompted the renewal of intermittent Sabbatarian efforts to deploy late eighteenth-century legislation to have Sunday lectures proscribed. As in previous episodes, although various forms of legal and informal pressure were successfully brought to bear at particular moments, they could not prevent the spread of the movement, or the steady dilution of its initial religiosity. By the 1890s the various Sunday Society lectures had in their turn become home to Sir Robert Ball, Frederic Villiers, Harry Furniss, and the other stars of the regular lecture platform.

Church Extension and Home Mission

By the 1880s the most dynamic element of the religious platform was elsewhere, in the Central Halls, settlement houses, and mission halls which were leading the outreach efforts of organized religion, drawing on many decades of varied experience in the use of lectures in church extension. From the early years of the century mission clergy in metropolitan episcopal chapels, such as the West Street Chapel in St Giles, had organized regular weekly lectures. By the 1840s bodies such as the Church

Pastoral Aid Society and the town and city missions were encouraging widespread attempts to develop lecturing. Around 1850 efforts to challenge the influence of secularist and 'infidel' lectures were redoubled: between 1851 and 1854 the Congregationalist minister Brewin Grant undertook a dedicated three-year mission to the working classes, giving anti-secularist lectures across the country. By the mid-1850s contemporaries sensed a new cross-denominational lecture 'movement'. Popular series, such as the Monday night lectures at the Surrey Chapel, sought to broaden the reach of the churches. From the 1850s mission stations were frequently designated lecture rooms or halls and lectures were presented as a central element of their outreach. Scripture readers and district visitors would distribute free tickets and in rural areas occasionally tour with their own lectures. Take the 'outlying mission rooms, lectures and cottage meetings scattered over the parish' of William Pennefather of Drogheda. On moving to Aylesbury in 1852, Pennefather established a lecture centre in a house previously used as a Catholic chapel; and on moving to St Jude's Church, Mildmay Park in London, he encouraged one of his curates, W. H. Aitken, to commence a series of Sunday evening lectures in the room which became known as the Lecture Hall, King Henry St (Braithwaite).

Often these lectures mixed secular and religious subjects. Biblical themes jostled with practical lectures on hygiene and sanitary matters. A primary purpose was to establish a sense of sympathy with the audience. Considerable attention was given to effective illustration, literal and figurative. Mission lecturers were urged to cultivate the power of analogy; the most successful, like G. W. McCree, were praised above all for their vividness and descriptive power. Pictorial aids were widely used, including diagrams, maps, and—as they became more effective and practical—lantern slides. In the 1850s the Working Men's Educational Union produced series of pictorial illustrations for use in popular lectures. Propagandist organizations, such as the various ultra-Protestant associations and the missionary societies, followed on, creating numerously illustrated lectures addressing their primary message, which could be delivered by various organizing secretaries or local agents across the country. By the 1880s 'dissolving views' or lantern lectures, in which the spoken matter was subordinated to the illustrations, were becoming the norm, opening up a whole new field for modest speakers who could exploit the ready-made sets of slides with accompanying text that were appearing in larger numbers, or could produce slides from their own amateur photography. As one London missionary noted, 'Such...subjects as "The Thames and its Scenery", "Animal Sagacity", "The Wonders of the Universe" etc, never fail to command large and appreciative audiences, and many may be attracted to such meetings who are habitual neglecters of the means of grace' (Pike: 14).

Despite this, lecturing was rarely central to 'mission' work as conventionally understood. Even here, where the demands of drawing in a congregation were foremost, workers feared the secularizing tendencies of lectures. Most active missionary itinerants, like Charles Richardson, the 'Lincolnshire Thrasher', avoided the nomenclature of 'lecture', preferring either preaching, or giving addresses. Likewise, revivalist evangelists generally sought a more direct and emotional appeal than was suitable for the lecture form.

Lectures were an occasional feature of the parochial missions which became popular from the 1860s, but generally—as in the Catholic parish missions of the Redemptorists, which focused on mass and the sermon, with occasional meetings for men or for parents—lectures were not employed. Nevertheless, periodically schemes for reaching the working classes returned to lectures. In the 1870s Samuel Barnett experimented with alternate lectures and concerts ('the oratorios will reach the emotions, the lectures the reason of the people'), lecturing on great men as diverse as Carlyle, Chaucer, John Brown, Savonarola, Marcus Aurelius, and Sir Harry Vane. Barnett was convinced that: 'It is by knowing grand lives, by feeling their hearts bow before men who have been heroes in daily life, that men now living will themselves live higher lives and find out God.' At Toynbee Hall, he adopted a more specialized approach. Thursdays with debates; popular Saturday evening courses; Sunday morning teaching 'of the poets and their ideals, of the artists and their works'; Sunday afternoon Ethical Society lectures; and Sunday evening lectures which brought in religious leaders. It was a difficult furrow: at times audiences numbered no more than 20 (Barnett: 1:93, 97, 367–71; 2:99).

The final decades of the century saw a pronounced shift: both a greater reference to contemporary affairs from the pulpit and a congruent interest in engaging the unchurched via lectures and discussions on social problems and their solutions. Stopford Brooke's preaching 'on public events and national policy; strikes, riots, wars, trade unions' at the Bedford Chapel in the 1870s and 1880s was said to have 'mark[ed] a distinct turning point in the history of English preaching' (Jacks: 2:450). For figures like the Congregationalist R. F. Horton at Hampstead, the lecture became an accepted means of articulating the church's developing commitment to social reform. Horton's monthly Sunday afternoon lecture to working men became a forum even for scrutinizing the conduct of the Prince of Wales. In such hands the lecture did not seek to convert, or even to minister; but rather to manifest and direct the social conscience of the church. Over time the discussion became more important than the address, and lectures transmuted into 'conferences' and discussion forums. Under Hugh Price Hughes's leadership of the Wesleyan Central Mission, St James Hall on Sunday afternoons became a centre for the consideration of great public questions that bore on the life of the Church: the evils of wealth and poverty, gambling, militarism, and drink (Lunn).

Significance

The importance of all this lecturing is difficult to ascertain from the generally uninformative accounts of hearers and readers. As contemporary diaries show, the religious lecture, like its secular counterpart, was a noteworthy event (especially in rural areas), but rarely prompted any extended reflection. Although there are a number of autobiographies which emphasize the importance of lectures in their author's intellectual formation, including Thomas Cooper's, anodyne nostalgia was the most common register. Many accounts recalled long evening tramps to listen to lectures; 'sermons', Silas

Hocking noted, 'did not interest me much, but a speech...warmed my blood and quickened my imagination' (Hocking: 1–2). Even the reminiscences of popular preachers rarely have anything to say about lecturing and when it came to their own careers confessions of failure were common. According to the Revd Francis Courtney, the Sunday Evening Lectures in his church had become a site of mischief and licentiousness:

> Parties talked and young girls flirted there—young people had been seen making signals to each other across the gallery, and many young females had been ruined by their attendance at these Sunday evening lectures. You might have thought that he was speaking of the vestibule or a brothel, or one of the dancing saloons of the metropolis, from the description which he gave of this sorrowful scene of levity, irreligion and demoralization. ('The Riot in a Church in Exeter': 8)

It was common for the transience of the lecture to be regretted, but an enormous amount of lecturing activity found its way into print. Newspaper and periodical accounts, summaries, even the full texts of lectures, the collected volumes of the YMCA Exeter Hall courses, and the steady flow of pamphlet publications, made religious lectures much more visible than sermons. Lectures formed the basis for many articles and books; as Archbishop Tait told Dean Lake in 1869, 'The easiest way of writing books is by delivering them as lectures' (Lake: 215). Many published lectures had substantial circulations. Binney's YMCA lecture 'Is It Possible to Make the Best of Both Worlds', went through nine editions within three years, and fifteen editions in all. Stowell's lecture on infidelity was distributed as a tract by London City Mission missioners. Such publications formed a staple of pious reading in domestic circles, but also a means of public propaganda. Canon Barnett read F. D. Maurice's *Lectures on the Epistles* to his new wife on their honeymoon, while Joseph Parker sent a copy of one volume of his Sunday lectures on public topics 'to every member of both Houses of Parliament, to many dignitaries of the Church of England, and other distinguished people' (A. Dawson: 49).

The life of a popular itinerant lecturer was not an easy one; 'Hardly sleeping in the same bed two nights running, lecturing or preaching five evenings out of six...fighting often against positive illness, almost always against weariness and exhaustion', as the Unitarian Charles Wicksteed encapsulated it (Wicksteed: 86). That so many were committed to the labour suggests a profound belief in its utility. Many of the Sunday lecturers traced an impact both in the augmentation of their congregation and in drunkards reformed. Robert Stainton claimed that over the ten seasons of his Sunday afternoon lectures he added 1,081 new members to his congregation in Sheffield, while Thomas Cooper trusted to his success in shoring up wavering faith. Individual affirmations of gratitude for the instruction or inspiration received by lecture audiences were not surprisingly a common feature of lecturers' biographies. 'We were lifted to a higher plane, and led to yearn more than we had ever yearned for a higher, truer, holier life', was the recollection of one of those hearing William Landels's first YMCA lecture at Exeter Hall (Landels: 88). Charles Garrett kept a bill announcing a lecture from John Cassell at Shaftesbury all his life; he described it as 'one of the most sacred things I have' (Broadbent: 7).

The broader intellectual impact is particularly difficult to assess, but it was certainly at its strongest earlier in the period, when lecturers like Thomas Chalmers were making defining statements of a controversial position, demanding attention. David Masson noted that Chalmers's lectures on the relations of religion and astronomy delivered in Edinburgh in 1815–16, 'after holding that city in a stage of intellectual excitement for a year, ran through the country in edition after edition to the extent of 20,000 copies, dividing attention with Scott's early novels' (Masson: 71). Gladstone confessed in *The State in its Relations with the Church* that Chalmers's lectures 'drove me' into writing the book. Thereafter the claims of the lecture platform as a basis for significant intellectual work probably rested primarily on the great lecture foundations like the Boyle Lectures, the Bampton Lectures, and the other eighteenth- and nineteenth-century additions and imitations (the Congregational Lecture, the Wesleyan Methodist Fernley Lecture, the Unitarian Hibbert Lectures). Although not all were like the Bampton lectures delivered within the universities, these aimed more at being 'academic prelections' (Grant: 154) rather than 'popular addresses', and for this reason lie outside the scope of this chapter.

At a more local level, in the towns and villages of rural England, itinerant lecturers offered at least a welcome novelty, at times a transformative awakening. For Joseph Parker, 'lectures and other agencies created an atmosphere which awakened intellectual life, leading the generous and thoughtful to meditate on the moral, social and political condition of the masses' (A. Dawson: 19). In 1880, Yarmouth was hardly unusual in that the town's largest public room was the Congregational Church Lecture Hall. The lecture, not least because it could be stretched to partake of many of the functions of a public meeting, with motions put and passed, offered a means of energizing communities and stirring up activity. The lecture platform provided figures with a cross-denominational profile; encouraged interdenominational interchange and cooperation. Hook was convinced that the public lectures he delivered in Leeds in the 1850s gave him a connection with the community, especially the working classes, that purely parochial work could not have achieved (Stephens: 2: 314–20). And beneath all this were the enormous financial benefits. The proceeds of lectures funded the wider ambition of Victorian religion. The £120,000 fund-raising credited to Peter Mackenzie may have been exceptional, but time and again reluctant lecturers were dragged to the platform by the financial difficulties of brother ministers and the endless demands of chapel debts, school buildings, and missions.

The role of the lecture in the evolution of preaching styles more generally is even more difficult to tease out. Given the clear overlap of sermon and lecture, and the diversity of practice that the pulpit surveys during the century reveal, the question of influence is perhaps a false one. There was convergence, perhaps most obvious in preaching outside the morning service, where the alternative lecturing modes were inexorably adopted even where the performance remained styled a sermon. Hence Samuel Pearson's evening preaching: 'more concrete, parabolic, biographical and free in style and method' than his regular sermons (Pearson: 30).

One strain of late Victorian preaching in which the influence of lecturing was visible was the popular Sunday afternoon sermon of which Scott Holland's St Paul's Cathedral sermons were a good example, in which religious messages were made to resonate powerfully with contemporary debates and concerns about national life, social justice, and similar concerns. Inevitably popular lecturers were likely to adopt the style in the pulpit; it was said of Paxton Hood's sermons that they were 'lectures, rather than sermons. They abound in anecdotes and historical allusions—not to mention imaginative descriptions and scraps of poetry. They contain dreams and allegories, quaint fictitious impersonations, and other novel devices for producing pulpit effect' (*The Congregational Pulpit*). Sermons adopted the freer structure, became less doctrinal, more practical, more worldly. There was also much greater 'action' in the pulpit. H. R. Haweis 'walk[ed] about the pulpit as if it were a small stage; [throwing] his head and arms about as though he felt that the success of his preaching depended on the violence of his gesticulations' (An Anglican Layman: 317). By the end of the century there was a growing concern that preaching was coming to be dominated by contemporary events, by the newspapers rather than the Bible. Even the morning sermon came under this influence. Tellingly, complaints about contemporary preaching styles offered an uncanny echo of the criticisms of Sunday lecturing forty years before: 'clap trap' titles, preoccupation with transient public affairs, an over-heated rhetoric, the sacrifice of lasting impact in the search for momentary excitement ('Sensational Preaching').

References

An Anglican Layman. (1877). *Pulpit and Pew. Sketches of Popular Preachers of the Period*. London: William Tegg and Co.
Bamford, J. S. (1900). 'Peter Mackenzie as I Knew Him'. *Wesleyan Methodist Magazine* 123: 108–11.
Barnett, H. (1918). *Canon Barnett*...London: John Murray.
Bebbington, D. W. (1989). *Evangelicalism in Modern Britain*...London: Unwin Hyam.
Braithwaite, R. (1878). *Life and Letters of Rev William Pennefather BA*. London: J. F. Shaw and Co.
Broadbent, J. W. (n.d.). *People's Life of Charles Garrett*. Leeds: James Broadbent.
Carpenter, W. B. (1911). *Some Pages of My Life*. London: Williams and Norgate.
The Congregational Pulpit. (1859). 8: 279.
Conway, D. M. (1894). *Centenary History of the South Place Society*. London: Williams and Norgate.
Cunliffe-Jones, J. (1992). 'A Rare Phenomenon: A Woman's Contribution to Nineteenth Century Adult Education'. *Journal of Educational and Administrative History* 24-1: 1–17.
Dawson, A. (1901). *Joseph Parker, D.D., His Life and Ministry*. London: S. W. Partridge.
Dawson, J. (1896). *Peter Mackenzie*...London: Charles H. Kelly.
—— (1897). *Lectures and Sermons of Peter Mackenzie*. London: Charles H. Kelly.
'Death of the Rev. Robert Halley, D.D.' (1876). *The Sheffield Independent*, 21 August: 3.
Dorling, W. (1879). *Henry Vincent. A Biographical Sketch*. London: J. Clarke and Co.
Ellison, R. H. (1998). *The Victorian Pulpit*...Selinsgrove, PA: Susquehanna University Press.
'English Correspondence'. (1858–9). *The Southern Spectator*, n.s. 1: 24.
Farningham, M. (1907). *A Working Woman's Life*...London: J. Clarke and Co.

The Freeman (17 June 1863).
Garrison, W. L. (1836). *Lectures of George Thompson*... Boston: Isaac Knapp.
Grant, B. (1869). *The Dissenting World*... London: W. Macintosh.
Guthrie, D. K. and Guthrie, C. J. (1874). *Autobiography of Thomas Guthrie, D.D.* London: Isbister.
Guttridge, J. (1884). *Life Among the Masses*... Manchester: Brook and Chrystal.
Halley, R. (1879). *A Short Biography of the Rev Robert Halley, D.D.*... London: Chilworth.
Harrison, A. J. (1901). *An Eventful Life*... London: Cassell and Co.
Hocking, S. (1923). *My Book of Memory*... London: Cassell and Co.
Jacks, L. P. (1917). *Life and Letters of Stopford Brooke*. London: John Murray.
James, J. A. (1861). *Discourses Addressed to Ministers*. London: Hamilton, Adams and Co.
Jennings, H. J. (1920). *Chestnuts and Small Beer*. London: Chapman and Hall.
Jerram, J. (1855). *The Memoirs and A Selection from the Letters of the Late Rev Charles Jerram, M.A.* London: Wertheim and Macintosh.
Johnson, D. A. (1981). 'Popular Apologetics in Late Victorian England...'. *Journal of Religious History* 11: 558–77.
Lake, K. (1901). *Memorials of William Charles Lake*... London: Edward Arnold.
Landels, T. D. (1900). *William Landels, D.D. A Memoir*. London: Cassell and Co.
'The Late Dr Halley'. (1876). *Congregationalist* 5: 641–50.
Leach, C. (1887). *How I Reached the Masses*... London: James Nisbet and Co.
'Lecture on Passages in the Life of the Apostle Paul'. (1856). *Huddersfield Chronicle*, 9 February: 6.
Lunn, H. S. (1918). *Chapters from My Life*... London: Cassell and Co.
McCree, C. W. (1893). *George William McCree*... London: James Clarke and Co.
McCullagh, T. (1881). *Rev. William Morley Punshon, LL.D.: A Memorial Sermon*. London: Wesleyan Conference Office.
Masson, D. (1911). *Memories of Two Cities, Edinburgh and Aberdeen*. London: Oliphant, Anderson and Ferrier.
Manchester Courier, 25 November 1837.
'Multum in Parvo: The Rev T. Binney's Early Struggles'. (1869). *Lancaster Gazette*, 25 December: 6.
Myers, F. (1856). *Lectures on Great Men*. London: J. Nisbet and Co.
Paget, S. (1921). *Henry Scott Holland: Memoir and Letters*. London: John Murray,
Paz, D. G. (1992). *Popular Anti-Catholicism in Mid-Victorian England*. Stanford, CA: Stanford University Press.
Pearson, S. (1891). *Service in Three Cities*. London: James Clarke and Co.
Pike, G. H. (1885). *Saving to the Uttermost*. London: Hodder and Stoughton.
Pond, J. B. (1887). *A Summer in England with Henry Ward Beecher*. New York: Fords, Howard and Hulbert.
'The Rev. D Macrae on Character and Characters'. (1879). *Daily Gazette*, 2 April: 4.
'The Riot in a Church in Exeter'. (1848). *Newcastle Courant*, 17 November: 8.
'Sensational Preaching'. (1892). *Church Times*, 19 February: 169–70.
Smith, A. O. (1882). *Rev Gervase Smith*... London: T. Woolmer.
Stephens, W. R. (1878). *Life and Letters of Walter Farquhar Hook*. London: R. Bentley and Son.
Stock, E. (1909). *My Recollections*. London, James Nisbet.
Stowell Brown, H. (1858). *Lectures to the Men of Liverpool*... Liverpool: Gabriel Thompson.
'Such is Popularity'. (1884). *Tuapeka Times* (NZ), 17 September: 6.

Waddel, J. N. (1860). 'The Lecture System—Its Influence on Young Men'. *Southern Presbyterian Review* 12–2: 258–88.
'W. B.' 'A Representative Man' (1892). *The Queenslander*, 27 May: 658. <http://nla.gov.au/nla.news-article19784475> accessed 15 June 2011.
Wicksteed, P. H. (1886). *Memorials of the Rev Charles Wicksteed*. London: Williams and Norgate.
Williams, D. R. (2008). *Cornubia's Son. A Life of Mark Guy Pearse*. London: Francis Boutle Publishers.
[Woodd, B.] (1834). *A Family Record or Memoirs of the Late Rev Basil Woodd*. London: R. B. Seeley and W. Burnside.
'The Working Men's Sabbath Addresses', *Cheshire Observer* 20 June 1857: 6.
Yeo, S. (1976). *Religion and Voluntary Organisations in Crisis*. London: Croom Helm.
Young, D. T. (1904). *Peter Mackenzie as I Knew Him*. London: Hodder and Stoughton.
—— (1920). *Stars of Retrospect*... London: Hodder and Stoughton.

CHAPTER 6

THE BRITISH QUAKER SERMON, 1689–1901

MICHAEL GRAVES

From their first appearance in the middle of the seventeenth century, the Quakers have made direct spiritual experience central to their teachings, resulting in a belief system that heralded and defended immediate revelation from God, a radical claim that fit hand in glove with their embrace of preaching that was radically impromptu in its practice and claimed to be immediately divinely inspired. For example, George Fox, one of the key founders of Quakerism, while clearly aided in the impromptu preaching challenge by his impressive knowledge of scripture, reveals in key passages of his *Journal* his astonishing claim of direct revelation, leading first to his salvation and later inspiring his sermons. What other Christians called the Holy Spirit, Fox and the early Quakers called the 'Inward Light' of Christ (Nichols: 11, 15, 27, 29, 33).

Quaker impromptu preaching from the 1650s into the 1800s has been the subject of scholarly exploration in books and monographs (Barbour; Bauman; Beamish; Gwyn; Graves). One result of these investigations is the development of an understanding of early Quaker preaching practice and a clear picture of the evolution of late seventeenth-century and early eighteenth-century Quaker sermons.

This chapter will briefly explore the effects of early Quakers' belief in immediate revelation on their incipient homiletic 'theory', a tenet that became a point of reference in the evolution of their sermons over the next two centuries. It will sketch some basic notions of early Quaker homiletics and deal with the development of the British Quaker sermon through three rough chronological divisions: the early 'quietistic' period, which preceded the Act of Toleration in 1689 and progressed until the early 1700s; the later 'quietistic' period, which spanned the eighteenth century and progressed into the early 1800s; and the period of Quaker diversity, which began in the 1820s and influenced Quaker theology and sermonizing throughout the nineteenth century. The state of scholarship focused on English Quaker sermons of each period will be considered as well as pointing towards possible future research.

Quaker Homiletic Writing

It is important to review the Quaker understanding of impromptu preaching prior to a consideration of the extant Quaker sermons from each period because the same principles continued to inform Quaker preaching.

In their journals and other writings early Quakers revealed a programme of advice for novice preachers, especially younger ones, those who were initially encountering the particular challenges of impromptu preaching (Punshon: 138–9). In his *Journal*, Fox recognized that young preachers might 'bubble forth' and 'go beyond their measure', but warned elders to deal gently with fledgling ministers and to 'be careful how that you do set your feet among the tender plants' (Nichols: 282, 312). Fox's own habits of preaching, which served as a model for others, included, first of all, frequent admonitions for hearers to turn to the source of life, the Inward Light of Christ. Secondly, he also placed great emphasis in his preaching on the hermeneutical use of Bible passages, particularly the use of Old Testament typology. Fox habitually stressed an interpretation of Old Testament events and persons seen as types, which anticipated analogous examples of New Testament fulfilment in Christ and the Church, as well as crucial applications of the types to the lives of his hearers (Nichols: 108–9). Thirdly, Fox also frequently interpreted scripture in ways that exposed or discredited other Dissenters and the Established Church, including particular attacks on their pre-planned and rehearsed sermonizing. Thus Fox modelled at least three possible approaches for other preachers to follow.

Margaret Fell, who became Fox's spouse, defended women's right to preach in her now famous *Women's Speaking Justified* (1666), which is important because the ranks of Friends' vocal ministers, or Public Friends, always included women. In addition, Anglicans and Puritans alike called for a well-educated clergy, but Fox, Fell, Robert Barclay, the Quaker apologist, and numerous other Quaker writers, such as Quaker preacher, Rebecca Smith, in her *The Foundation of True Preaching Asserted* (1687), rejected the need for university training or even ordination to become a minister, a universal and continuing theme among British Quakers from 1689 to 1900. Yet, as will be seen, the process of recognizing who had received the divine call to be a minister became a matter of great concern in the eighteenth century.

In 1676 27-year-old Robert Barclay published a theological justification of Quaker theology, which included 'Propositions' dealing specifically with immediate revelation, the ministry, and worship in his *Apology for the True Christian Divinity*. In the *Apology*, Barclay argued that silent group waiting is the core of acceptable worship, but that speaking prompted by the Spirit might also be helpful to the gathered meeting under conditions when 'every one puts that forth which the Lord puts into their hearts: and it is uttered forth not in man's will and wisdom; but in the evidence and demonstration of the Spirit and of power' (Barclay: 329). Barclay's work was hugely influential and the majority of Quakers during the eighteenth and nineteenth centuries attested to this principle.

As the last three decades of the seventeenth century unfolded, Quakers continued to accumulate a fairly consistent pattern of advice for novice preachers. Sociologically and theologically, even prior to the Act of Toleration in 1689, Quakers were losing the radical evangelical and 'revivalistic' edge of the earliest Friends, and their advice to neophyte preachers became increasingly conservative. For example, the Bristol Quaker, Charles Marshall, wrote his influential 1675 public letter, *An Epistle to Friends Coming forth in the Beginning of a Testimony*, which advocated a conservative 'passive' approach not only to what was said, but also to the very prospect of daring to speak aloud in a Quaker meeting for worship. He stressed the importance of silent waiting in the Spirit and also warned his readers about the deceitful spiritual 'Enemy' who sought to undermine true Christian worship by means of self-promoting expression prompted by the minister's ego instead of the Inward Light (Marshall: 5-6). This sort of negative warning by a highly respected elder Friend tended to have a dampening effect on impromptu preaching.

This conservative and cautionary approach found ultimate expression in Samuel Bownas's very significant *Description of the Qualifications Necessary to a Gospel Minister*, which was essentially a manual on impromptu preaching. It was written from the perspective of Bownas's long experience as a Public Friend, but also reflected the accumulated teachings of previous ministers and elders, including their warning to be certain that the message one heard inwardly was in fact a message to be uttered aloud. Bownas reiterated Fox's admonition for elders to be tender when rebuking young preachers, those who seem to go beyond the Spirit's leading (Bownas: 20-1). Bownas also added significant reflections and advice not discovered in earlier Quaker writings about vocal ministry. For example, regarding delivery, Bownas warned against speaking too fast or too loud. On style, he wrote in favour of terseness rather than copiousness: 'guard against superfluous words... which add nothing to thy matter, spoiling its coherence and beauty and expression' (Bownas: 38, 42). Bownas laced these pieces of advice with admonitions not to imitate other preachers, either in delivery or composition. He even warned against using original material on more than one speaking occasion (Bownas: 58-9), advice that, if followed, must have significantly reduced the impromptu preacher's fund of available material (or 'commonplaces') for potential use in the travelling ministry.

Bownas's chief original contribution to the development of a Quaker impromptu homiletic was his presentation of a checklist of the 'Matter and Manner of Expression', which amounted to an accumulation of six ways the young preacher might expect the Spirit to work in any given sermon. Bownas included the following categories: parables, allegories, narration of history, personal testimony, relation of another person's testimony, and application of biblical typologies (Bownas: 48-59).

This brief review of seventeenth- and eighteenth-century Quaker writing on impromptu preaching reveals that early on, Quakers attempted to lead their fledgling preachers down a conservative path of fruitful vocal ministry. By their published guidance they may have acted in ways that seemed overly cautious and paradoxical to their commitment to an ostensibly impromptu and immediately 'inspired' vocal ministry, a 'prophetic' strain of sermonizing that might at any moment, under Divine encouragement, fly in the face of the reticent, conservative, decorum offered by the published advice of elders.

British Quaker Sermons in the Early Quietistic Period

Quaker sermons from the period immediately prior to and following the Act of Toleration in 1689 until the early 1700s have attracted scholarly attention and are well mapped in studies by Bauman, Beamish, and Graves. Under the conditions of the conservative approach to preaching, it is not surprising that the number of sermon manuscripts available for study during any historical period is limited. All of the sixty-seven surviving printed and manuscript sermons for the early 'quietistic' period (1687–1700)—the majority of them delivered in London—are the products of anonymous auditors with shorthand skills, in most cases probably not Quakers (Graves: 313–21). The characteristics of these sermons persist into the eighteenth and nineteenth centuries, thus they offer readers a representative snapshot of what Quaker preaching became as the sect moved from seeing itself as the new and only church, to what John Punshon called 'a "little seed," a "Remnant," preserved from destruction by the special grace of God' (Punshon: 101).

Unfortunately, no sermons by women survive from the period prior to 1700. However, on the positive side, the list of preachers from whom we have sermons includes notable early Friends such as Robert Barclay, Charles Marshall, Benjamin Coole, Stephen Crisp, William Penn, and George Whitehead. Careful study of these extant sermons leads to the formulation of empirically grounded generalizations about seventeenth- and eighteenth-century Quaker impromptu sermon practice during the period of increasing 'Quietism'. Ben Pink Dandelion has offered a description of Quietism: 'Key to Quietism is the idea that the path to God is based in retreat from the world and the self. There is a supernatural plane and a natural one. The natural one is corrupt and corrupting and the faithful in their aspiration towards the supernatural need to guard themselves against the worldly...' (Pink Dandelion: 59). Notwithstanding the earlier, more outward and 'evangelical' sermons of the late 1680s and 1690s by Stephen Crisp, Robert Barclay, and William Penn, a careful review of the surviving sermon texts from this period indicates a gradual deepening into the concerns of Quietism described by Pink Dandelion. A survey of these sermons' rhetorical characteristics sets a benchmark for comparison of sermons from later periods.

With respect to the sermons of the early Quietistic period, the following characteristics are significant: themes or topics touched on by the preachers; the preachers' reliance on conceptual metaphors; their use of spatial terms; the use of rhetorical questions and the development of the 'catechetical' style; and (5) the growing significance of sharing personal testimonies.

Themes/Topics

Quaker sermons do not concentrate on raising doctrines from scripture and presenting their application or use, although occasionally some of the sermons do 'raise' and apply biblical doctrine. For the most part, though, these later Quaker sermons are best described as mosaic rather than linear in their organizational format, with some exceptions. Typically, a number of topics or themes are mentioned in each sermon, although sermons by Crisp, Penn, and others reveal the preachers' ability to sustain an argument and deal with a smaller number of topics or themes.

Many of the sermons' themes are squarely theological, employing the familiar biblical language of grace, truth, salvation, perfection, love, peace, faith, joy, justification, regeneration, and so forth, but these terms were often mixed with themes or topics more foundational to Quaker beliefs, such as 'the Inward Light' or 'silent waiting' (Graves: 322–36). Several of the sermons focus on specific Quaker beliefs regarding the proper manner of worship—for example, emphasis on the Quaker meeting convened in group silence—and the rejection of typical Protestant (and Catholic) rituals of worship, including water baptism and communion. Occasionally, compulsory tithes to the Anglican Church were also criticized (Graves: 176).

Furthermore, the sermons reveal that the preachers were concerned with guiding the behaviour of their listeners, sometimes to the extent of presenting specific behavioural injunctions against, for example, becoming too materialistic or giving way to anger when correcting children (Graves: 170–71), both themes receiving increased attention as Quietism deepened. With some frequency the sermons turned listeners to the Inward Light, seen as the direct source of guidance for moral behaviour. Some of the sermons stressed sexual morality, honesty, or truth-telling (without recourse to oaths), and the habitual use of 'plain' and unostentatious language. These references to proscribed behaviour all increased as the eighteenth century wore on, enforced by the prospect of 'disownment', or being 'read out of the meeting', a practice that 'was about the maintenance of spiritual purity to avoid contamination from worldly ways and the presentation of this purity to the outside world to obviate criticism and as a model of the gathered community' (Pink Dandelion: 69).

On occasion, the sermons make reference to some of the sectarian conflicts of their day. After the Act of Toleration in 1689, reflection on the past persecution of Protestant dissenters became a topic for some preachers. Also, a negative stand toward the Roman Catholic Church occasionally emerged as a theme (Graves: 176).

Some of the sermons took up quasi-secular topics, such as: presenting a distrust of secular learning, repudiating contentious public debate, appropriating the language of the new science with reference to their own 'experimental' and empirically grounded experience of faith, and expressing an utter rejection of the theatre (Graves: 177–79).

One of the radical social themes not frequently discovered in the sermons of early Quietism, the position against war as a way to resolve international conflicts, became increasingly important as the eighteenth century progressed (Graves: 179–81).

Key Conceptual Metaphors

George Lakoff and Mark Johnson have asserted that 'human thought processes are largely metaphorical' (Lakoff and Johnson: 6). Early Quietistic Quaker sermons illustrate this insight exceptionally well, as do most extant Quaker sermons in the nineteenth century. As has already been seen, these sermons were not typically characterized by rigorous scriptural explication according to doctrinal themes. Instead, they frequently rehearsed, accumulated, combined, and even juxtaposed language that featured five key conceptual metaphors or 'clusters' of related terms which grouped themselves into something like 'families'. Working together in linguist familial relationship, they captured an image of the early Quaker worldview. The five clusters of metaphors, arranged sequentially by their numerical prominence in the sixty-seven sermons from 1687 to 1700, included: the light/dark family metaphor; the voice or sound/silence metaphor; the seed metaphor; the hunger/thirst metaphor; and the journey/pilgrimage metaphor (Graves: 337–47). Each of these metaphors entailed a group of recurrent terms. For example, the light/dark family included the following terms: light, sun, day, sparks, fire, star, beacon, lamp, candle, day of visitation, day of the Lord, voice of the Light, darkness, night, clouds, fog, mist, shadows, veil, and chains of darkness. The five families of conceptual metaphors taken together helped early Quakers identify with each other through the rehearsal of imagery familiar to the group. Using the terms of the metaphors, they saw themselves as 'children of light', one of the first names they gave themselves, people who were led by the 'Inward Light of Christ'. They met in silence in order to hear and attend to the 'Voice' of the Lord. Christ the 'Word' was also seen as the 'Seed' that might take root, grow, and bring forth fruit in an individual's life. Naturally, a person needed spiritual water and bread for nourishment, refreshment, and health just as literal water and bread were necessary for sustenance in their daily lives. Lastly, early Quakers saw themselves as people on a spiritual journey, a pilgrimage full of tests and hardships, but also on a trek with a discernable destination ahead toward which they took daily steps. In important and sometimes surprising ways the five metaphors acted as a conceptual spine in sermons. They also functioned as a rhetorical tool in the invention process for speakers operating in the challenging impromptu situation. Preachers could turn to one or more of the metaphors to elaborate on a biblical concept or provide a familiar exhortation like this from Penn, which he offered at the memorial service for revered Quaker minister, Rebecca Travers: 'We are travelers here in this Vale of Tears, in this Earthly Pilgrimage, into the Land of Rest the Heavenly Canaan.... O Blessed are they that are waiting for their Lot and Portion in that Heavenly Country to which Abraham had his Eye, the City, the New Jerusalem' (Penn 1711: 6).

Spatial Terms

Another discernable feature of Quietistic Quaker sermons, but also a prominent linguistic feature of most Quaker sermons until the twentieth century, was the use of spatial terms. Maurice A. Creasey observed: 'On almost every page in the writings of early Friends the reader feels that he is being challenged to recognize a contrast. This contrast is expressed in spatial terms by such correlatives as "inward" and "outward", "within" and "without", "internal" and "external"' (Creasey: 3). This propensity in their writings is likewise a prominent linguistic feature of their sermons (Graves: 216). Generally, the sermons used spatial terms to express the difference between *experienced* faith and a mere intellectual commitment, or rationally based Christian belief. For example, preaching in 1694, Penn maintained: 'They only have the Benefit of what Christ hath done and suffered in his Outward Coming in the Flesh, that believe in him, and see the Necessity of his Inward Appearance and Coming in the Spirit' (Penn 1696: 48). Here Penn did not obviate the historical record of Jesus Christ's death to accomplish human redemption, but rather stressed the necessity of a personal, inward response to the living Christ. Penn's usage was typical of spatial terms in the early Quietistic sermons. The concept of the 'inward' or spiritual dimension versus the 'outward' or worldly dimension gained increasing importance in the life of eighteenth-century Friends and in the language of their sermons. Perhaps it is appropriate to end this brief discussion of spatial terms with a reminder that one of the key expressions of the light/dark conceptual metaphor in early Quaker sermons is the *Inward* Light.

The Catechetical Style

Early Quaker Quietistic preachers also relied heavily on the use of an ancient strategy: the venerable rhetorical question. This figure of thought (or 'scheme') has been popular since the dawn of rhetorical study in the fifth century BC, but early Quaker sermons present two rhetorically adroit adaptations of the common rhetorical question. First, the extant sermons reveal the development of the rhetorical question into its placement in narrative dialogues, thus producing a greater dramatic impact. For example, in a 1688 sermon, Crisp dealt with the Quaker position that living a holy and sin-free life was not only possible, but expected, a position greatly amplified and stressed in the evolution of discipline in the eighteenth century. In the sermon he stressed a key theological difference between Puritans and Baptists, who asserted that no one could be pure, and Quakers who demanded purity of themselves. To make his point, Crisp used dialogical rhetorical questions:

> Go to one place and another place, and ask them what is your way? Our way (say they) is the right way... But wither will it lead me? It will lead to the Kingdom of God: That is it I would have; but will it lead me to Holiness? No, never in this World, you must never come to Holiness... Do you hold out that in your way? Yes; then I have done with that. (Crisp: 114)

Forty of the extant sermons used the mini-dialogue format (Graves: 213). In a culture that followed the Puritan rejection of elegant, 'elevated' diction, the mini-dialogue probably tended to increase the hearers' attention and provided the preacher with another avenue of potential development and elaboration of a topic in the impromptu situation.

The second Quaker extension of the common rhetorical question fit their turn toward introspection in the last two decades of the seventeenth century and increasing throughout the eighteenth century. From 1680 on, Quaker sermons began to anticipate the development of a strategy for self-examination in their meetings, which became known as 'the Queries', a series of questions read aloud to oneself or in meeting in order to spur individual reflection, inward response, and behavioural correction, if need be (Graves: 401). The development of query-like rhetorical questions is best seen in this example from one of Crisp's sermons:

> if men would...answer the principle of Truth in themselves, they would put the question to themselves, Shall I take up my Daily Cross, or no? Shall I deny my self those Pleasures that my Conscience doth condemn; and those ungodly Gains that I seek after by Falsehood, by Lying, Prevaricating and Departing from the Truth? Shall I do this, that I may be Rich and Great in the World, or shall I not? (Crisp: 78)

Use of Personal Testimony

It is not unexpected that Bownas's checklist of the 'Matter and Manner of Expression' included the use of personal testimony. Approximately one-third of the sermons from early Quietism featured the preachers relating some aspect of their personal lives to the subject at hand (Graves: 222). Thomas Chalkley offers an apt example. He visited the American colonies where, on one occasion in 1698, his words were recorded in a sermon that included this defense of his youth and inexperience at preaching: 'some persons may say...but how doth though know these things, for thou art but a Youth, I speak nothing Friends, but what I have Experienced. I have felt the word of God enter into my Soul, &...I have known what it is, to be born again' (Chalkley: 9–10).

BRITISH QUAKER SERMONS IN THE LATER QUIETISTIC PERIOD

Pink Dandelion has concluded that the Quietistic period of Quakerism is neither adequately researched nor fairly evaluated:

> This period of Quakerism is not popular, either with the Quakers who worked against its continuing influence or amongst later scholars and historians. It remains under-researched and misunderstood. People see the rules and the disownments and a view of the self difficult to comprehend in today's psychologised world and fail to see the rich and deep spirituality of the journals, of the life underpinning the

> testimony... These Quakers too continued to campaign for reform and justice... particularly against slavery but also in the more mundane such as fixed-price trading which eventually became normative. Quietism represents the longest single period of Quaker theology to date, an enduring and distinctive interpretation of Quaker faith and practice. (Pink Dandelion: 77)

The sermons delivered by Quakers during the eighteenth century constituted an important aspect of Quietism that is 'under-researched'.

It is important before considering the British Quaker sermons that survive the period spanning the eighteenth century and into the early 1800s to acknowledge that Quakers at this time constituted a transatlantic community. This is important because extant eighteenth-century Quaker sermons reflected a remarkably unified transatlantic culture. Pink Dandelion has noted that 'in terms of the socio-political dynamic, Quakerism was always different on the two sides of the Atlantic. In terms of spirituality and of course kinship, Quakerism remained a single transatlantic community until the Great Separation of 1827 divided Quakerism in North America' (Pink Dandelion: 52). The presence of a strong tradition of travelling in the ministry helped to reinforce the common bonds. Thus, consideration of surviving sermons from the period will range over the transatlantic culture of Friends during the period.

Additionally, prior to considering the Quaker sermons of the period, it is important to note that the practice of Quaker ministry evolved during the period so that the sermons can be seen as arising from their evolving sociological context. The earliest Quakers grew rapidly in numbers through the efforts of itinerant 'Public Friends' who travelled energetically to minister and evangelize. Similarly, in later periods travelling ministers voyaged across the Atlantic (in both directions), to evangelize and minister to Quaker meetings.

Although Quakers rejected the necessity of ordination to preach, they eventually did 'record' God's call of ministry on individual Friends as the frequency of their public ministry grew and their special role as 'Public Friends' became obvious to the local meeting. Recording was not an instantaneous act upon one's first rising to speak in meeting, and it was never automatic in any case. It was, rather, the result of a period of effective vocal ministry and serious consultation with other ministering Friends, as was described in Bownas's important manual mentioned above. Most recorded ministers would stay in their local meeting, giving public voice from time to time as moved by the Spirit. However, some recorded ministers felt the call to travel in the ministry. Punshon observed that as the seventeenth century closed, one can discern 'a loose distinction between Friends who traveled in the ministry and those who stayed at home to care for their local meetings' (Punshon: 140).

Gradually Quaker ministry itself began to evolve. Eighteenth-century Friends began to see themselves differently from the way early Friends perceived themselves. Margery Post Abbott and Peggy Senger Parsons have captured the essential difference:

> The initial fervor was gone, as was the intense persecution. Friends were becoming respectable. They focused inwardly rather than believing that they were the forefront

of a movement that would change the entire world. The 'Lamb's War' against evil using only the 'weapons' of Christ, which was so central to first generation Quakers, had already become muted as Friends focused more on the preservation of a holy remnant. (Abbott and Parsons: 252)

Eventually, as Quietism deepened, and the need for additional spiritual oversight in meetings began to be seen as crucial to maintaining the purity of Friends' testimonies to the outside world, the role of Elder tended to became more important than Public Friend in local meetings, the Elders having been charged with the weighty task of 'moral oversight of the membership'. In addition, the office of 'Overseer' began to develop as separate from Elder or Minister as the century passed its halfway mark, and by 1789, Elders and Overseers were distinct offices. Punshon writes: 'There was thus established a spiritual aristocracy within a wider spiritual aristocracy with a steadily declining membership. The effects were profound' (Punshon: 143). Public ministers, whether travelling or settled, were at the bottom of the ministry hierarchy.

The development of a serious and conservative process of being recognized and eventually 'recorded' as a minister has been noted, but for potential travelling ministers, the process of approval became even more careful as the century progressed. Travelling ministers needed to secure a 'travelling minute' before they could embark. The minister shared his or her 'concern' to travel in the ministry to such and such meeting with his or her monthly meeting, who would, upon examination and prayer, grant a travelling minute, which the Public Friend would present to the meeting which the minister felt called to visit. He or she would have the minute endorsed by the visited meeting and return it to the original monthly meeting. This was no easily dispatched matter, especially when the travel might involve visiting numerous Quaker meetings in several countries, sometimes involving long sea voyages. Punshon noted that the travelling minute became 'the proudest passport a Quaker can carry' (Punshon: 142).

In sum, there were challenges to the impromptu preaching ministry in the long Quietistic period, with its emphasis on achieving moral purity and adherence to Quaker 'peculiarities', such as plain speech and dress. For the Public Friend, both from the point of view of initial recording as a minister, continued oversight by a system of Elders determined to preserve the 'remnant', and the conservative yet reassuring rigor of the approval to travel in the ministry, the calling was not an easy vocation. Nevertheless, Quaker preaching survived and a collection of later Quietism sermons is extant.

The extant sermons of eighteenth-century Quakers have not been as systematically collected, catalogued, and examined rhetorically as those from the period 1687–1700 (Graves: 318–20). The current one-volume histories of Quakers by Barbour and Frost, Punshon, and Pink Dandelion make frequent and insightful references to Quaker ministry, but rarely mention specific sermons or comment on the rhetorical choices made by the ministers. Similarly, in her fastidiously researched volume on Quaker women ministers, Rebecca Larson relies on journals and letters to unfold the story of ministry by women during the period. Larson mentions two 1765 sermons by Rachel Wilson (from Kendal) preached in the colonies, but offers no analysis of the sermons or comments on Wilson's rhetorical habits.

Beamish went further by referencing sermons by Stephen Crisp, Francis Stamper, and Richard Ashby (Beamish: 24–33), all from the earlier period, but failed to comment on Ashby's sermon preached in 1710, which is extant. Encouragingly, Beamish also provided brief commentary, mostly theological in nature, on twelve sermons by Thomas Story (1670–1742) and three sermons by Samuel Fothergill (1715–72), mentioning Fothergill's 'love of exhortation by means of queries', his preference for the Old Testament over the New Testament, and his habit of taking 'a recondite passage from Scripture and build[ing] a sermon on it' (Beamish: 33–8, 95, 97). These observations of Fothergill's rhetorical habits, empirically based in the sermon texts she references, may guide the future rhetorical critic through the additional ten or more sermon texts that survive from Fothergill. Moreover, Beamish mentioned the ministry of several eighteenth-century female Friends ministers, including Catherine Phillips, Mary Moore, May Drummond, Mary Kirby, and Lucy Bradley (Beamish: 84–91).

My own collection of eighteenth-century sermons numbers seventy-five, consisting mainly of full sermons taken down in shorthand and later printed, but also including some visions, prayers, and prophecies delivered on city streets and preserved in manuscript form. In addition to the two by Rachel Wilson mentioned above, the list includes nine sermons by women, for example: a sermon by Sarah Baker (1707); Deborah Bell's sermon on the Lord's Prayer (no date); one sermon by Lydia Lanchester (1738); one by Benjamina Paddley (1738); and two sermons by Catherine Phillips (1779 and 1780, and a prayer taken down in 1782). The list also includes sermons by numerous men, for example: Thomas Colley (1787) and George Dillwyn (preached in England in 1796), both colonists; one vision and at least twelve sermons by Samuel Fothergill, including sermons preached while travelling in North America; a prophecy by John Hall (1713); one sermon by Abraham Hodges (1708); two sermons by Benjamin Kidd of Banbury (1739); twelve sermons by Thomas Letchworth preached in 1737 or prior; nine sermons by William Savery from the 1780s and 1790s; one sermon by colonist Job Scott, preached in England the year he died (1793); one sermon by Samuel Scott (1737); ten sermons by Thomas Story (1737–8); and sermons by thirteen others (Graves MSS).

This partial list indicates that there is a substantial body of stenographic impromptu sermons yet to be examined rhetorically. In addition the list includes two or more sermons by five preachers, three men and two women, a situation that offers the rhetorical analyst the opportunity to undertake comparisons and contrasts of each individual's sermonizing and also affords comparison and contrast across preachers, including comparisons of rhetorical choices between genders. All of this careful analytical work remains to be undertaken.

Furthermore, it is clear that this list of sixty-seven sermons is incomplete. The sermon texts were gathered over a period of years at major Friends research libraries, including the Library of the Religious Society of Friends, London; the Bevan–Naish Collection of early Quaker materials at the Library of Woodbrooke Quaker Studies Centre, Birmingham, England; Friends Historical Library of Swarthmore College and the Quaker Collection of Haverford College Library, both located near Philadelphia. None of these resources has been exhausted. Other potential sources of additional eighteenth-century (and nineteenth-century) sermons are manuscript journals and commonplace books, which have been perused in my own research. In addition, the libraries of individual Friends meetings may prove to be valuable resources for shorthand sermon notes.

Perusal of the seventy-five eighteenth-century sermons indicates that they continue and deepen the tendencies of the early Quietistic period. As a whole, the preachers sought to preserve a holy, separated remnant, while holding forth a positive testimony to the 'world'. These ministers were Christians through and through and employed the standard lexicon of Christian theology: 'justification', 'sanctification', 'redemption', etc. They offered behavioural guidance on matters of morality and Quaker 'peculiarities', such as plain speech and dress. They stressed *purity* and how it can be attained. Everywhere, the personal *experience* of spiritual reality—their own and that of others—was overtly championed.

The surviving sermons continued to feature extensive quotation (from memory) of Scripture and frequent application of Scripture to the personal lives of the hearers, especially when the passages deal with moral strictures and attaining personal holiness. Like early Quaker sermons, most of these sermons did not rest on a base of theological argument. Rather, the conceptual spine of the sermons remained the world of the five key Quaker metaphors from the earlier period: light/dark, sound/silence, seed, hunger/thirst, and journey/pilgrimage.

Spatial terms were ubiquitous in the sermons, as preachers in the century attempted to move meetings toward the 'inward' reality of spirituality prompted by the 'Inward Light'. The 'outward' material matters were seen as transient and not to be esteemed.

The 'catechetical style' continued apace, with abundant use of rhetorical questions to prompt self-examination. As noted above, Beamish observed Fothergill as centering many of his appeals in the queries, questions individuals and meetings employed to facilitate introspection, behavioural self-scrutiny, and change.

Finally, the ministers chose personal testimony as a crucial rhetorical choice in many of the sermons.

British Quaker Sermons During the Period of Quaker Diversity

A period of strong theological disagreement began to emerge among Friends in the 1820s and eventually resulted in the 1827 schism in the Philadelphia Yearly Meeting known as the Hicksite Separation, a rending of Quaker unity that influenced Quaker theology and sermonizing on both sides of the Atlantic throughout the nineteenth century. Subsequent years saw further, less catastrophic 'separations' that eventually facilitated remarkable diversity among British Quakers. Interestingly, their surviving sermons reveal a diversity of theological content and style, but an essential core of shared vocabulary and impromptu tradition persists into the 1870s.

The historical, theological, and sociological contexts of nineteenth-century English Quaker sermons are complex and variegated. It is well beyond the scope of this chapter to sort through the threads of discord, but a general overview of the most important diverse paths is necessary for this discussion. The various paths of disagreement, diversity, and schism have been clearly presented by historians and sociologists. Friends were influenced from two sources, according to Punshon: Deism and the Evangelical Revival, the former questioning the deity of Christ, the authority of Scripture, and the need for personal salvation, while upholding Friends traditions such as group silence and the quest for inward experiential spirituality. On the other hand, ardent Quaker Evangelicals saw sin as 'total distortion of the human personality'; the Bible as 'inspired and infallible'; personal conversion as absolutely necessary; 'mission', or evangelization, as a high priority, as their name suggests. Quakers also emphasized the possession of a personal faith that was doctrinally sound, for example, the belief 'that Christ has accepted the penalty for your sin' (Punshon: 165).

However, rising evangelicalism was resisted by Quakers who had been influenced by Deism and rationalism its bed-fellow, the latter existing as an approach that placed 'reason above faith, or rational authority above scriptural'. Pink Dandelion writes that 'Deist, rationalist, and extreme Quietist ideas flew in the face of growing evangelical influence' (Pink Dandelion: 84).

There are many paths of nineteenth-century Quaker diversity, but one that came after the Hicksite Separation merits mention here. In the 1830s, Orthodox Friends—those who opposed the Hicksites—manifested disagreements between those in their number who held a primary allegiance to Quaker tradition and those who developed a strong attachment to the broader category, evangelical Christianity. Pink Dandelion writes: 'These two positions were epitomized by John Wilbur and Joseph John Gurney and they became the leading protagonists in a second wave of schism that rent Orthodox Yearly Meetings' (Pink Dandelion: 95). Eventually, Orthodox Yearly Meetings separated into Wilburite and Gurneyite Yearly Meetings, beginning in 1845 (Punshon 197). In America, the Gurneyites were strong in the burgeoning west and later were greatly influenced by the holiness revivals in the last half of the century. At length, because of the large influx of new members produced by the revivals, they embraced a system of 'released' ministry, a pastoral system, which eventuated in 'programmed' worship services (Pink Dandelion: 102–12; Punshon: 199–202). This truncated review of Quaker schism is important because the known extant sermons of the period include the essential 1826 sermons which fomented the Hicksite Separation, as well as the core of Joseph John Gurney's sermons in America that both revived the evangelical branch of American Orthodox Friends and prodded the intense response of the Wilburites.

In the overview of the extant sermons from the two previous historical periods, the accumulated corpus of seventeenth-century and eighteenth-century sermons is relatively large given their impromptu nature. However, the number of extant Quaker sermons from the nineteenth century is even more impressive. Currently I have uncovered sources for 163 Quaker sermons for the period, both printed and manuscript, copying many of them for future analysis. Most of these sermons are from auditors' notes, but a few are from the preachers' reconstructions of what they said. Further searches at major Quaker research libraries, with particular attention to handwritten journals and commonplace books, will produce more than 200 sermons with fairly complete texts to analyse. The majority of the sermons in this group are by American ministers, largely for two reasons: the holiness revivals in America in the second half of the century encouraged preaching rather than silence; and the turn towards the pastoral system in many American Gurneyite Quaker meetings encouraged sermons that were prepared in advance and sometimes written down.

Of the present 163 known sermons, seventy were either preached in Britain (by British or American Friends) or by British Friends speaking in America. The figure includes the names of key American figures in the Separation of 1827, such as Elias Hicks, the majority of which were preached in America. If we remove the sermons preached in America during the Hicksite Separation, the number drops to fifty-five.

The seventy-five sermon list includes the following: one sermon by William Allen (1833); two sermons by James Backhouse (prior to 1832); four sermons by Robert Barclay of Reigate, not the author of the *Apology* (1869, 1872, 1876, and one undated sermon published in 1878); one sermon each by Richard Barrett (prior to 1832), Hannah Braithwaite (1833), Elizabeth Dudley (published in 1832), Thomas Evans (1851), and Elizabeth Fry (published in 1832); two sermons by Stephen Grellet (1829 and 1832); four sermons preached in England by Sarah Grubb (no dates); twelve sermons by Joseph John Gurney (from 1832 to 1838, five of which were preached during his American visit); twelve sermons by Elias Hicks preached in America (all 1826); two sermons by Ann Jones (1832 and 1836); one sermon by Sybil Jones of Maine, which she preached in England (1853); two by Samuel Tuke (1840 and c.1848); five sermons by John Wilkinson (four in 1832 and one in 1834); and several more.

The list of preachers includes significant Quaker luminaries Grellet, Jones, Fry, Gurney, Grubb, Tuke, and Barclay of Reigate. This is an impressive list and offers the rhetorical analyst the opportunity to examine, for example, how the tensions of theological disagreement and sociological change were managed rhetorically by select ministers over several decades. In particular, the sermons of the Hicksite Separation are well represented in the surviving sermons by Hicks and others. Similarly, Gurney's important 1838 visit to America is captured in five sermons. Also of note, Robert Barclay's extant sermons provide a sample of preaching at a 'Mission Hall Service', which Punshon described as developing from an educational programme to address illiteracy by British Friends, a Quaker experiment with ministry among poor, under-educated non-Quakers (Punshon: 192). The list of seventy-five sermons also exposes several chronological gaps in the record of English Quaker preaching, particularly the last two decades of the century when English Quakerism took a turn toward modernism (Pink Dandelion: 117–28). In sum, much of the basic work of collecting sermon texts from both sides of the Atlantic lies ahead.

Despite the fact that many sermon texts are currently available, preached by significant Friends ministers, some quite well known, scholars have paid little attention to nineteenth-century English Quaker sermons, although some have commented on preaching. For example, Beamish mentions the preaching of Mary Stokes (later Dudley), Thomas Shillitoe, David Sands, and Stephen Grellet (Beamish: 102–16).

Perusal of the sermons in my collection indicates that the free play of theological concepts and the interweaving of scripture, exhortations to find spiritual meaning in silence, rehearsal of Quaker metaphors, and reliance on rhetorical questions, all characteristics discovered in earlier periods, survive in some of the later sermons. For example, in her 1853 sermon delivered in Birmingham, England, Sybil Jones of Maine wove together a series of scriptural quotations beginning with the Lord's Prayer, quoted in toto, and continuing with her own opening prayer. The sermon that follows featured an interlacing of exhortations to 'draw near in silent waiting' and 'silent adoration', peppered with direct quotations from the Psalms and the Book of Revelation. As evidenced above, she relied on the power of the Quaker metaphor family of sound/silence, but she also employed the light/dark family: 'the Sun of Righteousness may disperse the mist and darkness now prevailing'. Later in the sermon she employed the journey metaphor, as in the following: 'pass through the wilderness of this world' and the 'foot of a mountain of great difficulty'. Her evangelical orthodoxy was overtly revealed late in the sermon with these words: 'may sinners come, more and more, unto Zion, and ask, what shall we do to be saved? Let these come unto Jesus, "the Lamb of God, who taketh away the sin of the world," who died and rose again, the just for the unjust' (Jones: 1–2).

The contrast in styles and approaches in nineteenth-century Quaker sermons is easily seen by turning to Gurney's sermon preached in Liverpool on 6 May 1832. Here Gurney employed some of the rhetorical strategies of his Quaker predecessors, such as the rhetorical question, which he used with great skill:

> Where is our penitence, then, friends? where is our broken heart? where is our humiliation? where is our trembling? where is our godly fear? Are you baptized into the name of the Father? Why do you not then tremble? Why are you not amazed? Why are ye not broken down under the sense of the terrors of his law? Why are ye not humbled under the blessed tidings that 'God is love?'

Here we see a classic appeal by a Quaker preacher to have the hearers enter into an *experiential* spirituality. The thematic heart of Gurney's sermon, though, was apologetic and centered on defending the divinity of Christ, one of the points of contention during the Hicksite Separation:

> [T]he doctrine of the divinity of our saviour is not a doctrine of speculation... it does not belong, as some suppose, to the mere theory of religion, and therefore may be laid on one side without inconvenience and without mischief; or, if not disbelieved, be disregarded as a matter of theory alone. My friends, there never was a greater proof of human blindness and ignorance than this particular error. (Gurney: 5)

As is evidenced in this brief comparison, there are rich veins to mine, both theologically and rhetorically, in surviving nineteenth-century English Quaker sermons.

Conclusion

The more than 217 extant English Quaker sermons from the period 1787 to 1901 constitute the rhetorical products of a Christian sect that practised the intentionally impromptu sermon prompted, ostensibly, by immediate divine inspiration. While the corpus of extant sermons remains incomplete at this time, we cannot draw any hard and fast conclusions about sermon content and style over the entire period, especially with respect to the last two decades of British Quakerism's turn toward modernism. However, we can venture the following tentative conclusions. The earliest sermons are multi-thematic mosaics, which occasionally comment on quasi-secular topics, a characteristic of some of the later sermons as well, although the sermons of evangelical Quakers like Fothergill and Gurney tend to zero in on a single topic and venture into apologetic argumentation. In all periods the sermons show a propensity of the ministers to quote passages of scripture verbatim throughout the sermons, often achieving a seamless interplay of scripture and their own words. Several of the sermons from the second and third period begin with and focus on a text from scripture, a choice that was rare in the earlier period. Most of the sermons continue to interweave language drawn from the five conceptual metaphor clusters so prominent in the early period. Also, the sermons in all periods tend to exhibit the use of spatial terms and reliance of rhetorical questions.

Surviving Quaker sermons reveal a distinct genre of sermonizing that can be studied, critiqued, and appreciated within the constraints of its own evolving theologically and socially motivated context.

References

Abbott, M. P., and Parsons, P. S. (eds.) (2004). *Walk Worthy of Your Calling: Quakers and the Traveling Ministry*. Richmond, IN: Friends United Press.

Barbour, H. (1964). *The Quakers in Puritan England*. New Haven: Yale University Press.

Barbour, H., and Frost, J. W. (1988). *The Quakers*. Richmond, IN: Friends United Press.

Barclay, R. (1867). *An Apology for the True Christian Divinity*. Philadelphia: Friends Book-Store.

Bauman, R. (1983). *Let Your Words be Few: Symbolism of Speaking and Silence among Seventeenth-Century Quakers*. New York: Cambridge University Press.

Beamish, L. K. (1967). *Quaker Ministry, 1691–1834*. Oxford: By the Author, Woodstock Road.

Bownas, S. (1750). *A Description of the Qualifications Necessary to a Gospel Minister*. London: Luke Hinde.

Chalkley, T. 'Mr T. Chalkley's Sermon & Prayer'. Swarthmore College, Friends Historical Library.

Creasey, M. A. (1962). *'Inward' and 'Outward': A Study in Early Quaker Language'*. London: Friends' Historical Society.

Crisp, S. (1711). *Scripture-Truths Demonstrated: In Thirty-Two Sermons or Declarations of Mr. Stephen Crisp*. London: J. Sowle.

Fell, M. (1989). *Women's Speaking Justified, Proved and Allowed of by the Scriptures*, in C. Trevett (ed.), *Womens Speaking Justified*. London: Quaker Home Service.

Graves MSS. Private collection of manuscript sermons.

Graves, M. P. (2009). *Preaching the Inward Light: Early Quaker Rhetoric*. Waco, TX: Baylor University Press.

Gurney, J. J. (1832). *Sermons and Prayers, Delivered by Joseph John Gurney, In the Friends Meeting House, Liverpool, 1832*, 2nd edn. Liverpool: Thomas Hodgson, 1832. The Quaker Homiletics Online Anthology <www.qhpress.org/quakerpages/qhoa/jjg101.htm> accessed 6 June 2011.

Gwyn, D. (1984). *Apocalypse of the Word: The Life and Message of George Fox*. Richmond, IN: Friends United Press.

Jones, S. (1853). *Recollections of a Prayer and Sermon, by Sybil Jones, of Maine, New England, U.S., at the Friends' Meeting House, Birmingham, on 1st Day Morning, 1st of 5th Month, 1853*. Birmingham: B. Hudson and Son.

Lakoff, G., and Johnson, M. (1980). *Metaphors We Live By*. Chicago: University of Chicago Press.

Larson, R. (1999). *Daughters of Light: Quaker Women Preaching and Prophesying in the Colonies and Abroad, 1700-1775*. New York: Alfred A. Knopf.

Marshall, C. (1775). *An Epistle to Friends Coming Forth in the Beginning of a Testimony and of the Snares of the Enemy Therein*.

Nichols, J. L. (1975). *Journal of George Fox*. London: Religious Society of Friends.

Penn, W. (1696). *The Harmony of Divine and Heavenly Doctrines*. London: J. Sowle.

—— (1711). *The Concurrence and Unanimity of the People Called Quakers*. London: J. Sowle.

Pink Dandelion, B. (2007). *An Introduction to Quakerism*. New York: Cambridge University Press.

Punshon, J. (1984). *Portrait in Grey: A Short History of the Quakers*. London: Quaker Home Service.

Smith, R. (1687). *The Foundation of True Preaching Asserted*. London: Andrew Sowle.

CHAPTER 7

THE SERMONS OF THE EIGHTEENTH-CENTURY EVANGELICALS

BOB TENNANT

PERHAPS the most remarkable thing about the resurgence of evangelicalism in the eighteenth century is that it did not in the event tear apart a society still mindful of the Civil War. Across the country Christian witness was manifested by the intense silence and attentiveness usual, although not universal, in mass outdoor gatherings, while indoors there were often intensely noisy assemblies, mass faintings, glossolalia, women walking with their legs in the air (in a period before closed underwear). *The World Turned Upside Down* is a title long ago appropriated for the mid-seventeenth century (Hill) but if the mid-eighteenth century was not a world turned upside down it was because the Established Church was sufficiently confident, robust, and flexible not to precipitate a crisis and had leaders uneasy but not completely unsympathetic to the public witness of transforming faith. The Establishment survived the phenomenon of a network of hundreds of lay preachers, tightly organized in circuits, superimposed on the parishes, women preachers gaining significant followings and even within the core of the Church, the emergence of new modes of extroverted organization: missionary and anti-slavery societies, women's committees, dedicated fund-raising, model resolutions for agitational purposes. Ironically, it was Methodism rather than the Established Church that was to be badly divided in the years after 1795, even if it was felt necessary, in 1750, for Parliament to reaffirm the sixteenth- and seventeenth-century statutes inhibiting the practice of religion in non-canonical forms (23 Geo. II Cap. xxviii).

The recent literature of British evangelicalism is very large. David Bebbington, whose *Evangelicalism in Modern Britain* provides the spine of current historical discussions, has identified biblicism, crucicentrism, conversionism, and activism as its four main characteristics (Bebbington 1993: 5–14) and these are fundamental to a critical engagement with the sermon literature, most of which is designed to promote changes in states of mind, personal behaviour, and readings of the Scriptures. In *Lay People and Religion in the Early Eighteenth Century* W. M. Jacob regretted the predominance in the historical record of 'zealots and enthusiasts, who tend to define the "godly" in narrow terms, so as to exclude all those with whom they disagree. The average lay person is often perceived as a passive receptacle for religious truth communicated by a religious elite': he sketched how an account of popular religious beliefs and practices might look (Jacob: 7, 112–20). Kenneth Hylson-Smith noted that the Christian religion extended, then as now, beyond churches: folk and cultic religion, cultural religiosity, more or less spontaneous popular revivalism (Hylson-Smith: 2:119–22). John Lenton has charted the emergence of Methodist lay preachers from the general population as well as their career trajectories (Lenton: chapter 3), and Ann Taves the phenomena associated with awakenings (Taves). One of the ordained clergy's duties was to mediate theologically and accommodate practically these strains of witness. 'Evangelistic' and 'evangelical' were thus intimately related.

To avoid becoming viciously circular or merely anecdotal, all critical writing depends on definitions of corpora, and this is especially acute in the present case. The term 'evangelical' seems to call for several different and not obviously cooperating or even compatible criteria: biographical, theological, sociological, political, and rhetorical, quite beside literary issues about any generically distinctive methods of generating texts and any kinship between the 'evangelical' sermons of different periods. The Victorian Baptist Charles Haddon Spurgeon published 3,600 sermons, twentieth-century evangelicals like Billy Graham filled stadia, televangelists like Pat Robertson are omnipresent, at least in the USA, and the Evangelical wing of the modern Anglican communion flourishes globally. Are these facts so big as to compel us to define the eighteenth-century genre with hindsight? It is reassuring that the Evangelicalism and Fundamentalism in Britain Network, a project which initially reported in 2009, considered all but the critical elements in the above list and took a pragmatic approach to the question of definition: people's self-identification as 'evangelical' and 'fundamentalist' was respected, at least as a starting point (Bebbington 2009). This seems tactful as well as empirically rich and offers the present chapter a release from the attempt at a survey of denominational or party histories.

What follows will therefore be drastically selective and attempt a critical narrative of sermon rhetoric. This is set with deliberate irony in the context of Kelly Oliver's thesis of witness and the claim to 'recognition' being placed in an oppressive subject–object hierarchy (Oliver: 85–106). Pulpit preaching is a big-voiced literary genre, and evangelical rhetoric, often intended for an audience of thousands, is architectonic and not always subtle. Critical tools may therefore be appropriately broad-brush and this makes them peculiarly suitable for computer-based statistical treatment, which is the basis for much of the present chapter. As performance texts designed for large spaces sermons might fruitfully be approached through the body of critical theory developed to discuss theatre plays; Jeanne Halgren Kilde is especially stimulating in her exploration of the interactivity and roles of preacher, congregation, and architecture while, in the British context, T. Friedman has recently provided a mass of potentially helpful architectural material (Kilde: 22–55; Friedman). Sermons, however, are performance texts of a very peculiar kind: *only one of the cast of hundreds or thousands actually speaks*. One vital critical tool, therefore, investigates directionality: the lines of sight in the church and the patterns of reference among the various parties in the liturgical situation. It does so by examining the use of the families of personal pronouns (for example, the 'me' family comprises *I, me, mine, my*, and *myself*). Thus, a sermon might be 'me' preaching to 'you', often about how 'he' (God) asks 'us' (Christians, humankind) to conduct ourselves towards 'them' (some third party). Arrow symbols are used below to indicate the statistically predominant directional relationships of these persons. A more elaborate methodology has been published elsewhere (Tennant 2010). The default directional mode, of course, is structured by the duality and mutuality of 'I [preacher] ↔ you [congregation]'. Departures from this most fundamental of strategies will be assessed.

The other special feature of the texts considered here is the relationship between the sermon as delivered and as published. This is not to confuse criticism with history—the texts we possess were produced for precise and usually recoverable reasons and are legitimate objects of analysis—but to explore rhetoric. In the eighteenth century most sermons were published from the author's written copy, more or less heavily revised. Evangelical preachers, however, usually performed extemporarily, or from brief notes. When published, many of these sermons were written up from these notes (in critical terms, the sermon, at first realized as a phatic object, was realized afresh as a material object for a new purpose). Other texts were generated by redaction from shorthand notes taken by an amanuensis or a member of the congregation, and printed 'exactly as delivered', or some such formula, or by the author's recreation of his performance. The introductory exordium and concluding peroration or prayer might, or might not, be included or recreated in the published version. A sermon which extended over three or four hours (perhaps twenty-five thousand words) might appear as a text of five thousand words. However, in the pulpit, length of time matters: the quantities of repetition and expansion, and of simply being there, were and remain essential parts of the congregation's experience. Further, reading these texts questions insistently the nature of the corpus: were sermons the projection of evangelical ministries into the population, or were they called into being by public demand, in popular 'conversion narratives' riding on rapidly developing communications infrastructures (Hindmarsh: 74–87)? I have suggested elsewhere that, considered critically rather than historically, Wesley's preaching edged towards this latter, and that the Connexion's separation from the Established Church might have been for organizational rather than theological reasons (Tennant 2011: 138). By contrast, Whitefield's may be seen as of the former type: he engages dynamically with gatherings which, as we will see, he treats more like congregations than does Wesley.

George Whitefield and John Wesley

The narrative string of this chapter must begin with George Whitefield, perhaps the most vigorous and appealing preacher yet produced by the Church of England, and John Wesley, a lesser preacher but a great organizational genius. Whitefield (1714–70) was born in Gloucester in a vintage year for evangelicals. He became known to, and was ordained by, his diocesan, Martin Benson, a member of the circle around the Talbot family, which included William Talbot, Bishop of Durham, Charles Talbot, Lord Chancellor, the philosopher-parson Samuel Clarke, Bishops Joseph Butler, Thomas Secker, Martin Benson, John Conybeare, and George Berkeley, and many others who were notable both as intellectuals and churchmen. Whitefield's ministry thus originated in, and never wholly rejected, the Church of England's doctrinal mainstream and he managed fairly successfully to conduct an uninhibited itinerant mission with a minimum of conflict with the Church's canons and its complex patterns of patronage and property.

Whitefield's sermons are notable for their stripped-down quality, both stylistically and theologically: their vigorous prose has dated less obviously than that any of his contemporaries. 'The following Sermons, I think I may say were given me by the Lord Jesus Christ; and according to my present Light, are agreeable to the Form of sound Words delivered to us in the lively Oracles of God' was his claim (Whitefield 1742: Preface). He possessed remarkable vocal equipment: we must acknowledge the conclusion of Benjamin Franklin's on-the-spot investigation that he was able to address thirty thousand people in the open air. His preaching was shaped by the fact that he had no parochial congregation to which to minister: whether he addressed ad hoc crowds or borrowed congregations from others it was necessary for him to prepare them afresh on each occasion for the reception of his understanding of the gospel. Preaching from a minimum of notes (rather than extemporarily), he varied his rhetorical structures little. For this reason we will discuss only one of his seventy-eight published sermons, *The Kingdom of God* (Whitefield 1991: 1:7–25).

The sermon is based on Romans 14:17, 'For the Kingdom of God is not meat and drink; but righteousness, and peace, and joy in the Holy Ghost'. It presents an extended paraphrase and commentary on the text. Whitefield argues that the early Jewish converts 'thought themselves obliged, notwithstanding they believed in the Lord Jesus Christ, to abstain from such meats and drinks as were forbidden, and to submit to such festivals as were enjoined by the [Mosaic] law', in other words, and by implication, that national cultural practices were inevitable and valid, as long as they were seen as contingencies— 'indifferent' in contemporary terminology: note the force of 'thought themselves obliged... and... submit'. By contrast, Gentile converts 'could not submit to them... they ate what was set before them'. It was Paul's achievement to mediate between the two and distinguish the religious from the cultural. Whitefield's rhetoric is conversational and familiar: 'If we will, therefore, look to the 1st. verse... we shall find...'; 'As though he had said, My dear friends, beware of disputing...'; 'This is a short, but when I read it, I think it is one of the most comprehensive verses...' (Whitefield 1991: 1:8–10). This intimacy of tone is sustained across Whitefield's entire published corpus and we must accept it as a feature of all his preaching, whatever the size of his audience. The only rhetorical theories available to him and his contemporaries were Classical, and they provided no model for gradations of intimacy which could be applied to sermon construction: as potential analysts of their own rhetoric, eighteenth-century preachers were not equipped to think of it in this sort of way. In this intimacy of tone, the turn from a concern primarily with doctrinal exposition to the provoking of alterations in states of mind, and providing the individual congregant with a secure environment for such alterations, Whitefield provided the personal exemplar and the stylistic model for his successors. Moreover, his commentary was framed entirely in biblical cross-references, so that his audience (in contrast to Wesley's, as we will see) could be drawn into the enterprise of investigating the sacred texts rather than being distanced from them by elite scholarship. Whitefield alternated between 'me' and 'us', establishing his own position and drawing his audience together with him, but eschewed 'you', which would have given shape to the congregation as a separate entity: he preached as a member of the gathering, albeit one who had given greater thought to his topics than could be expected of the majority: again, he was the exemplar, for a widening circle of preaching lay people, women as well as men. Only in one respect is 'you' acknowledged in Whitefield's preaching: 'some of you perhaps may think I have not reached you yet...' (Whitefield 1991: 1:15): here the unconvinced remnant, scattered and isolated among the crowd, are addressed directly and receive his promise that even they will come to accept Christ's invitation. '[Y]ou moral gentlemen, who are for talking so much of your morality... you [should] not think you are Christians because you are not vicious... But if you depend on morality, if you make a Christ out of it... you are building on a rotten foundation' (Whitefield 1991: 1:15). What seems like a developing sneer ('you moral gentlemen') is checked. Whitefield's rebuke remains direct, but by the vivid grotesquery of 'make a Christ out of it' and the homeliness of 'rotten foundation'—most houses had wooden frames sitting on wooden piles—the rebuked are diverted to consider aspects of their conduct as simultaneously perverse and entertaining. Whitefield has developed a method of inclusiveness with a minimum of offence and a maximum of good humour. Thus the last third of his sermon links this remnant 'you' to Paul:

> Are you a Christian, do you think, because you are of this or that sect? Paul was a Jew and a Pharisee. Are you a Christian because you are baptized, and enjoy Christian privileges? Then Paul was circumcised. Are you a Christian because you do nobody hurt, and are sincere? Paul was blameless before his conversion; and was not a Gallio in religion, as many of us are: he was so zealous for God, that he persecuted the church of Christ. (Whitefield 1991: 1:17)

Again, the humorously but passionately grotesque. Whitefield accelerates towards his conclusion; now, having captured his listeners, he allows 'you' to become more prominent in the rhetorical dynamics: 'O my dear friends' is a many times repeated phrase. 'My dear friends, I would preach with all my heart till midnight, to do you good, till I could preach no more...I know that many of you come here out of curiosity: though you come only to see the congregation, yet if you come to Jesus Christ, Christ will accept of you... Will you come to Christ, and list under the banner of the dear Redeemer?' (Whitefield 1991: 1:24–25). Note again the humorous admission of his obsessiveness, marinated in the urgency of his mission. The mass of the crowd is caught up in a rhetorical and theological complex which generates the utmost urgent seriousness of purpose and the sense that the remnant's self-importance is unimportant. The reader's pleasure and excitement at his vivacity of style and economy of means is an analogue, if a pale one, of his congregations' reactions to the oral version.

Although a Calvinist, Whitefield was the great master of lightness and joy. John Wesley, founder of the *Arminian Magazine*, was a contrast in almost every possible way. Wesley's published sermons were no more remarkable than those of almost equally prominent Methodists like Charles Wesley and John Fletcher, but limitations of space preclude discussion of them.

Wesley preached indefatigably and usually extemporized: so total was his absorption in his mission that evidence exists of his refusal, or inability, to respond to events around him: in his Journal for 3 March 1788, for example, he notes that the meeting erupted like 'a city taken by storm. The people rushed upon each other with the utmost violence, the benches were broken in pieces...In about six minutes, the storm ceased...I went on without the least interruption' (Ward and Heitzenrater: 69–70). His standard published collection of sermons was carefully reworked for domestic use and as theological reference points for his followers, but during rewriting, as we have suggested of Whitefield, the contemporary lack of tools for linguistic analysis would have prevented his being aware of his own fundamental rhetorical structures. His preaching was somewhat distinct from his organizational work: a peculiarity of his theology was that it opposed the concept of an 'Awakening'. In his sermon, *Original Sin*, he supposes the experiment of children growing up without human contact:

> They would have no religion at all: they would have no more knowledge of God than the beasts of the field, than the wild ass's colt. Such is *natural religion*! abstracted from traditional, and from the influences of God's Spirit. And having no knowledge, we can have no love of God...God heals our atheism by the knowledge of himself, and of Jesus Christ whom he hath sent; by giving us faith, a Divine evidence. (Wesley: 213-14, 218)

The urgency of Wesley's need for evangelical assistants led him, after initial hesitation, to the institution of lay preachers. These were itinerants, disciplined members of teams each with its circuit, and without the security of tenure and the intellectual independence which the ordained clergy enjoyed in a Church of England where patronage and benefices were often independent of diocesans' appointment and, in the case of peculiars, even beyond the diocesan bishop's rights of visitation. Anglican clergy possessed a vocation, whereas the lay preachers were largely, although not entirely, subordinate to personal leadership (Lenton: 408–12). Even Selina, Countess of Huntingdon, who worked chiefly with ordained and non-itinerant Anglican clergy, placed them in proprietary chapels, under her personal influence, if not her full control.

Only twenty-four of the 426 lay preachers who left the Methodist circuits before retirement became ordained Anglican ministers (Lenton: 317). Wesley's itinerants expounded the Scriptures morning and evening, extemporarily, concentrating, like Wesley himself, on the New Testament and on the positive message of gospel redemption and on moving the audience spiritually—Wesley condemned emotionalism as such, even if he used it in his preaching (Heitzenrater). Very few sermons by the itinerants were published. Wesley's own indefatigable dominance of the movement, moreover, subordinated the preaching even of his fellow ordained ministers: whatever the merits of the sermons of Charles Wesley, John Fletcher, and their colleagues, to overemphasize them here would be to revise the future history which Wesley determined for the 'Connexion'.

Somewhat separate from the itinerant lay preachers was the resurgence of the mid-seventeenth-century phenomenon of preaching and public witness by women. This was almost entirely in what might loosely be called the Methodist movement, and chiefly in Wesley's 'Connexion'. John Lenton has detailed the more prominent of these women, from Elizabeth Thomas and Sarah Perrin in the 1740s, who supplied the initial lack of male preachers, to Sarah Crosby, Betsy Hurrell, Ann Cutler, and Mary Barritt in the last quarter of the century, who gained followings as personalities. Their activities are distinguished from those of their male counterparts, who were under the discipline of the preaching circuits (Lenton: 33–5). Moreover, their preaching was not only unlicensed but, precisely because they were women, uncanonical. More generally, women's contribution to evangelicalism was substantial—Hannah More, active in most literary genres and a large number of societies, is the great figure—and it should be remembered that at least by the early nineteenth century women predominated in congregations and local Christian activities (Davidoff and Hall: 107–8), even in the local activities of the Church of England's two official Societies, for the Promotion of Christian Knowledge and the Propagation of the Gospel in Foreign Parts. Modern scholarship is increasingly focusing on the special nature of the sermon, rather than assuming that it was the predominant religious vehicle.

Strategies of Rhetoric in Anglican Evangelicalism

It is in this context that, turning to the preachers active wholly within the Church of England, we approach the career of Samuel Walker (1714–61). Walker's evangelical, as opposed to clerical, career was short: although ordained in 1737 and appointed curate of Truro in 1746, he only developed gradually as an evangelical. His preaching achieved enormous local popularity, emptying the streets during his services and permanently closing the playhouse and cock-pit. He formed a religious society for his converts, providing a strengthened context for their conduct, organizing his fellow clergy into another society which met monthly, and publishing several handbooks, notably *A Short Instruction and Examination for the Lord's Supper* (1761), as well as collections of sermons, some practical (*The Christian*, 1755; *The Refiner*, 1790) and others more generally expressing an evangelical theology. He sought to persuade Wesley against separation from the Church and strongly opposed lay preachers. His influence continued to spread posthumously, works and editions being published in London and Hull.

Walker's ministry had its origin in a developing sense of social and spiritual mission: he was motivated not only by the 'Infidelity [but also the] Licentiousness' of the times. 'Brethren,... Nor can I forget the Ministerial Vows that are upon me, and how fearful my Doom, if any of you *die in your* Sins without Warning', runs *The Christian*'s 'Preface to the Inhabitants of Truro' (Walker 1755: v, iv–v). He worked to generate rather than to shape religiosity and religious practice, expounding the sinfulness and helplessness of humankind, the redemptive love of Christ, the socially and psychologically transformational symptoms of the 'new Creature', and a practical belief that 'the *one Thing needful*' is the 'Care of his Soul' (Walker 1755: 111). Like evangelicals generally, but in contrast to the bishop-philosopher Joseph Butler (Butler), Walker emphasized the extrovert love of Christ and one's fellow-creatures rather than the creative dynamic between the person in the private and the social capacities. He saw social grace, however important, as a by-product rather than an objective. This is seen clearly in his sermons' rhetorical structures, which are generally sequential, linear arguments directly addressed ('→ you ...') to a parochial congregation with which he had a didactic and diachronic relationship:

> Give me leave to hope, that amidst the various Concerns which have engaged your Attention since we last parted, the important one of your Souls Salvation may have had a peculiar Place: That you are come hither again desirous to have *the Way of God expounded to you more perfectly*...But I would ask you beforehand; Is it out of *Curiosity* you would hear if it, to amuse a critical Head?...Alas, I shall but lose my Labour upon you... (Walker 1755: 73–4)

Walker adopted the classic Tillotsonian method of announcing his topics by numbering them, in what a word-processing generation knows as 'outline style'. This gives a sense of weight and logical inevitability to his sequence of arguments and illustrations, building his doctrinal exposition on the shaping of daily experience by a minimum of theological axioms:

> You *are undone in yourself*: A Sinner, and Dishonorer of GOD; liable to his Wrath, which you have no Power to avert; fallen from the Purity of Man's Primitive Nature, which you have no Strength in you to recover. If left to yourself, you must abide under the Dominion of your Lusts, and at last perish in deserved Vengeance.—This Charge I suppose you to allow. (Walker 1755: 74–5)

Each of the elements of this sentence was elaborated and reworked in other sermons. As with most evangelicals, Walker's theology was narrow in range and sharply focused, but the power of his pulpit ministry lay in the subtly varied contexts, which were the rhetorical all: the repetitions of ruthlessly stripped-down doctrines of grace and redemption were set not only in an over-arching, strategic narrative but also in the experiences of the community's daily life. When he asked, 'Whatever Difficulties lie in the Way, in Life and Death, are you fully persuaded that he is able and faithful?', the ground had been laid, in pulpit, streets, and group discussions: gambling, the playhouse, the prevalence of casual blasphemy. Walker spoke in short sentences, with a minimum of subordinate clauses and a maximum of rhetorical questions of his congregation. The individuals' psychological ability to say 'no' to his questions was decisively inhibited by the presence of hundreds of their peers: the implied answers were automatically 'yes'—the congregation did not need to pause to work out the correct response—so that the outcome was a massive, collective affirmation of faith in the saving power of Jesus Christ.

Walker's ministry, like that of John Wesley, was evidently influenced by the work of the Societies for the Reformation of Manners, whose activity was just past its height at this time (Portus: 107–56). Having a broader social base than was achievable after the full flowering of Methodism, the Societies escaped the bitterness of tone and strenuousness of aim of later similar campaigns: Vincent Perronet, the 'bishop of Methodism', in no way more relaxed than Wesley about licentiousness, was able to deploy the same sort of irony which we find in Butler's occasional sermons:

> we ought to resolve never to furnish out a [dining] Table, which there was sufficient Cause to believe, must...be succeeded by a bitter Repentance [of gluttony]...It must be owned, that such a Resolution, though highly becoming a true Christian, might render us something Unpopular as well as Unfashionable. (Perronet: 15–16)

Walker was less urbanely ironical than this, but always kept a sense of proportion: licentiousness was a symptom, suppression being pointless without a strategy for spiritual rebirth. The reformation of his parishioners' manners was a consequence of their commitment to his religious societies.

Walker's method of systematic parish visiting was an adaption of the seventeenth-century 'High' Puritan practices, whose continuity, as illustrated by William Gibson, is more noticeable in the old, non-metropolitan Puritan power-bases (Gibson: 71–93). Thus,

> It was the frequent practice of Mr. WALKER, after preaching his Sermons on the Lord's day, to gratify some of his hearers with the perusal of them in the course of the following week, yielding them full liberty to copy them out, for their more effectual remembrance and edification. (Walker 1794: i–ii)

Evidently, his sermons were prepared, written out in full, not in notes. This practice must have greatly strengthened his standing among his parishioners, as his texts acquired the authority of text-books.

It should however be emphasized, that, theology aside, it is rhetoric which makes Walker's ministry evangelical. A slightly older contemporary in the West Country was John Fisher, a collection of whose parochial sermons was published posthumously in 1741, for the benefit of his widow. We find Fisher dismissing 'the Right which some claim of judging for themselves, exclusive of all foreign Aid and Assistance whatsoever'. The individual is 'not thoroughly acquainted with the Nature of any one Thing in the Universe; he knows little of himself, and less of the Being above him'. The aggregations of wider society, the individual, the parochial community and the liturgy and the Church cooperate to achieve a more sufficient body of religious knowledge. 'This natural Reason is not the reason of an individual Person, but the Reason of Mankind' (Fisher: 310–11, 314). Fisher stood apart from the evangelical movement rising around him in the West

Country but Walker shares his concentration on the collective enterprise of parochial worship and civil conduct.

James Hervey (1714–58) was Walker's and Whitefield's exact contemporary. After a number of curacies he inherited his father's rectory at Weston Favell in Northamptonshire. His ministry had distinct similarities to Walker's, although his rhetoric could hardly have been more different.

Hervey was an undergraduate during John Wesley's residence as a fellow and tutor of Lincoln College, Oxford, and acknowledged his debt, although his posthumous *Eleven Letters* (Hervey 1765) maintained his Calvinism against Wesley's attacks. Like Walker, he devised a set of rules for the regulation of religious lay societies; unlike Walker's, his prescribed groups of no more than twelve. He required long meetings (typically noon until about 4 p.m.) and a compulsory charitable donation of half a crown per meeting (Hervey 1802: 228–30). This was a day's pay for a labourer and both these requirements would have excluded non-gentry. He also engaged with what can be called cultural religiosity through the publication of his famous and best-selling collection, *Meditations and Contemplations* (1745–7). 'Meditations among the Tombs', 'Reflections on a Flower Garden', and 'Contemplations on the Starry Heavens' are sample titles. These may be seen as excursions into purely literary rhetoric, or prose poetry, which established the palette of emotional responses to the natural world and the numinous which were legitimate for the cultivated Christian to display, a palette considerably paler and more restrained than those permitted, or even encouraged, by the Methodist itinerants (Mack: *passim*). The role of emotionalism in purely Anglican ministries is at present virtually unexplored, despite documented evidence of mass, high-intensity congregational involvement in some localities, both metropolitan and provincial, and the scandal of the public witness of the Anglican poet, librettist, and humorist Christopher Smart, whose late religious work achieved permanency and even greatness.

Although not primarily noted as a preacher, Hervey's few published sermons are of great interest. They are clad in visually florid imagery. In *The Ministry of Reconciliation* he preaches of the love of God as 'a sacred flower, which, in its early bud, is happiness, and, in its full bloom, is heaven'; his ministry is 'To plant this noble principle in the breast, to cultivate its growth, and bring it to maturity.' Toplady remarked that for Hervey, 'Angels are happier than me, because they are better'. The sense of wonder which his rhetoric projects moves from the lighter to the darker without changing its method: 'Would Ahasuerus abdicate his imperial diadem, or the great ruler of Babylon forego the honours of his enlarged dominions, to attend on the welfare of some ignoble captive that grinds at a mill, or of some infamous malefactor that is chained in a dungeon?' (Hervey 1802: 23, 23 n., 27).

Typically, Hervey's sermons were structured 'I [Hervey] → you [congregation]' but with visual imagery clogging the directionality. They rely less than Walker's on a display of engagement with his congregation—'Many of my hearers, *I observe*, are husbandsmen' (Hervey 1802: 99, italics supplied)—and this more remote rhetoric, always reminding the listener, and reader, of the distinction between minister/author and congregation/reader, seeks to persuade by a more topical and less strategic method. His strategy is always to bring together a Calvinistic presentation of Luther and a sense of the numinous inhabiting the natural. The material of the latter is mainly provided by the *Meditations*. More than Walker, Hervey presents himself, the evangelical preacher, as an object of spiritual and operative interest, as here, where he speaks of himself in the third person:

> [His] usual subjects are, the absolutely-free grace of GOD, and the immensely-rich merits of CHRIST; the infinite atonement, and everlasting righteousness of the REDEEMER. But because he generally enlarges upon these doctrines, is he throwing away his words? does he...*disregard* the interests of *holiness*? Far from it. He is sowing the seed of vital holiness...without which...holiness will never...bring forth fruit in your lives; any more than your ploughed lands would produce a crop of corn, without receiving the appointed grain...Religious, yet neglect prayer!...Can a man live without food? can he breathe without air? (Hervey 1802: 99)

It will be noticed that Hervey's rhetorical questions here, as in *The Ministry of Reconciliation*, call for the answer, 'no', for, that is, a rejection of attacks on his own ministry: his parishioners are asked to unite behind him, to validate his ministry through a communal consent to his being their spokesperson. We noticed Walker, by contrast, mentioning his ministerial vocation (in a preface, not a sermon) as his motive for preaching, his 'yes' questions uniting the congregation in a communal, spiritual, and civic activity, largely conducted outside the walls of the church. Thus Hervey is distinctly more 'priestly' than Walker, his status (elaborated in the ostentatiously personal *Meditations*) being an offering by the congregation and his person presented as a Sentimental Hero—something which is identified elsewhere as subsequently being transferred to the person of Christ as Romantic Hero (Tennant 2009). Walker's outline structure is intended to convince doctrinally; Hervey's, with a glance towards the disastrous Lisbon earthquake, to suggest that the preacher's sensibility and special insight is a viable model for spiritual leadership—a point of contact with Wesley's strategy:

> We have now shewn...Give me leave to ask...He [Christ] sends his ministers to *invite* you...He bids earthquakes tear the foundations of nature, and turn mighty cities into ruinous heaps, that you may be built on that Rock which shall never be shaken...Is any of you still inclined to [reject my call]...? (Hervey 1802: 112–13)

An emphasis on the sacred nature of the institution of the Church and the development of sacerdotalism—a word for which the Oxford English Dictionary's earliest citation is 1847—can, in the context of British political life, hardly be separated from political conservatism.

Hervey's syntax is spacious: its sentences are complex, the subordinate clauses expand by elaborating adjectival phrases which crescendo slowly in rhetorical questions directed to the congregation. This is a high-risk strategy: the slightest flaw in composition or delivery could induce ridicule—provoking the wrong answers to the questions. But although Harvey's rhetorical and theological range is narrow, within it he is masterly.

Conveniently for our purpose, Hervey's funeral sermon was preached by the greatest of the strictly Anglican eighteenth-century evangelicals, William Romaine (1714–95), who was much the longest-lived of the brood of 1714. Romaine's method, of which the following is a fair example, is much closer to Walker's than to Hervey's. He begins by setting his chosen text, and his human subject, firmly in the liturgy: not only, he says, were Hervey's last words those of Simeon in the Luke text ('Mine eyes have seen thy salvation', Luke 2:29) but the text itself is closely related to a text 'to which our church referred you this afternoon', that is, the Nunc Dimittis in the Evening Prayer, upon which Romaine proceeds to elaborate, in a consideration of 'light...sight...sin...darkness' (Romaine 1759: 7). He moves to discuss the combination of the numinous and the physical in the incarnate Christ, referring to Hervey's *Theron and Aspasio* (and defending him against Wesley), then to his familiar topic of the sinner's breaches of the holy law (Romaine 1759: 11–12), and thence to the theological circumstances of Hervey's death. Like Simeon, Hervey 'knowing that he was prepared, therefore desired to depart...His great love to his Saviour's glory made him wish for death'. Then Romaine introduces the first of several episodes where he turns directly to his audience: 'I suppose some weak in the faith are thinking thus within themselves: 'well, is it so, that true believers die in peace and joy? I am sure I could not at present: for I am dreadfully afraid of death' (Romaine 1759: 15, 17, 18). There is a hint of exclusivity—some of '[them] thinking within themselves' might be in the congregation. The remainder of the sermon is a sequence of episodes, moving between Hervey's death and the congregation's spiritual state, plotted rhetorically on the two axes 'he [Christ] ↔ he [Hervey]' and 'I [Romaine] → you [congregation]'. Thus Romaine's mediatorial perspective is omnipresent, but his practice of care and charity towards the unregenerate prevents the rhetoric from becoming spiritually invasive: he appeals to his listeners to come to him and does not threaten or browbeat them. 'And none are rejected, because of their unworthiness: *Mary Magdalen* was pardoned; and so may you: for all the gifts of God flow from his free grace...Stop not short, but try to get beyond him [Hervey]...And above all, forget not what supported him in his last moments; it was the clear view he had of his interest in the great salvation of God...' (Romaine 1759: 41, 43). A concluding prayer unites ('...we...') all those present.

Romaine's Calvinistic and evangelical aims and methods are fairly uniform throughout his published sermons, so that we need not extend this discussion. His use of the rhetoric of grammatical persons (the interplay of 'I', 'we', 'you', 'he', and 'they') is consistent in its strategy of inclusiveness. The congregation is always invited to despair of its own resources of strength and capability, to throw itself on God's mercy and participate in the evangelical mission. Until quite late in his ministry Romaine was in the difficult position of not having a parish: he was appointed, through the patronage of Richard Terrick, the Bishop of London, to two metropolitan lectureships, which were strenuously opposed by the parochial clergy and churchwardens, in the law courts and occasionally by physical force in the church. He was successful in asserting his prerogatives and mobilizing the skilled workers around Fleet Street—his ministry coincided with the establishment of Britain's first modern trade union, among the print workers—and he seems later to have had great success in stimulating the taking of communion as vicar of

St Anne's, Blackfriars, a living which, significantly, was in the gift of the parishioners and which he secured only in 1766. In one of the sermons he delivered as an evening lecturer he reveals that he had earlier that day organized a mass communion, which must have been conducted by one of the clergy who vigorously opposed his lectureship (Romaine 1821: 3:61–92). Although totally dedicated to his vocation, he was, however, also steadfastly respectful of the terms and conditions under which he exercised his ministry within the Church of England.

The uncompromisingly Evangelical Thomas Haweis (1734–1820) was Romaine's biographer (Haweis 1797). He was educated in Truro (and at Christ Church, Oxford), so that it is difficult to imagine that he was uninfluenced by Samuel Walker. Because of his association with Methodism, his ministry suffered various difficulties, but he settled as the rector of All Saints, Northampton. Unusually, he was also very closely connected with the Countess of Huntingdon, managing her college in Trevecca, and then serving as her trustee and executor, and undertaking the general management of her network of chapels. For our purpose, his most significant work is his collection *Evangelical Principles and Practice: being Fifteen Sermons Preached in the Parish-church of St. Mary Magdalen in Oxford*, originally published in 1762 (Haweis 1775), which shows signs of being composed rather than extemporized or redacted and might be seen as a textbook for the teaching mission which was to be fulfilled at Trevecca. *Evangelical Principles* was 'sent into the world, to obviate the manifold misconceptions and misrepresentations which the Author of them has lain under', Haweis proclaiming his acceptance of the 'Articles and Homilies, which he was required solemnly to subscribe, [and which] he professes himself to be conscientiously attached to' (Haweis 1775: iii). Despite his success as a popular preacher, Haweis, a major late-century figure, was a Calvinist whose ministry tilted decisively from the evangelistic to the Evangelical, a distinction which could hardly be made with earlier Calvinists like Whitefield, Walker, Romaine, or even Hervey, let alone Anglican ministers like John Berridge (1716–93), who moved to Calvinism apparently as a consequence of his preaching in a functionally evangelical mission and whose funeral sermon was preached by Charles Simeon.

Haweis's sermon *On the Nature of True Holiness* expounds Ephesians 2:10: 'For we are his workmanship, created in Christ Jesus unto good works, which God hath before ordained that we should walk in them.' Like his other surviving works, it keeps within the core of eighteenth-century English Calvinism: the theological and practical relationship between grace and works. Of all the preachers we consider here, however, Haweis is the most consistently measured in his tone. The exegetical and doctrinal part of his sermon reads like a lecture, in 'I → you' form, until, reaching the application section, the rhetorical direction switches to a 'we ↔ he [God]' structure, which develops into a unidirectional 'you → he'. Previously, the exposition of doctrine had explained the relationship of God and humankind. Now, the human duty of attempting to follow the Law (and the attempt's inevitable failure) makes God more remote. The minister withdraws from the congregants, to emphasize their solitude (Haweis's first person singular sometimes emerging temporarily as a rhetorical pole: 'I → you') and the individualist nature of their duty and the God, with whom 'we' had previously engaged, becomes the object of longing.

An Evangelical Party

Running in parallel with the preachers discussed so far was the expansion of Wesley's organization and, in reaction, an assertion of Calvinist evangelicalism. We have already noticed that Augustus Toplady edited some of Hervey's works posthumously. Toplady (1740–78) was an Anglican Calvinist educated at Trinity College Dublin, notable as a hymn-writer and controversialist, and the object of language by John Wesley which fell well below eighteenth-century standards of civility. Toplady replied in kind and died maintaining his theological position and his opposition to Wesley, partisan slanders reaching such a pitch that his friends were forced to refute in detail rumours of his deathbed despair, clearly designed to destroy his legacy. He was the preacher who best exemplifies the emergence of an Evangelical party. Thus his sermon *Free-will and Merit Fairly Examined; or, Men not their Own Saviours* from 1775 led up to the conclusion that

> Some Christians are like decayed Mile Stones; which stand, 'tis true, in the right Road, and bear some Traces of the proper impression: but so wretchedly mutilated and defaced, that they, who go by, can hardly read or know what to make of them. May the blessed Spirit of God cause all our Hearts, this Morning, to undergo a fresh Impression...! (Toplady 1775: 40)

He had, however, arrived at this prayer from a starting point which grossly breached the convention that a sermon is doctrine expounded exegetically:

> I dare say, that, in such an Auditory as this, a Number of ARMINIANS are present. I fear, that all our public Assemblys have too many of 'em...[witnessing] that degrading Representation of the *true* God, which Arminianism would palm upon Mankind. (Toplady 1775: 4)

This sermon was preached in Romaine's church, St Ann's, Blackfriars, which was to become the locus for the annual sermons of the Church Missionary Society and other Evangelical societies. Its aggressive exclusivity, even in a congregation from which one may assume that Arminians had long withdrawn, demonstrates an approach to preaching and exegesis directly at odds with the theology and culture of the 1688 Settlement. It offers a rare example of the rhetorical third person ('they') being identified as the enemy actually within the church's walls, like a fifth column, and in effect asserts new definitions of basic concepts like 'congregation' and 'liturgy'.

In this the sermon was not aberrant. Already, in 1770, Toplady had preached at St Matthew, Bethnal Green. In his sermon he had remarked that

> The Rights of Conscience are inviolably sacred; and Liberty of private Judgment is every Man's Birth-right. If, however, Any, like *Esau*, have *sold* their Birth-right for a Mess of Pottage, by subscribing to Articles they don't believe in, merely for the sake of temporal Profit or Aggrandisement; they have only themselves to thank, for the little Ceremony they are entitled to. (Toplady 1770: 17)

Of course, if Toplady meant his remark sincerely (and we should assume he did), his definition of 'conscience' had only a contingent, not a necessary, relationship to human psychology, since it denoted only the conscience of those reborn in the Spirit. Toplady took opposition as a sign of spiritual corruption and it invariably provoked abuse of others' persons and culture. Haddon Smith, the incumbent of St Matthew's, found it necessary to protest against this rather brutal intervention in his parish ministry by preaching a corrective sermon the following Sunday. This is revealed in Toplady's sneering Postscript, addressed, over the incumbent's head, to the St Matthew's parishioners: 'It would render that Unthinking, but, I would hope, well-meaning Gentleman, much too considerable, were I... to address him by Name' (Toplady 1770: 65). Toplady's account of the practice of Paul as exemplified in his chosen text (1 Timothy 1:10) as support for his intervention in parish affairs, and his denial of the rights of the vicar, had no foundation in the canonical terms under which he preached as a guest in the parish. Indeed, his rhetoric suggests that he took upon himself, like Wesley, not only an 'indeterminate commission' (Tennant 2011: 132–35), but one encompassing theological enforcement.

After Toplady it might be suggested that the Anglican clergy did not demonstrate the same intensity of commitment to active evangelism, which merged with, and was subsumed by, the theology and culture of Evangelicalism. This greatly influenced the overseas work of the Church, extending from a power-base in Cambridge. A loose group including Henry Venn, John Newton (a close friend of the poet-priest William Cowper), and Thomas Scott served the transitional phase. Cowper's sermons are unworthy of a great poet, and Newton was not above using the glamour of his slave-trading past in the service of his ministry, and, as a stunt, published in 1786 a two-volume set of sermons on the passages of Scripture used in Handel's *Messiah* (Newton). This movement has been documented and analyzed by Isabel Rivers (Rivers). The sermons of Venn and Scott, however, have points of critical interest.

Henry Venn (1724–97) was the founder of the Evangelical Clapham Sect through his long curacy there and his influence on the Thorntons, Simeon, and William Farish, who was a leading light in the Church Missionary Society (CMS). Venn's ministry was almost entirely parochial and educational and is epitomized in his early *Complete Duty of Man... Designed for the Use of Families*, designed to be read through by the assembled household over a sequence of fourteen Sundays (Venn 1765). His sermons are notable for imagery which is the result of an intensely visualized contemplation of displays of sin and witness. The occasional sermons present persons with a static and considered quality. On Whitefield's death he preached that 'every living member of Christ's church, is both himself an instance of the grace of God, and holds forth to others the word of life' (Venn 1770: 4), and at the Kingston assizes, 'Jesus... suffered poverty and contempt, reproach and persecution, all his life; and in his death he endured torment of body, general execration of men, and inconceivable anguish of soul, whilst the sword of eternal justice cut him off, for the transgression of GOD's people' (Venn 1769: 6). This develops into full-blown visualized rhetoric which parallels the imagination of the sculptor John Flaxman: '... the *death of Christ*. By it, ... a fountain was opened, whose precious streams will flow to the end of time, to cleanse men from all unrighteousness' (Venn 1785: 5). This proto-Romantic style of imagery, directed principally towards culturally elite audiences, although sometimes ostentatiously in the hearing of the masses, such as the to-be-condemned prisoners in the assize sermon ('the agonies of a violent death [seize] upon their devoted bodies', Venn 1769: 6), was to emerge powerfully in the early nineteenth century.

Historically, the career of Thomas Scott (1747–1821) is most notable for his inauguration of a training programme for potential missionaries, and for his work in translating missionary resources into West African languages. Thus, even more than Venn, his ministry served a project within the Church's structures rather than extroverted, popular evangelism. If in Venn we see the beginnings of the rhetoric of theologically Evangelical aestheticism, in Scott there is the emergence of sacerdotalism, something which is understandable in a preacher concentrating on developing the special qualities needed to prepare individuals for the isolated witness of faith in non-Christian cultures. Thus, for his sermon on the death of John Charles Barneth, a German CMS missionary candidate who died before being shipped abroad, he selected Acts 20:24 as his text ('neither count I my life dear unto myself, so that I might finish my course with joy... to testify the gospel'). In critical terms, the sermon was not addressed to the congregation: '... you...' is absent from the rhetorical structure. Instead, those present merely overheard Scott's musings about the inadequacies of Barneth's life and ministry, a curious offering to God of institutional and personal self-examination:

> [Barneth] always seemed, without affectation, ready to sit down in the lowest place... I never entertained a hope, that he would ever appear eminent in the character of an author, or a translator of the Scriptures, into the African languages; (as I hope, concerning some under my care)... [but] I am confident [that his spirit] would have made him a valuable monitor and counsellor, especially to his junior brethren. (Scott 1810: 24)

In Scott's imagination stands the ideal Missionary Hero: priest, polymath, robust ascetic, leader of men, and potential martyr. Missionary candidates usually fell short of adequacy, let alone of the ideal, and this sermon, like the discussions minuted in many Society for the Propagation of the Gospel in Foreign Parts (SPG), Society for Promoting Christian Knowledge (SPCK), and CMS General Meetings and committees over the decades, expresses institutional anxieties and frustrations. The element of personal and institutional self-justification in this sermon is remarkable and unprecedented: the sermon was subordinated to the Committee's decision-making. Barneth, a working-class man, and his family had been the subject of lengthy discussions between the CMS and the Berlin seminary. At one stage he had been shipped back to Germany for further preparation and was the subject of the most careful scrutiny by the CMS's General Committee (CMS: 328).

No less than John Wesley's Connexion, the Evangelical societies required absolute obedience. Ironically, this effected gendered changes in them. The SPG had already found, and the CMS was to learn, that the overseas missions were not simply a matter of ordained clergy sermonizing the heathen but of multi-disciplinary teams, consisting of one or more missionaries, catechists, schoolmasters (sometimes unmarried schoolmistresses), doctors, craftsmen, and their wives. It was a matter of policy that mission personnel be married, so that half of the European missionary workforce was female, and the suitability of wives—perhaps we should call them 'marital candidates'—was scrutinized minutely: even the locally contracted marriages of manual labourers were conditional on reports and decisions at committee level in London. Apart from administration of the sacraments these wives served in the same roles as the men but included work with groups of women inaccessible to men. It is inconceivable that they did not preach exegetically and very likely that the relative informality and intimacy of their gatherings influenced the theologically and rhetorically reductionist sermons which began to appear in mid-Victorian times. Women produced large quantities of the text of missionary magazines, propaganda pamphlets, and Sunday School material; the linguistic kinship between these and their sermons may cautiously be assumed (Semple: *passim*). The limitations placed on women's witnessing and ministering of their religion may be termed patriarchal but it was also part of this growing sacerdotalism, which tended to assume that if a man had something to say about Christianity he would seek ordination: in the second half of the eighteenth century examples of laymen producing theology are rare compared with earlier and later periods, and even where the need for clergy was greatest, for example in the missions, it was very difficult for working-class men to achieve Anglican ordination. Thomas Scott himself, originally a grazier, was very unusual.

When Scott stood on London's dockside his thoughts went far beyond the usual celebration of the evangelical opportunities offered by Britain's merchant marine: he saw in the ships, crowded in the port and scattering across the ocean, an analogue not only of the proliferation of missionaries but even of the quasi-economic laws driving wholesome competition between missionary societies. The following sermon was one of four preached by clergy of different denominations at the London Missionary Society's 1804 General Meeting:

> The [missionary] societies may *seem*...to crowd and interfere with each other in London...Thus the ships, by which our extensive commerce is carried on, are greatly crowded together in the river; but not so on the vast seas and oceans which they severally navigate. Nay,...the approach of a vessel, though belonging to a rival company or merchant, gives the most heart-felt joy, that can almost be conceived...Perhaps the comparison may hold still further: and as a greater number of ships of moderate size are generally preferred to a few that are inconveniently large. (Scott 1804: 109)

With an eccentric exception, our narrative can end with Charles Simeon (1759–1836), whose entire career was spent at King's College, Cambridge and in ministering to the local parish of Holy Trinity. He exerted great influence on at least two generations of graduates, including the Evangelical centres in Hackney and Clapham, and hence on the Church Missionary Society and the British and Foreign Bible Society. Simeon's sermons are not of prime interest in the present context—and one wonders what was effected by the posthumous circulation, under the terms of his will, of his sermon *Evangelical Religion* to every household of his parish (Simeon 1837)—but he published 500 skeleton sermons up to 1818, and between 1819 and 1828 a further 2,536, by intention a commentary on the entire Bible, while exerting patronage systematically in favour of Evangelicals (Simeon 1801; Simeon 1855). With him we see a culmination of the question of the authenticity of the text as delivered. While strenuously opposing 'that disgraceful traffick in printed Sermons, which instead of meeting with encouragement from the clergy, ought to have excited universal indignation', he considered that his skeleton sermons 'cannot possibly be used at all, unless a considerable degree of thought be bestowed upon them. Nor does he think that any person, who has ever found the pleasure of addressing his congregation in his own words, will be satisfied with reciting the compositions of another' (Simeon 1801: vii). The skeletons, he thought, required the user to think in an Evangelical way and thus reinforce the Church. But the term 'Evangelical' by now refers to a type of theology, not to a genre of preaching. The link between theology and rhetoric, intrinsic to Whitefield's ministry, has definitely been broken:

> Now I am far from intimating that this call, which every candidate for Orders professes to have received, resembles that which was given to the Apostles: it is certainly not to be understood as though it were a voice or suggestion coming directly from the Holy Ghost...but it disposes the mind in a gradual and silent way to enter into the service of God; partly from a sense of obligation to him for his redeeming love, partly from a compassion for the ignorant and perishing multitudes around us, and partly from a desire to be an honoured instrument in the Redeemer's hands to establish and enlarge his kingdom in the world. (Simeon 1812: 87–8)

The elitist force of the last sentence's 'us' will be appreciated.

The eccentric exception mentioned above is the Scottish preacher Edward Irving (1792–1834), a protégé of the future 'Wee Free' Church of Scotland secessionist Thomas Chalmers. Irving's colourful ministry—he achieved the distinction of expulsion from a church he actually founded—need not concern us. What is relevant is the target of his mission. Irving was one of the most popular preachers of his day, but he became convinced that

> the chief obstacle to the progress of divine truth over the minds of men, is the want of its being properly presented to them...We must...lay our hand upon the press as well as the pulpit...[U]ntil...ministers...do pass the limits of pulpit theology and pulpit exhortation, and take weapons in their hand, gathered out of every region in which the life of man or his faculties are interested, they shall never have religion triumph and domineer in a country, as beseemeth...her eternity of freely-bestowed well-being. (Irving: v, vi–vii)

Thus he sought to diversify from preaching to gatherings where enthusiasm and glossolalia were usual to creating polite, even fashionable, literature: a non-exegetical genre of 'oration', revived from the classical model of Aelius Aristides, whose own *Oration XXVI, Regarding Rome* lent nineteenth-century Britain the concept of an empire 'on which the sun never sets'.

Irving's venture into the production of gilded and marbled literature and the Cambridge Evangelicals' concentration on their missions and church reform seem of a piece: a withdrawal from the market-places where Whitefield and Wesley, Walker and Romaine had laboured. To read any literature, religious or secular, is to encounter the opinions of the most opinionated and of those privileged few who could gain access to the printing press. We look somewhat cautiously, therefore, at the criticisms of the Church launched by nineteenth-century Tractarians, Evangelicals, liturgical innovators, educationalists, anti-slavery campaigners, and social improvers in general. Their diagnoses of Churchly ills seem increasingly the product of exaggeration, made to 'point a Moral, or adorn a Tale', to validate a project, or to serve in intra-church and inter-party struggle.

Conclusion

This chapter has suggested a narrative arc which originated in a popular religious revival. Preaching was the predominant clerical activity, and directly stimulated administrative innovations, ending, for the Church of England, in the emergence of an Evangelical party with a developed theology and a programme extending into the cultural life and policy of the State itself. The Anglican Evangelicals founded the CMS as a direct challenge to the SPG and, as described in Chapter 22 ('Hard Labour'), rival theories of education and Bible Societies competed for support.

In discussing the evangelical sermon as a genre it has not appeared feasible to suggest a defining set of stylistic parameters. The sculptural and floral imagery of Harvey and Venn shared little common ground with the austerities of Walker and Haweis. Sentence structures might be simple or extremely complex, the tone humorous, even playful, if far more often portentous or urgent. The rhetorical direction, as revealed by our study of person families, was saturated either with the communality of 'us', or the introversion of 'me', or the fluctuating interplay—whether stately or rapid—between God and congregation. Rather, a critical definition must be in terms of the sermons' fitness to function within strategies of disturbing and transforming the listeners' states of mind, and the harnessing of all rhetorical and literary considerations to this task. Systematic linguistic analysis, which should become a research priority, would reveal much about these preachers' strategies of inclusiveness and exclusiveness in relation to their congregations and about the dynamics which typified Victorian religion and politics. While the habitual violence of Augustus Toplady and the rugged discourtesy of John Wesley were, one suspects, characteristic of their personalities rather than of contemporary theorizing of preaching as a transformational medium, they did exemplify the rejection of the workaday and emotionally low-key. In this they stood consciously opposed to the Whig nation-building project. The preachers sought to provoke intensified experiences, but also sometimes preached, over their listeners' shoulders, to an England increasingly seen in terms of commercial and maritime expansion into areas where various meanings of 'darkness' coagulated: cultural primitivism, philosophical superstition, scientific ignorance, spiritual ill-health, and the physical and moral pollution of urban development. They wished to suggest that the most important things were the most psychologically and socially questioning, and here is where is seen their transcendence of the contemporary Sentimental sensibility and their development of an heroic and proto-Romantic ideology and aesthetic, developing rapidly into the full-blown version.

The strongly Pauline Church of the mid-eighteenth century—and the lists of sermon texts confirm Paul's dominance in the period's literature (Spaulding)—theologized the relationship of the individual, Church, and State as a form of corporate holiness; the phrase is William Warburton's (Warburton: 1:153–4). This concerned the liberty to live and worship according to conscience as mediated by social duty, the latter implying the predominance but not hegemony of the Church of England. By contrast, the Anglican Evangelical sermon was developed to intensify social organization. It sought to bind congregations by emphasizing distinctions of social activity and even liturgy. Because of this, the Evangelical sermon has proved to be self-perpetuating to an extent not equalled by other eighteenth-century sermon genres.

REFERENCES

Bebbington, D. (1993). *Evangelicalism in Modern Britain*. London: Routledge.
—— (2009). 'Evangelicalism and Fundamentalism in Britain', University of Stirling Department of History (8 July 2008). <http://www.eauk.org/efb/> accessed 27 June 2011.
Butler, J. (1729). *Fifteen Sermons*, 2nd edn. London: Knapton.
CMS. *Church Missionary Society, General Committee Minutes*. University of Birmingham Library, CMS/G/C/2/1.
Davidoff, L., and Hall, C. (1987). *Family Fortunes: Men and Women of the English Middle Class, 1780–1850*. London: Hutchinson.
Fisher, J. (1741). *Sermons on Several Subjects*. Sherborne: Score.
Friedman, T. (2011). *The Eighteenth-Century Church in Britain*. New Haven: Yale University Press.
Gibson, W. (2007). *Religion & the Enlightenment, 1600–1800: Conflict and the Rise of Civic Humanism in Taunton*. Oxford: Peter Lang.
Haweis, T. (1775). *Evangelical Principles and Practice*. London: Dilly.
—— (1797). *The Life of William Romaine*. London: Chapman.
Heitzenrater, R. (1998). 'John Wesley's Principles and Practice in Preaching', in R. Sykes (ed.), *Beyond the Boundaries*. Oxford: Applied Theology Press, 12–40.
Hervey, J. (1765). *Eleven Letters . . . to the Rev. Mr. John Wesley*. London: Rivington.
—— (1802). *Sermons and Tracts*, ed. A. Toplady. Edinburgh: Ogle and Aikman.
Hill, C. (1972). *The World Turned Upside Down*. London: Maurice Temple Smith.
Hindmarsh, D. B. (2005). *The Evangelical Conversion Narrative*. Oxford: Oxford University Press.
Hylson-Smith, K. (1997). *The Churches in England from Elizabeth I to Elizabeth II*. London: SCM Press.
Irving, E. (1823). *The Oracles of God, Four Orations*. London: Hamilton.

Jacob, W. M. (1996). *Lay People and Religion in the Early Eighteenth Century*. Cambridge: Cambridge University Press.

Kilde, J. H. (2002). *When Church Became Theatre*. Oxford: Oxford University Press.

Lenton, J. (2009). *John Wesley's Preachers*. Milton Keynes: Paternoster.

Mack, P. (2008). *Heart Religion in the British Enlightenment*. Cambridge: Cambridge University Press.

Newton, J. (1786). *Messiah. Fifty Expository Discourses*. London: J. Buckland and J. Johnson.

Oliver, K. (2001). *Witnessing: Beyond Recognition*. Minneapolis: University of Minnesota Press.

Perronet, V. (1745). *Some Thoughts on the Divine Hospitality of the Gospel; And on Hospitality Falsly so Called*. London: Knapton.

Portus, G. V. (1912). *Caritas Anglicana, or An Historical Inquiry into those Religious and Philanthropic Societies that Flourished in England between the Years 1678 and 1740*. London: Mowbray & Co.

Rivers, I. (1991, 2000). *Reason, Grace, and Sentiment*. Cambridge: Cambridge University Press.

Romaine, W. (1759). *The Knowledge of Salvation Precious in the Hour of Death...Preached...on the Death of...James Hervey*. London: Worrall and Withers.

—— (1821). *The Works*. London: W. Baynes.

Scott, T. (1804). *A Call to Prayer for the Sending forth of Labourers*, in *Four Sermons, preached...at the Tenth General Meeting of the [London] Missionary Society*. London: Williams.

—— (1810). *The Spirit and Principles of a Genuine Missionary*. London: Seeley and Hatchard.

Semple, R. (2003). *Missionary Women*. Woodbridge: Boydell Press.

Simeon, C. (1801). *Helps to Composition*. Cambridge: Deighton.

—— (1812). *The Excellency of the Liturgy in Four Discourses*. Cambridge: Cadell and Davies.

—— (1837). *Evangelical Religion. A Sermon Preached Before the University of Cambridge*. Cambridge: Parker.

—— (1855). *Horae Homileticae*. London: Bohn.

Spaulding, J. G. (1996). *Pulpit Publications, 1660–1782*. New York: Norman Ross.

Taves, A. (1999). *Fits, Trances, & Visions*. Princeton: Princeton University Press.

Tennant, B. (2009). 'On the Good Name of the Dead: Peace, Liberty, and Empire in Robert Morehead's Waterloo Sermon'. *Religion in the Age of Enlightenment* 1:251–77.

—— (2010). 'Enlightenment Sermon Studies: A Multidisciplinary Activity'. *Religion in the Age of Enlightenment* 2:323–41.

—— (2011). *Conscience, Consciousness, and Ethics in Joseph Butler's Philosophy and Ministry*. Woodbridge: Boydell Press.

Toplady, A. (1770). *A Caveat against Unsound Doctrines*. London: Joseph Gurney.

—— (1775). *Free-will and Merit Fairly Examined; or Men not their Own Saviors*. London: Mathews and Keith.

Venn, H. (1765). *The Complete Duty of Man*. London: J. Newbery.

—— (1769). *Man a Condemned Prisoner, and Christ the Strong Hold to Save Him*. London: Dilly.

—— (1770). *A Token of Respect to the Memory of the Rev. George Whitefield, A. M.* London: Dilly.

—— (1785). *The Deity of Christ*. London: Dilly and Matthews.

Walker, S. (1755). *The Christian. Being a Course of Practical Sermons*. London: Owen and Dilly.

—— (1794). *Christ the Purifier*. London: Matthews.

Warburton, W. (1753). *The Character and Office of the Messiah*. London: Knapton.
Ward, W. R., and Heitzenrater, R. P. (2003). *The Works of John Wesley*, vol. 24. Nashville: Abingdon Press.
Wesley, J. (1823). *Sermons on Several Occasions*, 8th edn. London: J. Bumpus.
Whitefield, G. (1742). *Nine Sermons*. London: Samuel Mason.
—— (1991). *Sermons*. New Ipswich, NH: Pietan Publications.

CHAPTER 8

SERMONS IN BRITISH CATHOLICISM TO THE RESTORATION OF THE HIERARCHY (1689–1850)

GEOFFREY SCOTT

DETAILS of sermons preached to British Catholics are not as easily uncovered as those preached to Reformed congregations. Few were delivered in public until the grant of Catholic Emancipation in 1829. Catholic sermons were, furthermore, only preached by the clergy; lay preaching as such was forbidden by canon law.

Although the Revolution of 1688–9 abruptly ended the series of published court sermons by English preachers, at least one royal chaplain, William Hall, accompanied James II to Ireland and in 1689 preached on 'the General Judgement' before the king which led to his expulsion (Clancy: 481–2). Published Catholic sermons in the years after the Revolution are a great rarity, only one seems to have survived, a sermon for Corpus Christi published in London in 1695 (Clancy: 180), and probably by the English Benedictine court preacher and Anglo-Gallican, James Maurus Corker. The preacher here expected his audience to be conversant with Aquinas's *Fomes Peccati*, or 'disordered concupiscence' and urged the inculcation of the state of 'disinterested love' of the Quietists as well as the prayer of 'abstraction and solitude', a key teaching of the English Benedictine mystical writer, Augustine Baker, whose disciple Corker was. After 1688, Jacobitism inevitably grew within British Catholic circles and what few sermons survive reflect this commitment, such as the panegyric preached in 1694 at the funeral of Sir Thomas Clifton, the Lancashire Jacobite rebel tried in Manchester in 1690 (Gillow 3:40, 608). The Revolution also made Catholics renew their European links. Thus a Carmelite preacher at the Portuguese Embassy chapel, London, in the 1680s, was in Paris by 1696, preaching on St Justin to the English canonesses who had received the saint's relics from Queen Mary of Modena (Ware: 33).

Evidence for British Catholic sermons in the early eighteenth century when the penal laws were renewed is scanty. Published panegyrics on leading Catholics, such as James II and Cardinal Fleury, must really have been collectors' curios, as was probably a translation of Pope Clement XI's 1717 sermon preached before the Old Pretender (Blom: 721, 1124, 2480). Except in Ireland, where congregations were numerous, sermons were preached either in England to small, mostly rural, congregations or in Europe to religious communities in exile. In Warwickshire, a family chaplain produced three 'discourses' for his 'Christian auditors' around 1740 which introduced them to the trials of witches in France over the past two centuries and lumped the witches of old alongside contemporary enemies of Christian truth, 'Socinians, Free-Thinkers and Latitudinarians' (Marshall and Scott: 182–3). Sermons to such gentry households often derived from published sermons on the Four Last Things and the art of dying happily by famous Italian and French missionary preachers such as Giovanni Pietro Pinamonti, the elder Paolo Segneri, and Jean Croiset. Thus, Robert Manning preached informally on the Four Last Things to his patron, Lord Petre, in 'a private assembly' at Ingatestone (Manning 1:A4r). Thomas Clayton, missioner in Norwich, edited for his city congregation the sermons originally given to the household of the Duke of Norfolk by the family chaplain (Clayton). These liturgical sermons conformed to the usual Catholic form: an Introduction, *Ave Maria*, and two points for commentary. There is a great deal here on sin and the sacrament of penance, and 'ladies of fashion' with trains and 'high heads' treating chapels like 'public places'. Significantly, some of these sermons were based on works by preachers abroad criticized for Jansenist tendencies, such as the English theologian Thomas Witham and the French Oratorian, Jean Le Jeune (1592–1672), known as Père l'Aveugle, a popular itinerant preacher and catechist who would have been attractive to English missionary priests. Bonaventure Giffard, the vicar apostolic of the London District, who had been a court preacher in James II's reign, abided by the Tridentine instruction that preaching was an episcopal duty, and with vigorous voice and gesture, delivered sermons in embassy and other private chapels, although he preferred to preach outside the capital (Hemphill: 54).

In London itself, where the congregation was more sophisticated and perhaps more aware of its minority status, sermons, often again recycled, quoted Seneca, allowed for mitigations of the Lenten fast, noted a common Catholic and Protestant interest in the primitive church, and described the Petrine primacy without any mention of the pope. John Gother remained the principal inspiration for London sermons, but by this period the popular liturgical *Méditations* of the Lazarist and opponent of Jansenism, Louis Abelly (1604–91) had become fashionable (Ware). At the Portuguese embassy chapel, Francis Blyth preached a response to William Whiston's doubts as to whether hell's torments were indeed eternal (Blom: 280–2, 286). Later, Thomas Meighan's important *Select Collection of Catholick Sermons* (1741) had an overtly proselytizing aim in republishing the court sermons of the 1680s for 'all well-disposed and disinterested Persons'. He had been arrested in 1737 and was to be imprisoned in 1747 for publishing controversial Catholic works.

Abroad, English exiled nuns were encouraged in sermons by their English chaplains to strive for Quietist 'disinterested love' and to embrace new Continental devotions such as that of the Sacred Heart. They were taught to eschew the vices of the age, described in detail, and to take comfort in the fact that Christ, 'perfect man' and 'Master of Nature', had had no interest in science, for he 'never spoke a word of all the sciences which he knew of and never taught his disciples any art or science' (Bishop: 13).

In Ireland, where Catholics were the majority, there seems to have been no tradition of sermons in private gentry chapels, but on account of possible recriminations preachers' names could still be blacked out by a printer (Fenning 1999: 99). Ireland had a particular tradition from around 1721 of publishing Good Friday sermons (Blom: 2224–5; Fenning 1997–98: 126–27). The sermons of James Gallagher, a fugitive missioner who became a bishop in 1725, throw some light on the educational levels of peasant congregations and their priests at this time. They were 'in an easy and familiar style' in Irish-Gaelic, but used words borrowed from English and employed 'English characters, as being the more familiar to the generality of our Irish clergy' (Blom: 1136–41).

During the second half of the eighteenth century, British Catholics witnessed important improvements in their national status, following the passing of two Catholic Relief Acts for England in 1778 and 1791, followed by similar Acts for Ireland and Scotland. These brought Catholics some degree of religious toleration and helped increase the publication of more sermons especially in Ireland. Model sermons or 'prones', some translated from French, were provided for preachers and the lazy habit of preachers repeating the same sermon annually continued (Parfitt). The Sunday sermon was now generally delivered at Vespers, rather than at Mass, because of the proliferation of Masses following the 1791 Act by means of which more new chapels were opened, accompanied by sermons from visiting preachers. Sermons were now regularly preached by vicars apostolic at mass Confirmations.

At the end of the century, pulpit oratory reflected concerns about the spread of rationalist thought and the effects of the French Revolution which forced religious communities back to England, thus ending the tradition of preaching to exiles. The Revolution also forced into England hundreds of French émigrés who brought with them their distinctive homiletic methods. Sermons to English monks and nuns actually in France during the Revolution, which showed some discomfort at the use of the term 'Supreme Being', emphasized the service of God as the end of reasonable creatures, the spirit of renunciation needed in a free-thinking age, and encouraged a return to the fervour of the apostolic age. Princess Louise Marie, daughter of Louis XV, who had become an enclosed Carmelite nun, was cited as an inspiration (Walker: 14). By the 1790s, English Catholic sermons began to reflect establishment ways: public sermons were delivered on days of General Fasts, at the consecration of vicars apostolic, and at the obsequies of the great and good. The many sermons of thanksgiving at the return to health of George III in 1788 are a striking example of Catholicism's new status. The ex-Jesuit, Charles Plowden, broadcast in 1798 that he preached loyalty to the government every Sunday (Coghlan: 216).

In the late eighteenth century, a new generation of popular preachers appeared, like the Franciscan Pacificus Baker and the secular priests, James Appleton and James Archer. Both Appleton and Archer published, in competition with each other, a set of volumes of their collected sermons in 1786. This was a new venture by Catholic homilists and one designed to instruct 'the lower orders, who compose the major part', although a critic noted they were here merely following Laurence Sterne's example (Banister: 78). Appleton, who had poor health and was chaplain to four recusant households in turn, persuaded his wealthy patrons to cover the cost of his volumes. He admitted his 'familiar and easy' sermons were heavily dependent on contemporary French collections, notably the *Dictionnaire Apostolique* (1755) of Hyacinthe de Montargon, court preacher to Louis XIV, which was designed as a manual for pulpit orators of town and country. Archer, whose preaching career would bring him some notoriety in the early nineteenth century, had been recruited as a seminarian when a pot-boy in The Ship Inn, Lincoln's Inn Fields, and had returned to preach there immediately after the Gordon Riots in 1780 when he also became chaplain at the Bavarian Embassy. In The Ship, he preached in the club-room while pots of beer were placed on the tables as a blind. Short, but with a silvery, musical voice, Archer was credited as the most eloquent preacher in England, although to his critics he provoked anti-Catholic public opinion and preferred 'ink-horn phrases' to simpler expressions. By the end of the century, however, conscious of Britain being at war with France, Archer urged 'love of our country' in a general fast sermon at Moorfields chapel in London. According to the leading Catholic lawyer, Charles Butler, Archer pleased, charmed, and instructed Reason by his sermons which were read by a large number of priests to country congregations and which found their way 'to many a protestant toilet' (Coghlan: 64; Banister: 202; Gillow 1:55-6). The heavy emphasis on sin and repentance in many Catholic sermons of this time parallel similar themes in the sermons of the Evangelical Revival which was then burgeoning in England.

In Scotland, the end of the eighteenth century was notable for some distinguished preachers, including Bishop George Hay who believed preaching was an 'indispensable duty' and who himself 'spoke in a plain, familiar and unaffected style' in the old Scottish dialect. His published catechisms and devotionary writings are numerous. In his domestic chapel in Edinburgh and elsewhere, Hay could be 'peculiarly animated' through his resort to 'the *percussio furoris* and the stamping of his right foot... he gesticulated with his hands, in the Italian manner'. He had a tendency to chide those who moved about during his sermon and distracted the congregation. Protestants who attended his sermons were reduced to tears, admitting if they knew Hay was preaching, they 'would never go anywhere else'. In 1777 Hay appointed the young priest, Robert Menzies, to preach sermons in Gaelic on Sunday afternoons in Edinburgh's Highland chapel to the Catholic peasantry who had descended on Lowland towns after the Highland clearances and when the War of Independence in America had blocked any hope of emigration. Hay had less success with Alexander Geddes, the wayward radical firebrand and biblical scholar who eventually found more sympathetic patronage in England. As early as 1769, Geddes was 'attracting a good deal of popularity as a Preacher', and what he said around 1778, of his fellow Scot, William Guthrie, he might have applied to himself: 'he preached terrification, and his words were like the voice of thunder.' Geddes, in turn, introduced a new oratorical genre to British Catholicism, the burlesque sermon. His sermons in the late 1790s *On the Day of the General Fast, A Sermon Preached before the University of Cambridge*, and *Something like a Sermon, in Defence of the Present War, Preached on the Day of Public Thanksgiving*, lampooned the Anglican establishment and are clear evidence that British society had become sufficiently tolerant of Catholicism for Geddes to poke fun at the establishment in this manner (Hay: xix; Gordon: 56, 177, 185, 273, 190).

In Ireland, poor preachers were offered a 'prone' or sample sermon to deliver to their congregations, but sermons were kept deliberately simple. William Gahan (1732–1804), an Augustinian friar, adopted such a style in his Dublin sermons, published in 1799. He added a preface to his 1796 edition of the liturgical sermons of the ex-Jesuit, Joseph Morony, in which he approved of the criticisms of Jean Grou, then exiled in England, against 'frivolous and profane' literary sermons: 'O Paul, where art thou?' These years saw the transfer of allegiance by Irish Catholic preachers from the Jacobite cause towards support for the Hanoverian government, especially in the fraught period of the French Revolution when anxiety over political instability and republicanism made such preachers wax eloquent on the virtues of patriotism. Panegyrics in honour of Louis XVI and Marie Antoinette were heard in Cork in 1793, and the publisher for Protestant Trinity College, Dublin, happily printed a loyalist homily of the Catholic pastor of Edgeworthstown in 1794 warning his flock against French guile. This shift in allegiance is most clearly illustrated in the homilies of Arthur O'Leary (1719–1802), 'a mixture of goodness, solemnity and drollery' who preached controversial discourses in 'a broad spirit of toleration' in Cork from 1771. O'Leary went on to harangue rural congregations against the Whiteboys during which the old women stopped coughing, and the old men desisted from spitting as he 'described the afflictions which had befallen our poor country… and painted our folly in expecting a remedy from illegal means'. O'Leary was persuaded by the British government, 'fearful of his ascendancy over the Irish peasantry', to become a chaplain at the York Street chapel of the Spanish Embassy in London in 1789 and it was O'Leary who built St Patrick's, Soho in the 1790s. From this pulpit he preached on the need for further Catholic relief and 'our common Christianity'; he called attention to the desperate condition of the French émigrés and preached a panegyric on the death of Pope Pius VI. On a day of public fast and humiliation in March 1797, he fanned Christian hatred against the French revolutionaries on whom he was 'very severe—with now and then a stroke of pleasantry, sarcasm, and rough wit, happily fitted to fortify the audience against any attacks of drowsiness'. In London O'Leary moved in the Whig circle of Edmund Burke and Charles James Fox, as did the senior chaplain at the Spanish Embassy, Thomas Hussey, another Irishman, whose relations with O'Leary were sometimes strained. Hussey, who had 'a great head, a small body, and little tail', preached on toleration at the opening of the new Spanish Embassy chapel in 1791. As he was loath to write out his sermons, some of the congregation took down shorthand notes as he spoke. In his oratory he 'rather subdued than satisfied reason' through 'theatrical tones'. He copied the French homilist, Jean Baptiste Massillon (1663–1742), well known for tugging at the heart-strings but also for his Jansenist severity. There was a hint of the latter in Hussey also, for in declaiming with some severity that the elect would be few, Hussey's 'audience was agonized...there was a general shriek,—and some fell on the ground' (Butler: 4:437–43; Blom: 1499–1502; Coughlan: 362).

From the time of the 1791 Relief Act until full Catholic Emancipation in 1829, steady progress was made by Catholics in Britain. Translations of well-known French manuals of the art of preaching and sermon collections of the great French pulpit orators circulated during these years. Thus, Edward Peach translated and adapted Massillon's sermons between 1807 and 1808 so that from once appealing to the voluptuous and irreligious votaries at Versailles they might now prove attractive to the new English Catholic middle class. Peach noted Massillon's 'awful' warning that the elect would be few had hit the Versailles courtiers like 'an electric shock'. These hedonists leapt from their seats and pleaded with him to desist, as was to happen also with Thomas Hussey's London congregation. Besides translations, these years saw an increase of published public sermons at chapel openings, episcopal consecrations, and requiem masses, extracts of some of these becoming broadsheets popular with Irish immigrants. In Ireland itself, members of committees regularly delivered runs of published sermons to subscribers. Preaching by invited clergy, some from Ireland, to raise funds for charity and Sunday schools, 'houses of recovery' and orphanages was a new and striking initiative in this economically depressed period, and these sermons were programmed to ensure major benefactors, including Protestants, were present (Carter 2001*a*: 487–510, 2001*b*: 648–69).

The advance in toleration caused some tension within the Catholic community, reflected in the sermons, between those who were prepared to be more cooperative with the English establishment in return for further measures of relief and those opposed to any surrender of Catholic principles. Thus, hatred of the French revolutionaries balanced by a loyal gratitude to the British government for providing sanctuary for the émigrés is evident in some sermons. James Archer was severely criticized by Bishop John Milner for 'his affected liberality', and in his sermon on universal benevolence to liberal congregations in Bath and London, Archer attacked the atrocities of contemporary fellow Catholics in Nîmes against Protestants and insisted Christianity was 'a social system, calculated to unite man to his fellow-man'. Equally offensive to the conservatives was another preacher at the Spanish embassy chapel, Peter Gandolphy (1779–1821), whose sermons were denounced by Bishop William Poynter of the London District and who published a trans-denominational book of common prayer(s). Gandolphy's apologetic sermons to 'my British Countrymen' have an eighteenth-century texture, and although they vaunted Roman Catholic claims, their dilution of papal authority and their doubts about papal infallibility, together perhaps with the statement, popular throughout the nineteenth century, that the constitution of the Roman Catholic Church was the prototype of the British constitution, prompted their condemnation. The firebrand priest, Joseph Berington, who had scant regard for the quality of current Catholic sermons and believed Bishop John Milner's sermons needlessly offended Protestants, was invited to preach in Dissenters' chapels (such as Joseph Priestley's Birmingham Unitarian chapel). Another preacher, John Fletcher (died 1856), whose early sermons were 'less calculated for the pulpit than the closet' and which deserved 'the perusal of every protestant', became more of a conservative apologist in later life (Berington 1820, 1800; Gillow: 2:298–300, 365–8; Nockles: 193–236).

By contrast, other sermons of these years deliberately exploited the recent toleration for Catholics by emphasizing Catholic claims to the truth and seeking to make more converts. Of these, John Milner (vicar apostolic of the Midland District, 1803–26), despite being a patron of Gandolphy, followed Fletcher's path in that he too moved from early accommodation towards stiff-necked militancy, demanding full Catholic Emancipation, but not on the government's terms. Milner, who modelled himself on Bossuet, blamed the lack of fluency among English priests on their early seminary education in Europe. As a young preacher, he was given elocution lessons by the lexicographer and convert, John Walker, author of the famous pronouncing dictionary, who, according to Milner, 'discovered the scale of speaking sounds, by which reading and delivery are now reduced to a system'. 'Argumentative' is how his biographer describes Milner's extempore preaching. To country congregations, he preached simply and bluntly, illustrating, for instance, the vice of profane swearing by uttering as an example the 'dreadful imprecation from the pulpit: "G-d d-n you!"'. Milner, 'the English Athanasius', tried to stem 'the torrent of innovation' by blasting Cisalpinism and its liberal successors as well as inveighing against Anglican claims so as to demonstrate Catholic orthodoxy triumphant. In his later years, he developed an incipient polemical ultramontanism in his sermons, professing his patriotic allegiance to the Crown while insisting on the spiritual prerogatives of the papacy (Husenbeth 1862; Nockles).

Peter Augustine Baines, another vicar apostolic (Western District, 1823–43) took over Milner's baton and, as a guest preacher at the opening of new chapels, used his homilies not so much to congratulate and celebrate but publicly to hammer home basic Catholic doctrine, another indication of how confident Catholicism had become by this time. Baines was perhaps the first Romantic English Catholic homilist. He preached extempore in a Lancashire accent, with pathos and a tremulousness in his voice, and his persuasiveness lay in his delivery, for he often wept. Shorthand copyists prepared his sermons for publication. The Benedictine Baines painted vivid pictures of events in church history and put a huge emphasis on the new gothic architecture and liturgy and their impact on the emotions. One senses that he only had one sermon. His pre-Emancipation sermons were generally benign; that given at Sheffield in 1816 paying tribute to Anglican dignitaries for recently restoring ruinous cathedrals, and thanking Protestant neighbours for help to Catholics in the erection of chapels and schools. Between 1827 and 1829, he preached Sunday afternoon sermons in Rome from the English pulpit in the church of Jesus and Mary in the Corso, an event initiated by Pope Leo XII for English visitors, including Protestants (Gilbert).

The Anglican Evangelical Revival coincided with Catholic Emancipation, and in the 1820s Protestant Reformation Societies everywhere raged against Romish superstition. A sermon of 1822 in the Sardinian Embassy chapel on the Real Presence shocked one Protestant into firmly endorsing the government's continuing opposition to Catholic Emancipation (Ackroyd). By this time the sermons of Baines and others were becoming more aggressively apologetic as the temperature rose. Baines's most famous controversial sermon *Faith, Hope and Charity*, delivered in 1825 at the opening of the Catholic chapel in Bradford, was frequently republished at home and abroad. It stoutly defended proselytism but being pre-Emancipationist, recommended Protestants show charity to their Catholic neighbours. Even so, its apologetic tone produced howls of protest from Anglican clergymen, from the British Reformation Society, and from Methodist ministers. Baines's final sermon, just before his death in 1843, at a church recently purchased from the Irvingites, was a full-scale attack on Protestantism.

Manchester played a key role in economic, political, and religious troubles of the 1820s, and here, in the capital of laissez-faire, Catholic preachers were sucked into the prevailing storms and their sermons appropriately reflected the troubles. Thus, as a pamphlet war among the denominations developed in the city, Joseph Curr's sermons went on the defensive. Curr had three aims: to defend the faith of a rapidly expanding English and Irish Catholic working class, mostly involved in the local textile industry, to rebuff the attacks on Catholicism by local Evangelical and Dissenting Bible Associations seeking converts from the labouring poor, and, thirdly, to uncover the insidious dangers of rationalist atheism or 'deism', which Curr maintained lay behind the Peterloo Massacre of 1819, although he refused to be drawn into an opinion on that affray. His sermons are a reminder, then, that during that agitated time, there were new and more complex issues involving British Catholics than merely the continuing campaign for Catholic Emancipation.

Sermons often developed into courses of public lectures during the two decades after Emancipation and reflect the expansion and new self-confidence of British Catholics. Larger and grander urban churches were built, religious publications and associations increased, and from 1840 the number of vicars apostolic in England was doubled. Italian missionaries and Tractarian converts introduced their own homiletic styles into English Catholicism. In Ireland, the sermons of John Meany included the first sermon printed in Irish Gaelic characters. But Ireland also provided the mainland Catholicism with a new working-class base as immigrants fled the recurrent Irish potato famines to find work in new industrial centres.

Unsurprisingly, British Catholic pulpit oratory burgeoned from 1829 and many manuscript sermons from England, Ireland, and Scotland survive from this time. There were increasing numbers of sermons now published in the annual *Laity's Directory*. *The Catholic Pulpit*, a compilation of over sixty sermons sponsored mainly by clergy educated at the English College, Lisbon (first edition 1839/40, second edition 1850), acquainted English readers with popular contemporary European preachers such as the French Jesuit Gustave Xavier Lacroix de Ravignan (1795–1858). Further translations of famous orators such as Alphonsus Liguori and Louis Bourdaloue were also published in these years and served as preaching manuals. Of particular importance for the day's sermon culture is the preface by Bernard Ullathorne to his *Sermons* (Ullathorne). Ullathorne, an English Benedictine and first Bishop of Birmingham, had returned from Australia in 1841 where he had been vicar general and prison chaplain, and at the time of publication of these sermons was a parish priest in Coventry. Actually, the volume introduced an English readership to many sermons he had delivered in New South Wales. In his preface, Ullathorne pleaded with British Catholics for a new 'quickening spirit in our sacred eloquence' to suit 'the restless and dissatisfied spirit of our times' and to help large urban congregations 'in commotion' and dissatisfied with 'Protestantism and Socialism'. In demanding proper training in sacred eloquence for 'our young ecclesiastics', Ullathorne strongly objected to continuing the use of the seventeenth-century classical preachers of the French court as models who were, he said, polite but hardly challenging, and taking his cue from Cicero, 'it is the listening multitude which makes the great orator', Ullathorne demanded all sermons should address the paşions as Daniel O'Connell had successfully done in Ireland. The 'multitude' wanted emotional sermons so that it might come to yearn for 'the mysterious and the supernatural'. English Catholic congregations had for too long been subjected to the 'conventional ideas of the fashionable class...indifferent to all feeling', so Ullathorne believed sermons should primarily preach the religious and passionate spirit of charity. He was convinced that the theologian Philippe-Olympe Gerbet (1798–1864), whose doctrinaire mennaisianism was currently giving way to ultramontanism, was absolutely right to teach that the affections could be enlivened by means of sermons on central Christian doctrines. Thus charity was to be defined 'as the mysterious joy of sacrifice'. Ullathorne abhorred Catholics copying the flat Anglican practice of reading out sermons: 'We tesselate words and sentences instead of fusing ideas', and believed instead that even the hardest Australian convict had 'an appetite for profound emotion' which could be awakened. Preachers should therefore dispense with secondary authorities and have recourse to the 'giants' of the early church and to the mystics in whom Ullathorne was himself deeply interested. If the multitude found undiluted mysticism beyond them, then Ullathorne, like William Frederick Faber before him, advocated preaching on the saints who were 'too much neglected in the pulpit lately'. Ullathorne therefore believed sermons preached by him in old gaols and other temporary locations in Australia were ideal for delivering secondhand to English Catholic congregations just emerging from the catacombs. He thus colonized urban, industrial England by means of sermons earlier delivered to Catholics and convicts in the Australian backwoods, his most famous, 'The Drunkard', being first heard in Australian public houses but now enthusiastically adopted by the English temperance movement (Ullathorne: 1–66, 109–26).

Cathedrals, seminaries, and monasteries made an official appearance after 1829, often with sermons in 'new pulpits' to commemorate their emergence from the penal shadows, though they continued to draw protests from the Protestant Reformation Societies. Nicholas Wiseman's sermon, at the dedication of St Chad's, Birmingham (1841), saw this Pugin masterpiece as the resuscitation of a degraded medieval cathedral, and the aristocratic George Spencer, who converted in 1830 and was professed as a Passionist missioner in 1848, used his sermons at St Mary's College, Oscott, and again at his appeal in Manchester for Catholic schools and at the new Cistercian monastery of Mount Saint Bernard, Leicestershire, to promote his ideal of Christian unity. His preaching at the laying of the foundation of Pugin's church in Derby in 1838 coincided with Queen Victoria's coronation, a nice patriotic gesture. The rapid expansion of Catholicism, however, still required the help of wealthy aristocratic patrons to build these prestigious ecclesiastical buildings. The panegyric at the funeral in 1831 of Lord Clifford, member of the Catholic Institute and a great aristocratic benefactor to new churches, typically paid tribute to him as an advocate of civil and religious liberties and welcomed his return to the House of Lords. Eulogies preached at the funerals of other aristocratic church builders, like the Stafford Jerninghams, portrayed them as models of nineteenth-century philanthropy (Oliver; Husenbeth 1832).

After 1829 published funeral and anniversary eulogies for vicars apostolic across Britain became more frequent and often contained a new emphasis on the episcopal office, a sign of things to come. Most striking were the deeply moving panegyrics following the death in 1847 in Rome of the Irish layman Daniel O'Connell, 'the Liberator'. These funeral orations introduced Catholic, especially Irish, public opinion to the new phenomenon of liberal ultramontanism then making headway in Europe, but in Ireland's case they attached respect for the universal primacy of the pope to that fervent Irish patriotism which O'Connell had himself championed. Dr Miley, O'Connell's chaplain, paid tribute to his success in liberating the Irish nation and Catholicism whilst acknowledging the Liberator's love and reverence for the pope. Miley drew attention to the fact that the recently elevated Pius IX had chosen Gioacchino Ventura (1792–1861), a disciple of Lamennais, as O'Connell's panegyrist in Rome. Ventura, whose eulogy was published in Dublin in 1847, advocated the union of the forces of religion and liberty and later predicted that ecclesiastical disestablishment would become the norm.

One should not, therefore, underestimate the influence of contemporary sermons in promoting a popular cult of the papacy throughout Britain. Priests like Charles Michael Baggs and Nicholas Wiseman, both to become bishops, were already preaching sermons on papal authority in Rome in the 1830s, and once in England they found a perfect setting for creating a liberal Ultramontane ideology amongst a recently emancipated religious minority which sought leadership and inspiration from the pope and, in return for patriotic loyalty, generosity from the government. While Bishop James Gillis, coadjutor vicar apostolic in Scotland's Eastern District from 1838 to 1852, whose substantial collection of manuscript sermons is still extant, could preach in 1850 the necessity of a crude temporal sovereignty to ensure the 'kingly independence' of the pope, Wiseman's early sermons reflected his more sophisticated position on this topic. He was a universalist in his ultramontanism and a liberal imperialist in his politics, perhaps even a one-world Tory. With a background in Oriental languages and culture, his sermons at the Gesù in Rome during 1831, when he was rector of the English College, reveal him citing Anglican scholars on 'the salvability of the Heathen' and musing on the oft-repeated claim that Islam was merely a branch of Christianity. In his funeral oration of 1837 celebrating the life of Cardinal Thomas Weld, an aristocratic philanthropist and patron who had supervised religious affairs in America, India, and Australia, and later settled in Rome, Wiseman noted how his elevation to the cardinalate had broken down the barriers between Rome and England (Wiseman 1831, 1837).

Not long after Wiseman had returned to England in 1840 the Irish immigration began. He was aware of this fundamental demographic change when he preached his appeal sermon in Salford, Manchester, in July 1850, noting how little was being done for the poor, a sentiment he repeated in another sermon at Southwark in August of the same year. But the Salford sermon, on the Pharisee and Publican, also revealed his patriotism; for England, he argued, had made more social and intellectual progress than any other nation, and Manchester, where factory and church stood united, was 'the very centre of that restless activity of the human mind' and above it 'the banner of industry ever streams in the wind'. In its mercantilism it was to be compared with Venice, but whereas the latter had built St Mark's in gratitude for the blessings of providence, Manchester had left its blessings unrecorded (Wiseman 1850: 7, 9, 15–16).

The increased prominence given in sermons of Catholic preachers to the ills of contemporary British society resulted as much from the new security granted to Catholics by Emancipation as the evil effects of industrialization and famine. Sermons induced clergy and laity to found and maintain 'confraternities' or associations, sometimes imported from abroad, to support the distressed. Thus, charity sermons began to seek contributions to help members of the St Vincent de Paul Society's work among the poor, the Society being established in England from France in 1844, and in London the Associated Catholic Charities organization funded annual charity sermons throughout the 1830s. By far the most popular Catholic moral crusade which involved preaching in these years was, however, that of the Irish Capuchin Theobald Mathew's Total Abstinence Society. The 'Apostle of Temperance' had been converted to temperance by a Quaker shopkeeper in Cork in 1838 and having preached total temperance throughout Ireland, Mathew, attractive by the earnestness of his preaching and his reputation for apparently working miracles, went on circuit in Scotland and England between 1842 and 1843. He would preach a charity sermon and then administer the pledge to thousands of individuals in a public, usually open-air, meeting throughout the day until dusk in what was the most obvious example of Catholic Revivalism. Although he inevitably suffered some rowdy opposition, from, for instance, hooligans of the 'Hop and Malt Society' at a meeting organized at Blackheath in 1843 by the West Kent Temperance Societies, Mathew had the respect of senior churchmen and politicians.

Mathew's apostolate had parallels with the famous Italian itinerant preachers at work in England during the 1830s and 1840s. They belonged to a new wave of international missionary endeavour which characterized the pontificate of Gregory XVI (1831–46) whose patronage for the newly founded Association for the Propagation of the Faith was welcomed enthusiastically by Catholic preachers throughout Britain including Luigi Gentili, the Italian Rosminian. Wiseman petitioned the pope in 1839 to found a body of travelling missionaries in England to preach and give retreats to Catholics and non-Catholics throughout the land (Wiseman 1839). After Catholic Emancipation, preaching to make converts across Britain became more popular than ever, with numerous confraternities being established with this as their first objective, and conversion became the central concern of missionaries from Italian religious orders whose track record had already been proven through their successful *svegliarini* or 'street preaching' in Italy (Gilley: 136).

The Passionist missioner, Dominic Barberi, and the Rosminian preacher, Luigi Gentili, were the most famous of these latter-day Italian friars. Barberi's early enthusiasm to come to preach in England had been warmed by his acquaintance with John Milner, George Spencer, and Nicholas Wiseman who brought him to Staffordshire in 1842. Barberi firmly believed, like Bernard Ullathorne, that a high level of education was not required to appreciate the Christian creed, so his sermons on 'Christ crucified' were always simple and practical, but delivered with some emotional force: he spoke 'almost like a child'. Despite some early noisy opposition, Barberi began preaching in barns and hotels and by 1844 his sermons were delivered at Corpus Christi processions and at outdoor conventions throughout England and Ireland. His sermons to children included dramatic impersonations of the devil doing his rounds as well as inspections of tongues to reveal the black spots of sin. His English was never fluent, indeed he sometimes required a prompter, but crowds, including Methodists, flocked to watch him gesturing, fascinated by his austere Passionist habit and sandals. As he himself said: 'We do more preaching here with bare feet and religious restraint and modesty than with the tongue.' Despite orders from his superiors, he refused to abandon his sandals. Barberi's most distinguished converts were the Tractarians John Henry Newman and John Dobree Dalgairns, whom he received into the Catholic Church towards the end of 1845 (Wilson: 260, 263).

Luigi Gentili, a revivalist like Barberi, had, however, a more elevated appearance and his sermons were more rhetorical. Gentili adopted the Spiritual Exercises of St Ignatius of Loyola as the basis of his preaching. Coming to England in 1835, he conducted his main missions in the East Midlands and the North, preaching and involved five daily sermons. He established confraternities and temperance societies, preached incessantly, made numerous converts, and inspired Italian immigrant communities. With his biretta, Roman collar, cloak and crucifix, Gentili also possessed an exotic attraction for the curious. More than Barberi, however, he was committed to deepening the education of the English clergy and using sermons to dampen potential unrest from Chartist rioters or Irish immigrant stockingers in Leicestershire. Like Wiseman, Gentili worried about the effects of the nation's increasing wealth, commenting in Liverpool that 'as long as business and money are in such abundance, I do not see how England can be converted to God'. His introduction into England of the Italianate *Quarant' Ore* and devotion to the Immaculate Conception of the Mother of God found some resistance among English Catholics of an older and more austere tradition. But Gentili had little time for high ritualism itself especially when it reduced the importance of the sermon, and his personal sobriety produced consternation at Newcastle-upon-Tyne when he inveighed against public dances like the indecent waltz and polka 'recently imported from France' (Leetham: 239).

Barberi and, to a lesser extent, Gentili were both aware of how influential Tractarian converts would be in their adopted church. Convert clergy brought with them a formal Anglican homiletic style honed over the centuries and distinguished by its theological sophistication and eloquence. The preaching of the aristocratic convert, George (Ignatius) Spencer, Anglican priest and Passionist from 1847, began before the Oxford Movement and continued until his death in 1864. Respected for his sanctity, Spencer's sermons in England, Europe and Ireland, where he was promised a Gaelic translation, were generally extempore, though his delivery was 'cold, dry and tame'. 'When will he have done talking and begin to preach?' was the question of one auditor. His idea of England's conversion to the Roman Church, a key theme, was more nuanced and ecumenical than other Anglican converts, for he offended Catholic susceptibilities by suggesting in a Manchester sermon of 1839 that Catholics, as well as Protestants, should be prepared to lay down some of their beliefs if they were proved untrue (Pius: 258–9, 273). By contrast, the early Catholic sermons of the ex-Tractarian Frederick William Faber were emotionally charged and theatrically colourful. Like the convert Richard Waldo Sibthorp, whose brief flirtation with Catholicism inspired his Birmingham sermon in 1842 on English Catholicism coming out of the shade, Faber was fascinated with the idea of holiness, which explains the frequency of his recourse to the lives of saints, his dualist perspective regarding the world (viewed by the saints as 'a howling wilderness'), and his repetitive promotion of Christian asceticism in contrast to his lack of interest in modern scientific endeavour. Faber's interest in hagiography paralleled his promotion of famous mystical texts of the medieval and early modern period by which, like Ullathorne, he hoped popular devotion and awareness of a continuing Catholic inheritance would spread (Wilkinson: 247).

The most distinguished Tractarian convert, John Henry Newman, preached his Catholic sermons between 1845 and 1850. They comprise some published occasional sermons, his discourses for mixed congregations, and some unpublished seasonal sermons, and they culminated with his *Christ upon the Waters* preached in 1850. As a Catholic, Newman moved away from the Anglican tradition of reading sermons and began to deliver his sermons from written notes or extempore. He had a distinctively self-effacing manner of delivery: a text rapidly spoken in a calm tenor voice without any histrionics, followed by a pause, and then the lesson rammed home. The result was that he managed to attract and keep the attention of each individual auditor, and through the frequent use of rhetorical questions Newman believed that the listener would later go on to 'realize' the lesson by means of the power of the will, a favourite theme of Newman's. He was always uncomfortable at being invited to preach occasional and special sermons to fashionable congregations, and his first, at a funeral in Rome in 1846 before his ordination, which dwelt on the subject of conversion, was reckoned to have been 'plain and cold' and was even criticized by the pope who felt that Newman should not have provided *aceto* but *miele* instead. Seven of his seasonal sermons survive for 1848 given in St Chad's Cathedral, Birmingham, and in delivering them he doffed his biretta at every mention of the Holy Name (Trevor: 400; Newman 1957: 6). They are brief, without ornament, and to the point; they condemned 'diseased curiosity' and drunkenness, and a falling into the way of the world which had dignified sin 'by new names', avarice becoming care of one's family and pride being termed independence. Newman's models for mortification of the reason and the will were Saints Philip Neri and Ignatius of Loyola. His sermon on Our Lady had recourse to his patristic background to show how Catholic devotion to Mary was in the tradition of the Fathers, and he encouraged his listeners to 'enter into the warmth of foreign books of devotion' (Newman 1957: 9, 73–6, 84, 93, 103).

Discourses Addressed to Mixed Congregations, dedicated to Nicholas Wiseman in 1849, was Newman's first volume of published Catholic sermons, delivered to a congregation of Catholics and Protestants in central Birmingham. These echoed many of the themes found in his seasonal sermons of 1848 and expounded essential beliefs such as grace, faith, sin, judgement, salvation, the search for truth and the avoidance of worldly standards. In their exploration of judgement and sin, and in their attack on smugness, these sermons were reckoned to be rather severe—Faber called them 'savage'—but they are more Italianate in style than his earlier Anglican sermons, St Alphonsus Liguori providing a model (Newman 1961–77: 13:340; Ker: 342). In them Newman consciously paraded his new faith by quoting from the Jesuit theologian Juan de Lugo's treatise on the incarnation, by making a passing reference to the recently promulgated dogma of the Immaculate Conception of the Virgin Mary and by ending one sermon with a prayer to the Sacred Heart (Newman 1849: 325, 361). Newman also published at this time a new Catholicized edition of his Anglican *Parochial Sermons*.

Finally, *Christ upon the Waters* was delivered in October 1850 at the installation of Ullathorne as the first Bishop of Birmingham as a storm raged outside over the restoration of the Catholic hierarchy, concerning which Newman protested he had never been involved. In his determination to teach a bold lesson, highlighting the indolence of the English character, he hoped that this sermon would not be seen as 'very violent' by Ullathorne. It was an apologia for the continuity of English Catholicism, now coming out of its prison: 'What an awful vitality is here!' The sermon must be a rare instance of the Catholic Church being likened to a railway in its complexity, popularity, pleasantly smooth travel and in its returns, but pre-eminently in its safety record: there is no mention of punctuality. Newman concluded 'the rail is safer than road (travel)' on a Wesleyan, Anglican, or Dissenting coach (Newman 1850: 7, 16, 23). *Christ upon the Waters* echoes themes in his 1848 sermon to mixed congregations on Christ's command over the winds and the sea and it formed a prelude in its central message to his most famous sermon on the Second Spring in 1852 which also celebrated the re-establishment of the Catholic hierarchy.

References

Ackroyd, H. (1822). Letter. Derbyshire Record Office, ref. D239 M/F/8484.
Banister, R. (1995). *The Revival of English Catholicism: The Banister-Rutter Correspondence*, L. Gooch (ed.). Wigan: North West Catholic History Society.
Berington, J. (1800). Letter to Edward Jerningham dated 31 December 1800. Archives of the Archdiocese of Westminster, ref Ware, p.87/4/11.
—— (1820). Letter to John Kirk dated 7 June 1820. Birmingham Diocesan Archives, ref C1843 Hier. no. Z5/3/99/12/77.
Bishop, D. (n. d.). Manuscript Sermons. Lille, Archives du Nord, ref. 20 H 13.
Blom, F. et al. (1996) (eds.). *English Catholic Books 1701–1800: A Bibliography*. Aldershot: Scolar Press.

Butler, C. (1822). *Historical Memoirs of the English, Irish, and Scottish Catholics, since the Reformation*... London: John Murray.

Carter, B. (2001a). 'Catholic Charitable Endeavour in London, 1810–1840, Part I'. *Recusant History* 25-3: 487–510.

—— (2001b). 'Catholic Charitable Endeavour in London, 1810–1840, Part II'. *Recusant History* 25-4: 648–69.

Clancy, T. H. (1996) (ed.). *English Catholic Books, 1641–1700: A Bibliography*, revised edn. Aldershot: Scolar Press.

Clayton, T. Manuscript Sermons. Bodleian Library, Oxford, ref. MSS. Eng. e. 2760–9.

Coghlan, J. P. (2007). *The Correspondence of James Peter Coghlan (1731–1800)*, ed. F. Blom et al. Woodbridge: Boydell and Brewer.

Fenning, H. (1997–98). 'Dublin Imprints of Catholic Interest: 1701–39'. *Collectanea Hibernica* 39/40: 106–54.

—— (1999). 'Dublin Imprints of Catholic Interest: 1740–59'. *Collectanea Hibernica* 41: 65–116.

Gilbert, P. J. (2006). *This Restless Prelate: Bishop Peter Baines*. Leominster: Gracewing.

Gilley, S. (1969). 'The Roman Catholic Mission to the Irish in London'. *Recusant History* 10-3: 123–45.

Gillow, J. (1885–1902). *A Literary and Biographical History or Bibliographical Dictionary of the English Catholics*... London: Burns & Oates.

Gordon, J. F. S. (1867). *Journal and Appendix to Scotichronicon and Monasticon*. Glasgow: Tweed.

Hay, G. (1871). *Works of the Right Rev. Bishop Hay of Edinburgh*. Edinburgh: William Blackwood & Sons.

Hemphill, B. (1953). *The Early Vicars Apostolic of England 1685–1750*. London: Burns & Oates.

Husenbeth, F. C. (1832). *Discourse Pronounced at the Funeral of the Right Hon. Frances Xaveria Stafford Jerningham*... Norwich: Bacon and Kinnbrook.

—— (1862). *The Life of the Right Rev. John Milner*... Dublin: James Duffy.

Ker, I. T. (1990). *John Henry Newman: A Biography*. Oxford: Oxford University Press.

Leetham, C. (1965). *Luigi Gentili: A Sower for the Second Spring*. London: Burns & Oates.

Manning, R. (1742). *Moral Entertainments of the Most Important Practical Truths of the Christian Religion*. London: Thomas Meighan.

Marshall, P., and Scott, G. (eds.) (2009). *Catholic Gentry in English Society*... Farnham: Ashgate.

Meighan, T. (ed.) (1741). *Select Collection of Catholick Sermons*. London: Thomas Meighan.

Newman, J. H. (1849). *Discourses Addressed to Mixed Congregations*. London: Longman, Brown, Green, and Longmans.

—— (1850). *Christ upon the Waters*... Birmingham: M. Maher.

—— (1957). *Catholic Sermons of Cardinal Newman*, Birmingham Oratory (ed.). London: Burns & Oates.

—— (1961–77). *The Letters and Diaries of John Henry Newman*, ed. C. S. Dessain. London: Thomas Nelson & Sons.

Nockles, P. B. (1998). '"The Difficulties of Protestantism": Bishop Milner, John Fletcher and Catholic Apologetic against the Church of England in the Era from the First Relief Act to Emancipation, 1778–1830'. *Recusant History* 24-2: 193–236.

Oliver, G. (1831). *Address Delivered in the Catholic Chapel, Ugbrooke, at the Funeral of Lord Clifford*... Exeter: T. Howe.

Parfitt, C. (1768). Inserted Manuscript Sermon. Clifton Diocesan Archives, ref. Maire: Prior Park Papers, MI59.
Pius, Father (1866). *The Life of Father Ignatius of St. Paul*...Dublin: James Duffy.
Trevor, M. (1962). *Newman: The Pillar of the Cloud*. London: Macmillan & Co.
Ullathorne, W. (1842). *Sermons, with Prefaces*. London: T. Jones.
Walker, A. MS Sermons. Lille, Archives du Nord, 20 H 14.
Ware Manuscript Sermons. Archives of the Archdiocese of Westminster, ref Ware 18/21.
Wilkinson, M. J. (2007). *Frederick William Faber: A Great Servant of God*. Leominster: Gracewing.
Wilson, A. (1967). *Blessed Dominic Barberi: Supernaturalized Briton*. London: Sands & Co.
Wiseman, N. (1831). *Two Sermons Delivered at Rome*...London: Keating and Brown.
—— (1837). *Funeral oration on Cardinal Weld*...London: Booker and Dolman.
—— (1839). Printed petition. Ushaw College Manuscripts, ref.4, 372.
—— (1850). *The Social and Intellectual State of England Compared with its Moral Condition*...London: T. Richardson.

CHAPTER 9

PREACHING IN THE CHURCHES OF SCOTLAND

ANN MATHESON

Background

The starting date for this review of the British sermon, 1689, was the year before the formal establishment of Presbyterianism in Scotland in 1690. The Scottish Reformation had considerably influenced the style of pulpit oratory from 1560. One of the most significant developments was the recognition that the sermon could serve as a unique medium for conveying the new truths of reformed religion to the layman. It could serve a useful purpose both in religious and in civil society as a medium for reformed ideas. This new thinking developed largely from Protestant recognition that if the new doctrine was to be successfully transmitted, the established corpus of the new faith must be conveyed from generation to generation. The sermon delivered in public and the written sermon were obvious choices. This presented little difficulty in the seventeenth century since the exercise of writing theses had been part of the normal medieval curriculum. Very little separated preachers and educated laymen since preparing and defending theses and pronouncing orations were taught in common: only the preacher's concern with conveying his religious message marked him out from his lay counterparts.

The need for sermons to create an indelible and lasting impression on their hearers led to prolonged discussions on the best medium through which to convey the message. In seventeenth-century Scotland this led to a reaction in favour of a more ascetic mode of preaching in which the sermon's effectiveness would depend solely on the essential message of Christianity. If the message was true, what further embellishment was required?

The over-reliance on scriptural quotation in seventeenth-century Scottish contemporary sermons was most vividly presented in the well-known satire on Presbyterian sermons, *Scotch Presbyterian Eloquence*: 'The most of their Sermons are Nonsensick

Raptures, the abuse of Mystick Divinity, in canting and compounded Vocables, oft-times stuffed with impertinent and base Similes, and always with homely, coarse and ridiculous Expressions, very unsuitable to the Gravity and Solemnity that becomes Divinity' (*The Scotch Presbyterian Eloquence*: 22). Later on in the eighteenth century, Edward Burt commented: 'I really think that there is nothing set down in the Book called *Scots Presbyterian Eloquence*, but what, at least, is probable' (Burt: 1:213). He did soften his comments later to admit that younger preachers were at that time 'introducing a *Manner* more decent and reasonable' (Burt: 1:214), a pertinent comment since it was made at the time when there was a shift in sermon taste from the older forms of pulpit rhetoric to a new respect for refinement in sermons.

The Episcopalian Gilbert Burnet had made the case for improvement as early as the end of the seventeenth century: 'Preaching has passed through many different forms among us, since the reformation... But without flattering the present age... it must be confessed, that it is brought of late to a much greater perfection than it was ever before at amongst us... Our language is much refined, and we have returned to the plain notions of simple and genuine rhetoric' (Burnet: 120). Despite these claims, the evidence suggests that the bulk of sermons from this period are of Covenanting zeal, delivered extempore at conventicles and wherever temporary meeting places presented themselves. The sense of urgency of these sermons was reflected in their form. Evangelical in intent, they were collections of spiritual phraseology with numerous biblical quotations. Form was sacrificed to content and sermons relied for their appeal on a direct confrontation between God and man and an appeal to souls. As the nineteenth-century preacher Robert Rainy commented, 'A man who preached as he could and *when* he could, in a house or on a hillside, was not likely to take much care of his style' (Rainy: 77). Where the fear that they might never have another opportunity to address their flocks was a real one, there was a strong incentive to crowd as much material as possible into a single discourse.

The Early Eighteenth-Century Scottish Pulpit

The tradition passed on to the eighteenth century by the pulpit in Scotland did little to assist in the search for a simple and genuine rhetoric. Surviving sermons are strongly Evangelical, elaborate, and heavily structured. In the eighteenth century they continued to fulfil the role of models for Evangelical preachers. The sermons of Alexander Peden, for example, were frequently reprinted: his *The Lord's Trumpet* had been reprinted three times by 1750 (Peden). On the other hand, a different tradition was also handed down in the sermons of men like Robert Leighton and Henry Scougal, Episcopalians whose sermons were 'moderate' both in content and expression. Their sermons were frequently reprinted: Scougal's *Life of God in the Soul of Man* was reprinted sixteen times between

1700 and 1800, four of these editions in Scotland. It was also widely circulated in Scotland: W Miller's catalogue of books attached to John Bonar's sermon before the Society for the Propagating of Christian Knowledge in 1752 lists it for sale along with the works of Tillotson and Barrow. Their sermons also influenced Scottish preachers such as William Wishart (who wrote a preface to Scougal's 1742 edition), William Leechman, George Wishart, and Robert Wallace.

From the 1730s onwards there was a growing divergence of views within the Church of Scotland on the nature of the message and how best to convey it. By the 1750s, one wing of the Church was being popularly identified as 'Moderate'; and the other 'Evangelical' or 'anti-Moderatism'. The Moderates accommodated the tenets of good taste in their sermons while, in contrast, the Evangelicals clung to the old verities of the message based on doctrinal truth. The nature of sermons in Scotland began to change quite significantly from the 1740s with the rise of the Moderates. As sermons began to be associated in the public mind with reflecting good taste, they became a popular genre, particularly with those who wished to demonstrate their cultivated interests. From mid-century onwards, Scottish ministers were preaching sermons that contained many of the fashionable ideas in vogue in contemporary society: stress on the moral virtues; benevolence; charity and candour; the sympathetic emotions; and the links between religion and civilized society.

Scottish Sermons and their Reception

From the middle of the eighteenth century Scottish sermons began to appear on the market in increasing numbers. They were generally met with a negative response from the *Critical Review* and the *Monthly Review* while the *Scots Magazine* usually took a much more generous view of them. Reviewing John Farquhar's *Sermons* in 1772, the *Critical Review* condemned them for their affectation of language and style while the *Scots Magazine* commended them in lavish terms: 'in these sermons a good judge will be at no loss to discern, in the preacher, an eminent clearness of apprehension, a correctness of taste, a lively imagination, and a delicate sensibility to all the finest feelings of which human nature is susceptible' (Review of *Sermons on Various Subjects*: 488). To be fair, this was not true of all Scottish reviewers. For example, the *Critical Review* and the *Edinburgh Magazine and Review* were united in their criticism of Robert Walker's *Sermons on Practical Subjects*.

There was unanimity between reviewers in Scotland and England on the need for standards in sermon-writing: they stressed the importance of a clearer distinction between the requirements of the sermon delivered in the pulpit and the demands of the published sermon; and they were agreed on the need for greater refinement of language in Scottish sermons and, in particular, on the expunging of Scoticisms from the sermons of Scottish ministers. This latter point was made very strongly from the 1760s onwards in regard to its corrupting effect on sermon quality. In an advertisement in the *Critical Review* in 1775 William McGill's sermon *On the Death of Jesus* is referred to as 'in some places... a little disfigured with Scotticisms' (Advertisement for *A Practical Essay*: 580). The same charge was levelled even at the *Sermons* of Dr Hugh Blair and those of George Hill, Principal of St Mary's College in St Andrews. The need to eradicate Scoticisms from printed sermons was very closely in line with a general trend in Scottish writing as a whole, which sought to divest itself of parochialism and limited aspirations. Sermon-writers had to consider the needs of a wider market outside Scotland; and the new requirements for polite writing in the fields of philosophy and belles-lettres must equally apply to sermons.

There was also agreement among reviewers on the differing needs of delivered and printed sermons, between the demands of small, generally receptive audiences for sermons delivered from the pulpit and those of the wider considerably more critical audiences for printed sermons. Sermons from the pulpit were primarily intended for the edification of their immediate congregations and their success principally depended on the oratorical style in which they were delivered. When sermons were submitted to the press, on the other hand, they lost any critical immunity and were judged by the same standards as applied to other forms of polite literature. Success in the pulpit was no guarantee of similar success on the literary market: in the *Critical Review's* 'Monthly Catalogue' of new books a reviewer commented of Robert Walker's sermons 'in the former case they address themselves to a popular congregation; in the latter to the learned world' (Review of *Sermons on Practical Subjects*: 392).

Throughout the eighteenth century, however, a difference of opinion persisted between the Evangelical and Moderate wings of the Church of Scotland on how sermons should be delivered. To Evangelicals, sermons delivered extempore were divinely inspired and sermons that were read lacked divine conviction. This view continued into the nineteenth century with numerous contemptuous dismissals of 'paper-ministers'. In his novel *Stronbuy*, James Cameron Lees put the matter clearly: 'Och, if ministers canna remember their ain sermons, how can they expect us to remember them?' (Lees: 313).

Early Eighteenth-Century Scottish Models

In a footnote to his translation of the Abbé Maury's *Principles of Eloquence*, John Neal Lake commented on the state of contemporary pulpit oratory: 'The Divines of the last century, wanted, it is true, that accuracy and refinement of taste, which characterise some of our more modern discourses... in the present day the names of PORTEUS, DAVIS, GERRARD, OGILVIE, LEECHMAN, BLAIR, FORDYCE, HUNTER and many others' (Maury: 191–2). The strong representation of Scottish names reflects the improvement in the quality of sermons in Scotland over the second half of the eighteenth century. How did this come about?

One of the principal models for early eighteenth-century Scottish preachers was John Tillotson, the English divine. There were three dominant themes in his preaching: the need for an appeal to reason in matters of religion; a distrust of spiritual intuition; and a stress on the imperfection of man's knowledge of God. The popularity of

Tillotson's sermons in Scotland can be deduced from the number of editions of his works: four editions of the *Works* had been published by 1772. His sermon *His Commandments are not Grievous* was far and away the most popular sermon of its day and its sentiments were particularly welcome to the Church of Scotland. A Church that was attempting to put behind it the embroiled religious disputes of the seventeenth century and was coming to terms with a society that was more mercantile would have grasped thankfully at John Tillotson's view that two things made the course of life easy: present pleasures and the assurance of a future reward. Hugh Blair, first holder of the Chair of Rhetoric and Belles Lettres in the University of Edinburgh in 1762, cited Tillotson as 'to this day, one of the best models we have for preaching' (Graham: 94): Blair himself was referred to as the Scottish Tillotson. Later on though, imitation of Tillotson began to attract criticism as evidence of a lack of ability on the part of Scottish preachers. In the poem *The Kirkiad*, Archibald Bruce satirized Tillotson's influence on preaching in Scotland:

> O *Tillotson*! Illustrious name!
> Can I forbear to sing thy fame?
> Dear *Tillotson*! soft rest thy head!
> Great pattern of the preaching trade!
>
> (Bruce: 21)

The Mid to Late Eighteenth Century

Teachers in Scottish Universities

Much of the influential thinking that changed preaching in Scotland in the eighteenth century came through Scotland's four ancient universities (St Andrews, Glasgow, Aberdeen, and Edinburgh). The influence of Lord Shaftesbury and his teaching had begun to percolate into Scottish thinking from England in the early part of the century. The publication of his *Characteristicks* in 1711 had introduced the view that man was essentially virtuous and that his basic aim was to live a reasonable life within a reasonable society. In Scotland, Shaftesbury's thought was responsible for injecting ideas of virtue and benevolence into the older more punitive-based system of moral conduct.

Frances Hutcheson matriculated at the University of Glasgow in 1711, the year in which the *Characteristicks* were published. Some years later in 1720 Hutcheson was introduced to Shaftesbury's work by Lord Molesworth, a Dublin acquaintance; and in 1725 Hutcheson published his own *Inquiry* and in 1728 his *Essay on the Passions*. The following year he was appointed to the Chair of Moral Philosophy at Glasgow. The most significant aspect of Hutcheson's philosophical *credo* was his belief in a morality accessible to and attainable by all. His ideas were quite new to Scotland and he was aware of the novelty of his thought, stating that 'I am called "New Light" here' (Scott: 257).

Hutcheson's work at Glasgow was built upon by William Leechman, who was appointed to the Chair of Divinity in 1742. One of his innovations was the introduction of a course of lectures on the composition of sermons (Reid: 254). Leechman's influence on sermon design and style can be seen both from his innovations and his extension of earlier practice. As an innovator, his system of lectures offered the first structured method on how to prepare sermons and provided practical guidelines for sermon-writers. His suggestions were complemented by practical examples from his own sermons; and he directed students on how to prepare for sermon-writing. Leechman's view that sensibility of mind was an essential component was to influence later sermon-writing and literary writing. Phrases such as 'moving the passions' and 'knowledge of the human heart' were measures deployed in Scotland not only in sermons but in literary criticism in the latter half of the eighteenth century. Leechman's decision to institute his lectures suggests a growing acceptance in Scotland that pulpit oratory was a skill that could be taught and that students could be instructed through formal courses in sermon composition at Scottish universities. Leechman's lectures attracted large numbers of students, not just from Scotland but from England and Ireland, itself a signal that divinity students were willing to learn the craft of sermon-writing.

In Edinburgh, training in sermon-writing was continued by John Stevenson who held the Chair of Logic and Metaphysics (to which the teaching of rhetoric was assigned) from 1730 to 1775. He gave lectures on the cardinal points of criticism in which he gave instruction on the rules of composition with examples and critical comment. Divinity students attended Stevenson's classes since it was a requirement for candidates for the ministry of the Church of Scotland to have completed a course in philosophy before enrolling for the divinity class. Stevenson's lectures were highly influential and many ministers who became eminent in the Church of Scotland, including Alexander (Jupiter) Carlyle, Thomas Somerville, William Robertson, and Hugh Blair, subsequently reflected on the influence of Stevenson's lectures and the gain they received from them. Although he was not an innovator like Hutcheson, Stevenson instilled in his students 'a relish for works of taste, and a love of elegant composition' ('Account of the Public Life and Character': 76).

Equally influential were the lectures by Adam Smith, first in Edinburgh and then in Glasgow, where he gave the Logic course in 1751 and succeeded to the Chair of Moral Philosophy the following year. Robert Watson and Hugh Blair succeeded Smith as lecturer in Logic at Edinburgh in 1756 and 1759 respectively. In his lectures Smith was primarily concerned with developing a style of composition that was plain and simple. He advised students to guard against having more than five subordinate propositions when composing a piece of writing since the human mind could not easily comprehend numbers in excess of five. Apart from these comments, Smith's lectures do not contain specific references to sermon-writing although many of the points he discusses could equally well apply to composing sermons. Smith's lectures are important because they deal not only with morality but also with criticism and taste. In this, he was central to the movement by which rhetoric ceased to be interpreted as a narrow discipline and became expanded in scope to encompass concepts of literature, taste and literary criticism.

Another very influential figure was William Wishart the Younger, minister of New Greyfriars and later appointed Principal of the University of Edinburgh in 1741. As Principal, Wishart took a keen interest in the progress of divinity students and, unlike his predecessors, he made a practice of attending classes and listening to and criticizing students' essays. He suggested that as an exercise they should make extracts of the best sentiments of sermon-writers such as Tillotson and translate them into a different form of English. His interest in composing sermons was further encouraged by his attendance at literary clubs. He was, for example, a member of the Rankenian Society which debated religious topics. Many of these Moderate figures had to steer a delicate course between advocating the breadth of thought that they considered appropriate to a forward-looking Church of Scotland while at the same time remaining within the bounds of orthodoxy. This continued to be a constant source of criticism from the Evangelical side of the Church.

After the last Jacobite Rising in 1745 and the aftermath of Culloden in 1746, greater political stability ensued in Scotland. Coupled with expanding commercial prosperity, a desire arose for a revised interpretation of the aims of man. The transition from a stern to a more generous vision of man and to the doctrines of benevolence, charity, and candour began to gain acceptance within society. Religion began to be seen as a binding force connecting men together in society.

An important step forward was the appointment of Hugh Blair to the newly founded Chair of Rhetoric at Edinburgh in 1762. As part of his syllabus Blair included lectures on the eloquence of the pulpit and its improvement. His lecture on the eloquence of the pulpit set down as the four criteria of a good sermon: just sentiments; a proper order of sentiments; elegance of style; and novelty. Blair's lectures are important since they were the first in Scotland to lay particular stress on the part that the sensibilities and the emotions had to play in persuasive oratory. They also equated the concept of taste with a central code of goodness. To Blair, the principal aim of preaching was a moral one and to him a man must be a good man to be a good preacher. He was sympathetic to Adam Smith's views on simplicity of style. However, he was opposed to sermons being read in pulpits, a practice which he considered had contributed to the poor standards of Scottish pulpit oratory. In this, however, he was out of touch with contemporary thinking since by mid-century the reading of sermons had become generally accepted practice among Moderate preachers. In his own lectures, Blair's models were those of the French school, including Bourdaloue, Massillon, Fénélon, and, in particular, Bossuet whom Blair regarded as the most 'nervous and sublime' of all preachers (Blair: 3:13). Blair saw a close link between rhetorical improvement and the polite society, and between sensibility and good taste and moral excellence. No man could be eloquent who was not virtuous.

In his 'Treatise on Taste' Robert Wallace gave an assessment of the eloquence of the Scottish pulpit. In his view it was deficient in good taste, and he offered guidelines for raising its quality and its reputation. Wallace's views were very similar to those of his contemporaries: he emphasized the need for unity in sermon design; the sermon should be adapted to the needs of its audience; and he stressed simplicity of language and style. How Wallace differed was in the precise language in which he defined the aim of preaching. He accepted that the primary aim of the preacher was to reform men but he wanted preachers to combine religious principles with realism and a practical understanding of how mankind behaved. He thought that preachers should inculcate industry, honesty, and contentment in the poor and encourage the wealthy to exercise humility, humanity, and generosity to their inferiors. He advised that 'a judicious instructor will not deliver a wild and visionary system...but will be contented to prove that external advantages are much less important to happiness than is commonly imagined' (Wallace: 609).

At the same time as Hugh Blair was launching his Edinburgh lectures, James Beattie was beginning to lecture in Aberdeen where he had succeeded Alexander Gerard in the Chair of Moral Philosophy and Logic in 1760. A set of Beattie's lectures is in Aberdeen University Library. The lectures underline that to have good taste one must be a good man; and they include a lecture on reading in public and one on speaking in public. Alexander Gerard, who was appointed to the Chair of Divinity in Marischal College, Aberdeen in 1760, won the Select Society prize that year for his 'Essay on Taste'. In his lectures he set out the characteristics necessary for ministers: 'The most important qualifications...are those of the heart. Sincere desire for goodness, a good heart, with a moderate degree of understanding & parts will enable a minister to do much greater service in the church than higher abilities with a vicious character would' (Gerard: f. 318). He classified the aims of preaching as belonging to one or other of these categories: to instruct, to convince, to please, or move or persuade. He assembled the classes of sermons that fulfilled these aims as instructive sermons, probatory sermons, panegyrics, and persuasive sermons. Gerard's successor in the Chair of Divinity in Marischal College in 1771 was George Campbell, who on his arrival in Aberdeen founded a literary club. George Skene Keith described how he had received an account of the club from Campbell where there was often talk of pulpit eloquence. Campbell was also a founding member of the Philosophical Society of Aberdeen (1758), which gave him a ready platform for rehearsing his lectures on pulpit eloquence, later published in *The Philosophy of Rhetoric* in 1776.

The evidence that most of the improving ideas on preaching were being produced by men like Leechman, Blair, Campbell, Stevenson, and Gerard suggests that shifts in the role of preaching and the sermon were closely related to developments in eighteenth-century Scottish universities. By this period a number of significant figures were combining dual functions as university teachers and ministers of the Church. As teachers, they were well equipped to absorb and present their students with the new conventions of taste and morality; and as preachers, they had a ready-made platform from which to disseminate these new ideas to their congregations. They were also in a strong position to influence the character of the Church of Scotland. They could wield influence on doctrine through their supervision of the divinity course but they could also exert organizational influence since, unlike other ministers, they were automatically returned year after year to the General Assembly of the Church of Scotland. The universities provided a useful platform for ideas on the progress of society; and the pulpit offered a convenient rostrum from which to air these views publicly and to maximum effect. The pulpit in Scotland was well positioned to fulfil the role of catalyst for improving ideas since adherence to it was strong and its influence was still extensive. It was the single guaranteed position in Scottish society from which a firm hold on public opinion could be obtained and from which public weekly addresses could regularly be made. The Moderates in the Church of Scotland believed that the end of preaching was the improvement of man. Preachers began to see that in an age of improvement the pulpit was well placed actively to assist. In his sermon to the Society in Scotland for the Propagating of Christian Knowledge, David Plenderleath made this point explicitly: 'Such is the friendly harmony and agreement betwixt religion and learning...they conspire together to promote the good of society' (Plenderleath: 15). By 1785 the *Edinburgh Magazine or Literary Miscellany* noted with pride that in Scottish preachers 'we have now a few whose compositions equal even those that are the most respectable pulpit orators of any establishment in Christendom' (R: 230–1).

Treatises on Sermons

In addition to new thinking in Scottish universities, Scottish preachers also drew on contemporary treatises on preaching and sermon composition. Robert Dodsley's *The Art of Preaching* was published by the Foulis Press in Glasgow in 1746. A few years later, *Theodorus: a Dialogue Concerning the Art of Preaching* by David Fordyce, Professor of Moral Philosophy in Aberdeen, was posthumously published in 1752 by his brother, James Fordyce. Fordyce's treatise was a dialogue between Philonous, the questor, Agoretes, a student of divinity, and Theodorus, 'the best Model of Preaching, and the noblest Example of Living' (Fordyce: 81). Fordyce's thesis was that preaching depended more on taste and sentiment than on reasoning and rules. He advocated a complete break with the earlier tradition of textual division and sub-division which, he argued, fractured the sermon into a series of parts and destroyed the overall effect for the congregation. James Fordyce published his own essay on *The Eloquence of the Pulpit* in 1752 as an appendix to his brother's *Theodorus*. He classified the natural talents of preachers as a sound and clear understanding, a warm and lively imagination, a retentive memory, and a natural elocution or gift of utterance. Among the acquired skills Fordyce listed were knowledge of religion, knowledge of the Scriptures, knowledge of men, and a competent knowledge of books.

In 1750 Fénélon's *Dialogues Concerning Eloquence* were published by the Foulis Press in Glasgow; and Charles Rollin's *Method of Teaching and Studying the Belles Lettres* was issued in Edinburgh in 1759, the year in which Hugh Blair began his lectures. Rollin's method, which included a discussion of pulpit eloquence, had a significant influence in Scotland. It was commended by Hugh Blair, and John Erskine noted that the flimsy taste of Scottish preachers had been checked 'by the translation of Fénélon and Rollin's writings, and the just sentiments of eloquence which they inculcated' (Erskine: 455). Jean Claude's *Essay on the Composition of a Sermon* was also a popular manual in Scotland. It had been translated by Robert Robinson, a Baptist minister in Cambridge, who paid a visit to Scotland in 1780 and met many of the literati, including William Robertson, the historian. However, Claude's *Essay* was known to Hugh Blair and to other Scots *literati* in the original French. S. T. Sturtevant points to its influence on Blair's sermons: 'It is supposed that Dr Blair, of Edinburgh, obtained his high reputation, which spread over both Scotland and England, by adopting the rules of that celebrated Essay' (Sturtevant: 1:3).

The Influence of Scottish Sermons

In addition to the influence of university teachers and treatises, sermons themselves were a vehicle for conveying ideas on preaching in Scotland. This practice first appears from the 1730s with the publication of James Dick's *Duties of a Minister of the Gospel* (1732); William Leechman's *The Temper, Character and Duty of a Minister of the Gospel* (1741), which had run into six editions by 1755; John Erskine's *The Qualifications Necessary for Teachers of Christianity* (1750); George Campbell's *The Character of a Minister of the Gospel as Teacher and Pattern* (1752); and Robert Traill's *The Qualifications and Decorum of a Teacher of Christianity Considered* (1755). It is important to observe that there is very little discussion of language in these sermons. Sermons in the pulpit continued to be delivered in Scots but in preparing sermons for the press there was a noticeable move away from the use of Scots. The desire was to refine the content and style of printed sermons, and this was considered synonymous with the use of English. This may have been a deliberate policy in that sermons delivered in the pulpit were intended to maintain a broad and popular base within congregations while printed sermons were now competing for a more specialized and demanding market. The English poet Samuel Rogers complained that in the pulpit Hugh Blair's 'broad Scotch accent offended my ears greatly' (Rogers: 46). Henry Cockburn refers to John Erskine's language in the pulpit as 'good honest natural Scotch' (Cockburn: 54-5). Alexander Carlyle is one of very few Church of Scotland ministers in the eighteenth century to draw attention to the desirability of substituting English for the vernacular in the pulpit (Carlyle: 8).

The Highlands and Gaelic

In 1709 the Society in Scotland for the Propagation of Christian Knowledge was established with the purpose of spreading knowledge of the Scriptures through the Highlands. The Highlands was Gaelic-speaking and in the eighteenth century it was a part of Scotland that was to a large extent still unknown. The New Testament in Gaelic was first published by Balfour, Auld, and Smellie in Edinburgh in 1767. The translator was the Reverend James Stewart of Killin, assisted by the poet Dugald Buchanan. Ten thousand copies were printed, and many of them were distributed free to Gaelic-speaking parishes in Scotland. The Old Testament was published in four volumes over the period 1783 to 1801 by William Smellie in Edinburgh. Dr Stuart of Luss undertook the translation of the first, third, and fourth volumes and the Reverend Dr Smith from Campbeltown the second volume. In spite of attempts to introduce English, preaching in the pulpit in Gaelic-speaking Scotland was mainly in Gaelic but there was no eighteenth-century tradition of sermon publication in Gaelic. It was not until the end of the century that the first sermons in Gaelic (*Searmoin, a Chuaidh a Liobhairt aig an Raft-Swamp*) by the Reverend Dugald Crawford were published in 1791, not in Scotland but by Sibley, Howard and Roulstone in Fayetteville in North Carolina in the United States. During the eighteenth century the staple reading material was Gaelic translations of the works of Evangelical divines, including Richard Baxter's *Gairm an Dé mhóir do'n sluagh neimh-iompoichte* (*Call to the Unconverted to Turn and Live*) (1750); Joseph Alleine's *Earail dhurachdach do pheacaich neo-iompaichte* (*Alarm to the Unconverted*) (1781);William Guthrie's *Còir mhòr a Chriosduidh* (*The Christian's Great Interest*) (1783); and John Willison's *Leabhar-ceist na màthair* (*The Mother's Catechism*) (1758) and his *Eisempleir shoilleir ceasnnuighe air leabhar aithghearr nan ceist* (*An Example of Plain Catechising upon the Assembly's Shorter Catechism*) (1773).

The Influence of Eighteenth-Century Theological Clubs

Theological clubs were of significant benefit to reforming preachers in eighteenth-century Scotland. The terms 'club' and 'society' were to a large extent synonymous with ideas of moral, cultural and economic improvement. Clubs enabled members to examine and discuss theoretical ideas and sharpen their wits by constant debate; and the clubs' affairs were always conducted in English. There were specialist clubs in the fields of literature, philosophy, and criticism, all of which were well-attended by the clergy, but there were also specialist theological clubs where all the religious issues of the day were debated. A Theological Club was set up in Edinburgh in 1759 and continued until 1764. Thomas Somerville, who attended it, contended that it was 'a school of improvement' and a 'nursery of brotherly love and kind affection'. A second Theological Club was founded in Edinburgh in 1776 for ministers and divinity students, primarily to discuss topics of interest to students. In 1785 the Adelpho-Theological Society was founded in Edinburgh with the stated aim of 'improvement in the composition and delivery of pulpit discourses' (Matheson: *passim*). Each meeting of the Society included two sermons and members were not allowed to deliver discourses that had already been given at the Divinity Hall or in the Church History class.

The Printed Sermons of Hugh Blair

Hugh Blair was by far the most successful sermon-writer in eighteenth-century Scotland. When he first approached William Strahan with a proposal to publish his sermons he received a rather cool response, but the publisher took the precaution of sending the sermons to Samuel Johnson, whose favourable opinion was instrumental in advancing their publication. Most eighteenth-century Scottish sermons were published with few realistic hopes of commercial success and Blair's own initial approach was a cautious bid for a small edition in order to assess its commercial prospects. In 1776, Alexander Kincaid, publisher and H M Printer in Scotland, offered Blair £100 for an edition of sermons to be jointly undertaken by Kincaid and Strahan. On Kincaid's death in 1777, William Creech took over the task, and the first volume appeared in 1777 under the imprint of Creech, Strahan, and Cadell. Although Blair described his sermons as of the 'sentimental sort' when he first submitted them to Strahan, he rapidly demonstrated his acute business sense in negotiating tough contracts with his publishers. By August 1779, Blair was busily engaged on preparing his second volume, with the aim of going to press in January 1780. In June 1790, with commercial success assured by the publication of the first two volumes, Blair wrote to Thomas Cadell pointing out that men of taste considered his third volume published to be his best; and in October 1793, Blair informed Thomas Cadell that he was preparing a fourth volume of sermons, which appeared in 1794. The fifth and final volume was published in 1801. Blair's published sermons had outstanding success in their day, both at home and abroad. In America, the *Sermons* had run into their sixteenth edition by 1792. His *Select Sermons* were published in New York by Hodge, Allen & Campbell and sold at their several bookstores. Blair's success was equally great at home: in his *Memoirs* in 1827, the bookseller James Lackington commented: 'Sherlock's Sermons had a very great sale, as had Dr White's and many others, but none ever sold as well as Dr Blair's, and the sale of them is as great as ever' (Lackington: 221).

Blair gave careful attention to preparing his sermons. In the *Tour to the Hebrides* James Boswell recorded that Robert Watson, Blair's predecessor as lecturer in Rhetoric, had told Samuel Johnson that it took Blair a week to compose a sermon (Boswell 1963: 45); and the anonymous author of *Letters on Dr Blair's Sermons* referred to the 'long-laboured revisal of the author' (*Letters*: 5). Blair circulated his sermons in manuscript to his literary colleagues in 1776 for advice but he still wrote to his publisher Strahan: 'If your corrector be a good judge of language, and if he notices any thing he takes to be a Scoticism or an impropriety, let him mark it on the Margin with a q- and I shall attend to it' (Schmitz: 82).

In addition to the sermons of distinguished *literati* such as Blair, Alexander Carlyle, Alexander Gerard, and James Beattie, large numbers of individual parish ministers published sermons, or selections from sermons, which had usually first been delivered in the pulpit. It was also common to publish occasional sermons delivered on public 'occasions'. Benefit sermons were often published for a deceased minister's widow and children, usually edited by the minister's colleagues and friends. This practice was fairly widespread in the eighteenth century, as a glance at prefaces will reveal. Sermons on political subjects were also very common: John Erskine's *Shall I go to War with my American Brethren* and *The Equity and Wisdom of Administration: in Measures that have Unhappily Occasioned the American Revolt*, both published in 1776, are examples of these. James Murray in his satire *Sermons to Asses* complained: 'There are now sermons to young men; and sermons to young women... Almost every subject is exhausted and sermonized to death' (Murray: v–vi).

Evangelical Sermons

While the Moderate wing of the Church of Scotland developed its new ideas, the Evangelical quarter of the Church remained irrevocably opposed: to them these ideas were the harbinger of decline in the national church. Decline in the Church would be closely followed by decline in national prosperity. Evangelical preachers saw themselves as 'preservers of the faith'. In 1733 a group of ministers headed by Ebenezer and Ralph Erskine left the Church of Scotland to form the Secession Church, an act which reinforced the Evangelical wing's determination to adhere to the past in opposition to modern ideas and philosophies. They had a brief flirtation with the Methodists in the wake of the Methodist movement which swept through Lowland Scotland. George Whitefield was invited to Scotland in 1741 by the Secession Church but it was very shortly discovered that there was little common ground between them.

Evangelicals roundly criticized the printed sermons of Moderates, and sought instead to get their own into print. Unlike Moderate sermons, there was very little difference between Evangelical sermons delivered in the pulpit and their printed versions. This was deliberate: printed sermons of this period often carry a note in the preface explaining that no attempt has been made to polish or refine the sermon for the press. James Ramsay stated that 'Elegance and refinement made no part of his design, and may not therefore be expected. He meant to say plain things, without affected ornaments' (Ramsay: iii). In his preface John Ker stated triumphantly, 'If the reader expects in the following pages elegance of composition, and a display of the powers of oratory, or if he expects a philosophical harangue, he will be disappointed' (Ker: iv).

Evangelical sermons followed a standard format comprising a number of heads which were sub-divided in turn. Sermon style was cumbersome and prolix but the content could sometimes be dramatic and imaginative. The sermons of Samuel Rutherford and Alexander Peden were frequently reprinted throughout the eighteenth century with the addition of the sermons of later preachers such as Thomas Boston and Ebenezer and Ralph Erskine.

The attraction of these sermons was that although their structure was complex, the imagery was simple and easily understood by formally uneducated but spiritually edified congregations. In terms of training, eighteenth-century Evangelicals drew their inspiration from their own and their predecessors' sermons, but in 1736 the Associate Presbytery appointed William Wilson of Perth to teach theology and the Theological Academy organized itself to provide formal training for student ministers of the Associate Synod. Sermons were generally written down but were then committed to memory and delivered extempore: they were never read.

Throughout the eighteenth century Evangelical opposition to the refined sermons of the Moderates did not waver. In his 1753 *Ecclesiastical Characteristics* John Witherspoon set out the *credo* of the new Moderates in society (Witherspoon: 211). For Moderate preachers, the sermon had to reflect contemporary changes in the canons of taste in Scottish society. Where the prevailing view was in the essential virtue of man, it was logical that sermons should shift from the older concepts of reward and punishment to stressing the benefits of virtue. As was said of Hugh Blair's sermons, they 'lighted things up so finely, and you get such comfortable answers' (Boswell 1928–1937: 7:16–17). Sermons stressed the positive virtues of benevolence, charity and candour, which were later to become the armour of the sentimental movement in Scotland. By 1803 the *Scots Magazine* commented on the improvement in sermon quality between 1742 and 1798 that, 'At the former period, sermons abounded with diffuse illustrations, and were disgraced with colloquial phrases, and vulgar provincialisms. In these later years, pulpit composition has attained a dignity and elegance of which our forefathers had no conception' ('Account of the Public Life and Character': 78). At the same time, of course, Evangelical preachers continued to criticize what John Howie of Lochgoin described as the Moderates' 'flights of fancy and terms of art, pronounced in a South British accent' (Howie: xxvi).

By the end of the eighteenth century the Moderates still held sway, but the zenith had passed and by the 1830s the situation in Scotland had changed very significantly. In 1834 the Moderates lost control of the General Assembly to the Evangelicals, who then set about transforming the whole basis of the Church of Scotland, leading in due course to the Disruption of 1843 when a third of ministers, mostly young men, left to form the Free Church of Scotland. As the century continued, the Church of Scotland faced continuing erosion of the Calvinism on which it was based and increased competition from other denominations. There was a rise in the number of Methodists, Baptists, and Congregationalists; the influence of the Episcopal Church increased; and the Catholic Church was resurgent following the arrival of large numbers of people from Ireland to work in Scottish mills and factories. In addition, the Church of Scotland was under pressure from competing calls on people's leisure time and from the effects of social pressures. By the end of 1880s the Church of Scotland was in a state of flux and Scotland was no longer uniform in its religious allegiance.

NINETEENTH-CENTURY SERMONS

In nineteenth-century Scotland, the sermon continued to be the central tenet of worship in the Church of Scotland but more and more it was great oratory that drew the crowds. As the power of the Evangelicals increased there was much greater emphasis on extempore sermons and as a result printed sermons no longer formed a very reliable source for the preaching of the day. For many, listening to great preachers was often the only form of entertainment available to them. The Free Church of Scotland had exceptional preachers in men like Thomas Chalmers, Thomas Guthrie, Robert Scott Candlish, James Begg, John Caird, and Norman MacLeod.

Thomas Chalmers (1780–1847) read his sermons but with great effect. His most popular sermon was *The Expulsive Power of a New Affection*. John Caird's most outstanding sermon was *Religion in the Common Life*, which was preached before Queen Victoria in 1855, and was frequently reprinted. In comparison, the United Presbyterian Church, for example, legislated to prevent the reading of sermons in order to maintain a high standard of popular preaching. As the century progressed, the need for ministers to have excellent pastoral abilities began to eclipse the former emphasis on good preaching.

In the early decades of the nineteenth century, the Evangelical movement had begun to manifest itself in the Highlands, possibly as Highland people retreated into religion following the major historical vicissitudes that had afflicted Highland society in the aftermath of the Jacobite Risings. This would be further accelerated in the nineteenth century through widespread emigration, some of it forced, and severe penury through bad harvests. The Evangelistic tours of the Perthshire-born Robert and James Haldane had a very significant effect in the Highlands and Islands and this was extended by later revivals.

The number and the themes of nineteenth-century sermons in Scotland were very extensive. Sermons were preached on contemporary social evils such as strong drink and in support of the temperance movement. Numerous sermons were preached on the ideas behind the Disruption and the principles of the Free Church of Scotland. Occasional sermons such as funeral sermons and ordination and farewell sermons for ministers were commonplace, as were sermons to mark public events.

By the end of the nineteenth century, the Church of Scotland had lost a large part of its influence and the Church as a whole had become fragmented and schismatic. The publication in 1880 of *Scotch Sermons* by a group of thirteen Church of Scotland ministers led by the Reverend John Caird was a significant moment since in this volume they set out to chart the direction of the Church's current thinking. Over the decades the Church had to try to adjust to scientific and critical attacks on its traditional beliefs and practices and *Scotch Sermons* set out the extent to which the Church was prepared to compromise.

References

'Account of the Public Life and Character of the Late Dr Erskine, of Edinburgh'. (1803). *Scots Magazine* 65: 76–86.
Advertisement for *A Practical Essay on the Death of Jesus Christ*, By William McGill, D.D. (1775). *Critical Review* 66: 580.
Blair, H. (1801). *Lectures on Rhetoric and Belles Letters*. Paris: James Decker.
Boswell, J. (1928–37). *Private Papers of James Boswell from Malahide Castle*, ed. G. Scott and F. A. Pottle. New York: privately printed.
—— (1963). *Journal of a Tour to the Hebrides*. New York: privately printed.

Bruce, A. (1774). *The Kirkiad; or, Golden Age of the Church of Scotland*. Edinburgh: W. Drummond.

Burnet, G. (1692). *A Discourse of the Pastoral Care*. London: R. Chiswell.

Burt, E. (1759). *Letters from a Gentleman in the North of Scotland to his Friend in London...* London: J. Pottinger.

Carlyle, A. (1793). *The Usefulness and Necessity of a Liberal Education for Clergymen*. Edinburgh: William Creech.

Cockburn, H. (1856). *Memorials of His Time*. Edinburgh: A. and C. Black.

Erskine, J. (1798). 'The Character of the Late Principal Robertson'. *The Edinburgh Magazine or Literary Miscellany*, new series 11: 452–9.

Fordyce, D. (1752). *Theodorus: a Dialogue Concerning the Art of Preaching*, ed. J. Fordyce. London: R. Dodsley.

Gerard, A. (n. d.). 'Dr Gerard's Lectures upon Theology'. Aberdeen University Library, MS. K.174.

Graham, H. G. (1901). *Scottish Men of Letters in the Eighteenth Century*. London: A. and C. Black.

Howie, J. (1779). *A Collection of Lectures and Sermons*. Glasgow: John Howie.

Hutcheson, F. (1725). *An Inquiry into the Original of our Ideas of Beauty and Virtue*. London: J. Darby.

—— (1728). *An Essay on the Nature and Conduct of the Passions and Affections*. London: J. Darby and T. Browne.

Ker, J. (1775). *Obedient Believers the Friends of Christ*. Glasgow: Robert Chapman and Alexander Duncan.

Lackington, J. (1827). *Memoirs of the Forty-Five First Years of James Lackington, Bookseller...* London: James Lackington.

Lees, J. C. (1881). *Stronbuy: or, Hanks of Highland Yarn*. Edinburgh: MacNiven & Wallace.

Letters on Dr Blair's Sermons. (1779). Edinburgh: n. p.

Matheson, A. (1995). *Theories of Rhetoric in the 18th-century Scottish Sermon*. Lampeter: Edwin Mellen Press.

Maury, A. (1793). *The Principles of Eloquence...*, trans. J. N. Lake. London: T. Cadell and C. Dilly.

Murray, J. (1800). *Sermons to Asses*, 6th edn. Paisley: R. Smith.

Peden, A. (1682). *The Lord's Trumpet Sounding an Alarm against Scotland by Warning of a Bloody Sword*. Glenluce: Alexander Peden.

Plenderleath, D. (1754). *Religion a Treasure to Men, and the Strength and Glory of a Nation: A Sermon*. Edinburgh: Hamilton, Balfour and Neill.

R. (1785). 'An Improvement Proposed'. *The Edinburgh Magazine, or Literary Miscellany*. 1: 230–1.

Rainy, R. (1872). *Three Lectures on the Church of Scotland*. Edinburgh: John Maclaren.

Ramsay, J. (1781). *The Character of the True Minister of Christ Delineated: a Sermon*. Glasgow: J. Bryce.

Reid, H. M. B. (1923). *The Divinity Professors in the University of Glasgow, 1640–1903*. Glasgow: Maclehose, Jackson & Co.

Review of *Sermons on Practical Subjects*, by Robert Walker. (1766). *Critical Review* 22: 392–3.

Review of *Sermons on Various Subjects*, by John Farquhar. (1772). *Scots Magazine* 34: 488.

Rogers, S. (1887). *The Table Talk of Samuel Rogers*. New York: D. Appleton & Co.

Schmitz, R. (1948). *Hugh Blair*. New York: Kings Crown Press.

The Scotch Presbyterian Eloquence: or, the Foolishness of the Teaching Discovered from their Books, Sermons and Prayers. (1692). London: Randall Taylor.

Scott, W. R. (1900). *Francis Hutcheson*. Cambridge: University Press.

Shaftesbury, Lord. (1711). *Characteristicks of Men, Manners, Opinions, Times.* London: n. p.

Sturtevant, S. T. (1834). *The Preacher's Manual…* London: Richard Baynes.

Wallace, R. (1770). 'Treatise on Taste'. Edinburgh University Library, MS. Dc.1.55.

Witherspoon, J. (1754). *Ecclesiastical Characteristics…* Glasgow: n. p.

CHAPTER 10

THE SERMON AND POLITICAL CONTROVERSY IN IRELAND, 1800–1850

IRENE WHELAN

In the annals of Ireland's long record of denominational conflict, the first half of the nineteenth century was remarkable for sectarian controversy. At its core was the centuries-old dispute between Protestantism and Rome, given a new lease of life by the revolutionary upheaval of the late eighteenth century and the demands of the Catholic Irish for political equality. Conducted mainly through journalistic and oratorical combat, this long drawn out ideological conflict had profound and lasting consequences. Since religious affiliation, belief, and practice were at the heart of the issue, it is no surprise that the sermon became a prime instrument for the dissemination of impassioned views on both sides of the denominational divide. When the Emancipation campaign began to gather force in the 1820s, the lines between religion and politics became increasingly blurred. Preaching became even more highly politicized and enormously significant in shaping the political culture that evolved around the issue of equality for Catholics. Whether it took place in a church or a public platform, preaching provided an ideal opportunity for the most committed, and often the most extreme, exponents of the rival churches to engage in fiery rhetoric as they exchanged opinions on everything from ecclesiastical history to political economy. This chapter considers the role of the sermon as a conduit through which religion was inserted into the political debate in Ireland and its contribution to the growth of sectarianism and political polarization.

The sheer volume of sermons and sermon-related commentary in print is the most obvious testimony to the importance of preaching in Irish religious life during the period under review. Important and well-publicized sermons received immediate coverage in national and provincial newspapers, they were commented on in the literary reviews, and printed and sold in pamphlet form as well as in collected volumes. The most popular preachers enjoyed celebrity status, and their printed sermons could be extremely lucrative for the publishing houses that held the rights to their work in print. Accounts of preaching tours and biographies of famous preachers were also staples of the reading public long into the nineteenth century. The task of the scholar in search of a starting point from which to unravel the mountain of material that has survived from this period, mercifully, is facilitated by the significance of one particular sermon that stands above the rest as an identifier of the moment when religion became the dominating issue in Irish political life. This is what became known as the famous 'antithetical' sermon; it was technically a 'charge' following a sermon, delivered by Archbishop William Magee at his inauguration as Archbishop of Dublin on 24 October 1822. Its importance as a watershed moment was recognized immediately by contemporaries and its place in the history of Protestant–Catholic relations has assumed legendary proportions. One historian, Desmond Bowen, has gone so far as to call it a 'declaration of religious war' (Bowen: xi). Its contemporary significance was perhaps best captured by Richard Lalor Shiel, next to O'Connell the most important organizer in the Catholic Association and a playwright of talent besides. In a witty vignette in which he had Archbishop Magee taken to Clongowes College to undergo an exorcism in order to rid him of the 'Devil of Polemics' Shiel, describing the condition of the country since Magee had issued his famous charge, lamented that

> ...all religions have gone amiss
> Since he flung his fierce antithesis
> If discord rages through the land
> If controversy's furious band
> From north to south and east to west
> The country with their howls infest
> The doctor has the fearful merit
> Of having raised this frantic spirit
> That long has set, and will for years
> Still set the people by the ears.
>
> (Fitzpatrick: 2:22–3)

As a preacher Magee was famous for his use of antithesis as a rhetorical device, and he made liberal use of it in his description of the two other traditions on the island (Presbyterian and Roman Catholic) which he described in the following language:

> We, my Rev Brethren, are placed in a station in which we are hemmed in by two opposite descriptions of Christians: the one possessing a Church without what *we* can call a religion, and the other possessing a Religion without what *we* can call a Church: the one so blindly enslaved as to suppose infallible Ecclesiastical authority, as not to seek in the Word of God a reason for the faith they possess; the other so confident in the infallibility of their individual judgment as to the reasons of their faith that they deem it their duty to resist all authority in matters of religion. We, my Brethren, are to keep free of both extremes, and holding the Scriptures as our great charge, whilst we maintain the liberty with which Christ has made us free, we are to submit ourselves to the

authority to which he has made us subject. From this spirit of tempered freedom and qualified submission sprung the glorious work of the Reformation, by which the Church of these countries, having thrown off the slough of slavish superstition, burst into the purified form of Christian renovation. (Magee: 22)

Leaving aside the intemperate and provocative language used to describe Catholics and Presbyterians, it was the substance of his famous charge—that the Church of Ireland should assert its claim as a national church because it alone could claim apostolical succession—that really caused the furore. In the controversy that followed he expressed surprise at the response to his sermon, claiming he had said nothing he had not said publicly many times before, and that furthermore such opinions were common currency among the Protestant community. In this he was correct. What his charge represented, in retrospect, was a vision of Protestant Ireland that had been taking shape since the early years of the century and was now being expressed in a coherent form by the head of the Dublin archdiocese in the hallowed confines of St Patrick's Cathedral. It was a synthesis that had developed over the previous two decades and reflected the changed circumstances of the Irish Protestant world since the passing of the Act of Union of 1800.

Less attention has been paid to the religious than to the political terms of the Act of Union, but in some ways the religious dimension was the more important, especially in the years immediately following 1800. Besides providing for the union of the two parliaments, the Act had also brought about an ecclesiastical union between the Church of England and the Church of Ireland. For Ireland's Protestant population this meant that they were now an integral part of a United Kingdom, a single administrative unit populated overwhelmingly by their co-religionists. Where formerly they had been a minority in a 'sister kingdom'—albeit one in which, as a landowning aristocracy, they had enjoyed an iron grip on the country's political life—now they were part of an ascendant empire that was bracingly assertive both of its religious identity and its status as a great international power. The first twenty years of the new century in consequence witnessed a surge of confidence among the laity, and especially the clergy, of the Church of Ireland, expressed mainly through the growing importance of religion in social and cultural life. The building of new churches and an increase in church attendance was a clear manifestation of this trend, as was the rise of voluntary philanthropy manifested in a multitude of societies designed to improve society through everything from Bible distribution to the education of the poor. In line with the heightened religiosity that came surging back in reaction to the extremes of the French Revolution, the Anglican Church comprising the united churches of England and Ireland now appeared poised to assert its claims to be a truly national church that could assert its influence over the whole population of the British Isles, including the Catholics of Ireland. The various component parts of the kingdom would thus be welded, in the words of Stewart J. Brown, into 'a single Protestant nation-state—homogeneous, benevolent, paternalistic, communal, traditional' (Brown: vii). The appointment of men of vision and commitment to the Irish episcopal bench resulted in the tightening of discipline and improvement in diocesan administration. The Irish Protestant community became more sober and responsible and strongly defensive of its religious tradition, thus enabling the development of a 'distinctly Protestant political culture' that took shape during the first two decades of the century (D'Alton: 55).

Much of the inspiration for the idealism and innovation that took root in the Church of Ireland at this time came from the example set by Methodists and Evangelicals of the Independent churches, especially Baptists and Congregationalists. In the Celtic fringe of Britain, especially in those parts of Wales and Scotland where the vernacular language was used, Methodists and Independent evangelical missionaries had won serious ground at the expense of the Church of England. With an eye on the multitudes of Irish speakers who appeared prime candidates for evangelization, they hoped to repeat the process in Ireland. Such energy and enthusiasm posed a challenge to the Church of Ireland and inspired its most ardent supporters to defend its status as the legally established State Church, as well as its doctrinal purity. The most influential defender of episcopal orthodoxy was the Revd William Phelan (1782–1830) whose famous treatise *The Bible Not the Bible Society* (1817) perfectly captured the self-image of the Church of Ireland: a body that espoused biblical Christianity but kept its distance from the interdenominationalism of the pan-Protestant evangelical movement. A convert from Catholicism, Phelan was well placed to draw on the history of early Christian Ireland to provide historical legitimacy for the claim that the Church of Ireland was the modern inheritor of the mantle of the early Celtic church. He argued that because the Celtic church had remained free of Roman influence until the twelfth century, its pure form of Christianity was more properly represented by the doctrines of the reformed faith (Hill: 25). Nothing evinced the Church of Ireland's aspiration to fulfil its status as a national church more than the intellectual drive to locate its theological origins in the ancient Celtic church of St Patrick and St Columcille.

The great challenge to this vision of historical legitimacy and aspiration to become the *de facto* church of the majority population came not, of course, from the Independents and Methodists, but from the Catholic Church with its implicit claim to the leadership of the majority population who outnumbered Protestants by about four to one. Alongside the Church of Ireland it was on a parallel track of renaissance and renewal at this time, and extremely well positioned to make a claim for its own place in the life of the nation. Following the lifting of the injurious penal laws relating to education in the late eighteenth century, Catholics had been free to open their own colleges and seminaries. French educational pedagogy adapted for the education of the poor was introduced by Nano Nagle whose Presentation Sisters had established a network of girls' schools that were a source of admiration to all observers. Her example was consciously imitated by Edmund Rice, who founded the Irish Christian Brothers in 1802 and introduced the educational philosophy of Jean Baptiste de la Salle (1651–1719) as the basis of his system. Rice typified the sort of personality likely to emerge as a leader of the Catholic community: a wealthy businessman who devoted his life and his resources to building a teaching order to train poor youths for 'useful' trades and middle management (Keogh: 110–15). In the view of the Catholic clergy and the upwardly mobile urban middle classes who were their main supporters, men like Edmund Rice were the natural leaders of the

Catholic 'nation-in-waiting' whose numbers betokened their strength, and their self-confidence their material progress.

Irish Protestants were no less wedded to the vision of education as the great panacea for the country's problems; for advocates of renewal and moral reform, indeed, no cause was more important than the education of the poor. In the first two decades of the nineteenth century, therefore, the relationship between the rival denominations, particularly on the subject of education, resembled two locomotives headed towards a collision. The rivalry might have been managed and a collision avoided if the right balance of state support and toleration for the rights of different denominations to provide for their own religious instruction could somehow have been agreed to. The Quakers who founded the Society for the Education of the Poor (the Kildare Place Society) in 1810 had aspired to create just such a system, and they were successful to a large degree, especially in the acquisition of government money to support the expansion of their schools which were spreading across the country in the second decade of the century. The use of the Protestant Bible in the schools had become a serious issue for Catholics around 1819, however, and the future progress of the Kildare Place system already looked to be in doubt.

Whatever fragile prospect existed of peaceful coexistence between the denominations was blown out of the water by Magee's sermon in 1822. The timing of the event could hardly have been more inopportune. A combination of trends that included a severe economic downturn, agrarian rebellion, and frustrated political ambition among the Catholic population had combined in the early 1820s to produce a dangerous atmosphere in which sectarian division was already pronounced. Stalwarts of polemical discourse like Sir Harcourt Lees and the Revd John MacHale were already in arms, so to speak, stoking the flames of controversy. The actual date on which Magee's charge was delivered, 24 October, was hardly an accident. The date immediately preceding, 23 October, had a powerful resonance in the Irish Protestant calendar. As the date which marked the beginning of the Great Ulster Rebellion in 1641, its imprint in the collective memory of Irish Protestants kept alive the fear of dispossession and massacre. In the eighteenth century the annual commemoration of this event, with its theme of the eternal danger of the Catholic threat and deliverance by a providential God, played a fundamental role in the construction of Irish Protestant national identity (Barnard). In choosing this date Magee was making an implicit statement of survival and triumph that had brought the Church of Ireland to the point where it could now look to completing the Reformation and bringing itself (and the country) into line with the Church of England. The overarching purpose of his charge was to initiate a revolution, what he called on a later occasion 'a glorious Second Reformation', to accomplish in religious culture what the Union had already accomplished politically: the complete integration of Ireland into a United Kingdom in which the Protestant religion formed the bedrock of its value system and way of life.

The implication of Magee's sermon was recognized immediately. The most politically opinionated of the Irish newspapers, the liberal Protestant *Dublin Evening Post*, registered the following opinion on 29 October, less than a week after the event:

> Had this charge, expressed as it was, in no very courteous or measured language, come from an individual less elevated in character and station than Archbishop Magee, it would have passed without any comment from us… That he will be answered by Disciples of Calvin and Knox, we believe… That he will awaken the slumbering Polemics of the Roman Catholic Church in Ireland we apprehend… To us the charge Presents itself as a political document of great importance.

The newspaper editorial was completely accurate in highlighting the danger for an episcopal dignatory like Archbishop Magee to enter the fray of religious controversy. As another of its caustic editorials noted in retrospect the following 24 January: 'Archbishop Magee had given the view hollow, and all the little dogs of the village, Tray, Sweetheart, and the rest, joined in the cry.' However, it was not the small fry rushing out in support of Archbishop Magee's charge who attracted the headlines in the weeks immediately following 24 October, but the entry into the lists of the formidable Catholic Bishop of Kildare and Leighlin, Dr James Doyle, writing under the pen name of 'JKL' (James of Kildare and Leighlin). Doyle had been appointed to the diocese in 1819 at the age of 33 and had already made a name for himself as a defender of Catholic principles and an advocate of the poor. The *Dublin Evening Post* was his newspaper of choice when it came to politics, and it was here that his reply to Magee first appeared on 7 November. The tone of this reply sent shock waves through the religious and political world. In an unapologetic and hard-hitting rhetorical style he landed a sequence of hammer blows against the claims made by Magee on behalf of the Church of Ireland. Beginning with the issue of Church property, Doyle underlined that the Church of Ireland held its possessions in Ireland 'not by deed or conveyance, not… by prescription, not by right of conquest, nor put in possession by any treaty, but held by the law and the law alone… not the Divine Law nor the Law of the Church… *but only by only by virtue of the civil law and that law is penal, and highly penal*'. He then went on to attack its economic foundation which rested on the tithes paid by Catholics to whom it offered nothing in return 'and there is not a peasant in Ireland who does not know, as well as Ulpian, that commutative justice demands that something be given in exchange for what is received'. Finally, as the *coup de grace*, he scorned Magee's claim for universalism on behalf of a Church 'that was not known outside these islands' (Doyle 1822).

The ferocity of Doyle's language and his fearlessness in attacking the establishment was reminiscent of the great propagandists of the revolutionary age, Thomas Paine and the Abbé Sieyes. There is no evidence that he was consciously imitating these giants of an earlier period, whose writings had launched revolutions in America and France. Given his opinion of the French Revolution he would no doubt have repudiated the comparison. Nevertheless, the consequence of his impassioned rhetoric tells its own story. Within a month of publication the printed pamphlet of his reply to Magee went through eight editions (McGrath: 107). And it was only the first of a stream of critical assaults on the establishment of church, state, and society that would flow from his pen in the following year. In all of them, to one degree or another, the defence of Catholic religious principles was conjoined with the cause of the Catholic poor and an attack on what he considered the sources of their oppression: the Protestant landed classes and the

Church of Ireland. In June 1824, by cleverly manipulating a controversy over miracles wrought at long distance by a German Catholic aristocrat, Prince Hohenlohe, he managed at one and the same time to defend the place of mystery in the belief system of Catholicism and to impress the Catholic Irish that their cause was going to prevail because God was on their side. This was so, he assured them, because of all they had suffered and endured for the faith, above all because His church on earth was coming forward as the instrument of their deliverance. He also spelled out that success was going to depend on proper conduct, the use of the constitutional system of government and adherence to the law (Fitzpatrick: 1:251). In November of the same year he produced the famous *Vindication of the Catholics of Ireland*, a lengthy pamphlet which he addressed to the Marquis of Wellesley (Lord Lieutenant for Ireland and brother of the Duke of Wellington) that drew together many of the themes he had dealt with in the previous year. It also marked a critically significant departure from the defensive tone that had characterized his earlier writings towards one that was more pointedly offensive as well as radical.

More than any of his earlier writings, the *Vindication* revealed how dangerously close to the wind Bishop Doyle was willing to sail in his embrace of the ideology of the revolutionary era. His criticism of the Protestant establishment clearly invoked the leading social ideals of the revolutionary period: the principle of 'utility' and the 'career open to talent'. In language frighteningly evocative of Sieyes's celebrated *What Is the Third Estate?* he described the aristocracy as an arrogant and parasitical elite unfit to be leaders of society:

> Their *esprit de corps*—the prejudices which encompass them—their family circumstances—the insolence, often, and immorality of their sons—the pomp and vanity of their wives and daughters –their ephemeral and transitory rank unfit them for the office of gentry. Lighten the pressure on the country, give good and equal laws, and talents and industry will produce a gentry. (Doyle 1823: 38)

Describing the Church of Ireland as an establishment 'as should not be suffered to exist in any civilized country' he claimed it enjoyed its patrimony at the expense of the sufferings and degradation of the Catholic population. Without going so far as to embrace the principles of radical democracy, he reminded the Marquis of the claims of Ireland's six million Catholics:

> do they imagine they can stifle the complaints of six millions of men?... We will never cease, my Lord, whilst our tongues can move, or our pens can write, to keep alive in the whole empire, as well as in our own people, a sense of the wrongs we suffer, and to exhibit to an indignant world, all the privations we endure. Our fetters are too galling, our chains are too closely riveted, our keepers are too unfeeling, for us to remain silent, or permit them to enjoy repose. (Doyle 1823: 4)

What really places Doyle in the same company as Paine and Sieyes, however, is the acuity with which he caught the precise moment in history where his particular analysis of what was needed to effect change galvanized his readers and pointed the entire country in a new and different direction. His concern for social justice was the real driving force behind his political activism. As a self-professed admirer of John Locke and the English constitutional tradition (as opposed to the absolutism he had witnessed in Portugal where he was educated) he believed in state support for education and the provision of a Poor Law. But it was the eternal and immutable truths of universal Catholicism that he looked to as the bedrock of his moral vision, as opposed to the secular philosophy of the radical Enlightenment that had inspired Paine and Sieyes. What he produced in 1822–3 in response to Magee's 'Protestant synthesis' was an alternative synthesis that provided Catholic Ireland with a consciousness of its history, a vindication of its religious tradition, and a sense of its future destiny and how it could be reached. The way forward would be accomplished by faith in the leadership of the Church and adherence to peaceful constitutional action as a means to redress grievances and advance the cause of Catholic freedom. He was, in effect, providing a script for a revolution in Catholic consciousness that was about to unfold, as Sieyes had done with his famous defence of the Third Estate in 1788 (Sewell: 64–5).

The realization of Bishop Doyle's vision began to take shape with the new and radical departure undertaken by the Catholic Association between 1823 and 1826 when Daniel O'Connell refashioned it into an engine of popular mobilization that shook the political world to its foundations. These years saw extraordinary developments in Irish political life. The restructuring of the Catholic Association and its transformation into a mass organization set the stage for the events leading up to the general election in 1826. In the two years before this election a revolution in popular politics took place. People were enrolled in a penny-a-month subscription, the Catholic Rent, collected after Sunday Mass, usually by the local priest. It was a process that united priests and people giving both an investment in the political process. Money thus collected allowed the Association to support candidates in the general election of 1826. Its electoral victories in that year sent a clear message to Westminster that the Catholic Association could repeat this process in every constituency in the country that had a Catholic majority. When the results of the 1826 general election came through, the most telling comment was made by John Jebb, the Church of Ireland Bishop of Limerick, who described the event as something 'we of this generation have never before witnessed...In truth an Irish revolution has in great measure been effected' (Reynolds: 22).In the eighteen-month period before the 1826 election the airing of sectarian arguments in sermons and great public debates played a fundamental role in changing the Irish political landscape. It was a time when preaching broke loose from the traditional mooring of the pulpit and followed the purveyors of religious controversy the length and breadth of the country. In the autumn of 1824 a well-coordinated effort was made to use anniversary meetings of voluntary societies like the Hibernian Bible Society and the Sunday School Society for public debates on the issues that were central to the Protestant–Catholic division, such as the right of private judgement in the interpretation of the scriptures, the use of the Bible in schools, state payment of the clergy, and so on. In cities and towns around the country the public was treated to the spectacle of teams of Protestant clergymen and Catholic priests facing off against each other in debates that could last for hours, and sometimes days, and that were often accompanied by physical violence and the presence of the military. The episode, quickly dubbed the 'Bible War' by the popular press, was clearly planned with a view to drawing the Catholic clergy into debates on religious controversy. The preachers around whose presence the event was organized were Independent evangelicals with strong Scottish connections who were already famous for their anti-Catholic sentiment. 'Baptist' Wriothesley Noel and Captain James Edward Gordon of the Royal Navy arrived in the country in September and made their way from one venue to the next to attend a sequence of public meetings that had already been organized and advertised locally. Christened 'the Scotch Captain' and 'the schoolboy' by the *Freeman's Journal*, their progress lent no end of amusement to the political satirists. At each venue the aim was to invite the local Catholic clergy to engage in a debate on points of controversy between the denominations. The assumption was if the priests stayed away, as was believed would be the case, then the Catholic cause would appear to have lost face. If, on the other hand, the priests did accept, it was assumed that the moral strength of the Protestant position would easily win the day (Whelan: 204).

As it happened, the Catholic clergy not only accepted the invitations but were accompanied in some cases by the most prominent political figures of the day such as Daniel O'Connell and Richard Lalor Shiel. Besides featuring debates on spiritual questions, the lay defenders of the Catholic position ensured that the debates covered major political issues, including the tithe system, the causes of the country's poverty, and especially Catholic Emancipation. O'Connell's manipulation of the opportunity for publicity and support was clearly political. He gloried in lambasting the Protestant establishment for its bigotry and hypocrisy and countered it by promoting the superior moral virtue of the Catholic Irish. Wherever he and his lieutenants decided to appear an audience could be guaranteed. The whole affair lasted three months and received extraordinary coverage in the newspapers. Its impact on political events can hardly be overstated. In one town after another where the 'roving show of controversialists' (as the *Freeman's Journal* caustically described the visiting preachers and their supporters) took their crusade, they were followed by organizers of the Catholic Association who signed up supporters by the hundred. Newspaper coverage provided free publicity that was particularly advantageous to the Catholic clergy if they were considered to have successfully defended their positions in the face of the Protestant challenge (Whelan: 203–4).

The debates of the Bible War clearly worked to mobilize priests and people behind the Catholic Association. A commentary in the *Dublin Evening Post* on 28 September underlined what might be the consequence of the episode:

> We admit that those things are constantly done in pamphlets and newspapers, charges and in sermons; but this is the first time in Ireland or in any country that two sets of orators have been found discussing knotty points of scripture in an aggregate assembly. The Catholics of Ireland, the priests of Ireland, have long been accustomed to outrage and insult; this is the first time that the experiment has been tried of rousing a whole population into madness.

It was not only Catholics who were brought into the camp of O'Connell and the Catholic Association by the debates of the Bible War. Protestant liberals, angered and disgusted at what they considered unprovoked attacks on the Catholic religion, also joined ranks with O'Connell and the Catholic Association. Without their support O'Connell would never have broken the hold of conservative landlords on electoral politics in 1826 (Whelan: 215).

The Bible War also marked the arrival of the controversial sermon as a regular feature of religious and political life in Ireland. Over the following five or six years, roughly between the period of the Bible War and the passing of the Catholic Relief Act of 1829, the practice of controversial sermons spread all over the country. There was no fixed prescription as to form or venue. A controversial sermon could be delivered within the confines of a church by an individual clergyman, or presented in a great public arena like the Rotunda in Dublin. In the provinces, town halls and rural schoolhouses were used if churches were not available. Controversial sermons could be presented in weekly instalments, much like a lecture series, or in public debates between rival preachers, either individually or in teams. The latter were most popular with the public and the press. Their proceedings were often carried verbatim in newspapers and later published in pamphlet form. These great public spectacles between especially gifted orators could be relied upon to attract huge audiences. Preachers capable of these marathon sessions soon acquired the status of champions, long-distance performers who could keep going for hours, and sometimes days, and whose stamina was seen to reflect the strength of the community that backed them. The most famous combatant on the Protestant side was the Revd Richard Pope, who had earned his reputation during the Bible War debates of 1824 in which he debated tirelessly on behalf of the Protestant cause, winning national recognition as a result. Not until 1826 did the Catholics discover a preacher capable of rivalling him in public debate. This was the celebrated Fr Thomas Maguire from County Leitrim, who raised the art of polemic to a new level with his colloquial style and verbal wit. The event that made a national hero of Maguire was a marathon debate with Pope held in the Sackville Institute in Dublin in 1827. Lasting all of six days, it proved to be the most publicized event since the great debates of 1824. It ended in a resounding victory for Maguire, and Pope was said to have lost his health as a result. Maguire went on to fame and notoriety as one of the most famous and memorable of the great Catholic champion preachers, the bane of Protestant contestants and a source of some embarrassment to his own clerical superiors (Whelan: 224–7).

The intensity of the controversial sermons increased with the official launching of the Second Reformation crusade on the estate of Lord Farnham in January of 1827. This was an attempt at giving actual form to the crusade that Archbishop Magee had called for in 1822 and to which he had given a name when he was examined by a government commission in 1825. It was aimed at effecting mass conversions among Catholics and providing a spark that would spread the momentum across the country. The Farnham estate had also been the scene of an experiment in estate management known as the 'moral agency' system, in which the tenants were supervised in their conduct and special attention paid to Bible distribution and education. In the electoral victories won by the Catholic Association in the 1826 election Cavan stood out as the exception, the one place where the landlord was able to hold the fort against a candidate supported by the Catholic Association. The combination of the success of the moral agency system and the defeat of the emancipation candidate in the general election convinced Lord Farnham that the time was ripe to proclaim a Reformation crusade. It was a move that the Catholic clergy could not afford to ignore and the register of sectarian controversy was increased accordingly.

Between 1826 and 1828 as O'Connell and the Catholic Association worked to press home the advantage won at the ballot box, sectarian controversy appeared to have taken over the country's religious life. The regular scheduling of controversial sermons in Protestant churches became widespread. One series begun at Ballymahon in Co. Longford in the spring of 1827 was said to have been 'well attended by Roman Catholics' and another was begun at Newtownmountkennedy in Co. Wicklow in December of the same year (Whelan: 227–8). Thomas McGrath has provided an account of the 'Protestant crusade' as it took place in Carlow (the seat of Bishop Doyle's residence) in January of 1827. Sermons were delivered on eight successive Sundays and controversial discussions organized in the middle of the week. Placards announcing the crusade posted in the surrounding countryside were guarded by the police (McGrath: 135). The overt purpose of the sermons and discussions was to impress the superiority of the Protestant faith, but they made little impact on the local Catholic population beyond arousing anger and indignation. The era was marked by increasing unity among different Protestant denominations. This was not especially remarkable among Baptists and Congregationalists in the southern counties, who had a similar stake with the Church of Ireland in the Reformation crusade. But a note of alarm was sounded in 1827 when the Presbyterian clergy of the north began to take up the practice on the eve of Catholic Emancipation (Whelan: 228). By the time emancipation was won in 1829 the country was divided into two mutually hostile camps. The division would only grow more extreme as Catholics consolidated their success and continued their push for equality in social and economic affairs.

In connection with the spread of controversial sermons in the 1820s, preaching tours became important in the Irish religious landscape. Visiting preachers from England and Scotland had always been a feature of the Irish Protestant world. Now the practice would become more organized as well as more frequent. Within Ireland itself preaching tours were used to mobilize the clergy and the lay congregations in the provinces in defence of the Protestant cause. A famous tour of Munster by the Revd John Gregg in the late 1820s sowed the seeds of local developments that would eventually take shape in missionary installations in the remote Irish-speaking areas of the Dingle and Beara peninsulas. Another significant consequence of this period of religious controversy was the dispatching to England and Scotland of experienced preachers to broadcast news of what was taking place in Ireland. The two most famous personalities connected with this traffic were both Church of Ireland clergymen, the Revd Robert McGhee and the Revd Mortimer O'Sullivan, who began this practice in the late 1820s and continued it through the 1830s. This helped to strengthen a trend where the religious controversy that had enveloped Ireland was now spreading beyond its shores. A popular account of their sermons, *Romanism as it Rules in Ireland* by Mortimer O'Sullivan, brought their exploits as well as their information to audiences on both sides of the Irish Sea.

By the 1830s religious controversy had woven itself into the fabric of national life in Ireland. The themes remained the same as those laid down by Archbishop Magee, primarily that the Anglican Church was the true inheritor of apostolical succession and the Catholic Church the renegade which, though the Council of Trent, had removed itself from the general Christian community. Catholic defenders were much more disposed to underline the loss and degradation suffered by the Irish Catholic Church as a result of conquest and colonization and the depredations of a colonial aristocratic class and its episcopal arm. Inevitably they were also forced to defend Catholic teaching on the proper use of the scriptures and the authority of the Pope in moral and ecclesiastical affairs. It was hardly surprising that the doctrine of papal infallibility received such scrutiny in Ireland, or that an Irish ecclesiastic, Cardinal Paul Cullen, should have made such a contribution to its definition as Catholic dogma later in the century.

In spite of the distaste of Catholic bishops for priests getting involved in religious controversy, there is no disputing that the Protestant challenge forced the Catholic Church to pay more attention to preaching. In the eighteenth century the effects of the penal laws had fostered a cautious attitude among the Catholic priesthood and hierarchy that inhibited the practice of passionate and animated sermons. It is instructive that, of the clergy trained in the classic tradition of French oratory in the eighteenth century, the ones who achieved lasting reputations—Walter Blake Kirwan and Thomas Lewis O'Beirne—were converts to the Church of Ireland. In the 1830s it was the religious orders that tended to fill the breach when it came to the organization of series of sermons. In the urban areas, particularly in Dublin and the larger provincial cities like Waterford and Galway, the religious orders had already been established in the 1820s to counter the effect of proselytizing schools among the urban poor. In the 1830s they began to do the same thing with preaching. Those who initially came to the fore, the Vincentians and the Redemptorists, had established reputations as preaching orders. The first preaching mission outside Dublin was organized by the Vincentians in 1842 in Athy in Co. Kildare. In 1846 they arranged to send a team of preachers to conduct a mission in the town of Dingle, which had gained notoriety as the location of a Protestant colony that was reporting widespread success in winning converts. Before taking up this counter-offensive the Vincentian preachers were trained to use an informal tone of address that would be understood by uneducated country people (Purcell: 115–18). They were to conduct a mission lasting two weeks where all local Catholics would be directed to attend daily Mass and receive the sacraments. This is one of the clearest instances of how Catholic religious practices were shaped by the Protestant challenge. The type of mission that the Vincentians led in Dingle in 1846 became a prototype for the entire country in the post-famine period. Unlike the Station Mass that had its origins in the eighteenth century, the parish mission was a new departure in Irish provincial life. In the period between 1850 and 1875, according to Emmet Larkin, it grew into an institution that became a standard bearer of the Devotional Revolution (Larkin: 29–30). Nothing represented the power of the Catholic Church in the post-famine period so effectively as the Jesuit, Redemptorist, and Vincentian missionaries who introduced the strict Tridentine standards that transformed the culture of rural Irish Catholicism.

A final comment on the role of the sermon in political controversy might be made in relation to the Irish in the international world. As emigration from Ireland increased throughout the 1820s and 1830s the culture of sectarian controversy tended to accompany the emigrants. The substance of the controversy did not change but moved alongside the emigrant current to work itself out on a broader international canvas. The flashpoints of sectarian controversy in Britain and the United States were often linked to what was happening in Ireland. In 1844, for example, it was the uproar over the prospect of the Westminster government increasing its grant to Maynooth that was the root cause of anti-Catholic rioting in Philadelphia. At the height of the potato famine the importance of the sermon as an instrument of religious and political controversy was illustrated to an extraordinary degree in two famous sermons delivered on either side of the Atlantic within weeks of each other. On 28 February 1847 a sermon preached in Liverpool entitled 'The Famine. The Rod of God' by a well-known Anglican evangelical, the Revd Hugh McNeile was responded to within weeks on the other side of the Atlantic. McNeile was married to a daughter of Archbishop William Magee, and shared many of the same leanings as his famous father-in-law. The ostensible purpose of the sermon on this occasion was to raise money for famine relief. However, in accounting for the occurrence of famine at this particular time in Irish history, McNeile stressed its providential design and suggested it was God's judgement on the wickedness of the Catholic Irish for persisting in their loyalty to the Church of Rome (McNeile). Within three weeks, this theme was taken up in New York by the Catholic Archbishop, the combative John Hughes, who explicitly rejected the interpretation of the famine as providential. Instead he laid the blame at the door of the laissez-faire economic policies of the Westminster government which chose to let Ireland starve rather than interfere with the workings of the free market. Archbishop Hughes's comments on the morality (or lack of it) of this particular policy would have done justice to Karl Marx. He saved his savage comments for the conclusion of the sermon, the better to hammer home his point and leave it fresh in the minds of his listeners. But the body of the sermon dealing with the 'antecedents' of the famine was wholly devoted to an outline of the centuries of conquest and dispossession, with particular emphasis on the degradation suffered by the Irish Catholic Church, the theft of its property and the destruction of its institutions (Hughes). The 'antecedent' for this interpretation of history, indeed the example of the type of clerical activism that Hughes specialized in, and for which he became famous, could be traced back directly back to the example of Bishop Doyle in 1823–4. It was a testimony to the strength of the links that joined religion and politics in the Irish world, across generations as well as across oceans. It was also a testimony to the role of the sermon in providing a medium (from the pulpit as well as in print) through which this culture was spread, nationally as well as internationally.

References

Barnard, T. C. (1991). 'The Uses of 23 October 1641 and Irish Protestant Celebrations'. *English Historical Review* 421: 889–920.

Bowen, D. (1978). *The Protestant Crusade in Ireland, 1800-70*. Dublin: Gill and MacMillan.

Brown, S. J. (2001). *The National Churches of England, Ireland, and Scotland, 1801-1846*. Oxford: Oxford University Press.

D'Alton, I. (1980). *Protestant Society and Politics in Cork, 1812-1844*. Cork: Cork University Press.

Doyle, J. (1822). *A Letter to His Grace, the Protestant Archbishop of Dublin, in Consequence of Unjust Animadversions against the Roman Catholic Religion, Delivered by Him in a Charge to the Clergy of his Archdiocese, on the 24th of October, 1822, in St. Patrick's Cathedral, Dublin 1822*. Dublin: R. Coyne.

—— (1823). *A Vindication of the Religious and Civil Principles of the Irish Catholics in a Letter Addressed to His Excellency, the Marquis Wellesley, K.G. Lord Lieutenant General and Governor General of Ireland, etc. etc.*, by J.K.L, 2nd edn. Dublin: R. Coyne.

Fitzpatrick, W. J. (1880). *The Life, Times, and Correspondence of the Right Rev. Dr. Doyle, Bishop of Kildare and Leighlin*. Dublin: J. Duffy & Son.

Hill, Jacqueline (2010). 'The Church of Ireland and Irish Church History c. 1790-1869', in T. Dooley (ed.), *Ireland's Polemical Past. Views of Irish History in Honour of R. V. Comerford*. Dublin: University College Dublin Press, 9-31.

Hughes J. (1847). *A Lecture on the Antecedent Causes of the Irish Famine Delivered under the Auspices of the General Committee for the Relief of the Suffering Poor of Ireland, at the Broadway Tabernacle, March 20th, 1847*. New York: Edward Dunigan.

Keogh, D. (2008). *Edmund Rice and the First Christian Brothers*. Dublin: Four Courts Press.

Larkin, E. (2011). 'Paul Cullen: The Great Ultramontane', in D. Keogh and A. McDonnell (eds.), *Cardinal Paul Cullen and his World*. Dublin: Four Courts Press, 15-33.

McGrath, T. (1999). *Politics, Interdenominational Relations and Education in the Public Ministry of Bishop James Doyle of Kildare and Leighlin, 1786-1834*. Dublin: Four Courts Press.

McNeile, H. (1847). *The Famine, a Rod of God, its Provoking Cause, its Merciful Design: a Sermon Preached in St. Jude's Church, Liverpool, on Sunday, February 28th, 1847*. Liverpool: Seeley, Burnside & Seeley.

Magee, W. (1822). *A Charge Delivered at His Primary Visitation in St. Patrick's Cathedral, on Thursday the 24th of October 1822*. Dublin: Grierson and Keene.

O'Sullivan, M. (1838). *The Church Never Forsaken. A Sermon Preached at the Visitation of the Clergy of the Diocese of Armagh, on Wednesday, September 5th, 1838 and Published by Desire of His Grace the Lord Primate by the Rev. Mortimer O'Sullivan, D. D.* Dublin: William Curry.

Phelan, W. (1817). *The Bible, Not the Bible Society: Being an Attempt to Point Out that Mode of Disseminating the Scriptures Which Would Most Effectually Conduce to the Security of the Established Church and the Peace of the United Kingdom*. Dublin: John Cumming.

Purcell, M. (2003). *The Story of the Vincentians*. Naas: The Leinster Leader.

Reynolds, J. A. (1970). *The Catholic Emancipation Crisis in Ireland, 1823-9*. Westport, CT: Greenwood Press.

Sewell, W. H., Jr (1994). *A Rhetoric of Bourgeois Revolution. The Abbe Sieyes and 'What is the Third Estate'*. Durham, NC: Duke University Press.

Whelan, I. (2005). *The Bible War in Ireland. The Second Reformation and the Polarization of Protestant–Catholic Relations in Ireland, 1800-40*. Dublin: The Lilliput Press.

CHAPTER 11

SERMONS IN WALES IN THE ESTABLISHED CHURCH

JOHN MORGAN-GUY

The Long Eighteenth Century

NEITHER the Order for Morning Prayer nor that for Evening Prayer in the 1662 Book of Common Prayer made any provision for the preaching of a sermon. That was reserved to the Order for the Administration of Holy Communion, when, after the recitation of the Nicene Creed, there was inserted a rubric which read: 'Then shall follow the Sermon, or one of the Homilies already set forth, or hereafter to be set forth, by Authority.' At a time when the full morning service was likely to be Morning Prayer, followed by the Litany, and then by the Holy Communion—at least as far as the Offertory—then it can be said that there was an expectation that a sermon would be preached or homily read on every Sunday in the year. Even when the service was shortened to just the Order for Morning Prayer that expectation remained.

Bishops were concerned that their parochial clergy fulfilled the obligation of regular preaching to the congregations in their charge. In 1763 Bishop John Ewer of Llandaff, in his Primary Visitation, enquired of his clergy: 'How often, and on what days is Divine Service perform'd in your church? If not twice every Lord's Day, with a sermon in the morning, for what reason?' (Guy 1991: appendix). That the duty of preaching was, in the main, faithfully discharged by his parochial clergy is revealed in the Returns which they made to his Queries. For example, Henry Jones, curate of Llancarfan, reported that Divine Service was performed there twice every Sunday, with a sermon in the morning, as did Moses Mitchell, rector of Machen (Guy 1991: 59, 127). Even in the smallest of parishes the duty could be conscientiously performed. The parish of Gileston in the Vale of Glamorgan was of very small extent; in 1771 Bishop Shute Barrington of Llandaff recorded in his Diocese Book that the whole community consisted of the rector and his family, 'a Farmer and his wife, with one child and four servants, one old man, one ancient widow'. The rector was also the squire, living in the manor house adjoining the church. Yet even with so small a population, there were two Sunday services, with a weekly sermon preached in the morning (Guy 1981: 123). Where a weekly sermon was not preached at Morning Prayer, the reason was usually provided. In some parishes where there was single duty (Morning or Evening Prayer on alternate Sundays) the sermon, as at Merthyr Mawr, was delivered in association with whichever Order was being read (Guy 1991: 43). In very few parishes was a weekly sermon omitted. Elias Thomas, curate of Llansoy, rather defensively reported that a sermon was only preached there fortnightly 'according to custom immemorial' (Guy 1991: 150). In this instance the fact that Thomas was serving four other churches in the vicinity may have had more to do with the reduced frequency of a sermon at Llansoy than immemorial custom.

This information is valuable so far as it goes. However, it leaves a number of unanswered questions. In parishes in which the population in the late seventeenth and throughout the eighteenth century was predominantly Welsh-speaking—and in many cases monoglot—in what language and in what manner was the sermon delivered? What was its duration and content? Was there any relationship between the subject matter and the biblical readings appointed for the service? (There is only one definite recorded example of this, in 1741 at Machen, when John Wesley preached at Evening Prayer, not on a Sunday but a Friday, taking as his text words from the appointed second lesson for that day, as set down in the 1662 Prayer Book. By contrast, Daniel Rowland, who also preached at the same service, presumably in Welsh rather than Wesley's English, chose a text unrelated to the office of the day (Morgan-Guy: 171, fn. 95)). It has to be said that for the four Welsh dioceses in which more than a thousand sermons would have been delivered on any given Sunday, only limited and sometimes anecdotal evidence survives to help us answer these questions.

There is evidence for the eighteenth century that efforts were made to provide for the service of the church in the predominant language. John Leach, appointed through family influence to the living of Raglan, Monmouthshire in 1746, did not speak Welsh, but services in Raglan were regularly held in that language. Leach's solution—and it was one that was regularly adopted by incumbents in his position—was to appoint a Welsh-speaking assistant curate to serve there in his place (Morgan-Guy: 150). That having been said, there is evidence of sermons being delivered in English to congregations which did not understand a word of them. The evangelically-minded Griffith Jones, founder of the Welsh Circulating Schools and rector of Llanddowror, Carmarthenshire (1716–61), in his annual published reports of the work of the Circulating Schools, was forthright in his condemnation of this practice. 'We cannot help thinking', he thundered, 'that English sermons to Welsh congregations are neither less absurd, nor more edifying than Welsh preaching would be in the centre of England, or Latin service in the Church of Rome' (Williams: 45). On another occasion he pointed out that English sermons to Welsh congregations were 'full as edifying to the walls and pews of the church, as to them that sit within them' (Williams: 65). It is no small wonder that Jones discerned a widespread ignorance of the fundamental tenets of the Christian faith in communities where this practice prevailed.

Where there was preaching in the vernacular, there was an enthusiastic response. William Richards in 1682 noted how far the Welsh 'are fain to trudge for a little homily' (Jenkins: 14) and Erasmus Saunders, who knew the diocese of St Davids well, writing nearly forty years later, said more or less the same thing. What he described as 'the poor inhabitants of these mountains' were avid sermon-tasters. 'They don't think it too much ... to travel three or four miles, or more, on foot to attend the public prayers, and sometimes as many more to hear a sermon' (Saunders 1949: 32). They could on occasion be disappointed. When the Reverend Thomas Bowens, newly appointed to the living of St Fagans in 1769, preached there for the first time, it was 'much to the disliking of the Inhabitants, being of a mean utterance and of a stammering tongue' (Denning: 228). By contrast, when a gifted preacher of the calibre of Griffith Jones was advertised, then congregations of upwards of four hundred were known to assemble. Jones could, and on occasion did, preach in English, but, fluent in Welsh as he was, he usually delivered his sermons in the vernacular (Jenkins: 15). Clergy whose command of Welsh was less certain, or who had, however conscientiously, attempted to learn the language, could not compete with such facility. However, whatever the preacher's limitations, there was in Wales what Geraint Jenkins has described as 'a taste for sermons' which long pre-dated the so-called 'Great Awakening' of the 1730s (Jenkins: 13), even if it was nourished by it thereafter. Congregations, as in the case of the unfortunate Thomas Bowens, could be severely critical. Revivalists of the calibre of Daniel Rowland, Howell Harris, and Williams Pantycelyn may have been notable preachers, drawing, like Griffith Jones, large congregations, but the evidence is there to show that Sunday by Sunday, in parishes throughout Wales, a less scintillating but perhaps more systematic preaching ministry went steadily on.

The diary of William Bulkeley of Brynddu, covering most of the years between 1734 and 1760, bears this out. It provides a vivid insight into church life on Anglesey, and especially in his home parish of Llanfechell, where a relative, Richard Bulkeley, was the rector. The Reverend Richard was clearly no star performer when it came to preaching. In company with most of his *confrères*, he either could or would not preach other than from a fully written text—on one Sunday in July 1735 he forgot his sermon, 'he went to ye Pulpit, read ye usuall Prayer before sermons, and when he should have begun there was nothing in Church but a general Silence for 3 or 4 minutes' (G. N. Evans: 19). Here is an insight not just into the patient docility of the congregation, but also into the fact that the Bidding Prayer enjoined by Canon 55 (1604) 'Before all Sermons, Lectures and Homilies' was still in regular use at Llanfechell in the 1730s (Lowther Clarke and Harris: 769–70).

Llanfechell Church was, if Bulkeley is to be believed, well attended, and even adverse weather was no disincentive. On 10 December 1749, when the river that ran through the village was in flood, and covered the bridge, three horses were employed to carry people through the water so that they could attend the morning service (G. N. Evans: 19). Richard Bulkeley—with occasional lapses, such as that mentioned above—was conscientious in his pastoral, liturgical and preaching ministry, occupying his pulpit even at the traditional—it had survived the upheavals of the Reformation—very early morning service on Christmas Day, the *Plygain*. At Llanfechell this took place at five o'clock in the morning and was attended by 'a prodigious number of people' who had risen at an even earlier hour to make their way in the winter darkness to an unheated church for the service of carols and their Christmas sermon (G. N. Evans: 38).

Sundays and major Holy Days were not the only occasions on which sermons were preached from parochial pulpits. Little known or recorded are the sermons delivered under the terms of a local charitable endowment. One such existed at Llanfechell, where a sermon for the feast of the Presentation of Christ in the Temple 'commonly called The Purification of St Mary the Virgin' (2 February) was endowed. William Bulkeley was assiduous in seeing to it that his rector discharged that duty (G. N. Evans: 29). Another endowment for an annual sermon existed at Chepstow in Monmouthshire, and it is to be suspected that such sermons were linked in some way with the provisions of parochial charities for the poor, for education or for reparation of the parish church (Guy 1991: 180). How well supported such sermons were, it is difficult to tell. The Reverend John Carne (1732–1798), normally resident on his estate at Nash in the Vale of Glamorgan, but an occasional visitor to his rectory of Plumtree in Nottinghamshire, recorded in his diary for 1773 preaching a charity sermon in St Mary's, Nottingham on 20 June on behalf of the Blue Coat School. He commented: 'The largest congregation I ever preached to, computed to be above 4000 people, or as some said, 5000' (Guy 1973: 57). Such numbers seem unbelievable, especially as Carne was no visiting bishop but merely a largely non-resident local incumbent, but as his diary was not written with publication in mind, there is little reason to doubt his veracity. None of the other entries show any tendency towards exaggeration. If a collection was taken up from such a congregation, then the benefit to the Blue Coat School would have been considerable. The sermon itself does not survive, but Carne's record of it and of the numbers who were present when it was preached serves to put in context the numerous charity sermons preached by bishops and subsequently printed, such as that by John Ewer, Bishop of Llandaff on 10 April 1766 in St Lawrence Jewry in the City of London on behalf of the London Hospital (the president of that institution, Edward, Duke of York, younger brother of George III, and the Board of Governors, being present) or that on 20 February 1767 at St Mary-le-Bow on behalf of the Society for the Promotion of Christian Knowledge (SPCK) (Guy 1991: 18–19). One can presume that these were equally fashionable, well-attended, and lucrative occasions.

It has to be said, however, that the distinction between serious purpose and entertainment could be a fine one on such occasions. Recording in March 1765 a gathering at Cowbridge of the 'Society of the Free Masons', the gossipy and acerbic Glamorgan diarist William Thomas, having described the procession to the church of the masons in full regalia, for a sermon by the Reverend John Williams, Master of the Grammar School, commented: 'A great croud admiring and looking at the sight, being the like never before seen here' (Denning: 133). The occasion for the sermon, rather than the sermon itself, especially if it involved spectacle (as at Cowbridge) or proximity to one or more celebrities (as at St Lawrence Jewry), could draw the curious as well as the committed, and might sometimes, at least, account for the size of the gathering.

Griffith Jones did not believe that sermons in the vernacular on their own would suffice, however well prepared or delivered. A primary purpose of his Circulating Schools was to provide the students—of all ages and both sexes—with a basic Christian education; the text-books were the Bible and the Book of Common Prayer, and especially the Catechism appended to it. Writing in *Welch Piety* in 1740, he said 'without catechising... preaching is in a manner lost and thrown away' (Jenkins: 33). Literacy was the key. Jones would have agreed with Samuel Ward who as far back as 1621 had said that sermons were 'as showers of rain that water for the instant, books are as snow that lies longer on the earth' (Jenkins: 33). The printed sermon could be read, and read again; it could also be read out loud to others, and thus over many years reach a far wider audience than the congregation to which it had been delivered. The religion of the hearth and home was of signal importance. Erasmus Saunders was only one author who emphasized this (Saunders 1701: 56–7) and the rehearsal of the main points of the Sunday sermon, or a precis of it, was widely acknowledged as one of the responsibilities of the head of a household. The reading of a printed sermon, or extracts from it, might serve just as well. The more prosperous, gentlemen-farmers, merchants and retail traders, members of the professions, were in a position to buy books, both in English and, more often, in Welsh, and sufficiently well educated to read them. Among their purchases were collections of sermons, such as those of Bishop Beveridge of St Asaph to be found in the library of Tristram Matthews of Llansilin, Denbighshire, who died in 1735 (Jenkins: 271). With such an understanding some clergy in Wales laboured to translate English-language sermons into Welsh and publish them. Robert Lloyd, rector of Hirnant, for example, in 1716 printed his translation of a sermon entitled *The Christian's Way to Heaven*, first composed in 1700, so that, as he said, 'it might dwell longer in the minds and hearts of men' (Jenkins: 33).

The foundation of the SPCK in 1698 gave a great boost to the publication and dissemination of sermons in Welsh. Four of the 'founding fathers' of the SPCK had Welsh connections, and very early on correspondents were recommending works for translation and publication. In November 1708 Sir John Philipps of Picton Castle—who was to be a strong supporter and patron of the work of Griffith Jones—suggested a sermon on Joshua 24:15, preached by the Radnorshire-born canon of Westminster, Richard Lucas, and in February 1709/10 the archdeacon of Carmarthen, Edward Tenison, recommended thirty of the sermons of Bishop William Beveridge of St Asaph (Clement: 16, 27).

Access to sermons, heard or read, was one thing; comprehension was another. Here the bishops of the Welsh dioceses in the late seventeenth and early eighteenth centuries were in agreement; intelligibility was of paramount importance for those occupying parochial pulpits. George Bull, Bishop of St Davids (1705–10), himself a theologian of international stature, nonetheless intensely disliked 'empty and frothy and trifling sermons'; his contemporary at St Asaph, William Fleetwood (1708–15), counselled his clergy to use plain speech and temper their sermons to the level of the greater part of their congregations—eschewing the temptation, it is to be suspected, of directing their discourses primarily at the occupants of the squire's pew; and Richard Smallbrooke, one of Bull's successors at St Davids (1724–31), 'advised his clergy to present their message to the meanest orders in such a way that there would be "no overshooting of them by fine speculations, or too close and elaborate reasonings"' (Jenkins: 16). Fleetwood in particular condemned obsequiousness to occupants of the squire's pew, warning his clergy, 'I cannot possibly approve of this respect and complaisance to a few' (Jenkins: 10–11), especially if that meant preaching a sermon in English to those few persons present who understood the language, whilst leaving the rest of the congregation in ignorance of its content.

Human nature being what it is, such warnings were no doubt necessary for some, and, though there were exceptions, it would seem they were largely heeded. A recently discovered manuscript book in the library of the Episcopal residence at Bangor contains six sermons preached in 1686 and 1687, probably by one of the vicars-choral of Bangor Cathedral, John Buttree. It reveals both the strength and the weakness that Bishop Fleetwood was to discern in preaching only a decade or so later. The sermons are in English, and were delivered in the cathedral, with some being repeated in the chapelry at Pentir (to all intents and purposes the proprietary chapel of the Williams family of Plas Pentir, who no doubt would not have objected to the use of the English language, though their tenantry and dependants might have thought otherwise). Their date is interesting, for as recently as 1684 Bishop Humphrey Lloyd had directed that in the cathedral Morning and Evening Prayer should be said or sung in English on Sundays and Holy Days, and duplicated in Welsh, thus abandoning the bi-lingual services which had been introduced at the Restoration (Clarke: 61). As the Welsh morning service was held between eight and ten in the morning, followed by the choral English service, we can be confident that these sermons were composed with the principal cathedral service in mind.

In his analysis of these sermons, Kenneth Padley has remarked that their value lies in their rarity—although there is some survival of parochial manuscript sermons in Wales, the record of those preached in the cathedrals is scanty—and in their ordinariness. They were preached, if the attribution to Buttree is correct, by a non-graduate minor cathedral dignitary, and only one was composed for a major festival (Christmas). If preached as written, then they would have lasted approximately half an hour; Padley notes that their 'overall message…underlines the necessity of godly living' but also that they are cast in 'terms that are general rather than specific'. There is little that is contentious, and, considering that they were preached at a time when the reign of James II was approaching its crisis, are singularly lacking in religious or political polemic (Padley 2010: 7, 8, 9, 10). This is preaching, however doctrinally sound, at its most uncontroversial.

In his analysis of sermons preached in the Established Church in the four Welsh dioceses prior to 1730, Geraint Jenkins found that most were, like Buttree's, well-constructed, straightforward discourses clearly expressed. He notes the anonymous sermons contained in Bangor University MS.54, for example, being in a style at once 'colloquial and homely, with each point carefully explained in the minister's local dialect', and those of Robert Wynne, vicar of Llanddeiniolen, as 'always well-organised, logical and relevant to the needs of his locality' (Jenkins: 18). These were clergy who were well aware of their pastoral responsibilities.

They were also men of their time, and Jenkins notes of the same Robert Wynne that 'he preached the duty of pious submission as sedulously as his Elizabethan forebears'. 'What is poverty but having to wear homespun clothes, live on modest fare, eat frugally, drink water from wooden bowls, earn bread by the sweat of one's brow, sit at the lowest end of the table, and tug one's forelock in gentle company?' (Jenkins: 19). The one surviving sermon of the Reverend John Carne, on the choice of friends, struck a very similar note:

> The first and greatest regard is to be had to the inward qualities of a man we choose for an intimate friend; some respect is to be had to outward circumstances: I mean such circumstances of life and station and fortunes as suit best and are most equal to our own. Not that a man should never court the friendships of any that are above him, nor stoop to an intimacy with any below him. For the apostle spoke well and meant well to Christians—but in general 'tis most true that there is a suitableness of stations and ranks of life that will best promote the confidence and advantages of friendship. 'Tis a known point that there cannot be that ease and freedom between unequals as may be between such as are nearer upon the level. (Guy 1973: 64)

Mrs C. F. Alexander could not have put it better. Always mindful of the social upheavals of the Civil Wars, fearful of the potentially disruptive influence of dissent (and especially of 'enthusiasm' and that to which it might lead), the Welsh clergy of the Established Church, in common with their English counterparts, largely stood firm on the necessity of a stable and static social order, of godly discipline and morality, of modest living and sobriety, and the paramount need for genuine, deep repentance of sin. The finer points of doctrine, what Griffith Jones called 'scholastical or controversial divinity above the reach of ordinary capacities' may have had its place, but that place was the study and not the pulpit (Jenkins: 17).

There were, however, from the 1730s onwards, those who sounded a more strident note of urgency; those clergy who were motivated by evangelical zeal and whose preaching ministry was built on foundations already firmly laid. The leaders of the Welsh 'Awakening', men of the calibre of Daniel Rowland, Howell Harris, and Williams Pantycelyn are well known; others of a subsequent generation who also exercised an effective and influential preaching ministry, such as David Jones of Llangan and Thomas Davies of Coity, probably less so. Davies, a protégé of Lady Charlotte Edwin, herself a confidante of the Countess of Huntingdon, was nominated by Lady Charlotte to the living of Coity, near Bridgend in Glamorgan, in 1769, and remained there until his death in 1819. It has been said of him that, like John Wesley, 'he preached as never certain to preach again, and he preached for conversion' (Fenn: 54). A manuscript volume of his sermons, dating from the years 1766–8, when he was curate of Llangorse in Breconshire—and subsequently preached again later in his churches at Coity and Nolton—is now on deposit at the Glamorgan Record Office, and reveals that careful preparation went into their composition. They are, nonetheless, characterized by freshness and immediacy: 'As a person upon a Pool, when the ice breaks under him, sinks down to the Bottom, is drowned, so an obdurate unrepented sinner after death sinks into utter darkness and there perisheth everlastingly' and 'Let me tell you, a cold wish never reached heaven, nor regenerate any man. Everyone must experience the pangs of conviction before he passes through the gate of regeneration' (Fenn: 54). As Roy Fenn put it, for Davies

> when judgement did come it was irrevocable, and eternal Hell as much a reality as Heaven... [T]he nation's disdain of judgement and hellfire was the origin of its moral degradation, political misfortunes, and of its social problems. Their solution and the ultimate reform of society lay, not in Parliament nor in agitation and unrest, but in the transformation of the will of the individual, in fact, in conversion. (Fenn: 54–5)

For Davies, the purpose of the ordained ministry, to either the diaconate or the priesthood in the Established Church, was to prioritize and authorize the ministry of the Word. Writing to his patron, Lady Charlotte Edwin, he said:

> Seeing the deplorable Darkness and Misery that the World lieth in, I think it incumbent upon me, as the Lord shall enable me, to spread the knowledge of Jesus & publish the glad tidings of salvation far and near and endeavour to pluck sinners as Brands out of the burning, & knowing the terrors of the Lord, to persuade men to be reconciled to God thro' the blood of his Son. (Fenn: 57)

For all his evangelical fervour, Davies remained an Establishment man, and lived and died as a priest of the Church of England. He did not see his espousal of 'vital religion' as anything other than a contribution to that church's ministry. In other respects, he did not differ greatly from John Carne (a fairly near neighbour) or Robert Wynne. He was a high Tory, who opposed the repeal of the Test and Corporation Acts, and was forthright in his condemnation of Protestant dissent, radical and otherwise. As Fenn put it, for Davies

> non-conformity was nothing more than an expression of discontent and jealousy, and he was unable to conceive of true religion outside the Established Church... [His] theology of the Church made secession impossible, Church and State are a unity, and as such are inseparable... The outward and visible sign of this unity was the King, who though head of the constitution, is also a communicant member of the Church of England. Consequently Dissenters, in leaving the Established Church, had thereby rebelled against the constitution, and their secession was as much treachery as it was schism, for any form of wilful division, political or religious, is sinful. As he himself wrote 'Division is commonly the forerunner of destruction'. (Fenn: 64–5)

Davies, although personally acquainted with John Wesley, who had preached for him at Coity and Nolton, did not approve of his presbyteral ordinations which precipitated the Methodist estrangement from the Established Church, nor the 1811 move into a separate 'denomination' in Wales of the Calvinistic Methodists. He is an important figure in the story of 'vital religion' in Wales, as he is a reminder of the danger of labels. He preached an uncompromising evangelical doctrine, but he preached it within the boundaries of the Established Church.

The same can be said of his close neighbour, David Jones, the rector of Llangan, who drew vast crowds to his services. (He is said to have preached to a congregation of between eight and ten thousand on one visit to Anglesey, and to a similar number at Lady Huntingdon's Spa Fields Chapel in London.) Like Davies, his sermons are characterized by plain speaking rather than eloquence, by directness and sincerity. By all accounts, he was a man of singular charm and compassion, and the evident power of his preaching sprang from his personal qualities and convictions (Granville: 142–6). A native of rural Carmarthenshire, fluent in Welsh, and, like Griffith Jones of Llanddowror, a non-graduate, Jones possessed an instant rapport with and attraction for the rural artisan and labouring classes, to whom so many of his sermons were addressed.

Of the first generation of the Evangelical revival, perhaps the greatest impact was made by the curate of Llangeitho, Cardiganshire, Daniel Rowland. Weighty in content, biblical, the fruit of wide reading, Rowland's sermons were nonetheless invigorating and arresting in their presentation, shot through with a sense of urgency. Although he could preach extempore, his usual practice was to use notes. His biographer Eifion Evans drew attention to the wide variety of biblical texts upon which he built his sermons, believing that preaching should embrace 'the whole counsel of God' (Acts 20:27) (E. Evans: 168). Of Rowland it was said 'he makes the devil's kingdom shake wherever he comes', but, despite the seriousness of his message, like David Jones, he was recognized as a 'chearfull man … clear of understanding, without Bigotry' (Denning: 235).

In this they differed from the other prominent revivalist, the frustrated ordinand Howell Harris. It would be wrong to doubt Harris's religious conviction, or to minimize the effect of his preaching, at least in the short term, but his arrogance is inescapable. His most recent biographer, Geraint Tudur, has highlighted his stubbornness and intransigence, 'impervious to criticism and deaf to advice' (Tudur: 233). He was, in spite of his manifest weaknesses, a powerful preacher, spontaneous in his oratory, only latterly basing his message on a specific text; initially he spoke 'in submission to whatever divine guidance he believed himself to be receiving at the time' (Tudur: 6). Certainly before 1750 travelling long distances on preaching tours and, being a layman and therefore barred from the pulpits of the parish churches, he was forced to deliver his message either in unconsecrated buildings or in the open air. His sermons were intensely personal in their application, challenging the consciences of his hearers, convincing them of the reality of sin and judgement, but also of the promise of salvation held out by the Gospel. He condemned the selfishness and greed of his day, and was censorious of anything he felt to be undermining of morality, such as sport and dancing (Tudur: 6–7). Convinced he was a 'chosen vessel of God', he was also a showman, as an officer in the Breconshire Militia between 1756 and 1762 preaching in his uniform and, as the diarist William Thomas recorded, travelling in 'his shaize and two horses, written on the same, God is my peace etc' (Denning: 129). Thomas, strong Calvinist as he was, thought little of Harris, criticizing his 'spirit of super authority' (Denning: 145), and maintaining that he 'went about as

Zinzendorf, the Moravian of Germany, in his chaise, being he himself have swallowed much of that doctrine' (Denning: 176). Here again we have to ask whether it was the content of the message alone, or the presentation and self-advertisement of the preacher, which drew the large crowds that undoubtedly gathered around Harris.

Whatever his faults, and the doctrinal heterodoxy of which he was sometimes accused, Harris, like David Jones and Thomas Davies after him, remained in communion with the Church of England. He was steadfast in his opposition to any Methodist secession from the Established Church and, had he lived (he died in 1773) would doubtless have opposed John Wesley's ordinations and the 1811 breakaway by the Calvinistic Methodists. Evangelical revivalist he may have been, and defiant of Episcopal authority as he undoubtedly was, his preaching was intended to rekindle the spiritual life of the church of which he was a communicant, and not create a schism within it.

The Nineteenth Century

In respect of sermons and preaching, the nineteenth century saw both the continuity and the development of much of what we have seen and discerned in the 'long' eighteenth century, since 1689. Sermons of half an hour or more's duration, read from a carefully prepared manuscript, continued to be preached throughout Wales. Kenneth Padley has drawn attention to the ministry of the Reverend William Hewson, vicar of Swansea from 1813 to 1845, years in which the character of that town was undergoing rapid and fundamental change. On the one hand there was the industrialization of both the town and its hinterland, with a concomitant rise in population, and on the other, and intimately linked with it, the proliferation of denominational meeting houses and chapels. Hewson and his 'highly respectable congregation' at St Mary's seem to have been, if contemporary comment is anything to go by, either oblivious or indifferent to the changing world around them. Preaching before his fellow clergy in the deanery of Gower in April 1820, Hewson indulged in 'a solid defence of tory values, in particular the alliance of Church and State against the forces of mischief and insubordination that would undermine them jointly' (Padley 2007: 36). Kenneth Padley summed up the sermon as 'just rhetoric, bringing little or no practical and theological help to the problems of the age' (ibid.). This is a glimpse of a largely moribund church, unaware of and unresponsive to the challenges and needs of the society that it was there to serve, determinedly anxious to maintain the status quo.

Similar attitudes can be discerned a generation later in the sermons of two successive vicars of the principal church in the Pembrokeshire town of Haverfordwest, St Mary's. Thomas Watts held the living from 1843 to 1859. He had some experience of the wider world, having been a chaplain on the Codrington Plantation in Barbados, but at Haverfordwest he was a cautious conservative, restoring his church in 1844 in a manner more suited to the previous century. On 18 November 1852, the day of the funeral of the Duke of Wellington, Watts preached on Psalm 103:15–16 ('The days of man are but as grass …') at a civic service, during which he descanted on the duke's 'strict and punctual attention to his religious duties' (Barker: 22). Wellington, the highest of high Tories, would have been a role-model for Watts; no mention was made of the duke's weaknesses, his snobbishness, his treatment of his wife, or his philandering—though admittedly in his lifetime the latter two were more a matter of informed rumour than established fact. The actual funeral in London has been described as 'floridly pompous' and this is not an unfair verdict on the sermon at Haverfordwest.

Watts's successor was the Reverend John Henry Alexander Gwyther Philipps, half-brother of Lord Milford and heir to his estates at Picton Castle. Here, four miles from his parish, he made his home. Despite his aristocratic connections, he was less hidebound than his predecessor, but still suspicious of the social, political and religious climate of his time. Philipps, at least until illness overtook him, was an energetic pastor and an assiduous preacher, mindful of the wide social mix of his parish. (In 1862, the publicity leaflet for a series of evening services, aimed specifically at his working-class parishioners, contained the exhortation, 'Working People Come In Your Ordinary Clothes' (Barker: 25)). However, in many ways Philipps's pulpit ministry was, by his day, old-fashioned. He preached from a written text, often for half an hour or more—one sermon, on John 10: 14, is thirty-two pages long—and had no qualms about repeated delivery. The same sermon was preached three times between 1847 and 1849 in his previous parish of Madeley, Salop, and twice between 1858 and 1862 at St. Mary's. Presumably over fifteen years he saw no reason to modify what he had to say in expounding 'I am the good shepherd…' (Barker: 25).

The rapid increase in church-building and restoration that marked the middle and later years of the nineteenth century, in Wales as in England, had one perhaps unlooked-for outcome. It made the person of the diocesan bishop more familiar to the parishioners than he had been hitherto. Bishops travelled to all corners of their dioceses to consecrate or re-hallow church buildings, and took such opportunities to preach to the assembled congregations. Such sermons seem to have been more respectfully than enthusiastically received. In 1854 Bishop Ollivant travelled to Nantyglo, in the heartland of Monmouthshire's industrial landscape, to consecrate a new church there. The *Cardiff and Merthyr Guardian* dutifully recorded that he preached 'a good, plain, practical sermon, appropriate to the occasion'. Ollivant had some acquaintance with, but no fluency in, the Welsh language, and it is likely that his consecration sermon was delivered in English—the service had been conducted throughout in that language. (It was not until 1870, with the elevation of Joshua Hughes to the bench as Bishop of St Asaph, that a native Welsh speaker, confident and fluent in the language, was to occupy any of the four Welsh sees.) The newspaper reserved its encomium of praise for the preacher in the evening, a local incumbent, the Reverend Mr Jones of Tredegar: 'We have had the satisfaction of frequently hearing this celebrated Welsh orator; but we have never heard him to greater advantage or when his discourses were more acceptable to the people than on this occasion' (Brown 2001: 101–2). Eighteen years before the consecration celebrations at Nantyglo, and the reaction to Ollivant's sermon, there had been a similar response when in November 1836 Bishop Edward Copleston had preached at the consecration of

St Paul's, Newport. (His sermon was on the text Matthew 11:4–5, 'Jesus answered and said unto them, Go and shew John again those things which ye hear and see: The blind receive their sight, and the lame walk, the lepers are cleansed, and the deaf hear, the dead are raised up, and the poor have the gospel preached to them'—on the face of it an ideal choice for such an occasion.) The sermon was damned in the press with rather faint praise as 'eloquent and interesting' (Pryce: 20–1). The higher clergy, however assiduous they were in the performance of their duties, seem to have lacked the common touch, preaching sermons on such major public occasions that were more abstract theological discourses than speaking to the needs of the particular congregations that had gathered to hear them. That was certainly true of the afternoon preacher at the consecration celebrations at Nantyglo. Archdeacon Crawley delivered 'a valuable sermon, but the congregation not yet in sufficient tone to appreciate or to receive its good qualities' (Brown 2001: 102). In other words, it had gone way over their heads.

At the other end of the scale were some of the non-graduate clergy; men like David Davies, a candidate for priest's orders in 1874, who was described by the Bishop of St Davids examining chaplain as 'weak and defective with much error' as regards his understanding of Christian doctrine, and the manner of his preaching as 'sing-song' (Knight: 345). On this question of preaching style, there is fairly plentiful, if sometimes rather anecdotal, evidence. John Stacey, the long-serving curate until 1861 of Cardiff's town-centre church, St. John's, was described as 'eloquent and impressive' in the pulpit, 'gifted with a sonorous voice, he filled the church clearly and easily'. This does, however, sound more like a description of oratory than parochial preaching (Brown 2005: 24). His contemporary, the evangelical vicar of the neighbouring parish of St Mary's, William Leigh Morgan, may have been guilty of the same vice, as his obituary recalled 'his ability to send home to the hearts of his hearers the riches of the Gospel expressed in polished and vigorous Anglo-Saxon'. This is not exactly how he himself saw it, recalling that in 'preaching the truth of the everlasting Gospel, I have not shunned to declare unto you all the counsel of God, [warning] everyone night and day. As far as I have known the truth, I have conveyed it sincerely to each of you without respect of persons' (Brown 2005: 89, 98). It has to be admitted that the preaching of men like Stacey and Morgan was very acceptable to the large congregations that attended upon their words, but these congregations were overwhelmingly of the respectable middle class. St John's at this date, as Roger Brown has pointed out, 'had the reputation of being a society church where "physical comforts were not altogether neglected"' (Brown 2005: 24). Both St John's and the newly-built St Mary's were fashionable preaching auditoria, with fashionable, reasonably well-educated congregations. Unfortunately St Mary's was sited in Cardiff's docklands, surrounded by mean streets, public houses, and brothels, whose denizens were untouched by its presence or the ministry of its clergy. In 1852 the senior curate 'complained that many would-be worshippers at the Sunday evening service…felt unable to attend because they lacked the courage to push themselves through the crowds lining the streets, with prostitutes "unblushingly" calling out their services, and having to hear foul language and expressions of the "vilest description"' (Brown 2005: 90).

The vigorous exposition of 'vital religion' was not, however, lacking elsewhere. John Griffiths, rector of Neath and archdeacon of Llandaff, was a gifted extempore preacher— 'he would pour forth a torrent of eloquence which held the listeners spell-bound' for anything up to three quarters of an hour—and he was convinced of the necessity of 'simple, warm, energetic preaching of the pure Gospel of Jesus Christ' (Brown 2005: 120). He was at his best, in either Welsh or English, when preaching extempore to informal gatherings. On one occasion, preaching at an outdoor temperance meeting at Pontardawe, he was 'able to draw in the thousands of scattered people into a packed group before the platform as soon as he started' (Brown 2005: 120).

Griffiths was an Evangelical, but the gift of holding the attention of large numbers of working people was not confined to preachers of his persuasion. Charles James Thompson, vicar of St John's, Cardiff from 1875 to 1901, had strong Tractarian and Anglo-Catholic sympathies. His preaching drew large congregations, never more so than in 1889, when major rebuilding and restoration of St John's necessitated the use of a local music hall. Here Thompson was in his element, as a report in the *Cardiff Argus* recorded. Preaching a series of evening sermons on 'The Person of Christ', Thompson addressed his congregation, largely composed of working men and women, extempore.

> He moves a few steps this way and that, sometimes speaks with arms folded, at others with one hand raised, but he does not saw the air or thump the Bible. He does not refer to a single note for guidance, and yet his subject is evolved with the care of a written discourse. He never stops for an idea, or falters for a word, and from the opening of his address to the close he retains the attention of his hearers, keeps them as it were spell-bound, and scarcely a sound breaks out from the mass of people before him. He brings into play a kind of influence over his listeners, makes them think as he thinks, and transplants his ideas, and fixes them in their minds. He reasons with them, and gives them his reasons for thinking as he does. Mr Thompson is something more than a preacher, he is a teacher, and he has the power of transferring to those who listen to him the knowledge he has acquired by long study. (Read: 61–2)

Too little attention, perhaps, has been paid to the place of preaching within the Anglo-Catholic revival, yet many of its luminaries set great store upon it, and were outstanding exponents of it. Priests of the calibre of Arthur Stanton of St Alban's, Holborn could draw crowds of working people, especially to the informal mission services they conducted. Stanton himself was a brilliant and challenging extempore preacher (Russell: 120–1). Such mission services were not, of course, the preserve of Anglo-Catholics; they were eagerly adopted by Welsh evangelicals as well. The long ministry of the Reverend J. Tinson Wrenford at St Paul's, Newport (1855–1904) saw many such occasions, with upwards of two thousand people crowding the church to hear preachers who were not always in Holy Orders—the noted evangelical Lord Radstock took part in one mission there (Pryce: 42–3).

Churches where the Catholic Revival took root were not just centres of liturgical splendour and excellence, but also of systematic preaching and teaching. The patronal feast was often the occasion for an octave of special services, each with a guest preacher, often a priest of proven ability in the pulpit. Thus in October 1888 one preacher at the patronal festival of St German's Church, Roath, a parish in south Wales, was Charles Smythies, Bishop of Zanzibar, then on leave in England, and a former curate in the mother parish of Roath. Here was not only a preacher of stature, but also, in one respect 'a local boy made good'. Smythies drew some 1,500 people to the church that night (Warner and Hooper: 40). Visiting clergy for such occasions often travelled considerable distances to fulfil their engagement; four years earlier, in 1884 the patronal festival preacher at St German's was the vicar of Petrockstow in Devon, who would have had to make a lengthy train journey, probably from Exeter, to take part in the celebration in a parish which was then on the outskirts of Cardiff (Warner and Hooper: 35). Such a journey also involved the kind of expense that could only be contemplated by a priest of independent means, as neither his benefice income nor the resources of a working-class parish like St German's would have been sufficient to underwrite it.

In one area Evangelicals and Anglo-Catholics were united, and that was the need for powerful preaching to be linked with social action. John Griffith, the evangelical rector of Merthyr Tydfil from 1859 to 1885, often outspoken and controversial, was committed to a vision of what he called, in an undated sermon to members of the Taff Battalion of the Rifle Volunteer Force, 'a living, practical Church, doing God's work to rich and poor, masters and men, instead of being what it is now—a grand, sepulchral old Church, existing only for the upper and middle classes, who consider themselves dignified and elevated by belonging to her' (Brown 2007: 228). Good and clear preaching, Griffith strongly believed, had to be 'united with, or le[a]d to, social concern. It was no good preaching about hygiene… "if this was not put into practice in the hutches they inhabited or with the vile stinks they inhaled"' (Brown 2007: 205). Here he was not only at one with priests like Arthur Stanton, but also with many Welsh nonconformists of his and of later generations.

There is plentiful evidence to suggest that the Established Church in Wales was undergoing something of a revival in the latter part of the nineteenth century, a revival in which both Evangelicals and Anglo-Catholics played a significant part. What Densil Morgan has called 'missionary fervour, practical holiness and preaching abilities' were coming to characterize that church, and not just among its evangelical members, as he suggests (Morgan: 27). The days of rhetoric and pulpit oratory, of Hewson, Watts, Stacey, Philipps and even Leigh Morgan, were long gone, as to a lesser extent were the formal, set-piece utterances of bishops of the calibre of Copleston and Ollivant. Frank Morgan, layman and tutor in history at Keble College, Oxford, was to say to the Welsh Church Congress in 1914 'that the Church, by its maintenance of a definite standard of religious belief enshrined in its Creeds and its Prayer-Book, by the importance it attaches to pastoral ministrations, and by its inculcation of a true spirit of reverence, is contributing to the religious life of Wales what no Nonconformist body has been able to contribute' (Morgan: 30). He did not have to mention the contribution to those standards, that pastoral care and concern, that spirit of reverence, which the sermon and the catechetical ministry made; that was, as he reviewed the previous half-century, something of a given.

To some extent the hope of Bishop Vowler Short of St Asaph, expressed in 1852, had been fulfilled. 'Clearly it is not within the power of any one generation to alter the tone and temper of a country... but if it pleases God to enable us, by increased exertions, to raise that tone and temper even in a comparatively small degree, I believe a work will have been effected far beyond any numerical account' (Jones: 30). The sermon in the Established Church in Wales, be it in English or—and this would not have particularly pleased Bishop Short—in Welsh, had no small part to play in the raising of that tone and temper. It had done so in the 'long' eighteenth century, and it had done so again in the nineteenth, at least from its middle years.

REFERENCES

Barker, P. A. (2002). *A History of St Mary's Parish Church Haverfordwest in the Nineteenth Century*. Haverfordwest: The Friends of St Mary's Church.

Brown, R. L. (2001). *Reclaiming the Wilderness. Some Aspects of the Parochial Life...* Welshpool: Tair Eglwys Press.

—— (2005). *Ten Clerical Lives. Essays Relating to the Victorian Church in Wales*. Welshpool: Tair Egwlys Press.

—— (2007). *John Griffith. The Unmitred Bishop?* Welshpool: Tair Eglwys Press.

Clarke, M. L. (1969). *Bangor Cathedral*. Cardiff: University of Wales Press.

Clement, M. (1952). *Correspondence and Minutes of the S.P.C.K. relating to Wales 1699–1740*. Cardiff: University of Wales Press.

Denning, R. T. W. (ed.) (1995). *The Diary of William Thomas 1762–1795*. Cardiff: South Wales Record Society.

Evans, E. (1985). *Daniel Rowland and the Great Evangelical Awakening in Wales*. Edinburgh: The Banner of Truth Trust.

Evans, G. N. (1953). *Religion and Politics in Mid-Eighteenth Century Anglesey*. Cardiff: University of Wales Press.

Fenn, R. W. D. (1963). 'Thomas Davies, Rector of Coity 1769–1819'. *Journal of the Historical Society of the Church in Wales* 13: 41–70.

Granville, N. (2009). Review of R. Brian Higham, *The Revd David Jones, Llangan, 1736–1810, and his Contribution to Welsh Calvinistic Methodism* (Lampeter: The Edwin Mellen Press, 2009). *Morgannwg* 53: 142–6.

Guy, J. R. (1973). 'The Reverend John Carne of Nash'. *Journal of the Historical Society of the Church in Wales* 23: 36–70.

—— (1981). 'Bishop Barrington's Book'. *Morgannwg* 25: 112–29.

—— (1991). *The Diocese of Llandaff in 1763*. Cardiff: South Wales Record Society.

Jenkins, G. H. (1978). *Literature, Religion and Society in Wales 1660–1730*. Cardiff: University of Wales Press.

Jones, I.G. (1987). *Communities. Essays in the Social History of Victorian Wales*. Llandysul: Gomer Press.

Knight, F. (2007). 'Part IV, 1850–1920', in G. Williams et al. (eds.), *The Welsh Church from Reformation to Disestablishment 1603–1920*. Cardiff: University of Wales Press, 309–98.

Lowther Clarke, W. K., and Harris, C. (eds.) (1964). *Liturgy and Worship. A Companion to the Prayer Books of the Anglican Communion*. London: SPCK.

Morgan, D. D. (1999). *The Span of the Cross. Christian Religion and Society in Wales 1914–2000*. Cardiff: University of Wales Press.

Morgan-Guy, J. (2009). 'Religion and Belief, 1660–1780', in M. Gray and P. Morgan (eds.), *The Gwent County History. Volume 3, The Making of Monmouthshire, 1536–1780*. Cardiff: University of Wales Press, 146–73.

Padley, K. (2007). *Our Ladye Church of Swanesey. A History of St Mary's*. Swansea: The Friends of Swansea St Mary.

—— (2010). 'Six Bangor Sermons from the 1680s'. *The Welsh Journal of Religious History* 5: 1–16.

Pryce, T. P. (1936). *One Hundred Years of Evangelical Witness, 1836–1936*... Newport: George Bell.

Read, J. C. (1995). *A History of St John's Cardiff and the Churches of the Parish*. Cardiff: Pauline House.

Russell, G. W. E. (1917). *Arthur Stanton. A Memoir*. London: Longmans Green and Co.

Saunders, E. (1701). *A Domestick Charge; or the Duty of Household-Govenours*... Oxford: L. Lichfield.

—— (1949). *A View of the State of Religion in the Diocese of St. David's*..., reprinted edn. Cardiff: University of Wales Press.

Tudur, G. (2000). *Howell Harris. From Conversion to Separation 1735–1750*. Cardiff: University of Wales Press.

Warner, M. and Hooper, A. C. (eds.) (1934). *The History of Roath St German's*. Cardiff: Western Mail and Echo.

Williams, W. M. (ed.) (1938). *Selections from the Welch Piety*. Cardiff: University of Wales Press.

CHAPTER 12

PREACHING IN THE VERNACULAR: THE WELSH SERMON, 1689–1901

D. DENSIL MORGAN

In his renowned assessment of the state of religion in the diocese of St Davids published in 1721, Erasmus Saunders, prebendary of Brecon and vicar of Blockley, Worcestershire, both lamented the penury of his native diocese and extolled the Christian virtues of its inhabitants. 'We the poor people of this obscure part of this church and nation' (Saunders: 3), he claimed, were afflicted by a raft of misfortune: bad communications, bishops abiding far away from their sees, an unacceptable number of indolent clergy, too many damp and near-derelict church buildings, yet despite everything there was a basic sympathy for the Established Church and a dogged faithfulness to its ministrations and mores. 'There is, I believe, no part of the nation more inclined to be religious and to be delighted with it than the poor inhabitants of these mountains.' Being 'naturally addicted to poetry', as well as composing their own pious verses, the *haslingod* and *carolau*, singing them spontaneously in close harmony, on Sundays the people would walk miles to dilapidated churches, often in the cold and the rain, awaiting the arrival of their clergy. Not only would they walk miles to partake of the liturgy, but 'sometimes as many more to hear a sermon' (Saunders: 32). Even before the advent of the Evangelical Revival, the Welsh, it seems, were addicted to the preaching of the Word.

All four Welsh dioceses were among the nine poorest in the provinces of Canterbury and York. In 1762 Bangor and St Asaph, both of which were in north Wales, were valued at £1,400 per annum, while the immense south Wales diocese of St Davids was worth £900 per annum and Llandaff, also in the south, was valued at as little as £500 a year (Jacob: 83), yet between them they supported hundreds of clergy who ministered to a population of some 400,000. The clergy themselves varied in quality. Owing to the fragmented nature of the Church of England in Wales at the time, there was an imbalance between some comfortably endowed parishes in the comparatively wealthier agrarian regions, invariably in the lowlands and border areas, and the vast patchwork of small and impoverished parishes in the hill country and mountain regions. Far from being sentiment or hyperbole, Erasmus Saunders's reference to 'those shepherdless flocks that stray upon the mountains' (Saunders: 52), described what was really true. Non-residency was a fact, pluralism was often a financial necessity yet despite the difficulty in providing adequate pastoral care for all, the church still functioned and there seems to have been no dearth of candidates for ordination. 'That there are still even in this obscure corner, many honest and good men, who labour under these difficulties, is too well known a truth to be denied' (Saunders: 72). Recent research has confirmed this truth (White; P. Jenkins; Williams). Even if only, or indeed as many as, a third of the Welsh clergy were graduates, many of the others had received a sound education in divinity and the classics in the sturdy network of reputable grammar schools which Wales possessed. The bishops were, for the most part, content to ordain worthy candidates from those schools. Along with being charged with leading worship according to the Book of Common Prayer and providing their flocks with pastoral care, it was taken for granted that these ordinands would be preachers.

By the end of the eighteenth century most Welsh parishioners could expect to hear a sermon at least once a fortnight. In the better off and more accessible parishes it was every week and even in the remoter areas it was rarely less than once a month (G. H. Jenkins: 12–13). The pattern for Anglican sermons, even in Welsh-speaking Wales, was the sober clarity of John Tillotson. In his diocesan charge of 1726, Richard Smalbroke, Bishop of St Davids, urged his clergy to master not only their content but their style: 'the best pattern that can be placed before us for completing a preacher, and which indeed includes all the precepts of that art, is that of the incomparable Archbishop Tillotson' (Smalbroke: 24). A Welsh version of Tillotson's *Persuasivity to Frequent Communion*, translated by George Lewis, a clergyman of the Diocese of St Asaph, as *Anogaeth i gymuno yn fynych* (1704), was popular, and its combination of moralism with an unambiguous sacramental thrust, set forth with unadorned clarity, typified the sermons of many of the clergy at the time. Although Puritanism had never made significant inroads into rural Wales—and post-Restoration Wales was overwhelmingly rural—Puritan convictions concerning the value of preaching and the need for clarity and immediacy had become the common currency of both Anglicanism and Dissent. Sermons were meant to be understood, hence plainness of style and directness of content were aimed at by all. Embellishments were eschewed, literary or classical references were, for the most part, avoided, and preachers were expected to preach the gospel simply, steering clear from abstruse or controversial doctrine. In an apologia for his zealousness in the preacher's task, Griffith Jones (1684–1761), rector of Llanddowror, assured Adam Ottley, Smalbroke's predecessor in the see of St Davids, that he avoided 'empty speculations, high and lofty or quaint phrases, scholastical or controversial divinity above the reach of ordinary capacities that they can't be the better nor the wiser for it' (G. H. Jenkins: 17). This was the ideal for all of the Welsh-speaking clergy and not confined to such gifted preachers as Griffith Jones.

Despite Wales being preponderantly Anglican, since 1689 the Dissenting tradition had been consolidated and was showing modest growth. As far as membership was concerned, in 1689 there can only have been some 12,000 Protestant Dissenters out of a population of 400,000, though congregations invariably contained many more adherents or 'listeners' than fully baptized communicant and committed members (Watts: 270). Unlike the Established Church, Dissent was only represented in parts of the country, mostly in south and south-west Wales and the north Wales border town of Wrexham. It was a small, select, and fairly middle class affair. Linguistically and culturally it was—like most of Wales' parish-based Anglicanism of the time—incontrovertibly Welsh. Preaching was of the essence of Dissenting faith. As the heirs of the Puritans, the Dissenting ministers had been emancipated from their liturgical fetters and saw their ministry in terms of prophecy or holding forth the Word of the Lord. Although set apart by their congregations to the ministry of word and sacrament, sacerdotalism was foreign to them and their staunch Calvinism gave absolute priority to the exposition of scripture. All Dissenting sermons aimed at exegetical clarity, doctrinal precision, and practical application. No heed was taken of the church year, with the systematic and cogently argued address based upon the text at hand. Never dominated by the pericope or reading for the day, the Dissenting minister was free to choose his text at will.

In Wales, the history of post-Restoration Dissent is that of its preachers: Enoch Francis, Miles Harry, Morgan Griffith, and Timothy Thomas were most renowned among the Baptists, while Philip Pugh, Edmund Jones, and Lewis Rees had prominence among the Congregationalists (Jenkins and Lloyd). Francis (1688–1740) fulfilled a distinguished ministry in Cardiganshire and the Teifi Valley; Harry (1700–60), the leader of the Monmouthshire Baptists and associate of the Methodist revivalist Howell Harris, ensured that the energies of the Evangelical movement would be channelled into the Older Dissent; Griffith (1699–1748), a zealous evangelist, led the movement in the eastern part of Glamorganshire; while Thomas (1720–68), minister at Aberduar, Carmarthenshire, combined literary gifts with a consummate doctrinal precision.

Following the Toleration Act of 1689, the Welsh Dissenting community knew itself to be both a minority and, with memories of the Great Rebellion still potent, politically suspect. Its exclusiveness was bolstered by church discipline, zealously upheld, and high Calvinist doctrine (D. D. Morgan 1990). For a small religious body, barely tolerated by law and held in fear and contempt by its opponents, the stratum of biblical teaching which emphasized that the elect would be few, the flock to which the kingdom was given was little, had a particular relevance. It made unpopularity, social ostracism, and even persecution bearable: it provided a rationale for the movement's comparative insignificance. Similarly, the theological conviction of irresistible grace guaranteed Dissenting churchmanship with a sense of psychic security which bolstered group solidarity. Welsh Dissenting sermons between 1689 and 1760 underpinned this exclusivity.

'We see here for whom Christ suffered,' reasoned John Jenkins, pastor of the Rhydwilym Baptist church in Pembrokeshire, in 1721.

It was for his elect, those given to him by the Father in the eternal covenant. He did not suffer for all men, for he says to some, 'You are not of my flock, nor do you recognize my voice'... It was on behalf of the elect that Christ suffered, the elect alone. (NLW 1059A)

Enoch Francis, a much more winsome preacher whose Calvinism was a good deal more moderate than his Rhydwilym colleague, also proclaimed the absolute sovereignty of God in salvation. 'The Lord', he maintained, 'gives grace only to those whom he wills, in the way he wills, when he wills' (NLW 1059A). 'Election', claimed Francis in a treatise of 1733, 'is that part of God's immutable, eternal and all-wise decree that he, of his free grace and immeasurable love, fore-ordained a certain number of men through Christ for eternal salvation' (Francis 1733: 5).

Within the churches there was some tension between High Calvinism, which was in danger of muting the general gospel call in the belief that God, through his absolute decree, would call his own come what may, and a much more open evangelicalism which balanced the divine sovereignty with the need for an unfettered human response. High Calvinism could degenerate into a speculative theory which limited preaching only to those who were thought (or thought themselves) to be the elect. At the Baptist Association meeting in Swansea in 1727, 'there was some debate...about preaching to sinners, and several reasons given for it' (J. Thomas: 43). The logic of the High Calvinist position was that if Christ's death had been sufficient for the redemption of the elect, then only they could justifiably be called upon to accept its saving benefits. Such logic was eschewed, the speculation which would sometimes bedevil the extreme doctrine was largely avoided, and following debate at the next association, in 1728, the principle of 'preaching to sinners' (J. Thomas: 44) became the accepted rule. The truth of the doctrine of election notwithstanding, the gospel was meant for all. High Calvinism gave way to 'moderate' or evangelical Calvinism which would characterize the movement throughout the Evangelical Revival and beyond.

In a rousing sermon on Ephesians 5:14, 'Awake, O sleeper, and arise from the dead', Enoch Francis's stress on man's inability to rise of himself is never used as an excuse for unbelief. The fact of spiritual death is squarely faced: 'The man who is dead in his sin...is like a corpse, he knows nothing of his state.' He must be touched by God: 'When the Lord...in his glorious salvation says, as he did to Lazarus, "Come forth", so he who is spiritually dead must first hear the call of Christ before he is made alive.' It was the sinner's duty to obey the call. 'Let us make sure that we are awake and not asleep' (NLW 1059A). In a sermon on Hebrews 10:22, the pastor of Pen-y-fai church in Glamorgan, Jacob Rees, issued a similar appeal. 'What prevents a man from turning to God?' he asked. 'A fear of losing the respect and friendship of carnal friends when starting out on the road to religion?' This, he claimed, was a small price to pay for eternal salvation. 'Remember', he said, 'that the ministers of the gospel are ready to do all they can to assist you; remember that the Spirit of God is yet at work!' (NLW Cwrt Mawr 68A). It was the Holy Spirit, active through the preaching of the gospel, which applied the benefits of Christ's death to the elect. 'The promise of salvation is for all who believe in the Son and who walk in his ways,' Enoch Francis insisted. 'There is no discrimination: God's revealed will is man's only rule' (Francis 1733: 29).

The basis of this promise and the evangelical Calvinists' rationale for calling all people to repentance was the all-embracing sufficiency of Christ's atonement. 'Christ's death', it was claimed, 'is sufficient to save all of mankind, though it is only effective for the elect; and the reason that it is only effective for them is due to the particular work of God's Spirit within' (Francis 1733: 77–8). The discrepancy between God's general desire for repentance and the melancholy fact that many reject the gospel (a rejection which, according to the logic of Calvinism, must also be rooted in God's design), was explained in terms of God's twofold will. God's revealed will was that all should repent and be saved. That some would seem not to be saved was due to God's *secret* design. It was the individual's duty not to pry. 'Who the elect are and who the reprobate are is part of God's secret counsel,' it was argued. 'And as his revealed will and not his secret will has been given to us as a rule of life, the door of hope is still held open for all people who, as sinners, come to Christ' (Francis 1733: 31). It was no part of the preacher's duty to anticipate God's secret will. The inscrutability was counterbalanced by an open offer of the gospel: 'It is not for us to look towards the decree of God as a rule of life but the word of the gospel' (Francis 1733: 27).

Unlike High Calvinism, which believed that humankind had inherited a natural inability to repent due to Adam's fall, the evangelical Calvinism of Welsh Dissent held to freedom of choice. The unregenerate were indeed free to turn to God. They simply refused to use that freedom. God had provided all men—and women—with every encouragement: conscience, commandments, the gospel itself. But people chose not to obey. Their problem was moral disobedience, not natural inability. Individuals were responsible for refusing the gospel offer. 'It is the sinner's duty to come to Christ when he hears his call,' emphasized Francis. 'But as Christ says, "No one can come unto me except that the Father, who sent me", attracts him. The comfort for those who admit their inability is that the virtue and grace of God's Spirit is sufficient to assist them' (Francis 1733: 109). Francis could implore his many hearers in south-west Wales to secure their own salvation: 'The man who rejects Christ', he said in a sermon preached in 1722, 'is the most pitiful of men.' It was man who rejected Christ, not Christ who has rejected man. 'Return to him for you have forsaken the best place of all' (Francis 1722: 19).

Just as this pertains to the Welsh Baptists of the Older Dissent, virtually the same is true of the Independents (R. T. Jones 2004A: 79–109): Philip Pugh (1679–1760) who did so much to preserve the doctrinal rectitude of Cardiganshire Independency in the face of the encroachment of Arianism and who became the virtual mentor of Daniel Rowland, the revivalist; Edmund Jones (1702–93), the so-called *Yr Hen Broffwyd* ('Old Prophet'), Miles Harry's nemesis in Monmouthshire and virtually an archbishop among the Congregationalists; and Lewis Rees (1710–1800), a native of the Neath Valley in Glamorgan who pastored the notable congregation at Llanbryn-mair, Montgomeryshire, before returning to oversee the significant growth of the Independent cause in the environs of Swansea. For the Older Dissent ecclesiastical purity, doctrinal precision, and evangelical zeal went hand in hand. An openness to the missionary task and a yearning for a fresh outpouring of the Spirit meant that the Evangelical Revival was afforded a cautious welcome during the 1740s and '50s, and would wholly transform Welsh Protestant Dissent from the 1780s onward.

The Evangelical movement began within the confines of the Established Church. In 1735, independently of each other, the Anglican layman, Howell Harris (1714–73) of Trevecca, Breconshire, and Daniel Rowland (1730–90), curate of the parish of Llangeitho, Cardiganshire, both in the diocese of St Davids, experienced evangelical conversion and began preaching (or in Harris's case 'exhorting') with startling effects. As a layman, Harris was never comfortable with the appellation of preacher as he believed that the preaching office should be fulfilled by the ordained clergy. 'I could never call myself a preacher', he said in 1763, 'but an exhorter, my gifts being so' (Nuttall: 14). Yet it was he who helped spearhead the Welsh Calvinistic Methodist movement's evangelistic drive which had spectacular results first in his native south Wales and latterly in the north (E. Evans 1974). 'When alone I was taken up wholly in reading, praying, or writing', he reminisced of the beginning of his ministry, 'and also continued to go on exhorting the poor people and they flocked to hear me every Sunday evening' (La Trobe: 21). An example of the 'awakening' nature of his exhorting has been preserved by John Thomas, a convert who later became an Independent minister. Addressing a congregation in Llanddeusant, Carmarthenshire, in 1746, he said:

> You may have turned the pages of your Bible for forty years or more, yet you know no more of God than a dog or a sow. You may have been on your knees praying many times thinking yourself to be a fine practitioner of your religion though you have never prayed from the heart once. If God does not own your heart, he will have the devils tearing at you body and soul at the hour of death and in the Day of Judgement. I know that my shafts are sharp, but may God drive his words like bullets to pierce your heart. (I. Thomas: 29)

By challenging formal religiosity the Methodists both enraged the religious establishment and scored massive success in evangelism, and by the 1760s had created a powerful body, still nominally attached to the Established Church but organized in two associations, one in south Wales and the other in the north, with their scores of 'societies' or local fellowship meetings functioning as gathered congregations administering discipline and choosing their own officers and leaders.

As a beneficed clergyman (though he was still in fact curate to his father in the parishes of Nantcwnlle and Llangeitho in Cardiganshire, and later to his brother and even to his own son), Rowland was more wedded to the parochial system, and though he travelled extensively addressing fellowship meetings and building up the societies, the scene of his most impressive labours was the parish church at Llangeitho. This became a mecca for the Methodists of south-west Wales, even attracting large crowds from north Wales who would cross Cardigan Bay by boat for the monthly 'sacrament Sunday', just as the parish church at Llan-gan in the Vale of Glamorgan, south-east Wales, would draw immense crowds during the ministry of David Jones (1736–1810), Welsh Calvinistic Methodism's last clerical leader before the final rift with the Established Church in 1811.

If Harris's genius was for exhortation and the organization of the Methodist body, preaching of a more formal kind was Rowland's forte. Whereas he, too, would challenge conventional religiosity, telling the people that they needed to be 'born again', his sermons were accomplished works carefully crafted according to the Puritan style. As well as individual sermons published in 1739 and 1762, his *Tair Pregeth a bregethwyd yn yr Eglwys Newydd gerllaw Llangeitho* ('Three Sermons Preached in the New Church near Llangeitho') (1772), his *Pum Pregeth* ('Five Sermons') of the same year, and *Tair Pregeth…a bregethwyd yn ddiweddar* ('Three Sermons…Preached Recently') (1775) are a distillation of the thousands that he delivered during his lifetime. A careful exposition of the text is followed by divisions, subdivisions and applications, all in the Puritan mode, though clarity, simplicity and directness are maintained throughout. Though it is difficult to square the dramatic descriptions of joyful exuberance and revivalistic paroxysms which were said regularly to accompany Rowland's preaching (E. Evans 1985: 69–80, 117–28) with the reasoned, polished style apparent on the printed page, there is no doubt that verve, order, and extraordinary spiritual power went hand in hand: 'The ecstasy and rejoicing which are contained in these sermons are eloquently controlled within a framework of reasoned doctrine' (D. L. Morgan: 500). It was Rowland's orations even more than Harris's organizational ability which became the benchmark for the view, prevalent throughout the nineteenth century, that Wales was the home of 'preaching second to no other under the sun' (Griffith 2001). 'Mark my words', wrote the Baptist Christmas Evans in 1838,

> The talent of periwigs (*dawn y perwigau*) [Evans's phrase for the formalistic preaching of the Older Dissent] is in danger of returning to Wales. That talent was dry and stilted, it made all the listeners fall asleep. Many of the old Presbyterians and the Baptists were able preachers but their style was so cold and lifeless that it froze everything that it touched. But when Rowland of Llangeitho…and others began preaching as though fired from heaven, the old periwigs were forced to pack their goods and dismantle their stalls for there was no-one left to listen to them in neither fair nor market from Holyhead to Cardiff. (Rowland: 180)

To mention Christmas Evans (1766–1838) is to link the preaching of Older Dissent with popular evangelicalism and the exuberance of eighteenth century revivalism with the advent, by the early nineteenth century, of 'Nonconformist Wales' (D. D. Morgan 2008). By 1790 both the Baptist movement and Welsh Independency were being revitalized, their high and corporate Dissenting ecclesiology being progressively weakened by the individualism of the Evangelical movement even as their effectiveness and popularity was being maximized to an unprecedented degree. The Welsh Baptists' 35 churches of 1790 had become 81 in 1815 and over 300 by mid-century while the Independents' 100 or so churches in 1790 had increased to 257 by 1815 and over 500 three decades later (D. D. Morgan 1988; R. T. Jones 2004b: 149). Equally significant was the fact that 1811 witnessed the secession of the Methodist movement from the Established Church to create the Welsh Calvinistic Methodist Connexion, now a Presbyterian body with a character and constitution of its own (Roberts: 281–376). By 1811 a significant portion of the Welsh people had become Nonconformists while the 1851 religious census showed that 80 per cent of the nation's worshippers or some 400,000 people, in a much expanded population, practised their religion, namely evangelical Protestantism, outside the pale of the Established Church (I. G. Jones). According to its principal apologists, it was by preaching that this 'nonconformist nation' perpetuated itself (T. Rees: 24–9). 'There can hardly have been a time in the history of Wales', noted R. Tudur Jones, 'when so many people were exposed to so much public speaking of which the sermon was the most common form' (R. T. Jones 2000: 240). Consequently, within Nonconformist Wales the preacher reigned supreme.

If there were poor preachers, the charlatans and mountebanks that the Anglican satirist David Owen, 'Brutus' (1795–1866), delighted in lampooning, not least in his rollicking 'novel' *Wil Brydydd y Coed* ('Will the Poet of the Woods') which appeared month by month in the Church publication *Yr Haul* ('The Sun') between 1863 and 1866 (Owen), there were also those who brought huge distinction to the Welsh pulpit. The three whose names are invariably mentioned as exemplifying the best in pulpit oratory at the beginning of the nineteenth century are Christmas Evans, a Baptist, John Elias (1774–1841), a Calvinistic Methodist, and William Williams of Wern, near Wrexham (1781–1840), an Independent.

Evans began life in poor circumstances in Cardiganshire and his religious upbringing, such as it was, had been among the Arminian Presbyterians of the Teifi Valley who were even then veering towards rationalist Unitarianism. Converted during a local revival, he came to espouse the Baptist faith, was ordained into that denomination's ministry and held pastorates on the Lleyn peninsula and in Anglesey (1789–1826), and in the south, Caerphilly and Cardiff (1826–32), returning north once more, to the town of Caernarfon, for the last six years of his life. 'He was a natural orator, fluent and brilliant of speech, a master of metaphor, wit and sarcasm' (L. I. Evans: 319). Although he published many of his sermons during his lifetime, it was only at the end of the century that his whole oeuvre was brought together in three bulky volumes (Davies). The pattern of each sermon was uniform: the exposition of a text with an introduction, three points or headings leading to an oratorical climax. The many divisions and subdivisions that had characterized the Nonconformist pulpit during the previous century had yielded to a simpler form better adapted to the capacities of the multitudes which thronged to listen to the peripatetic preachers in the associations, gatherings and vast assemblies that had multiplied since the 1790s. 'Perhaps there has never been such a nation as the Welsh who have been won over more widely to the hearing of the gospel', Evans wrote in 1812. 'Meeting houses have been erected in each corner of the land and the majority of the common people, nearly all of them, crowd in to listen. There is virtually no other nation whose members have, in such numbers, professed the gospel so widely' (C. Evans: 13). The doctrinal scheme which underpinned his message was the evangelical Calvinism that had become the shared orthodoxy of the Welsh Nonconformist pulpit during the nineteenth century, though Evans had been tainted at different times by Sandemanism—a dry High Calvinism which balked at overt experientialism—and a concept of the atonement which evenly balanced the depth of Christ's passion with the amount of human sin as though it were a commercial transaction. His genius, however, was in his luxuriant parabolic imagination.

> The sermons of Christmas Evans are considered in Wales of unrivalled excellence, especially in regards the ingenuity and splendour of their imagery and the appropriateness and force of their application. The author displays extraordinary knowledge of human nature and great power of imagination in drawing pictures from scenes of real life for practical purposes, so that when he preaches his applications shock the congregation like electricity. (Davis: 3)

Uniquely for a Welsh language preacher of the time, he gained wide recognition in both England and America through the publication of more than one English translation of his memoirs along with selections from his sermons (Davis; Phillips; Stephen; Cross; D. M. Evans). The 'allegory of the graveyard' from a sermon on Romans 5:15 in which Mercy and Justice are personified, with Christ, the Seed of the Woman, providing surety for the lost posterity of Adam by dying in their place, illustrated the baroque and picaresque cast of his mind. Similarly a famous sermon on Luke 8:26–39, the story of the Gadarenian swine, transfers the biblical scene to the hills of Wales replete with a dialogue between the swineherds Morgan and Tom, who have to explain to their master why his prize pigs had rushed over a cliff into Cardigan Bay! This use of wit and humour, which would be perfected by the Calvinistic Methodist Edward Matthews in mid-century, was wedded to a seriousness of purpose which secured Christmas Evans's standing as the most inventive of Welsh preachers during the first part of the nineteenth century.

Humour is not a trait one associates with John Elias. If Evans's background was in the Older Dissent of south Wales, Elias was brought up in the Established Church in north Wales as it was being increasingly influenced by the evangelicalism of the Methodist movement. The son of a Caernarfonshire weaver and like Christmas Evans of humble circumstances, he was drawn towards Methodism and joined his local 'society' as a lad of fifteen. He began preaching five years later, in 1794, and soon won a reputation for gospel preaching of immense gravity, passion and effectiveness. According to Owen Thomas, the historian of Welsh preaching—whose biography of John Jones, Tal-sarn, is a classic of Welsh prose—, Elias's outstanding trait was 'a deep and solemn conviction of the divine nature of the gospel and of the immense importance of its content for a lost world' (O. Thomas: 857). Following marriage in 1799, he moved to Anglesey where he became a neighbour to Christmas Evans, and from then until the end of his life the island would remain his home.

It was as a peripatetic orator, however, via the ever growing network of Calvinistic Methodist associations and preaching assemblies, that he made his name. 'He became', according to Owen Thomas,

> the most popular preacher...who ever arose in Wales. He was so from the beginning, and he was so to the end. He was so at home, and elsewhere: in Anglesey as well as Gwent, in Llangefni as in Llangeitho or Carmarthen. He was so in the towns and in the countryside, amongst the rich, the noble and the learned, as with the poor, the uneducated and the ordinary folk. (O. Thomas: 854)

Of immense strength of personality, his authority over the north Wales Methodists steadily increased and following the death of Thomas Charles of Bala (1755–1814), the clergyman who had presided over the ordination which created the Welsh Calvinistic Methodist Connexion in 1811, and even more so after the demise of the movement's premier theologian, Thomas Jones of Denbigh (1756–1820), his rule became absolute. Yet it was as an evangelist, preacher and the means of conversion of thousands, that this authority was sustained. In a single sermon, during a harvest fair in Rhuddlan, Flintshire, on a Sabbath afternoon in 1802, not only was the fair terminated, but the whole institution of hiring fairs on Sundays was thereafter discontinued (E. Morgan: 86–90).

> It is…a matter of wonder that one preacher, facing a mob bent on pleasure and more than a little drunk, could destroy the institution of the Sunday fair in the whole county with one sermon. It is a remarkable proof of the power of the preached word in 1802—and of the stature of the preacher. (R. T. Jones 1975: 11)

A selection of Elias's sermons was published in two volumes in 1849, eight years after his death (Hughes). They are sternly doctrinal but give little insight into the power with which they were accompanied. Like Owen Thomas, as a young man the Welsh-American biblical scholar Llewelyn Ioan Evans heard him many times:

> His powers to give reality to all that he said was extraordinary… The action of his index-finger alone was a study and a marvel… Add to this the sweep, the rush, the thrust, the blow of the sinewy arm, the authoritative stamp of the foot— add a plain style of marvellous fitness for popular effect, homely, plain, at the same time pure, strong, nervous Welsh from the granite rock-bed of the language—add a wonderful gift in fitting such words together, so that they would strike home—add the perfect preaching temperament with its instinctive perception of the tone, the temper, the atmosphere of the congregation, and the exact point at which to get the mastery of it—add a holy audacity which shrank from no lawful expedient to arouse and hold the people—over and above all add a burning passion for souls, an awful intense earnestness which had in it all the solemnities of the eternities, and you may faintly conceive the power of the man. (L. I. Evans: 330–1)

In all, John Elias was the most powerful preacher that Wales produced during the nineteenth century.

The third member of this triumvirate, the Independent William Williams of Wern, is the one who became least familiar to succeeding generations. A Methodist by background and conversion, the fact that he sought membership in a Congregational church, a branch of the Old Chapel in Llanuwchllyn, near Bala, in 1796, signified the way in which the Evangelical Revival was permeating the Older Dissent. Although he undertook training in the Dissenting academy at Wrexham, according to the cerebral discipline of his adopted tradition, his ordination in 1803 before the end of his course showed how evangelistic pragmatism was gaining the upper hand over academic finesse. 'There was in his sermons', related Llewelyn Ioan Evans, a remarkable combination of clear and vigorous thought, with lucid and felicitous illustration. So perfect were his illustrations that it seemed as though they had an existence in the order of things, on purpose to set forth the truths with which they stood associated. Reflection made his hearers feel that it was the truth which glorified the emblem, and not the reverse. (L. I. Evans: 328)

According to R. Tudur Jones, Williams could

> wed the philosophical and theological interests of the Nonconformist sermon to the liveliness, intensity and warmth of Methodist preaching. He could reason exceptionally clearly and there were none better at explaining a complex doctrinal topic. For his hearers, his strength lay in his simple and memorable expositions. But he, too, would bring pressure to bear on the consciences of his congregation, 'he pursued them from every direction, he followed them to every refuge, he disarmed them of every counter-argument' and all…to bring them to the crisis of decision. The effect of his preaching can be measured…from the assessment of his contribution by William Williams (Caledfryn): 'His arising was a means to put new life into the Independent cause in North Wales'. (R. T. Jones 2004a: 120)

Although an early biography was published in 1842 (W. Rees), it was not until 1894 that a hefty commemorative volume including a diplomatic edition of his best sermons appeared (D. S. Jones).

With the death of Williams of Wern in 1840, it was apparent that preaching had become the single most powerful aspect of life in Nonconformist Wales. Those who followed on—the Calvinistic Methodists Thomas Richard (1783–1856), Ebenezer Morris (1790–1867), Morgan Howell (1794–1852), John Jones of Tal-sarn (1796–1857) and supremely Henry Rees (1789–1869); Baptists like Ellis Evans (1786–1864) and Independents like William Rees (1802–83), better known by his bardic name of 'Gwilym Hiraethog' (Jenkins and Lloyd)—maintained both the style, content, and effectiveness of their immediate predecessors. Of these Henry Rees was the most exquisite. According to Owen Thomas:

> In Henry Rees, the pulpit reached, in our judgement, the highest perfection it has ever attained in our country, and we know of no-one in any country or in any age, whose sermons, considered as compositions, we should be willing to acknowledge as being superior to his. (quoted in L. I. Evans: 334)

The three highly accomplished volumes, published between 1872 and 1881, give ample substance to this view (R. Edwards).

Under this constellation of sanctified talent, the whole nation, it seemed, had been transfixed by the preaching of the Word. 'Taking everything into consideration', noted Edward Matthews in a seminal essay on Welsh preaching published in 1863, 'Wales can take pride in the fact that although she is bereft of many things, she is the home to the best preaching in the world, and the strongest yearning among the people to listen to such preaching' (Matthews: xvi). According to his contemporary, the Swansea Independent Thomas Rees: 'While it appears that the bulk of the working classes of England never attend the means of grace, and that a large proportion of them are avowed infidels, fully ninety per cent of the corresponding classes in Wales regularly attend public worship, except in the large towns and the most Anglicized districts' (T. Rees: 24). The country was certainly changing: its population was expanding, industrialization had become more widespread and intense, not least in the south Wales coalfields which were opening up and the north Wales quarrying districts, while partial Anglicization was beginning to occur, but zealous and activist biblical religion was a constant. 'The working classes of Wales', claimed Rees, 'have been evangelized by a faithful preaching of the gospel, the whole gospel and nothing but the gospel' (T. Rees: 25). Whatever we make of the hyperbole, they prided themselves that their preachers were in a category of their own: 'It is Wales that has reared... the most original, talented and powerful preachers of any country in the world' (Matthews: xxxii).

The gospel preachers who retained prominence during the third quarter of the century were no less gifted: Lewis Edwards (1809–89), John Phillips (1810–67), Roger Edwards (1811–86), Owen Thomas (1812–91), Edwards Matthews (1813–92) and David Saunders (1831–92) among the Calvinistic Methodists; Robert Ellis 'Cynddelw' (1810–75), William Roberts 'Nefydd' (1821–78), John Jones 'Mathetes' (1821–78) among the Baptists; Thomas Rees (1815–85) and John Thomas (1821–92) among the Independents, and many more, were in continuity with those who had gone before, but there were signs by then that the civilization which had been moulded by gospel preaching would be challenged by ideals and philosophies which would call many of the old truths into question. The generation of preachers who were called to hold the field until the end of the century and beyond had to contend with a changing world and shifting expectations.

Thomas Charles Edwards (1837–1900), son of Lewis Edwards, principal of the Calvinistic Methodists' Bala College and scion of a family which included the denomination's founding father, Thomas Charles, was both an intellectual leader and a preacher of huge renown. A New Testament scholar of note and the first principal of the University College of Wales, Aberystwyth, '[t]he one central fact about him', remarked his student and another gifted pulpit orator, J. Puleston Jones (1862–1925), 'was that he was a great preacher' (J. P. Jones: 356). Yet it was he who analyzed most acutely the social and philosophical changes which would, by the twentieth century, undercut the effectiveness of the evangelical pulpit in Wales. 'In our fathers' days', he told the General Assembly of the Welsh Calvinistic Methodists, meeting in 1888, 'it could be taken for granted that theology was the abiding concern of a huge swath of the Welsh lay folk, but can that be said of today? Now it is politics or scientific theory, and is it not a fact that our young men not only have no theology but have no appetite for it at all?' (T. C. Edwards 1888*a*: 282). 'In the present condition of things in Wales', he informed the Pan-Presbyterian Council in London in that same year, 'you have a people actually weary of contending systems, keenly alive at the same time to the fascination of new ideas, political and scientific, and, for this reason, in danger of drifting away from theological truth altogether' (T. C. Edwards, 1888*b*:110). It was not that the gospel was failing to be preached. The basic soundness of the evangelical pulpit could not be faulted. What was new was that the listeners, still active in their chapels, were becoming more and more sceptical as to the reality of divine truth. 'In our age agnosticism has come to the front as a conscious phase of the human intellect and teaches our young men not that this or that solution to the problem is fallacious...but that the problem itself need not be solved either way' (T. C. Edwards 1888b: 111). If the Dissenting divines and the Methodist Fathers had debated passionately and at length about the extent of the atonement, the present generation hardly believed in any sort of atonement and thought that it was all a waste of time: 'The greatest danger that besets religion in Wales today is plain. The sense of sin is not keen' (T. C. Edwards 1888b: 109). What, therefore, was to be done? To preach Christ, certainly, but not Christ as the linchpin of a sacrificial theory, but Christ in the glory of his incarnate person, come into the world to share the joys and sufferings of an increasingly inquisitive and sceptical generation: 'Theology will come afterwards, and it will come with a greater force... [Then] comes the preacher's golden opportunity to proclaim the infinite atonement through the infinite sacrifice of the God-Man' (T. C. Edwards 1888b: 11). Edwards's sermons, published posthumously in 1900 (T. C. Edwards 1900), show the way in which the emphasis, even in Welsh language discourse, was changing. They were sacramentalist in tone and underpinned by a philosophical idealism that saw Christ as fulfilling all that was best in human life. 'By the turn of the century', wrote R. Tudur Jones, 'it was apparent that the focus of Welsh preaching was shifting from the atonement to the incarnation, to Bethlehem rather than Calvary' (R. T. Jones 2004b: 143). His exercise in kenotic theology, *The God-Man*, published in 1895 along with the Welsh version, *Y Duw-Ddyn*, two years later, shows how the tenor of Welsh theology was shifting, with immanence rather than the divine transcendence coming well to the fore (D. D. Morgan 2009).

Just as Edwards epitomized the doctrinally informed pulpit of the late Victorian and Edwardian eras, the preacher who best characterized the transformation which was occurring between an older religiosity and the more hesitant mood of the new century was the Congregationalist Howell Elvet Lewis (1860–1953). The sermons exemplified by those published in his enormously popular volume *Plannu Coed a phregethau eraill* ('Planting Trees and other sermons') (1898), a reference to the grove planted by Abraham at Beersheba in Genesis 21:33, established a new mode of discourse: lyrical, understated, non-dogmatic though still incontrovertibly evangelical. There was, alas, a feeling abroad that the age of the great preacher was drawing to a close. Despite the renewal in the Welsh Anglican Church (Knight; D. D. Morgan 2011: 23–37, 78–93), Nonconformity remained central to the Welsh experience (D. D. Morgan 2011: 9–23, 107–72) and as such the pulpit took preference over the altar. Whether the pulpit would be able to retain its hold on the nation was being questioned. The fact that prayer and praise rather than powerful preaching characterized the great religious revival of 1904–5 underscored that point (R. T. Jones 2004b: 283–369). There was a wistfulness abroad that a great tradition was coming to an end.

In summarizing the character of Welsh preaching during these years, R. Tudur Jones remarked:

> What we see in the period between 1890 and 1914 is that the preaching tradition that did so much to shape modern Wales was beginning to disintegrate. There was much excellent preaching of course, but it was no longer a formative influence on thought,

culture and morality of the nation. Doctrinal preaching maintained its pre-eminence but it was beginning to lose its vigour, either because it was turning into a weary repetition of worn-out theological truths or because it embraced opinions that dulled its spiritual force. In consequence there developed a reaction against doctrine and the undisciplined allegorization of fancy and poetic preaching began to undermine the pulpit's gravitas. Generally speaking the pulpit reneged on its responsibility to keep daily before Welsh eyes the gravity of sin and contented itself with mentioning general principles now and then. In all, there were definite signs of a crisis in the pulpit. (R. T. Jones 2004b: 160)

It was in the twentieth century that this crisis would register most fully (D. D. Morgan, 2011). For the most part between 1689 and 1901 the vernacular sermon retained its character as a formative influence on the history of the people of Wales.

References

Cross, J. C. (1851). *Sermons of Christmas Evans, a New Translation from the Welsh, with a Memoir of the Author.* Philadelphia: Leary & Getz.
Davies, O. (ed.) (1898–9). *Gweithiau Christmas Evans.* Caernarfon: Gwenlyn Evans.
Davis, J. D. (1837). *Sermons on Various Subjects by the Rev. Christmas Evans.* Beaver: W. Henry.
Edwards, R. (ed.) (1872–81). *Pregethau gan y diweddar Barchedig Henry Rees.* Treffynnon: P. M. Evans & Son.
Edwards, T. C. (1888a). 'Prif nodwedd yr adeg bresennol ar grefydd yn y Cyfundeb'. *Y Drysorfa* 58: 280–90.
—— (1888b). 'Religious Thought in Wales', in D. D. Williams (ed.), *Thomas Charles Edwards.* Liverpool: National Eisteddfod Transactions, 103–12.
—— (1900). *Pregethau y Parch. Thomas Charles Edwards.* Bala: Davies & Evans.
Evans, C. (1812). 'Cyflwr crefydd yng Nghymru (1812)', in Owen Davies (ed.), *Gweithiau Christmas Evans*, vol. 3. Caernarfon: Gwenlyn Evans, 9–14.
Evans, D. M. (1863). *Christmas Evans, a Memoir.* London: Bunyan Library.
Evans, E. (1974). *Howel Harris Evangelist, 1714–73.* Cardiff: University of Wales Press.
—— (1985). *Daniel Rowland and the Great Evangelical Awakening in Wales.* Carlisle, PA: Banner of Truth.
Evans, L. I. (1893). 'The Welsh Pulpit', in *Poems, Addresses and Essays.* New York: Christian Literature, 310–59.
Francis, E. (1722). Sermon on John 6:68, preached in Rhydwilym, 1722, in *Trysorfa y Bedyddwyr* 1 (reprinted 1828).
—— (1733). *Gair yn ei Bryd.* Caerfyrddin: John Ross.
Griffith, W. P. (2001). '"Preaching Second to No Other under the Sun": Edward Matthews, the Nonconformist Pulpit and Welsh Identity during the Mid-Nineteenth Century', in R. Pope (ed.), *Religion and National Identity: Wales and Scotland c.1700–2000.* Cardiff: University of Wales Press, 61–83.
Hughes, R. (1849). *Pregethau y diweddar…John Elias*, vols. 1 and 2. Liverpool: Owen.
Jacob, W. (2007). 'Part II: 1660–1780', in G. Williams, W. Jacob, N. Yates and F. Knight (eds.), *The Welsh Church from Reformation to Disestablishment, 1603–1920.* Cardiff: University of Wales Press, 65–164.

Jenkins, G. H. (1978). *Literature, Religion and Society in Wales, 1660–1730*. Cardiff: University of Wales Press.

Jenkins, P. (2003). 'Church, Nation and Language: the Welsh Church, 1660–1800', in J. Gregory and J. S. Chamberlain (eds.), *The National Church in Local Perspective*. Woodbridge: Boydell and Brewer, 265–84.

Jenkins, R. T., and Lloyd, J. E. (1959). *The Dictionary of Welsh Biography Down to 1940*. London: Honorable Society of Cymmrodorion.

Jones, D. S. (1894). *Cofiant darluniadol y Parchedig William Williams, o'r Wern yn cynwys pregethau a sylwadau o'i eiddo*. Dolgellau: W. Hughes.

Jones, I.G. (1976). *The Religious Census of 1851: A Calendar of the Returns Relating to Wales*, vols. 1 and 2. Cardiff: University of Wales Press.

Jones, J. P. (1905). 'Principal Thomas Charles Edwards MA, DD', in J. V. Morgan (ed.), *Welsh Religious Leaders of the Victorian Era*. London: J. Nisbet, 356–77.

Jones, R. T. (1975). *John Elias, Prince Amongst Preachers*. Bridgend: Evangelical Library of Wales.

—— (2000). 'Nonconformity and the Welsh Language in the Nineteenth Century', in G. H. Jenkins (ed.), *The Welsh Language in its Social Domains, 1801–1911*. Cardiff: University of Wales Press, 239–64.

—— (2004a). *Congregationalism in Wales*, R. Pope (ed. and trans.). Cardiff: University of Wales Press.

—— (2004b). *Faith and the Crisis of a Nation: Wales 1890–1914*, ed. R. Pope, trans. S. P. Jones. Cardiff: University of Wales Press.

Knight, F. (2007). 'Part IV: 1860–1920', in G. Williams, W. Jacob, N. Yates, and F. Knight (eds.), *The Welsh Church from Reformation to Disestablishment, 1603–1920*. Cardiff: University of Wales Press, 309–99.

La Trobe, B. (1791). *Brief Account of the life of Howell Harris Esq*. Trevecka: n.p.

Lewis, H. E. (1898). *Plannu Coed a Phregethau Eraill*. Bala: Davies & Evans.

Matthews, E. (1863). *Bywgraffiad y Parch. Thomas Richard*. Abertawy: Joseph Rosser.

Morgan, D. D. (1988). 'Smoke, Fire and Light: Baptists and the Revitalization of Welsh Dissent'. *The Baptist Quarterly* 32: 224–31.

—— (1990). 'The Theology of the Welsh Baptists, 1714–60'. *The Journal of Welsh Ecclesiastical History* 7: 41–54.

—— (2008). 'Christmas Evans (1766–1838) and the Birth of Nonconformist Wales', in *Wales and the Word: Historical Perspectives on Welsh Identity and Religion*. Cardiff: University of Wales Press, 17–30.

—— (2009). 'O'r Iawn i'r Ymgnawdoliad: cyfraniad diwinyddol Thomas Charles Edwards (1837–1900)'. *Diwinyddiaeth* 61: 6–27.

—— (2011). *The Span of the Cross: Christian Religion and Society in Wales, 1914–2000*, 2nd edn. Cardiff: University of Wales Press.

Morgan, D. L. (1978). 'Llenyddiaeth y Methodistiaid', in G. M. Roberts (ed.), *Hanes Methodistiaeth Galfinaidd Cymru*, vol. 2, *Cynnydd y Corff*. Caernarfon: Llyfrfa'r Methodistiaid Calfinaidd, 456–528.

Morgan, E. (1844, repr. 1973). *The Life and Letters of John Elias*. London: Banner of Truth.

National Library of Wales (NLW) MS 1059A, sermon preached at Rhydwilym, 24 February 1723
—— Cwrt Mawr MS 68A.

Nuttall, G. F. (1965). *Howel Harris (1714–73), the Last Enthusiast*. Cardiff: University of Wales Press.

Owen, D. (1949). 'Brutus', in T. Jones (ed.), *Wil Brydydd y Coed.* Cardiff: University of Wales Press.

Phillips, D. (1843). *Memoir...of the Rev. Christmas Evans.* New York: M. W. Dodd.

Rees, T. (1866). 'The Working Classes of Wales and Religious Institutions (1866)', in *Miscellaneous Papers Relating to Wales.* London: John Snow, 24–9.

Rees, W. (1842). *Cofiant y diweddar Barch. William Williams o'r Wern.* Llanelli: Rees & Thomas.

Roberts, G. M. (ed.) (1978). *Hanes Methodistiaeth Galfinaidd Cymru,* vol. 2, *Cynnydd y Corff.* Caernarfon: Llyfrfa'r Methodistiaid Calfinaidd.

Rowland, J. (1879). *Cofiant y Parch Daniel Davies DD.* Llanelli: James Davies.

Saunders, E. (1721, repr. 1949). *A View of the State of Religion in the Diocese of St David.* Cardiff: University of Wales Press.

Smalbroke, R. (1726). *A Charge to the Clergy of the Diocese of St Davids.* London: John Nicks.

Stephen, D. R. (1847). *Memoirs of the late Christmas Evans.* London: Aylott and Jones.

Thomas, I. (1810, repr. 1949). J. Dyfnallt Owen (ed.) *Rhad Ras.* Cardiff: University of Wales Press.

Thomas, J. (1795). *A History of the Baptist Association in Wales from the Year 1650 to the Year 1790.* London: Dilly and Button.

Thomas, O. (1874). *Cofiant y Parchedig John Jones, Tal-sarn.* Wrexham: Hughes & Son.

Watts, M. (1985). *The Dissenters: Volume I: From the Reformation to the French Revolution.* Oxford: Oxford University Press.

White, E. M. (1997). 'The Established Church, Dissent and the Welsh language, 1660–1811', in G. H. Jenkins (ed.), *A Social History of the Welsh Language: The Welsh Language Before the Industrial Revolution.* Cardiff: University of Wales Press, 208–35.

Williams, G., Jacob, W., Yates, N., and Knight, F. (2007). *The Welsh Church from Reformation to Disestablishment, 1603–1920.* Cardiff: University of Wales Press.

CHAPTER 13

ORDER AND UNIFORMITY, DECORUM, AND TASTE: SERMONS PREACHED AT THE ANNIVERSARY MEETING OF THE THREE CHOIRS, 1720–1800

ANDREW PINK

Each year the UK's Three Choirs Festival provides a rich musical feast, both sacred and secular, comprising choral and orchestral music, community events, and theatre productions, spread over a week of late summer. The Festival is held in rotation in the three cathedral cities of Hereford, Gloucester, and Worcester, and is generally accepted as the world's oldest music festival, dating to at least the second decade of the eighteenth century. Then it was known as the Anniversary Meeting of the Three Choirs, and was organized as follows:

> The time of meeting is the first Tuesday in September, on Wednesday is a Sermon, on Thursday Purcel's Te deum performed with instruments as are the Anthems on both days. The two evenings there are public Consorts for the gentry. (Bisse 1726: 39 n.)

Initially, this Meeting was seen in purely musical terms as an 'anniversary testimony of ... fraternal concord' (Bisse 1720: 63) among the assembled cathedrals' musicians and as making a contribution to 'the advancement and propagation of musick for [God's] Holy Temple' (Bisse 1720: 64). In 1724 a charitable dimension was added to this annual musical meeting, a 'new and blessed work of Charity' (Bisse 1726: 38), explained in these terms:

> Church-musick was the original design of our Meeting, antecedent to other additions. But as all human designs, however praise-worthy, and wherever executed, receive not only an improvement, but a sort of consecration, from charity; so those designs which are of themselves in a manner hallowed and promoted also in an holy place, among which Ours may be ranked, are more hallowed and advanced by the mixture of charity. (Bisse 1729: 19)

This charity provided for

> placing out the children of the poorer Clergy belonging to the Dioceses of Glocester, Worcester, and Hereford, or of the members belonging to the three respective choirs. To be equally divided and disposed of by six Stewards, two for each Diocese, a Clergyman and a gentleman, members of the Society, and the account to be entered at the annual meeting. The first Collection [1724] amounted to 32 l. The two last [1725, 1726] to 50 l. A sum sufficient to place out three children annually, which has been accordingly done. (Bisse 1726: 38–39n)

Funds for the charity were raised not only by the collection at the Meeting's cathedral services, but also from the sales of printed sermons preached at them and the sale of tickets for evening concerts. Stewards were appointed annually to be responsible for underwriting the costs of the Anniversary Meeting and overseeing the disbursing of its charity funds.

Those familiar with the Church of England at this time will notice a similarity between the charitable activities of the Anniversary Meeting and those of the Corporation of the Sons of the Clergy, a London-based charity established in 1655. It supported clergy in the London diocese impoverished as a result of sequestration from their livings during the interregnum. The similarity was no accident: the Corporation was the Anniversary Meeting's model, as was made clear in the Hereford sermon of 1729, when the Corporation was described as

> that renowned Society, incorporated for the relief of the widows and orphans of the poorer Clergy…begun by our Fathers escaped out of the universal wreck of the Rebellion: Who in remembrance of their brethren that escaped not, and in compassion to their widows and children, met together a few of them weekly to begin and to give into a fund for the relief of a few. This voluntary communication of friends when known abroad, soon grew up into this mighty Corporation, established with a Charter, Laws and Offices. And the Collection, which might at first be contained in a scrip or poors-box, is now received into a Treasury. And the celebration of its annual Festival, Of which this our day of rejoicing is an exact resemblance in smaller proportion, fills our *Jerusalem* with admiration and joy. (Bisse 1729: 16–17)

We shall return to the subject of the Corporation in due course.

The Local Context

The precise origin of the Anniversary Meeting of the Three Choirs is lost in the mists of time, but understood to have sprung from a very small and accidental origine...a fortuitous and friendly proposal between a few Lovers of harmony, and brethren of the correspondent Choirs, to commence an anniversary visit to be kept in turn: Which voluntary instance of friendship and fraternity, was quickly strengthen'd by social compact. (Bisse 1729: 10)

It is thought that this 'friendly proposal' may have originated in the music clubs then to be found in the three cities (Boden: 9), and the earliest dated reference to such 'an anniversary visit' is found in the *Worcester Postman* of 14–21 August 1719, where we read that

The members of the yearly Musical Assembly of these Parts are desired to take Notice, That, by their Subscription in September last at Gloucester they are obliged to meet at Worcester, on Monday the last Day of this instant August. In order to publick Performance, on the Tuesday and Wednesday following. (Boden: 12)

From this notice we also have the evidence of a previous meeting in Gloucester in 1718, and it is apparent that the Meeting was already taking place over two days. While there is no reference here to a sacred component it seems likely that even then the cathedral musicians took the opportunity to share in each other's liturgical performances, an opinion we have seen already expressed by the preacher of 1720. This position is reinforced by the fact that in 1709 we find evidence of such joint liturgical performance in that year's publication of a set of the Matins canticles *Te Deum* and *Jubilate* in E-flat, jointly composed by Henry Hall the younger (d. 1714), organist of Hereford Cathedral, and William Hine (1687–1730), organist of Gloucester Cathedral. Furthermore, the Gloucester Cathedral accounts for 1709 record a payment of the relatively large sum of £2 to the organist of Hereford to be at Gloucester during that year, enough to suggest the presence of other musicians too (Boden: 9). Retrospectively, the date of 1709 for a festival in Gloucester fits neatly the regular sequence of the locations of the known Anniversary Meetings from 1718—Gloucester in 1718, Worcester in 1719, Hereford in 1720, and so on.

Whatever their origin, these Annual Meetings might have remained an item of purely local interest except for the arrival at Hereford in 1716 of Thomas Bisse (1675–1731), the new cathedral chancellor whose brother Phillip (1666–1721) had been Bishop of Hereford since 1713. Thomas seems to have treated this appointment as a non-residentiary sinecure, as too his appointment to the local living of Cradley (Marshall 2004b). Both brothers were prominent High Church Tories under Queen Anne (Marshall 2004a), their careers helped in no small part by the fact that at this time the Tory leader at court—Robert Harley, Earl of Oxford and Mortimer—was their cousin.

The death of Queen Anne in August 1714 and the accession of George I ushered in a period of change in the fortunes of many Tory churchmen whose previous ascendancy at court was superseded by those with Whig loyalties (Speck). This meant an end for old assumptions in politics and religion, and for an ambitious man like Thomas Bisse this was set to be a frustrating time (Weber: 115): as proved the case, neither Thomas nor Phillip was to receive further preferment.

By the time the Bisse brothers arrived at Hereford they were already active supporters of the Corporation of the Sons of the Clergy, which, like them, was distinctly High Church and Tory in sympathy: even after 1723 when the Corporation was headed by a succession of Whiggish archbishops of Canterbury 'it was slow to lose its Tory streak' (Weber: 105). As part of its fund-raising, the Corporation organized an annual charity service of choral Matins at St Paul's Cathedral with the support of Chapel Royal musicians as well as those from St Paul's, and a standard feature of the event was the setting of the *Te Deum Laudamus* and *Jubilate Deo* in D by Henry Purcell. Among the Corporation's preachers were high-profile, high-church Tory figures such as Francis Atterbury and Henry Sachervell. Phillip Bisse preached at the Corporation's annual Festival in 1708, the first year an orchestra was used, and was its president from 1717 until his death in 1731. Thomas preached at the 1716 Festival.

It is well known that in the early decades of the eighteenth century the Corporation's annual festival service came to be regarded as a notable event in the social calendar, as much for who was to be seen in the congregation as for the cause of the charity, becoming increasingly fashionable once the use of an orchestra became a regular feature. Also of significance at this time was the fact that following the King's proroguing of the Convocations of Canterbury and York in 1717, in reaction to the lower house of Canterbury's censure of the Whig Bishop Benjamin Hoadly (Taylor), the Corporation provided the only opportunity for the nation's 'lesser clergy' to meet together on a formal occasion (Cox: 51). Despite its High Tory complexion, the Corporation pragmatically reached out to engage with leading Whig clergy, so that in the political and religious context of its day the Corporation was able to provide a degree of mediation to bridge Anglican divisions in place of Convocation (Weber: 103). However, its imitator in the West Country, the Annual Meeting of the Three Choirs, was to remain a largely Tory affair, reflecting the political and social interests of the local clergy, the local gentry, and the local Members of Parliament, from among all of whom its stewards were drawn (Weber: 119–20). While the government might impose Whig bishops, the majority of the parochial clergy in these dioceses was appointed by lay patronage—69 per cent in Hereford in the mid-century—and many were sons of clergy, or even 'plebeians' who were likely to support the politics of their patrons (Jacob: 78, 40). Positions which were entrenched in the dioceses were difficult to shift. The majority of the published preachers—twenty-five, in fact—held posts within the three dioceses. Three-quarters held degrees from nearby Oxford and some of the handful of Cambridge graduates had family ties to the dioceses (Foster; Venn and Venn) and even the Cambridge-educated Whig poet and pluralist Samuel Croxall came to his prebend and parish in Hereford via a position as chaplain in ordinary in the Chapel Royal.

At Hereford, Thomas and his brother found themselves facing a number of local financial problems common to many provincial dioceses, not least a cash-strapped cathedral Chapter still struggling to fully re-establish itself decades after the interregnum, and rural clergy poverty. Not only were the three adjacent dioceses of Gloucester, Hereford, and Worcester among the least wealthy in England, but they had also been the sites of some of the fiercest strife of the Civil War. As early as 1697, hoping to address the poverty of his clergy, Bishop Croft of Hereford had offered the Corporation £300 to be invested specifically to provide a fund to assist the clergy of his diocese, but eventually to no avail (Cox: 36–7). While the diocese of Hereford was unsuccessfully turning to

London for financial help, clergy elsewhere in the country had already begun to organize themselves locally on the model of the Corporation: Norfolk, 1684; Bristol, 1692; Chester, 1697; Suffolk, 1704; York, 1722; and Durham, 1726 (Cox: 36–9). So it was that in 1724, under the energetic leadership of Thomas Bisse, the dioceses and cathedral chapters of Hereford, Gloucester, and Worcester took the opportunity provided by the annual meeting of their cathedral musicians to follow this fund-raising trend. As Bisse himself noted in his Anniversary Meeting sermon of 1726, in Hereford,

> Having first proposed this Charity with success at Glocester [sic],1724, and recommended it at Worcester, 1725, I thought myself obliged to promote it in this way, in the Church and Diocese to which I belong. (Bisse 1726: 38–9 n.)

The Sermons

Just twenty-nine published sermons survive from the more than eighty Anniversary Meetings that took place in the eighteenth century. While the three cathedrals' libraries contain very few, all twenty-nine are to be found in the British Library and all are available online (ECCO). Apart from these we also know a few facts about some 'lost' Meeting sermons from references to them in newspaper reports. In some of these reports we have just the name of the preacher, as at Gloucester in 1736, when *The Daily Gazetteer* of 16 September reported

> the Service was perform'd to the great Satisfaction of all that were present, and an excellent Sermon suitable to the Occasion was preach'd by Rev. Dr. Ellis, one of the Prebendaries of the Cathedral Church of Gloucester. (*Daily Gazetteer*: 2)

In other cases we have what amounts to a brief review, such as the report in *The Gloucester Journal* on 13 September 1784, which noted that

> The occasional sermon was preached by the Rev. the Dean [Josiah Tucker], who, in a discourse, as well directed to the understanding as to the benevolent affections, pointed out the excellence of a charity instituted for the relief of a description of persons in peculiar circumstances. His text was well selected to animate us in the prosecution of these meetings, *Let us not be weary of well doing*. (*Gloucester Journal*: 3)

From some of the printed sermons we learn that their sale in print was to benefit the Meeting's charitable aims (that of 1755 was 'Printed for the Benefit of the Charity') and so it may be that a sermon was printed only where funds were available to cover the cost. In some cases a sermon is dedicated to an elite patron, and we can imagine that here the dedicatee, or one of their circle, may have promised to defray the expense of publication where no other source was available. A likely example is the 1724 sermon dedicated by Henry Abbot to Lord Bathurst, a staunch Tory, described by Abbot as: *'not only an Admirer, but a great Encourager of Musick; and to be a true Son of the*

Established Church, (where God is worshipped in the Beauty of Holiness)' (Abbot: i). At other times the sermon appears to have been 'printed for the Author', such as that of 1750 by Henry Procter.

It must not be overlooked that the publishing of the sermons would have been beneficial not only for the charity but also for the preacher, if not in financial terms then in terms of the exposure it gave him on a national stage, since they were almost always printed and sold in London, and often in Oxford, as well as in the Meeting's three cities, and occasionally in Bath and in Birmingham. Such publication announced the preacher's active association with the Meeting, and on occasion with an elite patron too, assuring recognition of the preacher's theological and social credentials.

A scriptural epigraph is a feature of all the sermons, and while in some cases these refer to charity they more commonly relate to music, for example, 'As well the Singers as the Players on instruments shall be there: Ps.88, v.7' (Croxall). It is notable that all twenty-nine surviving sermons are preached on different texts.

In some cases the sermon is also given a title, and once again the theme of music in worship predominates, for example, *The Use and Benefit of Church Music Towards Quickening our Devotion* (Abbot). On just a few occasions the title brings together the themes of music and charity: *The Pleasure of Gratitude and Benevolence Improved by Church-Musick* (Parker). However, regardless of their titles and texts, the charity and church music are invariably discussed to a greater or lesser extent in all the sermons.

The Sermons and Church Music

Repertoire

Concerning the music used during the eighteenth-century Anniversary Meetings' cathedral services, and church music more generally, the sermons directly tell us almost nothing of repertoire and very little about how it was performed. We know most about the music used for the period after 1752—settings and anthems—from pieced-together details given in newspaper reports (Shaw: 111). Then the music of Purcell and/or Handel (both Chapel Royal composers) most often provided the settings for *Te Deum* and *Jubilate Deo*, a pattern only occasionally interrupted by, for example, settings 'adapted from Italian Masters' performed at Worcester in 1775 and 1783, or by the long-forgotten Wainwright, also at Worcester, in 1776. The anthems were most often the coronation anthems of Handel (especially *Zadok the Priest*), and then the so-called charity anthems of another Chapel Royal composer, William Boyce: *Blessed is He that Considereth the Poor* in 1741 and *Lord, Thou Hast Been Our Refuge* in 1755 (Boden: 24). The latter was composed for the Corporation, and both anthems were a regular feature there also (Bartlett and Bruce). Although Boyce himself had participated in the 1737 Meeting at Worcester and was connected with Meetings until at least 1756, evidence for his visits is sparse. Other anthems by such little-known composers as 'Stephens, Norris, Alcock or Howard break in only sporadically' (Shaw: 12–13).

For the period before 1752, despite the paucity of contemporary information, we can see already that Purcell's *Te Deum* and *Jubilate Deo* (composed 1694) were a staple feature at the first day's Matins service, and it seems likely that, until 1736, settings by Chapel Royal composer William Croft featured at the second (Shaw: 8; Boden: 17). After 1736 Croft's setting was replaced by Handel's 'Utrecht' setting (composed 1713), itself superseded in the 1750's by his later 'Dettingham' setting (composed 1743). Furthermore, in 1784 the second day's service of choral Matins (including Purcell's *Te deum*) was phased out in favour of a concert of miscellaneous sacred music composed entirely by Handel (Boden: 32–3). Handel is also the only composer specifically referred to in a sermon, just once, as an example of great skill in setting text to music (Rawlins: 24).

William Croft and Thomas Bisse were on personal terms, having received their doctoral degrees at the same time (Bisse 1726: 3), and they would have worked together as part of the Corporation of the Sons of the Clergy. This may explain the dedication of Bisse's 1726 sermon to Croft, in which Bisse described him as the equal of his Chapel Royal predecessors, naming Thomas Tallis, William Byrd, Orlando Gibbons, William Child, John Blow, and Henry Purcell, all of whom 'if living, would readily admit Croft upon their Roll' (Bisse 1726: 4–5).

Into this list of composers Bisse also inserted the name Henry Aldrich (1648–1710), Dean of Christ Church, Oxford from 1689 to 1710. Although only a minor composer in his own right, Aldrich is now recognized to have been one of the most influential Tory churchmen of his day, who gathered round him an influential circle of elite young students such as Edward Harley (1689–1741), son of the Robert Harley already mentioned, who was at Christ Church from 1707 until 1711. With these young men Aldrich shared his collection of 'antient musick', which at the time was 'England's most important early collection of music from the sixteenth and seventeenth centuries' (Weber: 34). It is perhaps no coincidence that between 1714 and 1720 the Harley family employed the 'ardent Tory' (Spink) Thomas Tudway, organist of King's College, Cambridge from 1670 to 1725, to create their own collection of 'antient' English cathedral and Chapel Royal music in six thick quarto volumes, destined for the family library at Wimpole Hall, Cambridgeshire (Harleian Manuscripts). It was the 'antient' musical tradition that Aldrich established at Oxford—and which was embraced by those who experienced it—that would eventually establish the works of Blow, Byrd, Child, Gibbons, Purcell, and Tallis at the heart of the daily repertoire of Anglican cathedral music (Weber: 32–6, 115).

Although, with the exception of Purcell, none of these composers appear to have provided music for the Meeting's Matins canticles or anthems, their mention could be an indication that their work provided the music for other parts of the Matins service. Writing in 1715, Thomas Tudway had noted that: 'those few places or churches who still make any uses of responses on great days always use Mr Byrd's' (Wilson: 138). We also know that Blow wrote four short services—each with chants for the psalms—that were then in circulation (Wilson: 138), while Tallis's music, both for the Litany (prescribed to follow Matins on Wednesday, Friday, and Sunday), and for the preces and responses, was in use in many cathedrals, often in adapted versions made by Aldrich and Tudway (Wilson: 145–7). Notwithstanding, the overall picture of the music at the Annual Meeting is of a rather narrow repertoire, despite the frequency of Meetings and the fact that their purpose was, in part at least, to promote cathedral music.

Order and Uniformity

The degree to which music should be used in the performance of Prayer Book liturgies (including chanting, recitation, and response), as well as the suitability of metrical psalms, was much discussed by eighteenth-century churchmen: 'Clerical arguments for and against choral service, pronounced in sermons and treatises revolved around perceived requirements of public worship such as order and uniformity, decorum and taste, and, above all, comprehension' (Wilson: 132), concerns that we find discussed in the Meeting's sermons.

Of those preachers who discuss the details of liturgical performance—George Lavington in 1725, Thomas Bisse in 1726, and Richard Banner in 1737—it was Bisse who dealt with the matter at greatest length, advocating a fully sung ('chaunted') service:

> Chaunting the Service is found more efficacious to awaken the attention, to stir up the Affections, and to edify the understanding, than plain reading of it...wrought principally by the melody of the voice...That there be a modest and distinct song so used thro' all the parts of the Common-Prayers, that the same may be as plainly understood as if it were read without singing...[A]t the close of each Prayer or Collect a certain modulation, inflexion or change of voice, such as is accustomed, is both necessary and becoming...placed upon that constant close 'through Jesus Christ our Lord'...[I]t serves as a publick sign or warning to the Choir to join in the approaching Amen. For the same reason it is also necessary in Chaunting the Versicles and Responses distributed throughout the Liturgy. (Bisse 1726: 32–5)

He went on to say that such musical custom was not only born out of necessity, in order for the liturgy to be better heard and understood within the large interior expanse of a cathedral, but also out of uniformity since 'chanting unifies and orders the responses of the people' (Bisse 1726: 38–9). He also argued for the use of the organ to accompany the whole congregation in the Litany, and the Creed as a means to uniformity, and likewise the Psalms, which are

> pointed, so as to be Sung in Churches; which had they to have been said only, would have required a different punctuation...The like artificial pointing, for the like end, is given to the Hymns and the Athanasian Creed...that one uniform manner of pronunciation should be observed in all Churches, if not of singing or chaunting as in Cathedrals, yet of saying or reading the Service in one equable unvaried Tone. (Bisse 1726: 47–9)

Banner was the only preacher to address directly the use of metrical psalms in Anglican churches. For him such music was an unfortunate product of 'the Puritan faction' introduced into public worship with no ecclesiastical authority. It was, he said, a musical practice that had lessened regard for the music of the cathedrals. However, while he thought such 'rhyming Performance' (Banner: 13) was inappropriate for cathedral worship, metrical psalms were an entirely useful solution in parish churches that had no choir, where, with the addition of instruments, including the organ, such

> Use of singing Psalms may improve the harsh unpleasing voices and unskilled singing of the common People [with] grave and melodious Instrumental Musick which tends to regulate the Time, and rectify the Tune, checks and prevents the over eagerness of some, drowns and mollifies the clamorous Harshness and Untuneableness of others, and in short adds such a grave and decent Solemnity to the whole Performance as may make harmony and devotion meet together. (Banner: 14)

In a properly ordered church music there were to be no unintelligible words or unnecessary repetitions (Bisse 1720), and while it was agreed that music carefully chosen could be put to good use by religion to prepare the mind for worship, some preachers—Lavington in 1725, Bisse in 1726 and 1729, John Newton in 1748, and William Parker in 1753—warned that it was important to be aware of music's potential to mislead the passions:

> Seeing, then, that Music seizeth irresistibly upon the Affections, and, when duly attended to, can raise, and still govern the Passions, with an almost arbitrary Sway; who can doubt the Utility of it in religious Worship? Indeed, so subservient it seems to all the Purposes of Religion, and particularly to the Sacrifice of Praise, that Religion, at least this Part of it, can never be full and strong without it. (Morell: 21)

However, it was made clear that there should be a distinction between the serious uplifting music suitable for the use of the church and the frivolous music that inspires levity and immorality. So music in church must be solemn and majestic, 'raising a devout admiration in the hearers; and preparing the mind for the reception of sacred truth' (Glasse: 14), and 'regular and well-ordered' (Harper: 8). Certainly, music should be ordered according to the rubrics of the Prayer Book and injunctions of the Crown (Bisse 1720: 57–64) and performed without drunkenness (Lavington: 3), shouting, 'yellings, and vociferations' (Banner: 26), with high moral standards (Brooker: 25), and at all times maintaining a sense of the divine (Parker: 25). The substance of public worship is holiness and the form of it ought to be beautiful (B. Newton: 6).

A Theology of Music

Above all, the sermons make us aware that in eighteenth-century England the use of any music by the Established Church was not at all a matter to be taken for granted. In their discussion of church music, the preachers' overriding concern was to justify the use of music in worship.

Several preachers felt obliged clearly to state the fundamental propriety of using music in Christian worship as a direct response to the complaints of English Protestant Dissenters:

> It cannot but appear surprising to us, that the Sectaries of *this Island* shou'd so Industriously defend that Enmity, which they show to Musical Instruments in our Churches; when 'tis so Notorious that the Generality of the *Foreign Reform'd*, as well as Calvinists and Lutherans, continue to use, and therefore to Approve them. It can therefore be no way Accounted for, that our *British Dissenters* are so very Averse to a sort of worship, that Foreign Protestants can see no superstition in. (Harper: 20)

Bisse noted recent attacks based on Erasmus's criticism of the worship of Roman church, whose

> Hymns, as well as their Prayers, were performed in an unknown Tongue; so that their Singing was mere Noise, and could contribute nothing to Devotion. But this is no more an Argument against English Hymns, and Anthems, than against English Prayers...[in] our own happy Establishment. (Bisse 1724: 20)

Banner reassuringly pointed out that the Lutherans and Calvinists allowed singing and organs, even at the communion, a point reiterated the following year, apparently against ongoing claims by Dissenters that the Church of England's use of music was Popish (Payne). The point was returned to again in 1746 by Thomas Morell. The exasperated preacher of 1748, John Newton, asserted that the Church should no longer heed the claims of the Dissenters whose objections are simply 'the Dictates of a vicious or prejudic'd mind, the offence cometh from them' (J. Newton: 25). In 1773 John Rawlins told the Meeting simply to ignore such criticism as a 'dismal kind of Fanaticism' (Rawlins: 22).

In theologizing music in the Christian liturgy, the preachers also make clear that the use of music in worship always had divine approval. Discussion was dominated by the Old Testament and its references to the development and use of choirs and instrumentalists in Temple worship, begun by Saul and brought to fulfilment by David. Bisse, in 1720, Banner, John Newton, Robert Eden in 1755, John Rawlins, William Langford in 1788, and Thomas James in 1800 all contributed to this. Daniel Brooker, the preacher of 1743, pointed out that even God himself was willing to appear in the Temple (as a cloud of glory) when there were singers and instrumentalists present. There are several other examples of the direct approval shown by God towards music. Preachers noted that Moses was instructed to praise God with trumpets (Bisse 1720); that music in all its forms was already present in the antediluvian world, and yet God permitted it to survive the Flood (Bisse 1729); and that the Book of Revelation shows that instrumental music is acceptable to God (Harper).

The preachers pointed out that from the time of Christ—who himself, according to Banner, must have attended music services at the Temple—music was integral to the worship of the early church and encouraged by St Paul (Lavington; Cotes). Other New Testament church leaders using music in worship—specifically singing—were cited by Banner, such as James and Silas, and Banner also made use of Pliny's contemporary report that describes the use of music by early Christians. Indeed, it was reasoned that since the Church of God was at first Jewish, so the Christian Church was only the same but 'more Refin'd and Enlarg'd [as] is manifest in the whole tenor of the Gospel' (Harper: 12).

Coda

The importance of the sermons preached at the Anniversary Meetings lies not in their musical content, for indeed there is little of that, but in what they can tell us of the social, political and religious context of eighteenth-century English church music, and the attitudes of those who sought to uphold its continued use—specifically those concerned with the Annual Meeting of the Three Choirs. It is also clear from the sermons (though not discussed at length here) that despite the national interest shown in the Annual Meeting, as seen in the regular reports of it to be found in the London press, the organizers never lost sight of the Annual Meeting's local charitable concerns. What these sermons can reveal about the period's theology of charity, and attitudes towards clerical vocations in eighteenth–century England, remains to be explored.

References

Abbot. H. (1724). *The Use and Benefit of Church-Musick, towards Quickning our Devotion*. London: Jonah Bowyer.
Banner, R. (1737). *The Use and Antiquity of Musick in the Service of God*. Oxford: printed at the Theatre.
Bartlett, I. and Bruce, R. J. (n.d.). 'Boyce, William', Grove Music Online. Oxford: Oxford University Press.
Bisse, T. (1720). *A Rationale on Cathedral Worship or Choir-Service*. London: W. and J. Innys.
—— (1726). *Musick the Delight of the Sons of Men*. London: William and John Innys.
—— (1729). *A Sermon Preach'd in the Cathedral Church of Hereford*. London: William Innys.
Boden, A. (1992). *Gloucester, Hereford, Worcester, Three Choirs, A History of The Festival; with Annals of the Three Choirs by Christian Wilson*. Stroud: Sutton.
Brooker, D. (1743). *Cathedral Music, Skilfully and Religiously Performed, a Reasonable Service*. London: J. and J. Bonwicke.
Cotes, D. (1756). *Music a Rational Assistant in the Duty of Praise when United with Charity*. Hereford: James Wilde.
Cox, N. (1978). *Bridging the Gap. A History of the Corporation of the Sons of the Clergy over Three Hundred Years, 1655–1978*. Oxford: Becket Publications.
Croxall, S. (1741). *The Antiquity, Dignity and Advantages of Music*. London: J. Watts and B. Dod.
Daily Gazetteer. (16 September 1736).
ECCO (n.d). *Eighteenth-Century Collections Online*. Farmington Hills, MI: Gale Publishing.
Eden, R. (1755). *The Harmony of Benevolence*. London: W. Sandby.
Foster, J. (1968). *Alumni Oxonieneses: The Members of the University of Oxford, 1500–1886*. Nendeln, Liechtenstein: Kraus Reprint.
Glasse, S. (1778). *The Beneficial Effects of Harmony*. Gloucester: R. Raikes.
Gloucester Journal. (13 September 1784).
Harleian Manuscripts. British Library, 7337–42.
Harper, J. (1730). *The Natural Efficacy of Music to Prepare the Mind for Good Impressions*. Oxford: Richard Clements.

Jacob, W. M. (2007). *The Clerical Profession in the Long Eighteenth Century, 1680–1840*. Oxford: Oxford University Press.

James, T. (1800). *The Prophetic Office Connected with Poetry and Music*. Worcester: J. Tymbs.

Langford, W. (1788). *A Sermon, for the Relief of the Widows and Orphans of Clergymen, Belonging to the Three Dioceses of Worcester, Hereford, and Gloucester*. Worcester: J. Holl.

Lavington, G. (1725). *The Influence of Church-Music*. London: Knapton.

Marshall, W. (2004a). 'Bisse, Philip (*bap*. 1666, *d*. 1721)', *ODNB*. Oxford: Oxford University Press.

—— (2004b). 'Bisse, Thomas (1675–1731), Church of England Clergyman and Founder of the Three Choirs Festival', *ODNB*. Oxford: Oxford University Press.

Morell, T. (1746). *The Use and Importance of Music in the Sacrifice of Thanksgiving*. London: M. Cooper.

Newton, B. (1760). *The Church of England's Apology for the Use of Music in her Services*. Gloucester: R. Raikes.

Newton, J. (1748). *The Natural, Moral, and Divine Influences Of Musick*. London: E. Cave and T. Payne.

Parker, W. (1753). *The Pleasures of Gratitude and Benevolence Improved by Church-Musick*. Oxford: James Fletcher.

Payne, T. (1738). *A Defence of Church-Musick*. Oxford: James Fletcher.

Procter, H. (1750). *A Sermon Preach'd at the Cathedral-Church of Hereford*. Gloucester: the author.

Rawlins, J. (1773). *The Power of Musick, and the Particular Influence of Church-Musick*. Oxford: Clarendon Press.

Shaw, W. (1954). *The Three Choirs Festival. The Official History of the Meetings of the Three Choirs of Gloucester, Hereford and Worcester c.1713–1953*. London: Baylis & Sons.

Speck, W. (2004). 'Harley, Robert, First Earl of Oxford and Mortimer (1661–1724), Politician', *ODNB*. Oxford: Oxford University Press.

Spink, I. (2004). 'Tudway, Thomas (*c*.1656–1726).', *ODNB*. Oxford: Oxford University Press.

Taylor, S. (2008). 'Hoadly, Benjamin (1676–1761)', *ODNB*. Oxford: Oxford University Press.

Venn, J, and Venn, J. A. (1974). *Alumni Cantabrigienses: A Biographical List of All Known Students, Graduates and Holders of Office at the University of Cambridge, from the Earliest Times to 1900*. Nendeln, Liechtenstein: Kraus Reprint.

Weber, W. (1996). *The Rise of Musical Classics in Eighteenth-Century England: A Study in Canon, Ritual, and Ideology*. Oxford: Clarendon Press.

Wilson, R. A. (1996). *Anglican Chant and Chanting in England, Scotland and America 1660–1820*. Oxford: Clarendon Press.

PART III
OCCASIONAL SERMONS

CHAPTER 14

THE SERMON, COURT, AND PARLIAMENT, 1689–1789

PASI IHALAINEN

In all ages and societies the representatives of public religion and the secular authorities have cooperated in the field of preaching: ceremonies with religious content have been used to express and teach the supposedly shared values of political communities—or at least the norms the holders of power wished to propagate. This was increasingly the case in Protestant countries as from the Reformation onwards churches came to be regarded as spiritual extensions of the secular state. Medieval traditions of preaching at court and to representative institutions became regular events. It was not only celebrations of political anniversaries and extraordinary national events that gave rise to sermons on the shared values of the political community; such values were also constructed, reinforced, and gradually redefined in connection with ordinary Sunday services attended by members of the royal family and the estates of the realm.

Preachers on such occasions were customarily leading clerics. At court, royal chaplains or clergymen who held suitable views on the constitution and the reigning dynasty, or whom the monarch otherwise favoured, were invited to speak, while bishops or other (would-be) senior clergymen were engaged by leading political actors to preach at other institutions. The methods of appointing the preacher varied from country to country, but the orator always acted on an official invitation from a secular authority. Quite often his sermon was also based on a biblical passage determined by that authority and applied to the subject of the political occasion under the control of the same elitist audience. The preacher was well aware that some members of the audience had the power to decide whether he would be rewarded for his endeavours and his sermon would be printed. This decision was a vital one: the sermon would be either accorded the status of a model text with official approval or doomed to be forgotten amongst the ephemera of pulpit oratory.

These circumstances surrounding preaching at courts and estate and parliamentary meetings throughout early modern Europe meant that the sermons were not only—or even primarily—religious texts. Nor did they usually constitute media for excessively individualistic interpretations of either religious truths or contemporary political reality. Their delivery was essentially a political act concerning the norms, values, attitudes, and opinions that prevailed in a particular political culture, in which the preacher served the state by performing the role of a popularizing political theorist, a role given to him by the political community. Political sermons at court and in Parliament were used to define the collective political and social values of the community—or at least to propagate those of the majority of its current rulers. Alternatively, they could be used to deliver partisan messages designed to advance the politico-religious cause of the group whom the speaker and some of the audience represented. In England and Sweden, where clergymen were allowed to vote, they were engaged in politics especially when party disputes involved religion. In the predominantly political contexts in which they were speaking, they were certainly expected to have something to say that was relevant to their authoritative audience, and their comments had to be formulated carefully in order to please that audience. By giving a rational or moving expression to values shared by many members of the elite, a clergyman could avoid controversies that might harm his career. At the same time, as an interpreter of God's word, he possessed a special authority which allowed him the liberty to raise matters which were of concern to the community (Ihalainen 2005: 38–41).

Royal courts had become venues for preaching, and major celebrations of the royal family were occasions for delivering some of the most important political sermons in every realm. This was the case particularly in Protestant monarchies such as England, Scotland, Denmark, Sweden, and many German lands, where the nationalization of public religion had in practice made the monarch the highest prelate of the Established Church. England was essentially a Protestant monarchy in which the succession to the throne was settled on religious grounds in 1689 and again in 1701. The union between the Church of England and the Protestant monarchy, still endangered by Jacobite plots, was regularly reinforced by inviting leading clerics to preach at court and by printing their sermons as a form of royal communication to the subjects. Until 1717, the court rather than Parliament was the most frequent forum for the highest political preaching in England. However, the printing of such royal propaganda abated suddenly after 1717; in this respect, Britain differed from the other Protestant monarchies, most of which published court sermons uninterruptedly well into the nineteenth century.

Why did the originally Lutheran Hanoverians and their Whig allies, after experimenting in the years 1714–17 with court preaching of the type employed by their predecessors, reject this traditional medium, which had evidently served the construction of the Protestant monarchy's image well, and which continued to be used elsewhere in Protestant Europe? Rather than in some early 'secularization' of the British monarchy, an explanation may be found in the experiences of the Bangorian Controversy of the late 1710s: the Hanoverian dynasty and the governing Whig faction learned how risky it was to use court sermons for propaganda purposes, as they could also be employed for the presentation of excessively radical and partisan politico-religious views. By no longer printing them, the crown relegated court sermons to the status of ephemera. From then on, only coronations and occasional family events would associate the crown with printed sermons; this represents a major change from the practice during the reigns of William and Mary and Anne and is very different from those of the Protestant monarchies and republics on the Continent.

While the pulpits of the Hanoverian court were marginalized as forums for explicit politico-religious debate, British high-profile political preaching was 'parliamentarized' after the Revolution of 1688 and, in comparison with the court, increasingly after 1717. This may be considered a symbolic reflection of the rise of Parliament as the centre of political debate, even if preaching was not quite as central a feature of the British Parliament as it was in many European diets. British parliamentary preaching in itself was not unique: the practice was common in all countries whose representative institutions survived the seventeenth century. For centuries sermons had constituted a means of communication between the rulers and the ruled. The genre was quite similar everywhere: the preachers were appointed from among the best educated and informed members of each political community, namely the leading bishops, and the sermons were given under the supervision of the rest of the political elite. The chosen clerics looked for ways to express the normative values of the community in terms that were acceptable from the theological point of view of the public church but also designed to serve the secular interests of the ruler and the majority of the political elite. Furthermore, they attempted to make their message understandable to all, including those who were not members of the political elite.

It was likewise a general early modern practice for sermons such as those given at the opening and closing of the diet (in Sweden) or preached to local estates in connection with national events (in the Dutch Republic) to be printed and distributed to a wider audience. This practice promoted the survival of sermons as an important element of public debate throughout the eighteenth century. In any representative government, partisan considerations could play a role in the appointment of the preachers and the formulation of arguments, which made this a genre that was particularly prone to provoke controversy (Ihalainen 2005).

Britain was exceptional in the eighteenth century only in terms of the number of printed parliamentary sermons: at least two sermons were delivered each year on 30 January, the anniversary of the regicide of Charles I, at which time Parliament was always in session. In Sweden, only sermons at the opening and closing of the Diet were printed, after approval by the Clerical Estate. In the Dutch Republic, local regents might decide on the printing of sermons related to events concerning the House of Orange or delivered on days of prayer, but the clerics could also have their sermons printed independently. Thanks to the practice of printing, the sermons of clergymen who enjoyed the favour of monarchs and the majority of the estates have been more carefully recorded than political oratory in general. Even if the printed version does not register the authentic performance and the content may have been edited, the printed sermons survive as unique evidence of the prevailing, or at least expected, politico-religious attitudes of governing elites. Importantly, these were expressed in a sacred context—in connection with a symbolic encounter between a political community and its divinity. For the study of long-term change in political and social values, political sermons constitute a common European genre, the value of which cannot be overestimated.

Challenging the Secularist Paradigm

For much of the twentieth century, the social sciences and humanities were dominated by a simplistic secularization thesis which questioned the relevance of studying eighteenth-century 'religious' discourse, or left it for theologians to explore. Mainstream eighteenth-century studies consequently bypassed political sermons—together with many other 'religious' themes not related to outright dissent or anticlericalism—as irrelevant for research on an era of a supposedly secular Enlightenment. By the early twenty-first century, an awareness of the continuing importance of religion as a field of human thought and practice, within which seemingly secular values, too, are discussed and redefined, has grown again. This paradigm shift has opened up possibilities for a more authentic understanding of past political sermons, too.

Since the late 1980s, sermons have been rediscovered by historians in several countries and have been subjected to non-theological content analyses inspired by the linguistic, cultural, spatial, communicative, transnational, and even religious turns in historical research. These studies have demonstrated the anachronistic conclusions that an overwhelming secularization thesis can lead to: it can prevent us from accessing the very core of eighteenth-century debate not just on religious but also on social and political values. What started as a somewhat provocative revisionist reintroduction of religion to eighteenth-century studies in the 1980s (Clark) has by the 2010s turned into a balanced reintegration of sermons into the eighteenth-century public debate. The value of political sermons has also been reassessed by several scholars. Even if traditional religion was becoming less dominant in political theory in the course of the eighteenth century, religious practices and modes of discourse retained their role in political communication and need to be considered in an historical interpretation of the political cultures of the period.

As far as English court and parliamentary sermons are concerned, two scholars made significant reinterpretations in the field in the late 1990s. Tony Claydon focused on the highly developed court propaganda machinery of the reign of William III, arguing that printed sermons formed the most important medium for presenting the politico-religious ideology of the new establishment (Claydon 1996: 3, 18, 87). He even sees intentionality in the integration of Williamite propaganda into biblically based sermon discourses. Claydon also emphasized the contribution of the sermon pamphlets to the late seventeenth-century English print industry and the public sphere (Claydon 2000). They were easily available on the book market, cheap to buy, and discussed topical events that were easy for the reading public to understand. They were, in brief, a response to a genuine market demand. James Caudle has likewise pointed to the large number of sermons published in eighteenth-century Britain in comparison with political pamphlets, the form and content of which still often resembled those of sermons (Caudle 1996: 52, 118, 127–28, 132, 149; Caudle 2000). Caudle has emphasized the role of sermons as a medium that could be used to communicate the political theories, ideologies and discourses of the elite to the wider public and also to inculcate the key virtues of obedience and resistance. As rulers changed, the preachers were able to accommodate themselves quite well to the new circumstances—to the accession of the Hanoverians, for instance.

With regard to parliamentary sermons, Caudle has focused on the party-political interests that guided decisions to appoint particular preachers and to prevent others from speaking or from being published (Caudle 1996: 97–8, 119; 2000). In order to reveal these interests, he has explored the political connections of the MPs who officially invited and thanked the preachers and dealt with the publication and censorship of the sermons. While such contextualization helps us to interpret the sermons, there were not that many cases of parliamentary dispute and censorship: the most obvious disputes were linked to the days of thanksgiving in the early reign of Anne, to Sacheverell's trial in 1710, and to the Bangorian Controversy in 1717. In the last case, the majority of the Commons appointed a traditionalist preacher against the wishes of the Whig government. After 1730, parliamentary disagreements on sermons became rare, though there was one important exception that will be discussed below (Ihalainen 2005: 36–7, 42–4).

Research interests have been moving towards the ordering, organization, forms of prayer and rituals of state prayers, fasts and thanksgivings, more particularly in the British State Prayers Project coordinated at the University of Durham. At the same time, analyses of the content of political sermons given on particular days continue to be carried out by both historians and linguists. In Britain, political sermons were delivered not so much at the opening of Parliament as on major days of Anglican commemoration, for which specific liturgies had been formulated in the Restoration period: on 30 January for the anniversary of the execution of Charles I in 1649, on 29 May for the anniversary of the Restoration of 1660, and on 5 November for the double anniversary of the discovery of the Gunpowder Plot in 1605 and the Glorious Revolution in 1688. In the reign of Anne, her accession day (8 March) was also observed as it fell during the parliamentary session. Of these, the anniversary of the martyrdom of Charles I retained its status throughout the eighteenth century despite some controversy over the justification of its continued observance. January was a suitable time for such preaching because Parliament was then in session almost every year, and even though the themes of the anniversary were to some extent set by the liturgy, the preaching of sermons on 30 January and their printing can be considered the British equivalent of the sermons made at the opening of diets. While the tradition of preaching separately to both chambers on 30 January survived well into the nineteenth century, the sermons of 29 May and 5 November became rarer after the Hanoverian Succession. The Restoration was commemorated during the succession crisis of the mid-1710s, whereas the Jacobite risings and plots of 1715, 1722 and 1745 revived sermons on 5 November. Times of war still produced parliamentary sermons on days of prayer or thanksgiving for victories and peace treaties, and so did the rare coronations.

With regard to the sermons of 30 January, Françoise Deconinck-Brossard (2000) has emphasized the diversity of political opinions that could be expressed by preachers of various confessional and political backgrounds when preaching in different contexts. Generally speaking, these sermons, too, were also most likely to be printed in years which saw a particular political crisis, such as 1710, 1716, and 1745, thus creating a need to communicate political messages. As for their content, towards the mid-eighteenth century there was a decreasing tendency to view Charles I as a royal martyr and to preach sermons on the day of his execution. The parliamentary sermons that were given may then have had the specific purpose of providing models for parish clergy on how to preach.

Comparative international analyses of court and parliamentary preaching have also been undertaken. In *Protestant Nations Redefined* and related articles (Ihalainen 2005; 2007; 2009), I demonstrate that a considerable number of conceptual redefinitions took place in political preaching in Protestant countries such as England, the Netherlands, and Sweden during the eighteenth century. The common values expressed in sermons were being adapted to suit those of political elites who had been influenced by Enlightenment trends and the modernization of the national identity. Leading members of the clergy increasingly presented the national community itself as something that was collectively felt to be sacred rather than merely as a fallen nation like the people of Israel. They might even allow the nation and the people at large a more active role in the formation of the destiny of the national community. This phenomenon is one of the reflections of the continuing amalgamation of religion and national thought in a period when modern nationalism is generally considered to have emerged.

The potential for redefining the values of the nation varied from one Protestant country to another, however—and changes in Catholic countries are generally rather less evident. The introduction of various predominantly secular ways of thinking to political sermons led to more fundamental reformulations of the political values of the national community among the Whig bishops of the Church of England than among the Swedish Lutheran or the clerics of the Dutch Reformed Church, for instance. Even in the case of England, the shift was not a straightforward one, given the conservative reactions that followed the American and French Revolutions.

There is no denying the general trend, however: in England, the nation was increasingly described as able to advance the temporal common good rather than as a mere fallen nation awaiting divine judgement. This was the case even in the anniversary sermons in memory of Charles I, for which the usual point of departure had for so long been an Old Testament worldview. The relative relevance of the Israelite prototype of the nation thus declined. An equally noteworthy development is that religion came to be represented in nation-centred and broadly Protestant rather than discriminatively Anglican confessional terms, as had been the convention for so long. This meant that the nation was being gradually extended to include a degree of religious pluralism, even though prejudice towards Protestant Dissenters and especially against the Catholics would continue to appear in Anglican political preaching at least until the French Revolution. Even so, the concept of 'popery' as the stereotype against which to construct the collective identity weakened somewhat in the course of the eighteenth century.

As far as the institutions of the state are concerned, by the mid-eighteenth century the monarchy was defined in considerably less confessional terms than had been the case under William III and Queen Anne. While different personal attitudes to religion among monarchs certainly supported this weakening of depictions of the traditional Protestant monarchy, there is no denying the influence of Enlightenment thought in the background. This becomes particularly clear in comparison with Sweden, where it was still possible to reintroduce references to the monarchy as a specifically Lutheran institution after the coup of Gustav III in 1772.

Among the alternative secular political discourses, which had become dominant in the parliamentary and press debates of the political elite and which also increasingly found their way into political sermons, those of patriotism in its classical form, liberty, commerce, and scientific progress should be mentioned. The vocabularies of these expanding discourses of secular politics were incorporated much more strongly into the clerical definitions of the political values of the nation in Britain than in the Dutch Republic or Sweden. This was the case at least until the French invasion of the Netherlands in 1795 and the Swedish 'revolution' of 1809.

A comparative analysis of Protestant political preaching thus suggests that the rise of ways of thinking typical of modern nationalism (and to a much more limited extent even of representative democracy) took place not only parallel with and as an alternative to Protestant public religion but also within mainstream Protestantism as articulated on major political occasions. The transformation of political sermons thus appears as an aspect of the Enlightenment that occurred not only in opposition to but also within religion. Such an understanding of the Enlightenment not based on the exceptional case of France (Ihalainen 2008) may appear to challenge the long-dominant tendency to associate the eighteenth century, the Enlightenment, anti-Christian secularization, and the disappearance of religion from the European political debate with each other.

This thesis is supported not only by the findings of other scholars who have worked on political sermons and interaction between religion and the Enlightenment but also by some twenty-first-century social theory calling for the reconsideration of the secularization thesis (Sorkin). The findings of this and related analyses suggest that traditional religion was not simply replaced by modern national identities from the French Revolution onwards but actually turned into a source of support for a gradually secularizing civil religion of nationalism in the modern period, particularly in Protestant countries. This was by no means a simple transformation. While Anglican parliamentary preaching was adapting itself to changing political values especially in the 1760s and early 1770s, first the American War and then the French Revolution brought about the reintroduction of some of the more traditionalist descriptions of the nation. The relative importance of language referring to the nation seems to have declined, perhaps as a result of an increasing privatization of religion, and a certain weakening in feelings of national glory as a consequence of the defeat in the American War.

With regard to future trends of research on sermons, the following seems evident: despite the predominantly theological motivation of preaching and the obvious literary value of sermons, sermons given at courts and estate meetings should also be read as political texts. More particularly, they should be seen as texts within which considerable changes in content and revaluations of political values took place, particularly after the 1760s, despite the seeming continuity in the external forms of their production and performance. We can certainly find from much later times instances of sermons made to a representative institution that convey significant political messages. Such a reading of sermons calls for a rethinking of the conventional categorizations of religion and politics—something that is indeed going on both in early twenty-first-century social theory and in eighteenth-century studies. The study of political sermons might in fact become one of the areas in which the interdisciplinary rethinking of the post-Enlightenment categorizations can take place in a way that deepens our understanding of the rise of modernity.

Challenging the secularist paradigm, I argue that political sermons need to be seen as one of the key genres of the history of political and social discourse in the context of parliamentary institutions and the monarchy. Their analysis could indeed be made one of the focal areas of a 'new' political history motivated by linguistic, cultural, communicative, spatial, transnational, and religious turns in the study of political history. Parliamentary sermons should be seen as a major aspect of representative and parliamentary government, as a forum which brings the prevailing religious and political values of political communities together. Especially in Protestant contexts, they were adapted to the developing, increasingly parliamentary and democratic political cultures, albeit with some delay. This meant, for instance, a clearer distinction in this genre between separate religious and political spheres, even if the links between the sacred and secular continued to be cherished. In Britain, the genre actually fell into disuse earlier than in most other Protestant countries. In Sweden and Finland, for instance, it still exists.

In the rest of this chapter, I shall explore examples of British political preaching at court and in Parliament during the period 1689–1789, focusing on the years 1689–1717 at court and the years 1772–90 in Parliament. The selected cases lead us to consider in more concrete (albeit simplified) terms how and why the political and social values communicated in political sermons changed not only as a consequence of a shift in the prevailing forum of political preaching but also as a result of wider intellectual developments, including the rise of experimental science and the breakthrough of the moderate Protestant Enlightenment. How was it possible up to the accession of the House of Hanover to propagate successfully traditional conceptions of the church and the monarchy in the context of court sermons? Why was this practice discontinued around 1720? How was loyalty to Church and State constructed at the beginning and the end of the eighteenth century? How were traditional religion and the changing political, social, and intellectual realities reconciled by the Anglican preachers in the intervening period?

As the corpus of printed court and parliamentary sermons is so extensive in England, I am building on my previous analysis of the period 1685–1772 and supplementing it with a survey of court preaching for the period up to 1717 and with another of parliamentary preaching for the period 1772–90. The sermons from the former period illustrate continuity in early modern political values while those from the latter years manifest considerable Enlightenment redefinitions of the political community.

Constructing the Protestant Monarchy in Court Sermons in the Reigns of William and Mary, Anne, and George I

English political preaching became such a powerful medium in the Williamite and Augustan eras because of the existence of well-established traditions, including the model that William and Mary had observed in the Dutch Republic and as a result of the personal religiosity of the rulers. Sermons served the needs of a political nation divided into politico-religious parties: the Church of England was divided into High and Low and the political elite into Tories and Whigs as a result of divergent conceptions of the church and its relations to the state and the monarchy, differing interpretations of the Revolution of 1688, and conflicting attitudes to Catholic and Protestant nonconformity. A further explanation may be a transformation within the genre which had recently started in England: the significance of sermons increased as a result of changes in their form, style, and content that allowed the discussion of subjects of contemporary relevance rather than the continuation of old controversies about dogma (Ihalainen 2011).

Under William and Mary and Anne, the printing of sermons preached at court developed into a full-blown industry. The large numbers of published court sermons ensured their importance within printed literature, but their political significance is more difficult to estimate. Sermons were preached and published not only in accordance with the Anglican calendar but also in connection with a variety of minor events and on ordinary Sundays and holidays. A satisfied monarch could order any sermon he or she heard to be printed. Many of the ordinary sermons did not deliver a particular political message, though general social values were certainly discussed in them as well.

William and Mary attended services and had a plethora of sermons printed. Seven sermons were printed in 1689 in addition to the three conventional anniversaries, including one delivered by William Wake, Chaplain in Ordinary, on 21 May entitled *An Exhortation to Mutual Charity and Union among Protestants*. Appealing to the Gospel, Wake urged the British people to unite spiritually in their everyday actions in a fight for the Protestant monarchy established by the Glorious Revolution. They should have disregarded minor issues of disagreement on notions of religion and followed Christian teachings calling for unity. Thereby, the Church of England and the Protestant Dissenters would continue to cooperate 'in a common Charity, but, if it be possible, in a common Worship of God too'. Wake defined the dogmatic common denominators of all Protestants as opposed to Catholics in such a flexible manner that even a vision of a national church that included the Dissenters became possible. Nor, in the aftermath of an anti-Catholic revolution, did he give up the polemic against the errors of Catholicism (Wake: 5–6, 10–11, 22–3, 26–7).

Nine court sermons were published in 1690, three in 1691, five in 1692, three in 1693, when William was absent for much of the year, and nine in 1694, when Lent and Easter became particular occasions for preached propaganda. As William III was engaged in fighting wars in Ireland, Mary took over the sponsoring of sermons, thus leading the spiritual battle on the home front. The repeated message of the sermons was a call for support for the Protestant monarchy and William's warfaring activities, sometimes formulated in a title like Thomas Comber's *The Reasons of Prayer for the Peace of Our Jerusalem* (1694). There was also an ongoing preaching ritual in the form of national fast days and occasional thanksgiving days, which by 1691 had become monthly events and in March 1692 reached seven per month. Queen Mary also attended services and frequently had sermons printed outside the established days of Protestant political worship, particularly when leading clergymen were preaching (Claydon 1996: 94–6, 100–1): four times in February and March 1689; six times in 1690; fifteen times in 1691; sixteen times in 1692; ten times in 1693; and nine times in 1694. William ordered only a couple of sermons delivered on the battlefield to be printed. After the death of his wife, he sponsored the printing of extraordinary court sermons in a much more selective manner.

Even though the number of extraordinary court sermons was also considerable under Queen Anne (1702–14), the figures of the early 1690s were never again attained. Under Anne, too, many of the sermons were related to warfare. A special feature was the combination of court and parliamentary preaching when thanksgiving sermons for victories in the Spanish War of Succession were delivered to the Queen at St Paul's—altogether six times between 1702 and 1708—and in some cases to both Houses of Parliament as well. On 1 May 1707, the Union of England and Scotland gave rise to a major thanksgiving service. From 1708 onwards, the queen preferred to attend thanksgiving services at court, which may reflect not only the state of her health but also her unhappiness with the lengthy war.

Anne liked to observe her birthday, accession day, and lesser occasions by attending a sermon. She willingly had sermons printed which either communicated a message that was to her liking or which were given by a clergyman who had earned her patronage. The subjects of the sermons were predominantly related to Christian life and general social virtues rather than politics (Claydon 1996: 96–7). In 1702–3, for instance, Archbishop John Sharp delivered a sermon entitled *A Serious Exhortation to Repentance and a Holy Life* and several others on the nature of Christianity. Mid-career clergymen like Samuel Clarke and White Kennett could also enjoy the royal favour of being invited to preach at court and getting published in 1705 and 1706 respectively.

Accession Day services provided suitable occasions for reinforcing the Protestant monarchy and frequently included sermons like Bishop Ofspring Blackall's *The Divine Institution of Magistracy, and the gracious Design of its Institution* (1708). In this sermon, which was reprinted four times, Blackall's point of departure was St Paul's teaching on the natural and necessary submission of the subjects: 'both Submission to the Authority of their Governours, and Obedience to their Laws'. Blackall presented monarchs as ultimately appointed by God to be his ministers and to exercise the authority derived from him. Rulers were by no means servants of the people or the state and were hence not accountable to human beings even when the people had nominally elected them. In Blackall's traditionalist political theory, no man was entirely free-born, had authority over others, or could delegate any power to the ruler. It followed that all suggestions about sovereign power being derived from the people were contrary to the Gospel. Blackall's sermon demonstrates how Augustan court sermons continued to counter Lockean contractual theories and thereby made for ideological tensions in the political community. Blackall's High-Church monarchy promoted the cause of religion and aimed at the realization of God's will on earth. Its subjects were to obey all monarchical orders in so far as they did not violate the divine law (Blackall: 6–8).

As has been seen, the choice of preacher and the decision to print parliamentary sermons sometimes became a matter of ideological dispute in the reign of Anne. One sermon demonstrates the political potential of the medium: Henry Sacheverell's anti-dissenting and anti-republican sermon of 5 November 1709 to the leaders of the City of London resulted in his prosecution by the Whig government in 1710, which led to widespread popular and electoral protests and ultimately to a change of government. While Sacheverell's original sermon was neither a court nor a parliamentary one it led to him being invited to deliver a sermon to Parliament, too: after the three-year preaching ban imposed at his impeachment was over, the Tory majority in the House of Commons ostentatiously invited the polemical clergyman to preach to them on Restoration Day, 29 May 1713. In his sermon entitled *False Notions of Liberty in Religion and Government Destructive of Both*, Sacheverell and his High Church allies had an opportunity once again, now in a parliamentary context, to denounce views that they regarded as detrimental.

In a rather similar vein to Blackall and other High Church clerics, Sacheverell emphasized that it was the duty of subjects to be obedient to their government. Referring to the lesson to be learnt from the Restoration, he suggested that the Dissenters, Republicans and Whigs continued to constitute a united group who had claimed to be fighting in the Civil Wars 'in Defence of Religion, and for Liberty and Property' but who actually aimed at subverting Christianity. Associating seventeenth-century experiences with current controversies on freethinking and party disputes, Sacheverell attacked alleged abuses of the ambiguous concept of liberty, which appeared to be undermining all established politico-religious order. Instead, he offered an alternative 'Christian' definition which allowed no disobedience to the monarchy or the authority of the church. According to Sacheverell, freethinking (and Whig) suggestions that all men were freeborn, possessed natural rights, and created government by contract were simply inconsistent with both reason and religion. The Tory majority in the Commons had no problem in having published this extreme formulation of High Church political theory, which stated that no one in or outside Parliament had 'any Coercive Power over the Persons of the Kings of this Realm' and urged the House to defend the monarchy, church, and country against a conspiracy of Whigs, Republicans, and Atheists (Sacheverell: 6–7, 9–10, 13, 15, 21). The accession of the Hanoverians and, later on, Enlightenment redefinitions of the values of the British political community would bring about a considerable change in the kind of political theory sanctioned by Parliament.

When George I (1714–27) arrived in London in the autumn of 1714, his Whig allies kept the institution of court preaching alive while changing its party-political content. Gilbert Burnet, who had been the leading figure of Williamite providentialist courtly propaganda (Claydon 1996: 30–1), was given the honour of defining Protestant politics under the new ruler in a welcoming sermon given on 31 October, suitably the anniversary of the Reformation. Protestant providentialism constituted the grand narrative for this Whig bishop: providence had been on the side of the Reformation throughout the history of Protestantism, including the Protestant winds that had blown William III to Britain in 1688 and the successful transition of power in 1714. Burnet depicted the Hanoverian Succession as a religious event that allowed the free expression of 'the true Spirit of the Nation, and its Zeal for the Purity of Religion'. For him, kings remained 'the defenders of the faith, both at Home and Abroad', which reveals the early modern confessional understanding of the political community that still dominated the sermon. In this sermon, politics continued to be discussed in religious terms in an Augustan party-political spirit (Burnet: 8, 15–16, 23, 32; Ihalainen 1999).

However, the era of the most unashamed party-political preaching was drawing to its close. In 1717, four court sermons were still printed, including the royal chaplain and Bishop of Bangor Benjamin Hoadly's *The Nature of the Kingdom, or Church, of Christ*, preached before the King on 31 March, which directly contributed to an ongoing theological argument about the government of the church. Only one court sermon was published in 1718 and, after this, only two ephemeral ones, one in 1730 and the other in 1752. This would suggest that Hoadly's sermon created such an unpleasant controversy that the entire genre was thereafter practically suspended, like Convocation. The controversy was still one dominated by the Augustan party spirit, but it also demonstrates the potential for innovation in the genre of the political sermon.

The Bangorian Controversy, which raged for the following five years, concerned Hoadly's tolerant attitudes to Protestant Dissent, his contractual notions of the monarchy, and his views of the Church as a national institution separated from the State. Hoadly seemed to regard the Church as a voluntary organization of believers that was independent of the control of the secular authorities (Hoadly: 10–11, 13, 20). He appeared to reject the traditional institution of episcopacy, to be calling for a further reformation of the Church, and to radically extend the freedom of conscience of believers (Gibson: 149–51; Starkie: 3). Apart from Hoadly's background as a Whig polemist, the ambiguity of his arguments, and the ongoing disagreements about toleration of Protestant Dissenters, the conflict was particularly acerbated by the use of the royal court as a forum to put forward such notions. Scholars disagree as to whether Hoadly's thoughts were enlightened and advanced for their time or heterodox and marginal; there are also divergent interpretations about which church party won the controversy in the short term (Gibson: 15, 36–40, 198; Starkie: 9–11, 16–17, 188–90). One consequence is obvious, however: the Hanoverian monarchy refrained from printing further court sermons after 1718. This removed the political relevance of court preaching and contributed to the moderation of party-political pulpit discourses. But political preaching was by no means over and done with: political sermons would find other forums and go through further modifications in content and style in the Age of Enlightenment.

Defining the Ideal Enlightened National Community in Parliamentary Preaching, 1772–90

The focus of British elite political preaching thus shifted from court to Parliament. From 1718 on, the parliamentary sermons of 30 January and extraordinary days of fasting and thanksgiving remained the only occasions for political preaching attended by members of the political elite. While gradual transformations in the content of parliamentary preaching towards more secular vocabularies of politics had taken place throughout the period 1720–1770 (Ihalainen 2005), the changes in emphasis are most visible after the Seven Years' War, when the era of confessional propaganda and strife seemed to be over throughout Western Europe and moderate Enlightenment thinking was already influencing most Protestant churches. To illustrate the effects of these trends on British parliamentary preaching, we can take two sermons that were given simultaneously in the Lords and the Commons on 30 January 1772—in the aftermath of extensive parliamentary and public debates related to Wilkite radicalism and before the escalation of the American Crisis. We shall conclude with two parliamentary sermons delivered at the time of the outbreak of the French Revolution in 1789–90.

An illustrative example of the effects of the transformation is provided by a parliamentary crisis in 1772 following a sermon given by Thomas Nowell, Regius Professor of Modern History at Oxford, to a handful of MPs. The sermon was inspired by a very pessimistic conception of human nature and complained about the 'madness' of the people acting against the divinely delegated monarchical power. Nowell's understanding of political authority was in line with the ideology of the Restoration liturgy (Nowell: 5–7, 10). He denied all contractual notions and called for submission to a God-given monarchy: 'The sword of the Magistrate is drawn to execute wrath upon the children of disobedience; to be a terror to evil works;…' Nowell extended his attack on the principles of the republican and dissenting rebels of the 1640s to include opposition to George III (1760–1820) and the party confrontations of his time:

> And while we behold the bright resemblance of those princely virtues, which adorned the royal martyr, now shining forth in the person of our gracious sovereign, let us earnestly address the throne of mercy, that the guilt of an ungrateful abandoned people may not cause this sun to be withdrawn from us, nor quench the light of Israel. (Nowell: 23)

By 1772, parliamentary sermons had generally been transformed into discussion of general political values which combined moderate Protestantism with secular political idioms. In this context, Nowell's High-Church Tory parallel between George III and Charles I and his rejection of opposition to the monarchy represented such an anomaly that a reaction was inevitable—particularly as the opposition had recently accused the government of tyrannical tendencies. Nowell's defence of non-resistance and passive obedience were denounced in the press as attacks on the British free constitution, and his suggestions about collective national guilt were likewise questioned (Ihalainen 2005: 46–7). In the Commons, speeches were made deploring the decision to print the sermon in hindsight, denouncing its denial of the right to oppose the monarch, questioning its suggestions of divine punishment following from collective guilt, and calling for the prevention of similar future cases. Nowell's defenders recalled the tradition of similar sermons, whereas his opponents maintained that the liturgy of 30 January should no longer be taken as a norm and that the entire practice of preaching then be discontinued. They failed to obtain a majority, however, and hence the controversial practice of parliamentary preaching continued in Britain until 1859 (*Parliamentary History*).

In contrast, Bishop Shute Barrington's sermon given to the Lords on the very same day illustrates what the majority of the parliamentary elite would have preferred to hear: it opened with contemplations about the principles of the good life supported by biblical references and then extended these principles to include social virtues that were beneficial to political communities as demonstrated by Greek, Roman, and British history (Barrington: 10–13, 15–17). Barrington set the proper degree of liberty and military glory as goals, denouncing divine-right monarchy and religious persecution on the one hand and the questioning of all authority and excessive innovations in religion on the other. In the spirit of the Protestant Enlightenment, he praised the religious and civil liberty established by the Revolution of 1688 and rejected all calls for reform of such an 'unparalleled' and 'perfect' constitution.

British parliamentary preaching was obviously well accommodated to support the established political order and the values of the ruling elite. The sermons of 1789–90 likewise reflect the prevailing optimism. On 23 April 1789, just two weeks before the summoning of the French Estates in Versailles, the British political elite celebrated the recovery of George III with Beilby Porteus, Bishop of London, giving expression to their feelings (Porteus: 21–2). While the sermon did contain traditional references to the Church of England as the leading Protestant church in Europe and the British nation as an object of special providence, the predominant theme was a belief in progress derived from scientific discoveries. According to Porteus, such progress supported 'rational piety' as opposed to the materialism of the radical Enlightenment. Naturally enough, Porteus continued to link religiosity and membership of the political community, the goal being 'a contented, a thankful, a united, a virtuous, a religious people'. This seemed within reach as Britain appeared to be an ideal society with the purest religion, the best constitution, equal laws and protected liberties, a thriving economy and widespread prosperity, and hence a respected international standing.

In the early phase of the French Revolution, an ideal Enlightenment nation still appeared to the Whig bishops to be an attainable goal. In January 1790, John Douglas—undisturbed by Richard Price's sermon of 5 November 1789 or the emerging more radical aspects of the Revolution which Edmund Burke was starting to criticize—considered that the opposition to Charles I had been based on 'right sentiments about the duty of rulers'. Charles's opponents, expressing 'the sense of the nation', had contended 'manfully for that freedom which their enlightened minds instructed them they had a right to enjoy'. Douglas distinguished between the French and the British, to be sure, pointing out that the wealthy Britons already lived 'in a terrestrial paradise' and were in no need of revolution (Douglas: 6–7, 18). The tone of sermons would become much more conservative as a reaction to the radicalization of the French Revolution, but still it is noteworthy how far the revaluation of the values of the British political community had advanced by 1790. In many ways, a transition to temporal, future-oriented and optimistic modernity had already taken place within the genre of the British parliamentary sermon.

REFERENCES

Barrington, S. (1772). *A Sermon... January 30, 1772....* London: W. Bowyer & J. Nichols.
Blackall, O. (1709). *A Sermon... March 8. 1708....* London: H. Hills.
Burnet, G. (1714). *A Sermon... 31st. of October 1714.* London: J. Churchill.
Caudle, J. (1996). 'Measures of Allegiance: Sermon Culture and the Creation of a Public Discourse of Obedience and Resistance in Georgian Britain, 1714–1760'. PhD dissertation, Yale University.
—— (2000). 'Preaching in Parliament: Patronage, Publicity and Politics in Britain, 1701–60', in L. A. Ferrell and P. McCullough (eds.), *The English Sermon Revised: Religion, Literature and History 1600–1750.* Manchester: Manchester University Press, 235–65.
Clark, J. C. D. (1985). *English Society 1688–1832: Ideology, Social Structure and Political Practice During the Ancient Regime.* Cambridge: Cambridge University Press.
Claydon, T. (1996). *William III and the Godly Revolution.* Cambridge: Cambridge University Press.
—— (2000). 'The Sermons, the "Public Sphere" and the Political Culture of Late Seventeenth-Century England', in L. A. Ferrell and P. McCullough (eds.), *The English Sermon Revised: Religion, Literature and History 1600–1750.* Manchester: Manchester University Press, 208–35.
Deconinck-Brossard, F. (2000). 'Sermons commémorant la mort de Charles Ier', *Confluences* 17: 149–67.
Douglas, J. (1790). *A Sermon... January 30.* London: T. Cadell.
Gibson, W. (2004). *Enlightenment Prelate: Benjamin Hoadly 1676–1761.* Cambridge: James Clarke & Co.
Hoadly, B. (1717). *A Sermon... March 31, 1717.* London: J. Knapton.
Ihalainen, P. (1999). *The Discourse on Political Pluralism in Early Eighteenth-Century England.* Helsinki: Finnish Literature Society.
—— (2005). *Protestant Nations Redefined: Changing Perceptions of National Identity in the Rhetoric of the English, Dutch and Swedish Public Churches, 1685–1772.* Leiden: Brill, 495–516.
—— (2007). 'Svenska Kyrkan och det, moderniserande nationella tänkandet, 1789–1810'. *Sjuttonhundratal* 3: 25–48.

—— (2008). 'Taivaan filosofiaa ja alkuperäistä demokratiaa. Claude Fauchet'n vallankumouksellinen kristinusko 1789–1791'. *Historiallinen Aikakauskirja* 106–2: 26–39.

—— (2009). 'The Enlightenment Sermon: Towards Practical Religion and a Sacred National Community', in J. van Eijnatten (ed.), *Preaching, Sermon and Cultural Change in the Long Eighteenth Century*. Leiden: Brill, 219–64.

—— (2011). 'The Political Sermon in an Age of Party Strife, 1700–20: Contributions to the Conflict', in H. Adlington, P. McCullough, and E. Rhatigan (eds.), *The Oxford Handbook to the Sermon in Early Modern Britain*. Oxford: Oxford University Press.

Nowell, T. (1772). *A Sermon...January XXX, 1772*. London, Henry Hughs.

Parliamentary History (1806–20). Vol. 17: 1771–1774. London: Bagshaw.

Porteus, B. (1789). *A Sermon...April 23d, 1789,...* London, J. F. & C. Rivington.

Sacheverell, H. (1713). *A Sermon...May 29. 1713*. London: Henry Clements.

Sorkin, D. (2008). *The Religious Enlightenment: Protestants, Jews, and Catholic from London to Vienna*. Princeton: Princeton University Press.

Starkie, A. (2007). *The Church of England and the Bangorian Controversy, 1716–1721*. Woodbridge: Boydell Press.

Wake, W. (1689). *A Sermon Preached...May 21. 1689*. London: Richard Chiswell & W. Rogers.

CHAPTER 15

THE DEFENCE OF GEORGIAN BRITAIN: THE ANTI-JACOBITE SERMON, 1715–1746

JAMES J. CAUDLE

The materials that survive for reconstructing the rhetoric of sermons against the Jacobites are necessarily partial, and an incomplete, though sufficiently representative, sample. We will never know precisely how many anti-Jacobite sermons were preached. The discussion here is limited to printed sermons because the dataset for this genre is near-complete, especially when contemporary lists are used as a cross-check. By contrast, the survival of manuscript sermons must necessarily be random, and it is questionable whether archival survivals can be considered equally representative. Moreover, this chapter is interested in the use of print media as a way of expanding the sermon's reach.

In the Glorious Revolution and the subsequent conflicts, there were some anti-rebellion fasts, notably those proclaimed on 20 February 1690 for the success of William's 'arms in Ireland' and the 'Day of Thanksgiving for Victory in Ireland'. The campaign against the Jacobite 'Fifteen', by contrast to William's Irish expedition, was quite brief—the major Jacobite field armies were eliminated after Sheriffmuir and Preston, only two months after the rebel royal standard had been raised. Because of this quick victory, the major proclamation was for a thanksgiving 8 May 1716 'for the successful suppression of the Pretender'. It was anomalous: a thanksgiving, as custom dictated, should have followed fast for victory against the rebels. God's reward was supposed to follow the nation's contrition, on the principle that you have to beg for divine mercy before you obtain it and give thanks. The second Jacobite conflict fought on British soil, The 'Forty-Five', lasted rather longer, with a decisive victory against the rebels achieved at Culloden, eight months after the rebellion had begun. This protracted struggle left more time for a measured spiritual defence, including Scottish fasts on 5 September 1745 and 8 April 1746 and a national general fast on 18 December 1746, followed by a Scottish thanksgiving on 26 June and the general thanksgiving on 9 October 1746 (Steele; Lindesiana). There was a subtle art to scheduling these fasts and thanksgivings. The thanksgivings had to be in recognition of signal victories, decisive battles, preferably that forced the foreign enemy to the peace conference, or in the case of a rebellion, broke the rebels' ability to sustain any armies of note. In their commissioners' minds, these fasts and thanksgivings were meant to please God; their goal was to influence God to change his mind if he was punishing Britain, or keep his goodwill if he was rewarding it. The fasts were intended to beg God's forgiveness for the sins that had brought about the punishment of rebellion; the thanksgivings were designed to express gratitude to God for sparing the penitent nation; they strove both to express and to steel the nation's resolve to live more righteously to avoid further chastisements. In this respect, despite the intrusion of the rhetoric of Enlightenment, they were remarkably similar to the fasts and thanksgivings of Elizabethan or Commonwealth times, and utterly unlike anything in modern Britain or the United States.

In the supernatural economy of Divine providence, the British Israel/Judah would be rewarded if it prayed fervently and repented for and turned away from its past sins such as luxuriousness, gambling, sexual immorality, boozing, unbelief, and religious laxity. By contrast, they would be punished, like Israel and Judah, if they failed to repent, did not express their gratitude and thanks, presumed themselves the true authors of the national victory, or abused the thanksgiving. With great mercy came a great duty of reform, as Edward Lewis pointed out in *Mercy and Judgment* (1747). Sermons such as those by Bellinger, Gill, Blackwell, Horsey, Whitefield, Clarke, J—H—, and Newman all admonished the listeners to use the thanksgiving for moral reformation rather than mere cheering, fireworks, and intoxication (Ippel). In this element, the Anti-Jacobite sermon was consonant with the post-1688 amplification of moral seriousness and reform (Bahlman).

Instrinsic to all of these fasts and thanksgivings was the concept which I term—with a nod to Carlyle and Abrams (Carlyle)—natural supernaturalism, a belief in a personal and superintending Divine providence, acting through natural and non-miraculous second causes. The hypothesis that the Enlightenment and allied movements in 1660–1800 caused a rapid and unilateral secularization of public debate and private belief has been undermined and discredited for the past decades (Morris: 967; Worden; Porter). The case that meaningful secularization was delayed into the nineteenth and twentieth centuries is certainly undermined by the strong current of Providentialism in these sermons. The discourses may not have seen the world as enchanted and frequented by miracles and wonders, but sermons by Ashton, Berrow, Doughty, and Milner saw it as guided by an invisible hand (Deconinck-Brossard 2005; Guyatt).

Certainly on the evidence of the anti-Jacobite sermons, the interpretation of the rebellions was spiritualized. Sermons such as that of Harvest argued for the divine economy of rewards and punishments. Whereas individuals could be rewarded with Heaven and punished with Hell, nations, by contrast, had no afterlife, and had to be rewarded with being spared conquest from invaders or rebels, or punished by falling prey to them.

The 'Fifteen'

The rise and progress of the 'Fifteen' as a viable invasion was incredibly short. There were only five months between the commencement of the 1715 rebellion and the final evaporation of the Jacobite force. Abbott, the best published article on the 'Clerical responses to the Jacobite rebellion in 1715', though it notes that the riposte to the 1715 rising was more coherent and concerted than previous accounts had argued, errs in presuming that the relative weakness of the response in 1715 when compared to that of 1745 chiefly resulted from less organization and skill in mobilizing opinion (Abbott). In fact, the extreme brevity of the 'Fifteen' itself meant that it was essentially over before the clerical responses could be properly organized; there was not even time for a fast before the thanksgiving. All the same, there were stories of clerical bravery, such as that of Samuel Peploe: 'While Preston was in the hands of the Jacobites, tradition says that a party of rebels entered the church while the vicar was reading the prayers, and threatened him with instant death unless he ceased praying for the "Hanoverian usurper". With great self-possession Peploe continued the service, only pausing to say, "Soldier, I am doing my duty; do you do yours"' (Sanders; Baskerville). The weekend of 7–10 June 1716 demarcated both the thanksgiving for the victory over the rebels and the Pretender's birthday. The thanksgiving occasioned over forty printed sermons preached throughout southern England, whereas the 'Pretender's' birthday was made into an ecclesiastical charivari of mockery, a sermonic anti-masque to the thanksgiving's solemn masque. The geographical range of these sermons was not broad, and more than 50 per cent of them were confined to the circle of counties around London, with exception of Dublin and Barbados, though there was some representation of Hampshire, Devon, Oxfordshire, Cambridgeshire, Worcestershire, Huntingdonshire, and Staffordshire.

As almost all of these thanksgiving sermons were given on the same day, so preachers in 1716 did not have first-rank models to use in their compositions. Their only guide was the wording of the proclamation itself, the various letters of instruction by bishops of which they may have been aware, and the sermons against the rebellion published to that date.

The 'Forty-Five'

While there were approximately sixty-nine sermons preached and printed throughout the 'Fifteen', there were about two hundred and four given throughout the 'Forty-Five'. This almost threefold increase reflects the general increase in pro-Hanoverian opinion over the years 1715–45, as the nation grew used to the dynasty, and it became more British and less foreign (Chastel-Rousseau; Hanham). It cannot be explained by reference to the growth of printed matter during the period 1710–50, since the best estimates of press production suggest—counter-intuitively—that print output actually declined in the middle decades of the century (Raven; Suarez and Turner).

In a number of published sermons, the years 1745–7 set several records for the period 1660–1782. These years were second only to the years of the Seven Years' War in the total number of fast sermons published. They produced the single greatest number of published thanksgiving sermons of the period. And, perhaps surprisingly, they saw the single largest peak of published anti-rebellion sermons in the entire 122-year period, including the American War. There were probably more sermons printed against the rebels of the 'Forty-Five' in the fourteen months from September 1745 than there were printed against the American rebels from 1775 to the Peace Thanksgiving of 1784.

The three or so months of greatest peril in 1745–6 saw about as many sermons published in about as many varied locations as did the five or so months of thanks after Culloden. One might easily attempt to explain away the fifty-nine thanksgiving sermons as the efforts of place-hunters to curry favour with the triumphant Hanoverian government. Unfortunately, the multiplicity and range of sermons during the height of the crisis of late 1745—seventy-nine separate from the fast, thirty-five on the fast itself, 114 total—cannot be explained away in a like manner. No time-serving Vicar of Bray would have hitched his wagon to an embattled dynasty during the months of crisis, when the safest option possible would have been to keep quiet, and certainly not to publish anything definite on either side.

The vigorous work of Anglican preachers against the rebels in 1715 and 1745 was exceptionally effective. It ranged from a low of 67 per cent of the clergy to an anomalous high of 100 per cent in 1715; it ranged from a low of 55 per cent to a high of 82 per cent in 1745. The majority of Anglican preaching against the 'Fifteen' and the 'Forty-Five' did not emanate from bishops and fashionable preachers; the rank-and-file clergy did most of the cultural work. Furthermore, while several preachers published more than one sermon during the crises—Gloster Ridley (three), William Warburton (three), and several more publishing two—they were in the minority. Most of the sermons were 'single-speeches'.

What immediately strikes the bibliographer of these sermons is the number of insignificant villages whose parsons' opinions were thought worthy of publication. One would have expected to see sermons from the great provincial capitals with populations exceeding 10,000: Norwich (one), York (eight), Colchester (one), Great Yarmouth (one): flourishing towns with corporations eager to be loyal. Far more surprising are the constellations of sermons from villages like Cutcombe, North Reppo, Oumley, Colwal, Layton, Cockey, and Bexley.

Since one of the most distinctive traits of the eighteenth century is the rise of a vibrant provincial culture and the emergence of new centres of discussion outside the metropolis, it comes as no surprise to find that the provincial sermon, and its encouragement in print by local elites, became a more important component of political preaching. In the 1715 rebellion, the ratio of known printed sermons preached in London versus those in the provinces was 46–50 per cent London versus 47–53 per cent Provincial; in 1745 the proportions had shifted to 11–39 per cent London versus 60–88 per cent Provincial

(Caudle 1996: 2:826–7). The provincial shaded over into the Atlantic and the broadly imperial, with a sermon from Barbados in 1716, and Boston, Philadelphia, and St Petersburg, Russia in 1746.

There is something of a rough parity between the number of metropolitan and non-metropolitan sermons published. I have not been able so far to explain the apparent interest by publishers in culling such a broad geographical spectrum of opinion (or preachers or congregations in paying them to care through shouldering the cost of publication themselves). Thus far, there is no evidence of publishers' subsidies from the government or Crown. This leaves us with the impression that a large number of publishers expected the demand for sermons to bear the writings not just of the bishops and the foremost theologians of England, but also of obscure parsons.

The general pattern to be observed from 1690 to 1746 is a penetration of the political sermon into what might be called the Bourgeois Public Sphere. This process began with the linkage of the sermon to the county community and local elites. Francis Turner's effusions 'to Samuel Killet, Esq., Mayor, and the Justices, Aldermen, and Common-Councilmen, of Great-Yarmouth' are fairly typical of the sentiments that the desire to publish did not stem from the parson's vanity, but from a patriotic congregation (Turner: i).

We may haggle over the correct amplification in audience that a sermon achieved as a result of publication, but it is indisputable that the increase in the book trade after 1690 led to a broader reach for these arguments than simple one-time oral delivery could have; a multiplying effect, especially for well-known preachers whose names could help to sell their books. Sermons were bought and read in coffeehouses and in the emerging public libraries, and those of a less pious orientation might opt to read political sermons as they would pamphlets on affairs of state. Whereas the Restoration governments from 1660 to 1688 had attempted to regulate what could be preached and to limit publication through pre-publication press censorship, things were differently ordered after the Revolution, when the increase in single-sermon pamphlets meant that political messages could be carried beyond the pulpit where they had been preached. They could be read in bookshops, in coffeehouses, and eventually in lending libraries (Ellis). The prices, mostly from three and four pence (especially in 1715) to six pence (by 1745), meant that they were inexpensive.

Furthermore, the political sermon played an important role in the emerging book market, despite concerns that they were a specialist item that might prove a 'drug' on the market. We get a glimpse of this author–publisher haggling in the letters of John 'Estimate' Brown to Robert Dodsley (Tierney: 103–5). Although few sermons were likely to have been printed in more than one edition and more than five hundred copies, the very existence of five hundred or even fewer copies gave a sermon a lease on life outside the pulpit. In 1715, there were almost as many different London publishers involved in producing the sermons as there were preachers. Only a few in 1715–16 printed multiple sermons: notably Churchill (five), Clark (seven), Knapton (three), Lintott (four), Matthews (three), and Wyat (six). Roberts, while he had only three sermons 'printed for' him, sold four others. The similarly active London publishers in 1745 were Cooper (thirteen); Hett (eleven); Oswald (nine); Noon (eight); Knapton (seven); Clarke, Waugh, and Hodges (five each); Manby, Rivington, Whitridge, and Millar (four each); and Brotherton, Buckland, Dodsley, and Roberts (all published or co-published three).

Some of the publishers of these sermons were mainly religious booksellers, as shown by their shop signs. But many more, like Tonson, or Dodsley, were mainstream booksellers, suggesting the reach of the sermon into secular publishing houses. This despite the fact that the Brown–Dodsley exchange on the milder 'Profit of a *Sermon* Printer', when compared to one of 'Poetical Affairs', suggested that Dodsley was expected to think that 'Sermons above all other things are a mere Drug' on the market (Tierney: 103–5).

And the rise of a provincial press, congruent with the growing vitality of provincial towns, meant that messages preached outside London were increasingly heard through better regional distribution networks, or increasingly through local provincial printers printing 'their' clergymen. The only provincially printed sermons of the 'Fifteen' appear to be those by 'T_____ E_____' (Exeter), Waterland (Cambridge), and Goodwin (Dublin). By contrast, in 1745–6 there were sermons published in York (thirteen), Cambridge (twelve), Salisbury (three), Lincoln (two) and one each in Reading, Ipswich, Hull, Bristol, Derby, Norwich, Liverpool, and even three in High Tory Oxford. Edinburgh (four) and Dublin (three) were also well represented. Many of the sermons printed in London were distributed to provincial towns.

In contrast to later state propaganda, which was standardized and mostly dictated in content and theme from above, the calls for sermons were rather loosely organized. Politicians in State and Church were certainly aware of the need to marshal the clergy. As Lord Hardwicke wrote to Archbishop Herring on 31 August 1745, 'Is it not time for the Pulpits to sound the Trumpet against Popery and the Pretender?' Herring replied on 7 September that 'So far as my example or monitions can go, I shall not be wanting in my duty, but your Lordship will give me leave to observe, that Preaching will be of little avail, where the countenance of the Magistrate is wanting'; this being a veiled request for stringency against Catholics (Garnett: 532–3). The most energetic bishops in motivating anti-Jacobite sermons were not the archbishops of Canterbury. Rather, in 1715, Bishop Willis of Gloucester penned the declaration which Archbishop Tenison issued, and Bishops Lloyd of Worcester and Nicolson of Carlisle gave their variants. In 1745, when Archbishop Potter proved less enthusiastic than the Duke of Newcastle wished, Bishops Gibson of London, Sherlock of Salisbury and Archbishop Herring of York took up the slack with their own letters to their clergy (Smith: 165–6; Garnett: 535). Some of the most important top-down inspirations for sermons came from Bishops Gibson, Sherlock, and Herring. Herring's efforts were celebrated in his speech and association being 'Beautifully printed on a fine large Sheet of Writing Paper to hang up in a Frame' and sold for two pence. In Scotland, the impetus came from the General Assembly of the Kirk (Assembly), and from its constituent Synods (Synods).

But were these sermons simply generated by the 'top' clergy in the three kingdoms, and copied by the minor clergy, in the way the Elizabethan *An Homily Against Disobedience and Wilful Rebellion* had been? Demonstrably most of the sermons printed were not by top-ranking clerics. By eliminating the sermons preached at Court and at the 'Big Six' locations which were the traditional locations for government-sponsored sermons—Chapel-Royal, Westminster Abbey, St Margaret's, St Paul's Cathedral, Oxford University, and Cambridge University (seven sermons in 1715–16, ten in 1745–6)—we gain a clearer view of the small sermons, and their proportion to those at the top of the system. There were sixty-nine non-elite sermons in 1715–16, and an astonishing 194 non-elite ones in 1745–6, marking a relative decline in the predominance of elite sermons in the sample from 9 to 5 per cent. Including other elite venues like inns of court, cathedrals, or mayors and corporations would modify these numbers, but the overall trend would remain the same (Caudle 1996: 2:827–9).

One of the features of the sermons of 1745–6 is their consistency, given that they were preached miles away from each other. This was probably to some degree the result of the communication of ideas from the king's speeches and from bishops' letters—phrases are repeated from both—but, *contra* Deconinck-Brossard, was primarily due to the creation of a national political language of Loyalism from 1714 onwards. Deconinck-Brossard suggested that 'It cannot be a coincidence that all these preachers should have used the same example to illustrate their sermons. They were obviously defending an ideology...The bishops...passed on the message to the clergy of their diocese, and reminded them of their duty to preach' (Deconinck-Brossard 1983: 255–6). But it is far more likely that what she is hearing is a common language, a political lingua franca that had developed from 1714, and indeed from 1688.

This consonance of attitudes and high concepts cannot have been the result of post hoc revision, since most of them were published only a month or so after being preached; the political sermon's market value was largely dependent on appearance in bookstalls roughly six to twelve weeks after preaching. A fast sermon delayed as little as three months after the event was considered unsaleable (Tinker 2:461). Timing was everything in the occasional sermon market.

Emulation and inspiration, and reference to common memes, was not, however, 'copying'. Indeed, the sermon-reading public and congregations demanded originality from their preachers. Samuel Lewis, curate of Great Oakley, in Essex, was pilloried for his over-reliance on 'our public Papers' and a sermon against the 'Fifteen'. A manuscript note on the BL copy reads, 'from [Charles] Lambe's Sermon [of 16 October 1715] on this Text'. Lewis himself admitted in the Preface: 'I ingenuously confess that I am much indebted for it, to a Sermon preached on a like Occasion, by a Minister of the Established Church, in the Year 1715'. However, he attacked those who accused him of lack of originality. The claim 'that I took the greater, or any Part of it, from our public Papers, since the present Rebellion first broke out, as some Persons, who wish well to no body, have represented it, is what I do declare to be absolutely false' (S. Lewis: v, MS note). Furthermore, the text as printed was expected to match the sermon as preached, or some explanation was due. Thus William Best observed, 'In Justice to the *Audience* before whom this Sermon was delivered; it is here confessed, that several Pages of it immediately preceeding [*sic*] the Conclusion the *Service* beginning later than usual, and the *Weather* being very severe) were passed over unrepeated' (Best: 28).

Whereas in Jacobean England published Loyalist sermons had largely emanated from Court preachers and dignitaries in the Church, by 1715 and especially by 1745 'marginal' places and 'marginal' denominations played an important role. Just as the sermon to Parliament was pulling ahead of the sermon at Court in numbers printed (Caudle 2001), the regional and non-Anglican preachers were attaining a public platform as exponents and shapers of Loyal discourse.

Indeed, one of the more unusual characteristics of the anti-Jacobite sermon, and of Loyalist sermons between 1714 and 1760, was the strong and vocal participation by Protestant Dissenters. In contrast in Scotland, the largest group of Protestant Dissenters from the Church of Scotland, the 'Episcopalians', were overwhelmingly Jacobites, or at least Jacobite sympathizers (Pittock: 97–105). Whereas in the Restoration, and in the American War period, Protestant Dissenters were most known for their dissident preaching against the monarchy or crown policy (Bradley), in the anterior period of 1714–60 they were among the most ardent of Loyalists. In the sermons against the two major rebellions, there was a significant discrepancy between the large proportion of published royalist sermons by non-Anglicans, mainly English Dissenters (ranging from an anomalous low of 0 per cent to a high of 23 per cent in 1715 and from a low of 13 per cent to a high of 44 per cent in 1745), and the small proportion of Dissenters in the English populations, a number estimated at six per cent. The loudness of Dissent in favour of the Hanoverian regime was much greater than their numbers would suggest.

It should be made clear at this point that the anti-Jacobite sermons were, *au fond*, sermons of religiously grounded dynastic loyalism. Admittedly, they involved broader issues of the early modern 'state', and of 'secular' civil society and the public sphere, and the Establishment, broadly speaking. Civil and religious rights, Church and State, foreign policy independence, and economic prosperity were all portrayed as threatened by the Jacobites. However, the main arguments were dynastic, almost resembling a modern electoral campaign's message to vote for a particular candidate; that is, to stay loyal to or to become loyal to the Protestant line of the Stuarts (or, from 1714 onwards, the Protestant House of Hanover), and to reject the Jacobite Stuarts.

Whatever other issues may have been addressed, an account of sermon rhetoric in the Jacobite wars that omits dynastic loyalism as the primary topic is akin to an account of the American Civil War that omits slavery and abolitionism. Loyalty to the dynasty, I argue along with Browning and Colley—and by contrast to Smith's excellent work on Georgian monarchy which argued that loyalty to the Georges was true enthusiasm for their persons—was primarily structural-functional (Colley: 202; Smith: 92–3). The Hanoverian dynasty was a service monarchy as well as a constitutional monarchy, and though they were hereditary rather than elected monarchs, most of their preachers treated loyalty to them as a matter of running on their record, though with elements of divine covenanted rule involved as well: the ideological alliance of (defeasible) divine right and (mediated) popular right.

These Loyalist sermons resorted to the rhetoric of what we might call 'obedience for a reason' rather than 'obedience by automatic compulsion'. The rhetorical strategy that characterized political preaching of the Laudians and the Restoration High Church divines, an emphasis on passive obedience and nonresistance as the rationale for supporting the dynasty, was, if not entirely absent, less common—though there were traditionalist sermons such as those by Bradford, Holbrook and Gilbert.

Supplanting the old theology of obedience was a Tillotsonian strategy of persuasion. Congregations were given rationales for obeying the government: that it protected from foreign enemies, that it sustained religious liberties as Protestants (including Dissenters under the Toleration), that it served as a bulwark of their civil rights. In this genre, Church and State rationales were linked. The contract nature of these rationales for obedience was clear in the sermons of Anguish, Doddridge, Arnold, Nicholls, Ridley, Roberts, and Warburton.

Biblical Texts

The use of biblical texts by the sermons is somewhat counter-intuitive. One naturally finds the classic 'obedience texts' prescribed through the centuries, most prominently Proverbs 24:21, Romans 13:1, 1 Peter 2:17, and Titus 3:1, to inculcate subjects against rebellion, albeit in rather modest numbers in 1715–16 and 1745–6. However, the single largest number of citations in 1715–16 and in 1745–6 is from Psalms. Texts from the histories, or the historical sections of the Pentateuch or Prophets, also predominate.

The deployment of biblical narrative was integral to the arguments for Loyalism against the Jacobite challenge. Later Stuart and Hanoverian political rhetoric was transtemporal; it was not fully historicized nor seen in stadial terms, and most preachers presumed that historical examples from the Bible were as relevant to modern circumstances as those from medieval or from Tudor and Early Stuart history.

The focus of many of the historical texts chosen was on infamous Hebrew rebels against their own god-given rulers: Korah against Moses was preached by Rosewell; Absalom against David, by Farrell; and Sheba the Benjamite against David by 'T. E.' and Waterland. Other sermons drew on the history of rifts among the Israelites, the rivalry of Judah and Israel forming a theme of a once united kingdom divided against its own people. However, many other sermons chose instances of international warfare: Deborah and Barak's defeat of the Canaanites, Samuel's crushing of the Ammonites, David's victory against the Philistines, Hezekiah's miraculous victory against Rabshakeh's Assyrian invasion on behalf of Sennacherib, Jehoshaphat's resistance to the allied Moabites, Ammonites, and people of Mount Seir, and Ahaz of Judah's defence against the allied kings of Syria and Israel all formed tropes for comparison and contrast. The alliance of Syria and the 'northern kingdom' to set up their own king (the son of Tabeal) in place of Ahaz proved particularly apposite. The push to identify the Jacobites with foreign invaders, or the pawns of foreign invaders, rather than indigenous rebels, served to exoticize them and make them easier to hate.

Much of this is the relatively familiar turf, known to readers of Colley's *Britons*, of the 'British Israel' meme. But it is more complex than that (Ihalainen: 111–14). Britain in the 'Forty-Five' played the role of Judah as often or more so than it did Israel, so simply counting instances of the use of the term 'British Israel', or even 'Israel', will adequately represent the identification of British political thought with Old Testament history. The themes often addressed the conflict between the elements of a divided kingdom, where Judah represents England and Israel is the northern kingdom of Scotland, broken off from its brethren. These were civil wars, and although I and others have argued in the past that the Jacobites were hyper-alterized, turned into the Other, I have recently revised my conclusions to include the present aspect of the fraternal conflict, which prefigures the war of Benjamin against his brothers as a trope of the American War.

One of the more curious uses of biblical text was the recourse to Galatians 5:1, 'Stand fast therefore in the liberty wherewith Christ hath made us free, and be not entangled again with the yoke of bondage'. This devotional text, normally applied to spiritual liberty, was transferred to political liberty in sermons by Wiche, Delafaye, and Wingfield.

Rhetorical Strategies

What were the broad ideological strategies of the anti-Jacobite sermons? Caudle identified ten major groupings of rhetorical strategies. One could certainly add more, but these are sufficient in the brief compass of this chapter to give an idea of the ways in which support for Loyalism was solicited:

1) the discrediting of the Pretender's blood right
2) the unmasking of the Pretender as a foreign-born, Italian puppet attempting to destroy an English line
3) the connection of the Pretender with Popery
4) the demonstration that the Pretender's promises were false
5) the connection of the Jacobites with French Imperialism
6) the raising of fears about the foreign nature and volatile composition of the Jacobite party and army
7) the creation of a Jacobite 'Dystopia', a cogent and terrifying depiction of what life would be like under 'James III'
8) the demonstration that King George's government was the true defender of civil rights and religious liberties
9) the demonstration that the British constitution based on fiduciary and revocable consent and compact with the governed was superior to Absolutism and Arbitrary Power
10) the creation of a pro-Georgian mythology of the heroes of Loyalism, including portraying George II as Samuel, David, and Hezekiah, and making heroes of the Duke of Cumberland and Col. Gardiner. (Caudle 1996)

Each of these strategies appeared in a coherent form in 1715, but they were articulated to the highest degree in the longer rebellion of 1745.

Loyalist sermons dipped into a deep if poisonous well of anti-Catholic rhetoric. The Achilles heel of the Jacobite line was the steady Roman Catholicism of the heirs-male of James II (Chamberlain). While the British population as a whole were more able to tolerate and even embrace their Roman Catholic neighbours than they had been in 1558–1688, the No Popery rhetoric that set London aflame in 1780 was a strong theme in rhetoric in mid-century. Much has been made of the toleration of James II and his strategic embrace of Dissent, and many claims have been made that 'Prince Charles' could have, should have, and would have converted to Protestantism. This counterfactual discussion of Jacobite Protestantism ignores the failure of the Stuarts to convert, and the degree to which a conversion would have been distrusted. Thus, in the 'Fifteen', sermons appeared with strongly anti-Catholic titles (Topping), as they did in the 'Forty-Five' (Webster; Bruce; Crookshank; Liptrott; Newton; Peploe; Downes). These were often based on views of Catholicism as antichristian, as in sermons by Hill and Warburton. Preachers such as Forster, Benet, Howdell, and Pendlebury frequently argued the incompatibility of a free Protestant nation with a Catholic prince.

Many of the sermons painted a Jacobite Dystopia of what life would be like under James III or Charles III. Robert Blakeway, preaching at Little Ilford in Essex, argued *That the Pretender Neither is Nor Can Be Our King Agreeably to Either. And That If He Should Ever Come to the Imperial Crown of These Realms (which God Forbid) He Must be a Wicked and Tyrannical King* (Blakeway). This was the burden of the use of the biblical narrative (1 Kings 12:10-11, 14) in which Rehoboam tells the people, 'My Father made your Yoke heavy, and I will add to your Yoke. My Father also chastis'd you with Whips, but I will chastise you with Scorpions' (Downes; Kerrich). If James II had been bad, James III would be worse. Civil rights and liberties would vanish after his conquest, and the national churches and the toleration of Dissent would be undermined.

The defence of Britain's civil and religious liberty was a crucial plank in mobilizing popular support. Anti-Jacobite sermons often discussed the civil rights and religious rights that Britain had enjoyed since 1689, and especially since 1714 (Piers). It was easy to portray the Jacobites as absolutist. Still, the sermons had to address, and contradict, both the later Jacobite claims in the proclamations that Jacobitism was no longer based on indefeasible royal power, and the Loyalist but disgruntled Country and Patriot claims that the Hanoverians were taking on elements of continental absolutism, including the large standing army, the heavy taxation, and the manipulation of popular assemblies.

Sermons sought to show that the British constitution based on fiduciary and revocable consent by the governed was superior to Absolutism and Arbitrary Power. Ihalainen has drawn welcome attention to the dynamic presence of Patriotism in the English and Prussian war sermons (Ihalainen). Indeed, one of the notable trends in 1715–46 is the rise of patriot language with the anti-Jacobitism of the 'Forty-Five', in sermons by Stevenson, Hargreaves and Huddesford; and Zachariah Suger dedicated his *The Preservation of Judah* to Archbishop Herring in homage to his 'noble Patriotism'.

Only in the 1745 rebellion was a martyrology created in the sermons. The death of Col. Gardiner from wounds suffered at Prestonpans provided a Protestant hero at a gentleman's level, below George II or the Duke of Cumberland (Doddridge 1745 and 1747). Gardiner's death would have been as well-known to the public of the 1740s as the deaths of Gordon at Khartoum or Custer at the Little Bighorn.

Conclusion

It is impossible using social-science or historical methods to evaluate how successful the political sermons of 1715–16 and 1745–6 were in motivating the population to energetic Loyalism and active obedience, or at least encouraging them in passive obedience. After all, public opinion in the early Hanoverian era was an emerging concept. Moreover just because there were numerous anti-Jacobite and pro-Georgian sermons, and that subsequently the Loyalists won in the battlefield, does not mean that the political sermon was the chief cause of victory. Military historians have outlined the reasons for those victories, although they have frequently ignored the role played by efforts at mobilization of popular support.

It is more possible to judge how sermons helped either to build or occasionally to wreck careers for ambitious clergymen. A few rising stars saw their careers take off; men like Peploe and Herring, whose zeal in fighting the Jacobites gained the attention and patronage of the Crown. The legend of George I's punning response to Peploe's bravery at Preston and political sermons is probably only a folktale. 'George I... is reported to have said: "Peep-low, Peep-low is he called?" Then... he added: "But he shall peep high; I will make him a bishop"' (Sanders). However, this was an important reminder that clerical peeping would enable a clergyman to obtain local and national preferment. Yet zeal that was seen as intemperate and excessive could lead to criticism, as in the querelle between William Warburton and Henry Stebbing (Warburton 1746). Charles Kerrich faced so much criticism after his sermons in Redenhall and Harleston, Norfolk, that he felt he had to clear his name. In his preface, Kerrich noted: 'The following Discourse had never seen the Light, had it not been partially and frequently represented by many as founded upon neither Truth, Reason, nor Scripture.' Kerrich refused to excuse himself if there were '*Expressions*' that were '*too strong, and... bear a little too hard*' on the Jacobites. The sermon, he noted, was preached when '*Danger was at the* Height', leading him to speak his mind with 'more Freedom' than usual (Kerrich: i–iii).

It is also possible to judge the coherence of the ideas presented, and their prevalence. If our yardstick for success is the promulgation of mostly standard doctrine, in the absence of off-the-peg sermons such as the Homilies, then the sermons of 1715–16 and 1745–6 (the latter, in particular) were astounding successes. Paradoxically, at the same time as the sermons proliferated across the country in increasingly diverse religious settings (dissenting chapels) and other locales (provincial towns in Britain and the empire more broadly), a more homogeneous and uniform political rationale for support of the

Georges continued to develop. 'The provincialization of published sermons from 1714 to 1760, far from precluding a more unified political language, actually enabled its creation' (Caudle 1996: 2:829). Though the sermons against the Jacobites did not sing in unison, they formed a harmonious chorus.

References

Abbott, S. (2003). 'Clerical Responses to the Jacobite Rebellion in 1715'. *Historical Research* 76–193: 332–46.
Anguish, T. (1745). *A Sermon Preached..., September the 29th, 1745*. London: H. Whitridge.
An Homily Against Disobedience and Wilful Rebellion. (1571). London: R. Jugge and J. Cawood.
Arnold, E. (1745). *A Sermon Preach'd... October 6. 1745*. London: A. Millar.
Ashton, T. (1770). *A Sermon Preach'd... On Thursday the 9th Day of October, 1746*. London: J. and R. Tonson.
Assembly (1745). *A Seasonable Warning and Exhortation of the Commission of the General Assembly of the Church of Scotland, Met at Edinburgh the 15th November 1745*. Edinburgh: n. p.
Bahlman, D. (1957). *The Moral Revolution of 1688*. New Haven: Yale University Press.
Baskerville, S. (2004). 'Peploe, Samuel (*bap.* 1667, *d.* 1752)', *ODNB*. Oxford: Oxford University Press.
Bellinger, C. (1746). *A Sermon Preached,... Thursday the 9th of October, 1746*. London: The Author.
Benet, G. (1746). *... Two Sermons Preach'd... 9th of October...; and on the 5th of November* Lincoln: W. Wood.
Berrow, C. (1746). *A Sermon, Preached October 9, 1746.... London: W. Parker.
Best, W. (1746). *A Sermon Preached.... On Sunday, January 12. 1745–46*. London: A. Millar.
Blackwell, T. (1746). *A Sermon Preached... Thursday, October 9, 1746*. London: Daniel Browne.
Blakeway, R. (1715). *Two Sermons Preach'd... in November and December 1715*. London: Bernard Lintott.
Bradford, S. (1715). *A Sermon Preach'd... October 16, 1715*. London: John Wyat.
Bradley, J. (1990). *Religion, Revolution, and English Radicalism: Nonconformity in Eighteenth-Century Politics and Society*. Cambridge: Cambridge University Press.
Bruce, L. (1745). *A Sermon Preached..., October 20, 1745*. London: D. Browne.
Carlyle, T. (1833–4). 'Sartor Resartus'. *Fraser's Magazine* 8: 581–92.
Caudle, J. (1996). *Measures of Allegiance: Sermon Culture and the Creation of a Public Discourse of Obedience and Resistance in Georgian Britain, 1714–1760*. PhD dissertation, Yale University.
—— (2001). 'Preaching in Parliament: Patronage, Publicity and Politics in Britain, 1701–60', in L. A. Ferrell and P. E. McCullough (eds.), *The English Sermon Revised: Religion, Literature And History, 1600–1750*. Manchester: Manchester University Press, 235–65.
Chamberlain, J. (2005). 'The Jacobite Failure to Bridge the Catholic/Protestant Divide, 1717–30', in W. Gibson and R. G. Ingram (eds.), *Religious Identities in Britain, 1660–1832*. Aldershot: Ashgate, 81–97.
Chastel-Rousseau, C. (2006). 'The King in the Garden: Royal Statues and the Naturalization of the Hanoverian Dynasty in Early Georgian Britain, 1714–60', in P. Eyres and F. Russell (eds.), *Sculpture and the Garden*. Aldershot: Ashgate, 61–71.

Clarke, J. (1746). *A Sermon Preached at Twickenham in Middlesex, October 9, 1746*...London: R. Manby & H. S. Cox.

Colley, L. (1992). *Britons: Forging the Nation, 1707–1837*. New Haven: Yale University Press.

Crookshank, W. (1745). *A Sermon Preach'd September 22d, 1745,*...London: J. Oswald.

Deconinck-Brossard, F. (1983). 'The Churches and the "45"', in W. J. Shiels (ed.), *The Church and War*. Oxford: Basil Blackwell for the Ecclesiastical History Society, 253–62.

—— (2005). 'Acts of God, Acts of Men: Providence in Seventeenth- and Eighteenth-Century England and France', in K. Cooper and J. Gregory (eds.), *Signs, Wonders, Miracles: Representations of Divine Power in the Life of the Church*. Woodbridge: Boydell & Brewer for the Ecclesiastical History Society, 356–75.

Delafaye, T. (1745). *A Second Sermon Preach'd...13th of October*...London: J. Roberts.

Doddridge, P. (1745)....*A Sermon...Preached at Northampton, October 13*. London: J. Waugh.

—— (1746)....*Two Sermons, Preached at Northampton, February 9, 1745–6*...London: J. Waugh.

—— (1747). *Some Remarkable Passages in the Life of the Honourable Col. James Gardiner*...London: J. Buckland and J. Waugh.

Doughty, J. (1746). *A Sermon Preach'd..., October 9, 1746*...London: J. and J. Rivington.

Downes, J. (1745). *A Sermon, Preached...Sunday the 13th of October, 1745*. London: R. Dodsley.

Ellis, M. (2009). 'Coffee-House Libraries in Mid-Eighteenth-Century London'. *The Library: The Transactions of the Bibliographical Society* 10–1: 3–40.

Farrell, G. (1716). *A Sermon Preach'd...June 7, 1716*. London: J. Clark.

Forster, J. (1746). *A Sermon Preach'd, November the 10th, 1745*...London: H. Whitridge.

Garnett, R. (1904). 'Correspondence of Archbishop Herring and Lord Hardwicke during the Rebellion of 1745'. *English Historical Review* 29: 528–50, 719–42.

Gibson, E. (1745). *The Bishop of London's Pastoral Letter on the Present Rebellion*. London: Owen.

Gilbert, J. (1746). *A Sermon Preached...Thursday the Ninth Day of October*....Sarum: B. Collins.

Gill, J. (1746). *A Thanksgiving Sermon Preached...July 27, 1746*. London: R. Hett.

Guyatt, N. (2007). *Providence and the Invention of the United States, 1607–1876*. Cambridge: Cambridge University Press.

Hanham, A. (2004). 'Caroline of Brandenburg-Ansbach and the "Anglicisation" of the House of Hanover', in C. Campbell-Orr (ed.), *Queenship in Europe 1660–1815: The Role of the Consort*. Cambridge: Cambridge University Press, 276–300.

Hargreaves, R. (1746). *Two Sermons. The First Preached September the 22nd, 1745,*.... *The Second Preached December the 18th, 1745*.... York: J. Hildyard.

Harvest, G. (1746). *A Sermon Preached at Ditton upon Thames, in Surrey*...London: M. Cooper.

Herring, T. (1745). *A Speech Made by the Archbishop of York at Presenting an Association, Entered into at the Castle of York, 24th of September, 1745*. London: John Hildyard.

Hill, J. (1745). *A Sermon Preach'd in the Parish Churches of Thornton and Pickering, in Yorkshire*...York: J. Hildyard.

Holbrook, A. (1715). *A Sermon Preach'd upon Occasion of the Northern Rebellion*. London: J. Wyat.

Horsey, J. (1746). *A Sermon...; May 4, 1746*. London: The Author.

Howdell, W. (1745). *A Sermon Preached..., October 6, 1745*. York: J. Hildyard.

Huddesford, W. (1745). *A Sermon...Preached..., September 22, and St. Michael's in Coventry, September 29, 1745.* London: T. Osborne.

Ihalainen, P. (2009). 'Patriotism in Mid-Eighteenth-Century English and Prussian War Sermons', in G. Teulié and L. Lux-Sterritt (eds.), *War Sermons*. Newcastle upon Tyne: Cambridge Scholars, 107–29.

Ippel, H. (1980). 'Blow the Trumpet, Sanctify the Fast'. *Huntington Library Quarterly* 44: 43–57.

Kerrich, C. (1746). *A Sermon Preached...December 18, 1745.* Norwich: M. Chase.

Lewis, S. (1746). *A Sermon...Preached..., December 18, 1745....* London: H. Woodfall.

Lewis, E. (1747). *A sermon...On Wednesday January 7, 1746[/47].....* London: J. Oswald.

Lindesiana (1913). *Bibliotheca Lindesiana...Handlist of Proclamations Issued by Royal and Other Constitutional Authorities 1714–1910, George I to Edward VII, Together with an Index of Names and Places*. Wigan: Roger and Rennick.

Liptrott, B. (1745). *A Sermon Preached September the 29th,....* London: J. Newton.

Milner, J. (1746). *A Thanksgiving Sermon Preached..., October 9, 1746....* London: the Author.

Morris, J. (2003). 'The Strange Death of Christian Britain: Another Look at the Secularization Debate'. *The Historical Journal* 46-4: 963–76.

Newman, T. (1746). *A Sermon Preached on the Ninth of October, 1746...* London: R. Hett.

Newton, T. (1745). *A Sermon Preach'd,...October 1745.* London: J. and R. Tonson.

Nicholls, B. (1745). *A Sermon Preached..., October 13, 1745.* London: H. Whitridge.

Pendlebury, W. (1746)....*Two Discourses, Occasion'd By the present Horrid and Unnatural Rebellion*. York: J. Hildyard.

Peploe, S. (1745). *A Sermon Preached...13th of October, 1745.* London: J. Rowley.

Piers, H. (1746). *A Sermon, Preached...9th of October, MDCCXLVI.* Bristol: F. Farley.

Pittock, M. (2009). *The Myth Of The Jacobite Clans: The Jacobite Army In 1745.* 2nd edn. Edinburgh: Edinburgh University Press.

Porter, R. (2000). *Enlightenment: Britain and the Creation of the Modern World*. London: Allen Lane.

Raven, J. (2007). *The Business of Books: Booksellers and the English Book Trade, 1450–1850.* New Haven: Yale University Press.

Ridley, G. (1746). *Three Sermons Preached..., In September and October 1745.* London: J. Clarke.

Roberts, S. (1745). *A Sermon Preach'd..., October 6, 1745.* London: R. Hett.

Rosewell, S. (1716). *A Sermon..., Febraury 24, 1716.* London: M. Lawrence.

Sanders, R. (1895). 'Peploe, Samuel', *Dictionary of National Biography*. London: Smith and Elder.

Sherlock, T. (1745). *Thomas, by Divine Permission, Bishop of Salisbury. To the Dean and Chapter of our Cathedral Church of Salisbury...* Sarum: n. p.

Smith, H. (2006). *Georgian Monarchy: Politics and Culture, 1714–1760.* Cambridge: Cambridge University Press.

Steele, R. (1910). *Preview this item A Bibliography of Royal Proclamations of the Tudor and Stuart Sovereigns and of Others Published under Authority, 1485–1714.* Oxford: Clarendon Press.

Stevenson, W. (1746). *A Sermon Preach'd...9th of October, 1746.* London: J. & P. Knapton.

Suarez, M and Turner, M. (2010). *The Cambridge History of the Book in Britain, 5: 1695–1830.* Cambridge: Cambridge University Press.

Suger, Z. (1745). *A Sermon Preach'd... 29th Day of September 1745...* York: J. Hildyard..

Synods (1745). *Memorial and Admonition of the Reverend Synod of Glasgow and Air [sic], Met at Glasgow, the First of October, 1745...,* London: J. Roberts.

'T_____ E _____'. (1716). *A Sermon, Preach'd June 7, 1716.* Exon: J. Bliss.

Tierney, J. (1988). *The Correspondence of Robert Dodsley, 1733-1764.* Cambridge: Cambridge University Press.

Tinker, C. (1924). *Letters of James Boswell.* Oxford: Clarendon Press.

Topping, H. (1716). *A Sermon... Preach'd..., upon New-Year's day....* London: J. Knapton.

Turner, F. (1746). *A Sermon Preached... October 9, 1746...* London: J. Hodges.

Warburton, W. (1745a). *A Sermon Preach'd at St. James's Church, Westminster.* London: J. and P. Knapton.

—— (1745b). *A Sermon... Preached in Mr. [Ralph] Allen's Chapel at Prior-Park near Bath.* London: J. and P. Knapton.

—— (1746). *An Apologetical Dedication to the Reverend Dr Henry Stebbing.* London: J. and P. Knapton.

Waterland, D. (1716). *A Sermon Preach'd...7 June, 1716.* Cambridge: Cambridge University Press.

Webster, W. (1746). *A Sermon Preached at Ware in Hertfordshire...* London: J. Brotherton.

Whitefield, G. (1746). *A Sermon Preach'd... August 24, 1746.* London: J. Robinson.

Wiche, J. (1745). *A Sermon Preach'd..., October 6, 1745.* Salisbury: B. Collins.

Wingfield, T. (1745). *A Sermon Preach'd..., September 29, 1745.* London: T. Payne.

Worden, B. (2001). 'The Question of Secularization', in A. Houston and S. Pincus (eds.), *A Nation Transformed: England After the Restoration.* Cambridge: Cambridge University Press, 20–40.

CHAPTER 16

PREACHING, NATIONAL SALVATION, VICTORIES, AND THANKSGIVINGS: 1689–1800

WARREN JOHNSTON

From 1689 to 1800 there were more than thirty occasions of national thanksgiving officially instigated by the government. Although most often associated with military accomplishments such as important victories or the implementation of peace settlements, there was a variety of circumstances that prompted thanksgiving celebrations. These included the 'deliverance' of England from 'popery and arbitrary government' in 1689, William III's escape from assassination in 1696, the military successes in Queen Anne's reign, the Union of England and Scotland, the achievement of Hanoverian succession, the defeat of Jacobite rebellions, the Treaty of Aix-la-Chapelle, the victory at Quebec, several treaties of Paris, and the commemoration of naval victory at the Battle of the Nile. From these and other thanksgivings there are over 500 extant copies of sermons published in the late seventeenth century and throughout the course of the eighteenth century (Spaulding).

This chapter will analyse the published sermons that accompanied the thanksgivings from 1689 to 1800. As the list above indicates, these sermons were preached on a variety of occasions signifying developments in the course of over 100 years of British history. Though these commemorations were accompanied by official stipulations that included specific prayers, scriptural readings, and messages to be delivered, the sermons composed for these occasions contain a wide range of ideas regarding the nature of British society during the late seventeenth and the eighteenth centuries. This can be accounted for by the volume of printed sermons that remain, the variety of authors who composed them, and the changing circumstances over more than a century. The preachers represented differing positions on the political and religious spectrums, and their concerns were wide. So, within the framework of an officially mandated and structured worship, thanksgiving sermons allow some scope to analyse diverse topics and opinions. These concerns included the political and religious circumstances of Britain, the meaning of military victories and settlements, the place of Britain within a changing European and global context, and particular ideas of British national identity.

The government's intention in sanctioning thanksgiving services was to encourage the expression of gratitude for important achievements, whether victories, peace, or other events of national significance. 'The wisdom and piety of our superiors have commanded us to assemble this day, with one heart and with one voice, to send up our praises, and devoutest acknowledgements to him, who hath said, it is enough' (T. Forster: 226). The collective celebration was necessary because the benefits being acknowledged were 'publick and universal' and therefore did 'not so much concern us in a Private Capacity, as in being Partakers of a National Blessing' (Elstob: 3). Such a thanksgiving was a 'work…to employ ourselves in as a Nation: called to it by Providence, and by our Prince, on the account of a national deliverance wrought for us by the divine hand' (Newman: 9). Ministers noted that 'Publick National Deliverances and Blessings, require Solemn, Extraordinary Rejoycing, and Thanksgiving' (Shower: 3), and reminded their listeners of the obligation 'to recollect in your grateful Breasts, and thankfully attend to, each particular Blessing which, as Protestants and Britons, we have received' (Fortescue: 10–11).

The thanksgivings also provided a means to focus the kingdom and to emphasize unity. They allowed the people to 'join in a national Act of Praise…together in a Body, and in our respective Places of religious Worship' (Brooker: 4). For one minister 'to consider a whole People…breathing forth at the same Hour from all Quarters their thankful Acknowledgements to the Deity, hath something in it wonderfully pleasing to the Imagination' (Fothergill: 3). The celebration of accomplishments afforded the country a means to express 'our unanimous Satisfaction, our universal Gladness', to 'assemble our selves together in the Houses of God,…Here jointly in the Great Congregation' (Kennett: 2). For Samuel Bromesgrove, a preacher in Spitalfields, the commemoration of the victory at Blenheim made 'the Hearts of every one of us, like that of the Queen,…in every Lineament of our Faces to be entirely English…every Tongue seems of it self soluble' (Bromesgrove: 20).

Since religious rites were central to the occasions, it is not surprising that God was identified as the principal benefactor for the nation, and the appropriate object of praise and thanksgiving. The services were to 'stir up thoughtless Sinners to take Notice of the Hand from whence Deliverance comes' (Farmer: 13), to give a 'sense of our dependance upon God…to raise our thoughts above the immediate and visible causes of the national prosperity and glory; to restrain us from vainly idolizing or confiding in secondary or inferior agents' (Kiddell: 6–7). It could also be dangerous to not recognize those divine blessings: 'If God in an illustrious manner saves a people from ruine, if he favours them with peculiar priviledges, and advances them above their Neighbours…it will be the blackest ingratitude in such, to neglect his worship, or to put him off with a few Hypocritical devotions' (*A Sermon…*: 14).

These expressions of thankfulness to God also informed attitudes towards the place of Britain within the divine plan. Articulations of the role of 'Providence' and its influence on current and past events in British history are ubiquitous and permeate the thanksgiving sermons. It was argued that 'No nation...since the Jewish Government ceased has had such Deliverances, and remarkable Interposition of divine Providence in their Favour, as we in these Lands have been blessed with' (Moody: 3–4). Thomas Smith, lecturer at St Giles, Cripplegate and at Stratford Bow, maintained 'it may justly be said of England, that as the hills stand about Jerusalem, so the Lord standeth about his People, even so has the Almighty environed this kingdom, and defended it on all sides by his Providence' (Smith: 26). In a specific reference to the circumstances of 1688–9, Simon Patrick, soon to become the Bishop of Chichester and later Ely, proclaimed 'we cannot take notice of the several Wonderful Events that fall out in the World, beyond all Humane Expectation; the strange Changes (for instance) and unlookt for Revolutions that there are in our own Affairs; but it will dispose us to confess the Providence of God' (Patrick: 1). The country was God's 'darling Nation' (Jacob 1702: 41), the 'Favourite Island of Heaven' (Welton: 14) and 'he hath pour'd down upon us of this Island' mercies and blessings that were 'numberless, and beyond Expression' (Evans 1704a: 22). In 1759 Nathaniel Ball, minister of West Horsley in Surrey, declared the 'Providence of God has been constantly displayed in protecting this Nation against Popery and arbitrary Power' (Ball 1759: 17), while an Irish minister remarked on 'the extraordinary Protection which God has vouchsafed to his People in these happy British Isles' which were 'as remarkable as those He afforded his antient People of Israel' (Henry: 6). The Bishop of Gloucester, William Warburton, affirmed 'that the same gracious Providence would be now no less watchful, for the preservation of the British nation, than it was of old, for the Jewish' (Warburton 1766: 194).

As these last examples demonstrate, many references to God's providential care for Britain were something more than simply generic expressions of divine interest in the good of humanity. A clue to the interpretation of Britain's pre-eminent purpose in God's design for the world is found in the texts chosen for the sermons: a vast majority of them were Old Testament scriptural passages, and preachers used them—both directly and indirectly—to place Britons in the role of God's chosen people. On the occasion of William III's escape from an assassination plot, William Talbot, dean of Worcester, observed "Tis certain this Church and Nation have been for some time preserved...by little less than Miracle[s]; God has as plainly appeared for us as he did of old for his People whom he brought out of Ægypt with a mighty hand' (Talbot: 23). References to the British 'Israel' and 'Jerusalem' abound in the sermons, as do other applications of the correspondence between the ancient Jews and the British people. 'So shall our Victories be continued, our Success stable and permanent, and the Dread of us, as of the Israelites of old (having the same insuperable Conducter and Ally) shall fall upon the Nations round us' (Neale: 19–20). The 1707 union of Scotland and England was likened to the uniting of the kingdoms of Judah and Israel: 'We are all this very Day become one Body under One Government, from Dan to Beersheba, from the Orcades to the South-Channel' (Bates: 4). Britain was also 'chosen by Providence, in these latter Ages, to preserve the Memory of Civil Liberty amongst the degenerate Sons of Men; as the House of Israel was formerly, to keep alive True Religion amidst an Universal Apostacy' (Warburton 1746: 28–29).

The Hanoverian succession also provided an instance for comparison of Britain and Israel. One minister proclaimed his text (Psalm 3:8) 'may be apply'd as properly to the present state of our English Israel, as any People whatsoever', further arguing that no other nation could 'produce either more or greater Instances of God's Providence' (Foster: 5, 10). Another asked why 'May not the same God be call'd the God of Great Britain…as he was the God of Israel' (Harrison: 13), while still another declared that George I was 'made king over us by the same Divine Providence, and much after the same Manner as David was over Israel' (Hawtayne: 2). Samuel Billingsly, vicar of Horley and rector of Newdigate in Surrey, also used this comparison to justify George I's claim to the throne against the Jacobite challenge: 'change but the Names of Persons and Places, and it is in a great measure our own very story. Take for Instance, our most Gracious Sovereign King George instead of King David. Why not? For has not God the same Power now as he had then…to reject a Saul, and raise up a David, the Beloved of the Lord?' (Billingsly: 14). In the face of a renewal of the Jacobite threat thirty years later, the biblical transposition remained appropriate. Commenting on the text Deuteronomy 33:29 (which begins 'Happy art thou, O Israel'), John Dupont, vicar of Aysgarth in Yorkshire, asserted these

> encouraging and prophetick Truths, however adapted to the then Condition and Situation of the Jews, are not less remarkably applicable to our own Times, our present Circumstances and Condition; with this only Difference, that…the prophetick Part of 'em…is now happily and almost miraculously accomplish'd to us ward. (Dupont 1747: 7)

Other ministers drew similar parallels, expressing gratitude for the deliverance of God's 'British Israel' (Hall: 20), 'a Favourite and Beloved People' dwelling in 'a Land of Canaan…as much distinguished from all other Lands, by signal Blessings of Providence, as ever the Canaan of the Jews was by its Milk and Honey' (Harvest: 140, 143). The dissenting minister Thomas Craner argued that such biblical references aptly 'be applied to the British isles, which as another Canaan, are the glory of the whole earth, and the envy of all the nations in the world' (Craner: 2).

Perceptions of Britain's exceptional providential position were significant for British Christianity as well. In 1715 Elias Sydall, a prebendary of Canterbury and later Bishop of Gloucester, declared that 'there is not in all Christendom, nor ever has been since the first and purest Ages of Christianity, a better constituted Church' (Sydall: 19). By the mid eighteenth century British military success bolstered the claim that 'the Church of England, by means of the mighty power of its Imperial head, is become the Fortress and Bulwark of the Protestant profession throughout the world' (Warburton 1766: 194–5). It was seen as 'the Glory of Christendom…famous and venerable for its genuine Purity, extensive Charity, and its near Approaches and just resemblance to the Apostolical and Primitive Times' (Dupont 1747: 16).

Despite such claims, separation from the Church of England was still an issue of concern. Even with the implementation of toleration, Protestant dissent was criticized: 'would our Dissenters act like Men, and hearken to right Reason…consult their

Bibles,... they would find no just Ground to withdraw themselves from the Church of England'; the danger of separation, it was claimed, was that 'once Men separate from our Publick Assemblies, and meet in Private Conventicles, 'tis well known that Priests and Jesuits, under a Disguise, creep in amongst them, and by degrees instill their Poisonous Doctrines into the Minds of Unwary and Credulous Men' (Gregory: 18, 19-20). The 'Schismatical Enthusiast' was held up as the equally dangerous counterpoint to the 'Idolatrous Papist' (Prideaux: 16), and, even at the end of the eighteenth century, new forms of divergence from the Church of England became targets for fresh denunciations. Methodism was the 'flie among the Ointment, this Leven of Hypocrisy' (Piers: 15), 'a new species of Fanaticism... within the bosom of the Church' (Warburton 1766: 204).

Dissenters also found cause to denounce those compatriots who differed from them. In a sermon praising Marlborough's most recent military successes, in 1705 the Congregational minister Joseph Jacob railed against 'Apostaciz'd Professors... their Faces so hid with the Hair of Whores, that they do neither blush at, nor stick to commit such Abominations' (Jacob 1705: 3). John Withers described the destruction of Dissenting meeting houses as the acts of Jacobites (Withers: 24-5). John Milner argued that the political constraints on Dissenters stood 'not in the way of the Enemies of the Government; but in the way of its Friends' and deemed it 'a proper time to put away this Scandal to the Cross of Christ' by getting rid of the Test and Corporation acts (Milner: 44). Such restrictions on Protestant dissent were described as 'a Violation of the common Rights of Subjects', though it was admitted they were much better than those imposed on their nonconforming predecessors (Kennedy: 19).

Dissenting ministers used their participation in national commemorations to account themselves and their congregations among the most loyal subjects. The Presbyterian minister Daniel Williams explained the publication of his 1702 sermon as an effort to refute the rumour that 'the Success of her Majesties Arms was not pleasing to us Dissenters', contending that 'we had solemnly in the appointed Fast, and usually throughout the Campaign prayed for this Success', maintaining dissenters shared the same interests as 'all true English Protestants' (D. Williams: iii). Another Presbyterian minister, Thomas Newman, declared that, during the 1745 Rebellion, dissenters were the most responsive to government calls for prayers and fasts, having 'set apart more days for the same work, on behalf of our King, and Country' (Newman: 3-4). It could also be reported that the national services were being observed in London by 'the generality of the Protestant Dissenting Ministers', with dissenters 'as fervent in their Thanksgivings to God, and as zealous to inspire their respective Congregations... as any of our Brethren of the Established Communion could be' (Richardson: iii-iv).

Yet, while religious debate and criticism continued, a mood of toleration did take root. Though soon to conform to the Established Church himself, at the 1696 thanksgiving the Quaker apostate George Keith celebrated the new religious policy, 'that all in this Nation and all three Nations that are Sober and Godly and of tender Consciences may enjoy the happy Freedom and Liberty to serve and Worship God according to their Faith and Perswasion' (Keith: 15). In the same year, the dissenting minister Charles Nicholetts described the Toleration Act as dissenters having 'their Liberty not only granted but secured and made firm by a Law, and the moderate and sober part of the Church of England...therewith well satisfied' (Nicholetts: 13). In 1715 the Anglican Joseph Acres asked 'When will our Divisions be healed?... What have the Dissenters done, that such a Rage should be spirited up against them, as if they were not fit to live, and breath the common Air with true Britons?' Acres concluded by affirming dissenters' political loyalty, asserting they 'are to a Man hearty to the Constitution' (Acres 1715b: 28–9). By 1759 the policy of toleration was praised as a 'blessed providence' that allowed dissenters to 'enjoy our seasons of public worship, and forms of church government, that in their own nature never clash with, or disturb the civil or religious constitution... [dissenters] are protected by the just sword of common liberty, while we worship... according to the dictates of our own consciences' (Hitchin: 16).

While rents in the fabric of British Protestantism were still in the process of mending in the eighteenth century, one thing that British Protestants could agree on was their condemnation of Catholicism. Through the late seventeenth and much of the eighteenth century, anti-Catholicism was a principal theme found in almost every thanksgiving sermon. In the aftermath of James II's short reign, Catholic interests were portrayed as the 'Antichrist... to lay that Yoke upon our necks, which must in a small time have press'd us down with Sorrow to the Grave' (Welton: 5), and such descriptions flourished well into the next century. Catholics were 'the avowed and determined troublers of our Israel' (Milner: 34), its supporters an 'odious Swarm of Rome's Vermin' (Wood: 16), and 'a Religion which transforms Men into Monsters' (Norman 1746: 16). Jesuits were 'the devil's synod' (Hitchin: 14), and, as 'the Moabites hated the Israelites and their worship, so do the Papists hate us and our religion' (G. Williams: 27). Those who supported Stuart over Hanoverian claims to the throne 'dismiss the Shepherds, and commit the Care and Custody of their Flocks to Wolves', and 'would lay their Lives, Religion, and all that is Dear and Valuable to them, at the Feet and Mercy of one train'd up in the Maxims of Despotick Power' (Masters: 20).

It was not simply religious differences that prompted such anti-Catholic vitriol. British Protestants also held the belief that Catholicism went hand-in-hand with despotic rule. Popery and arbitrary power were depicted as 'Twins' (Watts: 16), and 'where ever Popery comes, it brings Idolatry into the Church and usually slavery into the state' (*A Sermon...*: 21). Nicholas Forster, Bishop of Killaloe, argued that Jacobite success would endanger civil rights and property because Catholicism was 'exactly calculated to serve the Purpose of Arbitrary Power, and rarely fails to introduce Slavery wheresoever it prevails' (N. Forster: 12). Similarly, John Barr, rector of Owmby in Lincolnshire, claimed it was 'not ecclesiastical Tyranny alone that would have been imposed on us; we should have felt the like despotick Power in civil Life; for one never exists but in Company with the other' (Barr: 14).

Concern over the implications and influence of Catholicism on politics also revealed attitudes regarding the fundamental principles of British government in the eighteenth century. Praise of 'liberty' was another of the predominant elements of the thanksgiving sermons. 'Love of Liberty is a Principle implanted and as deeply rooted in Human Nature as the Love of Life... All Men are born to it, and hold this Privilege by the same

Grant and Tenure they do their Lives' (Kennedy: 15). Heralding the triumph of William and Mary's taking the throne, Gilbert Burnet's thanksgiving sermon before the House of Commons in 1689 delineated the need to protect 'two Sacred Things, Liberty and Property, and the Constitution of this August Body, which is the great Fence to both' (Burnet: 15). Thomas Watts, rector of Orpington in Kent, celebrated the defeat of opposing principles: 'Arbitrary Power, absolute Monarchy, or Tyranny, are equally condemned, and disallowed by the Laws of this Nation, we may be well assured from the late necessary Proceedings, and from the occasion of this Thanks-giving-Day' (Watts: 15). Liberty was 'That sacred Plant (which flourishes no where as in our British Soil)', which was 'now fenc'd and hedg'd about with the most inviolable Laws and Constitutions' (Taylor: 15).

Like the Church of England, British political forms were held up as the best in the world. Developing his argument from Locke's theories, John Barr declared 'Ours is without Dispute one of the best contriv'd Modes of civil Polity in the World; because... the Height and fullest Extent of Liberty will be thought to consist... in being govern'd by Laws of their own making... to which every one... has given his Consent' (Barr: 7). Britons had 'the best Laws in the World' (Patrick: 27), 'not only that is but that ever was in the World... drawn from the Wisdom and Experience of all Ages and Nations' (Nichols: 26). 'The British Constitution' was 'so richly worth all the Blood and Treasure by which it has been defended from Age to Age' (Farmer: 7–8), and 'above any Government in the world... as effectually securing to each Individual his Property, and the enjoyment of it with Freedom' (Cowper: 5–6). The nation was 'blest with the Enjoyment of the greatest Liberty, and in consequence with the greatest Happiness of any Nation upon Earth' (Sykes: 10), the 'honoured Repository of sacred Freedom' (Warburton 1766: 193).

Thanksgiving sermons also praised the political resolutions achieved after 1689. The Presbyterian Vincent Alsop reminded his audience to be grateful for the balance in the constitution, with the nation having 'known Laws, that we know what we may expect from our King; that he knows what he may expect from us... that the King break not in upon our Properties, that we break not in upon his Regalities; that the Laws of the Land are to determine and arbitrate all matters between us' (Alsop: 27). The constitution balanced the powers of monarchy and the people, acting as 'a guard against tyranny, the breach of the conditions for our safety on the side of the crown, is a forfeiture to the right of allegiance:—as a guard against rebellion, when the people are guilty of a breach of their bounden allegiance, they forfeit their right to mercy' (King: 13–14). Britain was 'governed by Laws to which we all give our Consent by our Representatives; and any of which the Authority of Parliament can repeal, if they are found inconvenient or burthensome to the Community' (Allen: 8). Laws provided a 'Fixed Boundary, between the Princes Authority, and the Peoples Obedience... It being the Genius of all true Britons, to Love Monarchy, when Duely Regulated, and Legally Exerted' (Blennerhaysett: 11). The British system saw 'the Advantages of Monarchy, Aristocracy, and Democracy tempered in one, without the Inconveniencies of either of them' (Harding: 22).

The characteristics of the British constitution were not simply insular in their import, but were also prescribed for universal benefit. 'Our wise laws, and most excellent, civil constitution, our generous plan of liberty, and the secure possession of our lives and properties, have rendered us the admiration and envy of the surrounding nations' (Benson: 421). Britain was 'the protectress of liberty, an asylum to the distressed and persecuted' (Lowthion: 6), 'not only the Dwelling-place of sweet Liberty, but the Nurse and Tutor of it for the Advantage of Europe' (Allen: 9). By the end of the seventeenth century, the nation had embarked on the 'Defence of Men's undoubted Rights, and Properties, and the Common Liberties of Europe against Tyranny and Oppression' (Evans 1704a: 19). '[T]he present War with France is…for the Civil Liberties of Europe' (Kennett: 22), with the 'fate of the Empire, and the Liberties of Europe' hanging in the balance (Sherlock: 9). This cause linked Britain's military endeavours to its political ideals.

Given the main adversary in these conflicts throughout the eighteenth century, it is not surprising that British constitutional tenets were contrasted with the characteristics of French government. The return of Stuart monarchy after 1715 was to be feared because the Pretender had been 'instructed by a French Tyrannical Master, accustom'd to French Methods of Government, and assisted by French Power' (Pooley: 15), and the defeat of the 1746 uprising was 'the Redemption of our Liberty from French Tyranny and Slavery' (Piers: 8). By the end of the eighteenth century, ministers would attack the efforts of the French 'to plant in their countries, the pestiferous tree of bondage and despotism, by a misnomer called the tree of liberty, more baneful than the deadly poison-tree of Java' (Booth: 12). France was 'a Power which under the opposite forms of monarchical and republican [governments], hath always been hostile to the laws, the liberties, and the religion of Britain' (Abdy: 5).

The identification of France as the nation's chief foe, as well as the distinctions between the countries, was so well known 'that scarce the meanest Plow-man in England, but knows so much the difference, between English Liberty, and the slavery of the poor Vassals in France' (Nicholetts: 19–20). France was Britain's 'too powerful Rival in Foreign Trade, and the Dominion of the Sea' (Smedley: 24), a 'potent and cruel Enemy…that hates us with an implacable Hatred' (Slater: 8). France was also accused of aspirations to universal empire, 'To seize upon the Liberties of all People, Nations, and Languages around them…and to compass what they have often endeavoured…Universal Monarchy, and Absolute Dominion in Europe' (Kerrich: 13). 'Lewis XIV…laid the Plan for enlarging and aggrandizing the French Monarchy in Europe and America; And ever since, the Court of France has been making all possible Advances to universal Empire' (Adams: 17). Britain remained France's 'mortal Enemy' because 'We alone are, and have been often the Power, that breaks their Scheme of Universal Empire' (Kennicott: 14).

Britain's opposition to France, along with its patronage of proper political principles, came to define the nation's international role. The 'restless Endeavours of France have long been working to reduce us to the Model of his own Tyranny…England was that Place alone which could set Bounds to his Lust, and stop his hopes of Universal Tyranny, over the rest of Europe' (Lambert: 10). The island's isolated interests gave way to grander and more far-reaching concerns: 'The Fate of Great Britain is an Affair of too great Importance not to affect, not only the Men of Property at Home; but likewise all those foreign Nations that are Enemies to the exorbitant Power of France' (Ward: 10). One of the achievements of the Revolution of 1688–9 was 'that we have lived to see the British Monarchy once more balancing Kingdomes, restraining exorbitant Power and Opresion, giving Life to a noble, numerous, and most just Confederacy [against Louis XIV], putting a stop to proud triumphant Armies, full of Blood and Conquest' (Stanhope: 22). In this role, the kingdom would 'spread our Honour and Repuation over all the Habitable World, and be Courted for Friends, and Dreaded for Enemies' (Brady 1706: 423). Through military successes 'we return'd to be the Head and not the Tail among Nations', and came to hold 'the Scales of Europe' as 'the principal support of the common Cause, the Terror of France, and Refuge of Forreign Princes' (Evans 1704*b*: 18). George I was acclaimed as a king who could 'Maintain our Figure and Character Abroad, and Keep up the Reputation which this Nation has had, of holding the Balance, and being the Great Patrons and Preservers of the Liberties of Europe' (Sydall: 11).

Given the criticism of French intentions of universal domination, it is interesting to see ideas of empire developing in the thanksgiving sermons. Needless to say, these attitudes were far more positive towards Britain's growing global concerns. Military might demonstrated the potential 'both to the securing and promoting our own Welfare, Peace and Happiness at home; and the maintaining the Ballance of Trade and empire abroad' (Clarke: 25–6). Benjamin Woodroffe, a canon of Christ Church, Oxford, praised the territorial gains of Anne's reign, 'the singular Advantages, that offer to Your Majesty's Fleets, in the Island of Tobago (the very Key and Door to the West Indies), the Ambition of Trinidado, and the whole Carab-Nation, to come under Your Royal Protection' (Woodroffe), and Samuel Bromesgrove described Queen Anne as 'surrounded with the Acclamation of an Empire' (Bromesgrove: a2r). The consolidation of English and Scottish efforts in 1707 would also be advantageous: 'Our Plantations Abroad...will soon be better Peopled and more Fruitful' (Bates: 21), and the Scots provided 'the Addition of some Millions of warlike, hardy, and industrious People, capable and ready to supply our Plantations abroad with numerous Colonies' (Grant: 15). Europe was no longer 'a Theatre wide enough for the English Triumphs, they are extended to the remotest Regions' (Vaughan: 11). This burgeoning imperial strength was presented as a means to advance British values throughout the world. Empire provided the opportunity to 'send such Missionaries as may recommend Christianity to the Savage Indians' (Acres 1715*a*: 25), to 'enlarge the Dominion of Christ's Kingdom' (Brewster: 27), and 'communicate to the poor unenlightened Natives, who have yielded up the Possession of their country to us, the comfortable News of a Saviour that taketh away the Sins of the World' (Fortescue: 20). With the victory over the French at Quebec in 1759, the colonists there 'shall become the Subjects of Great-Britain, [and] will be advanced from Servitude to Freedom' (Henry: 13). Colonial acquisitions provided 'for the security of the lives of our fellow-subjects in the British colonies, and for extending the pure, reformed religion over large tracts of country' (Gerard: 8).

Despite the predominantly positive attitudes towards empire, there were some less enthusiastic responses. 'Success in War leads to Ambition; which...perhaps is carried on, to such an encrease of Dominion, that at last the Empire sinks, as it were oppress'd by its own Weight' (Blackburn: 22). These were especially apparent after the American

Revolutionary War. For Andrew Burnaby, vicar of Greenwich, this defeat demonstrated that 'Our national pride was become obnoxious to all the kingdoms of the earth', and the possibility that Britain's expansion of territory had become 'large and extensive, perhaps more than sufficiently so' (Burnaby: 13, 14). According to William Backhouse, rector of Deal and archdeacon of Canterbury, the accumulation of colonies had drained the nation of its fruitful population. He appealed for the abandonment of 'the Utopian system of extensive empire', comparing it to a 'human body…enlarged beyond the proportionable size…unweildy [sic], and too great a mass for the soul to direct, or even support' (Backhouse: 14–15, 16). Others asked 'Why may it not be good for Britain, gradually detached both from the Western and the Eastern world, to confine her attention to her own fields and seas?' (Cappe: 22). 'Have we navigated and conquered to save, to civilize, and to instruct; or to oppress, to plunder, and to destroy?' This preacher concluded, 'Let India and Africa give the Answer to these Questions…The one we have exhausted of her Wealth…by Violence, by Famine, and every Species of Tyranny and Murder. The Children of the other we daily carry off from the Land of their Nativity', and condemned the actions of 'enlightened Englishmen! reformed Christians!' (Wakefield: 16, 17). Yet, by the end of the century, there were still those who defended imperial power against such criticisms, arguing that Britain remained 'the protectress of virtue, the vindicatrix of injured innocence, and the guardian of genuine freedom and rational liberty' (Booth: 10).

In addition to empire, the recognition of Britain's economic identity was developing in connection with its expanding global interests. Even amongst the criticisms in the 1780s, Britain was identified 'as a great commercial Nation' and urged 'to establish a mutual intercourse and friendly alliance with every part of the Globe' (Popham: 40). 'Trade and Commerce is known to be the making and enriching of any Countrey and next to Religion, nothing adds to the Prosperity of a People like it' (Davidson: 8–9). Strong recognition and encouragement of British trade can be found all through the sermons of the period. 'Must not Trade flourish, Commerce be maintain'd and enlarg'd, the Reputation of a People rise, and their Wealth increase?' (Browne: 18). 'We are situated between the old wor[ld] and the new; whereby we are inabled to extend our trade and commerce to the most distant parts of the earth…and to receive in return a large and willing tribute from the most remote nations, and widely differing climes' (Benson: 420). It was 'the free Exercise of our Trade…That makes all Nations tributary to us…by Choice and Interest…makes us not only a rich and flourishing, but a generous and hospitable, a robust and active, a notable and sagacious, and a happy People too' (Nichols: 27). Commerce was Britons' distinguishing aspect, 'in which we have an evident Superiority over other People, namely, that of a trading Nation: For'tis to our extensive Trade and Navigation that we owe most of our Opulency and Grandeur' (Dupont 1751: 97). It was the 'nourishing Blood of the Body politic' (Ball 1749: 17).

Peace treaties were celebrated for their economic benefits, that 'when we are at Peace abroad…how cheerfully may our Merchants Transport their Goods beyond the Seas, and bring back their Ships richly laden with Silks, Silver, Gold and Diamonds' (Gregory: 13), setting 'all the Wheels and Engines of Trade, of Traffick, and Commerce, into a joyful Movement' (L.: 6). 'Now the Adventrous [sic] Merchant may pursue his Traffick, and make the Wealth of both Indies meet together in his Coffers' (Brady 1697: 7–8). The effect of peace would be the 'incouragement of Industry, reviving of Trade by Sea and Land, … multiplying our Stocks on the ground, improving of all sorts of Arts and Sciences, and in a word, [bring] Universal Prosperity, and a growing Wealth' (Comber: 7–8). '[I]n time of Peace, the rich Merchant may boldly send forth his Ships to Sea, and expect their safe Return, laden with all manner of Store; which fills his Purse, and furnishes our Houses and Tables with all the necessary and delicate Products of the remotest Parts of the World' (Bear: 8).

Both trade and empire were tied to Britain's identification with maritime strength, with economic, naval, and military success interdependent:

> The more Trade and Navigation flourishes…the greater Number of Hands will be at home usefully and industriously employed, the less Number of Poor shall we be encumber'd with, and the greater Number of able and experienced Sailors shall we have ready to man our Ships, to scour our Seas, and to defend our Country. (Harris: 12)

It was acknowledged that 'Trade keeps up the Art of Navigation, and (according to the nature of our Situation[)], Shipping is our best Bulwark against our greatest Enemies, so far it must be own'd that our Security depends upon it' (Page: 21). Similarly, John Dupont proclaimed British naval power 'the impreganable and safest Bulwark of the Nation … The late … Services of our Fleets … are Facts too recent not to be remember'd with suitable Encomiums and Veneration' (Dupont 1751: 108). By the middle of the eighteenth century, it could be asserted that Britain had become 'the Masters of the Deep, without an Enemy left in this wide Element that dared to encounter us' (Fothergill: 25). Naturally, Nelson's victory in 1798 was praised in suitable terms:

> ought we highly to esteem and value the blessing we enjoy as natives of Great-Britain, and make our boast … of those invaluable advantages to which we are naturally entitled, by being born in high and imperial Albion, a country, which the Almighty hath surrounded by the ocean, and on which he hath bestowed the empire of the main. (Booth: 9)

The thanksgiving sermons display a number of perceptions of what constituted British identity in the period 1689–1800. It is not surprising that these national ceremonies, implemented to focus the country on common causes where 'all true Britons and Protestants' were expected to join together (Farmer: 32), should do so. The sermons conveyed a sense of the nation as God's chosen people with a particular spiritual and providential role. They also presented the political values of the kingdom by holding up ideals of liberty, the constitution, and the law. In addition to these political and religious ideas, which to some extent carried over from an earlier period, the eighteenth century also saw new elements of national interest presented. British attention began to turn to emerging international rivalries, military successes, and the expansion of empire. Together these religious, political, martial, and imperial concerns reveal new facets of 'Britishness' that developed as the nation passed from early modernity into the nineteenth century.

References

Abdy, W. (1798). *A Sermon...November 29, 1798*. London: J. Hartnell.
Acres, J. (1715a). *A Sermon Preach'd...January the 20th 1714/5*. London: John Clark.
—— (1715b). *A Sermon Preach'd...August 1, 1715*. London: J. Baker.
Adams, A. (1759). *A Sermon...October 25, 1759*. Boston: Edes and Gill.
Allen, J. (1746). *A Sermon Preached...October 9, 1746*. London: J. Noon and R. Hett.
Alsop, V. (1695). *A Sermon Preach'd...Sept. 8. 1695*. London: John Barnes.
A Sermon Preached...April 16. 1696. (1696). London: Robert Osbourne.
Backhouse, W. (1784). *A Sermon Preached...July 29, 1784*. Canterbury: Simmons and Kirkby.
Ball, N. (1749). *A Sermon Preached...the 25th of April, 1749*. London: J. Buckland.
—— (1759). *A Sermon Preach'd...November 29, 1759*. London: J. Buckland.
Barr, J. (1746). *A Sermon Preach'd on the Ninth of October*. Lincoln: R. Dodlsey.
Bates, J. (1707). *Two (United)...A Thanksgiving Sermon...May 1. 1707*. London: Jonathan Robinson.
Bear, W. (1713). *A Sermon, Preached...July the 7th, 1713*. Exeter: Edward Score.
Benson, G. (1748). *Sermons on the Following Subjects*. London: J. Waugh.
Billingsly, S. (1716). *A Sermon Preach'd...June the 7th, 1716*. London: D. Midwinter.
Blackburn, J. (1749). *A Sermon Preached...April 25. 1749....* London: J. Waugh.
Blennerhaysett, T. (1715). *A Sermon Preach'd...January the 20th, 1714/15*. London: Benjamin Cowse.
Booth, J. (1798). *A Sermon, Preached...the Twenty-Ninth of November, 1798*. Huddersfield: Silvester Sikes and Co.
Brady, N. (1697). *A Thanksgiving-Sermon...Preach'd...Decemb the 2d, 1697*. London: Joseph Wilde.
—— (1706). *Fifteen Sermons*. London: S. Crouch and John Chantry.
Brewster, R. (1759). *A Sermon, Preached...the 29th Day of November*. Newcastle Upon Tyne: Printed by John White.
Bromesgrove, S. (1704). *A Sermon Preached...September the 7th, 1704*. London: Matthew Hotham.
Brooker, D. (1746). *A Sermon Preached...the 25th of May 1746*. Worcester: T. Olivers and Z. Humphries.
Browne, S. (1715). *A Sermon Preach'd...January 20, 1714/15*. London: John Clark.
Burnaby, A. (1784). *A Sermon Preached...July 29, 1784*. London: T. Payne and Son.
Burnet, G. (1689). *A Sermon Preached...the 31st of January, 1688*. London: John Starkey and Richard Chiswell.
Cappe, N. (1784). *A Sermon Preached Thursday the Twenty-Ninth of July, MDCCLXXXIV*. York: J. Johnson.
Clarke, E. (1703). *A Sermon Preach'd...December 3. 1702*. London: Edward Evets and Gervas Sulley.
Comber, T. (1697). *A Sermon Preached...the Second of December*. London: Robert Clavell.
Cowper, C. (1763). *A Sermon Preached...May 5, 1763*. York: A. Ward.
Craner, T. (1763). *A Sermon Preached...May 5th, 1763*. London: Joseph Johnson.
Davidson, R. (1707). *A Sermon Preach'd...May the 1st, 1707*. London: R. Tookey.
Dupont, J. (1747). *A Sermon Preach'd...October 9, 1746*. London: J. Hildyard.
—— (1751). *The Loyal Miscellany*. London: T. Read.
Elstob, W. (1704). *A Sermon...For the Victory Obtain'd...Near Hochstet*. London: Jacob Tonson.

Evans, J. (1704a). *A Sermon Preached on Septemb. 7*. London: S. Crouch.

—— (1704b). *A Sermon Preach'd at Chester and Wrexam. Septemb. 7th. 1704*. London: A. Baldwin.

Farmer, H. (1746). *A Sermon Preach'd... Thursday the 9th of October, 1746*. London: R. Hett and J. Buckland.

Forster, N. (1715). *A Sermon Preach'd... the First of March, 1714/15*. Dublin: J. Pepyat.

Forster, T. (1784). *Sermons Upon Various Subjects*, vol. 2. Tunbridge Wells: J. Sprange.

Fortescue, J. (1760). *A Sermon Preach'd... Thursday November the 29th, 1759*. Exeter: B. Thorn and E. Score.

Foster, T. (1715). *A Sermon Preach'd... January 20. 1714*, 2nd edn. London: J. Baker and Joseph Marshall.

Fothergill, T. (1749). *A Sermon Preach'd... April 25. 1749*. Oxford: Richard Clements.

Gerard, A. (1759). *A Sermon, Preached... November 29, 1759*. Aberdeen: J. Chalmer.

Grant, J. (1707). *A Sermon Preach'd... the First of May, 1707*. London: W. Rogers.

Gregory, F. (1697). *A Thanksgiving Sermon... Preach'd... the Second Day of December, 1697*. London: Richard Sare.

Hall, T. (1746). *A Sermon Preached October 9. 1746*. London: J. Oswald.

Harding, N. (1715). *A Sermon Preach'd... January the 20th 1714/5*. London: John Clark.

Harris, T. (1749). *A Sermon Preach'd... the 25th of April, 1749*. London: J. Roberts.

Harrison, T. (1715). *A Sermon Preach'd the 20th of January 1714/15*. London: J. Harrison.

Harvest, G. (1754). *A Collection of Sermons, Preached Occasionally*. London: J. and R. Tonson and S. Draper.

Hawtayne, W. (1715). *A Sermon Preach'd... the Twentieth of January, 1714*. London: Tim. Goodwin.

Henry, W. (1759). *A Sermon Preached... Thursday, November the 29th, 1759*. Dublin: Peter Wilson.

Hitchin, E. (1759). *A Sermon Preached... 29 November 1759*. London: J. Buckland.

Jacob, J. (1702). *A Sermon Preach'd... the 12th of the 9th Month, 1702*. London: A. Baldwin and S. Drury.

—— (1705). *A Sermon Preacht the 23d of the 6th Month, 1705*. London: J. D.

Keith, G. (1696). *A Sermon Preached... the 16th. of the Second Month, 1696*. London: B. Aylmer.

Kennedy, G. (1749). *A Sermon Preach'd... Tuesday, April 25th, 1749*. Belfast: James Blow.

Kennett, W. (1704). *A Sermon Preached... September VII. 1704*. London: Awnsham and John Churchill.

Kennicott, B. (1749). *A Sermon Preach'd... April 25, 1749*. London: S. Birt et al.

Kerrich, S. (1746). *A Sermon Preached... October 9. 1746*. Cambridge: W. Thurlbourn.

Kiddell, J. (1760). *A Sermon Preached... November 29, 1759*. London: J. Ward.

King, A. (1749). *A Sermon Preached... April 25, 1749*. London: John Brotherton.

L., R. (1697). *A Thanksgiving Sermon... Preached... the 2d. of December, 1697*. London: n. p.

Lambert, R. (1703). *A Sermon, Preach'd Nov. the 12th. 1702*. London: William Lucas.

Lowthion, S. (1763). *A Sermon Preached... Thursday, May 5, 1763*. Newcastle Upon Tyne: T. Slack and W. Charnley.

Masters, T. (1715). *A Sermon Preach'd... January 20, 1714/15*. London: Emanuel Matthews and J. Harrison.

Milner, J. (1746). *A Thanksgiving Sermon Preached... October 9, 1746*. London: J. Noon.

Moody, J. (1746). *A Sermon Preached... October the Ninth, 1746*. Belfast: James Magee.

Neale, W. (1696). *A Sermon Preached... the 23d of April, 1696*. London: Abel Swall and Timothy Child.

Newman, T. (1746). *A Sermon Preached on the Ninth of October, 1746*. London: R. Hett.

Nicholetts, C. (1696). *A Sermon/Preached... April 16th 1696*. London: William and John Marshall.

Nichols, N. (1746). *A Sermon Preached... the 9th of October, 1746*. Hull: n. p.

Norman, J. (1746). *A Thanksgiving Sermon... Preached... October 9, 1746*. London: G. Ferraby.

Page, T. (1715). *A Sermon Preach'd... January the 20th, 1714*. London: J. Roberts.

Patrick, S. (1689). *A Sermon Preached... Jan. XXXI. 1688*. London: Richard Bentley.

Piers, H. (1746). *A Sermon, Preached... the 9th of October, MDCCXLVI*. Bristol: J. Wilson.

Pooley, G. (1716). *A Sermon Preach'd... June 7th, 1716*. London: George Mortlock.

Popham, E. (1784). *Two Sermons, Preached... the Former on February 8, 1782... The Latter on July 29, 1784*. Bath: S. Hazard.

Prideaux, H. (1703). *A Sermon Preach'd... December the 3d, 1702*. Norwich: Frances Burges.

Richardson, J. (1763). *A Sermon Preached May 5th, 1763*. London: J. Buckland.

Sherlock, W. (1704). *A Sermon Preach'd... the Seventh of September, 1704*. London: W. Roberts.

Shower, J. (1696). *A Thanksgiving Sermon Upon Thursday the Sixteenth of April, 1696*. London: B. Aylmer and J. Lawrence.

Slater, S. (1693). *A Sermon Preached... the 27th Day of October, 1692*. London: John Lawrence.

Smedley, J. (1715). *A Discourse... Preached... January 20*. London: R. Burleigh.

Smith, T. (1760). *A Sermon Preached... November the 29th, 1759*. London: n. p.

Spaulding, J. G. (1996). *Pulpit Publications 1660–1782*. New York: Ross Publishing.

Stanhope, G. (1692). *A Sermon Preached... Novemb. the 26th. 1691*. London: Sam. Smith.

Sydall, E. (1715). *A Sermon Preach'd... August 1st, 1715*. London: John Wyat.

Sykes, A. (1746). *A Sermon Preached... on the 9th Day of October, 1746*. London: John and Paul Knapton.

Talbot, W. (1696). *A Sermon Preach'd... April 16. 1696*. London: T. Bennet.

Taylor, C. (1707). *A Thanksgiving-Sermon, Preach'd on the First Day of May, 1707*. London: John Lawrence.

Vaughan, T. (1746). *A Thanksgiving-Sermon, Preached... October the 9th, 1746*. London: n. p.

Wakefield, G. (1784). *A Sermon Preached... July 29th 1784*. London: J. Johnson.

Warburton, W. (1746). *A Sermon Preach'd... the Ninth of October*. London: J. and P. Knapton.

—— (1766). *Sermons and Discourses on Various Subjects*, vol. 3. London: J. and R. Tonson.

Ward, J. (1747). *A Sermon Preached... October 9, 1746*. London: n. p.

Watts, T. (1689). *A Sermon Preached Upon Febr. the 14th*. London: R. Wilde.

Welton, R. (1697). *A Sermon Preach'd... the Second of December, 1697*. London: B. Aylmer.

Williams, D. (1702). *A Thanksgiving Sermon... Preach'd... November 12, 1702*. London: John Lawrence.

Williams, G. (1763). *A Sermon Preached... May 5, 1763*. London: C. Henderson.

Withers, J. (1716). *A Sermon Preach'd... June the 7th. 1716*. London: John Clark.

Wood, W. (1746). *A Sermon Preached... October 9, 1746*. Newcastle Upon Tyne: R. Akenhead.

Woodroffe, B. (1703). *A Sermon Preached... Decem. 3. 1702*. Oxford: J. Crosley.

CHAPTER 17

SERMONS IN THE AGE OF THE AMERICAN AND FRENCH REVOLUTIONS

G. M. DITCHFIELD

By the last quarter of the eighteenth century, the sermon in Britain was not only a well-established literary genre but was broadening in scope and expanding in quantity. There was a continuing expectation that a sermon would be delivered at services in parish churches; some evidence suggests that parishioners were less willing to attend when no sermon was preached (Gregory: 256–7). Dr Johnson in 1772 thought that it was easier for churchgoers to 'fix their minds' on a sermon than on prayer (Boswell: 2:173). In addition to the regular weekly services, there were numerous special occasions in the Christian year, some of them incorporating significant national anniversaries, notably 30 January, 29 May, and 5 November. Robert Nelson's *A Companion for the Festivals and Fasts of the Church of England: With Collects and Prayers for Each Solemnity*, first published in 1704, remained in print throughout the eighteenth century, reaching a twenty-third edition in London in 1773 and a twenty-eighth edition in 1800; it was also published in Dublin. Royal birthdays, marriages, and deaths, together with military and naval victories and peace treaties, were all occasions which stimulated, and often required, the preaching and publication of sermons. Similarly, it was increasingly the practice for the sermons of much admired exponents of the art to be re-published in collected editions. John Tillotson, the first Archbishop of Canterbury to be appointed after the revolution of 1688–9, was much imitated during the eighteenth century for the polish of his style as well as for his Latitudinarian opinions. The ten-volume edition of his works which was published in Dublin in 1739 contained 254 of his sermons. A further ten-volume edition of Tillotson's works appeared in Edinburgh in 1772.

Moreover, the later eighteenth century saw a considerable boost to the number of occasions on which a sermon would be preached, and frequently published. In addition to well-established voluntary religious organizations such as the Society for the Propagation of the Gospel (SPG) and the Society for the Promotion of Christian Knowledge (SPCK), religion helped to inspire the growing numbers of national and local charities, notably infirmaries, orphanages, and charity schools, which in many cases occasioned a sermon at their foundation and at their anniversary meetings. The charity sermon became an increasingly important sub-division of the genre as a whole. The rapid growth of Sunday Schools from the 1780s exerted a similar effect. So did the series of missionary societies which were established in the final decade of the eighteenth century and the first decade of the nineteenth. The Particular Baptist Missionary Society (1792), the London Missionary Society (1795), the Church Missionary Society, founded by Anglican Evangelicals in 1799, and the British and Foreign Bible Society (1804) were reinforced by many county or other area associations among the Dissenting denominations, such as the Baptist Society in London for the Encouragement and Support of Itinerant and Village Preaching (1797). Each of these organizations was specifically formed for purposes of persuasion and exhortation, purposes which stimulated the composition and preaching of sermons of various types. At the same time, the advance of denominationalism and the secession from the main Wesleyan body of the Primitive Methodists in the late 1790s produced a remarkable (and to some a threatening) explosion of lay preaching, often undertaken by relatively uneducated men (and sometimes women). We should add the increasing publication of funeral sermons as means of commemoration and as means of moral instruction. When the well-regarded Cambridge Baptist minister Robert Robinson died in 1790, leading Dissenters vied to pay homage; Joseph Priestley preached a funeral sermon in his honour (Priestley 1790), while Abraham Rees preached and published two separate (and different) funeral sermons for Robinson on the same day (Rees). The deaths in 1791 of three religious leaders of international significance—John Wesley, Richard Price, and the Countess of Huntingdon—contributed substantially to the use of the sermon in the process of memorializing. John Whitehead's funeral discourse for John Wesley took as its text 2 Samuel 3:38, 'Know ye not, that there is a Prince, and a great man fallen this day in Israel?' (Whitehead: 1). On a happier note, the major national celebration for the recovery of George III from life-threatening illness on St George's Day, 23 April 1789, prompted sermons of thanksgiving all over the country. The most widely publicized was that of the Bishop of London, Beilby Porteus, to a crowded audience in St Paul's Cathedral (Porteus 1789), which soon reached a sixth edition. The royal jubilee of October 1809, although set in the rather more sombre conditions of war and domestic hardship, allowed Anglican clergy in particular to heap encomia upon the ailing, but symbolically valuable, George III.

During the War of American Independence (1775–83) and the war against Revolutionary France (1793–1801) the government regularly designated days, usually in Lent, for fasting and prayer for success; fast days were proclaimed for Scotland, Wales, Ireland, and North America, as well as for England. Special days of thanksgiving were set aside for victories, such as those of Camperdown (1797) and Aboukir Bay (1798). The formation in 1794 of the Volunteer Movement, a series of associations of armed civilians for defence against invasion, provided further opportunities for the preaching of hortatory and loyalist sermons (Gee: 182–88). For all these reasons, sermons remained the largest single item of religious literature in the eighteenth century. Such indeed was the extent of the expansion of the genre that there was a need for consolidation, a need met by the publication of John Cooke's two-volume *The Preacher's Assistant* in 1782–3, which provided details of sermons in print on a very large number of themes and biblical texts.

In the period covered by this essay, no single sermon, perhaps, proved quite as sensational as that of Henry Sacheverell in 1709 or that of Benjamin Hoadly in 1717, each of which had sparked a political crisis. Several sermons, however, achieved national prominence between 1770 and 1800. In particular, Thomas Nowell's sermon before the House of Commons on 30 January 1772; Richard Price's *Discourse* preached to the Revolution Society at the Old Jewry Chapel, London, in 1789; and Samuel Horsley's dramatic tirade against the French regicide on 30 January 1793 each provoked a significant response and each will require some consideration in this chapter.

I

Listeners, rather than readers, of sermons were of the most immediate importance to a preacher. The delivery of a sermon depended heavily on a clergyman's personality, articulation, command of language, accent, and even appearance. It was primarily an oral performance. Congregations judged what they heard, or hoped to hear, according to diction, elocution, and style, as well as substance. When the Church of Ireland clergyman Thomas Campbell, the chancellor of St Macartan's, Clogher, visited London in 1775, he was horrified by the manner of a sermon preached by Richard Harrison:

> Went to hear Harrison at Brompton chapel his discourse incoherent & delivered in the gout of a Spouter—It is ridiculous in these fellows, whose eyes are scarce ever off the book to affect the animation of extemporaneous warmth.—yet this Mans composition inclined to vehemence—Talking of the corruption of the present times he said Xtns professed a creed indeed, but acted as if they had no belief—they offered a public sacrifice as on this day, yet they lived as if they sacrificed to the Devil. (Campbell: 81)

The Unitarian attorney James Losh, a regular presence at the Hanover Square chapel, Newcastle upon Tyne, frequently praised the sermons of its long-serving minister, William Turner, as 'excellent', 'good and well arranged', 'very clear, impressive'. But he took a far less favourable view when the sermon there was preached by another Unitarian minister of that city, Edward Prowitt: 'Mr Prowet gave us a poor sermon, poorly delivered', 'a poor sermon, poorly delivered, by Mr Prowet' (Losh). Since most sermons that were preached were never published, it is difficult for the historian to verify such judgements. However, numerous unpublished sermons survived, at least for a time, in manuscript. Many, perhaps most, clergy possessed at their deaths a substantial collection of manuscript sermons. Sometimes they bequeathed them in their wills. Francis Blackburne, archdeacon of Cleveland, on his death in 1787 left his to his fellow-Latitudinarian and reformer Christopher Wyvill (Blackburne). Ten years earlier William Chambers, rector of Achurch, Northamptonshire, left his manuscript sermons to his friend Theophilus Lindsey, with the request that he burn them, 'as they can only be of use in my own small parish and are too negligently wrote in general to be of use or do me Credit hereafter' (Chambers). Only three escaped the flames. Substantial collections of Lindsey's own manuscript sermons, from the periods before and after his secession from the Established Church, and with the dates on which he preached them, are held at Dr Williams's Library, London, and at Harris Manchester College, Oxford.

The published sermon, nonetheless, remains the most accessible form of evidence for the historian of the subject. A point of considerable importance, therefore, is the number of copies per edition of each sermon which found its way into print. Publication in the later eighteenth century, often undertaken by a single publisher/bookseller, could be a hazardous enterprise, with the possibility of serious financial losses. A characteristic print run for a sermon was one in the region of a cautious 1,000 to 1,500 copies per edition in the first place (Raven: 305–6; Ippel 1980: 46), with the hope that demand would justify further editions. It is clear that the total of 10,000 coarse and 1,000 fine copies of George Hill's loyalist *The Present Happiness of Great Britain* which were circulated on its publication in Edinburgh during the counter-revolutionary phobia of 1792 (Macleod: 157) was highly untypical. But the market for printed sermons was consistent and broadly predictable. Certain publishers were already specializing in the production of sermons of a particular theological tendency. The firm of Rivington at St Paul's Churchyard became increasingly committed to High Church authors; that of Joseph Johnson at St Paul's Churchyard concentrated on sermons composed by heterodox Dissenters, including those of Joseph Priestley. Public access to the contents of sermons, moreover, was widening, as they were increasingly reviewed in the monthly literary periodicals. The extent to which a sermon was reviewed is as important a measure of its influence as the number of editions which it stimulated. The *Gentleman's Magazine*, which began publication in 1731, has been credited with a sale of 3,000 copies per monthly number in 1746, a figure which increased to approximately 4,450 by the end of the century (de Montluzin: 2–3). For the *Monthly Review*, founded by Ralph Griffiths in 1749 with a pronounced sympathy with Protestant Dissent, the number of copies sold per number was approximately 3,500 in 1776 and as many as 6,000–7,000 by 1785 (Forster: 999). Of course, circulation measured by sales bears no relationship to circulation by readership. A single copy could be read by several members of the same family, by the patrons of a coffee house, subscribers to libraries and members of the universities and law courts. Admittedly, statistics of this nature indicate an essentially elite readership; but the audience for sermons was by its very nature far wider than their readership. And although it was unusual for sermons to be reviewed in late eighteenth-century newspapers, their appearance was often heralded by advertisement in the London and provincial press.

II

The dissemination of the contents of sermons helps to underline their continuing importance as an index of the nation's aspirations and apprehensions, and as a medium for the pursuit of a public debate. The theme of this chapter is the adaptation of a familiar and well-established genre to the rapidly changing circumstances of an age of revolutions. Newer priorities for preachers and publishers thrust themselves forward. They included the fear of revolution on the one hand and the fear of excessive authoritarianism on the other, the stress upon national moral reformation with the abolition of the slave trade as its outstanding ambition, and a growing interest, no doubt precipitated by the overthrow of established authority in France and elsewhere, in eschatology. At the same time, many familiar concerns were still evident: some Anglican clergy were still worried about the popularity of Methodism, while evangelical values began to permeate elements of the Church's hierarchy. Many clergy, Anglican and Dissenting, excoriated what they thought a dangerous growth of anti-Trinitarianism. Sermons continued to lambaste immorality and corruption; to exhort the poor to avoid indulgence and to be contented with their blessings under a free constitution; and to urge the wealthy to set an example of religious conduct. The claim of religious sanction as justification for the exercise of human authority continued to be a matter of contention. George Horne in *The Christian King*, preached in 1761, four months after the accession of George III, and Horne's cousin and fellow-High Churchman William Stevens in his *Discourse on the English Constitution* (1776) placed a high premium upon monarchy as divinely ordained and requiring almost unconditional submission. A more widely accepted opinion among the clerical elite, however, was that divine sanction was applicable to the entire structure of government and society, not to the monarchy alone. This view went hand in hand with the assertion that each nation was entitled to choose its own form of government and that, once the choice was made, obedience was then to be required (Hole: 12–31). The debate serves as a reminder that for many clergy—and by extension, for many lay people—politics was a still a branch of theology. 'The Bible is my system of Politics', declared the Evangelical John Newton to his London congregation in 1781 (Newton 1781: 7).

Sermons from this period are replete with evidence of the persevering and perhaps increasing importance of a profound belief in the providential interventions in human affairs of a benevolent deity. William Backhouse, archdeacon of Canterbury, was expressing a commonplace when he declared in 1784 'I am persuaded that the world is governed by a PROVIDENCE, a WISE and BENEFICENT PROVIDENCE' (Backhouse: 10). It was easy to assume a special providential guidance for the British as a chosen people. The recovery of George III in 1789, after three months of political uncertainty, was widely credited to the workings of providence. James Bean, vicar of Olney, told his congregation on 23 April of that year that 'the almost instantaneous and unexpected recovery of our beloved Sovereign' should be 'entered among the records of that gracious Providence, through the care of which, Britain, with all her sins, is yet the land of liberty, prosperity and peace' (Bean: 26). Moreover, there was no shortage of opportunities for the invocation of providence during the age of revolutions. Military and naval service necessarily involved the constant risk of injury and death. The naval chaplain John Cooke assured his audience of seamen at Greenwich in 1789 that it was through providential intervention that they had 'been preserved amidst the tempest and the storm: in the midst of dangers and of death: God hath covered your heads in the day of battle'. As supporting evidence, he drew upon the account in Acts 28 of St Paul's shipwreck at Malta (Cooke

1789: 17). The war of the 1790s involved the recruitment into the armed forces of a higher proportion of the adult male population than ever before. Military and naval victories were attributed to, and thus could be legitimated by, the workings of providence. Martin Benson of Tunbridge Wells believed that in addition to the 'patriotic valour of individuals', Nelson's victory at Aboukir Bay had been won through 'the providential controul of the elements' (M. Benson: 22). Similarly, it was possible to turn to providence for aid when the war of the 1790s was going badly for Britain, and when events seemed to be beyond immediate human control. The ways of providence were inscrutable. Asking himself why the perpetrators of the slave trade had not been 'blasted' by the divine wrath, Peter Peckard, Master of Magdalene College, Cambridge, replied that 'We must not too curiously pry into the secret dispensations of Providence—these are amongst the things that require us to walk humbly with our God' (Peckard 1788: 40). The dispensations of providence could be cited as justification of the hierarchical nature of society, as an explanation of the problem of evil, and as a means of reconciling the reality of human suffering with the ideal of a merciful God.

The tone of sermons preached on fast days during the American war changed predictably as expectation of quick victory gave way to anxiety over the wider consequences of failure to crush the rebellion. On the fast day in December 1776 Richard Hurd, Bishop of Lichfield and a personal friend of George III, could afford to speak more in sorrow than in anger. 'Our most religious and gracious Sovereign', he declared, 'regards this necessary chastisement of his undutiful subjects as a matter of the deepest humiliation; and...Victory itself but redoubles his ardour to procure for us, and for all his people, the blessings of Peace' (Hurd: 10). On the same day, Samuel Stebbing, a chaplain to George III, declared that the Americans were 'deluded by knaves'. While offering prayers for British victory, however, he also detected dangers to domestic stability posed by challenges to authority across the Atlantic: 'Whilst rebellion and war are disturbing our colonies abroad, let us be particularly attentive for maintaining Loyalty and Unanimity at home' (Stebbing: 6, 8). As British fortunes in the war declined, and the colonial rebellion turned into a world-wide conflict, James Yorke, Bishop of St Davids and Dean of Lincoln, in his fast day sermon in 1778, lamented on 'the present separation and distraction of this once prosperous and renowned nation. Great vigour, prudence and temper are necessary to recover our former harmony. The want of which may yield us up a prey to our national enemies' (Yorke: 13). There was increasing emphasis, too, on an interpretation of the prospect of defeat as divine punishment for the British people's preference for luxury and indulgence over Christian duty. In 1780 James Cornwallis, Dean of Canterbury, explained British setbacks in the American war as the result of God's punishment for national sin (Cornwallis: 16–20). There was an expectation that all clergy would use the occasion for patriotic purposes, although they were thereby vulnerable to the accusation that they were exploiting the occasion to buttress the current ministry and its policies, and fast sermons help to illustrate divisions within public opinion (Ippel 1980: 57). Henry Ippel identified 180 fast sermons in print during the American War, the overwhelming majority of which, especially those preached by Anglican clergymen, were supportive of the war (Ippel 1982–3: 192 n. 8, 197). However, fast day sermons preached by Dissenting ministers, such as that of Newcome Cappe at York in February 1782, were far more likely to deplore the shedding of the blood of fellow-Britons in America and to question the legitimacy of parliamentary authority in America.

An important reason for the Anglican hostility to the American colonists was the fate of their Episcopalian brethren in the colonies. Many Episcopalian clergymen, on being driven to exile in England, made no secret of their bitterness. East Apthorp, for example, used his fast sermon of 1776 to denounce the rebellion (Apthorp). This sense of outrage was reflected in the annual sermons before the SPG, which had responsibility for the provision of clergy to North America. When William Markham, who became Archbishop of York in 1777, preached the sermon before the Society in that year he asserted, with some hyperbole, that 'The ministers of our church (are) pursued with a licentiousness of cruelty, of which no Christian country can afford an example, the neighbouring savages perhaps may' (Markham: 14). Markham became one of the most vehement of the episcopate in the crimination of the rebellion (Aston: 185–219). Andrew Burnaby, vicar of East Greenwich, Kent, and like Apthorp an Episcopalian exile, preaching before the House of Commons on the fast day in 1781, asserted that responsibility for the bloodshed lay firmly with the colonists and with the European powers which had cynically entered the war on their side (Burnaby: 13). After American independence, many clergy and laity, concerned by what they thought a national descent into luxury and corruption, became advocates of moral reformation and a renewal of religious observance. William Wilberforce helped to secure a Royal Proclamation against vice in 1787, and the Proclamation Society, which aimed to implement it, was established immediately thereafter; The Society for the Suppression of Vice was founded in 1802. Already Beilby Porteus, much admired by George III, had preached an *Exhortation to the Religious Observance of Good Friday* (Porteus 1776) and it was frequently reprinted. Rice Hughes used his sermon of 4 November 1789 before the ancient and honourable Order of Bucks to rail against prize-fighting, duelling, gaming, lotteries, seduction, and prostitution (Hughes: 13–19). Moral reformation had the further advantage of drawing attention from reform of the constitution; as George Berkeley put it in 1785, 'Infidelity and a careless neglect of religion and its duties, are the crying sins of the passing century. Let but these evils be done away, and we shall soon happily experience that for *political* reformations there will be no occasion' (Berkeley: 24).

III

It is frequently asserted that the French Revolution led to the infusion of a more conservative and loyalist tone into many of the sermons, especially those preached by the Anglican clergy, during and immediately after the 1790s. Such preaching was far from the exclusive preserve of the Church hierarchy. John Maule of Merton College, Oxford, asked rhetorically in 1794 'Have we not a constitution perfect as human wisdom can devise?' (Maule: 15). Eight years later, Robert Lascelles Carr, addressing the Lodge of Odd Fellows in Stamford Parish Church, reminded its members that 'The rules of your society are calculated to teach you those important lessons, "fear God, honour the King"' (Lascelles Carr: 15). It was also possible to deploy libertarian arguments to justify the existing state of affairs, as two well-known Methodist preachers demonstrated. In 1794 Samuel Bradburn claimed that 'A firm adherence to the principles of unlimited religious liberty, is perfectly consistent with a steadfast attachment to our King, whom I earnestly pray God to bless, and our civil constitution, which in itself is excellent, and of which I highly approve' (Bradburn 1794: iv). In 1798 Joseph Benson, in his fast day sermon on 7 March, praised British institutions and civil and religious liberty: God had planted the tree of liberty in Britain, 'and with a tree much preferable to that which the French are planting on the Continent'; he referred to the French as 'these Infidels' (J. Benson: 15). 'Infidelity' became a common target, associated as it was with French atheism and Trinitarian heterodoxy in Britain. Sermons propagated the view that Socinianism in particular led directly to atheism, and the subversion of traditional morality and political allegiance (Cleaver). Robert Chalmers, preaching before the General Associate Synod at Edinburgh in 1790, expressed horror that 'men have the daring effrontery, to attack the scripture-doctrine about the Trinity; the doctrine of the true God-head, and proper Priest-hood of Jesus Christ' (Chalmers: 23). In his visitation sermon in 1794, George Pretyman lamented that 'We, who live at the end of the eighteenth century, have seen the Disciples of Socinus amongst the most zealous abettors of Republican Principles' (Pretyman 1794: 14). Preaching before the House of Lords in March 1800, John Randolph, Bishop of Oxford, identified Socinianism as a cause of the French Revolution (Randolph).

Admittedly, these were not the only opinions expressed in the sermons of the French Revolutionary period. There was hostility in some quarters to the use of the fast day sermons for secular purposes. On the occasion of the first fast day in the French Revolutionary War (19 April 1793), the refusal of the Unitarian minister of the George meeting, Exeter, Timothy Kenrick, to preach such a sermon drew upon him much criticism and a protest from a section of his congregation (Brockett: 145). An anonymously published sermon of 1795, printed, perhaps significantly, by J. S. Jordan, the publisher of Part I of Paine's *Rights of Man*, blamed the 'disorders' in France upon the 'unjust interference' of foreign powers (*A Lesson for Kings*: ix). John Henry Williams, vicar of Wellesbourne, Warwickshire, unusually for an Anglican clergyman, preached two sermons which were critical of war, and added point to their effect by choosing fast days for their delivery and ensuring that they were published (Williams 1793, 1795; Haydon: 91–114). The Unitarian minister David Jones, the successor to Priestley at New Meeting, Birmingham, selected as his text Psalm 120:7 ('I am for peace') on the fast day in 1795 when denouncing the war as unchristian, an act of aggrandizement against French liberty and a disaster even in terms of its own objectives (Jones: 5–6, 42–3). However, the general tone of preaching during the 1790s was unmistakably supportive of the existing order and of the war as a necessary and just struggle.

One reason why this was so concerned the way in which the American Revolution, and even more the French, gave a stimulus to the predominantly (though not exclusively) High Church cult of Charles I as a martyr for religion and orderly government.

The 30 January sermon had since the later seventeenth century been a vehicle for the condemnation of rebellion. The onset of rebellion in the American colonies gave this anniversary a renewed relevance. Few went as far as Thomas Nowell, who, as Pasi Ihalainen (Chapter 14, above) shows, provoked such an outcry in 1772 by defending Charles I and exonerating him from any responsibility for the breakdown of authority in the 1640s that a motion in the House of Commons to abolish the anniversary service was only narrowly defeated. But the High Churchman George Berkeley used his anniversary sermon in 1785 to decry 'the fashionable cry for a *parliamentary reform*', shortly before a motion for its enactment was to be debated (and defeated) in the House of Commons in April 1785. Citing the Civil War of the 1640s, he asked rhetorically 'Why... should we hazard the consequences of an innovation, which it is *barely possible* might do some good; but which is much more likely to *create discord*, and to proceed to lengths which were never intended?' (Berkeley: 22). Admittedly, not all 30 January sermons were panegyrics to the memory of Charles I. In 1789, the Cambridge Whig George Pretyman, Bishop of Lincoln and confidant of Pitt the Younger, ascribed the disaster of the 1640s to the 'unfortunate and misguided Prince' who had 'imbibed notions of civil government totally inconsistent with the spirit of a limited monarchy' (Pretyman 1789: 13). By contrast, and in a manner more representative of the 30 January sermons of the 1790s, William Cleaver, Bishop of Chester, in 1791 used the text 1 Peter 2:17 ('Fear God, Honour the King') to excoriate 'those who, whilst they destroyed the dignity of the Crown, crushed the liberties of the subject' and to praise the decision of the House of Commons to reject the motion for the repeal of the Test and Corporation Acts the previous year (Cleaver: 9, 16). But the climax of the 30 January sermons was reached in 1793, immediately after the arrival in London of the news of the execution of Louis XVI; Westminster Abbey was filled with peers and MPs, including Pitt the Younger and the members of his cabinet (Lacey: 239). They heard a powerful discourse from the High Churchman Samuel Horsley, Bishop of St Davids, who in an emotional peroration lamented the English precedent of regicide which the French had followed (Horsley: 23–24). Three days earlier, Samuel Hayes had preached at St Margaret's Church, Westminster, on Romans 13:1 ('Let every soul be subject unto the higher powers'), a text used with increasing frequency by Anglican clergy in this period, and argued that 'He... that, without adequate cause, disavows allegiance, and refuses to submit to the ordinances of man, violates a fundamental principle of his religion' (Hayes: 5). Hayes's careful qualification, 'without adequate cause', reminds us that he and Horsley (unlike Nowell) eschewed the uncritical advocacy of a Stuart-like divine right of kings; rather, their purpose was to appeal to divine sanction as justification for the whole structure of government and social order, not the independent prerogative of the Crown. Nonetheless the cult of Charles I as taken up by the Oxford Movement would not have been possible without its renewal through the 30 January sermons in the 1770s and (especially) in the 1790s. The very small parliamentary attendances at the 30 January services, with the significant exception of 1793, should not obscure the continuing relevance of these services and sermons in the country as a whole, and the office for 30 January remained part of the Book of Common Prayer until 1859 (Lacey: 239, 244–46).

Although there was never a comparable cult of Louis XVI, eulogistic sermons on his death were preached in England. The exiled French professor P. V. Lenoir invoked divine vengeance upon the revolutionaries and declared 'C'est NE(C)KER; voilà le premier de tous les regicides' (Lenoir: 68, 37). When John Milner, the Catholic vicar apostolic of the Midland District and a leading clerical authority in his community, preached a funeral sermon for the deceased king at Winchester, he not only lauded his Christian virtues but drew attention also to the virtues of George III:

> Be pleased also, O most merciful Lord! To save and protect our most gracious Sovereign George the Third, with his illustrious family, and as thou has made him, like Louis, an example of morality to his subjects, in a wicked age, and hast given to him, as thou did to Louis, the heart of a father towards them. (Milner: 61)

This pledge of English Catholic loyalty was a shrewd move at a time when a significant measure of Catholic Relief had been enacted by Parliament in 1791 and further legislation of the kind was anticipated. Admittedly not all sermons on this subject were uncritical encomia of the fallen monarch. Henry Hunter, minister of the Scots Church, London Wall, reminded his hearers that Britain had 'no small ground of offence' against Louis XVI, who had 'severed America' from her. He added cynically that execution had greatly improved Louis's reputation, conferred upon him the martyr's crown, and saved him from the 'inglorious, unregretted' legacies of his ancestors (Hunter: 13–14). However, the idealization of George III as a patriotic father-figure, already evident before the French Revolution and exemplified in Milner's sermon of 1793, received considerable enhancement in the aftermath of the death of Louis. His escapes from assassination in 1796 and 1800 were used for purposes of national commemoration, thanksgiving and reassurance (Clarke; Daubeny). 'Exemplary has been his behaviour in every department connected with individual and social felicity', maintained John Evans at the time of the King's Jubilee in 1809 (Evans: 4). It was much easier to preach on the virtues of fearing God and honouring the king when the monarch himself could be depicted as a model of Christian piety and domestic rectitude.

IV

From the late 1780s a remarkable public campaign against the British slave trade, surpassing in its support all contemporary moves for constitutional reform, reached a series of climaxes with petitions to Parliament in 1788 and 1792. The sermon was central to the propaganda of anti-slavery because so much of its case rested upon morality and religion. Opposition to the slave trade, moreover, exerted a unifying influence across religious traditions and denominations. High Church and Evangelical Anglicans, Latitudinarians, Dissenters of various types and Methodists all joined in execration of the 'traffic'. It was one of the very few topics on which two inveterate theological opponents, the High Churchman Samuel Horsley and the Unitarian Joseph Priestley, could agree, albeit not for the same reasons (Priestley 1788; Mather: 235–44). While there was wide agreement that the slave trade was a crime in the eyes of God, however, there were differences of emphasis among those who preached on the subject. Evangelicals tended to depict the trade in terms of purging of national sin to appease an offended divinity, and to advocate abolition as an act of mercy to the victims of the trade. The Methodist Joseph Benson declared 'Methinks the bare thought of this unprecedented and unparalleled iniquity, committed by persons professing to be the disciples of Christ, is enough to chill one's blood, and fill one's soul with horror' (J. Benson: 23). Samuel Bradburn of Manchester extended his condemnation to slavery itself (Bradburn 1792). John Newton, drawing on his own involvement in the trade, told his listeners at St Mary Woolnoth 'If you are justly shocked by what you hear of the cruelties practised in France; you would perhaps be shocked much more, if you could fully conceive of the evils and miseries, inseparable from this traffic' (Newton 1794: 14). Latitudinarians and many Dissenters were more inclined to see abolition as an extension of civil liberty of a type which carried the potential for reform in Britain. The Latitudinarian Peter Peckard compared the slave trade to political tyranny, and deemed it even more barbarous than the rule of Nero. By denying, furthermore, that slaves were 'of lower intellectual abilities than the rest of mankind', repudiating 'the doctrine of Innate Ideas', and insisting that the debased condition of slaves was solely the result of the way in which they had been deprived of education, he opened up the possibility of political rights for the enslaved (Peckard 1788: 27, 31–2). In 1795, Peckard, by this time Dean of Peterborough despite his unorthodoxy over the doctrine of the Trinity, went further, reviling the trade as a form of international aggression and the violation of natural rights. 'We assail far distant nations who have not done us any injury: we attack the dwelling places of innocent and inoffensive men ... we force away their natural proprietors without distinction, men, women, children, to captivity, to torture, to public sale like beasts of burthen, to unceasing misery and to premature death' (Peckard 1795: 12–13). Sermons, by their oral and printed impact, played a major part in the winning over of a substantial proportion of public opinion to the abolitionist case, so that by 1800, defences of the slave trade were confined mainly to those who possessed a financial interest in its preservation (Anstey: 184–99).

The abolitionist campaign reached its highest levels of popular support at a time when, not coincidentally, public events appeared to justify scriptural prophecies as to the second coming of Christ and the dawn of the millennium. Perhaps appropriately, it was the abolitionist, John Newton, who helped to stimulate this interest in eschatology. In a sermon entitled 'The great advent', he warned his parishioners of St Mary Woolnoth to flee from the wrath to come, and spoke of 'the voice of the Archangel ... and that trump of God, which will shake the creation and raise the dead' as an imminent possibility (Newton 1789: 17, 14). Speculations of this kind were not solely the obsession of radical seekers such as Richard Brothers and Joanna Southcott. A High Church millenarianism was encouraged by Samuel Horsley and others as a sign of divine judgement (Mather: 260–68). To Unitarians such as Priestley, the French Revolution, by breaking with the tyranny and superstition of the past, was the herald of a new age of liberty (Priestley 1794). The peroration of Richard Price's celebrated *Discourse* to the Revolution

Society at the Old Jewry chapel on 4 November 1789 had a strikingly millenarian note:

> After sharing in the benefits of one Revolution, I have been spared to be a witness to two other Revolutions, both glorious. And now, methinks, I see the ardor for liberty catching and spreading, a general amendment beginning in human affairs, the dominion of kings changed for the dominion of laws, and the dominion of priests giving way to the dominion of reason and conscience. (Price: 49–50)

It is a tribute to the sustained ability of sermons to influence opinion that Price's *Discourse*, through the responses which it provoked, set the terms of the British debate over the French Revolution. The success of Edmund Burke's *Reflections* served to confer upon the *Discourse* a heightened public profile, helping to ensure that it remains in print, along with Price's other political writings, to this day. A concentrated academic focus upon sermon literature will naturally promote the conclusion that religious values still dominated public life. Other types of focus will point to an increasingly secularized society. But the widespread interest in evangelicalism, anti-slavery, and eschatology in the early nineteenth century—all relying heavily on sermons as means of propagating their views—suggest that the birth, or at least the advance, of secularization has been much exaggerated.

Acknowledgements

I am grateful to Professor William Gibson for valuable advice in the preparation of this essay. Part of the research was financed by a grant from the British Academy, which I acknowledge with gratitude.

References

A Lesson for Kings: or the Art of Loosing [sic] a Kingdom…A Sermon. (1795). London: J. S. Jordan.

Anstey, R. (1975). *The Atlantic Slave Trade and British Abolition 1760–1810*. London: Macmillan.

Apthorp, E. (1776). *A Sermon on the General Fast…Imploring Victory and Perpetuating Peace to the British Empire*. London: J. Robson and Co.

Aston, N. (2010). 'Archbishop Markham and Political Preaching in Wartime England, 1776–77', in R. D. Cornwall and W. Gibson (eds.), *Religion, Politics and Dissent, 1660–1832. Essays in Honour of James E. Bradley*. Farnham, VT: Ashgate, 185–218.

Backhouse, W. (1784). *A Sermon preached…July 29, 1784*. Canterbury: Simmons and Kirkby.

Bean, J. (1789). *A Thanksgiving Sermon, Preached…23d of April 1789*. London: J. Johnson.

Benson, J. (1798). *A Sermon, Preached…7th of March 1798*. London: G. Whitfield.

Benson, M. (1797). *A Sermon, Preached…on Occasion of Reading the Prayer of Thanksgiving for the Late Victory*. London: F. and C. Rivington.

Berkeley, G. (1785). *A Sermon Preached…31 January 1785*. Canterbury: Simmons and Kirkby.

Blackburne W. (1787). Borthwick Institute, University of York, Prerogative Court probate records.
Boswell, J. (1934). *Life of Samuel Johnson*, ed. G. B. Hill, rev. L. F. Powell. Oxford: Clarendon Press.
Bradburn, S. (1792). *An Address to the People called Methodists Concerning the Wickedness of Encouraging the Slave Trade*. Manchester: T. Harper.
—— (1794). *A Sermon...Preached...February 28, 1794*. Bristol: Lancaster and Edwards.
Brockett, A. (1962) *Nonconformity in Exeter 1650–1875*. Manchester: Manchester University Press.
Burnaby, A. (1781). *A Sermon Preached...February 21, 1781*. London: T. Payne and Son.
Campbell, T. (1775). *Dr Campbell's Diary of a Visit to England in 1775*, J. L. Clifford (ed.). Cambridge: Cambridge University Press.
Cappe, N. (1782). *A Sermon Preached on the Eighth of February 1782,...and Again on...the Twenty-Fifth of February 1795*. York: Wilson, Spence and Mawman.
Chalmers, R. (1790). *A Sermon Preached...April 29, 1789*. Edinburgh: Neill and Company.
Chambers, W. (1777). The National Archives: PRO PROB 11/1046, fos.118v–120v.
Clarke, T. (1796). *A Sermon, on a Day of Thanksgiving for the Providential Escape of His Majesty*. London: S. & J. Reed.
Cleaver, W. (1791). *A Sermon Preached...January 31, 1791*. Oxford: James Fletcher.
Cooke, J. (1782–83). *The Preacher's Assistant*. Oxford: Clarendon Press.
—— (1789). *A Sermon preached...20 September 1789*. London: C. Nicol.
Cornwallis, J. (1780). *A Sermon Preached in the Cathedral and Metropolitical Church of Christ, Canterbury, on Friday, February 4, 1780....* Canterbury: Simmons and Kirkby.
Daubeny, C. (1800). *A Sermon Occasioned by a Late Desperate Attempt on the Life of His Majesty*. London: J. Hatchard.
De Montluzin, E. L. (2002). *Daily Life in Georgian England as Reported in the Gentleman's Magazine*. New York: Edward Mellen Press.
Evans, J. (1809). *The Jubilee, a Source of Religious Improvement*. London: C. Whittingham.
Forster, A. (2004). 'Griffiths, Ralph (1720?–1803)', *ODNB*. Oxford: Oxford University Press.
Gee, A. (2003). *The British Volunteer Movement 1794–1814*. Oxford: Clarendon Press.
Gregory, J. (2000). *Restoration, Reformation and Reform, 1660–1828. Archbishops of Canterbury and Their Diocese*. Oxford: Clarendon Press.
Haydon, C. (2007). *John Henry Williams (1747–1829) 'Political Clergyman'. War, the French Revolution, and the Church of England*. Woodbridge: Boydell Press.
Hayes, S. (1793). *A Sermon Preached...January 27, 1793*. London: J. Bate, T. Cadell and W. Ginger.
Hill, G. (1792). *The Present Happiness of Great Britain*. Edinburgh: John Balfour & James Dickson.
Hole, R. (1989). *Pulpits, Politics and Public Order in England 1760–1832*. Cambridge: Cambridge University Press.
Horne, G. (1761). *The Christian King. A Sermon Preached...30 January 1761*. Oxford: S. Parker.
Horsley, S. (1793). *A Sermon Preached...January 30, 1793*. London: J. Robson.
Hughes, R. (1789). *A Sermon Preached...4th of November 1789*. London: Sewell, Johnson, etc.
Hunter, H. (1793). *A Sermon, Preached Feb. 3, 1793....* London: John Murray.
Hurd, R. (1776). *A Sermon Preached...December 13, 1776*. London: T. Cadell.
Ippel, H. (1980). 'Blow the Trumpet, Sanctify the Fast'. *Huntington Library Bulletin* 44: 43–60.
—— (1982–3). 'British Sermons and the American Revolution'. *Journal of Religious History* 12: 191–205.

Jones, D. (1795). *A Discourse... February 25, 1795*. Birmingham: Thomas Pearson.
Lacey, A. (2003). *The Cult of King Charles the Martyr*. Woodbridge: The Boydell Press.
Lascelles Carr, R. (1802). *A Sermon Preached... 14th of June, 1802*. Stamford: J. Drakard.
Lenoir, P. V. (1793). *Éloge Funère de Louis Seize, Roi de France et de Navarre... par M. Lenoir, Professeur de Lange et de Belles Lettres Françoises*. London: n. p.
Losh, J. Manuscript diary. Carlisle Library, entries for 2 February, 11 May, 2 November, 5 January, and 2 March, 1800.
Macleod, E. V. (1998). *A War of Ideas. British Attitudes to the Wars against Revolutionary France 1792–1802*. Aldershot: Ashgate.
Markham, W. (1777). *Sermon Preached... February 21, 1777*. London: T. Becket.
Mather, F. C. (1992). *High Church Prophet. Bishop Samuel Horsley (1733–1806) and the Caroline Tradition in the later Georgian Church*. Oxford: Clarendon Press.
Maule, J. (1794). *A Sermon, Preached... February 28, 1794*. London: F. and C. Rivington.
Milner, J. (1793). *The Funeral Oration of His Late Most Christian Majesty Louis XVI... April 22, MDCCXCIII*. London: J. Goghlan.
Newton, J. (1781). *A Sermon Preached... Feb. 21, 1781*. London: J. Buckland and J. Johnson.
——. (1789). *The Great Advent: A Sermon Preached...* London: J. Buckland and J. Johnson.
——. (1794). *A Sermon, Preached... on Friday the 28th of February 1794*. London. J. Johnson.
Nowell, T. (1772). *A Sermon Preached... January XXX, 1772*. London: Henry Hughs.
Peckard, P. (1788). *A Sermon Preached before the University of Cambridge*. Cambridge: J. Archdeacon.
——. (1795). *A Discourse Deliver'd... February 25, 1795*. Peterborough: Jacob.
Porteus, B. (1776). *An Earnest Exhortation to the Religious Observance of Good Friday*. London: J. and F. Rivington.
——. (1789). *A Sermon Preached... April 23d, 1789*. London: J. F. and C. Rivington.
Pretyman, G. (1789). *A Sermon Preached... January 30, 1789*. London: T. Cadell.
——. (1794). *A Charge Delivered in May and June 1794*. London: T. Cadell and W. Davies.
Price, R. (1789). *A Discourse... Delivered on Nov. 4, 1789*. London: T. Cadell.
Priestley, J. (1788). *A Sermon... Delivered to a Society of Protestant Dissenters, at the New Meeting, in Birmingham*. Birmingham: J. Johnson.
——. (1790). *A Sermon on the Death of the Rev. Robert Robinson of Cambridge*. Birmingham: J. Belcher.
——. (1794). *A Sermon Preached... February 28, 1794*. London: J. Johnson.
Randolph, J. (1800). *A Sermon Preached... March 12, 1800*. Oxford: Hanwell and Parker.
Raven, J. (2007). *The Business of Books. Booksellers and the English Book Trade 1450–1850*. New Haven: Yale University Press.
Rees, A. (1790). *Two Sermons, Preached at Cambridge... 27 June 1790*. London: H. Goldney.
Stebbing, S. (1776). *A Sermon on the Late General Fast*. London: W. Flexney.
Stevens, W. (1776). *A Discourse on the English Constitution*. London: G. Robinson.
Tillotson, J. (1739). *Works... Containing Two Hundred and Fifty Four Sermons and Discourses on Various Occasions*, 12th edn. Dublin: S. Powell for Edward Exshaw.
—— (1772). *The Works of the Most Reverend Dr John Tillotson Late Archbishop of Canterbury*. Edinburgh: Wal. Ruddiman & Co.
Whitehead, J. (1791). *A Discourse Delivered... Ninth of March 1791*. London: G. Paramore.
Williams, J. H. (1793). *A Sermon on the Late Fast*. Birmingham: John Thompson.
——. (1795). *A Sermon on the Public Fast, February 25, 1795*. London: G. G. and J. Robinson.
Yorke, J. (1778). *A Sermon Preached... February 27, 1778*. Lincoln: W. Wood.

CHAPTER 18

'THIS ITCHING EAR'D AGE': VISITATION SERMONS AND CHARGES IN THE EIGHTEENTH CENTURY

WILLIAM GIBSON

THERE is a tale of a farmer asking the purpose of an archdeacon's visitation. His neighbour replied that it was for parsons to meet together to swap sermons; to which the farmer retorted that, if so, their incumbent always got the worst of the exchange (Ditchfield: 145). In fact, of course, while visitation may have afforded parsons the opportunity to meet and exchange sermons with one another, their formal purposes were quite different. The specific nature and functions of archdeacons' and bishops' visitations in the long eighteenth century have been considered in a recent study (Jacob: 273–5). In general, visitations were occasions of accountability for the clergy. As Alexander Torriano, preaching an episcopal visitation sermon at Huntingdon, claimed, 'we meet here this day... not only to keep up and cultivate a good brotherly correspondence amongst ourselves in general; but also in particular to give a good account of ourselves, and of the state of our parishes to our proper superior; and then to consider of, and confer about the best methods of well-governing the people entrusted to our change' (Torriano: 5). Visitations were also seasonal: archidiaconal and episcopal visitations were sometimes known as the winter and summer visitations respectively because of the time of year at which they were usually held. At each visitation, a sermon was preached, and this essay considers visitation sermons as a form of pulpit literature in its own right, although not a wholly discrete one.

The sermon sat alongside, and was often similar to, the visitation charge and visitation discourses and letters sent by bishops to be read to the clergy. Such discourses and letters were often sent when the bishops were absent through attendance on parliament or illness (Fowler: 4). In colonial America, where there was no ecclesiastical hierarchy, the function of visitation had to be entirely undertaken by such circular letters to the clergy (Bray). However some bishops, like Gilbert Burnet in Salisbury diocese, sent both a charge to the clergy giving them specific directions and advice, and a visitation sermon addressing wider theological issues. As time went on the distinction between charges and sermons blurred, which was intensified by bishops and archdeacons who sometimes published their sermons and charges together, and attached other materials (Bull; Kennett). The nineteenth century charge has been termed a 'rhetorical hybrid', part-sermon, part-'managerial address' (Ellison: 25, 49).

Visitation sermons are valuable for the light they shed on the process of visitations. Historically, visitation sermons and charges were addressed to the clergy; some were specifically described as 'ad clerum' sermons (Burd). That these were private occasions was emphasized by requests for permission by some preachers to 'make publick' their charges in print (Fleetwood 1712). But by 1694, Henry Cornwallis preached his visitation sermon in Tunbridge Wells before a mixed congregation of clergy and laity. Mayors, magistrates, and corporations sometimes attended visitation services. In 1760 in Wakefield, the evangelical Henry Venn made his visitation sermon a discourse principally for 'the flock at Huddersfield committed to my charge' (Venn: 1). Others also attended: in 1750 at Lisburne in the Irish diocese of Connor and Down, John Grace, preaching the episcopal visitation sermon, saw that there were many Dissenters in the congregation and 'apprehended it might be of Service to the Church and the spiritual interests of the Dissenters themselves that they should think worthily, that is, very honourably of the Bishop and the rest of the established clergy who reside among them' so he abandoned his prepared sermon and improvised comments to the Dissenters in attendance (Grace: ii).

Visitation sermons grew in length in this period. In 1701, Richard Bynns indicated that his would take an hour (Bynns: 2). But the increasing length was cited as justification for their publication, since the pulpit version was necessarily restricted. In 1709, Bishop Wake of Lincoln commented that when he first drew up the charge, which ran to sixty-eight pages, 'this matter was too large an extent, and too weighty a nature to be either so fully spoken to by me, or so duly consider'd by you, as it ought to be, in the short time that could then be spared from our other business' (W. Wake: i). Consequently visitation sermons often ballooned when prepared for publication, as Henry Taylor's eighty-six page discourse showed. This raised the issue of how the published sermon differed from that preached at the visitation. In 1794 John Longe, who preached the Bishop of Norwich's visitation sermon, published his with brackets around those passages which he had inserted into the preached sermon.

Publication was also justified when bishops wanted clergy to refer back to visitation sermons or wanted to spend time on a particular issue, as William Talbot proposed in 1717: 'I have endeavoured to touch on most of the common subjects of an ordinary visitation charge: and as you may now have it always by you, it may save a good deal of time which may be usefully employ'd to other purposes' (Talbot: i). The assumption that clergy would keep copies of the published visitation sermons and charges was sometimes mentioned (Smalbroke; Clavering). And younger, less experienced, clergy were often the objects of some specific published visitation sermons (Hort). On occasion individual clergy were held up as models to others in visitations, as John Killingbeck, vicar of Leeds, was by the Archbishop of York (Oates: 54–5).

Other visitation practices are apparent from the sermons. They show the seriousness with which the Church regarded peculiar jurisdictions, since separate visitation sermons were sometimes preached in such parishes (Stubbs). Some bishops, like Jonathan Trelawny of Winchester, expected different sermons to be preached in each of the visitation centres in his diocese (Norse; Scott). Occasionally visitation sermons provide evidence of episcopal performance, such as Benjamin Hoadly's visitation at Hereford, which refutes accusations of his failure to visit that diocese (Salwey 1722). Some bishops were very specific in the way they treated visitations. For example Edmund Gibson of London, at his primary visitation, gave each clergyman a book of directions relating to their duties: consequently he could avoid preaching on routine matters in his visitation sermons (E. Gibson).

Often bishops wrote and preached their own visitation sermons but their choices of others to preach for them were significant. Many preachers were naturally clients of bishops or of aristocrats, often their chaplains. In 1716 Bishop Bisse of Hereford chose his brother, Thomas, to preach at his primary visitation. Fellows of Oxford and Cambridge colleges were common choices, especially when a scholarly or theological discourse was called for, as in 1766, when Thomas Rutherford preached. Rutherford was Professor of Divinity at Cambridge and his sermon was a major theological response to Francis Blackburne's *Confessional,* which had advocated freedom from the strictures of subscription to the Thirty-Nine Articles. In 1760 a layman preached the sermon for the provincial visitation of the Archdiocese of Dublin, though he was careful to justify this in the preface to the sermon (*Charge Given by the Vicar-General of Dublin*).

It was sometimes asserted that clergy were obliged to accept a request to preach by the archdeacon or bishop. In 1710, Archdeacon Cannon of Norfolk asked Charles Buchanan to preach for him; Buchanan expressed some surprise 'when I found that I could not be excused' (Buchanan). Equally Robert Ham in 1713 found himself 'commanded' to preach Bishop Blackall's visitation sermon in Exeter (Ham). Thomas Secker clearly regarded himself as able to call on any clergyman in his diocese and only acceptance of a living outside his jurisdiction was legitimate grounds for refusal to preach (Jenkins: 183).

Preachers acknowledged that visitation sermons were *sui generis.* In 1717 Roger Altham claimed that archidiaconal visitations were the remainder of 'ancient Diocesan Synods in which the affairs of the Church used to be managed by a common consultation…' (Altham: 4). In 1776 the visitation preacher in London claimed that at visitations 'the preacher should not confine himself to the common rules of the pulpit, and exhort his hearers on subjects which may be…familiar to the minds of most of them' (*The Morality of a Citizen*: 1). In 1756 the newly-appointed archdeacon of the East Riding of Yorkshire, Robert Oliver, modestly admitted that, as someone new to the archdeaconry, silence 'would best become me'. But he acknowledged that visitations 'also furnish the clergy at those times assembled, with proper opportunities of conferring together and concerting the most effectual methods of promoting Christian knowledge among their flocks; and contributing, as far as their influence extends to the preservation of the best and wisest constitution in Church and State' (Oliver: 1–2).

The content of visitation sermons illuminates the principal concerns of the Church and in particular those concerns that most exercised the bishops and clergy as a professional body. The contemporary religious controversies of the period were played out in these sermons. In the first two decades of the eighteenth century the related issues of the Church's relations with Dissent, the legitimacy of religious toleration, the position in which it placed the clergy, and the religious implications of the Glorious Revolution were the dominant concerns expressed in visitation sermons. These controversies also fuelled a sharp rise in the number of published visitation sermons; the *English Short Title Catalogue* and *Eighteenth Century Collections Online* both show that published visitation sermons in the period 1700–10 were more than double the number in 1690–1700. This suggests that such controversies were of particular significance to the clergy and matters on which sermons of record were required. Such sermons expressed the problems of living in an era of legal toleration. In 1704, Ofspring Blackall, preaching in the London diocese, argued that if the clergy taught the truth and thereby offended people, 'they will go elsewhere and make enemies of us' (Blackall: 9). Similarly, John Savage argued for unity at a time when Anglicanism was 'caught between fanaticism and popery' (Savage: 23). Schism, by which most meant the separation of Dissenters from the Church, was widely bemoaned; and some preachers used visitation sermons as a vehicle to attack Dissenters. In addition, the separate High and Low Church groupings were regarded by one preacher as 'blackening distinctions' (Fowler: 4).

Partisan feeling is easily detected in the visitation sermons of the decade; yet some denied this. Thomas Wise, having preached a visitation sermon at Canterbury in 1710, expressed surprise 'at hearing it spoken of as a Party-Sermon' (Wise: preface). These circumstances sometimes led clergy into hyperbole, designed to urge the clergy to greater exertions against Dissenters, but which should not perhaps be taken entirely at face value. For example, in 1708 Thomas Littell claimed:

> Never was there an Age wherein Religion had more malicious and dangerous enemies... not that there is any more in the arguements of our Modern Atheists or Dissenters and Scepticks, than what has formerly been urged. (Littell: 5–6)

Bishop Trelawny's visitation preacher was more measured when, in the same year, he claimed 'there is no Nation under heaven where these controversies have been sharper, or of longer continuance than in our own' (Norse: 1), though even this is a conspicuous overstatement. Bishop Wake of Lincoln was probably nearer the truth when he preached that there had been many cries of the Church in danger, but suggested to his audience 'a matter of real danger': the need for 'learning, prudence and piety' among the clergy (W. Wake: preface). Equally, John Jackson, preaching at the Archdeacon of Gloucester's visitation in 1711, said 'yet [it] must be remembered... that there are I hope more who love and respect the clergy and the Church' (Jackson). But too often partisanship and the desire to spur on the clergy to greater efforts were couched in exaggerated tones. Bishop Gilbert Burnet in 1714 claimed:

> There are grievous wolves who are now howling about us, and seem to be in full hope that they shall have us quickly in their power; and then we may be well assured that they will not spare the Flock. (Burnet: 7)

By the second decade of the eighteenth century the rise of deism featured heavily in visitation sermons. In 1714, Hugh Boulter claimed that there were 'too many professing atheism or deism' (Boulter: 21).

During the Bangorian controversy, clergy found its provocations too compelling to ignore and many visitation sermons were preached in strong support or opposition to Bishop Hoadly's claim that the kingdom of Christ had no earthly powers and therefore the Church could not persecute people for their beliefs. Visitation sermons witnessed some of the final reverberations of the debate, with interventions as late as 1724 and 1725 (Hawtayne; Conybeare). By the middle of the eighteenth century the question of the nature of miracles, revelation, and prophecy, a religious controversy which was the focus of the clergy much more than the laity, attracted considerable attention (Ingram: 85–111; Cooke). Towards the end of the century the running sore of the subscription controversy was also discussed in visitation sermons (Bellward; Burnaby). Visitation sermons were also the cause of significant controversies. In 1731 William Bowman's fiercely heterodox sermon at a visitation in Wakefield was so controversial that it went through six editions, and led to five replies (Bowman; Philanthropos; S. Taylor).

Since visitation sermons were preached by, or on behalf of, church dignitaries they might be expected to exclude theology from the fringes of the eighteenth-century Church. Yet in a few cases there is evidence of the growth of evangelicalism. Thomas Vivian, preaching in Plymouth for the archdeacon's visitation in 1754, advocated 'watching over each other in love. Observing each others conduct and by mutual reproof and advice, and assembling together for religious conference, building up each other in their most holy faith and admonishing one another'. He also attacked amusements such as drinking, gambling, 'merry making', and 'trifling discourse' (Vivian: 25, 28). Augustus Toplady preached a strong evangelical sermon at the 1772 Exeter visitation, in which he proclaimed himself wary of those who 'doubt lest he have not the grace of the Holy Ghost within', as did James Hervey at the Northampton visitation in 1753 (Toplady: 1; Hervey). Naturally opponents of evangelicalism raised concerns at this, as when John Balguy argued that 'When weak and ignorant mortals have once presumed to boast of an intimate commerce with the Deity, it is even dreadful to think to what extremes they may be carried of folly and fanaticism' (J. Balguy: 174).

The political circumstances of the age were also frequently discussed in visitation sermons. In 1715 and 1745 many denounced the Jacobite uprisings. In 1715 the clergy of the Irish diocese of Clogher used the occasion of the visitation to present an address to the King to prevent the assumption that Irish clergy were disloyal (*To the King's Most Excellent Majesty*). Bishop Waugh of Carlisle regarded it as a source of pride that the rebellion of 1745 had not interrupted visitations in his diocese (Waugh: 1). John Chapman used the same subject to stoke up anti-Catholic feeling in his sermon in the archdeaconry of Sudbury in 1745 (Chapman). Political issues led some clergy to court danger in their sermons: in 1718 Mr Craddock, preaching the Bishop of Gloucester's visitation sermon, took note of the 'exemplary advice' offered regarding those who would not swear oaths to the King. But he also pointed out that their late diocesan, Robert Frampton, had been a Non-juror 'yet ne'er would forsake the Church' (Craddock: iii).

Preachers took for granted that the clergy were interested in politics and vigilant on behalf of the state, for, as John Balguy preached in 1760: 'we cannot be too zealous for the British constitution and the Protestant succession; because we cannot set too high a value on the blessing we enjoy of civil and religious liberty' (J. Balguy: 179). But the unalloyed Erastian tone of seventeenth- and early eighteenth-century sermons was waning after the mid-century. Francis Potter preached in Wells: 'It must be acknowledged that it is not impossible for governors to err; and that it is the undeniable privilege and birthright of a free-people to give their opinions on all points of absolute and national importance' (Potter: 9).

Fierce political and theological debate sometimes led clergy into the temptation to impugn their superiors, and visitation sermons were occasionally used to do this. Bishop Burnet, a Latitudinarian bishop in the largely High Church diocese of Salisbury, felt insulted by the Dean of Salisbury's peculiar visitation. The preacher argued

> if he who should lead the blind be blind himself, no wonder if contempt be his lot... the times are perilous indeed when the wolves enter in amongst us; but never sure are worse times when the shepherds themselves prove the wolves. (R. Wake: 3, 25)

Burnet was later referred to as a 'Scottish bagpipe' (Buchanan). Benjamin Hoadly was similarly attacked by his fellow clergy. In 1731 the preacher at the archdeacon of Essex's visitation lamented,

> if we should ever unfortunately have a Prelate amongst us who shall concern himself with the State, instead of the Church, study the law more than the Gospel, and seek the earthly tabernacle of Canterbury and its revenues, before the Kingdom of God and his Righteousness... (Symonds 1731: 3)

Given free rein, some clergy chose to draw attention to idiosyncratic issues in visitation sermons and charges. The variety of such topics is remarkable, but includes: concern at the number of aristocrats travelling abroad for their education; support for Protestant churches in Transylvania and Poland; concern for the Jews of Britain; and anxiety that the universities were more concerned with politeness than religion and the promotion of Sunday schools (Burd; Fleetwood 1716; Hockin; Firebrace; Moore).

The material culture of visitation sermons was increasingly important. They became a form of theological literature in their own right and developed a strong readership, so that some classic examples were reprinted. Edward Symonds's visitation sermon of 1632 was reprinted in 1712 (Symonds 1712). In 1727 the Bishop of Rochester's sermon of 1695 was reprinted (Sprat). In 1744 Bishop Skinner's sermon of 1637 was reprinted. And similarly a Hereford sermon of 1722 was reprinted in 1790 (Skinner; Salwey 1790). Visitation sermons also afforded opportunities for printers to promote their wares. In 1726 Benjamin Hoadly's visitation sermon for the diocese of Salisbury included three pages of advertisements of the bishop's other publications, which presumably might be of interest to the clergy of his diocese; and Bishop Smalbroke of St Davids visitation sermon of 1729 included a similar advertisement (Hoadly; Smalbroke).

Some clergy formed their visitation sermons into collections which would have a life and reach beyond the specific circumstances of the moment. Daniel Waterland's sermons of 1731, 1739, and 1740 in the archdeaconry of Middlesex were frequently collected and published as a classic defence of the orthodox doctrine of the Eucharist and were widely read and used for many years. The same is true of Thomas Balguy's, which were published in a collection in 1785 (T. Balguy). Perhaps the most significant body of visitation sermons of the period was that of Thomas Sharp, Archdeacon of Northumberland (1723–57) and son of Archbishop Sharp.

Thomas Sharp was an exemplary archdeacon who used visitation sermons to inculcate the highest professional standards into his colleagues in the most northerly archdeaconry in the Church of England. On his entry to the archdeaconry, Sharp drew up 'An account of the parochial churches and chappels within the archdeaconry of Northumberland' based on his primary visitation (Sharp n.d.). Sharp's collection of archidiaconal charges and sermons was published in a single volume in 1753. They were preached annually between 1731 and 1752, except when there were diocesan visitations. The preface sheds some light on Sharp's approach to visitation sermons: they were addressed to the clergy alone—excluding the laity—and were published for their 'private and unmolested perusal... [and] cool deliberate examination', since visitations were 'often interrupted, or at least rendered very incommodious by circumstances unavoidable on these occasions' (Sharp 1753: iii–iv).

Perhaps aware that, as the youngest archdeacon of Northumberland in the history of the diocese, his charges might carry less weight than those of an older man, Sharp claimed

> I did not venture to pass my judgements on these subjects or to use the privilege of my station in discussing them in public, till I had been exercised myself above ten years in an extensive cure. (Sharp 1753: viii)

He proposed nothing that he had not found expedient in his own work. He also challenged the 'notion [which] too commonly prevails' that it was too difficult to enforce the Church's laws, and argued that the conduct of the clergy should be 'adjusted to our rule and rendered uniform and irreproachable' (Sharp 1753: x).

Sharp was aware that regional differences required clergy to respond to local circumstances. He did not speculate how the rubrics 'may appear to our Brethren in some other parts of this realm, and chiefly in those great and populous towns where customs repugnant to the Ecclesiastical Laws, and in manifest violation of them have unhappily prevailed...' but offered practical solutions which he knew would be effective in Northumberland but would 'scarce be said to be so... in some other places, particularly in the capital of this kingdom; where difficulties that the parochial clergy must necessarily meet with in their attempts to govern ministrations by the prescribed rules of the Church... are greatly to be lamented by them.' In contrasting London with Northumberland Sharp said

> The case is otherwise within this jurisdiction, where, although some irregularities have been occasionally committed, yet they have always been condemned as innovations upon Church Discipline... and they have never grown into an avowed or customary practice. (Sharp 1753: x–xiv)

Sharp's positive view of the clerical performance in his archdeaconry led him, in his first published sermon in 1731, to comment that 'not having at this time any thing in particular to charge you with, I shall assume a general topic'. This was a practice adopted by others in visitation charges, including his successor (Stubbs: 3; Robinson: 1; Yonge: 1). In this first sermon Sharp advocated absolute clerical obedience to the canons and reminded the clergy of their ordination vows; but he also drew a distinction between voluntary stipulations and those canons from which bishops allowed dispensations. Above all he commended the Thirty-Nine Articles of the Church as 'bulwarks against popery and fanaticism' (Sharp 1753: 2–15). In the three following charges, issued between 1733 and 1735, Sharp considered baptism, holy communion, and the liturgy respectively. He warned of the dangers of private baptism, lay baptism, and of practices other than affusion or pouring of water. He briefly touched on the 1712 debate on lay baptism and the Archbishop of Canterbury's official discouragement of it; he also advised the clergy that Bishop Chandler of Durham had expressly charged the archdeacons with instructing the clergy on baptism, and particularly to make a note of the age and circumstances of adult baptisms. This latter was often either a means of evading the Church's requirement for child baptism or of admitting dissenters into the Church—both of which required episcopal attention (Sharp 1753: 20–48).

Sharp's charge on Holy Communion paid special attention to the problem confronting the clergy of excluding notorious 'evil livers' from the Eucharist as enjoined by the canons. He recognized that this presented a problem if the clergy were not to be pursued in law. In addition, the Test Act 'which brings abundance of persons to the Communion to qualify themselves for offices... [does not] have any proviso to indemnify the minister for proceeding according to the rubrick in denying the sacrament' (Sharp 1753: 54). Sharp advised the clergy to act cautiously: to admit those who sought to qualify under the Test Act and unless they had direct evidence of people affected by 'hatred and malice' they should admit those accused of them to Holy Communion also (Sharp 1753: 55–64). Sharp's charge on the liturgy advocated daily services, proper use of the collects, public notice of the celebration of communion, and proper issuing of the banns of marriage. One topic stands out: his advice on the churching of women, often assumed to be declining at this time. Sharp said that: 'it is commonly performed on the weekdays, just before the general thanksgiving; on Sundays just after the Nicene Creed.' He explained that Bishop Chandler had directed that churching should be done during public services (Sharp 1753: 76–86).

The canons of the Church exercised Sharp in his 1738 and 1739 charges. He defended obedience to the canons but recognized that bishops' dispensations were reasonable, such as the 'customary prerogative' of ordaining men to the diaconate and priesthood on the same day. This was an important matter for those ordinands who were far distant from either London or the see city of the diocese, and was an example of the efficacy of setting aside the strictures of the canons (W. Gibson: 267). In 1739 Sharp reminded clergy of the injunctions of successive monarchs to avoid sermons on political matters and mentioned again the way in which the Test Act seemed to oblige the clergy to admit to Holy Communion those who were 'schismatics' (Sharp 1753: 99–126).

In 1742 Sharp focused on subscription, and adopted the view of Bishop Burnet of Salisbury that subscription did not require *belief* in each of the Thirty-Nine Articles, but *assent* to them. But he went beyond Burnet when he claimed that the key issue in subscription was conformity to the liturgy and the acknowledgement that the Thirty-Nine Articles were the word of God. This was an important assertion, walking a middle way between the Low Church minimizing of conformity to the Articles and the High Church requirement of specific assent to each and every one of them (Sharp 1753: 151–3). Despite, or perhaps because of, the alarms of the Jacobite rebellion of 1745 the charge of that year discussed relatively anodyne issues of the licensing of preachers and the canonical form of prayers to be read before sermons (Sharp 1753: 173–228).

Clerical apparel was a topic to which Sharp turned in 1752, when he argued that its objective was to make the clergy 'sufficiently distinguished from the laity'. For Sharp, apparel was linked to behaviour:

> There are certain places of innocent diversion and entertainment where clergymen without their proper habit are allowed to appear without offence. But whether their appearance there, habited as clergymen, might pass without censure is yet a question.

Sharp himself 'never thought any entertainment worth my seeking or receiving, if I were obliged to disguise myself while I partook of it'. He referred to alehouses and public games: 'the taste of the world is now much altered in this respect: nor are offences taken at the clergy as formerly for using these diversions, so long as they do it with moderation.' He insisted that the clergy were forbidden to join the army but they could study law, 'physick', and surgery. Trade was seriously frowned on but, aware of the poverty of some of his fellow clergy, Sharp argued 'I should imagine that a clergyman driven by meer necessity to support himself by industry and labour, though in a properly lay business, would stand absolved from all censure, especially if he did at the same time fulfil, to the best of his power, the common duties of his vocation' (Sharp 1753: 333–50).

Sharp's 1747 charge is unique in containing criticism of his fellow clergy for their failure to follow the canons on confirmation and the preparation of candidates: 'I could wish both these canons were more strictly and punctually observed than they are.' He also criticized the infrequency of confirmation. Additionally, he censured the clergy on solemnization of marriage, discouraging 'any man from attempting to revive the old practice of open solemnization in service times' (Sharp 1753: 254, 265).

In 1749, Sharp termed his charge 'a miscellany', discussing parish registers, touching on records of recusants, of baptisms, and of visitations of the sick. He also told the clergy that they could not refuse burial to any except excommunicants. He mentioned that the register of births of dissenters was not required by law but was 'a favour which, when asked, should never be denied' (Sharp 1753: 292–313). He discussed Dissent a year later when he said that Anglican clergy were 'cut off from all pretentions of acting agreeably to the Constitutions and Rules of this Church, if they either form or draw together separate congregations for doctrine or worship, or, by their pretence, encourage the same'. He warned against religious meetings in private homes, another sign of a preoccupation with Dissent (Sharp 1753: 329–31).

In 1757 Sharp published together three further visitation charges on the subject of preaching. This was a popular work which reached a third edition in 1787. His advice on preaching was designed particularly for 'the use of one who had just entered into orders' and he hoped it might help younger clergy in the archdeaconry. He laid down rules for composition, style, delivery, and pronunciation, advocating the avoidance of long sentences, not leaving the hearer in suspense until the end of the sentence, speaking in concrete rather than abstract terms, avoiding the pedantic, and remembering that 'tedious addresses cloy the mind' (Sharp 1787: 13–16). He advocated brevity, discouraged attempts to explain mysteries, and warned against extempore preaching which ran away from considered written texts. He also encouraged the use of examples and comparisons and exhorted preachers to pronounce their words clearly so that they could be heard (Sharp 1787: 31–40).

In 1751 Sharp was chosen to preach at Bishop Joseph Butler's primary visitation, on 24 July at Alnwick. In this, he exhorted the clergy to share their knowledge with the laity:

> Learning and knowledge are much increased from what they were in former times; and unless the improvements of the clergy bear some proportion to that of the laity, they must expect to suffer in their credit...and in the Esteem in which they ought to be held in by the world. (Sharp 1751: 21)

Sharp clearly held the view that the distance from London and urban centres preserved Northumberland from some clerical diversion from orthodoxy and from the sources of problems for clergy and laity, and there may be some truth in this. However, distance from London would not explain the fact that there is no mention of the neglect of duty arising from non-residence and pluralism. Nor would it explain the concerns, sometimes expressed in other archdeacons' visitations, of disrepair of churches and irreligion among the laity. Given Sharp's willingness to confront concerns in his charges it is unlikely that such problems were prevalent. If, therefore, the northernmost parishes of England were largely well served, it is to Sharp's credit that he did not simply allow his office to become a sinecure. His visitation sermons, though not needing to deal with pressing problems, became the eighteenth century equivalent of continuing professional development for the clergy. Sharp reminded the clergy of their duties and discussed with them the sort of problems that arose from them; he warned them of some of the pitfalls of their profession and encouraged them to the highest standards of their vocation. As the 'oculus episcopi' the archdeacon was responsible to the bishop, and on occasion Sharp drew the clergy's attention to issues held to be important by the bishops of Durham. The significance of Sharp's sermons is not simply that they are a useful corrective to the pessimists' view of the eighteenth-century Church of England. It is that a man who was a pluralist, and had obtained his offices due to nepotism, was an exemplary diocesan officer.

Toward the end of the eighteenth century some visitation charges signalled, and sought to quantify, perceptions of problems in the Church. Bishop Butler of Hereford in 1792 spoke bluntly to his clergy, comparing the 1789 returns of communicants with those of 1747, and concluded that

> the unhappy fact is that the communicants in the year 1747 appear to have been many more, so many more, than those reported in 1789, that I am unwilling to recite the numbers. Yet it is observable that the numbers of the year 1747 are not so considerable as might have been expected in a flourishing state of our Church, in which for nearly a century before, every man had been encouraged to attend his religious duties not only without molestation of any kind, but with the immediate reward of the reputation belonging to a good Christian. (Butler: 4–5)

Yet against such an alarm must be set the view of Bishop Pretyman-Tomline of Lincoln who, in 1800, claimed that having visited his huge diocese five times,

> I cannot with justice to your own merits or my own feelings, omit this opportunity of publicly expressing the genuine satisfaction I have experienced, particularly in the Visitation I have lately concluded from observing that attention to the several duties of your respective situations has greatly encreased, at a period when the enemies of the Established Church are too ready to accuse its ministers of encreasing negligence. (Pretyman-Tomline)

His evidence for this was a significant rise in the numbers of confirmations he had conducted.

Such differing perceptions of the performance of the Church in the eighteenth century should not, however, blind us to the evidence of visitation sermons. They are remarkable testimony to the energy, dedication, and professionalism of bishops, archdeacons, and their clergy. Consequently, collections of sermons like those of Thomas Sharp were widely used to train clergy in the nineteenth century. Others, such as White Kennett's episcopal visitation sermon of 1720, emphasized the reciprocal responsibilities of bishops and clergy, and are among the most impressive statements of clerical duty in the post-Reformation Church. Matthias Symson, preaching at the archdeacon of Lincoln's visitation in 1708, referred to the time as this 'itching ear'd age' (Symson: i), in which everyone could hear opinions that most reflected their own views; Symson advocated that the clergy should preach what they believed to be right. For the most part that is what sermons in general, and visitation sermons in particular, represent. Visitation preachers had an opportunity to draw the attention of the clergy to the most significant issues facing them in church, state, and society. In doing so they provide a window on the clerical concerns of the period; but it was a window which—using the medium of print—the laity could look through as well. For the historian, visitation sermons are, above all, a testimony to the variety of religious concerns in this period as well as to the diversity of religious experience and observance, as Thomas Sharp's sermons demonstrate.

Acknowledgements

I am grateful to the Director of the Armstrong Browning Library at Baylor University in Texas for appointing me as visiting research fellow in 2009 to undertake research on their sermons collection for this project.

References

A Full Justification of the Doctrines Advanced in Mr. Bowman's Visitation Sermon. (1731). London: H. Cooke.

Altham, R. (1717). *A Charge Deliver'd to the Clergy of the Arch-Deaconry of Middlesex.* London: John Morphew.

A Plain and Humble Address to the Clergy and Ministers in Great-Britain. A Sermon Occasioned by Reading Mr. Bowman's Visitation Sermon. (1731). York: Thomas Gent.

Balguy, J. (1760). *On the Character and Conduct of a Minister of the Gospel, Delivered at the Archdeacon's Primary Visitation in the Year 1760.* London: Hitch and Hawes.

Balguy, T. (1785). *Discourses on Various Subjects.* Winchester: Lockyer Davies.

Bellward, J. (1774). *A Sermon, Preached at the Archdeacons Visitation, Held at Beccles, in Suffolk.* Norwich: William Chase.

Bisse, T. (1716). *A Sermon Preached at the Primary Visitation of… Philip, Lord Bishop of Hereford.* London: Henry Clement.

Blackall, O. (1704). *A Sermon Preach'd at Brentwood in Essex, October the 7th. 1693. at the Visitation of… Henry Lord Bishop of London.* London: Will Rogers.

Boulter, H. (1714). *A Sermon Preach'd at the Visitation of the Clergy, Held at Kingston Upon Thames, on Wednesday, May 26. 1714.* London: Timothy Childe.

Bowman, W. (1731). *The Traditions of the Clergy Destructive of Religion:… A Sermon Preach'd at the Visitation Held at Wakefield in Yorkshire, June 25. 1731.* Belfast: James Blow.

Bray, T. (1701). *Several Circular Letters to the Clergy of Mary-land, Subsequent to Their Late Visitation, to Enforce Such Resolutions as Were Taken Therein.* London: William Downing.

Buchanan, C. (1710). *A Sermon Preach'd at Loddon [sic] April 26. 1710. At the Visitation Held There by the Reverend Dr Cannon, Arch-Deacon of Norfolk.* Norwich: F. Collins.

Bull, G. (1715). *The Archbishop of Cambray's Pastoral Letter Concerning the Love of God, … To Which is Added, a Circular Letter, by George Bull, … His Visitation Sermon, and His Charge to His Diocese.* London: Robert Nelson.

Burd, R. (1703). *A Sermon Preach'd at the Lord Bishop of Winton's Visitation at Andover in the County of Southampton, on the 27th of September, 1703.* London: Edward Brewster.

Burnaby, A. (1774). *A Sermon on the Nature of Subscription to Articles of Religion; Preached Before the Rev. John Law, A.M. Archdeacon of Rochester, at His Visitation.* London: T. Payne.

Burnet, G. (1714). *A Sermon Preach'd, and a Charge Given at the Triennial Visitation of the Diocese of Salisbury.* London: J. Churchill.

Butler, J. (1792). *The Bishop of Hereford's Charge to the Clergy of His Diocese, at His Triennial Visitation in the Year 1792.* Hereford: J. & W. Eddowes.

Bynns, R. (1701). *A Sermon Preach'd Before... John, Lord Bishop of Coventry & Lichfield, at His Primary Visitation*. London: J. Downing.

Chapman, J. (1746). *A Charge Delivered to the Clergy of the Archdeaconry of Sudbury, at a Visitation on May 12, &c. 1746*. London: Samuel Birt.

Charge Given by the Vicar-General of Dublin, on the Triennial Visitation of that Province. (1760). Dublin: G. Faulkener.

Clavering, R. (1730). *A Charge Given by the Right Revd Father in God, Robert Ld Bishop of Peterborough, at the Primary Visitation of His Diocese in the Year 1730*. London: William Innys.

Cooke, W. (1750). *A Sermon Preached at the Visitation Held at Beaconsfield, May 25, 1750*. London: C. Bathurst.

Conybeare, J. (1725). *A Sermon Preach'd at the Triennial Visitation of... John, Lord Bishop of Oxford*. Oxford: S. Wilmot.

Cornwallis, H. (1694). *A Sermon upon Hospitality, Preach'd at a Late Visitation at Tunbridge in Kent, on 2 Kings, IV. 38... By H. C.* London: n. p.

Craddock, W. (1718). *A Discourse of the Due Catechising, and Confirming of Youth: Preach'd at the Episcopal Visitation*. London: B. Tooke.

Ditchfield, P. H. (1908). *The Old Time Parson*. London: Methuen.

Ellison, R. (2010). 'The Tractarians' Sermons and Other Speeches', in Ellison, R. (ed.), *A New History of the Sermon: The Nineteenth Century*. Leiden: Brill, 15–57.

Firebrace, J. (1767). *A Sermon Preached at the Archdeacon's Visitation at Stowe-Market*. Cambridge: J. Archdeacon.

Fleetwood, W. (1712). *The Bishop of St Asaph's Charge to the Clergy*. London: S. Buckley.

—— (1716). *A Charge Delivered to the Clergy of the Diocese of Ely at Cambridge, August the VIIth. MDCCXVI. At his Primary Visitation, by William Ld. Bp. of Ely*. Cambridge: C. Crownfield.

Fowler, E. (1707). *The Charge of the Bp. of Gloucester, Deliver'd to the Clergy of His Diocese, in His Late Triennial Visitation, Held by Commission*. London: J. Wyat.

Gibson, E. (1742). *The Charge of Edmund, Lord Bishop of London, to the Clergy of His Diocese, in His Visitation Begun in... 1741, and Finish'd in... 1742*. London: Edward Owen.

Gibson, W. (2004). *Enlightenment Prelate, Benjamin Hoadly, 1676–1761*. Cambridge: James Clarke.

Grace, J. (1750). *A Sermon Preached in the Parish-Church of Lisburn, on the 21st of June, 1749; When the... Bishop of Down and Connor Held His Episcopal Visitation of His Dioceses*. Dublin: Joseph Leathley.

Ham, R. (1713). *A Sermon Preach'd at the Archidiaconal Visitation, Held by... Ofspring, Lord Bishop*. Exeter: S. Farley.

Hawtayne, W. (1724). *A Sermon Preached at the Primary Visitation of the Right Reverend... Richard Lord Bishop of Lincoln: Held at Welling in Hertfordshire*. London: Robert Knaplock.

Hervey, J. (1780). *A Sermon, Preached at the Visitation of the Reverend John Brown, Archdean of Northampton... on 10th May, 1753*. Glasgow: J. Robertson.

Hoadly, B. (1726). *A Charge Deliver'd to the Clergy, at the Primary Visitation of the Diocese of Sarum, in the Year, MDCCXXVI*. London: J. Knapton.

Hockin, J. (1764). *A Sermon Preached Before the Clergy in the Parish Church of Oakhampton, Devon, on Tuesday the Fifth Day of June, 1764; at the Primary Visitation of... Frederick,... Lord Bishop of Exeter*. London: J. & W. Oliver.

Hort, J. (1770). *Instructions to the Clergy of the Diocese of Tuam. By Josiah Hort,...at His Primary Visitation Held There on Wednesday, July VIII, MDCCXLII. 1770*. London: n. p.

Ingram, R. G. (2010). '"The Weight of Historical Evidence": Conyers Middleton and the Eighteenth-Century Miracles Debate', in R. Cornwall and W. Gibson (eds.), *Religion, Politics and Dissent, 1660-1832*. Aldershot: Ashgate, 85-110.

Jackson, J. (1711). *A Sermon Preach'd at the Archdeacon of Gloucester's Visitation, Held in the Town of Dursly, April 17, 1711*. London: Bernard Lintott.

Jacob, W. M. (2007). *The Clerical Profession in the Long Eighteenth Century*. Oxford: Oxford University Press.

Jenkins, A. P. (1991). *The Correspondence of Bishop Secker*. Oxford: Oxfordshire Record Society.

Kennett, W. (1720). *Monitions and Advices Deliver'd to the Clergy of the Diocese of Peterborough, at the Primary Visitation..., MDCCXX*. London: J. Wyat.

Littell, T. (1708). *A Sermon Preach'd at a Visitation Held at Boston in Lincoln-shire; April 23. 1708*. London: Jonah Bowyer.

Longe, J. (1794). *A Sermon Preached at the Primary Visitation of the Right Reverend Father in God Charles, Lord Bishop of Norwich*. Ipswich: G. Jermyn.

Moore, C. (1785). *A Sermon Preached in the Church of St. Nicholas, Rochester, on June 24, 1785*. Canterbury: Simmons and Kirkby.

Norse, P. (1708). *A Sermon Preach'd at Alresford, in the County of Southampton, August 31. 1708*. London: John Wyat.

Oates, J., (2006). *The Memorandum Book of John Lucas, 1712-1750*. Leeds: Thoresby Society.

Oliver, R. (1756). *A Charge Delivered to the Clergy of the Archdeaconry of the East-Riding of York, at a Primary Visitation...on the 4th June 1756*. London: W. Sandby.

Philanthropos. (1731). *A Second Plain and Humble Address to the Clergy of All Orders in Great-Britain. A Sermon from II. Cor. iii. 5....Occasioned by reading Mr. Bowman's Visitation Sermon, at Wakefield, in Yorkshire*. York: Thomas Gent.

Potter, F. (1763). *A Charge Delivered at the Winter Visitation Held for the Archdeaconry of Wells in the County of Somerset*. Oxford: Clarendon Press.

Pretyman-Tomline, G. (1800). *A Charge Delivered to the Clergy of the Diocese of Lincoln, at the Triennial Visitation of That Diocese in June and July 1800*. London: Cadell and Davies.

Robinson, T. (1761). *A Charge Delivered at a Visitation, Held for the Archdeaconry of Northumberland*. Newcastle: J. White.

Rutherford, T. (1766). *A Second Vindication of the Right of Protestant Churches to Require the Clergy to Subscribe...in a Charge Delivered at a Visitation in July MDCCLXVI*. Cambridge: J. Archdeacon.

Salwey, J. (1722). *Divine Worship Due to Christ*. London: W. & J. Innys.

—— (1790). *Divine Worship Due to Christ*. Manchester: Sowler and Russell.

Savage, J. (1704). *A Sermon Preach'd at the Yearly Visitation Held at Welwyn in Hertfordshire, May the 3d. 1704*. Cambridge: Edmund Jeffery.

Scott, J. (1708). *A Sermon Preach'd at the Primary Visitation of...Jonathan Lord Bishop of Winton, August 26. 1708*. London: George Strahan.

Sharp, T. (n.d.). 'An Account of the Parochial Churches and Chappels Within the Archdeaconry of Northumberland'. Durham University Library, AUC/1/169.

——(1751). *A Sermon Preached at the Primary Visitation of the Right Reverend Father in God Joseph by Divine Providence Lord Bishop of Durham...* Newcastle: J. White.

—— (1753). *The Rubricks in the Book of Common Prayer and the Canons of the Church of England...Considered in a Course of Visitation Charges by Thomas Sharp Archdeacon of Northumberland*. London: J. Knapton.

—— (1787). *Discourses on Preaching, Or Directions towards Attaining the Best Manner of Discharging the Duties of the Pulpit, Delivered in Three Visitation Charges*. London: B. White.

Skinner, R. (1744). *The Speech of Dr. Robert Skinner, Lord Bishop of Bristol, at the Visitation at Dorchester, September 18. 1637*. London: Jacob Robinson.

Smalbroke, R. (1728). *A Charge Delivered to the Reverend the Clergy of the Diocese of St. David's, in a Triennial Visitation of the Same in August, 1728*. London: J. Knapton.

Sprat, T. (1727). *A Discourse Made by the Ld Bishop of Rochester to the Clergy of His Diocese, at His Visitation in the Year 1695*. London: E. & R. Nutt.

Stubbs, P. (1723). *Advice to the Reverend the Clergy, of the Peculiar Jurisdiction of Saint Alban...Given in the Court-Consistorial Held There on Thursday, May 2, 1723*. London: J. Penn.

Symonds, E. (1712). *A Visitation Sermon Preach'd at Halstead in Essex, April 12. 1632*. London: S. Popping.

—— (1731). *A Visitation Sermon, Preach'd at Halstead in Essex*. London: J. Roberts.

Symson, M. (1708). *A Sermon Preached at Horncastle in Lincolnshire. At the Visitation of the Reverend the Archdeacon of Lincoln*. London: George Strahan.

Talbot, W. (1717). *The Bishop of Sarum's Charge to the Clergy of His Diocese, at His Primary Visitation Anno, 1716*. London: J. Bowyer.

Taylor, H. (1760). *An Essay on the Beauty of the Divine Oeconomy. Being the Substance of a Sermon...Preached at the Visitation of the Lord Bishop of Winchester*. London: J. Wilkie.

Taylor, S. (2010). 'The Bowman Affair: Latitudinarian Theology, Anti-Clericalism and the Limits of Orthodoxy in Early Hanoverian England' in W. Gibson and R. Cornwall (eds.), *Religion, Politics and Dissent, 1660–1832*. Aldershot: Ashgate, 35–50.

The Morality of a Citizen; in a Visitation Sermon; with a View to the Present Alarming Situation of Public Affairs. (1776). London: G. Kearsley.

The Traditions of the Clergy not Destructive of Religion. Being Remarks on Mr. Bowman's Visitation Sermon. (1731). London: Stephen Austin.

To the King's Most Excellent Majesty. The Humble Address of the Clergy of the Diocese of Clogher, at Their Triennial Visitation. (1715). Dublin: E. Waters.

Toplady, A. (1772). *A Sermon Preached at an Annual Visitation of the Clergy of the Archdeaconry of Exeter*. London: Joseph Gurney.

Torriano, A. (1706). *A Sermon Preach'd at the Visitation at Huntingdon, on the 16th Day of April, 1706*. London: James Round.

Venn, H. (1760). *A Sermon, Preach'd at a Visitation of the Clergy*. Leeds: G. Wright.

Vivian, T. (1754). *A Sermon Preached in the Church of St. Andrew in Plymouth, at the Archdeacon's Visitation*. Belfast: James Magee.

Wake, R. (1704). *A Sermon Preached at the Triennial Visitation of the Dean of Sarum,...May 12. 1704*. London: R. Clavel.

Wake, W. (1710). *The Bishop of Lincoln's Charge, to the Clergy of his Diocese, in His Triennial Visitation Begun at Leicester, June the 1st. 1709*. London: Richard Sare.

Waterland, D. (1731). *A Charge Deliver'd to the Clergy of Middlesex, at the Primary Visitation Held May 19, 1731*. London: J. Crownfield.

——(1739). *The Sacramental Part of the Eucharist Explain'd, in a Charge Delivered in Part to the Clergy of Middlesex, at the Easter-Visitation 1739.* London: W. Innys.

——(1740). *Distinctions of Sacrifice: Set Forth in a Charge Deliver'd in Part to the Clergy of Middlesex at the Easter-Visitation, 1740.* London: W. Innys.

Waugh, J. (1747). *A Charge Delivered to the Clergy of the Diocese of Carlisle, at the General Chapter of Visitation, Begun May 26, 1747.* London: E. Owen.

Wise, T. (1710). *The Faithful Stewards: or the Pastoral Duty Open'd: In a Visitation-Sermon Preach'd at St. Margaret's Church in Canterbury, June the First, 1710.* London: E. Curl.

Yonge, P. (1763). *The Charge of the Right Reverend Father in God, Philip, Lord Bishop of Norwich, Delivered to the Clergy of His Diocese, at his Primary Visitation.* Norwich: W Chase.

CHAPTER 19

CONSECRATION SERMONS

COLIN HAYDON

Introduction

EPISCOPAL consecrations were, as preachers on those occasions frequently observed, 'solemnities'. In the eighteenth century, four-fifths were conducted in the chapel of Lambeth Palace (Stubbs: 108–23), a very microcosm of the Church of England's history. Embellished by Archbishop Laud, desecrated during the Commonwealth, it was restored by Archbishop Juxon at the Restoration. Archbishop Parker's tomb commemorated the Church's sixteenth-century Reformation. Dating from the thirteenth century, the chapel also emphasized the Church's medieval heritage. But the consecration service itself proclaimed the Church's episcopal continuity, beyond the Middle Ages, back to apostolic times. Epistle or Gospel readings outlined a bishop's necessary qualities (1 Timothy 3:1–7), St Paul's charges to church elders (Acts 20:17–35), and Christ's commission: 'Feed my sheep' (John 21:15–17); 'As my Father hath sent me, even so send I you' (John 20:19–23); 'Go ye therefore, and teach all nations' (Matthew 28:18–20). The Form stressed that the bishop-elect was called by the Holy Ghost to his work. Robed in his full episcopal habit, he knelt before the archbishop/senior bishop and other bishops present (three were needed); they laid their hands on his head, the archbishop saying: 'Receive the Holy Ghost, for the Office and Work of a Bishop in the Church of God.' 'Be to the flock of Christ a shepherd', the archbishop charged, so that 'when the chief shepherd shall appear, you may receive the never-fading crown of glory'. Plainly the service was unforgettable. Rather touchingly, Bishop Crew of Durham, near to death, requested a sermon, duly preached before him on 2 July 1721, '[b]eing the *Anniversary* of His CONSECRATION, His *Lordship* having Then been FIFTY YEARS A BISHOP' (Lupton: title page).

The Preachers and Their Sermons

The consecration sermon was delivered after the readings and was an integral part of the 'solemnity'. Since the wording of the service was not greatly different from that for the ordination of priests, it usually behoved the preacher to extol eloquently the office and labours of a bishop. The bishop-elect chose the preacher; and the sermon might, therefore, also anticipate the character of, or a programme for, the new episcopate. That of a bishop's chaplain might pre-eminently do so: thus, Charles Henry Hall's 1794 sermon prefigured Bishop Courtenay's charge to his clergy the following year. An old friend, who shared the new bishop's outlook, might be likewise invited. William Parker, in the preface to his published sermon, acknowledged 'with due gratitude' his 'long friendship' with Bishop Lyttelton (Parker: iv). The friendship of Samuel Croxall and Bishop Egerton began at Eton and lasted until Egerton's death. William Paley and Bishop John Law were very close. Bishop Moss poignantly repaid William Dodwell's consecration sermon by composing his friend's monumental inscription in Salisbury cathedral. Further connections are noteworthy. Samuel Knight and Bishop Tanner were united by antiquarian interests. William Wake chose White Kennett, his steadfast ally in the convocation controversy, to preach at his consecration. Institutional (particularly college) links were important: as with Croxall and Egerton, institutions nurtured friendships. Thomas Waite was a lecturer at the Temple, Bishop Sherlock its Master. John Green and Bishop Keene were allies when Cambridge dons. Michael Lort was a Fellow and Bishop Hinchliffe Master of Trinity College, Cambridge. At Christ Church, Oxford, John Randolph and Lewis Bagot, as censor and dean respectively, worked together. Thomas Balguy was archdeacon of Winchester from 1759 and Jonathan Shipley dean from 1760 until obtaining the mitre in 1769. Most strikingly of all, bishops-elect might even persuade relatives to preach. Benjamin Hoadly chose his younger brother, John; Spencer Madan co-opted his son, also Spencer, who, in the sermon, engagingly remarked on '*my* peculiar situation' (Madan: 20).

Preachers could find the occasions daunting: Benjamin Newton, in 1779, bewailed 'the *Importance* of the *Occasion*, and the *Insufficiency* of the *Speaker*' (B. Newton: 8). They often expressed their apprehensions when addressing venerable and learned bishops. A desire to inform 'such an audience...would be attended with no small degree of presumption', stated Charles Jenner in 1753, and Newton contrasted the bishops' 'enlarged understandings' with his own 'imperfect and weak' reasoning (Jenner: 15; B. Newton: 11). Such comments—however unctuous—rarely seem mere convention. Yet to preach was a considerable honour, outweighing anxieties, and the preacher sought to justify the new bishop's confident expectations. Furthermore, the invitation presented a golden opportunity for career advancement. Preachers hoped to impress, by their erudition, keen arguments, and eloquence, those vastly influential potential patrons, the captive audience of Church dignitaries. Usually, they wanted their discourses published by order of the presiding archbishop. John Jortin greatly impressed Archbishop Herring, and so secured a valuable patron, by his sermon at Zachary Pearce's consecration in 1748 (Young: 711). Some preachers fawned: 'let us *love*... [the bishops], and honour them, as our Spiritual Fathers', declared Lewis Stephens, 'and let us endeavour to make their Names as sweet and delightful as the *precious Ointment*' (L. Stephens: 22–3). Most, more subtly, aimed to please by aligning their discourses to the episcopate's perceived thinking and sensibilities. Later, some consecration preachers themselves became bishops. This was true of Hugh Boulter, Nicholas Clagett, Edmund Gibson, John Gilbert, John Green, John Hoadly, William Jackson, White Kennett, Samuel Lisle, William Markham, Thomas Newton, John Randolph, William Sancroft, Elias Sydall, Edward Synge (1659–1741) and his son, also Edward (1691–1762), and John Waugh. Yoked to rising stars, the preachers were frequently ambitious.

The most natural texts for the sermons came from St Paul's two epistles to Timothy (on church order, likely problems when evangelizing, and the qualities needed in a bishop) and his letter to Titus (on what to teach and, again, a bishop's essential qualities). One wonders if some archbishops cringed inwardly when a preacher announced yet another sermon with a text from Timothy or Titus (such sermons constituted half those considered here)! But the preachers could use any appropriate text, and some, imaginatively, chose verses from St Paul's other epistles, the Gospels, or Acts. As for the sermons' contents, they were not formally prescribed. From the 1660s to the 1730s, deeply mindful of the Puritan revolution and the Church's regrouping enemies, preachers were chiefly—though not exclusively—concerned to defend episcopacy in the Church and emphasize the respect owed to bishops. Thereafter, they felt less constricted, as the memories of the 1640s and 1650s became less traumatizing, and attacks on the prelacy diminished: 'Episcopacy seems now to be no longer a stumbling-block', Francis Webber observed in 1750, 'with the generality even of those, who are upon other accounts disaffected to the establishment' (Webber: 29). A preacher might now discuss a range of topical issues; almost absurdly, a few barely mentioned bishops (e.g. Barton 1750; Thomas). It was indeed a privilege to be, though only for a day, a representative of the lower clergy, and voice that body's immediate hopes, concerns, and fears to the most powerful in the Church.

It is clear that some bishops-elect worked closely with the preachers on the sermons. The former might want the discourses to spotlight their particular strengths or priorities. Kennett's sermon stressed the need for efficient diocesan administration: hardly surprisingly, since Wake was a superb organizer. Likewise, in his sermon, Lewis Stephens anticipated a 'Diocese well regulated' (L. Stephens: 18), the formidable Samuel Peploe's aim at Chester. William Buller, as bishop of Exeter from 1792 to 1796, was anxious to improve poor curates' stipends; the consecration sermon, by John Sturges, had contended that diocesans needed more power to regulate them (Sturges 1792: 10–11). The dislike of Methodism shown in James Backhouse's sermon (Backhouse: 7) reflected the comparable animosity of the bishop-elect of Bristol, Philip Yonge. No doubt at the service, the other bishops found it interesting to glimpse or uncover a new colleague's manifesto dexterously woven into the discourse. Two sermons supremely anticipated the reputations of the bishops for whom they were preached. Like a prologue to his brother's coming controversies, John Hoadly asserted the necessity of obedience to the civil powers and an unswerving respect for conscience (W. Gibson 2004*a*: 133–4; Hoadly: 14, 16, 22–3); and the obligation of differentiating between 'the Essentials of Religion' and 'indifferent Ceremonies' (Hoadly: 12). It 'doth not become Men to improve upon God's Revelation', he observed (Hoadly: 19). Charles Peter Layard's near-hysterical sermon of 1788 inveighed against enthusiasm, anticlericalism, Socinianism, sceptics, and infidels. With 'vigilance, perseverance, and firmness', he maintained, 'the defenders of sound doctrine' had to defeat their opponents 'in numberless contests' (Layard 1788: 14). Layard's bishop-elect was Samuel Horsley, who, in the era of the French Revolution, was to prove the fiercest episcopal champion of conservatism and Church orthodoxy.

A Bishop's Role and Status

Some bishops quickly applied themselves, and continued to apply themselves, to the administrative or other tasks outlined in the consecration sermons. Kennett in his sermon at Wake's consecration opined that 'the Decay of Discipline is a general and too just Complaint', adding that 'it can never be redress'd without exerting that Authority which remaineth in the Bishops' (Kennett: 17). In particular, he noted the desirability of uniform visitation enquiries. From the outset, the forceful Wake was determined to govern the huge diocese of Lincoln effectively, and succeeded in so doing, with his visitation arrangements, and probing visitation enquiries, famously becoming models for other bishops' practice. Samuel Peploe, a firm Whig, comparably brought to heel the fractious diocese of Chester, as Stephens had expected. Not only did he break the Tories' control of the cathedral chapter and the bishopric's administration, but he also conscientiously performed his pastoral duties (Baskerville). Although dogged by poor health, William Buller fought to help the Church's impoverished curates, as Sturges's sermon indicated he would. He supported the (admittedly limited) 1796 Act which sought to increase their stipends and empowered a bishop to assist when a curate's accommodation was poor (Aston). Backhouse's contemptuous depiction of Methodism was equalled by Philip Yonge who, in his first visitation charge at Norwich in 1763, sharply forbade his clergy to foster the movement. Yonge denounced 'the wickedness of clergy-men in joining themselves to and encouraging' 'the lowest of lay-men', who presumptuously took 'upon themselves the ministry of the gospel of Christ'. How 'inconsistent the frequenting conventicles and field-preaching is', he exclaimed, 'with what was expected from... [clerics], and became their duty, at their ordination' (Yonge: 7).

Among Protestant churches, the Church of England was unusual in its retention of episcopacy. The consecration preachers therefore were frequently obliged to justify it, especially since, as John Oldershaw admitted in 1792, '[w]e have not indeed been commanded by Christ to adopt any specific mode of ecclesiastical government' (Oldershaw: 11). Furthermore, the Anglican bishops' apostolic succession needed defending too, partly because of the Roman Church denied it, partly because of Erastian claims that episcopal authority derived from the State. In the early eighteenth century, Richard Mayo contended that the '*Government* of... [the Church of England] is... most agreeable to the Directions of the Apostles, and the Practice of the Primitive Church', while Zacheus Isham crossly noted that the 'Apostolical *Hierarchy*... was never violated, till after a Possession of 1500 Years' (Mayo: 19–20; Isham: 17). Later, Paley defended episcopacy partly for its utilitarian value—the title of his 1782 sermon was *A Distinction of Orders in the Church Defended upon Principles of Public Utility*—but, in a sermon preached in 1790, the defence of George Berkeley, prebendary of Canterbury, was sharply scriptural: the New Testament showed 'the Government of the *primitive* Church was *prelatical*' (Berkeley: 25). Regarding the apostolic succession, Anglican bishops, John Waugh stated, 'derive their Authority in a continued Line from the first Institution of the *Apostleship*; who were ordained by their *Predecessors*, they by *theirs*; and so upwards, till they ascend to *Christ*' (Waugh: 15). Waugh was speaking at the consecration of George Bull, a cleric later esteemed by the Tractarians, and Berkeley, at the High Church George Horne's consecration, was equally forceful (Cornwall; Berkeley: 14). But Whig preachers, notably Gibson and Kennett, also emphasized the apostolic succession in the early eighteenth century, as did other, less partisan, speakers thereafter (E. Gibson: 9; Kennett: 8). Plainly, the bishops' authority did not derive from the State, Berkeley concluded (Berkeley: 40).

The role of the episcopate was naturally the subject of many consecration sermons. Kennett's sermon, indeed, was entitled *The Office and Good Work of a Bishop*. Clagett concluded his discourse by stressing the vital importance of bishops: 'the success of Religion amongst us so much depends' on their endeavours (Clagett: 32). Theirs was a huge commitment. 'Great, and tremendous at all times is the burthen of the Episcopal Charge', Isham pronounced, a view with which other preachers often concurred (Isham: 26). As St Paul stated in his epistle to the Hebrews, a bishop watched for the souls of others. Although called to his office by providence, he would, by neglect or failure, endanger his flocks' eternal wellbeing, and 'certainly forfeit' his own soul (Rye: 28; Rayner: 16). Fittingly at the consecration of Courtenay, an aristocrat, though the comments were generally applicable, Hall described a bishop as 'a ruler in the house of God': he had to lead, 'to direct, to controul, and to govern' (Hall: 19). Since only bishops could ordain, it fell to them to select men for the priesthood with the utmost care. Thereafter, they had to ensure that the lower clergy performed parish duties effectively. Christian ministers, Waite argued at Sherlock's consecration, should never ignite 'Turbulency and Disquiet' (Waite: 22). Nevertheless, bishops had to counter error (like Sherlock during the Bangorian controversy), preserve order and discipline, and rebuke when necessary. They therefore needed 'great Steadiness and Courage' (L. Stephens: 12). Considerable administrative abilities were indispensable for the proper discharge of their duties. The innate qualities of gifted men, such as diligence, discretion, clear judgement, and eloquence, required cultivation and extension. A satisfactory grasp of useful knowledge, such as canon, Roman, and civil law, necessitated careful study (Synge 1723: 30).

Other forms of knowledge were naturally needed too; and acquiring them required 'no common pains' (Lloyd: 20). Referring to any cleric, Philip Barton observed: 'LEARNING is the Armour, with which the *Man of God* is furnished, and without which it is impossible He should be successful in his Christian Warfare' (Barton 1750: 14). But bishops especially had to guide the teachers. Theological learning was requisite principally for the accurate interpretation of the Gospels, and was further needed to refute old heresies, new attacks on Christianity, and Popery. Languages and history supplemented it, preachers repeatedly noted. At Francis Hare's and Lyttelton's consecrations, Robert Kilborn and William Parker respectively extolled the value of linguistics and antiquarian studies when wrestling with the Scriptures: Hare excelled in the former, Lyttelton in the latter (Kilborn: 27–8; Parker: 22; Pettit; Nurse). Nonetheless, having spluttered at the notion of an 'illiterate Bishop', Markham proclaimed that love was more important than learned attainments (Markham: 7, 10). East Apthorp fervently agreed. How 'inferior are all these endowments of nature and erudition! how much more easily attainable, than those essential qualifications of divine grace, the Virtues of the Heart!' (Apthorp: 9). It was by the example of their holy lives that bishops could best lead the parsons. The sanctity of a bishop's person gave him authority (Barton 1750: 19). The episcopal character, as described by St Paul, 'approaches to the utmost perfection of the Christian life', declared Apthorp (Apthorp: 8). Dodwell chose as his text Titus 1:7–9, which enjoined that '*A Bishop must be blameless as the Steward of God*', and detailed the individual's necessary qualities: '*not self-willed, not soon angry…sober, just, holy, temperate*' (Dodwell: 1). Such qualities would inspire not only the lower clergy but laymen too. 'A good life is the best and most convincing sermon', observed Thomas Newton (T. Newton: 11). Here was a key to successful ministry.

Under William III and Anne, the convocation controversy destabilized the Church. The Canterbury Convocation's lower house was dominated by High Churchmen with non-juring or Jacobite sympathies, whose tribune was Francis Atterbury. Despite their esteem for episcopacy, these men were deeply suspicious of the Whiggish episcopate and particularly disliked prominent Whig/Latitudinarian prelates, including Archbishop Tenison (Marshall). Consequently, the conflict between the lower and upper houses was often open, sometimes strident. In the early eighteenth century, therefore, and well after Convocation's prorogation in 1717, the consecration preachers—Whigs awkwardly joining with High Churchmen—countered such disrespect by emphasizing the esteem owed by the parish clergy to diocesans. Gibson, at William Nicolson's consecration, preached on 1 Thessalonians 5:12–13: '*know them which…are over you in the Lord, and…Esteem them very highly*' (E. Gibson: 1). '*Bishops…ought, justly, to meet with very great Honour and Esteem*', echoed the elder Synge (Synge 1710: 28). The 'Order of Bishops', warned Isham loftily, is 'distinct from, and superiour to common Presbyters' (Isham: 10), and the latter, Lisle admonished, should 'always remember how dutifully…[they] ought to reverence and *highly esteem*' the episcopate (Lisle: 30). And not merely esteem but obey. George Rye took as his text Hebrews 13:17—'*Obey them that have the Rule over you, and submit your selves…*'—at the consecration of a future archbishop of Canterbury, John Potter, in 1715 (Rye: 3). John Russell cited this verse and other authorities similarly enjoining obedience (Russell: 30). Disobedience risked—probably, indeed, condemned the transgressor to—punishment in the afterlife (Sydall: 31–2; Rye: 30–1).

Defining the Church of England

The consecration preachers fervently praised the Church which the new bishops were to help govern. It was 'the best constituted Church in the World', second to none in disseminating pure Christianity (Rye: 16; Paley: 10). Its constitution was, thought Kennett, 'as near to *that* of the Apostolical Churches, as Time and Place can possibly allow' (Kennett: 23). From the Reformation, God had favoured the English (Randolph: 14). The reformers had taken great care in framing doctrine; Cranmer had rejected Popery's errors and corruptions and preserved the faith and ceremonies of antiquity; and God had safeguarded the Church thereafter (Jackson: 12; Grisdale: 8; Byrche: 16; Jortin: 13). Consequently, foreign Protestants praised the Church of England enormously. The 'Reformed Churches abroad begin more and more to admire' her, Kennett declared proudly in 1705 (Kennett: 25). By 1732, her bishops had made her 'the Envy of... [her] Sister-Churches' (Knight: 21). Her clerics' learning and piety were admired throughout the world, proclaimed Houstonne Radcliffe in 1788 (Radcliffe: 18). Furthermore, as Britain's wealth, military power, and empire grew, the State was portrayed as the guardian of international Protestantism. In February 1739, with anti-Spanish fury rising over Captain Jenkins's ear, John Chapman trumpeted that the Church was 'the Glory and chief Bulwark of the Protestant Religion' (Chapman: 19). Yet, despite their confident praise of the Church, the preachers recognized that Anglican doctrine was, in reality, often awkward or inexact. Were the Catholic-but-reformed claims convincing? Repeatedly, therefore, the sermons endeavour to define the Church's identity by sharply delineating what it was not.

First, the preachers stressed that the Church of England was the *via media* between Popery and Dissent.

The corpus of consecration sermons contains most of the stock charges against Popery, 'that Bloody and Superstitious Religion' (Boulter: 30)—though the attacks diminished in the later eighteenth century. Preachers deplored the post-apostolic church's corruption, and inveighed against priestcraft and the papacy's political claims, notably the pretended power of absolving subjects from their allegiance to their rulers. They denounced popish perversions of the Gospel, idolatries, the unwarrantable importance accorded to tradition, and particular theological errors, such as transubstantiation and purgatory; and derided the uselessness and selfishness of monks, the biblical ignorance of lay Catholics, and indulgences and pardons, held to encourage vice. They attacked popish cruelty and bloodshed—the Crusades, the persecution of Protestants, the savagery of the Inquisition—and the malevolence of the Jesuits. But besides such assaults on popish tyranny, both spiritual and temporal, there were naturally two more specific concerns at episcopal consecrations. First, there was the Catholics' refusal to recognize the apostolic succession of the Anglican episcopate and, consequently, their refusal to accept the validity of that episcopate's ordination of clergy. No issue was more troubling: as Gibson said, the Papists maintain 'that our Bishops are meer Lay-men, and our Church therefore can be no Church' (E. Gibson: 23). Those charges had to be vigorously rebutted, and the Roman Church's iniquities exposed. Secondly, the papacy's claims to supremacy demanded refutation. There was 'no Sovereignty peculiar to *Peter*' and his successors, it was retorted, and the Pope was 'an Usurper over the whole Flock and Church of Christ' (Russell: 12, 13). Christ gave his '*General* Commission to all his Apostles *Equally*', John Adams stressed in 1710; 'no one [was] set above the rest', Russell argued a decade later (Adams 1710: 1; Russell: 12). Papal 'infallibility' was absurd

(Apthorp: 5). It followed, therefore, that the English bishops, the Apostles' successors, were the equals of the bishops of Rome and independent of them.

Just as papal claims of supremacy needed rebutting, so did Dissenters' attacks on episcopacy. Naturally these concerns were strong in the late seventeenth and early eighteenth centuries, the 'Church in Danger' years. Gibson deplored the Presbyterians' claims that episcopacy was 'a mere *Human* Institution' (E. Gibson: 23). Dissenters' 'Classes, and Synods, and Elders...[were] utterly unknown to all Antiquity', Lisle argued in 1723 (Lisle: 14). At worst, the rejection of God-ordained episcopacy imperilled Dissenters' souls (Waugh: 27): should not the Established Church therefore continue to battle Dissent? Certainly, Brampton Gurdon thought, it had a duty to check Dissent's growth (Gurdon: 7). But, with slackened religious tensions from the 1720s, the decay of Old Dissent, and the greater social assimilation of Dissenters, attacks on the sects' theology diminished—though memories of the Civil Wars continued to stoke concerns about their politics (Seed: *passim*). Gilbert revealingly described dissenting criticisms of Church doctrine as 'peevish', not appalling, in 1724, and Lewis Stephens, shortly afterwards, saw the sects themselves as 'sullen', not dangerous (Gilbert: 19; L. Stephens: 16). In 1739, Chapman maintained that the Church's principal adversaries were Papists and sceptics, not Popery and Dissent (Chapman: 12). The bishop at whose consecration Chapman preached, Matthias Mawson, was famously tolerant of most Protestant sectarians, and, in 1748, Lisle, now himself a bishop, discussed with the great nonconformist Samuel Chandler the possible comprehension of Dissenters within the Established Church (Chamberlain; W. Gibson 2004b). 'The violence of our Sectaries is much abated,' Markham proclaimed in 1752 (Markham: 26). However, the rise of Rational Dissent, linked with political radicalism, rekindled hostility. 'It is the fashion of the present time', Radcliffe ominously intoned in 1788, 'for the advocates of the Church of England to grant too much, I think, to their adversaries' (Radcliffe: 9). Soon, after the French Revolution's outbreak, they ceased to do so. In particular, Berkeley's 1790 sermon was a scarifying denunciation of all Dissenters and their doctrines (Berkeley: *passim*).

The maintenance of orthodoxy and the combating of infidelity were priorities for the eighteenth-century Church (Ingram: 71–113); and bishops, pre-eminently, had to 'guard...[her] *Doctrine*, and *Order*' (Isham: 9). The consecration preachers deplored the age's 'open contempt of Religion', 'the Insults of the Libertine, the Taunts of the Scoffer, the Impieties and Blasphemies of the Prophane' (Isham: 26; Gilbert: 19). Still worse were the systematic attempts to root 'up the very Foundations of Christianity, and...[plant] nothing but Atheism and Irreligion', resulting, by mid-century, in the 'manifest Growth...of Infidelity' (Waite: 22; Trevigar: 24). The times' degeneracy was inseparably linked to atheism, for the 'Man that has no Expectation of *another* Life, has nothing to do, but to provide for his Happiness in *this*' (Thomas: 13). Specific censure was reserved for Edward Gibbon and David Hume, that 'great *Master* in the *School* of contumelious *Scepticism*' (Oldershaw: 4; B. Newton: 16). The more specific concern for the episcopate was the contamination of its clergy by heresy—Arianism or Socinianism—the product of an unfettered 'free enquiry' into Scripture. Following the Feathers Tavern petition, seeking a relaxation of clerical subscription to the Trinitarian

Thirty-Nine Articles, Balguy fiercely attacked the petitioners. It was the clergy's duty 'to conform to...[the Church's] liturgy and articles', he insisted: a cleric troubled by them had to 'resign his office, or obey his superiors' (Balguy 1775: 8, 11). John Disney responded tartly to this 'extraordinary Sermon' (he left the Church for Unitarianism in 1782), but other consecration preachers continued to defend the Articles and liturgy (Disney: 5; Randolph: 16–18; Grisdale: 8–9). Free enquiry, Layard concluded, 'generally consists of an insidious attack upon opinions, which have stood the test of ages' (Layard 1794: 12).

Enthusiasm was equally inimical to the Church of England's character, preachers repeatedly maintained, particularly as Methodism grew. In 1738, the year of John Wesley's Aldersgate Street 'conversion', John Heylyn castigated those who became 'rank enthusiasts' by exciting 'fond, passionate, or rapturous Sentiments...in themselves' (Heylyn: 21). Pretending 'to Inspiration and supernatural gifts and powers' (Backhouse: 7), their folly was as irrational as credulous superstition: indeed, the preachers often denounced 'enthusiasm' and 'superstition' in the same breath. For the episcopate, Methodism represented a challenge to its authority and the lawful order. John Briggs accordingly deplored 'the Mischief of Self-appointed, itinerant Preachers' and Parker attacked parishioners' abandonment of 'properly-appointed pastors' for 'rambling assumers of superior mission' (Briggs: 30; Parker: 14). The sheer vulgarity of Methodist worship—'tumultuary devotions in the field'—contrasted with 'decent devotion in the church' (Parker: 14). Since bishops watched for others' souls, they could not ignore, several consecration preachers claimed, the dangers which Methodism posed. Most at threat was the ignorant populace. Some Methodists, Backhouse sneered, '*running up and down*, draw after them the unthinking multitude, *truly deceiving and being deceived*' (Backhouse: 7). Furthermore, the 'wild extravagancies of Enthusiasm' (Bell: 12) posed a danger to the state. Enthusiasm 'in religion hath often given the signal to sedition in the State', Parker pronounced (Parker: 12). 'One thing is certain,' echoed Balguy, 'that the influence of enthusiasm has ever been fatal to all regular governments' (Balguy 1775: 8). Clearly the spiritual peers, embodying the Church–State alliance, should not ignore that danger.

Popery, Dissent, unorthodox doctrines, enthusiasm: for the consecration preachers, all were antithetical to the Church of England and hence negatively defined its strengths. Christianity was a rational religion, the preachers repeatedly insisted. Green spoke of 'the rational doctrines of Christ'; 'REASON', John Wills declared, 'is the Word of GOD, written in the Heart of Man' (J. Green: 15; Wills: 10). Next, the Church of England was a rational church. The 'Constitution of this National Church', it was confidently asserted, 'will sufficiently justify it self to all reasonable Men'; freed from 'the blindness of superstition, or the unruly zeal of enthusiasm', the prevailing 'system of religion is established upon rational principles, and supported by rational means' (Hargraves: 17; Parker: 1). It was accordingly the clergy's duty to propagate Christianity so as 'to shew the perfect harmony between the dictates of right Reason, and the precepts of the Gospel' (Bell: 12). Besides this rationality, the Church's splendid moderation was praised. Indeed, 'moderation...has ever been her characteristic', claimed Oldershaw in 1792 (Oldershaw: 10).

Moderate men charted the difficult course between superstition and freethinking, enthusiasm and lukewarmness; and supported both the legal toleration and the gentle restraining of their Church's foes. Dr Grisdale's entire 1787 sermon was a defence of moderate clerics. Moderation was 'the mark of a noble mind', not culpable timidity and a want of principle. It had, 'like the church which it characterizes and adorns', weathered the storms, civil and ecclesiastical, that had beset the nation since the Restoration. 'Moderation is an experiment in church government that has now been tried for above a century with complete success', Grisdale concluded (Grisdale: 8, 1, 13): he was confident that the bishops aimed to perpetuate it.

Church, State, and Society

Since bishops were appointed by the monarch, and sat in the House of Lords, preachers frequently discussed the Church–State alliance—unfailingly, during the eighteenth century, in glowing terms. The 'true Interest[s] of ... [Church and State] are inseparable', declared Henry Stephens; 'the *lawful Commands* of ... the Church and State ... can never be *contrary*', thought the elder Synge (H. Stephens: 20; Synge 1710: 12). The alliance was mutually beneficial. The State protected the Church from its religious rivals by maintaining mild, but firm, penal legislation. It upheld orthodoxy. It ignored anticlerical zealots. Consequently, it was the bishops' duty to support the State (Russell: 22). Above all, the prelates, and their clergy, had to teach a 'dutiful submission to government in all things lawful', as enjoined by the Scriptures (Radcliffe: 18). Here the key text was Romans 13:1: 'Let every soul be subject unto the higher powers ...' 'If we do but prevail with men to be good Christians,' Clagett assured his hearers, 'there is no fear but they will be Loyal and Dutiful Subjects to their Prince' (Clagett: 26). Successive monarchs, their work as the Church's supreme governor, and their piety, were repeatedly praised; the sovereign's choice of bishops was the guarantee of the Church's health. George I displayed 'Care and Wisdom' in his appointments, and his son likewise, preachers noted; and the exceptionally devout George III impartially rewarded the meritorious (Hargraves: 19; Spry: 19; Apthorp: 11). Overall, the royal supremacy seemed to promote the Church's interests highly effectively (Balguy 1769: 16). On the eve of the French Revolution, therefore, Radcliffe expressed most preachers' opinion in arguing that 'our civil and ecclesiastical constitution[s] are so interwoven, that they cannot be separated without mutual danger' (Radcliffe: 17).

Eighteenth-century praise for the alliance of Church and State contrasted with late-seventeenth-century ambiguities and concerns about the Church's relations with the Crown. At the Restoration, the re-establishment of episcopacy was quickly deemed necessary (I. M. Green: 81–98), but its form remained a matter of contention. Indeed, Restoration clerics, fearing open, inexpedient disunity, often proved reluctant to define precisely the scope and source of the restored episcopate's authority (Spurr: 158, 159–64); and this reluctance was noticeable respecting episcopal and royal jurisdictions in the

Church. At the consecration, in Westminster Abbey, of seven bishops in 1660, the preacher, William Sancroft, prayed for Charles II as supreme governor of the Church and thanked God for reinstating the '*Nursing Father*' (Sancroft: 5, 33). Yet, given his immense devotion to the restored monarchy, it is surprising that Sancroft said so little about the Crown–Church alliance (he focused on episcopacy's divine origin). John Spurr has discussed how satisfactorily the respective roles of the king and the bishops in the Church's governance could be defined, and noted that surprisingly few consecration sermons were published between 1660 and 1688 (Spurr: 145–47, 151). Possibly preachers feared they might raise awkward issues in print, even implicitly or accidentally, about episcopacy and politics, especially after Charles's ecclesiastical policies—notably the 1672 Declaration of Indulgence—alarmed Churchmen. King Charles's golden days were perhaps most happily recalled decades later by men distanced from the Restoration's uncertainties.

The crisis of Crown–Church relations under James II culminated in the crisis of the Revolution of 1688, which cast a disturbing shadow over the subsequent consecrations. If William III were a usurper, as Sancroft, now archbishop of Canterbury, maintained, was not the Williamite Church schismatic? Refusing to swear allegiance to William, Sancroft and five other bishops were deprived on 1 February 1690. Who were their valid successors, jurors or nonjurors? When in 1689, the bishop of Salisbury, Seth Ward, died, William nominated Gilbert Burnet, his chaplain when he invaded England. Understandably, Sancroft would not himself consecrate Burnet, but Anthony Horneck, in the service's sermon, provided a veneer of unity, maintaining that the new bishop was called by God, the King, and the Church (Grieg; Horneck: 35). Later, the eminent John Sharp refused to fill any bishopric vacant because of a nonjuror's deprivation (Till). After Archbishop Lamplugh's death, he accepted York, but, rather awkwardly, was consecrated with three bishops who were taking nonjurors' mitres. Joshua Clarke, the chaplain of one of these, Moore of Norwich, preached the sermon and, understandably, emphasized the unbroken apostolic succession, thereby refuting directly Rome's, and implicitly nonjurors', accusations of schism (Clarke: 8–9, 11–12, 30). Another possible tactic for a preacher in the 1690s was to bypass recent troubles and look ahead. William Stanley employed it when Thomas Tenison was consecrated bishop of Lincoln in 1692. Stanley urged the necessity for order in the Church and the pressing need to combat heresy, vice, and debauchery (Stanley: *passim*). Given the concern that Tenison was to show about Church discipline, Socinianism's spread, and the 'Reformation of Manners', the sermon was patently a blueprint for future exertions. Revealingly, in the later sermons sampled here, the Glorious Revolution was rarely mentioned, except when the Church's role in it seemed unequivocally praiseworthy (as with the Seven Bishops' opposition to James II or in comparison with the Dissenters' apparent collaboration with his regime) (Gilbert: 16–17; Radcliffe: 17–18). Painful and controversial matters were best eschewed.

Some consecration preachers sought to palliate the trauma of the Revolution by decrying Jacobitism. To combat the latter, Church solidarity and national unity were, they maintained, essential. '[T]*o be Divided, is to be Ruin'd*', Adams declared in June 1708, following the Old Pretender's attempted invasion in March (Adams 1708: 15). During the first three decades of the eighteenth century, some denunciation of the Pretender was *de rigueur* at the consecrations of leading Whig bishops including William Fleetwood, Gibson, Benjamin Hoadly, and Wake. The 'Fifteen threatened 'the certain Ruine of the Church', as did the Atterbury plot of 1722, it was argued (Boulter: 5; Synge 1723: 38). Simultaneously and flatteringly, Whig bishops were extolled as stalwart defenders against Jacobitism (H. Stephens: 7), as they sought to eradicate Stuart loyalties among stubborn parsons. By 1724, the year after the decision to exile Atterbury, James Hargraves felt confident that this drive was succeeding and that Jacobites among the clergy were few (Hargraves: 17–18). Preachers, as ever, interpreted politics in providentialist terms. The Hanoverians ruled by 'the Providence of God... [not just] the Laws of the Land', it was stressed after George I's accession (Boulter: 32); God's manifest favour, not just the bloodline, determined the succession, and, accordingly, John Hoadly ascribed the 'Fifteen's failure to God's intervention (Hoadly: 21, 22). Thirty years later, Edward Ballard saw God's hand in the Young Pretender's defeat by the 'Beloved and Admired' Cumberland (Ballard: 12, 24).

In the later eighteenth and early nineteenth centuries, it was radicals who excited alarm. Besides inculcating political obedience, the consecration preachers observed, the Church enjoined submission to the social order. Family, rank, and riches commanded regard (Sturges 1777: 13). The social hierarchy was ordained by God himself, and those seeking '*a peaceable, and quiet*' existence needed to observe and support 'the necessary Distinctions of Life' (Thomas: 15). This was clear from the Scriptures. John Sturges cited St Paul's comparison of Christian society with the human body: each functioned properly precisely because of 'the due arrangement and subordination of its parts' (Sturges 1792: 2). Christianity, insisted the younger Madan, 'inculcates a love of order, and a sense of subordination' (Madan: 24). It further taught 'constant lessons of... probity, benevolence, and the whole train of social virtues'; indeed, 'religious Impressions... [were] the firmest Foundation of every social Virtue; of Justice, Veracity, and Faithfulness; of Beneficence, Candour, and Compassion; of Sobriety, Industry, and public Spirit' (Webber: 23; Stinton: 11). Radical ideas corroded such qualities. Preachers repeatedly recalled the Civil Wars and the Cromwellian zealots' destruction of Crown and government, the bishops and the Church, and the social order. The late-eighteenth-century heirs of the puritanical saints' lacked respect for Church or secular authorities, the guarantors of hierarchy (Layard 1788: 17). Presbyterianism and democratic principles went together, but it was the Rational Dissenters, led by Joseph Priestley and Richard Price, who appeared especially dangerous by the 1780s. Their 'mode of waging war against the establishment' was 'savage', opined Grisdale (Grisdale: 10). Once the French Revolution—promoted by unbelievers' doctrines (Layard 1794: 7)—had erupted, Sturges wanted 'all the friends of tranquillity and order to unite... and to repell the approaches of confusion and anarchy' (Sturges 1792: 14). Sturges's depiction of his well-regulated society and its blessings was perhaps too optimistic—he was notably complacent about the poor's lot (Sturges 1792: 2–4)—but the consecration preachers, and the clergy generally, shared the ideal.

The Clerical Profession

By the later eighteenth century, the status of the clergy was rising, and consecration preachers both appreciated and justified this. University educated, increasingly recruited from gentry families, enjoying greater wealth than their predecessors, they were at ease in local landed society. A clergyman, stated Apthorp, is 'respectable as a country-gentleman on his own freehold' (Apthorp: 20). Exempted 'from the hurry and fatigue of secular Employments' (Lloyd: 19), he could cultivate the attributes of men of rank. The higher a man rose in the Church, the more gentlemanly would his manners be. Paley believed that those occupying elevated stations should provide civilized 'friends and companions... for the superior... orders of the community' (Paley: 13, 12). And the bishops themselves pre-eminently had to be gentlemen. It is unsurprising that this was stated quite unequivocally by George Stinton at the consecration of Shute Barrington in 1769: Barrington was the youngest son of the first Viscount Barrington; had married a duke's daughter; and numbered George III among his patrons. 'An Age of refined and polished Manners', Stinton pronounced, 'will be little disposed to esteem the Person, or consequently to respect the Office, or attend to the Precepts, of a Man remarkable for Rusticity, Awkwardness of Behaviour, and Ignorance of the Customs of the World, or the Forms of what is called good Breeding' (Stinton: 19). Other preachers shared Stinton's opinion, expressing it, albeit sometimes indirectly, when they discussed hierarchy, clerical and lay. No clergyman should ever be an object of contempt, observed John Briggs (Briggs: 30).

In order to support the dignity of a gentleman, a satisfactory income was required. All clergymen needed 'a sufficient Maintenance to disengage them from secular Cares' (Briggs: 30). But as clerical incomes, and clerical expectations, rose in the later eighteenth and early nineteenth centuries, attacks on the Church's privileges and wealth increased. At some consecrations, the preachers lamented that clergymen were portrayed as drones, their lifestyles 'a release from all business and trouble' and 'a state of indolence and inactivity' (J. Green: 12). 'Ecclesiastical Honours and Wealth may perhaps to the ears of many sound invidious', complained Sturges; 'many may be disposed to reprobate them'. Yet, were clerical incomes reduced, 'men, capable of excelling, [would]... betake themselves to other paths of life' (Sturges 1777: 12). Obviously the bishops, as the princes of the Church, were especially liable to accusations of greed (Paley: 13); though Barton exonerated them, dismissing such charges as mere envy (Barton 1766: 15). The bishops' wealth was the just reward for their labours, proclaimed John Spry (Spry: 19). Prefiguring the debates of the 1830s, it was held that equalizing clerical revenues was an 'Impossibility' (Briggs: 30): hopes of a bishopric, 'to which considerable dignity and emoluments are annexed', attracted 'men of the first talents' to the clerical profession (Sturges 1777: 13; Oldershaw: 11). Indeed, it was the clergy's duty to preserve its wealth so that it could be used effectively in later years. Fortunately, Randolph noted, Church possessions were fully protected by law (Randolph: 18).

Granted that a clergyman merited status and a satisfactory income, was it seemly for some clerics to seek *considerable* dignity and emoluments? Was ambition becoming in the successors of Galilean fishermen? Were not radicals right to deplore the wealth of the richer sees? Plainly bishops, apparently the most ambitious clergy, needed a defence. William Jackson, Student (i.e. Fellow) of Christ Church, Oxford's most elite and prestigious college, and later bishop of Oxford, provided one—almost brazenly. For him, 'feelings of ambition and the desire of eminence' were as 'natural ingredients' in clergymen as in 'other persons'. Since these were ineradicable, the civil polity gave ambitious clerics 'reasonable objects for those desires'—'[v]ery wisely', for 'otherwise [those desires] might attempt their own gratification to the disturbance of public tranquillity, and the general well being of society'(!). It was unjust to regard attentions to temporal interests as a defilement of the clergy's character. Such attentions were reprehensible only when they became 'base and inordinate': circumspection and '*moderation in all things*', Jackson thought, were needed (Jackson: 15–16). Other preachers made a virtue of necessity too. Given humanity's 'ill-governed passions', bishops could not simply be pious, remote, and impractical scholars. Some 'experience of the world,' Markham observed, 'some knowledge of mankind, is particularly requisite in those, to whom the government of the Church is committed' (Markham: 28). Spry, in an oddly worded phrase, implied the same: the bishops' 'Secular Advantages' were, he said, 'effectual Instruments of their Success' (Spry: 19).

Just as the consecration sermons defined the Church's theological character, the preachers, with the bishops' concurrence, defined the clerical profession in their discussions of rank, finance, and ambition. That definition was limpid. The clerical profession was one fit for a gentleman, and its duties were probably best discharged by gentlemen. A satisfactory income was an entirely valid expectation. A ladder of preferment, with emoluments suitably pinned to its rungs, was necessary. Ambition for advancement was perfectly proper, indeed desirable. Unless men of 'promising abilities' anticipated appropriate rewards, Paley warned, 'our profession will be composed of the refuse of every other' (Paley: 14). The bishops at their consecrations were the very embodiments of clerical success, of service fittingly rewarded. W. M. Jacob has recently anatomized the Church between 1680 and 1840 as a profession, with a recognized structure and agreed standards; and the clergy *qua* professionals, with a clear self-identify and shared aspirations (Jacob: *passim*). The consecration sermons illustrate the same themes.

Conclusion

For the historian, consecration sermons constitute a valuable source. Preached at a vital ceremony before some of the Church of England's leaders, they serve as a barometer of the changing concerns of the clergy. Those delivered in the Revolution's aftermath reveal the many fears of a 'Church in Danger'. Under the Hanoverians, they trace the development of an increasingly assured, though not untroubled, body. They delineate the Church's theological self-identity. Changes in thinking about enemies and rivals—Papists and Dissenters without, the heterodox or enthusiasts within—can be charted in them. The preachers outlined clerical perceptions of the Church's place in the body politic and in society. Some revealed new bishops' planned responses to clerical anxieties. Scholars have to date given this distinct category of sermons surprisingly little systematic consideration, and this short chapter merely skims the surface, conflating or blurring preachers' nuanced arguments. Even when interesting, unusual comments—like an anti-Semitic jibe occasioned by the 1753 Jew bill (Trevigar: 6)—are here mostly ignored. These are sermons, therefore, that warrant further, properly sustained, analysis.

References

Adams, J. (1708). *A Sermon Preach'd... June the 6th, 1708*. London: Hills.
—— (1710). *A Sermon Preached... November the 19th, 1710*. London: Bowyer.
Apthorp, E. (1781). *A Sermon... October 28, MDCCLXXXI*. London: Cadell.
Aston, N. (2004). 'Buller, William (1735–1796)', *ODNB*. Oxford: Oxford University Press.
Backhouse, J. (1758). *A Sermon Preached... June 29, 1758*. Cambridge: Merrill and Paris.
Balguy, T. (1769). *A Sermon Preached... February 12, 1769*. London: Davis and Reymers.
—— (1775). *A Sermon Preached... February 12, 1775*. London: Davis.
Ballard, E. (1746). *A Sermon Preached... May 11. 1746*. Eton: Pote.
Barton, P. (1750). *A Sermon Preached... Dec. 3. 1749*. Oxford: Clements
—— (1766). *A Sermon Preached... June 15, 1766*. London: Sandby.
Baskerville, S. (2008). 'Peploe, Samuel (*bap*. ,1667, *d.* 1752)', *ODNB*. Oxford: Oxford University Press.
Bell, W. (1774). *A Sermon Preached... November 13, 1774*. London: Robson.
Berkeley, G. (1795). *An Inquiry into the Origin of Episcopacy*. London: Rivington.
Boulter, H. (1716). *A Sermon, Preach'd... February 12. 1715-16*. London: Childe.
Briggs, J. (1777). *A Sermon Preached... February 9, 1777*. London: Payne.
Byrche, W. (1717). *A Sermon Preach'd... November 17. 1717*. London: Holland.
Chamberlain, J. S. (2004). 'Mawson, Matthias (1683–1770)', *ODNB*. Oxford: Oxford University Press.
Chapman, J. (1739). *A Sermon Preach'd... February XVIII, 1738-9*. London: Innys and Manby.
Clagett, N. (1718). *A Sermon Preached... On Whitsunday, MDCCXVIII*. London: Wyat.
Clarke, J. (1691). *A Sermon Preached... 5th of July, 1691*. London: Rogers.
Cornwall, R. D. (2004). 'Bull, George (1634–1710)', *ODNB*. Oxford: Oxford University Press.
Disney, J. (1775). *Remarks on Dr. Balguy's Sermon*. London: Johnson.
Dodwell, W. (1767). *A Sermon Preached... November 30, 1766*. London: White.
Gibson, E. (1702). *A Sermon Preach'd... June 14th, 1702*. London: Churchill.
Gibson, W. (2004*a*). *Enlightenment Prelate: Benjamin Hoadly 1676–1761*. Cambridge: James Clarke & Co.
—— (2004*b*). 'Lisle, Samuel (1683–1749)', *ODNB*. Oxford: Oxford University Press.
Gilbert, J. (1725). *A Sermon, Preach'd... December the 27th 1724*. London: Buckley.
Green, I. M. (1978). *The Re-Establishment of the Church of England 1660–1663*. Oxford: Oxford University Press.
Green, J. (1752). *A Sermon Preached... March 22. 1752*. Cambridge: Thurlbourn and Bathurst.

Greig, M. (2004). 'Burnet, Gilbert (1643-1715)', *ODNB*. Oxford: Oxford University Press.
Grisdale, B. (1788). *A Sermon Preached…November 18, 1787*. London: Cadell.
Gurdon, B. (1723). *A Sermon Preached…Nov. 3. MDCCXXIII*. London: Knaplock.
Hall, C. H. (1794). *A Sermon, Preached…May 11, 1794*. Oxford: Fletcher and Hanwell.
Hargraves, J. (1724). *A Sermon Preached…October the 18th, 1724*. London: Stagg.
Heylyn, J. (1738). *A Sermon Preached…December 3, 1738*. London: Rivington.
Hoadly, J. (1716). *A Sermon, Preach'd…March the 18th, 1715-16*. London: Childe.
Horneck, A. (1689). *A Sermon Preached…Easter-day, MDCLXXXIX*. London: Chiswell.
Ingram, R. G. (2007). *Religion, Reform, and Modernity in the Eighteenth Century*. Woodbridge: Boydell Press.
Isham, Z. (1704). *A Sermon Preached…Octob. 31. [1703]*. London: Clavel and Kettilby.
Jackson, W. (1783). *A Sermon Preached…July 6, 1783*. Oxford: Fletcher and Rivington.
Jacob, W. M. (2007). *The Clerical Profession in the Long Eighteenth Century 1680-1840*. Oxford: Oxford University Press.
Jenner, C. (1753). *A Sermon Preached…January 28, 1753*. London: Birt.
Jortin, J. (1748). *A Sermon Preached…February 21, 1747*. London: Whiston.
Kennett, W. (1706). *A Sermon Preach'd…Octob. 21. 1705*. London: Churchill and Sare.
Kilborn, R. (1728). *A Sermon Preach'd…Dec. 17. 1727*. London: Innys.
Knight, S. (1732). *A Sermon Preached…Jan. 23. 1731*. London: Crownfield.
Layard, C. P. (1788). *A Sermon Preached…May 11, 1788*. London: Walter.
—— (1794). *A Sermon Preached…January 12, 1794*. London: Walter and Rivington.
Lisle, S. (1723). *A Sermon Preach'd…August 11th, 1723*. London: Cowse.
Lloyd, P. (1762). *A Sermon Preached…December 28, 1761*. London: Barker.
Lupton, W. (1721). *A Sermon Preach'd…July 2. 1721*. Oxford: Wilmot.
Madan, S. (1792). *A Sermon Preached…June 3, 1792*. London: Faulder.
Markham, W. (1753). *A Sermon Preached…Dec. 10. 1752*. Oxford: Fletcher.
Marshall, W. (2004). 'Tenison, Thomas (1636-1715)', *ODNB*. Oxford: Oxford University Press.
Mayo, R. (1725). *A Sermon Preached…January 3. 1724*. London: Downing.
Newton, B. (1779). *Sermon Preached…September 19, 1779*. Gloucester: Mutlow and Evans.
Newton, T. (1760). *A Sermon Preached…January 20, 1760*. London: Tonson.
Nurse, B. (2004). 'Lyttelton, Charles (1714-1768)', *ODNB*. Oxford: Oxford University Press.
Oldershaw, J. (1792). *A Sermon Preached…April 8, 1792*. Cambridge: Merrill.
Paley, W. (1782). *A Sermon Preached…September 21, 1782*. London: Faulder.
Parker, W. (1762). *A Sermon, Preached…March 21, 1762*. London: Baldwin.
Pettit, A. (2004). 'Hare, Francis (1671-1740)', *ODNB*. Oxford: Oxford University Press.
Radcliffe, H. (1788). *A Sermon Preached…January 20, 1788*. London: Rivington.
Randolph, J. (1782). *A Sermon Preached…April 7. 1782*. Oxford: Fletcher and Rivington.
Rayner, W. (1717). *A Sermon Preach'd…February 24, 1716-17*. Exeter: Bishop.
Russell, J. (1722). *A Sermon Preach'd…December 3. 1721*. London: Wyat and Childe.
Rye, G. (1715). *A Sermon Preach'd…May 15. 1715*. London: Mortlock.
Sancroft, W. (1660). *A Sermon Preached…on the First Sunday in Advent 1660*. London: Beaumont.
Seed, J. (2008). *Dissenting Histories*. Edinburgh: Edinburgh University Press.
Spry, J. (1756?). *A Sermon Preached…July 4. 1756*. Oxford: Fletcher.
Spurr, J. (1991). *The Restoration Church of England 1646-1689*. New Haven: Yale University Press.
Stanley, W. (1692). *A Sermon Preached…Jan. 10. 1691/2*. London: Clavell and Smith.

Stephens, H. (1719). *A Sermon Preach'd...November 15. 1719*. London: Knapton.
Stephens, L. (1726). *A Sermon Preached...April 12, 1726*. London: King.
Stinton, G. (1769). *A Sermon Preached...October 1, 1769*. London: Hughs.
Stubbs, W. (1858). *Registrum Sacrum Anglicanum*. Oxford: Oxford University Press.
Sturges, J. (1777). *A Sermon Preached...May 25, 1777*. London: Cadell.
—— (1792). *A Sermon Preached...December, 2, 1792*. London: Cadell.
Sydall, E. (1706). *A Sermon Preach'd...June 30. 1706*. London: Churchill.
Synge, E. (1659–1741) (1710). *A Sermon...Preached...April 2. 1710*. London: Sare.
Synge, E. (1691–1762) (1723). *A Sermon Preach'd...September 30, 1722*. London: Sare.
Thomas, H. (1750). *A Sermon Preached...Feb. 18, 1749*. London: Bowyer.
Till, B. (2004). 'Sharp, John (1645?–1714)', *ODNB*. Oxford: Oxford University Press.
Trevigar, L. (1754). *A Sermon Preached...March 31, 1754*. London: Hawkins.
Waite, T. (1728). *A Sermon Preached...February 4th. 1727-8*. London: Pemberton.
Waugh, J. (1705). *A Sermon Preach'd...April 29. 1705*. London: Churchill.
Webber, F. (1750). *A Sermon Preached...Dec. 23. 1750*. Oxford: Fletcher.
Wills, J. (1747). *A Sermon Preached...October 4. 1747*. London: Oliver.
Yonge, P. (1763). *The Charge of...Philip, Lord Bishop of Norwich, Delivered...at his Primary Visitation, A.D. 1763*. Norwich: Chase.
Young, B. W. (2004). 'Jortin, John (1698–1770)', *ODNB*. Oxford: Oxford University Press.

CHAPTER 20

THE PROTESTANT FUNERAL SERMON IN ENGLAND, 1688–1800

PENNY PRITCHARD

THE Protestant funeral sermon occupies a unique position in the wider genre of religious literature in early modern England, not least because (according to the most stringent interpretation of Calvinist reform) it shouldn't exist at all. Technically, scriptural prohibition of priestly attendance at funerals made the act of burial a civil rather than ecclesiastical office (Leviticus 21:1). For Elizabethan precisians such as Henry Barrow and Thomas Cartwright, the burial service as set out in the Book of Common Prayer retained too much ritual from its Roman Catholic predecessor; moreover, expressing praise for the dead left Protestant ministers vulnerable to accusations of accepting bribery for spiritual endorsement (Tromly).

Virtually all of these objections to the Protestant funeral sermon had found resolution by the end of Elizabeth's reign. This was largely achieved through the adoption of an asymmetrical structure, the importance of which cannot be overstressed for the funeral sermon's successful transition into Protestant ritual. An earlier, almost always longer, section was dedicated to scriptural exegesis, usually with little or no reference to the deceased. A latter section served to commemorate the deceased's life and character, the manner of their death, and their spiritual legacy (Tromly: 301–2; Gittings: 137). Some exceptions to this template remain extant; John Wesley's 1770 sermon commemorating George Whitefield, for example, reverses both its order and proportions, but such instances are relatively rare during the period as a whole.

It is usually impossible to ascertain which—if any—aspects of the published funeral sermon are consistent with its original, oral, delivery; some works, such as Richard Gilpin's 1700 funeral sermon for Timothy Manlove, openly announce changes undertaken for publication (in this case, the not-uncommon addition of a 'character' of the deceased). Other ministers make clear that theirs was not the sermon delivered at interment. The overwhelming majority of published funeral sermons, however, remain silent regarding this subject, raising fundamental questions concerning the interpretation of the published document in relation to the original congregation's experience of hearing sermons *in situ*. Contemporary ministers were clearly conscious of the ambiguities and paradoxes inherent in the act of publication (Fox: 90; Smith: 25–9). The authority and durability so often associated with the written word are frequently invoked in these works, yet ministers' deep reluctance to publish their funeral sermons is expressed so frequently that such disavowals arguably constitute a commonplace of the genre itself.

Published funeral sermons remember individuals across the social spectrum. Although the ceremonial and material details of death among royalty were administered in a consistently lavish manner, the marked contrast between the number and emotional register of published funeral sermons for King William III and Queen Mary is particularly striking (Fritz: 292–3). Thomas Goodwin's funeral sermon is broadly representative of the public outpouring of grief that followed Mary's death in December 1694: '[s]he is gone, and hath left us to our Sighs and Tears, to bewail a Loss, of which every Day will make us more and more sensible' (Goodwin: 16). Even the Archbishop of Canterbury's formal commemoration describes the nation's loss as 'a very copious Subject... [in which] the difficulty consists not in finding out matter, but in keeping measure in speaking' (Tenison: 4). The relative paucity of published funeral sermons following William's death suggests, in contrast, a degree of public composure, apparent in Nicholas Brady's placid remark that this 'surprising calamity... is mitigated, and made tolerable, by the Happiness we look for under the Auspicious Influence of so excellent a [new] Queen' (Brady: 311). William's memory *is* commemorated, and defended with some rigour, in numerous works including Defoe's *The Mock Mourners* (Defoe 1702) but conspicuous by their absence are the published funeral sermons of religious dignitaries. Nicholas Tyacke has noted the Bishop of Salisbury's contemporary remark concerning the 'scarce decent' acknowledgement of the King's death in only sixteen published funeral sermons (Tyacke), yet despite attending the King's deathbed himself (along with Tenison), Gilbert Burnet, the Bishop of Salisbury, only published a brief biography of William in 1702 (Burnet 1702).

Beyond the example of royalty, the numbers and multiple editions of published funeral sermons help us gauge the public's emotional response to the deaths of notable figures. This is strongly evident in the prolific commemoration of prominent agents of the Christian evangelical movement. Selina Hastings, Dowager Countess of Huntingdon, is keenly mourned in at least eight published funeral sermons; in one, the otherwise notably irascible David Jones praises her as 'the greatest Woman, in the cause of the Gospel of Jesus Christ, that ever lived in the World' (Jones: 17). The death of Isaac Watts in December 1748 prompted four editions of David Jennings's funeral sermon, while George Whitefield's death in 1770 occasioned at least thirteen separate funeral sermons.

The ceremonial and commemorative functions of the published funeral sermon are frequently associated with the deaths of public figures, but the long eighteenth century also witnesses large numbers of works remembering less prominent, and even anonymous, members of the population at large. This includes sermons for babies or children, as well as those whose lives were marked by extensive suffering, or who died in violent or unexpected circumstances. Typical works for nameless subjects include Samuel Acton's

1699 funeral sermon for an infant (which the preface offers to readers as a comfort for grieving mothers' sorrows and an aid to their fears concerning infant salvation), Benjamin Mills's 1750 sermon preached 'on the occasion of the death of a Pious Young Person', and Samuel Walker's sermon (the second edition is in 1753) for 'a young man, who was drowned as he was bathing' (Acton; Mills; S. Walker).

Often apparent in such works is a distinct sense of the genre's purpose as spiritual succour in generic form. One anonymously-penned sermon, which makes no mention of the deceased beyond the title-page, urges on readers the need for repentance and instructs that '[i]f these weighty Considerations are not worth your Reading, keep it clean, and return it when called for' (*A Call from Heaven to the Unconverted*). More pointed in tone is James Ellesby, vicar of Chiswick, whose 1693 funeral sermon is published 'chiefly for the Sake of the ordinary sort of Inhabitants of that Parish' (Ellesby). In his dedication Ellesby explains that his remedy for the 'great Carelessness and Neglect' of those 'who seldom or never see the Inside of a Church' is to publish the funeral sermon of a nameless individual whose life should thereby serve as a 'Warning and Example'. While cautionary lives are often presented in the period's funeral sermons, this minister's very personal admonition of his congregation takes precedence over the common didactic principle in which such works normally attempt to appeal to as wide a readership as possible.

Ellesby's work also provides a very specific and poignant account of the deceased's last days, despite its suppression of any material detail that might identify its subject. Though the genre's role as a generic form of public service is often implicated in works featuring anonymity (for either the sermon's author *or* his subject), this function is not exclusive to anonymous works. The 1690 funeral sermon for the wife of eminent antiquarian and scholar Henry Sampson, for example, announces that it is 'principally for the use of such as languish under painful and Chronical diseases', and provides a detailed account of the deceased's Job-like suffering; *its* author is the highly eminent Presbyterian minister John Howe (Howe). One of the most prolific of London's dissenting ministers in this period, Howe was personally responsible for at least nine published funeral sermons (including one for Queen Mary).

In the case of murder victims' funeral sermons, any specific circumstances related to the subjects' deaths are generally confined to the works' title pages; it is exceedingly rare for funeral sermons to include any lurid or violent content. Bankes Crooke's 1698 funeral sermon for Hannah Bullivant, for example, goes no farther than to inform readers that the deceased was 'barbarously murdered by Edmond Audley in St Martin's le Grand' (Crooke). Rather more information is provided through the contemporary news article (quoted from the *Norwich Mercury*) which prefaces Joseph Parsons's 1763 funeral sermon for Susan Sporle, also 'barbarously murdered in her own House...in the Seventy-third Year of her Age', yet the sermon itself remains entirely tacit concerning this gruesome subject.

In this context, at least, it is possible to make a clear distinction between funeral sermons and other published works which share a predilection for lurid and eye-catching advertisement on their title pages. Published funeral sermons almost always maintain a decorum suitable to the gravity of the occasion (that is, the passage of a Protestant soul from death to life thereafter) and tend to dwell only briefly, or indirectly, on the material or 'worldly' considerations of the secular context in which the deceased subject lived their life. Indirect treatment of a subject, however, does not necessarily constitute indifference on the part of the author so much as an awareness that 'worldly' matters must finally and properly be put into perspective in the funeral sermon. As will be further discussed, the author's use of indirect language in the funeral sermon often invites the reader to try to glean additional levels of meaning concerning the deceased and the contemporary context in which their life took place.

Estimating the total number of funeral sermons produced in the long eighteenth century remains deeply problematic. Many works only appear in collected sermon anthologies which, in turn, are printed in multiple editions. Moreover, certain related forms of 'funeral literature' so closely resemble funeral sermons in scope and presentation that distinction between their formats becomes highly subjective. The vast majority of published funeral sermons per se employ the conventional asymmetrical structure while commemorating a named individual recognized, on either a local or national scale, for the exemplary nature of their Protestant virtues. Less frequently, the deceased's own character might be described in terms of its unique qualities. Burnet's funeral sermon for Robert Boyle observes that many men 'seem to have only a Mechanical Life, as if there were a moving and speaking Spring within them, equally void both of Reason and Goodness' (Burnet 1692: 6), although Boyle's intellectual prowess and piety

> sets a new Pattern to all that are sincerely zealous for their Religion. It shews them in the simplest and most convincing of all Arguments what the Humane Nature is capable of, and what the Christian Religion can add to it. (Burnet 1692: 39)

The 'rarity' of such a man (later described as 'less than one in a thousand') is emphasized by Burnet's depiction of Boyle's idiosyncratic habits, such as his tendency to pause when he mentioned the name of God. Few individuals command such carefully tailored encomium, however, and far more common among funeral sermons is the exemplar of an ideal 'type' of Christian virtue, such as the 'great and charitable benefactor' Edward Colston, broadly commended for his piety and generosity in hope that 'all others who are rich in Possessions would tread in his Steps' (Hargrave: 15). Others are praised in even more general terms; in 1772 Hannah Jarrold is lauded rather vaguely by Thomas Bingham as one 'who engaged the esteem, love and affection of all who had the felicity of being related to, or acquainted with her' (Bingham: iii). In some cases, it is apparent that the minister barely knew his subject at all; one grieving husband justifies supplementing his wife's somewhat brief and bland funeral sermon with a lengthier biography on account of the minister's 'small acquaintance with her' (*A Sermon Preach'd on the Occasion of the Funeral of Mrs Elizabeth Gibson*: 22).

Without exception, the most prolific category of eighteenth-century Protestant funeral sermons commemorates ministers or their wives. As such, certain apposite scriptural texts feature repeatedly in the sermons' first section. These include references to the fourth chapter of I Timothy (in the sixth verse, to 'a good minister of Jesus

Christ') as well as the poignant reminder of ministers' mortality to be found in the fifth verse of the first chapter of Zechariah ('Your fathers, where are they? And the prophets, do they live for ever?'). Paul's reference to 'treasure in earthen vessels', found in verse seven of the fourth chapter of the second epistle to the Corinthians, also proved particularly popular in this context. Rather more predictable, and in funeral sermons both for ministers as well as other members of society, is the frequent employment of scriptural texts which exhort congregations and readers to the Christian duty of resignation to God's will (notable examples may be found in John 18:2 or Rom. 6:13) or to attend to the superior qualities of the deceased's heavenly destination (Phil. 1:23 or Rev. 14: 13).

Prevalent among—though not exclusive to—Dissenters' funeral sermons is the inclusion of scriptural texts preselected by the deceased, a feature which further demonstrates this genre's capacity to tailor the expressive means by which these individuals might be remembered. In 1695, the Presbyterian Oliver Heywood notes in his Epistle Dedicatory that the two greatest legacies left by his friend and colleague Jonathan Denton were 'advice to his friends', and 'this Text', by which he means the preselection of the tenth chapter of Job, verse seven, as the principal text on which Denton wished Heywood to base his funeral sermon. In the sermon's second section, the expressive capacity of the funeral sermon to evoke the deceased's personality is further extended by a rich variety of literary forms employed to portray their lives and characters. In addition to third-person narrative, many funeral sermons contain elegiac verse, extensive excerpts from the deceased's correspondence, and in the example of Matthew Sylvester's 1705 sermon for Grace Cox, a diary synopsis. Appended as a Postscript to Benjamin Fawcett's funeral sermon for fellow minister Risdon Darracott (a fourth edition of which appears fifteen years after Darracott's death in 1759) is a solemn five-page 'farewell meditation' composed by the deceased during his last illness (Fawcett).

Such literary diversity provides the reader with invaluable scope for extended spiritual interpretation which can best be met by the act of independent reading. Henry Godman observes, in his preface to the 1688 funeral sermon for Elizabeth Kilbury, that the reader must 'act the part of a Pastor and Teacher unto thy self, and thy own Soul... [since t]he Minister's Application without thine own, will be little or no purpose' (Godman). As with other published sermons, textual interpretation is central to the cultural importance of the funeral sermon because it emphasizes the individualistic nature of Protestant spiritual responsibility. In this context at least, the published funeral sermon may have been valued in some quarters as 'superior' to its oral counterpart; Rivers has suggested that Richard Baxter's *Christian Directory* (1673) provides a particularly valuable analysis of the 'personal, domestic, social, economic, and political advantages of reading over hearing, with particular emphasis on the freedom of the individual reader to choose books most suitable to his or her condition' (Rivers: 116).

Numerous earlier (and some later) funeral sermons feature vivid deathbed scenes, complete with emotional dialogue, details of the subject's dying moments, and multiple eyewitness accounts from friends or relations. Such works find their precursors in popular martyrologies and deathbed repentance narratives such as Burnet's 1680 account of

Lord Rochester's conversion, a work that sustained its popular appeal throughout the eighteenth and well into the nineteenth century (Walker: 24, 28). The use of deathbed scenes in funeral sermons had waned by the end of the seventeenth century (Houlbrooke: 183–4) but remained popular in related works such as John Dunton's 1692 commemorative anthology of notable deaths from history entitled *The Mourning Ring*. Dunton's work is prefaced with an address to the reader which asserts that a book is more appropriate than the 'bisquets, Gloves, Rings, &c.' traditionally given to well-to-do mourners attending the burial (Dunton). Dunton's anthology is just one example of a significant corpus of contemporary works that might be termed 'funeral literature'; such works also encompass funeral sermons themselves, usually within a compendious form that invites readers to contemplate the universality of the spiritual journey that awaits all mortals. Multiple editions of these works, as well as the collected editions of funeral sermons themselves, suggest not only their general popularity but also their usefulness in providing sermon templates for busy or inexperienced ministers. Two popular examples were John Shower's 1692 anthology *The Mourners Companion* (a third edition was published by 1699) and Edward Pearse's *The Great Concern, or, A Serious Warning*, which reached its twenty-fifth edition in 1715.

The frequency of multiple editions, and the proliferation of enhanced or extended biographical narratives in funeral sermons, also suggests a reading public whose avid taste for didactic literature extended far beyond the works of fiction and spiritual biography more familiar to the present day. The published funeral sermon's second section provided a creative space in which the Protestant congregation—or individual reader—was invited to call upon its own interpretative and spiritual resources to glean useful moral lessons from the example of the deceased's life and death. Increasingly less problematic, the form's classical and Roman Catholic origins came to be more comfortably acknowledged in light of what the genre had to offer the reader, as Edmund Calamy makes apparent in his funeral sermon for fellow minister Samuel Stephens:

> Though Funeral Orations had their Rise from Heathenish Vanity, yet may they (provided all unjust Commendation of the Dead, and servile Flattery of the Living, be avoided) be exceeding useful, even among Christians, in helping to make the Survivers better; there being nothing that more promotes the Amendment of our Lives, than the serious Consideration and Improvement of the Departure of Others. (Calamy: 1)

Such an estimate clearly aligns the published funeral sermon with the spiritual biography, whereby the 'exceeding useful' content—that is, the spiritual and didactic value of biographical experience—justified its detailed inclusion. This is a general characteristic of early modern religious literature, as D. Bruce Hindmarsh has suggested, in which the period 'witnessed a significant anthropocentric turn as theology increasingly concerned itself with the sequencing of salvation and mapped this understanding onto experience as an order of conversion' (Hindmarsh: 15). In his preface to one of the most popular spiritual biographies of the seventeenth century, Baxter had observed that 'the Lives of Holy Men' provide the reader with 'God's Image...not only in Precept, but in Reality and Practice; not Pictured, but in the *Substance*... the real Impress and Holiness in the Soul, is that living Image of God' (Baxter: 13–14).

Although by no means an exclusive feature of Dissenters' literature, the investment of the details of everyday life with spiritual significance clearly has a special appeal for Dissenters. This factor may help to explain the disproportionately high number of published funeral sermons which can be attributed to dissenting ministers throughout the period. Though estimates vary widely, Michael Watts has suggested that Dissenters in this period comprised somewhere between 6 and 10 per cent of the English population, with higher concentrations living in urban centres (Watts: 267–89). Their minority representation in the population as a whole is not reflected in the extant body of published funeral sermons from this period, in which Dissenters' works are represented in approximately equal measures with those from the Church of England.

Numerous funeral sermons are penned by dissenting ministers who share the denomination of their deceased colleagues. Often the author is the deceased's successor and seeks to exhort his new congregation to follow the moral example of their now-departed spiritual shepherd. In one example, Presbyterian minister William Tongue ominously warns the congregation of the late Thomas Sherwell that

> [t]his dear Servant of Christ is not the first, nor the second, nor the third, nor fourth only, that you have followed to the Grave, having spent themselves in the Service of your Souls. In the Name of God beware lest the Blood of your Ministers lie at your Doors. (Tongue: 27)

Tongue does not indicate how long each minister actually survived in service. The prospect of their own culpability in four or more ministers' deaths, however, combined with the fact that Thomas Sherwell actually dropped dead in the pulpit, must have given this unfortunate congregation some pause for thought. Such admonitory content is not uncommon in Dissenting ministers' funeral sermons; pertinent scriptural allusions, such as Corah's attacks on Moses (Numbers 16) or the first chapter of Zechariah, feature repeatedly. In an example of the latter in 1691, John Quick describes the means by which congregations 'are the real Murderers of their most Faithful Pastors', either through overwork or underpayment, or the sin of persecution (Quick: 18). Similarly, Matthew Mead's Preface observes that 'God often takes away his Ministers as a punishment for the unthankfulness and unprofitableness of their hearers', thus indirectly warning the Rotherhithe congregation of the late Thomas Rosewell to avoid such transgressions towards their next minister (Mead).

Funeral sermons provide an intriguing glimpse into conflicts between ministers and their congregations. The Epistle preceding Thomas Milway's 1692 funeral sermon for Francis Holcroft, for example, recalls an incident when

> (notwithstanding the rude insolency of the absurd Scholars disturbing the whole Assembly at that time, and therein highly affronting the present Generous Government) [Holcroft] was much assisted by the Lord... Knowing assuredly, that his words of threatning [with] which he denounced will overtake the scorners that ridiculed the Saints at his Funeral, contradicting and blaspheming.

Holcroft's treatment at the hands of some members of his congregation may have been related to a style of preaching that even Milway has to defend, somewhat reluctantly, as 'less methodical, yet truly when I have sometimes considered it, it hath appeared to me (at least) Apostolical, Primitive and Divine... though sometimes he might seem to have too much of the Spirit and Power of Elias with him' (Milway: 19–20). The difficulty in understanding localized disputes often lies in the pointed obscurity of ministers' language. Samuel Slater is equally mysterious in his funeral sermon for fellow minister George Day:

> There are some, nay too too many, that would have no difference made by Ministers and Churches in their Gospel-Ministrations... And let Persons at this Day, who are of Loose Principles and Lives, please themselves as much as they will with their vain imaginations[.] It is a certain Truth, That there is not only in the World, but also in the visible Church, a vast difference between Men and Men. (Slater: 15)

Slater may be referring here to specific individuals within Day's congregation; he later goes on, however, to abhor the congregation's moral laxity and its too-liberal admission (with 'all admitted to the Lord's Table, Children and Swine too') so he might equally be questioning Day's own lack of rigour for Church discipline. This ambiguity illustrates the slippery nature of terms such as 'Presbyterian' and 'Congregational'; here, Slater's implication is that stricter standards of church membership are required on the basis of moral conduct (a view normally associated with Congregational tendencies and in opposition to mainline Presbyterianism), yet Slater was a Presbyterian while the deceased was a Congregational pastor.

It has already been noted that the mourning congregation's moral culpability in relation to their minister's death is a common theme in funeral sermons, but John Nesbitt's bitter reference to certain members of Thomas Gouge's congregation, with its opening lines derived from the sixth verse of the thirteenth chapter of Zechariah, alludes to a specific rogue element rather than the general populace:

> Was he not wounded in the House of his professed Friends; or did he not suffer more by divided Friends (as they pretended to be) than united Enemies?... [Gouge] had better things to employ his thoughts and time about, than to relate the noted Barbarities and unparaleil'd Cruelties of a Person, who was so very notorious that their [sic] needed no Historian to inform the World of him, or them. (Nesbitt: 39–41)

The 'Person' in question was Joseph Jacob, initially a member of Gouge's Three Cranes (Thames Street) meeting house, who launched a series of verbal attacks on his former minister before poaching a number of the congregation to attend his own weekly lectures in 1697. Despite the enmity with which Nesbitt depicts Jacob's conduct, it is clear that he has no wish to single him out by name but rather to portray the events which have taken place as a danger to all congregations. Nesbitt concludes that 'the best constituted Churches have not been exempted from such disturbances. Weeds will spring up in the most regular Gardens, Vermin will crawl amongst the sweetest Roses' (Nesbitt: 41).

His employment of this garden metaphor suggests that Nesbitt recognizes such conflicts as an inevitable feature of the Dissenters' spiritual landscape, a view broadly consistent with those of many other Protestant ministers both within and outside of the Established Church. Conflict has always commanded an avid readership. Publications contemporary with the Antinomian Controversy provide a resounding example of this; it is evident in multiple editions of funeral sermons as well as the more predictable exchanges found in published pamphlets, 'defences', 'vindications', and 'answers'. The publicity which accompanied such works tells the same story since sale catalogues attached to pamphlets advertised contemporary funeral sermons for relevant ministers, and vice versa. Thomas Gouge's funeral sermon advertises funeral sermons for Matthew Mead and Stephen Lobb in addition to all of the key pamphlets related to the Antinomian Controversy, as does the nine-page catalogue accompanying the second edition of Stephen Lobb's own funeral sermon, also from 1700.

Despite the apparent popularity of such content, most dissenting ministers repeatedly stress that worldly matters *should* play no part in the commemoration of the deceased. John Quick proclaims his desire to distance himself from such matters: 'I'll not meddle with that Controversie, whether in the Church there be such an Officer distinct from the Pastor, as the Ruling Elder, I have told my poor thoughts about it elsewhere' (Quick: 21). Such a remark is doubly useful because it depicts the author as a peaceable minister devoted to the commemorative task at hand while it also guides readers to Quick's other writings should they wish to learn more of 'that Controversie'.

The formal conventions of the published funeral sermon generally required that Protestant ministers of all denominations employed a mode of language suitably decorous for the mournful event which occasioned their discourse. Samuel Annesley's funeral sermon for fellow Presbyterian minister Thomas Brand, however, published in the near aftermath of the Happy Union's breakdown, invests pointed ambiguity into an otherwise straightforwardly didactic format; his cryptic language draws specific attention to 'other' meanings in the text:

> I have undertaken what I can in no way perform, so much as to my own, much less to others satisfaction, when the collecting of some Memorables of Mr. Brand's Life was desired of me I too suddainly consented, not sufficiently considering, what Difficulties beset me: Namely some things of greatest moment must not be mention'd at all, either some Persons, or Times will not bear it; in other things, Places and Persons, upon the same Reasons, must not be named: and of those things which may be spoken, where they can't be mention'd without commending of him, others of name, will count themselves reproach'd. (Annesley: 1–2)

Following the breakdown of London's 'United Brethren' of Presbyterian and Independent ministers, one of the primary 'Difficulties' that Annesley faced in publishing this funeral sermon was how to describe Brand's ministerial training. Many Presbyterians, including Annesley, supported the formal assessment of ministers by the synod of elders, while Independent ministers could be appointed solely by members of their congregation on the basis of their ministerial 'gifts' (not necessarily reinforced by formal education)

(Bogue and Bennett: 109–12, 123–9). It would have been virtually impossible to avoid this subject in the funeral sermon's biographical section, where congregations and readers alike had come to expect a portrait of the deceased's life. Combined with the close attention of a congregation and readership primed for partisan debate, this expectation loads further potential meaning into ministerial accounts of their colleagues' lives.

The second section of Annesley's funeral sermon amplifies the precise nature of Brand's spiritual and educational journey towards ministerial ordination through the use of lengthy descriptive passages and double-size print. Annesley surmises that Brand's 'wary entring into this Office presages a careful fulfilling of it'; his repeated references to the deceased's 'doubts and fears' implicitly defend Brand's Presbyterian standards of ministerial ordination as spiritually, as well as technically, rigorous. The conspicuously obscure language employed by Annesley differs markedly from John Nesbitt's more cautious tone in Thomas Gouge's funeral sermon; Nesbitt asks readers to

> Consider him *as a Minister*; his Soul was better taught, than to think the Ministry, a Work to be undertaken without, or with a meer superficial Tincture of Learning… If any would Query what was his Learning? I might answer in the several parts of it, both as to Words and Things, but that which was his Delight and his Honour, was to be intimately acquainted with the mystery of *God-man* his Redeemer. (Nesbitt: 32–4)

Notable in Nesbitt's eulogy is the absence of references to formal ministerial training, although Gouge is credited with 'Wisdom', a 'Penetrating Mind', 'Active Phancy', and a 'Tenacious Memory'. Nesbitt's careful phrasing changes the connotation of 'meer superficial Tincture of Learning' since it implies that formal education is 'superficial' compared to the more valuable spiritual qualities possessed by Gouge. Nesbitt thereby leaves unanswered altogether the question of Gouge's formal qualifications; the implication is that the question is mooted since, without spiritual integrity, such training is meaningless. In a later passage, however, Nesbitt implies that formal training *should* be undertaken in order to counteract attacks against 'unqualified' ministers:

> I am not such a superstitious Adorer of Learning, as to lessen or Exclude the Work of the Spirit, I know the Spirit can qualifie Persons for his Work; but then, what others must seek in an ordinary way, that he does by his extraordinary power; and when extraordinary Operations are not to be expected. (Nesbitt: 46–7)

Gouge's funeral sermon in 1700 provides a public platform for Nesbitt's carefully worded—if deeply complex and possibly contradictory—position on ministerial education. It also reflects the complexity of Nesbitt's specific allegiances within the closely-knit dissenting community of late-seventeenth-century London. Nesbitt's attendance was noted at Daniel Williams's lectures yet he also married the daughter of Isaac Chauncy, Williams's foremost denunciator in the Antinomian Controversy. Ultimately, Nesbitt's deep reluctance to exacerbate divisions within London's dissenting community is evident in his management of the Common Fund from 1692 (which served both Presbyterian and Independent ministers) as well as in his own funeral sermon, which describes him as 'a great lover of Peace' (Hurrion: 39).

For a period so marked by doctrinal dispute both within and outside the Established Church, it is notable that irenicism is the virtue most consistently praised in dead Protestant ministers of all denominations. Ministers' hatred and avoidance of controversy are universally applauded in contemporary funeral sermons; praise meted out for their valiant efforts to unite believers in the common Scriptural path is so very commonplace that, if all the funeral sermons were to be believed, it is astounding that any doctrinal disputes ever occurred at all. Even Burnet's 1694 funeral sermon for the Archbishop of Canterbury is therefore typical of the genre as a whole when he observes that Tillotson, like many great men of faith,

> thought the maintaining these Doctrines as they are proposed in the Scriptures, without entring too much into Explanations or Controversies, would be the most effectual way to preserve the Reverence that was due to them... He thought the less mens Consciences were entangled, and the less the Communion of the Church was clogg'd with disputable Opinions, or Practices, the world would be the Happier, Consciences the freer, and the Church the Quieter. (Burnet 1694: 31)

If irenicism is the most universally praised ministerial virtue, then other relevant qualities commonly feature in relation to other professions and social registers. Praise is generally fashioned, in the early modern funeral sermon, to unite the qualities of the virtuous Christian with more singular aspects of the individual's public identity. Joseph Harrison of Hatton Garden, for example, is portrayed as 'studious, diligent and indefatigable in his honourable profession as a physician... ever willing to deliver his healing balm to the poor and distressed without fee or reward' (Proud: 18). For a naval commander, patriotic, martial, and Christian values are seamlessly united, as in the figure of Sir Cloudesley Shovell (notwithstanding the disastrous and arguably ignominious shipwreck which took his and so many other lives), lauded for his efforts to 'rescue the Honour of God and Religion, and vindicate the Laws and Glory of our Nation' while exercising those talents which 'render'd him a Sanctuary to Friends, and a Terror to the Enemies of his Cause' (Butler: 6–7).

Though never its primary concern, the funeral sermon almost always acknowledges the nobility of its subject with more than passing deference. Sir John Skynner's funeral sermon for Baptist Noel, the fourth Earl of Gainsborough (seven editions of which had been printed by 1754), takes note of the Earl's gentlemanly love of 'polite and manly amusements' and 'knowledge in the principal arts and embellishments of elegant life' before it provides a more elaborate portrait of the Earl's universal Christian qualities as 'the tender husband, the generous father, and the affectionate friend' (Skynner: 7, 11). Directly in line with its reformed origins, however, the Protestant funeral sermon in the long eighteenth century *always* affords priority to the deceased's private piety, regardless of social position. In this context, White Kennett's funeral sermon for William Cavendish, first Duke of Devonshire, initially seems to adopt a revisionist stance, as much is made of the distinguished family tree from which the Duke derived 'an Hereditary Spirit of Grandeur and Magnificence' (Kennett: 12).

In direct contrast to most other contemporary funeral sermons, Kennett's spirited defence of Devonshire's noble pedigree even extends to a rejection of what he views as indecorous austerity in the contemporary funeral ceremony: 'The Truth is, our private and parsimonious Funerals of Honourable Persons have been but a late degenerate Custom, which our brave and pious Forefathers did disdain' (Kennett: 2). Further reading reveals, however, that Kennett's point is to draw a clear distinction between the (false) modesty implied by fashionably unadorned funerals versus the useful instruction to be gleaned from sincere praise for an exemplary life:

> Whence then came a modern way of interring our deceased Fathers (especially those of the highest Fortune and Figure) in an effected Secrecy and Silence, with no Praises of the Dead, no Instructions to the Living? Is it, that some modest People have forbid that Office, for fear of being flatter'd? Is it, that some Preachers have exceeded in Commendations and Characters beyond Truth and Decorum? Or has not that late Omission been rather a love of Novelty and Change... the affecting new modes, not in manner of Life only, but in that of Death and Burial? (Kennett: 3)

Kennett's aim here is to highlight the dangers of misinterpreting modesty or silence in burial rites as a *lack* of praise for the deceased; his funeral sermon seeks to vilify contemporary fashions in funeral ceremony. Such trends emerge, as the period progresses, as a means of signalling the social exclusivity of the 'better sort' of mourners through the adoption of seemingly modest and 'decorous' rituals such as night-time burial (Houlbrooke: 190–3). Regarding this tendency, both Ralph Houlbrooke and Thomas Laqueur have noted how William III's refusal to renew the College of Arms' commission for authorizing heraldic funerals meant that the lavish pomp and ceremony previously reserved for the nobility became increasingly available to anyone wealthy enough to hire the undertakers' trappings. The ostentatious public funeral came in turn not to represent tasteful decorum but instead, pretension and artifice; as Laqueur observes, 'undertakers were seen as purveyors of falseness... men who traded in lies and deception' (Laqueur: 113). Public ceremonies pertaining to Protestant funerals in the early modern period were therefore increasingly subject to contemporary accusations of hypocrisy. In this respect, published funeral sermons were in precisely the right place to receive the lion's share of criticism.

Such criticism reflects the form's origins in Roman Catholic ritual even as it anticipates the growing cynicism of a cultural period increasingly saturated by print. In the Duke of Devonshire's funeral sermon, Kennett does in fact remain entirely true to the spiritual ideals of the genre since his subject is principally remembered for his private virtues regardless of his family pedigree; William is 'a Noble and most Eminent Peer, [yet] as mortal as the meanest of us' (Kennett: 12). His observations concerning the discrepancy between the Duke's social position and his funeral ceremony bring into sharper focus the central paradox this genre attempts to encompass. As a highly popular and public medium, the published funeral sermon thereby compromises the very praise of private virtue itself.

Herein lies the greatest difficulty faced by authors of funeral sermons since, throughout the period, the genre remains consistently vulnerable to accusations of falseness and mercenary intentions. Regarding Kennett's own funeral sermon, John Dunton makes clear that, notwithstanding his obligatory respect for the Duke as 'a Noble Patriot, and a True English-man',

> I cou'd never endure Flattery, (especially in Funeral Sermons) and for that Reason have as boldly discover'd [the Duke's] Whoredoms, as Dr. K—(in his Funeral Sermon) endeavour'd to hide them. 'Tis true, the D[uke] was a Peer of the Realm, and the Birth and Quality of such Men does demand our Tribute of Respect and Veneration when they live... But neither their Birth nor Grandeur shou'd dazzle our Eye-sight; and those Ministers that Preach their Funeral Sermons are yet less excusable than other Men, if they lessen or conceal their Whoredoms. (Dunton 1708: i–ii)

Dunton was a vociferous critic of hypocrisy in funeral sermons, as is also reflected in his 1707 poem *The Pulpit-Fool*; Defoe, too, in his satirical *Hymn to the Funeral Sermon* remarks how 'Pulpit-Praises may be had | According as the Man of God is paid' (Defoe 1703: 2). If these authors' sentiments are far from uncommon, however, the most vicious attacks of this kind are levelled by other ministers. In 1701 Philip Stubs finds himself obliged to 'declare openly against all those who write themselves Ministers of the Blessed Jesus, and yet give such umbrage for Scandal to the Enemies of his Cross' (Stubs: 31). He defends the brevity of his own funeral sermon for Thomas Wright as a means of avoiding the production of 'a tedious Heap of foolish, fulsome, false daubings (the too common Entertainment in many such Discourses as this) which whilst they are made for every body, do indeed fit no body' (Stubs: 29). Hypocrisy in funeral sermons, Stubs continues, 'damns all Religion as Craft and Cheat, and Priests of all Perswasions for a Mercenary Tribe', while the corruption of the form has come to dissuade the 'honest well-meaning Parishioner' from even requesting a funeral sermon for his own burial since, '[h]aving seen the Sacred Place so often prostituted to the basest Flattery for filthy Lucre, [he] dares not run the risque of undue Mixtures in his Panegyrick' (Stubs: 30).

Stubs's lengthy diatribe makes clear that the very purpose of the form itself—the promotion of virtue and piety in surviving mourners, as inspired by ministerial praise for the deceased—has been perverted by false funeral sermons. Presented within a funeral sermon itself, however, the paradox of Stubs's position is that his arguments detract from the value of his own praise for Thomas Wright, forcing him to conclude, rather weakly, that

> If any of this Congregation knew of any remarkable Failings in him (which God knows the best of us are subject to) those ye should industriously avoid: If any Vertues which I have omitted, as unacquainted with them, those ye must endeavour to imitate now in this your Day, and that will be the best Application of this part of my discourse. (Stubs: 32)

In the published funeral sermon, the validity of the ministerial position becomes increasingly paradoxical as the genre simultaneously attempts to encompass self-effacement (in encouraging the reader to come to their own conclusions regarding the deceased) and self-promotion (through publication). In turn, accusations such those made by Stubs, Dunton, and Defoe are countered by increasingly strident ministerial apologetics or defences for publishing in the first place. The publication of funeral sermons is progressively depicted as an act undertaken only with great reluctance, usually under duress from the deceased's family or congregation, but so frequently repeated, appears instead as a case of 'the minister protesteth too much'.

This commonplace posture of ministerial modesty contrasts starkly with the sheer numbers of published funeral sermons in this period. There is little doubt that part of the genre's popular appeal is due to the fundamental truth that, as John Shower succinctly puts it, 'the Living know that they shall dye'. Only a few paragraphs later, however, and perhaps not without some personal sense of satisfaction, Shower (the author of at least ten published funeral sermons, plus *The Mourners' Companion*) goes on to conclude that since the nation 'abounds with good Books of practical Divinity... we may conclude that there are many thousands in England who relish and read such Books, or so many would never sell' (Shower). The Protestant funeral sermon stands as a unique testimony to the widespread popularity, as well as the inherent paradoxes, that such 'good Books of practical Divinity' faced during the course of the long eighteenth century.

References

A Call from Heaven to the Unconverted. A Sermon Preached at the F[un]eral of Mr. John Gaspine. (1698). London: John Williams.

Acton, S. (1699). *Dying infants sav'd by grace proved and the blessd man with his blessedness described in a sermon preached near Namptwich in Cheshire at the burial of a deceased infant, July 25, 1695.* London: A. Fabian.

Annesley, S. (1692). *The Life and Funeral Sermon of the Reverend Mr. Thomas Brand.* London: J. Dunton.

A Sermon Preach'd on the Occasion of the Funeral of Mrs. Elizabeth Gibson (1692). London: n. p.

Baxter, R. (1672). 'Introduction', in T. Alleine, *The Life and Death of Mr. Joseph Alleine.* London: Nevil Simons, 1–18.

Bingham, T. (1772). *The Honour and Happiness of Departed Saints. A Funeral Sermon on the Death of Mrs. Hannah Jarrold.* Colchester: W. Keymer.

Bogue, D., and Bennett, J. (1808). *The History of the Dissenters from the Revolution in 1688 to the Year 1808*, vol. 1. London: William and Smith.

Brady, N. (1706). *Fifteen Sermons Preach'd on Several Occasions*, vol. 2. London: S. Crouch.

Burnet, G. (1692). *A Sermon at the Funeral of... Robert Boyle.* London: Chiswell and Taylor.

—— (1694). *A Sermon at the Funeral of the Archbishop of Canterbury...* London: Richard Chiswell.

—— (1702). *A Compleat History of the Glorious Life and Actions of... William the Third.* London: E. Jones.

Butler, D. (1707). *A Sermon Occasionally Preached at the Funeral of Sir Cloudesley Shovel.* London: Thomas Smith.

Calamy, E. (1694). *A Funeral Sermon... on Samuel Stephens.* London: Abraham Chandler.

Crooke, B. (1698). *A Sermon Preach'd at the Funeral of Mrs Bullivant.* London: Joseph Wild.

Defoe, D. (1702). *The Mock Mourners. A Satyr, By Way of Elegy on King William.* London: n. p.

—— (1703). *A Hymn to the Funeral Sermon*. London: n. p.
Dunton, J. (1692). *The Mourning Ring*. London: John Dunton.
—— (1707). *The Pulpit-Fool, A Satyr*. London: n. p.
—— (1708). *The Hazard of a Death-Bed-Repentance, Fairly Argued*. London: n. p.
Ellesby, J. (1694). *The Great Danger and Uncertainty of a Death-Bed Repentance, as It Was Deliver'd at a Funeral Sermon*. London: W. Crooke.
Fawcett, B. (1759). *Christian Stedfastness : Or St. Paul's Affectionate Pleas with his Converts at Philippi, to Stand Fast in the Lord. A Sermon Occasioned by the Death of the Reverend Mr. Risdon Darracott; Who Departed this Life March 14, 1759 in the Forty-third Year of his Age*... Salop: Printed by J. Cotton and J. Eddowes.
Fox, A. (2000). *Oral and Literate Culture in England: 1500–1700*. Oxford: Oxford University Press.
Fritz, P. S. (1982). 'The Trade in Death: The Royal Funerals in England, 1685–1830'. *Eighteenth-Century Studies* 15: 291–316.
Gilpin, R. (1700). *The Comforts of Divine Love*. London: T. Parkhurst.
Gittings, C. (1984). *Death, Burial and the Individual in Early Modern England*. London: Croom Helm.
Godman, H. (1688). *A Funeral Sermon Preached... Upon the Occasion of the Death of Mrs. Elizabeth Kilbury*. London: N. Crouch.
Goodwin, T. (1695). *Of the Happiness of Princes Led by Divine Counsel: A Sermon Occasioned by the Death of... Queen Mary*. London: Jonathan Robinson.
Hargrave, J. (1721). *Riches Rightly Improved. A Sermon Preached at the Funeral of... Edward Colston*. Bristol: reprinted by H. Greep.
Heywood, O. (1695). *Job's Appeal. Being a Funeral Discourse... upon the Occasion of the Death of Mr. Jonathan Denton*. London: B. Aylmer.
Hindmarsh, D. B. (2005). *The Evangelical Conversion Narrative: Spiritual Autobiography in Early Modern England*. Oxford: Oxford University Press.
Houlbrooke, R. (1999). 'The Age of Decency: 1660–1760', in P. C. Jupp and C. Gittings (eds.), *Death in England: An Illustrated History*. Manchester: Manchester University Press, 174–201.
Howe, J. (1690). *A Funeral Sermon for Mrs Esther Sampson*. London: Thomas Parkhurst.
Hurrion, J. (1728). *The Christian's Hidden Life*. London: J. Clark.
Jones, D. (1791). *A Funeral Sermon Preached at Spa-Fields Chapel... on the Death of the Late Countess Dowager of Huntingdon*. London: Rice Jones.
Kennett, W. (1707). *A Sermon Preach'd at the Funeral of the Right Noble William Duke of Devonshire*. London: H. Hills.
Laqueur, T. (1983). 'Bodies, Death, and Pauper Funerals'. *Representations* 1: 109–31.
Mead, M. (1692). *A Funeral Sermon Preached Upon the Sad Occasion of the Death of... Thomas Rosewell*. London: John Lawrence.
Mills, B. (1750). *The Blessedness of True Christians in a Future State. A Funeral Sermon Preached at Uxbridge, June 24, 1750. On Occasion of the Death of a Pious Young Person*. London: James Buckland.
Milway, T. (1692). *A Funeral Sermon Preached Upon the Death of... Francis Holcroft*. London: William Marshall.
Nesbitt, J. (1700). *A Funeral Sermon Preached... Upon the Death of... Thomas Gouge*. London: John Marshall.
Parsons, J. (1763). *A Sermon Preached at the Funeral of Mrs Susan Sporle*. London: B. Dod.

Pearse, E. (1674). *The Great Concern, or, A Serious Warning.* London: J. Robinson and B. Aylmer.

Proud, J. (1798). *A Funeral Sermon on the Death of John Harrison MD.* London: E. Hodson.

Quick, J. (1691). *The Dead Prophet Yet Speaking. A Funeral Sermon... upon the Sad Occasion of the Decease of... John Faldo.* London: Thomas Philips.

Rivers, I. (1991). *Reason, Grace, and Sentiment: Volume I, Whichcote to Wesley: A Study of the Language of Religion and Ethics in England 1660–1780.* Cambridge: Cambridge University Press.

Shower, J. (1692). *The Mourners Companion, or, Funeral Discourses on Several Texts.* London: Dunton and Chandler.

Skynner, J. (1751). *A Sermon Preached at the Funeral of Baptist Earl of Gainsborough.* London: R. Dodsley.

Slater, S. (1698). *Enoch's Translation.* London: John Lawrence.

Smith, B. R. (1999). *The Acoustic World of Early Modern England.* Chicago: University of Chicago Press.

Stubs, P. (1701). *The Hopes of a Resurrection Asserted and Applied. In a Sermon Preached... at the Interment of Mr. Thomas Wright.* London: Henry Mortlock.

Sylvester, M. (1705). *Christian Hope, The Mourners Feast. Faithfully considered and Humbly offered to the Solemn Thoughts of the Mournful Relatives and Relicts of Mrs. Grace Cox of Ealing Common, Lately Deceased; As a Divine Antidote against the Excess of Funeral Sorrows...* London: J. Robinson.

Tenison, T. (1695). *A Sermon Preached at the Funeral of Her Late Majesty Queen Mary.* London: Richard Chiswell.

Tongue, W. (1693). *A Sermon Preached at the Funeral of the Reverend Mr. Thomas She[r]well.* London: Thomas Parkhurst.

Tromly, F. B. (1983). '"According to Sounde Religion": the Elizabethan Controversy over the Funeral Sermon'. *Journal of Medieval and Renaissance Studies* 13: 293–312.

Tyacke, N. (2008). 'Farewell to a Hero: Printed Responses in Prose and Verse to the Death of William III (1702)'. Unpublished paper, 13 February 2008. Dr Williams's Library, London.

Walker, R. G. (1982). 'Rochester and the Issue of Deathbed Repentance in Restoration and Eighteenth-Century England'. *South Atlantic Review* 47: 21–37.

Walker, S. (1753). *A Sermon Preached at Truro,...* 2nd edn. Falmouth: M. Allison.

Watts, M. R. (1978). *The Dissenters: From the Reformation to the French Revolution.* Oxford: Oxford University Press.

CHAPTER 21

THE VICTORIAN FUNERAL SERMON

JOHN WOLFFE

FUNERAL sermons marked both the literal beginning and ending of the Victorian era. Following the 18-year-old Victoria's accession to the throne on 20 June 1837, preachers responded to the death of her uncle, William IV, with sermons usually delivered either to coincide with his funeral at St George's Chapel, Windsor on 8 July, or on the following day, Sunday 9 July. Similarly, more than six decades later, Queen Victoria's own death on 22 January 1901 was followed by nationwide preaching of sermons reflecting on the event, normally delivered on either of the two following Sundays, 27 January and 3 February, or to coincide with the funeral on Saturday 2 February. Although only a small proportion of such sermons were published in full, it is apparent from the larger selection reported in local and national newspapers that clergy and ministers felt an obligation to deliver sermons on such events, and that their utterances were of interest to a wider public than the normal congregations at their respective churches and chapels. In an age before broadcast media facilitated a sense of actual participation in remote observances, for the great majority of the population attendance at such a sermon is likely to have provided their most tangible sense of participation in national mourning.

Many hundreds of funeral sermons were published in Britain during the Victorian period. Just as in relation to eighteenth-century funeral sermons (see Chapter 20 above) more precise calculation of the size of the surviving corpus would be an extensive research project in itself. Not only is it necessary to take account of anthologies and multiple editions, but catalogue searches using obvious keywords cannot guarantee comprehensive recovery of titles in which these words do not feature, and there is a need to survey numerous different collections. Funeral sermons that were privately printed or had a local provincial circulation did not necessarily find their way into the copyright libraries, and even some sermons by substantial figures were missed. For example, while the British Library holds eleven sermons on the death of the leading Scottish churchman Thomas Chalmers in 1847, two further ones can be found in the Chalmers papers at New College, Edinburgh.

The British Library holds only six sermons preached in response to the death of the Duke of Clarence in 1892, whereas the Royal Archives hold a further seven published sermons, including ones by the deans of York and Llandaff (Purey-Cust; Vaughan 1892) which, it would seem, were sent personally to Queen Victoria but not to the then British Museum library. The collection in the British Library, the main resource used in the research for this chapter, nevertheless provides a rich and broadly representative cross-section of Victorian funeral sermons. However, exhaustive research on the genre would also require systematic work in other major libraries as well as the investigation of religious periodicals, specialist collections, private papers, and newspaper reports of unpublished sermons.

Published sermons came from clergy of all major Christian denominations, as well as, late in the nineteenth century, a few leading Jewish rabbis. However, Methodist and Roman Catholic preachers were under-represented. Motives for publication varied widely: some well-known preachers regularly published sermons on this as on other themes; others did so on a 'one-off' basis as a particular tribute to the deceased (Gresley), as a mechanism for making a public statement on wider issues (Steane: 3–6), or in response to requests from a congregation, the family of the deceased, the local community or a particular individual (Falloon: insert; Richardson; Drummond). Publication arrangements did much to determine circulation: a sermon by a metropolitan preacher distributed by a major London publishing house would have been much more widely read than that by a provincial minister, published locally or privately. Hence provincial clergy preaching on national figures often obtained London publishers or co-publishers.

In contrast to the dauntingly copious primary material, secondary analysis of Victorian funeral sermons is limited. Moreover even scholars who otherwise make substantial contributions to an understanding of Victorian cultural and religious responses to death (Rowell; Wheeler; Jalland) fail significantly to exploit the potentialities of sermon evidence. The present author has endeavoured to map out some key themes through research on the sermons preached in response to the deaths of prominent people (Wolffe 1996, 2000, 2010) but the numerous published sermons relating to more obscure individuals have hitherto only received incidental attention. Hence, while in the current chapter I widen the scope of my earlier work, particularly by considering some funeral sermons on relatively unknown people as well as those on famous figures, the field remains a rich one for further research, by those interested in Victorian views of death as well as by those studying sermons.

The subjects of published funeral sermons ranged from major public figures to those who were otherwise wholly obscure. Two particularly high-profile individuals each inspired dozens of published sermons: the Duke of Wellington, who died in 1852, gave rise to at least the sixty-five listed in the British Library catalogue, exceeded only by the Prince Consort, whose premature death in December 1861 stimulated at least seventy preachers into print. Publication on this scale was only exceeded by that relating to two pre-Victorian figures, Princess Charlotte, who died in childbirth in 1817, with eighty-one, and George III (d. 1820), with seventy-five. By comparison, the numbers of published sermons on George IV (d. 1830) and William IV, both with eleven identified sermons in the British Library, and Victoria with twenty-one, look quite meagre. While the relatively small numbers of published funeral sermons on the last two Hanoverian monarchs reflect the temporary recession in royal prestige apparent in those years, the reduced numbers for Victoria compared with the equally long-lived and revered George III are indicative of a decline in the popularity of the genre itself. In contrast to royalty even major statesmen, such as Peel (d. 1850), Palmerston (d. 1865), Disraeli (d. 1881), and Gladstone (d. 1898), gave rise to no more than a handful of published sermons. Indeed, after William IV, Wellington, Albert, and Victoria, the most popular subjects for published funeral sermons were Thomas Chalmers, General Gordon (killed at Khartoum in 1885), and the Duke of Clarence, Queen Victoria's grandson who died tragically young in 1892.

The appeal of such subjects provides an initial indication of the motivations for preaching and publishing funeral sermons. Preachers favoured figures, such as royalty or the quasi-royal Duke of Wellington, who represented some kind of national consensus, or those, such as Chalmers or Gordon, deemed to offer exemplary inspiration to the living. The deaths in advanced old age of George III, Wellington, and Victoria inspired reflection on the inevitable passage of time, and the ending of eras, while the untimely, sudden or violent deaths of Charlotte, Chalmers (who suffered a heart attack), Albert, Gordon, and Clarence moved preachers to dwell on the fragility of earthly life and the possible imminence of death even for the young and healthy.

Among less prominent individuals who gave rise to published funeral sermons, clergy and ministers were, as in the eighteenth century (Chapter 20), much the most numerous category. Whereas Church of England and Church of Scotland clergy, conscious of the duties of an Established Church, more frequently published sermons on national figures, Nonconformists gave particular attention to their own ministers. Sermons on deceased Baptist and Congregationalist ministers were disproportionately numerous, but there were also many sermons on Anglican Evangelical clergy, for whom there was a classic model in a sermon preached in 1808 by Thomas Scott, the biblical commentator, entitled *The Duty and Advantage of Remembering Deceased Ministers*. However, Methodist ministers, Catholic priests and High Anglican clergy were relatively underrepresented among the subjects of sermons. Methodist itinerancy precluded the settled connections with a single congregation that caused other branches of Nonconformity to experience the death of long-standing ministers as personal bereavements requiring particular commemoration, while it can be inferred that the very association of the genre with Dissent and Evangelicalism was a disincentive to Roman Catholics and Anglo-Catholics. Alongside sermons on ministers there were numerous sermons on leading lay members of congregations, including many women, who were deemed of significance variously as noble patrons (Holme), wives of ministers (James), or on account of exceptional dedication to church work (Aveling).

A third significant category of funeral sermons related to individuals who while not especially conspicuous in either the nation, the locality, or the congregation, nevertheless attracted a preacher's attention either in order to draw lessons from the very ordinariness of their lives (Thornton; Lemm) or because of the sudden or otherwise memorable nature of their deaths. Thus the tragic drowning of two young men while swimming in the Thames gave rise to a funeral sermon at Sion Chapel, Whitechapel (Hewlett). Other preachers wrestled with the theological and pastoral problems posed, for example, by the death of a young mother (Martin), a suicide (Shindler), the untimely death of a devoted superintendent nurse who seemingly still had much to give to others (Smith), and the Tay Bridge disaster of 1879 (Talon).

In the analysis that follows, attention will initially be directed to the changes in the form and structure of the funeral sermon that occurred during the Victorian years. We shall then turn to an account of the attitudes of preachers to death and commemoration, considering first their treatment of the exemplary lives of the deceased, second their views of the nature and significance of death itself, and third their ideas regarding the afterlife. Finally sermons on the death of Queen Victoria will be revisited, as representing something of an apotheosis for the genre as well as for the Queen herself.

Form and Structure

Despite the commonalities of context and some superficial similarities in content—notably in reflection on the transience of human life and the timeliness of death in the case of monarchs who had both exceeded the biblical allotment of 'three score years and ten' (Psalm 90:10; Graham: 5)—the differences between the funeral sermons on William IV and those on Queen Victoria are striking. In the 1837 sermons, preachers (Mardon; Steane) normally focused for much of their time on the extended exposition of their chosen biblical text, which was appropriate to the occasion, but not initially explicitly applied to the immediate circumstances. Only in the closing part of their discourse did they turn to direct comment on the late King and his reign. Sermons that dwelt less on the text and gave more extended attention to the deceased monarch, such as that preached to the University of Cambridge by John Graham, later bishop of Chester (Graham), were rare. Preaching on the death of Thomas Chalmers in 1847 W. L. Alexander felt it necessary explicitly to excuse himself for discoursing 'from an event in God's providence' rather than 'from a passage in God's word' (Alexander: 5). At the other extreme it was possible at that period for a funeral sermon to focus so exclusively on the exposition of its text that no explicit reference was made to the deceased (Hutton). In normally giving priority to biblical exposition, funeral sermons preached at the beginning of the Victorian era thus still had much in common with those of the eighteenth century (see Chapter 20 above).

The 1901 sermons, however, are much shorter, normally ten to fifteen pages of printed text, as opposed to the thirty or more pages characteristic of sermons from the 1830s, which must have taken well over an hour to deliver. In the 1901 sermons the main content was extended panegyric on the dead Queen, linked to the drawing of moral, spiritual and patriotic edification from her life. Reference to biblical texts was often merely tokenistic. Indeed the text chosen by Joseph Hammond, vicar of St Austell, 'I sit a queen and am no widow, and shall see no sorrow' (Revelation 18:7), appeared incongruous in the light of Victoria's long widowhood, although Hammond justified it by romanticizing her reunion with Albert in death (Hammond: 3, 7). Nevertheless had he considered the context of the text the effusively loyal Cornish cleric might well have hesitated to apply to his deceased sovereign words originally uttered by the Whore of Babylon. Although other preachers avoided howlers of this kind, they resorted to bland short texts such as 'A Mother in Israel' (Judges 5:7; Eldridge: 3), 'The Memory of the Just is Blessed' (Proverbs 10.7; Henson: 5), or even the single word 'Remember' (Hebrews 13: 3; Knox-Little: 3), which avoided the need to constrain the direction of their eloquence by any systematic biblical exposition.

It is possible to discern a transitional phase, apparent particularly from the 1860s to the 1880s. Preachers still sought biblical inspiration, but contented themselves with brief exposition of the text (e.g. Liddon 1871: 4–6), or framed it by initial extended reference to the death in question, whereas their predecessors had normally expounded the text at length first, therefore ensuring that it emphatically set the tone for their observations on the deceased. Thus for example, the Wesleyan John Jeffreys, preaching in Rochdale on Prince Albert's death, spent the first part of the sermon reflecting on the unexpected nature of the event, and its impact on the nation, before eventually turning, on page fifteen of the printed sermon, to offer explicit observations on his text, 2 Samuel 3:38, 'Know ye not that there is a prince and a great man fallen this day in Israel?' (Jeffreys). In a funeral sermon in 1870, Edward White Benson, a future archbishop of Canterbury, explicitly excused his limited reference to Scripture by saying that 'the wisdom and goodness of our own day cannot become truly more sacred things than they are by being described in borrowed language' (Benson). In 1881 J. A. Atkinson, Rector of St John's, Longsight, mined the book of Esther for a text relating to Mordecai, who was, like the recently-deceased Disraeli, a naturalized Jew who rose to high office. However, despite commenting on the remarkable capacity of 'God's word' to provide an illustration for every circumstance, for the rest of his sermon Atkinson made little further explicit reference to it (Atkinson). The transition was complete in an 1895 sermon on the poet Christina Rossetti, for which the preacher took his text from Proverbs 31:31, 'Her own works praise her', thus ingeniously giving himself a scriptural justification for devoting the whole sermon to an account of the dead woman's life and writings without further attention to the Bible (Nash).

Although the tradition of the expository funeral sermon was maintained, especially by preachers of a more conservative theological outlook who were using a sermon on a particular individual to make more generic points about death (for example Bickersteth; Lemm), its decline during the Victorian era from being the normal to becoming very much the minority model was a significant transition. It seems that the majority of preachers—including many who subscribed to an evangelical standpoint—in practice lost confidence in the traditional Protestant belief that the literalistic exposition of biblical texts was the best way to provide consolation and edification in the face of human mortality and bereavement. Rather, they came to find their primary inspiration in the life of the deceased, as a starting point for more free-flowing spiritual and theological reflection. The shift was a telling indication of changing attitudes to the Bible.

EXEMPLARY LIVES

Although the exemplary function of the subject's life thus assumed much greater prominence as the period wore on, it was nevertheless a feature of almost all Victorian funeral sermons. In sermons on ministers and pious lay people well known to the hearers, it was normally a straightforward matter to present the subject as a model Christian, although the permutations of personality and theology produced significant variations of emphasis. For evangelicals this was a matter of demonstrating the saving faith of the deceased as an inspiration and challenge to the living. In the eyes of the Baptist Octavius Winslow, preaching in 1849 on James Harington Evans, it all came down to showing 'his close adherence to the Lord Jesus Christ' (Shepherd, Winslow, and Noel: 10). When the vicar of St Saviour's, Retford was drowned in a shipwreck in 1859 the preacher of his funeral sermon entitled *The Death of the Righteous* argued that righteousness came from faith in Christ and was demonstrated in the nature of a man's life not his death (Mitchinson: 8, 13). Such evangelical sermons were apt to close by calling unconverted hearers to repentance and saving faith, presenting the recollection of the life and witness of the deceased as an appeal from beyond the grave (Shepherd, Winslow, and Noel: 37; Mitchinson: 14). In a sermon on the death of a local benefactress, the vicar of Kirkleatham took the opportunity to urge children to be diligent in their study of the Scriptures out of respect for the memory of the lady 'who as an instrument under God gave you the bread of life, enabled you to read and wished you to learn and understand your Bibles that you might find the way to heaven' (Holme: 6).

Non-evangelical preachers focused more on outward observance. The High Church Benjamin Harrison, preaching in 1855 on the leading Anglican layman Sir Robert Inglis, built his case rather by dwelling on his subject's conspicuous manifestation of the cardinal Christian virtues of faith, hope, and charity (Harrison). Frances Mary Gresley was described as holding 'fast to the Faith, as a staunch member of the glorious Church of England being a regular and devout communicant, loving the Church Services with their ancient Prayers and Psalms and Creeds' (Gresley: 6). In a rare published Roman Catholic funeral sermon, the subject's devotion to God was evidenced by her love for her local chapel and her responsiveness in her last illness to the voice of the priest as the earthly representative of the Almighty (Proctor: 3–6).

Where subjects possessed virtues that were not exclusively religious they were presented in a Christian context. Thus in the eyes of Henry Liddon, preaching on a leading scholar and philosopher: 'That which in Dean Mansel appears to me especially to challenge your Christian homage and admiration is not the possession of high intellectual power, but its consecration to the service of God' (Liddon 1871: 9–12). Sermons on women were particularly liable to highlight practical virtues whether in energetic Christian service which hearers were explicitly urged to emulate (Aveling: 30), or in more unassuming qualities, as in the case of the wife of a fellow minister described by the leading Congregationalist John Angell James: 'Her course through life was not that of a rapid and roaring torrent, but of a gentle noiseless stream, attracting little notice, yet scattering benefits as it flowed onwards' (James: 30).

In sermons on major secular national figures preachers often found the exemplary function more problematic, as there were greater moral and spiritual ambiguities, and the great majority of preachers lacked first-hand knowledge of their subjects. These difficulties are well illustrated by funeral sermons on the Duke of Wellington in 1852. For example Francis Maude, preaching in Trinity Church, Ipswich, felt it necessary both to defend the morality of defensive war and to acknowledge that Wellington's standing as a statesman was inferior to that he had had as a soldier. He then went on to discuss at length the question of whether the Duke had been a Christian. He felt that those who spoke 'of our deceased hero, as of a lost soul' were judging hastily and harshly, but recognized that from lack of personal knowledge it was impossible to be confident about his eternal future. Nevertheless one could be a child of God without being a conspicuous saint, and Wellington had at least been a conscientious attender at divine service (Maude). Extant published sermons generally show a charitable or agnostic view of Wellington's spiritual state, but Maude had evidently encountered more negative views, perhaps in unpublished sermons. Most preachers therefore found firmer ground in highlighting the Duke's more mundane and patriotic virtues, such as his integrity, sense of duty, and loyalty (Blunt; Bowhay). The issue was most effectively stated by George Steward, preaching in Glasgow, who compared Wellington with his near namesake John Wesley, affirming that while Wesley was a 'saint' who had reformed the populace and roused the nation from spiritual slumber, Wellington was a 'hero' who had preserved it from thraldom and given it 'rank and glory in the scale of empire'. In the perspective of eternity, however, Wesley's had been much the greater work (Steward: 47–48).

Nine years later Prince Albert was a more straightforward subject for preachers, because his career lacked the moral and political ambiguities that had been inescapable in relation to Wellington. Nevertheless there was a sense that preachers who felt the need to speculate on his spiritual state were building bricks with very limited straw (Lord: 8). Hence they tended to dwell upon his outward virtues, his sound judgement, his patronage of the arts and sciences, and above all praised him for demonstrating that 'it was possible for the husband of a queen to be a virtuous man, an exemplary husband and parent' (Clark: 6–9) as well as for bringing about a 'moral revolution' that made royalty a normative pattern for family life (Vaughan 1861: 12).

In reflecting on the careers of their subjects, early Victorian funeral preachers were not afraid of injecting a controversial or partisan edge into their sermons. Nonconformist ministers preaching on the death of William IV celebrated the advance of liberty and equality during the reign, in a manner that must have seemed provocative to Tory and Anglican opponents (Hutton; Steane). A Unitarian preacher attacked Anglican evangelicals who, he asserted, while professing 'to be the most closely allied to the principles of Protestantism' actually 'retain much of the leaven of Popery' (Mardon: 18). The Duke of Wellington's political record was attacked from both sides, by Tories because he had conceded Catholic Emancipation, and by liberals because he had resisted Reform

(Croly: 43–4; Binney: 38–9). Similarly while some preachers on the Duke used their sermons as a basis for developing moral and theological justifications for war (Ottley; Steward), the radical Scottish cleric Patrick Brewster turned his sermon on the Duke into an attack on aggressive British foreign and imperial policies. He acknowledged that the nation was indebted to Wellington 'in so far as... he has contributed to the defence of his country against foreign aggression', but condemned him as 'the friend and ally of every despotic power in Europe' who had fought an unjust war to restore the Bourbons to the French throne (Brewster: 6, 13).

By the last third of the century, however, it had become conventional for preachers to avoid controversy. Thus in a sermon on Walter Kerr Hamilton, the first Tractarian bishop, Henry Liddon, despite his personal sympathy for his subject's more controversial actions in asserting his theological convictions, sought to reach out to his critics by setting them in the context of his 'transparent sincerity', and then moved on to highlight Hamilton's 'large heartedness', evidenced by charitable attitudes towards Nonconformists and a desire for Christian unity (Liddon 1870: 7–14). In 1885, published sermons on the death of General Gordon held aloof from the intense political storm arising from the Gladstone government's perceived abandonment of him to the forces of the Mahdi, and focused rather on his qualities as an exemplary Christian soldier (Fleming 1885; Hitchens). William MacDonald Sinclair highlighted the 'betrayal' of Gordon, but presented it as the collective treachery of the nation as a whole, rather than the fault of particular individuals (Sinclair: 20). As the importance of the Bible as a common point of reference declined, it became all the more important that exemplary lives affirmed consensus rather than division.

The Deathbed

For many Victorian preachers it was important that exemplary lives were shown to culminate in exemplary deaths. Thus, although some preachers deemed detailed accounts of a subject's 'departure' to be 'improper' (Green-Armytage: 3) others gave what, to present-day eyes, seems excessive and rather prurient attention to the subject's final illness. The purpose of doing so was to provide evidence of a positive spiritual state that would thereby inspire the living with knowledge that the subject's faith had withstood its final earthly test. Some subjects, especially ministers, had known exactly what was expected of them, and were careful to provide utterances that could be duly reported in sermons. Thus the dying James Harington Evans had said: 'Tell them [his church] that I stand accepted in the Beloved, notwithstanding all my sin, and infirmity, and hellishness. I never felt more than I do now my sin and hellishness; but in Jesus I stand—Jesus is a panacea' (Shepherd, Winslow, and Noel: 8–9). Ambrose March Phillips de Lisle, a leading convert to Roman Catholicism, suffered from a long and painful terminal illness, but according to Caesarius Tondini, who preached his funeral sermon, this only served 'to bring to light a new and yet undiscovered power of God's grace in his soul' as well as demonstrating the efficacy of the sacrament of extreme unction in enabling him to face death calmly (Tondini and Collins: 19, 24).

Preachers had various strategies to handle subjects where evidence of the ideal deathbed was not available. Some were of course too inarticulate or gravely ill to make spiritually uplifting utterances, but a calm uncomplaining disposition in a last illness could still be reported as evidence of the desired spiritual state (Thornton: 20–1). Preachers also faced a difficulty when responding to the deaths of national figures, because of their lack of detailed first-hand information regarding the deathbed scene: however, some could not resist the temptation to speculate on the basis of circumstantial or fragmentary information (T. F. Dibdin: 14–17; R. W. Dibdin: 12–13). A more unusual and poignant problem faced a minister who preached a funeral sermon for his own wife following her suicide. He argued against the view 'that a child of God will never be suffered to commit suicide when in a state of insanity' by describing not only the evidence for her authentic Christian experience before she became ill, but also the dying professions she made before the poison she had drunk took full effect (Shindler: 5, 43).

In the later Victorian period reference to the deathbed was liable to become much briefer (Gresley: 6) or to be omitted altogether (Nash), but for other preachers its appeal persisted, as evoked in 1883:

> Who could afford to miss the prayers, the counsel, the consolation of the dying, which are never so effectual as when they are breathed in pain, and never so wise and gentle as when they are spoken by one half over the border, almost in sight of the Far Land? (Cure: 12)

In 1898 following Gladstone's protracted and widely reported terminal illness a preacher could still observe that the eyes of the nation had been focused on Hawarden Castle 'where the old warrior was vanquishing death by submitting to it' (Garnett: 3).

If there was broad continuity of interest in drawing spiritual lessons from well-ordered deathbed scenes, preachers' views of sudden and untimely deaths changed significantly over the course of the period. Princess Charlotte's death in 1817 had been widely perceived as a judgement on the nation for its collective spiritual failings, and echoes of this view could still be found as late as the death of Prince Albert in 1861 (Wolffe 2010: 193–8). A variant on this view was the idea, based on Isaiah 57:1, that the death of a righteous man was a forerunner of impending judgement on the survivors (Hoare; Lorimer). Sudden deaths could also be viewed by preachers as providentially ordained warnings to the living causing them to highlight the need always to be spiritually prepared to die (Hewlett; Richardson). The death of a child was seen as intended by God to stimulate the spiritual growth of the bereaved parents:

> It was one part of His purpose in taking to Himself your treasure, that you should feel a void, an aching void; that so you might be brought to fill up that sense of vacuum with an enlarged and more vivid realisation of His own presence... when at any time your minds too fondly dwell on your gathered flower, let the certainty of her eternal blessedness create increase earnestness in the pursuit of your own heavenly prize. (Hose: 16)

From the 1860s, however, when faced with tragic deaths, preachers began to show greater perplexity and less readiness unhesitatingly to discern the intentions of providence. Thus in 1863 Samuel Martin, minister of Westminster Chapel, preaching on the death of the young wife of a nearby minister acknowledged:

> Many may ask—some do ask—Why did God permit to become a wife one whose time to die was within fourteen short months of her wedding day? Why did God permit to become a mother one who could retain her motherhood but a few days? Why did God permit work to be commenced and service to be undertaken which should so soon be left? This is mysterious and inexplicable to us all. God has a reason for this dispensation and a perfect reason; but to our question 'Why', echo answers 'Why'! We cannot say really for what intent our sister has been removed, but we *can* say, 'It is the Lord, let Him do that which seemeth good unto Him.' (Martin: 21–2)

Similarly in 1868, the Chaplain of the Liverpool Workhouse agonized over the death of the Lady Superintendent of the local Nightingale Nurses. He suggested that, like Paul in his text (Philippians 1:23–4), she might be glad to depart and be with Christ, but that her loss was a 'painful riddle' for those left behind. God, he suggested, might need her for an even nobler work in heaven, or might want to make others more aware of their dependence on him, but ultimately one could only affirm trust in the overriding Will of God (Smith: 10–12). The Tay Bridge disaster of 1879 stirred explicit sermon controversy between those who saw it as a judgement on Sabbath breakers and materialists, and those who ridiculed the idea that the Almighty had a specific purpose in destroying 'a poor remnant of railway travellers' (Wolffe 2010: 198). While in an earlier generation the Duke of Clarence's premature death in 1892 would have given rise to numerous sermons on divine judgement, to his contemporaries God's purpose in the tragedy was largely mysterious (Purey-Cust: 10).

Something of the transition may be illustrated in two funeral sermons, delivered nearly half a century apart, by the prominent Broad Churchman Charles John Vaughan. In 1849, as headmaster of Harrow, Vaughan preached on the death at the age of 16 of a boy at the school, Francis Ashley, son of the future Lord Shaftesbury; in 1892, now Master of the Temple and Dean of Llandaff, he preached on the Duke of Clarence's death. In both cases Vaughan was evidently moved and troubled by the tragedy of untimely death and unfulfilled promise, but whereas in 1849 he described young Ashley's death as a 'chastisement with circumstances of peculiar mercy' (Warner and Vaughan: 23) in 1892 he sought comfort rather from stressing Christ's sympathy with sorrow and suffering, and from the power of universal human sorrow (Vaughan: 3–6, 13). He ended his 1849 sermon in language that sounded almost evangelical, reminding his hearers of the possibility of unexpected and premature death and calling them to personal repentance (Warner and Vaughan: 25); in 1892 by contrast he concluded with an exhortation to pray for the bereaved to find comfort in sorrow (Vaughan: 15). While something of the contrast can be explained by Vaughan's sensitivity to the evangelical convictions of the Ashley family, it is nonetheless indicative of how the approach of one leading Victorian preacher changed between his early thirties and his mid-seventies.

The Afterlife

Early Victorian funeral preachers frequently made general references to judgement, eternity, heaven and hell, but they had little to say about the specifics of the afterlife. The Unitarian Benjamin Mardon rather quaintly visualized the deceased William IV exchanging 'an earthly for a heavenly crown' although 'not occupying one of the highest stations in the heavenly kingdom' (Mardon: 17–18). The leading evangelical Baptist Noel vividly evoked the gloomy nature of death from a purely human perspective, which was 'frightful' for the ungodly man, who carried with him to eternity all his lusts and passions. People of faith, however, could look forward to a very literal bodily resurrection at the Second Advent of Christ:

> The time is coming—God knows when the hour will be—when that poor body, which some of us lately saw consigned to the grave, to have the dull earth heaped on it—when that very body, radiant with immortality, shall spring forth from the cemetery where we laid it, and shall rise into the presence of a returning Saviour, when he comes again to judge the quick and the dead. (Shepherd, Winslow, and Noel: 29–30)

Noel, however, did not speculate on the intermediate state of the soul, perhaps because like other premillennialists of his day, he perceived the Second Advent as an imminent rather than distant prospect. He chose to challenge the unconverted with the prospect of facing divine judgement with their deceased minister as a witness against them, rather than by dwelling on the horrors of hell (Shepherd, Winslow, and Noel: 37).

In the 1860s and 1870s, however, preachers gave more attention to the intermediate state, reflecting both ongoing theological controversies over the nature of the afterlife (Rowell; Wheeler), and a surge in popular interest demonstrated by the large sales of works such as William Branks's three books on heaven, published between 1861 and 1863, and Edward Henry Bickersteth's epic poem, *Yesterday, Today and Forever* (1866) (Wolffe 2000: 204–5). In 1860 Samuel Ley Thorne's funeral sermon for his grandmother Catherine O'Bryan, wife of the founder of the Bible Christian Connexion, was indicative of the emerging trend. Taking his text from Revelation 14:13, Thorne expounded the idea of death for a Christian as deliverance from bondage and exemption from labour, in exchange for the physical perfection of a spiritual body in heaven. He suggested that the doctrine of the future state was gradually revealed in the course of Scripture from initial hints in Genesis to a full account of the glories of heaven in a literal reading of the final chapters of Revelation (Thorne: 14–19). In striking contrast to Noel in his sermon a decade before, Thorne's emphasis was thus on the immediate prospect of a spiritual heaven for those who had been 'in the Lord' in life rather than the expectation of bodily resurrection at the *parousia*. E. H. Bickersteth, preaching on the same text in 1872, believed he could have it both ways, and it was clear that for him the intermediate state of the blessed dead was one of conscious enjoyment of Paradise and perhaps continuing awareness of loved ones still in this world, rather than merely one of 'sleep' until the Second Advent:

> The hope, the glorious and blessed hope of the Church, is indeed the second advent of her Lord, when this corruption shall put on incorruption, and when death itself shall be swallowed up in victory. But TILL HE COMES, Paradise is the next stage of our delightful existence, that Paradise which has already received all who sleep in Jesus and which, if we die in Him, will shortly receive us into its blissful bosom of repose. How narrow the frontier line that separates that world and ours! (Bickersteth: 18)

Queen Victoria's known anxiety to be reassured of her continuing spiritual communion with Albert was influential in encouraging dissemination of views of a conscious afterlife where loved ones would be reunited, a belief reflected down to the 1890s in sermons on her subsequent bereavements (Fleming 1899; MacGregor). In particular James Fleming's sermon on the Duke of Clarence, entitled 'Recognition in Eternity' first preached in front of the Prince and Princess of Wales shortly after their son's death, sold over 50,000 copies and was still being reprinted in 1899 (Fleming 1899: 1). By the end of the century, moreover, Thorne's and Bickersteth's evangelical view that heaven was reserved for those who had been demonstrably converted to Christ in life was being eclipsed by universalist views of the afterlife, where the subject's eternal happiness was not necessarily dependent on his or her manifestation of saving faith before death. Just as published preachers on the Duke of Clarence's death in 1892 did not see it as a divine judgement on the nation, they did not feel it necessary to justify their expectations that he was enjoying a fulfilled afterlife by claiming that he was a truly converted Christian. Fleming quoted the Princess of Wales's view that her late son 'did cling to the Cross' but earlier preachers would have looked for less indirect evidence (Fleming 1899: 2).

THE END OF AN ERA

By the time Queen Victoria died in 1901, despite the continuing appeal of productions such as Fleming's that addressed a particular topic of widespread interest, the funeral sermon as a published genre was already in significant decline. The British Library holds less than forty funeral sermons from the 1890s, in contrast to over a hundred from the 1830s. Newspaper reports indicate that countless such sermons were preached in response to Queen Victoria's death, but the fact that far fewer of them were published than in 1852 or 1861 is indicative of the realization of both clergy and publishers that there was no longer a substantial market for them. After 1901 the decline became precipitous: a thorough search of the British Library catalogue yields only eighteen examples for the whole of the rest of the twentieth century, most of these from the first two decades (including five on Edward VII), and the last of them Bernard

Delany's sermon in 1943 on the leading Roman Catholic intellectual Father Vincent McNabb. It therefore seems apt to conclude this chapter by considering the published funeral sermons on Queen Victoria, both as representing the final significant flowering of the genre, and also because they may provide clues to the reasons for its subsequent rapid demise.

The dominant tone of the sermons on Queen Victoria was eloquently, even movingly elegiac. Preachers were conscious that they were mourning not only an individual but a woman who had come to symbolize a whole age, and who had been part of the fabric of life for longer than they or most of their hearers could remember (Buxton: 4; Hyamson: 2). They saw her as focal point of unity in nation and empire and highlighted her conscientious discharge of the duties of a constitutional monarch, in the face of personal sorrow (Hyamson: 4). They praised her for setting a high standard of morality and family life, and suggested that her motherliness was central to her public as well as her private role (Sturges: 7). Above all they presented her as an inclusive figure, someone with whom everyone could identify even though they had never met her and who gave potentially oppressed and excluded groups a sense of being part of the imagined national family. Thus a Jewish preacher affirmed: 'She loved all of us, both great and small, with a great love, and we loved her with a great love' (Adler: 4). This assertion of inclusivity helps to explain why a substantial proportion of the published sermons came from more marginal groups that wanted to assert their participation in the national community; there were four from Jews, two from Anglicans overseas (Sandford; Wirgman), and two from the clergy of the small Reformed Episcopal Church (Eldridge; Sturges), who claimed they had been driven out of the Church of England by ritualism. On the other hand, it seems that no Nonconformist minister published a funeral sermon on Queen Victoria, indicating that they no longer felt a need to use this medium to assert their civic role.

Thus by 1901 the funeral sermon's primary role had become one of constructing and affirming consensus, comfort, and participation in the context of bereavement. One looks in vain in these texts for any less than adulatory tone, or of any spiritual or moral challenge to the hearers beyond vague exhortations to be inspired by the memory of Victoria, and to affirm national solidarity in the face of her loss (Sturges: 14). It had been different in previous generations when preachers had purposefully sought applications to the situation from the text of Scripture, had readily acknowledged the human fallibility of their subjects, speculated provocatively on the Almighty's purpose in their deaths, or pointedly confronted their hearers with reminders of their own mortality and the prospect of divine judgement. The 1901 sermons are interesting to the historian as powerful articulations of an intense but transient mood of national grief, but once that phase had passed they could have had little to offer to contemporaries but nostalgia. Preachers also said little that was not said in similar ways by secular speakers and obituarists. They symbolize the apotheosis of the funeral sermon as of Queen Victoria herself, and its transition at the end of a long life into the conventional twentieth-century funeral eulogy, in which the speaker pays tribute to the deceased and comforts the bereaved, but seldom says anything that merits the attention of a wider audience.

References

Adler, S. A. (1901). *The Passing of Our Queen*. London: A. J. Isaacs.
Alexander, W. L. (1847). *A Discourse of the Quality and Worth of Thomas Chalmers*. Edinburgh: John D. Lowe.
Atkinson, J. A. (1881). *Lessons from the Life of the Earl of Beaconsfield*. Manchester: John Heywood.
Aveling, T. W. (1872). *We Are the Lord's*. London: Hodder and Stoughton.
Benson, E. W. (1870). ΣΑΛΠΙΕΙ. *A Memorial Sermon Preached After the Death of the Rt Rev James Prince Lee, First Bishop of Manchester*. London: Macmillan.
Bickersteth, E. H. (1872). *The Blessedness of the Holy Dead*. London: Rivington.
Binney, T. (1852). *Wellington*. London: Hamilton Adams.
Blunt, J. J. (1852). *A Sermon in Memory of the Late Duke of Wellington*. Cambridge: J. Deighton.
Bowhay, J. H. (1852). *A Pulpit Tribute to the Memory of…the Duke of Wellington*. Hertford: Stephen Austin.
Brewster, P. (1853). *Wellington 'Weighed in the Balance;' or War A Crime, Self-Defence a Duty*. Paisley: Caldwell.
Buxton, H. J. W. (1901). *Full of Days and Honour*. London: Skeffington.
Clark, W. R. (1861). *A Sermon…on the Day of the Funeral of HRH the Prince Consort*. Taunton: F. May.
Croly, G. (1852). *A Sermon on the Death of the Duke of Wellington*. London: Seeley.
Cure, E. C. (1883). *Sudden Death: Is It to be Deprecated?* London: Rivington.
Dibdin, R. W. (1865). *The Patriot Palmerston: Was He Saved?* London: James Nisbet.
Dibdin, T. F. (1837). *The Patriot King*. London: James Bonn.
Drummond, J. (1865). *The Holiness of Sorrow*. Manchester: Guardian.
Eldridge, P. X. (1901). *Our Mother Queen*. London: Vacher.
Falloon, W. M. (1862). *A Prince and a Great Man Fallen*. Liverpool: Adam Holden.
Fleming, J. (1885). *The Forsaken Hero*. London: Larner & Knight.
—— (1899). *Recognition in Eternity*. London: Skeffington.
Garnett, C. (1898). *Mr Gladstone: Scholar, Statesman, Saint*. Manchester: J. Heywood.
Graham, J. (1837). *A Sermon Preached before the University of Cambridge…[on] the Day of the Funeral of…King William IV*. Cambridge: Pitt.
Green-Armytage, J. N. (1857). *A Sermon…on the Occasion of the Death of the Rev. John Browne*. Cheltenham: Wight and Bailey.
Gresley, N. W. (1888). *Funeral Sermon Preached on the Sunday Following the Burial of Frances Mary Gresley*. Dursley: Whitmore.
Hammond, J. (1901). *A Queen Indeed!* London: Skeffington.
Harrison, B. (1855). *All Things Referred to God*. London: Rivington.
Henson, H. H. (1901). *A Sermon Preached in Westminster Abbey…on the Occasion of the Death of Queen Victoria*. London: Macmillan.
Hewlett, J. G. (1847). *The Sunset of Youth*. London: Ward.
Hitchens, J. H. (1885). *Dr H. Hitchens on the Death of General Gordon*. Chelsea: G. Shield.
Hoare, C. J. (1847). *The Blessed Death of the Righteous*. London: David Batten.
Holme, J. (1844). *A Sermon Preached After the Death of the Hon. Lady Turner*. Stockton: T. Jennett.
Hose, F. (1859). *The Following of the Holy Child Jesus*. London: Hamilton Adams.
Hutton, T. P. (1837). *A Funeral Sermon Preached at Sydenham on Sunday the 22nd October 1837*. London: Shaw.

Hyamson M. (1901). *In Memoriam Queen Victoria, 1837–1901.* London: Willis.
Jalland, P. (1996). *Death in the Victorian Family.* Oxford: Oxford University Press.
James, J. A. (1856). *The Antidote of Death.* London: Hamilton Adams.
Jeffreys, J. (1861). *Princes and Great Men.* Rochdale: E. Wrigley.
Knox-Little, W. J. (1901). *Remember: A Sermon Preached at the Solemn Requiem for Her Late Majesty Queen Victoria at the Church of S. Barnabas, Oxford.* London: Longmans.
Lemm, J. (1896). *Death Versus Life.* Chippenham, Wiltshire: S. Spinks.
Liddon, H. P. (1870). *Life in Death.* London: Rivington.
—— (1871). *The Day of Work.* London: Rivington.
Lord, A. E. (1862). *A Prince and a Great Man Fallen.* London: John Snow.
Lorimer, J. G. (1847). *The Righteous Man Taken Away from the Evil to Come.* Glasgow: W. R. McPhinn.
MacGregor, J. (1897). *The State of the Christian Dead.* Edinburgh: Blackwood.
Mardon, J. (1837). *The Evanescence of Human Glory.* London: Smallfield.
Martin, S. (1866). *Sunset Ere Noon.* London: John Snow.
Maude, F. H. (1852). *The Mighty Man of Valour.* Ipswich: J. M. Burton.
Mitchinson, H. C. (1859). *The Death of the Righteous.* London: Simpkin Marshall.
Nash, J. G. (1895). *A Memorial Sermon…for the Late Christina Georgina Rossetti.* London: Skeffington.
Ottley, L. (1852). *A Scriptural View of a Soldier's Office and Honours.* Richmond, Yorkshire: John Bell.
Proctor, J. (1877). *In Memoriam. A Sermon Preached on the…Funeral of Mrs. Charlotte Agnes Law.* Hinckley, Leicestershire: Brocklehurst.
Purey-Cust, A. P. (1892). *God's Ordering, Our Sufficiency.* York: n. p.
Richardson, J. (1861). *Are You Ready?* Bury St Edmunds: Thompson.
Rowell, G. (1974). *Hell and the Victorians.* Oxford: Oxford University Press.
Sandford, C.W. (1901). *The Queen and Mother of Her People.* Oxford: n.p.
Scott, T. (1808). *The Duty and Advantage of Remembering Deceased Ministers.* Buckingham: Seeley.
Shepherd, C. A. M., Winslow, O., and Noel, B. W. (1850). *Three Funeral Sermons Delivered December 9 1849, the Sunday after the Funeral of the Rev J. H. Evans.* London: James Paul.
Shindler, R. (1853). *The Saints' Choice of Christ, and Security in Him.* Cranbrook: R. Waters.
Sinclair, W. M. (1885). *Gordon and England.* London: Hatchards.
Smith, E. (1868). *The Strait betwixt Two.* Liverpool: T. Brakell.
Steane, E. (1837). *The Eternal King.* London: Thos. Ward & Co.
Steward, G. (1852). *The Duke of Wellington.* Glasgow: n.p.
Sturges, T. R. H. (1901). *Queen Victoria the Good.* London: E. Marlborough.
Talon, T. K. (1880). *The Tay Bridge Disaster: Was it Accident or Judgement?* Edinburgh: D. Douglas.
Thorne, S. L. (1860). *The Security of the Saints in Life and their Consolation in Death.* Shebbear: Samuel Thorne.
Thornton, T. (1863). *Religion in Humble Life.* London: Rivington.
Tondini, C., and Collins, H. (1878). *Two Sermons Preached on the Death of Ambrose Lisle March Phillipps de Lisle.* No place or publisher.
Vaughan, C. J. (1861). *The Mourning of the Land, and the Mourning of the Families.* Cambridge: Macmillan.
—— (1892). *The Sympathy of Jesus Christ with Sickness and Sorrow.* London: n.p.

Warner, G. T., and Vaughan, C. J. (1849). *The Axe Laid Unto the Root of the Trees*. Harrow: J. S. Crossley.

Wheeler, M. (1990). *Death and the Future Life in Victorian Literature and Theology*. Cambridge: Cambridge University Press.

Wirgman, A. T. (1901). *Queen Victoria of Blessed Memory*. London: Longmans, Green and Co.

Wolffe, J. (1996). 'Responding to National Grief: Memorial Sermons on the Famous in Britain 1800–1914'. *Mortality* 1: 283–96.

—— (2000). *Great Deaths: Grieving, Religion and Nationhood in Victorian and Edwardian Britain*. Oxford: Oxford University Press.

—— (2010). 'British Sermons on National Events', in R. H. Ellison (ed.), *A New History of the Sermon: The Nineteenth Century*. Leiden: Brill, 181–206.

PART IV
CONTROVERSIES, AND THE DEVELOPMENT OF IDEAS

CHAPTER 22

HARD LABOUR: INSTITUTIONAL BENEVOLENCE AND THE DEVELOPMENT OF NATIONAL EDUCATION

BOB TENNANT

> The children of country villages shou'd, I think, seldom or never be suffered to go to those schools that are set up in towns; lest by seeing the easier and more plentiful manner in which tradesmen live, they shou'd get an aversion to low diet and hard labour, and so become useless and lost to the publick.
>
> (Chandler: 37)

THE sermon is that part of the liturgy which both expresses and develops a communion's confession and guides its members in specific practical applications of faith (e.g. Lose: 3; Padgett: xiii). The creation of a Church-sponsored national system of basic education required the development of robust procedures in the charitable societies' sermons so that liturgy, doctrine, and pedagogy could combine effectively. Indeed, an estimated 5 per cent of the total published sermon output was devoted to this.

In exploring the characteristics of pulpit preaching as the English charity-schools developed from thinly-scattered, ad hoc local provision into a national system, this chapter first considers a sample case of sermon exegesis and then explores sermons' roles in three contrasting loci: the Gravel Lane Dissenting charity-school (Gravel Lane); the annual assemblies of the Cities of London and Westminster charity-schools, sponsored by the Society for Promoting Christian Knowledge (SPCK); and local fund-raising for the Incorporated National Society for Promoting the Education of the Poor in the

Principles of the Established Church (NS). The present chapter focuses on charity schools in England but it is believed that those in Ireland, Wales, and Scotland are compatible with this account.

In the earlier eighteenth century a large body of sermons, almost entirely Whiggish and, when occasion demanded, anti-Jacobite, explored the duty of mutual charity in the context of the Church–State relationship. Titles like these are self-explanatory: *Universal Benevolence... With... a Farther Justification of the Principles of the Whiggs* (Squires); *The Obligations of the Clergy to Promote a Legal Subjection to his Majesty, and Mutual Charity Among Their Fellow-Subjects* (Bean); *Mutual Charity the Most Perfect Bond of Christian Unity* (Hayley); and, from a Dissenter, *Moderation and Charity, Recommended* (Dodson). Promoting charity-schools, and loyalty within them, was a key component of these sermons and Whigs were alert to any suspicions of disloyalty or subversion in school managers (e.g. Lambe), with much effort put into developing and promulgating relevant theology.

The relations between the individual and society and between human ethical and biological nature were philosophized in Joseph Butler's *Analogy* of 1736 and his later sermons. They are limited by his use of the terms 'benevolence' and 'charity' (Tennant 2011a: ch. 3, 5). In this context, the terms 'society', 'charity', and 'benevolence' became loaded with political as well as philosophical and theological implications.

A word-search of sermon title pages offers to quantify the use of these terms. In Table 1, column A records the singly-published sermons catalogued by the British Library in four half-centuries, and column B the numbers and percentages of those in A which feature the string 'society' on their title page. The peak engagement of sermons with Societies was in the late eighteenth and early nineteenth centuries. Column C allows comparison of B's results with sermon title-pages containing the strings 'charity' (which may refer to organizations or the cardinal virtue) and/or 'benevolence'. While the frequency of hits on 'charity' declines chronologically, both absolutely and relatively to the populations of column A, the frequency of 'benevolence' features a high, century-long plateau (1750–1850). After 1851 the results of these searches are insignificant. Column D suggests that an initially strong collocation of philosophical terminology and charitable organization weakened through time.

As the table confirms, the eighteenth century began with intensive discussions about ideas of charity and continued with expositions of the concept of benevolence in relation

Table 1 Key word hits in titles of British Library holdings

Period	A: 'sermon'	B: ['sermon' & 'society']	C: ['sermon' & 'charity'] + ['sermon' & 'benevolence']	D: (C/B)%
1701–1750	6237	246 (3.9%)	216 + 8 = 224	92%
1751–1800	5785	515 (8.9%)	165 + 25 = 190	37%
1801–1850	12647	1148 (9.1%)	151 + 19 = 170	15%
1851–1900	10541	245 (2.3%)	28 + 3 = 31	13%

Note: Search performed 28/02/2010

to charitable societies, this being especially notable during the period of Butler's theological (as opposed to his later philosophical) pre-eminence.

Enlightenment theories of 'natural' humankind and 'self-evident' rights continued to develop through the eighteenth century, as did purely secular ideas about the relationships of nation, capital, and credit (Colley: *passim*; Brantlinger: ch. 3; Macdonald: chs. 6, 7) and about an imperialist policy (Black 1994; Black 2006: ch. 16). The SPCK, whose reach became global, was a part of this and its corporate discussions centred on this environment's moral dynamics. Turning first to the exegetical role of sermons, we will consider the use of the popular text Proverbs 22:6—'Train up a child in the way he should go: and when he is old, he will not depart from it'—as applied to charity-school children.

This might be supposed the biblical text of first resort for a sermon about educating children. It is therefore remarkable that in the first four decades of the eighteenth century it was used in this context only twice: by Daniel Waterland in a 1723 sermon for the SPCK and by John Hurrion in 1730 for Gravel Lane. Then, in 1745, it was used by Joseph Butler for the SPCK, in a powerful account of the psychological basis of society and the reinforcement of the natural affections by habituation and the educated conscience (Tennant 2011a: ch. 2) which exerted an immediate and profound effect on Protestant theology and conversation about moral and religious education. Thereafter, for ninety years, Proverbs 22:6 was a favourite text in the SPCK. Besides many provincial instances, it was used by Gloster Ridley (1757), Josiah Tucker (1766), Jonathan Shipley (1777), George Huntingford (1796), Herbert Marsh (1811a), and John Jenkinson (1828)—more frequently than any other text. All these SPCK preachers, and many of the Gravel Lane series, for example, Furneaux, Calder, Wilton, and Lewis, were either known followers of Butler or heavily influenced by him: they use Butlerian vocabulary in contexts which support the suggestion that it is used with terminological accuracy. In no case can a preacher be shown to use the key terms 'affection', 'conscience', and 'benevolence' in ways incompatible with Butler's account of human development. This thoroughgoing philosophizing created a most unusual sermons corpus: theorizing was its predominant characteristic.

In his sermon for the benefit of the London hospitals Butler had sketched a social theory combining the creation and distribution of wealth, the quasi-familial duties of employers, poor children's routes to citizenship, and economic emancipation. From this he had proposed that 'some Share of the [charity-school] Childrens Time [be employed] in easy Labour, suitable to their Age' (Butler 1740: 20). He had done this, however, in the context of a discussion of sanctions against criminal behaviour, holding that 'the only Purposes of Punishments less than capital, are to reform the Offenders themselves' (Butler 1740: 20), thus securing the intimate connection of the educational, the emancipatory, and the corrective. Now, in his SPCK sermon, Butler extended his argument to encompass the legal and ethical:

> in that legal Provision for the Maintenance of the Poor, poor Children must doubtless have had a Part in common with grown People...And...there must immediately

> have been Need also of some *particular* legal Provision in Behalf of poor Children for their Education; this not being included in what we call their Maintenance... In the mean Time, as the Poor still increased or Charity still lessened, many poor Children were left exposed. (Butler 1745: 10-11).

Thus works of charity came to be seen as an expression of the extrovert benevolence which complements introvert self-love and completes the sociable and good person. The total of applied benevolence must increase at least proportionately with the population and the naturally increasing imbalance of wealth distribution. In tying together dynamic economic reality with Acts of Parliament and people's ethical consciousness, Butler ('...some *particular* legal Provision...') in effect proposes education publicly funded under statute law. He argues that the Elizabethan statutes implied a duty, as yet unfulfilled, to educate poor children at public expense: 'the Education of poor Children was all along taken Care of, by voluntary Charities, more or less: but obliging us by Law to maintain the Poor, was new in the Reign of Queen *Elizabeth*' (Butler 1745: 10). While the full fruits were not seen until the 1870 Act—for which Gladstone credited Butler's legacy (Gladstone: 2:292)—it was, however, possible to approach this doctrine through the supply of charity-schools unsupported by statute, and this is what the SPCK started to see as its role (Jacob: 365–6 and *passim*). This is the context in which Butler acknowledged the need for charity children's 'easy Labour' and their placing-out into apprenticeships and domestic labour; he even suggests a prototype case conference system, each placement being 'approved by every one' (Butler 1745: 16)—clergy, managers, employer, child. Thus he confronts that most insidious and populist suggestion of the satirist Bernard Mandeville, which was to be given fresh currency by reaction against the French Revolution: that lower-class children, if educated, would be a socially disruptive force. We have already noted the position of Samuel Chandler, Butler's friend at the Tewkesbury Dissenting academy; a 1723 predecessor in the Gravel Lane series had argued that

> Our Design is not to advance these Children above the Necessity of hard Labour...nor are we in Circumstances to do it...How many Industrious People have we seen lye out of Business for want of a little Education[!] (Neal: 13)

It was Butler who provided the classic arguments for the SPCK against the twin objections that educating the poor made for social instability and a potential shortage of domestic and manual labour and that religious education was merely anti-rational indoctrination. This was accepted across a wide theological range in the Church of England. Thomas Ashton preached for the SPCK that charity-school education was necessary because reason did not direct children towards an effective ethics, while Christian acculturation was necessary because to leave ethics to children's free enquiry was to abandon them to the 'Seminary...[of] the Streets' (Ashton: 21–3, 24). Lewis Bagot, Bishop of Norwich, remarked that the human affections were supplied by the 'great Author of Nature' specifically to fit us as 'social creatures...bound to all that variety of relative duties [i.e. duties in relation to one another], which arise from a state of society, which constitute it's beauty and happiness, and are all comprehended in that one Evangelical term, Charity' (Bagot: 3). The sceptics are 'not supported by the evidence of fact'—this is Butler's chief forensic strategy in *The Analogy*—and the Christian's duty is 'to consider mankind, as they actually are' (Butler 1745: 4–5). The human condition is such that others' help, driven by feelings of charity, is required in infancy and old age; this is recognized by England's statute laws—'the only State upon earth, to it's honour be it spoken, that hath ever provided a fixed and permanent maintenance for the poor and helpless' (Butler 1745: 5–6). The defence, and by implication extension, of this statutory provision is the highest duty of charity.

The question of educating the poor resolved itself into two components: in order of priority, first, Christian acculturation and indoctrination; and second, the provision of basic work-related intellectual and manual skills. The common factor was the inextricably related concepts of liberty and citizenship. These implied offering orphan and destitute children (and, indeed, slaves—Butler 1739: 13–14) a route into the class of citizen, the wide social group which comprised both those who owned property (and could vote) and those who sold their labour (Butler 1748: 6–7; Tucker: 20; Deakin and Wilkinson: ch. 2). During the passage of the first of the Master and Servant Acts in 1747 Butler authoritatively theorized the citizenry as co-extensive with 'society' and analogous to an extended family (Butler 1739: 13–14; Butler 1748: 26–7), within which the citizen enjoyed not only political and economic but also religious liberties and duties of mutual charity. Without these the dispossessed would be the merely passive objects of others' donations, unable to reciprocate. The duty of the charity children towards their parents, guardians, trustees, and teachers was a constant theme of the various series' preaching. In this Butler was possibly drawing on his Dissenting background: '[Christians] are of the same [= a single] household', as a Gravel Lane preacher had put it (Price: 6). When Roger Flexman preached to Gravel Lane about Abraham's 'family' he included the wider household of servants as a matter of course (Flexman: 22–6).

In the nineteenth century Butler's reputation as a social thinker retreated before his advance as a moral philosopher and there was a resurgence of trite and *ad hominem* arguments, perhaps made disingenuously (e.g. Coulson: 12–15), that any such labour shortages could be made good by importing illiterate cheap labour from Ireland. The title of Thomas Garbett's 1832 NS sermon is self-explanatory: *The Existence of Rich and Poor a Necessary Condition of Society, and the Source of Reciprocal Obligations: a Sermon, for the Benefit of the Deptford National School and School of Industry*.

Irony aside, preachers consistently thought that children's gratitude should be expressed through their work at school: actual manual labour, to help fit them for adulthood, teach steadiness and concentration, and generate income towards the masters' salaries. This, of course, threatened to reverse the schools' priorities and emphasize the revenue stream over pedagogy. In practice, habituation in both '*general duties*, which we owe to all men, and every man alike' and 'the duties of *particular relations*' was 'inforced' (Furneaux: 14) by the catechism and external discipline.

The punitive seeps in readily: Samuel Chandler thought that the children's very clothing 'should...teach *them* humility' as a check on their 'sloth, intemperance and insolence' (Chandler: 27–8), a topic which recurs in Jonathan Edwards's preaching to children on such topics (Breckus: 315). 'Discipline'—habituation to routine—is not a euphemism for beating, as eighteenth-century charity-schools seem generally to have eschewed this, there being cases of masters dismissed for beatings. Thomas Secker, the future Primate and close friend of Butler, had already called for children to be engaged in suitable work, adopting the Irish hard labour model (Secker: 25–30). In his 1766 SPCK sermon Josiah Tucker discussed this in a long footnote (Tucker: 12–14). Starting with the consideration that raw materials should be 'cheap...so that the Loss occasioned by the Heedlessness of Youth...might not be heavy' he proceeded via considerations of design, marketing, and skill acquisition to avoiding restraint of trade and undermining apprenticeship practices. This led via the question of staff payments (to be a proportion of turnover) to proposed limitations on parents' right to abrogate the children's contracts: some parents had objected to children working for schools rather than for themselves (Jacob: 375).

The problem of reconciling charitable love and educationally effective discipline was, it seems, due to the poverty of available conceptual equipment, which extended beyond the pulpit. Thus Henry Fielding, in his 1753 *Proposal for Making an Effectual [workhouse] Provision for the Poor*, is greatly at odds with his humane novelistic creativity in displaying an almost Sadean relish for the minute administrative details of fifty-nine proposed rules. In Fielding's opinion, institutionalized idleness is intolerable for both operational and financial efficiency and its cure must be through the administration of a disjunctive shock. This contrasts oddly with the perhaps empirically better-grounded developments in theories of slave education. James Ramsay, noting that slave labour was only a third as productive as free, argued that the problem of demoralization could only be tackled in the very long term:

> Perhaps successive generations are necessary to make the faculties of savages capable of the present common European improvements; and our slaves are not yet arrived to the rank of savage. A savage...acts for himself, and the advancement of his proper concerns; but a slave...has nothing, he can call his own. (Ramsay: 221)

Thus a theory of acculturation was brought into the theology of charity and the philosophy of citizenship, with work and the acquisition of property being the keys to bringing the child, or colonized subject, into maturity as a social and ethical being. The Butlerian exegesis of Proverbs 22:6 had produced a doctrine of adult benevolence and juvenile hard labour: his caveat about the need for such labour to be 'easy' was insufficiently theorized to be effective within the prevailing culture.

A wider survey of the three corpora of sermons provides insight into the schools' more complex ideological environment. Charitable and benevolent organizations engaged society through the procedure of a published sermon with an appended Annual Report, generally supported by statistics. The reports gradually grew to full book-length, but the sermon always functioned as the theological anchor, engaging the Societies' mission with the developing situation.

It is convenient to take the Gravel Lane sermons first. During the reign of James II Dissenters established a free charity-school in the Southwark docklands to combat Roman Catholic missionary work locally. The Lane was named from the gravel handled in ballasting and unballasting ships; preachers were frequently mindful of the effect on morale of such heavy, poorly-paid, and filthy work. The school raised funds at Westminster, among sympathetic Whigs (Billingsley: 29), but the big event was the sermon delivered to the children and their largely Dissenting supporters each January 1st (very occasionally on the 2nd) in Southwark parish church. From 1714 to 1796 these were usually published, although less frequently after 1776. While some were clearly adapted from existing sermons, most were composed specially. Most include a stereotyped account, provided by the managers, of the school's history, anti-Romanist and educational missions, and achievements. There is no continuity of theme or common theological ground: an Arminian sermon on the text 'The Grace of our Lord Jesus Christ Considered' (Denham) is followed by a stoutly Calvinist 'This year thou shalt die' (Read) and by elegant 'Reflections in Human Life' (the grammarian John Milner). Thus there is no corporate conversation, a feature of the SPCK and the Society for the Propagation of the Gospel (SPG) series, and no diachronic revaluation of the school's mission. It is therefore not surprising that after growing from fifty to two hundred scholars by 1760, the school stagnated and lost confidence as the wider charity-schools movement grew (Lewis: 23; Walker: 22): whereas, for example, Butler always saw diversity and conflict as a resource for what he called 'the Cement of Society', John Hodge saw complexity in the human body (an analogue of society) as inimical to survival: 'the more numerous the parts are of which our frame consists, so much the more numerous must be the dangers to which it is continually exposed' (Hodge: 12).

It is notable that the Gravel Lane preachers very often addressed the assembled children directly: their, and the managers', accounts of charitable benevolence were thus linked with the children's duty of gratitude, which required training and enforcement. However, the preachers never associated themselves or the adults with sharing the children's specific moral duties. The heavily Butlerian John Calder observed in 1772 that '[W]e are not equally debtors to all. In Charity Nature dictates predilection, Reason distinguishes among its claimants, and Nature, Reason and Religion agree to appropriate the greatest kindness to the worthiest objects. These then are they, who are of the "Household of Faith"' (Calder: 9). Thus Butler's account of the psychological environment of ethics was used—ironically, given his Dissenting origins and his strategy of inclusiveness (Tennant 2011a: ch. 3)—to reinforce Dissenting sectarianism. Since the children, aged around 10, were most unlikely to have understood the preachers' theology, these sermons can only have served as encouragements to the managers and community to maintain and even intensify school discipline. Only rarely is there an attempt to preach a communality of interest of children and adults. Edmund Butcher preached that 'The religious services of the family, and especially those of a Lord's-day evening, are frequently so conducted as to give them [= the children] no pleasure...Whether they shall become the plagues or the ornaments of society; whether they shall be the staff or the disgrace of our old age' (Butcher: 9, 16). Such thoughts might perhaps have been better left unheard by street-wise children.

In general, both rhetorically and doctrinally, the adult and juvenile listeners were treated separately, to the extent that while preacher and adults were often joined in a community of interest by the preacher's use of the second person plural, this never once happened between preacher and children. Andrew Kippis unwittingly illustrated this with an abrupt syntactical switch: 'we [= adults] should be solicitous to imitate the character which is given of Jesus in the text...I [= preacher] would particularly urge it upon young persons, that they [= children] should endeavour to excel in these divine attainments' (Kippis: 23). Later in the series the children's perspective is acknowledged more frequently. With an eye on their Docklands origin Thomas Jervis inserted images of storms and seafaring and took up the traditional Dissenting theology of Jesus as the children's 'friend': 'while you continue diligent, peaceable, frugal, and honest, you will never want a friend. For...*the* LORD *will take you up*. If you are *good* children, GOD will bless, he will ever love you, and will ever befriend you' (Jervis: 13–14, 22–3).

With a single exception (Moody), the sermons were issued by a relatively stable series of publishers: predominantly John Clark up to 1729, mostly Richard Hett in the 1730s and James Waugh in the 1740s and 1750s. Then for twenty years a wide variety of printers was used, often with multiple publishers in ever-shifting groups—perhaps indicating an attempt at stronger marketing—until from 1776 the series passed almost exclusively to Goldney in Paternoster Row. Towards the end of the published series the venue changed from St Thomas's parish church to Salter's Hall (Collyer). Such a move to the centre, combined with a falling roll, is a sure sign that local support for the school was slackening in vitality.

The mode of publication of the Gravel Lane series contrasts sharply with the better-resourced and nationally organized SPCK: here the Society's regular printers were used and the sermon bound with the annual report, which progressively expanded from a dozen pages to two hundred. Both in its annual metropolitan series and those of its local committees, the contrast with the sermons for the single Dissenting school is immense. The SPCK and its sister Society, the SPG, had been designed to be complementary and there was a great deal of overlap in their lists of annual preachers. While, unlike the SPG's annual sermon, the SPCK's was never the perquisite of the bishops, nor a de facto requirement of candidates for the highest Church offices, nevertheless between 1702 and 1832 a majority of SPCK preachers were, or were to become, bishops. Indeed, of the 260 individual sermons preached in the two series, sixty-five men preached both, constituting 50 per cent of the total: these were all bishops or future bishops, including four of the six archbishops of Canterbury, from Hutton to Howley.

During its first century the SPCK had seen the numbers of charity-schools under its auspices in the three kingdoms rise to 1,850, but there were more than ten thousand parishes and even one school per parish would be inadequate provision. Apart from facilitating staff appointments and supplying books it had no control over charity-schools and was unfitted, even constitutionally precluded, from founding them. Its local structures—at parish, archdeaconry or diocesan level—developed late and largely as the result of central policy: with regard to charity-schools (but not its strategic mission) it inadvertently inhibited local initiative. Central administration was weak: the statistics presented in its annual reports were essentially unchanged from 1761 to 1799, when there were 43,275 children in SPCK-sponsored schools in the three kingdoms (10,061 of these were girls). Assuming a target group of the three-year age band from 8 to 10 years old, this certainly represents less than 10 per cent of the target population of working-class children.

Nevertheless, the SPCK sermons constitute a series in the full sense of the term, conforming to the disciplines of a literary sub-genre and sustaining and developing theological themes, so that, as we have discussed, sequences of preachers were consciously in conversation with each other; the series thus became the Society's forum for ideology and doctrine. The annual sermon was a great and unique occasion: until 1782 up to 5,000 children, with their masters, mistresses, and trustees, members of the SPCK and the Corporation of the City, crammed into a City parish church, St Sepulchre's, or Christ Church, 'A Spectacle so singular, of so many Thousand Children in such decent Array, and regularity of Behaviour, with one Heart and Mouth praising GOD in the Beauty of Holiness' (Burton: 25). In 1782 the meeting moved to St Paul's Cathedral where, in specially-constructed stands under the dome, up to 10,000 children could be accommodated, double the previous capacity, a tremendous and even triumphalist expansion of the occasion. It is notable that when the 25-year-old William Blake wrote his Song of Innocence about the occasion he set it, either by mistake or design, on Holy Thursday, a date which it had not occupied in his lifetime, but whose sacramental associations were artistically and theologically compelling. In contrast to the Gravel Lane series, but in keeping with its doctrinally strategic nature, no preacher addressed the children directly until, in the most dramatic moment in both series, Henry Whitfeld displayed a rhetorical switch, deeply emotional and revolutionary in its inclusiveness, from the adults to the children—'But as for *you*, My Children, for on this day, I think, I have some right to call you Mine' (Whitfeld: 22; Tennant 2011*b*: 335–6).

By the turn of the century strong but geographically uneven growth in population was challenging the existing parochial system. Preaching in Cambridge in 1834, Thomas Thorp put it thus:

> 19/20 of the people were without accommodation. The natural consequence was the alienation from the church of thousands against whom she was compelled to shut her doors... [The Church is] a great National Trust, earnestly engaged in doing her duty to those who belong to her Communion, and content to be answerable (if she be allowed the means) for those that belong to none. (Thorp: 17–18)

As they inherited the SPCK's charity-school responsibilities, NS preachers (e.g. Boone) debated whether the State itself should provide universal, and, in the new age of Catholic Emancipation and Reform Acts, necessarily secular education. That this debate was conducted in pulpits across the country, rather than in controversial pamphlets, had the effect—consciously and deliberately—of congregations' receiving the question into the witnessing and shaping of their faith. Thus James Pears, preaching to the Bath District Committees of the SPCK, SPG, and NS in 1827 about the secular Society for Promoting Useful Knowledge:

> the Society proposes to enter upon another branch of science, that of the human mind—the intellectual and moral faculties of man—and 'his duties both towards

himself as an individual, and towards others as a member of society.' Now this certainly is teaching religion, but not the religion of Christ. (Pears: 9-10)

The extrovert energies evident in the work of the SPCK and SPG, their ambition in remodelling the English expression of faith in public policy, demanded the cooption of the entire nation, but the inclusion of anti-Anglican groups was unacceptable for some: we see diagnoses like this one, of the notionally ecumenical British and Foreign Bible Society:

> *the 'Circulation of the Bible' has been confounded with the 'Diffusion of pure Religion,'* ... [but in] a Society, where one Party [the Church of England] can have but one Object [the diffusion of pure religion], and the other may not unfairly be presumed to have more [increasing affiliations], in which the former can have no Interest, it is evident, that a Connection will be formed on very unequal Terms ... [The Dissenters] have laboured to procure so many of the regular Clergy to join with them in an Association, the Operations of which they will be totally unable ... either to counter-act or controul. (*A Letter from a Rector*: 14-15, 34-5)

It became evident that to name a society 'national' was to issue a manifesto and thus enter an arena of bitter political and theological controversy, in which the SPCK suffered a strategic defeat at the hands of a movement built on the pedagogical work of the Quaker Joseph Lancaster. The NS was set up in 1811 specifically to remove the SPCK's organizational bottlenecks to expansion. The problem of human resources was solved by importing from India the 'Madras' system which Andrew Bell had developed for the acculturation, education, and conversion of Indian children and the mixed-race offspring of the East India Company's army. There were enthusiastic reports about its effectiveness and its producing responsible young monitors who, in emergencies, could run entire schools and ultimately become qualified teachers (Bell 1805: 37-9; National Society 1827: 26). One result of this was the foundation of teacher training for non-graduates, addressing the chronic shortage of teaching staff (Burgess: ch. 9; National Society 1813; National Society 1833; National Society 1839). However, Lancaster was shown to have borrowed his system from Bell, with minimum acknowledgement and maximum misrepresentation (Marsh 1811*b*) and was accused of reintroducing into the public sphere the deism which Butler had long before neutralized (Daubeny: 1-3, 13-15). The increasingly urgent debate provoked some of the most masterly SPCK sermons (Marsh 1811*a*; Landon). The monitor system maximized educational output at minimum cost, but its rigidity accelerated the transition from 'easy' to 'hard' labour, both Lancaster and the NS aiming to industrialize education, imposing on the children not only manual but pedagogical labour, enforced, as was appreciated by contemporaries, by the schoolmaster's all-seeing role in something like Bentham's favourite 'panopticon' prison system, with 'the hundred hands of Briareus, the hundred eyes of Argus, and the wings of Mercury' (Hollingsworth: title-page):

> Machinery has been contrived for spinning twenty skeins of silk, and twenty hanks of cotton, where one was spun before; but no contrivance has been sought for, or

devised, that twenty children may be educated in moral and religious principles, with the same facility and expense, as one was taught before. The fruits and flowers of our fields and gardens are multiplied and improved with great skill and labour; but the immortal spirits of our youths are suffered to languish and perish for ever for want of due culture, and Christian education. (Bell 1807: 17)

In contrast to the preaching- and theology-centred SPCK, the NS's organizational mode was distinctly original, giving financial incentives for localities to affiliate existing schools to it and stimulating new schools by grants disbursed solely through Diocesan Central Committees. This compelled the formation of a hierarchically structured national organization of dioceses, deaneries, and parishes. Expansion was achieved by setting the bar high for applicant boards of governors, so that affiliation and accreditation were high status privileges. By 1822 as many schools were still outside the union as inside it, but pupils joining the union numbered in the tens of thousands annually and the rate was accelerating. In 1829, a typical year, sixty grants were made, totalling £4,282 (National Society 1830: 7). By 1834, the Revd G. E. Whyley, preaching to the Dunstable District Committees of the SPCK and SPG, reported, as many as 900,000 children were in affiliated schools, secure in 'a National Church... [whose] saving sacraments of Christ [are] administered by a rightly ordained and divinely commissioned ministry' (Whyley: 14, 21).

Soon expressions of Marsh's and Landon's fears, that the Church of England, in moving so strongly towards the sacramental aspect of religious practice, had ceded ground in wider society, became more general. An anonymous minister lamented that 'It has, unhappily, become too much the fashion to consider preaching as the principal part of the Church service: people... eagerly run after what they deem fine preaching... Hence arises their fondness for the conventicle in preference to the Church' (*A Comparative View*: 16). By 1829 Henry Drummond was able openly to claim that 'The connexion between Religion and Civil Policy is at an end. The very idea of such a state is evaporated out of men's minds' (Drummond: 1). The NS was helping to create a secular polity, saturated in Christian ethics, but in which charitable activity and Christian duty had no necessary connection. Dickens satirized just this in *Bleak House*'s internationally-minded Mrs Jellyby, her neglected children running riot through a neglected house.

These fears were felt with especial force in the provinces. In 1824 Frances Merewether preached that home missions undermined the strengths and prerogatives of parishes. In Blackburn in 1841 Jackson Porter's sermon for the benefit of the NS argued that the identity of Church and State was defined by their sharing overlapping charitable aims, while in Norfolk in 1850 William Henry Henslowe published *Reasons for Not Preaching in Aid of [the NS] in the Parishes of Wormegay and Tottenhill* because he believed that such aims were not embodied in the Society's constitution. As so often at this time, conservative and constitutionalist arguments were theoretically strong but unable to resist the greater force of theological and organizational innovation to meet the opportunities for evangelism which were increasing at accelerating rates. All this was a sharp contrast with the optimism of the brief period of Anglican triumphalism between the battle of Waterloo and the 1819 King's Letter for the benefit of the SPG. When William Oxnam, preaching to the SPCK in Exeter, noted the presence of 1,500 charity children and his joy at their mass praise of God, he proclaimed that 'The great and the learned, no less than the poor and illiterate, stand equally in need of the help and comforts [Christianity] administers' and rejoiced, that '[the SPCK] has brought multitudes of *nominal* Christians, who lay in almost pagan darkness, to the knowledge of "the truth as it is in Jesus"' (Oxnam: 7, 12, 13). NS sermons, by contrast, celebrated more secular and statistically tangible achievements than this.

Indeed, it is notable that the NS was not driven by exegesis or preaching. There are no 'Baldwin's Gardens sermons' (the headquarters and central school of the Society) to correspond with the Gravel Lane and St Paul's sermons. There is not even a corpus identified with the pioneering teacher training college at Cheltenham, despite its winning support from the great Evangelical educator Francis Close, for many years the local rector. Indeed, this theological inertness is a point against the NS project made as early as Charles Daubeny's 1809 SPCK sermon. This may be the result of the NS's much greater initial reliance on State subventions; in its dash for growth it could not match the SPCK's or SPG's theological vitality.

In this context, Table 2, which records the biblical texts used in the corpora, using Spaulding as a comparator, provides interesting insights into charity-school sermons. The 'main books' column shows that Matthew, with its Christological resources, and Proverbs, with the 22:6 text, predominate and the exegetical basis of the corpora's theology is consequently distinct from the comparator's. In the balance between Old and New Testaments, however, the SPCK sermons, at both national and district levels, approximate closely to the norm. Thus, although their subjects are restricted by their occasions, and their theology specialized, they demonstrate a coherence with Church rhetoric as a whole.

Table 2 Texts of Societies' annual sermons

Society (date-range analysed)	Sermons tabulated	Old Testament	New Testament	Main books
Gravel Lane (1714–94)	52	46%	54%	Proverbs (12%); Matthew (10%) Ecclesiastes (10%)
SPCK (annual) (1733–1858)	121	37%	63%	Matthew (14%); Proverbs (12%); Luke (7%)
SPCK (district) (selected; 1733–1858)	172	38%	62%	Matthew (15%); Proverbs (12%); Isaiah (8%)
NS (selected; 1820–1833)	17	18%	82%	[Matthew; Proverbs; Acts]
[comparator: Spaulding, 1995]	[c.34,000]	[37%]	[63%]	[Matthew (10%); Psalms (9%); Luke (6%)]

Note: NS items are not annual sermons but those raising funds from King's Letters.

The SPCK sermons are firmly oriented around Christ's own ministry as the model of the Society's—the view of Christ as teacher hardly needs exemplifying, especially in the period of the Enlightenment—with exegetical consideration of the Old Testament, particularly Proverbs, supplementing it with texts which had traditionally provided a stabilizing theology of wisdom in both Jewish and Christian cultures (Deane-Drummond: 226). It is notable that the SPCK provincial sermons, in which Isaiah features prominently, are distinctly more concerned than the national series with discussing the local educational mission in the context of the liturgy as interpreted through the Prophetic books (Rogers).

The Gravel Lane series is not very dissimilar from the SPCK provincial sermons in this respect. In contrast, the NS sermons, whose relative scarcity prevents the presentation of significant statistics, are very heavily New Testament in nature, and distinctly less exegetical. An orthodox view of this would predict theological instability in the basic organizational fabric of the NS, the Word being presented in a decontextualized and therefore weakened way, despite the emphatic urgency with which its mission is presented. If, in the interest of expanding provision by stereotyping methods and theology, the NS retreated somewhat from the Word, it is also notable that it retreated somewhat from the word in a linguistic sense. From 1836, with the foundation of the Home and Colonial School Society, and its strong association with the brother-and-sister team of Charles and Elizabeth Mayo, Pestalozzi's object- rather than word-focused teaching system for younger children came to prominence (Mayo; Burgess: 66). This quintessentially non-theological educational medium was predicated on the thesis that personal and institutional piety was less important than the system of learning through sensory enrichment and experience (Heafford: 60–5 and *passim*). The sermon was consequently displaced to the ideological periphery.

Thus the NS revisited 'hard labour' from a different direction and a shallower theology. An elaborate, but not atypical, example is *On the Connection of Works of Manual Industry, with Religious Education*, an 1810 District Committee sermon by the archdeacon of Bath, Charles Abel Moysey, who argues that work emancipates spiritually and economically.

> At Bath...the elder boys are often employed...in a garden, the produce of which is sold for the benefit of the school; and in the manufacture of linen...which is easily made, in consequence of...simple and ingenious machines...machines which...render it easy for children to do the work...[This] is at once a reward to the scholars, and an instruction in useful labour; and supplies also, by the sale of the different commodities, a fund for rewards [to the children]. (Moysey: 17–18)

The cheapness of the Madras system was seen as one of its greatest assets, maximizing educational delivery by involving the children in a virtuous circle of activity—learning, helping their juniors, working (Spry: 15; Coulson: 19—another use of Proverbs 22:6). Its method revealed the empirical strength of the Butlerian insight that 'Human society is only a collection of families; and it is the concern of the whole that each part should be well governed' (Goddard: 12).

Moysey's sermon was dedicated to the Duke of Clarence, whose attending at least one meeting in Goddard's parish may be taken to symbolize the shift from missionary to secular in the ideological environment. The NS, a Church organization which in a single generation increased the pupil numbers in charity-schools from 50,000 to a million, did so by stereotyping both pedagogical methods and theology. Its elaborate annual reports and systems of quality assurance displaced from its institutional core the vivid sermons which we have found exemplified in the Gravel Lane and, especially, the SPCK series.

The SPCK and the NS brought the country to within sight of a comprehensive system of schooling with a minimum of governmental support. In the event, the Evangelicals' belief that teachers' individual witness of faith would suffice to maintain an element of moral sanctity in the public space was to prove mistaken. Nevertheless, well into the 1830s, the sermon proved a sufficiently powerful and flexible rhetorical medium to allow the theological and philosophical exploration of children's needs and to convene a public consensus on the once highly controversial proposition that a national system of education was a moral duty and an economic necessity.

References

A Comparative View of the Merits of the Society for Promoting Christian Knowledge, and the Bible Society. (1817). Oxford: Munday.

A Letter from a Rector to his Curate, on the Subject of The Bible Society. (1816). London: J. Hatchard.

Ashton, T. (1760). *A Sermon Preached [at] the Yearly Meeting of... the Charity-Schools.* London: B. Dod.

Bagot, L. (1788). *A Sermon Preached [at] the Yearly Meeting of... the Charity-Schools.* London: S. Brooke.

Bean, C. (1716). *The Obligations of the Clergy to Promote a Legal Subjection to His Majesty.* London: R. Knaplock.

Bell, A. (1805). *An Experiment in Education, Made at the Male Asylum at Egmore, Near Madras.* London: T. Cadell.

—— (1807). *Extract of a Sermon on the Education of the Poor.* London: T. Cadell.

Billingsley, S. (1759). *A Sermon Preached for... the Charity School in Gravel-Lane.* London: J. Waugh.

Black, J. (1994). *British Foreign Policy in an Age of Revolutions 1783–1793.* Cambridge: Cambridge University Press.

—— (2006). *George III: America's Last King.* New Haven, CT: Yale University Press.

Blake, W. (1789). *Songs of Innocence.* London: W. Blake.

Boone, J. S. (1833). *National Education. A Sermon.* London: Rivingtons.

Brantlinger, P. (1996). *Fictions of State: Culture and Credit in Britain, 1694–1994.* Ithaca, NY: Cornell University Press.

Breckus, C. A. (2001). 'Children of Wrath, Children of Grace', in M. J. Bunge (ed.), *The Child in Christian Thought.* Grand Rapids, MI: Eerdmans, 300–28.

Burgess, H. J. (1958). *Enterprise in Education.* London: National Society.

Burton, J. (1759). *A Sermon Preached [at] the Yearly Meeting of... the Charity-Schools.* London: B. Dod.

Butcher, E. (1794). *A Sermon Preached for… the Charity School in Gravel-Lane*. London: C. Whittingham.

Butler, J. (1739). *A Sermon Preached [at] the Yearly Meeting of… the Charity-Schools*. London: Knaptons.

—— (1740). *A Sermon Preached before the… Lord-Mayor*. London: Knaptons.

—— (1745). *A Sermon Preached [at] the Yearly Meeting of… the Charity-Schools*. London: B. Dod.

—— (1748). *A Sermon Preached… for the Relief of Sick and Diseased Persons*. London: H. Woodfall.

Calder, J. (1772). *A Sermon Preached for… the Charity School in Gravel-Lane*. London: S. Peyton.

Chandler, S. (1728). *A Sermon Preached for… the Charity School in Gravel-Lane*. London: J. Gray.

Colley, L. (1992). *Britons: Forging the Nation 1707–1837*. New Haven: Yale University Press.

Collyer, W. B. (1802). *A Sermon Preached for… the Charity School in Gravel-Lane*. London: T. Williams.

Coulson, H. (1823). *A Sermon, Preached in the Parish Church of Madron… in Aid of the Funds of the National Society*, in *Two Charity Sermons*. Penzance: T. Vigurs, 1826.

Daubeny, C. (1809). *A Sermon Preached [at] the Yearly Meeting of… the Charity-Schools*. London: Rivingtons.

Deakin, S., and Wilkinson, F. (2005). *The Law of the Labour Market*. Oxford: Oxford University Press.

Deane-Drummond, C. E. (2000). *Creation through Wisdom: Theology and the New Biology*. Edinburgh: T. and T. Clark.

Denham, J. (1738). *A Sermon Preached for… the Charity School in Gravel-Lane*. London: R. Ford.

Dodson, J. (1720). *Moderation and Charity… Preach'd… to the Associated Protestant Dissenting Ministers of Cumberland and Westmoreland*. London: E. Matthews.

Drummond, H. (1829). *A Christian View of the Present State of the Country, Its Causes and Consequences*. London: J. Hatchard.

Fielding, H. (1753). *A Proposal for Making an Effectual Provision for the Poor*. London: A. Millar.

Flexman, R. (1753). *A Sermon Preached for… the Charity School in Gravel-Lane*. London: J. Waugh.

Furneaux, P. (1755). *A Sermon Preached for… the Charity School in Gravel-Lane*. London: J. Waugh.

Garbett, T. (1832). *The Existence of Rich and Poor a Necessary Condition of Society, and the Source of Reciprocal Obligations*. London: Rivingtons.

Gladstone, W. E. (1897). *Butler's Works*. Oxford: Clarendon Press.

Goddard, C. (1820). *A Sermon… on Behalf of the National Schools of [St. John's] Parish*. London: Rivingtons.

Hayley, T. (1718). *Mutual Charity the Most Perfect Bond of Christian Unity*. London: T. Childe.

Heafford, M. (1967). *Pestalozzi*. London: Methuen.

Henslowe, W. H. (1850). *Reasons for Not Preaching in Aid of 'The National Society…' in the Parishes of Wormegay and Tottenhill, Norfolk*. Lynn: E. Longbottom.

Hodge, J. (1751). *A Sermon Preached for… the Charity School in Gravel-Lane*. London: J. Waugh.

Hollingsworth, N. J. (1812). *An Address to the Public...to which is added a Sermon*. London: Rivingtons.

Huntingford, G. (1796). *A Sermon Preached [at] the Yearly Meeting of...the Charity-Schools*. London: Rivingtons.

Hurrion, J. (1730). *A Sermon Preached for...the Charity School in Gravel-Lane*. London: R. Hett.

Jacob, W. M. (1994). 'The Eye of his Master: Children and Charity Schools', in D. Wood (ed.), *The Church and Childhood*. Oxford: Ecclesiastical History Society, 362–77.

Jenkinson, J. (1828). *A Sermon Preached [at] the Yearly Meeting of...the Charity-Schools*. London: SPCK.

Jervis, T. (1784). *A Sermon Preached for...the Charity School in Gravel-Lane*. London: J. Buckland.

Kippis, A. (1780). *A Sermon Preached for...the Charity School in Gravel-Lane*. London: H. Goldney.

Lambe, C. (1718). *An Account of a Charity School...in which the Disaffection to the Government of the Managers of it is Made Apparent*. London: B. Lintot.

Landon, W. (1812). *A Sermon Preached [at] the Yearly Meeting of...the Charity-Schools*. London: SPCK.

Lewis, G. (1789). *A Sermon Preached for...the Charity School in Gravel-Lane*. London: H. Goldney.

Lose, D. J. (2003). *Confessing Jesus Christ: Preaching in a Postmodern World*. Grand Rapids, MI: Eerdmans.

Macdonald, J. (2003). *A Free Nation Deep in Debt: the Financial Roots of Democracy*. New York: Farrar, Straus, and Giroux.

Mandeville, B. (1723). *Essay on Charity and Charity-Schools*. London: E. Parker.

Marsh, H. (1811a). *A Sermon Preached [at] the Yearly Meeting of...the Charity-Schools*. London: Rivingtons.

—— (1811b). *A Vindication of Dr. Bell's System of Tuition, in a Series of Letters*. London: Rivingtons.

Mayo, E. (1830). *Lessons on Objects*. London: R. B. Seeley.

Merewether, F. (1824). *Thoughts on the Present State of Popular Opinion in Matters of Religion in England...with a Postscript Respecting the Hone [sic] Missionary Society*. London: Rivingtons.

Milner, J. (1743). *A Sermon Preached for...the Charity School in Gravel-Lane*. London: J. Noon.

Moody, C. L. (1786). *A Sermon Preached for...the Charity School in Gravel-Lane*. Kingston: J. Buckland.

Moysey, C. A. (1820). *A Sermon on the Connection of Works of Manual Industry, with Religious Education. Preached...before the Bath and Wells Diocesan Society of the National Schools*. Bath: J. Barrett.

National Society. (1813). *National Society for the Education of the Poor*. London: Free-School.

—— (1827, 1830, 1839). *Annual Reports*. London: Rivingtons.

—— (1833). *The Practical Manual of the Madras, or National System of Education as practiced at the Society's central schools*. London: National Society.

Neal, D. (1723). *A Sermon Preached for...the Charity School in Gravel-Lane*. London: J. Clark.

Oxnam, W. (1818). *A Sermon Preached at St. Peter's Cathedral, Exeter*. Exeter: Risdon.

Padgett, A. G. (2003). *Science and the Study of God: a Mutuality Model for Theology and Science*. Grand Rapids, MI: Eerdmans.

Pears, J. (1827). *A Sermon Preached... at the Annual Meeting of the [SPCK, SPG and NS Bath District Committees]*. Bath: Rivingtons.

Porter, J. (1841). *Identity of Interest the Directive Principle of Christian and National Charity*. Blackburn: W. and C. Tiplady.

Price, S. (1726). *A Sermon Preached for... the Charity School in Gravel-Lane*. London: J. Clark.

Ramsay, J. (1778). 'Memorial [re] sugar plantations and slaves'. Lambeth Palace MSS, SPG XVII.

Read, H. (1739). *A Sermon Preached for... the Charity School in Gravel-Lane*. London: R. Hett.

Ridley, G. (1757). *A Sermon Preached [at] the Yearly Meeting of... the Charity-Schools*. London: B. Dod.

Rogers, J. (1826). *A Sermon Preached on the Anniversary of the Central School and West Cornwall Committee of the [SPCK]*. London: Rivingtons.

Secker, T. (1743). *A Sermon Preached [at] the Yearly Meeting of... the Charity-Schools*. London: M. Downing.

Shipley, J. (1777). *A Sermon Preached [at] the Yearly Meeting of... the Charity-Schools*. London: Rivingtons.

Spaulding, J. G. (1995). *Pulpit Publications*. New York: N. Ross.

Spry, J. H. (1823). *The Church Responsible for the Religious Education of Her Members. A Sermon Preached... on Behalf of the Incorporated National Society*. Birmingham: Beilby, Knott, and Beilby.

Squires, F. (1714). *Universal Benevolence, Together with a Preface Wherein is a Farther Justification of the Principles of the Whiggs*. Exeter: J. Marsh.

Tennant, B. (2011a). *Conscience, Consciousness and Ethics in Joseph Butler's Philosophy and Ministry*. Woodbridge: Boydell Press.

—— (2011b). 'Enlightenment Sermon Studies: a Multidisciplinary Activity'. *Religion in the Age of the Enlightenment* 2: 249–75.

Thorp, T. (1834). *On Religious Education*. Cambridge: Deightons.

Tucker, J. (1766). *A Sermon Preached [at] the Yearly Meeting of... the Charity-Schools*. London: Rivingtons.

Walker, S. (1790). *A Sermon Preached for... the Charity School in Gravel-Lane*. London: H. Goldney.

Waterland, D. (1723). *A Sermon Preached [at] the Yearly Meeting of... the Charity-Schools*. London: W. and J. Innys.

Whitfeld, H. (1798). *A Sermon Preached [at] the Yearly Meeting of... the Charity-Schools*. London: Rivingtons.

Wilton, S. (1775). *A Sermon Preached for... the Charity School in Gravel-Lane*. London: J. Buckland.

Whyley, G. E. (1834). *A Sermon Preached in the Parish Church of Dunstable*. London: Rivingtons.

CHAPTER 23

SERMONS FOR END TIMES: EVANGELICALISM, ROMANTICISM, AND APOCALYPSE IN BRITAIN

KEITH A. FRANCIS AND
ROBERT J. SURRIDGE

BRITAIN did not experience the same millennial fervour that gripped the United States, particularly in the 'Burned Over District' of Western New York (Cross; Barkun), in the 1830s and 1840s. There was no exact British equivalent of William Miller (1782–1849) who preached for more than a decade that the Second Advent would occur 'at some time' in 1843 or, after the failure of his first two predictions, 1844. The so-called Great Disappointment of October 1844 was a peculiarly American event which mainly affected a uniquely American group of people—those who agreed with Miller, usually called Millerites (Numbers and Butler; Dunton: 110). And yet the British were not immune to what George R. Knight has described as millennial fever: Britain experienced occasional bouts of millenarianism in the 1690s, 1700s, and 1750s (Knight; Shaw: 126–8, 177). In the nineteenth century ministers such as Edward Bickersteth (1786–1850), Edward Irving (1792–1834), and William Dodsworth (1798–1861) helped to bring premillennialism to the forefront of British Christianity, briefly, through their preaching and lecturing. A doctrine which had been prominent among Puritan groups in the seventeenth century—contributing both to the thinking which resulted in migration to the American colonies and to the radicalism of British religion during the Civil War and Restoration period—was revived after a century in abeyance.

This chapter is dedicated to the memory of Robert James Surridge (1957–2011), colleague and friend. His sudden death meant that he was unable to write this chapter as the editors had originally planned. His work on the history of the rhetorical argument in Revelation 3:14–22 was the foundation of the argument in this chapter.

As Hugh Dunton has noted, 'There may have been more excitement over October 1844 in Britain than Millerite sources reveal' (Dunton: 126). While it is true that no lurid stories have been told about British 'saints', Millerites, waiting for Christ's return on wind-swept hills dressed in ascension robes as was the case for the United States (Sears), Irving had his Irvingites and John Nelson Darby (1800–82), the father of modern dispensationalism and futurism, his 'Darbyites'. In 1843 Thomas Birks (1810–83), a curate of Edward Bickersteth and a future professor of moral philosophy at Cambridge University, published *First Elements of Sacred Prophecy: Including an Examination of Several Recent Expositions and of the Year-Day Theory* in which he discussed at length the time prophecies in the book of Daniel such as the 'seventy weeks' and 'two thousand three hundred days' (Birks: 163–81, 308–72)—the same prophecies which led Miller to choose the year 1843 as the probable year for the Second Advent. In 1844 Henry Drummond (1786–1860), the Tory politician and apostle of the Catholic Apostolic Church, published *Tracts for the Last Days*, a 399-page work in which he explained the importance and implication of the eschatological prophecies in Bible; Drummond wrote this after he, and others studying apocalyptic works in the 1830s, spoke in ecstatic utterances, 'outpourings of the Holy Spirit'. The activities of groups associated with Irving, Darby, and Drummond, as well as those of the British Millerites, suggests that 'the premillennial fervo[u]r which swept parts of the United States in the 1840s was not without its impact in Britain' (Billington: 72).

The British then were no strangers to premillennialism nor to the fervour 'generated' by interpretations of the apocalyptic biblical books such as Daniel and Revelation. Robert Surridge and others have noted the importance of the figures such as Thomas Brightman (1562–1607) and Arthur Dent (1552/3–1603) in disseminating the historicist hermeneutical approach to the book of Revelation (Surridge 2003)—an interpretation which resulted in them seeing their time, the end of the sixteenth century, as close to or the actual end of time (Ball: 55–125; Surridge 2000: 218–71). The context for their views was the ferment of the Reformation period and, for those who subscribed to Brightman and Dent's views in the seventeenth century, the Thirty Years' War and the Civil War. The kind of political and social discord which resulted in the growth of groups such as the Diggers and Fifth Monarchy Men had long since subsided by 1800 but the unrest highlighted by the Spa Fields Riots in London in 1816 and the so-called Peterloo Massacre in Manchester in 1819 were signs of significant dislocation in British society. Furthermore, and in contrast to the seventeenth century, there were two other movements which made the character of premillennialism of the nineteenth century distinct from its predecessor—Evangelicalism and Romanticism.

These two movements are notoriously difficult for historians to define precisely. In *Religion in England 1688–1791* Gordon Rupp highlighted the varieties of Evangelicalism. Evangelicals could be Arminians, Antinomians, Calvinists, and Pietists (Rupp: 454–85). However, since the publication of David Bebbington's *Evangelicalism in Modern Britain: A History from the 1730s to the 1980s* (1989) and Bruce Hindmarsh's *Evangelical Conversion Narrative* (2005) historians have made a special effort to explain what these groups had in common: one of these common characteristics was the emphasis on a (recognizable) conversion experience of the believer. In the same vein, if the emphasis of Enlightenment thinkers was on 'the people', Romantics distinguished themselves from that movement by their emphasis on the individual. It was the genius of the individual imagination which enabled a person to see the world in a new way. When Irving reminded his listeners, and readers, that '[Christ] hath gone before you to prepare [heaven's] mansion for your reception and he will come again for those who look for his appearing' it was the culmination of argument in which he had emphasized the choice each person had to make in accepting what the Bible taught about the Second Advent (Irving 1824: 92). When Irving enjoined the congregation, and those reading the sermon later, 'For his sake be ye reconciled to God, that ye may have a right to the tree of life, and enter by the gate into the city' he joined millennial expectation with the need for personal conversion (Irving 1824: 92).

Another element of Romanticism which fitted well with millenarian preaching was the Romantics' emphasis on the imagination. 'The Romantic artist believed the primary power of the mind to be the imagination' (Peckham: 66), and Romantic imagination made it easier to bring to life the imagery of apocalyptic books such as Daniel and Revelation. Multi-metallic statues, lamb-like beasts, dragons, flying horsemen, crashing seas, and golden cities—images portrayed in captivating fashion by American Millerites such as Charles Fitch (1805–44)—could just as easily have been motifs in a Romantic or Gothic novel as elements of a biblical prophecy. This imagery fascinated millennialists (Newport: 48–65). It is no surprise that Samuel Taylor Coleridge was interested in the writing of Manuel Lacunza (1731–1801), a Jesuit priest whose *La venida del Mesias en gloria y majestad Seleccion* (1811) also influenced the thinking of Edward Irving and many others. For Irving, who translated Lacunza's work and published it as *The Coming of Messiah in Glory and Majesty* (1827), and Coleridge the signs of the Second Advent had to be imagined as well as believed (Coburn and Harding).

Given that there was a millennial milieu in Britain, albeit not of the size of that in the United States, how then did the sermons of preachers such as Irving, Bickersteth, and Drummond reflect the concerns of the time? Could these sermons be described as Romantic and Evangelical? Equally important, did the preachers pay attention to and incorporate the social dislocation and political critique of the period to highlight the urgency of their message? In Romantic literature there were numerous examples of writers using the end-of-the-world motif to make a point about the state of society (and how to fix it)—Percy Shelley's *Prometheus Unbound* (1820) and Mary Shelley's *The Last Man* (1826) are two well-known examples of this genre. Answering the question whether sermons were used in a similar way—in this case to persuade individuals of the pressing need for repentance—will provide another clue as to the function of the sermon in British life.

Millennial Sermons in Printed Form: The Importance of Tracts

Historians' knowledge of the impact of the sermon is based on the fact that versions of these spoken orations were written down and then published in sufficient numbers to be an object of research. This point has already been made in several other chapters in this volume. Clearly sermons could appear as books, pamphlets, and leaflets; in the case of millenarian sermons the favoured printed form was the tract. In fact, although men such as Bickersteth, Irving, and Dodsworth were well known for their preaching, it is interesting to note that their printed sermons on the Second Advent were rarely advertised as such (and the same is true for the lesser-known preachers). While it was clear that the subject of a particular tract was some aspect of millennialism, it was much less obvious that it had its origins in a sermon. Reading the tract, and not having any knowledge of its source and production, the historian might conclude that such a tract was written for the specific purpose of arguing the case that political events had been foretold by biblical prophecy. For example, in 1825 Edward Irving preached a sermon before members of the Colonial and Continental Society, a missionary society which supported Anglican education outside Britain, on the end of the world. In print, and expanded substantially, the sermon appeared in 1826 and 1828 as *Babylon and Infidelity Foredoomed by God: A Discourse on the Prophecies of Daniel and the Apocalypse, which relate to these Latter Times*: apart from the word 'Discourse' in the title there is no indication in the tract that it was produced from a sermon (Irving 1826).

One reason for this representation as a tract rather than a sermon was the subject matter. Although Irving was notorious for preaching long sermons, as much as three hours according to one biographer (Brown), it could not have been easy to explain in any detail the interpretation of complicated prophecies such as the 'seventy weeks' in Daniel 9 or the 'seven seals' in Revelation 5–8. The sermon may not have contained everything that the preacher wanted to say or explain, but the tract provided a second opportunity to do so. Furthermore, the tract—easy to transport and to distribute at the lectures that these preachers of millennial sermons frequently gave—could also be expanded into a book. Dodsworth's *The Second Advent of our Lord Jesus Christ, with an appendix on Jesus Christ as the Destroyer of Anti-Christ* is an example of this, as is the Baptist minister Joseph Tyso's *An Inquiry after Prophetic Truth relative to the Restoration of the Jews and the Millennium...* (Dodsworth 1835; Tyso 1831). It is unlikely that Tyso's congregation saw the map of the new Temple, which was included in the book, while he preached his sermon on prophetic truth. Tyso's emphasis was probably on the sermon's themes of preparedness for the end of the age; nonetheless, the preparation of a tract from the sermon, and then a book, meant that there were multiple opportunities to study the prophecies about the future of the Jewish nation more thoroughly and at the reader's leisure. This transformation of the sermon from oration to book is another example of the sermon's malleability and further evidence of sermon ubiquity in the period 1689–1901.

Persuading to Convert: Millennial Sermons and Evangelical Themes

With regard to repentance, ministers preaching and lecturing about the Second Advent were not starting from nothing. Their sermons had a context: they were not the only ministers calling for their congregations, hearers, or readers of their work to be converted. Historians are increasingly contesting the terms 'Evangelical Awakening' and 'Evangelical Revival' preferring to point to 'movements' associated with Wesleyanism, Methodism, or the Baptists—William Gibson and others have argued convincingly that 'Awakening' and 'Revival' do an injustice to the pastoral care shown by ministers and the vigour of the eighteenth-century Church (Gibson 1994; Gibson 2001; Walsh, Haydon, and Taylor). However there were preachers who sought to persuade British people of their need to be truly converted well before the efforts of Irving and other premillennialist preachers. John Wesley, in his much-reprinted sermon *The Repentance of Believers*, emphasized the need for repentance throughout the Christian's life as well as at conversion more than two decades before Irving, Bickersteth, and Drummond were born (Wesley). George Whitefield's famous sermon on the conversion of Paul, *God's Free Grace in the Salvation of Sinners*, predates Wesley's by a further two decades (Whitefield). When Bickersteth asked members of his congregation about their standing before God in the sermon *Practical Remarks on the Prophecies, with Reference to Efforts to Spread the Gospel and to Personal Edification* he was not demarcating new territory (Bickersteth 1832).

The rhetorical strategy of Evangelical preachers such as John Wesley is discussed in Chapter 7 above and so it is not necessary to describe it here. As Robert Surridge has noted, the Apocalypse, particularly passages such as Revelation 3:14–22, the message to the Church of Laodicea, is ideal for use in a rhetorical strategy in which the preacher wishes to persuade hearers to repent (Surridge 2000: 160–217). What was new in the late eighteenth and early nineteenth centuries were the millennial and Romantic additions or underpinnings to the call for change.

One way to interpret the books of Daniel and Revelation is to treat them as dual, intertwined stories—that of the individual and that of the group. The books tell of the visions of two men concerning God's people, the nation of Israel and the Christian Church. But in Romantic style, the artists, in this case the seers Daniel and John, are intimately involved in the progress of the visions and the outcome of their prophecies. Daniel rescues the wise men of Babylon by relating and explaining Nebuchadnezzar's dream and, in his later visions, Daniel is transported to various locations to see the events unfold (Daniel 2:1–48, 8:1–2, 10:4–21). John is so involved in his visions that in one he is 'seen' weeping because no-one is worthy enough to open the scroll with seven seals and in another he is told to eat a little book that he will find sweet to taste but bitter in the stomach (Revelation 5:1–5, 10:8–11). In the same way, the preachers of millennial sermons made themselves as much part of the story as they were messengers and persuaders. Thus, when Bickersteth wrote 'It appears to *me* that we may now see in Switzerland, as elsewhere, the beginning of the predicted division of Christendom into three parts, as foretold under the seventh vial, Rev. xvi. 19, Infidels, Papists, and the true followers of Christ' he was acting in a similar fashion to Daniel and John (Bickersteth 1848: 11, my italics). He made the comment in the preface to a pamphlet entitled *The Present Crisis in Switzerland, and the Events which Led to It*. Bickersteth argued that the crisis, a dispute over the role of the Protestant and Catholic churches in Swiss government which resulted in the expulsion of the Jesuits from one canton 'Should be a loud call on all faithful

Christians to be more prayerful, more united, more decided, and more bold in the open confession of his name and his truth before the world, assured of his speedy coming and approaching triumphant kingdom' (Bickersteth 1848: 11–12). In other words, any change should apply to Bickersteth himself as well as his fellow believers.

The propensity of inserting themselves into the story because they were also participants in the events of the day was common among millenarian preachers. James A. Begg (1762–1845), the Church of Scotland minister, noted in the preface to the first edition of his *A Connected View of some of the Scriptural Evidence of the Redeemer's Speedy Personal Return* that 'A stricter investigation of the Scripture on the subject has compelled the author of the following pages to relinquish, as untenable, the sentiments he formerly entertained, and to rank himself among the number of those who are "looking for the blessed hope, and the glorious appearing of the Great God and our Saviour, Jesus Christ," as an event speedily to be realised' (Begg 1831: v). Begg described his change of mind as a conversion experience and expressed the hope that the reading of his book would facilitate a revival in the Church. If the reason for writing the book was still unclear to the reader, Begg's donation of the profits from the second edition to the work of the London Society for the Promotion of Christianity among the Jews left no doubt (Begg 1831: xiii–xiv). Irving, preaching in the newly opened National Scotch Church in Regent Square in 1827, prayed that God would 'send forth into my heart the Spirit of truth...that I may see afar off the coming night and the coming day, and acquit me of my charge as a watchman upon the walls of Zion'. Only God could give him the wisdom to interpret the prophecies correctly and lead others to repentance—but Irving did not want to lose his place among those saved by giving the wrong message (Irving 1828: 3:966–7). Dodsworth, although preaching a sermon whose title was 'The Christian's Attitude in Reference to the Signs of the Times', used the pronouns 'our' and 'we' throughout, clearly including himself as a person who needed to be ready for the Second Advent. And then, using the same storytelling device of the books of Daniel and Revelation, Dodsworth injected himself into the narrative: 'If, instead of seeing in the convulsions of the world...in the development of antichristian power—if, I say, instead of seeing in all this the disappointment of our hopes—the distraction of our counsels, and the triumph of our enemies, we see only so many steps towards the consummation of our hopes...how differently will our trials, whatever they be, then be felt!' (Dodsworth 1849: 67). It was the only occasion that Dodsworth used 'I' in the sermon but it highlighted that he was both observer of and participant in the history of the end of the world.

The excitement, for want of a better word, about the final events that Dodsworth wanted to create in his congregation was another important theme of preachers of millennial sermons. In various forms, the text in Luke 21:28, 'Lift up your heads, redemption draweth nigh', appeared as a regular motif: if it was not quoted directly it was referred to indirectly. The dramatic events associated with the end of the world and the Second Advent should make people rethink their relationship to God. In talking about the prophecies and the fate of the Jewish nation, James Bicheno (1752–1831), a Baptist minister from Newbury in Berkshire, noted that the 'wonderful fulfilment of prophecies', which were evidence of the intervention of God in human affairs, would lead to 'the greatest events that ever mankind witnessed'. But the important point was that these events would 'dispose men for repentance' (Bicheno 1807: 209). Edward Irving struck a similar theme in a series of four orations—he asserted that 'the very name [sermon] hath learned to inspire drowsiness and tedium' (Irving 1824: viii)—on the Bible in general and prophecy in particular. When God reveals His will through his 'oracles', the Christian, according to Irving, has three duties: to have a 'due preparation for receiving it', 'a diligent attention to it while it is disclosing', and 'a strict observance of it when it is delivered'. The objective of Irving's orations was not the 'exposition or enforcement of a doctrine of Scripture founded upon some particular text'—that being the definition of a sermon according to Irving—but to 'move and persuade men on a particular point' (Irving 1824: 9–10). The 'particular point' was that each person should repent: 'Come over, cast in your lot with the saints; you have everything to gain—peace of conscience, a divine joy, a fellowship with God, a special providence, a heritage of promise and blessing, a triumphant death, and a crown of everlasting life' (Irving 1824: 76).

In contrast to Evangelical conversion, millenarian repentance did not have to be a full-scale conversion; Irving's comments in the previously mentioned sermon were directed at a congregation which, in theory, was already converted. Another theme struck by preachers of millennial sermons was the need for their listeners, and readers, to be cognizant of the state of the world and, putting it in bland terms, to adjust their lives accordingly. John Hooper, a Catholic Apostolic minister at the church Drummond built in Albury, Surrey, worried that there was insufficient time during the service for adequate teaching of his 'flock'. In order to deal with this deficiency, Hooper preached a series of sermons which he subsequently published as a set of eighteen tracts. The last three concentrated on the Second Advent; Hooper spoke on 'The Appearing and Coming of the Lord', 'The Establishment of Christ's Kingdom on Earth', and 'The Nearness of the Lord's Advent'. In the preface to the tracts, Hooper commented that the members of his congregation did not need to repent as such—although he noted that some of the congregation missed opportunities for instruction due to the pressure of work, or absence from church (Hooper 1844: iii, Preface)—but that they needed to be shepherded in the right direction (Hooper 1844: 5–6). Readiness for the Second Advent required the right 'education' with regard to the prophecies as well as living a life that was consistently Christian.

For most preachers of millennial sermons, questions of repentance, conversion, or the 'aware' Christian life were reserved for the peroration at the end of the sermon. In the largest portion of the sermon they concentrated on explaining one or several prophecies or commenting on the present or future state of the world; in the peroration they gave injunctions similar to that found in 2 Peter 3:11: 'Seeing then that all these things shall be dissolved, what manner of persons ought ye to be in all holy conversation and godliness, looking for and hasting unto the coming of the day of God, wherein the heavens being on fire shall be dissolved, and the elements shall melt with fervent heat?' The future calamities which would befall the world were terrible but, as 'A Clergyman of the Church of England', probably Dodsworth, put it in two sermons, the prepared Christian would not worry or panic because these events would precede 'the blessed hope', the return of Jesus Christ (A Clergyman of the Church of England).

There was then a distinctive Evangelical emphasis in the sermons of preachers such as Irving, Bickersteth, and Dodsworth. The focus on premillennialism may have been new—or, more accurately, a revival of an element of Christian doctrine not emphasized for a century—but the hoped-for end result was the same as in all Evangelical sermons: the listener or reader should repent, be converted, and remain converted.

Apocalyptic Imagery in Millennial Sermons

While 'the blessed hope' should be a source of comfort to the Christian ready for the Second Advent, there is no doubt that preachers of millennial sermons did not want their congregations and readers to be comfortable. These preachers, Irving in particular, made full use of the spectacular, and frightening, imagery in Daniel and Revelation. In this sense they were Romantics. One biographer of Irving's has drawn attention to his 'gloomy premillennialism' (Brown), but Irving's descriptions of the events leading up to the Second Advent were only 'gloomy' in the sense that Coleridge's imagery in 'The Rime of the Ancient Mariner' is gloomy. A sense of foreboding, and the invoking of imagery to reflect this, was a classic trope of Romantic literature.

A favourite 'Romantic prophecy' of Irving's was Daniel's vision of the four beasts (Daniel 7). The deformities of the beasts was intriguing enough—a lion with eagle's wings, a lopsided bear with three ribs in its mouth, and so forth—but the fourth beast with its ten horns and a little horn with 'eyes of a man' and a mouth which spoke 'great things' was a source of continual fascination. Between 1827 and 1829, Drummond, Irving, and several other ministers published a large, three-volume work entitled *Dialogues on Prophecy* in which a group of characters discuss at length the meaning of prophecies such as the little horn (Drummond). (The characters had names such as Anastasius, Philalethes, Isocrates, and Sophron: these were avatars for the participants in a series of conferences held at Albury Park, the home of Drummond, from 1826 onwards.) Irving, probably in 1828, preached a sermon on the four beasts and published an expanded version of it the next year as *Daniel's Vision of the Four Beasts, and of the Son of Man Opened, and applied to our Present Crisis in Church and State*. Also in 1829, Irving published a book of eleven discourses—again avoiding the word 'sermon'—on the topic of the four beasts. Two of the discourses had the title 'Rome, and the Pope Her Little Horn' and a third he entitled 'The Words which the Little Horn Spake' (Irving 1829: 216–371).

Why was the fascination with the imagery of the four beasts and the little horn so considerable? Because in recent years, as Irving put it:

> That wicked order [the Jesuits] hath been restored; and, with it, the ambition of the Roman see hath been awakened, and hath prevailed in this kingdom over all the bulwarks with which our Fathers had defended the Protestant constitution of this our kingdom. Instead of any signs of repentance, there have been manifested against the Holy Word of God an inveterate opposition, and a deadly hatred, hitherto unexampled in the history even of the Papacy itself. (Irving 1829: 370–1)

The vision of the four beasts and the little horn was prophetic evidence that the rise of Catholicism in Britain, and the world, had been predicted. Roman Catholicism was regarded as a danger to the true (Protestant) Church and Christians needed to be aware of the danger. The future destruction of the little horn mentioned in Daniel 7:26—in other words, the destruction of the Papacy and all associated with it—was a warning of the dangers of allowing the State to interfere in the affairs of the Church and of the union of Church and State (Irving 1829: 518–75). Coming at the same time as the repeal of the Test and Corporation Acts, the congregations had potent evidence of the reality of the dangers to which millenarian preachers were alerting them.

The dissolution of the union of Church and State resulting in the creation of a false Church, Babylon, was another favourite image of premillennial preachers. This wordpicture does not appear in the book of Daniel and so preachers such as Irving used the imagery of Babylon when they wanted to demonstrate the danger posed by Roman Catholicism as illustrated in the book of Revelation. In his best-known sermon on the subject, *Babylon and Infidelity Foredoomed by God*, Irving explained that anyone who did not repent and turn to God could suffer the fate of the false Church. Furthermore, the fall and destruction of Babylon, and any other opponents of God, was not far in the future. Irving put this dramatically at the end of a sermon he preached in 1824:

> 'Tis written, 'tis written, 'tis sealed of heaven, and a few years shall reveal it all. Even so it is to happen to the despisers of holy writ... Terror hath sitten enthroned on the brows of tyrants, and made the heart of nations quake; but upon this peaceful volume there sits a terror to make the mute world stand aghast. Yet not the terror of tyranny neither, but the terror of justice, which abides the scorners of the most High God, and the revilers of his most gracious Son. And is it not just, though terrible, that He who brooked not in heaven one moment's disaffection, but launched the rebel host to hell, and bound them evermore in chains of darkness, should also do his sovereign will upon the disaffected of this earth, whom he hath long endured and pleaded with in vain? (Irving 1824: 66–7)

Had the story ended with the destruction of God's enemies it might give comfort to Christians but it would hardly constitute 'the blessed hope'. The Second Advent would precede the uninterrupted reign of Christ and so, unsurprisingly, that extended image— which was more than one event—was another favourite. In two sermons preached in December 1829, Dodsworth captured the full range of Christ's experiences as God and man entitling his sermons *Jesus Christ in His Three-fold State of Sub-Angelic Humiliation, Heavenly Glory, and Earthly Dominion* (Dodsworth 1830). Tyso focused on the notion in Revelation that Christ will be the true King David in his sermon entitled *The Throne of*

David, the Throne of Christ (Tyso 1842). In order to make the troubles of the end of the world worthwhile, the appearance of Christ had to be spectacular and, unlike any of the political and religious powers associated with the four beasts in Daniel 7, Christ's kingdom had to last forever. Begg reminded readers that the reign of Antichrist was limited by the fiat of 'The Ancient of Days'; after the destruction of the little horn, and quoting from Daniel 7:14, 'there was given Him [the Son of Man] dominion and glory and a kingdom…His dominion is an everlasting dominion, which shall not pass away, and His Kingdom that which shall not be destroyed' (Begg 1831: 166). Preachers of millennial sermons focused on the dramatic images and imagery in the apocalyptic prophecies—with the same gusto as Romantic writers—because the purpose of the rampaging beasts and so forth was clear: the events in the period before and after the Second Advent were dramatic and the warning about the imminence of those events had to be stated boldly.

SOCIAL UNREST AND MILLENNIAL SERMONS

Apart from Henry Drummond, whose ordination as an apostle in the Catholic Apostolic Church was a little unorthodox (Flegg), all of the best-known preachers of millennial sermons were ministers who had been ordained in one of the major churches in Britain—Church of England or Church of Scotland, for example. Although they were concerned about the past and the future, as described by the apocalyptic prophecies, it is clear from their sermons that they did not ignore the here-and-now. They were equally pastors and 'prophets'. Understandably, given their premillennial beliefs, a significant part of their ministry was spent describing the state of the world. Unsurprisingly, for these preachers a cursory review of contemporary events demonstrated that the world was in a state of pre-Advent turmoil. These events were 'signs of the times', a phrase which appeared in the title of several sermons (Bicheno 1803; Dodsworth 1849), and the discerning Christian knew what they meant.

In Europe, the French Revolution and the Napoleonic Wars dominated the last decade of the eighteenth century and the first decade of the nineteenth. These events were of marked significance to preachers of millennial sermons, particularly when Pope Pius VI had his temporal power removed by the armies of Napoleon, a sign to some of the fulfilment or near-fulfilment of the 1260-day prophecy of Daniel 7:25, 11:2–3, 12:7 and Revelation 12:6, 12:14, 13:5–8. Reflecting on these developments, Bicheno noted that an 'awful crisis is at hand, and that what we have seen is but the beginning of sorrows' (Bicheno 1807: 230). A decade later he would assert that the period after the Congress of Vienna was 'the present forced and hollow peace' (Bicheno 1817: xi). For preachers such as Bicheno, the death of Pius VI in exile was a sign that the Antichrist would soon be destroyed and, even though the Napoleonic Wars had ended, any hope that Europe, and the world, would enjoy a period of tranquillity was in vain. According to Bicheno, '*The great and decisive shaking of the nations, which is to prepare the way for the Kingdom of our Lord, is very near at hand*, if not already begun' (Bicheno 1817: ix–x, his italics).

The battles of the Napoleonic Wars may not have reached the shores of Britain but preachers of millennial sermons made it clear to their congregations, and readers, that Britain would not be spared the judgments of God. In 1817, Bicheno claimed 'the shaking of nations' had either already begun or would begin at some time between 1819 and 1822 (Bicheno 1817: 19–20). In the preface, Bicheno stated that he wanted to publish the book in order to

> yield some assistance towards rousing men's minds from that state of insensibility into which self-sufficiency and flattery have lulled too many; and to awaken their attention to a *religious* regard to what is passing on the great theatre of Europe in general, and to the perilous state into which our own Country is brought, in particular; and to which *religious* regard, not only the thoughtless multitude have been fatally estranged, but even the majority of the more serious Christians have also been possessed by an awful degree of the same apathy; something like judicial blindness indicative of some awful visitation (Bicheno 1817: v).

Here, in referring to 'judicial blindness', Bicheno applied the message to the Church of Laodicea to Britain; illustrating again the persuasive rhetorical power of the text that Robert Surridge has noted (Surridge 2000: 189–217). In his sermon *The True Cause of the Prevalence of Pestilence, and other Judgments of God; with the Divinely Appointed Means of Deliverance and Safety*, Begg noted that disasters such as the cholera outbreak in 1831 were signs that God had already 'visited' Britain (Begg 1832).

Another development watched keenly by preachers of millennial sermons was the declining power of the Ottoman Empire. In his sermon *A Connected View of some of the Scriptural Evidence of the Redeemer's Speedy Personal Return*, Begg explained that the Ottoman Empire had to collapse because this would facilitate the restoration of Israel to Palestine and, ultimately, the destruction of all anti-Christian nations (Begg 1831). In 1827, Irving argued in a sermon entitled 'The Drying up of the Euphrates' that this event, predicted in Revelation 16:12, was the collapse of the Turkish Empire 'not so much [because of] act of aggression or of violence from without, [but] as a process of inward decay and dissolution' (Irving 1828: 3:1015). The Serbian uprisings, the Greek war of independence, and the loss of Algeria to the French were all viewed as upheavals that would result in a 'striking' end to the Ottoman empire (Irving 1831; Begg 1831). There was some disagreement about the exact timing of the events—Tyso in a sermon which was published with the title *An Elucidation of the Prophecies, being an Exposition of the Books of Daniel and the Revelation, Shewing that the Seventy Weeks, the One Thousand Two Hundred and Sixty Days, and the Events Predicted under the Seven Trumpets and Seven Vials have not yet taken Place*... argued that the real collapse had not begun yet (Tyso 1838)—but all agreed that the political and social unrest in the world meant that Armageddon and the use of Israel as 'the instrument of [God's] wrath' were not far in the future (Irving 1828: 3:979–83).

Given their association of political upheaval with an imminent Second Advent, it is no surprise that preachers of millennial sermons interpreted all the nationalist and democratic revolutions of the 1830s and 1840s, not just those occurring in the Ottoman empire, as further evidence of an impending Second Advent. Hooper's *The Present Crisis considered in Relation to the Hope of the Glorious Appearing of the Great God, and our Saviour Jesus Christ* and Begg's *The Value of Prophecy as a Light to the Church in Evil Times* of 1830 were typical of sermons which took this approach. Commenting on the revolutions in Europe in 1848, Dodsworth noted in the preface to his four sermons on the signs of the times that 'the stirring events which have been occurring throughout almost the whole of Christendom during the last year, have naturally turned the minds of many thoughtful persons to the subject of Prophecy' (Dodsworth 1849: v).

As with their use of apocalyptic imagery, the preachers of millennial sermons had a specific objective when drawing attention to political and social events occurring in the world. Bicheno put it simply: 'In a word, let all repent and obey the Gospel' (Bicheno 1817: 251). Irving, with his flair for the dramatic, told his congregation to 'weigh well the terrors of apostatizing from the Christian faith: observe the consequences of war and revolution and bloodshed, which come against a people and nation that is heedless of the glory of Christ, and giveth to another that worship and service which is due to him alone' (Irving 1828: 3:1022). Neither Bicheno nor Irving were reticent in noting that the travails of the world should evince some fear in their congregations, but that fear should lead to a change of behaviour—a true conversion. Furthermore, conversion was an individual responsibility: each person had to choose God for him- or herself. In a sermon entitled 'The Kings of the East, or the Tribes of Israel', after a long explanation of the meaning of Revelation 16:12—it is more than eighty pages of text—Irving emphasized the individualistic nature of conversion and salvation. Having spent the majority of the sermon talking about the Church or the nation of Britain, using the pronoun 'we', in his peroration he eliminated completely the notion of a group. He used the pronoun 'I' fifteen times: 'I resolve to understand'; 'I am persuaded'; 'I would save my own flock'; 'I would save all who hear me'; 'I would arouse the church from its stupefaction'; and 'I will preach', being some examples. He also used the pronoun 'you' ten times as in 'I pray you to search the word for yourselves' and 'you shall never be able to hear' (Irving 1828: 3: 1197–8). Only after these appeals to himself and each member of the congregation was he willing to say: 'He will [save], dear brethren, if ye reject it not: but, oh, and if ye reject, having been warned, having been entreated, then it will be more tolerable for others than for you' (Irving 1828: 3:1198). It was a singular example of rhetorical persuasion: it was a classic case of an Evangelical call to action. Its focus on the individual also drew on classic Romanticism.

Conclusion

The sermons of premillennialists such as Irving are an example of a continuity in the history of British Christianity. In subject matter and thrust, the sermons are not a particularly new phenomenon. The return of Jesus Christ in the Second Advent is orthodox Christian doctrine and even during the time when premillennialist preachers were most active, 1820–60, ministers who were not premillennialists gave and published sermons on the Second Advent. John Puckle, the incumbent of St Mary the Virgin in Dover and a rural dean in the diocese of Canterbury, published *The Advancement of the Signs of the Times* in 1857, a series of four sermons which he had preached during Advent of 1856 (Puckle). A year later, James Hatherell, the vicar of St. James's, West End, Southampton, published *The Signs of the Second Advent of Our Lord: Collected from the Words of Jesus and Applied to our Times*, a collection of twelve sermons which he had preached during the Advent seasons of 1856 and 1857 (Hatherell). The Evangelical call to repentance was a feature of preaching associated with the Wesleyans, Methodists, and Lady Huntington's Connexion, to give three prominent examples. In the 1840s, the Congregational minister David Ford (1797–1875), who was not a premillennialist, even used the message to the Church of Laodicea in order to persuade his congregation of the need for repentance (Ford).

Equally, the sermons of premillennialists such as Irving are an example of discontinuity in the history of British Christianity. Bickersteth, Dodsworth, and Drummond were not one more group of ministers preaching Evangelical sermons or preaching about the Second Advent. The way their sermons utilized, almost embraced, the political and social unease of the eighteenth-century *fin-de-siècle* make them much more like the Fifth Monarchy Men of the seventeenth century than their contemporaries. The specificity of their use of prophecy in making predictions about the collapse of the Ottoman empire or associating the capture of Pius VI with the end of the 1260-day prophecy made them unique. 'The Romantic interest is a new way of looking at the past,' notes one historian of the movement, 'not in terms of development of stylistic tradition but rather in the emergence of stylistic breaks; and the Romantic saw the artists who made those breaks, those discontinuities, as his models—though he was attempting a greater stylistic break than the past had ever achieved' (Peckham: 66). Perhaps these preachers of premillennialist sermons might have been surprised to hear themselves described as Romantics but that is what they were. The discontinuity was their radical interpretation of the nearness of the Second Advent. Christians may not know 'the day or the hour' of Christ's appearing, admitted Bicheno, but an analysis of the 1260-day and 2300-day prophecies demonstrated that the 'time is near' (Bicheno 1817: 17–18). To project the beginning of the millennium as an event occurring in the next decade or two rather than a (no matter how certain) future was unique.

Given the failure of their predictions, did these preachers and their sermons leave any kind of legacy? Not a large one, it seems. The centenaries of Irving's birth and death were marked in Scotland, the Brethren, with whom Darby was associated, still exist, and dispensationalism still has a small following in Britain. In terms of theology, the obvious successor is the Seventh-day Adventist Church but John Loughborough, one of the founders of the Church in Britain, makes no mention of Millerites or believers in a soon-coming Second Advent in his diaries (Loughborough); John Nevins Andrews, another founder, made contact with Seventh-day Baptists and they became the first Seventh-day Adventists (Leonard).

Millenarian sermons captured the feeling of an age but they were not timeless. The age of millennial fervour and Romanticism passed and has not returned to British Christianity. Perhaps the same can be said for the Evangelicalism of the late eighteenth and early nineteenth century. The evangelical 'mood' of the age of Wesley, Whitefield, and Lady Huntington's Connexion dissipated. Unlike the Evangelicalism of the period, as already noted, the millennialism of Irving, Darby, and Hammond did not result in the creation of a movement or a prominent mode of thinking and worship in British Christianity. While there are Evangelicals and there is an Evangelical wing in the major British churches no such equivalent exists as a result of the millennial sermons of the early nineteenth century. It is another example of how time-specific sermons were. And it is not simply the case that the rhetorical argument in the millennial sermons of an Irving are not persuasive or relevant; rather, the whole sermon belongs to another age—an age in which premonitions of the Second Advent had a far greater effect on the psyche of those preaching, hearing, and reading them. These were sermons for end times but also sermons for that time.

REFERENCES

Ball, B. W. (1975). *A Great Expectation: Eschatological Thought in English Protestantism to 1660*. Leiden: Brill.
Barkun, M. (1986). *Crucible of the Millennium: The Burned-Over District of New York in the 1840s*. Syracuse, NY: Syracuse University Press.
Bebbington, D. W. (1989). *Evangelicalism in Modern Britain: A History from the 1730s to the 1980s*. London: Unwin Hyman.
Begg, J. A. (1831). *A Connected View of some of the Scriptural Evidence of the Redeemer's Speedy Personal Return...*, 3rd edn. London: James Nisbet.
—— (1832). *The True Cause of the Prevalence of Pestilence...* London: James Nisbet.
Bicheno, J. (1803). *The Signs of the Times...* London: J. Adlard, 1803
—— (1807). *The Restoration of the Jews, the Crisis of All Nations*, 2nd edn... London: J. Barfield.
—— (1817). *The Fulfilment of Prophecy farther Illustrated by the Signs of the Times...* London: Ogles, Duncan, and Cochran.
Bickersteth, E. (1832). *Practical Remarks on the Prophecies, with Reference to Efforts to Spread the Gospel and to Personal Edification*, 3rd edn. London: L. B. Seeley & Sons.
—— (1848). *The Present Crisis in Switzerland, and the Events which Led to It*. London: Partridge and Oakey.
Billington, L. (1993). 'The Millerite Adventists in Great Britain, 1840–1850', in R. L. Numbers and J. Butler (eds.), *The Disappointed: Millerism and Millenarianism in the Nineteenth Century*, 2nd edn. Knoxville, TN: University of Tennessee Press, 59–77.
Birks, T. R. (1843). *First Elements of Sacred Prophecy...* London: William Edward Painter.
Brown, S. J. (2004). 'Irving, Edward (1792–1834)', *ODNB*. Oxford: Oxford University Press.
A Clergyman of the Church of England (1829). *The Blessed Hope: Two Sermons, Preached in Advent 1829*. London: James Nisbet, 1830.

Coburn, K. and Harding, A. J. (eds.) (2002). *The Notebooks of Samuel Taylor Coleridge*, 5: *1827–1834*. Princeton, NJ: Princeton University Press.

Cross, W. R. (1950). *The Burned-Over District: The Social and Intellectual History of Enthusiastic Religion in Western New York, 1800–1850*. Ithaca, NY: Cornell University Press.

Dodsworth, W. (1830). *Jesus Christ in His Three-fold State of Sub-Angelic Humiliation, Heavenly Glory, and Earthly Dominion*. London: J. Nisbet.

—— (1835). *The Second Advent of our Lord Jesus Christ…* London: James Burns.

—— (1849). *The Signs of the Times. Sermons Preached in Advent, 1848*. London: Joseph Masters.

Drummond, H. (1827–9) (comp.). *Dialogues on Prophecy*, 3 vols. London: James Nisbet.

Dunton, H. I. B. (1984). 'The Millerite Adventists and other Millenarian Groups in Britain, 1830–1860'. PhD dissertation, University of London.

Ford, D. E. (1844). *Laodicea; or Religious Declension…* London: Simpkin, Marshall and Co.

Flegg, C. G. (2004). 'Drummond, Henry (1786–1860)', *ODNB*. Oxford: Oxford University Press.

Gibson, W. (1994). *Church, State, and Society, 1760–1850*. Basingstoke: Macmillan.

—— (2001). *The Church of England, 1688–1832: Unity and Accord*. London: Routledge.

Hatherell, J. W. (1858). *The Signs of the Second Advent of Our Blessed Lord…* London: T. Hachard.

Hindmarsh, D. B. (2005). *The Evangelical Conversion Narrative*. Oxford: Oxford University Press.

Hooper, J. (1830). *The Present Crisis Considered…* London: James Nisbet.

—— (1844). *A Word in Season…* London: W. E. Painter.

Irving, E. (1824). *For the Oracles of God, Four Orations…*, 3rd edn. London: T. Hamilton.

—— (1826). *Babylon and Infidelity Foredoomed by God…* Glasgow: Chalmers and Collins.

—— (1828). *Sermons, Lectures, and Occasional Discourses*, 3 vols. London: R. B. Seeley and W. Burnside.

—— (1829). *The Church and State responsible to Christ, and to One Another…* London: James Nisbet, 1829.

Knight, G. R. (1993). *Millennial Fever and the End of the World…* Boise, ID: Pacific Press.

Leonard, H. H. (1985). 'Andrews and the Mission to Britain' in H. H. Leonard (ed.), *J. N. Andrews, the Man and the Mission*. Berrien Springs, MI: Andrews University Press, 225–60.

Loughborough, J. N. (1878–1883). Diaries. Newbold College, E. G. White-SDA Research Centre, 922 JNL 1878 VAULT.

Newport, K. G. C. (2000). *Apocalypse and Millennium: Studies in Biblical Eisegesis*. Cambridge: Cambridge University Press.

Numbers, R. L. and Butler, J. (eds.) (1993). *The Disappointed: Millerism and Millenarianism in the Nineteenth Century*, 2nd edn. Knoxville, TN: University of Tennessee Press.

Peckham, M. (1986). *The Birth of Romanticism 1790–1815*. Greenwood, FL: The Penkevill Publishing Company.

Puckle, J. (1857). *The Advancement of the Signs of the Times…* London: Rivington's.

Rupp, E. G. (1986). *Religion in England 1688–1791*. Oxford: Clarendon Press.

Sears, C. E. (1924) *Days of Delusion: A Strange Bit of History*. Boston, MA: Houghton Mifflin Co.

Shaw, J. (2006). *Miracles in Enlightenment England*. London: Yale University Press.

Surridge, R. J. (2000). 'The Art of Apocalyptic Persuasion: The Rhetorical Dynamics and History of the Influence of the Letter to Laodicea (Rev 3:14–22)'. PhD dissertation, University of London.

—— (2003). '"An English Laodicea": The Influence of Revelation 3:14–22 on Mid-Seventeenth Century England', in D. J. B. Trim and P. J. Balderstone (eds.), *Cross, Crown and Community: Religion, Government and Culture in Early Modern England 1400–1800*. Berne, Switzerland: Peter Lang, 143–176.

Tyso, J. (1831). *An Inquiry after Prophetic Truth relative to the Restoration of the Jews and the Millennium...* London: Holdsworth and Ball.

—— (1838). *An Elucidation of the Prophecies, being an exposition of the Books of Daniel and the Revelation...* London: Wallingford.

—— (1842). *The Throne of David, The Throne of Christ...* London: Wallingford.

Walsh, J., Haydon, C., and Taylor, S. (1993). *The Church of England c.1689–c.1833: From Toleration to Tractarianism*. Cambridge: Cambridge University Press.

Wesley, J. (1767). *The Repentance of Believers...* Bristol: William Pine.

Whitefield, G. (1740). *God's Free Grace in the Salvation of Sinners...* London: C. Whitefield.

CHAPTER 24

RATIONALISM, THE ENLIGHTENMENT, AND SERMONS

NIGEL ASTON

The Rational Sermon and Its Varied Fortunes

EIGHTEENTH-CENTURY preaching was as varied as it was prolific and popular. If it was a self-consciously enlightened era within which religion was comfortably accommodated, it was also supremely the century of religious revival (Beales: 131), one that could be articulated in voices and idioms that were far from rational and incurred the heinous and unfashionable charge of 'enthusiastic'. Most parochial Anglican clergy had no desire to spoil their chances of preferment by running that risk, opting instead for preaching a rational orthodoxy from their pulpits that was both intellectually coherent according to contemporary criteria and, above all, accessible to their congregations. The 'perceived need' was, as Jeremy Gregory has stressed, 'to get the message across in a clear manner' (Gregory: 75–7). Sermons of this temperate kidney might not set their peoples' hearts alight yet they offered edifying instruction, based on scripture, and intended to promote personal morality and mutually useful conduct. As Bishop Horsley expressed it, 'Practical holiness is the end: Faith is the means; and to suppose Faith and Practice separable, is to suppose the end attainable without the use of means' (Horsley: 10). Similarly, there was some wariness about imposing a controversial line in divinity on the wrong sort of listener: a zealous controversialist, one cleric complained, ran 'the Risque of giving Offence to the most genteel Part of his Congregation' (*A Protestant's Address to the Protestants of Ireland etc.* [1757]: 13, qtd. in Leighton: 51).

If there was a predominant homiletic style prevailing in this era it was that of the *simplicitas evangelica*, which had a long pedigree dating back to those hugely influential

Restoration clergy Robert South and John Tillotson (Brown: 176–7; Reedy). In their plainness and their clarity, in their rejection of the orotund and the Baroque, in their downplaying the mysteries of faith in favour of an emphasis on the reasonableness of God's laws, these two figures confirmed a trend that would not be displaced for several generations. High Churchmen who detected an easygoing attitude to dogma that betrayed Socinian tendencies periodically assailed Tillotson, Archbishop of Canterbury from 1691 to 1694, and yet it was precisely this quality to his preaching that made him so popular. And Tillotson also possessed an eloquence that offset any dryness in his content. He was 'the model of prose-writers for decades to come' (Lessenich: 11), admired and commended by both Addison and Steele. For Tillotson, revelation had been supported both by rational evidence and sense observation: 'And to assure us, that these reasonings are true, we have a most credible revelation of these things, God having sent his Son from heaven to declare it to us, and given us a sensible demonstration of the thing, in his resurrection from the dead, and his visible ascension into heaven.' (Tillotson: 2:69).

Preachers in the Tillotsonian mould (and they included as many Dissenters as Anglicans) were not complacent about the moral failings of mankind but believed that the bulk of baptized believers were capable, through exhortation, of practising lives of benevolence that would win them salvation. Their sermons were scripturally based: indeed, an 'amazing similarity in the use of the Bible by Anglican and dissenting preachers' has been detected, '... as if they had been guided by the same political and religious blueprints' (Deconinck-Brossard 1993: 109). This faith respected the practice and precepts of the Gospel (and indeed was inspired by them) only locating them loosely within an overarching dogmatic framework. Tillotson's celebrated sermon on the text 'And his Commandments are not grievous' inspired countless thematic imitations. As the Revd Anthony Hastwell, a North Riding parson, observed before his rural congregation:

> God almighty, in the laws he gave us by Christ, never intended to require an exact and unsinning obedience to them; but in the Gospel sense we are said to obey God's laws when we use our sincere endeavours to obey them; when in the main of our lives we live up to them; when we do not indulge ourselves in any known, wilful course of sin'. (qtd. in Watson)

Such sermons were thus both accessible in an auditory sense as well as a pastoral one. They could be moderately learned, unashamedly so if the congregation was an academic one, yet recondite scholarship was never to obscure straightforward scriptural truths or confuse the average Christian. These views were held and practised by such leading exemplars of the pulpit arts as Thomas Secker, Archbishop of Canterbury (1693–1768), and Hugh Blair, doyen of the Moderate 'party' in the Church of Scotland, both in his *Lectures on Rhetoric and Belles Lettres* (1783) and in the four published volumes of his sermons. Thus whatever doubts were held about Tillotson's theology, his preaching style aroused close to universal admiration. There were other gifted preachers who were influenced by Tillotson while possessing homiletic capacities that were excitingly individual, such as the High Churchman Francis Atterbury. He had more interest in arousing the passions than many of his contemporaries, and won many female admirers (as well as Richard Steele and Jonathan Swift). Atterbury never lost sight of the weaknesses of rational Christianity and the need of mankind for God's free and mysterious gift of salvation proclaimed in scripture and the sacraments (Bennett: 36–8). As James Downey noted, 'in him can be observed the major stylistic trends of eighteenth-century preaching—the lucidity and immediacy of the moralists, the aggressiveness of the polemicists, and the passion of the evangelicals' (Downey: 29).

The Enlightenment and the Pulpit

Plain preaching was easily reconciled with a 'rational' Christianity. That adjective aroused few misgivings in the first half of the century and was unashamedly claimed by the national Churches of both England and Scotland. It sat easily within the Hookerian synthesis of scripture, reason, and tradition, all part of an enlightened religious understanding that was held to confer upon the Church of England a unique confessional lustre, for, as Roy Porter insisted (and most historians would concur), 'Enlightenment in Britain took place within, rather than against, Protestantism' (Porter: 99), forming part of a wider movement of spiritual and moral renewal in both Protestant and Catholic Europe (Rosenblatt). There was a firm tendency for dogma to be not uncritically received. As J. G. A. Pocock has said, 'The Trinity, the Incarnation, the divinity of Christ were understood to be doctrines arrived at through dialectic and disputation; it was proper for persons of integrity to dispute them among themselves, as churchmen frequently did in print as well as in speech' (Pocock 1995: 48). Men were to use their minds in hearing the Word of God and be guided by the clergy towards a correct understanding of the scriptures. God's purposes were inscrutable but they were prima facie reasonable. It was a commonplace, for example, that reason could establish the existence of God. The Revd John Lloyd (vicar of Epping, 1710–54) put it thus:

> That there is a supreme Being or God, who is the first cause and chief governor of all things, and who has a just right to our greatest veneration and worship, is a truth of which we have such certain evidence and knowledge, that it seems impossible for any thinking man to be either ignorant or doubtful of it. (unpublished sermon, qtd. in Sykes 1959: 181)

The created world provided abundant evidence of an intelligent, benevolent creator while the New Testament supplemented natural theology with the good news of Revelation. The triumph of Newtonianism across Europe in the first part of the century had reaffirmed the power of God, and Christian apologists had been quick to claim Newton as implicitly sanctioning the claims of their own revealed religion. Some attempts were even made to state Christianity in mathematical terms, as in *Theologiae Christianae Principia Mathematica* of John Craig, the Newtonian and prebend of Salisbury from 1708 (Sykes 1959: 153). The scientific interests of the age were taken to buttress the claims of Christianity not just on intellectual occasions, such as the delivery of the Boyle Lectures, but in churches up and down the country—witness Parson Woodforde: 'how little is all which we can comprehend of the works of God, when compared with the immensity of space without any possible limit or bound: I say, how inconsiderable all the works of God, that we know anything of when compared with this immensity and that Being who fills it!' (Sykes 1939: 97–106, 341–5). Of all his writings, Locke's *The Reasonableness of Christianity, as Delivered in the Scriptures* (1695) had a particular influence (Sell: *passim*). Reason was the supreme tribunal and Revelation, according to Locke's classic formulation, no more than 'natural reason enlarged by a new set of discoveries communicated by God immediately, which reason vouches the truth of by the testimony and proofs it gives that they come from God' (Locke: 4:4). Faith and reason were thus complementary, though faith is based on reason. It was when they attempted to justify the teachings of the Church that had only a limited or negligible basis in scripture that contentions arose. With Protestant Dissenters and Low Church Anglicans often working together for 'Christian liberty', their mid-century objective became to secure relaxation of laws requiring subscription to the Thirty-Nine Articles. It generated considerable tensions within the Established Church and by the 1770s those congregations (principally Dissenting ones) that would not pass beyond what was plainly contained in the Bible had more or less appropriated the term 'rational Christians' to themselves as the latitudinarian consensus broke down.

An emphasis on rational belief never sat entirely comfortably with classical Christian orthodoxy; the parting of the ways gradually occurred during the reign of George III. Even in its heyday from the 1730s to the 1750s, many orthodox Anglicans had never been entirely comfortable with an hortatory emphasis on reason and natural religion over revelation of God in Jesus Christ. And, on the other hand, rational Dissenters like Priestley and Price in the 1780s were determined to demonstrate that Trinitarian Christianity was firmly non-scriptural. These tensions had been prefigured much earlier in the century by anticlerical polemicists such as John Toland (1670–1723), the thrust of whose whole career was devoted to divesting the Churches of their institutional authority in the field of learning by a progressive assault on their intellectual credibility (Champion: *passim*). Toland was a free-thinker, determined to compromise the authority of Christian 'knowledge' as well as the political power of the Church (of England); although he was unsuccessful in his own time, his ideas had a corrosive effect in the medium term that weakened the Church's claims to rationality in its teaching ministry.

Toland's injection of a note of instability into notions of rationality became an inseparable element of what scholars following Jonathan Israel now customarily refer to as the 'radical Enlightenment'. After the lapse of the licensing laws in 1695, English clerics from all parties took to the pulpit regularly to deplore the growth of irreligion, anticlericalism, and libertinism, to declare afresh the exclusive rationality of Christianity (Redwood). The High Churchmen among them proclaimed repeatedly that the Church was 'in Danger', but Whig bishops or clergy such as Benjamin Hoadly who took their stand on the religious settlement of the Glorious Revolution and the Toleration Act of 1689 did not level such a charge. They were comfortable with the unfolding of Enlightenment values in post-Revolutionary England and its identification with clergy of latitudinarian values, especially those among them seeking further reformation. They included stellar names such as Queen Caroline's favourite clerical luminary, the Revd Samuel Clarke, rector of St James's, Piccadilly, and Boyle Lecturer in 1704 and 1705. One of the two theses he defended for his Cambridge DD in 1709 was ever his inspiration: 'No article of the Christian faith, delivered in the Holy Scriptures, is disagreeable to right reason.' Yet Clarke's assured ascent in the Church of England was stymied by his Newton-inspired propensity to Arianism (subtly evidenced in his *The Scripture-Doctrine of the Trinity* (1712)). His error appeared confirmed when he omitted the celebration of Holy Communion from the service he conducted on Trinity Sunday 1713. Presuming that he wished to avoid reading the Proper Preface, his conduct provoked a wave of complaints from the Lower House of Convocation in 1714 that he was subverting the Articles and the Book of Common Prayer (Stewart). Despite his extreme moral rationalism, Clarke was a preacher whose talents even his fiercest opponents could not deny however much they alleged that the heterodox and the anti-dogmatists were doing the work of anti-christian forces for them (Young: 24). Significantly, the incontrovertibly Athanasian Samuel Johnson regarded Clarke's as the best sermons in the English language for their sound biblical exposition, their emphasis on Christ's propitiatory sacrifice, and their eloquence, and he was ready to overlook the determination of Clarke and his followers to discount the unwavering faith of the western Church in defence of the Trinity. If parish clergy had difficulties making their own use of Clark's corpus of his sermons it was probably as much for their rather abstract discussion of theological doctrine as for their neo-Arianism. Clarke had a large following among non-Arian clergy though his two closest disciples, John Jackson and Arthur Ashley Sykes, received no State preferment. His career highlighted the capacity of rational Christianity to tip over into heterodoxy and the need for the clergy to be vigilant in offsetting that possibility. By and large, they were successful.

Deism in England and America

The problem was that rational criticism could question the authority of revelation. The danger in having a dominant theology in which reason was used to prove the existence of a distant deity before it could disclose the God of Abraham, Isaac, and Jacob is that faith might lose its top tier (Deconinck-Brossard 1991: 73–99). Those who sought to challenge the veracity of the Gospel as received by the western Church and to call into doubt its institutional importance made repeated polemical attacks that were at their height from the 1710s to the 1740s. What the Deists lacked in a popular following they made up for in terms of intellectual quality: protagonists of the stamp of Toland, Collins, Tindal, and Woolston presented Christian apologists with a serious challenge. As Roy Porter put it: 'the English Deists were novel, incisive and influential—Voltaire and other *philosophes* were deeply in their debt' (Porter: 98). The Deists privileged natural theology and depicted the Creator as largely detached from human affairs. They explicitly denied Christ's divine nature on the grounds of fable, historical misunderstanding, and the philosophically impossible and they accused the clergy of conspiring to bamboozle the laity. Deism was a 'complex and amorphous movement' that 'combined the assaults of traditional Christianity launched by natural religion, the comparative study of religion, deductions from the scientific movement and an incipient rationalistic criticism of the Bible itself' (Sykes 1959: 169); Deists saw themselves to be purifying the faith and defending reason against unthinking authority, as the talented gentleman-lawyer Anthony Collins tried to do in his *Discourse of Free-Thinking* (1713) (O'Higgins). Likewise, the candlemaker Thomas Chubb wanted a purified religion emptied of the 'corrupt doctrines' of Christianity: the Trinity, the atonement, and the Virgin birth. All had to go (Bushell: 18).

The Deists were not without friends in the first Whig governments of George I. The commonwealth values of the Stanhope-Sunderland ministry of 1717–20 gave them every prospect of eroding the privileges of the Church of England following the prorogation of Convocation in 1717. The institutional crisis died down temporarily after the bursting of the South Sea Bubble in 1720 and the determination of Sir Robert Walpole to buttress his government with Anglican support rather than destabilize it by antagonizing further the clerical establishment. Nevertheless, the Deists continued to publish their tracts of 'polemical divinity', and there were further assaults on the Church in the 1730s with plans to contest the value of tithes and scale back further the power of the ecclesiastical courts. Few clergymen, confronted with this antagonism, could forbear from having their say in the pulpit and the Deists faced a homiletic offensive that gradually countered their influence and curbed their effusiveness.

In the long-term it was arguably in British North America that the Deists had the maximum influence; witness that sizable proportion of the Founding Fathers whose explicit endorsement of Trinitarian Christianity was either withheld or grudgingly given. Benjamin Franklin never wavered in his persuasion that religious observance was a civil duty. Though a Deist, he attended the recently established Unitarian chapel on Essex Street when in London during the 1770s and took an interest in liturgical simplification, bringing out a *Preface to an Abridgement of the Book of Common Prayer* in 1779. That same year he produced a revised account of the Lord's Prayer and even proposed a new version of the Bible in modern language, in effect an exercise in stripping Christianity of its 'superstitious' elements while preserving its moral appeal. For Thomas Jefferson, 'the old Trinity was replaced by a new trinity, Newton, Locke, and Bacon' (Brodie: 98), and he read the Deists alongside them. He nurtured a respect for the person and ministry of Christ—in a letter of 1823 to John Adams he calls Jesus 'the most venerated reformer of human errors' (Ferguson: 77)—with a lifelong deprecation of sacerdotalism against which he frequently resorted to using the invective of the Enlightenment: 'My opinion is that there would never have been an infidel, if there had never been a priest', he wrote to Mrs Samuel Smith in 1816 (Ferguson: 73). Jefferson maintained an absolutist faith in the power of reason alongside an appreciation of the extraordinary vitality of the scriptures. Appropriately, he was the primary architect of the separation of Church and State and resorted readily to the language of civil religion as in his inaugural address. As has been well said of his generation of American republicans, 'Reason does not so much join revelation in the language of the political elite; it becomes revelation' (Ferguson: 75).

Defenders of Rational Religion: Berkeley, Butler, and Waterland

The Anglican response to the Deists from the 1690s onwards has been adjudged to be 'more widespread, more scholarly and polemically more effective' than has sometimes been allowed (Clark: 360). George Berkeley, Bishop of Cloyne (1685–1753), was renowned as an immaterialist metaphysician and a philosopher of the science of man in his time but he was also a subtle apologist for the claims of the Church. Berkeley met the critiques of free-thinkers unflinchingly to the point of denying them their descriptive name, used notably by Collins in his *Discourse of Free-Thinking*, and attempted to show that they were the bigoted, prejudiced ones, perversely unwilling to follow impartial reason. Whatever their apparent obscurities and difficulties, religious mysteries had their parallels in the received theories of Locke and Newton. Hence one must either accept these mysteries or reject them along with cherished philosophical and mathematical mysteries (Berman: 159). Berkeley was 'a preacher of power and distinction' (Downey: 87). Few of his sermons survive (and those only unpublished) but they all display an exceptional range of rhetorical devices to articulate his faith. He may have been a philosophical theologian and yet the sermons disclose his profound respect for religious mystery and the Church as the mystical body of Christ. Berkeley was in no doubt about the reality of sin and the need for all men to attend to their salvation. In the next generation, Philip Skelton appeared as the leading Irish critic of the Deists. In 1749 he published *Ophiomaches, or Deism Revealed* (1749), a book that contained a wide-ranging analysis of the different sorts of religious unbelief. Skelton had no truck with what he alleged was the essence of Deism, the belief that man can be self-sufficient, know the truth, and live a good life without external revealed authority (Berman: *Introduction to Skelton*). In 1754 two volumes (mainly of sermons) appeared with the title of *Discourses Controversial and Practical on Various Subjects* that cleverly and uncompromisingly reasserted core Christian doctrines of the Trinity and the Atoning work of Christ, leading some critics of his views to (mis)represent him as 'an orthodox bully' (Burdy: 128). Though their initial impact was small, Skelton's sermons came to be widely read by Anglican divines in the second half of the century. The orthodox Irish nonconformist minister, John Leland (1691–1766), produced a comprehensive *A View of the Principal Deistical Writers* in 1754. In his reading, theirs was not a complex historical phenomenon but a conspiracy to discredit the authority of revelation, Scripture, and the Church hatched by men who could not even agree on their principal beliefs. His was a Lockean view of Christianity and as such widely serviceable by other clergy, not discarding doctrine but insisting on its simple character and the need to transmit and uphold it. Four volumes of his selected sermons appeared posthumously in 1768–9 as *Discourses on Varied Subjects*. Their cumulative thrust was to present Christianity as a moral religion within a firmly redemptive framework. But if there was an authoritative Anglican response to Deism it was delivered by Joseph Butler, Bishop of Bristol and Durham, the product of a Dissenting Academy at Gloucester and Tewkesbury who converted to Anglicanism. It came in the form of his *Analogy of Religion, Natural and Revealed, to the Constitution and Course of Nature* (1736) in which he showed that the natural religion exclusively admitted by the Deists was 'as full of mystery and shadows as revelation' (Sykes 1959: 174). He was never slow to stress the limitations of man's spiritual and intellectual grasp. Butler already had a solid reputation as a preacher and moral philosopher thanks to the appearance in 1726 of the first edition of his *Fifteen Sermons Preached at the Rolls Chapel*, and the *Analogy* confirmed his standing as one of the supreme philosophical theologians of his age who was wholly orthodox in his creed. Butler was not primarily a preacher. His Rolls Chapel *Sermons* were addressed to a highly educated congregation to whom he offered a framework for what was really a theory of ethics. Though less abstract than either Clarke or Berkeley, he was not a popularizer. His pessimistic tone when combined with an absence of humour or irony limited his appeal; he also had a tendency in his sermons to choose texts which could lead him into minute discussions of doctrine resulting in obscurity, and even he admitted the defect (Lessenich: 48). Nevertheless, he was such a commanding presence in mid-eighteenth-century Anglicanism that he could not easily be ignored, and preachers drawing on him for inspiration took comfort from his argument that assertions about the content of natural religion had exactly the same epistemological status as assertions about the content of revealed religion.

Slightly less influential but hardly less gifted as a philosophical cleric was the Cambridge academic Daniel Waterland (1683–1740). Having initially made his name by arguing that orthodox Trinitarianism was the pure doctrine of the primitive Church in *A Vindication of Christ's Divinity* (1719), he made sure that a large Anglican audience were left in no doubt that their weekly profession of belief was historically justifiable in *A Critical History of the Athanasian Creed* (1724). Waterland, a High Church Whig, was determined to remind the Church that Christian rationalism as it was professed by Clarke and his disciples was uncomfortably close to Deism, and that the surest means of guarding the faith against philosophical contamination was by resorting to history and tradition within the Anglican Patristic inheritance. He used a range of communicative means to make his case, including the pulpit. His *Eight Sermons in Defence of the Divinity of our Lord Jesus Christ* (1720) were preached in the newly opened St Paul's cathedral and were partly in response to Clarke. Archidiaconal charges were another means of bringing home to the parish clergy the contemporary concerns of the higher reaches of the hierarchy in hopes that they would in turn act to guard their congregations against false teachers; Waterland (appointed to the Archdeaconry of Middlesex in 1730) did this with Deism in mind in his 1732 charge published as *Christianity Vindicated against Infidelity*. He denounced Deists for teaching moral corruption, derided their claims that Moses and Christ were false prophets, and denied that Christianity was just a confection of priestcraft, for it had been founded by Christ and his apostles (Holtby). Opponents of the Deists could all concur that Christianity must be presented as the necessary completion and complement of natural religion; where there was appreciable divergence among them was on how far (if at all) it should be simplified and purged of all save the fundamental articles of faith as contained in scripture (Sykes 1959: 161).

Hoadleians and Warburtonians

Other senior members of the early eighteenth-century hierarchy were less concerned to stay close to credal Christianity than Waterland. The greatest champion of Low Church Whiggism in the 1710s, Benjamin Hoadly, was an irrepressible and talented polemical divine who duly received reward in the shape of the see of Bangor two years after the accession of George I in 1714. He gained notoriety in 1717 after preaching before the king on 'The nature of the Kingdom or Church of Christ' and in effect denying the Church any visible presence or authority, thereby inaugurating the most intensive and long drawn out theological contest of the century, the Bangorian Controversy. His own extreme latitudinarian thinking elevated conscience to an extent that left minimal scope for ordained ministers to teach the Gospel as it had been received by the Church. It predictably incurred the misgivings of moderate Whig clergy and the fury of the High Church party almost as much as his ecclesiology: the non-juror and mystic, William Law, even thought he could substantiate the charge that Hoadly was an anti-Trinitarian (Law: 67) though that particular allegation could never be made to stick. Hoadly's championing of scripture as the supreme authority for Protestants and his repeated vindication of toleration made him the darling of dissenters, and his own distrust of anything that smacked of sacerdotalism did nothing to stunt his ascent in the Church of England and his enjoyment for twenty-seven years (after 1734) of the fifth highest place in the hierarchy, the bishopric of Winchester. He was energetically resourceful in promoting clergy who shared his theological outlook and usually combined it with some admiration of Clarke's highly rational sermons. John Balguy (1686–1748), vicar of Northallerton (awarded a prebend of Salisbury by Hoadly), for instance, published six tracts between 1726 and 1733 with targets that included Shaftesbury, Hutcheson, and Wollaston, and his *Twenty One Sermons* appeared posthumously in 1749 (in the first four years of his clerical career he claimed to have composed a sermon every week!). Balguy looked at ethical questions in the light of religion and attempted to map out a distinctively rational Christian position as opposed to a Deistic one. He had endeared himself to the bishop by weighing in in his favour during the Bangorian Controversy and his writings have been adjudged 'arguably the best apology for Hoadleian theology to be published in the controversy' (Starkie: 86). Pockets of 'Hoadleian' Anglicanism survived almost to the end of the century, especially in the

Winchester diocese, and echoes of his distinctive, 'enlightened' faith could be heard from country pulpits even when the orthodox largely held sway in the Church of England from the middle years of George III's reign and relations with Dissenters were steadily worsening. This was a distinctive school within eighteenth-century Anglicanism with a pervasive outreach. Many of his supporters granted Hoadly a status on a level with Bacon and Locke and lauded his achievement, Balguy thus fulsomely praising his Hoadly 'for demolishing the wild schemes of Patriarchal and Despotick Power; [and] for erecting in their stead that glorious Pile of solid Reasoning, and sound Politicks, which protects our just Liberties, and deserves to be reckoned among the principal Bulwarks of our Constitution' (Balguy: Introduction).

William Warburton (1698–1779), Bishop of Gloucester after 1760, was comparably apostrophized. He was both a religious polemicist and an authoritarian literary figure with a national influence and a 'Warburtonian following' (Evans). Though a distinctive Erastian in his ecclesiology, he stood at some distance to Hoadly's theological stance, defending the miracles of the early Christian centuries as necessary truths and attacking the Deistic materialism of Bolingbroke in his *A View of Lord Bolingbroke's Philosophy* (1754–5). Warburton had no time for the 'enthusiasm' he detected in Whitefield and Wesley, and his own neo-orthodox faith was always held to be open to rational persuasion. Indeed the whole point of his notorious *The Divine Legation of Moses Demonstrated* (1737) is that he claimed to have found a means of proving the truth of the Mosaic religion as the forerunner of Christianity. Warburton liked rarified congregations for his auditors. He found one at Lincoln's Inn for his *The Principles of Natural and Revealed Religion Occasionally Opened and Explained* (3 vols., 1753, 1767). Although he had a broad front of enemies, Warburton had a select group of vocal friends anxious to proclaim their loyalty, foremost among them George III's favourite bishop, Richard Hurd. They may have been latitudinarians and eirenic but they were still Trinitarian and orthodox. With their master dead, second-generation Hoadleians found the Warburtonians congenial allies, and there was scope for intellectual convergence and cooperation on the basis of theology and history, and an attachment to the Whig constitutional inheritance and to the Bible as the unassailable foundation of the Established Church. Interestingly it was John Balguy's son, Thomas, archdeacon of Winchester, who over time inspired this gentle convergence as Hurd's friend over many decades.

The Debate on Miracles

Any attempt to validate the authenticity of Christianity had to examine the status of miracles which, with prophecy, were foundational to the historic proofs of Christianity; a key part of this has been recently represented as the rise of a historically grounded apologetics (Pocock 2008: 83–96; Shaw: 144–73). These became a major field of combat between the orthodox and their adversaries. Warburton (*supra*) had taken part in it, although he was far from first in the field and perhaps a rather questionable defender of their veracity. Thomas Sherlock, Bishop of London and High Church Hanoverian Tory, published two influential defences of miracles and prophecies (Carpenter: 294–322) that gave the parish clergy a prized resource (just as he did in defence of the Test and Corporation Acts). Collins had insisted in his *A Discourse on the Grounds and Reasons of the Christian Religion* (1724) that the prophecies of the Old Testament should be interpreted allegorically. Not so, said Sherlock in *The Use and Interests of Prophecy* (1725): they betokened a progressive demonstration of divine purpose and were indubitably predictive, pointing the way towards the coming of Christ. Most preachers—insisting that the biblical examples of miracles and prophecy were literally and historically true—simply ransacked Sherlock, including the two volumes of his *Sermons* published in 1747 (Ingram: 287–8). His *Discourses on the Miracles of our Saviour* (1727–9) was a rejoinder to the Deist Thomas Woolston's attack on the credibility of miracles and was a definitive affirmation of the reliability of those witnesses to the miracles recorded in the New Testament. In the words of Leslie Stephen, it has a claim to be considered 'the concentrated essence of eighteenth-century apologetic theology' (Stephen: 1:243). The debate was far from ended. Conyers Middleton, the fiercely anti-Catholic polemicist, in *Free Enquiry into the Miraculous Powers* (1749) accepted the veracity of miracles though insisting that none had taken place beyond the confines of the apostolic age, and this was probably a position that commended itself to a considerable proportion of parish clergy. They would have sympathized with his presentation of the apostles as simple men and reliable eye-witnesses as opposed to the sophisticated Fathers.

Middleton was not per se sceptical about the existence of miracles; David Hume was. In Section X of his *Enquiry Concerning Human Understanding* (1748) he defined them as a violation of the laws of nature and put the case for denying the authenticity of all miracles, including necessarily those of Christ's as recorded in the Gospels. There was a limited clerical response, John Leland turning to it with some effect in his *A View of the Principal Deistical Writers* (1754) criticising Hume for the ambiguities in his use of the term 'experience': 'It is...a kind of cant term, proposed in a loose indeterminate way' (Leland: 1:286). The Master of Pembroke College, Oxford, William Adams, also published a rejection of Hume's arguments in *An Essay on Mr Hume's Essay on Miracles* (1752), first articulated as a visitation sermon the previous year. Hume reiterated his argument in a wider philosophical analysis of the psychological and social motives that make mankind believe in a higher power in *The Natural History of Religion* (1757). At the time it was of limited intellectual persuasion and a co-authored reply by Warburton and Hurd (*Remarks on Mr David Hume's Essay*) was believed to have been effective in belittling a man who had 'usurped to himself the name of Philosopher' (Young: 169–70, 210–11). Hume remained marginal to English intellectual life for much of the century though a minority of clergy were alert to the destructive importance of his work for both natural and revealed religion, with far more serious consequences for the former than for the latter (Aston). Subtle critics glimpsed the extent of the damage: in 1776 Soame Jenyns observed that miracles and prophecies 'must now depend for much of their credibility on the truth of that religion, whose credibility they were at first intended to support' (qtd. in Mossner: 294).

Paley

William Paley was an outstandingly gifted theologian who knew of Hume's work but considered it indirectly and offered a bold counter-statement in his *Evidences of Christianity* (1794), which, along with *Natural Theology* (1802), were standard readings for students throughout the nineteenth century. Paley confirmed the aptness and importance of John Locke for Anglican divines and placed an emphasis on natural theology that became a *locus classicus* even as a sizable body of religious (and philosophical) opinion was finding it unsatisfactory—for different reasons. He offered clergy a restatement of the argument from design (beginning with the famous analogy between the world and a pocket watch) that purported to show that the whole of nature had a single, divine author of infinite power, wisdom and goodness. And he was also defending Christian revelation directly from Hume's critique of miracles, returning to Leland's point that Hume fails to distinguish between a particular and general sense of the term 'experience' and had therefore failed to show that miracles were contrary to experience. If there is a probability of revelation, then this probability must extend to miracles also. Though placing reason at the centre of Christian ethics, Paley was critical of ultra-rational tendencies, declaring:

> We are...setting up a kind of philosophical morality, detached from religion and independent of its influence, which may be cultivated, it is said, as well without Christianity as with it; and which, if cultivated, renders religion and religious institutions superfluous. (Paley: 16)

Paley was vastly influential into the early nineteenth century as a moralist who defended the existing political and social order on the basis of its consistency with divine law (Clark: 154–6, 309–10). He enjoyed composing sermons and delivered them as he composed them, in an unaffected and unrhetorical style, influenced by Clarke and Hoadly. He never published a collection in his lifetime: his *Sermons on Several Subjects* (1808) was a popular resource but appeared three years after his death. His uses for the sermonizing clergy (especially those who had studied his works while undergraduates at Cambridge) were therefore manifold and various, though High Churchmen were not comfortable with his ecclesiology, which had echoes of Hoadly and Warburton in its denial that Christ had left any instructions regarding the form of Church government and that its authority rested on nothing more than utility to be altered as civil circumstances required. Neither did Paley's optimistic vision of the natural world commend itself to Evangelicals such as Thomas Gisborne, whose *Natural Theology* (1818) saw the world as fallen, a place of sin and death, a vale of tears precisely because of mankind's original disobedience. Coleridge, too, expressed his dissatisfaction from a different angle:

> *Evidences* of Christianity! I am weary of the word. Make a man feel the *want* of it; rouse him, if you can, to the self-knowledge of his *need* of it; and you may safely trust to its own evidence. (Coleridge: 272)

Conclusions

Paley's absence of spiritual fervour greatly reduced his currency for the Evangelicals who, by the beginning of the nineteenth century, were increasingly prominent in the Church establishment. Their emphasis on repentance, personal salvation, and spiritual revival could not be comfortably contained within the stylistic and doctrinal confines of Tillotsonian preaching (Ditchfield: 45). This theology catered for human needs, as an Evangelical like Gilbert Wakefield recognized, as he observed that the dry reading of dry sermons was always going to drive large numbers of Christians to seek out enthusiastic Methodist preachers (Wakefield: 184). Drawing on the rich rhetorical range of mystics, Moravians, and non-jurors, Wesley, Whitefield, and their followers offered their auditors a different experience to mainstream, 'rational' preaching, and it was never silenced at any point in Augustan England. George Whitefield, a preacher often derided by contemporaries for his ecstatic style and delivery, worked hard to take his hearers' passions by surprise and often reduce them to tears. He was ridiculed by the Revd Richard Graves in *The Spiritual Quixote* (1773) whose hero Geoffry Wildgoose had only a brief impact on his congregations: 'But, their affections only being moved, and their understandings not enlightened, nor their reason convinced, too many of them soon relapsed into their former dissolute courses' (Graves: 75). Graves was fingering a classic vulnerability of revivalism at the parish level (evangelists needed resident incumbents to keep the flame they had lit fanned) yet Whitefield's impact in England and colonial America is not to be underestimated. As Johnson tersely said of him: 'He would be followed by crowds were he to wear a night-cap in the pulpit, or were he to preach from a tree' (Boswell: 409). Whitefield combined the skills of a great actor with a voice of immense amplification and impressive media skills, reaching out to attract an even greater audience through advertisements and press coverage in newspapers (Lambert: 52–94; Lessenich: 143–5). The whole thrust of such preaching was to awaken a zeal against sinfulness, to leave no individual in any doubt of the need for conversion, and to restrict and sometimes deplore the emphasis on good works. Yet it was also solidly Trinitarian in its emphasis and repudiated Socinianism 100 per cent. As Ditchfield has noted: 'It was partly because of the success of the Revival that deism remained a minority affair and had lost much of its impetus by 1750, while Arianism and Socinianism,...never acquired popular followings' (Ditchfield: 34).

And yet precisely because of the excess to which it was liable as well as its pejorative cultural associations, emotional preaching carried to the point of enthusiasm remained a minority option for the clergy in the eighteenth century. Most tried to strike a balance between rationality and mystery, what could be said and what could not be said about the Christian faith, and here, once again one finds the moderate High Churchman, Bishop Thomas Sherlock, setting the tone. In his *Several Discourses Preached at the Temple Church* (1754), he attempted to define the distinctive spheres of reason and revelation, emphasizing both the limitations of human reason and the importance of revelation as the most sure guide to salvation. Preachers like the celebrated novelist Laurence Sterne may have been doctrinally light but they were appealing (with some success) not just to reason but 'to a combination of psychology and common sense, the idea that sinfulness is an unavoidable part of our fallen natures, but that the truth of the Gospel can redeem those failings' (Bowden: 133). Similarly, Samuel Johnson, for all his admiration of Clarke, concluded not that religion was unreasonable, but that human reason is limited (Chapin: 156–8). This was precisely the ground on which the Scottish Common Sense philosopher, James Beattie of Aberdeen, pitched his best-selling *Essay on the Nature and Immutability of Truth* (1770) in response to Hume. With its attempt to harmonize the rational and emotional aspects of man, it had an immense circulation among the higher clergy of the Anglican Church who could hardly commend Beattie sufficiently.

This tempered rationalism was the hallmark of the pre-Romantic sermon yet the importance of a figure such as Beattie in the emergence of Romantic sensibilities reminds us that cultural shifts and fashions were subtle and various. The 'rational' sermon may have been normative in Hanoverian Britain and yet its pitch, presentation, emphasis, and intellectual indebtedness were extraordinarily various. Temperate, moderate sermons could readily sound ponderous and lifeless in the wrong hands, becoming what the moralist and pedagogue Vicesimus Knox described as a 'dull, dry, torpid, languid, soporific style' (Knox: 1:180), yet these dangers did not offset the determination of the majority of eighteenth-century clergy to rejoice in the marriage of reason and religion (though the term 'rational' was generally dropped). What has been called the 'holy alliance' between Anglicanism and the new science endured throughout the century; Deism only revived well into the reign of George III by which time, it has been persuasively claimed, the Church 'was ever more clearly revealed as apostolical and sacerdotal rather than Erastian or rationalist' (Clark: 361). It would be within those former categories that refreshed apologetic discourses would be developed.

References

Aston, N. (1993). 'Horne and Heterodoxy: The Defence of Anglican Belief in the Late Enlightenment'. *English Historical Review* 108: 895–919.

Balguy, J. (1734). *A Collection of Tracts Moral and Theological*. London: J. Pemberton.

Beales, D. (2000). 'Religion and Culture', in T. C. W. Blanning (ed.), *The Eighteenth Century: Europe 1688–1815*. Oxford: Oxford University Press, 131–77.

Bennett, G. V. (1975). *The Tory Crisis in Church and State, 1680–1730. The Career of Francis Atterbury, Bishop of Rochester*. Oxford: Clarendon Press.

Berman, D. (1994). *George Berkeley. Idealism and the Man*. Oxford: Clarendon Press.

Boswell, J. (1980). *The Life of Johnson*. Oxford: Oxford University Press.

Bowden, M. (2007). *Yorick's Congregation. The Church of England in the Time of Laurence Stone*. Newark, DE: University of Delaware Press.

Brodie, F. M. (1974). *Thomas Jefferson: An Intimate History*. New York: Norton.

Brown, J. (1900). *Puritan Preaching in England*. London: Hodder and Stoughton.

Burdy, S. (1914). *Life of Philip Skelton*. Oxford: Clarendon Press.
Bushell, T. L. (1967). *The Sage of Salisbury. Thomas Chubb, 1679-1747*. New York: Philosophical Library.
Carpenter, E. (1936). *Thomas Sherlock, 1678-1761*. London: SPCK.
Champion, J. (2003). *Republican Learning. John Toland and the Crisis of Christian Culture, 1696-1722*. Manchester: Manchester University Press.
Chapin, C. F. (1968). *The Religious Thought of Samuel Johnson*. Ann Arbor, MI: University of Michigan Press.
Clark, J. (2000). *English Society 1660-1832. Religion, Ideology, and Politics During the Ancien Régime*. Cambridge: Cambridge University Press.
Coleridge, S. T. (1904). *Aids to Reflection*. London: Bell.
Deconinck-Brossard. (1991). 'L' Apologétique dans la prédication anglaise au XVIIIè siècle', in M. Pitassi (ed.), *Apologétique 1680-1740: Sauvetage ou Naufrage de la Théologie?* Geneva: Labor et Fides, 73-99.
—— (1993). 'Eighteenth-Century Sermons and the Age', in W. M. Jacob and N. Yates (eds.), *Crown and Mitre. Religion and Society in Northern Europe Since the Reformation*. Woodbridge: Boydell Press, 105-21.
Ditchfield, G. M. (1998). *The Evangelical Revival*. London: UCL Press.
Downey, J. (1969). *The Eighteenth Century Pulpit: a Study of the Sermons of Butler, Berkeley, Secker, Sterne, Whitefield and Wesley*. Oxford: Clarendon Press.
Evans, A. W. (1932). *Warburton and the Warburtonians: A Study in Some Eighteenth-Century Controversies*. London: Oxford University Press.
Ferguson, R. A. (1994). *The American Enlightenment, 1750-1820*. Cambridge, MA: Harvard University Press.
Graves, R. (1967). *The Spiritual Quixote or The Summer's Ramble of Mr Geoffrey Wildgoose. A Comic Romance*, ed. C. Tracy. London: Oxford University Press.
Gregory, J. (1993). 'The Eighteenth-Century Reformation: The Pastoral Task of Anglican Clergy after 1689', in J. Walsh, C. Haydon, and S. Taylor (eds.), *The Church of England c.1689-c.1833: From Toleration to Tractarianism*. Cambridge: Cambridge University Press, 67-85.
Holtby, R. T. (1966). *Daniel Waterland 1683-1740: A Study in Eighteenth-Century Orthodoxy*. Carlisle: C. Thurnam.
Horsley, S. (1791). *The Charge of Samuel, Bishop of St David's, to the Clergy of His Diocese, 1790*. Gloucester: R. Raikes.
Ingram, R. G. (2010). 'Nature, History, and the Search for Order: The Boyle Lectures, 1730-1785', in P. Clarke and T. Claydon (eds.), *God's Bounty? The Churches and the Natural World*. Woodbridge: Ecclesiastical History Society, 276-92.
Knox, V. (1788). *Winter Evenings or Lucubrations on Life and Letters*. London: Charles Dilly.
Lambert, F. (1994). *George Whitefield and the Transatlantic Revivals, 1737-1770*. Princeton, NJ: Princeton University Press.
Law, W. (1717). *A Second Letter to the Bishop of Bangor*. London: W. Innys.
Leighton, C. D. A. (1994). *Catholicism in a Protestant Kingdom. A Study of the Irish Ancien Régime*. New York: St Martin's Press.
Leland, J. (1757). *A View of the Principal Deistical Writers*. London: B. Dod.
Lessenich, R. P. (1972). *Elements of Pulpit Oratory in Eighteenth-Century England (1660-1800)*. Koln: Bohlau.
Locke, J. (1690). *Essay Concerning Human Understanding*. London: Thomas Basset.

Mossner, E. C. (1954). *The Life of David Hume*. Edinburgh: Nelson.
O'Higgins, J. (1970). *Anthony Collins: The Man and His Works*. The Hague: Martinus Nijhoff.
Paley, W. (1790). *A Charge Delivered to the Clergy of the Diocese of Carlisle, in the Year 1790*. London: R. Faulder.
Pocock, J. G. A. (1995). 'Within the Margins: The Definitions of Orthodoxy', in R. D. Lund (ed.), *The Margins of Orthodoxy. Heterodox Writing and Cultural Response 1660–1750*. Cambrdge: Cambridge University Press, 33–53.
—— (2008). 'History and Enlightenment: A View of their History'. *Modern Intellectual History* 5: 83–96.
Porter, R. (2000). *Enlightenment: Britain and the Creation of the Modern World*. London: Allen Lane.
Redwood, J. (1976). *Reason, Ridicule, and Religion 1690–1730*. London: Thames & Hudson.
Reedy, G. (1992). *Robert South, 1634–1716: An Introduction to His Life and Sermons*. Cambridge: Cambridge University Press.
Rosenblatt, H. (2006). 'The Christian Enlightenment', in S. J. Brown and T. Tackett (eds.), *Enlightenment, Reawakening and Revolution 1660–1815*. Cambridge: Cambridge University Press, 283–301.
Sell, A. P. F. (1997). *John Locke and the Eighteenth-Century Divines*. Cardiff: University of Wales Press.
Shaw, J. (2006). *Miracles in Enlightenment England*. New Haven, CT: Yale University Press.
Skelton, P. (1990). *Ophiomaches, or Deism Revealed*, ed. D. Berman. Bristol: Thoemmes.
Starkie, A. (2007). *The Church of England and the Bangorian Controversy, 1716–1721*. Woodbridge: Boydell Press.
Stephen, L. (1876). *History of English Thought in the Eighteenth Century*. London: Smith, Elder.
Stewart, L. (1981). 'Samuel Clarke, Newtonianism, and the Factions of Post-Revolutionary England'. *JHI* 42: 53–72.
Sykes, N. (1939). 'The Sermons of a Country Parson: James Woodforde in his Pulpit'. *Theology* 38: 97–106, 341–5.
—— (1959). *From Sheldon to Secker: Aspects of English Church History 1660–1768*. Cambridge: Cambridge University Press.
Tillotson, J. (1728). *Works*. London: J. Darby.
Wakefield, G. (1792). *Memoirs of the Life of Gilbert Wakefield… Written by Himself*. London: Hodson.
Watson, E. W. (1928). 'An Eighteenth-Century Clergyman'. *Church Quarterly Review* 105: 255–71.
Young, B. W. (1998). *Religion and Enlightenment in Eighteenth-Century England: Theological Debate from Locke to Burke*. Oxford: Clarendon Press.

CHAPTER 25

PREACHING THE OXFORD MOVEMENT

JEREMY MORRIS

INTRODUCTION

FROM its very beginning, the Oxford Movement courted controversy. If it was a movement seeking to renew the theology, devotional life, and liturgical practice of the Church of England, at the same time, like the Evangelical Revival, its forerunner in so many ways, it also raised time and again points of critical challenge against the Church. Its style seemed to many contemporaries polemical, harsh, sectarian, clerical, and exclusive. In its early years, its most notable publications were the *Tracts for the Times*, which asserted distinct points of controversy, and lent to the Movement one of its names, 'Tractarianism'. Other names, however, carried much the same overtone of *odium clericum*, especially 'Puseyite' and 'Newmanite' (Nockles 1994: 33–43). It propagated its views through house journals, above all the *British Critic* (Skinner: 33–64). It produced treatises of original—but controversial, nevertheless—divinity, which spared no one in their readiness to criticize the theological positions of its opponents. Beginning with a suspicion of the Whig government's 1833 proposals to reform the Irish Church widely shared amongst High Churchmen, its trajectory has commonly been seen as one of ever deepening isolation, until the catastrophic year of 1845, when Newman finally converted to Rome.

Yet it is often forgotten that the Oxford Movement was not so much written as *preached*. It was not merely or even predominantly an academic movement, but one which rapidly sought to embed itself in the parishes and to promote a reform of the Church's teaching and pastoral practice. With a few significant exceptions, most of its leading figures were at one time or another parish priests whose staple means of expression was the weekly sermon. Richard Hurrell Froude died young and Edward Pusey remained an Oxford professor for most of his life, but throughout the 'twelve years' (1833–45) characterized by Dean Church, following Newman, Keble was vicar of a country parish, and Newman himself both incumbent of St Mary's, Oxford, and also priest-in-charge of the hamlet of Littlemore on the outskirts of Oxford (Church). Almost all of the other Tractarians occupied pastoral positions for long stretches of their ministry, and were concerned as much to teach the principles of the Movement to their congregations as to participate in national theological controversy. For this, the principal vehicle was naturally the sermon. According to Francis Paget, preaching formed, with catechizing, 'the most efficient of all machinery for the purposes of Christian instruction' (Paget 1858: 77). And yet even contemporaries frequently overlooked this fact. The conventional impression of the Oxford Movement's attitude to preaching was summed up by Dean Goulburn's biographer, who claimed that its reaction against the 'sermon-loving proclivities of the old Evangelical school' unduly depreciated sermons altogether 'as having robbed liturgical observances of much of their proper honour' (Compton: 31).

Such a perception of Tractarianism as motivated by a critical reaction against the dominant religious trends of the age (and therefore, depending on whether one was an opponent or a sympathizer, as a distortion or a recovery of the essential spirit of the Church of England) has coloured its reception amongst scholars. Critical interest in the history of the Oxford Movement has been intense, sustained in part by the overlapping but distinct fascination with the theology and spirituality of John Henry Newman, and particularly by the campaign for his canonization. At the risk of simplification, it is possible to identify three main strands. The first is the 'heroic' interpretation of Tractarianism as a story of struggle by an embattled group of religious reformers, who pioneered the revival of High Church principles and practice and thus gave birth to what was, by the late nineteenth century, being called the 'Anglo-Catholic' wing of the Church of England. Though not the first of its kind, Dean Church's history of the Movement, which broadly followed Newman's chronology in his *Apologia Pro Vita Sua*, was perhaps the most influential historical account, but the basic interpretation was considerably buttressed by various texts which appeared in or around the 'centenary' year of 1933 (Chadwick: 146). With some qualification and nuance, this view has remained influential for some scholars, foremost amongst whom would be Geoffrey Rowell and Owen Chadwick (Rowell; Chadwick). But almost coincidental with it was an alternative stream of interpretation, which emphasized the alien character of the Oxford Movement in Anglicanism. Drawing in particular on contemporary Evangelicals' hostility, and on popular anti-Catholicism, this received its most notorious expression in the 'conspiracy' view of Walter Walsh's *Secret History of the Oxford Movement* (1898). Walsh's book was factually rich, but not critically astute. It was part and parcel, however, of a stream of historiography which never unquestioningly accepted the Oxford Movement's agenda (Toon; Wellings). In recent years, a third strand has proved increasingly influential. Signalled above all by the work of Peter Nockles, this has moved beyond Tractarian 'hagiography' to look much more critically at the Oxford Movement's relationship to Evangelicalism and traditional Anglican High Churchmanship, in the process widening both the focus of Tractarian studies to include many figures and aspects formerly neglected, and at the chronology of the Movement, to question the 'twelve years' mythology which Newman largely dictated, and which so strongly influenced Church and others (Nockles 1994; Skinner; Pereiro).

From the many recent studies clustering under this very broad theme of 'revisionism', a number of points have emerged which bear on the interpretation of Tractarian preaching. As Nockles has argued, it was not that Tractarianism simply recovered long-lost aspects of Anglican divinity, as it claimed, but rather that it represented an altogether new form of Anglican ecclesiology, placing so much emphasis on the doctrine of apostolic succession, on the authority of the ordained ministry, and on the sacramental system of the Church, that it also required altogether new or intensified considerations of practical devotion, including penance, sanctification, and communion (Nockles 1994: 146–83). However, in turn this has only served to throw up points of continuity with the existing High Church tradition of Anglicanism, and also with Evangelicals—indeed, the very notion that one can trace distinct church 'party' labels in early nineteenth-century Anglicanism has come under close scrutiny. Pastoral, parochial renewal was really at the heart of the Tractarian enterprise, and not incidental to it. But this was an agenda shared with others: studying Tractarian pastoral practice has brought to light again striking continuities with other Anglican efforts, as well as dissonances. Much Tractarian preaching displayed themes and moods highly characteristic of Evangelicalism, including a strong appeal to emotion and religious experience, a sharp contrast between the Church and the world, a belief in the importance of conversion, and reliance on the authority of the Bible. Yet it also appealed to what it called 'Church Principles' in a way characteristic of the older High Church tradition. What was not shared with others were the ritual and ceremonial changes that eventually issued out of the theological changes engineered by the Tractarians (Morris: 144–6). Tractarian preaching touched on these from time to time, though it is true—as often observed—that what became Ritualism was to some extent a development beyond what the Oxford leaders themselves practised (Reed: 14–6).

But this growing recognition of elements of continuity and discontinuity which cut across the main strands of both Tractarian and Evangelical historiography has raised, naturally, profound questions about the identity of the Oxford Movement. At the most basic level, what was it, and who composed it? Newman's *Apologia*, one of the most influential spiritual autobiographies in the English language, has cast a long shadow over these questions. His depiction of a movement generated in the Oriel Common Room, triggered by Keble's clarion call to defend the Church against the depredations of the State, and led above all by a small group of friends, has proved so attractive to subsequent generations that it has largely resisted revision. And yet even Newman's narrative—hastily constructed in a few fevered weeks in 1864—itself acknowledged a much wider, larger movement of opinion, which not only drew on changing currents of sentiment and intellectual life at the beginning of the nineteenth century, but also sought to gather wide support amongst the parochial clergy (Newman 1964: 43). If we follow Nockles's lead in accepting elements of continuity between the 'Church Principles' advocated by the Tractarians and the older High Church tradition, and in recognizing at the same time the ecclesiological innovations of the Oxford Movement, what emerges is a distinct group within High Church opinion, marked off by its wariness of the term 'Protestant' and of the Reformation heritage of the Church of England, by its readiness to accept loudly-condemned elements of Roman Catholic devotional practice, by the concentrated emphasis it placed on apostolical succession, and by its willingness to 'unchurch' non-episcopal churches. It was never a particularly large group, but it was a group that achieved significant geographical spread throughout the Church of England. The most detailed study of Tractarian numbers, in an unpublished thesis by George Herring, reckoned on some 950 clergy in all by the mid-nineteenth century, the vast majority of whom were parish clergy (Herring: 39). This estimate is close to the figure of 1,000 claimed by the influential *Edinburgh Review* article on mid-Victorian parties by W. J. Conybeare (Conybeare: 357). If the advocacy of 'Church Principles' and scepticism about the Reformation differentiated the Tractarians, on one side, from Evangelicals and those 'middle' Anglicans later to be termed the 'Broad Church', nevertheless it also differentiated them, on the other side, from those traditional High Churchmen with whom they otherwise had much in common.

Herring took his analysis well beyond 1845, and in doing so implied that no account of the Oxford Movement which accepted Newman's conversion as a *terminus ad quem* could hope adequately to explain the Tractarians' impact on the Church of England. There could be no chronological end-point as such, when, even leaving to one side the further difficulty that many of the later Anglo-Catholics traced a direct lineage from the Tractarians even as they embraced Ritual change with an enthusiasm from which Pusey and Keble shrank, many clergy in the late Victorian period continued to profess the principles of the Oxford Movement, not least Henry Liddon, Pusey's great friend and disciple, without whom no consideration of Tractarian preaching would be complete. But just as the end of the Movement is problematic, so too is the beginning. Here, Nockles above all has indicated how the decisive theological and ecclesiological opinions adopted by the leaders of the Movement really emerged in the late 1820s. The struggle over Catholic Emancipation in the University of Oxford was a decisive point of clarification for the ideas and personal connections of those later to be regarded as the 'leaders' of the Oxford Movement, though much recent scholarship, including Nockles's own, also recognizes distinct shifts of opinion even from the mid-1820s within the intellectual development of Pusey and Newman (Nockles 1997: 202). Keble's Oxford 'Assize Sermon' of 14 July 1833 may have been kept by Newman as the start of the Oxford Movement, but in practice any discussion of Tractarian sermons inevitably has to cover a much longer period of time, from roughly the mid or late-1820s, onwards into the late-nineteenth century.

These difficulties in the historiography naturally are reflected in the scope of this chapter. Whether or not there was ever something so characteristic and distinctive as a 'Tractarian sermon', there was certainly a distinct set of preoccupations commonly shared by those who followed the Oxford Movement. The preaching of Tractarian clergy is therefore an important lens through which to view the Movement's identity. The richness of Tractarian parochial sermons in particular has perhaps still to be exploited to the full by historians. Almost every volume yields myriad insights into the characteristic theological and devotional themes of the Oxford Movement. This chapter will thus not confine itself to considering the sermons of the handful of leaders, but will also encompass the preaching of some of the more minor Tractarian clergy, and its timeframe is broadly the middle quarters of the century. Of all the published sermons of the Oxford Movement, Newman's were in time to prove the most enduring and influential, read as much for their literary style as for their theological content. But consideration of Newman should not overshadow the preaching of others, and is therefore brief here.

Influences

As part of its professed revival of a historic, Catholic Anglicanism, the Oxford Movement naturally leant much upon the teaching and practice of the Early Church, as well as upon that of seventeenth-century churchmen. Patristic influences included the sermons of St Ambrose, St Augustine, and St Chrysostom. These were not usually present in explicit reference or quotation, but rather in the doctrinal content of Tractarian sermons, and perhaps also in the very conception the Oxford Movement sponsored of a Church whose liturgy, devotional practice, and sacramental discipline were of a piece with its teaching. The Patristic model, exemplified above all in St Augustine, of a priest or bishop teaching doctrine through pastoral engagement, and so adjusting their mode of preaching to suit a congregation, but never in the process compromising Church teaching, was echoed in the importance Tractarians attached to the sermon. Pusey even edited for the *Library of the Fathers* a collection of St Augustine's sermons on the New Testament (Pusey 1844). The much-vaunted principle of 'reserve', which the Tractarians traced back to Patristic sources, was in evidence here. As Isaac Williams put it in Tract 80, *On Reserve in Communicating Religious Knowledge*, 'the important practical conclusion' was that, if God at once concealed himself from human beings so that they should not speak lightly of him or obscure their faith in him by vanity and self-preoccupation, 'all the means of grace faithfully cherished will lead us, as it were, step by step, into all these treasures, inexhaustible in their nature'; in other words, proper teaching adjusted religious truth to the capabilities of those to whom it was addressed (Williams 1840: 82). A similar conception was present in Tractarian emphases on 'adaptation'. William Gresley, parish priest near Lichfield in the 1830s, who wrote an early Tractarian handbook on preaching, placed great importance on this principle: 'it is essential to the force... of a sermon... that [it] should be specially adapted to the character, capacity, circumstances, the habits, prejudices, mode of thinking, and degree of knowledge of the hearers' (Gresley 1835: 5). Whilst regretting excessive Evangelical emphasis on the preaching of the Word, to the neglect of the Sacrament and public prayer, the Tractarians highly valued the sermon, and sought to exploit it as a means of teaching 'Church Principles' along lines they considered to have been laid down in the Early Church.

Yet the Tractarians were heirs of Evangelicalism, nonetheless—many of them had passed through an Evangelical phase—and their conviction of the importance of preaching cannot but have been influenced by Evangelical models. Particular attention was paid to J. B. Sumner's *Apostolical Preaching*—it was specifically commended by

Gresley—and many would have been influenced too by John Wesley's sermons, and Charles Simeon's sermon outlines (Sumner; Wesley; Simeon). The readiness of Tractarian clergy to criticize Evangelicals for their emotionalism, and for their alleged elevation of 'private judgement' in interpreting Scripture above the authority of the Church, masks this debt. But grudging admiration was often present alongside condemnation. Francis Paget feared the degradation of the clergy if they aped 'the profane ribaldry of a Spurgeon', and yet he acknowledged that Spurgeon too would serve the Church of England well if he roused the younger clergy to learn the art of public speaking (Paget 1858: 82–3). He distrusted arguments drawn from the state of religious feelings: 'Religion does not consist in excitement, but in action' (Paget 1849: 56). But, as Yngve Brilioth acknowledged, the experiential elements of Evangelicalism were central to the religious sensibility of Tractarianism (Brilioth: 42–3). Gresley criticized 'modern Evangelicalism' for its lack of a spirit of Christian unity, but he shared many of its convictions, such as its emphases on the inward spirit ('It is the presence of Christian motive which sanctifies every faculty'), on conversion as well as regeneration as the proper task of the Church, and on the heart as the true seat of Christian character (Gresley 1839: iv, 21; Gresley 1848: 86). Pusey too stressed the heartfelt assent necessary to faith in asking that characteristic Evangelical question, 'Who or what is a Christian?', and in replying 'He who believes in Christ, who loves Christ, hopes in Him, and obeys Him; and...with all his mind and soul and strength, owning no other Lord, but only Christ', for 'whoso wilfully falls short of this, in faith, or love, or obedience, is *not* a Christian, is hanging on only to Christianity' (Pusey 1883: 55). Evangelical hearers of Tractarian sermons were likely, then, to detect a common mood, and a common sensibility.

Conventional High Church (or 'Orthodox') preaching was another influence. Gresley, like Newman in the *Apologia*, professed a deep obligation to the teaching of Charles Lloyd at Oxford, who urged his students to write their own sermons, rather than rely on the printed sermons of others (a common enough practice in the early nineteenth century) (Gresley 1835: 1–2). Yet time and again the Tractarians appeared to denigrate the preaching of the 'Orthodox'. Pusey claimed that, for all its earnestness, respectability, and loyalty in faith, the High Church school, antagonistic to Calvinism, was 'sadly wanting in depth and warmth' (Pusey 1848: vii). According to Liddon, in the early 1830s 'Orthodox' sermons of the day 'were wanting in that affectionate devotion to our Divine Lord which was inculcated by the earlier Evangelicals', so that Walter Kerr Hamilton, though brought up 'High and Dry' and later regarded as a 'Tractarian' bishop of Salisbury, found in Evangelical teaching 'a warmth which was then sought in vain elsewhere' (Liddon 1869: 11). Francis Paget evidently had the 'Orthodox High Church' in mind when he contrasted the weaknesses of those who had made 'outward forms, and their trust in Church privileges, a substitute for inward piety' with Evangelicals whose 'boast of Bible knowledge' and 'self-confident reliance on their own private judgment' had led them away from 'Scripture-truth, and Scripture holiness' (Paget 1849: 237–8). Yet others brought up in the High Church tradition, including Keble and Froude, even as they criticized the formalism of the 'High and Dry', at the same time proclaimed their loyalty to the ordinances of the Church of England and their trust in devotional habit. 'It is too plain', as Keble asserted in 1833, 'that those who pray least regularly have least devotion when they pray' (Keble 1868: 308). One of his earliest sermons, long predating the Oxford Movement, claimed in a manner quite characteristic of the Keble of twenty years later, that the doctrine of sanctification implied there could never be an excess of virtue or holiness (Keble 1868: 8).

A third possible area of influence is harder to assess, and that is the homiletic practice of Roman Catholicism overseas. When they travelled, Tractarians often took advantage of the opportunity to hear sermons in Catholic churches. In all his trips abroad, Henry Manning, for example, frequently attended sermons and, according to his biographer, kept copious notes on them (Purcell: 1:346). Thomas Allies, visiting Paris with Charles Marriott in July 1845, noted the Abbé d'Alzon's preaching without notes and his animated action (quite in contrast to 'our quiet manner'), and reflected that his people would find preaching from a prepared text quite insupportable (Allies: 61). What struck Tractarians, then, was a quite different preaching style from that common in England—extempore preaching (which of course was common enough with Evangelical preachers) married to a dramatic manner as a means for communicating Catholic theology, an approach sometimes characterized as 'Sulpician', from the great French seminary at St Sulpice in Paris. Summing up his experiences of Catholic preachers on the Continent, Allies noted again that they usually preached without a text, that their sermons were much more rhetorical than English ones, and appealed to the feelings 'rather than the understanding', but that, notwithstanding this, English clergy should try this approach (Allies: 344–5). Paget was another who affirmed himself not averse to extempore preaching, since 'an address delivered without book seems...to come more freshly from the heart than a written discourse' (Paget 1858: 81). Keble, Pusey noted, late in his ministry made a practice of preaching extempore (Pusey 1877: v). Significantly the more traditional-minded Christopher Wordsworth, perhaps more an 'Orthodox' High Churchman than strictly a Tractarian, was critical of the Continental practice of extempore preaching, which, he feared, could expose the preacher to 'the utterance of language in the pulpit, in the heat of a discourse, which he may afterwards regret in his calmer moments' (Wordsworth: 55).

Preaching Doctrine

The sheer notoriety of some of the best-known examples of Tractarian preaching has perhaps obscured the fact that the vast majority of surviving Tractarian sermons were aimed at ordinary parish congregations, and did not so much seek to assert long-lost doctrinal truths or to comment pointedly on particular questions of ecclesiastical governance and identity, as simply to build up the Christian character of their hearers. Though it is not a distinction which can be sustained in every case, nevertheless this suggests that a survey of Tractarian preaching has to reckon with two rather different categories of sermon. One was aimed at propagating for a wider audience the doctrinal principles central to the Oxford Movement. The other—to be covered in the next section—might be called 'pastoral' or devotional sermons, no less theological in content in that they built on, and articulated, a coherent set of doctrinal principles, but nevertheless produced in the main for ordinary parish congregations or for particular pastoral contexts. The former would naturally include Keble's 'Assize Sermon' which Newman hailed later as the start of the Oxford Movement, a number of Newman's own sermons, and particularly some of those subsequently included in his *Oxford University Sermons* (1843) such as that on 'The Theory of Developments in Religious Doctrine'. It could also include the most controversial of all, Pusey's 1843 sermon *The Holy Eucharist a Comfort to the Penitent* which, through its advocacy of the doctrine of the Real Presence, led to his condemnation by a committee appointed by the Oxford Heads of Houses and a two-year suspension from preaching, although the sermon itself, as Liddon pointed out, was practical and not intentionally controversial, having as its aim 'not the formal statement of disputed or forgotten truth, but the encouragement of a certain class of souls' (Liddon 1893: 2: 308). But these are only the best-known of what is after all a quite extensive literature of ecclesiastical controversy. Other examples might include, for example, William Gresley's sermons at St Paul's, Brighton, on *The Present State of the Controversy with Rome* (1855), or William Bennett's two sermons on the Gorham judgement, or again Bennett's 1842 course of sermons on the errors of Romanism (Gresley 1855; Bennett 1842; Bennett 1850). Whether these sermons can be said to have contributed to development of the art of preaching itself is doubtful, since in almost every case reportage and publication for a wider readership was perhaps the primary goal from the very beginning. But they certainly reflected the Tractarian concern not only to reassert a set of doctrinal principles they were convinced had been neglected by the Church of England, but also to promote and effect the reform of the Church as a whole along Tractarian lines.

The Tractarians were in two minds about religious controversy, since they both deplored it and frankly indulged in it with gusto. Paget could even claim that 'controversy is a sign of life' and yet at the same time admit that those who loved controversy for its own sake were 'hateful characters' (Paget 1849: 111). Like Evangelicals, a sense of urgency runs through these Tractarian sermons on disputed Church matters, as if the time was propitious for asserting Church principles because the Church was in dire straits without them. Dwelling on the trials of the Church, Paget, for example, could suggest that 'Churchmen' should 'keep close to the Catholic Faith, maintaining *that* whole and undefiled' (Paget 1849: 204). For Pusey, the proper response to the time of trial which the Church was undergoing was not to trust to any human project of chastisement, but to 'commit ourselves into the Hands of God, to chasten, correct, wound, heal, sift, cleanse, as He wills' (Pusey 1848: 95). Nor did many of them flinch from the divisive implications. Amongst the fiercest was the apparently mild-mannered Keble, for whom love of Christ required honouring friends and 'discountenancing and shrinking from His enemies' (Keble 1868: 319).

The sermon was thus a valued weapon in ecclesiastical combat, and as such was exploited to the full by the Tractarians. Their leaders' prominence in Oxford gave them access to an influential audience, assisted by sympathetic publishers such as Rivington's and Parker's (Fitzpatrick; Riddell). In these sermons, a particular theme could be expounded at greater length than would have been appropriate for a village context, with a supporting arsenal of authors and quotations.

The redoubtable Pusey is perhaps the example that springs most readily to mind. His bibliography includes many examples of sermons which were evidently preached for a wider audience than that of their immediate congregation. Especially in the years after Newman's secession to Rome in 1845, and after the furore caused by his own 1843 sermon on the Eucharist, the suspicion which followed Pusey around meant he attracted significant publicity for the causes he espoused. Not only the 1843 sermon, but others such as *This is My Body*, preached before the University in 1871, thus were almost guaranteed to attract a wide audience, if not always a sympathetic one (Pusey 1871). Pusey himself disavowed controversial intention ('he endeavoured, with deep conscientiousness, to avoid the bitterness of controversy'), but his position as Professor of Hebrew and Canon of Christ Church in the University of Oxford inevitably gave him a platform from which to address the Church as a whole, especially after Newman's conversion, when his name came to the fore as leader of those Tractarians who remained in the Church of England (Church: 222). The very fact that many of his sermons were addressed to congregations of undergraduates and Fellows, whether at Christ Church or at St Mary's, the University church, blurs the distinction between 'controversial' and pastoral sermons: this was Pusey's pastoral context, after all. But the educated nature of the congregations surely gave full rein at times to Pusey's inclination to complex and weighty argument and crushing evidential support. As published, *The Holy Eucharist a Comfort to the Penitent* was almost 8,000 words long, and would have taken almost an hour and a half to deliver. But this was not unusual for Pusey. His two sermons on 'The Church the Converter of the Heathen', preached for the Society for the Propagation of the Gospel (SPG) at Melcombe Regis in 1838 in the morning and afternoon of one day, amounted to almost 20,000 words, if the published texts are anything to go by (Pusey 1838). Each one must have taken almost two hours to preach. The course of sermons he inaugurated at St Saviour's, Leeds on its consecration in 1845 included no less than ten preached in a single week by various preachers, and although these were ostensibly aimed, not so much at clergy, but at ordinary churchgoers, they indicated the high and demanding standard of attention Pusey demanded of his hearers; his own contribution of three in that week amounted to almost 15,000 words (Pusey 1845).

Even the apparently self-effacing Keble, however, was capable of delivering sermons sharply angled towards a particular point of controversy, or with a wider audience in mind. The best-known of these, of course, was his sermon on 'National Apostasy', preached at St Mary's in Oxford to mark the start of the county assizes, and called by one biographer 'perhaps the most famous sermon in the history of English ecclesiastical writing' (Griffin: 82). The conventional connection historians have made is to the Whig government's proposals to reduce the number of Irish bishoprics—in this again they have largely followed Richard Church's lead—and undoubtedly this was one of Keble's targets, but it is not explicitly mentioned in the sermon, which dwells more generally on the danger of the State abandoning the Church (Church: 68). Given the date of the sermon—14 July—Keble surely cannot but have borne in mind the (for him) terrible example of Revolutionary France and its persecution of the Church. Parts read like a warning to the Church of England that it could face the same danger if it did not defend its spiritual integrity and authority, if necessary by separation from the State, fearing that it could 'happen... that the Apostolical Church should be forsaken, degraded, nay trampled on and despoiled by the State and people of England' (Keble 1833: 21). This was deliberately provocative language. The sermon was rushed into print, advertisements for it appearing within three weeks in various national newspapers such as the *Standard* and the *Morning Post*. Whatever the merits of Newman's judgement about the significance of the sermon, Keble certainly intended it to make a mark, and aimed at a national readership (Coleridge: 209–11). But far from shrinking altogether from national controversy thereafter, Keble from time to time repeated this foray into it. Another example was his 1836 sermon, *Primitive Tradition Recognised in Holy Scripture*. As published, this ran to over 12,000 words; since it was preached at a visitation, its congregation would have consisted mostly of clergy, and its content was proportionately more demanding than his parish sermons, with, for example, a detailed exposition of the Greek παρακαταθήκη, or 'trust' (Keble 1836: 14–16).

A Pastoral Vision

For all the attention these controversial sermons have attracted, they are a misleading guide to the general tenor of Tractarian preaching. For that, we must turn instead to sermons aimed largely at ordinary congregations. The dominant concern of Tractarian preaching was essentially pastoral, expressing Christian doctrine so as to continue the work of conversion, building up the believer in Christian faith and life. This was articulated time and again in the reasons Tractarian clergy gave for publishing their sermons, but perhaps nowhere more definitively than in the 'Advertisement' Isaac Williams drafted for the series of *Plain Sermons* he collected and published from 1839 (Williams 1839). His aim in persuading Newman, Keble, and others to contribute was to steady the Movement, by showing that its principles were set forth not 'as themes for disputation' but as 'truths of immediate and essential importance, bearing more or less directly on our every day behaviour, means of continual resource and consolation in life, and of calm and sure hope in death' (Williams 1839: 2). Williams feared the Movement was being distracted by those who had adopted Church principles superficially, and who were all the more 'noisy and voluble' as a result without feeling these principles to be deeply founded 'in divine and eternal truth' (Williams 1839: 1). Even these sermons, plain and practical as they were, therefore were not without a wider programmatic intent. They demonstrated a characteristically Tractarian determination to transform the life and worship of the Church of England in the parishes as much as in the universities and bishops' palaces.

This required, or rather dictated, an approach to preaching which was eminently practical and adaptive, recognizing the difficulties of particular pastoral situations and calibrating the teaching of Church principles accordingly. William Gresley's manual on preaching took its cue in this respect from Aristotle's *Rhetoric*, adumbrating 'general rules of the art of persuasion' which could be applied in many different contexts, since they were founded on human nature (Gresley 1835: 12). He emphasized the preacher's need to adapt his discourse to 'the peculiarities of those whom he addresses'; the 'varying circumstances' of readers were the justification for the continuous publication of new volumes of sermons (Gresley 1835: v–vi). The Tractarian system of divinity, for all its importance as a reassertion of Church principles, needed 'reasoning and analogy' to work out its implications in parishes (Gresley 1835: vi–vii). For Gresley, the parish system was as much of divine institution as was episcopacy (Gresley 1839: 72). Along with it went the value of pastoral visiting, something which Paget, for example, held to be crucial for people's willingness to listen to the preaching of their priest, for where 'the Parson sees little of his people, and knows little of their spiritual condition, he has no right to complain if he finds the post which he has deserted occupied by another' (Paget 1858: 89). Edward Monro was another whose vision of Church principles was wholly infused with a conviction of the integrated and interdependent character of all pastoral work. Preaching, along with teaching, was a vital means by which the people of a parish could be induced to take more seriously the sacramental provision through which their personal salvation and their pursuit of holiness could be assured: there could be 'no appreciation of sacraments or Church discipline until the people became alive to the need of personal religion' (Monro: 89; Davie: 9–12).

Such a vision of the place of preaching in parish life was reflected in the welter of pastoral sermons published by Tractarian clergy. If the *Plain Sermons* compiled by Isaac Williams could be seen as a model, nevertheless almost all the Tractarians published volumes of 'plain', or 'practical', or 'parochial' sermons. The plainness was reflected in simplicity of language, economy of construction, and relative brevity. In commending the sermons of his friend Robert Suckling, Williams appealed to their 'eminently plain, and practical, and full of life' character, which made them 'well suited for parochial use and edification' (Williams 1853*b*: iii). Pusey commended Keble's 'simple, earnest style', which aimed, following the pattern of St Frances de Sales, to send the hearer home saying 'God be merciful to me, a sinner' (Pusey 1877: vii). But even many of Pusey's own sermons attempted to emulate this ideal. Plainness or simplicity did not only mean short sentences and simple style, however: it also denoted a certain directness, a readiness to go straight to the point without getting distracted by speculative indulgence and rhetorical flight. As Gresley commented, there was no place for 'cutting sarcasm, nor fierce invective, nor cool and dignified irony', for all those 'spirit-stirring' devices should be avoided in order to confine oneself to 'the plain words of soberness and truth' (Gresley 1835: 25). In line with this commendation, most Tractarian pastoral sermons were not littered with references to the Fathers but were intensely and almost exclusively Scriptural, indeed almost severely so. Perhaps the most famous and influential of all these sermons, Newman's *Parochial and Plain Sermons*, were an outstanding example of this biblical concentration. In this, Tractarian preaching owed much to Evangelical expository homiletics. But, true to Tractarian instincts, the reading of Scripture assumed by preachers was one steered by the Church. As was hardly surprising from those who vaunted 'Church principles', Tractarian sermons took the calendar and liturgy as the framework within which Scripture would be interpreted, as shown again and again in sermon series to be read in concert with the believer's progress through the Church year. Keble's eleven-volume series *Sermons for the Christian Year* is a case in point (Keble 1877). But Pusey also published different volumes of sermons for Advent to Whitsuntide and later for Lent, Isaac Williams a volume tied specifically to the Book of Common Prayer Sunday lections, and J. M. Neale sermons for the Church's year, to name but a few examples (Pusey 1848; Pusey 1874; Williams 1853*a*; Neale).

The frequency with which Tractarian preachers insisted that sermons should be *practical* as well as 'plain' showed a concern to achieve a definite change in the religious life of the believer. The temptations that surrounded the Christian could be kept at bay by the proper cultivation of regular and frequent habits of prayer and contemplation. For Pusey, nothing but

> a continued active habit of directing our actions to God, such as results from offering them to God, morning by morning, for the day, and then renewing that direction often through the day, by some brief prayer ... will rescue some fragments of our acts from the unclean contact of those spiritual harpies, our besetting faults. (Pusey 1874: 100)

Gresley commended daily reading of the Bible, 'our familiar companion and friend' (Gresley 1848: 8). His list of practices for cultivating the Christian life included 'self-examination, self-discipline, regard to conscience, frequent prayer, devout communion, holy observance, and habitual watchfulness': all these things were necessary to cultivate 'that heavenly principle of faith which is the essence of the life of God in the heart of man' (Gresley 1848: 56). For Pusey, again, prayer, alms, and fasting formed 'one holy band, for which our Blessed Lord gives rules together, and which draw up the soul to Him' (Pusey 1848: 189). Keble even emphasized the importance of punctuality in prayer (Keble 1868: 307). For him, nothing less than Church principles, drawn above all from the Prayer Book, could save Church people, as otherwise 'we shall become heretics, or worse, before we are aware' (Keble 1868: 367). He was also a strong advocate of fasts as 'special helps' to bring the believer nearer to Christ, for by following Christ's own example in the wilderness even the poor might learn not to be tempted by their sense of need (Keble 1877: 48–9). The vision of the devotional life which emerges from consideration of these sermons is one in which the earnestness of Evangelical 'heart' religion has been translated into a no less earnest and attentive series of daily practices, guided by reflection on the Church's year, and designed to deepen the believer's understanding of, and dependence on, the Christian gospel.

But a precondition for a deepening of the spiritual life was a corresponding willingness to let go of many of the pleasures of contemporary life. Tractarian sermons accordingly displayed a startling austerity. Paget called his contemporaries 'a luxuriant, pampered, self-indulgent people, who have altogether got out of the way of bodily mortification and self-denial' (Paget 1849: 291). Pusey warned his Oxford hearers that 'the world is the enemy of the Gospel, in faith as well as in life' (Pusey 1874: 56). Keble even lamented that the 'whole Christian world is fallen and decayed' and that God 'has more or less withdrawn His grace and presence from us' (Keble 1877: 89). Tractarian sermons, no less than those of Evangelical clergy, were intended to sharpen up the believer's sense of urgency and dread, to the point at which a renewed commitment in faith would be produced. Again, it was Keble who urged his congregation to 'pray to God, day after day, that we may fear Him more and more', for if they did not seek continually to improve, they were, in practice, 'sure to go back' (Keble 1877: 131). And so the parochial sermons of Tractarian clergy mostly give the lie to the charge, sometimes made by Evangelicals, that they neglected or downplayed the significance of sin (Wilson; Pereiro: 65). Charles Marriott, for example, warned the congregation of St Saviour's, Leeds, against precisely that danger: 'A little sin may be made great by indulging such unholy weakness' (Pusey 1845: 27).

Devotional practice was not commended without an eye on wider doctrinal implications, however. Though the Tractarians' emphasis on a disciplined spiritual life, public prayer, and the sacraments could lead to Evangelical accusations of an undue emphasis on 'works', it was always situated within a broader theological perspective which modified Protestant teaching on justification through faith alone as traditionally understood, and attempted to emphasize the place of sanctification in the life of the believer (Nockles 1994: 262–9). This was most famously expressed in Newman's controversial *Lectures on Justification* (1838), which Brilioth called 'the most important attempt to find the theological expression of [the Oxford Movement's] piety' (Brilioth: 282). Here, Newman argued for a *via media* between what he took to be the Lutheran interpretation of justification by faith, and the 'Roman' position of justification by obedience, and asserted, on Patristic (especially Augustinian) grounds in effect a doctrine of justification through baptismal regeneration. Justification, Newman said, 'comes *through* the Sacraments; is received *by* faith; *consists* in God's inward presence, and *lives* in obedience' (Newman 1840: 216–17). Newman may have laid especial emphasis on obedience, but in a more general sense sanctification constituted the core doctrinal principle of the Tractarian system of devotion, and it was reflected and advocated forcefully in Tractarian sermons. It was depicted time and again as a necessary complement to justification. For Gresley, for example, 'the one would be incomplete without the other' (Gresley 1848: 32). There was a fine line between emphasizing the importance of sanctification, with appropriate devotional and ascetic practice, and claiming 'merit' for works rather than faith, and Tractarians were well aware of this. Francis Paget, for example, strove to maintain with equal strength the double proposition that salvation came from Christ alone, and that human beings would be judged for their deeds (Paget 1849: 4–11).

Evangelical suspicion of Tractarian devotional practice was countermanded, in part at least, by the prominence given to the sacraments, and to sacramentalism more broadly, in Tractarian preaching. Salvation, as the Oxford leaders iterated, was mediated to the believer through the sacramental life of the Church. There was, then, an intrinsic link between justification and the Church, which was not merely a gathered body of believers but the means whereby Christ's presence on earth was made real, not only in a general sense but also in the very particular sense of his presence in and through each of his followers. Pusey emphasized the unity of the gift of grace: the features or aspects of truth might appear to be manifold, but the one gift underlying them all was the incarnate Christ himself (Pusey 1848: 219). Christ himself was sanctification to us, and the sacraments were the 'channels whereby, through Union with Him, He conveys these Exceeding Gifts to us' (Pusey 1849: 220). Tractarian sacramentalism was thus disposed to a practical or devotional mysticism, in which the presence of the eternal life of God, itself in a sense beyond all human capacity for definition or comprehension, was made real and tangible for believers through the material means of the sacraments. Accordingly, the frequency with which Tractarian preachers spoke about the sacraments reflected not just—as some might have expected—a preoccupation with the authority of the ministry, but also, and perhaps more significantly, a concern for salvation. Tractarian sacramentalism was exactly coterminous with Tractarian soteriology.

This was particularly in evidence in the very great prominence given to baptism in Tractarian preaching. The salvation of the individual, in the Tractarian understanding, was achieved not merely through a conversion of the heart and soul of the believer, but through the medium of the Church. Here the Tractarians could draw, so they thought, on significant support from the baptismal liturgy of the Prayer Book, in which the regeneration of the child followed directly from his or her baptism—'[s]eeing now, dearly beloved brethren, that this child is regenerate, and grafted into the body of Christ's Church' (Thompson: 67–91). It was a matter of grave importance that the child (or baptized adult) subsequently lived up to their baptismal promises. An austere theology of baptismal regeneration thus ran through Tractarian sermons. The most notorious expression of this point of view was Pusey's three *Tracts for the Times* on baptism, which propounded such a severe understanding of post-baptismal sin that they caused F. D. Maurice to break off his association with the Tractarians (Maurice: 1:186). But Paget, for example, was equally fierce, asserting that, since in Baptism human beings received 'the gift of an in-dwelling grace to enable [them] to serve and please God', they were 'without excuse' if they forgot him (Paget 1849: 38). Baptism was especially prominent in Isaac Williams's sermons: it signified 'the unspeakable gift of the Holy Spirit imparted to you', and yet, as heaven opened at Jesus's baptism, so in ours we become heirs of the heavenly country, so that we then 'have nothing at all to do here but to fit and prepare ourselves for it' (Williams 1882: 38, 46). Keble was another for whom post-baptismal sin was a matter of the utmost gravity. He compared the behaviour of those who flouted their baptismal commitments to the nine lepers who failed to give thanks for their healing, for baptism, as a 'thorough spiritual cleansing', was the equivalent of physical healing (Keble 1868: 351).

Whilst there is too little space here to give a full account of the sacramental system encountered in Tractarian sermons, it is important to note the essential unity and coherence of the attention given to the place of sacraments in the life of the Church, following on from this conception of baptism. Tractarian preaching strongly emphasized the importance of frequent reception of communion as a vital means of deepening and sustaining the believer's faith. In his sermon on 'Increased Communions', Pusey dwelt on the growth in holiness which would flow from more frequent communion: God may have withdrawn communions from the Church in the past, he suggested, in case they damaged the weak of faith, but now he was calling his followers to new degrees of devotedness, and the weekly communion would become 'the very Centre, as it is the Fulness [sic] of your life' (Pusey 1848: 324). Again, the seriousness with which Tractarians viewed post-baptismal sin merely served to highlight the importance of regular confession, and the sacramental nature of penance and absolution by a priest—even though the Thirty-Nine Articles ruled out treating penance as a sacrament in the same sense as baptism and the Eucharist. Gresley, like many Tractarians, used the exhortations in the service of Holy Communion to argue that the Prayer Book in fact commended private confession; this was different from the compulsory, periodical confession required of Roman Catholics (Gresley 1848: 103–8). Pusey's advocacy of private ('auricular') confession is well known, and was deeply controversial, but Keble was no less vehement in his profession of the need for all Christians to make their confession regularly, and if need be in private. Even children had need of penitence, he said, and he too cited the Prayer Book in justification of the practice of regular confession (Keble 1877: 63, 66).

In addition to the sacraments, and corresponding to the importance of confession, Tractarian preachers also directed the attention of their hearers inwards, to a constant, prayerful examination of interior motives and states of mind. This was also a corollary of the renewed emphasis on sanctification. If justification brought with it union with God, and the presence of the indwelling Spirit, so that the life of the earnest believer would be marked by the development of an obedient heart, and of a life of devotion and discipline in accordance with the teaching and ordinances of the Church, it followed that the believer ought to be concerned above all with purity of motive, with humility and having an eye ever alert to temptation. Tractarian sermons displayed a constant awareness of the condition of danger in which the soul might find itself. 'Listen we then to every whisper of our conscience', Pusey urged his hearers, for '[it] is Jesus Who, within, is speaking to us by His Spirit'; and again, 'We may know His Presence by the deep, breathless stirrings of our hearts' (Pusey 1848: 285). Constant attention to the inward state of one's soul was needed. Keble especially emphasized the importance of 'consideration' in prayer (Keble 1868: 309). As Pusey commented, Keble's Lenten sermons were marked by a sense of sin as the 'malice of an unseen enemy', and aimed to 'unveil his hearers' hearts to themselves', so that they might turn to God in penitence and with renewed zeal (Pusey 1877: vi). Again, as Pusey said, 'Dare, my brother, to look into thyself; dare to see what that is in you, which still holds thee back from God' (Pusey 1874: 87). This attention to the cultivation of one's spiritual state, supported by the Tractarian conception of the priest as confessor, promoted the practice of what later came to be called spiritual direction, by which priests would seek to give regular guidance to those who came to them for advice. Both Pusey and Keble were to have collections of their letters of spiritual advice published posthumously (Keble 1870; Pusey 1901).

Anchoring Tractarian conceptions of interior contemplation and the spiritual life, and preventing their dissolution into subjectivism, was the strong emphasis preachers placed on the authority of the Church. As Keble argued, the Church, with its clergy and sacramental provision, was the safeguard appointed by God 'from the beginning' to defend us against new and false doctrine (Keble 1868: 328). The whole course of the world's history, he claimed, with regard to the Church 'is a scheme ordered by Almighty God to bring lost souls back into saving communion with Him' (Keble 1868: 334). Without the authority of the Church to direct and shape Christian discipleship, society itself was at risk. Gresley illustrated perfectly the conviction that the 'private judgment' of Scripture was the root of religious disunity and social disharmony, asserting that 'the want of sound views on church authority' underlay the present ills of the nation (Gresley 1839: 9). God had provided both Scripture and the Church, together, as safeguards against error (Gresley 1848: 7). Keble, again, taught his village congregation the importance of the apostolic authority of the Church: the presence of Christ's clergy, spiritually commissioned by their bishops, was not merely an external blessing, but an inward one too, 'a true token to faithful men of our exceeding nearness to Christ' (Keble 1876: 191).

Newman

The sermons of John Henry Newman stand in a class of their own, despite sharing many of the characteristics described above. Newman's notoriety—in Protestant circles—after 1845 seems not to have dented the popularity of his published sermons, especially the *Parochial and Plain Sermons*, which continued to appear in considerable numbers throughout his lifetime. Probably they attracted a new, predominantly Roman Catholic readership after his conversion, though almost certainly they continued to attract Anglican and other Protestant readers too. Ian Ker has called them 'one of the great classics of Christian spirituality' (Ker: 90). But he is not alone in his estimation of them. According to Brilioth, they represented a 'literary master-work belonging to the best productions of English prose', and were perhaps the best single introduction to Tractarian piety (Brilioth: 212). It is surely true that, great English stylist as Newman was, the readers of these sermons would have found in them not only a characteristically Tractarian scheme of doctrine and devotion, but also a remarkably penetrating analysis of elements of religious experience. Time after time, Newman could seem to have combined psychological realism with a demanding standard of devotion, as when he asserted that 'to pray attentively is a habit', for 'No one begins with having his heart thoroughly in [prayers]; but by trying, he is enabled to attend more and more, and at length, after many trials and a long schooling of himself, to fix his mind steadily on them' (Newman 1868: 1:42). Or again, preaching on the 'difficulty of realizing sacred privileges', he could suggest that 'Every act of obedience has a tendency to strengthen our convictions about heaven... This is a use, too, of the observance of sacred seasons; they wean us from this world, they impress upon us the reality of the world which we see not' (Newman 1868:

6:100). Many of the characteristic features of Newman's preaching are present here—the relative simplicity of language, the emphasis on obedience, the pervasive sense of human frailty, the boldness of assertion, the sacramental or mystical awareness of the dependence of the world of sense on that of spiritual reality. When placed in the context of Newman's quite explicit endorsement of the whole range of Tractarian doctrinal and devotional teaching, the popularity and penetration of these sermons in High Church circles perhaps comes as no surprise. But that depended also on an exceptional clarity of theological vision, which Ian Ker argues was secured above all by Newman's conception of the indwelling Spirit, a doctrinal but also spiritual and pastoral *locus* which cohered his very practical understanding of the spiritual life along with his sacramentalism (Ker: 91). 'The whole system of the Church, its discipline and ritual', he claimed,

> are all in their origin the spontaneous and exuberant fruit of the real principle of spiritual religion in the hearts of its members. The invisible Church has developed itself into the Church visible, and its outward rites and forms are nourished and animated by the living power which dwells within it. Thus every part of it is real, down to the minutest details. (Newman 1868: 5:41)

Even though so much of Newman's homiletic strategy appeared to be to stress the significance of obedience and discipline, from the human side, the persuasive power of his preaching surely lay in his articulation of human dependence on God, and so on the transfiguration of human religious activity by the love of God, for as he said memorably, 'Grace ever outstrips prayer' (Newman 1868: 5:351).

But Newman was also perfectly comfortable with controversial preaching of a kind which was not demonstrably 'plain' or 'parochial'. His *University Sermons*, published with numbered paragraphs, though addressing in some respects similar congregations (university ones) to those of his parochial sermons (for his parish was, after all, that of the University church, St Mary's), nevertheless showed a quite different conception of what preaching was for. He used them to assert or rediscover teaching which had been neglected in the Church of England, or to propose an idea which might seem needlessly speculative for a pastoral context, but which merited exploration. Sermons of this type were amongst his most famous, including those which helped to lay the foundations for his later work, such as 'The Nature of Faith in relation to Reason', preached in 1839 and anticipating aspects of *The Grammar of Assent* (1870), and 'The Theory of Developments in Religious Doctrine', preached in 1843 as Newman was already beginning work on what would become his *Essay on the Development of Christian Doctrine* (1845), the work which facilitated his conversion to Rome. The style of these sermons is clear and has moments of poetry, but in general it is detached and analytical, much more akin to that of a lecture. Just a brief example may suffice. Preaching on 'Implicit and Explicit Reason' in 1840, he could say of the 'science' of interpretation that

> in considering the imperfections and defects incident to such scientific exercises, we must carefully exempt from our remarks all instances of them which have been vouchsafed to us from above, and therefore have a divine sanction; and that such instances do exist, is the most direct and satisfactory answer to any doubts which

religious persons may entertain, of the lawfulness of employing science in the province of Faith. (Newman 1843: 265)

This is the formal register of the treatise or the lecture-hall. It is—even in comparison with Pusey and Keble—still relatively uncluttered, and marked with many of those epigrammatic moments which also clinch the style of the parochial sermons, and yet it is unafraid of careful distinctions and philosophical vocabulary. The sermon, in Newman's hands, was an effective, sharp foray into theological controversy.

There can be no question about the lasting impact of Newman's preaching. Brilioth, shadowing Wilfrid Ward, notes how a significant number of undergraduates were seduced by it, and references testimony from R. W. Church, always an admirer, and J. A. Froude, an admirer turned sceptic, as to its power (Brilioth: 212). But many others have done the same. Perhaps the most famous testimony was that of Matthew Arnold who, as an undergraduate at Balliol in the early 1840s, heard Newman at St Mary's:

> Who could resist the charm of that spiritual apparition, gliding in the dim afternoon light through the aisles of St. Mary's, rising into the pulpit, and then, in the most entrancing of voices, breaking the silence with words and thoughts which were a religious music,—subtle, sweet, mournful?...I seem to hear him still, saying: 'After the fever of life, after wearinesses and sicknesses, fightings and despondings, languor and fretfulness, struggling and succeeding; after all the changes and chances of this troubled, unhealthy state,—at length comes death, at length the white throne of God, at length the beatific vision.' (Arnold: 350)

But in the end it was not the sermons as heard but as *read* that influenced subsequent generations of High Churchmen, and read almost certainly through the lens of the post-1864 view of Newman, when his controversy with Kingsley and his *Apologia* transformed his popular reputation from that of suspicion to one of growing appreciation.

Postscript: Liddon

If Newman's sermons were to prove the enduring literary monument of Tractarian homiletics, the Oxford Movement's greatest heir as a preacher was Henry Parry Liddon. Liddon was born in 1829, the year that Peter Nockles claims as the real beginning of the Oxford Movement, and he was not an undergraduate until after Newman's conversion. Yet he entirely imbibed the Movement's theological and spiritual ideals, and in a life centred on Oxford and St Paul's, London, placed them at the very centre of his ministry.

There is more than an echo of Liddon's own estimate of the value of the sermon in his description of Bishop Hamilton's preaching, which became 'ever more fervent than before, and...was attended with larger results in the increased devotion of his people and in the conversion of sinners to earnest and living Christianity' (Liddon 1869: 14). The importance of adequate teaching and preaching was underlined in Liddon's approval of the Italian Catholic Rosmini's analysis of the lack of sympathy between clergy and people, the 'Wound of the Left Hand of the Crucified', according to Rosmini, which was due above all to 'the want of adequate Christian teaching' (Liddon 1883: xviii).

It is in Liddon's *Clerical Life and Work*, a collection of sermons and essays delivered over thirty years from 1856, that we see probably the most coherent, rounded interpretation of the place of preaching in the Tractarian conception of ministry. It is not a systematic description of clerical tasks, but it contains many references to the task of preaching, and above all helps to situate Liddon's conception of preaching in the context of his view of the clergyman's spiritual vocation. His chapter on 'The Priest in his inner life', for example, closely linked the practice of preaching to the saying of the daily offices of morning and evening prayer, since the saying of the latter—along with the whole life of the clergyman—would reflect the pattern of personal devotion; conversely, for Liddon, extempore preaching divorced from the recitation of the office would be disastrous (Liddon 1895: 18–19). Likewise, the daily, pastoral round of parish life inevitably would help to prepare a priest for preaching (Liddon 1895: 43). A preacher had to stand 'inside' the spiritual life: his sermons would be of a piece with his praying and his whole mode of life (Liddon 1895: 129). Preaching was thus an integral aspect of what Liddon called the 'moral value of a mission from Christ', for so enormous and responsible was the task, that it could only be undertaken on the basis of a belief in the reality of the Divine call and mission (Liddon 1895: 218). The aim of preaching was to assist in the work of conversion and sanctification; Liddon's models included St Augustine, St Francis Xavier and, perhaps more surprisingly, Henry Martyn (Liddon 1895: 99–100, 117).

All this was surely reflected in the seriousness with which Liddon himself took the responsibility for preaching. Like his great mentor, Pusey, at times Liddon's sermons were immense. One on 'Fatalism and the Living God', preached at an ordination in Salisbury Cathedral in 1866, was almost 12,000 words long in its printed form, for example, though the published version was likely to have been longer than that actually delivered during the service itself, since Liddon's practice seems to have been to preach from fairly extensive notes (Liddon 1895: 172–206; Johnston: 53–4). It was common for him to preach for an hour at St Paul's. The crowds he drew were such that the doors were opened fifteen minutes earlier than usual when he was in residence, though even then it was often difficult to hear him—despite the strength of his voice—unless one was standing under or around the central dome (Prestige: 101).

Liddon can stand as a thread of connection from the Oxford Movement down to the late Victorian Church, and on into the twentieth century. He died in 1890, revered for the quality of his preaching. Although by then he was increasingly associated in the popular mind with tenacious resistance to the critical concessions of liberal Catholicism, his coherence of spiritual, pastoral, and doctrinal vision remained influential. It was Liddon above all who helped to ensure that the legacy of the Oxford Movement was not to be defined by suspicion of the preached Word, but by a commitment to effective teaching as well as sacramental practice.

References

Allies, T. W. (1849). *Journal in France in 1845 and 1848, with Letters from Italy in 1847, of Things and Persons Concerning the Church and Education*. London: Longman, Brown, Green & Longman.
Arnold, M. (1903). 'Emerson', in *Works*, vol. 4. London: Macmillan.
Bennett, W. J. E. (1842). *Distinctive Errors of Romanism: A Series of Lecture-Sermons*. London: Cleaver.
—— (1850). *The Church, the Crown, and the State: Their Junction or Their Separation*. London: Cleaver.
Brilioth, Y. (1925). *The Anglican Revival: Studies in the Oxford Movement*. London: Longmans.
Chadwick, W. O. (1990). *The Spirit of the Oxford Movement: Tractarian Essays*. Cambridge: Cambridge University Press.
Church, R. W. (1970). *The Oxford Movement: Twelve Years, 1833–1845*, new edn. London: University of Chicago Press.
Coleridge, J. T. (1869). *A Memoir of the Rev. John Keble*. Oxford: Parker.
Compton, B. (1899). *Edward Meyrick Goulburn, D.D., D.C.L., Dean of Norwich: A Memoir*. London: John Murray.
Conybeare, W. J. (1999). 'Church Parties', in R. A. Burns and S. Taylor (eds.), *From Cranmer to Davidson: A Church of England Miscellany*. Woodbridge: Boydell Press/Church of England Record Society, 213–385.
Davie, P. (1997). *Raising up a Faithful People*. Leominster: Gracewing.
Fitzpatrick, B. L. (2004). 'Rivington Family (*per. c.*1710–*c.*1960)', *ODNB*. Oxford: Oxford University Press.
Gresley, W. (1835). *Ecclesiastes Anglicanus: Being a Treatise on the Art of Preaching, as Adapted to a Church of England Congregation*. London: Rivington.
—— (1839). *The Necessity of Zeal and Moderation: the Present Circumstances of the Church, Enforced and Illustrated in Five Sermons Preached Before the University of Oxford*. London: Rivingtons.
—— (1848). *Practical Sermons*. London: Joseph Masters.
—— (1855). *The Present State of the Controversy with Rome: Three Sermons Preached in S. Paul's Church, Brighton*. London: Joseph Masters.
Griffin, J. R. (1987). *John Keble: Saint of Anglicanism*. Macon, GA: Mercer University Press.
Herring, G. W. (1984). 'From Tractarianism to Ritualism: A Study of Some Aspects of Tractarianism outside Oxford, From the Time of Newman's Conversion in 1845 until the First Ritual Commission in 1867'. DPhil thesis. University of Oxford.
Johnston, J. O. (1904). *Life and Letters of Henry Parry Liddon*. London: Longmans, Green & Co.
Keble, J. (1833). *National Apostasy Considered*. Oxford: Parker.
—— (1836). *Primitive Tradition Recognised in the Holy Scriptures: A Sermon, Preached in the Cathedral Church of Winchester*. London: Rivingtons.
—— (1868). *Sermons, Occasional and Parochial*. Oxford: Parker.
—— (1870). *Letters of Spiritual Guidance and Counsel*. London: Parker.
—— (1876). *Sermons for the Christian Year*. Oxford: Parker.
—— (1877). *Sermons for the Christian Year. Sermons for Lent to Passiontide*. Oxford: Parker.
Ker, I. (1988). *John Henry Newman: A Biography*. Oxford: Oxford University Press.

Liddon, H. P. (1869). *Walter Kerr Hamilton; Bishop of Salisbury, A Sketch, Reprinted, with Additions and Corrections, From 'The Guardian'*. London: Rivington.

—— (ed.) (1883). *A. Rosmini, Of the Five Wounds of the Holy Church*. London: Rivington.

—— (1893). *Life of Edward Bouverie Pusey*, 4 vols. London: Longmans.

—— (1895). *Clerical Life and Work: A Collection of Sermons*, 2nd edn. London: Longmans.

Maurice, F. (1884). *Life of F.D. Maurice*. London: Macmillan.

Monro, E. (1850). *Parochial Work*, 2nd edn. Oxford: Parker.

Morris, J. N. (1996). 'The Regional Growth of Tractarianism', in P. Vaiss (ed.), *From Oxford to the People: Reconsidering Newman and the Oxford Movement*. Leominster: Gracewing, 141–59.

Neale, J. M. (1876). *Sermons for the Church Year*. London: Hayes.

Newman, J. H. (1840). *Lectures on Justification*, 2nd edn. Oxford: Rivingtons & Parker.

—— (1843). *Fifteen Sermons Preached Before the University of Oxford*. Oxford: Rivington.

—— (1868). *Parochial and Plain Sermons*, new edn. London: Rivington.

—— (1964). *Apologia Pro Vita Sua*, new edn. London: Oxford University Press.

Nockles, P. B. (1994). *The Oxford Movement in Context: Anglican High Churchmanship 1760–1857*. Cambridge: Cambridge University Press.

—— (1997). '"Lost Causes and...Impossible Loyalties": The Oxford Movement and the University', in M. G. Brock and M. C. Curthoys (eds.), *The History of the University of Oxford, 5: Nineteenth-Century Oxford, Part I*. Oxford: Clarendon Press, 195–267.

Paget, F. E. (1849). *Sermons on Duties of Daily Life*. Rugeley: John Thomas Walters.

—— (1858). *The Parish and the Priest: Colloquies on the Pastoral Care, and Parochial Institutions of a Country Village*. London: Joseph Masters.

Pereiro, J. (2008). *'Ethos' and the Oxford Movement: At the Heart of Tractarianism*. Oxford: Oxford University Press.

Prestige, G. L. (1955). *St Paul's in its Glory: A Candid History of the Cathedral 1831–1911*. London: SPCK.

Purcell, E. S. (1896). *Life of Cardinal Manning, Archbishop of Westminster*. London: Macmillan.

Pusey, E. B. (1838). *The Church the Converter of the Heathen: Two Sermons Preached in Conformity With the Queen's Letter on Behalf of the Society for the Propagation of the Gospel*. Oxford: Parker & Rivington.

—— (ed.) (1844). *Sermons on Selected Lessons of the New Testament, by S. Augustine*. Oxford: Parker.

—— (ed.) (1845). *A Course of Sermons on Solemn Subjects Chiefly Bearing on Repentance and Amendment of Life, Preached at St Saviour's, Leeds, During the Week of Its Consecration*. Oxford: Parker.

—— (1848). *Sermons during the Season from Advent to Whitsuntide*. Oxford: Parker.

—— (1871). *This is my Body: a Sermon preached before the University at St Mary's*. Oxford: Parker.

—— (1874). *Lenten Sermons*. Oxford: Parker.

—— (1877). 'Advertisement', in J. Keble, *Sermons for the Christian Year: Sermons for Lent to Passiontide*. Oxford: Parker.

—— (1883). *Lenten Sermons, Preached Chiefly to Young Men at the Universities*. London: Walter Smith.

—— (1901). *Spiritual Letters*. London: Longman, Green & Co.

Reed, J. S. (1998). *Glorious Battle: The Cultural Politics of Victorian Anglo-Catholicism*, new edn. London: Tufton.

Riddell, R. (2004). 'Parker (1806–1884) John Henry', *ODNB*. Oxford: Oxford University Press.

Rowell, G. (1983). *The Vision Glorious: Themes and Personalities of the Catholic Revival in Anglicanism*. Oxford: Oxford University Press.

Simeon, C. S. (1819–28). *Horae Homilecticae or, Discourses (Principally in the Form of Skeletons) Now First Digested into One Continued Series and Forming a Commentary Upon Every Book of the Old and New Testament*. London: Watts.

Skinner, S. A. (2004). *Tractarians and the 'Condition of England': The Social and Political Thought of the Oxford Movement*. Oxford: Clarendon Press.

Sumner, J. B. (1815). *Apostolical Preaching Considered in an Examination of St Paul's Epistles*. London: Hatchard.

Thompson, D. M. (2005). *Baptism, Church and Society in Modern Britain*. Milton Keynes: Paternoster.

Toon, P. (1979). *Evangelical Theology, 1833–1856: A Response to Tractarianism*. London: Marshall, Morgan & Scott.

Walsh, W. (1898). *The Secret History of the Oxford Movement*. London: Swan Sonnenschein.

Wellings, M. (2003). *Evangelicals Embattled: Responses of Evangelicals in the Church of England to Ritualism, Darwinism and Theological Liberalism*. Carlisle: Paternoster Press.

Wesley, J. (1964). *Standard Sermons: Consisting of Forty-Four Discourses*, new edn. London: Epworth.

Williams, I. (ed.) (1839). *Plain Sermons by Contributors to the 'Tracts for the Times'*, vol. 1. London: Rivington.

—— (1840). Tract 80, 'On Reserve in Communicating Religious Knowledge', in *Tracts for the Times*, vol. 4. London: Rivington.

—— (1853a). *A Series of Sermons on the Epistle and Gospel for each Sunday in the Year*. London: Rivington.

—— (ed.) (1853b). *Sermons, Plain and Practical, By the Late Rev. R.A. Suckling*. London: Joseph Masters.

—— (1882). *Plain Sermons on the Catechism*, new edn. London: Rivington.

Wilson, D. (1851). *Revival of Spiritual Religion the Only Effectual Remedy for the Dangers Which Now Threaten the Church of England*. London: Hatchard.

Wordsworth, C. (1854). *Notes at Paris, Particularly on the State and Prospects of Religion*. London: Rivington.

CHAPTER 26

SERMONS AND THE CATHOLIC RESTORATION

MELISSA WILKINSON

On 29 September 1850, Pope Pius IX restored the Roman Catholic Hierarchy of England and Wales. The Bull *Universalis Ecclesiae* created the Archdiocese of Westminster and the Dioceses of Birmingham, Beverley, Clifton, Hexham, Liverpool, Northampton, Nottingham, Newport and Menevia, Plymouth, Salford, Shrewsbury, and Southwark. These dioceses replaced the London, Eastern, Western, Northern, and Central Districts, which had administered post-Reformation Roman Catholicism in England and Wales. The vicars apostolic, who had supervised these Districts, were replaced by the Archbishop of Westminster, Cardinal Nicholas Wiseman, and twelve suffragan bishops, of whom at least one, W. J. Hendren of Clifton, had formerly been the vicar apostolic. Reaction to the Restoration of the Hierarchy was influenced by several hundred years' distrust of Rome; and the act of Restoration came to symbolize the heavy-handedness of the Pope in the popular imagination, hence its alternative title, the 'Papal Aggression'.

The Restoration of the Hierarchy was controversial at all levels of society. Those angered by the 'Papal Aggression' demonstrated by public protests and graffiti, as well as by more intellectual forms of public addresses such as lectures and sermons.

Of the corpus of documents generated by the Restoration of the Hierarchy (such as letters, articles, pamphlets, and Acts of Parliament), sermons are only a small portion. However, the significance of sermons is that they form the interface between the Church hierarchy and clergy on one hand, and the congregation and society as a whole on the other. Analysis of these sermons is, therefore, valuable; firstly, because they reveal the theological and ecclesiological debate which underpinned both sides of this controversy, and secondly, because of the multiplicity of ideas and opinions relating to the Restoration of the Hierarchy which are contained within them.

Church of England and Nonconformist Sermons, 1850–1851

The first part of this chapter is concerned with sermons about Roman Catholicism written between 1850 and 1851 and public reaction to them. Although their authors wrote the majority for use on Sundays, they also preached several of them on occasions such as diocesan meetings and church festivals. The most successful sermons exhibit skilful use of ideas and well-structured intellectual argument, whilst their language varies depending on whether the preacher addressed his parishioners or clergy. Popular protest, which was particularly active during November and December 1850, clearly influenced the tone and subject matter; and, despite differences of emphasis and opinion, these sermons are essentially vehicles for anti-Catholic polemic. (Published sermons sold for between one and three pence each, and were available in multiple copies for a reduced price, thereby widening their readership and ensuring that their ideas contributed to the debate.) These sermons exhibit a deep distrust of Roman Catholicism, which illustrates the scale of the negative reaction to the Restoration of the Hierarchy and the depth of feeling that it engendered. The most noticeable disparity is that between sermons written by clergy of the Church of England and Nonconformist clergy. Whereas the latter were generally critical of both the Church of England and the Roman Catholic Church, a number viewed Catholics as outsiders and nonconformists like themselves.

Several preachers presented Catholicism as anti-Christian, while others described it as a spiritual darkness outside the Christian Church, a superstition contrary to the religious freedom endorsed and encouraged by Protestantism. Protestant preachers at one extreme predicted damnation for all Roman Catholics (James: 45), while those at the other suggested caution regarding their ultimate fate, exhorting their congregations to exercise charity towards Catholics regardless of their wariness and negative views about Catholicism itself. Analysis of these sermons reveals several common criticisms of Catholic theology and practice; in particular, Protestant preachers focused on purgatory, transubstantiation, clerical celibacy, auricular confession, masses for the dead, and indulgences. They also condemned Roman Catholicism for allowing tradition to supplant scripture, for withholding free access to scripture to the majority, and for giving credence to unscriptural practices. In the context of these sermons, all of these practices seduce and enthral those who are weak, sentimental, and gullible, epithets used to characterize the majority of Catholics. Sermon writers also took advantage of the lack of knowledge of their listeners, by highlighting practices imputed to Catholicism in the popular imagination such as idolatry, Mariolatry, and excessive prayer to saints. E. J. Herbert criticized the use of Latin in Roman Catholic liturgy, using Article 24 of the Thirty-Nine Articles to defend the notion that Welsh and English should be used for worship in these countries (Herbert: 11).

The scriptural texts on which these sermons were based were diverse; and criticism of Catholicism was grounded in both the Old and New Testaments, particularly, but not exclusively, in the books of Daniel, Psalms, 2 Thessalonians, and Revelation. Protestant preachers identified the Antichrist with the Pope from texts that described the Man of Sin who 'denies God and defies Christ' (Wordsworth 1851: 7; Coleman 5). Because of this identification, God would ultimately destroy both Catholicism and the Papacy (James: 6). These preachers rejected the authority and primacy implied by the identification of the Pope with St Peter—and the argument that St Peter had no intrinsic pre-eminence in the primitive Church was popular. Other preachers noted that St Paul had been a more influential and important figure than St Peter throughout the history of the Church. Within the 'Papal Aggression' controversy, the language used to describe Pius IX and Cardinal Wiseman was characterized by epithets such as arrogant, aggressive, 'deluded', and 'dishonest' (Kilby: 9).

The preachers expressed the principles of the Protestant Reformation in phrases that exhorted individuals to 'vindicate protestant truth against Papal superstition, apostasy, and usurpation' (Coleman: 3). A recurring notion in these sermons was that the hierarchies of popery, ousted during the Henrician Reformation, should not be allowed to return. Those who defied Rome, martyrs such as Cranmer and Latimer, were presented as examples of the necessity of continuing to resist Roman influence during the nineteenth century. Preachers also highlighted internal debates within the Church of England, caused by influences such as Ritualism and the Oxford Movement. In this context, they characterized Tractarians such as E. B. Pusey and J. H. Newman as heretical crypto-papists who had demonstrated their disloyalty to Protestantism by encouraging Roman practices within the Church of England. They also directed opprobrium at those who converted from the Church of England to Roman Catholicism, particularly those who did so because of their involvement with the Oxford Movement. These preachers frequently honoured the reception of those who moved away from Roman Catholicism to the Church of England or Nonconformity. They also criticized Tractarian doctrines and liturgical emphases. These included the revival of monasticism for women, the use of relics, altar crosses, candlesticks, genuflections, and veneration of saints (Spencer: 7, 25). Preachers such as W. F. Williams considered the Tractarian appeal to the Fathers of the Church theologically suspect: 'It is not surprising to find much dubious and objectionable doctrine in the writings of the Fathers', he noted (Williams: 11). Other sermon writers emphasized the purity of the primitive Church, underscoring this as the route by which the Church of England acquired apostolic succession, thereby freeing it from the corrupt traditions and later modifications of Roman Catholicism.

Universalis Ecclesiae denied the Church of England the status of a Church and described its members as schismatic. A number of Anglican preachers countered this by noting that Christianity in England and Wales pre-dated the arrival of St Augustine from Rome (*Papal Aggression*: 4), a historical circumstance that removed them from the necessity of loyalty to Roman Catholicism and obedience to the Pope.

The 'Papal Aggression' has a civil dimension in these sermons, particularly in those that presented the resurgence of papal influence in England and Wales as an invasion by, and on behalf of, individuals whose allegiance to the Pope and to Rome was essentially loyalty to another country (James: 10). Protestant preachers interpreted this as an affront both to the Protestantism of the British empire and to Queen Victoria as head of State and Governor of the Church of England. Additionally, they construed acts of Parliament such as the Catholic Emancipation Act (1829), the Irish Church Temporalities Act (1833), and money given to Catholic education during the first half of the century as accommodating Roman Catholicism. Thus, they considered the Ecclesiastical Titles Act (1851) an attempt to counterbalance this, in order to discourage papal claims of sovereignty and supremacy.

Within wider society, people expressed antagonism towards the Restoration of the Roman Catholic Hierarchy in lectures, newspaper articles, and public meetings. A transcript of an address given by J. Cumming at the Hanover Square Rooms in London is significant because it contains printed notes indicating the number of people present, their comments and reactions and, significantly, the presence of professional troublemakers (Cumming). (Cumming, and others like him, reinforced the clergy's arguments in a popular setting and references to sermons are rare in these circumstances.) The majority of sermon writers were aware of the mob element in 'a nation drunken with religious excitement' (Eddrup: 14). It was, said W. R. Barker, a climate in which 'every sign-post becomes a ghost, and every glow-worm the eye of some infernal monster' (Barker: 6). Barker and several other preachers characterize the majority of the population as being 'ignorant and infidel, so far as religion is concerned' (Barker: 23). Barker's comments suggest that the debate was above the heads of the majority of its participants, with a professional, educated clergy writing to, and within, a society whose members believed that they had a right to contribute to theological arguments using words and concepts whose meanings they did not fully understand, if at all. These sermons amply demonstrate the depth of anti-Catholic notions ingrained in the collective psyche of educated and uneducated people in England and Wales. However, this is a multi-faceted and complex issue, fuelled by a real sense of grievance, which has its roots in the wider history of England and Wales as well as in historical events occurring during the latter part of the eighteenth century and the first half of the nineteenth century. It was also as much about the superstitions of the English and Welsh as those attributed to Roman Catholics.

Preaching on the Restoration of the Roman Catholic Hierarchy by those who were not Roman Catholic was not always negative. By no means all sermons encouraged civil disobedience and even some that were vehemently anti-Catholic emphasized the need for caution, toleration, charity, and fairness. Thus, in a sermon preached to clergy, J. F. Macarness noted that caring for individuals within society who are poor, destitute, and suffering was intrinsically more valuable than fighting against Rome (Macarness: 10–11). Some preachers suggested that individual Christians should remain aloof from quarrels and other matters that were essentially ephemeral, while others suggested that those who protested against the Restoration eventually denied everyone freedom of expression whatever their religious affiliation (Barker: 2). Several preachers acknowledged the right of Roman Catholics to have churches, archbishops, and dioceses in England and Wales—as long as they paid for them from their own purse and did not use public funds (Barker: 5). They also suggested that individuals were arguing about words that were meaningless because the Restoration of the Hierarchy resulted in a new series of titles—bishop for vicar apostolic and diocese for district—rather than a new institution (Barker: 4; Bowyer: 12).

Roman Catholic Sermons, 1850–1851

The majority of Roman Catholic sermons preached in the period 1850–1 were delivered during Sunday morning or evening services, at the consecration of new churches, or at associated locations abroad such as the English College in Rome. Collectively, these sermons demonstrate the considerable response of Catholic preachers to popular protest and the extent to which they engaged with those who were critical, not only of the Restoration, but also of Catholic theology, doctrine, and history. For this reason, the most significant points of history, ecclesiology, and theology in these sermons are worth noting.

Sermons written and published by Roman Catholic clergy during 1850 and 1851 presented the case for the Restoration of the Hierarchy. Analysis of these sermons illustrates the extent to which preachers were influenced by the criticism, suspicion, and distrust of Roman Catholicism exemplified by anti-Catholic and anti-papal polemic in speeches in Parliament, lectures, public addresses, newspaper articles, and the civil unrest endemic in mid-nineteenth-century society. The reaction of the clergy to this climate can be divided into two distinct approaches. In the first of these, preachers demonstrated an uncompromising assertiveness that engaged with popular protest while not allowing themselves to be influenced or compromised by it. In the second, preachers employed an approach seemingly calculated to change the attitude of their adversaries in order to create a climate of tolerance and understanding.

Mid-nineteenth-century sermon writers viewed the Restoration of the Hierarchy as a pivotal moment in the history of Roman Catholicism in England and Wales. H. E. Manning characterized it as the time when 'Catholics entered into the political and social life of England, as the early Christians emerged from the catacombs into the light of the sun' (Manning 1863: 47). Newman used metaphors of renewal from the *Song of Songs* in order to describe it as a second spring, a moral and spiritual revival that no one could have imagined or prophesied before it happened (Newman 1852: 14, 20). Newman also suggested that the Restoration marked the reacceptance and rediscovery of Roman Catholicism, an event that would allow Roman Catholics to regain their position of importance in English and Welsh society (Newman 1852: 14). In the sermon *Christ upon the Waters*, he drew attention to the resilience of the Church during periods of persecution, and its ultimate triumph over its aggressors (Newman 1850: 4). He portrayed the Restoration as the fulfilment of Catholic destiny, the impetus for which came not from Catholics inside or outside England and Wales, but from God. In this context, preachers were concerned to emphasize that God chose the moment for the return of Catholicism (Newman 1850: 16); and the implication is that the mid-nineteenth century was the proper moment. A number of clergymen mention the working of God in history; and this is the reason why they portrayed the passage of time between the Reformation and the Restoration as part of the measured movement of Divine grace, presence, and providence in history (Newman 1850: 8, 5).

Preachers counterbalanced the sense that Catholics were a marginalized minority within the society of the 1850s by highlighting historical details surrounding the arrival of Roman Catholicism in England. They presented this event as one that brought order out of chaos—Newman characterized the period before the arrival of Roman Catholicism as a period of moral darkness (Newman 1850: 5–6). To illustrate this, he applied the text from Matthew's Gospel, of the encounter between Jesus walking on water and Peter, to the meeting between the Roman Catholic Church and the English and Welsh (Newman 1850: 8). It is interesting to note the contrast between this, Roman Catholic, reading of the state of England and Wales before the arrival of Roman Catholicism, and the more positive view held by clergy of the Church of England, in which these countries were already Christian. Newman and others had a similar reading of the post-Restoration return of Roman Catholicism. For Manning, refusal to accept Roman Catholic truth causes a regression into moral and spiritual darkness (Manning 1873: 267).

In emphasizing Catholic history, preachers noted the pre-eminence of Roman Catholicism before the Reformation, and its contribution to society in the form of church building, the spread of monasticism, Catholic ritual, and ecclesiastical art (Newman 1852: 14–15). They also highlighted the Church's antiquity and authority and its unique position as the true religion (Newman 1850: 11), the only authentic church and the 'one fold of the one shepherd' (Cruikshank: 16, 9). A number of sermon writers stressed that 'Christianity and Catholicism are one' while others emphasized that Catholicism is distinguished from other churches by its familiarity with God (Newman 1850: 9; Cruikshank: 6). Manning took this a stage further, writing of the certainty of eternal damnation for those who do not believe in the revelation from God revealed through the Roman Catholic Church (Manning 1872: 23). In these sermons, preachers characterized churches outside Roman Catholicism as being purely human institutions. They frequently expressed the distinctions between the Catholic Church and other churches using contrasting epithets such as authentic and inauthentic or right and wrong, and their respective adherents as being saved or damned. In a sermon preached for the opening of St Marie's Church, Rugby, A. P. J. Cruickshank emphasized these distinct states of being by noting that there was no middle way between Roman Catholicism and unbelief (Cruikshank: 8). F. W. Faber, preaching at the London Oratory, noted the incompatibility of the Roman Church with other churches and civil institutions, opining that the latter are worldly and inconsequential. He also claimed that it was impossible for Roman Catholics to counter long-standing prejudices and argued that the discourtesy of anti-Catholic polemic highlighted the ineffectual and counterfeit nature of other churches (Faber: 297–8).

The authors of these sermons were also concerned with the history of the Reformation and the emergence of Protestantism, both of which they discussed from the perspective of their effect on Roman Catholicism. Several ideas recur. Newman described the Reformation as having been inspired by the devil and he criticized other churches for their subsequent replacement of the spiritual with the temporal and for private judgement in matters of religion, which he characterized as being both a Protestant and a national problem (Newman 1850: 12, 11, 25). He also warned of the danger involved in giving assent to any theological opinions that the Roman Catholic Church had not verified and refined (Newman 1850: 29). (Newman's command of the theology of his adversaries is evident in his use of reasoning, rather than provocation, to demonstrate that the devil encourages individuals to believe ideas such as the Pope is the Man of Sin prophesied in the book of Revelation (Newman 1850: 18–19).) Wiseman, in taking up, and disputing, an argument used by clergy of the Church of England, emphasized the theological and moral gravity inherent in believing that the Roman Church is Satanic, rather than from God (Wiseman 1850d: Lecture 3:8).

Discussion of the decay of Catholicism in England and Wales after the Henrician Reformation is central to these sermons; preachers who discussed post-Reformation history highlighted the hostile reception given to Catholics. Newman spoke about the fragmentation of Catholicism into small groups distant from the centre of national life (Newman 1852: 16–18), and noted the losses resulting from the rejection of Catholicism, particularly the destruction of monasteries, churches, and ritual (Newman 1850: 14). In answer to the accusations of critics, Wiseman noted that the majority of the population lacked a true theological understanding of Roman Catholicism (Wiseman 1850d: Lecture 1:14). Collectively, preachers suggested that God had abandoned the nations of England and Wales because of their peoples' desecration of their Roman Catholic heritage; and there is a distinct sense these preachers were aware that Catholicism was not, and never had been, part of the natural religious milieu of England and Wales. Such an understanding led to clergymen making a distinction between sermons written for those who were hostile and sermons written for those who possessed a shared understanding of Catholicism. A sermon preached by Wiseman in the chapel of the English College in Rome, written to encourage clergy returning to England after ordination, is an example of the latter (Wiseman 1854).

The most notable agreement between 'Papal Aggression' sermons by clergy of the Church of England and Restoration sermons by Roman Catholic clergy was in their discussion of persecution: both discussed similar issues from opposite standpoints. T. Burgess highlighted the persecution in the form of anti-Catholic polemic surrounding the Restoration of the Hierarchy by observing that 'the passions of mankind have been excited against our holy religion by every means that prejudice could devise' (Burgess: 4). Faber suggested that anti-Catholic controversy was caused by a deep-rooted fear of Roman Catholics which was inspired by the devil (Faber: 297–8). Although both interpretations are significant, it is interesting to note that Burgess viewed the intolerance of his contemporaries not just in terms of his own religion, but also as an attack on the ethical principles of Christianity as a whole which, if allowed to continue, would be detrimental to the stability of society (Burgess: 4). Roman Catholic preachers, like those in other churches, also discussed the extent to which adherents had been persecuted throughout history—and both groups frequently mention the personal history and significance of those who have been acknowledged as martyrs, either officially or unofficially. Roman Catholic clergy connected discussion of martyrdom with the ultimate victory of Catholicism over those who have persecuted it. Contemporary and historical examples of persecution come together in the notion that the Restoration of the Hierarchy provided 'recompense' for the sacrifice of those who have been persecuted (Newman 1852: 25), which would, 'make up to us in this our generation for all that our fathers suffered' (Wiseman 1850b: 30).

Another facet of these sermons was the presentation of the Restoration of the Hierarchy as a matter of social justice. In his Apostolic Letter, Pius IX wrote that it was the wish of Roman Catholics from all levels of society in England and Wales that the Hierarchy should be restored (Pius IX: 5). It is, however, difficult to say conclusively the degree to which this was the case, or to know the extent to which the majority of Roman Catholics were aware of the implications inherent in changing from vicars apostolic to diocesan bishops. The view that there was no legal or civil reason why the Church should not have diocesan bishops, as they had had a legal right to practise their religion since the Catholic Emancipation Act of 1829, is popular with preachers such as Wiseman (Wiseman 1850a: 14–15). Others asserted the right of the Pope to create bishops and dioceses in England and Wales, irrespective of the legal status of Catholicism or the opinion held by civil Government. In this context, they presented the Restoration as an event that would bolster the social status of Roman Catholicism, thereby giving it equality with other churches, each of which already possessed its own separate identity within civil law. Such debate highlights the strategic importance of theological controversy within the social and political life of England and Wales during the early and middle years of the nineteenth century. Catholic preachers also characterized anti-papal and anti-Catholic feeling as unfounded hysteria and, in an attempt to pacify critics, they stated that the new bishops would have no civil jurisdiction or power to affect civil or other ecclesiastical authority in England and Wales. In doing so, they also acknowledged that the temporal advantage was with the Church of England, which retained its position as the state religion (Wiseman 1850a: 16).

Several sermon writers noted that whereas laity, clergy, and bishops desired to revive Roman Catholic influence, spirituality, and hierarchy, they did not wish to create a Roman Catholic country; and they highlighted countries, such as Belgium, in which the government acted as an autonomous body, remaining free from Church influence (Wiseman 1850b: 10–12). Perhaps more important given, several preachers noted that the historical rejection of papal authority by the government in England and Wales, Catholics did not intend to usurp the authority of Queen Victoria (Wiseman 1850b: 21; *Declaration of the Roman Catholic Laity*: 4–5). Awareness of the wider climate of mistrust of Roman Catholicism led Wiseman to make the pertinent observation that the creation of dioceses elsewhere, such as Ireland and America, had not caused the same level of controversy as it had in England and Wales (Wiseman 1850a: 24).

The nineteenth-century debate between liberals and Ultramontanes is evidence of internal controversy within Roman Catholicism, although protagonists did not state these differences overtly in their sermons. Ultramontane defence of the Pope's Restoration of the Hierarchy was a response to the popular belief that the Pope had exercised an *aggressive* jurisdiction over England and Wales. However, Wiseman put this into context by noting that other countries were also suspicious of the interference of foreign powers (Wiseman 1850d: Lecture 1:8). Burgess argued that the world outside the Church was the adversary of the Church and the Pope (Burgess: 6) while Wiseman reassured the wider population of England and Wales that they had nothing to fear from the Pope's jurisdiction (Wiseman 1850a: 21). Wiseman also noted that the change from temporary vicars apostolic to a hierarchy of bishops was advantageous to the country because it was permanent (Wiseman 1850a: 23); there was historical continuity because the hierarchy had been restored, not created afresh (Wiseman 1850d: Lecture 1:8–9).

In engaging with critics of the Restoration, Wiseman argued that toleration of Roman Catholicism must be toleration of its entire religious outlook, not just parts of it (Wiseman 1850a: 14–15). In *An Appeal to the Reason and Good Feeling of the English People*, which commented on the state of relations between Roman Catholics and the public, Wiseman asked his listeners to apply the traditional British virtues of fair play and tolerance to Roman Catholics. Other preachers highlighted the need for Catholics to acquire the same virtues in their communication with other individuals. Thus, in a sermon at the London Oratory on the Ecclesiastical Titles Bill, Faber stressed the necessity for calm tolerance by English and Irish Catholics in the face of Protestant opprobrium (Faber: 297–8).

As to the wider British society, the empire, Catholic preachers commended its positive attributes such as its range, scope, and influence as well as the wealth associated with its trade and natural resources. Manning described it as a descendent of the Roman empire (Manning 1873: 8), and Wiseman argued that the intellectual and scientific discoveries associated with the empire were divine in origin (Wiseman 1850c: 11, 5). However, although these preachers associated themselves with the empire, they noted that Roman Catholicism had been a beneficial part of all of its constituent countries except England and Wales (Wiseman 1850a: 23). Catholic Emancipation and the Restoration of the Hierarchy were the means by which Catholicism benefited the whole of society; for example, Wiseman called church building an important expression of thanks to God for temporal prosperity (Wiseman 1850c: 18–19). He also contrasted Britain with Italy noting that, unlike Britain, Italy had preserved the association between art, economic success, belief in God, and membership of the Roman Catholic Church (Wiseman 1850c: 8–9).

Several preachers concerned about the Restoration also highlighted the negative attributes of the empire although with a lesser weight of emphasis than those writing about its success. Wiseman suggested that future historians, writing after the inevitable dissolution of the empire, would judge it to have been great in all aspects except its attitude toward religion, for which it had done nothing (Wiseman 1850c: 10). Cruickshank noted the contrast between temporal riches and spiritual poverty (Cruikshank: 8) at all levels of society and Wiseman the general lack of empathy with the economically poor (Cruikshank: 8; Wiseman 1850c: 16).

Study of these sermons illustrates the extent to which Catholic clergy thought it necessary to make their religion accessible to their contemporaries, by encouraging individuals to be enthusiastic in discussing its practices and theology in public and private (Wiseman 1850b: 29). They also impressed upon their congregations the importance of maintaining their faith and identity as an antidote to worldliness and persecution. An example of the important role played by converts in mid-nineteenth-century Catholicism is illustrated by the number of these sermons that were written by recent converts, several of whom had been part of the Oxford Movement. Conversions were undoubtedly important for a reinvigoration of the intellectual life of Roman Catholicism in England and Wales. Faber asserted that one of the proofs of the truth of Catholicism was the 'numerous conversions and growing trouble in thoughtful minds' (Faber: 298); in other words, Roman Catholic intellectuals stimulated and energized the intellectual life of the country. This is an important characteristic of sermons such as those of Wiseman; these form a successful corpus of intellectual apologia for Catholicism, thanks to their inventive use of argument and stylistic sophistication: the sermons exuded confidence without seeming arrogant or confrontational. In a sermon preached in Southwark in 1850, Wiseman observed, 'How many have joined us from every profession which naturally tends to make the intellect more keen, or to give greater power of logical deduction and accurate investigation' (Wiseman 1850b: 25).

According to the Religious Census of 1851, 5 per cent of the population of England and Wales were members of the Roman Catholic Church. Between 1851 and 1901, the number of Roman Catholic churches and chapels in England and Wales increased from 597 to 1,536, while the number of clergy increased from 826 to 3,298 (Cook and Keith: 223). Immigration from Ireland was one reason for the rise in Catholic numbers, and Catholic clergy preached several Restoration sermons at the consecration of churches built for congregations with a significant Irish population. Those who preached to Irish immigrants, or who discussed them, generally mentioned the material and economic poverty of the Irish, to characterize them as exiles or to describe them as faithful Catholics (O'Donnell: 13; Wiseman 1850a: 18). In one sense, the traditions and attitudes of Irish Catholics represented Catholicism to many of the population of England and Wales. Further, a number of these sermons create the impression that English and Irish Catholics were not close. In preaching about the circumstances surrounding the Ecclesiastical Titles Bill, Faber observed that persecution had created more empathy than had previously existed between these two groups (Faber: 298). In a sermon preached on St Patrick's Day 1852, M. O'Donnell drew similarities between the Irish, who brought Roman Catholicism to England and Wales, and St Patrick, who took Christianity to Ireland (O'Donnell: 4). O'Donnell compared the renewal of the Catholic Church in Ireland and the historical dislocation of the Catholic Church in England; he likened Protestant England and Wales to other heretical nations such as Calvinist France (O'Donnell: 10, 8). Although not overtly stated, O'Donnell clearly viewed these countries as being in the same state as that of the world before the advent of Christianity: places of darkness, spiritual uncleanness, idolatry, and superstition (O'Donnell: 5). His sermon gives the impression that the Irish had limited status during the early 1850s (although this could feasibly have been applied to the majority of society). However, O'Donnell, who was probably of Irish extraction, also noted that all Roman Catholics are protected by God and would, therefore, be saved, a boon denied to those outside the Church (O'Donnell: 10). O'Donnell's intention, presumably, was to boost the morale of his audience, thereby providing an antidote to popular opinion. However, despite its moral certitude, there is a strong element of introspection in this sermon, which comes close to becoming a self-satisfied smugness.

Sermons Preached during the Second Half of the Nineteenth Century

Among the many sermons preached by Church of England, Nonconformist, and Roman Catholic clergy in the latter half of the nineteenth century, several contain discussions of ecclesiological distinctions between churches. Three trends are visible in these sermons. The first is the subtle similarities and differences in the relationship between the Church of England, Nonconformity, and Roman Catholicism; the second, the consolidation of Roman Catholicism after the Restoration of the Hierarchy; and the third, particularly noticeable by the end of the century, the altered relationship between all churches and society as a whole. In this part of the chapter, we shall explore the extent to which each of these trends is discernible in sermons preached and published during this period.

The most notable change of emphasis in sermons preached by members of the Church of England and Nonconformists is that these preachers frequently emphasize the need for tolerance, despite the differences of opinion (Tyrwhitt: 3). In doing so, these sermons highlighted the changing nature of the relationship between the Church of England and other churches, a subject that became increasingly important during the latter part of the century. During this time, there was a distinct sense of co-existence with Roman Catholics at a social and religious level. The climate of anti-Catholicism also changed, in that violent anti-Catholic expression occurred only occasionally; and examples of anti-Catholic sermons, such as those that accompanied the Restoration of the Hierarchy, were exceptional rather than the norm. It is, however, significant that, although sermons became less critical, the fundamental critique of Roman Catholic theology and practice did not change during the second half of the nineteenth century. The Bible, the Thirty-Nine Articles, and pre- and post-Reformation history continued to inspire the refutation of Roman Catholicism and justification of Protestantism.

The distinction between the Restoration controversy and later attitudes towards Catholicism lies in subtle changes of emphasis, nuance, and circumstance. The controversy in connection with the Restoration of the Hierarchy continued after 1851, and there was a remarkable consistency in anti-Catholic and anti-papal polemic during the remainder of the century. Thus, whenever Protestant preachers interpreted something as an abuse of papal power, they referred to it as *papal aggression*, the definition of Papal

Infallibility and the First Vatican Council being two prominent examples. Preachers highlighted the connection between the actions of the Pope and the civil and religious climate in England, with clergymen such as M. J. Fuller emphasizing that the Pope had no legal rights over the country (Fuller). In these types of sermons, preachers did frequently mention the doctrinal differences between Protestants and Roman Catholics; Anglican preachers described the Church of England as the only authentic Church, a 'faithful witness in harmony with really primitive antiquity' (Tyrwhitt: 3). Popular criticisms of Roman Catholicism are evident in these sermons; objections to Roman Catholic errors and superstition are stated both overtly and indirectly (Tyrwhitt: 6). Some preachers commented on doctrines such as those related to the essence of Catholicism—purgatory, the Sacred Heart, the Eucharist, and the priesthood—while others questioned what they considered ethical issues such as whether Catholics were encouraged to read scripture. In discussing *Ineffabilis Deus*, which defined the doctrine of the Immaculate Conception in 1854, some charged Catholicism with idolatry and Mariolatry (Gore Tipper: 6); R. Tyrwhitt described the Immaculate Conception as the 'consummation of Mariolatry' (Tyrwhitt: 6). A number of preachers identified the Church of Rome with The Beast from the book of Revelation and with Babylon (Gore Tipper), while others characterized it as being cursed by God (Macneile: 14). The latter sermons are especially interesting as they are examples of a particular type of mind-set and provide the most excessive and vitriolic of anti-Catholic statements.

Unsurprisingly, in these sermons, preachers highlighted in a triumphal manner any conversions from Roman Catholicism as indications of the error of Rome. Conversely, they denounced converts to Roman Catholicism, whom C. Wordsworth characterized as misguided individuals, concerned only with glory and vanity; he suggested that Satan, who fell from grace due to spiritual pride, is an example of such an attitude (Wordsworth 1864: 5, 7). Drawing parallels between Christ's faithless contemporaries and those who have departed from the Church of England, he noted that there were historical precedents for individuals departing from the truth presented by Christ (Wordsworth 1864: 6). It is significant that Wordsworth blamed these conversions on 'dissentions of Protestants' (Wordsworth 1864: 13), observing that individuals joined the Roman Catholic Church because Protestants were not sufficiently interested in, nor serious about, the practice of religion, and neglected prayer and other services (Wordsworth 1864: 16). This sermon provides a good example of a reasoned anti-Catholic argument, illustrating that, although Catholicism was by this time established and flourishing, many Anglicans and Nonconformists considered it morally and doctrinally false.

An examination of sermons preached by Roman Catholic clergy during the second half of the nineteenth century reveals the consolidation and growth of Roman Catholicism in the years following the Restoration of the Hierarchy. These sermons were more measured and less defensive than those preached during 1850 and 1851. There was, however, consistency in their subject matter during this period, despite differences of emphasis and tone; this is particularly evident in discussions of Roman Catholic sacramental and moral theology and ecclesiology. Sermons written after the Restoration display a sense of the moral and spiritual excellence of Catholicism, and preachers highlighted its position as the only authentic church. For Manning, the nineteenth century was a time of 'triumph' for Roman Catholicism (Manning 1873: 222). He stressed the authority of the Church and the moral and spiritual consequences of rejecting an authority whose defining characteristic is that it 'imposes its doctrines on...men under pain of eternal death' (Manning 1872: 23). Other clergy expressed similar sentiments, viewing this period as one of unique promise for Catholicism and using epithets that highlight the power and invincibility of the Church; similar to sermons preached earlier in the century, a significant number of sermons noted the working of God in history particularly as it related to Roman Catholicism. For Manning, unity within Catholicism, shown by its rejection of arguments contrary to its doctrinal position, was the defining characteristic of the late nineteenth century (Manning 1873: 259).

In a stance that contrasted with the defensive position freely adopted in many Restoration sermons, Roman Catholic clergy looked back at the Restoration of the Hierarchy as an event that engendered a resurgence of Catholicism, leading to its position as an established part of the religious milieu of England and Wales. The Restoration was central in the formation of Catholic identity and status, enhancing the influence and contribution to society of Catholics. The Restoration was characterized as part of a wider history, affecting the future development of Catholicism in England and Wales. These sermons were also forward-looking in their aspirations for Catholicism, frequently extending their hopes beyond the end of the nineteenth century and into the twentieth century. Catholic preachers also demonstrated an awareness that post-Restoration Catholicism in England and Wales was a constituent part of the worldwide Catholic Church in a fuller sense than was possible with Districts and vicars apostolic.

Catholic preachers also referred to the Restoration of the Hierarchy in sermons preached after the deaths of the protagonists most responsible for it. J. Connolly called Wiseman an important Roman Catholic intellectual and 'the greatest man of the age' (Connolly: 16, 12, 6). This sermon illustrates both the affection in which Wiseman was held by his contemporaries and the extent to which they believed that Roman Catholicism in England and Wales had been shaped by his influence and personality. In a eulogy for Pius IX, W. B. Ullathorne referred to the Restoration as one of the successes of a Pontificate that included *Ineffabilis Deus* (1854), the First Vatican Council (1869–70), Papal Infallibility (1870), and the Restoration of the Scottish hierarchy (1875) (Ullathorne: 13, 11). This sermon is significant because Ullathorne was writing to a Church that was thriving and successful—rather than one that was apologetic about its position—and part of a larger whole, both temporally and spiritually.

Discussion of the Papacy was important to Ultramontane preachers in the context of events abroad, such as the wars in Italy that involved the Papal States, and at home, in the form of opprobrium directed against the Pope. In a collection of sermons published in 1873, Manning wrote of the importance of the temporal and spiritual power of the Papacy which is 'a power ordained of God' and therefore higher than secular authority (Manning 1873: 4, 5, 14). He also emphasized the importance of St Peter to the history of the Papacy in general (Manning 1873: 15), while Ullathorne used scriptural language to present the Pope as a leader and High Priest, a conqueror who counters the secular forces of the world, the majority of whom have rejected him (Ullathorne). Preachers such as Ullathorne frequently couched the Restoration of Roman Catholicism in highly symbolic terms, contrasting the Catholic elect with the misunderstanding of those who have rejected, and continued to reject, Catholicism. In discussing the latter, these preachers noted the extent to which residual anti-Catholicism, in subtle and overt forms, continued to affect Catholics later in the century; indeed, despite new churches and increased numbers of clergy, the characterization of Roman Catholics, by themselves and by their contemporaries, as persecuted was never entirely absent.

Many Catholic clergy repeated and enlarged upon criticisms of the British empire and the civil government made in the context of the Restoration controversy. In the introduction to *Sermons on Ecclesiastical Subjects*, Manning asserted that the English nation had always been essentially anti-Catholic, although he interpreted this attitude theologically by relating it to displays of 'insubordination to revelation and to divine authority' (Manning 1863: 71–2). It is, however, significant that, in a later sermon in the same volume, he conceded that there was a gradual on-going movement towards toleration of Roman Catholicism in England (Manning 1863: 79).

Criticism by Catholic preachers of anti-Catholic polemic, encountered throughout the century, now encompassed criticisms of philosophy, rationalism, atheism and 'individualism in religion' (Manning 1863: 72). The majority of Roman Catholic clergy were concerned that these movements affected not only their religion but also religion in general; they denounced all criticisms, not only of Roman Catholicism but also of Christianity itself. Commenting on the problems of the day, Manning noted that fragmentation had damaged Christianity because it had watered it down, thereby making it less believable (Manning n. d.: 15); in a sermon, Manning argued that rejection of Roman Catholicism leads towards 'sin, worldliness, indifference, unbelief [and] practical atheism' (Manning 1863: 108). A number of sermon writers suggest that there is less public hysteria about religious controversy and, equally noteworthy, that the contemporary controversies did not have the same power to influence society. One of the major differences in emphasis in these sermons is that the confrontation was no longer simply Catholic versus Protestant but Catholic and Protestant, still with their disagreements, against atheism. Much of Manning's sermon writing exhibits a particular awareness of this and he characterized atheism as 'a lower abasement of the intellect than was ever reached by the heathen world' (Manning, n.d.: 13).

Conclusion

A study of sermons preached before and after the Restoration of the Roman Catholic Hierarchy in England and Wales reveals the most important debates associated with the Restoration and the ways in which these both changed and stayed the same during the remainder of the century. As noted throughout this chapter, the subjects focused on by clergy of the Church of England and those of the Roman Catholic Church show both groups had similar as well as dissimilar priorities and preoccupations. For clergy of the Church of England, these included the use of and references to anti-Catholic polemic, discussions of the threat to the nation from the 'Papal Aggression', and the theology of Roman Catholicism, drawn from scripture and history. Sermons by Roman Catholic clergy focused on the importance of the Restoration controversy, by indicating the positive and negative reactions to it. The triumphalism evident during the latter part of the century replaced the defensiveness of Restoration sermons, thereby reinforcing the significance of the Restoration as an event that re-established Roman Catholicism in England and Wales. For this reason the Restoration of the Roman Catholic Hierarchy in England and Wales, or 'Papal Aggression' controversy, was one of the pivotal moments of nineteenth-century ecclesiastical history. In one sense, the subject matter of the sermons preached in the period around 1850 provides a view of the thinking of Catholics and Protestants that is a microcosm of the wider religious controversy of the age.

References

Barker, W. R. (1851). *Free Thoughts on Men and Things*... London: Green.
Bowyer, G. (1850). *The Cardinal Archbishop of Westminster and the New Hierarchy*. London: Ridgway.
Burgess, T. (1851). *A Pastoral by the Right Rev. Thomas Burgess DD*. Bath: Prior Park Press.
Coleman, J. N. (1851). *Papal Rome, the Foretold and Foredoomed Apostasy*... London: Jackson and Walford.
Connolly, J. (1865). *Sermon in Memory of Nicholas Cardinal Wiseman Archbishop of Westminster*. London: Duffy.
Cook, C., and Keith, B. (1975). *British Historical Facts 1830–1900*. London: Macmillan.
Cruikshank, A. P. J. (1857). *The Fullness of Christ's Mystical Body*... London: Burns and Lambert.
Cumming, J. (1850). *Dr Cumming's Lecture on the Papal Aggression*. London: Westerton.
Declaration of the Roman Catholic Laity of England. (1851). London: Henry Lucas.
Eddrup, E. P. (1850). *Papal Aggression*... London: George Kincombe.
Faber, F. W. (1866). *Notes on Doctrinal Subjects*, 3rd edn. London: Burns and Oates.
Fuller, M. J. (1896). *The Pope's Encyclical and the Papal Aggression*. London: J. Masters and Co.
Gore Tipper, J. (1867). *A Sermon Preached in St Stephen's Church Canonbury*... London: Hatchard and Co.
Herbert, E. J. (1850). *The Real Causes of the Papal Aggression*. London: Ollivier.
James, J. A. (1851). *The Papal Aggression and Popery Contemplated Religiously*... London: Hamilton Adams and Co.
Kilby, T. (1850). *A Sermon on the Late Papal Aggression*. London: Longman, Brown, Green.
Macarness, J. F. (1850). *A Plea for Toleration in Answer to the No Popery Cry*. London: Ollivier.
Macneile, H. (1868). *The Church of England and Her Attitude towards the Church of Rome*. London: W. Hunt & Co.
Manning, H. E. (1863). *Sermons on Ecclesiastical Subjects*, vol. 1. Dublin: Duffy.
—— (1872). *Sermons on Ecclesiastical Subjects*, vol. 2. London: Burns Oates and Co.
—— (1873). *Sermons on Ecclesiastical Subjects*, vol. 3. London: Burns Oates and Co.

—— (n.d.). *The Four Great Evils of the Day*, 9th edn. London: Burns and Oates.

Newman, J. H. (1850). *Christ upon the Waters*..., 2nd edn. London: Burns and Lambert.

—— (1852). *The Second Spring*. London: Thomas Richardson and Son.

O'Donnell, M. (1852). *A Sermon Preached at the Laying of the Foundation Stone of St Patrick's Church, Bradford*... London: Bradley.

Papal Aggression, or, Popish Priests versus the Word of God. (1852). London: Bosworth.

Pius IX, Pope (1850). *The Apostolic Letter of Pope Pius IX on the Re-establishment of the Roman Catholic Episcopate in England*... London: Gorbell.

Spencer, W. (1850). *Papal Aggressions Aided and Encouraged by Tractarian Movements.* Devonport: Heydon.

Tyrwhitt, R. (1874). *Catholic and Protestant; Discipline: Two Sermons.* London: Macintosh.

Ullathorne, W. B. (1878). *The Discourse Delivered at the Solemn Requiem for H. H. Pius IX.* Birmingham: Canning.

Williams, W. F. (1852). *The Antidote to Popery and Priestcraft*... London: Effingham Wilson.

Wiseman, N. (1850a). *An Appeal to the Reason and Good Feeling of the English People*... London: Thomas Richardson and Sons.

—— (1850b). *A Sermon Delivered at St George's Catholic Church, Southwark*... London: Richardson.

—— (1850c). *The Social and Intellectual State of England, Compared with its Moral Condition*... London: Thomas Richardson and Son.

—— (1850d). *Three Lectures on the Catholic Hierarchy*. London: Richardson and Son.

—— (1854). *A Sermon Delivered in the Chapel of the English College at Rome*... London: Richardson.

Wordsworth, C. (1851). *Is the Pope of Rome the Man of Sin?* 2nd edn. London: F. & J. Rivington.

—— (1864). *On Perversions to Rome*..., 2nd edn. London: Rivingtons.

CHAPTER 27

PALEY TO DARWIN: NATURAL THEOLOGY VERSUS SCIENCE IN VICTORIAN SERMONS

KEITH A. FRANCIS

Natural Theology, William Paley, and Charles Darwin

In crossing a heath, suppose I pitched my foot against a stone, and were asked how the stone came to be there, I might possibly answer, that, for any thing that I knew to the contrary, it had lain there forever: nor would it perhaps be very easy to shew the absurdity of this answer. But suppose I had found a watch upon the ground, and it should be enquired how the watch happened to be in that place, I should hardly think of the answer which I had before given, that, for any thing I knew, the watch might have always been there. Yet why should not this answer serve for the watch, as well as for the stone? Why is it not as admissible in the second case, as in the first? For this reason, and for no other, viz. that, when we come to inspect the watch, we perceive (what we could not discover in the stone) that its several parts are framed and put together for a purpose. (Paley 1802: 1–2)

So begins the argument of William Paley in *Natural Theology*, the best known exposition of natural theology in the nineteenth and twentieth centuries. In fact, its ideas and style of argument became the new orthodoxy in theological study. *Natural Theology* helped to cement Paley's reputation as one of the pre-eminent theologians of the eighteenth and nineteenth centuries. It was published in numerous editions, both by Paley and by subsequent editors after his death, and ensured that Paley's works were studied assiduously by aspiring students of theology for the next hundred years and more.

But Paley's teleological argument, popularly known as the 'argument from design', is no longer the standard explanation in theology for the existence of God or God's activity in the natural world. Except in Christian theologies labelled 'conservative' or 'fundamentalist' the ideas in *Natural Theology* are more of a historical curiosity than a subject of serious study.

How did this 'fall from grace' occur? Historians of nineteenth-century thought usually suggest the cause was the development of new ideas about science, particularly the growing acceptance of evolutionary theory for an explanation of the origin of life. As Robert J. Richards put it recently, 'the usual assumption is that [Charles] Darwin killed those barren virgins of teleology and purpose' (Richards: 10056). Observers saw the writing on the wall in the nineteenth century: 'It was Mr Darwin who first, by his discovery of natural selection, supplied the champions of science with the resistless weapon by which to vanquish, in this their chief stronghold, the champions of theology', noted James Houghton Kennedy in 1890 (Kennedy: viii).

If there is a real story, it is more complex than Darwin ushering in more modern thought than Paley's by the publication of *On the Origin of Species* in 1859. As Richards and others have noted, the language and style of Darwin's argument, and tropes underpinning it, are not a blanket repudiation of everything in *Natural Theology*. It may be better to think of Darwin reconstructing the design argument from the inside out. To extend the metaphor, Darwin was willing to use old bricks for his new building (Richards: 10056–60; Beer).

One way to tease out the impact of Darwin's writing and work on the development—or retardation—of natural theology in the nineteenth century is to examine what was happening 'on the ground'. As Henrik Alvar Ellegård showed in *Darwin and the General Reader*, it is possible to acquire a different, and more nuanced, perspective of the dissemination of Darwin's theory of evolution by examining the material that ordinary people, non-experts, were likely to read (Ellegård). And it would be a more-than-useful exercise to do the same for Paley's ideas. On the other hand, as the authors of several of the chapters in this volume have argued, a study of the sermon makes it possible to investigate in greater breadth the thinking and attitudes of ordinary folk. Preachers, whether they were Church of England bishops, country clergymen, Methodist circuit preachers, or Salvation Army captains, had the opportunity to comment on a wide range of topics by dint of having to preach regularly—more than three times a week in some cases—and though they mainly directed the thinking of their congregations they also reflected it. Furthermore, every social class was represented in their congregations. Queen Victoria heard sermons regularly, as did the agricultural labourer, the dock worker, or the bencher at Gray's Inn.

One major task of this chapter will be to examine what happened to Paley's 'theory' of natural theology in the years after the publication of *Natural Theology*. The sermon—what preachers said, to whom they said it, and how often—will be the tool used to highlight the development of this area of theology. Of course, such an examination would be limited without taking into account the new science of the nineteenth century, particularly the evolutionary ideas of Charles Darwin. A second major task of this chapter then will be to assess the extent of the impact of Darwin's ideas on the development of natural theology. Put simply, do the sermons preached after 1859 suggest that their authors were influenced by the discussions about *On the Origin of Species* and other contemporaneous formative works of science when they preached about nature and God's connection to it?

While historians such as John Hedley Brooke and James Moore have warned about the dangers of applying the conflict metaphor to developments in science and religion (Brooke; Moore), it is worth asking whether Darwin's ideas 'killed' natural theology or, with less emphasis on battle rhetoric, supplanted it. Is the infrequent use of the maxims of natural theology in the late twentieth and early twenty-first centuries causally connected to the rising importance of sciences such as geology, biology, and ecology in the nineteenth century? Posing the previous question a different way, to what extent did preachers in 1901 use the ideas of natural theology in their sermons differently from their counterparts in 1802 and can the influence of *On the Origin of Species* and other works be seen in this change? Equally important, although it will not be discussed in detail in this chapter, if Darwin's ideas did not deal a fatal blow to Paley's natural theology then who or what did?

It may be an exaggeration to talk of science as an antagonist of natural theology throughout the nineteenth century but it would be facile not to acknowledge the change in their relative positions, their perceived cultural value, by 1901. When Queen Victoria died, science—and technology—was far more important than it had been in 1802 or 1837 and natural theology was less important. How did preachers adapt to these changes in their sermons? Were there, for example, any attempts to frame a debate with two protagonists, natural theology and science? What did preachers expect their congregations to know about natural theology and science in 1901 and how was this expectation different from that of preachers in 1802? More important, given that the majority of sermons were part of some type of religious service, did the relative decline of natural theology have an impact on preachers' explanations of basic tenets of Christianity such as the birth, death, and resurrection of Christ or the attitudes towards prayer and miracles?

Natural Theology In Danger?

The number of sermons dealing with science and the natural world is not large, probably constituting less than one per cent of the total number of sermons published in the nineteenth century. Conversely, given the popularity of Paley's *Natural Theology*—eleven editions were published by 1807 and fourteen by 1813—one might expect a larger number of sermons on natural theology. It was, after all, theology; even though connected to science and the natural world, preachers would not have to make the case for appropriateness—as they might if they preached a sermon on evolution, for example. If nature was a handbook of God's creative activity, then the theology derived from this handbook ought to be a subject for the pulpit.

Interestingly, the terms 'natural theology' and 'natural religion' are used rarely in the titles of sermons. Not including a series of sermons on natural and revealed religion by William Watson English entitled *Faiths of the World in Relation to Christianity* (1888) and the American poet James Vila Blake's *Natural Religion in Sermons* (1892), the British Library catalogue lists only two each for both terms (Davies; Jackson; Thorp; Bradlee) and one of these is a sermon preached in Boston on 19 May 1878 (Bradlee). There are sermons on God and the natural world, seeing God in nature, the attributes of God as derived from nature, God acting through nature, and, most numerous, on providence (Mant; Lewin; Meeson; Dickson; Brownlow; Dowden; Lyttleton)—all standard tenets of natural theology—but virtually none using the phrases 'natural theology' or 'natural religion'.

The absence of the terms only applies to sermons: the number of books published using the terms was numerous. Taking the major university lectures as one example, 'natural theology' is the subject and title of Alfred Barry's Boyle Lectures in 1876, James Houghton Kennedy's Donnellan Lectures to the University of Dublin in 1888 and 1889, and Sir George Stokes's Gifford Lectures in 1891 and 1893 (Barry; Kennedy; Stokes 1891; Stokes 1893). 'Natural religion' was the subject and title of John Gorham Palfrey's Dudleian Lecture to Cambridge University on 8 May 1839 and Friedrich Max Müller's Gifford Lectures in 1888 (Palfrey; Müller). Taking as another example books on natural theology for the young, a category that to a twenty-first-century observer seems destined to generate little revenue, the choices are also numerous. William Enfield stated, by including it in the title, that his *Natural Theology* was 'arranged in a popular way for youth' (Enfield) and the title page of *Lectures on Natural Theology* drew readers' attention to the fact that the book was 'intended chiefly for the use of young persons' (Richardson). Other authors made similar claims of intending to teach the young or those unfamiliar with the subject (Rennie; Drummond). The Suffolk publisher T. Tippel, with an eye on the market for Paley's work, arranged for an abridged version of *Natural Theology* to be 'adapted for youth' (Paley 1820). Acquiring books on the subject was quite easy for anyone wishing to read about natural theology.

The study of natural theology was a thriving business. This is graphically illustrated by a survey of works on the subject. The best known of these were the frequently reprinted Bridgewater Treatises, a series of eight books commissioned by the Royal Society at the behest of the eighth Earl of Bridgewater, the Reverend Francis Henry Egerton (1756–1829), and first published between 1833 and 1836 (Bell; Chalmers; Kidd; Whewell; Prout; Roget; Kirby; Buckland). Furthermore, lecture series such as the Boyle and Gifford lectures certainly helped. Lord Gifford's bequest in order to create a lectureship for 'Promoting, Advancing, Teaching, and Diffusing the study of Natural Theology' at the universities of Edinburgh, Glasgow, Aberdeen, and St Andrews (Müller: viii–ix) did for Scotland in the 1890s what the Boyle Lectures had attempted to accomplish since the 1690s. While not all of the Boyle and Gifford lecturers addressed natural theology directly, it was the point of reference. Equally important, the tradition in the nineteenth century was for these lectures to be published as a book.

The field of study was wide: though dominated by Paley's teleological argument, natural theology also comprehended moral, ontological, and cosmological arguments for the existence of God, and was preached and written about by commentators from a broad spectrum of theological positions. The topics chosen by Edward Garbutt, clergyman, journalist, and uncle of the future Archbishop of York for his Boyle Lectures in the 1860s are an indication of the diversity of subject matter which could fit under the rubric of natural theology; Garbett's lectures were published as *The Bible and Its Critics* (1861) and *The Pentateuch and Its Authority* (1862). A more unusual example is *Theism as a Science of Natural Theology and Natural Religion* (1895) by the one-time Anglican clergyman Charles Voysey. Voysey, well-known for his series of sermons published under the title *The Sling and the Stone* (Wright), used his book as a vehicle to explain the main ideas of the Theistic Church, a church he founded after being deprived of his living for his heterodox views (Voysey).

If the standard used is the existence of a steady stream of publications on the subject then natural theology was hardly in danger in the nineteenth century, from the ideas of Darwin or anyone else. The subcutaneous view, as it were, provided by preachers and their sermons, makes it possible to assess whether the seemingly obvious analysis is in fact an accurate one.

Natural Theology in Paley's Sermons

The large number of books on natural theology and natural religion compared with the paucity of published sermons bearing those terms as a title suggests one distinction between what was preached in the pulpit and what was available elsewhere. Preachers may have talked about natural theology and natural religion in their sermons but almost never in a technical fashion. Preachers did not discuss natural theology in the pulpit in the academic manner used by the Boyle, Gifford, or Dudleian lecturers. (For example, they did not announce in the pulpit that the day's sermon was the teleological argument for the existence of God.) Neither did they preach about natural theology in the apologist fashion of the Bridgewater Treatises. They did discuss doctrines such as atonement in this way, discoursing on them in a manner which would befit a university lecturer, but not so for natural theology or natural religion: doing this was, seemingly, considered out of place for the pulpit. (Why this was the case will be addressed in the conclusion of this chapter.) Thus, even before Darwin published *On the Origin of Species*, natural theology had a particular 'place' in the religious life of Britain. It was the subject of academic analysis in public forums such as the university lecture hall on a regular basis but did not belong in the pulpit—except in a vulgar fashion, watered down to very simplistic ideas.

This is well illustrated by the sermons of William Paley himself. Although in several sermons he talked about God and nature, none of his published sermons is specifically about natural theology or natural religion, and certainly none has 'natural theology' or 'natural religion' in the title.

The impression one receives when reading Paley's sermons is that he was a sensible, pragmatic preacher. If his *Sermons on Several Subjects* reflects his preaching career well, Paley the preacher was far more interested in heaven and hell or sin and morality than natural theology (Paley 1808)—as befits a cleric who ministered to low-profile congregations for the first seventeen years of his career, not achieving a more senior position, the archdeaconry of Carlisle, until 1782. When Paley stated in a sermon entitled 'This Life a State of Probation' that 'Few things are easier than to perceive, to feel, to acknowledge, to extol the goodness of God, the bounty of Providence, the beauties of nature, when all things go well; when our health, our spirits, our circumstances, conspire to fill out hearts with gladness, and our tongues with praise. This is easy: this is delightful' he was stating the obvious: natural theology works well when all is right with the world—Paley did not need to state the converse (Paley 1808: 497). As a piece of apologetics it might be easy to say, as Paley did, 'once believe that there is a God, and miracles are not incredible' (Paley 1795: 1:11) but for most of his parishioners the problems of life were more pressing. Natural theology was more about surviving the daily dramas of life than proving whether God was, for example, omnipresent. As Paley, a man who suffered from intestinal problems, put it in 'This Life a State of Probation':

> Our own bodies only reflect how many thousand things must go right for us to be an hour at ease. Yet at all times multitudes are so; and are so without being sensible how great a thing it is. Too much, or too little of sensibility, or of action, any one of the almost numberless organs, or of any part of the numberless organs, by which life is sustained, may be productive of extreme anguish, or of lasting infirmity. A particle, smaller than an atom in a sunbeam, may, in a wrong place, be the occasion of the loss of limbs, of senses, or of life. Yet under all this continual jeopardy, this momentary liability to danger and disorder, we are preserved. (Paley 1808: 492–3)

Although Paley did not work in country parishes in the early part of his career—Greenwich and Dalston were close to London and Appleby was a market town in Cumbria—his congregations were not the Oxford University type and Paley's sermons probably reflected their concerns (and his?). The consequences of evil actions, what happened after death, or whether people would recognize their friends after the resurrection are common themes. That being the case, Paley's statements about natural theology assume an understanding of natural theology rather than explicitly defending or arguing a theological position. In a sermon entitled 'The Knowledge of One Another in a Future State', when explaining the post-resurrection form, Paley noted that 'in the magazine of God's Almighty creation, two very distinct kinds of bodies [subsist]...a natural body and a spiritual body...the natural body is what human beings bear about with them now; the spiritual body, far surpassing the other [is] what the blessed will be clothed with hereafter' (Paley 1808: 510). And in a sermon entitled 'On Filial Piety', Paley suggested that the story of Joseph was 'a strong and plain example of the circuitous providence of God...of his bringing about the end and purposes of his providence, by seemingly casual and unsuspected means' (Paley 1808: 147). This accidental providence Paley characterized as a 'high doctrine, both of natural and revealed religion' (Paley 1808: 147).

In his apologetics Paley seems so definitive. Commenting on his watch and watchmaker analogy, Paley describes the unwillingness to derive, to him, the obvious conclusion as 'atheism'. Such a strong word is necessary because 'for every indication of contrivance, every manifestation of design, which existed in the watch, exists in the works of nature; with the difference, on the side of nature, of being greater and more, and that in a degree which exceeds all computation' (Paley 1802: 17–18). Or, when defending miracles, Paley asks, almost incredulously, 'Ought we not rather to expect, that such [an intelligent] Being, upon occasions of peculiar importance, may interrupt the order which he had appointed, yet, that such occasions should return seldom; that these interruptions consequently should be confined to the experience of a few; that the want of it... in many, should be matter neither of surprise nor objection?' (Paley 1795: 1:10). Perhaps the failing was, and is, in Paley's acolytes. The previous two quotations are indeed Paley's but they are not a fair reflection of the subtlety of and nuance in his argument. God may be the creator of the natural world and may act in nature but such a statement was, at the minimum, problematic according to Paley. As he noted in one of the concluding chapters of *Natural Theology*:

> I have already observed, that, when we let in religious considerations, we often let in light upon the difficulties of nature. So in the fact now to be accounted for, the *degree* of happiness, which we usually enjoy in this life, may be better suited to a state of trial and probation, than a greater degree would be. The truth is, we are rather too much delighted with the world, than too little. (Paley 1802: 534)

Paley was no Pollyanna. The natural world and humankind's place in it was both amazing and disappointing. In fact, Paley conceded, the state of the world was an argument against design (Paley 1802: 534–5)—a point Darwin would have agreed with readily (Darwin 1859: 165–7, 184–86). As I have argued elsewhere, Paley and Darwin had more in common than most commentators are willing to concede (Francis). That there is a kind of dualism in the natural theology of Paley's sermons is less of a surprise when his arguments in *Natural Theology* and *Evidences* are reviewed. The beauty of God's design could be easily occluded; the certainty of God's providence could be, in a word, unreliable; humankind's sojourn on earth could be trying and unfulfilling. It should not be a surprise then that in his sermons Paley was cautious about God's providence and His activity in the natural world.

Natural Theology in the Sermons of Paley's Near Contemporaries

If it is fair to characterize Paley, and his sermons in particular, as more pragmatic than apologetic, the next question to address is whether this description can be applied to his near contemporaries. Did they realize that a natural theology which took little or no account of the bad in life and nature might not be relevant to most of the congregations to whom they preached?

On 18 May 1818, Richard Mant, the rector of St Botolph's, Bishopsgate and East Horseley in Surrey as well as a chaplain of the Archbishop of Canterbury, preached a sermon entitled 'The Sovereignty of God in the Natural World, and the Agency of Man, Practically Considered'. His congregation—perhaps audience is more appropriate?—comprised members of the Corporation of Trinity House including their titular head (known as the Master), the second Earl of Liverpool, and Prime Minister at that time. Mant's sermon was one element of the service held at the beginning of the Corporation's annual meeting. Part business meeting and part celebration of the Corporation's royal charter granted in 1514 so that its members 'might regulate the pilotage of ships in the King's streams' ('History: Henry VIII and Pilotage'), Mant's task was to commend the Corporation for its promotion of maritime safety and charitable work for sailors and their families.

Given the occasion, it is no surprise that Mant praised the Corporation for having 'regulated its proceedings by a devout sense of its dependence on the Almighty' and 'the bountiful and extensive relief which you supply for the feeble and defenceless' (Mant: 21, 24). Further, it is also not a surprise that Mant chose a maritime story, the shipwreck of the Apostle Paul (Acts 27:13–44), to illustrate the power of God over nature. What is interesting is that nowhere in the sermon does Mant attempt to prove that God acts in nature: he assumes it. As for providence, the first major point of the sermon was 'that the whole course of nature is under the control of Providence, and that all deviations from the uniformity of its course by the conflict of the elements, as well as every return to that uniformity by the restoration of tranquillity, are to be referred to his sovereign power' (Mant: 5). Any Corporation member expecting a defence of this proposition would have been disappointed because Mant continued by asserting that God was in control of the elements and his proof, such as it was, was that 'the dangers and difficulties, which arise from this order of things are themselves proof of God's goodness' (Mant: 6).

Was Mant more 'Paley' than Paley himself? Again, like Paley, such a characterization would do injustice to the subtlety of Mant's arguments. After several declaratory statements about God's power and providence, Mant stated: 'Sometimes the goodness of God may be less discernible. The evil may appear to our finite perception to preponderate over the good' (Mant: 9). Mant was less cautious than Paley, suggesting that the occasions to doubt God were 'far from numerous' (Mant: 9), but he seemed to recognize that men who knew much about the dangers of the sea would find it hard to believe that God controlled nature at every moment. In his second major point of the sermon Mant acknowledged that, despite a belief in providence, 'we ought...to be active in the exercise of the faculties intrusted to us, in order to [safeguard] our preservation and welfare' (Mant: 11–12). And for the rest of the sermon his argument can be summarized in the old truism 'God helps those who help themselves'. Thus, the Corporation of Trinity House had been successful because God had blessed its efforts to professionalize the training and work of sailors (Mant: 19–21).

This recognition of the vagaries of the world, a natural theology with caveats, was not unique to Paley and Mant. Charles Thorp, the rector of Ryton and chaplain to the future Prime Minister, Earl Grey, made the same point in a sermon preached five months earlier than Mant's. While urging his audience, the Gateshead Friendly Society, to praise God for His providence and care, he stated that the objective of his sermon was to give 'some arguments in favour of a discreet attention to the exigencies of life, and a reasonable provision against future want' (Thorp: 5). He wanted to convince those listening (and reading) that it was their civic and religious duty to create a system which provided for their future daily needs—in this case a savings bank. God would bless such an endeavour and it was not inconsistent with 'the sanctions of Christian law' (Thorp: 6).

It would be wrong to suggest, however, that the willingness of a Paley or a Mant to see shades of grey in natural theology held sway in the early part of the nineteenth century in the thinking about God's existence or God's actions in the natural world. Even though the controversy was kept out of the pulpit, there was clearly a healthy debate going on among those who chose to speak about natural theology. William Enfield, in his book on natural theology for the young, had these lines on the title page:

> Dull, atheist! Could a giddy dance
> Of atoms, lawless hurl'd
> Construct so wonderful, so wise,
> So harmoniz'd a world?
>
> (Enfield)

Had a reader skipped the title page for some reason the frontispiece contained a similar point:

> I read his awful name emblazon'd high
> With golden letters on the illumin'd sky
> Nor less the mystic characters I see
> Wrought in each flower, inscrib'd in every tree!
> In every creature own his forming power,
> In each event his providence adore.
>
> (Enfield)

It is unlikely that Enfield encountered many atheists in his travels; rather, his 'atheists' seemed to be those who had doubts about the natural world—could see the bad and evil in it—or God's omnipotent power and providence.

More than twenty years later the debate still continued. In 1836, in a series of lectures on the connection between science and religion, Nicholas Wiseman, at that time Principal of the English College in Rome, complained about 'the malice of superficial men' who, he claimed, 'had not patience or courage to penetrate into the sanctuary of nature, that [have] suggested objections, from her laws, against truths revealed'. 'Had they boldly advanced,' Wiseman argued, 'they would have discovered... that the depths which serve to conceal her darkest mysteries, may the soonest be changed into fittest places for profound admiration' (Wiseman: 1:261–2). Two years earlier, Richard Davies, the Archdeacon of Brecon, remarked in a sermon on natural theology that the study of nature only made sense if guided by the view that God was almighty, all wise, and had infinite knowledge; any other approach would result in the world being seen as 'incoherent and untenable' (Davies: 8). For Davies, the vastness and diversity of nature should leave the scientist or the student of nature with a 'lofty and magnificent' conception of God; if it did not the fault was the scientist's or the student's: he had not tied together his faith with his study of natural theology (Davies: 17, 6).

Not even the authors of the Bridgewater Treatises were immune from criticism. William Buckland, for pointing out that the Earth's surface had not been the same since eternity but had undergone a 'series of creative operations' (Buckland: 1:10–11), received a rebuke from the Reverend Fowler de Johnsone in the book *Truth, in Defence of the Word of God—Vanquishing Infidelity* (1838). The subtitle of the book made clear what had irked de Johnsone; it read, in part: 'Address to the Rev. William Buckland, D.D. Professor of Geology, etc., Christ Church, Oxford. Wherein his objections to the first chapter of Genesis are met—the stumbling stone removed—and the texts in the first three chapters fully explained' (de Johnsone). While some preachers like Paley were cautious and, perhaps, tentative, others were certain: any doubts belonged outside of the pulpit.

Sermons on Natural Theology in the 1840s and 1850s

With hindsight, the challenge that Darwin's theories were likely to pose to the orthodox thinking about natural theology seems obvious: at the time it was less so. The French naturalist Georges Cuvier's theory of multiple destructive global catastrophes—hinted at by William Buckland and condemned by Nicholas Wiseman—had been widely disseminated after its publication in English as *Discourse on the Revolutions of the Surface of the Globe* (1829). Charles Lyell had reignited the eighteenth-century debate about the age of the Earth in his *Principles of Geology* (1830–3). There had even been a controversy about evolution well before 1859; the publication of the *Vestiges of the Natural History of Creation* in 1844 sparked a public debate about science, humankind's place in nature, and God as creator. Put colloquially, Darwin was late to the party.

In fact, far more troubling, at least in terms of the natural theology posited by ministers such as Richard Davies, were the natural disasters which occurred in the 1840s and 1850s—a series of poor harvests and several outbreaks of cholera being most prominent. The way in which one clergyman, Charles Kingsley, now better known for his novel *The Water Babies*, addressed these problems provides some insight into the ways in which ideas about natural theology were already changing even before the publication of *On the Origin of Species*.

On 27 September 1849, Kingsley preached a sermon on the cholera outbreak which, at the time, was still spreading through the British Isles. Kingsley's objective was to counter the widespread belief, in Britain, that the cholera outbreak was a judgement of God. The outbreak should not be called God's judgement, according to Kingsley, when one could work out how to prevent it (Kingsley 1852: 177–8). Kingsley said his soul 'boils over with sorrow and indignation' at the unwillingness of British society to do those things which would prevent a cholera outbreak (Kingsley 1852: 183). The source of his anger was this:

> When... the Sanitary Commissioners proved to all England fifteen years ago, that cholera always appeared where fever had appeared, and that both fever and cholera always cling exclusively to those places where there was bad food, bad air, crowded bed-rooms, bad drainage and filth—that such were the laws of God and Nature, and always had been; they [the English] took no notice of it, because it was the poor rather than the rich who suffered from those causes. (Kingsley 1852: 176–7)

To Kingsley, the notion that God was acting in nature through the calamity of a cholera outbreak was wrong-headed. The actual calamity was the willingness of British society to ignore what Kingsley called God's order. God 'does not change His order to punish us', Kingsley noted, '*We* break His order, and the order goes on in spite of us and crushes us; and so we get God's judgment, God's opinion of our breaking His laws' (Kingsley 1852: 181). Repeating the point in a second sermon preached the next Sunday, Kingsley told his congregation that 'God has taught us what is right and wrong, and He will be judged by His own rules' (Kingsley 1852: 192).

If Richard Mant was suggesting caution with regard to God's providence—humankind should rely on its own ingenuity rather than waiting for God to act—Kingsley went a step further: most of what his congregation considered providence was simply natural law, the rules of science, at work. Thus, the draining of the marshes in Scotland had resulted in fewer fevers (Kingsley 1852: 187–8). And in a third sermon on the cholera outbreak, he blamed bad housing, poor diet, and improper drainage of sewage for the ease of the transmission of the disease (Kingsley 1852: 203). Further, on the day of thanksgiving marking the end of the outbreak, Kingsley counselled his congregation not to thank God for taking away the disease. Such a prayer would imply that God had 'gone away' whereas He is always present—in the laws of nature. In a subtle, but important, reworking of the natural theology usually associated with Paley, Kingsley noted that God had 'ordained' all the natural laws and took a keen interest in them: 'He never breaks [them], or allows us to break them' (Kingsley 1852: 222). Kingsley's God was omnipresent and even omnipotent—but limited by His unwillingness to interfere with the laws of nature He had created.

Kingsley was aware that he was doing something new. When another cholera outbreak occurred in 1854 he republished his four sermons on the previous outbreak in *Who Causes Pestilence?* In the preface Kingsley thanked Lord Palmerston, then the Home Secretary, for refusing requests for a national day of fasting thus preventing 'fresh excuses for the selfishness, laziness, and ignorance which produce pestilence... turning men's minds away from the real causes of this present judgment to fanciful and superstitious ones' (Kingsley 1854: 3). Later in the preface he rebuked the clergy for their lack of support for sanitary reform noting that such a step would 'interfere with their religious views' (Kingsley 1854: 5). In a sermon preached three years earlier entitled 'The Fount of Science' he had rebuked, mildly, the congregation for not giving sufficient glory to God for all the scientific discoveries of the era. Speaking about the Great Exhibition at Crystal Palace, Kingsley remarked:

> Our notion of God's blessing it seems to be God's absence from it; a hope and trust that God will leave it and us alone, and not 'visit' it or us in it, or 'interfere' by any 'special providences,' by storms, or lightning, or sickness, or panic, or conspiracy; a sort of dim feeling that we could manage it all perfectly well without God, but that as He exists, and has some power over natural phenomena, which is not very exactly defined, we must notice His existence over and above our work, lest He should become angry, and 'visit us'. (Kingsley 1852: 144–5)

For Kingsley it was useless to pray to God to fix a problem that humans had caused; it was equally foolish not to acknowledge that God was the architect of modern science and that he was pleased when humankind made discoveries which improved society. Kingsley's was a natural theology which lauded the laws of nature, (his version of) God's providence, and the science of Lyell, Cuvier, and, later, Darwin.

Was Kingsley unique? His thinking seems far ahead of his time—and all in sermons, not 'hidden' in academic lectures or books. A review of the sermons of the era suggests that the answer is 'no'. Not everyone agreed with Kingsley's approach but they were aware of it and acknowledged it implicitly in their own sermons.

On 4 November 1846, Charles Wagstaff, a junior minister at St Andrew's Chapel, Aberdeen, preached a sermon which commented on the recent crop failure in Scotland. In it he took exception to the 'infidel views' of those Christians who looked for 'secondary causes' for the crop failure instead of acknowledging that it was a divine visitation (Wagstaff: 13, 16). He suggested that the crop failure was 'of a character exactly suited to check [the] presumption' that advances in science could produce food in sufficient quantities to feed the nation (Wagstaff: 15–16). God's hand could, as it were, roll back the advances of science. And in a recitation of what seemed to be orthodox natural theology, he noted that 'All the circumstance seem to concur in leading to this view of the case; not the time only, but the unusual character of the calamity, its yet unexplained causes, its universal prevalence, and the failure of every attempt to check its progress. We may well ask, if the hand of God be not here, can such a thing as a divine visitation be?' (Wagstaff: 16).

Thirteen years later, on 9 November, less than two weeks before the publication of *On the Origin of Species*, Hugh McNeile, a future Dean of Ripon, preached at a memorial service for Jeremiah Horrocks. (Horrocks, a clergyman who died in 1641 at the age of 23, had discovered three major astronomical phenomena in his short life, including the transit of Venus.) McNeile told the congregation that he wanted to counter the opinion 'that any detailed attention to secular knowledge, or any prolonged study of physical science, is so foreign to all the ends and purposes of true religion, that a good Christian man ought not to suffer his thoughts...to be engaged in matters so comparatively worthless' (McNeile: 10). There was no antagonism between (supposedly) secular knowledge and true religion. In fact, noted McNeile, 'true religion...consecrates to the service of God all the powers of every description, ALL the talents entrusted to man'. He added, 'We would consider very defective the religion of a man who did not cultivate his intellectual powers, but was lacking in the study, according to his opportunities, of divers departments of science' (McNeile: 12). In an inversion of Wagstaff's approach, he asserted that natural theology, seeing God in the stars or searching for examples of divine visitation, would not result in the salvation of anyone—only revealed theology could do this—but the laws of science 'spoke' of the majesty and power of God (McNeile: 32). McNeile's natural theology was Paley-plus and Kingsley-lite.

What Did Darwin Contribute?

To state the obvious, *On the Origin of Species* was not about natural theology. (Given what has been said about Darwin's intentions both during his life and afterwards, this needs to be stated.) In his words, it was 'a volume on the transmutation of species' (Darwin 1887: 1:85). Nevertheless, Darwin did recognize that his theory of natural selection was not neutral on natural theology. As he wrote in the conclusion, 'It is so easy to hide our ignorance under such expressions as the "plan of creation," or "unity of design," &c., and to think that we give an explanation when we only restate a fact' (Darwin 1859: 481–2). Later in the chapter, when Darwin asked, 'Do they [naturalists] really believe that at innumerable periods in the earth's history certain elemental atoms have been commanded suddenly to flash into living tissues?' (Darwin 1859: 483) he could hardly have expected all the clergy to keep silent at the implicit challenge of his question.

Whether Darwin was or was not the 'Father of Evolutionary Theory'—the title on the plinth of the statue of the French naturalist Jean-Baptiste Lamarck (1744–1829)—he did focus the minds of naturalists. As Darwin put it, there were 'innumerable well-observed facts...stored...[and] ready to take their proper places as soon as any theory which would receive them was sufficiently explained' (Darwin 1887: 1:87). What occurred in nature could indeed be explained by scientific laws and, although Darwin did not state it explicitly in 1859, no person nor providence (nor chance) was needed in order for these laws to operate.

Sermons on Natural Theology after 1859

The clergyman-naturalist was a common phenomenon in 1860. For example, Samuel Wilberforce was asked to chair the meeting discussing Darwin's theory at the British Association for the Advancement of Science that year because he was both Bishop of Oxford, the city where the meeting was held, and a well-known amateur naturalist. Thus it is that, though there are few sermons with the terms 'natural theology' or 'natural religion' in them, there are several notable examples of sermons in which preachers accounted for the new science while discussing questions of natural theology.

On 1 June 1862, Thomas Boultbee, a theological tutor at Cheltenham and a former fellow of St John's College, preached a sermon before the University of Cambridge entitled 'The Imperfection of Human Knowledge'. The topic of the sermon was life beyond death and, it being the Sunday after Ascension Day, Boultbee tried to comfort those in the congregation whose relatives and friends had died by pointing out that the departed were closer to seeing the perfection of God. Perhaps intentionally, perhaps not, in trying to explain to the congregation what God was like Boultbee spent the majority of the sermon discussing natural theology. Fascinatingly, his attempt to state how nature proved the existence of God—which was really a restatement—demonstrates the impact of the 'old' new science on natural theology and, just two years after the publication of *On the Origin of Species*, the impact of Darwin's theory.

Starting with cosmology, Boultbee asked: 'To what do the arrangements of the host of heaven point?' His answer: 'Ultimately to God's wondrous poising of the nebulous bodies in space, to the errand of the comet, in short, to the creative act and purpose of God' (Boultbee: 6). Moving on to geology, he said it views God 'in the act of creation marvellously, and with *the patience of eternity* (so hard for the creatures of a day to conceive) fashioning this world, arranging age after age its stones, its earths, its minerals, until it was fit for man, a storehouse containing supplies for all his tastes and necessities' (Boultbee: 6). With its references to long durations of time, Boultbee's was a natural theology recognizable by its 1860s feel rather than 1810s.

Although Boultbee appeared to have incorporated the ideas of Lyell and Alexander von Humboldt in his natural theology he was not ready for Darwin. Throughout the sermon, particularly in relation to the origin of humankind, Boultbee mentioned the importance of the unity of knowledge and that some knowledge had not been blended into the whole as yet. No matter how impressive our knowledge, it was still imperfect and partial; scientists and biblical critics should not forget this—any other stance was presumptuous (Boultbee: 7, 8–9, 13, 15).

Where Boultbee feared to tread Kingsley strode boldly. Kingsley, whose guarded endorsement of the theory of natural selection Darwin had included in the second edition of *On the Origin of Species* (Darwin 1860: 481), was adamant that the new science posed no danger to natural theology. In a sermon preached to the Corporation of Trinity House in 1866 he noted that science and religion are 'twin sisters meant to aid each other and mankind in the battle with the brute forces of this universe'. While going further than Mant had done fifty years earlier, and perhaps with an eye to his mariner audience, Kingsley defended a classic tenet of natural theology—the intervention of God in times of distress:

> These are days in which there is much dispute about religion and science... Especially there is dispute about Providence, Men say...that the more we look into the world, the more we find everything governed by fixed and regular laws; that man is bound to find out those laws, and save himself from danger by science and experience. But

> they go on to say—'And therefore there is no use in prayer. You cannot expect God to alter the laws of his universe because you ask him...and the man who prays against danger, by sea or land, is asking vainly for that which will not be granted'. (Kingsley 1868: 23–4)

Kingsley rejected the latter proposition: sound science and sound religion were not mutually exclusive (Kingsley 1868: 24–5).

Lest anyone think Kingsley reserved his radicalism for cynical mariners, he made similar points in a sermon to his parishioners entitled 'Why Should We Pray for Fair Weather?' in August 1860 and in a sermon entitled 'The Temple of Wisdom' to the boys of Wellington College in 1866 (Kingsley 1860, 1866). However, in a sermon entitled 'God's World', preached before the Prince of Wales in 1866, he sounded a note of caution—perhaps for the benefit of his royal audience: Kingsley warned against the 'new idolatry'. The new science did not mean one had to give up the old faith that God ruled the earth; Kingsley thought 'too many seem to believe that the world somehow made itself, and that there is no living God ordering and guiding it [and] that a man must help himself as he best can in this world, for in God no help is found' (Kingsley 1868: 119). Again, Kingsley expected his congregations—whether local parish, schoolboy, or royal—to know that 'eternal laws', scientific ones, controlled the processes of nature but these laws were put in place and regulated by God; thus, God's existence as a person, intercessory prayer, and salvation from sin were still major components of Christian theology and the Christian's daily life.

Ten years later, preachers were still trying to balance what they knew about science and what they held as Christian doctrine. The Archbishop of York, William Thomson, posited the problem this way:

> Ought we to allow our minds to connect with the beauty of nature and with the symmetry of nature's laws...the thought of a Being who has caused all these, or ought we to seek nothing beyond the facts themselves, and to dismiss all thought of a wise and loving Being whom we have not seen, as unscientific, and as belonging to the vague region of metaphysics? (Thomson: 1–2)

Thomson was well-qualified to comment. He was a scientist and philosopher as well as a clergyman. He had written *An Outline of the Necessary Laws of Thought*—published in 1842, the year he was ordained—and *Design in Nature* (1871) and had been elected to the Royal Society and the Royal Geographical Society. In his sermon, entitled 'God a Personal Being, Not an Impersonal Force', Thomson argued that it was an artificial limitation on humankind's abilities to suggest that a person must choose between the laws of science and the argument from design for the existence of God (Thomson: 5).

Fatal to natural theology, according to Thomson, was the idea that the world was created solely for the benefit of humankind (Thomson: 9–11). Equally dangerous to the theory of evolution, he noted, was the idea that something without thought created something with thought. There were two opinions concerning the appearance of biological life on earth: one was 'that a Being of infinite wisdom contrived and effected it'; the other was 'that it evolved itself with no thought or contrivance at all, and that the thought that can understand and appreciate its marvel came first into being when man appeared—that, in a word, there is no conscious thought or wisdom but in man' (Thomson: 12). Thomson rejected the dichotomy. To accept the new science in place of the 'old' natural theology would mean 'no worship, no religious duty, no future hope, no providence, no God!' (Thomson: 24).

Bold though his resolution was, Thomson had not progressed much past Kingsley— and neither man had explained how exactly a Christian should integrate a belief in the existence of God with the science of evolution, for example. What was noteworthy was the person delivering the sermon: an archbishop as opposed to an ordinary clergyman (albeit a well-known one). In Anglican circles, at least, and in certain clergy in other churches—John Page Hopps (1834–1911), the Unitarian and Free Christian Church minister, being one notable example—the need to integrate the new science, including evolutionary theory, was the new orthodoxy.

Conclusion

Darwin did not create the challenge to ideas about natural theology. Archbishop John Tillotson (1630–94) preached a sermon entitled 'Of the Great Duties of Natural Religion' in which he discussed the relationship between natural theology and the scientific discoveries of his day (Tillotson). Paley was clearly dealing with similar problems in the late eighteenth and early nineteenth centuries. What Darwin did was to move the focus away from the laws of mechanics, cosmology, and geology to the origins of humankind. Even though *On the Origin of Species* was not about human evolution, the implications of his theory of natural selection were clear to anyone interested in science or natural theology. Whatever the thinking of clergy about dealing with 'secular matters' in the pulpit—the clergyman George Henslow began his sermon 'Genesis and Geology' with an apology and a defence of the topic's appropriateness for a religious service (Henslow: 1–3)—Darwin's work compelled some clergy to preach about it.

Unsurprisingly, the reactions were not limited to the pulpit. Frederick Le Gros Clark's *Paley's Natural Theology. Revised to Harmonize with Modern Science* (1875) and Joseph Morris's *A New Natural Theology based upon the Doctrine of Evolution* (1896) were reactions similar to the university lectures mentioned earlier. Perhaps Darwin did deal natural theology a fatal blow but the initial cuts occurred at least two centuries before 1859. One set of reactions were like Paley's, another set were like Kingsley's, and some reacted as did Arthur Winnington-Ingram, the future Bishop of London, in a sermon to a group of adolescent boys:

> Every law of nature, we are told by science, needs a continual application of force, and we can understand that, for when we whirl a stone round at the end of a string, we are bound to keep our hand moving or the stone falls; so as the little earth speeds

on its way, as the great suns flash along without colliding, they sing psalms to the marvellous power of God. (Winnington-Ingram: 35)

By the end of the twentieth century such a statement was mainly consigned to poetic licence.

REFERENCES

Barry, A. (1877). *What is Natural Theology? An Attempt...* London: Christian Evidence Committee of the Society for the Promotion of Christian Knowledge.
Beer, G. (2000). *Darwin's Plots ...*, 2nd edn. Cambridge: Cambridge University Press.
Bell, C. (1833). *The Hand: Its Mechanism and Vital Endowments as Evincing Design.* London: William Pickering.
Boultbee, T. P. (1862). *The Imperfection of Human Knowledge...* London: Macmillan and Co.
Bradlee, C. D. (1878). *Natural and Revealed Religion: A Sermon Preached...* Cambridge, MA: J. Wilson & Son.
Brooke, J. H. (1991). *Science and Religion: Some Historical Perspectives.* Cambridge: Cambridge University Press.
Brownlow, M. (1878). 'The Immanence of God in Nature', in *Theism and Christianity: Six Sermons...* London: SPCK.
Buckland, W. (1836). *Geology and Mineralogy Considered with Reference to Natural Theology.* London: William Pickering.
Chalmers, T. (1833). *On the Power, Wisdom and Goodness of God as Manifested in the Adaption of External Nature....* London: William Pickering.
Darwin, C. (1859). *On the Origin of Species...* London: John Murray.
—— (1860). *On the Origin of Species ...*, 2nd edn. London: John Murray.
—— (1887). *The Life and Letters of Charles Darwin*, F. Darwin (ed.). London: John Murray.
Davies, R. (1834). *A Sermon on Natural Theology...* London: J. G. & F. Rivington.
de Johnsone, F. (1838). *Truth, in Defence of the Word of God...* London: R. Groombridge.
Dickson, J. (1877). *God in Nature and Grace...* London: Rivingtons.
Dowden, J. (1884). *The Beauty of Nature a Revelation of God.* Edinburgh: D. Douglas.
Drummond, J. L. (1831). *Letters to a Young Naturalist...* London: Longman, Rees, Orme, Brown, and Green.
Ellegård, H. A. (1990). *Darwin and the General Reader ...*, repr. edn. Chicago: The University of Chicago Press.
Enfield, W. (1808). *Natural Theology...* London: Thomas Tegg.
English, W. W. (1888). *Faiths of the World in Relation to Christianity....* London: Walter Smith & Innes.
Francis, K. A. (2010). 'William Paley, Samuel Wilberforce, Charles Darwin and the Natural World: An Anglican Conversation'. *Studies in Church History* 46: 353–65.
Henslow, G. (1871). *Genesis and Geology...* London: Robert Hardwicke.
'History: Henry VIII and Pilotage'. The Corporation of Trinity House. <www.trinityhouse.co.uk/th/about/history.html> accessed 18 August 2011.
Jackson, W. (1870). *Right and Wrong: A Sermon...* Oxford: J. Parker.
Kennedy, J. H. (1891). *Natural Theology and Modern Thought.* London: Hodder and Stoughton.

Kidd, J. (1833). *On the Adaptation of External Nature to the Physical Condition of Man*. London: William Pickering.

Kingsley, C. (1852). *Sermons on National Subjects*...London: J. Griffin and Co.

—— (1854). *Who Causes Pestilence? Four Sermons*. London: Richard Griffen and Company.

—— (1860). *Why Should We Pray for Fair Weather? A Sermon*...London: John W. Parker and Son.

—— (1866). *The Temple of Wisdom*...London: Macmillan and Co.

—— (1868). *Discipline, and Other Sermons*. London: Macmillan and Co.

Kirby, W. (1835). *On the Power, Wisdom and Goodness of God as Manifested in the Creation of Animals*...London: William Pickering.

Lewin, S. (1844). *The Infinite Benevolence of God*...Hartlepool: J. Procter.

Lyttleton, W. H. (1871). *Following the Leadings of God in Nature and in Providence*...London: Strahan.

McNeile, H. (1859). *The Astronomer and the Christian*...Liverpool: Adam Holden.

Mant, R. (1818). *The Sovereignty of God in the Natural World*...London: F. C. & J. Rivington.

Meeson, H. A. (1844). *The Testimony of Nature to the Unity of God*. London: n. p.

Moore, J. (1979). *The Post-Darwinian Controversies*...Cambridge: Cambridge University Press.

Müller, F. M. (1889). *Natural Religion*. London: Longmans, Green, and Co.

Paley, W. (1795). *A View of the Evidences of Christianity*..., 3rd edn. London: R. Faulder.

—— (1802). *Natural Theology*...London: R. Faulder.

—— (1808). *Sermons on Several Subjects*, 3rd edn., George Stephenson (ed.). London: Longman, Hurst, Rees, and Orme.

—— (1820). *An Abridgement of Dr. Paley's Natural Theology*..., 'L. A.' (ed.). Halesworth, Suffolk: T. Tippel.

Palfrey, J. G. (1839). *The Theory and Uses of Natural Religion*. Boston, MA: Ferdinand Andrews.

Prout, W. (1834). *Chemistry, Meteorology and the Function of Digestion*...London: William Pickering.

Rennie, J. (1834). *Alphabet of Natural Theology*...London: Orr and Smith.

Richards, R. J. (2009). 'Darwin's Place in the History of Thought: A Reevaluation'. *PNAS* 106, suppl. 1, 16 June: 10056–60.

Richardson, J. (1855). *Lectures on Natural Theology and the Old Testament in General*. London: W. & F. G. Cash.

Roget, P. M. (1834). *Animal and Vegetable Physiology Considered with Reference to Natural Theology*. London: William Pickering.

Stokes, G. G. (1891). *Natural Theology. The Gifford Lectures*...London and Edinburgh: Adam and Charles Black.

—— (1893). *Natural Theology. The Gifford Lectures*...London: Adam and Charles Black.

Thomson, W. (1871). 'God a Personal Being, Not an Impersonal Force', in *Some Modern Religious Difficulties. Six Sermons*...London: Christian Evidence Society.

Thorp, C. (1818). *Economy, a Duty of Natural and Revealed Religion*...Newcastle: J. & R. Akenhead.

Tillotson, J. (1704). *Several Discourses*..., 3rd edn, R. Barker (ed.). London: R. Chiswell.

Voysey, C. (1895). *Theism as a Science of Natural Theology and Natural Religion*. London: Williams and Norgate.

Wagstaff, C. (1846). *The Judgment of God in the Recent Failure of One of the Principal Means of Subsistence*... Aberdeen: Brown & Co.

Whewell, W. (1833). *Astronomy and General Physics*... London: William Pickering.

Winnington-Ingram, A. F. (1901). *Addresses to Working Lads*. London: Society for Promoting Christian Knowledge.

Wiseman, N. (1836). *Twelve Lectures on the Connexion between Science and Revealed Religion*. London: Joseph Booker.

Wright, D. (2004). 'Voysey, Charles (1828–1912)', rev. K. D. Reynolds, *ODNB*. Oxford: Oxford University Press.

CHAPTER 28

PREACHING THE BROAD CHURCH GOSPEL: THE *NATAL SERMONS* OF BISHOP JOHN WILLIAM COLENSO

GERALD PARSONS

IN July 1866, Bishop John William Colenso, the first Anglican Bishop of Natal, famous—or, as many would have said, infamous—for his forthright application of biblical criticism to the text of the Pentateuch, wrote to the English Unitarian author, Frances Power Cobbe. In a letter from the Colenso family home in Natal, he discussed various aspects of the on-going controversies that surrounded him, including the demands made on his time by his regular preaching in St Peter's Cathedral in Pietermaritzburg. 'I need hardly say', he remarked, 'that it is a great test to be obliged to write two sermons a week upon *such* subjects, which cannot be treated in the old humdrum fashion. And the people now *expect* to be provided for with food convenient for them' (Colenso 1866*b*). The sermons to which Colenso referred were subsequently published, in four volumes, under the simple title *Natal Sermons*, subtitled 'Series 1' to 'Series 4'. For a variety of reasons, these sermons have received relatively little treatment from scholars (but see Hinchliff 1964: 173–6; Guy 1983*a*: 161–71; 1983*b*: 8–18; Parsons 1997: 162–4; 2011). They remain, however, a potentially valuable source, not only for understanding Colenso, but also for the way in which Broad Church theological ideas could be presented in sermon form and for the relationship between Broad Church Anglican theology and other trends within Victorian religious thought.

The present chapter will examine these sermons and consider their context within Victorian religious life. It will do so, first, by providing a case-study of Broad Church preaching—and thus of the presentation of Broad Church theology from the pulpit. By focusing on the content and range of the *Natal Sermons* of Bishop Colenso it will examine the way in which Broad Church ideas and themes could be translated into sermons presented to a weekly congregation—in this particular case a congregation in a colonial cathedral. Second, the essay will offer some contextualization of Colenso's weekly sermons to his colonial cathedral congregation, initially by brief comparison with the Oxford college-preaching of the Anglican Broad Church theologian Benjamin Jowett, and subsequently by consideration of their significance for the frequently noted, but much less often examined, relationship between the Anglican Broad Church tradition and Victorian Unitarianism.

The *Natal Sermons*: Origins and Content

The four volumes of Colenso's *Natal Sermons* contain ninety-six sermons preached in St Peter's Cathedral, Pietermaritzburg, at the regular Sunday morning or evening services, between November 1865 and December 1866, together with one sermon that he had written while in England in 1864. As Colenso explained in the Preface to the first series, the sermons were preached in the Cathedral Church of his diocese 'to large and attentive congregations' and were not 'written upon any set plan or system; but have been composed from week to week, upon subjects suggested either by texts occurring in the services of the day, or by some train of thought into which I had already been led by a previous Sermon'. They were printed in the colony, 'separately, as delivered, in accordance with the wish expressed by many of those who heard them' (Colenso 1867: Preface). The first two series were subsequently also published in England (Colenso 1867; 1868), but the third and fourth series (Colenso 1866c and d) were published only in Natal—apparently on the advice of Colenso's lawyers in London (Rees: 109, 119).

Colenso had returned to Natal in late 1865, having spent three years in England defending himself against charges of theological unorthodoxy, not only in respect of his critical treatment of the text of the Pentateuch, but also in relation to his rejection of both substitutionary interpretations of the doctrine of the atonement and the concept of endless punishment for the unconverted—views which he had expressed in his commentary on Paul's Epistle to the Romans, written 'from a missionary point of view', that he had published four years earlier (Colenso 1861; 2003). His return to Natal brought no respite from theological controversy. On the contrary, as Colenso knew only too well, whilst he had been in England the Bishop of Cape Town, Robert Gray, had been working hard to undermine Colenso's position in Natal, with the enthusiastic assistance of the Dean of St Peter's, J. R. Green. Indeed, on 7 January 1866—just hours before Colenso preached the ninth in the first series of his *Natal Sermons*—Dean Green had read out a 'Sentence of Greater Excommunication' pronounced on Colenso by Bishop Gray. According to Gray, Colenso had fallen into heresies that touched 'the very life and being of the Christian Church' and 'overthrow the faith of Christendom'. Colenso, he continued, had assailed the 'fundamental truths of our common Christianity', to the extent that, he asserted, 'It is with Christianity itself, as a revelation from God, that he is at war' (Gray: 2:249; Guy 1983a: 157; Parsons 1997: 136).

This context is important, not least because it explains Colenso's heart-felt protests in a number of the *Natal Sermons* against the oppressive use of ecclesiastical authority and the spirit of condemnation, denunciation, and excommunication that so often accompanied it (Colenso 1866c: 147–8; 1867: 66–7, 115–16, 289; 1868: 42–9). It was also a context which Colenso explicitly acknowledged in the Preface to the first series of his *Natal Sermons* where he noted that he had 'been compelled by the peculiar circumstances under which I returned to my Diocese, to deal with some of these subjects in a more controversial manner than I should have otherwise deemed best suited to the needs of my flock' (Colenso 1867). But the context of theological conflict—and accusations of heresy—within the Anglican Church in South Africa is also important because it locates the *Natal Sermons* firmly within the cluster of religious controversies during the 1860s that are conventionally referred to as the 'Victorian crisis of faith'. In relation to the controversy between 1860 and 1864, over *Essays and Reviews*, it has been argued, persuasively, that a key factor in the intensity of the crisis was the insistence of the orthodox opponents of the Broad Churchmen upon faith being a matter of 'either/or', 'all or nothing'; that faith must be held without reservation and that acceptance of the data of revelation must be total and uncritical; and therefore the Bible must be accepted in its entirety (Altholz: 38–40). While in England between 1862 and 1865, Colenso followed the *Essays and Reviews* controversy, and the associated legal case, with great interest, believing that the acquittal on appeal of Rowland Williams and Henry Bristow Wilson established his right to hold and to preach the views that he did (Rees: 82). Moreover, as key passages—and also the overall tenor—of the *Natal Sermons* make clear, Colenso understood his sermons to be a rejection and refutation of the 'either/or', 'all or nothing' approach to Christian belief.

As one of Colenso's most sympathetic modern interpreters has observed, the originality of his *Natal Sermons* lay in the synthesis that he achieved in them and in his determination to present 'a clear statement on the religious difficulties of the time' to as wide an audience as possible, 'and to show why, if approached in a proper manner, they offered no threat to faith' (Guy 1983a: 162). Indeed, in the *Natal Sermons* themselves, Colenso clearly stated his aim of providing an alternative—and in his view a vital and essential alternative—to the 'either/or', 'all or nothing' dichotomy proposed by the orthodox opponents of Broad Church theology. For example, in his sermon in Pietermaritzburg Cathedral in the evening of 22 April 1866, he explained to his congregation that it was part of his duty as a bishop to explore matters of biblical criticism with them because 'This is information, which as Christians, in these days especially, you should possess, in order that you may be able to form something like a reasonable judgement upon the nature of the great controversies of our times.' Thereby, Colenso continued, they would be able to 'see plainly how little ground there is for the popular notion, on which some are still insisting so vehemently, of the absolute infallibility of Scripture—and of its being placed by its very origin and history above the reach of all criticism.' They would be able to decide for themselves whether the truth was more likely to lie with those who refused to look at the facts of modern criticism, or those who 'desire to look the facts in the face, to strip away the mere accretions of ignorance and superstition, which have so long disfigured the true beauty, and hidden from us the true excellence of the Scripture, and to draw from these records of past ages those precious lessons of Eternal Truth, which shall endure for all times' (Colenso 1868: 194–5). Similarly, a month later, in his evening sermon for Pentecost, he assured his congregation that: 'The felt Presence of the Living God amongst us will deliver us from the terrors which assail those, who think that their whole religious system, their house of faith, and fortress of their souls, is in danger of falling at once to the ground, if one line or letter of the Bible should prove to be less than infallible' (Colenso 1868: 315).

Indeed, biblical criticism provided the most consistent theme of the *Natal Sermons*. Both Colenso's preaching *about* biblical criticism, and also his use of biblical criticism *in* his preaching, were founded on the conviction that, thereby, Christians were 'released from the thraldom of mere bibliolatry' (Colenso 1867: 18). Far from undermining its true status, Colenso assured his congregation, 'the more the Bible is studied, the more Divine it seems' and the more people were freed from 'a slavish adherence to the mere letter of Scripture' (Colenso 1867: 38). Far from destroying the authority of the Bible, recognition of its human origins and of the human fallibility of its authors enhanced its status as a record of the profound religious and spiritual experiences of those who wrote it (Colenso 1867: 59–63). The desire for either an infallible Bible or an infallible Church, Colenso argued, was a denial of the call to 'walk by faith and not by sight' (Colenso 1867: 67–8). Worse still, if the challenges of modern biblical criticism were simply ignored or suppressed, then there was a genuine risk that the enduring religious and spiritual value of the Bible as a whole would be lost. As Colenso put it in one of his most forthright sermons on this subject:

> The great danger and mischief of making an idol of the Bible is not perhaps fully realised at a first glance. Its teaching is for the most part so pure, so exalted... But shall we then stake the whole of that treasure, which the writings of the Old Testament and of the New contain for us, upon the super-human perfection of each and every page of these manifold documents?... the truth is that we cannot, [even] if we would, maintain any longer the old traditionary dogma of the infallibility of the Scriptures... We run the risk of losing the precious contents of the casket altogether, by putting it in a position where it cannot, where it is not meant to, stand. We must place it lower that it may be safe. (Colenso 1866d: 33–4)

By contrast, for those willing to 'abandon altogether the traditionary notion of the absolute infallible accuracy of every part of Scripture', there would be no difficulty in still maintaining the 'the general truth of the whole' (Colenso 1867: 293–4).

It was not only in order to protect 'the general truth of the whole', however, that Colenso urged his congregation to accept a critical approach to the Bible. A critical approach to the Bible, Colenso argued, was also a moral duty because it was wrong to deny the truth which God was now revealing through contemporary intellectual advances. As early as the fourth sermon in the entire series, Colenso had stated unambiguously that the new discoveries of Science, whether in Natural Philosophy or Biblical Criticism, *must* be received, indeed, and be received with joy and thankfulness as God's gifts, the gifts of a dear Father to his children...without any detriment to the vital principles of true religion, and the essential truths of Christianity'. (Colenso 1867: 37)

In subsequent sermons Colenso continued, from time to time, to show how the discoveries of modern science added to the perception of the greatness of God's creation. He referred to the work of the geologist Charles Lyell, and in particular to passages in his book *The Antiquity of Man*, published in 1863 (Colenso 1866c: 167, 198; 1868: 64), and he argued that geology and astronomy offered 'unceasing proofs of the Power, and Wisdom, and Goodness of our Great Creator' (Colenso 1868: 190). Similarly, he referred to 'God's newest revelations of Himself' in the 'Light of Modern Science' (Colenso 1866c: 14); asserted that contemporary Christians should accept all that God gives 'our Bibles on the one hand, the light of Science on the other' (Colenso 1866c: 207); and extolled the way in which 'the grand results of Modern Science—the immeasurable extension of the age of the earth—the unutterable vastness of the heavenly host, their size, their numbers... the infinite profusion of life which the microscope reveals to us' revealed the 'wonders on wonders of creative wisdom' (Colenso 1866c: 235).

Moreover, it was not only ideas of biblical infallibility that Colenso opposed in his *Natal Sermons*. Although he gave the subject somewhat less space in his sermons, relative to his rejection of 'traditionary' views of the Bible, he was also consistently and equally dismissive of any idea of the infallibility of creeds, all of which, he insisted, were but imperfect attempts to express complex religious insights through the limited means of human language and the concepts current in particular eras. It was impossible, Colenso stated in the eighth of the first series of *Natal Sermons*, that 'the essential truths of Christianity' should be 'compressed into any formulae of man's imagining', especially ones from an age ignorant of 'modern critical or physical science...Christianity, in order to show its Divine Original, must adapt itself to meet the circumstances of every age'—and this included the need to abandon 'whatever of its traditionary system will not stand the test of examination' (Colenso 1867: 111–12). Similarly, in one of the sermons in the second published series, Colenso said plainly that creeds were, 'but, at the most, approximations to the Truth' (Colenso 1868: 308), and in the final sermon of this series—preached on the day in the liturgical year when the congregation were required to recite the Athanasian Creed—he explained that he regarded it as good that the creeds should be read, as evidence of past formulations of faith, 'if only we regard them from a rational point of view as human compositions, at least as much liable to error as the text of the Scriptures itself on which they are based', and not as absolute and infallible statements (Colenso 1868: 332). The task of modern Christians, therefore, was 'to translate the language of the devout men of older ages into that of our own' (Colenso 1867: 84).

Colenso also consistently contrasted the spirit of Jesus, and also of Paul and the earliest Christians, with that of the Church's later dependence upon creeds and articles. 'Our hope for eternity cannot depend upon our believing implicitly in the absolute infallible truth of each word of the Bible,—much less, of each statement of the Athanasian and other Creeds, which fallible men have derived from the Bible...In fact we hear nothing from the lips of Jesus about creeds and articles, as necessary to salvation...He tells us nothing about systems of Church-Government—about Priests and Deacons, Bishops and Metropolitans, Synods and Councils' (Colenso 1868: 33–4). Paul similarly insisted on belief in the Truth, but did not require 'strict dogmatic precision, or lay down a creed' (Colenso 1867: 169). To assert that the first Christians all believed a single creed is 'mere fiction', because the Apostles 'never embodied their simple teaching in articles and creeds, enforcing their dogmas upon the consciences of their hearers by threats of everlasting damnation' (Colenso 1866d: 96). In two of the last sermons in the entire sequence, Colenso became, if possible, even more outspoken on the subject. Thus, in the seventeenth sermon of the fourth series he insisted that, 'The Christianity manufactured in Church Councils, amidst ignorance and prejudice, in dark ages', had killed both the bodies and the souls of men and brought 'heavy chains for the intellect and conscience' instead of liberty. Therefore, 'we must go back to the Fountain Head itself to find true Christianity, as taught by the life and death of Christ himself' and give priority to Christianity as taught by him over 'the Christianity of Church Articles and Creeds' (Colenso 1866d: 178–80). And in the penultimate of the *Natal Sermons*, again preached on the day set for the public recitation of the Athanasian Creed, he repeated that he thought it good to do so 'if only to make us feel from time to time the strong contrast which is here presented between the Christianity of the fifth century and that of the nineteenth,—yes, and I trust, the nearer approximation of the latter to that of the primitive age, when dogmatic creeds and damnatory clauses were unknown' (Colenso 1866d: 206).

This critical approach to both the Bible and the Church's creeds duly enabled Colenso to present a theologically liberal interpretation of an impressively diverse range of doctrines and issues. Literal belief in a devil and in demonic possession (Colenso 1867: 323–40; 1868: 1–24), or in Jesus' second coming (Colenso 1867: 72–86) was shown to be both incredible and unnecessary. The appeal to miracles as a support for belief was rejected as contrary to genuine faith (Colenso 1867: 150–82). Prophecy was explained as moral proclamation, not the prediction of the future (Colenso 1868: 220–42). The 'commonly entertained' idea that the 'main office of prophecy was to foretell the future, and that this is one of the great guarantees of the truth of revelation...has been distorted into a superstitious falsehood' (Colenso 1868: 224). Baptism and Holy Communion were both interpreted in a thoroughly symbolic manner (Colenso 1867: 128–49, 183–216). Strict sabbatarianism was rejected (Colenso 1867: 217–78). Substitutionary ideas of atonement (Colenso 1866d: 75–82; 1867: 109–10) and of eternal punishment (Colenso 1866c: 182, 251, 262–5; 1866d: 41–5, 106–11, 117–19, 245–6, 262–5; 1867: 22, 134–7, 147; 1868: 165–6) were also both rejected, not only on moral grounds but also on the basis of an informed exegesis of relevant biblical texts. Thus, on atonement, Colenso asserted the 'truth, that Christ suffered *on behalf of* his brethren, has been corrupted by many into the notion of his having offered what is called a vicarious sacrifice, having suffered *instead of* them' (Colenso 1868: 109–10), adding in another sermon, 'the fact is that, in the passages of Scripture which allude to this subject, the expression is always "he suffered on our behalf",—for our sake indeed, but not in our place' (Colenso 1866d: 80).

And on the concept of eternal punishment, he affirmed equally strongly that, because 'we refuse to ascribe to Him anything inconsistent with Justice and Mercy, Faithfulness and Lovingness', therefore, '... the old notion of the almost universal perdition of the human race...falls out of our creed as inconsistent with the free light of Gospel day... [and] as blasphemy against the God and Father of our Lord Jesus' (Colenso 1867: 165–6). Colenso also, therefore, frequently affirmed the presence of God's spirit among all peoples and in all eras (Colenso 1866c: 111, 237, 247–51, 264–5; 1866d: 37–9; 1867: 11, 38, 93–4). Jesus, meanwhile, was presented as the supreme revelation of a God whose character was, above all, that of a loving Father (Colenso 1866c: 4–7; 1867: 105–7; 1868: 73–4, 93–94, 324–5), and the 'essence of Christianity', Colenso asserted, was the enduring message of the 'Fatherhood of God' and the 'Brotherhood of Man' (Colenso 1866c: 135, 174, 179, 190; 1866d: 181, 221; 1867: 106; 1868: 200, 325, 343).

Arguably, however, it was in his application of a critical approach to the New Testament—and in particular his forthright recognition of the limits of the Gospels, historically speaking, as sources for the life of Jesus—that Colenso's liberal approach was most striking. Unsurprisingly, given the critical work on the Pentateuch that had made Colenso so controversial, many of his sermons addressed issues of Old Testament interpretation and accuracy—and, as ever, Colenso said plainly that particular passages were unhistorical or otherwise problematic, although he also always took care to show how the text might nevertheless have something valuable to teach, if understood in a critical manner (Colenso 1866c: 34–48, 61–72, 208–21; 1867: 58–62; 1868: 50–8, 61–2, 257–71). But, as early as the thirteenth of the first series of *Natal Sermons*, Colenso had also stated clearly: 'It is certain that in this age of ours every part of the New Testament, as well as the Old, will be subjected to a close and searching criticism'(Colenso 1867: 191), and later in that series, discussing the story of the Temptations, he asserted that 'it is impossible to regard this narrative as historically true', adding that it was 'probably one of those numerous mythical additions to the real history of the life of our Lord' (Colenso 1867: 301). In the second series, Colenso addressed the issue of Jesus' belief in devils, noting simply that this was the 'current view of the people of his time' and that he spoke 'in the language and according to the modes of thought of the age in which he lived' (Colenso 1868: 9, 12). Similarly, he acknowledged frankly not only that many of the resurrection narratives were of 'a legendary character' (Colenso 1868: 125), but also that there was little more than a 'slight sketch' of the 'life of Christ' in the Gospels (Colenso 1868: 327). Again, in the third series of sermons, Colenso spoke of Jesus' life being 'set before us, however imperfectly, in the Gospels' (Colenso 1866c: 4), and reminded his hearers that 'all we know of him is in the four Gospels, which record only a small part of his life, were written after his death, from unknown sources, the fourth probably being of an even later age' (Colenso 1866c: 120). Predictably, he also explained clearly the 'legendary' and 'mythical' nature of the narratives of the Nativity (Colenso 1866c: 54, 84).

It was in the later numbers of the final series of *Natal Sermons*, however, that Colenso's application of biblical criticism to the Gospels became most radical. The Gospels, composed in a later age, contained much that was legendary and could not be relied on as history, although the general impression was of one who 'went about doing good, and preaching the good news of God's Kingdom' (Colenso 1866d: 145). In the penultimate sermon, Colenso spoke of Jesus as 'that ideal which each devout mind forms of him from the scanty records of his life, enlarged and supplemented by the pious thought of ages' and asserted that, 'Whatever criticism may do with the documents relating to him—*must* do, as God's servant, as a minister of truth—it will never take from us this pure ideal, which they have helped us to realise,—this image of a perfect man, perfectly obedient, perfectly loving, the perfect type of our humanity' (Colenso 1866d: 207–9). Finally, in the last of his *Natal Sermons*, Colenso concluded with what amounted to a concise summary of his own faith. Fear that research into the Gospels and the life of Christ would sweep away Christianity, and leave only a few religious ideas that could be found elsewhere, might be justified if Christianity consisted in maintaining a system of dogmas, based on an infallible Book or Church, 'But if Christianity is a life...if by Christianity we mean that faith which Jesus taught, and in the exercise of which he lived and died...if Christianity consists in this recognition of the Fatherhood of God and of the Brotherhood of Man, and of this revelation of God in Man, going on through the ages...then this Christianity will never die' (Colenso 1866d: 220–1).

Colenso made no extravagant or lofty claims for the content of his *Natal Sermons*, although he did regard their origins and context as worthy of attention. Thus, in a letter to the Dutch Old Testament scholar Abraham Kuenen, written in November 1866, Colenso remarked that, 'my Cathedral sermons, though insignificant in themselves, are of some importance as having been actually preached by a Bp in a Cathedral, and printed by the desire of the people' (Colenso 1866a). Moreover, in the light of the positive reception of his sermons by the laity in Natal, he also believed—as he told Frances Power Cobbe in his letter to her of 27 July 1866—that: 'If only the clergy in England *could* speak as freely as I am able to do here, I am sure their churches would be equally filled. Numbers come regularly now to the Service, both Morning and Evening, who used to go nowhere' (Colenso 1866b). Whether Colenso was correct in the latter judgement it is impossible to say. It is possible, however, firstly, to compare Colenso's sermons in his cathedral in Pietermaritzburg with the sermons preached by Benjamin Jowett in the chapel of Balliol College, Oxford; and secondly, to consider what light they shed upon the relationship—and the proposed affinity—between Victorian Anglican Broad Churchmen and Victorian Unitarians.

The *Natal Sermons*: A Broad Church Comparison and a Broader Context

It is instructive to compare Colenso's preaching in his *Natal Sermons* with the preaching of another famous mid and late Victorian Anglican Broad Churchman, Benjamin Jowett. Like Colenso, Jowett had developed liberal theological views in the 1850s and had already attracted criticism for expressing these in his commentaries on the Letters of Paul to the Thessalonians, Galatians and Romans (Jowett 1855; Jowett 1859; Hinchliff 1987: 45–68). Controversy centred, in particular, on his stinging moral critique of traditional understandings of the doctrine of the atonement, which he described as revolting to human moral sensibilities (Hinchliff 1987: 62–3). Then, in the early 1860s, Jowett had become embroiled in even greater controversy because of his contribution, 'On the Interpretation of Scripture', to *Essays and Reviews* (Jowett 1860; Shea and Whitla). However, after the intense controversy over *Essays and Reviews*—indeed probably because of the intensity of that controversy—Jowett never again published any theology. His essay 'On the Interpretation of Scripture' proved to be his 'final venture into public theology' and instead 'he became a preacher' (Hinchliff 1987: 99, 114), preaching regularly in the chapel of Balliol College, Oxford—where he became Master in 1870—until his death in 1893. Three volumes of his sermons were eventually published—consisting mainly of sermons delivered in Balliol chapel, together with several others preached in either the University church in Oxford or in Westminster Abbey. All of them, however, were published only after his death (Jowett 1895; 1899; 1901).

As careful analysis of Jowett's sermons clearly reveals, a number of themes were not only central to these texts, but also demonstrated the continuity between the earlier theological liberalism of both his Pauline commentaries and his contribution to *Essays and Reviews* and the later theology of his preaching (Hinchliff 1987: 121–46). Together with a sermon on 'The Life of Jesus Christ' in the first published collection of his sermons (Jowett 1895: 309–25), these themes are particularly evident in the final published anthology of examples of Jowett's preaching, entitled *Sermons on Faith and Doctrine* (Jowett 1901). The Bible remained—as he had famously argued in his contribution to *Essays and Reviews*—a work that 'must be interpreted like any other book, according to the same laws of language and the same rules of evidence and criticism' (Jowett 1901: 207). As for traditional understandings of the atonement, just as he had argued in his Pauline commentaries, so again in his preaching, Jowett protested that 'Men will often advance the most monstrous doctrines respecting the character of God' and asked, 'how can a just God punish us for what we never did, for what another did, for the mere tendency to evil which is inherent in the nature which he has given us?' (Jowett 1901: 43, 50). But such specific continuities with his earlier theology were now accompanied by numerous other examples of characteristically liberal Broad Church theology.

Thus, Jowett also presented moral critiques of other traditional Christian beliefs, asking for example, 'Who can believe that the unbaptized infant is consigned to everlasting torments?' or that 'one mortal sin consciously committed after baptism, almost, if not altogether excluded the sinner from the hope of salvation?' (Jowett 1901: 51, 170–1). Similarly, in reflecting on the concept of hell, he also asked, 'Is the justice of God reconcilable with the everlasting damnation of a portion of His creatures?' (Jowett 1901: 168–9). Or again, he protested against 'actions being attributed to God which are at variance with our conceptions of His goodness, or His justice', whether these actions were in the biblical text or the result of later theological formulae (Jowett 1901: 161–2, 165–6).

Prophecy, rightly understood, was not 'the second sight of future events' but the proclamation of 'the truth and justice and mercy of God' (Jowett 1901: 143, 178–9, 287–90), whilst on the subject of prayer Jowett insisted that, since God's creation is governed by laws, and since God is just to all, Christians should not ask for special, miraculous interventions (Jowett 1901: 255, 258, 268, 272, 274). As to the relationship between the spirit and the letter, between the outward forms of the Christian religion—whether in doctrine or worship—and the inward truths which lay behind them, Jowett was clear: 'The greatest lesson which the religious history of mankind teaches us is that, laying aside the ceremonial and external, we should cling to the moral and spiritual' (Jowett 1901: 33, 155, 197–8). Similarly, he asserted that, '"To do justice and to love mercy and to walk humbly before God." These are the truths about which the minister of Christ should desire to speak with authority; not about baptisms or laying on of hands, or about rubrics or vestments or metaphysical controversies' (Jowett 1901: 222–3). Or again, 'the spirit of Christianity is not that we should maintain this or that opinion, or use this or that form of words, but that, maintaining any opinion and using any form of words, we should be like Him' (Jowett 1901: 313).

Jowett also referred frequently, and positively, to other religions, noting that in each great religious tradition there were individuals who 'have sought to pierce through the outward forms of religion to its true nature' (Jowett 1901: 31). He affirmed that God spoke to all peoples in different ways, times and places, so that no part of the human family was 'altogether banished or expelled from Him' (Jowett 1901: 32), rather, he argued, there were antecedents of the Christian faith in other religions, many of whose adherents were 'included in the invisible church' of those who, although not Christians, 'had the temper of Christ' (Jowett 1901: 34–5; Jowett 1895: 311). God, Jowett insisted, is the Father of 'all mankind. The heathen, as we sometimes disparagingly call them, are not His enemies but His children, whom, though at a greater distance from Him and by a longer path, He is guiding into His truth' (Jowett 1901: 103). 'For the love of God embraces all men everywhere and at all times' (Jowett 1901: 164). Unsurprisingly, Jowett also affirmed that new scientific discoveries revealed more of the glory of God, whether through the telescopic investigation of the heavens or the minuteness revealed by the microscope (Jowett 1901: 105). Thus, because God is truth, all inquiry honestly pursued is pleasing to God, 'the truths of science as well as the truths of religion or morals' (Jowett 1901: 111).

Above all, however, Jowett emphasized the absolute priority of the life of Christ, the example of Jesus, and, therefore of the call to 'return to the beginning of Christianity' (Jowett 1901: 24, 90–1). 'The simplicity of religion', he asserted, 'may be illustrated... from the life and example of Christ... The love of God, the love of man, the preference of the spirit to the letter' (Jowett 1895: 315–16). Jowett acknowledged the fragmentary nature of the Gospels (Jowett 1895: 317; Jowett 1901: 86), but nevertheless affirmed that we know that Christ 'went about doing good, because He was good, because He was love, because He was truth' and because 'He lived in communion with God' (Jowett 1895: 318). Moreover, he expressed the hope that the 'day may be coming when a larger idea of Christianity, the true religion of Christ, may win back the hearts of those who have been repelled by the perversions and disfigurements of it' (Jowett 1901: 235). Thus, for Jowett, it has been argued persuasively, 'essential Christianity lay in the simplicity of Christ himself' (Hinchliff 1987: 141), and because of this, '...he was determined to reject abstractions and assert that the ultimate truth was embodied in the person of Christ' (Hinchliff 1987: 124).

As the summaries presented above amply demonstrate, in terms both of their overall theological assumptions and orientations and also their perceptions of the essential nature of Christianity, the similarities between Colenso and Jowett, as revealed by their sermons, were extensive. Both were thoroughly convinced that Christianity had nothing to fear from honest engagement with modern thought, whether historical or scientific; both placed greater importance on the spirit than the letter; both presented a moral critique of traditional Christian doctrine and belief, especially in relation to the doctrines of the atonement and of eternal punishment; both were adamant that God's spirit was at work in other religions and among all peoples; both distrusted the power of outward ritual and the excessive claims made for creeds and definitions; and both insisted that the essence of Christianity lay in the life, teaching and example of Jesus, who was, in turn, interpreted as the clearest revelation of the true nature of God.

Unsurprisingly, both men took a positive view of the other's work. That Colenso had not only read Jowett but approved of his theology was clear from passages in his *Natal Sermons*. Thus, in the sixth in the first series of *Natal Sermons*—on the subject of the 'Second Coming of Christ'—Colenso quoted from the first volume of Jowett's commentary on *The Epistles of St Paul to the Thessalonians, Galatians and Romans*, citing him in support of the fact that the early Christians clearly believed in the imminent return of Jesus, resulting in statements in the New Testament that 'have in their letter been contradicted by the course of events in human history'. In particular, Colenso approved of Jowett's clear-eyed acceptance that this was, indeed, the case, and that it was futile to try to conceal it (Colenso 1867: 77). Then, in the next sermon in the series—this time on 'The Joy of Christmas'—Colenso again quoted from the same volume of Jowett's commentary on Paul's Epistles, but this time as part of an explanation of the evidence of interaction between Jewish and Platonic ideas in the New Testament, especially in the first chapter of John's Gospel (Colenso 1867: 104). Again, in the second series of *Natal Sermons*, when preaching on the subject of 'Prayer to Christ', Colenso quoted at some length from the second volume of Jowett's Pauline commentary, citing his exposition of the idea of the 'brotherhood of all mankind', a concept which Jowett maintained relieved Christians 'from anxiety about the condition of other men, of friends departed, of those ignorant of the Gospel, of those of a different form of faith from our own'—a point on which Colenso wholeheartedly agreed (Colenso 1868: 142–3).

Jowett, for his part, demonstrated his support for Colenso by inviting him to preach in Balliol College chapel when Colenso was again briefly in England in 1874. By this time, Colenso was even more isolated in Natal, having by then lost the support of many of those among the laity who had previously stood by him—although this subsequent loss of support was not due to his liberal theology but was the result of his defence of the rights of the Zulu people against the actions of the colonial government in Natal (Guy 1983a: 193–349; Parsons 1997: 166–70). Colenso had returned to England to present his protests concerning the treatment of the Zulu to the Colonial Office. Predictably, Samuel

Wilberforce, the Bishop of Oxford (who had been one of Colenso's fiercest opponents among the bishops a decade earlier) now refused to allow Colenso to preach in his diocese. Balliol College chapel was not under Wilberforce's jurisdiction, however, and Jowett, as Master, invited him to preach (Guy 1983a: 227; Hinchliff 1987: 108).

Despite their many similarities, however, in respect of their sermons, Colenso and Jowett also differed in significant ways. Colenso's *Natal Sermons* were the product of a regular cycle of preaching, week by week, following the readings specified in the official lectionary, to a cathedral congregation—but a colonial cathedral congregation which probably resembled a large parochial congregation rather than that of an English cathedral. They were published, by request and week by week, in Natal and then also in collected volumes. Jowett's sermons, by contrast, were preached almost always to university congregations and mainly in Balliol College chapel, were not intended for publication, and indeed were not published until after Jowett's death. The contrasting audiences—as well as the different temperaments of the preachers—may also account for the difference in the style and tone of the sermons. Jowett, although always using a biblical text, characteristically began in a predominantly philosophical manner by setting out an intellectual issue, then proceeding to explore the issue concerned by reference to appropriate biblical texts and ideas. Colenso characteristically started with a biblical text from the reading specified for the day, explored its context, bringing to bear a critical understanding of the text itself, and then often referred his hearers to the way in which the text had been treated by other Christian theologians and preachers—often with the aim of showing that the liberal theological position which he presented had precedents within the writings of earlier theologians and exegetes.

Comparison with the preaching of Benjamin Jowett is not, however, the only potentially revealing context in which to consider Colenso's sermons. It is also instructive to locate Colenso's preaching in the context of the often remarked upon, but much less frequently explored, 'affinity' between Victorian Anglican Broad Churchmen and Victorian Unitarians. The classic study of this phenomenon traced the similarities between Anglican Broad Churchmen and Unitarians in attitudes to biblical inspiration, biblical criticism, miracles, the doctrines of the atonement and everlasting punishment, the person of Christ, the use of traditional language, and mutual interaction around the idea of a Broad Church (Wigmore-Beddoes). Despite the many affinities thus identified, the possibility of a further affinity in the area of preaching and in the content of sermons remained largely unexplored. That such an additional affinity also existed is, however, suggested by an observation in the autobiographical reflections of Charles Kegan Paul who, in the 1850s and 1860s, had been an Anglican clergyman of Broad Church views. Whilst vicar of Sturminster Marshall in Dorset he had been a friend of Rowland Williams and H. B. Wilson (both of whom had been prosecuted for their contributions to *Essays and Reviews*) and also of their fellow Broad Churchman Robert Kennard. Writing in the 1890s, Paul remarked that:

> In my opinion the whole theology of the ... Broad Church party is simply Unitarian. Of course, when a distinction had to be made, it was possible to make it by quoting

Creeds and Devotions which had been retained by the Church of England... But what I mean is that the sermons preached in Broad Churches might have been delivered in any Unitarian pulpits. (Paul: 215–16)

Moreover, as well as sharing the general Broad Church affinity with liberal Unitarianism, Colenso was also indebted to Unitarians in more specific ways. As early as 1844, writing to his future wife, he quoted from the published sermons of the Unitarian James Martineau, saying that he had 'never seen a book... so full of brilliant and truthful passages' (Martineau; Wigmore-Beddoes: 101–2). Years later he disclosed in conversation with Frances Cobbe that his decision to return to England in 1862, to defend his commentary on Romans and publish his work on the Pentateuch, had been prompted, in part at least, by his reading of the biography of the Unitarian Blanco White—a text which includes many liberal theological ideas that subsequently feature prominently in the *Natal Sermons* (Thom; Cobbe: 97; Parsons 1998). Whilst in England between 1862 and 1865, Colenso then received the support and friendship of a number of prominent Unitarians, and also, in correspondence with Frances Cobbe, acknowledged the very high regard which he had for the theology of the American Unitarian Theodore Parker (Parsons 2000).

For those who, both in his own day and subsequently, found or continue to find Colenso's theology inadequate because of its liberalism and 'unorthodoxy', such contacts and affinities with Unitarianism will surely serve merely to confirm his shortcomings. They also, however, provide a vital clue to the character and nature of his preaching. In both the range of subjects and the consistently liberal theology presented, Colenso's *Natal Sermons* are an embodiment of the 'affinity' between Victorian Anglican Broad Churchmen and Unitarians. They were also central to Colenso's own understanding of the Christian faith. Although produced, week by week, for his cathedral congregation, the *Natal Sermons* were not merely a passing, incidental work. Writing in 1872, in the preface to the sixth volume of his study of the Pentateuch, Colenso observed that:

In four volumes of *Natal Sermons*... I have done my best to show that the central truths of Christianity—the *Fatherhood of God*, the *Brotherhood of Man*, and the *Revelation of God in Man*—are unaffected by these results of scientific enquiry, or rather are confirmed by the witness which the Pentateuch, when stripped of its fictitious character, gives of the working of the one Divine Spirit in all ages. (Colenso 1872: xv)

And eleven years later, in his last published sermons, preached in the year he died, Colenso presented the same themes and affirmed the same faith that he had proclaimed in his *Natal Sermons*: 'This doctrine of the Fatherhood of God to all, even to the publican and sinner, the outcast and the prodigal, is at all events the doctrine which Jesus taught... the truth which Jesus taught us when he bade us all to say "Our Father"' (Colenso 1883: 26).

Noting the reluctance of Colenso's lawyers to sanction publication of more of her husband's sermons in England, Frances Colenso remarked that she regretted this because 'he is so abominably calumniated in the so-called Church papers, that I am sure many would be quite astonished if they could see what he really does preach and teach, how far removed from infidelity, how absolutely the opposite of atheism' (Rees: 119). The Unitarian weekly paper, *The Inquirer*, was equally positive in its assessment of Colenso's preaching. His *Natal Sermons*, their reviewer suggested, might serve 'as a model of what preaching in these days ought to be and—if such preaching were not as rare as it is admirable—would go far to redeem the pulpit from the imputation that it falls behind the higher intelligence of the age and has become an obsolete institution'. Colenso's sermons, the reviewer continued, combined 'a readiness to receive all new facts in science and new conclusions in Biblical criticism, with a steadfast faith in Christianity as the religion of God for the conversion and redemption of the world'. They were, as a result, 'singularly bold, thoughtful, and critical theological treatises, and yet, instead of being dry and unattractive, as theological treatises often are, they are full of the warmth, piety and unction of a spiritual religion' ('Natal Sermons': 583). It was a fitting Unitarian tribute to the boldest of Broad Church bishops.

References

Altholz, J. L. (1982). 'The Mind of Victorian Orthodoxy: Anglican Responses to "Essays and Reviews", 1860–1864'. *Church History* 51: 186–97.

Cobbe, F. P. (1894). *Life of Frances Power Cobbe by Herself*. London: Bentley.

Colenso, J. W. (1861). *St Paul's Epistle to the Romans*... Cambridge: Macmillan.

—— (1866a). Letter to Abraham Kuenen, 27 November 1866. Kuenen Archive, University of Leiden.

—— (1866b). Letter to Frances Power Cobbe, 27 July 1866. Cobbe Collection, Huntington Library, San Marino, California.

—— (1866c). *Natal Sermons: Third Series*. Pietermaritzburg: P. Davis.

—— (1866d). *Natal Sermons: Fourth Series*. Pietermaritzburg: P. Davis.

—— (1867). *Natal Sermons. A Series of Discourses Preached in... St Peter's, Maritzburg*, London: Trübner.

—— (1868). *Natal Sermons. Second Series of Discourses Preached in... St Peter's, Maritzburg*, London: Trübner.

—— (1872). *The Pentateuch and Book of Joshua Critically Examined, Part VI*. London: Longmans.

—— (1883). *Three Sermons: Preached in... S. Peter's Pietermaritzburg in 1883*. Pietermaritzburg: City Printing Works.

—— (2003). *Commentary on Romans by John William Colenso; edited with an Introduction by Jonathan A Draper*. Pietermaritzburg: Cluster Publications.

Gray, R. (1875–1876). *Life of Robert Gray, Bishop of Capetown and Metropolitan of Africa*, C. Gray (ed.), 2 vols. London: Rivingtons.

Guy, J. (1983a). *The Heretic: A Study of the Life of John William Colenso 1814–1883*. Pietermaritzburg: University of Natal Press.

—— (1983b). 'The Religious Thinking of J. W. Colenso: The Theology of a Heretic'. *Religion in Southern Africa* 4: 3–20.

Hinchliff, P. (1964). *John William Colenso: Bishop of Natal*. London: Nelson.

—— (1987). *Benjamin Jowett and the Christian Religion*. Oxford: Clarendon Press.
Jowett, B. (1855). *The Epistles of St Paul to the Thessalonians, Galatians and Romans*. London: Murray.
—— (1859). *The Epistles of St Paul to the Thessalonians, Galatians and Romans*... 2nd edn. London: Murray.
—— (1860). 'On the Interpretation of Scripture' in *Essays and Reviews*. London: Parker: 330–433.
—— (1895). *College Sermons*, ed. W. H. Fremantle. London: Murray.
—— (1899). *Sermons: Biographical and Miscellaneous*, ed. W. H. Fremantle. London: Murray.
—— (1901). *Sermons on Faith and Doctrine*, ed. W. H. Fremantle. London: Murray.
Paul, C. K. (1899). *Memories*. London: Kegan Paul, Trench, Trübner.
Martineau, J. (1843). *Endeavours after the Christian Life*. London: Munroe.
'Natal Sermons. By the Right Rev. J. W. Colenso, D.D., Bishop of Natal. London: Trübner, 1868' (1868). *The Inquirer*: 583–5.
Parsons, G. (1997). 'Rethinking the Missionary Position: Bishop Colenso of Natal', in J. Wolffe (ed.), *Religion in Victorian Britain*. V: *Culture and Empire*. Manchester: Manchester University Press, 135–75.
—— (1998). 'A Forgotten Debt: John Colenso and the *Life* of Blanco White'. *Faith and Freedom* 51: 96–116.
—— (2000). 'Friendship and Theology: Unitarians and Bishop Colenso'. *Transactions of the Unitarian Historical Society* 22: 97–110.
—— (2011). '"Released from the Thraldom of Mere Bibliolatry": Biblical Criticism in the Sermons of Bishop Colenso'. *Modern Believing* 52: 22–9.
Rees, W. (1958). *Colenso Letters from Natal*. Pietermaritzburg: Shuter and Shooter.
Shea, V. and Whitla, W. (eds.) (2000). *Essays and Reviews: The 1860 Text and Its Reading*. Charlottesville: University of Virginia Press.
Thom, J. H. (ed.) (1845). *The Life of the Rev. Joseph Blanco White, Written by Himself*... London: John Chapman.
Wigmore-Beddoes, D. (1971). *Yesterday's Radicals: A Study of the Affinity between Unitarianism and Broad Church Anglicanism in the Nineteenth Century*. Cambridge: James Clarke.

PART V

MISSIONS AND IDEAS OF EMPIRE

CHAPTER 29

FROM BARBARISM TO CIVILITY, FROM DARKNESS TO LIGHT: PREACHING EMPIRE AS SACRED HISTORY

ROBERT G. INGRAM

THE MEANINGFUL PAST

IN spring 1773 Robert Lowth, Bishop of Oxford, preached a sermon at St Mary-le-Bow, London, in which he explained why the Irish lived in 'a state of darkness and barbarism'. The anniversary feast of the London society which corresponded with the Incorporated Society for Promoting English Protestant Working Schools in Ireland provided the occasion of Lowth's reflections, and his audience included many of the great and good in Church and State. The members of the London society, like nearly all eighteenth-century charitable foundations, gathered annually to conduct business, raise money and dine together. Before the dinner, a prominent cleric gave a sermon which he had tailored to the foundation's mission and which the society's governors hoped would encourage donations (P. Clark: 265–71; Lloyd: 187–9). The Incorporated Society existed, its royal charter noted, because Ireland had 'great Tracts of Land almost entirely inhabited by Papists, who are kept by their Clergy in great Ignorance of true Religion, and bred up in great Disaffection to the Government'. George II had chartered the society in 1733 to establish schools that would instruct children 'in the English Tongue, and in the Principles of true Religion and Loyalty' (Hansard: 3–4). By the time Lowth stepped into St Mary-le-Bow's pulpit to address this theme, the society's officers had gone over the accounts in the parish vestry room and the audience had navigated through a slalom of collection plates and boxes.

Once in their seats, they heard the familiar account of the war between 'true religion' and 'popery'. It was an old story, one which had long helped the English to make sense of themselves and their history. Lowth's story began where English sacred histories almost always began, at some point in the distant past. The Romans had never conquered Ireland, he noted, which had deprived the native Irish of the 'order, laws, civility, [and] cultivation' that usually came from a stint under Roman dominion. Neither did the Protestant Reformation alleviate things: 'When the light of the Gospel was relumined by the Reformation, the same pillar of fire, which gave a guiding light to England, [it] became a cloud of darkness to the Irish', Lowth lamented. '... It threw them more irrevocably into the arms of Rome; and made them seek alliances with every Popish nation, that could flatter them with promises of protection'. And it was this Irish religion—popery—which had cemented Irish 'barbarism'. 'Popery, that more than Egyptian darkness, still covers the greater part of the land', Lowth argued. '... It is the great obstacle, that stands in the way of every beneficial, every generous, design'. The Incorporated Society, then, had to

> awaken the Native Irish of the lower rank out of their torpid state, in which their prejudices have so long held them; to call them forth... from barbarism to civility, from darkness to light, from bigotry to religion, from a slavish subjection to their priests, and an abject vassalage to the Pope, to the glorious liberty of the Gospel, that they may become useful to themselves and to the community, good subjects, rational Christians, real Catholics, servants of God alone, and freemen of Christ. (Lowth: 5, 8, 9-10)

Robert Lowth's auditors and the contemporary readers of his sermon would have recognized his story and understood its applicability at a charity's anniversary feast: that was why he told it. For his story—a sacralized story of England's foreign possessions—was the way that many within the English establishment understood and articulated the nation's imperial project. This traditional—though capacious and accommodating—sacred history gave providential meaning to England's empire, yet it is a story which historians have largely missed. It was a story that mattered to contemporaries, though, and to understand what it meant to them requires that we reconsider sacred history of the sort Lowth preached in 1773 on its own terms, both as a manifestation of marrow-deep belief and as a method which could and was used for contemporary political and polemical purposes. To that end, this chapter examines the sacred histories expounded in the nearly one hundred anniversary sermons preached before the Incorporated Society for Promoting Protestant Working Schools in Ireland (henceforth 'Incorporated Society') (1735–83) and the Society for the Propagation of the Gospel in Foreign Parts (SPG) (1702–83). These sermons were members of a generic family—the charity sermon—and contained all of that genre's tropes. But, both individually and collectively, they also articulated a rationale for England's empire and argued for the established Church of England's participation in that imperial project by way of a particular sacred history.

Empires are bottom-line enterprises which involve the governance of lands by a power which does not initially have sovereignty over them. Those annexations are almost always justified publicly, and the reasons used to justify them tell us something important about the nature of the annexing power's political life and thought. In the case of eighteenth-century England, it has been argued that the 1730s witnessed the emergence of a new conception of the empire 'as a political community incorporating Britain, Ireland and the plantations', and, furthermore, that this transatlantic political community was conceived of as 'Protestant, commercial, maritime and free' (Armitage: 170–98; cf. J. C. D. Clark 2000; Claydon). While acknowledging a religious dimension to English imperial ideology, historians of empire have, in practice, paid it scant attention. The Incorporated Society and SPG feast sermons, though, illustrate how the leaders of the eighteenth-century established Church of England built their ideas about empire upon the foundation of sacred history. They do this by showing, perhaps not surprisingly, that sacred history framed the ways in which England's rulers understood Ireland's place within their empire. But they also illustrate how metropolitan religious leaders applied that very same framework to the North American colonies. In the end, the Enlightenment discourses of empire were not anathema to sacred history, but rather were easily subsumed within it. And that was surely one of the reasons that the Incorporated Society and SPG feast preachers employed it so regularly. But there were other reasons why the feast preachers might have constructed sacred histories of the empire: they moralized the imperial project and, in so doing, claimed a role for the established Church. The English were not just competing with other nations abroad, they were competing with the forces of Antichrist: for that task the state surely required the help of the established Church (Sirota).

The Generic Context: Charity Sermons

The Incorporated Society and SPG sermons were generic set-pieces (charity sermons) that open a window into the official mind of the English Church and State. During the eighteenth century, the British Isles abounded with charitable foundations—hospitals, asylums, orphanages, schools, and the like—thanks to the post-revolutionary 'moral revolution'. The English, inspired by this 'reformation of manners', gave generously and congratulated themselves for their generosity (Spurr 1993). Indeed, the best recent treatment of the subject goes so far as to argue that 'philanthropy became the ersatz religion of national life' (Sirota: 5). Charity schools proved particularly attractive to donors, and by 1734 London alone had more than 130 such schools which educated over 6,100 boys and girls. Financed by subscriptions and run by trustees, the charity schools manifested the increasingly confident and robust spiritual vigour of the eighteenth-century Church of England (Rose).

The charity school anniversary feast sermons, and particularly those of the Incorporated Society and the SPG, highlight the shared beliefs of the English establishment. The feast preachers for both organizations were almost always bishops, and their audiences were comprised of London's and Dublin's elite. Not only were the speaker and his audience drawn largely from the establishment in Church and State, but the sermons' content could not help but reflect elite attitudes and assumptions: off-base harangues were not the best way to convince anyone to give to a charity and to give to it annually. The printed versions of these anniversary charity sermons also revealed much. In the case of the Incorporated Society and SPG, each year's anniversary sermon prefixed the societies' annual reports, which listed the members, donors and the precise amounts of their donations. Not only did these lists publicly advertise the donors' benevolence, but they gave the donors' implicit imprimatur to the charity sermon which prefaced them (Farooq).

While these sermons reflected shared beliefs of the English establishment, they served simultaneously as tools to shape belief. In an age during which the relationship of Church and State came under both practical and theological stress, it hardly surprises that leaders of the established Church would try in these sermons to convince the public of the Church's proper role in governing the nation and its empire. That members of the English and Irish elite comprised the immediate audiences for these sermons also surely was not lost on the preachers.

So what did charity sermons actually argue? Most commonly, they made the case that God was the ultimate charitable donor, since He gave his only Son to redeem mankind. In turn, He enjoined man to provide charity to the needy here on Earth. Charity, then, was not so much an option as a religious duty. It was, furthermore, beneficial, both to the individual donor and to society more generally (Andrew). Charity school sermons extended these arguments, contending that the purpose of charity schools was, by teaching 'true religion', to inculcate loyalty to the established Church and State, on the principle that loyalty to the former necessarily ensured loyalty to the latter (Rose: 40–45; Lloyd: 47–50).

The Incorporated Society and the SPG were like any other eighteenth-century charity school foundations, then, in that they sought to bolster allegiance to Church and State by teaching 'real Christianity'. But in important respects, both were anomalous, for they had as their charitable 'objects' people beyond the pale of English civilization—'papists' and 'heathens'. With its main governing body in Dublin and a corresponding society in London, where many of the Irish Protestant ascendancy spent a large part of each year, the Incorporated Society ran schools which aimed to extirpate their students' popery. The SPG, a slightly older charitable society, was chartered in 1701 to combat 'Atheism and Infidelity' by providing the North American colonies with 'Learned and Orthodox Ministers to Instruct Our said Loving Subjects in the Principles of true Religion'. The need for such religious instructors was particularly acute, the royal charter continued, because 'divers Romish Priests and Jesuits are the more incouraged to pervert and draw over Our said Loving Subjects to Popish Superstition and Idolatry' (Pascoe: 1:932). Especially vulnerable to popish corruption were the native Indians on the imperial frontier, while the African slaves' 'heathenism' also made them appropriate objects for charity. Both the Incorporated Society and the SPG, then, confronted the problem of religious and cultural difference within the empire in ways that most charitable foundations did not. And they explained those differences to themselves and others by way of longstanding sacred narratives, narratives able to comprehend within themselves both traditional and contemporary themes and concerns.

The Intellectual Framework: Sacred History

What was sacred history? It was a style of historical writing that built a narrative human history and endued it with both secular and providential significance. That story had a beginning (the past, pure, though not for long), a middle (the present, degenerate and corrupt), and an end (the future, providentially redeemed from degeneration and purified from corruption). As applied to Ireland and North America by the Incorporated Society and SPG preachers, it both sacralized the English imperial project and justified the established Church of England's role in that project.

Sacred history's presence and prominent public use during the eighteenth century presents an interpretative problem for the modern historian. To be sure, English Protestants thought concertedly and publicly about the history of the English Church from at least the Reformation onwards (Champion; Levine 2003; Spurr 2006; Starkie). Yet sacred history, as distinct from ecclesiastical history, is reckoned to have been on the wane by the eighteenth century. In particular, biblical criticism, comparative chronology, and theories of human origins which challenged the biblical homogenetic account eroded the historical reliability of the Bible, the launching-off point for sacred histories. And, sacred history gave way to natural history, a science of religion in which 'religion' became a secularized category of analysis (Harrison 1990, 2001, 2007). This explanation of sacred history's decline, if not eclipse, fits nicely with modern accounts of the development of late seventeenth- and eighteenth-century historical practice—which emphasize the increasingly rationalist evidentiary standards and the development of cosmopolitan historical styles—and of early modern natural philosophy—which highlight the simultaneous, if paradoxical, re-emergence of scepticism and the rising confidence in human reason to understand and explain a mechanistic universe (Levine 1995; O'Brien; Israel; Popkin; Jacob and Stewart; Woolf; Griggs).

Yet the Incorporated Society and SPG sermons demonstrate that those at the very highest echelons of the established Church continued to explain the past, present and future of England and its empire by way of sacred history. In large part, sacred history's survival and use can be put down to its capacity to comprehend simultaneously within it traditional Christian themes (such as providence), core Protestant ones (anti-popery, for instance), and more recent Enlightenment sensibilities and concerns. And that should hardly surprise us because the transitions between the supposed 'stages' of history are neither neat nor complete. If we think about early modern English intellectual and religious history as the story of fission, not fusion, of adaptation and accommodation, not obsolescence and extinction, then we can appreciate more fully why sacred history remained a powerful explanatory tool for those trying to make sense of England's Atlantic empire (Gregory).

Ireland: 'Here Popery Reigns in Its Full Force'

Eighteenth-century Ireland was a colony, subjugated by the English in the sixteenth century and governed since by an Anglo-Irish elite who served at the behest and to achieve the ends of the King's government in London (McBride). In the minds of Ireland's governors, the greatest practical political problem facing them was ensuring the island's allegiance, and they inevitably tethered the problem of Irish political allegiance to the problem of Irish religious pluralism (Ingram). For Ireland was, to their way of thinking, a confessional dystopia, one in which papists accounted for 75–80 per cent of the population. Anglo-Irish governors approached the popish problem in a number of ways. On the one hand, they took punitive measures passing penal laws that accorded full civil, political, and religious rights only to members of the established Church of Ireland, itself representing only a small minority within the quarter of the island's inhabitants who were Protestants (Connolly: 263–313). On the other hand, though, there emerged during this period a 'creed' of 'improvement', a creed easily accommodated within the ideology of anti-popery. As Toby Barnard characterizes it, 'Devotees tended to be conquerors and colonizers. An article of their faith was the superiority of their culture: they and their ways epitomized civility. Believing this, adherents had a mission to spread their beliefs and practices. Others, presently inferior, would benefit—materially and morally—from being improved' (T. Barnard: 13). One of the aims of the eighteenth-century Irish improvers was the Protestantization of Irish papists, and the Incorporated Society—founded by Henry Maule, Bishop of Dromore, with the aim of converting papist children and teaching them industriousness—was part of the improving movement's efforts to address Ireland's popish problem (Milne; cf. Hayton). The society was a voluntary one, centred in Dublin but with an active corresponding society in London. While the society's royal charter spelled out its essential mission, the Irish and English bishops who preached the anniversary sermons in turns reiterated, distilled, and amplified upon the mission statement. They did so employing sacred history, one whose central theme was anti-popery and whose unfolding narrative charted a story of purity, declension and redemption.

Anti-popery emerged from and continued to thrive in a world which thought in terms of binaries and by way of inversion (Lake 1989, 2006; S. Clark: 43–79; cf. Shagan). The lineaments of English anti-popery were formed during the sixteenth century, as Protestant polemicists worked to distinguish the English Church from the Roman one. The Roman Church, in their view, was 'false' and foreign, and it was riddled with 'superstition' and 'idolatry' since it was a man-made religion which owed allegiance to the bishop of Rome, whom some believed to be the 'antichrist'. The Protestant English Church, by contrast, was the 'true' church, a native church which taught 'pure religion'—because it was a 'religion of the word'—and which had its authority from God alone (Lake 1989, 2006; Milton; Davies: 18–66). English Protestant polemicists also constructed an anti-popish narrative that had a beginning (the past, pure before popery's emergence), a middle (the present, corrupted by the popish religion), and an end (the future, redeemed from popery). By the eighteenth century, that story had long helped the English to understand, organize and explain their history (Scott). And it was a story applied directly to the Irish situation by the Incorporated Society feast preachers.

They began not with Ireland itself or even with the 'perversions' of popery, but with the origins of man. From the very beginning, man had perverted God's original 'pure' religion (Rubiés; Sheehan). 'The nations of the earth were idolaters before the coming of Christ', Thomas Sherlock argued, 'and their religious worship was not only directed at false objects, but was itself impure and corrupt, and tended to introduce great depravity of manners' (Sherlock: 9). Chiefly to blame for the degeneration of religion were the Jews, whose 'Idolatry... was a formal Act of High Treason against God' (Hayter 1754: 12). They worshipped false idols because they had been corrupted by 'prosperity' and as their 'corruption had made a separation between them and their God, his protection was withdrawn' and they were 'swallowed up under the dominion of the Romans' (Conybeare: 6). Neither, though, were early Christians blameless, for even after Christ had reinstituted the pure religion of God, his early followers soon fell into a degenerate state. Some argued, for instance, that early Christians were 'given over to their own Imaginations, when they no longer retained God and the Simplicity and Purity of his Religion in their Thoughts'. Instead of following God, they had a 'false Zeal for what ministered Strife and Contention' and evidenced a 'mutual Negligence and Lukewarmness to the weightier Matters, and indisputable Duties of Religion' (Rundle: 14). Others were even more specific. '[T]he Jewish Converts became Judaizing Christians, and thought the Practice of Virtue and Piety upon mere Gospel Principles barren and jejune, without the Addition of some of their own Legal Ceremonies,' Matthew Hutton reckoned. 'The Gentiles wanted to retain part of their Heathenish Superstition, and to partake of the Lord's Table at the same time with the Tables of their own Idols' (Hutton 1745a: 5). Within only a few centuries of Christ's appearance, then, the primitive purity of the early Church was gone.

The Church of Rome instantiated and promulgated the impure religion that was post-primitive Christianity. William Barnard, for instance, contrasted 'the genuine Truths of Christianity, the Precepts of Jesus Christ' with 'the vain Traditions of weak and unlearned and perhaps also wicked and designing Men'. Papists, he assured his audience, were

> blinded by Ignorance, and betrayed into dangerous Errors, thro' an implicit Obedience to such Guides as maintain their Influence over Men, by permitting them to commute for their Sins, and depend upon the Merits of those holy Men, who had learned no other way to Heaven than Christ and his Apostles had taught them. (W. Barnard: 6)

Many others likewise pointed to the corrupting influence of popish 'priestcraft' (Bulman). 'Implicit Faith, and a blind Devotion to the Will of their Priests, constitutes the Essence of their Religion,' Edward Young argued. 'In Proportion to the People's Ignorance must ever be their Bigotry and Superstition, and consequently the Power of their Priests' (Young: 6). In the Incorporated Society anniversary sermons, these long-standing anti-popish binaries and inverted realities appear again and again.

Having established that popery was uniquely awful, the preachers turned their attention to Ireland, a land which most argued was singularly degraded. In a sense, Ireland had little chance for hope, since its earliest dwellers were themselves barbarians. Robert Howard, for instance, detailed the reasons for Ireland's backwardness. 'Its remote Situation from the rest of Europe, made it later inhabited than most other Countries,' he began, 'and it had the ill Fortune to be neglected by the Roman Conquerors, whose indulgent Arms spread Labour and Industry, Arts and Improvement wherever they came, and made all their Provinces to feel the Blessings of Order and Government.' Instead, the Irish remained 'in a sort of State of Nature, broken and divided into Septs and Clans' (Howard: 17). Nearly half a century later, William Beresford took the same line, arguing that the remoteness of the Irish, their misfortune not to have been conquered by the Romans, and their internal tribal divisions made Ireland 'a Situation extremely unfavourable to Improvement' (Beresford: 5–6). Notably, where many early modern Protestants linked Rome and Romanism, by way of the Church's imperial corruption, the Incorporated Society preachers, by contrast, generally reckoned that the Romans were a civilizing force sadly absent in early Ireland (Bulman). In the end, it was little surprise that the Irish were 'a clan of... wretched creatures, scarce defended from the inclemency of the weather, in dismal cottages and huts of clay, almost naked, almost starting, under sad impressions of wild superstition, and in great barbarity of manners' (Maddox).

When popery was added to the native Irish barbarism the combination was noxious. 'It is the Spirit of Popery that keeps this Nation divided against itself, and therefore in a state of Desolation,' Michael Cox lamented. 'The Natives imbibe from their Infancy such prejudices against our Religion and Constitution that Supports it, as the very Principles of self-preservation are not able to overcome' (Cox: 11; Mann: 10–11). The Protestant Reformation, which had revived primitive Christianity, had made no headway in Ireland, thanks to popish priests, who teach 'a Popery refined with all the arts of policy, disguised under false colourings, and accommodated to the genius and manners of the people they hope to seduce' (Thomas 1743: 18–20). The result was that 'great Numbers of our Countrymen live in constant Enmity with us; [and] form a Schism in the Body Politic, of the most dangerous and destructive Kind' (Keene: 16).

The spectre of rebellion haunted Anglo-Irish relations, and for good reason. The seventeenth century, as many preachers noted, had shown what Irish papists unchecked might do to their English governors. 'Let us then look back on the last Century, and see Popery wantoning in the Blood of Protestants, unparalleled Massacres, unheard of Cruelties,' Philip Fletcher warned, 'and then let their Advocates say whether it were not reasonable in us to apprehend that the Spirit may still be willing, though the Flesh is weak' (Fletcher: 14). How best to neuter the rebellion inherent in Irish popery? Conversion to 'true religion' was the surest route. Coercion was out of the question—the 'Weapons of our Warfare are not carnal, but spiritual: Instruction, Conviction, Exhortation', Thomas Secker reminded his audience—and so the 'national reformation' would have to come from recapturing the 'zeal' of the primitive Church (Secker: 13). All the Protestant working-schools in the world would make little difference, unless the Church of Ireland was 'as solicitous for spreading Religion and Truth as [Catholics] are for propagating Error and Superstition' (Hutchinson: 13–14).

A properly pursued 'national reformation' taught that 'true religion' could redeem Ireland. It would then be a land freed 'from gross Superstitious, and Papal Tyranny', and, as a result, it would abound

> with every Convenience for Commerce, with Cattle innumerable of every useful King, with Lands yielding to none in their Fertility, with Villages full of industrious Inhabitants, with Ports crowded with Vessels to carry off the Necessaries of Life to other Kingdoms, whilst enough, even for the Elegancies of it, shall be retained at home. (Yonge: 12)

But the redemption had to be safeguarded, as Thomas Herring noted, by continued vigilance, so that the converted Irish papists would maintain 'a true sense of the Christian religion, as laid down in the Scripture'. Otherwise, he cautioned, 'the Irish Converts to Protestantism, may become like some of the American Converts to Christianity, not the Credit, but the Disgrace, not the Advantage and Security, but the Mischief and Ruin of their Benefactors' (Herring 1740: 25).

North America: 'the completion of Christ's kingdom on earth'

Thomas Herring was not unique in seeing parallels between the Irish and the American situation, for Ireland had long been the template for England's North American colonization (Canny). And many of the themes and subjects which pervaded the Incorporated Society sermons regarding Ireland similarly pervaded the SPG ones regarding North America. So, for instance, we encounter recurrent analyses of Christianity's degeneration from its primitive purity; of popery's malign influence in the past, present, and future; of Protestantism's revival of primitive Christianity; and of the redemptive possibility of a national reformation along primitive lines. Yet eighteenth-century America presented a markedly different set of practical challenges from Ireland, and those challenges coloured the SPG sermons (Stevens; Strong 2006, 2009). In particular, whereas the Irish were European peoples, Indians and African slaves joined a motley assortment of European colonists in populating British North America. This, in turn, presented a significant conceptual problem for European Christians, for America was home to peoples who were, prior to European colonization, wholly ignorant of both Christianity and

Christendom. Of course there were, as the eighteenth century unfolded, competing secular theories of human development—such as rationalistic natural history or Scottish conjectural history—which were available to explain the variegated American situation (Harrison 1990; O'Brien; Bickham: 171–205; Griffin: 19–94). Yet, the SPG preachers, no less than their counterparts who preached before the Incorporated Society, fitted America into a sacred narrative whose inflection was different from the Irish story but whose arc (purity, declension, redemption) remained precisely the same.

If colonial Ireland was about the extirpation of popery, colonial America was about the fulfilment of God's providential plan for the world (J. C. D. Clark 2003). Empire had mightily enriched England, and there were obvious material benefits to the metropolis from evangelizing in the American colonies since Christianity 'enjoins all those Virtues that make Commerce gainful, and prohibits all those Vices that bring Poverty in the Rear' (Benson: 10). Yet while these bottom-line considerations surely mattered, the SPG preachers situated them within a larger providential story. Not even trying to explain the origins of the indigenous American peoples, nearly all of the SPG preachers simply began by emphasizing that God had, from the very beginning, promised that salvation would be available to all. 'Salvation is in the Gospel offer'd to all Men, to all Nations without Distinction, not confined to one People, as was the Law given by Moses,' Francis Hare insisted (Hare: 3). Similarly, Samuel Lisle argued that the 'Kingdom of the Messiah' was aimed at 'teaching and enlightenment of Men's Understandings, and reducing them to the Love and Obedience of the Law of God, and consequently to be of a Spiritual Nature, and designed for the universal Good of Mankind, Gentiles, as well as Jews' (Lisle: 5). Indeed, Christian universalism had been foretold even in the earliest books of the Old Testament: 'the prophetic scriptures not only afford no solid grounds for this partial and contracted notion of it, but furnish numerous and incontestable proofs of its universality: that the Gentiles of every denomination would be entitled to an equal share with the Jews of all its rights and benefits' (Moss: iv). And yet there was much in human history that seemed to contradict the notion that God cared for all his creatures equally. '[T]here are some of the Divine Dealings with Mankind, which seem to contradict this general Declaration', John Thomas lamented, 'and have given Occasion for Expostulation and Complaint' (Thomas 1751: 3). God's original covenant with the Jews and the Gospel's limited diffusion especially begged for explanation. Both problems, in the hands of the SPG preachers, were transformed into lynchpins of a sacred narrative of England's North American empire.

The Jews they characterized as deluded proto-papists, employing precisely the sort of language to vilify popery that had been used throughout the early modern period. Mosaic law was 'a vain and haughty Casuistry', and 'peculiar Rites and Ceremonies...fetter'd and bound' the 'Jewish Religion' (Herring 1738: 5; Cresset: 6). The Jews, William George argued, 'were in a State of Childhood' so that the 'Knowledge of even the wisest among them was so partial and defective, that they were ignorant of the very first Principle of Religion, the Object of Worship'. Not surprisingly, they had 'concur'd, or at least acquiesc'd, in those childish and ridiculous Institutions, those obscene and cruel Rites, the Inventions of barbarous and absurd Superstition' (George: 6). Given their credulity, idolatry, and superstition, it was no wonder that the Jews had misinterpreted their original covenant with God, thinking that it was an exclusive covenant and that that God would send a militant Messiah to deliver the kingdom of Israel. Such beliefs, Matthew Hutton suggested, made the Jews 'blind...against every Truth, wherein the rest of Mankind were to have an equal Share and benefit with themselves' (Hutton 1745b: 4). Indeed, Thomas Hayter went so far as to contend that the Jewish rejection of Christ was providentially predestined: 'And thus the Jews, as God foresaw and intended, interpreted away the Messiah..... Upon this secret hinge of providence, the scheme of universal spirituality and redemption from sin and death, was directed to turn' (Hayter 1755: 10).

In the same way that the SPG preachers had reinterpreted the original Jewish covenant in a way easily conformable to English sacred history, so too did they reinterpret and recast the fact that over half of the world remained stuck in 'Pagan Ignorance or Mohammedan Superstition' (Rufford: 7). Most of the preachers acknowledged that God's providential plan was inscrutable, but that did not stop them from speculating about its agents, speed, or current course. Orthodox Protestants, they ruled out the supernatural (miracles, prodigies, the gift of tongues) as current providential agents and insisted, instead, that God had, since the primitive Church, worked only through secondary causes. 'God, by extraordinary means, and by his own immediate agency, often makes a beginning, and prepares matter for his creatures to work on,' Richard Newcome contended, 'but after that the rest is left to its ordinary course, to be effected by second causes, by human prudence and industry; and this especially seems to be the course he has taken for the dispersion of the knowledge of Christianity through the world' (Newcome: 16). Christian missionaries, then, were providential agents, agents whose evangelical efforts could even help bring about the end of time. On Charles Moss's reckoning, for instance, the world would, at some point in the future, 'exhibit an uninterrupted scene of peace, harmony and joy'. But, for that time to come, it fell to Christian missionaries 'to impart the light of the gospel to the Gentiles, and to promote that fullness, which must precede the conversion of the Jews, and the completion of Christ's kingdom upon earth' (Moss: xx). All of this meant that the SPG was more than a royally-chartered organization: it was a body fulfilling God's providential plan through its missionary efforts in North America. In that way, the SPG missionaries were like the original Apostles, yet the challenges facing them in America were, in some ways, even more daunting than those which faced the Apostles. For God had chosen to launch Christianity originally into a world that was highly civilized, steeped in the learning of classical Greece and Rome, and not rife with anticlericalism (Smalbroke: 41; Rufford: 13). The SPG missionaries, by contrast, enjoyed no such advantages in North America. Instead, they faced the task of civilizing, Christianizing and Protestantizing a land of barbarous 'heathens'.

North American Indians resembled the pagan heathens of antiquity. 'The condition of the rest of the nations, to whom the Gospel hath not been, and is not yet publish'd, has been, and is the very same deplorable condition, that it was in the Apostles' days,' Samuel Bradford reckoned (Bradford: 21). Some, like Philip Bisse, went even further to argue that, 'If the Gentiles under the Roman empire, were said to have sat in Darkness, these may be said to have sat in outer Darkness, as well as the shadow of Death: Ignorant not only of the Will of God, but of all the advantages and even conveniencies of Life' (Bisse: 9). To all it was clear that civilization and Christianity were the only sure remedies to this deplorable state, but there was disagreement over sequencing. Some, like Richard Terrick, contended that Christianity itself lessened barbarism and increased civilization: 'As it became more extended in its influence, the effects were seen in abating the Cruelty of the most savage Nations, in abolishing many barbarous customs, which were a disgrace to human nature in its Pagan State, and in making the Laws of every country... speak a language more mild and gentle' (Terrick: 20). Others, like Jonathan Shipley, though, countered that Christian evangelization amongst the Indians was impossible without civilization: 'I fear we have little reason to hope for their conversion, till some great change in their manners has made them abandon their savage vagrant life, and prepared them for the discipline of law and religion' (Shipley: 4). Whether the Indians needed civilizing first and Christianizing second, or the other way around, it was axiomatic for the SPG preachers that without both the Indians would remain stuck in darkness and barbarism.

African slaves were the other 'heathen' population in North America. They too, in the hands of the SPG preachers, became players in the providential scheme. Philip Bearcroft pointed out references to them in Genesis: 'Most remarkable is the Prophecy of the great Ancestry of this post-diluvian world, concerning the Fate of his Posterity; *Cursed be Canaan, a Servant of Servants shall be to his Brethren*. This the poor African Negroes of his Race prove in their hard Slavery to their great Sorry fulfilled' (Bearcroft: 21). William Beveridge went so far as to contend that God had actually allowed slavery to fulfil his providential design. 'I verily believe God would never have suffered, but that he designed they should be there taught all the Principles of the Christian Religion,' Beveridge insisted, 'and some so well, as to be sent back again into their own country, with full Instructions to preach the Gospel to those Nations, that they also may be brought over to Christ; by whom alone either they or we can be saved' (Beveridge: 20–1). Converting African slaves in America to Christianity, then, was a providential good.

Conclusion

The SPG sermons, like those preached before the Incorporated Society, displayed a remarkable consistency across the eighteenth century. Both were typical products of the charity sermon genre, but they tell us something important about how the eighteenth-century English thought about their past. In the age of Hume and Gibbon, enlightened clerics still constructed and employed sacred histories to explain the larger purpose of England's Atlantic empire and to claim a role for the established Church of England within that empire. When the sacred histories started to come apart at their logical seams—as they did for the SPG preachers during the 1770s and early 1780s—it was not because of the triumph of rationalism or natural history but because the antagonists in the sacred history were not papists, proto-papists, heathens or barbarians but Anglophone Protestants 'attempting new and impracticable systems under new and delusive names and appearances' (North: 17).

Acknowledgements

I thank Bill Bulman, Bill Gibson, and Patrick Griffin for their generous assistance with this chapter.

References

The following abbreviations are used in the References.
ISD sermon = *Sermon Preached in...Dublin, before the Incorporated Society for Promoting Protestant Working Schools in Ireland*;
SCISD sermon = *Sermon Preached before the Society Corresponding with the Incorporated Society in Dublin for Promoting Protestant Working Schools in Ireland*;
SPG sermon = *Sermon Preached before the Society for the Propagation of the Gospel in Foreign Parts.*
Andrew, D. (1992). 'On Reading Charity Sermons: Eighteenth-Century Anglican Solicitation and Exhortation'. *Journal of Ecclesiastical History* 43: 1–11.
Armitage, D. (2000). *The Ideological Origins of the British Empire*. Cambridge: Cambridge University Press.
Barnard, T. (2008). *Improving Ireland?* Dublin: Four Courts.
Barnard, W. (1752). *ISD Sermon*. Dublin: S. Powell.
Bearcroft, P. (1745). *SPG Sermon*. London: Edward Owen.
Benson, M. (1740). *SPG Sermon*. London: J. and H. Pemberton.
Beresford, W. (1783). *ISD Sermon*. Dublin: George Perrin.
Beveridge, W. (1707). *SPG Sermon*. London: Joseph Downing.
Bickham, T. (2006). *Savages Within the Empire*. Oxford: Oxford University Press.
Bisse, P. (1718). *SPG Sermon*. London: Joseph Downing.
Bradford, S. (1720). *SPG Sermon*. London: John Wyatt.
Bulman, W. J. (2009). *Constantine's Enlightenment: Culture and Religious Politics in the Early British Empire, c.1648–1710*. PhD dissertation, Princeton University.
Canny, N. (1973). 'The Ideology of English Colonization: From Ireland to America'. *William and Mary Quarterly*, 3rd series, 30: 575–98.
Champion, J. (1992). *The Pillars of Priestcraft Shaken*. Cambridge: Cambridge University Press.
Clark, J. C. D. (2000). 'Protestantism, Nationalism and National Identity, 1660–1832'. *Historical Journal* 43: 249–76.
—— (2003). 'Providence, Predestination and Progress; Or, Did the Enlightenment Fail?' *Albion*. 35: 559–89.
Clark, P. (2000). *British Clubs and Societies, 1580–1800*. Oxford: Clarendon Press.
Clark, S. (1999). *Thinking with Demons*. Oxford: Oxford University Press.
Claydon, T. (2007). *Europe and the Making of England, 1660–1760*. Cambridge: Cambridge University Press.

Connolly, S. J. (1992). *Religion, Law and Power*. Oxford: Clarendon Press.
Conybeare, J. (1752). *SCISD Sermon*. London: J. Oliver.
Cox, M. (1748). *ISD Sermon*. Dublin: George Grierson.
Cresset, E. (1753). *SCISD Sermon*. London: Edward Owen.
Davies, C. (2002). *A Religion of the World*. Manchester: Manchester University Press.
Farooq, J. (2008). *London Sermon Culture, 1702–1763*. PhD thesis, University of Reading.
Fletcher, P. (1759). *SCISD Sermon*. London: J. Oliver.
George, W. (1749). *SPG Sermon*. London: J. Roberts.
Gregory, B. S. (2005). *Catholicism and Historical Research*. South Bend, IN: Erasmus Institute.
Griffin, P. (2007). *American Leviathan*. New York: Hill and Wang.
Griggs, T. (2007). 'Universal History from Counter-Reformation to Enlightenment'. *Modern Intellectual History* 4: 219–47.
[Hansard, J.] (1735). *A Brief Account of the Proceedings of the Incorporated Society in Dublin*. Dublin: n. p.
Hare, F. (1735). *SPG Sermon*. London: S. Buckley.
Harrison, P. (1990). *'Religion' and Religions in the English Enlightenment*. Cambridge: Cambridge University Press.
—— (2001). *The Bible, Protestantism, and the Rise of Natural Science*. Cambridge: Cambridge University Press.
—— (2007). *The Fall of Man and the Foundations of Modern Science*. Cambridge: Cambridge University Press.
Hayter, T. (1754). *SCISD Sermon*. London: J. Oliver.
—— (1755). *SPG Sermon*. London: Edward Owen.
Hayton, D. (1995). 'Did Protestantism Fail in Early Eighteenth-Century Ireland? Charity Schools and the Enterprise of Religious and Social Reformation, c.1690–1730', in A. Ford, J. McGuire, and K. Milne (eds.), *As by Law Established*: the Church of Ireland since the Reformation. Dublin: Lilliput, 166–86.
Herring, T. (1738). *SPG Sermon*. London: J. and J. Pemberton.
—— (1740). *SCISD Sermon*. London: M. Downing.
Howard, R. (1738). *ISD Sermon*. Dublin: George Grierson.
Hutchinson, S. (1761). *ISD Sermon*. Dublin: S. Powell.
Hutton, M. (1745a). *SCISD Sermon*. London: John Oliver.
—— (1745b). *SPG Sermon*. London: Edward Owen.
Ingram, R. G. (2010). ' "Popish Cut-Throats Against Us": Papists, Protestants and the Problem of Allegiance in Eighteenth-Century Ireland', in S. Taylor et al. (eds.), *From the Reformation to the Permissive Society*. Woodbridge: Boydell, 151–209.
Israel, J. (2002). *Radical Enlightenment*. Oxford: Oxford University Press.
Jacob, M., and Stewart, L. (2004). *Practical Matter: Newton's Science in the Service of Industry and Empire, 1687–1751*. Cambridge, MA: Harvard University Press.
Keene, E. (1755). *SCISD Sermon*. London: J. Oliver.
Lake, P. (1989). 'Antipopery: the Structure of a Prejudice', in R. Cust and A. Hughes (eds.), *Conflict in Early Stuart England*. London: Longman, 72–106.
—— (2006). 'Anti-Puritanism: The Structure of a Prejudice', in P. Lake and K. Fincham (eds.), *Religious Politics in Post-Reformation England*. Woodbridge: Boydell, 80–97.
Levine, J. (1995). 'Deists and Anglicans: The Ancient Wisdom and the Idea of Progress', in R. Lund (ed.), *The Margins of Orthodoxy*. Cambridge: Cambridge University Press, 219–39.

—— (2003). 'Matter of Fact in the English Revolution'. *Journal of the History of Ideas* 64: 317–35.
Lisle, S. (1748). *SPG Sermon*. London: Edward Owen.
Lloyd, S. (2009). *Charity and Poverty in England, c.1680–1820*. Manchester: Manchester University Press.
Lowth, R. (1773). *SCISD Sermon*. London: W. Oliver.
McBride, I. (2009). *Eighteenth-Century Ireland*. Dublin: Gill and Macmillan.
Maddox, I. (1740). *SCISD Sermon*. London: M. Downing.
Mann, I. (1775). *ISD Sermon*. Dublin: S. Powell.
Milne, K. (1997). *The Irish Charter Schools, 1730–1830*. Dublin: Lilliput.
Milton, A. (1995). *Catholic and Reformed*. Cambridge: Cambridge University Press.
Moss, C. (1772). *SPG Sermon*. London: T. Harrison and S. Brooke.
Newcome, R. (1761). *SPG Sermon*. London: E. Owen and T. Harrison.
North, B. (1778). *SPG Sermon*. London: T. Harrison and S. Brooke.
O'Brien, K. (1997). *Narratives of Enlightenment*. Cambridge: Cambridge University Press.
Pascoe, C. F. (1901). *Two Hundred Years of the S.P.G.* London: SPG.
Popkin, R. H. (2003). *The History of Scepticism: from Savonarola to Bayle*. Oxford: Oxford University Press.
Rose, C. (1991). 'Evangelical Philanthropy and Anglican Revival: The Charity Schools of Augustan London, 1698–1740'. *London Journal* 16: 35–66.
Rubiés, J.-P. (2006). 'Theology, Ethnography and the Historicization of Idolatry'. *Journal of the History of Ideas* 67: 571–96.
Rufford, F. (1779). *SPG Sermon*. London: E. Berrow.
Rundle, T. (1736). *ISD Sermon*. Dublin: R. Reily.
Scott, J. (2000). *England's Troubles*. Cambridge: Cambridge University Press.
Secker, T. (1757). *SCISD Sermon*. London: J. Oliver.
Shagan, E. (2010). 'Beyond Good and Evil: Thinking with Moderates in Early Modern England'. *Journal of British Studies* 49: 488–513.
Sheehan, J. (2006). 'Sacred and Profane: Idolatry, Antiquarianism and the Polemics of Distinction in the Seventeenth Century'. *Past and Present* 192: 35–66.
Sherlock, T. (1738). *SCISD Sermon*. London: J. and J. Pemberton.
Shipley, J. (1773). *SPG Sermon*. London: Thomas and John Fleet.
Sirota, B. (2007). *The Christian Monitors: Church, State and the Voluntary Sector in Britain, 1690–1720*. PhD dissertation, University of Chicago.
Smalbroke, R. (1733). *SPG Sermon*. London: J. Downing.
Spurr, J. (1993). 'The Church, the Societies and the Moral Revolution of 1688', in J. Walsh, S. Taylor, and C. Haydon (eds.), *The Church of England, c.1689–c.1833*. Cambridge: Cambridge University Press, 127–43.
—— (2006). '"A Special Kindness for Dead Bishops": The Church, History, and Testimony in Seventeenth-Century Protestantism', in P. Kewes (ed.), *The Uses of History in Early Modern England*. San Marino, CA: Huntington Library, 313–34.
Starkie, A. (2006). 'Contested Histories of the English Church: Gilbert Burnet and Jeremy Collier', in P. Kewes (ed.), *The Uses of History in Early Modern England*. San Marino, CA: Huntington Library, 335–47.
Stevens, L. (2005). 'Why Read Sermons? What Americans Can Learn from the Sermons of the Society for the Propagation of the Gospel in Foreign Parts'. *History Compass* 3: 1–19.

Strong, R. (2006). 'A Vision of Anglican Imperialism: The Annual Sermons of the SPG, 1701–1714'. *Journal of Religious History* 30: 175–98.

—— (2009). 'Rescuing the Perishing Heathen: The British Empire versus the Empire of Satan in Anglican Theology, 1701–1781'. *Studies in Church History* 45: 323–35.

Terrick, R. (1764). *SPG Sermon*. London: E. Owen and T. Harrison.

Thomas, J. (1743). *SCISD Sermon*. London: M. Downing.

—— (1751). *SPG Sermon*. London: Edward Owen.

Woolf, D. (2006). 'From Hystories to the Historical: Five Transitions in Thinking about the Past, 1500–1700', in P. Kewes (ed.), *The Uses of History in Early Modern England*. San Marino, CA: Huntington Library, 33–70.

Yonge, P. (1765). *SPG Sermon*. London: E. Owen and T. Harrison.

Young, J. (1766). *ISD Sermon*. Dublin: S. Powell.

CHAPTER 30

EIGHTEENTH-CENTURY MISSION SERMONS

ROWAN STRONG

Context

In the sense of Christian conversion of non-Christians, British mission sermons in the eighteenth century were not very common until the Evangelical Revival turned its attention to overseas missions, following the foundation of the Baptist Missionary Society in 1792 and similar Evangelical societies in that last decade of the eighteenth century. The one exception to this was the Society for the Propagation of the Gospel in Foreign Parts (SPG) founded in 1702 (all dates are New Style) as a chartered organization within the Church of England. In contrast to the prevailing historiography (Stanley: 55–6; Bebbington: 12, 40–2) I have argued elsewhere that the initiation of the SPG marks the true beginning of British missionary attention to non-Christian peoples, rather than the Evangelical societies at the end of the eighteenth century (Strong 2007: 12–18). While in the same place I have found that the later Evangelical mission discourse had much in common with the mission theology of the SPG, in other ways these later missions marked a watershed in British missionary history. Rejecting the eighteenth-century model of operation with its reliance on patronage and support networks around the wealthy and influential, the Evangelicals went public. They quickly mastered the commercial arts of advertising and publicity, and used activist, broadly based, voluntary societies with developed local groups to spread their message and agitate for change. The history of British missions, therefore, is not well served by the commonly adopted 'long eighteenth century'. Rather, it is a case of the short eighteenth century, with the 1790s demarcating a major shift in British missions, with the advent of multi-denominational, evangelical, activist missionary societies alongside the older SPG. Consequently, this chapter examines the annual anniversary sermons of the SPG from the society's foundation until the 1790s, when the SPG ceased to be the only British ecclesiastical organization preaching a new sermon genre, the mission sermon.

The SPG had three missions stipulated in its royal charter. They were, first, to provide clergy and resources for the English (and then British) colonies. Then there were the heathen indigenous populations of America. Thirdly, attention was paid to the Black slaves of British colonies. The SPG funded and resourced a stream of Anglican clergy going to America in this period and of colonial young men coming to England for the necessary episcopal ordination before returning home, due to the lack of a bishop in North America. This aspiration to be ordained contained a significant element of risk as not a few of them died on one or other crossing of the Atlantic. These colonized and colonizing peoples all came in for attention in the SPG sermons and, as a result, the SPG preachers began a process of a theological construction of their identities. While the metropolitan urging of mission towards these non-Christian groups was reasonably constant throughout the eighteenth-century sermons, it was not entirely aspirational on the colonial ground. A small minority of the SPG clergymen did make substantial efforts at native American and Black conversions, though more were induced to concentrate their efforts on the less risky and lucrative colonial congregations (Pestana: 171–3).

The SPG sought to engender support for its work by recruiting the backing of the rich and powerful, and by going public by printing its proceedings for a select, largely clerical, audience at home and in the colonies. Along with these printed proceedings the society published its annual anniversary sermons, preached each year to mark its foundation, usually in the London church of St Mary-le-Bow. The preachers were always drawn from the episcopal or senior ranks of the Anglican clergy.

The Preachers

There were only fourteen occasions on which the anniversary preacher was not a bishop. This minority group consisted mostly of English deans, some from major cathedrals, including Lincoln and Canterbury. The only preachers other than deans or bishops over this century were Thomas Hayley, canon of Chichester, in 1717; Edward Waddington, fellow of Eton College, in 1721; Zachary Pearce, vicar of St Martin's in the Fields, in 1730; and Philip Bearcroft, secretary of SPG, in 1745. The preachers among this small group of higher clergy all came within the first half of the eighteenth century. After 1749, when the preacher was William George, Dean of Lincoln, the sermons were invariably preached by bishops. Among the bishops who preached, only once did an archbishop undertake the task, and that was William Markham, Archbishop of York, in 1777. There was a surprising number of bishops (twenty-two) from the poor Welsh sees, and one from the Church of Ireland—St George Ashe, Bishop of Clogher in 1715 (though George Berkeley, Dean of Derry, preached in 1732). The English bishops (other than those from Wales) were generally those from the lesser sees. Among the wealthiest and most powerful English sees, the Bishops of Salisbury, Worcester, and Ely preached twice in the period. Those most frequently represented were Litchfield and Coventry (six times),

Norwich, Oxford, Lincoln, and Gloucester (five times each), followed by Chichester and Peterborough (four times each). Other sees represented among the preachers were Chester, Hereford, Carlisle, Bristol, Exeter, and Rochester. Along with the Welsh bishops, this geographical spread suggests that the strongest supporters of the SPG were the bishops in the west of the country, where, of course, shipping for the American colonies was concentrated. The surprising omission was the Bishop of London, whose see was traditionally responsible for clergy in overseas and colonial positions. However, this was not from lack of interest in the society by incumbents of the see. Thomas Sherlock, Bishop of London from 1748–1761, preached for the society in 1716 when he was Dean of Chichester. Other Bishops of London who preached earlier in their episcopal careers included Richard Osbaldeston in 1752, Richard Terrick in 1764, Robert Lowth in 1771, and Beilby Porteus in 1783 (Pascoe: 2:833–4). The Archbishop of Canterbury, by convention president and chair of the SPG board, was thereby not an appropriate preacher on such an occasion.

Politically, the bishops were a mixed bunch, particularly in the first decades of the society when, under the reigns of William III and Anne, Whigs and Tories were alternately in power (Strong 2006: 180–1). Once the Whig stranglehold on power began with the advent of the Hanoverian monarchy, the SPG's preachers were mostly of that ilk, as few Tories were promoted to the episcopal bench. Theologically, none of the preachers in this era were Evangelicals. The first Evangelical to become a bishop was Henry Ryder who was appointed Bishop of Gloucester in 1815, though he did preach for the SPG in 1819. Eighteenth-century theology in the Church of England was broadly consensual, with few supporting the extreme Erastianism of Bishop Hoadly, and was generally supportive of the divine claims of the Church to apostolic succession, the necessity of the sacraments, episcopal ordination, preaching, and the pastoral importance of priestly ministry. High Church episcopal positions were strengthened in the last quarter of the eighteenth century, prompted by the rise of theological liberalism over subscription to the Thirty-Nine Articles (Jacob: 23–5).

Scriptural Interpretation: Old Testament

Between 1702 and 1793 there were ninety-two sermons preached and all but one, Charles Lloyd's in 1703, were published. Of the published sermons the overwhelming majority were preached from New Testament texts. There were eighteen preachers who chose an Old Testament text and, of these, the most common book of the Bible chosen was, inevitably, Psalms (five sermons), which had been a catch-all source of proof-texts for Christian preachers for centuries. After this came Malachi and Isaiah with four sermons using texts drawn from them. The most commonly used verses from the Old Testament were Malachi 1:11 ('"For from the rising of the sun even unto the going down of the same my name shall be great among the Gentiles, and in every place incense shall be offered unto my name, and a pure offering: for my name shall be great among the heathen," saith the Lord') and Malachi 1:2. Also with two sermons based on them were Isaiah 49:6, Psalm 2:8, and Daniel 12:3.

The three sermons on Malachi are useful to analyse as they extend across the whole period. The first was by Gilbert Burnet, Bishop of Salisbury, in 1704; the second by Martin Benson, Bishop of Gloucester, in 1740 (both on Malachi 1:11); and the third, on Malachi 1:2, by Edward Smallwell, Bishop of Oxford, in 1791. Malachi 1:11 was to become one of the favourite texts for mission sermons in the nineteenth century, appealing because of its prophecy of advancement amongst the heathen (Tennant: 149). However, in the eighteenth century, other mission proof-texts which were to become common, such as Matthew 28:18–20, hardly stood out amongst the choices made by SPG preachers.

Burnet's take on Malachi begins by recounting the history of prophecy and knowledge of God vouchsafed to the Jews. He saw Malachi as a prophet urging the return to the religious reforms of Nehemiah, after religious degeneration has again set in within the Jerusalem cult. More specifically, Burnet saw Malachi as proclaiming the possibility that God would cast off the corrupt Jews and bring about what the text prophecies—namely, that the truth of God would be preached to the whole human race. Using ancient allegorical exegesis (Young: 846–7) Burnet exegetes 'incense' in the text as 'prayer', and 'the pure offering' it refers to as 'oblation' or worship. 'So the meaning of this Prophetick passage is that whereas the Knowledge of God was then confined to one Nation, and restrained to one Place what was to be opened afterwards to all Nationals and in all Place' (Burnet: 8). He then rehearsed, as a fulfilment of this prophecy, the history of Christian extension, first in the Roman empire, and continuing, but in a debased way, from the purity of the first centuries of Christianity.

Burnet is therefore well within the longstanding Anglican tradition which ascribed to the first centuries of the Church a purity due to proximity to the apostolic age that gave that period a peculiar authority in the history of the Church, second only to scripture. It was also an interpretation of the Christian past drawn from Protestant historiography that, since Luther, had viewed the Gospel as generally debased, or even ultimately lost, by the corruptions and superstitions of the Church of Rome. Particularly, Burnet lamented the missions of Rome that the discoveries of the New World by Portugal and Spain had prompted.

> The methods of Providence are unsearchable: for here was a Harvest, and that a great one, if it had fallen into good hands. The poor ignorant Natives were struck with admiration of their new Masters, and disposed to an entire Submission to them in all things, and might have easily been brought to the Faith of Christ: but as the Christianity that was offered them was only a ritual matter, accompanied by no Instruction; so the unexampled Cruelties and barbarities that almost exceeded belief with which they were treated, as they destroyed the greatest part of them, so they possessed the rest which escaped that savage Treatment with such unconquerable Prejudices against a Religion, which they are not able to examine or to distinguish, but take it in the gross-

ness from what appeared in those who first came among them, that twill be a Miracle indeed if ever they come to have just Impressions of it. (Burnet: 11–12)

So at the very commencement of this Anglican public mission discourse comes the traditional trope of anti-Catholicism doing theological duty in a new mission sphere. It would be reiterated by a number of other SPG preachers. White Kennett in 1712 preached against the Spanish missions associated with conquest, and attention turned to French missions when France replaced Spain as the pre-eminent national enemy under William III, who used his English crown as a new foundation for his on-going struggle against Louis XIV. So, in 1729, Bishop Egerton of Hereford promoted the SPG missions as a counter to the spread of Roman error by French missions in North America. More positively, in 1740, Martin Benson of Gloucester believed SPG missions represented a primitive, and hence a pure, English Christianity as an antidote to superstitious popery in North America (Strong 2007: 77–81).

Burnet next turned to what methods might be used to convert the natives of North America, as they were wild, infidel, and savage, and opted, unsurprisingly 'for the moral part of the Christian Religion' as this was self-evident to every person. Moral reform was a preoccupation of the Anglican clergy at the turn of the century, from High Church London clergy to Archbishop Tillotson. Burnet was to the fore in stressing its unifying appeal to all Protestants, an invaluable tool for national unity from a leading advocate of the new Williamite monarchy (Claydon: 161–3). Religion could be judged truthful because it made people 'just and charitable, sober and modest, sincere and faithful, compassionate and generous'. But this self-evident test of a religion's truth was threatened by the immoral behaviour of poorly-instructed Christian colonists in English colonies. Consequently, mission to the natives had to begin with instructing and reforming the colonists by schools and books. Having made a good beginning at home with the institution of the Society for Promoting Christian Knowledge, this work now proceeded 'to the remote and dark corners of the Earth' in the mission of the SPG, supported by the new Williamite succession (Burnet: 16–24).

Finally, Burnet adduced a number of reasons for supporting the work of the SPG. They were a remedy to the reproaches of Rome for neglecting mission; a censure of neglect that Burnet acknowledged his Church deserved. It was a just return for the wealth generated by the colonies for many in Burnet's metropolitan audience, especially in the City of London, as well as something owing to God from whence those blessings of wealth ultimately derived. This would secure the English in divine favour (Burnet: 25–9). This anxiety about the security of England in the divine economy, as early as the third SPG sermon, mirrors the fear that John Spurr has concluded to be a characteristic of the post-Restoration Church of England (Spurr: 236–49).

Forty years later when Martin Benson turned his attention as a preacher to the same verse in the book of Malachi he preached a comparatively hard-hitting sermon. He confined his specific exegesis of the verse to a short introductory paragraph, concluding that it predicted the universality of the Christian Gospel, whose completion required the cooperation of human agency. This was requisite, first, because the Christian religion was for the universal benefit of all mankind and there was a commensurate duty to spread the knowledge of it. Benson unquestionably asserted what would now be called the globalization of Christianity as divinely proclaimed by the Old Testament prophets and by Jesus himself. Attacking the Enlightenment Deist writers with their own rationalist and universalizing weapons, Benson claimed that Christianity was the surest support for 'a more rational Rule of Private Life, and surer support of Publick Society' than anything devised by ancient philosophers or 'Modern Unbelievers'. Belief in eternal life based on divine judgement in this one made us both content in ourselves and prompted charity to others, compared with debased gods of polytheism who engendered the same immorality in those who worshipped them (Benson: 1–11).

But Benson confined most of his sermon to extrapolating on the second requirement of the Christian Gospel: that not only was it a general duty to spread the knowledge of it, but it was more particularly the obligation of the British in their American colonies, because it gave Britain an opportunity of making a spiritual return for the material wealth she derived from her colonies, and sowed loyalty among colonial populations. 'Do we imagine, that if these People have no Faith towards God, they will have any Fidelity to their King?' (Benson: 13). So, upon the merchant especially fell this obligation of promoting the cause of true religion, not only among English colonists but also among the native Americans to whom civil life needed to be shown, 'to make them *Men* before we can make them *Christians*' (Benson: 14). Arguing against those who claimed that bringing civilization to indigenous peoples also corrupted their rustic virtues with European vices, Benson maintained this was merely the innocence of brutes who only lacked the means for the indulgence of vice, not the will. Anglican SPG preachers would have little truck with the concept of the sinless, naturally virtuous savage, whose profile would be given such a boost by Rousseau in the 1760s.

What was lacking in the colonial world was a 'purity of morals' for effective mission, particularly because of the introduction of alcohol and disease. 'Who can blame a Savage, that when he observes the Cruelty, the Treachery, the Lewdness, the Baseness of one, who calls himself a Christian, he scorns to be called by the same Name, and become a Proselyte to such a Religion?' (Benson: 17). Instead of missionaries Britain sent America 'Our Felons and Convicts: Whom being too bad to be suffered to live here, we think however good enough for our *Colonies*' (Benson: 18). People risked life and limb to gain colonial wealth, but neglected their spiritual condition. So the colonial English, with their dubious morals and questionable trading practices, were, paradoxically, an obstacle to mission. Benson applied this discourse of colonial spiritual debasement particularly to slave owners; or, possibly he had in mind British slave traders with his remark about those who 'compass Sea and Land to gain even a small matter'.

> They will compass Sea and Land to gain even a small matter, but out of the great gains they will not contribute one farthing towards humanizing and instructing these poor Wretches. Nay even they oppose the Instruction of Those who are the most serviceable to them, the African slaves, upon a bare suspicion, lest their being instructed in what regards their eternal Interest, should prejudice the little worldly

interests of their masters. It is hard to say, whether the Wickedness or the Folly of these Men is greater. They have been assured by the ablest Lawyers... that the Law makes no Alteration in the outward State of these poor Creatures, on their becoming Christians: And the meanest Divine is able to shew them, that the Gospel makes none. Surely then it is not likely, that they should make the worse Servants for being taught to serve faithfully and diligently from a Principle of Conscience. And since for our Advantage they are treated with so great Rigour in this World, we ought to take great Care to lay before them the Prospect in Rest and Happiness in another. (Benson: 19–20)

Unlike the early Christians the English had grown weary of Christianity because they had had it so long. Making a disturbing point in the midst of the War of Austrian Succession, Benson stated that British weariness in the divine could also weary the patience of God, so that they could lose providential support in their war with the French (Benson: 22). He was drawing a decided divine conditionality over British commerce and slavery, without going as far as to condemn slavery or the slave trade outright.

Finally, Benson addressed himself to contemporary criticisms of the missionary methods of the SPG. As with Burnet, the lack of any direct or personal experience of mission did not prevent the SPG preachers from proposing ways in which mission should proceed in their society. Among the problems identified by Benson was the futility of sending out unqualified or morally unsuitable clergymen, though he distinguished the careful selection of SPG clergymen from those who went to the colonies of their own choosing. Even better candidates could be found if critics were to fund the society more bountifully. But the Church of England lacked the advantages of its Roman rival in not having religious orders to send missionaries where the need was. Neither did it have colonial bishops to supervise missionaries; nor was it able to use the coercion of the colonial power (Benson: 23–5).

Malachi was last preached on in this period by Bishop Edward Smallwell of Oxford in 1791. Again seeing Malachi's prophecy as relating to the coming Kingdom of God under Christ, in his comparatively short sermon Smallwell asserted that true believers would want to contribute to the promotion of this desirable end. But he was conscious of contemporary millenarian speculation and sectarian activity, and warned against improper speculations of those who wanted to identify the fulfilment time of God's designs (Smallwell: 4). The sermon predates the emergence of the millenarian prophets Joanna Southcott and Richard Brothers in England; the best-known millenarian sect in 1791 was the Buchanites of Dumfriesshire and Ayrshire in the 1780s (Söderstrom). The bishop went on to identify certain preliminary conditions for Christ's return. The Gentile had to be converted, along with Israel which would return to its promised land, and neither of these conditions looked like being fulfilled in the near future. Other obstacles included the far from adequate devotion to God around the world and general dissipation and worldliness. Then there were national hostilities and 'a desire for greater power, a thirst for further conquest'. Infidelity also, especially with regard to the Holy Trinity, and strife over revealed religion, were further factors in pushing the completion of God's purposes further off by promoting Christian disunity and discord. All these issues hindered the purposes of the SPG being achieved. But the bishop first exhorted his audience to begin at home, which must have been somewhat frustrating to supporters of an overseas focus for the society. 'Let us, as a nation, correct our own morals and our own faith, before we undertake to teach these duties to others.' Belatedly, in his final two paragraphs, the bishop got around to the real work of the society in a rhetorical exhortation in favour of the SPG, speaking of the joy consequent upon the conversion of the 'unenlightened Indians'. Probably Smallwell would have derived more joy from an increase of obedient English Christians, keeping at bay the political and social upheavals from France, than from any conversions of remote 'Indians'. Compared with his predecessors, Smallwell's focus on the SPG and its missionary purpose was slight.

Scriptural Interpretation: New Testament

Among the New Testament texts chosen by the society's preachers, the most popular books proved to be the Gospel of Matthew (eighteen sermons), Paul's Letter to the Romans (ten), and the Book of Acts (nine). Other New Testament books used more than twice were the Gospels of Mark, Luke, and John, and the Letter of Paul to the Galatians. The most frequently used texts from Matthew were 28:18–20 and 6:10 ('Thy kingdom come'), but both were only used three times. These were followed by texts used twice: Matthew 9:36–8 and 13:31–32. While the Gospel of Matthew was the predominant book of the New Testament used, there was no outstanding proof-text drawn upon by these eighteenth-century mission preachers to promote their cause. Even Matthew 28:18–20, a favourite of missionary preachers in the next century (known as the Great Commission from its ringing endorsement of proclaiming the Gospel to all nations) was used by only three preachers. The other equally used text, Matthew 6:10, will be explored here because of its greater chronological spread throughout the period. It was used for the anniversary sermon in 1725, 1747, and 1788.

Bishop John Wynne of St Asaph chose the text 'Thy Kingdom come' for his 1725 sermon. It was an average length homily of thirty-one printed pages. Commending the Lord's Prayer as a short compendium of Christian life grounded in dominical authority, Wynne set out to exegete the passage, then to apply it generally to Christian life, and finally more specifically to the occasion of the sermon. This was a general pattern of many of the SPG sermons, which overwhelmingly fell into an exhortatory mode. This is hardly surprising, as the fundamental purpose of the preachers was to exhort their London audience, and, in their published sermons, their wider public, to support the SPG cause, both financially and, among the clergy, to consider a colonial career.

The exegesis Wynne proposed was that the Kingdom of God had already come in its fullness in God's sovereign rule over all God's creation, but there was another kingdom, the rule of Jesus Christ through his Church. Consequently, to pray 'thy Kingdom come' was to desire the full establishment of Christ's kingdom over all the world, which entailed duties on the part of the Christian. Wynne spent considerable time advocating the necessity of personal commitment as the basis for the conversion of others (Wynne: 15–16). Just as the English were originally converted by the 'zealous Labours and travels of those, who came from very remote Countries', so they should bring to others the Gospel of redemption whose saving knowledge can only be known through revelation.

From that general exhortation to spread the Gospel by charitable actions which witness to the truth that is in us, Wynne applied his exegesis more specifically. Reviewing the Christian past he proposed the same theological history as Burnet before him; of a general decay of Christianity subsequent to the early Church. Countries formerly Christian had lost the Gospel, or had it 'depraved and adulterated', of which the Roman Church was the chief exemplar. From this degenerating Christianity the Church of England emerged at the Reformation purified and renewed: 'we had the happiness to be among the first that shook off the Papal Yoke, and all that mass of errors and Abuses, under which a great Part of the Christian World had long groan'd, and reduced our Doctrine and Worship to its primitive and original standard' (Wynne: 25). Preoccupied with defending itself from Roman attacks, or with internal disputes, the Church of England had neglected mission, or what Wynne called 'the common Cause of Christianity', but the extension of British colonies and commerce had opened a door for the Church to propagate the Gospel among infidels, though it continued to be hampered by inattention to domestic mission, and by a lack of organization. This latter obstacle had now been rectified by the founding of the SPG. So Wynne concluded with a peroration in which the infidel was overlooked in favour of the maintenance of religion among the colonizing incomers.

> But the many Labourers that have been sent into that harvest, by the Care, and under the Direction of this Society, a Spirit of Piety and Religion is stirr'd up among many of those, tho, for want of Teachers and Instructors, and of Persons and Places necessary for the due Celebration of the Publick Worship of God, had scarce anything left of Christianity, besides the bare name. The Effects of this are visibly seen, in the good Disposition of the People, in many Places, to receive Instruction; in the longing Desire they express to have more pastors and Ministers settled among them; in their Forwardness to contribute, according to their Ability, towards Building of Churches, and Erecting of Schools, for the Instruction of their Youth in the Principles and Duties of Religion, as well as other parts of useful learning. (Wynne: 29–30)

In 1747 Bishop John Thomas of Lincoln preached a short sermon (just twenty-one printed pages) on the same text. Like Wynne, Thomas posited two kingdoms—the eternal rule of God the creator over his creation, and that of Christ advancing on earth through the propagation of the Christian religion. Again, like his predecessor, he pointed out that Christ's kingdom advanced only insofar as Christians had an authentic belief in Christ (Thomas: 6). To pray this prayer and do nothing was an abuse of prayer, so Christians had a duty to promote the extension of genuine Christian faith. But a disjunction with this evangelistic duty was evident, Thomas proclaimed, in the way in which churches in England were 'almost deserted', while others attacked the prophecies and miracles that constituted the evidence of Christianity, so that there was a 'general lukewarmness, or Indifference in matters of Religion'. Only in the final section of his sermon, three pages before the end, did Thomas get round to overseas mission. But, like Wynne before him, he was more concerned with the maintenance of his Church among colonists than propagating the Gospel among non-Christian native Americans.

> This Society was erected for Receiving, Managing, and Disposing of Charity towards the maintaining of Missionaries, and making other necessary Provisions for the Propagation of the Gospel in Foreign Parts, upon Information received, that in many of our Colonies beyond the Seas, the Provision for Ministers was very mean; and in others of them, for lack of Support and Maintenance of a Ministry, many of His Majesty's Subjects wanted the Administration of God's Word and Sacraments, and seemed abandoned, some to Atheism and Infidelity, and others to Popish Superstition and Idolatry. (Thomas: 19)

It was only in the second to last paragraph that Thomas explicitly mentioned, in passing, 'the poor Negroes, and the native Indians bordering on our Settlements', while acknowledging the greater missionary efforts of the Church of Rome in 'spreading her Errors and Superstition, than we are in propagating a pure Religion'. Like a number of the SPG preachers, mostly bishops with pressing domestic diocesan responsibilities and too few resources to meet them, mission was primarily a matter of battling the Church's opponents at home, such as anti-miraculous, rationalist Deists, before it was involvement with colonial conversions (Gregory: 287–95). It was hard enough for the SPG, dependent like all missionary societies upon voluntary support, to develop the widespread consensus necessary for its work in colonial missions, always a case of 'out of sight, out of mind' for most politicians or ecclesiastics. Their case for support was not helped by some of their preachers for whom domestic concerns clearly outweighed foreign ones.

The last preacher using this petition of the Lord's Prayer as his text was the aristocratic James Cornwallis, Bishop of Lichfield and Coventry, in 1788. This episcopal fourth Earl Cornwallis was more attuned to the colonial mission of the SPG than some of his predecessors. He began immediately to identify populations which had lost sight of the spiritual Kingdom of God, which he defined as an obedience to divine directions. The first of these were the Heathen whose 'erroneous conclusions' about the divine, lacking revelation, produced idolatry and immorality, against which the Old Testament prophets witnessed, supported by the divine dispensation of reward and punishment for virtue and vice. This was evidenced in the history of the Jews, when national depravity brought about their national destruction, though Cornwallis was clear that this divine sentence only applied to the generation alive in the siege of Jerusalem in 70 AD. While the Kingdom of God was gradually moving toward its establishment in the history of the Jews, and in the moral ancient philosophers, it was accelerated by the advent of Christ (Cornwallis: ix–xi). Reaching the SPG in the middle of his sermon, Cornwallis believed that the work of the society in recovering new lands for Christianity balanced the loss of Christian lands to Islam (Cornwallis: xvi–xvii). In contrast to the Catholic expansion in the east and in America, the exertions of the SPG were guided by the 'true profession of Christianity, which Protestantism hath since extended' to 'our distant emigrants' and 'their savage neighbours' (Cornwallis: xviii). But, taking up a refrain of a number of the society's preachers since Bishop Charles Trimnell of Norwich in 1710, Cornwallis stated that the society's missionaries might have been even more effective had there been a bishop in America.

Finally, Cornwallis turned to the subject of 'heathen Indians' and 'the oppressed Negroes' and that 'degree of civilization' which was necessary for effective conversion. While agriculture may prove useful for the former it would not with the latter, who needed their suffering alleviated. 'Of what peculiar advantage then will the expounder of the Gospel be possessed, should the rigours of a servitude, repugnant to our best feelings, and degrading to human nature, happily subside!' (Cornwallis: xxiii). Would not slaves be interested in the religion of anyone who interested themselves in their welfare, Cornwallis asked rhetorically. But he ducked giving any answer to his own question, merely concluding his sermon by a general exhortation to ground their missionary work in Truth, but without identifying what exactly that was. Perhaps his hearers understood that the urging of the amelioration of the conditions of slavery was a self-evident lesson for the society with its own slave plantations? If so, the prompting fell fruitless upon the society as it ran up against the Scylla of inadequate supervision from London and the Charybdis of local planter culture supporting the slave economy (Strong 2007: 87–91).

Elaborated Sermons

We can be reasonably confident that, given their comparatively short length (twenty to thirty printed pages) these sermons were generally printed in the form in which they were delivered, with the exception of some footnotes. Like other sermons domestically, those of the SPG preachers varied in length (Jacob: 262–3). Most seem to have been about three-quarters of an hour long, if the printed editions are any guide; though some, those printed at sixteen to eighteen pages, were clearly shorter.

However, among these missionary sermons there were some much lengthier in their printed form and these were clearly substantially elaborated from their original spoken genre. Among the longest published sermons were those of John Moore in 1713 (forty-seven pages), and Richard Smallbroke in 1733 (forty-six pages); but these were dwarfed by the effort of John Denne, Archdeacon of Rochester, whose 1731 sermon ran to seventy-six printed pages. Both Smallbroke and Denne were clearly troubled by the rise of Deism in the 1730s, and they used their sermons to construct a particular view of the mission field of America in the light of this anxiety. This concern was clearly heightened by the publication of Matthew Tindal's *Christianity as old as Creation* in 1730, for Denne cites that work as early as page 7 of his sermon in support of the view that Christianity restored a rational understanding of monotheism to a polytheistic ancient world (Denne: 7n.), and cites the work as evidence for the existence of Deism throughout the sermon. Both preachers viewed the work of the SPG in America as creating the Christian conditions for that land to become an asylum for the Church of England and English Christianity should Deism overturn orthodoxy at home (Denne: 62; Smallbroke: 44). So length did not necessarily translate into a focus that benefited the core business of the society, which was the maintenance and promotion of Anglican Church extension to colonists and non-Christian populations in America.

But some of the lengthier sermons were by very strong supporters of the society, who did concentrate on the missionary imperatives of the Gospel as they understood it. Among such preachers whose sermons ran from thirty to forty-odd pages were White Kennett, Dean of Peterborough, in 1712; Thomas Secker, Bishop of Oxford, in 1741; William Warburton, Bishop of Gloucester, in 1766; and Beilby Porteus, Bishop of Chester, in 1783. All eventually rose to some of the highest positions in the Church of England. White Kennett became Bishop of Peterborough; Secker, liking the piety, if not the enthusiasm, of the Methodists, became Archbishop of Canterbury in 1758; William Warburton, who also disliked Methodistical enthusiasm, was the leading theologian of his day; while Porteus, Bishop of London from 1787, was a non-Calvinist supporter of both the Church Missionary Society and the British and Foreign Bible Society.

Kennett saw a commitment to mission in North America as a consequence of God allowing the English to 'discover' it. God gave them colonies and an empire; they were subsequently required to spread the Gospel in 'their' lands (Kennett: 31–2). Like many SPG preachers, he was preoccupied by Anglican competition with Catholic missions. Their Catholic rivals had created an obstacle to mission among the native Americans by disguising conquest with religion and ignoring their natural and hereditary right to their land. The English, on the other hand, merely took over '*Derelict Lands*' abandoned by their former inhabitants. But colonial trade also meant that material gain had become an end in itself, rather than religious goals, threatening, Kennett maintained, to make English colonization just like its rapacious Spanish rival (Kennett: 5–11, 12–17). Three decades later Indian conversion was also on the mind of Thomas Secker, who propounded in 1741 the view that the barbarous way of life of native Americans placed them at the opposite end of the (English) civilized scale. They were steeped in 'the vilest Superstitions', locked into warfare, and regarded human life cheaply (Secker: 9). This construction of a barbarous native American militancy was heedless of Britain's own contemporary involvement in the War of the Austrian Succession.

Warburton in his 1766 sermon also thought native Americans 'Savages without Law or religion' who needed to be civilized before they could be converted (Warburton: 17–18). However, he devoted most of his sermon to the Black slaves and the godless iniquity of the slave trade, which he saw as an idolatrous serving of the 'GOD of GAIN', and slave owners as 'worshippers of Mammon', flinging fury on them for conceiving of human beings as property.

> Gracious God! To talk (as in herds of cattle) of property in rational creatures! Creatures endowed with all our faculties, possessing all our qualities but that of colour; our BRETHREN both by Nature and Grace, shocks all the feelings of humanity, and the dictates of common sense. But alas! What is there in the infinite *abuses* of Society which does not shock them! Yet nothing is more certain in itself, and apparent to all, than that the infamous traffic for Slaves, directly infringes both divine and moral Law. Nature created Man, free: and Grace invites him to assert his Freedom. (Warburton: 25–6)

Warburton's tirade might have packed more punch if he hadn't gone on to excuse the SPG, which had been a slave owner itself since 1710 when General Christopher Codrington bequeathed them his slave estates in Barbados. The society, asserted Warburton, was only 'an innocent partaker of the fruits of this iniquitous traffic', and he tamely advised them to ameliorate slavery in the West Indies 'within the limits of our own property' (Warburton: 27–9). This advocacy of the Christianization of slavery was of a piece with similar views propounded by contemporaries such as the Quaker George Fox in Barbados, and Cotton Mather in Massachusetts, although a few, including some Quakers and the Anglican High Churchman Granville Sharpe, were by then publicly calling for the abolition of the slave trade (Brown 2006a: 521; 2006b: 172–3).

Porteus was preaching at the conclusion of the American War of Independence, and Britain's defeat in that conflict. He was able to speak about colonial conditions with some personal experience, as his parents had been tobacco planters in Virginia, presumably a slave estate. The bishop clearly wanted to refocus the attention of the society's supporters from the lost North American colonies to Britain's Caribbean possessions, so his sermon too was devoted to missions among the Black slaves there. He railed against slave owners' opposition to baptism, notwithstanding being assured the rite would not have the consequence of legal emancipation; and against the slaves' dehumanizing conditions, with too little leisure for religious instruction. As a result slaves were without God and given to gross immorality. Like Burnet and Benson before him Porteus was not reticent about giving practical advice to his mission society, a feature of mission sermons that began well before the nineteenth century (Tennant: 156). Porteus wanted to turn the slaves into smallholders, with secure legal rights, including marriage. He thought that the slaves should become accustomed to a life similar to that of English agricultural labourers, learning to appreciate monetary rewards for their labour. These practical reforms, plus the hope of gradual progress to freedom would make them more appreciative of the Anglican Christianity of their owners. The society should use its own slave plantations to implement this scheme as a model for others (Porteus: 15–16, 20–9).

> Let then our fellow countrymen make haste to relieve, as far as they are able, the calamities they have brought on so large a part of the human race; let them endeavour to wipe away the reproach of having delivered so many of their fellow creatures to a most heavy temporal bondage, both by contributing to sooth and alleviate that

as much as possible, and by endeavouring to rescue them from the still more cruel bondage of ignorance and sin. (Porteus: 33)

The key word here is 'alleviate' rather than 'emancipate'. By the late 1740s the SPG and its preachers were becoming uneasy about the slave trade, though not so much about slavery itself (Strong 2007: 95). They advocated a policy of amelioration of slavery, not its abandonment; a policy that was a dismal failure even on its own slave plantation in Barbados (Bennett: 221).

Conclusion

Lacking either the dedicated personnel of Catholic missions or the established mechanism of mission at the start of the eighteenth century, the SPG preachers were part of the process that Jeffrey Cox has labelled 'confessional improvisation' for its unprecedented missionary endeavour (Cox: 23). As they constructed a new missionary worldview a strong belief developed that the English, and later the British, had had their empire bestowed on them by providence. This corresponded with many non-missionary sermons which also detected the particular blessing of God upon the nation identified with the Glorious Revolution and safeguarding of liberty (Jacob: 264–5). But the SPG preachers saw this providential guidance of Britain as strictly conditional. It would continue as long as Britain spent some of the substance that it derived from the colonies upon evangelizing that empire and maintaining the Church of England there. Prior to the end of the American War of Independence in 1783, this divine requirement for support of the colonial Church became increasingly focused on the granting of a colonial bishopric in America, a condition that was never achieved before that date because of British political caution, colonial indifference, and the strength of Dissenting lobbying (Bridenbaugh).

Generally, throughout the eighteenth century, the SPG mission sermons constructed identities for the various colonial North American and, to a lesser extent, West Indian populations that were the targets of SPG missions. Colonists, by leaving England and the ministrations of the Church, were regarded as people at risk of lapsing into the non-practice of, or, worse, the non-belief in their metropolitan faith, as they slid from their English Christian identity. Consequently, Church extension to colonists was as much mission as maintenance (Strong: 71–6). The native Americans were heathens, immoral, and without God in the world. Consequently they were given to immorality that would eventually damn them, without the saving knowledge of the Gospel of Jesus Christ. Their burden of inferiority was compounded by their lack of 'civilization', understood as European economic life and culture. Until their reconstruction was achieved through conversion, commerce based on settled agricultural smallholding, and literacy, they were brutes needing to be made men, and then turned into Christians. While native Americans came to the attention of the society's preachers almost from the beginning, slaves did so particularly from the 1740s. Once the slaves had surfaced in the SPG's attention their condition was adjudged deplorable but redeemable, in a policy of Christianization and increasing advocacy of improving their material life but not abolishing their slavery; a policy that the SPG could not even successfully mandate on its own Barbados slave plantations.

REFERENCES

Bebbington, D. (1989). *Evangelicalism in Modern Britain: A History from the 1730s to the 1980s*. London: Unwin Hyman.
Bennett Jr, J. H. (1950). 'The Society for the Propagation of the Gospel's plantations, and the emancipation crisis', in S. C. McCulloch (ed.), *British Humanitarianism: Essays Honouring Frank J. Klingberg*. Philadelphia: Church Historical Society, 15–29.
Benson, M. (1740). *SPG Anniversary Sermon*. London: J. and H. Pemberton.
Bridenbaugh, C. (1962). *Mitre and Sceptre: Transaltantic Faiths, Ideas, Personalities, and Politics 1689–1775*. New York: Oxford University Press.
Brown, C. L. (2006a). 'Christianity and the Campaign Against Slavery and the Slave Trade', in S. J. Brown and T. Tackett (eds.), *The Cambridge History of Christianity: Enlightenment, Reawakening and Revolution 1660–1815*. Cambridge: Cambridge University Press, 517–35.
—— (2006b). *Moral Capital: Foundations of British Abolitionism*. Chapel Hill: University of North Carolina Press.
Burnet, G. (1704). *SPG Anniversary Sermon*. London: Joseph Dowling.
Claydon, T. (1996). *William III and the Godly Revolution*. Cambridge: Cambridge University Press.
Cornwallis, J. (1788). *SPG Anniversary Sermon*. London: T. Harrison and S. Brooke.
Cox, J. (2008). *The British Missionary Enterprise since 1700*. New York: Routledge.
Denne, J. (1731). *SPG Anniversary Sermon*. London: J. Downing.
Gregory, J. (2000). *Restoration, Reformation and Reform 1660–1828: Archbishops of Canterbury and Their Diocese*. Oxford: Clarendon Press.
Jacob, W. M. (2007). *The Clerical Profession in the Long Eighteenth Century*. Oxford: Oxford University Press.
Kennett, W. (1712). *SPG Anniversary Sermon*. London: J. Downing.
Pascoe, C. F. (1901). *Two Hundred Years of the SPG: An Historical Account of the Society for the Propagation of the Gospel in Foreign Parts 1701–1900*. London: SPG.
Pestana, C. G. (2009). *Protestant Empire: Religion and the Making of the British Atlantic World*. Philadelphia: University of Pennsylvania Press.
Porteus, B. (1783). *SPG Anniversary Sermon*. London: T. Harrison and S. Brooke.
Secker, T. (1741). *SPG Anniversary Sermon*. London: J. and H. Pemberton.
Smallbroke, R. (1733). *SPG Anniversary Sermon*. London: J. Downing.
Smallwell, E. (1791). *SPG Anniversary Sermon*. London: S. Brooke.
Söderstrom, J. (2002). 'Escaping the Common Lot: A Buchanite Perspective of the Millennium'. *Studies in Church History* 37: 243–54.
Spurr, J. (1991). *The Restoration Church of England 1646–1689*. New Haven, CT: Yale University Press.
Stanley, B. (1990). *The Bible and the Flag: Protestant Missions and British Imperialism in the Nineteenth and Twentieth Centuries*. Leicester: Apollos.

Strong, R. (2006). 'A Vision of an Anglican Imperialism: The Annual Sermons of the Society for the Propagation of the Gospel in Foreign Parts 1701–1714'. *Journal of Religious History* 30: 175–98.

—— (2007). *Anglicanism and the British Empire c.1700–1850*. Oxford: Oxford University Press.

Tennant, B. (2010). 'Missions, Slavery, and the Anglican Pulpit, 1780–1850', in Robert H. Ellison (ed.), *A New History of the Sermon: The Nineteenth Century*. Leiden: Brill, 139–80.

Thomas, J. (1747). *SPG Anniversary Sermon*. London: J. Roberts.

Warburton, W. (1766). *SPG Anniversary Sermon*. London: E. Owen and T. Harrison.

Wynne, J. (1725). *SPG Anniversary Sermon*. London: Joseph Downing.

Young, F. M. (2008). 'Interpretation of Scripture', in S. A. Harvey and D. G. Hunter (eds.), *The Oxford Handbook of Early Christian Studies*. Oxford: Oxford University Press, 845–63.

CHAPTER 31

THE SERMON IN THE BRITISH COLONIES

JOANNA CRUICKSHANK

This chapter is concerned with the sermon in the British colonies. As the other chapters in this volume demonstrate, within Britain the sermon was a long-established, highly theorized, and widely propagated form of public speech and published text. What happened to this genre when preachers and publishers began to develop and deliver sermons in the widely varying contexts of the colonies? How were sermons disseminated and received across the empire? The answers to these questions have the potential to tell us much, not only about the global history of the modern British sermon, but also about the place of Christianity in colonial life.

The primary focus of this chapter is on sermons delivered to, read by, or intended for British colonists, which distinguishes it somewhat from that dealing with sermons preached about the British empire and that examining sermons preached by British missionaries. There are, of course, areas of overlap, as British preachers in the colonies often addressed congregations of both colonists and colonized. However, this chapter is concerned with those sermons which were preached to colonists by visiting and colonial clergy and lay preachers of all kinds, as well as those disseminated among colonists in print form by local and metropolitan publishers.

Given the scattered nature of existing scholarship on this topic, the purpose of this chapter is neither to provide a lengthy literature review nor an exhaustive overview of colonial sermons. Rather, the aim is to open up this potentially vast field of study by demonstrating the value of the sermon as a source for understanding colonial life and culture. The chapter begins with a general discussion of the sermon in the British colonies, drawing on existing studies to identify key themes and areas of investigation that may be fruitful for further study. This discussion draws on examples from the North American colonies, from 1688 until independence, and from India in the eighteenth and nineteenth centuries and the Cape Colony in the nineteenth century. Following these broader reflections, the remainder of the chapter is devoted to a case study of the sermon in early colonial Australia.

Scholarship on the Sermon in the British Colonies

Colonial sermons receive little attention in most existing scholarship on either the sermon or colonialism. The notable exception to this is in the case of the Puritan colonies in North America. Puritan colonists brought with them from Britain a theology in which the sermon was of great importance, understood as what Cotton Mather would in 1726 call 'a nett of salvation' (Bosco: 158). In New England, the settlers were able to develop a society which reflected this conviction, placing preaching at the heart of communal life (Gordis: 9). Into the eighteenth century, the sermon was seen as the focus of Sabbath services and preaching as the key task of the minister. Sabbath sermons were complemented by a wide range of weekday sermons, which might be preached at fast days, election days, days of thanksgiving, or executions. In weekday sermons, ministers were more likely to go beyond the central theme of salvation to comment on public events and the life of the community (Butler: 172).

The obvious political and cultural importance of the sermon in colonial New England has led to many studies of the Puritan sermon, particularly since the publication of Perry Miller's two-volume work *The New England Mind*. Miller used the changes he identified in Puritan sermons to chart developments in colonial culture and identity. Miller's reliance on the printed sermon divided historians and literary scholars over the value of sermons as an indicator of broader social realities, but also stimulated interest in the Puritan sermon, reflected in a stream of books and articles, some of which are discussed below (see for example Elliot; Bercovitch; Lowance; Gordis). In *The New England Soul*, Stout made an important intervention in this debate by examining 2,000 manuscript sermons, where previous scholarship had focused almost entirely on published sermons.

Other North American colonies have received less attention from scholars, though scholarship on the 'Great Awakening' includes some substantial studies of revival preaching, discussed in more detail below. This is partly a consequence of the availability of sources, as far fewer printed sermons were produced by colonists other than New England Puritans. In the eighteenth century, sermons made up nearly 13 per cent of all domestic publishing in the North American colonies and more than half of these were published in Massachusetts (D. D. Hall: 155). However, a lack of printed sermons does not necessarily imply that sermons were unimportant in these colonies. In colonial Virginia, for example, church attendance was compulsory and preaching was seen as the first and most important of the Anglican parson's duties (Nelson: 278, 201; Bond).

Beyond North America, preaching among colonists receives little or no attention in recent major surveys of English-language preaching in the modern period (Old 2006, 2009; Edwards 2004), though Old discusses some African preachers, like Bishop Samuel Ajayi Crowther, who preached to colonists (See Old 2009: 204–15). Similarly, a focus on sermons remains rare among colonial historians and literary scholars as a whole. In part, this may reflect contemporary concerns and realities about the irreligion of colonists in much of the British empire. Regular church attendance was patchy across the North American colonies during the eighteenth century—varying from around two-thirds of New England adults to only 15 per cent of adults in New York in the middle of the century (Gould: 22). In India and Australia, clergy and devout colonists repeatedly lamented the low rates of church attendance, to which freedom from social expectation, low numbers of clergy, and lack of church buildings could contribute (Neill: 23). In Australia, of which much more will be said later, in the middle of the nineteenth century only around 20 per cent of the settler population attended church regularly (Breward: 166). In India, where church attendance was difficult to quantify, although major centres such as Madras and Calcutta were regularly supplied with chaplains by the East India Company, British people living further from the centres of colonial power might have few opportunities to hear sermons preached (Neill: 106, 112; O'Connor).

Nonetheless, as Indian examples show, colonists were exposed to sermons not only in church services, but also in printed form, through open-air preaching or in congregations gathered outside churches. When the Lutheran missionary Philip Fabricius visited the small military station of Vellore in 1773, he discovered that English soldiers were meeting for Bible reading and prayer. During his visit, he preached in English at a parade service, in Tamil to the Indian Christians, and in German to some German soldiers. Fourteen years later, a surgeon named Duffin wrote from Vellore to Fabricius's colleague C. F. Schwartz, asking him to supply a volume of sermons, apparently for use at the Vellore meetings. Schwartz obliged by sending him two volumes of Isaac Watts's sermons (Neill: 104–5). Such accounts suggest that the reach and influence of sermons must be traced beyond formal church services and those who attended them.

Even with regards to the Cape Colony, however, where church attendance and other religious observances appear to have been far more common throughout the nineteenth century than in India or Australia (Ross: 43–5, Davenport: 52–5), historians have written little about the sermons that colonists listened to each week or the role of preaching in colonial life. More broadly then, this lack of attention to preaching and sermons among colonists reflects a general lack of scholarly interest in religion among colonists in the British empire. Etherington noted that the *Oxford History of the British Empire* gave little detailed attention to the role of religion in the colonies (Etherington: 1–2). Though the last twenty years have seen an explosion of scholarship on missions and missionaries this has focused largely on missionary work among indigenous peoples in (and beyond) the colonies. In the remainder of this section, therefore, a number of aspects of the sermon in the colonies that demonstrate its value for scholars of colonialism and colonial religion are identified.

The Sermon as Colonial Text

First, as the existing studies of colonial sermons show, the history of the sermon in its colonial context reveals much about changes and continuities in colonial culture and society. Perhaps the most famous example of this is found in the long-running debate around the 'jeremiad' sermons that Puritan preachers delivered on the annual election day holiday, identifying the corporate sins of the colonists and the divine judgement that would result barring repentance. The 'jeremiad' was a genre inherited from European preachers, which had taken on new form and purpose in the colonial context (Bercovitch: 9). For Miller, these sermons provided evidence of Puritan anxieties over the declining state of the colony (Miller 1953: 28), whereas Bercovitch has argued that they were a means through which foundational notions of American identity were established (Bercovitch: 176–210). More recently, Silva has focused on election sermons at the time of the Glorious Revolution, tracing the emergence of new constructions of colonial leadership with a transatlantic focus (Silva: 50). This ongoing discussion demonstrates the ways in which the colonial transformation of European sermon types, in both structure and content, could reflect broader changes within colonial society.

In 1699, the formation of the Brattle Street Church in Boston under Benjamin Colman marked a substantial shift in Puritan practices of preaching. Moving towards more traditional Anglican practice, Colman introduced set prayers and Bible readings at Brattle Street and preached 'elegant literary sermons in the English latitudinarian tradition of polite sensibility' (Gustafson: 43). As Gustafson has shown, these more 'literary' practices linked the Church to transatlantic print networks, which sustained a growing American literary culture, especially in the eastern colonies. Shifts in rhetorical and homiletic practice were thus connected to the emergence of new commercial and cultural networks across the empire.

As these examples demonstrate, studying shifts in homiletic theory and practice also has the potential to reveal the imperial networks which linked colonies and metropole. This second important aspect of the colonial sermon is nowhere more obvious than in the development and spread of Evangelical influence through the colonies from the 1730s onwards. In the case of the North American colonies, Evangelical revival was encouraged and sustained through a transatlantic network of correspondents, which included key preachers like Jonathan Edwards and Benjamin Colman of New England, Isaac Watts and George Whitefield in England, and John Erskine of Scotland, as well as other preachers, printers, and supporters of the revivals. Their correspondence included descriptions of preaching, discussions of significant issues related to preaching such as the adoption of itinerant preaching, and copies of sermons (O'Brien: 819). During the revivals, the sermons of Whitefield and other British Evangelicals were published in the American colonies, while the sermons of American preachers were also published back in Britain (D. D. Hall: 415).

Not surprisingly therefore, the preaching of these revivalists reflected and promoted the exchange of ideas and practices across the Atlantic. Arriving in the American colonies after revival had already broken out under the preaching of men like Edwards and Gilbert Tennant, Whitefield preached in an emotive, extemporaneous style, which was partly shaped by his reading of Edwards's grandfather Samuel Stoddard's sermon 'Defects of Preachers Reproved'. In turn, Whitefield's extraordinary success brought to crisis point debates among American preachers, who showed their allegiance to the new Evangelical movement by throwing away their notes and adopting the extemporaneous style

(Gustafson: 46 n. 10, 47). Similarly, Timothy Hall has argued that the widespread adoption of Whitefield's example of itinerancy by American preachers during the revival was both a response to the increasingly mobile and pluralistic transatlantic world and a means by which colonial communities were connected to this broader world (T. D. Hall).

Another transatlantic preaching network was formed by those inveterate travellers, the Quakers. Throughout the eighteenth century Quaker preachers, both men and women, travelled from Britain to North America and vice versa. These preaching networks served to cultivate a transatlantic Quaker culture and provided conduits for new ideas to spread rapidly (Larson: 185–6, 189). In 1750, for example, the Pennsylvania Quaker John Churchman and companions arrived in England and began preaching reform through new structures for discipline and renewal. His preaching had a substantial impact, with many English Quaker meetings adopting the new structures he promoted. Three years later, an Irish preacher named Mary Peisley and an English preacher named Catharine Payton, who had been preaching for some years in England, in turn took the message of reform back to America (Larson: 203–8). These examples also remind us that, if not always highly visible in the historical records of this period, women were active in colonial networks in both the delivery and reception of sermons (Brekus: 23–67).

Sermons in other colonies also travelled across imperial networks. From 1866, the controversial Bishop of the Church of England in Natal, John Colenso, published four series of *Natal Sermons*, which are discussed in far more detail in Chapter 28 of this volume. In these sermons, Colenso taught that the Bible was a valuable but fallible book, that salvation was not gained through 'the unquestioning reception of this or that particular dogma' (Colenso: 197) but was attained as people lived out the life of justice, mercy, and charity that God revealed to their hearts. These sermons, originally preached in Natal, were read across the empire and became part of the broader controversy during this period over the impact of higher criticism. And though Colenso was preaching to colonists, his sermons included discussion of metropolitan matters, such as a wholesale critique of strict Sabbath regulations in England and Scotland (Sugirtharajah: 108–9).

A preacher of very different theological persuasion, the Scottish-trained Dutch Reformed minister Andrew Murray, who led a revival in 1860 in the Cape Colony, was also influential in Britain, contributing to the development of the 'holiness movement'. His sermons were widely disseminated in Europe and he preached at the Keswick Convention (Fiedler: 218–19). Other collections of sermons by colonial preachers, like those of George Cotton, Bishop of Calcutta, were also published and circulated in Britain (Cotton). As R. S. Sugirtharajah (one of the few scholars of colonialism to pay close attention to the sermon) has shown, sermons preached by colonial preachers could take part in wider debates about the nature of empire itself, as when Bishop Daniel Wilson preached on the 'Indian Mutiny' to a Calcutta congregation as part of the empire-wide 'day of humiliation' (Sugirtharajah: 66–70).

These examples demonstrate the value of studying sermons as part of the imperial networks of people, objects, and ideas that spread across the colonies. Recent scholarship on imperial networks has shown how significant, diverse, and complex these connections were. Imperial networks could be formal or informal; military, humanitarian, religious, scientific or familial (and often several of these); these networks could function to sustain and promote empire, to critique it and occasionally to subvert it (see Lester 2001, 2006; Elbourne). A hint of the ways in which sermons could take on a subversive role is seen in a sermon preached by the native American preacher Samson Occom, apparently delivered in 1787. Occom's sermon, directed at white colonists, contains a wide-reaching discussion of the impact of European colonization, including a damning account of the devastation wrought to indigenous people by the arrival of white people in Tahiti and an unflattering portrayal of the relative morality of white settlers compared to native Americans (Occom 1787). Though by this stage Occom was no longer preaching within the British empire, his sermon demonstrates the ways that sermons could become a vehicle for critique of the empire and its impact.

This example leads to a third and final aspect of sermons in the British colonies that seems worthy of particular attention. The colonial context, because it was one of cultural encounter and exchange (however exploitative), created opportunities in which new voices were heard in the history of the British sermon. Occom, a Presbyterian clergyman, preached during the colonial period both to his own people and to colonists, undertaking a hugely successful preaching tour of England and Scotland in 1765–6 (Krupat: 106). In his most famous sermon, preached at the execution of a native American named Moses Paul in 1772 and published shortly afterwards, Occom defended his intention to add yet another sermon to the many others already published. Most sermons, he claimed, were delivered in language that was too complicated for the average listener, whereas his own language was 'common, plain, every-day talk', comprehensible to 'little children', 'poor Negroes' and 'my poor kindred the Indians'. 'Further', Occom noted, 'as it comes from an uncommon quarter, it may induce people to read it, because it is from an Indian' (Occom 1772: 2). Though the deprivations and betrayals of Occom's life illustrate the injustices of colonialism, his preaching exposed thousands of British people to the voice and (often critical) opinions of a native American, delivered in the authoritative form of a sermon.

While recent work on the history of missions has emphasized the role played by indigenous converts in preaching to their own people, Occom provides a rarer example of an indigenous convert who preached to the British. While unusual, this happened at times in all the colonies as well as in Britain itself (see for example, Killingray and Edwards: 55–71, Cruickshank: 47–8, Carretta and Reese: 9–23; Old 2009: 204–9). The impact of these indigenous voices on the genre of the sermon has yet to be studied in any detail.

A Case Study: Sermons in Colonial Australia

Having argued for the importance of the sermon as a source for studying British colonies and colonial networks, the following discussion provides a case study of preaching and sermons in the Australian colonies. Beginning by examining the arrival and dissemination of the sermon in Australia, the discussion will then turn to the question of change and continuity in the sermon, considering both colonial discussions of the sermon and a selection of sermons preached in the early period of colonization. The analysis focuses primarily on the period 1788–1850, but also draws on material from later periods where it provides a perspective on this earlier period.

The British sermon arrived in the land which the colonizers called Australia on 3 February 1788. On that first Sunday after the arrival of the First Fleet, the new settlement's Evangelical chaplain, Richard Johnson, preached on the beach at Sydney Cove to a crowd of soldiers, sailors, and convicts. He took as his text Psalm 116:12, 'What shall I render unto the Lord for all his benefits towards me?' According to one observer, the behavior of the hearers, who were compelled to be in attendance, was 'equally regular and attentive' (Macintosh: 49).

Not surprisingly, Johnson brought with him a large collection of religious reading matter provided by the Society for Promoting Christian Knowledge (SPCK). Among the Prayer Books, Bibles, and many tracts provided, Johnson brought 100 copies of Stephen White's *Dissuasives from Stealing*, a sermon preached in Suffolk and first published in 1747. While there are massive gaps in historians' knowledge of the books which those sailing on the First Fleet brought, some of those who travelled brought religious books and it seems likely that devout colonists may have brought published sermons to a situation where they knew they would have limited opportunities to hear preaching (see Steele and Richards).

Though it is difficult to know exactly which sermons were brought to the colonies in the early years, sermons were not prominent among the literature advertised for sale by local merchants in the periodicals that were published in profusion from the 1830s onwards. Those collections that were offered catered to a wide variety of theological preferences. Colonists in the 1820s, 30s and 40s were offered collections of sermons by Andrew Thomson, John Jortin, Hugh Blair, Jean Baptiste Massillon, Isaac de Beausobre, John Tillotson, and George Whitefield among others (*Sydney Gazette* 22 September 1821; *Hobart Town Gazette and Van Diemen's Land Advertiser* 29 September 1821, 29 March 1823; *The Sentinel* 8 January 1845; *The Sydney Protestant Magazine* 15 April 1840). In the 1840s and 50s, colonists recorded reading or receiving volumes of sermons by Robert Murray McCheyne, George Burder, James Archer, and—in Irish—James Gallagher. Both men and women were among those who recorded purchasing and reading sermons (Willson: 54–5).

Easier to follow is the development of sermon publication in the Australian colonies. In 1792, Richard Johnson's *Address to the Inhabitants of the Colonies, Established in New South Wales and Norfolk Island*, which is usually described as a sermon, was sent back to England for publication. Not until the arrival of William Grant Broughton, first archdeacon, later bishop of the colony, did sermon publication begin to occur more frequently. One of Broughton's sermons was published in 1830; another in Hobart, in Van Diemen's Land, in 1833; and another two in Sydney in 1834 (Ferguson). In the same year, Charles Pleydell Wilton, the chaplain of Newcastle, published *Twelve Plain Discourses Addressed to the Prisoners of the Crown in the Colony of New South Wales*.

In the following six years, there were ten sermons published by Anglicans, as well as a few by Presbyterians and Independents, one Methodist and one Quaker, evidence of the growing diversity in the religious life of the colonies (Ferguson 1945–51). The tensions created by this diversity emerge in some sermons of these early years, such as Broughton's 'Take Heed', preached to the women convicts at the Female Factory in Parramatta in 1844. Horrified by the baptism of four Anglican convicts into the Roman Catholic Church, Broughton preached on the text 'Take heed that no man deceive you', accusing the Catholics of attempting 'to seduce away from their own Church poor uneducated persons, placed under circumstances which peculiarly expose them to a misleading influence' (Broughton: 5). Only one Roman Catholic sermon was published in Australia before 1850. The first Jewish sermons were published in 1877 (Brodzky).

In many ways, the developing culture of sermon publication in Australia appears to mimic practices of sermon publication in Britain. The majority of sermons published prior to 1850 were Anglican sermons and the majority of these had been preached to mark events in the life of the Church, such as the laying of foundation stones for new churches, ordinations, confirmations, funerals, and visitations; as well as events in the life of the nation, such as the national day of thanksgiving held in 1829 and the national fast day in 1838. After the establishment in Sydney of the diocesan committee of the SPCK and the Society for the Propagation of the Gospel (SPG) in 1836, an anniversary sermon for these societies was preached every year, just as such sermons were preached for the metropolitan societies in London.

Yet these unremarkable similarities mask some deeper differences in the reasons for sermon publication and distribution in the Australian colonies. Johnson, in the foreword to his aforementioned *Address*, explained to his readers that as a result of the rapid spread of the colony and his own failing health:

> I feel it impracticable, and impossible for me, either to preach, or to converse with you so freely, as my inclination and affection would prompt me to do. I have therefore thought it might be proper for me, and I hope it may prove useful to you, to write such an Address. (Johnson: iv)

Wilton made similar comments in the introduction to his *Twelve Plain Discourses*, explaining that the size of his parish meant his flock did not have the access to public worship they would have had in Britain. It therefore occurred to him, he wrote, 'that were he to draw up a small Collection of Sermons, suited to the circumstances of the Prisoners in his Chaplaincy, to be given to them to read themselves, or to be read to them...a desirable object would be gained' (Wilton: v). This remained the primary motivation for publishing collections of sermons during this period. In 1843, a Presbyterian minister, William Hamilton, published *Practical Discourses Intended for Circulation in the Interior of New South Wales*, noting that his pastoral responsibilities covered a thousand people living scattered across an area stretching 500 miles to one side of his church and eighty-five on the other (Hamilton: iv).

While the idea of preaching sermons for those who could not attend public worship was not new, these publications show preachers seeking solutions to the practical problems of distance and lack of personnel and property, problems which they confronted far more urgently in the colonies than in Britain. Such challenges were particularly hard for Anglican clergy, with their traditional attachment to the parish model. Johnson initially preached weekly in Sydney, but as the colony expanded he began to travel fortnightly to the neighbouring settlement of Parramatta, where he would preach three times in different locations. Samuel Marsden, his colleague and successor, was left to follow the same pattern after Johnson's departure. Robert Knopwood, the first chaplain in Van Diemen's Land, rode to the far reaches of his enormous parish on horseback, travelling 160 kilometres at times to preach and conduct services (Monks: 66–7). Such clergy were mobile but not itinerant, retaining a parish centre where they spent the majority of their time.

By contrast, Rowland Hassall and William Pascoe Crook, the London Missionary Society (LMS) missionaries who arrived in the early 1800s, as well as the Methodists who began to arrive from 1815, brought with them itinerant models of ministry that more easily allowed them to minister to a far-flung flock. Methodism grew rapidly in the colony during this period, as zealous lay Methodists began preaching wherever they settled, building and maintaining congregations until clergy arrived (Clancy; Thompson: 8).

These examples confirm that in Australia as in other colonies, we need to look beyond the clergy and church buildings to track the circulation and use of sermons. In 1838, when Broughton visited the settlement of Melbourne, he found that morning and evening prayers were being conducted by a respected settler named James Smith, who also read a 'printed sermon' every Sunday in the building used as a schoolhouse (Lake: 210). In the 1830s, a leading Anglican colonist assembled his convict servants every fortnight to read them a sermon by the Roman Catholic William Ullathorne, 'On Drunkenness' (Ullathorne: 127). In the late 1840s, an isolated settler named James Murray recorded that he read 'a chapter and a sermon' for household worship each Sunday; and other colonists recorded reading sermons together on Sunday afternoons (Willson: 42–3). The periodical *Melbourne Christian Record* was established in 1870 to publish the sermons of the minister at Collins Street Baptist Church in Melbourne, in order, the editors explained, 'to some extent, to meet the constant demand for sermons to read in the bush' (*Melbourne Christian Record*: ii).

Preachers in the early years of the colony, raised and educated in Britain, brought with them theological and homiletic traditions, so it is not surprising that these traditions were both maintained and critiqued in the new colonial context. Evidence of this is found in the 1870s, when a Melbourne journalist named Howard Willoughby published a popular series of articles on the preachers of that city, providing a 'critic's' overview of their style and content. Willoughby, born and educated in England, evaluated the preachers in part against his expectation of the preaching tradition of their denomination. The sermons of Charles Perry, the evangelical Anglican Bishop of Melbourne, were described as 'religious essays on "the whole duty of man"—more especially, a Low Churchman' (Willoughby: 2–3). Of Mr Bickford, the lay preacher at Wesley Church, Willoughby commented that 'like most Wesleyans he has a fund of genial anecdote' but that his sermons were 'more cold and formal than one might expect from a Wesleyan divine' (Willoughby: 31). The preaching at the Roman Catholic St Francis's, about which Willoughby was enthusiastic, was described as 'distinct from that of the Protestant communion', being far shorter, more vivid, and more emotional (Willoughby: 39). These comments show a strong sense of denominational traditions of preaching being maintained in the colonial context.

It is also clear, however, that such traditions were also being critiqued and examined within denominations. During 1862, for example, the Sydney-based *Presbyterian Magazine* contained two critiques of preaching within the denomination, by different authors. Both lamented the tendency of Presbyterian sermons to hold too closely to outdated historical forms. One author, identified only as 'W. G.', complained of the 'dry essay style, and the tiresome and never ending divisions and uses of the Puritans—which, like the bones in Ezekiel's vision, were very many and very dry' ('W. G.': 72). The other author, identified as 'A. C. G.' (presumably Archibald Geikie, a prominent Presbyterian of the time) lampooned the 'old-fashioned' technicality of many of his colleagues, writing:

> We have known men who loved 'division' for its own sake, who talked 'division', who dreamed 'divisions' and who seemed far better pleased with peculiarly disposed *firstly, secondly* and *thirdly*, than with the grandest of sermons where these familiar figures did not, like a policeman, do duty at the head of every section. (Geikie: 235)

A survey of published Presbyterian sermons from the early years of the colony suggests some justification for this complaint, as such sermons rarely strayed from the conventional form of introduction, divisions, and application (see Hamilton; McGarvie; Cairns; Lang; Fraser).

Another example of colonial reflection on homiletic traditions can be seen in the Roman Catholic Church. The influential Benedictine William Ullathorne, who returned to England in 1840, published a collection of eight sermons, seven of which he had preached during his five years in the colony. In the lengthy introduction to this collection, Ullathorne criticized what he saw as the 'favorite method of preaching by handling objections, by keeping up a constant reasoning with the fallacies of the passions' (Ullathorne: 7). This tendency among Catholic preachers he blamed partly upon the influence of the French 'courtly' preachers (Edwards 2009: 10–11) but more directly upon the Anglican homiletic tradition, which saw the English mind as 'too calm and rational to draw profit from a greater and more glowing eloquence' (Ullathorne: 10).

Against this 'Anglican' tendency, Ullathorne argued that his experience in the colonies confirmed his belief that all human beings were moved by impulse as well as reason:

> In the guiltiest and hardiest criminals I ever met, during my experience of New South Wales and Norfolk Island... I have ever found the same pliant human nature, moved by the same reasons, swayed by the same motives, and accessible to the same feeling with their fellow-men. (Ullathorne: 12)

In order to reach such an audience, Ullathorne argued, the preacher must draw on the resources of the Church, becoming familiar with the Church Fathers, especially Chrysostom, and making constant use of metaphor, allegory, and 'dramatic dialogue'.

His own sermons, some of which are discussed below, were rich in imagery and quotation, as well as emotive description.

Ullathorne's comments show again that the colonies could provide a context for the practice as well as the conscious development and renewal of particular traditions of preaching. The collection as a whole is also an example of the interaction between colony and metropole in relation to sermons. Though Ullathorne preached most of these sermons to his colonial flock, they were published in England and were presumably intended primarily for an English audience. His experience in the colony was used as evidence for his philosophy of preaching; the description of the varied and unusual locations in which the sermons had been preached added credibility to Ullathorne as heroic preacher and added interest to his sermons.

As is obvious, in addition to reflecting upon the homiletic traditions which had been imported from Britain, many preachers, including Ullathorne, sought to address their sermons to the specific audiences and situations presented by colonial life. In 1867, a Presbyterian minister named Thomas McKenzie Fraser, based in the colony of Victoria, published a volume titled *Sermons for Colonists*. In the preface, Fraser lamented that although single sermons had been published in Victoria, 'so far as I know, there is no volume of discourses expressly composed for colonists, pervaded by colonial illustrations, and suited for family reading in Victoria. All our collections of sermons are importations from the mother country' (Fraser: v). Fraser clearly saw a pressing and as yet unfulfilled need for truly 'colonial' sermons which addressed the specific conditions of colonial life.

Examining those sermons which were presented as directly addressing the situations of colonists in the early years provides some indication of how sermons were adapted to local conditions and congregations. Johnson's *Address to the Inhabitants of the Colonies*; Wilton's *Twelve Plain Discourses Addressed to the Prisoners of the Crown*; Hamilton's *Practical Discourses* and Ullathorne's *Sermons* provide good examples of such sermons. John Dunmore Lang's famous sermon on the fast day in 1838, called in response to a terrible drought, is also important.

Johnson's *Address* was not a conventional sermon, but an extended appeal to the colonists of New South Wales to consider the state of their souls, repent, and believe the gospel. 'To endeavour to bring you, my dear friends' he wrote, 'to a saving knowledge of what is contained in this gospel, is not only my duty and inclination as a minister, but also my earnest desire and pleasure' (Johnson: 7). The text reflects Johnson's evangelical convictions: the first half, thick with biblical quotations, is an explanation of the gospel along classic evangelical lines, emphasizing the fall of man, the atoning death of Christ, the gift of repentance, faith, and the starkly different eternal fates which awaited those who accepted this gift and those who did not.

The address then moves to practical matters, providing an outline of those activities which Johnson believed would assist the colonists in living a godly life. Johnson advised his parishioners to adopt regular Bible reading, Sabbath-keeping, and prayer and avoid swearing, adultery, theft, idleness, and disrespect to social superiors. In discussing these behaviours, Johnson addressed many aspects of life for colonists, including the lack of time available to convicts and what he saw as the colonial proclivity for swearing, sexual promiscuity, and theft. He also touched briefly on the convict background of many of his flock:

> I do not mean, my friends, to reflect harshly upon you for what is past, and cannot be recalled. I pity your past misconduct; I sympathize with you under your present sufferings. And therefore I admonish and caution you to abstain from this course for the time to come. (Johnson: 61)

In seeking to motivate his readers to a transformation of their lives, Johnson pointed not only to their own future welfare, but also the 'affectionate, tender and serious' friends and relations they had left behind in Britain, who would rejoice to hear of their reformation. Finally, Johnson urged them to consider the example they were setting to 'the poor unenlightened savages' who were observing them (Johnson: 65, 68).

As noted, Johnson's *Address* was not a conventional sermon. However, it provides an excellent introduction to the published collections which followed it, containing many of the themes and emphases which appear throughout the colonial sermons studied here. Wilton, who did not share Johnson's evangelical convictions, was equally keen to urge the importance of repentance and reformation in his *Twelve Plain Discourses*. Unlike Johnson, however, he reminded his hearers at every opportunity of their past wrongdoings (Wilton: 2, 5, 11, 14, 21, 22, 58–9). In a sermon on the 'Fall of Man', for example, Wilton questioned his hearers:

> What was it that stirred you up to commit that sin and wickedness against God and your neighbor, which was the cause of your being banished from your native country and sent away, as a punishment for your crime, into this far distant land? Was it not the Devil? (Wilton: 11)

In calling his readers to reform their lives, Wilton also addressed what he saw as the particular vices of colonials. Like Johnson, he urged the convicts to read their Bibles, addressing particularly the issue of free time for convicts. A sermon 'On Keeping Holy the Sabbath-Day' lamented the irregularity of Sabbath-keeping and church attendance in the colony and remonstrated particularly against drunkenness on Sundays. In 'On Keeping the Commandments' Wilton cautioned against stealing and in 'The Fear of God, and Obedience to the Laws of the Land' he urged reverence for the king and conformity to his laws. The latter sermon dealt particularly with the recent execution of a group of local bushrangers, whose deaths Wilton used as an example of the wages of sin. (Wilton: 1–7, 24–30, 19–23, 58–63).

The moral concerns of these Anglican preachers, who focused on matters such as Sabbath-keeping, swearing, theft, and drunkenness, may seem to reflect the broader preoccupations of many nineteenth-century British preachers. In general, however, these preachers claimed that they were addressing sins that were particularly predominant in Australia. In the sermons discussed above, the prevalence of theft was linked to the convict background of much of the population. William Hamilton, like the other preachers noted here, preached on the importance of keeping the Sabbath holy and of attendance at public worship 'on the Lord's Day', questioning how 'to account for the so general forsaking of ordinances which are well observed in our native land?' (Hamilton: 163). Hamilton provided a lengthy response to this question, pointing to the relaxation of social constraints in the colony, the problem of distance, the danger of leaving land and property unattended and the lack of state support for clergy.

Drunkenness was seen as similarly acute in the colonies. Hamilton preached on this topic in obedience to a directive by the Presbyterian Synod of Australia for all ministers to preach a sermon against drunkenness because of the prevalence of the problem in the colony. Ullathorne wrote that he had preached his sermon on drunkenness at a time when there had been a 'great prevalence' of that vice in New South Wales, but the introduction of Catholic clergy and temperance societies had led to significant improvement (Ullathorne: 109).

Fewer preachers demonstrated Johnson's concern for the situation of the indigenous people of the colony. An exception was Hamilton, who discussed the plight of indigenous people in two sermons. His sermon 'Thou shalt not kill' dealt at length with the application of this commandment to the question of colonization, justifying colonization but condemning violence and greed among colonists (Hamilton: 61). Another sermon in his collection was dedicated to urging colonial Presbyterians to make greater missionary efforts among the Aboriginal people of the territory (Hamilton: 135–50).

A far stronger statement is found in Lang's fast day sermon, which identifies the 'blood-guiltiness' of colonists against Aboriginal people as the first of the sins for which God is judging the colony. Lang proclaimed:

> not only have we despoiled them of their land, and given them in exchange European vice and European disease in every foul and fatal form, but the blood of hundreds, nay thousands of their number... still stains the hands of many of the inhabitants of the land! (Lang: 14).

To this 'enormous' sin against Indigenous Australians, Lang added two more which he believed were particularly prominent in the colony: oppression of the poor (especially convicts) and the profanation of the Sabbath.

This brief survey of the main sermon collections published in Australia before 1850 provides insights into the concerns of colonial preachers, as they condemned what they saw as the particular vices produced by colonial conditions and urged individual and corporate repentance. If such sermons provide some justification for long-standing Australian suspicions about the 'wowserism' of the devout and their leaders, they also show preachers reflecting with greater or lesser degrees of sophistication upon the impact of colonial life on individuals, the nature of colonial society, and the imperial project itself. There is evidence too that colonial preachers, who carried with them ancient homiletic traditions, both continued and critiqued these traditions in their new environment. They did so in a growing field of sermon publication and dissemination, driven not only by the concerns of religious leaders to minister to colonists in a society where distance and freedom from social conventions created new challenges to religious observance, but also by the demand for sermons and preaching among colonists themselves.

Conclusion

In 2007, while providing an overview of the recent proliferation of studies and anthologies of Australian speeches, historian Ken Inglis commented that the sermon, 'the genre most productive of public speech for most of Australian history', was barely represented in these works (Inglis). The same may be said for most of the British empire. With the exception of scholarship on North America, sermons have yet to be studied in detail as an important source for understanding colonial society and culture. However, examples from throughout the British empire show the importance of sermons in the life of many colonists, the role of sermons and preaching as part of colonial networks, and the value of sermons as a source for understanding the development of colonial culture, including processes of cultural exchange. Studies of reception of sermons in the colonies, a matter only briefly touched on here, will reveal much about colonial practices of orality and aurality. Issues of race, gender and class in relation to both preachers and sermons also deserve further attention. Further scholarship in these areas will expand our understanding of both the sermon and colonialism.

References

Bercovitch, S. (1978). *The American Jeremiad*. Madison, WI: University of Wisconsin Press.

Bond, E. L. (2004). *Spreading the Gospel in Colonial Virginia: Sermons and Devotional Writings*. Lanham, MD: Lexington Books.

Bosco, R. A. (1978). 'Lectures at the Pillory: The Early American Execution Sermon'. *American Quarterly* 30: 156–76.

Brekus, C. (1998). *Strangers and Pilgrims: Female Preaching in America, 1740–1845*. Durham, NC: University of North Carolina Press.

Breward, I. (2001). *A History of the Churches in Australasia*. Oxford: Oxford University Press.

Brodzky, M., et al. (1877). *Historical Sketch of the Two Melbourne Synagogues... Together with Sermons*. Melbourne: A. & W. Bruce.

Broughton, W. G. (1844). *Take Heed: A Sermon Preached in the Female Factory at Parramatta, on Tuesday the 4th of June, 1844*. Sydney: Kemp and Fairfax.

Butler, J. (1990). *Awash in a Sea of Faith: Christianizing the American People*. Cambridge, MA: Harvard University Press.

Cairns, A. (1857). *Sermon by the Rev. Adam Cairns: at Chalmers' Church, Melbourne*. Melbourne: Goodhugh and Hough.

Carretta, V., and Reese, T. M. (eds.) (2010). *The Life and Letters of Philip Quaque, the First African Anglican Missionary*. Athens, GA: University of Georgia Press.

Clancy, E. G. (1981). 'Rural Methodism in New South Wales, 1836–1902', in J. S. Udy and E. G. Clancy (eds.), *Dig or Die: Papers Given at the Wesley Heritage Conference, University of Sydney, 10–15 August 1980*. Sydney: World Methodist Historical Society, 89–113.

Colenso, J. W. (1866). *Natal Sermons: A Series of Discourses Preached at the Cathedral Church of St Peter's, Maritzburg*. London: N Trübner and Co.

Cotton, G. E. L. (1867). *Sermons Preached to English Congregations in India*. London: Macmillan and Co.
Cruickshank, J. (2010). 'Race, History, and the Australian Faith Missions'. *Itinerario* 34: 39–52.
Davenport, R. (1997). 'Settlement, Conquest and Theological Controversy: The Churches of Nineteenth-Century European Immigrants', in R. Elphick and R. Davenport (eds.), *Christianity in South Africa: A Political, Social and Cultural History*. Oxford: James Currey, 51–67.
Edwards, O. C. (2004). *A History of Preaching*. Nashville, TN: Abingdon.
—— (2009). 'Varieties of Sermon: A Survey of Preaching in the Long Eighteenth Century', in J. van Eijnatten (ed.), *Preaching, Sermon and Cultural Change in the Long Eighteenth Century*. Leiden: Brill, 3–54.
Elbourne, E. (2003). 'The Eastern Cape and International Networks in the Early Nineteenth Century'. *Fort Hare Institute of Social and Economic Research Working Paper Series,* 43. Alice, South Africa: University of Fort Hare.
Elliot, E. (1975). *Power and the Pulpit in Puritan New England*. Princeton, NJ: Princeton University Press.
Etherington, N. (2005). 'Introduction', in N. Etherington (ed.), *Missions and Empire*. Oxford: Oxford University Press, 1–18.
Ferguson, J. A. (1945–51). *Bibliography of Australia 1784–1850*, vols. 1–4. Sydney: Angus and Robinson.
Fiedler, K. (1997). *The Story of Faith Missions*. Oxford: Oxford Centre for Mission Studies.
Fraser, T. M. (1877). *Sermons for Colonists*. Geelong: Wise and Downie.
Geikie, A. C. (1862). 'Preaching'. *Presbyterian Magazine*, December: 227–41.
Gordis, L. M. (2003). *Opening Scripture: Bible Reading and Interpretive Authority in Puritan New England*. Chicago: University of Chicago Press.
Gould, E. H. (2005). 'Prelude: The Christianizing of British America', in N. Etherington (ed.), *Missions and Empire*. Oxford: Oxford University Press, 19–39.
Gustafson, S. (2000). *Eloquence is Power: Oratory and Performance in Early America*. Durham, NC: University of North Carolina Press.
Hall, D. D. (2000). 'The Atlantic Economy in the Eighteenth Century', in H. Amory and D. D. Hall (eds.), *The Colonial Book in the Atlantic World*. Cambridge: Cambridge University Press, 152–62.
Hall, T. D. (2004). *Contested Boundaries: Itinerancy and the Reshaping of the Colonial American Religious World*. Durham, NC: Duke University Press.
Hamilton, W. (1843). *Practical Discourses Intended for Circulation in the Interior of New South Wales*. Sydney: Kemp and Fairfax.
Hobart Town Gazette and Van Diemen's Land Advertiser (29 September 1821).
—— (29 March 1823).
Inglis, K. (2007). 'Speechmaking in Australian History'. The 2007 Allen Martin Lecture. <http://www.theaha.org.au/awards/martin/speeches/inglis.htm> accessed 20 February 2011.
Johnson, R. (1792). *Address to the Inhabitants of the Colonies, Established in New South Wales and Norfolk Island*. Port Jackson, Aus.: n. p.
Killingray, D., and Edwards, J. (eds.) (2007). *Black Voices: The Shaping of our Christian Experience*. Nottingham: IVP.
Krupat, A. (1994). *Native American Autobiography: An Anthology*. Madison, WI: University of Wisconsin Press.

Lake, M. (2008). '"Such Spiritual Acres": Protestantism, the Land and the Colonisation of Australia 1788–1850'. PhD Thesis, University of Sydney.

Lang, J. D. (1838). *National Sins the Cause and Precursors of National Judgments: A Sermon*. Sydney: James Tegg.

Larson, R. (2000). *Daughters of Light: Quaker Women Preaching and Prophesying in the Colonies and Abroad, 1700–1775*. Durham, NC: University of North Carolina Press.

Lester, A. (2001). *Imperial Networks: Creating Identities in Nineteenth-Century South Africa and Britain*. London: Routledge.

—— (2006). 'Imperial Circuits and Networks: Geographies of the British Empire'. *History Compass* 4: 124–41.

Lowance, M. I. (1980). *The Language of Canaan*. Cambridge, MA: Harvard University Press.

Macintosh, N. K. (1978). *Richard Johnson, Chaplain to the Colony of New South Wales*. Sydney: Library of Australian History.

McGarvie, J. (1842). *Sermons Preached in St Andrew's Church, Sydney*. Sydney: Kemp and Fairfax.

The Melbourne Christian Record. (1870).

Miller, P. (1939). *The New England Mind: The Seventeenth Century*. Cambridge, MA: Harvard University Press.

—— (1953). *The New England Mind: From Colony to Province*. Cambridge, MA: Harvard University Press.

Monks, L. (1967). 'Knopwood, Robert (1763–1838)', *Australian Dictionary of Biography* Melbourne: Melbourne University Press.

Neill, S. (1985). *A History of Christianity in India 1707–1785*. Cambridge: Cambridge University Press.

Nelson, J. K. (2001). *A Blessed Company: Parishes, Parsons and Parishioners in Colonial Virginia*. Chapel Hill, NC: University of North Carolina Press.

O'Brien, S. (1986). 'A Transatlantic Community of Saints: The Great Awakening and the First Evangelical Network, 1735–1755'. *American Historical Review* 91: 811–32.

Occom, S. (1772). *A Sermon Preached at the Execution of Moses Paul, an Indian*. New Haven, CT: T. & S. Green.

—— (1787). 'Untitled Sermon' Papers of Samson Occum; Correspondence 1727–1808; Sermons; Diary, 7/5-9/16. Connecticut Historical Society, microfilm 79998.

O'Connor, D. (2011). *The Chaplains of the East India Company, 1601–1858*. London: Continuum.

Old, H. O. (2006). *The Reading and Preaching of the Scriptures in the Worship of the Christian Church, 6: The Modern Age*. Grand Rapids, MI: Eerdmans.

—— (2009). *The Reading and Preaching of the Scriptures in the Worship of the Christian Church, 7: Our Own Time*. Grand Rapids, MI: Eerdmans.

Ross, R. (1999). *A Concise History of South Africa*. Cambridge: Cambridge University Press.

Silva, A. J. (1999). 'Increase Mather's 1693 Election Sermon: Rhetorical Innovation and the Reimagination of Puritan Authority'. *Early American Literature* 34: 48–77.

Steele, C. and Richards, M. (1988). *Bound for Botany Bay: What Books Did the First Fleeters Read and Where Are They Now?* Canberra: Australian National Library.

Stout, H. (1998). *The New England Soul: Preaching and Religious Culture in Colonial New England*. Oxford: Oxford University Press.

Sugirtharajah, R. S. (2005). *The Bible and Empire: Postcolonial Explorations*. Cambridge: Cambridge University Press.

Sydney Gazette (22 September 1821).
The Sentinel (8 January 1845).
The Sydney Protestant Magazine (15 April 1840).
Thompson, R. C. (2002). *Religion in Australia: A History*. Oxford: Oxford University Press.
Ullathorne, W. (1842). *Substance of a Sermon Against Drunkenness Preached to the Catholics of Divers Parts of New South Wales*. Dublin: R Coyne.
W. G. (1862). 'The Pulpit'. *Presbyterian Magazine* July: 70–4.
Willoughby, H. (1872). *The Critic in Church or Melbourne Preachers and Preaching*. Melbourne: George Robertson.
Willson, R. J. (1986). 'Colonial Preaching and Piety: Aspects of the Religious History of the Colony of New South Wales, 1836–1862'. MA Thesis, Australian National University.
Wilton, C. P. N. (1834). *Twelve Plain Discourses Addressed to the Prisoners of the Crown in the Colony of New South Wales with An Appendix Containing a Manual of Prayers for their Use*. Sydney: Stephens and Stokes.

CHAPTER 32

CHURCH OF IRELAND MISSIONS TO ROMAN CATHOLICS, C.1700–1800

ANDREW SNEDDON

The Church of Ireland and Religious Literature

Eighteenth-century Irish Church historians have revised the traditional picture of the Church of Ireland as materially poor and unable to perform its pastoral role because of clerical nepotism, non-residence, pluralism, and general negligence. Revisionists have demonstrated that it was a relatively well-run and well-staffed institution, able to meet the spiritual needs of its own communicants, if not the nation as a whole. Long criticized for claiming the privileged position as the state Church but doing little to make it such, it is now largely agreed that it made serious attempts during the century to convert the majority, Catholic population to Protestantism.

Despite our increased understanding of the functions of this relatively dynamic institution, comparatively little work has been done on the voluminous literature produced by it in this period. This was era of expanding print culture in Ireland, both in terms of production and consumption, and religious texts became of tremendous importance to printers, sellers, authors, and readers alike. For example, before the 1790s they far outstripped controversial and secular works in terms of numbers, titles, and edition sizes. The Church of Ireland and affiliated charities and institutions published English translations of the Bible, biblical commentaries, Catholic convert testimonies, and religious pamphlets. More importantly, the 1690s saw an explosion in the publication of the printed sermon, reflecting a growing market and greater official enthusiasm for the genre. Collectively, devotional texts aimed, along with preaching and pastoral care, to demonstrate that the Established Church's particular brand of Protestantism was the truest form of Christianity, and the only one to guarantee salvation (Mandlebrote: 115–31).

Church of Ireland Sermons

Apart from the pioneering, and much cited, studies by Raymond Gillespie, S. J. Connolly, and T. C. Barnard of late-seventeenth and early- to mid- eighteenth century Anglican sermons (Gillespie 2001; Connolly; T. C. Barnard 1991), and the passing references made in the first major survey of the Irish book in English, *The Oxford History of the Irish Book*, the study of Established Church sermons remains an under-researched area of Irish Church history. Such an omission is lamentable because sermons are guides to Protestant moods and reactions to the changing social, political, and religious agenda of the State Church in a century of intense change (T. C. Barnard 1991: 889).

The work of the aforementioned historians has given us a clearer picture than ever of the religious and political content of Anglican sermons. However we still know very little about their structure, form, and style, and little research has been done on provincial sermons, as few manuscript examples exist and most printed sermons originate in Dublin churches (T. C. Barnard 1991: 890 n. 1). In any case, printed sermons probably represent but a small fraction of those actually preached. This may have something to do with the fact that many clergy were reluctant to have their words put down in a permanent and widely distributable form. It may even be that we have overestimated the frequency of sermon preaching in parish churches, especially in the first half of the century, and that they were delivered only on special occasions. The style of preaching adopted, and the topics broached in parochial sermons, which in common with their English counterparts were probably endlessly recycled, may even have been copied from a preacher's diocesan or from printed, Dublin sermons. Access to Church of Ireland Bibles, Common Prayer books, commentaries, and sermons, was, by the late seventeenth century, relatively easy for most Protestant laity and clergy (Gillespie 2001: 128–9; Gillespie 2005: 132–44, 152; Deconick-Brossard: 111–12).

Printed Sermons

In eighteenth-century Ireland, printed sermons were preached on a variety of occasions, such as days of local or regional importance. For example, up until the 1720s, a number of sermons were delivered in Cork and Kinsale to celebrate the expulsion in the late seventeenth century of Jacobite troops from the area (T. C. Barnard 1991: 913).

Surprisingly, printed County Assize sermons, preached before Grand Juries and Judges, were extremely rare in Ireland. As the majority of the six surviving Assize sermons were preached after 1714, on a Sunday, by higher clergy, it might be that they were only preached if the opening of the Assizes occurred on that day, or if there was a particular issue that the preacher or the audience wanted to give wider exposure to. Given that they were preached before local and national legal elites, it is unsurprising that the main themes covered in them were the need for campaigns to reform manners, the importance of individual and collective morality, and the obligation of subjects to their government, its laws, officials and magistrates. Within this remit, topical issues were debated, such as the need to combat crypto-Jacobite toasting during the party-torn, final years of the reign of Queen Anne, and the politically radical nature of agrarian protest in Ulster in the early 1770s (French; Mathews; Radcliffe; Clayton 1739; H. Hamilton; T. Barnard).

Other surviving printed sermons were first aired at Episcopal visitations (Shaw; F. Hamilton; Lyster), or at the funerals of monarchs or influential clergymen and laity (Choppin; Connor). Thanksgiving sermons celebrating the accession of George I were also published, as were those praising God and the government for the deliverance of Protestants from Jacobite invasion or rebellion, especially in 1715 and 1745–6. The higher clergy also used occasional sermons, preached before important audiences (the Lord Justice, Lord Deputies, MPs and peers), to give wider exposure to certain views, topical issues or events, which are too varied to be adequately categorized here. Finally, religious societies and charities affiliated to the Established Church published sermons to raise money and increase public support for their particular cause. Chief among these were the societies to reform manners in the 1690s and early 1700s (T. C. Barnard 1992: 807–9, 812, 817, 826–7), the Incorporated Society for the Propagation of the Gospel in Foreign Parts (formed in 1701), and the Charity and Charter School systems.

However, the most ubiquitous sermon genre in the early- to mid-eighteenth-century in Ireland, and upon which most work has been done, was the semi-ritualized, metropolitan, celebratory sermons of 30 January, 29 May, 23 October, and 5 November: dates set by the Established Church in the late seventeenth and early eighteenth centuries. The vast majority of these were preached by the aspiring or higher clergy in the smarter churches of Dublin, before elite audiences (T. C. Barnard 1991: 889–90, 912–13).

Sermons preached on 29 May celebrated the return of Charles II at the Restoration, while those of 30 January commemorated Charles I's execution in 1649. At a height of popularity in the Restoration era, sermons preached on 30 January proved contentious among the generation after the 'Glorious Revolution', as they had to 'tip-toe' around the issue of the legitimacy of William III's removal of James II from the throne in 1688, while simultaneously condemning civil war rebels and regicides. This task was made easier by the appropriation by the Hanoverian regime in Britain and Ireland of traditional Anglican rhetoric of obedience to authority in the form of the ideology of order and the theory of divine right of governors (Mischler; Connolly: 484–85). On the other hand,

5 November sermons were preached as a thanksgiving for the discovery of the Gunpowder Plot in 1605 and William III's landing in England in 1688. The subjects for these commemorations had their origin in England, and in the late seventeenth and early eighteenth century gave Irish Protestants the opportunity to advertise their English heritage and allegiance to the Crown (T. C. Barnard 1991: 890).

Sermons preached on 23 October have survived in the greatest number, possibly because they were devoted to a uniquely Irish event and were instituted by an Act of Parliament of 1662. They commemorated the date in 1641, before the subsequent (alleged) massacre of Protestants, when Dublin Castle narrowly averted capture by Catholic rebels. These sermons, in both Anglican and Presbyterian churches, followed a sin-deliverance-repent paradigm, in that thanks were given for Protestant deliverance by God, and deliberation made upon the sins which had provoked God's wrath in the first place. The most popular explanation was that God had punished Protestants for their indolence in dealing with the Catholic threat, but irreligion and immorality were also considered major contributing factors (Connolly: 484–5, 488; T. C. Barnard 1991: 889–90, 895–6; Blackstock: 103).

Sermons and Conversion

Another area of eighteenth-century Anglican sermons that warrants further investigation is the extent to which they figured in missions to convert Roman Catholics to Protestantism. It will be suggested below, using a wide cross-section of eighteenth-century printed sermons, that most Irish Protestants regarded the mass conversion of the Catholic population as laudable for religious, economic, and political reasons, and that they took a position on how this would be best achieved on a continuum between the binaries of coercion and conciliation. Each approach, and the specific conversion scheme that was adopted to realize it, was advertised, justified (and sometimes criticized) in printed sermons.

The complexity of this issue clearly confused some Low Church Whig preachers, who stated, in typical Low Church terms, that it should be achieved through persuasion, by convincing Catholics of the errors of their religion. Crucially, however, they failed to detail how this would be achieved practically (Lambert: 16; Story: 27–9; R. Downes: 15; Cumberland: 14–16). Others however adopted a more pragmatic approach. Some believed that penal legislation alone would bring the Reformation to Ireland, while others suggested that this approach should be coupled with Protestant education in Charity Schools. For a committed minority, however, evangelizing in the vernacular, the Irish language, was the only way to create mass numbers of sincere converts. These methods were popular at different times during the long eighteenth century, reflecting the changing attitude to Roman Catholicism within the Established Church and Protestant society at large.

Sermons, Conversion and Anti-Catholicism

Just as it was in the nineteenth and twentieth centuries, during the long eighteenth century, Ireland was a Catholic country. Although the precise numbers of the three main denominations fluctuated over time, in particular provinces (especially in Ulster) and in individual dioceses, on average Roman Catholics comprised around 80 per cent of the Irish population, Presbyterians around 9 per cent, and communicants of the Church of Ireland around 11 per cent in a country that contained 2.5 million people in 1700 and 5.5 million in 1800 (Yates: 19, 30). For most of the century, Irish Protestants, especially the clergy, acknowledged publicly, even if some harboured private reservations, the worthiness of the conversion of the mass of the population. The reasons proffered as to why this was a worthwhile endeavour differed from individual to individual, from decade to decade, and according to a rapidly changing religious climate. Nevertheless they were articulated, in sermons at least, using popular, political, economic, and religious anti-Catholic rhetoric, which by the beginning of the century was an ingrained part of British and Irish Protestant elite and popular culture.

Conversion was regarded by Anglican clergymen as forming a central duty for good Protestants and Christians, as it saved the benighted souls of an otherwise damned Roman Catholic population. Catholics were widely believed to be beholden to a rag-bag of superstitions, unscriptural doctrines, and sacraments, which collectively resembled a political system more than a religion. In a 23 October sermon of 1703, preached before the House of Lords, Edward Smyth attacked the Catholic doctrines of 'Christ's corporal presence' (or transubstantiation), and 'Purgatory' (Smyth: 17), while twelve years later, John Richardson, champion of evangelizing in Irish and Rector of Belturbet, Co Cavan, condemned 'the virtue of relicks, consecrated beads' and 'pilgrimages to places of pretended sanctity' (Richardson 1716: 41, 25–37). Robert Downes, Bishop of Ferns and Leighlin, in a House of Lords sermon, lamented the fact that the 'Church of Rome teacheth to pray to…Saints and Angels' (R. Downes: 8); while in a more fiery denunciation, the Dean of Ferns, John Alcock, in a House of Commons sermon, lambasted 'the priests…speaking lies in hypocrisy, when they pretended the Honour of Christ' (Alcock: 14). In 1769, William Newcome, Bishop of Dromore, in a flourish of Reformation rhetoric, attacked the Catholic Church for 'offering up public prayers in an unknown tongue' (Newcome: 7).

Roman Catholicism was also perceived by many Protestants as a barrier to economic and social development, as it discouraged individual responsibility, while a proliferation of holy days, combined with a parasitic clergy, who profited from pilgrimages, relics, and masses for the living and dead, drained the coffers of their already impoverished flock. Although economic anti-Catholicism was not nearly as common in sermons as its theological or political variant, when discussed in the early part of the century it was often couched in improvement rhetoric. During the eighteenth century, the Irish

Protestant landowning elite fostered agricultural improvement, developed the linen industry (especially in Ulster), facilitated urban modernization, and constructed polite, conspicuous country houses and demesne parks; at the same time the established clergy initiated moral programmes to reform manners and suppress vice and disseminated the culture of social and economic improvement (T. C. Barnard 1992, 1995; Sneddon 2007). In a sermon preached on the occasion of his first Episcopal visitation in 1721, economic improver Francis Hutchinson, Bishop of Down and Connor, stated that the Church of Ireland, in contrast to Roman Catholicism, did 'not draw money out of their purses, with pretences that we can deliver the sufferers out of them by our bought prayers and masses' (Hutchinson 1721: 11). In the later eighteenth century economic anti-Catholicism became one of the ideological weapons for Charter School propagandists.

Irish Catholics were, more importantly, regarded in British and Irish culture as inherently disloyal to Protestant monarchs, being required to give their spiritual and religious allegiance to the Pope, who was committed to the extirpation of all Protestants. This temporal allegiance was made particularly frightening due to two medieval doctrines that successive Popes laid claim to up until the 1770s: dispensing powers, which allowed Catholics to dispense with any obligation or oaths made to 'heretic' monarchs; and deposing powers, which imparted the right to depose or murder any monarchs excommunicated by the Pope.

This political anti-Catholic rhetoric informed Established Church sermons (especially in State thanksgiving sermons of 23 October and 5 November) up until the 1770s. It was complemented with explorations of concrete examples of Irish Catholic disloyalty: the Irish rebellion of 1641; the Irish phase of the Williamite wars, fought principally between England and Catholic France, 1688–97; the various Jacobite risings of the early part of the century; and the War of Spanish Succession, 1701–14 (Higgins: 14; H. Downes 1719: 19; Bolton 1721: 42–3; W. Hamilton 1723: 14; Bacon: 2, 7; Maurice: 15).

Robert Howard, the Irish-born and educated, Whig rector of St Bride's in Dublin, and later Bishop of Killala and Anchonry, on 23 October 1723 warned of the security threat posed by the Jacobite-supporting, Catholic Irish: 'Thus encouraged from abroad, and hoping for like success, they have fixed their eyes on Rome and a Popish successor, to whom only, they acknowledge their civil and religious allegiance is due' (Howard: 25). In a sermon preached before the House of Commons on 5 November 1759, treasurer of St Patrick's Cathedral, Dublin, Richard Chaloner Cobbe, mirrored the anti-Catholic sentiments of previous decades, albeit in more measured language: 'For popery is not only at, but within, our doors: whatever may be its disguise, the materials of its composition are the same: it has the same zeal; the same attachments to foreign powers, and interests; the same arts, and the same designs' (Cobbe: 11). For established clergymen, conversion to their brand of Protestantism, by whatever means, was the surest way to achieve the political pacification of the mass of the population.

Sermons containing a less structured, more popular brand of popular anti-Catholicism were employed pragmatically by the Hanoverian state in its first tentative years of existence, and at a time when loyal Whig clergy were more likely to be chosen to preach the four main celebratory sermons, especially in the House of Lords. In the aftermath of the 1715 rebellion, which in common with every uprising and plot in the British Isles since 1688 contained a majority of Catholics, both in rank and file as well as in positions of command, thanksgiving sermons poured forth from Dublin presses celebrating a further deliverance by providence from the halters of 'Popery'. Along with the new conservative political ideology of order, the Whig and Hanoverian regime in Britain and Ireland used anti-Catholic propaganda to forge political legitimacy among a riot-prone populace, who had not immediately taken to their new masters. Consequently, Irish printed sermons, in common with their English counterparts, informed their audiences of the consequences of a successful Stuart rebellion, namely a return to the late 1680s, an absolute monarchy, the restoration of Roman Catholicism as the state religion, and the persecution of Protestants (Tyrrell: 16–19; Godwin: 12; Ashe 1716: 15–18; Bolton 1717: 36–7, 40).

Means of Conversion

Premised on the belief that the Catholic population, with or without French or Jacobite assistance, was a continuing security threat to the Established Church and State in Ireland, the Penal Laws were introduced piecemeal by the Irish parliament between 1695 and 1750 to strip Irish Catholics of many of their property and civil rights, as well as their right to an organized Church. The Penal Laws were enacted in two waves: the first intense wave of measures was introduced between 1695 and 1709, almost on a yearly basis. These laws were concerned with Catholic solicitors, the prohibition of arms, foreign education, intermarriage, and the banishment of clergy and registration of secular priests. The second wave, introduced between 1716 and 1750, saw the sporadic passing of measures in response to certain concerns such as the sincerity of Catholic converts working in the legal profession. By forcing converts not only to take communion according to the liturgy of Established Church, but to produce a certificate of conformity and take oaths and declarations specified in the relevant legislation, collectively speaking, the Penal Laws, either indirectly or directly, aimed at encouraging conformity.

The Penal Laws relating to Catholic worship and the registration and expulsion of ecclesiastics, in contrast to those connected with political activity and land ownership, were rigorously enforced at a national and local level only at times of political crisis. It was at these times that Irish Protestants' sense of Catholic threat became almost hysterical in intensity and calls within the Irish parliament to enact new Penal Laws, or to toughen existing ones, became particularly audible. Among the strongest advocates for toughening the Penal Laws were the numerous English-born, Whig bishops were who, after the Hanoverian succession transported to Ireland by the Whig political and religious ascendancy to tame an incalcitrant Irish House of Lords.

During the reign of Anne, when religious politics in Britain and Ireland were divided along Low Church Whig and High Church Tory lines, the Tories, who comprised the majority of the parish clergy, argued that Whigs had exaggerated the Catholic threat and that this had allowed a greater threat to the established church—namely, Presbyterianism—to flourish in the North of the Island (Travers: 17–18). Furthermore, Tories tended to support the Penal Laws and conversion by means of Protestant education, while Whigs were more likely to support evangelizing in Irish. When penal legislation was discussed in sermons in this period, either negatively or positively, it was usually within this ideological framework.

Although penal legislation was sporadically enacted by the Irish parliament until the 1750s, to all intents and purposes attempts to enforce the Penal Laws ended by the third decade of century, after nearly forty years of internal peace. There was a general feeling among Irish Protestants that although Catholics were superior in number, they lacked arms, leadership, and the political will to threaten the Protestant state by internal rebellion; and even if they did rebel, British diplomatic relations were such that it was unlikely they would be assisted by a French-backed, Jacobite invasion. It was also generally accepted that Ireland would remain a Catholic country, a prospect which some members of the Anglican laity welcomed, as it ensured their continuance as a political and social elite. That the Penal Laws had failed to convert Ireland to Protestantism was obvious by the 1720s, as Catholics were to all intents and purposes able to practise their religion. By the 1730s, the country was well supplied with mass houses, schools, convents, and friaries and the numbers of secular and regular Catholic clergy were increasing steadily. Not only had the Penal Laws failed to disable the Catholic ecclesiastical structure, they had worked to convert only those with anything to lose by them: landowning Catholics, those with political aspirations, and the minority of worldly priests after the annual stipend paid by Grand Juries to clerical converts. In other words, the mass of the poor population of Ireland remained Catholic, while a new entrepreneurial merchant and yeoman middle class sprang up to fill the social and economic gap left by the disappearance of Catholic landowners.

The general softening of Protestant attitudes towards Irish Catholics in the mid-century, together with an increasing realization that the Penal Laws had not brought and probably would never bring the Reformation to Ireland, was reflected in most celebratory sermons, if not all. In other words, the opposition to conversion by coercive means, first voiced by the Whig Low Church clergy, was by the late 1720s a mainstream position. Although still convinced that Roman Catholics were inherently disloyal, the Irish-born chancellor of St Patrick's Cathedral and later Archbishop of Cashel, Theophilus Bolton, stated in a Commons sermon preached on 23 October that in matters of religion, 'coercion can contribute nothing' (Bolton 1721: 42–3, 31). The parliamentary sermons preached on 5 November 1731 by Whig bishop of Down and Connor, Francis Hutchinson, and Henry Jenney, chaplain to the Irish House of Commons, suggested that politically docile Catholics should be allowed to practise their religion (Jenney; Hutchinson 1731, 27–9). Edward Synge senior, Archbishop of Tuam, and his son and namesake, Edward junior, having passed through the whole gamut of conversionary schemes on offer, were by the 1720s calling for liberty of conscience, if not full civil toleration, to be extended to those Catholics willing to pledge allegiance to George I (Synge: 7, 12–23).

In a House of Commons sermon of October 1743, Benjamin Bacon, Archdeacon of Derry, stated that, 'whatever our laws relating to property may have put upon the better sort, they have had, nor ever can, have any effect on the vulgar'. Convinced that their 'deplorable condition', both economically and spiritually, was the result of their adherence to Catholicism, he believed, in common with an increasing number of clergy, that cultural assimilation of Catholic children in Charter Schools was the only way to make Ireland Protestant (Bacon: 15, 14–17). These were sentiments repeated by Bishop Edward Maurice of Ossory in his debut Lords sermon of 23 October 1755. Bishop Maurice however was also at pains to point out the continued security threat posed by the Catholic majority (Maurice: 15). Echoing Bishop Hutchinson's sermon three decades earlier, one preacher in 1763 suggested that the Penal Laws should be kept on the statute book unenforced, not because they would produce converts but as a deterrent against future Catholic aggression (Young: 7); while another, two years later, suggested that to use force to convert Catholics was not only un-Christian but reeked of intolerant, heretic burning, 'Popery' itself (Cumberland: 14, 15–16).

The reason that this retreat from clerical advocacy of coercive conversion increased in the second half of the century was because the political will which maintained the Penal Laws was slowly ebbing away. In the 1756–7 session of the Irish parliament unsuccessful attempts were made to pass a registration law legitimizing the secular priesthood. Between 1774 and 1793, a series of Catholic relief bills were passed relaxing laws on property ownership, while repealing those relating to the registration of priests, and allowing Catholics to marry Protestants, practise law, and vote in parliamentary elections. This legislation was the result of a number of factors: parliamentary lobbying by various societies, committees, and activists, some more radical and religiously inclusive than others; the decline of Jacobitism as a force in Irish and European politics; a growing number of Catholic clergy, gentry, professionals, and merchants increasingly willing, from the 1750s onwards, to align themselves to the Hanoverian regime; and pressure from the British government, especially on issues such as re-enfranchisement, in the early 1790s.

Evangelizing in Irish

The second method of conversion was the use of key religious texts printed in Irish, combined with the provision of Irish-speaking ministers and teachers. The rationale behind this was that most Catholics were illiterate and spoke only Irish. Thus if they were evangelized in the vernacular, as Scripture (as interpreted by Protestants) insisted, they would discover the errors of 'popery' for themselves, becoming more sincere converts in the process.

Between the sixteenth and early eighteenth centuries there had been various attempts to convert in this manner, none of which were successful. In 1571, two hundred copies of a government-sponsored, Church of Ireland catechism were printed in Irish, followed by five hundred copies of a Gaelic New Testament in 1602, and the Book of Common

Prayer in 1608. In the 1620s, William Bedell, Provost of Trinity College, Dublin and later Bishop of Kilmore and Ardagh, learnt Gaelic, initiated a lecture at the University in Irish, and ensured that on Holy Days prayers were given in Irish. He spent the 1630s translating the Old Testament, but abandoned the project during the 1641 uprising. These schemes to proselytize in print were not however accompanied by the provision of an Irish-speaking clergy. By the 1670s, the 1602 version of the New Testament was out of print, and in that decade and the early part of the next the natural philosopher Robert Boyle, aided by Narcissus Marsh, Archbishop of Dublin, printed the Anglican catechism and the Old and New Testament in Irish. Archbishop Marsh also encouraged several Protestant ministers to preach in Irish. The project was carried out against a backdrop of Protestant clerical and political opposition to Gaelic evangelizing. Some argued that Irish should be suppressed because it encouraged and maintained linguistic differences, thus preserving cultural and religious divisions in the country. It was further suggested that only by banishing the Catholic clergy from Ireland would the illiterate, native population be released from the bondage of 'popery'. Boyle and Marsh's project was discredited further in the 1680s as emerging Gaelic-speaking graduates from Trinity College, along with the scribes employed to do their translation work, backslid into Catholicism. The majority of the print-run was dumped in Scotland, as only a few copies were sold, and the project was finally abandoned at the onset of more confessional violence during the Irish stage of the Williamite Wars. In the aftermath of the bloodshed of 1689–91, several Irish clergymen who had supported the 1680s Gaelic campaign, such as Archbishop March, and Anthony Dopping, Bishop of Meath, now stood in opposition to it. Archbishop Marsh for example appropriated the arguments of his opponents in the 1680s, an outlook which underlay the Heads of a Bill by James Lanes, Viscount Lanesborough, to ban Irish, which he presented to the House of Lords in September 1697 (T. C. Barnard 1993: 244–53; FitzSimon: 159–68).

Despite such high-placed opposition, preaching in Irish was still pursued by some Established Church clergy. Between 1708 and 1729, a Catholic convert, Charles Lynegar, was employed in Trinity College to teach Irish to divinity students who were expected to become future agents of conversion. The fact that his stipend was not paid using college funds, but by the voluntary contributions of his students, indicates the still controversial nature of his undertaking. Furthermore, in 1703 and again in 1709, both the lower and upper houses of the Irish Convocation gave their tacit approval to preaching in Irish. In June 1709, the Lower House of Convocation, 'resolv'd that some person be appointed to prepare a short catechisme particularly fitted for the instruction of Papish recusants', and that 'some fit persons be provided and encouraged to preach, catechise and perform divine service in the Irish language' (Journal of the Upper House of Convocation 1708–13: 50–1).

It was John Richardson, Rector of Belturbet, who in 1710 set in motion a full-scale Gaelic conversion programme. Richardson took a multifaceted approach, suggesting that Irish-speaking clergy were to be provided with newly printed Gaelic Bibles and simple religious manuals and catechisms to enable them to preach to adult Irish Catholics. Catholic children, on the other hand, were to be converted in English-speaking Charity

Schools. Only by concentrating on all ages, reasoned Richardson, could Ireland be converted quickly and easily; and once they were they would abandon their language and culture, becoming indistinguishable from the English. However, party political animosity soon infected the scheme. The majority of Tory bishops in the Upper House objected to Richardson's plan because by its very nature it implicitly supported the Whig, Low Church, voluntary approach to tackling the Church's problems, rather than the coercive methods envisaged by High Churchmen to restore the Anglican Church's religious monopoly. The old arguments of the 1680s were marshalled once again, and it was even suggested erroneously that monoglot Irish speakers were few and English was fast becoming Ireland's main language. The Tory view was the prevailing one in Established Church sermons in this period (Richardson 1711a: ii–iii). The Whiggish Lower House on the other hand broadly supported Richardson's scheme, along with Archbishop Synge of Tuam, Bishop Edward Wettenhall of Kilmore, and Archbishop William King of Dublin. Supporters of preaching in Irish were in the vanguard of the realization that the Williamite Penal Laws had failed to deliver on their promise of a Second Reformation. In his 23 October sermon preached in London, the Whig Bishop of Clogher, St George Ashe, stated that, since 'Penal Laws and severity have hitherto proved ineffectual...let us endeavour to gain them...by allowing them the word of God, our excellent liturgy, and other pious Protestant books in their own language' (Ashe 1712: 22).

Using government money and donations from the Society for Promoting Christian Knowledge (SPCK) in London, between 1711 and 1712 Richardson published a new Irish-language version of the Book of Common Prayer, a catechism, and a selection of five sermons (T. C. Barnard 1993: 254–7). The sermons were designed to be used by Irish-speaking clergy in their efforts to convert Catholic adults. This collection, printed in traditional literary Irish—which bore little resemblance to eighteenth-century spoken Gaelic—contained sermons by Protestant clergy like Richardson himself and Seon Ó Maolchonaire and Philip Mac Brádaigh. Ó Maolchonaire translated a sermon (appropriately enough) by Welsh evangelizer and early supporter of the SPCK, William Beveridge, Bishop of St Asaph; while Mac Brádaigh presented an Irish version of a sermon (from 1689) by the Latitudinarian Archbishop of Canterbury, John Tillotson (O' Dochartaigh: 178; Richardson 1711b). In Richardson's conversion scheme, sermons took centre stage, forming a core part of its proselytizing machinery.

Richardson made little headway in furnishing the Established Church with Gaelic-speaking minsters, and by 1717 most of the massive print runs for these expensive texts were left unused and unwanted. Despite Richardson's frequent reports to the SPCK regarding progress made, it gradually backed away from evangelizing in Irish—as did the Irish government and any support the missions had mustered in Ireland. With the tide of public opinion turning against him, Richardson continued to use the printed sermon to publicize evangelizing in Irish. In 1716, he published a sermon in English and Irish that had been first heard in his parish church of Belturbet the previous year. It was printed, in two facing columns, one in English and one in traditional, literary Irish, and provided a highly subjective history of Ireland, from biblical times onwards, to demonstrate how Catholicism had kept the country spiritually and materially poor. He went on to suggest that conversion could reverse these trends, both on an individual and collective level (Richardson 1716).

The Bishop of Down and Connor, Francis Hutchinson (1661–1739), was another prescient Whig clergyman and Gaelic evangelizer who pointed out in the early 1720s that the Penal Laws had served only to convert rich Catholics. In common with Richardson, Hutchinson maintained that an essential part of any Gaelic conversion programme was to ensure that public worship was conducted by Irish-speaking clergy. In practice, he made no effort to promote the activity. A typical, Low Church, English reformer, he stressed the value of the written word, believing those converted by it were likely to be more committed to their new religion than those made Protestant by oral instruction. Consequently he focused his efforts on the young, in particular those Catholics attending Charity Schools. He argued that these children could be converted using custom-made, Anglican texts, written in a new easy-to-read, phonetic, form of Irish. This new way of presenting Gaelic was unveiled in his bilingual *Irish Catechism* of 1722. Its casual disregard for traditional typographical and orthographic conventions of literary Irish, and to a much lesser extent, English, was almost universally condemned by the Irish Protestant clerical and lay elite. Undeterred, he published a bilingual, phonetic almanac two years later in 1724, which marked the end of Anglican print in Irish for the next sixty-six years (Sneddon 2004: 37–56).

Despite the ignominy into which Richardson and Hutchinson had plunged evangelizing in Irish, a minority continued to support the project. William Hamilton, Archdeacon of Raphoe, in a sermon preached on 5 November 1725, championed Irish preaching in conjunction with limited liberty of conscience (W. Hamilton 1725: 18–23). George Berkeley, the Bishop of Cloyne, in his *Querist*, published in Dublin between 1735 and 1737, called for a solution to the Catholic problem that could have come directly from the lips of Richardson: Irish-speaking clergy for the conversion of Catholic adults, and Protestant education conducted in English for their children (Sneddon 2008: 152). If the majority of established clergy were, in both in the later Stuart and early Georgian periods, deeply divided over the use of the vernacular, their denominational rivals, the Presbyterian and Roman Catholic Churches, held no such qualms, promoting Irish preaching and printing sermons, catechisms and other Gaelic devotional material (Blaney: 20–7; McCaughey: 47–62; O'Ciosain: 134–6, 145).

English Protestant Education

By the second decade of the eighteenth century, Charity Schools were the symbol of hope for those worried about Protestantism. Clerical and lay reformers poured their time and money into the scheme and schools were established in increasing numbers, first through private and parish initiatives and then under the auspices of a national society located in Dublin. The Dublin Society for Charity Schools was set up in 1717 and modelled on the SPCK in England. In Charity Schools, Catholic children were to be made Protestant through a slow process of linguistic and cultural assimilation. They promised the children they educated would be made to be Protestant and deferent to their social superiors, as well as mannered, moral, and industrious. In practice, Charity Schools catered primarily for the educational needs of Protestants and did little to convert the Catholic Irish.

As has been mentioned, in their sermons, enthusiasts in the period before 1720 regarded Charity Schools as a supplement to the Penal Laws, although some leading Tories, such as Bishop Nathanael Foy of Waterford and Bishop Thomas Lindsay of Killaloe, seemed more committed to attacking what they saw as their main competitor evangelizing in Irish (Foy: 25–30; Maule: 17–20). The failure of Richardson's scheme vindicated this Tory opposition of Gaelic evangelizing.

Sermons preached annually on behalf of the Dublin Society for Charity Schools were a useful way to relieve influential congregations of their money, as donations were collected publicly and refusal was deemed unsociable and uncharitable. They also furnished those listening with a ready supply of reasons why they should support the charity, with each motivational speech weighted according to the preacher's particular prejudice. Bishop Peter Browne of Cork emphasized the utility of the schools, as they taught poor children 'such things as may qualify them for trades and callings' (Browne: 36). Archbishop Synge of Tuam, on the other hand, played the religious card, stating that conversion in Charity Schools would save a generation from growing up 'in ignorance and wickedness' and from 'eternal damnation hereafter' (Synge: 17). In 1721, the Bishop of Elphin, Henry Downes, suggested that the Charity Schools would carry on where the 'Reformation of Manners' societies of earlier decades had left off, by inoculating poor children against idleness, predilection to vice, and disobedience to parents and elders (H. Downes 1721: 6–16).

As David Hayton points out, 'In 1733 the Charity Schools were reborn with a different set of priorities: proselytization first; moral reformation, social discipline and economic reconstruction all given a subsidiary role' (Hayton: 181). The Irish Charter School system, whose official title was the Incorporated Society for Promoting English Protestant Working Schools in Ireland, was a national organization that attracted widespread support from the lower and higher clergy alike, as well as the Protestant laity. It was set up primarily through the efforts of the vehemently anti-Catholic, English-born, Whig Archbishop of Armagh, Hugh Boulter. By 1748, the Incorporated Society was operating thirty schools scattered throughout Ireland, educating 900 children, of whom 500 were apprenticed (Milne: 12, 22–5). Despite the priority given to proselytization in the Charter School system, it simply represented a face-saving exercise by the Anglican ascendancy, aware as it was that Ireland would remain Catholic.

Sermons that promoted Charter Schools were for the most part preached before the Incorporated Society, and were designed to raise both its profile and revenue levels. As with Charity School enthusiasts, Charter School promoters suggested their institutions would create a new generation of sincere Protestants who were hardworking, sober, honest, and trained in useful industries. Bishop Beresford of Ossory suggested that if Catholic children were taken from their families and placed in Charter Schools, and therefore 'rescued from hereditary error and parental influence', they would 'acquire Christian Knowledge, together with the habits of decency and useful industry' (Beresford: 9). This concentration on Catholic children was justified because, in the words of the Reverend Benjamin Bacon, 'there is a certain time of life, when few of any sort will suffer their religious principles to be called into question' (Bacon: 15).

This motivational rhetoric was elaborated upon using economic and religious anti-Catholicism, as well as appealing to Christian charitableness. In May 1764, the audience of Christ Church Cathedral Dublin were told by Dean Woodward that by supporting the Incorporated Society they were demonstrating Christian charitableness, as Charter Schools targeted the deserving poor (destitute children), unlike the Roman Catholic Church on the continent which distributed charity indiscriminately (Woodward: 3–4, 14). Woodward went on to suggest that conversion of Catholic children was worth pursuing because 'there is a constant connexion between Popery, despotick power, idleness and immorality' (Woodward: 14). Bishop Beresford of Ossory reiterated this popular and economic anti-Catholicism by suggesting in his Incorporated Society sermon that Irish Catholics were, and have historically been, 'in a situation extremely unfavourable to improvement...their religion, instead of disposing them to social connections and industrious pursuits...encouraged sloth, and condemned the arts of life as incompatible with their spiritual interests' (Beresford: 5). For others, conversion in Protestant working schools was to be pursued for religious reasons, as it delivered poor children from 'all the errors, and destructive principles' of the Catholic religion (Clayton 1740: 21; Woodward: 14).

During the final phase of the Penal era, the 1750s and 1760s, support for the schools as conversionary agents was couched in political as well as religious and economic anti-Catholicism, with the Catholic majority regarded as inherently rebellious and a potential security threat (Cobbe: 11; Woodward: 9, 14). In an Incorporated Society sermon of 1775, Isaac Mann, Bishop of Cork and Ross, stated that the 'lower rank of the people' were condemned by their 'popery' to live in 'sullen discontent against the government they live under, ready to join in open hostility with any invader' (Mann: 5). By the 1780s, however, political anti-Catholicism was no longer deployed in Charter School sermons, and in keeping with Protestant discourse as a whole at that time, the traditional terms of 'popery' and 'papist' were replaced by 'Roman Catholick', 'Romanist', or the 'Church of Rome' (Percy: 15, 16; Cleaver: 9–10, 13–14, 17–18; Beresford: 7).

Conclusion

Given the almost wholesale destruction of Church of Ireland records in 1922 during the Irish Civil War, sermons are an important way to gauge the views of the higher clergy and to a lesser extent the Protestant Ascendancy as a whole. This is especially true if one takes the approach adopted here, by considering all types of sermon and not just those dedicated to the four state preaching days.

Anglican sermons provide a significant insight into changing views of Irish Catholics within the Church of Ireland during the course of the eighteenth century, and in particular how and why their conversion should be pursued. They also contradict the view that the hierarchy of the Established Church in that period rested content with the fact that their religion was that of a small minority of the inhabitants of Ireland. In fact, the higher and influential parish clergy consistently and publically wrestled with the problem of how to convert Ireland to Protestantism in front of audiences they knew possessed the political influence and wealth to realize their adopted conversion scheme.

In the first half of the long eighteenth century, the main motivation for conversion was the political pacification of the Catholic majority. This was most prevalent in those celebratory sermons (23 October and 5 November) whose purpose it was to discuss the Catholic question through the distorted historical lens of past acts (or perceived acts) of Catholic aggression towards the Protestant Church and state in Ireland. Although the sense of the perceived threat was contingent on the preacher and the audience, broadly speaking they followed the base-line of the level of Protestant fear in the country as a whole at that time. This was at its height during the rage of party and Jacobite invasion scares of the first thirty years after the 'Glorious Revolution', subsided somewhat in the 1720s and 1730s (a period of de-facto toleration), and fell further in the 1750s, when Irish Catholics were seen more as a potential rather than as an immediate threat. The era of the Catholic relief, the 1770s onwards, saw the end of political anti-Catholicism in sermons. Although economic and religious reasons for conversion, centring on utility and salvation respectively, were mooted alongside political ones in the earlier period, they became more pronounced in the later eighteenth century, particularly in Charter School sermons. With the demise of celebratory sermons after 1770, Charter School sermons became the new debating forum for the Catholic problem.

Sermons not only discussed the problems created by Catholicism but how they were to be solved, by the conversion of the population to Protestantism. Sermons were used to help fund and raise the profile of particular conversion schemes, as well as to recruit the support of the influential and wealthy. Furthermore, in John Richardson's scheme, sermons formed part of his conversionary apparatus.

In the first decades of the century, when political fear of the Catholic population was at its height, sermons supported and disseminated the culture of conversion in three main, often interrelated ways: the passing, tightening and enforcement of the Penal Laws; evangelizing in Irish; and social, linguistic, religious, and cultural assimilation by means of Protestant education for the young. By the mid-1710s, Irish language enthusiasts, who pronounced that only by teaching the Word of God as interpreted by the Church of Ireland in print and from the pulpit could Ireland be made Protestant, began to suggest that the Penal Laws had failed as a conversion tool, as they had worked to convert only the rich and influential and not the mass of the population. This position became mainstream, in the late 1720s and early 1730s, as Protestant attitudes to Roman Catholics began to soften and the political will that maintained the Penal Laws began to dissipate. Controversial by its very nature, evangelizing in Irish foundered on the rocks of party conflict in the 1710s and early 1720s, with those Whigs who had originally supported it fleeing to the rival programme of English Protestant Charity Schools, once the province of the committed Tory. Of all conversionary measures, Protestant education was the only one considered viable by the Established Church for most of the eighteenth century, even during the Catholic relief era. Charter Schools, however, were an Anglican face-saving exercise performed by a clerical and political elite all but resigned to the fact that Ireland would remain a Catholic country. Less able to accept this than the laity, the established clergy continued to champion this cause in their sermons, which both publicized and helped fund them. One wonders however if the Incorporated Society did not have the attendant, utilitarian goal of producing a passive, pliable, hardworking, semi-skilled workforce, if the Protestant gentry, especially in the later period, would have lent it their support.

References

Alcock, J. (1747). *Sermon...23 October*. Dublin: S. Hyde.
Ashe, St George. (1712). *Sermon...23 October*. London: S. Buckley.
—— (1716). *Sermon...30 January*. London: A. Rhames.
Bacon, B. (1743). *Sermon...23 October*. Dublin: R. Owen.
Barnard, T. (1772). *Sermon...London-Derry, 13 September*. Londonderry: George Douglas.
Barnard, T. C. (1991). 'The Uses of 23 October 1641 and Irish Protestant Celebrations'. *English Historical Review* 106: 889–920.
—— (1992). 'Reforming Irish Manners: the Religious Societies in Dublin during the 1690s'. *Historical Journal* 35-4: 805–38.
—— (1993). 'Protestants and the Irish Language, c.1675–1725'. *Journal of Ecclesiastical History* 44-2: 243–72.
—— (1995). 'Improving Clergymen, 1660–1760', in A. Ford, J. McGuire, and K. Milne (eds.), *As by Law Established: the Church of Ireland since the Reformation*. Dublin: The Lilliput Press, 257–65.
Beresford, W. (1782). *Sermon...4 August 1782, before the Incorporated Society*. Dublin: George Perrin.
Blackstock, A. (2007). 'Armed Citizens and Christian Soldiers: Crisis Sermons and Ulster Presbyterians, 1715–1808'. *Eighteenth-Century Ireland* 22: 81–105.
Blaney, R. (1996). *Presbyterians and the Irish Language*. Belfast: Ulster Historical Foundation.
Bolton, T. (1717). *Sermon...30 January 1717*. Dublin: J. Pepyat.
—— (1721). *Sermon...23 October 1721*. London: W. Taylor.
Browne, P. (1716). *Sermon...15 April...Charity School*. Dublin: E Waters.
Choppin, R. (1729). *Funeral Sermon...Death of Rev'd Mr Joseph Boyse*, reprinted edn. London: John Gray.
Clayton, R. (1739). *Sermon...Cork...15 April*. Cork: Andrew Welsh.
—— (1740). *Sermon...Incorporated Society*. Dublin: George Grierson.
Cleaver, E. (1792). *A Sermon Preached at Christ-Church, Dublin...* Dublin: George Perrin.
Cobbe, R. C. (1759). *Sermon...5 November*. Dublin: A. James.
Connor, J. (1783). *Sermon...Funeral of Richard Malone*. Dublin: William Watson.

Connolly, S. J. (2003). 'The Church of Ireland and the Royal Martyr: Regicide and Revolution in Anglican Political Thought, c.1660–c1745'. *Journal of Ecclesiastical History* 54(3): 484–506.

Cumberland, D. (1765). *Sermon...House of Lords...5 November*. Dublin: Samuel Price.

Deconick-Brossard, F. (1993). 'Eighteenth-Century Sermons and the Age', in W. M. Jacob and N. Yates (eds.), *Crown and Mitre: Religion and Society...*Woodbridge, Suffolk: Boydell Press, 105–22.

Downes, H. (1719). *Sermon...23 October*. Dublin: J. Pepyat.

—— (1721). *Sermon...7 May...Charity Schools*. Dublin: John Hyde.

Downes, R. (1747). *Sermon...5 November*. Dublin: M. Owen.

FitzSimon, B. T. (2005). 'Conversion, the Bible, and the Irish language: the Correspondence of Lady Ranelagh and Bishop Dopping', in M. Brown, C. I. McGrath, and T. P. Power (eds.), *Converts and Conversion in Ireland, 1650–1850*. Dublin: Four Courts Press, 157–82.

Foy, N. (1698). *Sermon...23 October 1698*. Dublin: Samuel Adey.

French, M. (1712). *Sermon...Assizes...Carrickfergus...23 April*. Dublin: John Hyde.

Gillespie, R. (2001). 'The Reformed Irish Preacher: Irish Protestant Preaching 1660–1700', in A. J. Fletcher and R. Gillespie (eds.), *Irish Preaching, 700–1700*. Dublin: Four Courts Press, 127–43.

—— (2005). *Reading Ireland: Print, Reading and Social Change in Early Modern Ireland*. Manchester: Manchester University Press.

Godwin, T. (1716). *Sermon...26 February*. Dublin: n. p.

Hamilton, F. (1739). *Sermon...Visitation [of]...the Lord Primate*. Dublin: George Grierson.

Hamilton, H. (1772). *Sermon...Armagh...12 April*, reprinted edn. London: J. Nourse.

Hamilton, W. (1723). *Sermon...5 November 1722*. Dublin: Samuel Fairbrother.

—— (1725). *Sermon...5 November*. Dublin: Samuel Fairbrother.

Hayton, D. (1995). 'Did Protestantism Fail in Early Eighteenth Century Ireland? Charity Schools and the Enterprise of Religious and Social Reformation, c.1690–1730', in A. Ford, J. McGuire, and K. Milne (eds.), *As by Law Established: the Church of Ireland since the Reformation*. Dublin: The Lilliput Press, 166–86.

Higgins, F. (1707). *Sermon...28 August*. London: B. Barker.

Howard, R. (1722). *Sermon...23 October*. Dublin: J. & S. Pepyat.

Hutchinson, F. (1721). *Sermon...Primary Visitation...Lisburn, 3 May*. Dublin: E. Dobson.

—— (1731). *Sermon...23 October*. Dublin: George Grierson.

Jenney, H. (1731). *Sermon...5 November*. Dublin: Robert Owen.

Journal of the Upper House of Convocation (1708–13). Public Record Office of Northern Ireland, DIO 4/10/3/3.

Lambert, R. (1709). *Sermon...23 October*. Dublin: A. Rhames.

Lyster, J. (1793). *Sermon...Archbishop of Cashell's Triennial Visitation*. Dublin: William McKenzie.

McCaughey, T. (1998). 'General Synod of Ulster's Policy on the use of the Irish Language in the Early Eighteenth Century: Questions about Implementation', in K. Herlihy (ed.), *Propagating the Word of Irish Dissent, 1650–1800*. Dublin: Four Court Press, 46–62.

Mandelbrote, S. (1997). 'John Baskett, the Dublin Booksellers, and the Printing of the Bible, 1710–1724', in A. Hunt, G. Mandelbrote, and A. Shiel (eds.), *The Book Trade and Its Customers*. Winchester: St Paul's Bibliographies, 115–31.

Mann, I. (1775). *Sermon Preached...5 November*. Dublin: W. Sleater.

Mathews, E. (1714). *Sermon...Assizes...Carrickfergus 17 July 1713*. Dublin: John Hyde.

Maule, H. (1733). *Sermon Preached...23 October*. Dublin: George Grierson.
Maurice, E. (1755). *Sermon...23 October*. Dublin: Richard James.
Milne, K. (1997). *The Irish Charter Schools, 1730–1830*. Dublin: Four Courts Press.
Mischler, G. (2001). 'English Political Sermons 1714–1742: A Case Study in the Theory of Divine Right of Governors'. *British Journal of Eighteenth-Century Studies* 24–1: 33–61.
Newcome, W. (1769). *Sermon...5 November*. Dublin: Samuel Price.
O'Ciosain, N. (2010). *Print and Popular Culture in Ireland, 1750–1850*, reprinted edn. Dublin: Irish Academic Press.
O'Dochartaigh, C. (1976). 'The Rathlin Catechism'. *Zeitschrift fur Celtische Philologie* 35: 175–233.
Percy, T. (1790). *A Sermon Preached...*Dublin: George Perrin.
Radcliffe, S. (1714). *Sermon...Assizes...Kildare, 6 April*. Dublin: John Hyde.
Richardson, J. (1711a). *A Proposal for the Conversion of the Popish Natives of Ireland to the Established Religion...*Dublin: E. Waters.
—— (1711b). *Seanmora Ar Na Priom Phoncibh na Chreideamh...[Sermons on the Principal Points of Religion]*. London: n. p.
—— (1716). *Sermon...Belturbet, 23 October 1715*. Dublin: n. p.
Shaw, F. (1705). *Sermon...before...Archbishop of Tuam...at a Visitation*. Dublin: n. p.
Smyth, E. (1703). *Sermon...23 October 1703*. Dublin: Eliphal Dobson.
Sneddon, A. (2004). ' "Darkness must be expelled by letting in the light": Bishop Francis Hutchinson and Conversion of Irish Catholics by means of the Irish Language'. *Eighteenth-Century Ireland* 19: 37–55.
—— (2007). 'Bishop Francis Hutchinson: a Case Study in the Culture of Eighteenth-Century Improvement'. *Irish Historical Studies* 35–139: 289–310.
—— (2008). *Witchcraft and Whigs: the Life of Bishop Francis Hutchinson, 1660–1739*. Manchester: Manchester University Press.
Synge, E. (1731). *Sermon...23 October*. Dublin: Robert Owen.
Story, J. (1733). *Sermon...23 October*. Dublin: Stearne Brock.
Travers, J. (1711). *Sermon...5 November*. Dublin: John Hyde.
Tyrrell, D. (1716). *Sermon...29 January*. Dublin: J. Pepyat.
Yates, N. (2006). *The Religious Condition of Ireland, 1770–1850*. Oxford: Oxford University Press.
Young, E. (1763). *Sermon...23 October*. Dublin: Samuel Price.
Woodward, R. (1764). *Sermon...13 May...Incorporated Society*. Dublin: S. Powell and Son.

CHAPTER 33

'GO YE THEREFORE AND TEACH ALL NATIONS.' EVANGELICAL AND MISSION SERMONS: THE IMPERIAL PERIOD

JESSICA A. SHEETZ-NGUYEN

INTRODUCTION

MISSIONARY literature and sermons published between 1851 and 1901 show how spiritual expatriates incrementally expanded their influence in proportion to British commercial, political, military, and cultural power around the world. Andrew Porter's 'Religion, Missionary Enthusiasm, and Empire' in *The Oxford History of the British Empire: The Nineteenth Century* captures well this Victorian missionary milieu (Porter). More specifically, *The British Missionary Enterprise since 1700* by Jeffrey Cox offers a monumental undertaking that addresses key missionaries and their work, from William Carey to Bishop Crowther, the first native African bishop. Cox also delineates three research fields, 'imperial history, ecclesiastical history, and mission studies' (Cox: 5); the different approaches adopted by scholars in these sub-fields are essential to understanding the role played by the spoken and published sermon in the activities of British missionaries and their supporters. Conversely, to understand the missionary impulse itself and the literature at the foundation of it, Esther Breitenback's essay 'Religious Literature and Discourses of Empire' in *Empires of Religion* offers insight into one of the pressing scholarly questions regarding the study of missions: why did the British, and others, feel the need to evangelize the so-called heathen?

While this essay represents the beginnings of an exploration of the answers to the aforementioned question, it is important to note at the outset the importance of the sermon. Robert Ellison has argued convincingly about the persuasive power of the sermon in the nineteenth century (Ellison 1998): his theory certainly applies in the case of sermons preached as part of the nineteenth-century British missionary enterprise. Furthermore, the collection of essays headed 'Sermon and Society in the British Empire' in *A New History of the Sermon: the Nineteenth Century* are among the first to explore the value of published sermons as historical and cultural artefacts (Ellison 2010). It is in reviewing these 'artefacts' that the rationale for British missionary activity becomes clearer. These sermons demonstrate that it was possible to mix a genuine concern for the evangelization of the world with a rampant triumphalism and imperialism.

The World Missionary Conference in 1910 was perhaps both the apogee of this approach to missions as well as a clear indication of its coming nadir. The close connection between imperium and the Gospel is explained clearly in Brian Stanley's *The World Missionary Conference, Edinburgh 1910*. The empire of Christian churches sent workers into the spiritual battlefield spreading the good news as well as education and medicine (Stanley). And yet, as an analysis of some of the sermons preached in the nineteenth century demonstrates, the philosophy of equality underlying ideas of brotherliness guaranteed that the attitude of superiority adopted by many British missionaries could not be sustained. 'Native' Christians would begin to consider themselves the equals of the British, and other foreigners, wishing to run their churches themselves. With regard to Christianity, the civilizing mission of the British became, inadvertently, an egalitarian and democratic enterprise.

Again, the sermons described in this essay are exemplary, not widely representative. This analytical review of missionary sermons does not pretend to be exhaustive, but rather offers a sampling to illustrate the value of the sermon as an historical artefact for the interpretation of imperialism.

Sermons and the Missionary Ethos

In 1888, when the British empire neared its zenith, Benjamin Broomhall, secretary of the China Inland Mission prepared a table illustrating the estimated worldwide population for his publication, *Evangelisation of the World*. On it, each square shaded in tones from white, to grey, to black, represented one million souls. At the top of the graph, in white, Protestants accounted for 135 million, Greek Orthodox Christians 85 million, Roman Catholics 195 million, Jews—shown in light grey and occupying the centre of the graph—equalled 8 million in count. Mohammedans or Muslims, situated between Catholics and heathens, appeared a tone darker than members of the Church of Rome and ranked at 173 million, but the darkest blocks comprising more than half the graphic represented 874 million un-churched 'heathens' (Broomhall: 102). By 1900, twelve mission groups were working in China alone. From Africa to India to China, missionary activity accelerated after the 1850s, particularly with the opening of the Suez Canal and new ocean-going steam-powered ships that carried Europeans to far-flung parts of the world. On the frontiers of empire British cultural and spiritual power was articulated in homilies, letters, and journals. Measuring the extent to which Christianity had spread round the world by translating it onto a graph speaks to a mentality that lacks tolerance for, if not appreciation of, other cultures and people. Taking sermons as historical artefacts, significant milestones in cultural and political expansion may also measure the process by which Christianity extended its reach across the globe through homilies.

The imperial ethos, best theorized by Norbert Elias in *The Civilizing Process,* created a platform for British sermon givers in the home country and across Africa, India, and China. According to Elias, religion, the belief in the punishing or rewarding omnipotence of God, is as 'civilized' as the society or class that upholds it (Elias: 169). Christian preachers set out to change the world, but to do this they conceptualized themselves as purveyors of the truth and the indigenous as Others. The concept of 'Otherness' explained by Edward Said in his ground-breaking work, *Orientalism,* provides a second useful text that partially explains British cultural perceptions. By distinguishing the mother culture from newly encountered spiritual and social practices, missionary thinkers clarified their own deeply held values, helped others to grasp similarities and differences, and ultimately reflected on their experiences as a kind of spiritual warfare. Analytical complexities in addressing these issues include cross-fertilization of cultures and a sense of pride in their own culture and admiration for others. An element of self-satisfaction or a sense of accomplishment for some missioners also reveals a military spirit that aimed to conquer the Other world, not physically but spiritually. As Elias claimed, communal discussions about the place and meaning of religious values and practices carried as much weight as the spread of democratic ideals and economic development (Elias: 24).

In effect, the sermons explored in this chapter mirror the ways in which mid- to late Victorian Protestant beliefs changed over time. By stepping back and examining the world of the international sermon giver, scholars may feel they are in a panopticon, trying to see all things at once. Recognizing the futility of this exercise, the following analysis selects missionary sermons on a continent-by-continent and mission-by-mission basis to assess the significance of religion and its power to wage spiritual warfare.

This study relies on published and preached sermons that may lose something in the transition from the experiential domain to the printed page. Obviously, reading a text cannot be comparable to the lived experience of sitting in a pew and listening to a preacher, because one loses the chance to assess the nuances of facial expression and body posture of the preacher and the reactions of the congregation. On such occasions, the preacher will extend his broad knowledge of the Bible and its practical application for his listeners. An imperial missionary sermon may be defined as a message calling people to action in a geographical setting that extended beyond the boundaries of the British Isles. The purpose of the language is to persuade for success in terms of morality. The structure of the missive, whether delivered at home in the British Isles or abroad, included a selection of precepts, from both Old and New Testament verses, which offered thematic guidance. The exhortation, or call to action, set the stage for supporting arguments explaining why the faithful needed to carry on with imparted pious recommendations. The explication of the verse and the call to action unfolded through a set of syllogisms and/or analogies integrated to form a convincing argument pointing to truth. Finally, an injunction or call to action ended the discourse. All sermons had a message, but among the category of imperial sermons, those preached in Great Britain generally focused on a request for prayers, missionaries, or financial support, while the sermons given in Africa, India, or China explored the many challenges of building God's spiritual kingdom on earth in distant lands.

Among the numerous talented preachers of the mid-nineteenth century, Charles Spurgeon inspired many through his sermon entitled 'The Divine Call for Missionaries'. He opened with a quotation from Isaiah 6:8: 'Also I heard the voice of the Lord saying, "Whom shall I send, and who will go for us?" Then said I, "here am I; send me"'. In this homily, Spurgeon relied on repetition of the message to reinforce his theme, 'Whom shall I send? Who will go?' Using the method of Socratic dialogue with himself, the preacher queried, where are the volunteers to take the message across the seas to heathen lands? Not to let others off the hook, Spurgeon observed, 'Here are multitudes of professing Christians, making money, getting rich, eating the fat, and drinking the sweet. Is there not one to go for Christ?' Ask yourselves, he chided, 'What position do I occupy towards this work for God?' Then the speaker turned to visualization, 'I see the skirts of His garments as he reveals himself to me.' Moving to auditory senses, Spurgeon exhorted listeners to 'hear the rush of seraphic wings as I perceive how near heaven is to earth'. Then he focused on emotions: 'I feel in my soul I must give myself up to God' by seeing the need of the heathen (Broomhall: 89). Spurgeon explained what willing servants would encounter if they chose to heed the call. They must know they will be sent to the wildest region, to the 'jaws of death', to 'lie in the trenches at the head of my regiment'. Painting one last scenario of a capsizing ship, not lost to a population living on an island with many relatives who ventured across the seas, he asked: 'Who will leap in and take the oar for the love of Jesus?' In closing he urged, let those who love the Lord consider the 'world's dire need' and 'cry in the agony of Christian love, "Here I am, send me"' (Broomhall: 90).

Spurgeon, also known as the 'Great Teacher', was not without his critics. Nonetheless, others echoed Spurgeon's call to action in churches and town halls, where the impetus to induce change in 'heathen lands' inspired many young men and some women to go forth and teach all nations. The London Missionary Society, for example, took Spurgeon's charge to heart through 'preaching with power'. Missioners went forward as ambassadors of God to preach forgiveness, to bring the Saviour to those who did not understand, to battle with error, 'iron systems of priest craft, inhumanity, and wrong'. They set out through preaching, to stop crime, lay a hand on the slaveholder, appeal to the drunkard, clear out vice, and provide hope and gladness to those in despair (*Fruits of Toil*: 10–11). By addressing the five senses in the sermon explicated above, Spurgeon prepared his listeners for a choice to serve in the mission fields; wide stretches of Africa presented this great opportunity. Spurgeon's inspiration 'travelled' far.

Africa, 1851–1901

In South Africa by 1890, over four hundred ordained European and colonial missionaries, joined by sixty-five native followers, preached in over seventeen languages in 271 districts, including the Kimberley diamond fields (Tucker: xiv). Although the Society for the Propagation of the Gospel (SPG) expressed frustration that few attended church in South Africa, within a year of their arrival churchmen held Sunday services in Dutch, 'Kaffir' (a highly derogatory term), Zulu, and Sechuana. Churchmen believed they had made a start to bringing the word of God to the indigenous. Again, the Victorian penchant for counting appeared as Jesse Page, the biographer of Samuel Crowther, the first African ordained as Anglican bishop in Nigeria, claimed the population stood at 200 million, with the wider majority living as 'utter heathens' in the 'densest darkness of superstition and sin' (Page: 16). Missionaries like Crowther anxiously hoped to take responsibility for ameliorating the distressing spiritual condition of the Africans. To do this, the bishop petitioned and received support from the Church Missionary Society (CMS), Macgregor Laird, a London merchant engaged in the West African trade, and a government steamer to explore the many tributaries of the Niger River delta (Page: 85).

The civilizing initiative commenced decades earlier in conjunction with the end of the slave trade, when missionaries began to spread the good news of salvation through the sacraments and the promise of eternal life after death. In a sermon preached by John Weeks, the Anglican Bishop of Sierra Leone, at the ordination of four indigenous pastors, the impetus behind the language of the spiritual and civilizing mission becomes clear. First, he explained the relationship between a pastor and his spiritual charges who trusted his guidance towards meeting the 'concerns of eternity'. Drawing an analogy, the bishop did not see himself as the ultimate translator of power, rather he claimed true authority depended on the relationship between a man and his 'Maker, Redeemer, Sanctifier'. This association went deeper than that of a parent and child. Highlighting the transformative power of Christ's relationship to humanity, he noted that the path to salvation came through the bread of life. Through ordination, the new ministers would take the pledge to work for the 'solemn and awful charge' of spiritual formation (Weeks: 161).

The first indication that this charge had a missionary bent to it appeared well into the sermon. Weeks believed that one had to 'know' Christ to 'preach' Christ in order to impart that 'knowledge to those to whom he is sent' (Weeks: 162). To emphasize the idea that he spoke from a pulpit in a distant land, Weeks drew from St Paul, the first missionary to the Gentiles. (Many missionary sermons frequently mention the Epistles to bring comfort and confidence to carriers of the Word.) Comparing the true risks and struggles of living in a distant land such as Sierra Leone to those of Paul in Ephesus or Corinth, Weeks further humanized the future trials facing the new pastors by comparing the blessings with pain and distress inflicted on the human body, and pointed to the Christ-like sacrifice of life for this mission. Invoking 2 Corinthians 4:12, his text for the sermon, he remarked of the pain, 'We had the sentence of death in ourselves', and asked rhetorically about the sacrifice, 'Who shall deliver me from the body of this death?' It was true, Weeks noted, that 'death worketh in us' (Weeks: 165). These were words of encouragement to the four men ordained on that day with a 'high commission' to accept death with resolve and confidence, knowing the promise of life after death. Weeks ended the sermon by comparing the situation in the African town to John's visions in Revelation by bringing his listeners to hear the 'voice that spake to me' and the eyes that saw 'seven golden candlesticks'. He 'who walketh in the midst of the seven golden candlesticks…will own the church of Abbeokuta as one of the brightest of them all, and yourselves [are] as stars in His right hand, to shine…as the stars forever and ever' (Weeks: 165). Drawing on Paul's travels and church building in Ephesus, Weeks had looked to the future when he quoted Revelation 1:12. Little did he know that spreading the promise of spiritual life everlasting would be aided by gunboats, and that commercial interests would trump African culture and mores (Sheetz).

India, 1851–1901

In India, British missionaries recognized two strains of religion, Islam and Hinduism, and acknowledged a multitude of languages. The CMS divided India by north and south, with Muslims most represented in northern provinces, while Hinduism held sway over the south. Reviewing the history of British activities in India, Edward Jacob Boyce prepared a sermon of thanksgiving at Godalming Church. However, in the preface to the published version, *Christian England and Her Fellow Subjects in India*, he criticized missionary failures on the sub-continent (Boyce). In 1757, after Robert Clive assumed power at the Battle of Plassey, support for the spread of Christianity had simmered rather than boiled, he complained. In 1814, the first Bishop of Calcutta arrived to oversee the entire sub-continent, a large geographical region for one man to administer. Further, the special challenges and legal proscriptions against conversion to Christianity discouraged British missionaries from going to India. For example, local laws disqualified men who converted to Christianity from service with the Sepoys, Indian soldiers in service to a European power. Psychologically and intellectually prepared in advance for what they would encounter upon arrival in India, readers understood that Indians lived in a 'degraded state to which ignorance and superstition' reduced human morals ('The Sepoy Convert and the Authorities': 220).

In the autumn of 1856 the Bishop of Calcutta, George Edward Lynch Cotton, delivered a sermon in the Chapel Royal, Whitehall, celebrating the consecration of Archibald Campbell Tait, Bishop of London and Henry Cotterill, Bishop of Grahamstown (now South Africa) entitled *The True Strength and Mission of the Church*. While the sermon attracted considerable attention for the comparisons it drew between metropolitan London and an African colony, *The Colonial Church Chronicle* dismissed it as having little value for missionary purposes because although 'written in good spirit' it took a limited view of the 'unity' as described by John 17:20–21. *The Ecclesiastic* witnessed 'peculiar' if disappointed interest in the Cotton sermon because of an absence of scriptural references; Bible verses such as 'That they all may be one; as thou, Father art in me, and I in thee' provided one of the clearest statements of ecumenism available. Editors noted a fundamental error in the injunction, whereby Cotton compared unity in Christ with the 'communion of our spirits with God'. The foul chord prompted the editor to charge Cotton with Deism, or belief in God whose existence was based on reason and natural phenomena ('The Strength and Mission of the Church': 19). With the outbreak of social and political unrest in India, London clerics called for infighting to cease and issued a clarion call to advance missionary activities for spiritual and cultural conversions.

After the Indian Mutiny, the British government settled political and military issues by an Act of Parliament, transferring the government of India to the Crown. At that time, the British Raj issued an order forbidding missionary activity in the regions surrounding North Indian military stations, where the massacres had occurred (Boyce: 4–5). In the aftermath, Charles Spurgeon announced a church service to be held at the Crystal Palace. Observers recounted that the event probably drew one of the largest congregations ever assembled. Spurgeon preached the sermon for the Indian Mutiny Relief Fund. By noon on the day of the event, no less than 24,000 persons had assembled. Young at the time, Spurgeon stepped up to the 'portable pulpit' and opened with an invocation followed by a hymn, 'Before Jehovah's Awful Throne', composed by Isaac Watts based on the Psalms of David. Framing the sermon, the lyrics 'He can create and He destroys' set the tone (Spurgeon: 2). A reading from Daniel 9 supplied further background to a prayer, in which the preacher called on God to witness the horrible scenes in India and prayed that England might be preserved from the further scourge. He asked God to give soldiers strength to 'execute the doom which justice demanded'. The British troops must remember the Sepoys were not only warriors, but executioners of innocents. Who, he asked, will destroy the enemy that defiled Britain? (Spurgeon: 3). Then congregants sang 'Our God, Our Help in Ages Past'. The stanza 'In vain the sons of Satan boast | Of armies in array | When God has first despised their host | They fall an easy prey' was particularly pertinent.

Spurgeon's selection of the hymn, focusing on the spiritual powers of Satan's army, resonated with the congregation and refocused the sermon's tone, turning the event from questions about the causes of the uprising to opportunities for national redemption. Spurgeon read from Micah 6: 9, 'Hear ye the rod, and who hath appointed it?' and followed this by one question after another. Who holds the power in this world? Why did this massacre happen? Was it because the world was a place for punishment for sin? 'Not usually,' Spurgeon remarked (Spurgeon: 3). For his part, he believed the episode represented a judgement or chastisement for 'national sins'. The mutiny offered Britain's people an opportunity to humble themselves, to repent, and to recover from transgressions against God. Spurgeon lamented over the 'revolted subjects', who he regarded as fellows in armed rebellion against the government. Fortunately, Spurgeon concluded, the British constitution protected against revolution (Spurgeon: 3).

In a Surrey parish located southwest of London, Edward Jacob Boyce, a lesser-known preacher, also published his sermon on the Indian Mutiny to raise funds for victims (Boyce: Preface). Boyce compared and contrasted Christian England with 'subjects in India' on 7 October, the day appointed by royal proclamation for fasting and prayer. Boyce clearly regarded British subjects working in India as unhelpful to the spread of Christianity, even going so far as to accuse expatriates of being ashamed of their faith. The best and brightest men—civilians or soldiers—may have tried to 'spread the word of Christ', but, he claimed, they almost ignored or placed less emphasis on their faith than did Muslims, Jains, and Hindus (Boyce: preface).

Boyce compared the status of the followers of Christ in India with Saint Peter in Rome and Saint Paul in Athens. The experiences of these church founders, both martyred by the Romans, offered a handy trope. The patriarchs of Christianity had battled Rome and its state religion. Similarly, missionaries in India encountered a large and powerful cultural enterprise that blocked advance of their belief system. (The pastor's knowledge of Greece and Rome demonstrated his classical education and training for the ministry, and therefore served as a platform for analogies between the classical world and India.) Further, Boyce compared victims of the mutiny to St Peter's incarceration by the Romans in the Mamertine Prison, overlooking the Forum; quoting Acts 12: 5, he said they needed 'the prayer [that] was made without of the Church unto God for him' (Boyce: 1). He exhorted parishioners to recognize how the sub-continent suffered from famine and pestilence. Echoing Spurgeon, Boyce claimed that the Lord had spared Britain bloodshed at home, because troops, trained for battle and prepared to die, had defended rights and inflicted punishment on the Sepoys for their wrongs. Yet, from childhood, Boyce reminded listeners, students learned about the 'Black hole of Calcutta'. Analogizing, Boyce turned to the Old Testament and compared the plight of the British living in India to the Israelites living under the Egyptians, where they struggled through famine, pestilence, and war. God had observed a breach of trust because 'Christian England' denied her 'Hindu and Mohamedan subjects' the true word of God, suggesting the need to remedy this deficiency (Boyce: 4). Three generations of Indians had been permitted to 'sink into the dust... without having made any effort to save their souls from death'. He further argued the Hindu community had been denied the *right* to become Christian subjects, because, he noted, the concept of religious toleration did not exist in India (Boyce: 6).

Turning his attention to contemporary missionary activity, Boyce reminded the congregation of the story of Paul preaching on Mars Hill—the Areopagus, the meeting place of the Athenian supreme court. In Acts 17:22–31, Paul recounted walking past many Greek statues to deliver the sermon, even by an altar to 'the unknown god'. Earlier, Paul had taught about the power of the God of Israel who, while omnipresent, did not dwell in Greek man-made temples. Although many of Paul's listeners had not known God, primarily because of their ignorance, they had a chance to repent. By analogy, Boyce claimed that Indians deserved the same as the Athenians. Resting his case on statistics, Boyce noted that over 170 million heathen subjects suffering from England's 'notorious commercial profligacy' remained beyond the word of God, making them vulnerable to the fires of Hell (Boyce: 6, 7).

Boyce's fire and brimstone warning directly linked divine and national power as a means for building the 'kingdom' on earth. 'God gives, to a man or to a nation, power; He expects that power to be used directly and indirectly for His Glory...and furtherance of His Kingdom' (Boyce: 8–9). Voicing a realistic perspective, Boyce asserted that it hardly seemed possible that fasting, humiliation, and prayer could allay the suffering in India. Then Boyce turned to visualization recalling images of vulnerability, where powerless and helpless individuals found themselves surrounded by 'savage rebels thirsting for their blood'. British soldiers withstood and bore the cross. Do not forget, Boyce admonished, contemporary Christians had as much power to help as did St Paul (Boyce: 9).

Boyce suggested that his parishioners should use the same strategy as Hezekiah when he prayed for help against Sennacherib; they should 'entreat the Lord of hosts' to send His angel to 'cut off the mighty men of valour, and the leaders and captains in the camp of the rebels, even before our brave soldiers shall have reached the scene of bloodshed in sufficient numbers to inflict just punishment upon them' (Boyce: 11–12). In the injunction, Boyce called on parishioners to remember 'the conduct of the Church when Peter was in prison, and to pray constantly, earnestly, and reverently for India and fellow countrymen living there and for the government of that benighted land...that God would now rule this heartrending calamity to the furtherance of His Glory' (Boyce: 11–12). For the British, Boyce asserted the Indian Mutiny would prove providential, bringing forward a rising generation of wealth and splendour based on a successful military enterprise (Boyce: 14–15).

After the debacle in the sub-continent, the hierarchy translated missionary churches there into permanent establishments. A set of published sermons delivered by George Edward Lynch Cotton between 1858 and 1866 expressed a wide array of concerns, from the proper consecration of a church to celebrations of the liturgical year. The best characterization of these sermons is that they offer examples of ecumenical teachings for Christians. Thus, for example, Cotton drew from Ephesians 6: 24, 'Grace be with all them that love our Lord Jesus Christ in sincerity', as the foundation for the first sermon titled 'Apostolic Blessing', in which he discussed how Paul first became a Roman citizen and then a spiritual warrior. Placing himself in the shoes of Paul, he compared Calcutta to Ephesus located in Asia Minor, where 'pagan multitudes' surrounded the ancient missionary. Taking on 'defective views of Christian truth', the sermon reassured listeners that Paul offered affection and hope for the 'brethren in Christ' (Cotton 1867: 1, 2).

Cotton, like Paul, drew upon personal experiences that required his congregation to remember a time when they found themselves in unfamiliar territory, not just physically, but spiritually. Think what it meant to be a stranger 'surrounded on all sides by millions of unbelievers', even in their own English homes (Cotton 1867: 4). Drawing lines between non-believers and believers, and noting the theological differences amongst various communities of Christians, Cotton pointed out that while not all Christian 'modes' could be 'equally true' and acceptable to God, the differences were trifling, when compared to the chasm that separated Christians in India from those who did not 'know the Lord Jesus' (Cotton 1867: 5). The preacher asked people to think about the bonds that united them on that Sunday, and to consider how they would 'cleave to' one another, when compared to those who had no knowledge of redemption and sanctification. The English found themselves confronted by those who rejected God and worshipped deities from whom they gained favour by the practice of 'wicked rites and grovelling superstitions', and these foreign gods assumed human forms that exemplified 'fraud, and lust, and cruelty' (Cotton 1867: 6). To manage the problems facing him as bishop, he asked for prayers because the Lord had sent him forth to 'do battle against every form of ungodliness'. In this injunction to action, he asked for strength to 'live and die as devoted servants of Christ'. Finally, he asked, 'God be merciful to me a sinner' (Cotton 1867: 11).

In a sermon entitled 'Proselytism and Conversion', delivered in Delhi in 1865, Bishop Cotton referred to the injunction in Matthew 28: 19, 20, 'Go ye therefore, and teach all nations, baptizing them in the name of the Father, and of the Son, and of the Holy Ghost: teaching them to observe all things whatsoever I have commanded you.' Again invoking the loneliness of Christians living outside their community of believers, Cotton asserted that they were living 'in the midst of heathen, called upon constantly to support missionary efforts, and yet sometimes hearing them spoken of in terms of disparagement as a mere form of proselytism' (Cotton 1867: 119). Addressing the congregation as messengers of God, he reminded them that 'in this pagan land, a common faith in the Lord Jesus Christ should unite us all far more closely than differences of opinion on church government, or on certain parts of Christian doctrine' (Cotton 1867: 120). In his view, the Gospel of peace commanded the work of missionaries; and their toil could never end until the entire world had been evangelized (Cotton 1867: 119). Further, missionaries must lay claim to a 'burning desire to make others partakers in blessings which we have learned to regard as inestimable'. A goal of the movement was to bring others to know 'His will and commandments' and to teach 'truth, and righteousness, and purity...found in Christ Jesus', even if there seemed no particular desire for it (Cotton 1867: 122). Reminding parishioners that Christ commanded his disciples to go forth, baptize, and teach all nations, Cotton provided the motivation to fulfil the commandment (Cotton 1867: 124).

China, 1851–1901

Although the London Missionary Society (LMS) had been operating on a small scale from 1807, it had been impossible to make inroads into China's vast interior. Arthur H. Smith, in his essay 'A Centennial of Protestant Missions in China', divided missionary work in China by regions, events, and people. First arrivals landed in one of the five treaty ports between 1807 and 1842, Guangzhou (Canton), Hokkien (Amoy), Fuzhou (Foochow), Ningpo and Shanghai. These cities had been opened to the West through the East India Company and the office of Foreign Trade. The second era extended from 1842 to 1860, during which time the Taiping Rebellion broke out, the British and French captured Peking, and British officials executed ratification of the Treaty of Tientsin, opening all of China to Christianity (Smith: 7). After 1860, a steady rise in mission groups permitted H. W. Tucker to report that missionaries working across Asia from India to Burma to China served thirty-three races and 'half castes', in twenty-seven different languages and dialects. Over 380 ordained preachers carried on the work with the help of almost two hundred 'native' or 'dark races' supplementing the initiative. During the long nineteenth century, the SPG had expended over £2 million to spread the word of God in Asia (Tucker: xiv).

Early arrivals knew little about manners, language, customs, and literature; and expensive and arduous voyages caused the deaths of many missioners who had given up a comfortable life in London to serve God. Upon arrival, most recognized the need to cross the cultural bridge. The uniformity of language helped these 'spiritual warriors' make inroads. For example, Scottish missionary James Legge translated Confucian classics while he worked with the LMS in Malacca, before going to open a seminary in Hong Kong in 1843. He believed Chinese natural theology contained elements of Christian truth. Legge's openness to the host culture bespeaks an alternative approach to the missionary enterprise. After completing assignments in China, Corpus Christi College, Oxford, appointed him fellow and then first professor of Chinese studies. Legge's translations contributed to the propagation of Christianity; in fact, the China Inland Mission concluded that no Church work could have been attempted without a translation of the Bible, the compilation of a Chinese and English dictionary, and numerous books and tracts, which began in Malacca and whose completion coincided with the Treaty of Nanjing in 1842 (Smith: 7).

The SPG began working in China under the auspices of the Bishop of London after the French ambassador had signed treaties permitting freedom of access for Christian missionaries. As in any enterprise, money was essential for operations, thus a fund was opened at the office of the SPG for the explicit purpose of bringing Christianity to Asia (Grant: Preface). In a sermon preached at Camden Church, Camberwell, Anthony Grant opened with a reading from Acts 16: 6–8 that addressed the question of preaching in Asia. According to the homily, Paul and Silas had received orders not to enter Asia. Drawing on the history of the biblical era, Grant told his parishioners that the Apostles would have borne the tidings of salvation to Asia, but the Holy Ghost stopped them and so they redirected their efforts to Bithynia. Why, the preacher wished to know, did the Trinity offer such guidance, with one choice preferred to another? Most importantly, he asked, why were some parts of the world enlightened by God's truth, but not all? In answer to his query, Grant argued that where faith in God could and did exist, missionary efforts were wasted. In reality, the Chinese were without religion. Indeed, much work needed to be done, because of the three forms of worship, the first, Daoism, scarcely rose above superstition, being a form of idolatry, the second, Buddhism, offered ceremony and 'dreamy atheism', while the third, Confucianism, provided a system of ethics. Although Confucius promoted 'the doctrine of the learned', such a creed could not provide the peace of Christianity (Grant: 20).

By 1869, the LMS occupied seven principal stations and employed twenty-one English missionaries. From Amoy, the Reverend John Stronach reported on his work in distant

San-io and the village of Tang-son where he set up schools. Positioning himself as a teacher, a scholar, with outreach to the poor, Stronach encouraged conversion to Christianity. When he asked for proof, families brought their 'idols' to the school and 'decapitated' them and broke the statues into pieces. He then baptized four new Christians. In Amoy, preaching took place in a church with few members, showing, he wrote, that 'the Gospel though productive in one place had little influence elsewhere' (*Fruits of Toil*: 63). The Reverend G. John returned the following information on preaching to London from Hankow, located up river on the Yangtze. Between 1861 and 1868, he had baptized fifty-one converts, including thirteen women, eleven of whom were wives of new Christians. Of significance for those interested in outreach to women, John reported that his preaching aimed to impress on new Christians that they had a duty to bring their wives under the direct influence of the Gospel but that the men maintained that bringing wives to 'church' was against custom; if they did this, it would bring communal contempt upon themselves and their family (*Fruits of Toil*: 64). John also wrote that he hoped the 'whole Empire may be influenced from this grand centre' that comprised 'different grades of society', including scholars, tradesmen, artisans, and barbers (*Fruits of Toil*: 65).

The Reverend John Griffith, who lived in China for over fifteen years, offered a firsthand account of life for missionaries in a sermon entitled *Hope for China! or, Be Not Weary in Well-Doing*. In his tellingly prejudicial sermon he observed, 'I have never met a heathen who seemed to be troubled with a sense of sin, or appeared to have the least desire to be delivered from its dominion' (Griffith: 2). Obviously frustrated, Griffith described the Chinese as impenitent and godless; because, he argued, their society had been in decay for a long time. The 'friends of Missions', he warned, needed to moderate expectations, and yes to even observe the state of Christianity at home and recognize how slowly Christian truth moulded everyday life. This, he believed, would aid in understanding how little had been 'accomplished in heathendom' (Griffith: 2).

In *Missionaries after the Apostolical School* (1825), by the Reverend Edward Irving, which was also included in Hudson Taylor's *China's Millions* (1885), readers learned about spiritual travellers crossing Greece and Asia Minor on their way to Rome who 'had nowhere to lay their heads' (Hudson Taylor: 119). They took as their charge not speeches, but speaking the truth. The injunction called the faithful to disavow material belongings, to leave families, and to become followers of Christ. Drawing an analogy between the original disciples who carried the good news and contemporary preachers, Irving reminded his listeners that missionaries should not expect to be welcomed, but to be prepared to go forward as 'sheep in the midst of wolves' (Hudson Taylor: 120). Comparing the work of a missionary to engagement in war, he offered this stark observation: 'If ye have a heart for the extremes of human sufferings, and a soul above the fear of man, ye need not undertake this work—more perilous than war ... more important to the earth than any sacred legation that ever went forth on behalf of suffering' (Hudson Taylor: 121).

The years 1895–1900 marked the prelude to the Boxer uprising, when indigenous rioting attempted to expunge 'foreign devils'. Christians provoked a violent backlash from the 'Boxers' who lived in Shansi province. One assessment of the uprising might be that this group of individuals suffered delusional ideas; but it is also fair to say that Boxers attempted to return the assault on their culture by taking spiritual warfare to a new level of reality. A Boxer poster revealed their view of Christians: to the Boxers, Christians had neither ethics nor morals. Missionaries had caused the ills of bad weather resulting in famine and pestilence and their churches blocked access to the gates of heaven. Finally, preachers not only taught the word of God, but they also brought railroads, ships, and other components of modern technology. At the same time, it was also true that missionaries challenged the long held structures of rank and cultural practices in small and large communities. They took on the mantle of scholar bureaucrats, even going so far as to adopt the clothing styles of the elite. Perhaps, more disturbing to the elite, westerners promoted individuals who ranked on the lower rungs of society. In short, in an effort to find converts, western missionaries offered different promises to peasants, who, may or may not have grasped the spirituality and intellectual modalities of Western traditions. By removing the strictures of the examination system and many other social constraints as the escalators to wealth and success, Europeans presented themselves as instrumental counter-cultural beings. Therefore, the foreigners, according to the Boxers' worldview, had to die to ensure longevity of the Qing Dynasty (Zao).

Writing in 1907, A. H. Smith described the exercise of spiritual power in China as a 'missionary war' replete with wire entanglements, manholes, and sharp stakes. He observed that it required a 'higher order of courage to face the terrible ordeal of hatred, suspicion, and contempt' (Smith: 9). Those 5,860 missionaries who experienced this suffering, and had even died 'forgotten in the city' where they worked, had now been 'recalled with gratitude to God' (Smith: 9).

Conclusion

The ending of the slave trade in Africa, the Indian Mutiny in India, and the Opium Wars in China facilitated the expansion of Christian missionary work. Today the world is witnessing rapidly moving tides of change and interplay of ideas in far-flung quarters of the globe. In the nineteenth century, a far less democratic milieu, the concept of spiritual warfare at the local and international level operated as a component of the imperial project. 'Heathens' offered a *raison d'être* for learning languages other than English, travel to distant lands at considerable risk to the lives of the missionaries and their families, and the establishment of mission stations in urban and remote areas of regions far from home. Missioners measured success by the number of baptisms, confirmations, and other rites of passage performed in the Church community. Although not directly mentioned, sermon-giving across the British Isles describing experiences in Africa, India, and China had one goal: to raise funds to bring the others under the sacred dome of Christianity. Missionaries imagined their work as part of 'foreign relations', seeing themselves as diplomats of God's Holy Word; when they required actual military intervention, they willingly called on the home country's troops for assistance. For the most part, however, the travelling vessels of the Word of God tried to accomplish their aim without use of force.

Clearly, the present chapter only scratches the surface of this historical arena. More research, analysis, and writing remains, especially as more missionary publications become available through digitized collections. Sermons provided a platform for social criticism both at home and abroad. Some preachers recommended the British organize their affairs first, before going elsewhere. On-going debates amongst Christian faith communities travelled to the far reaches of empire, despite calls for ecumenism among some. Preachers clearly compared the work of the mission with that of the soldier, the civilizing processes with conversion of heathens, and the spread of Christianity with civilization and respectability.

REFERENCES

Boyce, E. J. (1857). *Christian England and Her Fellow Subjects in India*... London: Bell and Daldy.
Breitenback, E. (2008). 'Religious Literature and Discourses of Empire: The Scottish Presbyterian Foreign Mission Movement', in H. M. Carey (ed.), *Empires of Religion*. Basingstoke: Palgrave Macmillan, 84–112.
Broomhall, B. (1887). *The Evangelisation of the World. A Missionary Band* ..., 2nd edn. London: Morgan & Scott.
Cotton, G. E. L. (1856). *The True Strength and Mission of the Church*... London: Rivingtons.
—— (1867). *Sermons Preached to English Congregations in India*. London: Macmillan and Co.
Cox, J. (2010). *The British Missionary Enterprise Since 1700*. New York: Routledge.
Elias, N. (2000). *The Civilizing Process* ..., reprinted edn., E. Dunning, J. Goudsblom, and S. Mennell (eds.). Oxford: Blackwell Publishing.
Ellison, R. (1998). *The Victorian Pulpit*.... Selinsgrove, PA: Associated University Presses.
—— (ed.) (2010). *A New History of the Sermon: the Nineteenth Century*. Leiden: Brill.
Fruits of Toil in the London Missionary Society... (1869). London: John Snow.
Grant, A. (1859). *The Church in China and Japan: A Sermon Preached*... London: Bell and Daldy.
Griffith, J. (1872). *Hope for China! or, Be Not Weary in Well-Doing*. London: John Snow.
Hudson Taylor, J. (ed.) (1885). *China's Millions: China Inland Mission*. London: Morgan and Scott.
Page, J. (1892). *Samuel Crowther: The Slave Boy who became Bishop of the Niger*. New York: Fleming H. Revell Company.
Porter, A. (1999). 'Religion, Missionary Enthusiasm, and Empire', in A. Porter (ed.), *The Oxford History of the British Empire: The Nineteenth Century*. Oxford: Oxford University Press, 222–46.
Said, E. (1978). *Orientalism*. New York: Pantheon Books.
'The Sepoy Convert and the Authorities'. (1856). *The Church Missionary Intelligencer, A Monthly Journal of Missionary Information* 7: 217–30.

Sheetz, J. A. (1990). 'Ja Ja, Chief of the Opobo and the British Annexation of the Niger Delta, 1857–1891'. Unpublished MA thesis, Millersville University, 1990.

Smith, A. H. (1907). 'A Centennial of Protestant Missions in China', in Centenary Conference Committee (ed.), *China Centenary Missionary Conference. Addresses: Public and Devotional...* Shanghai: Methodist Publishing House, 1–33.

Spurgeon, C. H. (1857). *The Sermon at The Crystal Palace on 7 October 1857*. London: J. A. Berger.

Stanley, B. (2009). *The World Missionary Conference, Edinburgh 1910*. Grand Rapids, MI: Eerdmans.

'The Strength and Mission of the Church'. (1857). *The Ecclesiastic and Theologian* 19: 19.

Tucker, H. W. (1894) (ed.). *Digest of the Records of the Society for the Propagation of the Gospel in Foreign Parts, 1701–1892*, 4th edn. London: SPG.

Weeks, J. W. (1852). 'First Ordination Sermon Preached at Sierra Leone by the Right Rev. Bishop...'. *The Church Missionary Intelligencer: A Monthly Journal of Missionary Information* 3: 161–5.

Zao, Yang Feng. (1901). *Boxer Rebellion in Beijing and Tianjin*, vol. 3. Hong Kong: Hong Kong Publishing House.

PART VI
SERMONS AND LITERATURE

CHAPTER 34

THE POET-PREACHERS

KIRSTIE BLAIR

In 1851, reviewing Charles Kingsley's poem *A Saint's Tragedy* alongside a volume of his sermons for the *North British Review*, the reviewer (Francis Russell) took the opportunity to reflect upon the connection between the two genres: 'What sort of sermons are we to look for from a poet? or, in other words, What relation does the gift of poetry bear to the gift of preaching?' (Russell: 229). Espousing a standard Romantic view of the 'poet' as fundamentally different from other men, possessing 'peculiar mental structure and powers', Russell suggests that the term 'poet' implies an innate gift, whereas preaching is part and parcel of the recognized office of a clergyman and in itself requires no special powers (Russell: 229, 233). Sermons, he argues, are not works of art, nor should they be.

Yet Russell's review nonetheless notes the powerful forces that come into play when poetry and preaching interact, highlighting several areas that were crucially important in nineteenth-century perceptions of this interaction, and are hence the primary focus of this essay. First, he observes that preaching may have particular force in that it can exert 'rather a physical than a rational influence' (Russell 233). To Russell this signifies a lower form of preaching, which he defines as 'oratory' and associates, for instance, with the rhetoric of the temperance preachers. But his comment is also significant in that it emphasizes a key difference between poetry and the sermon—the latter is predominantly an oral form addressed to specific audiences, the former most often, though not exclusively, written—while introducing the concept of somatic affect, a notion which was to prove vital in connecting rather than separating the two genres. Indeed, Kingsley himself was deeply concerned in his own reviews of the 1850s with the dangerously affective power of poetry, decrying the works of Byron and Shelley in terms which speak to the physiological as well as mental influence of poetry on the reader (Kingsley 1890a: *passim*).

While Russell associates a higher form of preaching with reflection rather than affect, he does go on to argue that a key characteristic of the poet-preacher will be 'sympathy', which will make him better able to convey the emotional force of historical events and characters to his listeners (Russell: 236). Sympathy is implicitly designated a more subtle and ultimately more powerful affective force than the crude physical emotions produced by fiery rhetoric, and Russell views it here as perhaps the most important quality that a poet can bring to sermon-writing. As we shall see, it was the perceived (and felt) sympathetic force in the great nineteenth-century sermon writers examined below, primarily John Henry Newman, Frederick W. Robertson, and Kingsley himself, that made their sermons seem 'poetic' to their listeners and readers, while many nineteenth-century preachers also deliberately deployed poetry in their sermons in part because of its assumed value in conveying sympathy. Finally, Russell's argument defends the connection between sermons and poetry by noting the presence of poetic qualities in Christ's teaching and in biblical prophecy (Russell: 234). Stylistic and formal qualities associated with poetic language, such as parallelism and repetition, rhythm, symbolism, and simile and metaphor, were thus authorized for use in religious language, particularly when it had a pedagogical function. This was again a common link made by nineteenth-century writers, as in John Keble's well-known comment in his lectures as Oxford Professor of Poetry:

> Poetry lends Religion her wealth of symbols and images: Religion restores these again to Poetry, clothed with so splendid a radiance that they appear to be no longer merely symbols, but to partake... of the nature of sacraments. (Keble 1912: 2:481)

Religion, this suggests, can sanctify the artifices and ends of poetry. Newman's even better-known comment, in the essay on Keble's poetics that served as a defence of the poetry of Roman Catholicism, states that 'the very being' of the Catholic Church is 'poetry', in part because the Church is so 'rich in symbol and imagery', though he is thinking much less of sermons than of ritual ordinances and non-verbal performance (Newman 1871: 2:442).

In the mid-nineteenth century it was the leading Tractarians, themselves heavily influenced by Romantic poetics and Wordsworth in particular, who did much to solidify and confer a High Anglican tinge to the position that poetry and religion could not be considered as separate discourses. In terms of the sermon, this ideological stance fed into varied conceptions of the 'poet-preacher'. Perhaps most obviously, poets in the Romantic and Victorian period were often credited as religious teachers in their own right. F. D. Maurice, in a series of early essays on contemporary poets written before he himself became a leading preacher and Broad Church controversialist, argued that the 'real and perfect poet [...] is indeed of as high and sacred a function as can belong to man', and continued by explicitly comparing the role of poet and minister of God:

> It is not the black garment, nor the precise and empty phrase, which makes men ministers of God: but the communion with that Spirit of God, which was, in all its fullness, upon those mighty poets, Isaiah and Ezekiel; which unrolled its vision over the rocks of Patmos, and is, in larger or smaller measure, the teacher of every bard. (Maurice: 351)

Poets and preachers are equivalent in that both may rely on external appearances and the clever but hollow use of language in their careers, but without divine inspiration and belief, they will not be true to their calling.

Over half a century later, the view of great poets as natural religious teachers was still in evidence in the Revd H. R. Haweis's series of lectures on *Poets in the Pulpit*, which surveys the religious thought of Herbert, Wordsworth, Keble, Tennyson, Browning, and Longfellow. Haweis specifically argues that ministers like himself ought to deploy poetry, because poets have the 'deepest hold over, and insight into, the thoughts and feelings of their age' (Haweis: 5). It is writers such as Longfellow, with his extraordinarily wide cross-denominational and cross-class appeal, who serve as 'minister[s] of hope and the stay of faith in this artificial and doubt-tossed age' more effectively than an ordained minister could ever aspire to do (Haweis: 7).

Wordsworth, Browning, and Tennyson were probably the most important British poets to be appropriated for this branch of the poet-preacher tradition (despite the persistent hints of unorthodoxy associated with each of their careers), with numerous publications attempting to assess their religious teaching. In a different category were those poets like George Herbert and Keble who were ordained ministers, and whose poetry was directly related to their explicit religious mission. Before considering this grouping, it is worth noting that Samuel Taylor Coleridge falls mid-way between the two camps. His early career as a Unitarian preacher was overshadowed by his later reputation as poet and theologian, but although he abandoned the idea of preaching as a career, he remained attached to the form of the sermon. In his political and religious 'Lay Sermon', *The Statesman's Manual or The Bible the Best Guide to Political Skill and Foresight* (1816), he states that 'When I named this Essay a Sermon, I sought to prepare the inquirers after it for the absence of all the usual softenings... of all compromise between truth and courtesy' (S. T. Coleridge: 35–6). This suggests that the sermon is a plainer, more direct and more critical form of prose. Yet Coleridge also included 'poetic' images of nature, cited both his own poetry and that of others, and suggested in the second of these Lay Sermons that the superiority of religion lay in the fact that it incorporated the best aspects of poetry: 'Religion is the Poetry and Philosophy of all mankind' (S. T. Coleridge: 197). This was perhaps defensive given that at least one hostile reviewer, in the conservative *Edinburgh Review*, sneered at the Lay Sermons precisely because they were too 'poetic', singling out an image of the sun from *The Statesman's Manual* (very reminiscent of similar imagery in Coleridge's poetics) as 'a very pretty Della Cruscan image: and we really think it a pity that Mr Coleridge ever quitted that school of poetry... to lose himself in the depths of philosophy' ('The Statesman's Manual': 452). For a poet, someone for whom writing 'sermons' was no longer part of his profession, to produce prose works in this genre was to risk a lack of credibility.

For nineteenth-century Anglican religious poets, Herbert was probably the most important instance of a poet who was also a professed minister, more so than the leading 'poet-preacher' of the eighteenth century, Charles Wesley, whose poems and hymns remained popular throughout the nineteenth century, but who did not inspire any major Evangelical poets to follow his lead. Like Keble, whose *Christian Year* was the most influential volume of religious verse published in the nineteenth century, Wesley appears to have seen his ministerial function as more important than his poetic productions, but both writers were fated to be known primarily as poets rather than sermon writers. In Wesley's case, this is partly because he tended to deliver sermons extempore and relatively few have survived. But even Kenneth Newport, in his detailed and well-contextualized introductory account to those that remain, also admits that their quality as literary texts is 'somewhat mixed', although the spoken delivery was apparently highly effective (Newport: 47). Similarly, Keble's sermons attracted little negative criticism but, despite Keble's near saint-like status in the late nineteenth century, were never considered as classics of the genre. Like Wesley, Keble deliberately adopted a plain style of exposition and in at least one early sermon ('Favour Shown to Implicit Faith', delivered 1822), he self-consciously rejects the importance of 'originality of intellect', literary graces and the 'rhetorical exhibition of truth in its most inviting form' as alien to Biblical teaching, suggesting that 'literary and intellectual advantages' are 'precious, but dangerous' to the possessor (Keble 1847: 6, 13, 22).

Such language suggests that Keble, who was always anxious about his decision to publish his poems and actively disliked the praise and adulation of his contemporaries, set out in effect to make his sermons as unpoetic as possible. He also published relatively few sermons during his lifetime, and after his death the major collection of his sermons clearly highlighted the greater reputation of his poems when the editors titled it *Sermons for the Christian Year*. Indeed, Keble's friend and biographer, John Taylor Coleridge, suggested that *The Christian Year* had superseded any possible function of Keble's sermons, describing the poems as each containing 'an excellent skeleton of a sermon' and reporting: 'I have heard of a clergyman in a rural parish in Worcestershire who was in the habit of reading, and explaining from the pulpit, in lieu of an afternoon sermon, the poem for the Sunday' (J. T. Coleridge: 2:157). Only Keble's 'Assize Sermon' of 1833, 'National Apostasy', is still well-known, and more because Newman characterized it as the opening volley of the Oxford Movement in *Apologia Pro Vita Sua* rather than on its own merits.

From the Roman Catholic tradition, Gerard Manley Hopkins is, of course, by far the most important example of a poet-priest. To a much greater extreme than Keble, however, Hopkins, whose relatively few sermons were never published and who shared with his superiors an anxiety about his gifts as a preacher, is remembered as a poet rather than a sermon writer. Although his sermons were collected and printed in the twentieth century and do certainly contain striking passages, they are deployed by critics for their insights into Hopkins's poetry and theology, and few would consider them the equal of his other unpublished prose writings in letters and journals.

Any survey of nineteenth-century religious verse suggests that for the clergymen of the period, particularly—though by no means exclusively—those within the Church of England, writing and attempting to publish poetry was commonplace. Indeed, given the difficulties of making a career as a poet, entering the Church could be a desirable option for a well-educated literary man with poetic aspirations, but without the independent income to support them. Tennyson was threatened with a ministerial career by his grandfather, and his brother Charles did end up as a reluctant Anglican minister, as well as a notable sonnet writer and minor poet. Richard Chenevix Trench and Henry Alford, both student colleagues and friends of Tennyson at Cambridge, achieved a significant reputation as religious poets (and also published quite successful sermon collections) while gaining high status within the Church. Other notable British religious poets who were also clergymen include Isaac Williams and Frederick Faber from the early Tractarian tradition (the latter followed Newman into the Roman Catholic Church in 1845); R. S. Hawker, a famously eccentric clergyman and poet from Morwenstow in Cornwall; and Richard Watson Dixon, admired by the Pre-Raphaelites and now primarily remembered for his epistolary correspondence with Hopkins.

Combining the roles of poet and minister was not always easy. One anonymous satirical poem on the Public Worship Regulation Act mocked the literary pretensions of High Church clergymen, advising parishioners to keep a suspicious eye on their new incumbent: 'People say he's rather clever—writing poetry, you know,— | And he's what they call aesthetic—that is, he goes in for show!' (*Spirit of the Age*: 32). The dangers of being perceived as overly-invested in the aesthetic qualities of verse, and of appearing too much of a poet as opposed to a man of God, were particularly evident in the reputation of Robert Montgomery. A considerable celebrity in his day but now totally forgotten, he was the author of various blockbuster religious epics and bestselling verse collections from the 1820s to the 1840s. 'Satan' Montgomery (so named after his best-known epic) became a popular and fashionable clergyman on the strength of his poetic writings, so that in his case the poetic career enabled his clerical ambitions. But heavy criticism of Montgomery's poems for their lofty yet ultimately meaningless rhetoric and their over-ambitious bombast, not to mention criticism of Montgomery himself for his attempts to pose as a Byronic poet, fed into perceptions of his preaching career as dependent on 'show'. John Ross Dix, describing his encounters with various well-known public figures of the 1840s, attended one of Montgomery's sermons in his fashionable Charlotte Street church and typically commented on the careful arrangement of the preacher's curls, his eyebrows that seemed pencilled on, and the 'snowy whiteness' of his gown, sardonically adding 'I have heard that Mr Montgomery sometimes sports ruffles, but I did not observe them on this occasion' (Dix: 213). For Dix, this staged outward effect is mirrored by the artificial content of a sermon containing 'a tissue of laborious conceits' and clearly learnt by heart in order to appear spontaneous, while actually being carefully contrived (Dix: 214). Montgomery's poetic persona and the increasingly negative critical opinions of his poems tarnished his clerical role and prevented him from being taken altogether seriously.

These poets and ministers were important in establishing an image of the nineteenth-century clergyman, and particularly the Anglican clergyman, as someone who could be expected to have literary, poetic interests and who might well be at least a competent versifier, if not more. For the remainder of this chapter, however, I will focus on three leading figures—Newman, Kingsley, and Frederick William Robertson—from the last and, in the context of a study of sermons rather than of poetry, the most significant group of 'poet-preachers': those whose sermons were in themselves 'poetic', in their modes of address, use of language, or actual citation of poetry, and who were thus 'poets' less because they wrote in metrical verse than because they possessed the power (as identified in Russell's review) of creating sympathy and of using language vividly to convey emotion to an audience. The writers listed above could be categorized as poets who also wrote sermons, or preachers who wrote poetry on the side, while these three in contrast serve as examples of ministers who wrote generically hybrid poetic sermons. Of this triumvirate, Newman has the most lasting reputation for his sermons, although in the Victorian period Robertson arguably competed with him as Britain's most widely read and admired sermon writer. Margaret Oliphant's survey of a century of religious prose in *The Victorian Age of English Literature* listed Newman and Robertson as the two writers whose sermons were still generally known and read in the 1890s, and also discussed Kingsley's sermons in some detail, though she suggested that unlike the first two, his collections had not 'taken any place in literature' (Oliphant: 2:36). F. W. Head, lecturing to aspiring ministers at Cambridge in 1927 on their eminent predecessors, again selected Newman and Robertson as the two figures whose sermons remained widely available and advisable to read (Head: 160); he also included a talk on Kingsley though without special mention of his sermons. One of the few twentieth-century literary critics of the Victorian sermon, E. H. Mackerness, suggests that Kingsley's collections are 'unrewarding to the modern reader' in comparison to Robertson's works (Mackerness: 48). Yet if Kingsley's prose style did not attain the poetic, affective force widely assigned to the other two, he nonetheless stands with Robertson—as the frequent comparisons of the two suggest—in his high valuation of the poetic, and in his deliberate incorporation of poetic quotations into his sermons.

Mackerness comments that in Newman's Anglican sermons (which tended to attract far greater critical praise than those he wrote later as a Roman Catholic), 'there are many occasions when [he] admits a modicum of "poetic prose" into his expositions' (Mackerness: 12). This sounds rather grudging, as opposed to J. C. Shairp's well-known and enthusiastic celebration of the poetry of Newman's sermons in his essays on 'John Keble' and on 'Prose Poets: Cardinal Newman'. In the first, Shairp introduced a long digression on the glories of hearing Newman preach before turning to his primary subject, Keble and the *Christian Year*, exclaiming that 'To call these sermons eloquent would be no word for them; high poems they rather were, as of an inspired singer, or the outpourings as of a prophet, rapt yet self-possessed' (Shairp 1886: 249). Shairp depicted Newman's famous silvery tones as a 'fine strain of unearthly music', recalling how 'Through the stillness of that high Gothic building the words fell on the ear like the measured drippings of water in some vast dim cave' (Shairp 1886: 249). This accords Newman's eloquence a natural power of musicality, and as a simile, tends to imply that the content of the words was less important than their delivery. Matthew Arnold, in another famous account of Newman's poetic preaching, similarly focused on delivery and on Newman himself as a scarcely-human figure:

> Who could resist the charm of that spiritual apparition, gliding in the dim afternoon light through the aisles of St Mary's, rising into the pulpit, and then, in the most entrancing of voices, breaking the silence with words and thoughts which were a religious music,—subtle, sweet, mournful? (Arnold 1885: 139–40)

But while these recollections by actual hearers of the sermons seem to attribute their poetic force to peculiarities of tone and delivery, Shairp was careful in his essay on Newman as a 'prose poet' to indicate that their musicality was inherent in Newman's prose style, which demonstrated that 'the mellow cadence and perfect rhythm of the

Collects and Liturgy' survives in English, in the 'soothing harmonies' of Newman's sermons (Shairp 1881: 444, 456). They 'fall on the heart like dew, and soothe it, as only the most exquisite music can' (Shairp 1881: 459)—and crucially, they do so in printed as well as oral form. Shairp emphasized that even when reading alone, in 'the retirement of their rooms', men felt their affective power: 'the printed words of those marvellous sermons would thrill them until they wept "abundant and most sweet tears"' (Shairp 1886: 256). Given his expertise on the Oxford Movement, Shairp would have been well aware that 'soothing' in particular was a key word in Keble's poetics, both in his lectures as Oxford Professor of Poetry and in the Preface to the *Christian Year*, where he describes his poems as an intentional effort to recreate the '*soothing* tendency of the Prayer Book' (Keble 1827: I; emphasis in the original). To excite, to thrill and then to soothe and calm: these are the shared functions of poetry and religion in both Keble's writings and in Newman's view on religious emotion, as expressed in sermons such as 'The Religious Use of Excited Feelings' from *Parochial Sermons* (1834).

For another important commentator, R. W. Church, Newman's ability to bring theology into 'immediate relation to real feeling' lay in the 'directness and straightforward unconventionality' of his prose style as well as its 'purest English' (Church: 2:455, 443, 447). As Robert H. Ellison observes in his important study of the Victorian sermon, this period saw 'the culmination of a shift from an ornamented oral rhetoric to a plainer, more natural, more literary approach to sacred speaking' (Ellison: 28). This may seem a contradiction in terms—how can a 'plainer' style also be more 'literary'? In fact, it is so in the sense of Wordsworth's famous definition of poetic language in the Preface to *Lyrical Ballads* as 'a selection of the language really spoken by men...made with true taste and feeling' (Wordsworth and Coleridge: 254). As Church observes, Newman specialized in the arresting and immediate opening to sermons, as when he states in the first lines of 'The Immortality of the Soul': 'I suppose there is no tolerably informed Christian but considers he has a correct notion of the difference between our religion and the paganism which it supplanted' (Newman 1844: 2:17). 'I suppose' makes the statement seem hesitant, but it is also a challenge, with a touch of irony in 'tolerably informed' and a tinge of doubt in 'considers', which invites the listener or reader to question the correctness of his or her own notions. Newman's use of 'our' invokes his common strategy of appealing to his audience as one of them, rather than someone set above, but it also contrasts with 'he' in implying that perhaps the speaker is less assured of the difference between Christianity and paganism than the average Christian. The next sentence seems to reassure in asserting that 'we' all know that the doctrine of the soul's immortality supplies the crucial difference:

> Every one, if asked what it is we have gained by the Gospel, will promptly answer, that we have gained the knowledge of our immortality, of our having souls which will live for ever; that the heathen did not know this, but that Christ taught it, and that His disciples know it. (Newman 1844: 2:18)

But the purport of the sermon is that while this is common knowledge, it is not commonly *felt*:

> I have said that every one of us is able fluently to speak of this doctrine, and is aware that the knowledge of it forms the fundamental difference between our state and that of the heathen. And yet, in spite of our being able to speak about it ... the greater number of those who are called Christians in no true sense realize it in their own minds at all. Indeed, it is a very difficult thing to bring home to us, and to feel, that we have souls; and there cannot be a more fatal mistake than to suppose we see what the doctrine means, as soon as we can use the words which signify it. (Newman 1844: 2:18)

For the benefit of listeners, this recaps the first paragraphs of the sermon, and now includes the speaker himself in 'every one of us', before turning the argument in 'And yet' towards the difficulty of actually appreciating what it means to have an immortal soul. 'Those who are called Christians' nicely implies the importance of Newman's topic, in that it may be the 'true sense' of the soul that distinguishes the true Christian, while 'fatal' also adds to this urgency. A sermon that opened almost casually is now dealing with a matter of more than life and death. By its close, the tone has shifted from conversational to anguished and impassioned, as Newman implores:

> Oh that there were such a heart in us, to put aside this visible world, to desire to look at it as a mere screen between us and God, and think of Him who has entered in beyond the veil, and who is watching us, trying us, yes, and blessing, and influencing, and encouraging us towards good, day by day! (Newman 1844: 2:29)

Exclamations ('Oh', 'yes') and exclamation points express the speaker's growing excitement, as do longer sentences containing short repetitive clauses separated by commas, which serve to quicken the pace of the line. Again, it is vital that there is no separation between preacher and listeners or readers here: part of the great mastery of these sermons is their ability to create both a sense of Christianity as a shared communal endeavour, and ongoing effort, and a sense of the inevitable loneliness and bitter alienation of those shut out of that endeavour. They both emphasize and enact the importance of sympathy and feeling in religion.

Newman's sermons were linked to Robertson's because both used, as Church notes on Robertson, 'keen, free, natural language' and both presented a persona which conveyed what Oliphant describes as 'sadness and wistful reflectiveness', hence inspiring 'sympathetic attraction' in listeners and readers (Church: 2:266; Oliphant: 2:30). Newman is discussed elsewhere in this volume, and his career and writings remain familiar to scholars and are widely treated. Robertson, in contrast, has had a limited impact in the twentieth and twenty-first centuries. His early death meant that he never acquired high status within the Church, and his disinclination to link himself to any one party (though contemporaries tended to place him firmly in the Broad Church camp), meant that his published works arguably had less influence on wider movements in his time. During his lifetime, his period of fame as a hugely popular preacher in Trinity Chapel, Brighton, lasted for only six years. Yet we must not underestimate the extent to which Robertson was a household name in mid-Victorian Britain. Amongst the many accolades he received posthumously, Charles Dickens described

Robertson as 'one of the greatest masters of elocution I ever knew' (qtd in Beardsley: xxi), while the *Saturday Review* suggested that many found his published sermons 'the most stable, satisfactory and exhaustless form of religious teaching which the nineteenth century has given' (qtd in Robertson 1863: 7). Tennyson described them to Queen Victoria as 'the most spiritual utterances of any minister of the church in our times', strong words for a writer often ambiguous about the value of the Anglican clergy (Tennyson 1987: 238). Arthur Stanley compared the sermons to the *Christian Year* and *Pilgrim's Progress* in that they appealed to all denominations, describing Robertson as 'accepted as the chief of English preachers by almost every phase of English religious thought' (Stanley: 245). Of course, Tennyson and Stanley were both sympathetic to Broad Church opinions (and the former was unlikely to have remained unmoved by Robertson's passionate advocacy for his poetry), but the repeated calls for new editions of the sermons, and their inclusion in Tauchnitz's series of English classics alongside major works of literature, does suggest that they were very highly valued in the decades after Robertson's death (Beardsley: xxii).

Robertson had started out as strongly Evangelical and remained sceptical about High Church ideals, although according to his biographer, Stopford Brooke, he 'read Newman's sermons with profit and delight till the day of his death' (Brooke: 1:126). He was also an immense admirer of Keble's poetry, and had memorized much of the *Christian Year*. Indeed, while Robertson, unlike Newman, did not write poetry (or at least wrote none that has survived), he was potentially a stronger advocate for its importance. His widely circulated lectures on 'the Influence of Poetry on the Working Classes' emphasized the vital role that poetry had to play in everyday life in Kebleian terms of emotional release and recovery, and he stressed that poetry should teach all men 'not to...think accurately, but to feel truly' (Robertson 1858: 146). The poetry of the Bible, in the Psalms for instance, should operate exactly as Keble indicated in his *Lectures on Poetry*, offering 'relief for feeling' and 'soothing power': 'they express for us indirectly those deeper feelings which there would be a sense of indelicacy in expressing directly' (Robertson 1855: 156–7). Robertson also argued, moreover, that poetry was not limited to rhythmic words but could be found in nature and in the grandest of human actions: 'Whatever wakes up sensibilities, puts you for a moment into a poetic state' (Robertson 1858: 105). By his own definition, then, Robertson's sermons, which were known for their affective power—Christina Beardsley cites reports of women frequently fainting in the electrically-charged atmosphere of his church—participated in this poetic enterprise (Beardsley: xxi).

Throughout the sermons, Robertson stressed that feeling (and sympathy in particular) was vital to a true understanding of Christianity. In 'The Good Shepherd', for example, he argued that Christ's comparison of himself to a shepherd was deliberately chosen to appeal not just to the lived experience of his historical contemporaries but to their emotional associations, touching 'strings which would vibrate with many a tender and pure recollection of their childhood' (Robertson 1855: 288). In order to understand the impact of this image, Robertson continued, nineteenth-century Christians must try to recreate these feelings:

> And unless we try, by realizing such scenes, to supply what they felt by association, the words of Christ will only be hard, dry, lifeless words to us: for all Christ's teaching is a Divine Poetry, luxuriant in metaphor, overflowing with truth too large for accurate sentences, truth which only a heart alive can appreciate. More than half the heresies into which Christian sects have blundered, have merely come from mistaking for dull prose what prophets and apostles said in those highest moments of the soul, when seraphim kindle the sentences of the pen and lip into poetry. (Robertson 1855: 288)

Robertson takes a liberal view of the Bible by suggesting that its words should not be taken literally or read with an analytical view to their meaning, but should be *felt* as poetry. In fact, Robertson repeatedly returned to the crucial importance of feeling, both in interpreting Christ's words and actions and in acting as a Christian. A sermon on 'The Sympathy of Christ' argues that sympathy—which, in his view, always required a personal understanding of pain and suffering—is one of the most important attributes of humanity, and especially of the priest. It does not consist of feeling alone, but of feeling that spurs to action, and it can take place either between individuals, or as a communal experience of emotion: he specifically uses public worship as an example of this 'electric touch of sympathetic feeling' (Robertson 1856: 127, 123). The opening sermon in his first published collection, 'God's Revelation of Heaven', also stresses the importance of 'the mysterious union of heart with heart' as 'the purest, serenest ecstasy of the merely human', though in itself it is only a dim shadow of union with God (Robertson 1856: 10–11).

In the same sermon, Robertson is careful to emphasize that although poetry might seem to offer a valuable instance of 'a rare power of *heart*' (Robertson 1856: 10) in men, the creative spirit as found in works of imaginative literature is inferior to the spirit of love that any of his listeners could access. Moreover, in clear references to Byron and Shelley he mentions two unnamed poets who, while producing 'some of the deepest' utterances ever spoken, failed to appreciate Christianity. Taking actual poetic productions as a guide to Christian sympathy and morality, this suggests, might be dangerous. In the light of the frequent references to poetry throughout his sermons, however, this passage might seem a little disingenuous. As Mackerness suggests, 'quotations from Wordsworth and adaptations of the Lake Poet's most notable lines are...ubiquitous in [Robertson's] works', as are allusions to Shakespeare and Tennyson (Mackerness: 38). Robertson seldom explicitly cites these writers, but their words are bound up with his, either in direct quotations, as when Wordsworth's 'Getting and spending we lay waste our powers' is compared to St Paul's 'Let us eat and drink, for tomorrow we die', or more subtly into his prose (Robertson 1855: 148). After 1850 Tennyson's *In Memoriam*, for example, which Robertson greatly admired and described as 'the most precious work published this century', makes a number of appearances in his work while rarely being openly cited (Brooke: 2:83). A sermon existing only in note form, 'Views of Death', suggests that in spoken form it included a detailed analysis of *In Memoriam* II ('Old Yew, which graspest at the stones | That name the under-lying dead' (Tennyson 1989: 346)), but if so it would be a rare example of Robertson deliberately assessing a poet's work in a sermon (of course, his lectures did this in detail for both Tennyson and Wordsworth). More frequent is a sense that his prose rests on Tennyson's verse. In 'Spiritual Knowledge', which again restates the doctrine of feeling, Robertson reaches the high point of the sermon in comparing the wise Christian to an innocent child, stating:

> And there are few more glorious moments of our humanity than those in which Faith does battle against intellectual proof: when, for example, after reading a sceptical book, or hearing a cold-blooded materialist's demonstration, in which God, the soul, and life to come, are proved impossible—up rises the heart in all the giant might of its immortality to do battle with the understanding, and with the simple argument 'I *feel* them in my best and highest moments to be true,' annihilates the sophistries of logic. (Robertson 1855: 150)

This clearly alludes to the climactic section of *In Memoriam*, CXXIV, when Tennyson chooses to adopt a child-like stance and rely on feeling rather than rationalism or materialism:

> I found Him not in world or sun,
>   Or eagle's wing or insect's eye;
>   Nor through the questions men may try,
> The petty cobwebs we have spun:
>
> If e'er when faith had fallen asleep,
>   I heard a voice 'believe no more'
>   And heard an ever-breaking shore
> That tumbled in the Godless deep;
>
> A warmth within the breast would melt
>   The freezing reason's colder part,
>   And like a man in wrath the heart
> Stood up and answered 'I have felt'.
>
> (Tennyson 1989: 470)

Tennyson's views on human love as echoing the divine, his emphasis on moments of emotional connection with God, and his generally liberal views on Christianity were so much in tune with Robertson's religious opinions that Tennysonian imagery and language is fully integrated into his prose style. Indeed, the key images in lines 9–12 above of the feeling heart and the breaking of waves on the shore, potent and recurring throughout Tennyson's poetics, are also used in some of the most powerful passages of Robertson's prose. As I have discussed at more length elsewhere, these two thinkers came to represent loosely defined Broad Church liberalism to the mid-Victorian reader; although in the production of the sermons the influence ran one way, from Tennyson to Robertson, Tennyson became a devoted reader of Robertson and had the latter lived longer, it is likely that he would have exercised the kind of personal and reciprocal influence on Tennyson that Benjamin Jowett or F. D. Maurice achieved (Blair).

Reverence for Wordsworth and Tennyson, and the direct and indirect use of English poetry in sermons, provides a strong link between Robertson and his contemporary (and at least acquaintance if not friend) Charles Kingsley. Kingsley, who unlike

Robertson was an esteemed literary critic and poet during the period when his sermons were delivered, is remarkable for his direct reliance on the words of the poets, citing among others Milton, Pope, Coleridge, Wordsworth, Longfellow, and Tennyson, besides the poems and hymns of Newman and Charles Wesley. Kingsley is much less anxious than Keble, Newman, or Robertson about the potential dangers of literature, and indeed, while Robertson warns that aesthetic beauty cannot always be trusted, Kingsley tends to celebrate its benefits. He describes a chapter from Isaiah in 'Ezekiel's Vision', for instance, as valuable for the 'very sound of the words', and believes that the poetic pleasures of melodious language will draw men to the sense:

> Yes—I believe that the beauty of this chapter has made many a man listen to it, who had perhaps never cared to listen to any good before; and learn a precious lesson from it, which he could learn nowhere save in the Bible. (Kingsley 1890b: 91)

Kingsley's poetic quotations operate in a similar way: to highlight particular issues to his audience through their enjoyment of the heightened language of poetry. He seldom refers to poets by name, either citing a passage directly without attribution, or referencing the author as a 'wise man'; so 'The Victory of Life' suggests that sceptics can be answered 'in the words of the wise man' before citing Milton's 'On Time' in entirety, or 'Pride and Humility' asks 'What is our wisdom? What does a wise man say of his?' before citing *In Memoriam*. By presenting poets as a repository for 'wisdom' (a word with strong biblical resonance) as well as beauty, Kingsley seems to take an Arnoldian view of poetry as a 'touchstone' for what is best in human civilization and comes nearest to the inspired language of the Bible—though he is perhaps more interested in the unconscious religion of poetry rather than Arnold's unconscious poetry of religion (Arnold 1888: *passim*). Moreover, for those who were frequent hearers or readers of his sermons, it would have been clear that Kingsley was fond of invoking particular passages repeatedly, and that he was doing so from memory, as his own language slides into citation:

> All things, as the Psalmist says, come to an end. All men's plans, men's notions, men's systems, men's doctrines, grow old, wear out, and perish.
> 'The old order changes, giving place to the new:
> But God fulfils himself in many ways.' (Kingsley 1861: 315)

Although the quotation marks in the text separate these words of Tennyson's (from the 'Morte D'Arthur') from Kingsley's own speech, the distinction might not have been so evident in spoken delivery, and because Tennyson's lines are anonymized they hold in effect the same status in this passage as the words of the unknown Psalmist. Moreover, as often happens in these sermons, Kingsley misquotes his source. Tennyson's published lines read 'The old order changeth, yielding place to new | And God fulfils Himself in many ways' (Tennyson 1989: 162). By removing the archaic 'changeth' and substituting the five-syllable 'giving place to the' for Tennyson's 'yielding place', Kingsley modernizes Tennyson's language and disturbs the metrical beat of line 240, effectively translating the lines into more contemporary prose. The fact that Kingsley did not check and revise his quotations before the sermons were published suggests that accuracy was not his primary aim. Indeed, in misquoting, Kingsley is actually highlighting his familiarity with selected poets and emphasizing that he recalled them off-the-cuff, as though their words had already become proverbial and could be easily integrated into the 'simple straightforwardness' of his style (Oliphant: 2:32).

The 'generous sympathy' that Oliphant recognized in Kingsley's sermons was both created by the impression of spontaneity and immediacy in his style—not least his use of misquotation—which might designedly give the impression of the speaker as overcome by feeling; and is evident in the sympathy that he extends towards other writers (Oliphant: 2:34). By including voices from the English and American poetic traditions in his sermons he gives the impression of a community of writers engaged in a shared aim of making Christianity both more attractive and more understandable. Like Robertson, but perhaps to an even greater extent, he does much to elevate English poetry into a religious discourse and emphasize its usefulness to Christianity in general, and to the sermon in particular. Like Newman, his readers' awareness that he was himself a poet and critic would also feed into their interpretation of his prose sermons, though in Kingsley's case readers were almost disappointed not to find his own prose more 'poetic'. In common with many other preachers not discussed here, these three figures engaged with the affective connections between poetry and the sermon and used the sermon form as a means to negotiate the vital, but at times vexed, relationship between poetry and religion in the long nineteenth century.

References

Arnold, M. (1885). *Discourses in America*. London: Macmillan.
—— (1888). *Essays in Criticism, Second Series*. London: Macmillan.
Beardsley, C. (2009). *Unutterable Love: The Passionate Life and Preaching of F. W. Robertson*. Cambridge: Lutterworth Press.
Blair, K. (2012). *Form and Faith in Victorian Poetry and Religion*. Oxford: Oxford University Press.
Brooke, S. A. (1865). *Life and Letters of Frederick W. Robertson*. London: Smith, Elder.
Church, R. W. (1897). *Occasional Papers, Selected from the Guardian, the Times and the Saturday Review 1846–1890*. London: Macmillan.
Coleridge, J. T. (1869). *A Memoir of the Reverend John Keble*, 2nd edn. Oxford: James Parker.
Coleridge, S. T. (1972). *Collected Works of Samuel Taylor Coleridge, 6: Lay Sermons*, ed. R. J. White. Princeton, NJ: Princeton University Press.
Dix, J. R. (1846). *Pen and Ink Sketches of Poets, Preachers and Politicians*. London: David Bogue.
Ellison, R. H. (1998). *The Victorian Pulpit: Spoken and Written Sermons in Nineteenth-Century Britain*. London: Associated University Presses.
Haweis, H. R. (1880). *Poets in the Pulpit*. London: Sampson Low, Marston, Searle and Rivington.
Head, F. W. (1929). *Six Great Anglicans*. London: SCM.
Keble, J. (1827). *The Christian Year*. Oxford: J. H. Parker.
—— (1847). *Sermons, Academical and Occasional*. Oxford: J. H. Parker.

—— (1912). *Keble's Lectures on Poetry, 1832–1841*, trans. E. K. Francis. Oxford: Clarendon Press.

Kingsley, C. (1861). *Town and Country Sermons*. London: Parker, Son & Bourn.

—— (1878). *All Saints' Day, and Other Sermons*. London: C. Kegan Paul.

—— (1890a). *Literary and General Lectures and Essays*. London: Macmillan.

—— (1890b). *The Water of Life, and Other Sermons*. London: Macmillan.

Mackerness, E. H. (1959). *The Heeded Voice: Studies in the Literary Status of the Anglican Sermon, 1830–1900*. Cambridge: W. Heffer.

Maurice, F. D. (1828). 'Sketches of Contemporary Authors. No XII: Lord Byron'. *Athenaeum* 23: 351.

Newman, J. H. (1844). *Parochial Sermons*. London: Rivington.

—— (1871). *Essays Critical and Historical*. London: Basil Montagu Pickering.

Newport, K. G. C. (2001). *The Sermons of Charles Wesley: A Critical Edition, with Introduction and Notes*. Oxford: Oxford University Press.

Oliphant, M. (1893). *The Victorian Age of English Literature*. Leipzig: Heinemann and Balestier.

Robertson, F. W. (1855). *Sermons Preached at Trinity Chapel, Brighton, Second Series*. London: Smith, Elder.

—— (1856). *Sermons Preached at Trinity Chapel, Brighton, First Series*, 2nd edn. London: Smith, Elder.

—— (1858). *Lectures and Addresses on Literary and Social Topics*. London: Smith, Elder.

—— (1863). *Sermons Preached at Trinity Chapel, Brighton, Fourth Series*. London: Smith, Elder.

Russell, F. (1851). 'Kingsley's Saint's Tragedy, and Sermons'. *North British Review* 16: 229–38.

Shairp, J. C. (1881). *Aspects of Poetry, Being Lectures Delivered at Oxford*. Oxford: Clarendon Press.

—— (1886). *Studies in Poetry and Philosophy*, 4th edn. Edinburgh: David Douglas.

The Spirit of the Age, and Other Rhymes for the Times. (n. d.). London: Bemrose and Sons.

Stanley, A. (1870). *Essays, Chiefly on Questions of Church and State*. London: John Murray.

'"The Statesman's Manual; or the Bible the Best Guide to Political Skill and Foresight: A Lay Sermon, Addressed to the Higher Classes of Society" by S. T. Coleridge, Esq'. (1816). *Edinburgh Review* 27–54: 444–60.

Tennyson, A. (1987). *The Letters of Alfred Lord Tennyson, Vol II: 1851–1870*, ed. C. Y. Lang and E. F. Shannon, Jr. Oxford: Clarendon Press.

—— (1989). *The Poems of Tennyson: A Selected Edition*, ed. C. Ricks. London: Longman.

Wordsworth, W., and Coleridge, S. T. (1991). *Lyrical Ballads*, ed. R. L. Brett and A. R. Jones, 2nd edn. London: Routledge.

CHAPTER 35

TRADITION, PREACHING, AND THE GOTHIC REVIVAL

STEPHEN PRICKETT

The 'Gothick' was always a hydra-headed monster; nor did it make its shambling appearance unaccompanied. From wherever one cares to date its beginning, it was always loosely (sometimes very loosely) associated with religious mysticism, a feeling for the numinous, the irrational and mysterious—not to mention a much more practical and down-to-earth revulsion against the squalid and degrading conditions of the early industrial revolution. From the Palace of Westminster to London's St Pancras Station or Keble College, Oxford, the nineteenth century saw a resurgence of Gothic plots, emotions, aesthetics, and architecture. In the case of churches and sermons, its association with Ritualism and the Anglo-Catholic movement turned this style into a theological as well as an aesthetic statement.

Horace Walpole (1717–97) is often credited with having begun the Gothic revival with his extraordinary architectural fantasia at Strawberry Hill, and his outrageously bad—and best-selling—novel, *The Castle of Otranto*, which was set in a vastly inflated version of his own bijou residence, and gave (literally) an inner life to his own stucco-Gothic creation. But in fact a taste for the Gothic long predates him. Indeed, it is arguable that it had never really died out in England, but lingered on from the fifteenth century, like Walpole's giant Otranto ghost in the Enlightenment machine. For many it only reached its apogee in King's College Chapel in Cambridge in the sixteenth century—already a neo-classical age in the rest of Europe. Indeed it is hard to say if St John's College library, dating from the middle of the eighteenth century, is the first example of the Gothic revival, or the last of the original (Clark: 77 n.). All the great classical architects, including Sir Christopher Wren, Sir John Soane, Nicholas Hawksmoor, and James Gibbs had also tried their hands at Gothic designs—Soane, indeed, had produced a standardized design for a church in Classical, Egyptian, or Gothic as desired (Pevsner: pl. 35/36). In 1753, when

Walpole had only just completed his first modest alterations to Strawberry Hill, a columnist in *The World*, a magazine devoted to taste and fashion, declared that the Gothic was already altogether passé:

> A few years ago everything was Gothic; our houses, our beds, our book cases, and our couches were all copied from some parts or other of our old cathedrals... This, however odd it might seem, and however unworthy of the name of TASTE, was cultivated, was admired, and still has its professors in different parts of England. There is something, they say, in it congenial to our old Gothic constitution; I should rather think to our modern idea of liberty, which allows every one the privilege of playing the fool, and making himself ridiculous in whatever way he pleases. (*The World*, 22 March 1753, qtd. in Ketton-Cremer: 136)

But if Walpole was already falling behind the avant-garde in 1753, it was nevertheless he, more than any other single person, who turned the Gothic into 'Gothick', from fashion into a movement, creating from an architectural fad a quite new kind of emotional and aesthetic sensibility. 'I almost think,' he wrote to a friend,

> there is no wisdom comparable to that of exchanging what is called the realities of life for dreams. Old castles, old pictures, old histories, and the babble of old people make one live back into centuries, that cannot disappoint one. One holds fast and surely to what is past. The dead have exhausted their power of deceiving—one can trust Catherine of Medicis now. (Ketton-Cremer: 231–2)

Nevertheless, a cult of age, dreams, magic, and the supposed certainties of the dead does not account for the wild popularity of the Gothic, in all its many manifestations, throughout the last quarter of the eighteenth century. What turned novels of extraordinary silliness—Beckford's *Vathek*, Lewis's *The Monk*, etc—into something much more substantial was the fact that the Gothic, for all its faults, provided a vocabulary of the unconscious—a way of describing dreams, nightmares, even forms of mental illness with which the official language of the Enlightenment had no way of coping (Prickett 2005: 71–108). It is no accident that so many eighteenth-century writers and artists, from Samuel Johnson to William Cowper, felt themselves—rightly or wrongly—to be teetering on the edge of breakdown, despair, and even madness. There is here a real paradox. Walpole himself, like the 'Gothic' architect James Wyatt, the former stage-set designer who built the flamboyant and catastrophically unstable Fonthill Abbey for his client William Beckford, for all his interest in 'dreaming', seems to have seen it as an essentially *outward* process leading to a recapture of the past. There is no evidence that he saw the giant ghost within the crumbling castle of Otranto in the psychological terms that have become almost second nature in our post-Freudian world. Similarly, neither he, nor Wyatt, understood, or were apparently interested in understanding, the serious engineering and constructional principles on which medieval Gothic architecture actually depended. Such an internalization of the Gothic belongs to a later generation of poets whom we now (in retrospect) call the 'Romantics'—most notably, of course, Samuel Taylor Coleridge (1772–1834) with poems such as the 'Ancient Mariner' and 'Christabel', or John Keats's (1795–1821) 'Eve of St Agnes', not to mention such novels as Mary Shelley's *Frankenstein* or Emily Brontë's *Wuthering Heights*.

It is, therefore, one of the freaks of intellectual history that what had started as such an unreal literary extravaganza should have given rise not merely to a new sense of the unconscious, and therefore opened the door to a new science soon to be labelled 'psychology', but also to a new literary genre, that of the seriously-researched and scholarly historical novel, most notably by Walter Scott (1771–1832). Still missing from this potent brew, however, were two of what were to prove its most explosive elements: politics and, above all, religion.

Inevitably any attempt to imitate fourteenth-century architecture had to draw on ecclesiastical models. Though Fonthill Abbey, with its tower and spire, its (unheatable) 80-foot-high great hall, and pointed Gothic windows, was designed as a house, and had never been an abbey, every feature, however exaggerated, was 'borrowed' from a medieval church. Yet if Beckford, like Walpole, yielded to no one in his passion for ecclesiastical fantasy, it remained just that—fantasy. But Walpole was at least prophetic in associating the Gothic with age, and its religious concomitant: Catholicism. 'If only because it is so ancient,' wrote Dorothea Mendelson, wife of the German Romantic Friedrich Schlegel, on their conversion to Rome in 1808, 'I prefer Catholicism. Nothing new is of any use' (Eichner: 106). It was left to a much more devout successor, however, to turn the Gothic into an effective political and religious totem: the architect Augustus Welby Northmore Pugin (1812–52), who had become a convert to Catholicism in 1833—the same year as the foundation of the Oxford Movement. Anticipating the fusion of ritualism and social conscience that was to power his Tractarian contemporaries, Pugin's book *Contrasts* (1836) set out, in a series of architectural drawings, to display the 'Christian' architecture of the Middle Ages against what he saw as the brutal utilitarian functionalism of his own day. One double-page spread contrasts a city of the fourteenth century, dominated by graceful Gothic dreaming spires, with its 'reformed', smoky, stunted, factory-begrimed nineteenth-century counterpart; another illustrates housing for the poor contrasting a fourteenth-century monastery dispensing Christian charity with a nineteenth-century workhouse. A picture was worth a thousand words. *Contrasts* was an instant sensation, and a new edition with more material followed in 1841. 'It was not until the advent of Pugin,' writes the architectural critic H. A. N. Brockman, 'that the use of Gothic architecture became the passport to salvation' (Brockman: 69).

By mid-century easy assumptions of progress, and of the obvious advantages of the present age over its predecessors, could no longer be taken for granted. The superior moral qualities of the Middle Ages, or even earlier, had become, if not a generally accepted fact, a point of controversy and distinct literary trope. It provided the polemical mainspring for Carlyle's *Past and Present* (1843) and for the plot in Disraeli's political novel, *Sybil: or the Two Nations* (1845), and for a whole genre of historical novels thereafter—perhaps the most remarkable of which was E. Nesbit's children's book, *The Story of the Amulet* (1906). Here, the children, who through a rather grumpy sand-fairy, the Psammead, are in possession of magic means of time travel, try to work out what should be done with a homeless orphan they find crying in St James's Park, because she is about to be taken into the workhouse. With an ironic echo of Shakespeare's *Cymbeline*—shortly to be explained—she is called Imogen. When someone they consult wishes they 'could find a home where they would be glad to have her' they find themselves transported to pre-Roman Britain. 'Why *here*?' says Anthea in astonishment. 'Why *now*?' (That 'now' has a touch of brilliance—because, of course, her 'now' is (or rather *was*) really 'then'.)

> You don't suppose anyone would want a child like that in *your* time—in *your* towns?' said the Psammead in irritated tones. 'You've got your country into such a mess that there's no room for half your children—and no one to want them.' (Nesbit: 183)

Though pre-Roman Britain could not by any stretch of imagination be 'Gothic,' for Nesbit, a member of the Fabian Society, and a friend of Bernard Shaw and H. G. Wells, historicism has become a potent factor in contemporary politics. The 'sorry present' is under perpetual silent judgement from the moral achievements of the past.

Again, there was nothing essentially new in this re-evaluation of history. It was, in effect, only the latest manifestation of the battle of the 'ancients' and the 'moderns', which had been raging intermittently at least since the Renaissance. But from the late eighteenth century onwards, even architectural style had been a way of making an ideological statement. A magnate who built his country house as a Gothic pile was making one kind of public assertion of his religion, politics, and worldview; a neoclassical country seat usually made another. The former implied a High Church, Tory, and conservative outlook, often coupled with care for the tenantry and a sense of responsibility towards the countryside; the latter, a more 'progressive', deist, or even free-thinking religion, Whig politics, and sometimes also a more mercantile financial outlook. Since most great houses were, of course, inherited not built, and religion (if not political party) might vary from one generation to the next, such statements were frequently retrospective, but the same polarity underpins much public architecture of the nineteenth century. New College, in the University of Edinburgh—the city that prided itself on being 'the Athens of the North'—is a fine neoclassical building; when its great rival, Glasgow, moved to new premises on Gilmour Hill in the 1860s it was no less natural for it to be built in a flamboyantly Gothic style. As we have seen, St John's College, Cambridge, commissioned a 'Gothic' library at the height of the neoclassical revival. When money was raised for the construction of an Oxford college to commemorate the life and work of John Keble, founder of the Tractarians, it was natural for it to be in contemporary, red-brick, Gothic.

The hypothesis that Gothic might have had an influence not merely on the shape of ecclesiastical architecture, but on the form and content of sermons, is a more problematic idea. Unlike many Nonconformist ones at the time of the French Revolution, eighteenth and nineteenth-century Anglican sermons were hardly epicentres of radicalism, political or aesthetic—especially at a time when the Church of England was sometimes known as 'the Tory Party at prayer'. Nor, until the Tractarians, were they likely to appeal to pre-Reformation virtues. Nevertheless, whatever their official purposes in expounding the Gospel, sermons inevitably had other functions as well. In an age when church attendance was still (nominally) compulsory, and the King James Bible was 'appointed to be read in Churches', the sermon was the weekly centrepiece of an act of dramatic rhetoric in every parish in England. In the eighteenth century this weekly 'drama' was sometimes devoted to social or philanthropic purposes—Laurence Sterne (1713–68) once raised the astounding sum of £64-11s-8d (£5,500 in today's money) in a charity sermon on the text of 'Elijah and the Widow of Zarephrath' at St Michael le Belfry, in York, in 1747 (Cash: 216). But, as might be expected, the author of *Tristram Shandy*, and a man who was Walpole's exact contemporary, is already treading the boundary between traditional biblical exegesis and a much more startling 'novelistic' reading of the same material.

Sterne's sermons have usually been quarried by literary critics seeking—and often finding—clues to the development of the mature novelist's style. Neither of the two major studies of them, by Heyden Hammond and Melvyn New, addresses this new novelistic rhetoric in his preaching (Hammond; Sterne). The former is largely concerned with the sources of the sermons; the latter with arguing for the orthodoxy, indeed, the conventionality, of Sterne's preaching. So far as I know, only Françoise Deconinck-Brossard's magisterial study of mid-eighteenth-century sermons in the North of England has attempted to set Sterne's work in the context of other contemporary sermons, and even she has only a few pages on matters such as hermeneutics and modes of biblical interpretation (Deconinck–Brossard). Yet to any reader familiar with eighteenth-century hermeneutic style what is most striking about the sermons of Mr Yorrick is not what they contain, but what they do *not* contain. Even a cursory knowledge of biblical commentaries and homilies of the period reveals the degree to which they were still overwhelmingly dominated by traditional typological and figural readings. Though the pioneering work of Benjamin Kennicott (1718–83) or Robert Lowth (1710–87) might be affecting small groups of avant-garde intellectuals, such groups typically tended to be Nonconformist or Unitarian rather than Anglican. Even Lowth makes it clear in his notes to his *New Translation of Isaiah* (1778) that in the last resort the prime purpose of textual criticism, with its concentration on the literal and historical sense of the passage, is not to produce a univocal reading, but rather to place figural and allegorical readings on a sounder historical base. Though the sermons of Joseph Butler (1692–1752) are atypical in their reliance on philosophical reasoning from first principles, they make it equally clear that the prime purpose of the Old Testament is to point figuratively to the New (Butler: 324–5). For instance, a standard exegesis of Sterne's charity sermon, 'Elijah and the widow of Zarephath', mentioned above, reveals that it signified 'the holy Mystery of the Incarnation, wherein the Divine living Body was applied to our dead Bodies, to quicken them from the Death of Sin' (*History of Old and New Testaments*: 136).

Sterne's sermons, in contrast, are aimed at affecting and moving the reader in ways that if not Gothic, are openly appealing to its contemporary concomitant: sentiment. His re-telling of the story of Elijah and the widow, for instance, is, in his own later sense of the word 'sentimental', emphasizing the nature of the widow's plight, and Elijah's pity for her. Even more dramatic, however, is the rhetoric of Sermon 18, on the story of the Levite and his concubine (Judges 19). Here we encounter something more like a conversation between an increasing babel of voices:

> —A CONCUBINE!—but the text accounts for it, *for in those days there was no king in Israel*, and the Levite, you will say, like every other man in it, did what was right in his own eyes,—and so, you may add, did his concubine too—*for she played the whore against him, and went away.*—
>
> —Then shame and grief go with her, and wherever she seeks a shelter, may the hand of justice shut the door against her.—
>
> Not so; for she went unto her father's house in Bethlehem-Judah, and was with him four whole months.—Blessed interval for meditation upon the fickleness and vanity of this world and its pleasures! I see the holy man upon his knees,—with hands compressed to his bosom, and with uplifted eyes, thanking heaven, that the object which had so long shared his affections, was fled.—
>
> The text gives a different picture of his situation; *for he arose and went after her to speak friendly to her, and to bring her back again, having his servant with him, and a couple of asses; and she brought him unto her father's house; and when the father of the damsel saw him, he rejoiced to meet him.*—
>
> —A most sentimental group ! you'll say: and so it is, my good commentator, the world talks of everything: give but the outlines of a story,—let *spleen* or *prudery* snatch the pencil, and they will finish it with so many hard strokes, and with so dirty a colouring, that candour and courtesy will sit in torture as they look at it.—
>
> …Here then let us stop for a moment, and give the story of the Levite and his Concubine a second hearing: like all others much of it depends upon the telling; and as the Scripture has left us no kind of comment upon it, 'tis a story on which the heart cannot be at a loss for what to say, or the imagination for what to suppose—the danger is, humanity may say too much. (Sterne: 1:167–8)

The story of the Levite and his concubine is one of the nastiest in the entire Bible—involving betrayal, the gang-rape and eventual murder of the woman by Benjamites. It was to lead to one of the worst inter-tribal conflicts in the entire Old Testament, with—according to Judges 21—a total of 85,130 dead. Sterne, however, only hints at this macabre context. What concerns him here is the relationships of the Levite, his concubine, and her father—and the voices of scandal surrounding them.

There seem to be several dialogues going on at once in this passage. The most obvious is that between 'I' and 'you': the preacher and his hearers, who are no mere passive auditors, but interject with their own opinions and comments. But that initial dialogue is, in turn, subverted by another voice, seemingly that of the so-called 'good commentator' whose contribution begins 'Then shame and grief go with her'. But this shadowy voice is not the last of the phantom speakers, for no sooner has 'I' indulged in his wonderful fantasy of the Levite on his knees thanking God that the woman in his life has left him than we get the deadpan corrective: 'The text gives a different picture…'. By the end all the qualities of the reader's mind are crowding into the pulpit as separate personifications: Spleen and Prudery, Candour and Courtesy, Heart and Imagination have all arrived to give us their unasked-for opinions—not to mention arguing among themselves. At every point the innocent reader is wrong-footed, shown over and over again that he has misread the clues in his text.

Perhaps we should pay closest attention to that 'good commentator' with whom so much of the debate is conducted. Though Sterne is careful to deny us a clear foothold, it would seem that the voice of the bumbling commentator—the conventional critic—shifts its ground to a new cliché each time Sterne renders the last one untenable. As Sterne concludes, 'the world talks of everything'. So, of course, does he. In place of traditional polysemous readings is a dramatic dialogue. Instead of trying to eliminate individual or idiosyncratic reactions, he takes it for granted that, subject to the authority of the text, it is the personal response of heart and imagination that is all-important—more, that it is in some sense the purpose of holy Scripture to awaken the emotions and imagination to their proper functions. Indeed, 'Humanity may say too much': there is a point beyond which over-meticulous commentary may get in the way of the immediacy of our own responses.

We could say more—the whole passage is an extraordinary assemblage of many disparate influences (Prickett 1996: 122–9)—and it may even be that Sterne is obliquely defending himself against scandals in his own life. What I want to call attention to here, however, is Sterne's use of that word 'sentimental'. For the man who was within a few years to write *A Sentimental Journey*, and thereby create a Europe-wide best-seller, this is a key word, and one that offers what one might call the reverse face of the Gothic—just as Sterne has taken one of the most violent horror stories of the Old Testament, and chosen, ironically, almost brazenly, to look for a kind of false empathy instead. For Sterne, 'sentimental' has none of its feeble enervated modern connotations, but rather represents a spontaneous overflow of sympathetic emotion. Of course, this also has its richly comic aspects—*A Sentimental Journey* ridicules self-conscious emotion as much as it celebrates it as Yorrick stumbles his well-intentioned and philandering way across Europe.

None of this, of course, is Gothic in the later sense of the word, but we miss much of the attractive force of what is happening if we fail to recognize in this novelistic and empathetic approach to scripture elements that will later be central to the new style of nineteenth-century sermon. But to complete the formula one other element was still necessary, and this, strangely enough, was perhaps the final development in all the improbable descendants of Walpole's mad extravaganza—the idea of tradition.

Given the attempt by the Council of Trent to appropriate the tradition of the Catholic Church to aid its claims to Papal Supremacy, it is hardly surprising that at the beginning of the nineteenth century 'tradition' was not exactly a popular concept in the English-speaking world. When, in the previous century, the word was used at all—and it usually wasn't—it referred only to the beliefs and stories of the remote (pre-Tridentine) past. Swift scarcely uses it. In all his voluminous writings John Wesley only uses the word nine times (seven in one piece) and always pejoratively (Prickett 2009: ch. 2). Robert Lowth, perhaps the man who knew more about scriptural tradition in a scholarly, rather than a polemical, sense than any other man alive, uses the word only three times in some 500 pages—and then only to suggest the doubtful authority of some of his sources (Prickett 2009: 43). Perhaps more surprising, Burke, in what is perhaps the most influential piece of conservative polemic in the entire eighteenth century, his *Reflections on the French Revolution*, only invokes the concept twice, and then in the form of 'traditionary', making it clear that it is an antique, even obsolete, idea, belonging to the pre-1688 world. By and large, tradition was a dirty word and an empty concept in 1800.

How then did a word whose original meaning was largely confined to law and religion, and only later, by extension, to politics, come to be a vital part of that quality of the historical imagination that we take for granted in the modern self-understanding? Though it, too, had roots in the Gothic, and the new emerging sense of history at the beginning of the nineteenth century, the word's slow climb back to respectability did not start with Walpole, or even with the 'Romantics'—the very people whose modern name seems like a claim to be reviving the aesthetic and moral qualities of a past age. Or, to be exact, it did not start with the *English* Romantics, who were almost as wary of using the word as Burke and Paine, but rather with one of their closest admirers—the man who has every right to the title of Coleridge's greatest American disciple—James Marsh.

James Marsh (1794–1842) was a key figure in the introduction of Coleridge's philosophy to American readers, producing in quick succession editions of *Aids to Reflection*, *The Friend*, and *The Statesman's Manual*. In 1833 he produced a translation of Herder's *Spirit of Hebrew Poetry*. This, he tells us, contained

> the traditions of the patriarchs, which, as among all nations, so peculiarly among this people, were the source from which were derived all the peculiarities of their modes of thinking, consequently also the genius of their poetry. To set forth these, and unfold them correctly, was here so much the more necessary, since most traditions of this kind have themselves more or less of poetical colouring, and what is worse, are often misapprehended. (Herder: 17)

In fact, however, Marsh is being less than candid here. The word 'tradition' exists in German, stems from the same Latin root, has and had much the same meaning as in English—and is used by Herder at some points. But this is *not* the word that Herder commonly uses. That word is 'sage'—as in the English 'saga' or, more straightforwardly, 'legend'. If Marsh had consistently translated 'sage' as 'legend' instead of 'tradition', the whole flavour of his translation would have been different. Rather than being essentially unreliable, traditional legends are, instead, the source of the poetic genius of the race. So far from being a source of unreliable fact, mythology is the source of ineffable sublimity.

> Among the Hebrews, history itself is properly poetry, that is the transmission of narratives, which are related in the present tense, and here too we may discover an advantage derived from the indefiniteness or fluctuation, of the tenses, especially in producing conviction, and rendering what is described, related or announced, more clearly and vividly present to the senses. Is not this in a high degree poetical? (Herder: 37)

'History is poetry'. Tradition is thus nothing less than the voice of the poetic genius of the race This is not a definition that would have been understood by Bossuet or any other Roman Catholic expositor of the period. It does not consist of the accretion of commentary and extra-canonical assumptions central to the imperial claims of the

Vatican. Nor is it the essentially unreliable process of oral transmission treated with such contempt by most contemporary eighteenth-century writers. Neither Burke nor Paine would have recognized it. The claim that traditions (at least of the Bible) provide a guide both to lost truths—now almost certainly inaccessible to other kinds of investigation—*and*, even more significantly, to the unique sublimity of the poetic traditions of the Hebrews, is a reading-back of Herder's own aesthetics into the ancient world. What Herder and Marsh have between them created is an appeal to the wisdom of the past totally consonant with the new 'sentimental' and Gothic spirit of the age—both a guide towards a greater understanding of history, and a way of perceiving the present.

What distinguishes this new approach to tradition is a changed sense of history itself. Herder had been writing in the 1780s—before the French Revolution. For a generation that had grown up with its traumas and violent aftermath, it was no longer possible to assume that things were very much as they always had been. The events of recent European history had made the irony of Gibbon's Enlightenment epigram that history was little more than the record of the 'crimes, follies, and misfortunes of mankind' begin to look very threadbare. History could never again be a record of particular events against a background of stasis, but from henceforth had to be about change itself. The translation of Niebuhr's massive *History of Rome* by Julius Hare (1795–1855) and Connop Thirlwall (1797–1825) in 1827 has (in retrospect) sometimes been seen as a watershed in British historiography but, in truth, it would be no less accurate to see it as a 'sign of the times'—itself a phrase adopted as a title by Carlyle. It was the first modern history to attempt to go beyond the accretions of myth and tradition handed down by the Latin authors themselves, and to search for documentary evidence. Where that was impossible, Niebuhr looked for explanations in areas not necessarily always obvious to contemporary observers, such as institutions, laws, class, culture, and even race. Carlyle's own titles, from his *Signs of the Times* (1829) to *Past and Present* (1843*)*, hammer home the message of historical flux and transformation—a theme central to his monumental history of *The French Revolution* (1837) itself, which explored change not so much as process but apocalypse.

Marsh's translation of Herder was published in 1833, the same year as Keble's July Assize Sermon, which, undramatic in itself, proved to be the rallying cry for the Tractarians. For those like Keble, and his Oxford associates, Richard Hurrell Froude, H. P. Liddon, John Henry Newman, or Edward Bouverie Pusey, the questions raised by Keble were vital to the future of their Church, and it was to answer them that the Oxford series, 'Tracts for the Times' (1833–41) together with a more substantial historical series, 'The Library of the Fathers' (begun in 1835), were created. Explicitly designed to remind Anglicans of their Catholic inheritance from the early Church, the Tracts were intended as a defence against the excesses of Reformation Protestantism and contemporary Evangelical neglect for the traditions of the institutional Church (Wheeler). Though both enterprises were couched in the language of the Vincentian canon, claiming to be about the very central doctrines of the historic Church—following the formula of Vincent of Lerins: *Quod semper, quod ubique, quod ab omnibus* (what all Christians at all times everywhere had believed)—one aspect of this, at least, was very untraditional:

Newman and his associates supported their claims on a solid basis of detailed historical scholarship. In a time of epistemological crisis they were, like all their predecessors in search of tradition, reading back into the past their own concerns, and finding in the Gothic spirit of medieval Catholicism the seeds of a new synthesis on which the Anglican settlement might be based.

What was less immediately noticed in the years of ecclesiastical and legal turmoil of the 1830s and 1840s was that the idea of 'tradition' was itself again coming under radical re-examination. Catholic architecture pointed towards Catholic doctrines. Though it seems an obvious point, it is worth noting the inexorable progression by which what was initially an essentially legal dispute moved into a debate over the nature of the Church itself. The idea of tradition, which had begun largely as an assumption of the Apostolic Episcopal succession, rapidly involved not merely the Tracts themselves (with their own internal dynamic that was to lead many to Rome before Newman's eventual reception—or, in contemporary jargon, 'perversion'—in 1845), but the interpretation of Church history implicit in such projects as the 'Lives of the English Saints', and the aesthetics of worship. All the elements of this idea of tradition—Apostolic succession, Church history, architecture, and aesthetics—were widely caricatured and misunderstood, then as now. It is easy, for instance, to mock the author of the 'Life of St Neot', who concluded, with an honesty even more commendable than his piety, '... and that is all, and, indeed, rather more than all that is known about the life of the blessed St Neot'; or the 'smells and bells' of ritualists—which were nearly as much despised by Keble and Newman as by their Evangelical critics. Yet there was behind such ecclesiastical kitsch a genuine thirst for historical truth about the Church that had been missing for generations—and which was, in the end, to affect the Catholic Church as much as its Protestant rivals.

Moreover, with the coming of the Tractarians in the 1830s, there was renewed emphasis on dogma and theological debates. The mere exposition of conservative doctrines contained within itself the seeds of change. Since, for Anglicans, there had been little theological training for clergy, beyond the expectation of a university degree, until the coming of the Clapham Sect in the eighteen-teens, genuine theological debate as distinct from sectarian polemic had been comparatively rare. As George Eliot points out in *Felix Holt*, Nonconformists were usually better educated. Now for almost the first time, many Anglicans were being challenged to know what they believed—and this, as much the specifics raised by Keble in his Assize Sermon, intensified the theological debates of the 1830s and 1840s. For some, the outcome was ultimately a matter of 'perversion' to Catholicism (Newman and Manning); for others it involved a new stress either on 'tradition' (Keble, Hampden or Blomfield), or on more radical social ideas (Kingsley, Maurice, and the Christian Socialists). At the same time, Coleridge's notion of 'lay sermons', still on theological issues, spread to the opposition, and was to be taken up by Huxley and Cooper.

Not everyone, of course, was seduced by the aesthetics of tradition. For the Tractarians' opponents tradition was unreliable hearsay—exposing the essential weakness of the position of Roman Catholics and Tractarians alike. As early as 1819, Edward Hawkins

(1789–1882), a fellow, and later to be Provost, of Oriel College, had staked out his position in his *Dissertation upon the Use and Importance of Unauthoritative Tradition*. (Hawkins, 1818). Tradition, though not valueless, is taken throughout with all its eighteenth-century connotations of primitiveness and historical unreliability. This is a point he returned to in a sermon of 1830. 'We [unlike the Romish Church], acknowledge the Scriptures as the only rule of faith, and appeal to no uncertain traditions in proof of Christian doctrines' (Hawkins 1830: 15).

For Newman, writing in his still-Protestant 1837 *Lectures*, building on an image used (though not originated) by Lowth, and taken up by Coleridge, tradition is akin to the river of life flowing down the years, as a kind of collective unconscious, flowing through the mind and imagination of the Church:

> If we ask, why it is that these professed Traditions were not reduced to writing, it is answered that the Christian doctrine, as it has proceeded from the mouth of the Apostles, is too varied and too minute in its details to allow of it.... It is latent, but it lives. It is silent, like the rapids of a river, before the rocks intercept it. It is the Church's unconscious habit of opinion and feeling; which she reflects upon, masters, and expresses, according to the emergency. We see then the mistake of asking for a complete collection of the Roman Traditions; as well might we ask for a collection of a man's tastes and opinions on a given subject. Tradition in its fullness is necessarily unwritten; it is the mode in which a society has felt or acted during a certain period, and it cannot be circumscribed any more than a man's countenance and manner can be conveyed to strangers in any set of propositions. (Newman 1837: 40–1)

In his 1845 *Essay on the Development of Doctrine* Newman, now defending the position of the Catholic Church which he had not yet joined, elaborated on this image of tradition as a river by attacking Lowth's idea that a stream becomes progressively polluted the further it is from its original source (Lowth 1:84–6).

> It is indeed sometimes said that the stream is clearest near the spring. Whatever use may fairly be made of this image, it does not apply to the history of a philosophy or belief, which on the contrary is more equable, and purer, and stronger, when its bed has become deep, and broad, and full. It necessarily rises out of an existing state of things, and for a time savours of the soil. Its vital element needs disengaging from what is foreign and temporary, and is employed in efforts after freedom which become more vigorous and hopeful as its years increase. Its beginnings are no measure of its capabilities, nor of its scope. At first no one knows what it is, or what it is worth. It remains perhaps for a time quiescent; it tries, as it were, its limbs, and proves the ground under it, and feels its way. From time to time it makes essays which fail, and are in consequence abandoned. It seems in suspense which way to go; it wavers, and at length strikes out in one definite direction. In time it enters upon strange territory; points of controversy alter their bearing; parties rise and fall around it; dangers and hopes appear in new relations; and old principles reappear under new forms. It changes with them in order to remain the same. In a higher world it is otherwise, but here below to live is to change, and to be perfect is to have changed often (Newman 1989: 40).

In 1838 Hawkins came out against the whole notion of ecclesiastical tradition in even stronger terms:

> On observing how common it is for men of all countries and names, whether Christians, Jews, or Mahometans, to receive the religion of their fathers, I have again and again asked myself, whether I too was not a slave? whether I too was not blindly walking in the path of tradition, and yielding myself as passively as others to an hereditary faith? (Hawkins 1838: 29)

By 1842, no doubt as the result of almost a decade of polemical struggle with the Tractarians, this metaphor of a false trail had hardened still further into the actual suggestion of 'false report'.

> It is no act of Christian faith to believe a point of Ecclesiastical History which cannot be proved. How many are there in England who have heard the traditionary rumour of an objection to the Succession of Bishops in this Reformed Church, who know not, and cannot know, any thing of its refutation. And what if, many centuries later, the tradition of the objection should outlive the historical evidence by which it is disproved? (Hawkins 1842: 15)

For others, however, the flow of tradition, while not necessarily leading towards Rome, provided an irresistible image of progress. Thus for Renn Dickson Hampden (1793–1868), Regius Professor of Divinity in Oxford at the time, tradition was also a constantly flowing river: 'in the stream of Tradition, as in the successions of Time itself, there may be no pause'. In this sense it becomes a metaphor for the unfolding of revelation, from 'the passing, ever-flowing Tradition of the truth' (Hampden: 3).

Meanwhile, yet another term had been added to the Gothic–sentimental appeal to the traditions of the past: the 'poetic'. It is important to remember that Keble and Newman, the two most important religious leaders of the Tractarians, were also both published poets. Keble was already famous as the author of *The Christian Year* (the best-selling poetry book of the century) well before the Assize Sermon of 1833, and any account of his thought that fails to stress the importance of both *Tract Eighty Nine*, and the *Lectures on Poetry*, misunderstands the degree to which the tradition of the Church had always been for Keble as much a poetic as a legal or theological one. Newman, the author of such popular poems as 'Lead Kindly Light' and, later, 'Praise to the Holiest in the Height' from the longer poem, *The Dream of Gerontius*, was no less aesthetically inclined. Both had been heavily influenced by their Romantic predecessors, especially Coleridge and Wordsworth—and had inherited from them an idea of the Church which, in their terms, was essentially 'poetic' (Prickett 1986: Chs. 4, 7). Religion and aesthetics met not merely in forms of worship, but also in the belief that the unity of the Church itself was best understood by means of aesthetic analogies.

'It would be hard to believe', declares Keble in his *Lectures on Poetry*, that poetry and theology 'would have proved such true allies unless there was a hidden tie of kinship between them' (Keble: 2:479–80). 'Poetry...supplies a rich wealth of similes whereby a pious mind may supply and remedy, in some sort, its powerlessness of speech' (Keble:

2:581). It is the proper medium or vehicle of religious experience because it does not make direct statements (which the limitations of human language would render impossible) but through its symbols, which express the hidden inwards of religion. 'In short, Poetry lends Religion her wealth of symbols and similes: Religion restores these again to Poetry, clothed with so splendid a radiance that they appear to be no longer merely symbols, but to partake (I might almost say) of the nature of sacraments' (Keble: 2:481).

The echoes of Coleridge's description of symbols in the appendix to *The Statesman's Manual*—published less than twenty years before—are obvious (Coleridge 1972: 28–9, 30). So, indeed, is Newman's gloss on this idea written now not as a Tractarian, but as a Catholic.

> It is sometimes asked whether poets are not more commonly found external to the Church than among her children; and it would not surprise us to find the question answered in the affirmative. Poetry is the refuge of those who have not the Catholic Church to flee to and repose upon, for the Church herself is the most sacred and august of poets. Poetry, as Mr Keble lays it down in his University Lectures on the subject, is a method of relieving the overburdened mind: it is a channel through which emotion finds expression, and that a safe regulated expression. Now what is the Catholic Church, viewed in her human aspect, but a discipline of the affections and passions? (Newman 1890: 2:442)

Small wonder that Bishop Blomfield in his *Charge to the Clergy of the Diocese of London* in 1846 should have inveighed as much against those—especially apparently women— who 'seem to have been misled by the treacherous light of a poetical mysticism, following the guidance, not of their reason but of imagination', as against those who (he alleged) had remained in the Anglican Church with the express purpose of making converts to Rome (Blomfield: 20, 15).

Blomfield's fears may have been exaggerated, but even his turn of phrase, in suspecting 'a treacherous light of a poetical mysticism', a will o'-the-wisp from a more primitive past, reveals how close he is to Gothic terrors of a resurgent and sinister Catholicism. He was right at least in realizing that the nineteenth century's rediscovery of an emotional and aesthetic pre-Enlightenment past had had profound implications for his own day. Even for those like Keble, Liddon, or Pusey, who were to resist the siren-song of Rome, the landscape had been transformed. To try and distinguish architecture from ritual, superstition, literary fad, sentimentality, politics, a sense of history or attachment to tradition is to seek a false clarity where none is possible. Nor does the much-disputed title of 'Romanticism' (a term dating back in England only to the 1880s) help. But in harking back to its roots—in many cases as much imaginary as real—religion in England had acquired not merely a new aesthetic, but a new self-awareness, and a new emotional depth.

REFERENCES

Blomfield, C. J. (1846). *Charge to Clergy of Diocese of London*, 2nd edn. London: B. Fellowes.
Brockman, H. A. N. (1956). *The Caliph of Fonthill*. London: Werner Laurie.
Butler, J. (1749). *Fifteen Sermons Preached at the Rolls Chapel to which are added Six Sermons Preached on Publick Occasions*, 4th edn. London: John and Paul Knapton.

Cash, A. H. (1975). *Laurence Sterne: The Early and Middle Years*. London: Methuen.
Clark, K. (1964). *The Gothic Revival*. Harmondsworth: Pelican.
Coleridge, S. T. (1972). 'The Statesman's Manual', in R. J. White (ed.), *Lay Sermons*. London: Routledge.
Deconinck-Brossard, F. (1984). *Vie Politique, Sociale et Religieuse en Grande-Bretagne d'après les Sermons Prêchés ou Publiés dans le Nord d'Angleterre 1736–1760*. Paris: Didier Erudition.
Eichner, H. (1970). *Friedrich Schlegel*. New York: Twayne.
Hammond, Lansing Van der Heyden (1948). *Laurence Sterne's 'Sermons of Mr Yorrick'*. New Haven, CT: Yale University Press.
Hampden, R. D. (1842). *A Lecture on Tradition, Read at the Divinity School, Thursday, March 7, 1839*, 5th edn. London: B. Fellowes.
Hawkins, E. (1818). *A Dissertation upon the Use and Importance of Unauthoritative Tradition as an Introduction to the Christian Doctrines; Including the Substance of A Sermon Preached before the University of Oxford, May 31, 1818*. Oxford: W. Baxter.
—— (1830). *Christianity Not the Religion Either of the Bible Only, or of the Church: A Sermon Preached at Maldon, July 28, 1830, at the Primary Visitation of Charles James Blomfield, Bishop of London*. Oxford: Parker.
—— (1838). *The Duty of Private Judgement, A Sermon Preached before the University of Oxford, Nov. 11, 1838*. Oxford: J. H. Parker.
—— (1842). *The Apostolical Succession, A Sermon Preached in the Chapel of Lambeth Palace, Sunday, February 27, 1842*. London: B. Fellowes.
Herder, J. G. (1833). *The Spirit of Hebrew Poetry*, trans. J. Marsh. Burlington, VT: Edward Smith.
The History of the Old and New Testaments Extracted from the Sacred Scriptures, the Holy Fathers, and Other Ecclesiastical Writers… (1712). 4th impression. London: Jeremiah Bright.
Keble, J. (1912). *Lectures on Poetry*, trans. E. K. Francis. Oxford: Oxford University Press.
Ketton-Cremer, W. R. (1964). *Horace Walpole: A Biography*, 3rd edn. London: Methuen.
Lowth, R. (1787). *Lectures on the Sacred Poetry of the Hebrews*, G. Gregory (trans.). London: J. Johnson.
Newman, J. H. (1837). *Lectures on the Prophetical Office of the Church, Viewed Relatively to Romanism and Popular Protestantism*. London: J. G. & F. Rivington.
—— (1890). *Essays, Critical and Historical*, 9th edn. London: Longman.
—— (1989). *Essay on the Development of Doctrine*, 6th edn. Reprinted with Foreword by Ian Ker. Notre Dame, IN: University of Notre Dame Press.
Nesbit, E. (1959). *The Story of the Amulet*. Harmondsworth: Penguin.
Pevsner, N. (1956). *The Englishness of English Art*. London: Architectural Press.
Prickett, S. (1986). *Romanticism and Religion: the Tradition of Coleridge and Wordsworth in the Victorian Church*. Cambridge: Cambridge University Press.
—— (1996). *Origins of Narrative: The Romantic Appropriation of the Bible*. Cambridge: Cambridge University Press.
—— (2005). *Victorian Fantasy*, 2nd edn. Waco, TX: Baylor University Press.
—— (2009). *Modernity and the Reinvention of Tradition*. Cambridge: Cambridge University Press.
Sterne, L. (1996). *The Sermons of Laurence Sterne*, ed. M. New. Gainesville, FL: University Press of Florida.

The History of the Old and New Testaments Extracted from the Sacred Scriptures, the Holy Fathers, and Other Ecclesiastical Writers… (1712). 4th impression. London: Jeremiah Bright.

Wheeler, M. (2006). *The Old Enemies: Catholic and Protestant in Nineteenth-Century English Culture*. Cambridge: Cambridge University Press.

CHAPTER 36

THE SERMON AND THE VICTORIAN NOVEL

LINDA GILL

Quoting several representative Victorian preachers in his investigation of the Victorian sermon, Robert H. Ellison points out that by and large Victorians believed the sermon's 'main business' was 'to plead and persuade' and that the sermon was to 'be solemn and affecting, loving and urgent, full of persuasion, warning and rebuke' (Ellison: 18). When one unpacks what the Victorian sermon's 'business' was, then, one unpacks the fact that the sermon's objective was to convey the truth or truths to its listeners. After all, 'persuasion' implies truths one must be persuaded by just as 'warning' and 'rebuke' imply untruths one must be warned and rebuked against. In short, the Victorian sermon was and was intended to be monologic; it claimed (like most sermons, past and present) to present an ontology based on a God-given authoritative text. It purported to present, for the layman's understanding, the biblical 'grand narrative' as interpreted by a particular church. The sermon was thereby seen to be predicated upon—even as it was a producer of—a defined, central first principle which generated values, hierarchies, categories of identity, and the way to give meaning to the world. The epistemology being ontological, the sermon invited no rebuttal. Given the above premise, each member of the congregation should have known who he/she was in the grand scheme of things and what his/her purpose was. To reject the sermon was to reject truth. Why, then, one is left to ask, does so much Victorian literature, the vast majority of which was written and read by church-goers and sermon-listeners, articulate doubt and uncertainty?

In the wake of liberal humanist education, the ideas of the Enlightenment, the growing interest in German philosophy and the higher criticism of the Bible, geological and other scientific discoveries, utilitarianism, the societal destabilization of the Industrial Revolution, and an irrevocably splintered and splintering church, even Victorian churchgoers could hardly be unaware that a belief in any sort of grand narrative—even a religious one—was proving to be uncomfortably tentative if not outright fictional.

Long-held first principles and the ontology they generated were proving not to be so. Categories of identity were proving to be porous. Hierarchies were falling apart or being sometimes violently rearranged. Categories of meaning were deconstructing. In short, values were shifting and meaning was becoming uncertain as industry, individualism, and science displaced agriculture, communal identity, and authority—authority which was once based upon God, His Word, and a Church that defined what each meant. The result could hardly help but be a crisis in identity and purpose. Unlike later postmodernists, the Victorians were not ready to embrace chaos with enthusiasm.

Many of the accepted philosophical and religious thinkers, as well as those who turned to them for guidance, responded by rearticulating old or creating new epistemes which in turn generated categories, values, and hierarchies of meaning. For instance, in *Past and Present* (1843), Thomas Carlyle, the culturally proclaimed 'Sage of Chelsea', employed a fictionalization of an historical abbey as a model for social construction. In his appropriation of the abbey's religious society, Carlyle articulates a hierarchy of people based on capability and talent, insists that every individual should have a purposeful duty which benefited the whole, and declares all should be infused with the spirit of God and interconnected by love. This model is, in short, an iteration of the Great Chain of Being, but it is ultimately emptied of religion, if not the 'Divine Idea of the World' (Tennyson: xxv). He argues that captains of industry, the leaders of the working, producing class, should create the organizing principle around which society and meaning would cohere—not religious authorities. Institutionalized religion, Carlyle argues in his earlier *Sartor Resartus* (1833), is no longer capable of teaching morality or conveying the idea of God: it is empty clothing. History and its heroes, he goes on to explain, have supplanted the Bible as the text of transcendental truths. Recorders of this history are, then, the new preachers. In like vein, Matthew Arnold responded to what he termed social 'anarchy' by giving up writing poetry of sorrow and loss in order to write social criticism which he felt could fix society (both in terms of repair and anchorage). In 'Culture and Anarchy', he devotes himself to organizing nearly everything and everyone into tidy, knowable categories which could, therefore, be identified, contained and, when need be, corrected. Like Carlyle he did not submit religion as the anchoring pillar around which to ward off chaos but instead insisted what was needed was the 'sweetness and light' literature ('the best that was known and thought in the world') provided through the mediation of disinterested criticism (Arnold 1961a).

Many others responded to the perceived destabilization of social order by reasserting religious principles. John Henry Newman, as part of the Oxford Movement, helped lead the charge to reform the Church of England in order to unite the people of God, and then, in what many felt was an apocalyptic event, turned to the ancient creeds of the Catholic Church and its papal authority as the answer to a society in crisis. The irony is that the myriad attempts to create or re-establish a grand narrative predicated on ontological givens only reiterated how impossible it was to do so. There were just too many voices, too many points of view, too many ideologies at play.

This is the context in which the novel spins out its webs of discourse and matures during the Victorian period. If the sermon is monologic, from the very beginning, the novel has been and continues to be dialogic. Its very form and structure create the battle ground for vying ideologies. The novel is, as Mikhail Bakhtin argues, a carnival of voices (Bakhtin). Even in the most didactic novels, various characters, their experiences and discourses continually puncture the dominant narrative and offer alternative possibilities; even if these possibilities are subsequently rejected, they are not erased.

It follows, then, that in the novel, when sermons are represented or reported, they only have value as part of a dialectic. The sermonizer, and even the novelist who creates the sermonizer and the sermon, may intend that the sermon be the conveyer of God-given truths and unimpeachable lessons, but because the sermon is only one voice in the midst of others, it cannot help but be modified or even undermined by the multi-voiced context in which it appears. Anthony Trollope, in *Barchester Towers* (1857), implicitly argues this point when Mr Slope, the chaplain of the new bishop of Barchester, preaches a sermon intended to correct the Church's use of music as an integral part of its religious services. The narrator points out that the music-loving congregation 'had to sit through [the sermon]! None of them...could close his ears, nor leave the house of God during the hours of service. They were under an obligation of listening, and that too without any immediate power of reply' (Trollope 1987: 45). In pointing out that the listeners are forced to endure in silence a sermon with which they ardently disagree, the narrator provides the reply the congregation cannot give. In Charles Dickens's *Bleak House* (1852–3) when the Revd Chadband launches into several impromptu sermons at the dinner table—homilies consisting of 'piling verbose flights of stairs, one upon another' and repetitive rhetorical questions meant to teach what he feels are profound truths—the narration in which these sermons are embedded ensures that these supposed revelatory truths are read as hilariously obvious and even ridiculous (Dickens: 247). In George Eliot's *Adam Bede* (1859) when the Revd Irwin's replacement condemns him for being worldly as he himself self-righteously preaches doctrine, the narrator points out that the sour-tempered sermonizer liked nothing better than to punish and scold people from the pulpit. He may have been, the narrator notes, knowledgeable about doctrine but, unlike the doctrinally lax Irwin, is woefully ignorant of the people he is meant to serve (Eliot 1981: 178–9). When in Charlotte Brontë's *Jane Eyre* (1847) Mr Brocklehurst preaches a condemnatory sermon defining Jane as a liar to her school mates and teachers (C. Brontë: 69), it is in the context of Jane's proven integrity. Miss Temple, the headmistress of the school, then invites Jane to her own rooms, tells Jane she will ignore Brocklehurst's condemnation and let Jane prove herself truthful or otherwise (C. Brontë: 71–3). The narrator in *Barchester Towers* may lament that 'there is, perhaps, no greater hardship at present inflicted on mankind in civilized and free countries, than the necessity of listening to sermons' because 'no one but a preaching clergyman can revel in platitudes, truisms, and untruisms, and yet receive, as his undisputed privilege, the same respectful demeanour as though words of impassioned eloquence or persuasive logic fell from his lips' (Trollope 1987: 45–6), but embedded in this lament is the transparent condemnation of such monologic discourse.

To a large degree, the fault of the preacher is not that he expresses an opinion but that he presents his opinions as ontological givens: he does not recognize the dialectic in which he is participating. Thus, Dickens writes of the Revd Chadband, 'Mr Chadband—of whom the persecutors say that it is no wonder he should go on for any length of time uttering such abominable nonsense, but that the wonder is that he should ever leave off, having once the audacity to begin' (Dickens: 252). Having gained the bully pulpit, such a preacher tyrannizes his hearers by refusing to acknowledge possible opposition.

On this note, because the sermon-giver refuses to acknowledge contrary opinion, and his sermon is presented as God-given truths, in the Victorian novel the sermon often becomes a vehicle for the sermon-giver's self-aggrandizement and empowerment as much as a vehicle to convey God's word or even the creeds of the Church. Further, in the sermon's ability to render the listeners voiceless, the novel often makes clear that this empowerment is only achieved by disempowering the listeners. As Trollope puts it in *Barchester Towers*, 'a preacher is encouraged in the vanity of making his [voice] heard by the privilege of a compelled audience. His sermon is the pleasant morsel of his life, his delicious moment of self-exaltation' (Trollope 1987: 47). When in *Jane Eyre* St. John Rivers insists Jane must accompany him to the mission field he does so in the form of a sermon, for he feels he is presenting the will of God (C. Brontë: 420–1). When Jane then prays and subsequently rejects St. John and his plans for her, the reader, as well as Jane, understands St. John's desires are his own, not God's (C. Brontë: 422–3). When Mr Slope defines music in church as a sin, in essence he defines his parishioners as sinful while elevating himself to the position of God's elect. Likewise in Emily Brontë's *Wuthering Heights* (1847) one of the ways Joseph establishes his power over the otherwise rebellious Cathy and Heathcliff is through the three-hour Sunday sermons to which he subjects them and to which they are forced to listen (E. Brontë: 16). In *Bleak House*, when one of the Revd Chadband's listeners attempts to interject a response to one of his many rhetorical questions, Chadband immediately frowns the man down with contempt (Dickens: 245). Chadband is not open to sharing even a modicum of power. True to its dialogic form, in all these cases, while the sermon-givers jam their ideological positions down the throats of their listeners, the novels reveal that the empowerment these sermonizers achieve is undeserved, unmerited, and unwarranted.

Certainly this is true in Samuel Butler's *The Way of All Flesh* (1903). Primarily written during the 1870's, the novel spans five generations of the Pontifexes from the late eighteenth century to 1867 (Mason: xviii). As a satire of religion, the ideological position of the novel is in opposition to the sermons it presents. Narrated in the first person by Edward Overton, a spokesperson for Butler's own views, the narrative's weight falls on the shoulders of the earnest Anglican preacher, Ernest Pontifex—another avatar of Butler himself (Mason: xxx)—who loses his faith and embraces a self-possessed, self-assured existentially phenomenological hedonism. Throughout Ernest's spiritual journey, the sermon is presented primarily for the purpose of unmasking it as a weapon the preacher uses to establish a despotic reign over his God-fearing hearers. Ernest is raised by a clergyman father who was raised by a religious publisher, both of whom are representatives of what Butler viewed as a middle-class Victorian ideology which established patriarchal tyranny predicated on religious authority. 'Sinful' children, therefore, were to be physically beaten into submission. Everyone else was to be verbally beaten into submission. Accordingly, Theobald, Ernest's father, beats Ernest for the most innocent of errors which the former defines as sins. When, for instance, four-year-old Ernest pronounces 'Come' as 'Tum' while reciting a hymn at the close of a tediously observed Sabbath (Butler: 73), Theobald, accusing his son of being 'self-willed and naughty' rather than allowing him to be a vebally imperfect child (Butler: 74), mercilessly beats him much to the horror of the on-looking and recording Overton. Immediately after beating Ernest for committing the sin of speaking like a child, still 'red-handed' (Butler: 74), Theobald calls in his wife and servants for worship. He reads to them Numbers 15, a chapter in which God commands Moses to stone a man for having gathered sticks on Sabbath, a reading which Overton includes in its entirety (Butler: 75). Overton notes Theobald undoubtedly chose the chapter according to 'some system of his own' (Butler: 74), and, indeed, it is a system meant to bolster his own authority as the Moses of the household carrying out punishments at the command of the Lord God Almighty for seemingly trifling disobediences. The implied subtext of the service Theobald conducts is that those beneath Theobald in terms of power—and according to the religious ideology he espouses everyone is beneath him in terms of power—must obey or die—so says God and so Theobald earnestly believes and therefore preaches. Unsurprisingly, he believes so earnestly because this is an ideology which validates his complete 'devotion' to himself (Butler: 52). By directly juxtaposing the physical beating with the verbal beating, Butler, through Overton, implies that sermons—the verbalization of religion—are merely culturally accepted forms of torture. The verbal beating is hardly more palatable than the physical one. In both cases, the reader, cued by Overton, is meant to recoil from them as manifestations of the cruel brutality of a preacher who uses his voice as well as his fists as a weapon. Both are meant to elicit submission and confirm dominance. The fact that both are mandated by God, at least as far as Theobald, and Butler, would have us understand, renders them unimpeachable. The fact both are, as Butler would also have us understand, wrong, is equally unimpeachable.

Paradoxically, the text also suggests that both physical and verbal violence may not be effective as a means for inculcating ideology. Ernest does master the 'k' sound enabling him to say 'come' rather than 'tum', but this ability undoubtedly has little to do with his father's physical or verbal beatings of him and everything to do with his growing verbal skill. And, in fact, Ernest ultimately rejects everything his father stands for and preaches about, including his ideological position on God and religion. There is little evidence to suggest the servants are anything but obedient to Theobald, but the fact that Overton records he had never seen 'more absolute vacancy...upon the countenances of human beings' than that of the servants during the worship service (Butler: 74) suggests this obedience has nothing to do with the Sabbath sun-down reading's implicit warning.

And yet, the psychological impact a sermon can have, at least temporarily, suggests that the sermon is a means of forcing a particular ideology down the throats of its listeners and resisting all rebuttals and emendation. This is made clearest in Overton's inclusion of Mr Hawke's sermon in its entirety. Just as clear is the dismissal of such discourse and the ontology it assumes. Overton points out that such 'a state of mind [as Hawke's] in another generation or two will seem to stand sadly in need of explanation' (Butler: 168). That is, Hawke's ideology is an ideology which no longer has validity.

This is not to suggest that at the time it is received the sermon does not profoundly affect its listeners, including Ernest, or is not given in earnest. Even Overton acknowledges Hawke sermonizes with 'simplicity and obvious earnestness' (Butler: 171). Nevertheless, Hawke's sincerity does little to change the fact that he is engaging in psychological warfare; he is simply nimbler, gentler, and more persuasive in his use of emotional and psychological manipulation than others—at least as far as the text is concerned. In this he is not unlike Ernest's mother whose 'loving' and explicitly religious counsel is described by Overton in the language of warfare (Butler: 179–84). Ernest's recommitment to the Church after hearing Hawke's sermon, like his commitment to his mother's counsel, finally and utterly fails, and Ernest declares himself independent from his religious masters in order to be master of himself. A representative of the modern subject, Ernest ultimately defines himself as 'free' (Butler: 234), a subject whose definition is generated from within rather than imposed upon him from without.

While in the Victorian novel the sermon is often represented as a means of establishing or maintaining power, it is just as often represented as the accidental, narrow-minded, or uneducated means of disseminating falsehoods. For instance, while Mr Slope, in *Barchester Towers*, bases his condemnation of music in church on seemingly sincere belief, the text's narration very obviously represents him and his sermon on the subject as wrong. *Barchester Towers*, and *The Warden* (1855) before it, represent music as a God-given gift and a means for praising God. In *Wuthering Heights* Joseph's homilies are not only nearly literally incomprehensible, but he lopsidedly represents God as (only) wrathful and vindictive. Thus, the second generation of characters in the novel abandon him to the vacated Wuthering Heights estate while they move into Thrushcross Grange.

Often the sermon-giver's errors are compounded by his hypocrisy. In Winwood Reade's *The Outcast* (1872), when the clergyman and main narrator becomes convinced the Bible is a literary masterpiece consisting of 'profane and ridiculous fables' (Reade: 49), his mentor actually temporarily convinces him to embrace hypocrisy as a moral good (Reade: 53–5). Again, in *Wuthering Heights*, Joseph is described as 'the wearisomest, self-righteous Pharisee that ever ransacked a bible to rake the promises to himself, and fling the curses on his neighbours' (E. Brontë: 34). In *The Way of All Flesh*, Dr Skinner, Ernest's schoolmaster, writes a pamphlet, which was supposed to have 'shown great learning' about the gross idolatry found in the Catholic Church based on the inscription 'A.M.D.G.' which Skinner 'had seen outside a Roman Catholic chapel' and which, based on no evidence whatsoever, he assumes must stand for '*Ad Mariam Dei Genetrice*' (To Mary mother of God). 'Could', he rhetorically asks the reader of his pamphlet, 'anything be more idolatrous?' (Butler: 91). But Skinner is wrong. Not only does Overton point out that Skinner is using 'bad' Latin—thereby dismissing his 'great learning'—but 'A.M.D.G.' actually 'stood for nothing more dangerous than Ad

Majorem Dei Gloriam', or 'to the greater glory of God' (Butler: 92). Nevertheless, Skinner's errors do not stop him from preaching them to the naive and susceptible young Ernest (Butler: 92).

Likewise, Ernest's father is often as hypocritical as he is tyrannical. For instance, Overton makes sure to point out that he preaches 'a less feeble sermon than he usually preached, upon the horrors of the Inquisition' (Butler: 142) only then to conduct his own 'Inquisition' on his son in order to discover the 'sins' of Ernest's classmates (Butler: 141–2). In *Bleak House*, after the Revd Chadband finishes congratulating the homeless Jo for being a 'gem' and reminding him of how 'glorious' it is 'to be a human boy!', he leaves Jo to run off and be swallowed by his poverty. Meanwhile, the narrator tells the reader, Chadband 'sits munching, and gnawing, and looking up at the great Cross on the summit of St. Paul's Cathedral' (Dickens: 252). In the context of Dickens's text, it is not 'glorious' to be a boy when self-satisfied Revd Chadbands let boys starve to death in homeless destitution. In *Jane Eyre*, Brocklehurst self-righteously preaches that his 'mission' at the Lowood institution 'is to mortify in these girls the lusts of the flesh; to teach them to clothe themselves with shame-facedness and sobriety' (C. Brontë: 67). As Brocklehurst earlier sermonizes, their role models were to be 'the sufferings of the primitive Christians...the torments of martyrs...the exhortations of our blessed Lord himself, calling upon His disciples to take up their cross and follow Him' (C. Brontë: 65). Meanwhile his wife and two daughters look on wearing 'velvet, silk and furs', their hair done up in the latest fashion (C. Brontë: 67). While Brocklehurst and his family live in the lap of luxury, under his supervision, 'forty-five out of eighty' malnourished and deprived girls are infected with typhus (C. Brontë: 79). If in Dickens the hypocritical Chadband is set up to be mocked and if in Charlotte Brontë the equally hypocritical Brocklehust is set up to be despised, in both cases their hypocrisy is instrumental in leading to others' deaths.

William Hale White's *The Autobiography of Mark Rutherford* (1893) provides a representative novel in which the sermon is primarily presented as an exercise in hypocrisy, cant, or both. Mark Rutherford, White's pseudonym and ideological representation, is raised as a dissenter and as such is subject to an endless number of sermons, all of which follow a traditional pattern: 'It generally consisted of a text, which was mere peg for a discourse, that was pretty much the same from January to December. The minister invariably began with the fall of man; propounded the scheme of redemption, and ended by repeating in the morning the blessedness of the saints, and in the evening the doom of the lost' (White: 14). Subject to an interminable monotony of sermons, Rutherford finds himself unmoved, literally and figuratively, falling asleep at services to which no one listens (White: 14). Nevertheless, for vague, largely unexplained reasons, Rutherford prepares himself to become a dissenting clergyman, even feigning the expected 'conversion' which he in no way feels: he is, he acknowledges, a hypocrite (White: 16).

Rutherford's real 'conversion', and in this he validates Arnold's assertion that literature, not religion, is the centre for morality and right social conduct, is when, 'by chance', he reads William Wordsworth's 'Lyrical Ballads'. In Wordsworth's verses he feels

> by degrees, all the systems [of doctrine] which enveloped me like a body gradually decayed from me and fell away into nothing. Of more importance, too, than the decay of systems was the birth of a habit of inner reference and a dislike to occupy myself with anything which did not in some way or other touch the soul, or was not the illustration or embodiment of some spiritual law. (White: 22)

He finds in Wordsworth a 'living spirit' to replace 'the old deity, once alive but gradually hardened into an idol' (White: 23). However, when, in accordance with his new belief, Rutherford determines to preach only what he feels is right and does so, the principal of his theological college reprimands him, not for preaching untruths, but for preaching a sermon which might 'perplex and disturb' his congregation. Sermons, the principal argues, should not demand 'any exercise in thought' but repeat the 'old story' (White: 25), the old ideology which suffers no contradiction or problematization despite profound ideological shifts in culture. Close on the heels of his Wordsworthian 'conversion', the principal's response to Rutherford's new and deeply felt beliefs further propels the slow breaking of Rutherford's tenuous hold on the creeds of the Church.

Though for a number of years Rutherford struggles to fulfil his duties as a clergyman to a congregation utterly uninterested in the religion he still attempts to preach, because he becomes increasingly convinced of the Church's errors, he finds it increasingly difficult to live with his own hypocrisy. As painful as it is to him, in the face of what he sees as irrefutable arguments he no longer believes in the immortality of the personal soul or the deity of Jesus (White: 47–8). For a short time he dallies in Unitarianism, preaching rather flabby sermons about 'Scripture characters, amplifying them from hints in the Bible and neglecting what was supernatural' in order to avoid dogma altogether (White: 63). Ultimately, however, he cannot continue the pretence of being a believer. Refusing to continue to be a hypocritical preacher like a very popular preacher acquaintance of his (White: 92), he finds he is morally obliged to give up being a clergyman and preacher. Unlike Ernest Pontifex, however, once he gives up his faith, he does not embrace hedonism but rather a kind of Carlylean transcendentalism: he believes in a God as an Intelligence (White: 70); he believes in the immortality of the soul, not as an identifiable personality (this he identifies as 'egotism'), but an energy; he believes in Jesus as a sacrificial hero worthy of emulating and taking comfort in if not worshipping; as for the rest he is 'content to rest and wait' (White: 104), 'to live each moment as it passed' (White: 47). In other words, Rutherford's spiritual journey, recorded in his sermons, moves him away from institutional religion and towards a belief in something that cannot be readily defined.

Echoing Butler's sentiments in *The Way of All Flesh*, what White is suggesting is that Rutherford's loss of faith in religion is inevitable because religion is no longer a viable epistemology. In his loneliness Rutherford laments, 'If I had been born a hundred years earlier, I should have transferred this burning longing [for a true friend] to the unseen God and become a devotee. But I was a hundred years too late' (White: 85). In Rutherford's insistence that meaning must come from within rather than be enforced from without, like Ernest Pontifex, Rutherford reflects Victorian culture's shift toward modern subjectivity, a subjectivity which places value on personal agency and responsibility rather than in the words of a preacher's sermons. But religion also so utterly fails Rutherford due to its complacency, with its lazy assumption that everyone believes, and therefore its preachers preach the truth because they say they do. As in Butler's novel, religion, like the sermons it generates, refuses to engage in the ever-evolving cultural dialectic, eschewing rather than confronting opposition. But unlike in Butler's novel, in White's novel this is not as much about establishing power as it is about resting easy in it. Thus, Rutherford points out his religious training is worthless in preparing him 'to meet the doubts of the nineteenth century' (White: 18) because the arguments he is given to meet them, the arguments 'which were supposed to be a triumphant confutation of the sceptic, were mere sword of lath' (White: 19).

The result is that Rutherford's religious beliefs cannot stand in the face of any real opposition. When he is confronted with the arguments of an atheist, he is utterly confounded. As he recalls, 'This negative criticism… was all new to me' (White: 45). Like the Church, he responds by avoiding any further contact with the opposing party (White: 45–6). And yet, if Wordsworth's verses show him he must believe only in what he feels, it is his failed argument with the atheist which enables him to finally admit his foundational beliefs have crumbled (White: 48) and he is only then able to formulate what he believes rather than what he has been taught by his religious teachers to say. The dialectic—not a monologic insistence on an unproven and unprovable ontology—provides him with a synthesis, as provisional as this synthesis may be. According to Rutherford's autobiography, then, the clergyman who preaches religion as truth can only be a hypocrite or a superficial thinker. Rutherford exposes the former and has no time for the latter. The implied message to the reader is that if he/she does otherwise then he/she is in collusion with hypocrites or idiots.

Of course, the sermon in the Victorian novel is not always an example of hypocrisy, meaninglessness, or the abuse of power. Sometimes a sermon in the novel is used to emphasize the overall ideological position of the novel. And, to be sure, Victorian novels, like all novels, like all discourse, are every bit as ideological as the sermon. Most Victorian novels are obviously and openly intended to teach and advise, to 'declare and enforce common rules for the right government of life', as the sermon was intended to do (Ellison: 19). Indeed novels are, as Terry Eagleton convincingly argues, perhaps more effective vehicles of ideology because they work through the tactics of hegemony: they 'present a specific [fictional] situation as though it were universal truth' (Eagleton: 13). At the same time, paradoxically, because the novels' plots and themes interweave warring discourses they suggest the possibility of coherence despite the warring discourses. In other words, the novel proposes that there is no need to fear dialogic discourse as a one way ticket to social chaos and anarchy. Instead dialogic discourse via the dialectic is represented as ensuring personal and social evolution (Eagleton: 5–7).

Certainly this is true for Mark Rutherford who only learns what he thinks after engaging in a healthy debate with an atheist. The clergyman who inhabits the novel—and the Victorian novel is replete with them—did not need to mount the pulpit to preach because his life, his daily conversations, his interactions with other characters and, when he did preach, even his sermons, become strands of the novel's thematic concerns, the moral lessons the novel represents. Indeed, in her 'Silly Novels by Lady Novelists', George Eliot attacks overtly religious novels which attempt to be monologic in their intent to indoctrinate as 'frothy', 'prosy', and 'pedantic' and goes on to argue that novels such as these are written by novelists whose ability 'to describe actual life and her fellow-men, is in inverse proportion to her confident eloquence about God and the other world' (Eliot 2000: 1465). Thus, in *Adam Bede*, Eliot chastises the reader for expecting her to create a sermonizing rector for, she argues, sermons are not the province of novels (Eliot 1981: 174). Instead, she goes on to assert, the novel's province is to create life as it really is, and thereby create sympathy with our fellow men and women through empathy rather than argument (Eliot 1981: 174–75). As far as she was concerned, and as the assistant editor of *The Westminster Review* and a well-respected philosophical novelist her opinions carried weight, representations *of* life, not narratives *about* life, were the province of the novel and the means through which morality and proper social conduct were to be conveyed. And at least some of the leaders in the Church agreed. For instance, in 1870 from the pulpit of Westminster Abbey, Benjamin Jowett said that Dickens's novels were 'great instructors of the world' because *unlike* sermons, they did not 'directly...instruct' but rather indirectly 'led us through our better feelings to sympathize with the good, the true, the sincere, the honest English character of ordinary life' (Jowett: 274). In other words, Jowett proclaims Dickens is a blessing from God not for the sermons his novels record—which are very few—but because his novels *are* sermons.

And yet, while George Eliot actually stops the story in her novel *Adam Bede* in a chapter entitled 'In Which the Story Pauses a Little' to explain why the novel is not and should not be a sermon, *Adam Bede* includes a complete sermon. As such, it serves to illustrate that the novel itself functions as a sermon—the sermon in it does not; it merely serves to underscore the novel's themes and the preacher's character. Eliot introduces Dinah, the novel's Methodist preacher, via the experience of a travelling stranger whose main purpose in the novel is to register his reactions to Dinah and the sermon she gives. As an outsider and stranger, the traveller is uniquely positioned to experience Dinah's sermon with disinterested objectivity unfettered by self-interest or personal prejudice. One of the first things the traveller notes is that Dinah's sermon is in no way an exercise in self-elevation. Dinah mounts the cart from which she will preach without the 'smile of conscious saintship' or 'denunciatory bitterness' which he expected (Eliot 1981: 33). The traveller is surprised that she is as utterly 'unselfconscious' as a 'boy': 'There was no keenness in her eyes, they seemed rather to be shedding love...they had the liquid look which tells that the mind is full of what it had to give out' rather than what it might take in (Eliot 1981: 33). Despite the fact that Dinah could easily claim the position of the empowered orator, she casts herself as part of the working class; she refuses to be placed above her listeners, for, she says, she is one of the 'we', who are 'poor' and have to do 'hard work to make a living' and who, therefore, are most in need of 'a friend as will help 'em' (Eliot 1981: 35–6). This friend, she says, is the Jesus and saviour of the gospel, and the 'good news' of the gospel is that if they are penitent, her listeners, like her, can experience 'joy', 'peace', and 'love' amidst their toil (Eliot 1981: 41).

While Dinah's sermon enraptures her audience who push close to the cart upon which she preaches to catch her every word, while it 'chain[s]' the traveller 'to the spot against his will', and while Dinah temporarily convinces Bessy to throw away her earrings as a worldly distraction, the purpose of the sermon in the context of the novel is not to convert the reader to Methodism. As the narration makes clear, Dinah's sermon is part of the 'after glow' of Wesley which 'has long faded away' and given way to a Methodism of 'sleek grocers, sponging preachers and hypocritical jargon' (Eliot 1981: 47). The sermon functions as an illustration of Dinah's character, to highlight her simple faith and her selfless devotion to God and her fellow man.

Dinah, as a character, is the articulation of one of Eliot's perpetual themes: the need for men and women to shed their egoism in order that they might empathize, understand, and better other men's and women's lives. As such, Dinah does not preach to fulfil any personal ambition but because she feels called by God to 'minister to others, not to have any joys or sorrows of my own, but to rejoice with them that do rejoice and weep with those that weep' (Eliot 1981: 45). Dinah's sermonizing is merely another way in which she serves others. She enacts as well as preaches empathy and loving understanding, and it is in the former that she does the most good. After all, Bessy puts her earrings back on, the traveller rides off before the closing hymn is over, and it is a safe bet that readers rarely turn Methodist. However, everyone Dinah touches benefits from her unselfish and tender service—the reader, Eliot intends, will be compelled to emulate her selfless kindness. Dinah is the sermon she preaches just as the novel is the sermon in which she preaches.

At the same time, one cannot escape the fact that while Eliot does not preach religion in *Adam Bede* and in her other novels, her narrations are 'preachy': her novels are not only ideological, but she unabashedly pushes her ideological agenda. Using an editorializing narrator, the narrative often draws explicit moral lessons from various characters' behaviours and thoughts rather than allowing readers free play to come to their own conclusions. At the same time, however, this 'preaching' is not explicitly religious; even though it is inscribed with religious signifiers, it is of a liberal humanist bent. In this Eliot is not unlike most Victorian novelists. Thomas Hughes, in *Tom Brown's School Days* (1857), expresses what most Victorians felt was the moral requisite of the novel when, in response to a reader who felt his novel had too much preaching in it, wrote in the preface to the second edition, 'My sole object in writing was to preach to boys... I can't see that a man has any business to write at all unless he has something which he thoroughly believes and wants to preach about' (Hughes: 14). This being said, the 'something' which he 'preaches about' is emptied of religious content except in the most general sense. And, as in Eliot and the majority of Victorian novels which continue to be read, the 'preaching' narrator articulates a general moral good as defined by the middle classes regardless of their specific religious affiliation or even lack thereof.

It is important to acknowledge again that Victorian, middle class ideology is inscribed by Protestantism. But even this ideological 'preaching' is always a part of a dialogue; given the dialogic nature of the novel, it cannot help but be so. Furthermore, in the novel, ideology is increasingly represented as a construct rather than an ontology founded on the word of an omnipotent God. The reader may enter into a contract with the author in which the fiction presented is, for the time the novel is being read, conceived of as a factual story told by a truth-telling narrator, but this willing suspension of disbelief does nothing to change the fact that the reader understands that the author is creating a fictional narrator who is telling a fictional story. This is a far cry from the sermon during which the congregation listens to a clergyman who claims to be speaking the words of God from the Word of God.

At this point, a gesture must be made toward the overtly religious novel of the nineteenth century. As Eliot's 'Silly Novels by Lady Novelists' suggests, the number of proselytizing Victorian novels was large enough that she felt the need to write an attack on them in the widely read *Westminster Review*. In these overtly religious novels, specific religious creeds or only one side of a religious issue is presented positively. For instance, Newman wrote two novels defending and celebrating Catholicism for the Catholic Popular Library series: *Loss and Gain* (1848) and *Callista: A Sketch of the Third Century* (1856) (Fraser: 106). And yet, like his *Apologia Pro Vita Sua*, these novels must be read in the context of a dominant Protestant culture which was often actively engaged in attacking Catholicism in general and Newman, as a notable Catholic convert, in particular. In fact, Newman wrote his second novel *Callista* in response to Charles Kingsley's anti-Catholic novel, *Hypatia: or, New Foes with Old Faces* (1853) (Fraser: 106). But again, in these novels the opposition is represented, and even if it is represented only so that it might be argued against, this dialogic debate underscores the dialogic nature of the novel.

It is also worth pointing out that these overtly dogmatic, doctrinal, and religious novels are no longer widely read. Their audience is particular and narrow; they did not and do not resonate with the general reader. In fact, many novelists predicted the demise of the importance of religion in modern life. Thus, Eliot places Dinah and her Methodism in the past and more than once reminds the reader of the fact. Butler and White overtly state religious arguments will soon no longer have validity. In Emily Brontë, the local church is literally a ruin. In short, as the Victorian period progresses, religion in the novel becomes an increasingly irrelevant and remote part of life.

And yet, religion is represented in the Victorian novel as so fundamental to Victorian culture and ideology that even when it is introduced merely to be deconstructed, it is a kind of omnipresence. A case could be made, then, that there are so few sermons mentioned in the novels simply because the reading public already knew them; they knew what would be said and if they 'forgot' there would be another sermon the next Sunday.

But sometimes, the sermon is conspicuous by its absence. This is true of Thomas Hardy's very late novel *Jude the Obscure* (1895) where the sermons profoundly affecting the characters are only implied through the characters' reactions and reiterations. Initially Jude is a religious man who is a scholar of religious works and the Bible. And yet, though Jude spends much of his time doing stone-work on, sitting in, studying about, and attending services at church, curiously and significantly, the novel records no actual sermons. There are numerous references to doctrine, religious figures, and religious texts, but the only words of a church service to which the reader is privy are a reading of a Psalm and snatches of choral songs. One is tempted to conclude this is because after Jude's first marriage fails and he falls in love with the irreligious Sue, that through Sue's influence he comes to see religion and its doctrines as 'old husks of prejudice' (Hardy: 370). Although he is speaking about his literal stone-work on a church he might very well be talking about his spiritual life when he tells Sue, 'The Church is no more to me. Let it lie!... My point of bliss is not upward, but here' (Hardy: 249).

On the other hand, after her children with Jude are murdered by Jude's eldest son by his first wife, in her grief and looking for some comprehensible reason for her children's deaths, Sue embraces religion; she attends church services alone and she becomes convinced her marriage to Jude is a sin and the cause of her children's tragic end. Reminded of the biblical injunction against certain marriages, she insists Jude and she must separate and remarry their first spouses. The result is their tragic unhappiness. In Hardy, the Church and the sermons it generates become the means of creating needless human misery. The reason, it would seem, no sermons are represented in *Jude the Obscure* except through the grieving Sue is that sermons only have meaning in the individual's interpretation of them. In and of themselves they are merely 'old husks of prejudice'. In other words, Hardy's novel represents modern subjectivity as a fait accompli; Hardy proves to be the gateway to modernism and the modern reader.

It is hardly surprising that, apart from those which explicitly intended to convert to or reassure confirmed believers in the truth of a specific religious creed, as the Victorian period progresses, the way the sermon is used in the novel increasingly reflects modernity and the modern subject. In George Eliot's *Adam Bede* the narrator states, matter-of-factly, that Adam's understanding of the past has altered for 'no story is the same to us after a lapse of time—or rather, we who read it are no longer the same interpreters' (Eliot 1981: 498). In Butler's *The Way of All Flesh*, Ernest must learn to listen to his 'inner' self and the 'real' Ernest rather than aping the Ernest religious authorities have defined him to be. In his maturity, as the 'real' Ernest, he writes essays which argue that while it would be too 'inconvenient' to change 'the words of our prayer book and articles, it would not be inconvenient to change in a quiet way the meanings which we put upon those words' so as to come nearer to representing the evolution of culture (Butler: 412). Likewise, in White's *The Autobiography of Mark Rutherford*, Rutherford's belief that meaning must be generated from within as it engages with an evolving culture suggests a phenomenological subjectivity. In *Wuthering Heights*, the obvious unreliability of the narrators suggests meaning-making is subjective. In *Jane Eyre*, Jane leaves Rochester and resists his arguments that she stay with him because 'I care for myself' (C. Brontë: 319). In Hardy's *Jude the Obscure*, sermons mean only what the listener personally hears: the listener fills the 'husks' with his/her own understanding.

In short, the way the sermons are used in these representative novels illustrates that the individual is rapidly coming to be seen as the centre of meaning-making—not outside authorities. Thus, there can be no God-given ontology. Meaning is individually defined. Truth is relative. Humans have the freedom, burden, and responsibility of individual agency. The sermon can no longer be a valid discourse because it is a monologue, predicated on an infallible truth, whereas the novel, through its use of dialogue (including sermons), is.

The Victorian novel, therefore, suggests the path the sermon in the novel will take in early twentieth-century novels. In James Joyce's *Portrait of an Artist* (1916) the novel includes a disproportionately long sermon which works to temporarily recommit Stephen to Catholicism. However, Stephen's 'conversion', like Ernest Pontifex's, is temporary, and he ultimately rejects Catholicism as one more ideological construct he must escape. In Evelyn Waugh's *A Handful of Dust* (1934), the two sermons the Rector gives are hilariously irrelevant as he repeats the sermons he wrote during Victoria's reign while he worked as a missionary in India. Significantly, the congregation does not seem to mind. The point is that the sermon, like the Church, may be comforting in terms of tradition and connecting the parishioners to their past, but it has no other value. Carlyle's assertion that religion is but empty clothing, a signifier pointing to nothing, has come to be accepted by the dominant culture as a norm.

The Victorian novel, the product of a culture where religion is its wallpaper, rarely goes as far as its twentieth-century successors. Nevertheless, the Victorian novel, whether consciously or unconsciously, works to deconstruct the whole notion of a monologic discourse of truth which the sermon represents; the Victorian novel suggests *truths* are to be found in *fictions* which represent voices in ideological conflict. In other words, 'truth' becomes something one constructs in dialogue with others rather than something one learns and then preaches to a silently submissive and obedient congregation.

References

Arnold, M. (1961a). 'Culture and Anarchy', in A. D. Culler (ed.), *Poetry and Criticism of Matthew Arnold*. Boston: Houghton Mifflin, 407–18.
—— (1961b). 'The Function of Criticism at the Present Time', in A. D. Culler (ed.), *Poetry and Criticism of Matthew Arnold*. Boston: Houghton Mifflin, 237–58.
Bakhtin, M. M. (1981). *The Dialogic Imagination: Four Essays*, M. Holquist (ed.). Austin: University of Texas Press.
Brontë, C. (1982). *Jane Eyre*. New York: Signet Classic-New American Library.
Brontë, E. (1956). *Wuthering Heights*. Boston: Riverside-Houghton Mifflin.
Butler, S. (2004). *The Way of All Flesh*. New York: Dover Publications.
Carlyle, T. (1984). 'Sartor Resartus', in G. B. Tennyson (ed.), *A Carlyle Reader*. Cambridge: Cambridge University Press, 124–331.
—— (2009). *Past and Present*. Rockville, MD: Arc Manor-Serenity Press.
Culler. A. D. (1961). 'Introduction', in A. D. Culler (ed.), *Poetry and Criticism of Matthew Arnold*. Boston, MA: Houghton Mifflin, ix–xx.
Cunningham, V. (1975). *Everywhere Spoken Against: Dissent in the Victorian Novel*. Oxford: Clarendon Press.
Dickens. C. (1985). *Bleak House*. New York: Bantam Classics.
Eagleton, T. (2005). *The English Novel: An Introduction*. Oxford: Blackwell.

Eliot, G. (1981). *Adam Bede*. New York: Signet Classic-New American Library.

—— (2000). 'Silly Novels by Lady Novelists', in M. H. Abrams et al. (eds.), *The Norton Anthology of English Literature*, 7th edn. New York: Norton, 2:1461–9.

Ellison, R. H. (1998). *The Victorian Pulpit: Spoken and Written Sermons in Nineteenth-Century Britain*. Selinsgrove, PA: Susquehanna University Press.

Fraser, H. (2005). 'The Victorian Novel and Religion', in P. Brantlinger and W. B. Thesing (eds.), *A Companion to the Victorian Novel*. Malden, MA: Blackwell, 101–18.

Hardy, T. (1985). *Jude the Obscure*. Oxford: Oxford University Press.

Hughes, T. (1986). *Tom Brown's School Days*. New York: Signet Classic-New American Library.

Jowett, B. (1899). *Sermons Biographical and Miscellaneous*, ed. W. H. Fremantle. London: John Murray.

Joyce, J. (1964). *A Portrait of the Artist as a Young Man*. New York: Penguin.

Mason, M. (1993). 'Introduction', in S. Butler, *The Way of All Flesh*. New York: Oxford University Press, vii–xli.

Newman, J. H. (1995). *Apologia Pro Vita Sua*. New York: Penguin Books.

Reade, W. (2003). *The Outcast*. New Delhi: Rupa.

Tennyson, G. G. (1984). 'Introduction', in *A Carlyle Reader*. Cambridge: Cambridge University Press, xiii–xxxviii.

Trollope, A. (1987). *Barchester Towers*. New York: Penguin.

—— (1998). *The Warden*. Oxford: Oxford University Press.

Waugh, E. (1934). *A Handful of Dust*. Boston, MA: Back Bay-Little Brown.

White, W. H. (2009). *The Autobiography of Mark Rutherford*. Champaign, IL: Book Jungle.

PART VII
CONCLUSION

CHAPTER 37

SERMON STUDIES: MAJOR ISSUES AND FUTURE DIRECTIONS

KEITH A. FRANCIS

Suffering from Neglect?

COMMENTING on the attitude of modernist writers, particularly novelists, in the early twentieth century, Philip Waller remarked that 'authors who had no religion conspicuously failed to grasp a significant source of inspiration in others. More than that, this carelessness cut them off from the past' (Waller: 1046). Leaving aside the question of secularization for the moment—this will be discussed later in the chapter—Waller's assessment could be applied to the sermon in the period 1689–1901. Sermons, as opposed to preaching, have 'escaped' scholarly scrutiny until the last decade. As the preceding chapters have shown, the varieties of sermons and the ways in which they were used mean that there is, putting it metaphorically, a rich seam of material that scholars ought to mine.

Even those scholars aware of the potential of published sermons have not really utilized them. Waller noted that 'the principal literary means of getting across the Christian message to the mass of people was via journals, pamphlets, and printed sermons, not books', but there is only one other reference to sermons in his magnum opus of a thousand plus pages: namely his summary of an article in the *Fortnightly Review* of December 1892 entitled 'The Traffic in Sermons' in which the author complained about clergy buying from 'hacks with stocks of sermons' (Waller: 1017, 181). Waller mentioned preaching in two other places—an American literary agent wanting to use Charles Spurgeon as a lecturer, after hearing about Spurgeon's ability to fill the 5,000-seat Metropolitan Tabernacle regularly, and the fact that several well-known preachers used the religious novelist Marie Corelli's books in their sermons (Waller: 577–9, 779)—but otherwise the sermon as an object of study remained unexplored.

As William Gibson demonstrates in Chapter 1 of this volume, Waller is not alone in his omission. Scholars have studied religious and non-religious journals, pamphlets, and books in an attempt to describe the phenomenon of British religion in the modern era but sermons have been neglected. Given the preceding chapters, why this has been the case is a question worth asking.

Ironically, one possible reason why scholars of the period 1689–1901 have ignored sermons is the sheer number of documents to consider. Even though the number of 'sermon events' was vast compared to those published—and it is lamentable that so many of these sermons went unrecorded, unpublished—the corpus of printed sermons is still very large and, unfortunately, amorphous. Estimates are possible but no precise count is available. A scholar wishing to study the sermon confronted, and confronts, an unknown corpus: without the discipline of Sermon Studies there would not be a systematic way to do the research and any examination would be fragmentary or an investigation of the margins: even a study of one thousand sermons probably represents no more than one-eightieth of the corpus.

Their very ubiquity is a challenge. How can one make sense of material that exists in such fecundity? Because sermons are everywhere, the notion of them as 'background noise', as William Gibson suggests in Chapter 1, or as 'wallpaper', the description used by Linda Gill in Chapter 36, is appropriate. Scholars can be forgiven for ignoring material which is so obvious that it is 'hiding in plain sight'. Furthermore, other factors—there is no large-scale collection of sermons in a single set of volumes, no summary bibliographic listing of sermons apart from John Gordon Spaulding's effort, and no group of libraries or archives which has all the published sermons—make the neglect even more understandable. It has been a great deal easier to concentrate on great preachers, preaching styles, and theories of preaching.

Social changes in Britain—perhaps more accurately described as changes in literary tastes—also contributed to the lack of attention to the sermon as a form 'worthy' of study. The greatest threat probably came from the novel in its various forms even though, as Linda Gill notes in Chapter 36, the clergyman was a regular character in Victorian novels. The decline of the funeral sermon and its last gasp in 1901, to which John Wolffe draws attention in Chapter 21, is emblematic of sermons in general: they were still of some importance but the art form needed revivification. (Twentieth-century advances in communication such as public address systems, radio, and television did breathe new life into the sermon form after the 1950s.) Furthermore, as Martin Hewitt notes (Chapter 5), the challenge posed by the religious lecture—in evolutionary terms the sermon's nearest rival—complicated matters: the religious lecture could be used in settings where the sermon was inappropriate and by those who were not qualified—either because they could not or did not want to join the ranks of the clergy—to preach sermons. All of these were perfectly plausible reasons for not studying the sermon.

Some of the ways that sermons had been used were off-putting also. Just as, for example, the study of the work of Francis Galton in the area of eugenics declined after the Second World War, so some of the polemical and nationalist uses of the sermon in the modern era seem out of place in a study of British social and religious history. Sermons defending the monarchy and the need for good, stable government preached at the accession of the Hanoverian monarchs were already unfashionable in 1837 and were definitely an oddity by 1910. The reaction of an early-twentieth-century congregation to the kind of anti-Jacobite sermon described by James Caudle (Chapter 15) is hard to imagine. Frankly, though substantially milder in tone than some of the anti-Jacobite thunderings, the sermons celebrating victories such as Trafalgar would have resulted in some uncomfortable squirming in a congregation listening after 1918, and that is despite the sobering national experience of the Boer War and the Great War. The kind of political sermon that was commonplace for half of the period 1689–1901 has not been studied enough in the past precisely because it was a 'child' of the late seventeenth and the whole of the eighteenth century.

Neither is the nineteenth-century sermon less anachronistic. The connection of the sermon with empire, almost a rhetorical weapon in the mouths of some preachers, hardly made the study of the sermon de rigueur in an age when Britain was retreating from empire. Even the attachment of the sermon to 'missions' was problematic in an age of twentieth-century ecumenism or, as in the case of Ireland, a period of national self-determination. Emerging 'young churches' wanted to develop their own sermon culture and colonial sermons, with their emphasis on preaching Britishness to 'colonial subjects', were hardly good models. In the cases of Ireland and Wales, no 'mission' ought to have been necessary when there was a thriving indigenous culture of sermon creation and preaching. Again, the tone of these sermons would make scholars think twice about making them the object of study.

And yet, as the essays in this volume have shown, there is a richness in these sermons that scholars can no longer ignore. A history of the churches in Ireland in the nineteenth century is incomplete without a consideration of the mission sermons coming from the mainland and the kinds of sermons that were already being preached in those churches. Equally, it would be unwise to write about eighteenth-century religious history and not mention the ways in which Jacobitism was counteracted in the sermons of the day. The sermons preached by Charles Spurgeon and Edward Boyce after the Indian Mutiny while strange to contemporary ears, and ethical values, are essential reading for a clearer understanding of Britain's imperial history. Quaint and embarrassing these sermons may be, but also worthy of further integration into the British historiographical record.

SERMON STUDIES AND THE SECULARIZATION THESIS

'Faith and doubt in Victorian Britain', the 'Victorian crisis of faith', 'the decline of religion' are all terms which have been used to describe one important development in British religious history from the late eighteenth century onwards—secularization, the phenomenon of the British becoming less religious or less observant in the period from the Industrial Revolution onwards. (As more scholarly research is done on the period, 'religious' and 'Industrial Revolution' have become contested terms also.) There have been attempts to begin the period of secularization earlier in the eighteenth century or later in the twentieth century (Chadwick; Brown), but the descriptor itself, though controversial, has remained.

Despite challenges to the secularization thesis—to take three examples, Timothy Larsen has shown that significant figures famed for their doubt returned to Christianity; Geoffrey Cantor has explained that a supposedly secular event such as the Great Exhibition was steeped in religion; and Jonathan Clark has suggested that it fails as a 'grand narrative' (Larsen; Cantor; Clark)—the term seems helpful. How should scholars incorporate into British religious history novels such as John Henry Newman's *Loss and Gain* (1848), J. A. Froude's *Nemesis of Faith* (1849), or Charles Kingsley's *Alton Locke* (1850), which deal with questions of faith and doubt so explicitly, particularly when these are written by 'insiders', as it were? Poems such as Matthew Arnold's 'Dover Beach' and Alfred Tennyson's 'In Memoriam' also suggest some kind of generational turn away from religious faith. Then there are the examples of direct challenges to the old ways of understanding Christianity best exemplified by *Essays and Reviews* (1860) and *Lux Mundi* (1889). How to believe was not the same in 1901 as it was in 1837, never mind 1689, and secularization has seemed an appropriate way to describe this change.

Furthermore, the new science of the nineteenth century raised even more questions than the 'scientific revolution' of the seventeenth century. The efforts of George Berkeley or David Hume to incorporate the ideas of Isaac Newton and his fellow natural philosophers appeared to be a relatively easy task compared to what was required to rationalize the ideas of Charles Lyell in *Principles of Geology* or Charles Darwin in *On the Origin of Species*. When Francis Galton claimed that 'It is therefore a fact, that in proportion to the pains bestowed on their education generally, the sons of clergyman rarely take a lead in science. The pursuit of science is uncongenial to the priestly character', he seemed to be demanding that readers take seriously the idea that Christianity and religion were no longer important when it came to the serious scholarship of the day (Galton: 24). Galton made his claim despite the well-known Christian commitment of contemporaries such as the clergyman-biologist George Henslow and the physicist-engineer Sir William Thomson, the future Lord Kelvin. Again, it seems to make sense to use the term secularization for these developments.

On the other hand, given what authors of the chapters in this volume have written, is the descriptor 'secularization' appropriate? The ubiquity of the sermon may be a source of scholarly complaint in that it makes the study of the sermon difficult, but surely something so universal is evidence that the idea of secularization is inadequate? Jeffrey Chamberlain's analysis of parish preaching (Chapter 3) and Frances Knight's review of the village sermon (Chapter 4)—sermons being preached up and down the country, with no fanfare, from Sunday to Sunday—render it difficult to think of Christianity declining in the nineteenth century or before. As Linda Gill has shown (Chapter 36), not even in the novel—the newcomer in literature compared to other forms such as the poem—is the sermon eliminated completely. The sermon is pervasive. And if the sermon is a universal phenomenon in the nineteenth, and earlier, centuries, then it seems logical to argue that Christianity was everywhere too.

Consequently one conclusion to draw from Sermon Studies is that the British were very religious in the period 1689–1901. Human culture is not static and so there were differences in emphasis and differences between regions, but the character of being religious remained. The Scots were not religious in the same way as the English, and Welsh religious practices were very different from those in colonial America or Australia. Equally, religiosity changed over time but did not diminish; so that religion in 1700 meant different things to ordinary Britons than it did in 1900, but it is inaccurate to describe those living at the beginning of the twentieth century as 'secularized' any more than to apply that description to Britons living at the beginning of the eighteenth century. The willingness of publishers, whose interest was mainly commercial, to put out collections of sermons, and to continue doing so well into the early years of the twentieth century, supports the view that secularization is a dangerously inaccurate term for the changes that occurred in British religious life during the eighteenth and nineteenth centuries. Publishers were not, in the main, trying to turn the British back to an older form of observance or religiosity but they did, in the case of Passmore and Alabaster, publish Charles Spurgeon's Metropolitan Tabernacle Pulpit series of sermons until 1917 even though Spurgeon died in 1892; and they did, in the case of Hodder and Stoughton, publish the sermons of Alexander MacLaren until 1906, just four years before his death in 1910 at the age of 84.

Not only do the essays in this volume illustrate the wide variety of British religious experience in the period 1689–1901 but they also add detail—depth and contour—to the British social experience. Clergymen preached sermons in expected and unexpected contexts. It is no surprise, for example, that sermons were one tool used to disseminate the Oxford Movement but it is surprising that sermons were part of the debate that led to the formation of a national education policy. The notion that bishops and others preached sermons during their visitations is not strange but the idea that scholars must consider sermons when researching the Gothic Revival is. Clearly, to talk of the secularization of British religion is unwise when so much of British life is permeated by the sermon and the sermon is an essential component of the religious experience of most Britons in the period 1689–1901.

The Laity and Sermons

The close connection of the sermon with the clergy—they preached them and, in general, they allowed them to be published or submitted them for publication—makes it easy to forget the major consumers of sermons, the people in the various congregations. Although clergy might have to listen to a visitation sermon or read it later, they were not the object of most sermons. Indeed, the ubiquity of the sermon and the way it could be adapted for use in so many parts of the life of the British means that the history of the sermon has to be far more than a history of the clergy. Joseph Jowett's musing that he would suppose, charitably, that the objective of clergy who published their sermons was 'the spiritual improvement of their readers rather than self-interest or fame' was worth expressing given the money both publisher and author could make (Jowett: 1:v), but it could be countered by a totalling of the prefaces and dedications in which a group stated their desire for the publication of a particular sermon or collection of sermons. The words 'Published at the request of many of his hearers' were evidence of a tri-partite symbiotic relationship between clergyman, laity, and publisher: one preached, another heard and demanded more, and the third supplied the demand. Whether observers looked back upon the relationship with some cynicism, as Jowett seemed to do, is not important. Congregations were the consumers of sermons in their first iteration and, for those who could and wanted to afford it, they could also possess a version of the spoken sermon in perpetuity. Whatever their motivation, 'the hearers' were the apex of a relationship which resulted in the sale of hundreds of thousands of sermons which were preserved for later generations to read.

The overwhelming majority of the sermons extant for the period 1689–1901 were preached by clergy of the Church of England, and if not Anglican in origin were published in England. The authors of essays on sermons and sermon culture in Scotland, Wales, and Ireland or on Catholics and Dissenters/Nonconformists have had a more difficult task of recovery than their fellow authors. If there is a group of spoken but not published sermons that future scholars will wish appeared more often in print it is those outside of England and its national church. The episodes described by Irene Whelan (Chapter 10) and Densil Morgan (Chapter 12) reveal a culture different from the English and Anglican: discovering more about these differences is a harder task than, for example, an analysis of charity sermons preached by Anglican clergy.

Another seemingly absent voice is that of women. The clergy was a male-dominated profession in Britain and women preachers were few. In the period 1689–1901 there were times when women were noticeable as preachers—Methodism in the later years of the eighteenth century and the Salvation Army in the latter half of the nineteenth century are two well-known examples—but little evidence of their preaching remains in the form of printed sermons. Despite this lacuna, it is important to recognize that if the laity were the audience and purchasers of sermons then women were their consumers too. When William Harper, chaplain to Viscount Malpas, preached a sermon entitled 'The Antiquity, Innocence, and Pleasure of Gardening' to a meeting of gardeners and florists in the parish church of Malpas in the diocese of Chester on 18 April 1732 he clearly had the female members of the gardeners' society in mind; and women were certainly the intended audience of Uriah Davies, perpetual curate of St Matthew's in Islington, who preached a sermon entitled 'Woman's Influence' to the 'young women' who attended his church on 14 September 1890 and James Fordyce, the Church of Scotland minister, who had preached fourteen sermons for women and published them in two volumes entitled *Sermons to Young Women* in 1766 (Harper; Davies; Fordyce). Whether women purchased a significant number of these types of sermons is not known but the specific targeting of women does mean that whoever did buy these printed sermons had another reason to do so.

As John Wolffe has noted in Chapter 21, women were the object of funeral sermons. Obviously queens such as Mary II, Anne, and Victoria had more sermons preached at their death than other women but other royal figures were also commemorated, particularly if they died unexpectedly or young as in the cases of Princess Anne of Orange, the daughter of George II, Princess Charlotte, the daughter of the future George IV, and Princess Alice, the daughter of Victoria. Equally important, in terms of recovering the influence of women on the development of the sermon, the clergy regularly used the funeral sermon as an opportunity to memorialize ordinary women, particularly those whose 'virtuous lives' had had a significant impact on the local community. The popularity of such sermons is illustrated by the publication of the sermon preached on 10 June 1866 by Albert Augustus Isaacs, entitled *The Path of the Just*. The sermon commemorated the life of a Mrs Hoskin, the wife of the Reverend P. C. M. Hoskin, the minister of Trinity Church, North Malvern. Perhaps it was the stress and emotion surrounding her death, but whatever the reason no-one arranged for a reporter to record the sermon. Thus it transpired that only the 'substance' of the sermon was available. Even after this unfortunate eventuality there were still sufficient requests for the sermon to be printed that both a London firm, William Macintosh, and a local dignitary, a Mrs Hartley, published the summary sermon (Isaacs).

Women were the object of sermons, the distributors of sermons, and the consumers of sermons. Peeresses' chaplains, for example, provided sermons for women from the highest social stratum. Selina, Countess of Huntington, who employed a 'connexion' of Evangelical ministers, was also a great patron of preachers and routinely judged the incumbents of her proprietary chapels on the basis of their sermons and preaching.

Leaving aside examples of women in the Bible—unsurprisingly, there are sermons on well-known figures such as Ruth, Esther, and Mary the mother of Jesus—the work of women was also a subject of sermons. Charities for the benefit of women, and run by women, regularly asked clergy to preach on their behalf in order to raise funds or raise awareness of their work as did other charities: the same is true of various missions run by women. The sermons of Peter Hall, the minister of Tavistock Chapel, Drury Lane, in 1837 for the London Female Mission and Henry William Burrows, a canon of Rochester, for the Parochial Mission Women Association in 1867 are examples of these (Hall; Burrows). These sermons were preached in the nineteenth century in the main, when women's charities and missions became a standard feature of British religious life.

The nineteenth century was also the period of the first women's movement both inside and outside the churches. The desire for a greater role for women in Christian ministry and in British society in general occurred at the same time with some of the same women involved in both. These trends did not pass unnoticed in the pulpit. Sermons with titles such as 'A Woman's Place' were preached with regularity from the 1850s onwards. One such sermon, preached by John William Burgon, the conservative vicar of St Mary's, Oxford, in 1871 was controversial enough that it 'received' a reply in print by an anonymous author entitled *A Woman's Reply to a Sermon Preached by the Rev. J. W. Burgon* that included a review of the Woman Question (Burgon; *A Woman's Reply*). A sermon more sympathetic to the women's movement such as R. W. Church's 'The Ministry of Women', preached at the Festival of the Community of St Mary the Virgin in 1875, recognized that women had always held important roles in the ministry of the Church (Church 1895: 264–77). Pamphleteering of the kind seen during the Bangorian Controversy did not occur as a result of these sermons but neither did supporters nor opponents of women's rights allow them to pass without comment. The sermon, though focused mainly on living the Christian life in the latter half of the nineteenth century, still had the power to provoke and annoy as was the case in the previous two centuries: it was only the subject matter that had changed.

The Work Ahead

Despite the fact that the sermon was still culturally important in British life at the beginning of the twentieth century, Solomon's admonition about 'the making of books' has not been applicable to the study of the sermon in the modern era. Perhaps 'much study is a weariness of the flesh' (Ecclesiastes 12:12) but scholars of Sermon Studies have much to do before they can claim to be exhausted by their work. (Furthermore, the term 'scholars of Sermon Studies' is a misnomer when applied to the period 1689–1901. 'Sermon Studies' is a developing area of study for this period and the formation of a scholarly community is a recent development.) The publication of Robert Ellison's *The Victorian Pulpit* in 1998 is clearly an important marker. Taking an interdisciplinary approach to the study of the sermon—not just homiletics or theology or literature or rhetoric or history, but all of these—represented an important step in the making of the 'discipline' of Sermon Studies in the 1990s. Ellison did for the nineteenth century what had been done for the medieval and early modern periods since the 1930s. The publication of *Preaching, Sermon and Cultural Change in the Long Eighteenth Century* (2009) and *A New History of the Sermon: The Nineteenth Century* (2010) represent important additions and continuations of Ellison's work. With the publication of the *Oxford Handbook of the Early Modern Sermon* (2011) there is now a scholarly 'bridge' between the work of more established scholars of Sermon Studies, in the medieval and early modern eras, and those who are beginning a systematic examination of the impact of the sermon on British life in the modern era.

In his opening chapter William Gibson states that the *Oxford Handbook of the Modern British Sermon* represents a beginning, not an end. In a field that has no boundary markers and no clear agreement among scholars as to the parameters of the 'discipline', this book is an attempt, continuing the metaphor, to put down some stakes and provide a helpful outline of the property. Scholars in the future may find new areas that need to be explored which have not been covered in the book. In this volume, for example, more could have been said about the economics of the production of sermons, particularly given the prolific output of preachers such as the Baptists Charles Spurgeon and Alexander McLaren. Outlines of McLaren's sermons were published as late as late as 1954 so that a new generation of preachers could learn from the great man, and the Metropolitan Tabernacle Pulpit was reproduced in full by different publishers more than once in the twentieth century (McLaren; Spurgeon 1969; Spurgeon 1974). Other topics that deserve more discussion in the future include the relationship between the sermon and homiletics, the sermon and intellectual thought or philosophy, and literary analyses of particular groups of sermons. Furthermore, future scholars may recognize the importance of sermons in cultural movements such as the Gothic Revival. More research will provide greater clarity (as has been the case with the study of the sermon in earlier eras). The object of the essays in this volume is to stimulate more work on the sermon as well as define some avenues of further study. In discussing the future of Sermon Studies for the period 1689–1901, the objective is to be suggestive. While appreciating that there is much work still to be done on the history of the sermon in the modern era, after producing a volume such as this one, it is clear that there are some tasks and some topics of research which ought to be part of the next stage in the development of Sermon Studies. These are areas which seem a natural extension of what has been accomplished thus far.

Defining the 'Real' Sermon

At the conclusion of a volume of essays on the sermon, it may seem a little perverse to ask the question 'What is a Sermon?' but, as William Gibson points out in Chapter 1, the definition of 'sermon' was flexible during this period. Lectures, discourses, and talks could all be sermons. When Thomas Griffith, the incumbent of Ram's Chapel, Homerton, had published his *The Leading Idea of Christianity Investigated in a Series of Discourses* in 1833 the discourses were supposed to be a group of seven sermons; in fact, the printed version of these sermons were organized in summary form that read more like the outline of lectures than sermons (Griffith). In the same year John Hoppus, the Independent minister and professor of logic and philosophy of the mind at the University of London, preached a sermon entitled 'The Difficulties of Infidelity' in Tonbridge Chapel, Somers Town which was 'one of series of discourses': the published version ran to fifty-seven pages (Hoppus). Gone were the days of the previous century when a minister could preach a fifty-seven-page sermon: this sermon was the edited, 'cleaned-up', version of the original. That being the case, which was the real sermon: the one preached, the one published, or both versions? The problem of defining the sermon is not simply a question of recognizing that there were various types of sermons—discourse, lecture, and sermon; it is also the case that scholars in Sermon Studies confront multiple copies of the same sermon with each claimed, by the person who preached it, as the 'actual' sermon. Thus, when R. H. Goodacre, the curate of Ipstones, near Stoke-on-Trent, and a former chaplain at Stafford County Prison, published a series of six sermons entitled *The Fruits of Sin* (1860) he admitted that,

> The following Sermons were preached in the chapel of the Stafford County Prison, during Lent, 1856, and were announced for publication shortly afterwards, but were not published. They have been now entirely re-written; and in the revision of them,

the Author has left out all allusions to Prisons and Prisoner; and so altered or modified their applications, as to adapt them to an ordinary congregation. (Goodacre: Preface)

The published version of Goodacre's sermons had been preached during Lent of 1860 (Goodacre). Arthur Roberts, the rector of Woodrising in Norfolk, made a similar admission to Goodacre in 1850 when Roberts's two-volume edition of *Village Sermons*, originally published between 1835 and 1845, was published by the Religious Tract Society. In order to adapt his sermons to fit the objectives of the Society and to make them 'more suitable for family worship or cottage reading', Roberts had removed 'such peculiar phraseology as would be suited only to the pulpit or to a minister of the established church' (Roberts: Introduction). Busy ministers of whatever church stripe could be forgiven for seizing the opportunity to reuse a sermon preached previously; furthermore, even if rehashing were considered a form of clerical indolence, there was clearly a demand for adapted sermons to be published. Multiple versions of the 'actual' sermon could and did exist. John Wesley's published sermons rarely bore any resemblance to those he preached since he heavily edited all that he published.

Even more confusing, there were various kinds of 'phantom sermons'. One was a printed sermon that had never been preached. Arthur Baker, the rector of Kemerton in Gloucestershire, admitted that his sermon 'The Blessedness of Motherhood and Childhood' had never been 'delivered to a congregation in its present form, but is made up of passages from two or three detached ones bearing upon the subject, together with some additional matter' (Baker: 1). R. W. Church's sermon 'The Peace of Christ' was written for the Easter Day service of 1886 in St. Paul's Cathedral but never preached because Church was ill on that day: nevertheless, it was still published in Church's *Cathedral and University Sermons* (Church 1892: 144–53). Another type of 'phantom sermon' was a spoken sermon that became something else. A sermon of the Unitarian minister Joseph Dobell was published as a tract in 1813 by the Kent & Sussex Unitarian Christian Association and some of Henry Edward Manning's Anglican sermons were published as devotional readings in 1868, by which time he had been Archbishop of Westminster for three years (Dobell; Manning). A third type of 'phantom sermon' was a lecture or discourse that masqueraded as a sermon: R. W. Church's lectures on Bishop Andrewes and Bishop Butler given in 1877 and 1880 but published in his *Pascal and Other Sermons* are examples of these (Church 1895). Because the sermon form was so adaptable, its malleability necessitates that future scholars think carefully about the definition of 'a sermon'.

This point seems particularly appropriate for the case of sermons which only exist in manuscript form. While the authors in this volume have mainly concentrated their investigation on printed and published sermons, some have drawn attention to important manuscript sermons which enable scholars to have a better understanding of Catholic preaching, parish sermons, and culture—for example in the eighteenth century. These sermons are not 'phantom' in the sense that they are masquerading as something else but rather because they are even more elusive than published sermons 'hidden' in volumes where scholars might not expect them. Finding manuscript sermons requires trawling through archives without the guarantee of success, but such research is necessary if the case of Samuel Wilberforce, bishop of Oxford and then Winchester, is considered. A popular speaker and active diocesan, Wilberforce often volunteered to preach at events because, as people knew, he was able to speak well extemporaneously once he had made a few brief notes (Wilberforce: 285–6). A one-word note made on the back of an envelope, as Wilberforce once used as a prompt for a sermon, is not much research material but the same cannot be said for manuscript notes. Equally important, to what extent are such notes a sermon? Taking into account the number of published sermons, the difficulty of finding manuscript sermons, and the need for Sermon Studies in the modern era to become a discipline, scholars must consider whether every sermonic form should be studied equally. Are there, for example, some types of sermons which merit more scholarly investigation because their authors or themes are more important or because they represent, quintessentially, what the experience of a sermon was?

Mapping the Sermon—How Many?

If it seems contrarian to consider the definition of 'sermon' at the end of a volume examining the sermon in its historical and cultural context, it may be equally odd to talk about mapping the sermon at the end of a series of essays which have suggested numerous ways to begin to think about the corpus of sermons preached and published in the modern period. Its strangeness aside, such a discussion is vital: how many sermons is one of the critical questions facing future scholars of Sermon Studies. Several authors have drawn attention to the number of sermons preached, 'sermon events', and the number of sermons published. While it is important to acknowledge the gap between the two, scholars of Sermon Studies must not be distracted by the discrepancy to the extent that they ignore a more pressing problem—the need for a clearer idea of the number of published sermons extant.

Both introductory essays have already drawn attention to one of the difficulties facing scholars who ask the question 'How many?' There is no simple way to search for sermons. The only consistency is inconsistency. Sermons are discourses, lectures, published individually and in collections; some are recognized as such by cataloguers and some are not. Put simply, the absence of 'rules of the game' means that it will require a major collaborative effort on the part of scholars to turn estimates and educated guesses to a precise number of published sermons.

The authors in this volume are not the first to recognize the scope of the task. Commenting on the difficulty of choosing the best sermons of the nineteenth century, in 1940 Gaius Glenn Atkins observed:

> Naturally, in editing an anthology of master sermons the choice of master preachers is determinative. If one should begin with the sermons themselves he would...end

by spending his life in the proper alcoves of the libraries of theological seminaries, trying, with an impossible mass of material, to reach conclusions for which there are really no final objective tests. (Atkins: vii)

For the modern period, Sermon Studies as a discipline will progress far more usefully, in terms of contributing to a more complete picture of British history, if this 'impossible mass of material' is rendered into something much less inchoate.

Some aids for this task are already in place. Databases such as Early English Books Online (EEBO), covering the period 1475–1700, and Eighteenth Century Collections Online (ECCO), covering the period 1701–1800, contain large numbers of printed sermons for the seventeenth and eighteenth centuries. Google's digitization project, while not targeting sermons specifically, has resulted in the addition of sermons including, for the nineteenth century, some not even found in book form in libraries of record such as the British Library and the Bodleian Library. There is also the work of John Gordon Spaulding which has been mentioned previously—and Spaulding's work will be even more useful when it is converted into a searchable database. Furthermore, there already exist online collections of the sermons of well-known preachers such as John Henry Newman and Charles Spurgeon. The problem with all of these collections is that they are disparate; it is not possible, for example, to compare easily the sermons of John Tillotson and William Paley, found in EEBO, ECCO, and Google books respectively, with those of Newman found at the Works of John Henry Newman web site (www.newmanreader.org).

One way forward is to create a database of sermons beginning with, but ultimately not limited to, the modern era (or even British sermons). Such a database would follow standard cataloguing rules and be accessible to all scholars, professional or 'lay'. The information about the sermon would contain some basic elements—name of the preacher, title of the sermon, Scriptural text used, title of the book/collection in which the sermon is found, publisher of the sermon or collection, date and place in which the sermon or collection was published. Complementing this basic information would be details, if known, such as the date the sermon was preached, the place in which the sermon was preached (both the building and the village, town, or city), the occasion of the sermon, and the audience who heard the sermon. A database containing the estimated 85,000 sermons for the modern period catalogued in this way would be a major step forward in providing a common research aid for scholars of Sermon Studies; a more precise answer could be postulated to a question such as which Bible texts were most used in sermons preached during the Jacobite uprisings of the eighteenth century, for example. A database containing 80,000 to 100,000 sermons could revolutionize the understanding of the development of British religion in the period; broader themes such as the sermon topics of Evangelicals in the eighteenth and nineteenth centuries could be investigated in a systematic fashion.

Given the argument proffered by several authors in this volume that the sermon was an essential component of British life in the modern era, it is better to say that the creation of a database of sermons is as necessary as a database of Anglican clergy or the works of Charles Darwin. Delineating the corpus of modern British sermons numerically—and, ultimately, to provide access to the texts of these sermons—would be the real achievement of Sermon Studies for the period 1689–1901. Scholarly assertions about the sermon would certainly be less speculative. Who was the most prolific publisher of sermons in the modern era (and why)? Perhaps such a question can never be answered definitively, but the creation of a database would increase substantially the likelihood of giving an accurate answer.

Going further and outside the scope of this volume, if a sermons database were extended beyond the period of this volume, the linking of the work of modern scholars with that of scholars of the early modern and medieval period would represent an even larger step forward. While it is an exaggeration to describe the sermon as the ultimate research tool in British history, there is no doubt that as a common feature of British life for centuries the sermon has been severely under-utilized as an object of research: a large and comprehensive database could change this omission.

The Sermon and the Liturgy

As Bob Tennant notes in Chapter 7, the liturgical setting of the sermon implies that the sermon should not only be seen as a speech directed by a preacher towards an audience but as an episode in the wider liturgical drama—as a time during which the minister steps forward and speaks to, and on behalf of, the congregation. Further, the congregation may be supposed to consist predominantly of baptized and catechized Christians not altogether ignorant of the religion. In this model the sermon event may be visualized as a scene from a play where only one of the actors has a speaking part: this actor addresses, speaks for, and shapes the experience of the congregation. In cases where the sermon is the high point of the liturgy the preacher issues a kind of rallying cry: his words are intended to sustain the congregation, as a community, until the next service. In cases where the act of communion is the high point of the service the preacher guides the communal experience in anticipation of the climax of the liturgy. What was said—and, when known, how it was said—is of crucial importance in the study of the sermon.

Drama criticism, itself a multidisciplinary activity, is very well established and its methods could be usefully applied to the published sermon. Just as, for example, a Shakespeare play as it exists in printed form has a certain relationship to its original performance on the stage—not a redaction but a re-creation in a different form—so are printed sermons realized afresh in new performances, be they in the pulpit or in the domestic circle or in the private study. Such an extension of Sermon Studies would also help to bridge the chasm between literary criticism and religious and historical studies of the modern era. This line of investigation would be of mutual benefit—breaking down the separation between 'religious' and 'secular' literature, for example—and would enable a better balanced account of the reality of Britain's, and the Anglophone world's, history. Scholars of Sermon Studies, whether historians, sociologists, or literary critics, could begin to explore the cultural conditions and conditioning of the sermon and its exponents. For example, how might a mission sermon be performed differently in the slums of London as compared to a village in Ireland? Or, moving further afield in terms of time and distance, how might a sermon on good government (and empire) be performed differently in India in 1800 as compared with 1900? In these cases the answers must include information about the context of the sermon, the cultural conditioning of the preacher, and the expectation and cultural conditioning of the audience.

To tease out motivation and emotion from a text is always a difficult task for scholars: avoiding imposing their own cultural conditioning is the problem continually faced. With regard to Sermon Studies, mapping the sermon may lead to some fruitful discoveries. (And here the assumption is that the database of sermons also includes access to the text.) Putting the sermon in the context of a liturgy means that the task is to discover how language is used in a sermon as compared to others rather than calculating how many sermons there are. Do the preachers regard themselves as authority figures set above the congregation or are they making a different kind of connection with their hearers? Bob Tennant's examination of the use of the personal pronoun by Evangelical preachers is one example of the way this research could be conducted. Done on a large scale, such mapping would provide greater understanding of British culture to several areas of study. Liturgical scholars would be able to examine changing patterns of worship. Sociologists of religion would be able to examine closely the ways in which the British changed their understanding of clerical authority in particular and all religious authority in general. Linguists and literary critics would be able to detect the shifts in the use of the English language. Such research will only be possible if scholars of Sermon Studies take on the task of cataloguing the modern British sermon systematically.

Recovering 'Silent' Voices

Though it may not rank as chief among the tasks for the future of Sermon Studies, an interesting project will be the recovery of those voices which seem quiet as compared to the collective noise of, for example, sermons preached by clergy of the Church of England. As noted earlier in this essay, two of these 'voices' are women and the preachers who were not clergy. An additional 'voice' is that of people of religious faith who were not Christians.

In the case of women, to the question 'Did women preach?' the answer is clearly 'yes'. It is impossible to construct a history of religion in Victorian Britain without some reference to the Salvation Army and it is equally impossible to talk about the origins of the Salvation Army movement without reference to the leadership, which included the preaching, of Catherine Booth. It is no surprise, for example, that the public speaking career of Maude Royden (1876–1956), which by 1920 had become a preaching career, began in 1902 with her ministry at the parish of South Luffenham, Leicestershire;

Royden was a prominent rather than a unique phenomenon: her preaching was possible because other women had done so before her (Heeney; Fletcher).

Royden's predecessors may not be easy to find but neither is the task impossible or impractical. By 1901 women had found numerous ways to preach even if they were barred from the pulpit. Edith Harvey Brooks, for example, was one of several woman lay workers attached to the Society for the Promotion of Christian Knowledge (SPCK) in the 1890s. In 1900 the SPCK published one of her tracts—it ran to more than ninety pages. Taking the text 'Consider the lilies of the field' (Matthew 6:28), Brooks drew spiritual lessons from the anatomy of the plant. The six petals of a lily provided material for brief sermons on motherliness, trustfulness, unworldliness, patience, reverence, and wisdom (Brooks: 40–83). What is fascinating about Brooks's tract is the sermonic tone she adopted throughout. Commenting on the responsibilities of the mother as the foundation of a Christian family, she remarked:

> Dear mothers, is it a distressing thought to you, that you have this great responsibility always? Does it frighten you to realize that whether you will or no, your life is silently producing an unseen effect all the time, and that nothing you can do will prevent it? It would indeed be a terror to contemplate, if it were not that He Who made the lilies made you also. (Brooks: 92)

Brooks had cultivated a preaching style: it is not stretching the boundaries of credulity to suggest that this style had been developed by engaging in actual preaching. Finding the sermons of women preachers such as Brooks will add variety and contour to what scholars of Sermon Studies already know about the modern British sermon.

Equally important, if specific sermons were directed at women, rather than a congregation of which women were a part, then applying the techniques that scholars such as Beth Barr have used for the medieval period will also add depth to what is known about the sermon in the modern period (Barr). The gendered sermon, a sermon directed at women although not apparent from the title nor a cursory reading of the text, to which scholars subject careful literary analysis of characteristics such as word usage and style, will no doubt reveal much about the intended and unintended uses of the sermon by the clergy.

As authors of the essays in this volume have commented on the multifarious uses of the sermon, another area of future investigation must be non-clerical, or lay, sermons. The lay sermon gained popularity in the latter half of the nineteenth century. The British Library catalogue lists thirty-one titles of these sermons for the period 1850–1901. Of the various contributors the best known is Samuel T. Coleridge, whose two sermons are commentaries on issues of class and economics: *The Statesman's Manual* was addressed to 'the higher classes' and *'Blessed are ye that sow beside all Waters!'* was addressed to 'the higher and middle classes' (Coleridge 1816; 1817). The titles of the other sermons range from the standard sermon title, such as Joseph Drew's *The Mystery of Creation*, to the quixotic, as in James More's *A Lay Sermon on Clubs and their Doctors* (Drew; More). The 'preachers' of these sermons tackled matters of spiritual reform, such as *Quousque tandem? A Lay Sermon to the Clergy*, and matters of political reform, as in John Morrison

Davidson's sermon on land usage entitled *Politics for the People* (Laicus; Davidson). And, although not too surprising given the increasing involvement of women in various kinds of Christian ministry, there is even a sermon by 'A Lady' entitled *New Lamps for Old Ones* (1882).

There is no evidence that any of these lay sermons were preached in a formal religious setting, but their existence is evidence that by the end of the nineteenth century laity did not consider the sermon a prerogative of the clergy alone. The growth of the lecture as a form of public communication, and entertainment, no doubt accelerated the trend of people who were not clergy adopting another type of lecture, the sermon, as a vehicle to disseminate their ideas, religious or otherwise. Given these two trends, it is unlikely that the thirty-one entries in the British Library catalogue are the complete corpus of lay sermons. Recovering and discovering these sermons will help to explain how the sermon form was changing before the twentieth century began.

For communicating religious, moral, and ethical ideas the pulpit was still king in 1850 though it was facing serious challenge from the lecture stand and the serial novel. The same can be said of the sermon as entertainment: if venues such as the theatre had not surpassed the pulpit by 1901, the signs were apparent that this would soon be the case. While that cultural shift is noteworthy, there was an enduring quality about the sermon which explains why its use did not cease even in the supposedly secular late twentieth century. One of the best illustrations of the reason for the persistence of the sermon form is its use by other religions such as Jews and Muslims in the nineteenth century.

Judaism and Islam were preached about, particularly during missions at home and abroad (Bickersteth; Crawford; Stowell; Moslem Mission Society), but Jews and Muslims also preached their own sermons. By 1800 there was a thriving Jewish community in Britain and several strands of Judaism had adherents who were ministered to and worshipped together. The number of Muslims in Britain was much smaller than that of Jews in 1800—it took until 1860 for a mosque to be registered as a religious building—but the numbers increased steadily throughout the nineteenth century (Ansari: 24–40).

For Muslims there is anecdotal evidence of imams preaching sermons but none of these are listed as published in the British Library catalogue. In the case of Jews, several of the major figures in Judaism in the nineteenth century published their sermons: Nathan Marcus Adler, the Chief Rabbi of Ashkenazi Jews from 1845 to 1890, Adler's son Hermann, Chief Rabbi from 1891 to 1911, and Benjamin Artom, *haham* or leader of Spanish and Portuguese Jews in London from 1866 to 1879, are three prominent examples (H. N. Adler; N. M. Adler 1891; Artom 1873). A search for sermons preached to and for Jewish congregations reveals that a strong tradition of Jewish preaching had been established by 1901; in the case of the Adlers these sermons were also preached with an eye towards the Christian churches (N. M. Adler 1892; H. N. Adler). Again, it is unlikely that the sermons listed as Jewish in the British Library catalogue represent the total number preached and published by Jewish rabbis. How those who were not a part of Christian Britain viewed the state of religion, their own and that of Christianity, in the country of their domicile is one question that can be answered better if more of these sermons are found and studied. That interesting line of research aside, for scholars of

Sermon Studies the existence of any Jewish and Muslim sermons is another reminder of the universal appeal of the sermon.

The Production of Sermons and Its Impact

While the focus of the essays in this volume has been on the sermon as text, the varieties of sermon—Anglican, Catholic, Evangelical, Jewish, lay, political, philosophical, and so forth—suggest that the economics of the sermon, particularly questions of production, is another fruitful area of research for Sermon Studies. Unless really committed to a cause, a publisher would not publish a sermon if his, or her, company could not make a profit from the sales. With a precise figure for the number of sermons published it will be possible to calculate the amounts of revenue being generated by publishers and, even more challenging and interesting, the percentage of their income being spent by those who purchased sermons. Conducting these lines of research is another way to answer questions about the impact of the sermon on daily life: for example, how popular was the sermon?

Sermon production and sales had an important impact on the religious life of Britain. Though the content of the numerous sermons on the Bangorian Controversy was the catalyst which prolonged the debate between the protagonists, publishers profited from the on-going dispute (and were probably unhappy when it dissipated!). Charles Spurgeon funded the building of his new church, the Metropolitan Tabernacle, and his college, by the sales of his books, particularly sermons. Charles Kingsley was able to stay afloat financially by having his writing published—a significant portion of which was sermons. In the publishing and selling of sermons, economic activity engaged with religious activity resulting in the promotion of both: God and Mammon could be joined together.

Turning to matters of economics, how the sermon affected the production of the book is another area of investigation likely to provide insight into the development of British society in the modern era. There clearly were significant effects. That the Brighton publisher Charles E. Verrall had to advertise for workers who wanted to learn shorthand to staff his growing business is evidence of one area of the book trade that was affected by the sermon (Bidder: 160). More sermons being published meant more people were needed to take accurate notes of those sermons, which meant more people had to learn shorthand. And the practice of taking sermon notes even affected the form of stationery. In the case of three late seventeenth-century sermon notebooks in the Folger Library, the books are hinged along the top edge, rather than the left-hand side, for ease of use. Perched on a knee when in church, scribbling notes as the parson preached, the notebook was much easier to use when opening vertically (Sherrard).

When it came to the publishing of their sermons, clergy had to think like businessmen. They had to consider the format that would make their sermons most appealing to consumers (which also explains why clergy spent time editing their sermons rather than having the spoken version of the sermon published). More research is needed but the records in the catalogues of major libraries seem to suggest that the single sermon was the more popular format in the eighteenth century and collections of sermons were more popular in the nineteenth century. By investigating the aforementioned questions, scholars of Sermon Studies can certainly make contributions to the history of the book and the history of publishing.

Conclusion: Why was the Sermon Popular?

While it may be tempting to think of the sermon as an instrument of oppression, that temptation must be resisted. It is true that, with regard to extant sermons, the form is dominated by the Church of England. It is also true that the large majority of sermons in the period originated—either preached or published—in England. Furthermore, the overwhelming majority of sermons involved men speaking authoritatively to women, with few examples of the reverse, for all of the period. Scholars of Sermon Studies must not allow these facts to cause them to forget the universality of the sermon in its appeal and the many ways in which the form was used and was useful. Sermon Studies encompass the history of preaching and the history of rhetoric as well as, for example, the history of publishing and the history of social movements such as mass education. The fact that a woman such as Rebecca Burleigh could be the publisher of sermons during the Bangorian Controversy is a reminder that consumption was as important as delivery in the history of the sermon. In addition, the fact that women took advantage of situations such as being at sea to preach is a reminder that no group controlled the form (Morgan-Guy)—not men, not the English, not Anglicans, not Christians, and not even believers. Women, like Elizabeth Howland, directed their patronage to deserving preachers such as Benjamin Hoadly, who in turn commemorated their qualities in funeral sermons (Gibson: 115–16); Benjamin Artom, an Italian who spoke no English at the time, could preach a sermon on the duties of a Jewish pastor to his London congregation of Spanish and Portuguese Jews in French (Artom 1866); George Eliot could use the words and style of a woman preacher in *Adam Bede* to put forward a description of a sincere Christian; and the scientist Thomas Huxley could 'preach' a lay sermon on 7 January 1866 entitled 'On the Advisableness of Improving Natural Knowledge' (Huxley: 3–22). In the period 1689–1901 the sermon was indeed all things to all persons.

References

Adler, H. N. (1848). *The Jewish Faith. A Sermon*... London: Effingham Wilson.
Adler, N. M. (1891). *The Ideal Jewish Pastor. A Sermon*... London: Wertheimer & Lea.

—— (1892). *The Functions of the Jewish Pulpit. A Sermon*...London: A. J. Isaacs & Sons.
Ansari, H. (2004). *'The Infidel Within': Muslims in Britain Since 1800*. London: C. Hurst & Co.
Artom, B. (1866). *The Duties of the Jewish Pastor in the Present Age. A Sermon*...London: Wertheimer, Lea & Co.
—— (1873). *Sermons Preached in Several Synagogues*. London: Trübner & Co.
Atkins, G. G. (ed.) (1940). *Master Sermons of the Nineteenth Century*. Chicago: Willett, Clark & Company.
A Woman's Reply to a Sermon by the Rev. J. W. Burgon...(1871). Oxford: George Shrimpton.
Baker, A. (1847). *Sermons on the Holy Joy*...London: Francis and John Rivington.
Barr, B. A. (2008). *The Pastoral Care of Women in Late Medieval England*. Woodbridge, Suffolk: Boydell & Brewer.
Bickersteth, R. (1851). *A Sermon Preached on Behalf of the Operative Jewish Converts' Institution*...London: Operative Jewish Converts' Institution.
Bidder, W. (1860). *Second Number: Containing Six Sermons Preached by Mr. William Bidder*...Brighton: C. E. Verrall.
Brooks, E. H. (1900). *Fair as a Lily*. London: Society for the Promotion of Christian Knowledge
Brown, C. (2009). *The Death of Christian Britain* ..., 2nd edn. London: Routledge.
Burgon, J. W. (1871). *Woman's Place. A Sermon*...Oxford: J. Parker & Co.
Burrows, H. W. (1867). *Parochial Mission-Women Association. A Sermon*...Oxford: J. Parker & Co.
Cantor, G. (2011). *Religion and the Great Exhibition of 1851*. Oxford: Oxford University Press.
Chadwick, O. (1975). *The Secularization of the European Mind*...Cambridge: Cambridge University Press.
Church, R. W. (1892). *Cathedral and University Sermons*. London: Macmillan and Co.
—— (1895). *Pascal and Other Sermons*. London: Macmillan and Co.
Clark, J. C. D. (2012). 'Secularization and Modernization: The Failure of a "Grand Narrative"'. *Historical Journal* 55, 1: 161–94.
Coleridge, S. T. (1816). *The Statesman's Manual*...London: Gale & Fenner.
—— (1817). *'Blessed are Ye that Sow Beside All Waters!' A Lay Sermon*...London: Gale & Fenner.
Crawford, T. J. (1847). *An Argument for Jewish Missions, being a Sermon*...Edinburgh: Myles Macphail.
Davidson, J. M. (1887). *Politics for the People*...London: William Reeves.
Davies, U. (1890). *A Woman's Influence*...London: John Kensit.
Dobell, J. (1813). *The Exaltation, Dignity & Dominion of Jesus. A Sermon*....Cranbrook Samuel Waters.
Drew, J. (1879). *The Mystery of Creation*. Printed for Private Circulation.
Fletcher, S. (1989). *Maude Royden: A Life*. Oxford: Basil Blackwell.
Fordyce, J. (1766). *Sermons to Young Women*, 2nd edn. London: A. Millar and T. Cadell.
Galton, F. (1874). *English Men of Science*...London: Macmillan.
Gibson, W. (2004). *Enlightenment Prelate: Benjamin Hoadly 1676–1761*. Cambridge: James Clarke & Co.
Goodacre, R. H. (1860). *The Fruits of Sin. A Course of Six Plain Sermons*...London: Longman, Green, Longman, and Roberts.
Griffith, T. (1833). *The Leading Idea of Christianity Investigated in a Series of Discourses*. London: T. Cadell.

Hall, P. (1837). *The Woman Taken in Adultery. A Sermon*...London: London Female Mission.
Harper, W. (1732). *The Antiquity, Innocence, and Pleasure of Gardening*...London: Thomas Edlin.
Heeney, B. (1988). *The Women's Movement in the Church of England*. Oxford: Clarendon Press.
Hoppus, J. (1833). *The Difficulties of Infidelity*...London: Jackson and Walford, 1833.
Huxley, T. (1870). *Lay Sermons, Addresses, and Reviews*. London: Macmillan and Co.
Isaacs, A. A. (1866). *The Path of the Just*...London: William Macintosh.
Jowett, J. (1828). *Sermons, Preached before a Village Congregation*. London: R. B. Seely and W. Burnside.
A Lady (1882). *New Lamps for Old Ones. A Lay Sermon*. London: W. Poole.
Laicus (1881). *Quousque Tandem? A Lay Sermon to the Clergy on Public Worship*. London: E. W. Allen.
Larsen, T. (2006). *Crisis of Doubt*...Oxford: Oxford University Press.
McLaren, A. (1954). *Sermon Outlines*, ed. S. B. Quincer. Grand Rapids, MI: W. B. Eerdmans.
Manning, H. E. (1868). *Devotional Readings. Being Select Passages*...London: Simpkin, Marshall and Co.
More, J. (1878). *A Lay Sermon on Clubs and their Doctors*. London: J. & A. Churchill.
Morgan-Guy, J. (1989). 'Fishing for the Soul "No'ard of the Dogger"', in W. J. Sheils and Diana Wood (eds.), *Studies in Church History*, vol. 26: *The Ministry: Clerical and Lay*. Oxford: Basil Blackwell, 415–22.
Moslem Mission Society. (1873). *A Plea for 75 Members of a Church of England Missionary Brotherhood*...London: Moslem Mission Society.
Roberts, A. (1850). *Village Sermons*. London: The Religious Tract Society.
Sherrard, T., MSS: Sherrard Sermon Notes V.a.40, Folger Shakespeare Library, Fairfax Sermon Notes V.a.14; V.a.15.
Spurgeon, C. H. (1969). *Metropolitan Tabernacle Pulpit*...London: Banner of Truth Trust.
—— (1974). *Metropolitan Tabernacle Pulpit*...Pasadena, TX: Pilgrim Publications.
Stowell, H. (1847). *Jewish Claims on Christian Sympathy. A Sermon Preached*...London: London Society for the Promotion of Christianity Amongst the Jews.
Waller, P. (2006). *Writer, Readers, and Reputations*...Oxford: Oxford University Press.
Wilberforce, R. (1888). *Life of Samuel Wilberforce*...London: Kegan Paul, Trench, & Co.

Index

Abbot, Henry 219
Abbott, M. P. and Parsons, P. S. 105–6
Abbott, S. 247
Abelly, Louis 137
Aberdeen University 159, 160
Abney, Lady 12
abolitionist sermons/lectures 37, 84, 284–5; *see also* anti-slavery sermons
accession day sermons 233, 238, 267, 532
acculturation 360, 361, 366
Acres, Joseph 266
Act of Toleration (1689) 97, 99, 101, *see also* Nonconformists
Act of Union (1707) 238, 261, 263
Act of Union (1800) 171, 173
Acton, Samuel 323–4
Adams, John 311, 315–16, 395
Adams, William 400
Addison, Joseph 391
Adler, Nathan Marcus 626
advertisements for sermons 23, 31, 82, 88, 92, 154, 278, 295, 324, 330, 415
Africa 514–15, 549, 552–3, 560, *see also* Natal Sermons; colonial sermons
African slaves 484, 489, 492, 502–3, 506, 507, 508, 511
afterlife 348–9, 449, 457
Aitken, W. H. 90
Albert, Prince 67, 339, 340, 342, 344, 346, 349
Alcock, John 534
alcohol 502; *see also* temperance movement
Aldrich, Henry 221, 222
Alexander, Mrs C. F. 189
Alexander W. L. 341
Alford, Henry 65, 568
allegories 99, 207, 500, 522
Alleine, Joseph 162
Allen, George 81

Allen, William 110
Allies, Thomas 412
Alsop, Vincent 267
Altham, Roger 291
American Civil War (1861–65) 85, 252
American colonies/United States of America:
  anti-Jacobite sermons in 249
  Catholics in 435
  church attendance in 515
  circular letters in 290
  deism in 395–6
  Evangelical Revival in 516
  impact of colonization on 518
  lecture tours in 85
  millenarianism in 374, 375
  popularity of sermons by Hugh Blair in 163
  publishers of Gaelic sermons in 162
  Puritan sermons in 514, 516
  Quakers in 105, 108, 109, 110, 517
  sectarian controversy in 181
  SPG mission sermons 18, 484, 485, 489–92, 498, 501, 506–10
  Spurgeon's printed sermons in 20–1
American War of Independence (1775–83) 139, 234, 235, 248, 254, 270, 276, 280–1, 283, 509, 510
analogies 72, 82, 90, 401, 416, 444, 450, 551, 552, 555, 559
Ancient Greece 555
Andrewes, Lancelot 3, 620
Andrews, John Nevins 386
Anglicanism:
  Broad Church 463–76
  evangelicalism and 120–32, 142, 340, 344
  lampooned 140
  lecturers 86

Anglicanism (*cont.*)
   parochial model 67–8, 81
   reading pews and pulpits 19
   sermon lectures 81; *see also* Church of England; Church of Scotland
Anglo-Catholicism 195–6, 407, 409; *see also* High Churchmen
Anne, Queen 217, 231, 233, 235, 238–9, 269, 617
Anne of Orange, Princess 617
Annesley, Samuel 330–1
anti-Catholicism 84, 139, 143, 235, 237, 255, 407, 435, 438, 439, 482, 486–8, 500–1, 543
   consecration sermons 311–12
   Evangelicalism and 177
   lectures 86
   in novels 605
   Quakers and 101
   rhetoric 534–6, 540–1
   riots 139, 181, 255
   sermons 429–33, 520
   thanksgiving sermons 261, 263, 266
Anti-Corn Law League 84
anti-Jacobite sermons 245–57, 315–16, 358, 532, 613
anti-Methodist sermons 308, 313
anti-Protestant sermons 142–3
anti-revolutionary sermons 281–3
anti-Semitism 319, 487
anti-slavery movement and sermons 4, 24, 37, 252, 284–5
anti-Trinitarianism 279, 395, 398
Antichrist 266, 383, 430, 483, 487
anticlericalism 393, 491
Antinomian Controversy 330, 331, 375
antithetical sermons 170–81
apocalyptic imagery 381–3
apostolic succession 308–9, 311–12, 315, 408, 499, 588
Appleton, James 138–9
Apthorp, East 310, 317
Aquinas, Thomas 136
Archer, James 138–9, 141, 519
architecture 18, 579, 580, 581, 582, 588
Arianism 203, 312, 394, 402
Aristotle 416
Arminian Magazine 119

Arminian Presbyterians 71, 127, 206, 363, 375
Arnold, Matthew 423, 570, 595, 614
Arnold, Thomas Kerchever 65
Artom, Benjamin 626, 628
Ashby, Richard 107
Ashe, St George 498, 540
Ashton, Thomas 360
assize sermons 13, 128–9, 409, 413, 414, 532, 568, 587, 588
astronomy 455, 467
Athanasian Creed 68, 222, 394, 397, 467–8
atheism 282, 441, 450
Atkins, Gaius Glenn 37, 621–2
Atkinson, J. A. 342
atonement, doctrine of 206–7, 211, 448, 464, 468, 471, 473
Atterbury, Francis 16, 218, 310, 391–2
Atterbury plot (1722) 316
Augustine, St 54
Australia 143–4, 515, 518–25
awakenings 115, 119, 185, 189, 204, 514

Backhouse, James 110, 307, 313
Backhouse, William 270, 279
Bacon, Benjamin, Archdeacon of Derry 538, 543
Bacon, Francis 395
Baggs, Charles Michael 145
Bagot, Lewis 306, 360
Baines, Peter Augustine 142–3
Baker, Arthur 620
Baker, Augustine 136
Baker, Pacificus 138
Baker, Sarah 107
Bakhtin, Mikhail 596
Balfour, Clara 87
Balguy, John 293, 294, 295, 306, 313, 398–9
Balguy, Thomas 399
Ball, Nathaniel 263
Ball, Sir Robert 89
Ballard, Edward 316
Bampton lectures 7, 93
Bangorian Controversy (1717–25) 36, 230, 233, 240, 293, 398, 618, 627, 628
Banner, Richard 222–3, 224

baptism 296, 419–20, 468, 471
Baptiste de la Salle, Jean 172
Baptists 104, 276
   funeral sermons 340, 343
   in Ireland 172, 179
   lecturers 86
   in Scotland 165
   Seventh-day 386
   in Wales 201, 203, 205, 206–7, 209, 210
Barbados 509, 511
Barberi, Dominic 146–7
Barclay, Robert 98, 100, 110
Baring-Gould, Sabine 65
Barker, W. R. 431
Barnard, T. C. 486, 531
Barnard, William 487
Barneth, John Charles 129
Barnett, Samuel 91, 92
Barr, Beth 625
Barr, John 266, 267
Barrett, Richard 110
Barrington, Shute 183–4, 242, 317
Barritt, Mary 120
Barrow, Henry 322
Barry, Alfred 447
Barton, Philip 309, 317
Bathhurst, Lord 219
battlefield sermons 238
Baxter, Richard 17, 162, 326, 327–8
Baynes, Robert 41
Beamish, L, K. 100, 107, 108, 111
Bean, James 279
Bearcroft, Philip 498
Beardsley, Christina 573
Beattie, James 159, 163, 403
Beausobre, Isaac de 519
Bebbington, David 114, 375
Beckford, William 580, 581
Bedell, William 539
Beecher, Henry Ward 86
Begg, James A. 166, 378, 383, 385
Bell, Andrew 366–7
Bell, Deborah 107
Bennett, William 413
Benson, Edward White 342
Benson, Joseph 282, 285
Benson, Martin 117, 280, 500, 501–3

Bentham, Jeremy 366
Bercovitch, S. 516
Berens, Edward 65, 68, 73–4
Beresford, William 488, 542–3
Berington, Joseph 141
Berkeley, George 49, 117, 281, 283, 309, 312,
   396, 541, 614
Berridge, John 126
Best, William 251
Beveridge, William 21–2, 187, 492, 540
Bible 399
   Anglicans/Dissenters use of 391
   apocalyptic imagery in 376, 378,
      381–3, 384
   Chinese translations of 558
   Christian universalism predicted by 490, 501
   eschatological prophecies in 375
   female figures in 617
   Gaelic translations of 161–2, 538–9
   lectures 86, 87, 90
   on music in worship 224
   poetry of 573, 574, 576
   Quakers and 98, 109
   rationalism and 392–4, 395, 400
biblical criticism 485, 594
   Colenso 464, 465–7, 469–70, 476, 517
   Jowett 471
   literary 599–600
biblical exegesis 3, 81, 322, 583
biblical exposition 72, 341–2, 394
biblical texts in sermons 48–9, 51–2,
   55–9, 309
   anniversary sermons 283
   anti-Catholic sermons 429–30, 439
   anti-Jacobite sermons 253–4
   charity-school sermons 359, 362, 368–9
   colonial sermons 519, 523
   consecration sermons 305, 307, 310, 314
   court sermons 229
   funeral sermons 276, 325–6, 328, 341, 342,
      345, 346, 347, 348
   Gothic Revival sermons 583–4
   mission sermons 499–507, 550–1, 552–3,
      554, 555, 556–7, 558
   national thanksgiving sermons 263–4, 279
   naval sermons 451
   parliamentary sermons 242

biblical texts in sermons (*cont.*)
    Quaker sermons 108, 111, 112
    satire of 152–3
    Tractarian sermons 416–17
    village sermons 69, 70, 72–5, 76, 77
    Welsh sermons 191, 202, 207
Bicheno, James 379–80, 383–4, 385, 386
Bickersteth, Edward Henry 348–9, 374, 375, 377, 378–9, 381, 386
Bickersteth, Robert 80
Bingham, Thomas 325
Binney, Thomas 80, 83, 86, 92
Birch, Thomas 57, 58
Birks, Thomas Rawson 65, 375
Birmingham:
    St Chad's Cathedral 144, 148, 149
    Sunday afternoon lectures 89
    Unitarian chapel 141
bishops 316–18, 498–9, 506–7, 508, 514, 552; *see also* consecration sermons; visitation sermons
Bisse, Phillip 217, 218, 291, 491–2
Bisse, Thomas 217, 218, 219, 221, 222–3, 224, 291
Blackall, Offspring 238–9, 291, 292
Blackburne, Francis, Archdeacon of Cleveland 277
Blair, Dr Hugh 13–14, 20, 155, 156, 157, 158, 160, 161, 162–4, 165, 391, 519
Blake, James Vila 447
Blake, William 365
Blakeway, Robert 255
Blomfield, Charles James 591
Blow, John 221
Blunt, J. J. 69, 70, 72
Blyth, Francis 137
Bolton, Theophilus 536
Bonar, John 154
Book of Common Prayer 55, 75, 141, 183, 200, 283, 322, 394, 395, 417, 531, 538
booklets 48, 49
booksellers/book trade 20, 23, 26, 249, 250, 627, *see also* publishers
Booth, Catherine 624
Bossuet, Jacques-Bénigne 158
Boston, Thomas 164
Boswell, James 13, 20, 163

Boultbee, Thomas 457
Boulter, Hugh 293, 307, 542
Bourdaloue, Louis 143
Bowen, Desmond 170
Bowens, Thomas 185
Bowman, William 293
Bownas, Samuel 99, 104, 105
Boxer uprising (1899–1900) 559–60
Boyce, Edward Jacob 553, 555–6, 613
Boyle, Robert 325, 539
Boyle Lectures 7, 93, 393, 394, 447, 448
Bradburn, Samuel 282, 285
Bradford, Samuel 491
Bradley, Lucy 107
Brady, Nicholas 323
Braithwaite, Hannah 110
Brand, Thomas 330–1
Brank, William 348
Breitenback, Esther 548
Brewster, Patrick 345
Bridge, Stephen 39
Bridgewater Treatises 447, 448, 453; *see also* natural theology
Briggs, John 313, 317
Bright, George 35
Brightman, Thomas 375
Brilioth, Yngve 411, 418, 423
British and Foreign Bible Society 130, 276, 366, 508
British Association for the Advancement of Science 456
British constitution 268, 271, 279, 281, 294
British Critic 406
British Empire 8, 431, 441, 513, 515, 518, 526, 549, 613, *see also* colonial sermons; missionaries/missionary sermons
'British Israel' meme 234, 246, 253–4, 264
British Library 338–9, 349, 358, 447, 622, 626
'Britishness' 271, 613
Britten, Emma Hardinge 87
Broad Church 463–76, 566, 572, 573, 575; *see also* Latitudinarians; Church of England
Bromesgrove, Samuel 269
Brontë, Charlotte, *Jane Eyre* 596, 600, 606
Brontë, Emily, *Wuthering Heights* 580, 597, 599, 605, 606

Brooke, John Hedley 446
Brooke, Stopford 91, 573
Brooker, Daniel 224
Brooks, Edith Harvey 625
Broomall, Benjamin 549
Brothers, Richard 285, 503
Broughton, William Grant 518, 519, 521
Brown, Hugh Stowell 13, 86
Brown, James Baldwin 4, 83
Brown, John 'Estimate' 249, 250
Brown, Roger 194
Brown, Stewart J. 171
Browne, Peter 542
Browning, Robert 567
Bruce, Archibald, *The Kirkiad* 156
Buchanan, Charles 291
Buchanan, Dugald 161
Buckland, William 453
Bulkeley, Richard 185–6
Bulkeley, William 185–6
Bull, George 187
Buller, William 307
Bunting, Jabez 36
Burder, George 65, 71, 519
Burgess, Daniel 10
Burgess, T. 434, 436
Burgon, John William 617
Burke, Edmund 140, 243, 286, 585–6, 587
Burleigh, Rebecca 628
burlesque sermons 139–40
Burnaby, Andrew 270, 281
Burnet, Gilbert 11, 13, 37, 153, 240, 267, 290, 292–3, 294, 297, 315, 323, 325, 326–8, 332, 500–1
Burns, Jabez 65
Burrows, Henry William 617
Burt, Edmund 13
Burt, Edward 153
Butcher, Edmund 363
Butler, Charles 139
Butler, George 64
Butler, Joseph 37, 41, 117, 121, 122, 298, 299, 358, 359–61, 363, 366, 397, 583, 620
Butler, Samuel, *The Way of All Flesh* 597–600, 601, 602, 606
Buttree, John 188
Bylaugh, Norfolk 18

Bynns, Richard 190
Byrd, William 221
Byron, Lord 565, 574

Cadell, Thomas 163
Caird, John 166
Calamy, Edmund 41, 327
Calder, John 363
Calvinism 13, 119, 123, 125, 126, 127, 165, 375
Calvinistic Methodists 190, 192, 201, 202–3, 206, 207–8, 209, 210;
 see also Presbyterianism; Wales
Cambridge University 13, 218, 251, 280, 291, 306, 341, 375, 447, 457
Campbell, George 159, 161
Campbell, Thomas 277
Candlish, Robert Scott 166
Cannon, Archdeacon of Norfolk 291
Cantor, Geoffrey 614
Cape Colony 515, 517
Cappe, Newcome 281
caricatures 24–5, 588
Carlyle, Alexander 157, 161, 163
Carlyle, Thomas 581, 587, 595
Carne, John 186, 189
Carr, Robert Lascelles 281–2
Cartwright, Thomas 322
Cassell, John 92
catechetical sermons/lectures 12, 15, 35, 55, 81
catechisms 12, 55, 139, 162, 187, 361, 538–9, 540, 541
cathedral sermons 68, 620
Catholic Association 170, 176, 177–9
Catholic Emancipation (1829) 136, 141, 178, 344, 409, 431, 435
Catholic Relief Acts (1778 and 1791) 138, 141, 538
Catholics/Catholicism 68, 136–49, 255, 588, 591
 apocalyptic imagery and 382
 apostolic succession 308–9, 311–12, 315, 408, 499, 588
 church music 224
 controversy within 434, 435–6
 conversion to Protestantism 489, 533–41
 devotional practice 409

Catholics/Catholicism (*cont.*)
  and Gothic Revival 581
  Irish sectarian controversy 172–81
  New World 500–1
  novels defending and celebrating 605
  Penal Laws 536–8, 540, 541, 544
  poetry and 566, 568
  Restoration of the Hierarchy 428, 429–32
  sermons 137, 284, 343, 345, 350, 412, 432–42, 522
Caudle, James 232–3, 613
celebratory sermons *see* anniversary sermons
censorship 233, 249
Chadwick, Owen 407
Chalkley, Thomas 104
Chalmers, Robert 282
Chalmers, Thomas 92, 131, 166, 338, 340, 341
Chamberlain, Jeffrey S. 7, 614
Chambers, William 277
Chandler, Edward 296
Chandler, Samuel 312, 360, 361
Chapel Royal 218, 220, 251, 553
Chapman, John 293–4, 311, 312
Charity School system 481–8, 489, 492, 532, 533, 542–3, 545
charity sermons 15, 24, 25, 41, 146, 186, 276, 357–70
  sacred histories in 481–93
  for women 617
Charles, Thomas 208
Charles I, King 243
  commemoration of death of 20, 231, 233, 234, 241, 242, 275, 277, 283, 532
  ecclesiastical policies 315
Charles II, King 13
  Restoration Day sermons (29 May) 233, 239, 275, 532
Charlotte, Princess 339, 346
Chauncy, Isaac 331
Chesterfield, Lord 17
Child, William 221
children:
  funeral sermons for 324, 346, 347
  monitor system 366, 369
  sermons for 361–2, 363–4, 458, 459
  'sinful' 597–8, 600
China, missionaries in 549, 557–60

cholera epidemics 453–4
Christianity 430, 433, 437, 470
  civilizing mission of 492, 502, 507, 508
  criticism of 467–8, 471–2
  degeneration from original purity of 485, 487, 489, 505
  doctrine of feeling 573–5
  fragmentation of 441
  global spread of 550
  miracles 12, 146, 175, 399–400, 450, 468, 506
  rationalism and 392–7
  slavery and 508–10, 511
Chrysostom, St John 54
Chubb, Thomas 395
Church, R. W. 41, 64–5, 76, 414, 423, 571, 572, 617–18, 620
Church Missionary Society 127, 128, 129, 130, 132, 276, 508, 552, 553
Church of England 7, 117, 367–8, 616
  Act of Union and 171–2
  catalogue of printed sermons 8
  clergymen as educators 83
  consecration sermons defining 310–14
  convocation controversy 306, 310
  convocations 218, 240, 395
  Dissenters won back to 12–13
  evangelical preachers 120–6
  imperialism and 481–93
  internal debates 430
  licensing of preachers 5
  Methodist secession (1811) 204, 205
  relationship with other churches 438–9
  relationship with the state 314–16, 319, 367, 382, 395, 415
  retention of episcopacy by 308
  schism 292
  Thirty-Nine Articles of 55, 291, 296, 297, 313, 393, 394, 420, 429, 437, 499
  use of the Bible 391
  in Wales 10, 188–97, 199–200, 204
  written sermons preferred by 14, 16, 48; *see also* Anglicanism
Church of Ireland:
  mission to convert Catholics 531–44
  and religious literature 530–1
  sectarian controversy 170–81

Whig government's reform of 406, 414
Church of Laodicea 378, 384, 386
Church of Scotland:
    clerical training 157
    Disruption (1843) 164-5, 166
    Episcopalians 252
    fragmented 154, 155, 158, 166
    influence of universities on 159-60
    Tillotson's sermons 156, 158
Church Pastoral Aid Society 89-90
Churchdown, Gloucestershire 11
churches:
    acoustics 18-19
    attendance 515, 524-5, 582
    building 19, 436, 437, 627
    Catholic 143, 144-5
    fashionable 194
    lighting 23
Churchman, John 517
civil liberty 255, 266-7, 268, 282
Civil Wars 18, 34, 189, 218, 239, 316
Clagett, Nicholas 307, 309, 314
Clarence, Duke of 339, 340, 347, 349, 370
Clark, Frederick Le Gros 459
Clark, Jonathan 614
Clarke, Adam 17, 22
Clarke, Joshua 315
Clarke, Samuel 117, 238, 394, 397, 398
Claude, Jean 160-1
Claydon, Tony 232
Clayton, Thomas 137
Cleaver, William 283
Clement XI, Pope 137
Clements, Henry 6
clergymen:
    accessories and accoutrements for 23, 297
    anti-Jacobite sermons and 250-1
    buying sermons 611
    and church music 222-4
    clerical obedience 296-9
    as educators 83
    Episcopalian exiles 281
    farewell sermons by 40-1
    funeral sermons commemorating 325-6, 328-9, 340, 343
    handwriting of 48
    impoverished 216, 217-19, 308
    intensive work writing sermon 54
    Jacobite uprisings and 247-8
    manuscript sermons destroyed by 47
    pastoral responsibilities of 188-9
    on the pervasiveness of sin 57-8
    plagiarism 23
    poetry and 568-9
    politics and 230-1
    printed sermons by 21
    prosecuted for too few sermons 11
    publishers and 41-2
    regionality 295-6, 298
    rising status of 317-18
    royal chaplains 229
    sanitary reform and 454-5
    sectarian controversy in Ireland 176-80
    sermon guides for 21-2, 48-9, 66-7, 69, 71, 75
    sermon studies and 615-18
    and sermon trade 22-3, 71
    Tractarian 409, 420, 424
    travelling 196
    village sermons 64-6
    Welsh 199-200
clerical training 144, 157, 164, 180, 588
Clifford, Lord 145
Clifton, Sir Thomas 136
Clive, Robert 553
Close, Francis 41-2, 368
Clubbe, John 13
Cobbe, Frances Power 463, 470, 475
Cobbe, Richard Chaloner 535
Cobden, Edward, Archdeacon of London 35
Cockburn, Henry 161
Codrington, General Christopher 509
coffee houses 23, 26, 249, 278
Colenso, Frances 475-6
Colenso, John William 65, 463, 517
    compared with Benjamin Jowett 470-4
    origins and content of sermons 464-70
    and Unitarians 474-6
Coleridge, John Taylor 568
Coleridge, Samuel Taylor 376, 381, 401, 567, 576, 580, 586, 588, 589, 590, 591, 625
Colley, Linda 254

Colley, Thomas 107
Collins, Anthony 394, 395, 396, 400
Colman, Benjamin 516
Colonial and Continental Society 377
colonial sermons 7, 8, 34, 39, 513–14, 514–15, 515–18, 518–25, 526, 613
colonies 143–4, 269–70, 281, 509–11, 515, 518–25, 549, 552–3, 560; *see also* American colonies
colonization 505–7, 508, 518, 525
Comber, Thomas 238
commemorative sermons 233, 234, 240
    French Revolution 415
    Gunpowder Plot (5 November 1605) 242, 275, 532, 533, 541, 544
    Irish Rebellion (23 October 1641) 532, 533, 534, 535, 537, 538, 544
    martyrdom of Charles I (30 January 1649) 20, 231, 233, 234, 241, 242, 275, 277, 283, 532
    Restoration Day (29 May 1660) 233, 239, 275, 532
    sacred histories in 481–93
    SPCK 520
    SPG 498–511, 520
commonplace books 54, 108
communion 420, 468, 623
conduct lectures and literature 36, 86, 88
Confucianism 558
Congregationalists 4, 329, 343
    funeral sermons 340
    in Ireland 172, 179
    lecturers 86, 89, 90, 91, 93
    national salvation 265
    repentance 386
    in Scotland 165
    in Wales 201, 211
congregations/audiences:
    of Anglican evangelists 125
    comprehensibility of sermons 187–8, 194, 200, 390, 391, 414, 518
    conflicts between ministers and 328–9
    for consecration sermons 306–7
    discriminating 11–13
    disempowerment of 597
    disorder amongst 13, 119
    and dramatic sermons 17
    emotionally overwhelmed 139, 140–1, 573
    for evangelical sermons 116, 118–19
    for farewell sermons 40–1
    fashionable 194, 532
    for funeral sermons 328
    genteel parts of 390
    illiterate 17
    Jewish 626
    lampooned 11, 24–5
    for lecture series 81–2, 83–4, 86–7, 90, 92
    length of sermons 10–11, 23, 69
    and printed sermons 249, 278–9
    requesting copies of sermons 39–40
    size of 186, 191, 195, 196
    for village sermons 69–71
    for visitation sermons 290
    Welsh 185–8, 199, 209–10, *see also* emotionalism; note-taking; preaching performances
connexionalism 116, 120, 129, 205, 208, 386, 387, 617; *see also* Methodism
Connolly, J. 440
Connolly, S. J. 531
consecration sermons 193–4, 305–8, 318–19
    bishop's role and status 308–10
    Catholic churches 437
    Church-State alliance 314–16
    clerical profession 317–18
    course of sermons 414
    defining Church of England 310–14
convicts 524, 619–20
Conybeare, John 55, 117
Conybeare, W. J. 409
Cooke, John 8, 21, 277, 279
Coole, Benjamin 100
Cooper, Thomas 84, 85, 91
Copleston, Edward 193–4
copyright 20, 21
Corelli, Marie 611
Corker, James Maurus 136
Cornwallis, James 280, 506–7
coronation sermons 11, 233
Corporation of the Sons of the Clergy 216, 217–18, 220, 221
corruption 100, 128, 277, 279, 281, 311, 334, 349, 397, 430, 484, 485, 487, 502

Cotterill, Henry 553
Cotton, George Edward Lynch 517, 553–4, 556–7
court preachers 136, 137, 139
court sermons 35–6, 229, 234, 235–6, 237–41, 250, 252, 398, 458
Courtail, John 58
Courtenay, William 306, 309
Courtney, Francis 92
Cowper, William 128, 580
Cox, Jeffrey 510, 548
Cox, Michael 488
Crabbe, George 12
Craddock, W. 294
Craig, John 392
Craner, Thomas 264
Cranmer, Thomas 311, 430
Crawford, Dugald 162
Creasey, Maurice A. 103
Creech, William 163
Crew, Nathaniel 305
Crisp, Stephen 100, 101, 103, 104, 107
Critical Review 154, 155
Croft, Herbert 218
Croft, William 221
Croiset, Jean 137
Crooke, Bankes 324
Crooke, William Pascoe 521
Crosby, Sarah 120
Crowther, Samuel Ajayi 514, 552
Croxall, Samuel 218, 306
Cruickshank, A. P. J. 433, 436
Cruikshank, George 19, 25
Culloden, battle of (1746) 158, 245, 248
Cumberland, Duke of 254, 256
Cumming, J. 431
Curr, Joseph 143
Cutler, Ann 120
Cuvier, Georges 453, 455

Daily Gazetteer 219
Dalgairns, John Dobree 147
Dallas, Alexander 64
Dalton, Daniel 55
Dalton, Thomas 57, 58–9
Darby, John Nelson 375, 386

Darracott, Risdon 326
Darwin, Charles 31, 445–6, 448, 450, 453, 455, 456, 457, 459, 614
Daubeny, Charles 368
Davidson, John Morrison 625–6
Davies, David 194
Davies, Richard 452–3
Davies, Thomas 189–91
Davies, Uriah 616
Dawes, Francis 11
Dawes, William 17
Dawson, George 83, 85
Day, George 329
De Johnsone, Fowler 453
Deconinck-Brossard, Françoise 234, 251, 583
Defoe, Daniel 323, 334
deism 89, 109, 143, 293, 366, 394–8, 399, 400, 402, 403, 502, 506, 507, 508, 554
Delany, Bernard 350
Denne, John 507–8
Dent, Arthur 375
Denton, Jonathan 326
Devonshire, William Cavendish, first Duke of 332–3
diaries 55, 58, 91–2, 185–6, 326
Dickens, Charles 572–3, 603
  Bleak House 367, 596, 597, 600
Dicks, James 161
Dillwyn 107
directionality 116, 118, 123–4, 125, 126, 129, 132, 624
disease 10, 454, 502, 525
disestablishment movement 84, 145
Disney, John 313
Disraeli, Benjamin 340, 342, 581
Dissenters 3, 48, 59, 98, 114, 237, 239, 240, 298, 393
  anti-Jacobite sermons 252
  anti-slavery sermons 284–5
  attacks on episcopacy 312
  charity schools 357, 359, 360–1, 362–4, 368, 369, 370
  church music 223–4
  fast day sermons 281
  funeral sermons 324, 326, 328, 329–31, 340
  lectures 80, 81, 82, 85

Dissenters (*cont.*)
  missionary societies 276
  national salvation and 264–6
  number of sermon events 7
  printed sermons by 8, 21–2, 278
  Rational 316
  spiritual biographies 327–8
  'testing' of candidates 5
  use of the Bible 391
  visitation sermons 290, 292
  in Wales 201
  won back to Established Church 12–13
Divine judgement 285–6, 347, 454, 455
Divine providence 246, 262–3, 279–80, 347, 449, 450, 452
Dix, John Ross 569
Dixon, Richard Watson 569
Dobell, Joseph 620
Dodsley, Robert 160, 249, 250
Dodsworth, William 374, 377, 379, 381, 382, 385, 386
Dodwell, William 306, 310
Donne, John 3, 20
Dopping, Anthony 539
Douglas, John 242–3
Dowden, J. 41
Downes, Henry 542
Downes, Robert 534
Downey, James 392
Doyle, Dr James 174–6, 181
Drew, Joseph 625
Drummond, Henry 367, 375, 381, 383, 386
Drummond, May 107
Dublin Evening Post 173–4, 177–8
Dublin Society for Charity Schools 541–2
Dublin University 447
Dudley, Elizabeth 110
Dunton, Hugh 375
Dunton, John 327, 334
Dupont, John 264
Dutch Reform Church 517
Dutch Republic 231, 235, 237

Eagleton, Terry 602
East India Company 515

Easter sermons 49, 76, 77, 238, 620
Ecclesiastical Titles Act (1851) 431, 436, 437
Edinburgh, lecture series 93
Edinburgh Magazine and Review 154, 160
Edinburgh Review 409, 567
Edinburgh University 157, 158
education 628
  Charter School system 532, 535, 538, 539–40, 542–3, 544, 545
  in Ireland 172, 173, 180
  lecture series and 83–5, 91
  National Society 357–8, 365–8, 369–70
  Quaker programme of 110, 173
  sermons for families 128
  in Wales 187
Education Act (1870) 360
Edward VII, King 349
Edwards, Jonathan 361–2, 516
Edwards, Thomas Charles 210–11
Edwin, Lady Charlotte 189, 190
Egerton, John 47, 59, 306, 501
election day sermons 514, 516
Elias, John 206, 207–8
Elias, Norbert 550
Eliot, George 604
  Adam Bede 596, 603–4, 605, 606, 628
  Felix Holt 588
  Middlemarch 63
  'Silly Novels by Lady Novelists' 603, 605
Ellegård, Henrik Alvar 445
Ellesby, James 324
Ellison, Robert H. 68, 77, 549, 571, 594, 618
Emerson, Ralph Waldo 83
emotionalism 50, 51, 87, 90, 123, 326, 551, 599
  Catholicism and 140–1, 142, 144, 147–8
  Evangelicalism and 16, 119–20, 408, 411
  George Whitefield and 402
  poetic 569, 571, 573, 574–5
  sympathetic 585
  Ullathorne and 523
endowment sermons 186
Enfield, William 22, 447, 452
English, William Watson 447
Enlightenment 56–7, 232, 234, 235, 236, 239, 242, 246, 358, 392–5, 485, 580
episcopacy 240, 307–10, 312, 314–16, 416, *see also* bishops

Episcopalians 153, 165, 281, 350
Erastianism 294, 308, 399, 403, 499
Erskine, Ebenezer 164
Erskine, John 160, 161, 163, 516
Erskine, Ralph 164
eternal damnation 55, 76, 433, 464, 468, 469, 471, 473
Etherington, N. 515
Eucharist 295, 296, 414, 420, 439
eulogies 51, 145, 440
eulogistic sermons 41, 193, 284, 350
Evangelical Revival 139, 142, 191, 192, 202, 204–5, 378, 406, 497, 516
evangelicalism 3, 4, 6, 114–16, 375–6
    Anglican 120–32, 340, 344
    anti-slave trade 285
    Calvinism and 203–4, 206
    criticisms of 411
    emotionalism 16, 119–20, 408, 411
    extempore preaching 16
    extreme preachers 11
    first bishop 499
    funeral sermons 340, 343, 348
    in Gaelic 538–41, 544
    interpretation of Scriptures 411
    in Ireland 172, 177
    lampooned 25, 206, 402
    millennial sermons 377–81
    and the Oxford Movement 407, 408, 410–11, 413, 417, 418
    poetry and 567
    preachers 59, 120–6, 128, 132
    preaching of the Word 410
    Quakers and 109, 112
    religious lectures 80
    repentance and 386
    in Scotland 153, 154, 158, 164–5, 166
    Simeon's *Horae Homiletica* 22
    village sermons 65
    visitation sermons 293
    in Wales 195, 196, 201:
      see also Whitefield, George; Wesley; John
Evangelicalism and Fundamentalism in Britain Network project 115
Evans, Christmas 205, 206–7
Evans, Eifion 191
Evans, James Harington 343, 345

Evans, Lllewelyn Ioan 208
Evans, Thomas 57, 110
evolution 445, 453, 456, 459
Ewer, John 183, 186
excommunication 464–5
Exeter Hall lectures (London) 5, 19, 85–6, 87, 92
existence of God 392, 448, 452, 457, 458
extempore preaching 13–14, 16, 116, 119, 142, 148, 424, 621
    Continental 412
    English Evangelicals 516–17
    Scottish Evangelicals 153, 155, 164
    Welsh Evangelicals 195

Faber, F. W. 433, 434, 436, 437, 569
Faber, William Frederick 144, 148, 149
Fabricius, Philip 515
Faithful, Emily 87
family sermons 128, 620
famine 146, 555, 560
farewell sermons 40–1
Farnham, Lord 178–9
Farningham, Marianne (Mary Anne Hearne) 87
Farquhar, John 154
fast-day sermons 49–50, 51, 139, 140, 241, 245, 246, 276, 280–2, 454, 520, 523, 525
Fawcett, Benjamin 326
Fell, Margaret 98
Fénélon, François 158, 160
Fenn, Roy 190
Fielding, Henry 362
    Joseph Andrews 20
    Tom Jones 12
Finkelstein, Lydia von 87–8
Finland 236
Fisher, John 122
Fitch, Charles 376
Flaxman, John 128
Fleetwood, William 187–8, 316
Fleming, James 349
Fletcher, John 119, 120, 141–2
Fletcher, Philip 488
Fleury, André Hercule de 137
Folds, James 24

Ford, David 386
Fordyce, David 160
Fordyce, James 16, 17, 160, 616
Forster, Nicholas 266
Fortnightly Review 611
Fothergill, Samuel 14, 107, 108, 112
Fox, Charles James 140
Fox, George 97, 99, 509
Fox, W. J. 83, 84
Foy, Nathanael 542
Frampton, Robert 294
France 268–9, 270, 280, 282, 500; *see also* French Revolution
  sermons 137, 138, 139, 141, 144, 158, 160
Francis, Enoch 201, 202–3
Franklin, Benjamin 18, 117, 395
Fraser, Thomas McKenzie 523
Fraser, William 40
Free Church of Scotland 165–6
free-thinking 137, 138, 393, 395, 396, 582
Freeman's Journal 77
Freemasons 186–7
French Revolution 138, 140, 171, 174, 234, 235, 241, 242–3, 277, 281–4, 285–6, 308, 312, 316, 383, 415, 587
French Revolutionary War (1792–1802) 270, 280, 282
Frewen, John 55
Frewen, Thomas 58
Friedman, T. 115
Froude, J. A. 411, 423, 614
Froude, Richard Hurrell 406, 587
Fry, Elizabeth 110
Fuller, M. J. 439
fund-raising sermons:
  benefit sermons 163
  charities 532, 583
  charity schools 363, 481
  controversial sermons 181
  and Indian Mutiny 554
  lecture series 93
  printed sermons 24, 41, 141, 146, 186, 216, 219–20, 627
funeral sermons 13, 15, 17, 41, 51, 125, 145, 148, 276, 284
  afterlife 348–9
  anonymous 323–4
  biographical and spiritual narratives 326–8, 331
  clergy and wives 325–6, 328–9, 340, 617
  deathbed scenes in 326–7, 345–7
  decorous language of 330–1
  end of Victorian era 349–50
  exemplary lives 340–1, 343–5, 617
  form and structure 341–2
  hypocrisy and flattery in 333–4
  for murder victims 324
  for national figures 340, 344–5, 346
  praise and deference in 325, 332
  Protestant 322–35, 532
  quantifying 325
  Victorian 338–50
  for women 340, 343–4, 617, 628
Furniss, Harry 89

Gaelic language 161–2
Gahan, William 140
Gainsborough, Baptist Noel, fourth Earl of 332
Gallagher, James 138, 519
Galton, Francis 612, 614
Gandolphy, Peter 141, 142
Garbett, Edward 448
Garbett, Thomas 361
Gardiner, Colonel 254, 256
Garibaldi, Giuseppe 85
Garrett, Charles 92
Garrick, David 17
Gavazzi, Alessandro 84
Geddes, Alexander 139–40
Gentili, Luigi 146, 147
Gentleman's Magazine 278
geology 453, 457, 459, 467, 614
George, William 490, 498
George I, King 217, 218, 240, 256, 264, 314
George II, King 35, 254, 256, 481
George III, King 138, 241, 242, 279, 281, 399
  and bishops 314, 317
  funeral sermons 339, 340
  idealization of 284
  illness and recovery of 50, 276, 279
Gerard, Alexander 159, 163
Gerbet, Philippe-Olympe 144

Gibbon, Edward 312, 492, 587
Gibbons, Orlando 221
Gibbs, James 579
Gibson, Edmund 14, 250, 291, 307, 309, 310, 316
Gibson, William 122, 378, 612, 618, 619
Giffard, Bonaventure 137
Gilbert, John 307, 312
Gilfillan, George 86
Gill, Linda 612, 614
Gillespie, Raymond 531
Gillis, James 145
Gilpin, Richard 322
Gilpin, William 48, 55
Girdlstone, Charles 23
Gisborne, Thomas 401
Gladstone, William 93, 340, 345, 346, 360
Glasgow 19, 85
Glasgow University 156–7
Glorious Revolution (1688–9) 3, 9, 34, 136, 231, 233, 237, 242, 245, 269, 315, 393, 510, 532
Gloucester, diocese of 215, 217, 218, 219
Gloucester Journal 219
Godman, Henry 326
Good Friday sermons 73, 138, 281
Goodacre, R. H. 619–20
Goodwin, Harvey 69–70, 71, 72
Gordon, Captain James Edward 177
Gordon, General 340, 345
Gordon, Sir Adam 50
Gordon Riots (1780) 139, 255
Gother, John 137
Gothic Revival 579–91, 615, 619
Gouge, Thomas 329, 330, 331
Gough, John B. 86
Goulburn, Edward Meyrick 407
Grace, John 290
Graham, John 341
Grant, Anthony 558
Grant, Brewin 84, 90
Gravel Lane Dissenting charity school 357, 359, 360–1, 362–4, 368, 369, 370
Graves, Richard 17, 402
Gray, Robertx 4645
Great Awakening (1730s) 185, 514
Great Exhibition (1851) 67, 455, 614

Great Ulster Rebellion (1641) 173
Green, J. R. 464
Green, John 306, 307, 313
Gregg, John 179
Gregory, Jeremy 390
Gregory XVI, Pope 146
Grellet, Stephen 110, 111
Gresley, Frances Mary 343
Gresley, William 70, 71, 75–6, 410, 411, 413, 416, 421
Grey, Earl 452
Griffith, John 196, 559
Griffith, Morgan 201
Griffith, Thomas 619
Griffiths, John 195
Grisdale, Dr B. 314, 316
Grotius, Hugo 54
Grou, Jean 140
Grubb, Sarah 110
Gunpowder Plot (1605) 233, 242, 275
Gurdon, Brampton 312
Gurney, Joseph John 109, 110, 111, 112
Gustafson, S. 516
Gustav III, King 235
Guthrie, Thomas 80, 166
Guthrie, William 139, 162
Guttridge, Joseph 84

Haldane, Robert and James 166
Hall, Charles Henry 306, 309
Hall, Henry (the Younger) 217
Hall, John 107
Hall, Peter 617
Hall, Timothy 517
Hall, William 136
Halley, Robert 81, 82
Ham, Robert 291
Hamilton, Walter Kerr 345, 411
Hamilton, William 520, 523, 524–5, 541
Hammond, Heyden 583
Hammond, Joseph 341
Hampden, Renn Dickson 590
Handel, George Frideric 128, 220, 221
Hanovarians 230–1, 233, 236, 239–40, 247, 252, 256–7, 264, 316, 318, 499, 538, *see also* George I; George II; George III

Harbin, Charles 41
Hardwick, Charles 68
Hardwicke, Lord 250
Hardy, Thomas, *Jude the Obsure* 605–6
Hare, Francis 309, 310, 490
Hare, Julius 587
Hargraves, James 316
Harley, Edward 221
Harper, William 616
Harris, Howell 185, 189, 191–2, 204, 205
Harrison, Benjamin 343
Harrison, Joseph 332
Harrison, Richard 10, 277
Harry, Miles 201, 203
Harvest, G. 246
Hassall, Rowland 521
Hastwell, Anthony 391
Hatherell, James 386
Haweis, Hugh R. 86, 94, 566–7
Haweis, Thomas 13, 126, 132
Hawker, R. S. 569
Hawkins, Edward 588–9, 590
Hawksmoor, Nicholas 579
Hay, George 139
Hayley, Thomas 36, 498
Hayter, Thomas 491
Hayton, David 542
Head, F. W. 570
Headlam, Stewart 89
Hendren, W. J. 428
Henslow, George 459, 614
Henslowe, William Henry 367
Herbert, E. J. 429
Herbert, George 567
Herder, Johann Gottfried 586, 587
Hereford, diocese of 215, 216, 217, 218, 219
Herring, George 409
Herring, Thomas 250, 255, 306, 489
Hervey, James 13, 123–5, 127, 132, 293
Heurtley, Charles 65, 67, 71, 76, 77
Hewitt, Martin 612
Hewlett, John 55
Hewson, William 192
Heylyn, John 313
Heywood, Oliver 326
Hicks, Elias 110
Hicksite Separation (1827) 108, 109, 110, 111

High Calvinism 202–3, 206
High Churchmen 65, 217–19, 221, 237, 239, 282, 283, 285, 292, 297, 310, 340, 391, 401, 407, 411, 536–7, 540, 542, 569, 582; *see also* Anglicanism; Church of England
Hill, George 155
Hills, Henry 21
Hinchliffe, John 306
Hindmarsh, D. Bruce 327, 375
Hine, William 217
historical lives, sermons and lectures on 42, 91
historicism 581–2
history 99, 586–91, 595
Hoadlians 398–9
Hoadly, Benjamin 21, 22, 36, 41, 218, 240, 277, 291, 293, 294, 295, 306, 316, 393, 398, 401, 499, 628
Hoadly, John 306, 307, 316
Hocking, Silas 80, 91–2
Hodge, John 363
Hodges, Abraham 107
Hogarth, William 11, 24
Hohenhohe, Prince 175
Holcroft, Francis 328–9
Holden, Lawrence 39
Holland, Henry Scott 82, 93–4
Holland, William 25
Home and Colonial School Society 369
homilies 7, 126, 140, 142, 183, 185, 256, 550, 583, 596, 599
Hood, Edwin Paxton 85, 86
Hood, Paxton 94
Hook, Walter 81
Hooper, John 380, 385
Hopkins, Ellice 87
Hopkins, Gerard Manley 568, 569
Hopps, John Page 33, 459
Hoppus, John 619
Horne, George 279, 309
Horneck, Anthony 315
Horrocks, Jeremiah 455
Horsley, Samuel 11, 277, 283, 284, 308, 390
Hort, F. J. A. 65, 69, 72–3, 75, 76
Horton, R. F. 91
hospital sermons 4, 10
hospitals 7, 10, 18, 67, 186, 359, 483

Houlbrooke, Ralph 333
House of Commons/House of Lords 11, 241–2, 242–3, 534, 535, 536, 538, 538; *see also* parliamentary sermons
Howard, Robert 488, 535
Howe, John 324
Howie, John 165
Howland, Elizabeth 628
Hughes, Hugh Price 91
Hughes, John 181
Hughes, Joshua 193
Hughes, Rice 281
Hughes, Thomas 604
Humboldt, Alexander von 457
Hume, David 312, 400, 401, 492, 614
humour in sermons 38, 49, 86, 88, 118, 207, 397
Hunter, Henry 284
Huntingdon, Selina, Countess of 119, 126, 189, 276, 323, 386, 617
Huntingford, George 359
Hurd, Richard 15, 280, 399
Hurrell, Betsy 120
Hurrion, John 359
Hussey, Thomas 140–1
Hutcheson, Frances 156–7
Hutchinson, Francis 535, 538, 540
Hutton, Matthew 491
Huxley, Thomas 89, 628
Hylson-Smith, Kenneth 115
hymns 15, 65, 222, 224, 554, 567, 576, 604
hypocrisy 74, 177, 333, 334, 534, 599–602

ideology and Victorian novels 595–605
idolatry 439, 486, 487, 491, 558, 559
Ihalainen, Parsi 255
imperialism 254, 269, 481–93, 549
impromptu preaching *see* extempore preaching
Incorporated Society for Promoting English Protestant Working Schools in Ireland, *see* Charter School system
Independents 203, 205, 206, 208–9, 210, 330
India 366, 517
 church attendance 515
 missionaries in 549, 553–7, 560
Indian Mutiny (1857) 517, 554–5, 556, 560, 613

individualism 441, 595
Industrial Revolution 614
industrialization 146, 192, 210, 594, 595
Inglis, Ken 526
Inglis, Sir Robert 343
Ippel, Henry 280
Ireland 34, 137, 169–81, 435, 437–8, 613
 Act of Union 171, 173
 Catholic Relief Acts 138
 Catholic sermons 138, 140, 141, 143, 144
 charity schools/charter system 481–9, 492, 532, 533, 535, 538, 539–45, 542
 education of the poor 172–3
 evangelizing in 538–41
 famine in 181
 Jacobite uprising in 245
 Magee's sermon 170–1, 173–4
 migration from 143, 145, 181, 437
 mission sermons 613
 nationalism in 145, 173
 parliament in 537–8
 preaching tours in 179
 Second Reformation crusade (1827) 178–9
 sectarian controversy in 173–81
 socio-economic reform in 534–5
 visitation sermons in 293, *see also* Church of Ireland; Catholics/Catholicism
Irish Church Temporalities Act (1833) 431
Irving, Edward 131–2, 374, 375, 376, 377, 380–2, 384, 385, 559
Isham, Zacheus 308, 309, 310
Islam 145, 626, 627
Israel 384, 503
Italy 146, 436
itinerant preachers/lecturers 84–5, 92–3, 119–20, 137
 Dissenting 276
 George Whitefield as 117, 516, 517
 Italian 146–7
 Methodist 340
 Quaker 105, 106
 in Wales 207–8

Jackson, John 292, 394
Jackson, William Walrond 39, 69, 74–5, 307, 318

Jacob, Joseph 265, 329
Jacob, W. M. 114–15, 318
Jacobite rebellions 9, 34, 166, 245–6
   (1715) 247, 248, 255, 293, 535, 536
   (1745) 247–53, 255, 256, 265, 293–4, 535
Jacobitism 136, 230, 266, 268, 531, 532, 538,
   544, 613
Jago, John 17
James, John Angell 79, 80, 343
James II, King 136, 137, 188, 255, 266, 315
Jarrold, Hannah 325
Jebb, John 176
Jefferson, Thomas 395–6
Jeffreys, John 341
Jenkins, Geraint 185, 188–9
Jenkins, John 201–2
Jenkinson, John 359
Jenner, Charles 306
Jennings, David 323
Jenyns, Soame 400
'jeremiad' sermons 516
Jerram, Charles 81–2
Jervis, Thomas 364
Jesuits 311, 376, 378
Jewish sermons 339, 350, 520
Jews 379, 487, 490–1, 500, 506, 626, 628
John, G. 559
Johns, B. G. 23
Johnson, Joseph 278
Johnson, Richard 519, 520, 521, 523–4
Johnson, Samuel 16, 20, 162, 275, 394, 402, 403, 580
Jones, Ann 110
Jones, David 189, 191, 204, 282, 323
Jones, Edmund 203
Jones, Griffith 184–5, 186, 189, 200
Jones, Henry 183d
Jones, J. Puleston 210
Jones, John 207
Jones, R. Tudur 206, 209, 211–12
Jones, Sybil 110, 111
Jones, Thomas 24, 208
Jortin, John 306, 519
Jowett, Benjamin 42, 464, 470–4, 575, 603
Jowett, Joseph 40, 616
Joyce, James, *Portrait of an Artist* 607
Judaism 626
Juxon, William 305

Keats, John 580
Keble, John 65, 408, 419, 421, 566
   assize sermon (1833) 409, 413, 414–15, 568,
     587, 588
   extempore preaching by 412
   Lenten sermons by 420
   and poetry 566, 567–8, 570–1, 573,
     590, 591
Keene, Edmund 306
Keith, George Skene 159, 265
Ken, Thomas 13
Kennard, Robert 474
Kennedy, James Houghton 447
Kennett, White 238, 299, 306, 307, 309,
   310–11, 332–4, 501, 508
Kennicott, Benjamin 583
Kenrick, Timothy 282
Ker, Ian 421, 422
Ker, John 164
Kerrich, C. 256
Kidd, Benjamin 107
Kilborn, Robert 309–10
Kilde, Jeanne Halgren 115
Killingbeck, John 291
Kincaid, Alexander 163
King, William 540
Kingsley, Alton, *Alton Locke* 614
Kingsley, Charles 38, 41, 423
   educational lectures 83–4
   Hypatia 605
   income from printed sermons 627
   natural theology 453–5, 457–8
   as poet-preacher 570, 575–7
   A Saint's Tragedy 565, 566
   Town and Country Sermons 68
   village sermons 65
   village welfare schemes 67
Kingsley, Fanny 38
Kippis, Andrew 364
Kirby, Mary 107
Kirwan, Walter Blake 180
Knight, Frances 614
Knight, George R. 374
Knight, Samuel 306
Knopwood, Robert 521
Knox, Vicesimus 403
Kuenen, Abraham 470

Lackington, James 163
Lacroix de Ravignan, Gustave 143
Lacunza, Manuel 376
Laird, Macgregor 552
Lake, Dean 92
Lake, John Neal 155
Lakoff, George and Johnson, Mark 102
Lamarck, Jean-Baptiste 456
Lamplugh, Thomas 315
Lancaster, Joseph 366
Lancaster, Peter 56
Lanchester, Lydia 107
Landels, William 86, 92
Landon, W. 367
Lang, John Dunmore 523, 525
Lankester, Edwin 86
lantern displays 84, 90
Laqueur, Thomas 333
Larkin, Emmet 180
Larsen, Timothy 614
Larson, Rebecca 106
Latham, John 54
Latimer, Hugh 87, 430
Latitudinarians 58, 137, 275, 277, 284, 285, 294, 310, 393–4, 398, 399, 516, 540; *see also* Tillotson, John; Broad Church
Laud, William 54, 305
Lavington, George 222, 223
Law, John 306
lay preachers/sermons 6, 115, 118, 119, 191, 204, 276, 588, 625–6, 628
Layard, Charles Peter 308, 313
Le Jeune, Jean 137
Leach, Charles 89
Leach, John 184
lectures 7, 79–94, 178, 447, 566, 612
  catechetical 55, 81
  Catholic 143
  church extension and home mission 89–91
  education and 83–5, 91
  intellectual impact of 93
  on natural theology 447
  'phantom sermons' 620
  printed 88, 92
  religious 79–94, 125
  science and religion 452
  on sermon composition 157–9

  significance of 91–4
  Sunday afternoon 88–9, 91, 92
  Sunday evening 80–1, 82, 83, 89, 90, 92
  YMCA (Young Men's Christian Association) 85–8, 92
Lee, Dowden 41
Leechman, William 154, 157, 161
Leeds 17, 18, 19, 41, 83, 93
Lees, James Cameron 155
Lees, Sir Harcourt 173
Legge, James 558
Leighton, Robert 153
Leland, John 396–7, 400, 401
Lenoir, P. V. 284
Lenten lectures and sermons 76, 81, 82, 97, 137, 276, 420, 619–20
Lenton, John 115, 120
Leo XII, Pope 142
Letchworth, Thomas 107
Letsom, Sampson 21
Letsome, J. 8
Lewis, Edward 246
Lewis, George 200
Lewis, Howell Elvet 211
Liberation Society lectures 84
libraries 20, 26, 67, 107–8, 110, 249, 278, 622
Liddon, Henry Parry 41, 343, 345, 409, 411, 423–4, 587
Lightfoot 42
Liguori, Alphonsus 143, 149
Lincoln's Inn, London 13, 139
Lindsay, Thomas 542
Lindsey, Theophilus 277–8
Linneaus, Carl 34
Lisbon earthquake (1755) 20, 124
Lisle, Samuel 307, 312, 490
Littell, Thomas 292
Liverpool 88, 111
Lloyd, Charles 411, 499
Lloyd, David 18
Lloyd, Humphrey 188
Lloyd, John 392
Lloyd, Robert 187
Lobb, Stephen 330
Locke, John 239, 267, 393, 395, 396, 401
Lombe, Sir John 18
London:

anti-Jacobite sermons in 248–9
anti-ritualist disturbances in 13, 80
auditory churches in 18, 19
bishops of 499
Catholic sermons in 137, 139, 140, 146
charity schools in 357
charity sermons in 186
City of 501
Corporation of the Sons of the Clergy 216, 217–18, 220, 221
Dissenting community in 330–1
earthquake (1750) 20
embassy chapel sermons in 136, 137, 140, 141, 142
Evangelical centres in 130
fashionable preachers in 10, 19, 22, 24
Gordon Riots in 255
Great Exhibition (1851) in 67, 455, 614
'hospital Sunday' sermons 4
Hyde Park sermons 17–18
lecture series in 11, 80, 81, 82, 83, 84, 89, 90, 91, 125, 126
published guides on preachers in 22
Sacheverell sermon and trial (1709) 5, 6, 8, 24, 233, 239, 277
sermon publishers in 21, 32, 33, 249–50, 339
town sermons in 68
YMCA lectures in 85
London City Mission 92
London Female Mission 617
London Missionary Society 130, 276, 521, 551, 557, 558
Longe, John 14–15, 54–5, 290
Longfellow, Henry Wadsworth 567, 576
Lord's Prayer 107, 111
Lort, Michael 306
Losh, James 277
Louis XIV, King 139
Louis XVI, King 140, 283, 284
Louise Marie, Princess 138
Low Churchmen 297, 393, 398, 521, 533, 535–7, 540, 541
Lowth, Robert 481–2, 499, 583, 585, 589
loyal sermons 140, 251–7, 265, 281–2, 282, 284
loyalty 138, 141, 144
Lucas, Richard 187

Lyell, Charles 453, 455, 457, 467, 614
Lynegar, Charles 539
Lyng, William 39–40
Lyttelton, Charles 306, 309, 310

Macarness, J. F. 431
McCheyne, Robert Murray 519
McCree, George W. 85, 90
McCullough, Peter 33
McGhee, Robert 179
McGill, William 154–5
MacHale, John 173
Mackenzie, Peter 82, 83, 93
Mackerness, E. H. 570, 574
MacLaren, Alexander 42, 615, 618–19
MacLeod, Norman 166
McNabb, Vincent 350
McNeile, Hugh 181, 455–6
Macrae, David 86
Madan, Martin 10, 316
Madan, Spencer 306
Madras system 366, 369
Magee, William 170–1, 173–4, 178, 181
Maguire, Thomas 178
Manchester 144
    Catholic preachers 143
    Catholic sermons 145–6
    lecture series in 81, 82, 88, 89
Manlove, Timothy 322
Manning, Henry Edward 412, 432, 433, 436, 440, 441, 620
Manning, Robert 137
Mansel, Henry 343
Mant, Richard 451, 452, 454
manuscript sermons 7, 14, 15, 22–3, 48, 49, 163, 620–1
    bequeathed 277–8
    Catholic 143, 145
    paucity of 47–8
    Puritan 514
    Quaker 100, 109–10
    references and notations 53, 54
    sources 54–5, 71
    Welsh parochial 188
Mardon, Benjamin 348
Marie Antoinette, Queen 140

Markham, William 281, 307, 310, 318, 498
Marriott, Charles 412, 418
Marsden, Samuel 521
Marsh, Herbert 359, 367
Marsh, James 586, 587
Marsh, Narcissus 539
Marshall, Charles 99, 100
Martin, Samuel 347
Martineau, James 37, 475
martyrdom 233, 234, 241, 282, 435, 555
martyrology 256, 326
Marx, Karl 181
Mary II, Queen 11, 13, 24, 35, 231, 237–8, 267, 323, 617
Mary of Modena, Queen 136
Massillon, Jean Baptiste 140, 141, 519
Masson, David 93
Master and Servants Acts (1747) 361
Mather, Cotton 509
Mathew, Theobald 146
Matthews, Edward 207, 209
Maude, Francis 344
Maule, Henry 486
Maule, John 281
Maurice, Edward 538
Maurice, F. D. 65, 76, 92, 566, 575
Mawson, Matthias 312
Maynooth grant (1844) 181
Mayo, Charles and Elizabeth 369
Mayo, Richard 308
Mead, Matthew 328, 330
Meany, John 143
memento mori 51
Mendelson, Dorothea 581
Menzies, Robert 139
Merewether, Frances 367
metaphors 522, 590
   Baptists 206
   Catholic Restoration 432, 433
   Quaker 102, 103, 108, 111, 112
Methodism 11, 48, 120, 126, 190, 279, 282, 508
   in *Adam Bede* 604, 605
   anti-slave trade and 285
   in Australian colony 521
   criticism of 313
   female preachers 616
   field preaching 5
   in Ireland 172
   lampooned 25, 206
   lay preachers 6, 115, 119
   lecture culture in 82, 86
   preachers 59, 616
   schism within 114
   in Scotland 164
   secession 192
   in Wales 204–5
   Wesley's guidance on preaching 17
Middleton, Conyers 400
Miley, Dr 145
millenarianism 285–6, 503
millennial sermons 386–7
   apocalyptic imagery in 381–3
   conversion and 377–81
   printed sermons 376–7
   social unrest and 383–6
Miller, John C. 86
Miller, Perry 514, 516
Miller, William 374
Millerites 374, 375, 376
Mills, Benjamin 324
Milne, Colin 24
Milner, John 141, 142, 147, 265, 284
Milton, John 576
Milton, William 40–1
Milway, Thomas 328
miracles 12, 146, 175, 399–401, 450, 468, 506
missionaries/mission sermons 4, 7, 34, 510–11, 513, 518, 548–61, 553–60, 613, 624
   in Africa 549, 552–3
   in Australia 521
   Catholic 137
   Catholic/Anglican rivalry 503, 508
   in China 549, 557–60
   elaborated 507–10
   evangelical societies 129–30
   at home 89–90, 146–7
   in India 515, 549, 553–7
   in Ireland 180
   Italian 143
   New Testament interpretation 504–7
   Old Testament interpretation 499–504
   preachers 498–9
   training programme for 129; *see also* SPCK; SPG

missionary societies 127, 128, 129, 130, 132, 276, 377, 508, 521, 551, 552, 553, 557, 558, 617
Mitchell, Moses 183
Molesworth, Lord 156
monarchy:
    Catholic allegiance to 535, 537
    episcopacy and 314
    religious authority and 239, 241, 242, 252, 279, 283, 532
    royal propaganda 230-1, 232
    secularization of 234-5
Monro, Edward 416
Montgomery, Robert 569
Monthly Review 5, 20, 154, 278
Moore, James 446
Moore, John 507
Moore, Mary 107
moral agency system 178-9
moral conduct 85, 101, 156, 158, 238, 279
moral reform 246, 281, 501, 523-5, 534, 542-3
More, Hannah 120
More, James 625
Morell, Thomas 224
Morgan, D. Densil 196, 616
Morgan, Frank 196-7
Morgan, William Leigh 194
Morony, Joseph 140
Morris, Joseph 459
Morris, T. M. 42
Moss, Charles 306, 491
Moysey, Charles Abel, archdeacon of Bath 369-70
Müller, Friedrich Max 89, 447
Munro, Edward 13
Murphy, William 84
Murray, Andrew 517
Murray, James 13, 164
Murray, John 31
Mursell, Arthur 88, 89, 96
music for worship 220-5, *see also* hymns
music hall venues 5, 19, 195
mysticism 144, 148, 175, 402, 419, 579, 591

Nagle, Nano 172
Napoleonic Wars 383-4
Natal Sermons 463-76, 517

national education 357-70, 615
National Society for Promoting the Education of the Poor in the Principles of the Established Church 357-8, 365-8, 369-70
nationalism 145, 173, 234, 235, 384
native Americans 484, 489, 490, 491-2, 506, 507, 510-11, 518
natural disasters 20, 37, 50, 124, 453-4, 455, 523
natural history 485, 490
natural selection 459
natural theology 401, 450-60
    books published on 447
    Chinese 558
    Darwin and 456
    sermons by William Paley 444-5, 446, 448-50
    study of 447-8
naval sermons 4, 279-80, 451, 457-8
Neale, J. M. 417
Nelson, Admiral Horatio 271, 280
Nelson, Robert 275
Nesbit, E. 581-2
Nesbitt, John 329-30, 331
New, Melvyn 583
New England 514, 516
Newcastle-upon-Tyne (Northumberland) 147, 277
Newcome, Henry 15
Newcome, Richard 491
Newcome, William 534
Newhouse, Thomas 47
Newman, John Henry 37, 41, 147, 148-9, 421-3, 430, 434, 566, 573, 587, 588, 622
    Apologia Pro Vita Sua 407, 408, 411, 423, 568, 605
    Christ upon the Waters 148, 149, 432
    destabilization of social order 433, 595
    novels 605, 614
    and Oxford Movement 406, 409, 410, 413, 414, 415, 416, 418
    as poet-preacher 569-72, 576, 577, 590, 591
    on tradition 589
Newman, Thomas 265, 408
Newport, Kenneth 567-8
newspapers:

advertisements 23, 278, 415
Irish 'Bible War' 177–8
lectures 92
sermon critique 193, 194, 521–2
Newton, Benjamin 306
Newton, Isaac 392, 395, 396
Newton, John 11, 128, 223, 224, 279, 285
Newton, Thomas 307, 310
Nicene Creed 183
Nicholson, William 310
Niebuhr, Barthold Georg 587
Nockles, Peter 407–8, 423
Noel, Gerald 10
Noel, Wriothesley Baptist 177, 348
Nonconformists 237
   chapels with two pulpits 19
   clerical training 588
   funeral sermons 340, 344, 350
   lectures 85
   relationship with other churches 438–9
   village sermons 65
   in Wales 205–6, 211
Norfolk, Duke of 137
North British Review 565
note-taking 3, 12, 32, 41, 108, 116, 126, 140, 412, 627, *see also* shorthand notes
novels 5, 6, 26, 614
   Gothic 579, 580, 581, 583
   religious history 614
   and sermons 594–607, 612, 628
Nowell, Thomas 241–2, 277
Numa Pompilius 54

Oakes, John 13
O'Beirne, Thomas Lewis 180
O'Bryan, Catherine 348
occasional sermons 7, 9, 35–8, 514
   Australian colonies 520
   Catholic 148
   Church of Ireland 531–2
   for families 128
   gardening 616
   memorialization 40–1
   Scotland 163–4
   timing crucial for publication 251, *see also* anniversary sermons; assize sermons; charity sermons; consecrations sermons; court sermons; funeral sermons; parliamentary sermons; thanksgiving sermons; visitation sermons; university sermons
Occom, Samson 518
O'Connell, Daniel 144, 145, 176, 177, 178, 179
O'Donnell, M. 437–8
Old, H. O. 514
Oldershaw, John 308, 313
O'Leary, Arthur 140
Oliphant, Margaret 570, 572, 577
Oliver, Kelly 115
Oliver, Robert 291–2
Ollivant, Alfred 193
Opium Wars 560
ordination 17, 98, 105, 130, 142, 424
Osbaldeston, Richard 499
O'Sullivan, Mortimer 179
Ott, John Henry 54
Ottley, Adam 200
Ottoman Empire 384–5, 386
outdoor sermons 5, 19
   Catholic Revival 146
   sectarian lecturers 84
   vocal projection 17–18, 19, 117
   Wales 195
Owen, David 206
Owenism 81
Owst, Gerald 33
Oxford and Mortimer, Robert Harley, Earl of 217
Oxford Dictionary of National Biography 65
Oxford Movement, *see* Tractarians
Oxford University 218, 251, 291
   Balliol College 54, 471, 473, 474
   Bodleian Library 622
   Christ Church 306, 318, 414, 453
   Keble College 196, 582
   Lincoln College 123
   Pusey's sermon 414
   struggle over Catholic Emancipation 409
Oxnam, William 368

pacifism 101, 282
Paddley, Benjamina 107
Padley, Kenneth 188, 192

Page, Jesse 552
Paget, Francis 407, 411, 412, 416, 417–18, 418
Paine, Thomas 174, 175, 282, 586, 587
Palestine 384
Paley, William 39, 306, 309, 317, 318, 401–2, 622
   Feathers Tavern petition 312–13
   natural theology 444–5, 446, 448–50
   watch and watchmaker analogy 444, 450
Palfrey, John Gorham 447
Palmerston, Lord 340, 454
pamphlets 33, 88, 92, 143, 174–5, 178, 232–3, 249, 378, 618
panegyrics 42, 136, 137, 140, 145, 159, 283, 334, 341
papacy 145, 430–1, 434, 435, 436, 440–1, 535, 595
'Papal Aggression' controversy 428, 430, 434, 438–9, 442
papal infallibility 180
parish preaching 4, 8, 614
   anti-Jacobite sermons 248
   Catholic sermons 142
   delivery style of 59
   in Ireland 138, 140
   Irish religious orders 180
   long eighteenth century 47–60
   printed sermons 63–77, 163
   religious lectures 80–1
   rotated/recycled sermons 53–4
   Samuel Walker and 122
   themes in 54–9
   Tractarian 412, 415–21
   in Wales 183–5
Parker (publisher) 414
Parker, Joseph 92, 93
Parker, Theodore 475
Parker, William 223, 306, 309–10, 313
parliamentary sermons 231, 233–6, 238, 239, 241–3, 252, 267, 277, 281, 282, 534, 535, 538
Parochial Mission Women Association 617
parodies 19, 24–5
Parsons, Joseph 15, 324
Particular Baptist Missionary Society 276
Patrick, Simon 263
patriotic sermons 139, 142, 145, 255, 280
Patristics 148, 397, 410, 418

Patterson, John 22
Pattison, Mark 14
Paul, Charles Kegan 474–5
Paul, Moses 518
Payton, Catharine 517
Paz, Dennis 84
Peach, Edward 141
Pearce, Zachary 306, 498
Pears, James 365
Pearse, Edward 327
Pearse, Mark Guy 87
Pearson, Samuel 93
Peckard, Peter 280, 285
Peden, Alexander 153, 164
Peel, Robert 340
Peisley, Mary 517
Penn, William 100, 101, 102, 103
Pennefather, William 90
Peploe, Samuel 247, 256, 307, 308
periodicals 54, 92, 278
Perrin, Sarah 120
Perronet, Vincent 122
Perry, Charles 521
Peterloo Massacre (1819) 143, 375
Petre, Lord 137
'phantom sermons' 620
Phelan, William 172
philanthropy 145, 171, 483
Philipps, John Henry 193
Philipps, Sir John 187
Phillips, Catherine 107
Phillips de Lisle, Ambrose March 345
philosophy 41, 155, 156, 157, 162, 176, 441, 567, 586, 589, 594, 619
pilgrimages 102, 108, 534
Pinamonti, Giovanni Pietro 137
Pink Dandelion, Ben 100, 104–5, 106, 109
Pitt, William (the Younger) 283
Pius IX, Pope 145, 428, 430, 435, 440
Pius VI, Pope 140, 383, 386
Plenderleath, David 160
Plowden, Charles 138
Pocock, J. G. A. 392
poet-preachers:
   Charles Kingsley 570, 575–7
   Frederick William Robertson 84, 566, 569, 570, 572–6, 577

John Henry Newman 569–72, 590
poetry 34, 565–77, 580, 590–1, 595, 600–1, 614
political sermons 34, 84, 163–4, 230, 231, 232–4, 279
　anti-Jacobite 245–57, 315–16, 358, 532, 613
　penetration into 'Bourgeois Public Sphere' 249
　secularization of 234, 235–6; *see also* parliamentary sermons
Pope, Alexander 576
Pope, Richard 178
Porter, Andrew 548
Porter, Jackson 367
Porter, Roy 392, 394
Porteus, Beilby 242, 276, 281, 499, 508, 509–10
Portugal 20, 124, 500
Postlethwayte, Matthew 14
Potter, Francis 294
Potter, John 15, 310
Poynter, William 141
prayers 12, 15, 107, 111, 185
preachers' guides and manuals 247
　Archdeacon Sharp's 298, 299
　The Preacher's Assistant 277
　on pulpit performance 17, 22, 516
　Quaker 98, 99–100
　sermon writing 21–2, 48–9, 157–61
　Tractarian 410, 416
　for village sermons 66–7, 69
preaching performances 3, 9–18
　adaptable 416
　of catechetical sermons 12
　Catholic preachers 139, 412
　clergy judged on 71
　critiques of 277
　disappointing 13
　dramatic and sensational 17, 87, 94, 139, 412
　elocution training for 142
　guides on 17, 22
　lampooned 569
　lectures and 88, 93
　length of 10–11, 116, 178, 377, 414, 424, 507
　marathon debates and 178
　memorized sermons 16
　Newman's 423
　parish preachers 59

popular/fashionable preachers 10–13, 19, 569
Quaker preachers 99
reading sermons *v.* extempore preaching 13–16
'showmanship' 190–1
spellbinding 195, 208, 402
Tractarians 148, 416
vocal projection 18, 194; *see also* spoken sermons
premillennialism 375, 381, 383, 385–6
Presbyterianism 152, 265, 316, 329, 330–1, 522, 534
　in Australia 523, 525
　in Ireland 179
　lectures on biblical history 81
Pretyman-Tomline, George 282, 283, 299
Price, Richard 242, 276, 277, 285–6, 316, 393
Priestley, Joseph 141, 278, 284, 285, 316, 393
Primitive Methodists 276
printed sermons 4, 14, 37, 616
　accuracy of 22, 32
　adaptability of 37
　advantages of 187
　anti-Jacobite sermons 245–57
　battlefield sermons 238
　of Benjamin Jowett 471–6
　Catholic sermons 136, 138–9, 141, 143–4, 145, 149
　charity-school sermons 363–70
　charity sermons 24, 41, 186, 484–93
　Church of Ireland 531–2, 540–1
　Church of Scotland 166
　colonial sermons 516, 518–26
　controversial 55, 178
　court sermons 136, 229, 231, 232–3, 237–41, 252
　Dissenters' 278
　drama criticism and 115, 623
　evangelical 116, 123
　explosion in numbers of 530–1
　of Frederick William Robertson 573
　funeral sermons 51, 276, 322–3, 338–50, 617
　in Gaelic 162
　growing importance of 33
　of Hugh Blair 162–4
　of John Wesley 119
　lampooned 25
　literary criticism of 570, 583

printed sermons (*cont.*)
  market penetration of 6, 9
  memorialization and 40–1, 276
  millennial sermons 376–7, 386
  mission sermons 499–511
  Natal Sermons 463–76
  parish sermons 63–77
  parliamentary sermons 231, 242, 252
  pedagogical use of 35, 40
  'phantom' 620
  prefaces to 32, 35, 38–40, 71, 121, 124, 140, 143–4, 163, 164, 251, 256, 291, 295, 306, 324, 326–8, 379–80, 384–5, 454, 464–5, 475, 484, 523, 553, 571, 616
  print runs of 278
  production of 627–8
  publishing industry and 20–1
  Puritan sermons 514
  purpose of 38–42, 38–43
  Quaker sermons 100, 106–7, 109–10
  quantifying 7–8, 621–2
  readership of 71–2
  relationship with spoken sermons 116, 154, 155, 187, 290, 550, 619–20
  requested by congregation 39–40
  revised and edited 619–20
  scholarship and 611
  Scottish 153–4, 161
  self-centred reasons for 41–2
  targeting of women 616–17
  thanksgiving sermons 261–71, 276
  topical sermons 9
  Tractarian sermons 410–24
  trade in faux sermons 22–3
  vernacular 540–1
  visitation sermons 290–1, 292, 294–9
  Welsh 205, 206, 207, 208, 209, 211
Proclamation Society 281
Procter, Henry 219
prophecy 399–400, 468, 471–2, 500, 506
prostitution 194, 281
Prowitt, Edward 277
public school sermons 68
Public Worship Regulation Act 569
publishers 278, 364, 447, 615, 627–8
  Australian colonies 519–20
  clergymen and 41–2

  provincial 250, 339
  sympathetic to Tractarians 414
  Verrall 31–3
Puckle, John 386
Pugh, Philip 203
Pugin, Augustus Welby Northmore 144, 581
Punshon, John 100, 105, 106, 109
Punshon, William Morley 86–7
Purcell, Henry 218, 220, 221
Puritans 103, 200, 204, 514, 522
  'jeremiad' sermons 516
  premillennialism 374
  religious lectures 80
  sermon note-taking 3, 12
Pusey, Edward Bouverie 10, 19, 406–7, 409, 410, 412, 413, 414, 416, 419, 420, 430, 587
Pyle, Edmund 21

Quakers 15, 112, 265, 509
  catechetical style 100, 103–4, 108
  diversity sermons 108–11
  Early Quietistic period sermons 97, 100–4
  education for the poor 110, 173
  Hicksite Separation (1827) 108, 109, 110, 111
  homiletic writing 98–100
  Later Quietistic period sermons 97, 104–8
  ministry hierarchy 105–6
  North American colonies 105, 517
  personal testimony 99, 104
  schism 108–9
  transatlantic community of 105
Quick, John 328, 330
Quietism 100–8, 109, 136

Radcliffe, Houstonne 311, 312, 314
Radstock, Lord 195
Rainy, Robert 153
Ramsay, James 164, 362
Rand, Samuel 51–3
Randolph, John 282, 306, 307, 317
rational sermons 390–403
  debate on miracles 399–400
  defenders of 396–8
  deism 394–6

Enlightenment and 392–4
Hoadleians and Warburtonians 398–9
Paley 401–2
rationalism 392–4, 441, 485, 490
Rawlins, John 224
Rawlinson, Richard 48
recycled sermons 14, 15, 36–7, 53, 137
Rees, Henry 209
Rees, Jacob 202
Rees, Lewis 203
Rees, Thomas 209–10
Reformation 240, 433–4, 482, 488, 505
regicide 231, 277, 283, 284, 532
relics 136, 430, 534
religious censuses 88, 437, 549
religious controversy 9, 35, 36, 55, 423, 441
    Antinomianism 330, 331, 375
    Bangorian Controversy 36, 230, 233, 240, 293, 398, 618, 627, 628
    Down-Grade controversy 36, 38
    Essays and Reviews 465, 471, 614
    funeral sermons 345
    in Ireland 170–1, 173–4
    Sacheverell sermon 5, 6, 8, 24, 233, 239, 277
    Tractarians and 413, 414, 415
    and 'Victorian crisis of faith' 465
    visitation sermons and 292, 293
religious conversion 74, 147, 148, 208, 385, 397, 411, 414, 591
    Catholic to Protestant 489, 533–44
    Chinese 559
    education and 532, 535, 538, 539–40, 542–3, 544, 545
    in fiction 600–1, 607
    millennial sermons 377–81
    Protestant to Catholic 430, 437, 439;
        see also missionaries/mission sermons
religious festivals 7, 49–50, 75, 76, 81, 138, 275
religious freedom 255, 282
religious orders 180, 503
religious tolerance 141, 142, 436, 438, 441, 555
Religious Tract Society 620
Religious Worship Act (1855) 88
Renaud, Daniel 53–4, 55, 56, 58, 59
Renaud, David 50, 53–4, 57, 58
repentance 37, 49, 50, 53, 56, 189, 246, 324, 368, 382, 386, 523, 524

republicanism 140, 239, 241, 282, 396
Restoration 13, 188, 249, 314–15
Restoration Day sermon (29 May 1660) 233, 239, 275, 532
rhetoric 77, 94, 116–19, 123, 127, 129, 131, 153, 157–8, 170, 174, 196, 252–6, 378, 385, 396, 412, 516, 534, 569, 571, 628
rhetorical questions 16, 124, 148, 283, 507, 553, 596, 597, 599
    Anglican evangelicalism 121–2, 124
    Newman 148
    Quakers 100, 103–4, 108, 111, 112
Rice, Edmund 172
Richards, Robert J. 445
Richards, William 185
Richardson, Charles 90
Richardson, John 534, 539–40, 541, 544
Ridley, Gloster 359
riots 84, 139, 255, 375
Ritualism 13, 80, 430, 579
Rivers, Isabel 128, 326
Rivingtons (London publisher) 21, 32, 278, 414
Roberts, Arthur 620
Robertson, Frederick William 84, 566, 569, 570, 572–6, 577
Robertson, Pat 115
Robertson, William 157, 161
Robinson, Robert 161
Robinson, Thomas 12–13
Rochester, Lord 327
Rogers, Samuel 161
Rollin, Charles 160
Romaine, William 125–6
Roman empire 68, 482, 487, 488, 492, 555
Romanticism 375–6, 378, 381, 383, 385, 386, 403, 565, 566, 580, 581, 586, 591
Rome 142, 145, 148, 434, 452
Rosmini, Antonio 146, 424
Rossetti, Christina 342
Rousseau, Jean-Jacques 502
Rowell, Geoffrey 407
Rowland, Daniel 10, 184, 185, 189, 191, 203–4, 204
Royden, Maude 624–5
Rupp, Gordon 375
Russell, Francis 565–6

Russell, Jack 23
Russell, John 310, 311
Rutherford, Samuel 164
Rutherford, Thomas 291
Ryder, Henry 499
Rye, George 310

Sabbatarianism 89, 468, 517, 523, 524
sacerdotalism 124, 129, 130, 201, 395, 398
Sacheverell, Henry 5, 6, 8, 24, 233, 239, 277
sacramentalism 418–20, 499
Said, Edward 550
St Anne's, Blackfriars 126, 127
St Augustine 410, 430
St Bonaventure 54
St James, Piccadilly 10, 18
St Justin 136
St Margaret's Church, Westminster 251, 283
St Martins in the Fields, London 18
St Matthew's, Bethnal Green 127, 128
St Patrick's Day sermon 437
St Pauls (periodical) 23
St Paul's Cathedral, London 4, 251, 276, 600, 620
  charity services 218
  Liddon's sermons 423, 424
  SPCK sermons 365
  Sunday afternoon sermons 93–4
  Waterland's sermons 397
St Paul's Churchyard, London 278
St Sulpice, Paris 412
St Vincent de Paul Society 146
Salisbury Cathedral 306, 424
Salmon, George 41
salvation 385, 418, 490, 514
Salvation Army 616, 624
Sampson, Henry 324
Sancroft, William 307, 315
Sands, David 111
satire 11, 24–5, 152–3, 156, 164, 367, 569
Saturday Review 573
Saunders, Erasmus 185, 187, 199, 200
Savage, John 292
Savery, William 107
Schlegel, Friedrich 581
Schwartz, C. F. 515

science 138, 242, 392–3, 403, 445, 452, 454–60, 467, 594, 595, 614
scientific sermons and lectures 83, 445–60
Scotland 10–11, 34, 152–66, 254
  Catholic Church in 165, 440
  Catholic Relief Acts 138
  Catholic sermons in 139–40, 146
  contemporary thinking in 154, 158
  critical reception of sermons 154–5
  crop failures in 455
  disappointing Calvinist preaching in 13
  eighteenth-century sermons in 153–65
  Evangelical sermons in 164–5
  Gaelic translations 161–2
  Gothic public architecture 582
  Highlands 166
  influence of sermons in 161
  Jacobite rebellions 245–6
  lecture series in 81, 85
  millennialism legacy 386
  nineteenth-century sermons 165–6
  printed sermons of Hugh Blair 162–4
  removing vernacular from sermons 154–5, 161, 163, 165
  theological clubs in 162
  treatises on sermons 160–1
  university courses in sermon-writing 156–60
Scots Magazine 154
Scott, Job 107
Scott, Samuel 107
Scott, Thomas 65, 128, 129–30
Scott, Walter 581
Scottish Reformation Society 84
Scougal, Henry 153–4
scriptural epigraphs 220
Secker, Thomas 10, 12, 37, 117, 291, 362, 391, 489, 508
Second Advent 348–9, 374, 375, 376, 377, 379, 380, 381, 382, 383, 384–7
Second Reformation crusade (1827) 178–9
secularization 26, 230, 232–6, 241–2, 246, 286, 611, 613–15
Seed, Jeremiah 54
Segneri, Paolo 137
Seneca 137

sentiment 133, 158, 160, 583–5, 587, 590, 591
sermon events 7, 8–9, 34, 40, 612, 621
sermon studies 611–12, 618–19
    clergy and 615–18
    defining the sermon 5–6, 619–21
    female preachers 624–5
    Jews and Muslim sermons 626–7
    lay sermons 625–6
    liturgy and 116, 623–4
    production of sermons 627–8
    quantifying 7–8, 621–2
    secularization and 613–15
Seven Years' War (1757) 50, 241, 248
Seventh-day Adventist Church 386
Shaftesbury, Lord 156
Shairp, J. C. 570–1
Shakespeare, William 574, 581, 623
Sharp, John 14, 51, 238, 295, 315
Sharp, Thomas 15–16, 21, 295–9
Sharpe, Granville 509
Shelley, Mary:
    Frankenstein 580
    The Last Man 376
Shelley, Percy Bysshe 565, 574
    Prometheus Unbound 376
Sherlock, Thomas 20, 22, 250, 306, 309, 400, 402–3, 487, 499
Sherlock, William 12, 14
Sherwell, Thomas 328
Shiel, Richard Lalor 170, 177
Shillitoe, Thomas 111
Shipley, Jonathan 306, 359, 492
Short, Vowler 197
shorthand notes 12, 15, 107, 108, 116, 140, 142, 627
Shovell, Sir Cloudesley 332
Shower, John 327, 335
Sieyes, Abbé 174, 175, 176
Silva, A. J. 516
Simeon, Charles 22, 126, 128, 130–1
Sinclair, William MacDonald 345
skeleton sermons 131, 140
Skelton, Philip 396
Skinner, John 10, 11, 12
Skinner, Robert 294
Skynner, Sir John 332
Slater, Samuel 329

slave trade 279, 280, 284–5, 492, 502, 508–10, 511, 552, 560
Smalbroke, Richard 200, 295
Smallwell, Edward 500, 503–4, 507
Smart, Christopher 123
Smellie, William 162
Smith, Adam 157
Smith, Arthur H. 557, 560
Smith, Dr (of Campbeltown) 162
Smith, Gervase 86
Smith, Haddon 128
Smith, Rebecca 98
Smith, Sydney 65
Smith, Thomas 263
Smyth, Edward 534
Smythies, Charles 196
Soane, Sir John 579
social movements 4, 34–5
social order 59, 189, 196, 316, 383–6, 594–5
Society for Promoting Useful Knowledge 365
Society for the Promotion of Christianity among the Jews 378
Society for the Reformation of Manners 122
Society for the Suppression of Vice 281
Socinianism 55, 137, 282, 308, 312, 315, 391, 402
Somerville, Thomas 157, 162
South, Robert 391
South Sea Bubble (1720) 395
Southcott, Joanna 285, 503
Southey, Robert 11, 16
Spa Fields Riots (1816) 375
Spain 500–1
Spaulding, John Gordon 8, 368, 612
SPCK (Society for Promoting Christian Knowledge) 19–20, 120, 129, 154, 275, 362, 363, 501
    in Australia 519, 520
SPCK (Society for Promoting Christian charity schools 357, 359–60, 364–5, 370
    female workers 625
    in Ireland 540
    in Scotland 160, 161
    sermons 186, 364–6, 367, 368–9
    in Wales 187
Spencer, George 144, 147–8

SPG (Society for the Propagation of the
    Gospel in Foreign Parts) 7, 120, 129, 132,
    275, 281, 363, 364, 366, 368, 497–511, 532
  African colonies 552
  Australian colonies 520
  China 558
  North American colonies 484, 485, 489–92
spiritual biographies/autobiographies
    327–8, 408
spoken sermons 42, 166
  adaptability of 37
  Catholic 138
  controversial 173–81
  court 35–6
  critical tools 115–16
  frequency of 183–4, 200, 531
  intelligibility of 187–8, 194, 200
  length of 414
  memorizing 16, 569
  musicality 570–1
  by Newman 148, 570–1
  with notes 191
  numbers of 612
  'phantom' 620
  reading 13–14, 158
  recycling 36–7, 53, 193, 531
  relationship with printed sermons 116, 154,
      155, 187, 290, 550, 619–20
  vernacular 138, 139, 161, 184–5, 187, 193;
      see also preaching performances, 539–41;
      see also preaching performances
Sporle, Susan 324
Sprat, T. 5
Spry, John 317, 318
Spurgeon, Charles Haddon 4, 5, 17, 19, 37, 411,
    613, 618, 622
  collected sermons of 21
  Down-Grade Controversy 36, 38
  fund-raising sermon after Indian
      Mutiny 554
  funding new church 627
  on missionaries 551
  Penny Pulpit 33
  popularity of 611
  preaching out-of date sermon 23
  printed sermons 20–2, 41, 115, 615
  requests for sermons from 39

The Sword and the Trowel 36
Stacey, John 194
Stainton, Robert 89
Stamper, Francis 107
Stanley, Arthur 573
Stanley, Brian 549
Stanley, Francis 53
Stanley, William 315
Stanton, Arthur 195, 196
Stanton, Robert 92
Stanton, William 54, 57
Stebbing, Henry 6, 20, 35, 38, 256
Stebbing, Samuel 280
Steele, Joseph 391, 392
Stephen, Leslie 400
Stephens, Henry 314
Stephens, Lewis 312
Stephens, Samuel 327
Stephenson, George 39
Sterne, Laurence 20, 139,
    403, 583–5
Stevens, William 279
Stevenson, John 157
Steward, George 344
Stewart, James 161
Stinton, George 317
Stock, Eugene 81
Stoddard, Samuel 516
Stokes, Mary 111
Stokes, Sir George 447
Story, Thomas 107
Stout, H. 514
Stowe, John 22
Stowell Brown, Hugh 86, 88–9
Strahan, William 162, 163
street preaching 146
Stronach, John 558–9
Stuart, Dr (of Luss) 162
Stuart, John 59
Stubs, Philip 334
Sturges, John 307, 308, 316
Sturtevant, S. T. 161
Sugar, Zachariah 255
Sugirtharajah, R. S. 517
Sumner, J. B. 410–11
Sunday School Society 176
Sunday schools 87, 88, 276

superstition 58, 142, 437, 486, 487, 488, 489, 490–1, 508, 558, 591
Surridge, Robert James 375, 378
Sweden 230, 231, 234, 235, 236
Swift, Jonathan 10, 13, 392, 585
Switzerland 378
Sydall, Elias 264, 307
Sykes, Arthur Ashley 394
Sylvester, Matthew 326
Synge, Edward 307, 310, 314, 537, 540, 542

Taiping Rebellion 557
Tait, Archibald Campbell 92, 553
Talbot, William 263, 290
Talbot family 117
Tallis, Thomas 221
Tanner, Thomas 306
taste 158, 159, 160
Tatham, Edward 10
Tatler 11
Taves, Ann 115
Tay Bridge disaster (1879) 341, 347
Taylor, Hudson 559
Taylor, Robert 83
Taylor, Robinson 32
temperance movement 67, 84, 85, 86, 144, 146, 147, 166, 195, 521, 524, 525, 565
Tenison, Edward 187
Tenison, Thomas 310, 315
Tennant, Bob 623, 624
Tennant, Gilbert 516
Tennyson, Alfred Lord 567, 568, 573, 574–5, 576, 614
Terrick, Richard 125, 492, 499
Test and Corporation Acts 190, 265, 283, 382, 400
Thackeray, William Makepeace, *Vanity Fair* 2
thanksgiving sermons 50, 51, 138, 233, 241, 261–71
  British constitution 267–8
  Church of Ireland 532
  health of the monarch 242, 276, 279
  imperialism 269–71
  national 261–71, 520
  naval power 271

peace treaties 248, 261, 270–1
royal jubilee 276
victories 238, 245–6, 247, 248, 261, 265, 276, 280, 532, 613
theatres 5, 19, 626
Theistic Church 448
theological clubs 162
Thirlwall, Connop 587
Thomas, Elias 184
Thomas, Elizabeth 120
Thomas, John 204, 490, 505–6
Thomas, Owen 207, 209
Thomas, Timothy 201
Thomas, William 186, 191–2
Thompson, Charles James 195
Thompson, George 84
Thomson, Andrew 519
Thomson, Sir William 614
Thomson, William 458–9
Thorne, Samuel Ley 348, 349
Thornton, Spencer 82
Thornton, William 36
Thorp, Charles 452
Thorp, Thomas 365
Three Choirs 215–17, 219, 220, 225
Tillotson, John 3, 13, 37, 41, 54, 253, 332, 402, 501, 519, 622
  disastrous attempt at extempore preaching 16
  dominant themes in preaching 155–6
  on justification and sanctification 56
  as model for other preachers 54, 155–6, 158, 200, 275, 391
  natural theology 459
  'outline style' 121
  preaching to the illiterate 17
  printed sermon sales 20
  recycling old sermons 14
Times, The 4
Titcomb, Jonathan 19
Toland, John 392, 393
Toland, Matthew 507
Toleration Act (1689) 201, 265, 393
Tondini, Caesarius 345
Tongue, William 328
Toplady, Augustus 23, 123, 127–8, 132, 293
Torriano, Alexander 289

Tractarian sermons/Tractarianism 13, 35, 76, 143, 195, 283, 309, 345, 406–24, 430, 581, 582, 587–8, 615
   authority of the church 421
   contemplation and spiritual life 420
   converts 147, 148
   doctrine 412–15
   Henry Parry Liddon 423–4
   influences on 410–12, 424
   John Henry Newman 421–3
   pastoral 415–21, 424
   poetry and religion 566, 568, 569, 589–91
   practical and plain style of 416–18
   private confession 420
   village 65, 68
tracts 376–7, 398, 620
trade and commerce 270–1, 502–3, 508
trade unions 125
Traill, Robert 161
transubstantiation 311, 429, 534
Travers, Rebecca 102
Trelawny, Jonathan 291
Trench, Richard Chenevix 568
Tresidder, H. J. 33
Trimnell, Charles 507
Trinitarianism 282, 312–13, 394, 397
Trinity House, Corporation of 451, 457–8
Trollope, Anthony:
   Barchester Towers 596, 597, 599
   The Warden 599
Trusler, John 5, 19, 22
Tucker, H. W. 558
Tucker, Josiah 219, 359
Tudur, Geraint 191
Tudway, Thomas 221, 222
Tuke, Samuel 110
Turner, Francis 249
Turner, Thomas 12, 52, 58
Turner, William 277
Tyacke, Nicholas 323
Tyndall, John 89
Tyrwhitt, R. 439
Tyso, Joseph 377, 382–3, 384

Ullathorne, Bernard 143–4, 147, 148, 149
Ullathorne, William 440–1, 521, 522–3, 525

ultramontanism 144, 145, 435–6, 440
Unitarians 81, 92, 277, 282, 285, 459, 474–6, 601, 620
United Presbyterian Church 166
universities 156–60, 160–1, 447, 459
university sermons 4, 10, 13, 17, 68, 414, 422, 457, 471–6, 620
urbanization 66, 133

Vaughan, Charles John 347
Venn, Henry 128–9, 132, 290
Ventura, Gioacchino 145
Verrall, Charles E. 31–3, 39, 627
vicars apostolic 138, 143, 145, 428, 435, 436, 440
Victoria, Queen 36, 431, 435, 445, 573, 617
   coronation of 144
   death of 3, 4, 42
   funeral sermons for 338, 339, 340, 341–2, 350
   sermons preached to 166
   spiritual communion with Albert 349
Victorian funeral sermons 338–50
village sermons 63–77, 614; *see also* parish preaching
Villiers, Frederic 89
Vincent, Henry 85
visitation sermons 68, 282, 289–94, 295–9, 308, 415, 532, 535, 615
visual aids 90
Vivian, Thomas 293
Voltaire 394
Volunteer Movement 276
Voysey, Charles 21, 448

Waddington, Edward 498
Wagstaff, Charles 455, 456
Waite, Thomas 306
Wake, William 237, 292, 306, 308, 309, 316
Wakefield, Gilbert 402
Wales 11, 18, 34, 184–9, 193, 209, 210, 613
   chapels with two pulpits 19
   Dissenters in 201–12
   Established Church in 10, 188–97, 199–200, 204

nineteenth century 192–7, 205–12
    printed sermons 21
    vernacular preaching 199–212
    working class 209–10
Wales, Prince of 91, 349, 458
Wales, Princess of 349
Walker, James 40
Walker, John 142
Walker, Robert 154, 155
Walker, Samuel 120–3, 124, 125, 126, 132
Wallace, Robert 154, 158–9
Waller, Philip 611, 612
Walpole, Horace 13, 25, 579–80, 581
Walpole, Sir Robert 395
Walsh, Walter 407
War of Austrian Succession (1740–8) 311, 503, 508
War of Spanish Succession (1701–14) 535
Warburton, William 256, 263, 399–400, 508–9
Ward, John 57–8
Ward, Samuel 187
Ward, Wilfrid 423
Wardlaw, Ralph 81
Waterland, Daniel 295, 359, 397–8
Waterloo, Battle of (1815) 8
Watson, Robert 157, 163
Watts, Isaac 323, 516
Watts, Michael 328
Watts, Thomas 192–3, 267
Waugh, Evelyn, *A Handful of Dust* 607
Waugh, John 293, 309
Weeks, John 552–3
Weld, Thomas 145
Wellesley, Marquis of 175
Wellington, Duke of 192–3, 339, 344–5
Wellington College 458
Wells Gardner, Darton & Co. 42
Welsh, John 14
Welsh Calvinistic Methodist Connexion 205–6, 208, 210
Wesley, Charles 15, 16, 119, 120, 567–8, 576
Wesley, John 11, 22, 38, 41, 116, 118, 119–20, 122, 123, 127, 132, 344
    'Aldersgate Street' conversion 313
    celebrity of 17
    commemorative souvenirs 24
    criticism of other preachers 14, 16
    death of 276
    editing printed sermons 620
    found disappointing by some 13
    guidance on preaching 17
    length of sermons 10
    printed/spoken sermons 22
    on repeating sermons 7
    on repentance 378
    sermon commemorating George Whitefield 322
    sharing sermons 15
    time spent composing sermons 14
    use of portable pulpit 19
    use of 'tradition' 585
    vocal power of 18
    in Wales 184, 190
Wesley, Samuel, Sr 16
West Indies 509, 510
Westcott, B. F. 65, 72
Westminster Abbey, London 4, 251, 315, 603
Westminster Review 603, 605
Weston, Edward 6
Wettenhall, Edward 540
Whately, Richard 4
Whelan, Irene 616
Whigs 140, 230, 239, 240, 310, 358, 363, 395, 406, 414, 499
Whiston, William 137
White, Blanco 475
White, Stephen 519
White, William Hale 600–2, 606
Whitefield, George 11, 14, 16, 22, 116–20, 128, 131, 322, 516, 519
    commemorative medal 24
    on the conversion of Paul 378
    death of 323
    funeral sermon for John Wesley 276
    The Kingdom of God sermon 117–19
    and Secession Church 164
    sensational sermons 17–18
Whitehead, George 100
Whitfeld, Henry 365
Whyley, G. E. 367
Wicksteed, Charles 92
Wilberforce, Samuel 38, 41, 456, 473–4, 621
Wilberforce, William 36, 281

INDEX

Wilbur, John 109
Wilde, Oscar 66
Wilkinson, Edward 41
Wilkinson, John 110
William and Mary, *see* William III; Mary II
William III, King 35, 231, 232, 235, 237–8, 245, 267, 501
   coronation sermon 11
   Crown-Church relations 315
   escape from assassination 261, 263
   printed funeral sermons 323
   refusal to renew College of Arms 333
William IV, King 338, 339, 341, 344
Williams, Daniel 265, 331
Williams, Isaac 410, 415, 416, 417, 419, 569
Williams, John 186
Williams, John Henry 282
Williams, Rowland 474
Williams, W. F. 430
Williams, William (Pantycelyn) 185, 189, 206, 208–9
Willison, John 162
Willoughby, Howard 521–2
Wilson, Daniel 517
Wilson, H. B. 474
Wilson, Rachel 106
Wilson, William 164
Wilton, Charles Pleydell 519, 520, 524
Winnington-Ingram, Arthur 42, 459–60
Winslow, Octavius 343
Wise, Thomas 292
Wiseman, Nicholas 144, 145–7, 428, 430, 434, 435, 436, 437, 440, 452, 453
Wishart, George 154
Wishart, William 154
Wishart, William (the younger) 158
witch trials 137
Witham, Thomas 137
Withers, John 265
Wolffe, John 612, 617
women:
   churching of 296
   congregation members 573
   lecturers 87–8
   missionaries 129–30
   preachers 6, 98, 102, 106, 107, 110, 111, 118, 120, 517, 616, 624–8
   sermons for 343–4, 346, 348, 617, 625
Woodd, Basil 81
Woodforde, James 58, 393
Woodroffe, Benjamin 269
Woodward, George (clergyman) 53, 55
Woodward, George Moutard (caricaturist) 24, 25
Woodward, Richard 543
Woolston, Thomas 394, 400
Worcester, diocese of 215, 216, 217, 218, 219, 220
Worcester Postman 217
Wordsworth, Christopher 412, 439
Wordsworth, William 566, 567, 571, 574, 575, 576, 590, 600–1
Working Men's Institutes 84
World Missionary Conference (1910) 549
Wren, Sir Christopher 18, 579
Wrenford, J. Tinson 195
Wright, Thomas 334
Wyatt, James 580
Wynne, John 504–5
Wynne, Robert 188–9

YMCA (Young Men's Christian Association) 85–8, 92
Yonge, Philip 307, 308
Yorke, James 280
Young, Edward 488

Zulu people 473